Praise for Mark Sobell's Previous Books

D1556281

The beauty of GNU/Linux and the open source movement is that at some stage, everyone will need the help of someone else, and therefore those people will generally not hesitate to help others when asked.

—Darrell Esau

A Practical Guide
to Red Hat® Linux® 8

Psyche

A beautiful princess who shared a love with Eros and
was united with him after overcoming Aphrodite's
jealousy. She is the personification of the soul.

See www.geocities.com/Athens/Forum/6946/mythology/psyche.html
for more on Psyche.

A Practical Guide
to Red Hat® Linux® 8

Mark G. Sobell

✦✦Addison-Wesley

Boston • San Francisco • New York • Toronto • Montreal
London • Munich • Paris • Madrid
Capetown • Sydney • Tokyo • Singapore • Mexico City

Many of the designations used by manufacturers and sellers to distinguish their products are claimed as trademarks. Where those designations appear in this book, and Addison-Wesley was aware of a trademark claim, the designations have been printed with initial capital letters or in all capitals.

"Red Hat" is a registered trademark of Red Hat, Inc. Used with permission.

The author and publisher have taken care in the preparation of this book, but make no expressed or implied warranty of any kind and assume no responsibility for errors or omissions. No liability is assumed for incidental or consequential damages in connection with or arising out of the use of the information or programs contained herein.

The publisher offers discounts on this book when ordered in quantity for special sales. For more information, please contact:

U.S. Corporate and Government Sales
(800) 382-3419
corpsales@pearsontechgroup.com

For sales outside of the U.S., please contact:

International Sales
(317) 581-3793
international@pearsontechgroup.com

Visit Addison-Wesley on the Web: www.aw.professional.com

Library of Congress Cataloging-in-Publication Data

Sobell, Mark G.
    A practical guide to Red Hat Linux / Mark G. Sobell.
        p. cm.
    ISBN 0-201-70313-0
    1. Linux.   2. Operating systems (Computers). I. Title.
    QA76.76.O63 S59485 2002
    005.4'469—dc21

                                                      2002018544

ISBN 0-201-70313-0
Text printed on recycled paper
1 2 3 4 5 6 7 8 9 10—CRS—0605040302
First printing, December 2002

for my mom,
Dr. Helen L. Sobell
1918–2002

Brief Contents

Contents

5 The Shell I   137

8   KDE Desktop Environment   267

9 Networking and the Internet   351

10   The vim Editor   413

11   The emacs Editor   473

12 The Shell II: The Bourne Again Shell   541

13 **Programming the Bourne Again Shell**   **625**

14 The TC Shell   681

15   The Z Shell and Advanced Shell Programming   735

16 Programming Tools   837

17 Red Hat Linux System Administration   895

PART III   The GNU/Linux Utility Programs   1081

PART IV   Appendixes   1381

A Regular Expressions   1383

Preface

This is a straightforward, easy-to-read, logically organized book about GNU/Linux[1] by an author who has been writing successful books on UNIX/Linux operating systems for more than 20 years. This book is a *practical guide* because it uses tutorial examples to show you how each command works, each step of the way. Your screen mimics what you see in the book as you learn about GNU/Linux in general and Redhat Linux version 8 in particular.

The book is uniquely designed for both beginners and experienced users, including introductory and more advanced chapters. Although this book targets Red Hat version 8, most of it applies to all GNU/Linux distributions.

Parts I and II of *A Practical Guide to Red Hat® Linux® 8* show you how to

- Log in on and get familiar with your system—Chapters 2–5
- Use and customize graphical user interfaces (GUIs)—Chapters 6–8
- Understand and use networks—Chapter 9
- Master the vim and emacs text editors—Chapters 10–11
- Work with the bash, tcsh, and zsh Shells—Chapters 12–15
- Write complex shell programs (scripts)—Chapters 13–15

---

1. Proper credit is owed the Free Software Foundation/GNU for its contribution to the operating system commonly referred to as *Linux*. Thus this book uses the name *GNU/Linux* in places where others use *Linux* by itself. Red Hat Linux is a distribution of GNU/Linux. Refer to the beginning of Chapter 1 for more information on the development of GNU/Linux.

- Use sophisticated software development tools—Chapter 16
- Perform system administration—Chapter 17

Part III is a *reference guide* to more than 85 GNU/Linux utilities. Part IV includes appendixes, a glossary, and the index.

You do not have to read this book in page order. Once you are comfortable using GNU/Linux, you can use this book as a reference: Look up a topic of interest in the table of contents or index and read about it. Or think of this book as a catalog of GNU/Linux topics: Flip through the pages until a topic catches your eye. This book has many pointers to Web sites where you can get additional information: Consider the Web as an extension of this book.

Red Hat Version 8

Red Hat version 8 release provides users and administrators (who are sometimes one and the same) with tools and an environment that make setting up, maintaining, and using a GNU/Linux system more straightforward than ever before.

Red Hat has wrapped the GNOME and KDE GUIs in its Bluecurve theme, making the two principal graphical desktop environments look and perform similarly. Under Red Hat's setup, GNOME runs utilities designed for KDE, and KDE does the same with GNOME utilities. By providing a uniform environment and key tools that work across many platforms, Red Hat is working toward corporate acceptance of desktop GNU/Linux, which benefits all users. For the user who needs to communicate and exchange documents with users on other platforms, Red Hat 8 includes

- OpenOffice.org office suite, formerly Sun's StarOffice and now an open source project (runs on MS Windows, GNU/Linux [x86 and PPC], Solaris, Mac OS X)
- Mozilla, which includes a Web browser, e-mail and news reader programs, and an IRC chat client (runs on MS Windows, GNU/Linux x86, Mac OS X, Mac OS 9.x)
- Evolution, an e-mail and calendar application (runs on GNU/Linux and Solaris 8)

For the system administrator, Red Hat Linux version 8 provides new configuration tools including

- A package management utility that facilitates adding packages to and removing them from your system using the installation CD-ROMs
- Graphical configuration tools that help you set up the simpler aspects of Apache (HTTP), Samba, firewalls, network settings, system services, and more

- An upgrade of Red Hat Network (RHN) that not only enables you to keep your system software up-to-date automatically but allows you to query, download, and install over the Internet any package that Red Hat provides
- The Logical Volume Manager (LVM) that provides high-level manipulation of disk storage, allowing you to grow and migrate partitions without interrupting system users

Also, by including the latest software and conforming to the LSB (Linux Standards Base) 1.2, Red Hat helps software developers focus on designing and implementing applications, not dealing with nonconformance issues.

Audience

This book appeals to a wide range of readers; it does not require programming experience, but some experience using any general-purpose computer is helpful. This book is appropriate for

- **Students** taking a class in which they use GNU/Linux
- **Home users** who want to set up and/or run GNU/Linux
- **Professionals** who use GNU/Linux at work
- **System administrators** who need an understanding of GNU/Linux and the tools that are available to them
- **Computer science students** studying the GNU/Linux operating system
- **Programmers** who need to understand the GNU/Linux programming environment
- **Technical executives** who want to get a grounding in GNU/Linux

Benefits

A Practical Guide to Red Hat® Linux® 8 gives you a broad understanding of many facets of GNU/Linux, from using it through customizing it. Whether you are a programmer/developer, a systems administrator, or an end user, this book gives you the knowledge you need to get on with your work: You will come away from this book understanding how to use GNU/Linux, and this book will remain a valuable reference tool for years to come.

Scope of Coverage

A Practical Guide to Red Hat® Linux® 8 covers a wide range of topics, showing you how to use Red Hat Linux from your screen and keyboard.

- **Part I**, Chapters 1–5, introduces new users to Red Hat Linux: introduction, logging on, basic utilities, filesystem structure, and the shell. Part I contains step-by-step tutorials covering the most important aspects of the GNU/Linux operating system.

- **Part II**, Chapters 6–17, covers intermediate and advanced aspects of Red Hat Linux: GUI interfaces, networking, the vim and emacs editors, the Bourne Again, TC, and Z Shells and shell scripts, programming tools, and system administration.

- **Part III** offers a comprehensive, detailed reference to more than 85 GNU/Linux utilities, with numerous examples. If you are already familiar with UNIX/Linux, this part of the book will be a valuable, easy-to-use reference. If you are not an experienced user, you will find Part III a useful supplement while you are mastering the subjects and tutorials in Parts I and II.

- **Part IV** includes appendixes on regular expressions, where to find help on the Web, system security, POSIX, and the definition of free software. This part also includes a glossary and the index.

Experienced Users May Want to Skim Part I || tip

If you have used a UNIX/Linux system before, you may want to skim over or skip some or all of the chapters in Part I. All readers should take a look at "Conventions" (page 24), which explains the typographic and layout conventions that this book uses, and "Documentation" (page 42) which points you toward both local and remote sources of GNU/Linux and Red Hat documentation.

The more advanced material in each chapter is presented in sections marked "Optional," which you are encouraged to return to after mastering the basic material presented in the chapter. Review exercises are included at the end of each chapter for readers who want to hone their skills. Some of the exercises test your understanding of material covered in the chapter, whereas others challenge you to go beyond the material presented to develop a more thorough understanding. Answers to some exercises are at www.sobell.com.

Features by Chapter

- The history and background of GNU/Linux (Chapter 1)

- Conventions used in this book, how to log in on your system, and using the documentation systems (Chapter 2)

- Basic utilities (Chapter 3)

- The GNU/Linux filesystem structure (Chapter 4)

- The (generic) shell (Chapter 5)

- An introduction to GUIs, including the X Window System (Chapters 6)

- The X Window System: use and customization (Chapter 6)

- The GNOME 2 desktop environment (GUI interface, Chapter 7)

- The KDE 3 desktop environment (GUI interface, Chapter 8)

- Networks: concepts, terminology, and practical instructions for setting up a secure network (Chapters 9 and 17)

- Secure utilities: ssh, scp, gpg, lokkit, and more (Chapter 9, Part III, and Appendix C)

- The vim and emacs text editors (Chapters 10 and 11)

- Using the shells interactively and as programming languages: the Bourne Again Shell—bash—(Chapters 12 and 13), the TC Shell—tcsh—(Chapter 14), and the Z Shell—zsh—(Chapter 15).

- Programming tools: C, make, source code management—RCS and CVS—(Chapter 16)

- System administration (Chapter 17)

- More than 85 utilities, including many examples (Part III)

- Appendixes covering

    - Regular expressions (Appendix A)

    - Finding software and pointers to useful Web pages (Appendix B)

    - Security: an overview of this important topic (Appendix C)

    - POSIX: standards that specify a standard UNIX/Linux (Appendix D)

    - GNU's Free Software Definition (Appendix E)

- A comprehensive glossary of more than 500 words and phrases

- A complete index

Features by Concept

- Concepts illustrated by practical examples throughout
- A security-conscious perspective: security boxes throughout the book noting where you can improve system security, including network security
- Key topics with tutorials: pico, vim (vi improved), and emacs text editors; pine mail and news reader, and more
- Resources for finding and installing software: Web sites, rpm, and the GNU Configure and Build System
- Resources for finding online documentation—both local and on the Internet
- Important GNU tools, including gcc, gdb, GNU Configure and Build System, gawk, gzip, and many others

Assistance

- Many examples throughout
- Comprehensive index
- Caution boxes warning you of the consequences of taking certain actions
- Security boxes alerting you to security issues
- Tip boxes helping you avoid pitfalls
- Help in obtaining online documentation from many sources including your local system, the Red Hat documentation CD-ROM, the Red Hat Web site, GNU, and other locations on the Internet
- Many useful URLs (Internet addresses) where you can obtain software, security programs and information, and more

Tutorials

- pico text editor
- emacs text editor and programmer's environment
- vim (vi improved) editor
- pine as a mail program
- pine as a newsreader

Features by Topic

Red Hat Linux

- *A Practical Guide to Red Hat® Linux® 8* is based on Red Hat version 8, although much of it is compatible with other versions and distributions of GNU/Linux.

- A complete chapter and more covers the GNU/Linux filesystem and Red Hat's implementation: structure, types of files, links, pathnames, permissions, locations for common files, as well as utilities that change filesystems.

- Red Hat has built and contributed to many tools for system administration, including rpm (Red Hat Program Manager), which makes it a simple matter to install or remove program packages; RHN (Red Hat Network), which can keep your system programs and files up-to-date automatically as well as install new ones; redhat-config-users (sets up users on the system); printconf-gui (configures printers); and many more.

- A chapter each is devoted to the GNOME version 2 and KDE version 3 graphical desktops as configured by Red Hat with the Bluecurve theme.

Networking, the Internet, and the World Wide Web

Chapter 9 explains what a network is, how it works, and how you can use it. This chapter covers types of networks, various network implementations, distributed computing, using the network for communicating with other users, and using various networking utilities (such as ssh, scp, telnet, ftp, pine, host, and more).

- Broad Internet coverage includes firewalls, network services, types of networks and their operation, network protocols, and IPv6.

- Complete instructions are given on using free software: finding, downloading, and installing free software from the Internet, using a variety of tools.

- Guidance is provided on using networking tools, including ping, host, dig, traceroute, swat (Samba), and more.

- Distributed computing, including DNS, NIS, NFS, proxy servers, Internet services, and more, is also covered.

Organizing Information

Chapters 2, 3, and 4 explain how to create, delete, copy, move, and search for information by using GNU/Linux utilities. You also learn how to use the GNU/Linux file structure to organize the information you store on your computer.

Electronic Mail and Telecommunications

Chapters 2 and 3 and Part III include information on how to use utilities (pine, mail, talk, write) to communicate with users on your system and other systems. Chapter 9 details how to address electronic mail to users on remote, networked systems. Chapter 17 has a section on using sendmail.

The Shells

Chapter 5 introduces the concepts of standard input, standard output, redirection, pipes, background processes, filename generation, and builtin commands. It shows you how to redirect output from a program to a printer or a file simply by changing the command line. The chapter also demonstrates how you can use pipes to combine utilities to solve problems right from the command line.

Shell Programming (Shell Scripts)

Once you have mastered the basics of Red Hat Linux, you can use your knowledge to build more complex and specialized programs, using a shell as a programming language. Chapter 12 picks up where Chapter 5 leaves off, covering more advanced aspects of working with a shell, using for examples the Bourne Again Shell—bash, the shell used almost exclusively for system shell scripts. Chapter 13 shows how to use bash to write scripts composed of GNU/Linux system utilities. Chapter 14 covers the TC Shell—tcsh, an improved version of Berkeley's C Shell. Chapter 15 covers the Z Shell—zsh, similar to the Korn Shell—extending the concepts of shell programming introduced in Chapter 13 into more advanced areas, including more information on the locality of variables, recursion, and the coprocess. The examples in Part III also demonstrate many features of the utilities you can use in shell scripts.

Job Control

The job control commands, which originated on Berkeley UNIX, allow you to work on many jobs at once from a single window and to switch back and forth between the jobs as desired. Job control is available under the three major shells.

Shell Functions

Shell functions available in the bash and zsh Shells enable you to write your own commands that are similar to the aliases provided by the TC Shell, only more powerful.

The X Window System and Graphical User Interfaces (GUIs)

Chapter 6 discusses the X Window System and how to open and control windows, customize your X work environment, and use some of the features common to GNOME and KDE. Chapter 7 covers GNOME and Chapter 8 covers KDE.

X Window System

- Window managers
- Bringing up and shutting down the X Window System
- Setting X resources
- Using the X Window System
- Customizing the X Window System
- Remote computing and local displays

GNOME Graphical Desktop

- Main panel: control center of the GNOME desktop
- Menus: the key to using GNOME, including details of the GNOME (Main) menu
- Metacity window manager: how to use and customize this new, simple, compact window manager
- Bluecurve theme: its icons and buttons
- Nautilus file manager: the cornerstone GNOME utility, including the use of control bars and establishing properties
- Start-Here window: an alternative way of setting preferences
- GNOME utilities: search, terminal emulator, pick a font, pick a color, MIME types, and much more
- Customizing GNOME: Nautilus, panels, and menus
- Sawfish window manger: window operations, menus, and configurator

KDE Graphical Environment

- Main panel (kicker): control center of the KDE desktop
- Menus: the key to using KDE, including details of the K (Main) menu, Desktop menu and menubar, Taskbar, Window List menu, and Operations menu
- Bluecurve theme: its icons and buttons
- Konqueror browser and file manager: views, toolbars, find files, shortcuts, Navigation panel
- Start-Here window: an alternative way of setting preferences
- How to get help: What's this?, KHelpcenter, Help menu
- Window manager: using and modifying kwin
- Customizing KDE: Control center, panels, toolbars, K Menu editor, autostart, and sound.

Utilities

Linux includes hundreds of utilities. Part III contains extensive examples of how to use many of these utilities to solve problems without resorting to programming in C or another language. The example sections of gawk (more than 20 pages, starting on page 1185), sed (page 1310), and sort (page 1326) give real-life examples that demonstrate how to use these utilities alone and with other utilities to generate reports, summarize data, and extract information.

Secure Utilities

Many newer utilities establish secure connections, encrypt data, and verify the identify of the creator/sender of files. Appendix C discusses security issues and solutions; Chapter 9 and Part III explain the use of secure utilities, including ssh, scp, and pgp.

The vim Editor

Red Hat Linux supplies the vim text editor, an "improved" version of vi. The vi editor was originally a part of Berkeley UNIX and is still one of the most widely used text editors. Chapter 10 starts with a tutorial on vim and goes on to explain how to use many of the advanced features of vim, including special characters in search strings, the general-purpose and named buffers, parameters, markers, and executing commands from vim.

The emacs Editor

Red Hat Linux supplies the popular GNU emacs editor. Chapter 11 includes information on emacs and the X Window System, allowing you to use a mouse and take advantage of such X Window System features as menus and cut-and-paste with emacs. This chapter explains how to use many of the features of this versatile editor, from a basic orientation to the use of the META, ALT, and ESCAPE keys; key bindings, buffers, the concept of Point, the cursor, Mark and Region, incremental and complete searching for both character strings and regular expressions; using the online help facilities, cutting and pasting from the keyboard and with a mouse, and using multiple windows and frames; and C mode, which is designed to aid programmers in writing and debugging C code. The chapter concludes with a summary of emacs commands.

Regular Expressions

Many UNIX utilities allow you to use regular expressions to make your job easier. Appendix A explains how to use regular expressions so that you can take advantage of some of the hidden power of your GNU/Linux system.

System Administration

Chapter 17 explains how to set up, control, and keep secure a Red Hat Linux system. The chapter details the responsibilities of the Superuser and explains how to bring up and shut down a Red Hat Linux system, add users to the system, back up files, set up new devices, check the integrity of a filesystem, and more. This chapter goes into detail about the structure of a filesystem and explains what administrative information is kept in various files. In addition, this chapter presents an *overview* of installing Red Hat Linux, information on rebuilding the GNU/Linux kernel, and managing user accounts, and it provides security boxes throughout:

- Use the Superuser (**root**) account
- Download Red Hat Linux from the Internet and burn a CD-ROM
- Find/add/remove rpm software packages with rpmfind and rpm
- Install non-rpm software with the GNU Configure and Build System
- Understand and manage basic security issues with secure programs including ssh (secure shell) and GnuPG (GNU Privacy Guard)
- Add and remove users with redhat-config-users and kuser
- Use RHN (Red Hat Network) to keep your system software up-to-date automatically and to download new packages from Red Hat's Internet site.

- Build a firewall with gnome-lokkit
- Manage local and remote printers with printconf-gui and KDEPrint
- Use graphical system administration tools, including GNOME Start Here, GNOME and KDE menu systems, KDE Control Center, and KDE Control Panel
- Understand system operation, including the boot process, **rc** scripts, emergency mode, single- and multiuser mode, and what to do when the system crashes
- Learn about files, directories, and filesystems, including types of files and filesystems, **fstab**, automatically mounted filesystems, filesystem integrity checks, filesystem utilities, and how to tune filesystems
- Use backup utilities, including tar, cpio, dump, and restore
- Use the **/proc** filesystem
- Configure network services: proxies, NFS (Network Filesystem), DNS (Domain Name Service), automount filesystems, Samba server, OpenSSH
- Rebuild the kernel
- Plan disk layout and partition disks
- Run system reports
- Use the Logical Volume Manager (LVM) to grow and migrate partitions without interrupting users
- Manage printers
- Connect to the Internet
- Configure PAM (pluggable authentication modules)
- Use administration utilities

Programming Environment

Chapter 16 introduces you to GNU/Linux's exceptional programming environment. This chapter explains how to use some of the most useful software development tools: gcc (the GNU C compiler), the gdb debugger, make, and the CVS and RVS source code management tools. The make utility automates much of the drudgery involved in ensuring that a program you compile contains the latest versions of all program modules. CVS and RVS help you manage source code by tracking multiple versions of files on various types of projects.

- Manage source code with RCS or CVS
- Use make to keep a set of programs current
- Use the GNU C compiler (gcc) and debugger (dbg)
- Work with shared libraries
- Understand system calls

POSIX

The IEEE POSIX committees have developed standards for programming and user interfaces, based on historical UNIX practice, and new standards are under development. Appendix D describes these standards and their direction and effect on the UNIX and GNU/Linux industry.

Supplements

The author's home page (www.sobell.com) contains downloadable listings of the longer programs from the book, pointers to many interesting and useful GNU/Linux sites on the World Wide Web, a list of corrections to the book, answers to selected exercises, and a solicitation for corrections, comments, suggestions, and additional programs and exercises.

Thanks

A big "Thank You" to the folks who read through the drafts of the book and made comments that caused me to refocus parts of the book where things were not clear or were left out altogether. Thanks to Carsten Pfeiffer, Software Engineer and KDE Developer; Dustin Puryear, Puryear Information Technology; Gabor Liptak, Independent Consultant; Bart Schaefer, Chief Technical Officer, iPost; Michael J. Jordan, Web Developer, GNU/Linux Online Inc.; Steven Gibson, owner of SuperAnt.com; John Viega, Founder and Chief Scientist, Secure Software, Inc.; K. Rachael Treu, Internet Security Analyst, Global Crossing; Kara Pritchard, K & S Pritchard Enterprises, Inc; Matthew Miller, Boston University; Glen Wiley, Capitol One Finances; Karel Baloun, Senior Software Engineer, Looksmart, Ltd.; Matthew Whitworth; Dameon D. Welch-Abernathy, Nokia Systems; Josh Simon, Consultant;

Stan Isaacs; and Dr. Eric H. Herrin, II, Vice President, Herrin Software Development, Inc.

Thanks to Doug Hughes, who gave me a big hand with the sections on system administration, networks, the Internet, and programming.

Thanks also to the folks at Addison-Wesley who helped bring this book to life: My editor Karen Gettman; Tyrrell Albaugh, production manager, who gave me guidance and much latitude in producing the book; and everyone else who worked behind the scenes to make this book happen.

Thanks to the Texan, JFP (Dr. John Frank Peters), for his many hours on the emacs chapter. His understanding of this editor gives this chapter a depth and breadth that makes you want to dive right in. Fred Zlotnick, author of *The POSIX.1 Standard*, did a lot of work on Appendix D.

I am also indebted to Denis Howe, who edits *The Free On-line Dictionary of Computing*. Dennis has graciously permitted me to use entries from his compilation. Be sure to look at the dictionary at foldoc.doc.ic.ac.uk/foldoc.

Thanks to Lorraine Callahan and Steve Wampler, who researched, wrote, analyzed reviews, and coordinated all the efforts that went into the first Linux book. Thanks for help on my first Linux book to Ronald Hiller, Graburn Technology, Inc.; Charles A. Plater, Wayne State University; Bob Palowoda, Tom Bialaski, Sun Microsystems; Roger Hartmuller, TIS Labs at Network Associates; Kaowen Liu, Andy Spitzer, Rik Schneider, Jesse St. Laurent, Steve Bellenot, Ray W. Hiltbrand, Jennifer Witham, Gert-Jan Hagenaars, and Casper Dik.

A Practical Guide to Red Hat® Linux® 8 is based in part on two of my previous UNIX books: *UNIX System V: A Practical Guide* and *A Practical Guide to Linux*. Many people helped me with those books, and thanks here go to Pat Parseghian, Dr. Kathleen Hemenway, and Brian LaRose; Byron A. Jeff, Clark Atlanta University; Charles Stross; Jeff Gitlin, Lucent Technologies; Kurt Hockenbury; Maury Bach, Intel Israel Ltd.; Peter H. Salus; Rahul Dave, University of Pennsylvania; Sean Walton, Intelligent Algorithmic Solutions; Tim Segall, Computer Sciences Corporation; Behrouz Forouzan, DeAnza College; Mike Keenan, Virginia Polytechnic Institute and State University; Mike Johnson, Oregon State University; Jandelyn Plane, University of Maryland; Arnold Robbins and Sathis Menon, Georgia Institute of Technology; Cliff Shaffer, Virginia Polytechnic Institute and State University; and Steven Stepanek, California State University, Northridge, for reviewing the book.

I also continue to be grateful to the many people who helped with the early editions of my UNIX books. Special thanks to Roger Sippl, Laura King, and Roy Harrington for introducing me to the UNIX system. My mother, Dr. Helen Sobell, provided invaluable comments on the original manuscript at several junctures. Also thanks to Isaac Rabinovitch, Professor Raphael Finkel, Professor Randolph Bentson, Bob Greenberg, Professor Udo Pooch, Judy Ross, Dr. Robert Veroff, Dr. Mike Denny, Joe DiMartino, Dr. John Mashey, Diane Schulz, Robert Jung, Charles

Whitaker, Don Cragun, Brian Dougherty, Dr. Robert Fish, Guy Harris, Ping Liao, Gary Lindgren, Dr. Jarrett Rosenberg, Dr. Peter Smith, Bill Weber, Mike Bianchi, Scooter Morris, Clarke Echols, Oliver Grillmeyer, Dr. David Korn, Dr. Scott Weikart, and Dr. Richard Curtis.

Dr. Brian Kernighan and Rob Pike graciously allowed me to reprint the **bundle** script from their book *The UNIX Programming Environment.*

Finally, thanks to the brothers at JumpStart for providing nourishment through the final push. As Peter said, "You wouldn't have finished that book until 2010 if it weren't for us!"

I take responsibility for errors and omissions. If you find one or just have a comment, let me know (mark@sobell.com), and I'll fix it in the next printing. My home page (www.sobell.com) will contain a list of errors and those who found them, as well as copies of the longer scripts from the book and pointers to many interesting GNU/Linux pages.

Mark G. Sobell
San Francisco, California

PART I
GNU/Linux Basics

IN THIS CHAPTER

GNU/Linux: A Product of the Internet

1

The Linux *kernel* was developed by Finnish undergraduate student Linus Torvalds, who used the Internet to make the source code immediately available to others for free. Torvalds released Linux version 0.01 in September 1991.

The new operating system came together with a lot of hard work. Programmers throughout the world were quick to extend the kernel and develop other tools, adding functionality matching that found in both Berkeley UNIX (BSD) and System V UNIX (SVR4) and adding new functionality as well.

The new operating system, developed through the cooperation of many, many people around the world, is a *product of the Internet* and is a *FREE* operating system: All the source code is free. You are free to study it, redistribute it, and modify it. As a result, the code is available free of cost—no charge for the software, source, documentation, or support (via newsgroups, mailing lists, and other Internet resources). As The GNU Free Software Definition (reproduced in Appendix E, also at www.gnu.org/philosophy/free-sw.html) puts it:

> "Free software" is a matter of liberty, not price. To understand the concept, you should think of "free" as in "free speech," not as in "free beer."

The GNU/Linux Connection

An operating system is the low-level software that schedules tasks, allocates storage, and handles the interfaces to peripheral hardware, such as printers, disk drives, and your screen, keyboard, and mouse. An operating system has two main parts: the *kernel* and the *system programs*. The kernel allocates machine resources, including memory, disk space, and *CPU* (page 1462) cycles, to all other programs that run on the computer. The system programs perform higher-level housekeeping tasks, often acting as servers in a client/server relationship. *Linux* is the name of the kernel that Linus Torvalds presented to the world in 1991 and that many others have worked on to enhance, stabilize, expand, and make more secure.

Fade to 1983

Richard Stallman[1] announces[2] the GNU Project for creating an operating system, both kernel and system programs, and presents The GNU Manifesto,[3] which begins as follows:

> GNU, which stands for Gnu's Not UNIX, is the name for the complete UNIX-compatible software system which I am writing so that I can give it away free to everyone who can use it.

Some years later Stallman added a footnote to the preceding sentence when he realized that it was creating confusion:

> The wording here was careless. The intention was that nobody would have to pay for *permission* to use the GNU system. But the words don't make this clear, and people often interpret them as saying that copies of GNU should always be distributed at little or no charge. That was never the intent; later on, the manifesto mentions the possibility of companies providing the service of distribution for a profit. Subsequently I have learned to distinguish carefully between "free" in the sense of freedom and "free" in the sense of price. Free software is software that users have the freedom to distribute and change. Some users may obtain copies at no

---

1. www.stallman.org

2. www.gnu.org/gnu/initial-announcement.html

3. www.gnu.org/gnu/manifesto.html

charge, while others pay to obtain copies—and if the funds help support improving the software, so much the better. The important thing is that everyone who has a copy has the freedom to cooperate with others in using it.

In the manifesto, after explaining a little about the project and what has been accomplished so far, Mr. Stallman continues.

Why I Must Write GNU

I consider that the golden rule requires that if I like a program I must share it with other people who like it. Software sellers want to divide the users and conquer them, making each user agree not to share with others. I refuse to break solidarity with other users in this way. I cannot in good conscience sign a nondisclosure agreement or a software license agreement. For years I worked within the Artificial Intelligence Lab to resist such tendencies and other inhospitalities, but eventually they had gone too far: I could not remain in an institution where such things are done for me against my will.

So that I can continue to use computers without dishonor, I have decided to put together a sufficient body of free software so that I will be able to get along without any software that is not free. I have resigned from the AI Lab to deny MIT any legal excuse to prevent me from giving GNU away.

Next Scene, 1991

The GNU Project has moved well along toward its goal. Much of the GNU Operating System, except for the kernel, is complete. Richard Stallman later writes:

By the early '90s we had put together the whole system aside from the kernel (and we were also working on a kernel, the GNU Hurd,[4] which runs on top of Mach[5]). Developing this kernel has been a lot harder than we expected, and we are still working on finishing it.[6]

---

4. www.gnu.org/software/hurd/hurd.html

5. www.gnu.org/software/hurd/gnumach.html

6. www.gnu.org/software/hurd/hurd-and-linux.html

...[M]any believe that once Linus Torvalds finished writing the kernel, his friends looked around for other free software, and for no particular reason most everything necessary to make a UNIX-like system was already available.

What they found was no accident—it was the GNU system. The available free software[7] added up to a complete system because the GNU Project had been working since 1984 to make one. The GNU Manifesto had set forth the goal of developing a free UNIX-like system, called GNU. The Initial Announcement of the GNU Project also outlines some of the original plans for the GNU system. By the time Linux was written, the [GNU] system was almost finished.[8]

The Present

The question is, What should we call this operating system composed of the Linux kernel and the GNU operating system (sans kernel)? Because of the events that led up to the "new" operating system, it is commonly referred to as Linux. But that name belies its lineage. This book uses the alternative name, which is becoming more popular: GNU/Linux.

The Code Is Free

Part of the tradition of free software dates back to the days when UNIX was released to universities at nominal cost, which contributed to its success and portability. This tradition died as UNIX was commercialized and as manufacturers regarded the source code as proprietary and made it effectively unavailable. Another problem with the commercial versions of UNIX was complexity. As each manufacturer tuned UNIX for a specific architecture, it became less portable and too unwieldy for teaching and experimentation. Two professors created their own stripped-down UNIX look-alikes for educational purposes: Doug Comer created XINU[9] and Andrew Tanenbaum created MINIX.[10] It was Linus Torvalds's experience with MINIX that led him on the path to creating his own UNIX-like operating system.

---

7. See Appendix E or www.gnu.org/philosophy/free-sw.html.

8. www.gnu.org/gnu/linux-and-gnu.html

9. www.cs.purdue.edu/research/xinu.html

10. www.cs.vu.nl/~ast/minix.html

You can obtain GNU/Linux at no cost over the Internet (page 906). You can also obtain the GNU code via U.S. mail at a modest cost for materials and shipping. You can support the Free Software Foundation by buying the same (GNU) code in higher-priced packages, and you can buy commercial packaged releases of GNU/Linux (called *distributions*), such as Red Hat, that include installation instructions, software, and support.

Linux and GNU software are distributed under the terms of the GNU General Public License (GPL, www.gnu.org/licenses/licenses.html). The GPL says that you have the right to copy, modify, and redistribute the code covered by the agreement, but that when you redistribute the code, you must also distribute the same license with the code, making the code and the license inseparable. If you get the source code for an accounting program that is under the GPL off the Internet and modify it and redistribute an executable version of the program, you must also distribute the modified source code and the GPL agreement with it. Because this is the reverse of the way a normal copyright works (it gives rights instead of limiting them), it has been termed a *copyleft*. (This paragraph is not a legal interpretation of the GPL; it is here only to give you an idea of how it works. Refer to the GPL itself when you want to make use of it.)

Have Fun!

Two key words for GNU/Linux are, "Have Fun!" These words pop up in prompts and documentation. The UNIX—now the GNU/Linux—culture is steeped in humor that can be seen throughout the system. For example, less is more—GNU has replaced the UNIX paging utility named more with an improved utility named less. The utility to view PostScript documents is named ghostscript, and one of several replacements for the vi editor is named elvis. While machines with Intel processors have "Intel Inside" logos on their outside, some GNU/Linux machines sport "Linux Inside" logos. And Torvalds himself has been seen wearing a T-shirt bearing a "Linus Inside" logo.

The Heritage of GNU/Linux: UNIX

The UNIX system was developed by researchers who needed a set of modern computing tools to help them with their projects. The system allowed a group of people working together on a project to share selected data and programs while keeping other information private.

Universities and colleges played a major role in furthering the popularity of the UNIX operating system through the "four-year effect." When the UNIX operating system became widely available in 1975, Bell Labs offered it to educational institutions at nominal cost. The schools, in turn, used it in their computer science programs, ensuring that computer science students became familiar with it. Because UNIX is such an advanced development system, the students became acclimated to a sophisticated programming environment. As these students graduated and went into industry, they expected to work in a similarly advanced environment. As more of these students worked their way up in the commercial world, the UNIX operating system found its way into industry.

In addition to introducing students to the UNIX operating system, the Computer Systems Research Group (CSRG) at the University of California at Berkeley made significant additions and changes to it. They made so many popular changes that one of the versions of the system is called the Berkeley Software Distribution (BSD) of the UNIX system (or just Berkeley UNIX). The other major version is UNIX System V, which descended from versions developed and maintained by AT&T and UNIX System Laboratories.

What Is So Good about GNU/Linux?

In recent years GNU/Linux has emerged as a powerful and innovative UNIX work-alike. Its popularity is surpassing that of its UNIX predecessors. Although it mimics UNIX in many ways, the GNU/Linux operating system departs from UNIX in several significant ways: The Linux kernel is implemented independently of both BSD and System V, the continuing development of GNU/Linux is taking place through the combined efforts of many capable individuals throughout the world, and GNU/Linux puts the power of UNIX within easy reach of business and personal computer users. Today, skilled programmers submit, over the Internet, additions and improvements to the operating system to Linus Torvalds, GNU, or one of the other authors of GNU/Linux.

A rich selection of applications is available for GNU/Linux—both free and commercial, as well as a wide variety of tools: graphical, word processing, networking, security, administration, Web server, and many others. Large software companies have recently seen the benefit in supporting GNU/Linux and have programmers on staff whose job it is to design and code the Linux kernel, GNU, KDE, or other software that runs on GNU/Linux. GNU/Linux conforms more and more closely to POSIX standards, and some distributions and parts of others meet this standard. See "Standards" on page 10 and Appendix D on page 1427 for more information. These facts mean that GNU/Linux is becoming more and more mainstream and is respected as an attractive alternative to other popular operating systems.

Another aspect of GNU/Linux that is appealing to users is the amazing breadth of peripherals that are supported and the speed with which new peripherals are supported.

Frequently GNU/Linux supports a peripheral or interface board before any company does. Also important to users is the amount of software that is available—not just source code (which needs to be compiled) but also prebuilt binaries that are easy to install and ready to run. These include more than free software—Netscape has been available for GNU/Linux from the start and included Java support before it was available from many commercial vendors. Now its sibling, Mozilla, is also a viable browser, mail client, newsreader, performing many other functions as well.

GNU/Linux is not just for Intel-based platforms but has been ported to and runs on the Power PC—including Apples (MkLinux), the Compaq (nee DEC) Alpha-based machines, MIPS-based machines, Motorola 68K-based machines, and IBM S/390. Nor is GNU/Linux just for single-processor machines: As of version 2.0 it runs on multiple processor machines (SMPs).

Finally, GNU/Linux supports programs, called *emulators*, that run code intended for other operating systems. By using emulators you can run some DOS, MS Windows, and MacIntosh programs under GNU/Linux.

Why GNU/Linux Is Popular with Hardware Companies and Developers

Two trends in the computer industry set the stage for the popularity of UNIX and GNU/Linux. First, advances in hardware technology created the need for an operating system that could take advantage of available hardware power. In the mid-1970s minicomputers began challenging the large mainframe computers because, in many applications, minicomputers could perform the same functions less expensively. More recently powerful 64-bit processor chips, plentiful and inexpensive memory, and lower-priced hard-disk storage have allowed hardware companies to install multiuser operating systems on desktop computers.

Second, with the cost of hardware continually dropping, hardware manufacturers can no longer afford to develop and support proprietary operating systems. A *proprietary* operating system used to be written and owned by the manufacturer of the hardware (for example, DEC/Compaq owns VMS). Manufacturers need a generic operating system that they can easily adapt to their machines. A *generic* operating system is written outside of the company manufacturing the hardware and is sold (UNIX, MS Windows) or given (GNU/Linux) to the manufacturer. GNU/Linux is a generic operating system because it runs on different types of hardware produced by different manufacturers. Of course, if a manufacturer can pay only for development and avoid per unit costs (as they have to pay to Microsoft for each copy of MS Windows they sell), developers are much better off. In turn, software developers need to keep the prices of their products down; they cannot afford to convert their products to run under many different proprietary operating systems. Like hardware manufacturers, software developers need a generic operating system.

Although the UNIX system once met the needs of hardware companies and researchers for a generic operating system, over time it has become more proprietary as each manufacturer adds support for specialized features and introduces new software libraries and utilities.

GNU/Linux has emerged to serve both needs. It is a generic operating system that takes advantage of available hardware power.

GNU/Linux Is Portable

A *portable* operating system is one that can run on many different machines. More than 95 percent of the GNU/Linux operating system is written in the C programming language, and C is portable because it is written in a higher-level, machine-independent language. (The C compiler is written in C.)

Because GNU/Linux is portable, it can be adapted (ported) to different machines and can meet special requirements. For example, GNU/Linux is used in embedded computers, such as the ones found in the cable box on top of many TVs. The file structure takes full advantage of large, fast hard disks. Equally important, GNU/Linux was originally designed as a multiuser operating system—it was not modified to serve several users as an afterthought. Sharing the computer's power among many users and giving them the ability to share data and programs are central features of the system.

Because it is adaptable and takes advantage of available hardware, GNU/Linux now runs on many different microprocessor-based systems as well as mainframes. The popularity of the microprocessor-based hardware drives GNU/Linux; these microcomputers are getting faster all the time, at about the same price point. GNU/Linux on a fast microcomputer has become good enough to displace workstations on many desktops. And the microcomputer marketplace is totally different from the workstation and mainframe marketplaces. GNU/Linux also benefits both the users, who do not like having to learn a new operating system for each vendor's hardware, and the system administrators, who like having a consistent software environment.

The advent of a standard operating system has aided the development of the software industry. Now software manufacturers can afford to make one version of a product available on machines from different manufacturers.

Standards

Individuals from companies throughout the computer industry have joined together to develop a standard named POSIX (Portable Operating System Interface for Computer Environments), which is based largely on the UNIX System V Interface

Definition (SVID) and other earlier standardization efforts. These efforts have been spurred by the U.S. government, which needs a standard computing environment to minimize training and procurement costs. Now that these standards are gaining acceptance, software developers are able to develop applications that run on all conforming versions of UNIX, GNU/Linux, and other operating systems. Refer to Appendix D for more information on POSIX.

The C Programming Language

More than 95 percent of the GNU/Linux operating system is written in C. Ken Thompson wrote the UNIX operating system in 1969 in PDP-7 assembly language. Assembly language is machine-dependent: Programs written in assembly language work on only one machine or, at best, one family of machines. Therefore, the original UNIX operating system could not easily be transported to run on other machines (it was not portable).

To make UNIX portable, Thompson developed the B programming language, a machine-independent language, from the BCPL language. Dennis Ritchie developed the C programming language by modifying B and, with Thompson, rewrote UNIX in C in 1973. After this rewrite the operating system could be transported more easily to run on other machines.

That was the start of C. You can see in its roots some of the reasons why it is such a powerful tool. C can be used to write machine-independent programs. A programmer who designs a program to be portable can easily move it to any computer that has a C compiler. C is also designed to compile into very efficient code. With the advent of C, a programmer no longer had to resort to assembly language to get code that would run well (that is, quickly, although an assembler will always generate more efficient code than a high-level language).

C is a good systems language. You can write a compiler or an operating system in C. It is highly structured, but it is not necessarily a high-level language. C allows a programmer to manipulate bits and bytes, as is necessary when writing an operating system. But it also has high-level constructs that allow efficient, modular programming.

In the late 1980s a standards organization, the American National Standards Institute (ANSI), defined a standard version of the C language, commonly referred to as *ANSI C*. The original version of the language is often referred to as *Kernighan & Ritchie* (or *K&R*) C, named for the authors of the book that first described the C language. Another researcher at Bell Labs, Bjarne Stroustrup, created an object-oriented programming language named C++, which is built on the foundation of C. Because object-oriented programming is desired by many employers today, C++ is preferred over C in many environments. The GNU project's C compiler (named gcc), and its C++ compiler (g++) are integral parts of the GNU/Linux operating system.

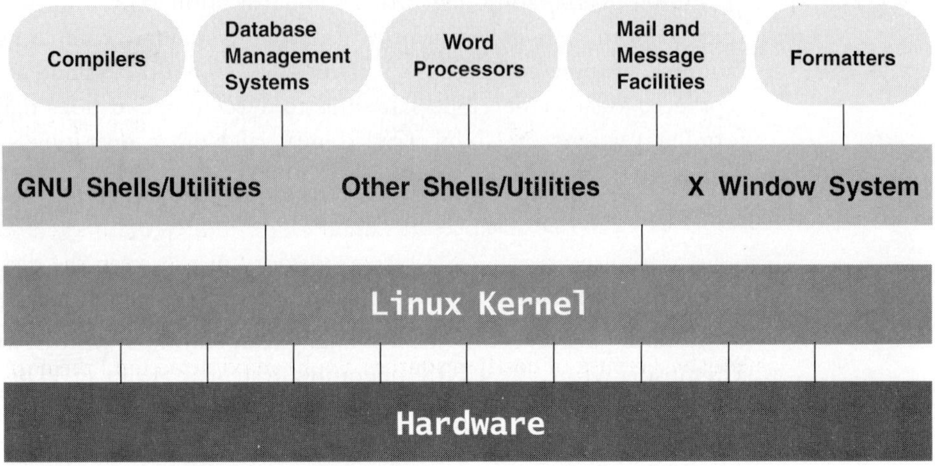

Figure 1-1   A layered view of the GNU/Linux operating system

Overview of GNU/Linux

The GNU/Linux operating system has many unique and powerful features. Like other operating systems, GNU/Linux is a control program for computers. But like UNIX, it is also a well-thought-out family of utility programs (Figure 1-1) and a set of tools allowing users to connect and use these utilities to build systems and applications.

Linux Has a Kernel Programming Interface

The Linux kernel, the heart of the GNU/Linux operating system, is responsible for allocating the computer's resources and scheduling user jobs so that each one gets its fair share of system resources, including access to the CPU; peripheral devices, such as disk and CD-ROM storage; printers; and tape drives. Programs interact with the kernel through *system calls*, special functions with well-known names. A programmer can use a single system call to interact with many kinds of devices. For example, there is one **write** system call, not many device-specific ones. When a program issues a **write** request, the kernel interprets the context and passes the request to the appropriate device. This flexibility allows old utilities to work with devices that did not exist when the utilities were originally written, and it makes it possible to move programs to new versions of the operating system without rewriting them (provided that the new version recognizes the same system calls).

GNU/Linux Can Support Many Users

Depending on the hardware and what types of tasks the computer performs, a GNU/Linux system can support from 1 to more than 1000 users, each concurrently running a different set of programs. The cost of a computer that can be used by many people at the same time is less per user than that of a computer that can be used by only a single person at a time. The cost is less because one person cannot generally use all the resources a computer has to offer. No one can keep the printers going constantly, keep all the system memory in use, keep the disks busy reading and writing, keep the modems in use, and keep the terminals busy. A multiuser operating system allows many people to use all the system resources almost simultaneously. The use of costly resources can be maximized, and the cost per user can be minimized. These are the primary objectives of a multiuser operating system.

GNU/Linux Can Run Many Tasks

GNU/Linux is a fully protected multitasking operating system, allowing each user to run more than one job at a time. Although processes can communicate with one another, they are also fully protected from one another, just as the kernel is protected from all processes. You can run several jobs in the background while giving all your attention to the job being displayed on your screen, and you can switch back and forth between jobs. If you are running the X Window System (page 17), you can run different programs in different windows on the same screen and watch all of them. With this capability, users can be more productive.

GNU/Linux Provides a Secure Hierarchical Filesystem

A *file* is a collection of information, such as text for a memo or report, an accumulation of sales figures, an image, or an executable program created by a compiler. Each file is stored under a unique identifier on a storage device, such as a hard disk. The GNU/Linux filesystem provides a structure whereby files are arranged under *directories*, which are like folders, or boxes. Each directory has a name and can hold other files and directories. Directories in turn are arranged under other directories, and so forth, in a treelike organization. This structure helps users keep track of large numbers of files by grouping related files into directories. Each user has one primary directory and as many subdirectories as required (Figure 1-2).

With the idea of making it easier for system administrators and software developers, a group got together over the Internet and developed the Linux Filesystem Standard (FSSTND), which has evolved into the Linux Filesystem Hierarchy Standard (FHS). Before this standard was adopted, key programs were located in different

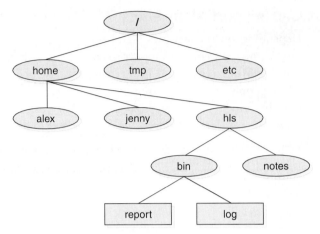

Figure 1-2   The GNU/Linux filesystem structure

places in different GNU/Linux distributions. Today you can sit down at a GNU/Linux machine and know where to expect to find any given standard program (page 112).

Another mechanism, *linking*, allows a given file to be accessed by means of two or more different names. The alternative names can be located in the same directory as the original file or in another directory. Links can be used to make the same file appear in several users' directories, enabling them to share the file easily. MS Windows uses the term *shortcut* in place of *link*.

As with most multiuser operating systems, GNU/Linux allows users to protect their data from access by other users. GNU/Linux also allows users to share selected data and programs with certain other users by means of a simple but effective protection scheme. This level of security is provided by file access permissions which limit which users can read from, write to, or execute a file.

The Shell: Command Interpreter and Programming Language

The shell is a command interpreter that acts as an interface between you and the operating system. When you enter a command at a terminal, the shell interprets the command and calls the program you want. A number of shells are available for GNU/Linux; the three most popular ones are

- The Bourne Again Shell (bash), which is an enhanced version of the Bourne Shell, one of the original UNIX shells

- The TC Shell (tcsh), which is an enhanced version of the C Shell, developed as part of Berkeley UNIX

- The Z Shell (zsh), which incorporates features from a number of shells, including the Korn Shell

Because users often prefer different shells, multiuser systems can have a number of different shells in use at any given time. The choice of shells demonstrates one of the powers of the GNU/Linux operating system: the ability to provide a customized user interface.

Besides its function of interpreting commands from a terminal or workstation keyboard and sending them to the operating system, the shell is a high-level programming language. Shell commands can be arranged in a file for later execution (DOS and MS Windows call this a *batch* file). This flexibility allows users to perform complex operations with relative ease, often with rather short commands, or to build elaborate programs that perform highly complex operations with surprisingly little effort.

Filename Generation

When you are typing commands to be processed by the shell, you can construct patterns using characters that have special meanings to the shell. These patterns are a kind of shorthand: Rather than typing in complete filenames, users can type in patterns, and the shell expands them into matching filenames. A pattern can save you the effort of typing in a long filename or a long series of similar filenames. Patterns can also be useful when you know only part of a filename or cannot remember the exact spelling.

Device-Independent Input and Output

Devices (such as a printer or terminal) and disk files all appear as files to GNU/Linux programs. When you give the GNU/Linux operating system a command, you can instruct it to send the output to any one of several devices or files. This diversion is called output *redirection*.

In a similar manner a program's input that normally comes from a terminal can be redirected so that it comes from a disk file instead. Input and output are *device independent*; they can be redirected to or from any appropriate device.

As an example, the cat utility normally displays the contents of a file on the terminal screen. When you run a cat command, you can easily cause its output to go to a disk file instead of to the terminal.

Shell Functions

One of the most important features of the shell is that users can use it as a programming language. Because the shell is an interpreter, it does not compile programs written for it but interprets them each time they are loaded in from the disk. Loading and interpreting programs can be time-consuming.

Many shells, including bash and zsh, include shell functions that the shell holds in memory so it does not have to read them from the disk each time you want to execute them. The shell also keeps functions in an internal format so it does not have to spend as much time interpreting them.

Job Control

Job control is a shell feature that allows users to work on several jobs at once, switching back and forth between them as desired. When you start a job, it is frequently in the foreground, so it is connected to your terminal. Using job control, you can move the job you are working with into the background and continue running it there while working on or observing another job in the foreground. If a background job needs your attention, you can move it into the foreground so it is once again attached to your terminal. The concept of job control originated with Berkeley UNIX, where it appeared in the C Shell.

A Large Collection of Useful Utilities

GNU/Linux includes a family of several hundred utility programs, often referred to as *commands*. These utilities perform functions that are universally required by users. An example is sort. The sort utility puts lists (or groups of lists) in alphabetical or numerical order and thus can be used to sort by part number, last name, city, zip code, telephone number, age, size, cost, and so forth. The sort utility is an important programming tool and is part of the standard GNU/Linux system. Other utilities allow users to create, display, print, copy, search, and delete files, as well as to edit, format, and typeset text. The man (for manual) and info utilities provide online documentation of GNU/Linux itself.

Interprocess Communication

GNU/Linux allows users to establish both pipes and filters on the command line. A *pipe* sends the output of one program to another program as input. A *filter* is a special form of a pipe that processes a stream of input data to yield a stream of output data. A filter processes another program's output, altering it. The filter's output then becomes input to another program.

Pipes and filters frequently join utilities to perform a specific task. For example, you can use a pipe to send the output of the cat utility to sort, a filter, and then use another pipe to send the output of sort to a third utility, lpr, that sends the data to a printer. Thus in one command line you can use three utilities together to sort and print a file.

System Administration

The system administrator, who on a GNU/Linux system is frequently the owner and only user of the system, has many responsibilities. The first responsibility may be to set up the system and install the software. *This book does not discuss specific system installation* but does cover the topic in general.

Once the system is up and running, the system administrator is responsible for downloading and installing software (including upgrading the operating system), backing up and restoring files, and managing such system facilities as printers and terminal ports. The system administrator is also responsible for setting up accounts for new users on a multiuser system, bringing the system up and down as needed, and taking care of any problems that arise. This book *does* cover postinstallation system administration in Chapter 17 and throughout the book.

Additional Features of GNU/Linux

The developers picked features from both BSD and System V, as well as features developed by Sun Microsystems for its versions of UNIX. Also, features not found in any previous version of UNIX were added to GNU/Linux. Finally, although most of the tools found on UNIX exist for GNU/Linux, in many cases these tools have been replaced by more modern counterparts. The following sections describe many of the popular tools and features available under GNU/Linux.

GUI: Graphical User Interfaces

The X Window System, also called X, was developed in part by researchers at the Massachusetts Institute of Technology and provides the foundation for the GUIs available with GNU/Linux. Given a terminal or workstation screen that supports X, a user can interact with the computer through multiple windows on the screen, display graphical information, or use special-purpose applications to draw pictures, monitor processes, or preview typesetter output. X is an across-the-network protocol that allows a user to open a window on a workstation or computer system that is remote from the CPU generating the window.

Usually two layers run under X: a desktop manager and a window manager. A *desktop manager* is a picture-oriented user interface that enables you to interact with system programs by manipulating icons instead of typing the corresponding commands to a shell. Red Hat includes GNOME (Figure 1-3) and KDE.

A *window manager* is a program that runs under the desktop manager and allows you to open and close windows, start programs running, and set up a mouse so it does various things, depending on how and where you click. It is the window manager that gives your screen its personality. Microsoft Windows allows you to change the color of key elements in a window, but a window manager under X allows you to change the overall look and feel of your screen: change the way a window looks and works (you can give a window different borders, buttons, and scrollbars), set up virtual desktops, create menus, and more.

Figure 1-3   A GNOME workspace

Several popular window managers run under X and GNU/Linux. Red Hat gives you a choice of window managers: Metacity (default under GNOME), kwin (default under KDE), Sawfish, and WindowMaker. Chapters 6 through 8 have more information on GUIs.

(Inter)networking Utilities

GNU/Linux network support includes many valuable utilities that enable users to access remote systems over a variety of networks. Besides giving you the ability to send e-mail to users on other machines, you can access files on disks mounted on other computers as if they were located on your machine, make your files available to other computers in a similar manner, copy files back and forth, run programs on remote machines while displaying the results on your local machine, and perform many other operations across local area networks (LANs) and wide area networks (WANs), including the Internet.

Layered on top of this network access is a wide range of application programs that extend the computer's resources around the globe. You can carry on conversations with people throughout the world, gather information on a wide variety of subjects, and download new software over the Internet quickly and reliably. Chapter 9 gives more information on using the network facilities of GNU/Linux.

Software Development

One of the strengths of GNU/Linux is its rich software development environment. You can find compilers and interpreters for many computer languages. Besides C and C++, other languages available for GNU/Linux are Ada, Fortran, Java, Lisp, Pascal, Perl, Python, and many others. The bison utility generates parsing code that makes it easier to write programs to build compilers (tools that parse files containing structured information), whereas flex generates scanners, code that recognizes lexical patterns in text. The make utility and GNU's automatic configuration utility (configure) make it easy to manage complex development projects; source code management systems, such as RCS and CVS, simplify version control. Several debuggers, including ups and gdb, help in tracking down and repairing software defects. The GNU C compiler (gcc) works with the gprof profiling utility to let programmers determine where potential bottlenecks are in a program's performance. The C compiler includes options to perform extensive checking of C code that can make the code more portable and reduce debugging time. These and other software development tools are discussed in Chapter 16 and are described in detail in Part III.

Text-Based Editors

Full-screen-oriented text-based editors (for example, vi, emacs, pico) are an advance over their line-oriented predecessors (ed, teco). A screen-oriented editor displays a context for editing; where ed displayed a line at a time, vi displays a screen of text. The xcoral utility uses multiple X windows.

This book starts by teaching you to create and edit files by using pico (page 49). Because the pico editor is easier to learn than vi or emacs, it allows you to work with files in the process of learning GNU/Linux without getting bogged down in the specifics of a more complex editor. Chapter 8 explains how to use vi in stages, from a tutorial introduction (page 414) through "Advanced Editing Techniques" (page 455). Chapter 9 is dedicated to emacs, the do-everything editor written by Richard Stallman.

GUI Editors

The GNU/Linux environment provides many graphical editors to choose from: some free and some commercial. Some stand alone, whereas others are part of extensive suites of office applications. A few of these editors are AbiWord, Applixware Office, KOffice, OpenOffice, Xcoral, and WordPerfect. See Table on page 1401 for more details.

Electronic Mail

Choosing a mail program is largely a matter of personal preference. This book focuses on pine because of its free licensing, popularity, availability, stability, and ease of use, providing tutorials on using pine as a mail program (page 88) and a news reader (page 401). Mozilla is also popular yet more powerful (and complex) than pine. Mozilla is free and similar to Netscape because of its origin and close connection to Netscape.

Many other mail programs are available for GNU/Linux, both with graphical and text-based interfaces. Popular mail programs are mail, xmh, exmh, elm, mutt, emumail, twig, basilix, squirrelmail, imp, and mail through emacs.

Chapter Summary

The GNU/Linux operating system grew out of the UNIX heritage to become a popular alternative to traditional systems (that is, MS Windows) available for microcomputer (PC) hardware. UNIX system users will find a familiar environment in GNU/Linux; at least one version has been POSIX certified. Distributions of GNU/Linux contain the expected complement of UNIX utilities, contributed by programmers around the world, including the set of tools developed as part of the GNU project. The GNU/Linux community is committed to the continued development of the system. Support for new microcomputer devices and features is added soon after the hardware becomes available, and the tools available on GNU/Linux continue to be refined. With many commercial software packages available to run on GNU/Linux platforms and many hardware manufacturers offering it on their systems, it is clear that the system has evolved well beyond its origin as an undergraduate project to become an operating system of choice for academic, commercial, professional, and personal use.

Exercises

1. What is *free software?* List three characteristics of free software.

2. Why is GNU/Linux popular? Why is it popular in academia?

3. What are multiuser systems? Why are they successful?

4. What is the Free Software Foundation/GNU? Linux? Which parts of the GNU/Linux operating system did each provide? Who else has helped build and refine this operating system?

5. In what language is GNU/Linux written? What does the language have to do with the success of GNU/Linux?

6. What is a utility program?

7. What is a shell? How does it work with the kernel? With the user?

8. How can you use utility programs and a shell to create your own applications?

9. Why is the GNU/Linux filesystem referred to as *hierarchical?*

10. What is the difference between a multiprocessor and a multiprocessing system?

11. Give an example of when you would want to use a multiprocessing system.

12. How many people wrote GNU/Linux (approximately)? Why is this unique?

13. Who owns GNU/Linux? What are the key terms of the GNU General Public License?

14. Your system has a utility named cut. Find out what it does, and give an example of how you might use it.

IN THIS CHAPTER

Getting Started 2

This chapter gets you started using Red Hat Linux. Read this chapter in front of a computer running GNU/Linux so that you can experiment as you read. If you are using a *GUI* (page 1469), you will need to use a terminal emulator to run many of the examples. Refer to "Graphical versus Character-Based Interface" on page 28. If you are familiar with the items in the "In This Chapter," you may want to skip this chapter or skim through it.

This chapter leads you through a session with GNU/Linux and covers two utilities that you can use to get help with GNU/Linux commands: man (or xman), which displays the online manual, and GNU info, which displays different/additional information about commands. Next is a tutorial on pico, a compact, easy-to-use text editor. Finally, this chapter introduces other utilities that manipulate files and describes how to find additional documentation on the machine you are using, on the Red Hat Documentation disk, and on the Internet.

This Book Does Not Cover Red Hat Linux Hardware or Installation || tip

This book does not discuss hardware selection; nor does it go into detail about the installation of GNU/Linux. Refer to page 905 for a limited discussion about installing GNU/Linux. Refer to the Red Hat Installation manual (www.redhat.com/docs/manuals/linux) for more information.

Before You Start

The best way to learn is by doing. You can read and use Chapters 2 through 17 while you are sitting in front of a screen and keyboard attached to a system running GNU/Linux. Learn about GNU/Linux by running the examples in this book and by making up your own examples. Feel free to experiment with various utilities. The worst thing that you can do is erase one of the files that you have created, but because these are only practice files, you can easily create others.

The source code for GNU/Linux and many GNU/Linux applications is free; Red Hat Linux is available on CD-ROM from Red Hat and other sources (such as the ones in this book) and from the Internet.

Conventions

This book uses conventions to make its explanations shorter and clearer. The following paragraphs describe these conventions.

Text and Examples

The text is set in this type, whereas examples are shown in a `monospaced font` (also called a *fixed-width* font) either within a text line or between paragraphs as follows:

```
$ cat practice
This is a small file that I created
with a text editor.
```

See the next section for a discussion of why part of the first line is in boldface.

Items You Enter

Everything that you enter at the keyboard is printed in boldface: Within the text, **this bold typeface** is used; within examples and screens, **this one** is used. See the previous section for an example: In the first line the dollar sign ($) is a prompt that GNU/Linux displays, so it is not bold; the remainder of the first line is entered by a user, so it is in boldface.

See the first line of Figure 2-1 on page 30 for another example. The word `login:` is displayed by GNU/Linux and therefore is not bold. The word **jenny** is bold to show that the user entered it and it would appear as **jenny** within the text.

Utility Names

Names of utilities are printed in this bold sans serif typeface. This book references the emacs editor, the ls utility or ls command (or just ls) but instructs you to enter **ls –a** on the command line. The text distinguishes between utilities, which are programs, and the instructions you give on the command line to invoke the utilities.

Filenames

Filenames appear in the text font but in **bold**. Examples are **memo5, letter.1283,** and **reports**. Filenames may include upper- and lowercase letters; however, GNU/Linux is *case sensitive* (page 1459), so **memo5, MEMO5,** and **Memo5** name three different files.

Characters and Character Strings

Within the text, characters and character strings are marked by putting them in a `monospaced font`. This convention avoids the need for quotation marks or other delimiters to surround a string. An example is the following string, which is displayed by the `passwd` utility: `Sorry, passwords do not match`.

Buttons and Labels

In the sections of the book that describe a GUI (graphical user interface), you will see words in a display typeface. This font indicates that you can click your mouse on these words where they appear on the screen or on a button with this name.

Keys and Characters

This book uses SMALL CAPS for three kinds of items:

- Important keyboard keys, such as the SPACE bar and the RETURN,[1] ESCAPE, and TAB keys.

- The characters that keys generate, such as the SPACEs generated by the SPACE bar.

- Keyboard keys that you press with the CONTROL key, such as CONTROL-D. (Even though D is shown as an uppercase letter, you do not have to press the SHIFT key; enter CONTROL-D by holding the CONTROL key down and pressing **d**.)

---

1. Different keyboards use different keys to move the *cursor* (page 1463) to the beginning of the next line. This book always refers to the key that ends a line as the RETURN key. Your keyboard may have a RET, NEWLINE, Enter, RETURN, or other key. Some keyboards have a key with a bent arrow on it. (The key with the bent arrow is not an arrow key. Arrow keys have straight shafts.) Use the corresponding key on your keyboard each time this book asks you to press RETURN.

Shell Specifier

This book covers three shells: the Bourne Again Shell (bash), the TC Shell (tcsh), and the Z Shell (zsh). The book discusses shell builtin programs, shell variables, and shell functionality, each of which is specific to one or more of the three shells. Where appropriate, these items are followed by a small rectangle containing the names of the shells the item is available in. For example, the box 〔bash tcsh zsh〕 means that the item preceding the box is available in bash, tcsh, and zsh. In Chapter 15, covering zsh, the box in the following sentence means that the readonly builtin is available in both bash and zsh: "You can use the readonly builtin 〔bash zsh〕 in place of **typeset –r**."

Prompts and RETURNs

Most examples include the *shell prompt*—the signal that GNU/Linux is waiting for a command—as a dollar sign ($) or sometimes a percent sign (%). The prompt is not in boldface, because you do not enter it. Do not enter the prompt on the keyboard when you are experimenting with examples from this book. If you do, the examples will not work.

Examples *omit* the RETURN keystroke that you must use to execute them. An example of a command line is

```
$ pico memo.1204
```

To use this example as a model for running the pico editor, type **pico memo.1204** and then press the RETURN key. (Press CONTROL-X to exit from pico.) This method of entering commands makes the examples in the book correspond to what appears on your screen.

Menu Selection Path

The menu selection path is the name of the menu or where the menu is located, followed by a colon, a SPACE, and the menu selection(s) separated by ⇨s. The whole menu selection path is in display type. You can read Konqueror: Tools⇨Find as "From the Konqueror menubar select Tools and from Tools select Find."

Definitions

All entries marked with FOLDOC are courtesy of Denis Howe, editor, the Free Online Dictionary of Computing (www.foldoc.org) and are used with permission. This site is an ongoing work containing not just definitions but also anecdotes and trivia. (Denis always needs help. Contact him through the site if this type of project interests you.)

Optional

Optional Information

Passages marked as optional are not central to the concepts presented in the chapter but often involve more challenging concepts. A good strategy when reading a chapter is to skip the optional sections and then return to them after you are comfortable with the main ideas presented in the chapter. This is an optional paragraph (and if you are not reading it, . . .).

URLs (Web Addresses)

Web addresses, or URLs, have an implicit `http://` prefix unless `ftp://` or `https://` is shown. You do not normally need to specify a prefix when the prefix is `http://`, but you must use a prefix from a browser when you specify an FTP or secure HTTP site. The result is that you can specify a URL in a browser exactly as this book specifies it.

As an example, the following sentence appears later in this chapter: "Red Hat has many **mailing lists** that you can subscribe to (https://listman.redhat.com) and mailing list archives that you can review (www.redhat.com/mailing-lists)." You must enter the `https://` prefix before the name of the Web page in the first URL but there is no need to enter a prefix with the second URL.

Tip, Caution, and Security Boxes

The following boxes highlight information that may be helpful while you are using or administrating your GNU/Linux system.

This Is a Tip Box || tip

A tip box may help keep you from repeating a common mistake or may point you toward additional information.

This Box Warns You about Something || caution

A caution box warns you about a potential pitfall ahead.

This Box Marks a Security Note || security

A security box marks a potential security issue. These notes are usually for system administrators, but some apply to all users.

Graphical versus Character-Based Interface

When you work with a GNU/Linux system, you will work with a *character-based* interface (page 1459) or a GUI (page 1469). When you log in on the *system console* (page 1496), you can usually use a GUI and can always use a character-based interface. When you are not on the system console, your ability to use a GUI depends on the hardware and the connection. You can always open a terminal emulator window (page 35) to run a character-based interface on a GUI. The following sections explain how to log in on each type of interface.

GUI? Use a Terminal Emulator to Run Command Line Examples || tip

Except for Chapters 6, GNOME Desktop Manager, and 8, which discuss GUIs, most of the examples in this book work with a character-based/command line interface. When you work within a GUI, you can run all the character-based examples from a terminal emulator window (page 35), which presents you with a character-based interface within a GUI.

Whenever this book refers to a character-based interface, you can use a terminal emulator window.

Red Hat Linux

This section leads you through a brief session using Red Hat Linux, explaining how to log in, change your password, and log out.

Always Use a Password || security

Unless you are the only user of your system, your system is not connected to any other systems, the Internet, or a modem, and you are the only one with physical access to your system, it is a bad idea to allow any user to log in without a password.

Keep Your Password Secure

Enter your password in response to the `Password:` prompt, and then press RETURN as the user has done in Figure 2-1. For security the characters you enter do not appear on the screen. For more information refer to "`passwd`: Changes Your Password" on page 40.

Logging In

Before you can work with a GNU/Linux, system you must log in on a computer. Because multiple users can (and some people may not be permitted to) log in on a GNU/Linux system, you must identify yourself before GNU/Linux allows you to give it commands. In order to log in, you must provide your user name and usually your password.

Chapter 17 Covers System Administration

When you are running on a system you are administrating, that is, you are responsible for setting up users (such as yourself), making backups, and have other administrative responsibilities, refer to Chapter 17. Specifically see the introductory paragraphs starting on page 895.

Once your system is up and running, GNU/Linux presents you with a GUI login window or a character-based login prompt. Figure 2-1 shows a character-based login. Figure 2-2 on page 31 shows a GUI login window with a welcome message in the middle of the screen. You may be able or want to use either of the interfaces. Table 2-1 lists how to bring up the display you want.

Character-Based Interface

(Skip to "GUI: Graphical User Interface" on page 31 if you are using a GUI.)

Figure 2-1 shows what a typical character-based login procedure looks like. Your login screen may look different. If you are using a *terminal* (page 1497) and your screen does not display the word `login:`, check whether the terminal is plugged in and turned on, and then press the RETURN key a few times. If `login:` still does not appear, try pressing CONTROL-Q. If you are using a *workstation* (page 1502), make sure it is running. Run ssh (page 374), telnet (page 35), or whatever communications/emulation software you have to log in on the system.

In Figure 2-1 the line that starts with bravo shows the GNU/Linux `login:` prompt followed by the user's response. Jenny enters **jenny**, her *login name* (also

```
Red Hat Linux release 8.0 (Psyche)
Kernel 2.4.18-17.8.0 on an i686

bravo login: jenny
Password:
Last login: Wed Sep 25 17:20:08 from lightning
You have mail.
[jenny@bravo jenny]$
```

Figure 2-1   A typical login sequence on a character-based terminal

Get the Display You Want		‖ table 2-1
Display You Have	**Display You Want**	**What to Do**
Graphical	Graphical	Log in (page 31).
Graphical	Character-based	Log in and use a terminal emulator (page 35) or switch to another virtual console (on the console only—page 36) and log in on the character-based display.
Character-based	Character-based	Log in.
Character-based	Graphical	Log in and run **startx**. Refer to "Bringing a GUI up from a Character-Based Display" on page 33.

called her *username*), and a RETURN. The next line of Figure 2-1 shows the Password: prompt. The system never displays passwords, so no one can steal your password by looking at your screen. Try logging in, making sure that you enter your login name as it was specified when your account was set up; the routine that verifies the login name and password is case sensitive.

Next, the *shell prompt* (or just *prompt*) appears, indicating that you have successfully logged in; it indicates that the system is ready for you to give it a command. The shell prompt line may be preceded by one or two short messages called the *message of the day*, or **motd** (page 961) and *issue*. These messages generally identify the version of Red Hat Linux that is running, along with any local messages placed in either the **/etc/motd** or the **/etc/issue** file. The usual prompt is a dollar sign ($) ᵇᵃˢʰₜ꜀ₛₕ or a percent sign (%) ᵤₛₕ. Red Hat establishes a prompt of *[user@host directory]$*,

Did You Log in Last? || security

The line following the password line gives you information about the last login on this account, showing when it took place and where it originated. In Figure 2-1 the last access came from a machine named **lightning**. You can use this information to see whether anyone else may have accessed this account since you last used it. If someone has, perhaps an unauthorized user has learned your password and has logged on as you. In the interest of security, advise your system administrator of the circumstances that made you suspicious, and change your password (page 40).

where **user** is your login name, **host** is the name of your computer, and **directory** is the name of the directory you are working in. For information on how to change your prompt, refer to page 579 `bash`, page 749 `tcsh`, or page 708 `zsh`.

GUI: Graphical User Interface

When your system is set up so that you log in directly on a GUI (Figure 2-2), you will, by default, log in on the GNOME desktop manager. (The welcome message can be set locally so your message will differ from the illustration.) To log in on a different desktop manager, see "Choosing a Desktop Manager" following.

Make sure that the *text cursor* (the [blinking] thin vertical bar that indicates where the next character you type will appear) is in the text box under the word username (Figure 2-3). If necessary, position the text cursor by left clicking the mouse while the mouse pointer is in the text box.

Figure 2-2   The Red Hat login screen

Figure 2-3   The Red Hat login Session menu

Enter your user name, press RETURN, and enter your password before pressing RETURN again. Your password does not appear on the screen as you type it. Once you have logged in, you are presented with a GUI desktop session. For information on using GNOME, see Chapter GNOME Desktop Manager; for KDE see Chapter 8.

Choosing a Desktop Manager

The Login menubar at the bottom of the Red Hat login screen allows you to choose the type of session that you want to log in on. Click Login menubar: Session to display the Session menu window (Figure 2-3). After you make a selection, click OK, and log in as usual. Table 2-2 describes the choices on the Login menubar.

Optional

Even when your system supports a GUI, you do not have to log in as described here. You may find it more convenient to log in on a character-based system; you can always start the GUI after you have logged in. Under GNU/Linux you can log in on either, allowing you access to both a GUI and a non-GUI environment. When you have applications that work only in one environment or the other, it is useful to have access to both environments. When you set up one virtual console with a GUI and another with a character-based interface, it is easy to switch between them (page 36).

Red Hat/GNOME Login Menubar

|| table 2-2

Language	When you want to change the language of the window titles, prompts, error messages, and so on, select the language you want by first selecting the range containing the letter it starts with and then the language itself.
	Just after you log in, you will be asked whether you want to make this change in languages permanent or whether it is a one-time change. The language changes affect GNOME and KDE and may affect applications.
Session	
Last	The window manager you used last time you logged in.
Failsafe	Brings up an **xterm** window without a desktop manager. This setup allows you to log in on a minimal desktop in case your standard login does not work well enough to allow you to log in to fix a login problem.
Default	As shipped by Red Hat, the default is GNOME.
Window Maker	Brings up the Window Maker desktop manager (www.windowmaker.org).
GNOME	Brings up GNOME, the default desktop manager.
KDE	Brings up the KDE Desktop Environment.
System	
Shut down the computer	Shuts down the system and turns off the power if the hardware permits.
Reboot the computer	Shuts down and reboots the system.

Bringing a GUI up from a Character-Based Display

Once you have logged in on a virtual console, you can start a graphical display by giving the following command to bring up your default desktop manager:

```
$ startx
```

Refer to "GUI: Graphical User Interface" on page 31 for continuing information. If startx does not work, give one of the following commands, depending on whether GNOME or KDE is installed on your system (and when both are installed, which you want to use), and then try startx again:

```
$ switchdesk GNOME
```

or

```
$ switchdesk KDE
```

Refer to page 173 for a detailed description of how the X Window System starts up.

Incorrect Login

When you enter your username or password incorrectly, the login utility displays the following message after you finish entering both your login name *and* password on a character-based display:

```
Login incorrect
```

On a GUI you will see

```
Invalid username or password!
```

This message tells you that you have entered either the login name *or* password incorrectly or that they are not valid. The message does not differentiate between an unacceptable login name and an unacceptable password, in order to discourage unauthorized people from guessing names and passwords to gain access to the system.

See page 40 when you want to change your password.

Login Name and Password Are Case Sensitive   ‖ tip

Make sure the CAPS LOCK key is off and that you enter your name and password exactly as specified or as you set them up.

Make Sure Your Login Name Is Valid   ‖ tip

Another reason the login/password combination may not be valid is that you have not been set up as a user. If you are administrating your machine, refer to "Configuring User and Group Accounts" on page 992. Otherwise, check with the system administrator.

The Shell

Once you log in on a character-based system or open a terminal emulator window, you are communicating with the command interpreter known as the *shell*. The shell plays an important part in much of your communication with GNU/Linux. When you enter a command at the keyboard in response to the shell prompt on the screen, the shell interprets the command and initiates the appropriate action. This action may be executing your program, calling a compiler or a GNU/Linux utility or another standard program, or giving you an error message telling you that you entered a command incorrectly. When you are working on a GUI, you bypass the shell and execute a program by clicking an icon or name.

Terminal Emulation and telnet

A terminal emulator is software that produces on your screen a window that looks and acts like a character-based terminal. Because a character-based terminal uses a simpler interface than a graphical display, terminal emulators have been written for almost all computers, including Apples and PCs. Once you bring up a GUI, you can open a terminal emulator window on a graphical display (page 177).

When you do not have your own terminal, workstation, or X terminal, you are likely connected to a GNU/Linux machine, using a terminal emulator. The terminal emulator, running on your computer, connects to a GNU/Linux machine via a network (Ethernet, asynchronous phone line, PPP, or other type) and allows you to log in on the GNU/Linux machine.

Make Sure TERM Is Set Correctly | caution

No matter how you connect, make sure you have the **TERM** variable set to the type of terminal your emulator is emulating. For more help, see "Specifying Your Terminal" on page 1402.

When you log in via a dial-up line, the connection is straightforward: You instruct the emulator program to contact the computer, it dials the phone, and you get a login prompt from the remote system. When you log in via a directly connected network, you use telnet or ssh[2] (page 374) to connect to the computer. Like the terminal emulator, telnet is a program that has been implemented on many machines, not just on GNU/Linux systems. Most user interfaces to TELNET include a terminal emulator. From your Apple, PC, or UNIX machine, give the command **telnet**

---

2. The telnet utility is not secure. Use ssh if it is available.

followed by the name or IP address (a number that has four segments separated by periods; refer to "Host Address" on page 362) of the machine that you want to log in on. For examples and more detail, refer to "**telnet**: Logs in on a Remote Computer" on page 376 and "Terminal Emulator/Shell" on page 177.

Logging Out

Now try logging out and logging back in again. From GNOME, click the red hat to display the GNOME menu. Choose Logout. GNOME displays a `Really logout?` window. Choose Logout, Halt, or Reboot,[3] and click Yes. If you are using a character-based interface, press CONTROL-D $\begin{smallmatrix}\text{bash}\\\text{tcsh}\\\text{zsh}\end{smallmatrix}$, and give the command **exit** $\begin{smallmatrix}\text{bash}\\\text{zsh}\end{smallmatrix}$ or **logout** $\begin{smallmatrix}\text{tcsh}\end{smallmatrix}$ in response to the shell prompt to log out.

Superuser

While you are logged in as the user named **root**, you are referred to as *Superuser* and have extraordinary privileges. You can read from or write to any file on the system, execute programs that ordinary users cannot, and more. On a multiuser system you may not be permitted to know the **root** password, but someone, usually the *system administrator*, knows the **root** password and maintains the system. When you are running GNU/Linux on your own computer, you will assign a password to **root** when you set your system up. Refer to "System Administrator and Superuser" on page 896 for more information.

Do Not Experiment While You Are Superuser || caution

Do not experiment with the system while you are logged in as **root**. Superuser *can* do a lot of damage quite quickly and easily on a GNU/Linux system. Work as Superuser only when you have need for special permissions.

Virtual Console

When running GNU/Linux on a personal computer, you frequently work with the display and keyboard that are attached to the computer. Using this physical console

---

3. The Halt and Reboot choices appear only if you are logged in on the system console.

you can access up to 63 *virtual consoles* (also called *virtual terminals*). Some are set up to allow logins, whereas others act as X displays. You switch between virtual consoles by holding down the CONTROL and ALT keys and pressing a function key corresponding to the console you want to view. For example, CONTROL-ALT-F5 displays the fifth virtual console. This book refers to the console that you see when you first boot your computer (or press CONTROL-ALT-F1) as the *system console,* or *console.*

By default, six virtual consoles are active and have text login sessions running. When you want to use both a character-based interface and a GUI, you can set up a character-based session on one virtual console and an X session on another. Whichever virtual console you start an X (graphical) session from, the X session finds the first unused virtual console (number seven by default).

Correcting a Mistake

This section explains how to correct typos and other errors you may make while you are logged in on a character-based display. Because the shell and most other utilities do not interpret the command line or other text until after you press RETURN, you can correct typing mistakes before you press RETURN.

You can correct typing mistakes in several ways: erase one character at a time, back up a word at a time, or back up to the beginning of the command line in one step. After you press RETURN, it is too late to correct a mistake; you can either wait for the command to run to completion or abort execution of the program (page 38).

Erasing a Character

While entering characters from the keyboard, you can back up and erase a mistake by pressing the *erase key* once for each character you want to delete. The erase key backs over as many characters as you wish. It does not, in general, back up past the beginning of the line.

The default erase key is BACKSPACE. If this key does not work, try DELETE or CONTROL-H. If these keys do not work, give the following stty[4] command to set the erase and line kill (see "Delete a Line" second section following) keys to their defaults

```
$ stty ek
```

---

4. The command stty is an abbreviation for *set teletypewriter,* the first terminal that UNIX was run on. Today stty is commonly thought of as *set terminal.*

> ### CONTROL-Z **Suspends a Program** || tip
>
> Although not a way of correcting a mistake, you may press the suspend key (typically CONTROL-Z) by mistake and wonder what happened (you will see a message containing the word Stopped). You have just stopped your job, using job control (page 554). Give the command **fg** to continue your job in the foreground, and you should be back to where you were before you pressed the suspend key. Although not usual, it is possible to change the suspend key (page 1339). For more information, refer to "**bg**: Sends a Job to the Background" on page 556.

If you would like to use another key as your erase key, refer to "Examples" on page 1338. You can use any key you like, but some choices are more convenient than others.

Delete a Word

In many shells you can delete a word you entered by pressing CONTROL-W. A *word* is any sequence of characters that does not contain a SPACE or TAB. When you press CONTROL-W, the cursor moves left to the beginning of the current word (as you are entering a word) or the previous word (when you have just entered a SPACE or TAB), removing the word. The stty utility uses **werase** for controlling the character that performs this function (page 1336).

Delete a Line

Any time before you press RETURN, you can delete a line you are entering by pressing the *line kill* key, or *kill key*. When you press this key, the cursor moves to the left, erasing characters as it goes, back to the beginning of the line. The default line kill key is CONTROL-U. If this key does not work, try CONTROL-X. If these keys do not work, give the following command to set the erase and line kill keys to their defaults:

```
$ stty ek
```

If you would like to use another key as your line kill key, refer to "Examples" on page 1338.

Abort Execution

Sometimes you may want to terminate a running program. A GNU/Linux program may be performing a lengthy task such as displaying the contents of a file that is several hundred pages or copying a file that is not the one you meant to copy.

To terminate a program from a character-based display, press the *interrupt key* (CONTROL-C or sometimes DELETE or DEL). When you press this key, the GNU/Linux operating system sends a terminal interrupt signal to the program you are running and to the shell. Exactly what effect this signal has depends on the program. Some programs stop execution immediately, whereas others ignore the signal. Some programs take other actions. When it receives a terminal interrupt signal, the shell displays a prompt and waits for another command. If these keys do not work or if you would like to use another key as your interrupt key, see page 1338.

If these methods do not terminate the program, try stopping the program with the suspend key (typically CONTROL-Z), giving the **jobs** command to verify the job number of the program, and using kill to abort the program. The job number is the number within the brackets at the left end of the line that **jobs** displays ([**1**]). The **kill** command uses **–TERM** to send a termination signal[5] to the job specified by the job number, which is preceded by a percent sign (%1):

```
$ bigjob
^Z
[1]+  Stopped                 bigjob
$ jobs
[1]+  Stopped                 bigjob
$ kill -TERM %1

[1]+  Stopped                 bigjob
$ RETURN
[1]+  Killed                  bigjob
```

The **kill** command returns a prompt; press RETURN again to see the confirmation message. For more information on job control, refer to "Running a Program in the Background" on page 154.

Killing a job that is running under a GUI is straightforward. At the upper-right corner of most windows is a button with an **X** on it. Move the mouse pointer so that the its tip is over the **X**. If you leave the mouse stationary for a moment, instructions on how to kill the window appear. With the mouse pointer still over the **X**, kill the window by clicking the left mouse button. You may need to click several times.

Repeating/Editing Command Lines

To repeat a previous command, press the UP ARROW key. Each time you press it, you see an earlier command line. To reexecute the displayed command line, press RETURN. Press DOWN ARROW to browse through the command lines in the other direction.

The RIGHT and LEFT ARROW keys move you back and forth along the displayed command line. At any point along the command line, you add characters by typing them. Use the erase key to remove characters from the command line.

These instructions work for any of the three major shells. For more complex command line editing, see page 591 `bash`, page 696 `tcsh`, or page 791 `zsh`.

---

5. When the terminal interrupt signal does not work, use the kill (–KILL) signal. A running program cannot ignore kill; it is sure to abort the program (page 901).

passwd: Changes Your Password

If someone else assigned you a password, it is a good idea to give yourself a new one. A good password is seven or eight characters long and contains a combination of numbers, upper- and lowercase letters, and punctuation characters. Avoid using control characters (such as CONTROL-H) because they may have a special meaning to the system, making it impossible for you to log in. Do not use names, words from English or other languages, or other familiar words that someone can easily guess.

For security reasons none of the passwords that you enter is ever displayed by any utility.

Protect Your Password || security

Do not allow someone to find out your password: *Do not* put your password in a file that is not encrypted, allow someone to watch you type your password, give it to someone you do not know (a system administrator never needs to know your password), or write it down.

Choose a Password That Is Difficult to Guess || security

Do not use phone numbers, names of pets or kids, birthdays, words from a dictionary (not even a foreign language), and so forth. Do not use permutations of these items.

You can change your password under a GUI or character-based interface; the process under each interface is virtually the same. Under a character-based interface, use the passwd utility. Under a GUI, run passwd from a terminal emulator window.[6] Figure 2-4 shows the process of using the passwd utility to change a password.

Give the command **passwd** in response to a shell prompt. This command causes the shell to execute the passwd utility. The first item passwd asks you for is your *old* password. The passwd utility verifies this password to ensure that an unauthorized user is not trying to alter your password. Next, passwd requests the new password.

Your password should meet the following criteria to be relatively secure. Only the first item in the list is mandatory.

---

6. You can also choose K menu: Utilities⇨Change Password under KDE or GNOME menu: Utilities⇨Change Password under GNOME.

```
$ passwd
Changing password for jenny
(current) UNIX password:
New UNIX password:
Retype new password:
passwd: all authentication tokens updated successfully
$
```

Figure 2-4   The passwd utility

- It must be at least six characters long (or longer if the system administrator sets it up that way).
- It should not be a word in a dictionary of any language, no matter how seemingly obscure.
- It should not be the name of a person, place, pet, or other thing that might be discovered easily.
- It should contain at least two letters and one digit.
- It should not be your login name, the reverse of your login name, or your login name shifted by one or more characters.
- If you are changing your password, the new password should differ from the old one by at least three characters. Changing the case of a character does not make it count as a different character.

Refer to "Keeping the System Secure" on page 1070 for more information about choosing a password.

After you enter your new password, passwd asks you to retype it to make sure you did not make a mistake when you entered it the first time. If the new password is the same both times you enter it, your password is changed. If the passwords differ, it means that you made an error in one of them, and passwd displays the following message:

```
Sorry, passwords do not match
```

After you enter the new password, passwd—as it did before—asks you to re-enter it. If your password is not long enough, passwd displays the following message:

```
BAD PASSWORD: it is too short
```

When it is too simple, passwd displays this message:

```
BAD PASSWORD: it is too simplistic/systematic
```

When it is formed from words, passwd displays this message:

```
BAD PASSWORD: it is based on a dictionary word
```

Enter a longer or more complex password in response to the New password: prompt.

When you successfully change your password, you change the way you log in. You must always enter your password *exactly* the way you created it. If you forget your password, Superuser can straighten things out. Although no one can determine what your password is, Superuser can change it and tell you your new password.

Documentation

Distributions of GNU/Linux often come without hardcopy reference manuals. However, online documentation has always been one of GNU/Linux's strengths. The manual (or man) and info pages have been available via the man utility since early releases. With GNU/Linux and the advent of the Internet, the sources of documentation have expanded. The following sections discuss some of the places you can look for information on various aspects of GNU/Linux in general and Red Hat Linux in particular.

---

man and info Display Different Information || tip

The info utility (page 45) displays more complete and up-to-date information on GNU utilities than does man. When a man page displays abbreviated information on a utility that is covered by info, the man page refers you to info. The man utility frequently displays the only information on non-GNU utilities; when info displays information on non-GNU utilities, it is frequently a copy of the man page.

---

man and xman: Display the System Manual

The character-based man (manual) utility and GUI xman utility display pages, known as man pages, from the system documentation. This documentation is useful when you know what utility you want to use but have forgotten exactly how to use it. You can also refer to the man pages to get more information about specific topics while reading this book or to determine what features are available with GNU/Linux. Because the descriptions in the system documentation are often terse, they are most helpful if you already understand basically what a utility does. When a utility is new to you, the descriptions provided in this book are typically easier to understand.

To find out more about a utility, including the man utility itself, give the command **man**, followed by the name of the utility. For example, the following command displays information about the who utility:

```
$ man who
```

The command **man man** displays information on man. The man utility automatically sends the output through a *pager*, usually less (page 54), which allows you to view a file one screen at a time. When you display a manual page in this way, less displays a prompt (:) at the bottom of the screen after each screen of text and waits for you to request another screen by pressing the SPACE bar. Pressing **h** (help) displays a list of the less commands that you can use. Pressing **q** (quit) stops man and gives you a shell prompt. You can search for topics covered by man pages by using the apropos utility (page 79 or give the command **man apropos**).

Under the X Window System (running GNOME or KDE, for example), you can use xman, which provides a GUI to the manual pages. Start xman by giving the command **xman** from a terminal emulator. Use **xman&** when you want xman to run in the background (page 154) so that the shell gives you another prompt and you can use the window while xman is running. Either way, a small xman window appears. When you move the mouse pointer over and click Manual Page at the bottom of the window, xman displays a larger window, named Manual Page, that contains xman Help (Figure 2-5).

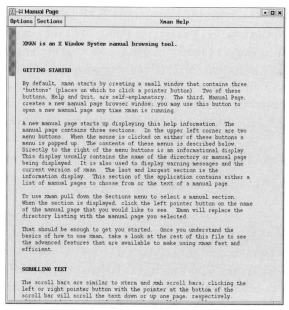

Figure 2-5   xman Help page

Other graphical tools for reading the GNU/Linux manual are the GNOME help system (page 204) and the KDE KHelpcenter (page 269). These browsers are more sophisticated than xman and include such features as the ability to move quickly from one page to another by using *hypertext* (page 1472) links.

Based on the FHS (Filesystem Hierarchy Standard, page 112), the GNU/Linux system manual and the man pages are divided into ten sections. Each section describes related tools:

1. User Commands

2. System Calls

3. Subroutines

4. Devices

5. File Formats

6. Games

7. Miscellaneous

8. System Administration

9. Local

10. New

This layout closely mimics the way the set of UNIX manuals has always been divided. Unless you specify a manual section, man displays the earliest occurrence in the manual of the word you specify on the command line. The xman utility requires that you specify the manual section you want to look in. Most users find the information they need in sections 1, 6, and 7; programmers and system administrators frequently need to consult the other sections.

In some cases there are manual entries for different tools with the same name. For example, the following command displays the manual page for the write utility (page 84) from section 1 of the system manual:

```
$ man write
```

To see the manual page for the **write** system call from section 2, enter

```
$ man 2 write
```

This command instructs man to look only in section 2 for the manual page. Use the –a option[7] (press **q** to move to the next section) to view all the man pages for a given subject; use **man –a write** to view all the man pages for write.

Figure 2-6   The first screen that info displays

info: Displays Information

The character-based info utility is a menu-based hypertext system developed by the GNU project and distributed with Red Hat Linux. You can call this utility from within the emacs editor or as a stand-alone program as described here. The info utility includes a tutorial on itself (give the command **info info** or go to www.gnu.org/manual/info/html_mono/info.html) and documentation on many GNU/Linux shells, utilities, and programs. Figure 2-6 shows the screen that info displays when you give the command **info**. Because the information on this screen is drawn from an editable file, you may see a different display. When you see the initial info screen, you can press

- **h** to go through an interactive tutorial on info
- **?** to list info commands
- SPACE to scroll through the menu of items you can get information on
- **m,** followed by the name of the menu item you want to go to
- **q** to quit

The notation that info uses to describe keyboard keys may not be familiar to you. At the bottom of Figure 2-6 are the words "C-h" for help: Hold down the CONTROL key and press **h** to get help. Similarly, M-x means hold down the META or ALT key

---

7. An option modifies the way a utility or command works. Options are specified as one or more letters that are preceded by one or two hyphens (there are exceptions). The option appears following the name of the utility you are calling and a SPACE. Any other *arguments* (page 1454) to the command follow the option and a SPACE. For more information, refer to "Options" on page 139.

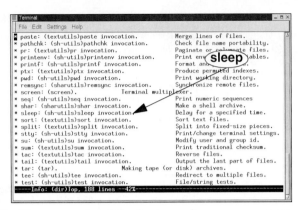

Figure 2-7   The screen that **info** displays after you press SPACE a few times

and press **x**.[8] Refer to "Keys: Notation and Use" on page 482 for more information on this notation.

After starting info, press the SPACE bar a few times to scroll the display. Figure 2-7 shows the entry for **sleep**. The asterisk at the left end of the line means that this entry is the beginning of a menu item. Following the asterisk is the name of the menu item, followed by a colon, the name of the package (in parentheses) that the menu item belongs to,[9] other information, and, on the right, a description of the item.

The name of the menu item is what you type in a menu command to view information on that item. To get information on **sleep**, give the command **m sleep**, followed by a RETURN. When you type **m** (for *menu*), the cursor moves to the bottom line of the window or screen and displays Menu item:. Typing **sleep** displays sleep on that line, and pressing RETURN takes you to the menu item you have chosen.

Figure 2-8 shows the *top node* of information on **sleep**. A node is one group of information that you can scroll through with the SPACE bar. To get to the next node, press **n**. Press **p** to get to the previous node. You can always press **d** to get to the initial menu, shown in Figure 2-6.

As you read this book and learn about new utilities, you can use man or info to find out more about the utilities. Although you may have access to a *hardcopy* (paper) GNU/Linux manual, the electronic copies are generally more up-to-date. If you can print PostScript documents, you can print a manual page with the man utility using the **–t** option (for example, **man –t echo | lpr**). Better yet, use your browser to look at the documentation on the Red Hat Documentation CD-ROM (page 48), www.redhat.com and www.tldp.org, and print the information from your browser.

---

8. On some systems you need to press ESCAPE and then **x** to duplicate the function of META-x.

9. In most cases this name corresponds to the name of the rpm package (page 928) containing the file.

Figure 2-8   The info page on the sleep utility

HOWTOs

A HOWTO document explains in detail how to do something related to GNU/Linux, from setting up a specialized piece of hardware to performing system administration to setting up specific networking software. Mini-HOWTOs offer shorter explanations. As with GNU/Linux software, one person or a few people generally are responsible for a HOWTO document, yet many people contribute to it.

The Linux Documentation Project (LDP) site houses all the HOWTO and mini-HOWTO documents. From a GUI, use your browser to go to www.tldp.org, click HOWTOs, and pick the index you want to use to find a HOWTO or mini-HOWTO. Or use the LDP search feature on its home page to find HOWTOs and more. From a character-based interface, use ftp (page 378) to open ftp.ibiblio.org and go to **/pub/Linux/docs/HOWTO** to download character-based versions of the HOWTOs.

Other Sources of Help

KDE and GNOME provide tooltips (page 182), which display context-sensitive help in a GUI environment. GNOME provides an integrated help system (page 204), and KDE provides a What's This? button (page 269), the KHelpCenter (page 269), and Help Menu selections (page 270).

Your System

The **/usr/share/doc** and **/usr/src/linux✳/Documentation**[10] directories often contain more detailed and different information about a utility than does man or info.

---

10. Only present if you installed the kernel source code.

Frequently this information is meant for people who will be compiling and modifying the utility, not just using it. These directories hold more than 500 files and directories, each containing information on a separate topic.

Red Hat Documentation CD-ROM

Unless it mounts automatically, the easiest way to work with the Red Hat Documentation CD-ROM is to mount it from a terminal emulator window with

```
$ mount /mnt/cdrom
```

Then point your browser toward **/mnt/cdrom** and click **index-*xx*.html** (*xx* is the language code, such as **en** for English). From there you can choose the manual and format you want.

Documentation CD-ROM Useful Only from GUI || tip

The files on the Red Hat Documentation CD-ROM are useful only from a GUI. They cannot be read on a character-based terminal.

You can read the Documentation CD-ROM on another system, such as MS Windows, and use the tools there to open the files. Click the **index-*xx*.html** file to get started.

Internet

The Internet provides many helpful sites. Aside from sites that carry various forms of documentation, you can enter an error message that you are having a problem with in a search engine such as Google (www.google.com). Enclose the error message within double quotation marks to improve the quality of your results. You will likely find e-mail concerning "your" problem and how to solve it.

The Red Hat Home Page

The Red Hat home page (www.redhat.com) has a wealth of information. Click Support and Docs to view a lot of online documentation specifically for Red Hat. All the manuals are online at www.redhat.com/docs.

- **Support forums** are online discussions about any Red Hat–related issues that people want to raise. One forum is dedicated to new users; others to Apache, X Window System, and so on. From the Red Hat home page, click Support and Docs and then Support Forums (upper left). Choose About these forums and then A Guide to Web Crossing for a tutorial on using the support forums.

- **Hardware help** is available by going to Support and Docs⇨ Support Resources⇨Hardware Compatibility (see the Support Links).

- Red Hat has many **mailing lists** that you can subscribe to (https://listman.redhat.com) and mailing list archives that you can review (www.redhat.com/mailing-lists).

GNU

GNU makes many of its manuals available at www.gnu.org/manual. In addition, go to the GNU home page (www.gnu.org) for more documentation and other GNU resources. Many of the GNU pages and resources are available in a wide variety of languages.

Linux Documentation Project

The Linux Documentation Project (www.tldp.org), which has been around for almost as long as GNU/Linux, houses a complete collection of guides, HOWTOs, FAQs, man pages, and GNU/Linux magazines. The home page supports English, Brazilian, Spanish, and French and is easy to use, supporting local text search. It also has a complete set of links (Figure 2-9) that can help you find almost anything you want related to GNU/Linux (click Links/Resources in the Search box or go to www.tldp.org/links). The links page has sections on general information, events, getting started, user groups, mailing lists, and newsgroups, each containing many subsections.

Tutorial: Using pico to Create/Edit a File

A file is a collection of information that you can refer to by a *filename*. A file is frequently stored on a disk. *Text* files typically contain memos, reports, messages, program source code, lists, or manuscripts. An *editor* is a utility program that allows you to create a new text file or change an existing one.

Many editors are available for Red Hat systems. These editors range from small and simple character-based text editors (pico, joe, and others) to more full-featured text editors (vi; see the tutorial on page 414) and complete working environments (emacs; see the tutorial on page 475) to GUI word processing applications that format your text (Kate, Kword, Applix, WordPerfect, AbiWord, TeX, and so on).

This section demonstrates how to use pico, an easy-to-use, interactive, visually oriented text editor, to create and edit a file. Alternatively you can start with vi (page 414) or emacs (page 475). If you are familiar with one of these or another text editor, skip over this section on pico and continue with "ls: Lists the Names of Files" on page 53.

The pico editor does not format text, center titles, or provide the output formatting features of a word processing system. The emacs editor provides some of these features, but when you want different sizes and types of fonts, you must use a word processing application.

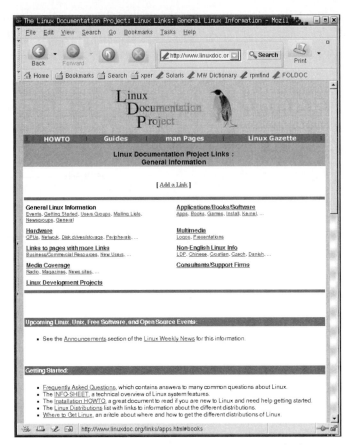

Figure 2-9   The Linux Documentation Project links page

The pico editor has a layout that is similar to that of the pine mail program (see the tutorial on page 88); both were developed at the University of Washington. The top line of the display is the status line, which shows the name of the file you are editing and the word Modified if there are changes that need to be saved. (Have you typed anything since the last save?) The third line from the bottom is the message line, which displays messages and accepts command input. The bottom two lines list the commands that you can use in the current context.

Starting pico

Give the following command to start pico so you can edit the file named **practice**:

```
$ pico practice
```

Figure 2-10 shows an X Window System window running the konsole terminal emulator (part of KDE) which is running pico. If you are working on another type of terminal or emulator, your display will be similar. If pico complains about the

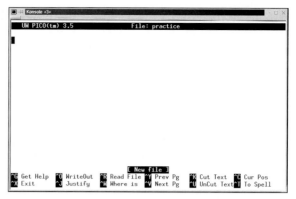

Figure 2-10   The first screen that pico displays

terminal type, your display is garbled, or the display is not stable as you use pico (words jump around or disappear), set your **TERM** variable according to the instructions in "Specifying Your Terminal" (page 1402).

The words New file on the message line indicate that you are creating a new file, not editing an existing file. These words disappear as soon as you write out the buffer (write what you can view to the disk). The name of the file that you are editing is at the center of the status line. If you do not specify a filename on the command line, pico displays New Buffer. Once you have typed something and changed the file, the word (Modified) appears to the right of the filename on the status line (Figure 2-11).

Entering Text

Now you are set: Type whatever you want to appear in the file. Press RETURN when you finish a line, or just keep typing and allow pico to put RETURNs in for you. If you notice a mistake just after you enter it, use the erase key to remove it and then retype it correctly. The section titled "Correcting Text" (page 52) contains instructions on moving the cursor and correcting other mistakes.

Figure 2-11   The screen after typing some text

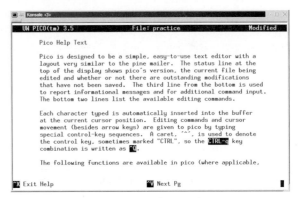

Figure 2-12   The pico Help window

Getting Help

For people who are learning how to use it or using commands they are not familiar with, one of the most useful features of pico is the Help window. Press CONTROL-G (there is a reminder at the left of the top command line at the bottom of the screen), and the Help window appears (Figure 2-12).[11] Any text you have entered is displaced by the Help window but is not lost. At the bottom of the Help window is a reminder telling you ^X Exit Help, meaning press CONTROL-X to remove the Help window and restore your text.

The Help window contains four pages of text. You move to the next page of help by pressing CONTROL-V and to the previous page with CONTROL-Y.

Correcting Text

Using the commands described in the Help window, you can move the cursor to any point in the file. Pressing CONTROL-D deletes the character under the cursor, whereas CONTROL-H or the erase key deletes characters to the left of the cursor.

You can enter new text at any point in the document. Use the ARROW keys to move the cursor to the location you want to enter new text and start typing the new text.

Ending the Session

To end your editing session, you can either save your work and exit or not save your work and exit. Normally you want to save your work. You might not want to save your work if you made some changes to an existing file and decided you liked it better as it existed before the last time you wrote out the buffer.

---

11. The commands are not case sensitive. You can enter CONTROL-G, CONTROL-g, CONTROL-X, or CONTROL-x to open or close the Help window.

Press CONTROL-X to exit from pico. You are given the option of saving the buffer to a file: **Y** saves the buffer and **N** discards it. If you choose to keep the buffer, you can then enter or change the filename that the buffer is written to.

Basic Utilities

One of the important advantages of GNU/Linux and other variants of UNIX is that they come with several hundred utilities that perform many functions. You will use utilities whenever you use GNU/Linux, whether you use them directly by name from the command line or indirectly from a menu or icon. The following sections discuss some of the most basic and important utilities that you need to know. They are available from a character-based interface. Some of the more important utilities are also available from a GUI, and some are available only from a GUI.

The term *directory* is used extensively in the next sections. A directory is a resource that can hold files. On other operating systems, including MS Windows, a directory is referred to as a folder, which is a good analogy: A directory is a folder that can hold files. When you log in on the system, you are working in a directory that is called your *home directory*. In this chapter that is the only directory you use: All the files you create in this chapter are in your home directory.

ls: Lists the Names of Files

Using the editor of your choice, create a small file named **practice** in your directory. After exiting from the editor, you can use the ls (list) utility to display a list of the names of the files in the directory. The first command in Figure 2-13 shows ls listing the name of the **practice** file. (You may also see files listed that were put there by your system administrator or automatically created by a program you ran.) Subsequent commands in Figure 2-13 display the contents of the file and remove the file. These commands are described next.

```
$ ls
practice
$ cat practice
This is a small file that I created
with a text editor.
$ rm practice
$ ls
$ cat practice
cat: practice: No such file or directory
$
```

Figure 2-13   Using ls, cat, and rm on the **practice** file

Filename Completion || tip

After you enter one or more letters of a filename on a command line, press TAB and the shell completes as much of the filename as it can. When only one filename starts with the characters you entered, the shell completes the filename and places a SPACE after it. You can keep typing or press RETURN to execute the command at this point. When the characters you entered do not uniquely identify a filename, the shell completes what it can, beeps, and waits for more input. When pressing TAB does not change the display, press TAB again to display a list of possible completions. Refer to "Completion" on page 599 **bash**, "Filename Completion" on page 693 **tcsh**, or "Pathname Completion" on page 792 **zsh**.

cat: Displays a Text File

The cat utility displays the contents of a text file. The name of the command is derived from *catenate*, which means to join together one after the other. (Figure 5-8 on page 147 shows how to use cat to string together the contents of three files.)

A convenient way to display the contents of a file to the screen is by giving the command **cat**, followed by a SPACE and the name of a file. Figure 2-13 shows cat displaying the contents of **practice**. This figure shows the difference between the ls and cat utilities. The ls utility displays the *name* of a file, whereas cat displays the *contents* of a file.

less Is more: Displaying a Text File One Screen at a Time

When you want to view a file that is longer than one screen, you can use either the less or the more utility. Each of these utilities pauses after displaying a screen of text. Because these files show one page at a time, they are called *pagers*. Although they are very similar, they have subtle differences. At the end of the file, for example, less displays an **EOF** (end of file) message and waits for you to press **q** before returning you to the shell, whereas more returns you directly to the shell. In both utilities you can press **h** to display a help screen that lists commands you can use while paging through a file. Give the commands **less practice** and **more practice** in place of the **cat** command in Figure 2-13 to see how these commands work. Use the command **less /etc/termcap** instead if you want to experiment with a longer file. Refer to page 1226 in Part III for more information on less.

rm: Deletes a File

The rm (remove) utility deletes a file. Figure 2-13 shows rm deleting the file named **practice**. After rm deletes the file, ls and cat show that **practice** is no longer in the directory. The ls utility does not list its filename, and cat says that it cannot open the file. Use rm carefully.

Safer Way of Removing Files || tip

You can use the interactive form of rm to make sure that you delete only the file(s) you intend to delete. When you follow rm with the −i option (see footnote 7 on page 45) and the name of the file you want to delete, rm displays the name of the file and asks you to respond with y (yes) or n (no) before it deletes the file. The −i option is set up by default for the **root** user on Red Hat Linux:

```
$ rm -i toollist
rm: remove 'toollist'? y
```

Optional: You can create an alias (page 602) and put it in your startup file (page 109) so that rm always runs in interactive mode.

---

hostname: Displays Your Machine Name

The hostname command displays the name of the machine you are working on. Use this command if you are not sure that you are logged in on the right machine.

```
$ hostname
bravo
```

Special Characters

Special characters, which have a special meaning to the shell, are discussed in Chapter 5. These characters are mentioned here so that you can avoid accidentally using them as regular characters until you understand how the shell interprets them. For example, avoid using any of these characters in a filename (even though emacs and some other programs do) until you learn how to quote them (next). The standard special characters are

      & ; | * ? ' " ` [ ] ( ) $ < > { } ^ # / \ % ! ~ +

Although not considered special characters, RETURN, SPACE, and TAB also have special meanings to the shell. RETURN usually ends a command line and initiates execution of a command. The SPACE and TAB characters separate elements on the command line and are collectively known as *whitespace,* or *blanks.*

If you need to use as a regular character one of the characters that has a special meaning to the shell, you can *quote* (or *escape*) it. When you quote a special character, you keep the shell from giving it special meaning. The shell treats a quoted special character as a regular character.[12]

---

12. A /, however, is always a separator in a pathname, even when you quote it.

To quote a character, precede it with a backslash (\). When you have two or more special characters together, you must precede each with a backslash (for example, enter ✳✳ as \✳\✳). You can quote a backslash just as you would quote any other special character—by preceding it with a backslash (\\).

Another way of quoting special characters is to enclose them between single quotation marks, as in '✳✳'. You can quote many special and regular characters between a pair of single quotation marks, as in 'This is a special character: >'). The regular characters remain regular, and the shell also interprets the special characters as regular characters.

The only way to quote the erase character (CONTROL-H), the line kill character (CONTROL-U), and other control characters (try CONTROL-M) is by preceding any one with a CONTROL-V. Single quotation marks and backslashes do not work. Try the following:

```
$ echo 'xxxxxx CONTROL-U'
$ echo 'xxxxxx CONTROL-V CONTROL-U'
```

Chapter Summary

As with many operating systems, your access to the system is authorized when you log in. You enter your login name at the login: prompt, followed by a password. You can use passwd to change your password at any time. Choose a password that is difficult to guess and that conforms to the criteria imposed by the passwd utility.

The system administrator is responsible for maintaining your system. On a single-user system, you are the system administrator. On a small multiuser system, you or another user is the system administrator, or this job may be shared. On a large multiuser system or network of systems, there is frequently a full-time system administrator. When extra privileges are required to perform certain system tasks, the system administrator logs in as the **root** user by entering the user name **root** and the **root** password. While logged in this manner, this user is called Superuser. On a multiuser system, several trusted users may be given the **root** password.

You use a RETURN to terminate commands entered at the keyboard. Until you press RETURN, you can make corrections to the command line by backing over typed characters with the erase key or deleting the entire line with the line kill key. You can delete the current word by typing CONTROL-W.

The following table lists the CONTROL characters usually defined for correcting command line mistakes, as well as some other useful CONTROL characters.

Command Line CONTROL Keys

CONTROL-C	Is the default interrupt key: It aborts execution of the program you are running (page 38).
CONTROL-D, **logout**, or **exit**	Logs you off the system from a character-based interface or out of a shell from a GUI interface (page 36).
CONTROL-H or BACKSPACE	Is the default erase key. It erases a character on the command line (page 37).
CONTROL-R or CONTROL-L	Refreshes the screen.
CONTROL-U	Is the default line kill key: It deletes the entire command line (page 38).
CONTROL-W	Is the default erase key: It erases a word on the command line (page 38).
CONTROL-Z	Is the default suspend key: It stops execution of the command you are running and returns you to the shell. For more information, refer to "**bg**: Sends a Job to the Background" on page 556.

Once you press RETURN, a program called the shell interprets the words of the command. By default, accounts under Red Hat Linux are set up to use the Bourne Again Shell (bash), and many users stay with bash. Other shells are available, including the TC Shell (tcsh) and the Z Shell (zsh). The shells know to treat many special characters differently from regular characters; when you want one of these characters to represent itself, you must quote it. One way to quote a character is to precede it with a backslash (\).

You often use an editor to create a file in the GNU/Linux filesystem. Among the editors available on Red Hat Linux systems are vi, emacs, and pico. Chapters 10 and 11 cover vi and emacs. The pico editor is popular and easy to learn and use. The pico Help feature provides a short summary of the key sequences for the main editing commands. You can refer to the Help window as necessary when practicing with pico.

The man (or xman) utility provides you with online documentation on system utilities. This utility is helpful to new GNU/Linux users, as well as to experienced users who must often delve into the system documentation for information on the fine points of a utility's behavior. The info utility helps the beginner and expert alike. This utility includes a tutorial on its use and documentation on many GNU/Linux utilities.

After reading this chapter and experimenting on your system, you should be comfortable using the utilities listed in the following table. Part III has more information on less, ls, rm, man, and cat. Appendix B has a list of resources that you can use to obtain more information.

Utilities Covered in This Chapter

passwd	Changes your password (page 40)
man and xman	Displays pages from the online GNU/Linux manual (page 42)
info	Displays documentation on GNU/Linux utilities (page 45)
pico, vi, and emacs	Creates and edits text files (pages 49, 414, and 475)
ls	Displays a list of files (page 53)
cat	Catenates the contents of files and displays them on the screen (page 54)
less and more	Displays the contents of a text file one screen at a time (page 54)
rm	Deletes a file (page 54)

Exercises

1. The following error message is displayed when you attempt to log in with an incorrect username *or* an incorrect password:

   ```
   Login incorrect
   ```

   This message does not indicate whether your username, your password, or both are invalid. Why does it not tell you?

2. Give three examples of poor password choices. What is wrong with each? Include one that is too short. Give the error message displayed by the passwd utility.

3. Is fido an acceptable password? Give several reasons why or why not?

4. When you start pico and your screen looks strange, what might be wrong? How can you fix it?

5. How can you get help from pico while you are using it?

6. What pico command(s) would you use to

   a. Delete a line

   b. Undo your last command

   c. Leave the pico editor

7. What are the differences between the cat and ls utilities? What are the differences between less or more and cat?

8. What is special about the shell special characters? How can you cause the shell to treat them as regular characters?

9. Experiment with the xman utility to answer the following questions:

   a. How many man pages are in the Devices section of the manual?

   b. What version of xman are you using?

   c. What happens when you search for a man page that does not exist?

Advanced Exercises

10. Four of the following five filenames contain special characters:

    ```
    "\abc
    "abc"
    'abc'
    ab*c
    abc
    ```

    a. Show how to create files with these names.

    b. Give commands to remove the first four files, leaving only **abc**.

11. You saw that man pages for write appear in sections 1 and 2 of the system manual. Explain how you can determine what sections of the system manual contain a manual page with a given name.

    a. Using man

    b. Using xman

    Which do you think makes this task easier: man or xman? Explain.

12. How many man pages are in the Devices subsection of the system manual? (*Hint:* Devices is a subsection of Special Files.)

IN THIS CHAPTER

Introduction to the GNU/Linux Utilities

3

The GNU/Linux utility programs allow you to work with GNU/Linux and manipulate the files you create. Chapter 2 introduced the shell, the most important GNU/Linux utility program, and passwd, the utility that changes your password. Chapter 2 also introduced some of the utilities you can use to create and manipulate files: ls, cat, less, more, and rm. This chapter describes several other file manipulation utilities, as well as utilities that find out who is logged in; communicate with other users; print, compress, and decompress files; and unpack archived files. This chapter provides many jumping-off points in the form of page references for the curious or more advanced reader. Part III covers many of these utilities, as well as others, more concisely and completely.

Working with Files

The following sections describe utilities that copy, move, and print files.

cp: Copies a File

The cp (copy) utility makes a copy of a file. This utility can copy any file, including text and executable program (binary) files. You can use cp to make a backup copy of a file or a copy to experiment with.

```
$ ls
memo
$ cp memo memo.copy
$ ls
memo memo.copy
```

Figure 3-1   cp copies a file

A cp command line uses the following syntax to specify source and destination files:

cp source-file destination-file

The ***source-file*** is the name of the file that cp is going to copy. The ***destination-file*** is the name that cp assigns to the resulting—new—copy of the file.

cp Can Destroy a File   ‖ tip

If the ***destination-file*** exists *before* you give a cp command, cp overwrites it. Because cp overwrites (and destroys the contents of) an existing ***destination-file*** without warning, you must take care not to cause cp to overwrite a file that you need. You can use the cp interactive (−i) option; it checks with you before it overwrites a file. Options are discussed on page 139. The following example assumes that the file named orange.2 exists before you give the cp command. The user answers y to overwrite the file:

```
$ cp -i orange orange.2
cp: overwrite 'orange.2'? y
$
```

The command line shown in Figure 3-1 copies the file named **memo** to **memo.copy**. The period is part of the filename—just another character. The initial ls command shows that **memo** is the only file in the directory. After the cp command, the second ls shows both files, **memo** and **memo.copy**, in the directory.

Sometimes it is useful to incorporate the date in the name of a copy of a file. The following example includes the date January 30 (0130):

```
$ cp memo memo.0130
```

Although it has no significance to GNU/Linux, the date can help you find a version of a file that you created on a certain date. The date can also help you avoid overwriting existing files, by providing a unique filename each day. Refer to "Filenames" on page 103.

Use scp (page 376) or ftp (page 378) when you need to copy a file from one system to another on a common network.

```
$ ls
memo
$ mv memo memo.0130
$ ls
memo.0130
```

Figure 3-2   mv renames a file

mv: Changes the Name of a File

The mv (move) utility can rename a file without making a duplicate, or copy, of it. The mv command line specifies an existing file and a new filename using the same syntax as cp:

> *mv existing-filename new-filename*

The command line in Figure 3-2 changes the name of the file **memo** to **memo.0130**. The initial ls command shows that **memo** is the only file in the directory. After you give the mv command, **memo.0130** is the only file in the directory. Compare this to the earlier cp example.

The mv utility can be used for more than changing the name of a file. Refer to "mv, cp: Moves or Copies a File" on page 117.

lpr: Prints a File

The lpr (line printer) utility places one or more files in a print queue for printing. GNU/Linux provides print queues so that only one job gets printed on a given printer at a time. A queue allows several people or jobs to send output simultaneously to a single printer with the expected results. On machines with access to more than one printer, you can use the **–P** option to instruct lpr to place the file in the queue for a specific printer, including one that is connected to another machine on the network. The following command prints the file named **report**:[1]

```
$ lpr report
```

The next command line prints the same file on the printer named **mailroom**:

```
$ lpr -Pmailroom report
```

---

1. Because this command does not specify a printer, the output goes to the default printer, which is *the* printer when you have only one printer. Refer to "Printing" on page 1005 for information on setting up a printer and defining the default printer.

```
$ cat memo
Helen:

In our meeting on June 6th we
discussed the issue of credit.
Have you had any further thoughts
about it?

                    Alex
$ grep 'credit' memo
discussed the issue of credit.
```

Figure 3-3   grep searches for a string

You can see what jobs are in the print queue by using the lpq utility:

```
$ lpq
lp is ready and printing
Rank  Owner   Job Files               Total Size
active alex      86 (standard input)      954061 bytes
```

In this example Alex has one job that is being printed; no other jobs are in the queue. You can use the job number—86 in this case—with the lprm utility to remove the job from the print queue and stop it from printing:

```
$ lprm 86
```

You can send more than one file to the printer with a single command. The following command line prints three files on the printer named **laser1**:

```
$ lpr -Plaser1 05.txt 108.txt 12.txt
```

grep: Finds a String

The grep (global regular expression print[2]) utility searches through one or more files to see whether any contain a specified string of characters. This utility does not change the file it searches but displays each line that contains the string.

The grep command in Figure 3-3 searches through the file **memo** for lines that contain the string credit and displays a single line. If **memo** contained such words as discredit, creditor, or accreditation, grep would have displayed those lines as well because they contain the string it was searching for. You do not need to

---

2. Originally it was a play on an ed—an original UNIX editor and available on Red Hat Linux—command: g/re/p. In this command the g stands for global, re is a regular expression delimited by slashes, and p is for print.

```
$ cat months
Jan
Feb
Mar
Apr
May
Jun
Jul
Aug
Sep
Oct
Nov
Dec

$ head months
Jan
Feb
Mar
Apr
May
Jun
Jul
Aug
Sep
Oct
```

Figure 3-4   head displays the first lines of a file

enclose the string you are searching for in single quotation marks, but doing so allows you to put SPACEs and special characters in the search string.

The grep utility can do much more than search for a simple string in a single file. Refer to grep on page 1215 in Part III and Appendix A, Regular Expressions, for more information.

head: Displays the Beginning of a File

The head utility displays the first ten lines of a file. You can use head to help you remember what a particular file contains. If you have a file named **months** that lists the 12 months of the year in order, one to a line, head displays Jan through Oct (Figure 3-4).

The head utility can display any number of lines, so you can use it to look at only the first line of a file or at a screen or more. To specify the number of lines head displays, include a hyphen followed by the number of lines in the head command. For example, the following command displays only the first line of **months**:

```
$ head -1 months
Jan
```

The head utility can also display parts of a file based on a count of blocks or characters rather than lines. Refer to page 1222 in Part III for more information on head.

tail: Displays the End of a File

The tail utility is similar to head but by default displays the *last* ten lines of a file. Depending on how you invoke it, the tail utility can display fewer or more than ten lines, use a count of blocks or characters rather than lines to display parts of a file, and display lines being added to a file that is changing. The following command causes tail to display the last five lines, Aug through Dec, of the **months** file shown in Figure 3-4:

```
$ tail -5 months
Aug
Sep
Oct
Nov
Dec
```

The ability to display lines as they are added to the end of a file is a useful feature. You can monitor lines as they are added to the end of the growing file named **logfile** with the command

```
$ tail -f logfile
```

Press the interrupt key (usually CONTROL-C) to stop tail and return to the shell prompt. Refer to page 1340 in Part III for more information on tail.

sort: Displays a File in Order

The sort utility displays the contents of a file in order by lines but does not change the original file. If you have a file named **days** that contains the name of each day of the week on a separate line, sort displays the file in alphabetical order (Figure 3-5).

The sort utility is useful for putting lists in order. The **–u** option generates a sorted list in which each line is unique (no duplicates). The **–n** option puts a list of numbers in order. Refer to page 1326 in Part III for more information on sort.

uniq: Removes Duplicate Lines from a File

The uniq (unique) utility displays a file, skipping adjacent duplicate lines but does not change the original file. If a file contains a list of names and has two successive entries for the same person, uniq skips the extra line (Figure 3-6).

```
$ cat days
Monday
Tuesday
Wednesday
Thursday
Friday
Saturday
Sunday
$ sort days
Friday
Monday
Saturday
Sunday
Thursday
Tuesday
Wednesday
```

Figure 3-5   sort displays a file in order

If a file is sorted before it is processed by uniq, uniq ensures that no two lines in the file are the same. (Of course, sort can do that all by itself with the **–u** option.) Refer to page 1368 in Part III for more information on uniq.

diff: Compares Two Files

The diff (difference) utility compares two files and displays a list of the differences between them. This utility does not change either file and is useful when you want to compare two versions of a letter or report or two versions of the source code for a program.

```
$ cat dups
Cathy
Fred
Joe
John
Mary
Mary
Paula
$ uniq dups
Cathy
Fred
Joe
John
Mary
Paula
```

Figure 3-6   uniq removes duplicate lines

```
$ diff -u colors.1 colors.2
--- colors.1    Fri Nov 21 15:45:32 2003
+++ colors.2    Fri Nov 21 15:24:46 2003
@@ -1,6 +1,5 @@
 red
+blue
 green
 yellow
-pink
-purple
 orange
```

Figure 3-7   diff displaying the unified output format

The diff utility with the **–u** (unified output format, Figure 3-7) option first displays two lines indicating which of the files you are comparing will be denoted by a plus sign (**+**) and which by a minus sign (**–**). Figure 3-7 shows that a minus sign indicates the **colors.1** file; a plus sign, the **colors.2** file.

The **diff –u** command breaks long, multiline text into *hunks*. Each hunk is preceded by a line starting and ending with two at signs (**@@**). This hunk identifier indicates the starting line number and the number of lines from each file for this hunk. In Figure 3-7 this line indicates that the hunk covers the section of the **colors.1** file (indicated by a minus sign) from the first line and continuing for six lines (for a total of seven lines). Similarly, the +1,5 indicates that the hunk also covers **colors.2** from the first line through five subsequent lines.

Following these header lines, **diff –u** displays each line of text with a leading minus sign, plus sign, or nothing. The leading minus sign indicates that the line occurs only in the file denoted by the minus sign. The leading plus sign indicates that the line is from the file denoted by the plus sign. A line that begins with neither a plus sign nor a minus sign occurs in both files in the same location. Refer to page 1149 in Part III for more information on diff.

file: Tests the Contents of a File

You can use the file utility to learn about the contents of any file on a GNU/Linux system without having to open and examine the file yourself. In the following example file reports that **letter_e.gz** contains data that has been compressed in a particular way:

```
$ file letter_e.gz
letter_e.gz: gzip compressed data, deflated, original filename, last
modified: Tue Oct  8 16:02:25 2002, os: Unix
```

Refer to page 1163 in Part III for more information on file.

| (Pipe): Communicates between Processes

Because pipes are integral to the functioning of a GNU/Linux system they are introduced here for use in examples, Pipes are covered in detail in on page 151.

A *process* is either the means by which GNU/Linux executes a utility or other program or is the utility/program as GNU/Linux executes it (page 142). Communication between processes is one of the hallmarks of UNIX/Linux. A *pipe* (written as a vertical bar, l, on the command line and appearing as a solid or broken vertical line on keyboards) provides the simplest form of this kind of communication. Simply put, a pipe takes the output of one utility and sends that output as input to another utility. Using UNIX/Linux terminology, a pipe takes standard output of one process and redirects it to become standard input of another process. Most of what a process displays on your screen is sent to standard output. Without being redirected, this output appears on your screen. Using a pipe, you can redirect that output so that it does not go to the screen but goes instead to standard input of another utility. (See page 142 for more information on standard input and output.) A utility such as head can take its input from a file whose name you specify on the command line following the word **head**, or it can take its input from standard input. For example, you can give the command shown in Figure 3-4 as

```
$ cat months | head
Jan
Feb
Mar
Apr
May
Jun
Jul
Aug
Sep
Oct
```

You can use the following command to see the first line of the **months** file:

```
$ cat months | head -1
Jan
```

Four More Utilities

The echo and date utilities are two of the most frequently used from the large collection of GNU/Linux utilities. The script utility helps you record part of a session in a file, and mcopy makes a copy of a text file that can be read on an MS Windows machine.

```
$ ls
memo   memo.0714   practice
$ echo Hi
Hi
$ echo This is a sentence.
This is a sentence.
$ echo star: *
star: memo memo.0714 practice
$
```

Figure 3-8   echo copies the command line (but not the word echo) to the screen

echo: Displays Text

The echo utility copies anything you put on the command line after **echo** to the screen. Some examples are shown in Figure 3-8. The last example shows what the shell does with an unquoted asterisk (*) on the command line: expands it into a list of filenames in the directory.

The echo utility is a good tool for learning about the shell and other GNU/Linux programs. Some examples on page 158 use echo to illustrate how special characters, such as the asterisk, work. Throughout Chapters 12–15 echo helps explain shell variables and how to send messages from shell scripts to the screen.

date: Displays the Time and Date

The date utility displays the current date and time. An example of date is

```
$ date
Wed Mar 13 08:00:38 PST 2002
```

You can choose the format and select the contents of the output of date as in the following example. Refer to page 1141 in Part III for more information on date.

```
$ date +"%A %B %d"
Wednesday March 13
```

script: Records a GNU/Linux Session

The script utility records all or part of a login session, including your input and the system's responses. This utility is useful only from character-based devices, such as a terminal or a terminal emulator. The utility does capture a session with vi, but because vi uses control characters to position the cursor and display different typefaces, such as bold, it will be difficult to read and may not be useful. When you cat a file that has captured a vi session, you will see the session pass before your eyes in a great hurry.

By default, script captures the session in a file named **typescript**. To use a different filename, follow the **script** command with a SPACE and the filename you want to use. To append to a file, use the **–a** option after **script** but before any filename; otherwise, script overwrites an existing file. Following is a session being recorded by script:

```
$ script
Script started, file is typescript
$ date
Wed Mar 13 08:10:51 PST 2002
$ who am i
alex       pts/4     Mar  8 22:15
$
$ apropos mtools
mtools                 (1)   - utilities to access DOS disks in Unix
mtools.conf [mtools]  (5)   - mtools configuration files
mtoolstest             (1)   - tests and displays the configuration
$ exit
Script done, file is typescript
$
```

Use the exit command to terminate a script session. You can view the file you created with cat, less, more, or an editor. Following is the file that was created by the preceding script command.

```
$ cat typescript
Script started on Wed Mar 13 08:10:47 2002
$ date
Wed Mar 13 08:10:51 PST 2002
$ who am i
alex       pts/4     Mar  8 22:15
$
$ apropos mtools
mtools                 (1)   - utilities to access DOS disks in Unix
mtools.conf [mtools]  (5)   - mtools configuration files
mtoolstest             (1)   - tests and displays the configuration
$ exit
Script done on Wed Mar 13 08:11:07 2002
$
```

If you will be editing the file with the vi, emacs, or another GNU/Linux editor, you can use tr (translate) as shown in the following command to get rid of the ^M characters that appear at the ends of lines in the **typescript** file.

```
$ cat typescript | tr -d '\r' > typescript.good
```

Refer to page 1362 in Part III for more information on tr.

mcopy: Converts GNU/Linux Files to MS Windows Format

The mcopy utility (part of the set of Mtools) converts a GNU/Linux text file so that it can be read by a DOS or MS Windows system. Give the following command to convert a file named **memo** (created with pico, vi, emacs, or another text editor) to a DOS-format file on the floppy in drive **a:** named **memo.txt**. The **–t** option converts the line-ending characters so that they are appropriate to the operating system that will read the file.

```
$ mcopy -t memo a:memo.txt
```

The original file is not changed. You can e-mail the new file as an attachment to someone on an MS Windows system. You can also use mcopy to convert DOS files so they can be read on a GNU/Linux system:

```
$ mcopy -t a:memo.txt memo2
```

In order to change the format of a file with mcopy, you must read from or write to a DOS-format floppy disk. Refer to page 1256 in Part III for more information on Mtools.

You can also use tr to change a DOS file into a GNU/Linux text file. In the following example the **–d** option causes tr to remove RETURNs (represented by \r) from the file.

```
$ cat memo | tr -d '\r' > memo.txt
```

Converting a file the other way without Mtools is not as easy. Refer to page 1362 in Part III for more information on tr.

Compressing and Archiving a File

Large files use a lot of disk space and take longer than smaller files to transfer from one system to another over a network. If you do not need to look at the contents of a large file very often, you may want to save it on a magnetic tape, CD-ROM, or other medium and remove it from the hard disk. If you have a continuing need for the file, retrieving a copy from a tape may be inconvenient. To reduce the amount of disk space you use without removing the file entirely, you can compress the file without losing any of the information.

You frequently get a compressed file when you download files from the Internet. The utilities described following compress and decompress files by using various tools.

gzip: Compresses a File

The gzip (GNU zip) utility compresses a file by analyzing it and recoding it more efficiently. The new version of the file looks completely different. In fact, the new file contains many nonprinting characters, so you cannot view it directly. The gzip utility works particularly well on files with a lot of repeated information, such as text and image data, although most image data is already in a compressed format.

The following example shows a boring file. Each of the 8,000 lines of this file, named **letter_e**, contains 72 e's and a NEWLINE character marking the end of the line. The file occupies more than half a megabyte of disk storage.

```
$ ls -l
-rw-rw-r-- 1 alex    speedy  584000 Jul 31 06:07 letter_e
```

The –**l** option causes ls to display more information about a file. Here, it shows that **letter_e** is 584,000 bytes long.

The **––verbose** (or **–v**) option causes gzip to report how much it was able to reduce the size of the file; in this case, it shrank the file by more than 99 percent.

```
$ gzip -v letter_e
letter_e: 99.6% -- replaced with letter_e.gz

$ ls -l
-rw-rw-r-- 1 alex    speedy    2030 Jul 31 06:07 letter_e.gz
```

Now the file is only 2,030 bytes long. The gzip utility also renamed the file, appending **.gz** to the file's name. This naming convention helps to remind you that the file is compressed; you would not want to display or print it, for example, without first decompressing it. The gzip utility does not change the modification date associated with the file, even though it completely changes the file's contents.

In the following, more realistic example, the file **card2.bm** contains a complex computer graphics image:

```
$ ls -l
-rw-rw-r-- 1 jenny   speedy  131092 Jul 31 10:48 card2.bm
```

Here gzip can reduce the disk storage for the file by about only 20 percent:

```
$ gzip -v card2.bm
card2.bm:       19.7% -- replaced with card2.bm.gz
$ ls -l
-rw-rw-r-- 1 jenny   speedy  105261 Jul 31 10:48 card2.bm.gz
```

A second utility, compress, can also compress files but not as well as gzip. The compress utility marks a file it has compressed by adding a **.Z** to its name.

gunzip and zcat: Decompress a File

You can use the gunzip (GNU unzip) utility to restore a file that has been shrunk with gzip or compress:

```
$ gunzip letter_e.gz
$ ls -l
-rw-rw-r--  1 alex      speedy   584000 Jul 31 06:07 letter_e

$ gunzip card2.bm.gz
$ ls -l
-rw-rw-r--  1 jenny     speedy   131092 Jul 31 10:48 card2.bm
```

The zcat utility displays a file that has been compressed with either gzip or compress. The equivalent of cat for **.gz** and **.Z** files, zcat decompresses the compressed data and displays the contents of the decompressed file. Like cat, zcat does not change the source file. The pipe in the following example redirects the output of zcat so that instead of being displayed on the screen, it becomes the input to head, which displays the first two lines of the file:

```
$ zcat letter_e.gz | head -2
eeeeeeeeeeeeeeeeeeeeeeeeeeeeeeeeeeeeeeeeeeeeeeeeeeeeeeeeeeeeeeeeeeeeee
eeeeeeeeeeeeeeeeeeeeeeeeeeeeeeeeeeeeeeeeeeeeeeeeeeeeeeeeeeeeeeeeeeeeee
```

After zcat is run, the contents of **letter_e.gz** is unchanged; the file is still stored on the disk in compressed form.

gzip versus zip   ‖ caution

Do not confuse gzip and gunzip with the zip and unzip utilities. These last two are used to pack and unpack zip archives containing several files compressed into a single file that has been imported from or is being exported to MS Windows. The zip utility constructs a zip archive, whereas unzip unpacks zip archives. The zip and unzip utilities are compatible with PKZIP, an MS Windows compress and archive program.

bzip2: Compresses/Decompresses a File

The bzip2 utility (sources.redhat.com/bzip2) is a highly efficient compression program that does a better job than any of the programs discussed previously. Its flags and operation are very similar to those of gzip (previous sections), and it supports limited recovery from media errors (bzip2recover). Use bzip2, bunzip2, and bzcat just as you would use gzip, gunzip, and zcat. Refer to the bzip2 man page and the *Bzip2 mini-HOWTO* (see page 47 for help finding this) for more information.

tar: Packs and Unpacks Files

The tar utility performs many functions. Its name is short for *tape archive*, as its original function was to create and read archive and backup tapes. Today it is used both to create a single file (called a *tar file*) from multiple files or directories containing any level of subdirectories and files and to extract files from a tar file.

In the following example ls first shows the existence and sizes of the files **g**, **b**, and **d**. Next, tar uses the −**c** (create), −**v** (verbose), and −**f** (write to or read from a file) options[3] to create an archive named **all.tar** from these files. Each line of the output from tar starts with the letter **a** to indicate that it is appending to the archive. This letter is followed by the name of the file.

The tar utility does add overhead when it creates an archive. The next command shows that the archive file, **all.tar**, is about 9,700 bytes, whereas the sum of the sizes of the three files is about 6,000 bytes. This overhead is more appreciable on smaller files, such as the ones in this example:

```
$ ls -l g b d
-rw-r--r--   1 jenny     jenny          1302 Aug 20 14:16 g
-rw-r--r--   1 jenny     other          1178 Aug 20 14:16 b
-rw-r--r--   1 jenny     jenny          3783 Aug 20 14:17 d
$ tar -cvf all.tar g b d
a g
a b
a d
$ ls -l all.tar
-rw-r--r--   1 jenny     jenny          9728 Aug 20 14:17 all.tar
$ tar -tvf all.tar
-rw-r--r-- jenny/jenny    1302 2003-08-20 14:16 2003 g
-rw-r--r-- jenny/other    1178 2003-08-20 14:16 2003 b
-rw-r--r-- jenny/jenny    3783 2003-08-20 14:17 2003 d
```

The final command in the preceding example uses the −**t** option to display a table of contents for the archive. Use −**x** in place of −**t** to extract files from a tar archive. Omit the −**v** option if you want tar to do its work silently.

You can use compress or gzip to compress tar files and make them easier to store and handle. Many files you download from the Internet are in one of these formats. Files that have been processed by tar and compressed by gzip frequently have a filename extension of **.tgz** or **.tar.gz**. Those processed by tar and compress use **.tar.Z**.

You can unpack a tarred and gzipped file in two steps. (Follow the same procedure if the file was shrunk by compress, but use uncompress in place of gunzip.) The next example shows how to unpack the GNU make utility after it has been downloaded:

---

3. Although the original UNIX tar did not use a leading hyphen to indicate an option on the command line, it now accepts them. GNU tar described here will accept tar commands with or without a leading hyphen. This book uses the hyphen for consistency with most other utilities.

```
$ ls -l mak*
-rw-r--r--  1 sam      sam           634229 Oct 17 15:01 make-3.76.1.tar.gz
$ gunzip mak*
$ ls -l mak*
-rw-r--r--  1 sam      sam          2344960 Oct 17 15:01 make-3.76.1.tar
$ tar -xvf mak*
x make-3.76.1, 0 bytes, 0 tape blocks
x make-3.76.1/Makefile.in, 19129 bytes, 38 tape blocks
x make-3.76.1/AUTHORS, 1391 bytes, 3 tape blocks
.
.
.
x make-3.76.1/make.info-8, 42472 bytes, 83 tape blocks
x make-3.76.1/make.info-9, 10289 bytes, 21 tape blocks
```

The first of the preceding commands lists the downloaded tarred and gzipped file:
make-3.76.1.tar.gz (about 0.6 megabytes). The asterisk (*) in the filename matches
any characters in any filenames (page 158), so you end up with a list of files whose
names begin with **mak**—in this case only one. Using an asterisk saves typing and
can improve accuracy with long filenames. The gunzip command decompresses the
file and yields **make-3.76.1.tar** (no **.gz** extension), which is about 2.3 megabytes.
The tar command creates the **make-3.76.1** directory in the working directory and
unpacks the files into it:

```
$ ls -ld mak*
drwxr-xr-x  4 sam      sam             2048 Sep 19  2003 make-3.76.1
-rw-r--r--  1 sam      sam          2344960 Oct 17 15:01 make-3.76.1.tar
$ ls make-3.76.1
total 4196
-rw-r--r--  1 sam      sam             1391 Aug 27  2003 AUTHORS
-rw-r--r--  1 sam      sam            18043 Dec 10  2002 COPYING
-rw-r--r--  1 sam      sam           153710 Sep 19  2003 ChangeLog
...
-rw-r--r--  1 sam      sam             5586 Jul 25  2002 vmsfunctions.c
-rw-r--r--  1 sam      sam            15653 Aug 27  2003 vmsify.c
-rw-r--r--  1 sam      sam            16320 Aug 27  2003 vpath.c
drwxr-xr-x  5 sam      sam              512 Sep 19  2003 w32
```

After tar extracts the files from the archive, the working directory contains two
files whose names start with **mak: make-3.76.1.tar** and **make-3.76.1**. The **–d** option
causes ls to display only file and directory names, not the contents of directories,
which it normally does. The final ls command shows the files and directories in the
make-3.76.1 directory.

You can combine the gunzip and tar commands on one command line with a
pipe (|), which redirects the output of gunzip so that it becomes the input to tar:

```
$ gunzip -c make-3.76.1.tar.gz | tar -xvf -
```

tar: –x Option May Extract a Lot of Files | caution

Some tar archives contain many files. Run tar with the –t option and the name of the tar file to list the files in the archive without unpacking them. In some cases you may want to create a new directory (mkdir [page 106]), move the tar file into that directory, and expand it there. That way the unpacked files do not mingle with your existing files, and there is no confusion. It makes it easier to delete the extracted files if you choose to do so. Some tar files automatically create a new directory and put the files into it. Refer to the preceding example.

tar: –x Option Can Overwrite Files | caution

The –x option to tar overwrites a file that has the same filename as a file you are extracting. Follow the suggestion in the preceding caution box to avoid overwriting a file.

The –c option causes gunzip to send its output through the pipe instead of creating a file. Refer to "Pipes" (page 151), gzip (page 1219), and tar (page 1343) for more information about how this command line works.

A simpler solution is to use the –z option to tar. This option causes tar to call gunzip (or gzip when you are creating an archive) directly and simplifies the preceding command line to

```
$ tar -xvzf make-3.76.1.tar.gz
```

In a similar manner the –j option calls bzip2 or bunzip2.

Locating Commands

The whereis and apropos utilities help you find a command whose name you have forgotten or whose location you do not know. When there are multiple copies of a utility/program, which can tell you which copy you will run. GNU made a utility named locate more secure and renamed it slocate. This utility builds a compressed database that speeds up searches. Refer to the slocate man page.

---

which **versus** whereis   **|| tip**

Give it the name of a program you want to run, and **which** looks through the directories in your *search path,* in order, and locates the program. If more than one program with the name you specify is in your search path, **which** displays the name of only the first one (the one you will execute).

The **whereis** utility looks through a list of *standard directories* and works independently of your search path. Use **whereis** to locate a binary (executable) file, any manual pages, and source code for a program you specify.

---

which, whereis: Locate a Utility

When you type the name of a utility on the command line (that is when you give GNU/Linux a command), the shell (Chapter 5) searches a list of directories for the program. This list of directories is called a *search path*; the chapters that describe each shell explain how to change this path. If you do not change the search path, the shell searches only a standard set of directories and then stops searching. There are other directories on your system that contain useful utilities.

The which utility helps you locate utilities (commands) by displaying the full pathname to the file for the utility. (Chapter 4 contains more information on pathnames and the structure of the GNU/Linux filesystem.) There may be multiple commands that have the same name on your system. When you type the name of a command, the shell searches for the command in your search path and runs the first one it finds. You can find out which copy of the program the shell runs by using which. In the following example which reports the location of the tar command:

```
$ which tar
/bin/tar
```

The which utility can be helpful when a command seems to be working in unexpected ways. By running which, you may discover that you are running a nonstandard version of a tool or a different one than you expected. (Refer to "Important Standard Directories and Files" on page 112 for a list of standard locations for executable files.) For example, if tar is not working properly and you find that you are running **/usr/local/bin/tar** instead of **/bin/tar,** you might suspect that the local version is broken.

The whereis utility also searches for copies of a utility by looking in a few standard locations instead of using your search path. For example, you can find the locations for versions of the tar command:

```
$ whereis tar
tar: /bin/tar /usr/include/tar.h /usr/share/man/man1/tar.1.gz
```

> ## which, whereis, and Builtin Commands   ‖ caution
>
> Both the **which** and **whereis** utilities report only the names for commands as they are found on disk and do not report shell builtins (utilities that are built into a shell; see page 161). When you use **whereis** to try to find out where the **echo** command (which exists as both a utility program and a shell builtin) is kept, you get the following:
>
> ```
> $ whereis echo
> echo: /bin/echo /opt/../bin/echo /usr/man/man1/echo.1
> ```
>
> The **whereis** utility does not display the **echo** builtin. Even the **which** utility reports the wrong information:
>
> ```
> $ which echo
> /bin/echo
> ```

This whereis utility finds three references to tar. If it can find any man pages for the utility, whereis lists those too. In this case the whereis utility has located tar, a tar header file, and the man page.

apropos: Searches for a Keyword

When you do not know the name of the command you need to carry out a particular task, you can use a keyword and the apropos[4] utility to search for it. This utility searches for the keyword in the short description line[5] of all of the man pages and displays those that contain a match. The man utility, with the **–k** (keyword) option, gives you the same output as apropos (it is actually the same command).

Figure 3-9 shows the output of apropos when you call it with the who keyword. The pipe redirects the output of apropos so that it becomes the input of sort, yielding a sorted list. The pipe includes the name of each command, the section of the manual that contains it, and the brief description from the top of the man page. This list includes the utility that you need (who) and also identifies other, related tools that you might find useful.

The whatis utility is similar to apropos but finds only complete word matches on the name of the utility. Try giving these commands to see the difference: **apropos grep** and **whatis grep.**

---

4. The **whatis** database has to be set up with makewhatis in order for apropos to work. Refer to "Initializing Databases" on page 923.

5. The top line on a man or xman page.

```
$ apropos who | sort
at.allow [at]         (5)  - determine who can submit jobs via at or batch
at.deny [at]          (5)  - determine who can submit jobs via at or batch
fwhois [whois]        (1)  - query a whois or nicname database
w                     (1)  - Show who is logged on and what they are doing
who                   (1)  - show who is logged on
whoami                (1)  - print effective userid
whois                 (1)  - query a whois or nicname database
```

Figure 3-9   apropos displays man page headers that match a string

Obtaining User and System Information

This section covers utilities that display who is using the system, what most of the users are doing, and how the system is running. If you are running GNU/Linux on a workstation that is not connected to a network, you may want to skip the rest of this chapter. (If you are set up to send and receive e-mail, read "E-Mail" on page 87).

To find out who is using the computer system, you can use one of several utilities that vary in the details they provide and the options they support. The oldest utility, who, produces a list of users who are logged in on your system, the terminal connection each person is using, and the time the person logged in.

Two newer utilities, w and finger, show more detail, such as each user's full name and the command line each user is running. You can use the finger utility (page 370) to retrieve information about users on remote systems if your computer is attached to a network.

Following these utilities, Table 3-1 on page 84 summarizes their output.

who: Lists Users on the System

The who utility displays a list of users who are logged in. In Figure 3-10 the first column of who shows that Alex and Jenny are logged in. (Alex is logged in from two locations.) The second column shows the designation of the terminal, workstation, or terminal emulator that each person is using. The third column shows the date and time the person logged in.

The information that who displays is useful when you want to communicate with a user at your installation. When the user is logged in, you can use write (page 84) to establish communication immediately. If who does not list the user or if you do not need to communicate immediately, you can send that person e-mail (page 87).

```
$ who
root         console      Mar 27 05:00
alex         pts/4        Mar 27 12:23
alex         pts/5        Mar 27 12:33
jenny        pts/7        Mar 26 08:45
```

Figure 3-10   who lists who is logged in

If the output of who scrolls off your screen, you can redirect the output through a pipe (l [page 151]) so that it becomes the input to less, which displays the output one page at a time. You can also use a pipe to redirect the output through grep to look for a specific name.

If you need to find out which terminal you are using or what time you logged in, you can use the command **who am i**:

```
$ who am i
bravo.tcorp.com!alex        pts/5          Mar 27 12:33
```

finger: Lists Users on the System

You can use finger to display a list of the users who are logged in on the system. In addition to login names, finger supplies each user's full name, along with information about which terminal line the person is using, how recently the user typed something on the keyboard, when the user logged in, and information about where the user is located (if the terminal line appears in a system database). If the user has logged in over the network, the name of the remote system is shown as the user's location. In Figure 3-11, for example, the user **hls** is logged in from the remote system named **bravo**. The asterisk (*) in front of the name of Helen's terminal (TTY) line indicates that she has blocked others from sending messages directly to her terminal (refer to "**mesg**: Denies or Accepts Messages" on page 87).

```
$ finger
Login      Name            Tty   Idle  Login Time   Office       Office
Phone
root       root            1     1:35  May 24 08:38
alex       Alex Watson     /0          Jun  7 12:46 (:0)
alex       Alex Watson     /1    19    Jun  7 12:47 (:0)
jenny      Jenny Chen      /2    2:24  Jun  2 05:33 (bravo.tcorp.com)
hls        Helen Simpson   */2   2     Jun  2 05:33 (bravo.tcorp.com)
```

Figure 3-11   finger I: lists who is logged in

You can also use finger to learn more about a particular individual by specifying more information on the command line. In Figure 3-12, finger displays detailed information about the user named Alex. Alex is logged in and actively using his terminal; if he were not, finger would report how long he had been idle. You also learn from finger that if you want to set up a meeting with Alex, you should contact Jenny at extension 1693.

Most of the information in Figure 3-12 was collected by finger from system files. The information shown after the heading Plan:, however, was supplied by Alex. The finger utility searched for a file named **.plan**[6] in Alex's home directory and displayed its contents. You may find it helpful to create a **.plan** file for yourself; it can contain any information you choose, such as your typical schedule, interests, phone number, or address. In a similar manner, finger displays the contents of the **.project** file in your home directory. The **.forward** file contains the address that Alex's mail is forwarded to. If Alex had not been logged in, finger would have reported the last time he logged on, the last time he read his e-mail, and his plan.

---

finger Can Be a Security Risk || security

On systems where security is a concern, the system administrator may disable finger. This utility can give information that can help a malicious user break into the system.

You can use finger to display a user's login name. For example, you might know that Helen's last name is Simpson but might not guess that her login name is **hls**. The finger utility can search for information on Helen, using her first or last name. (The finger utility is not case sensitive.) The following commands find the information you seek, along with information on other users whose names are Helen or Simpson.

```
$ finger HELEN
Login: hls                              Name: Helen Simpson.
.
.
$ finger simpson
Login: hls                              Name: Helen Simpson.
.
.
```

---

6. Filenames that begin with a period are not normally listed by ls and are called invisible filenames (page 106).

```
$ finger alex
Login: alex                              Name: Alex Watson
Directory: /home/alex                    Shell: /bin/ksh
On since Wed Jun  7 12:46 (PDT) on pts/0 from :0
    5 minutes 52 seconds idle
On since Wed Jun  7 12:47 (PDT) on pts/1 from bravo
Last login Wed Jun  7 12:47 (PDT) on 1 from bravo
New mail received Wed Jun  7 13:16 2000 (PDT)
      Unread since Fri May 26 15:32 2000 (PDT)Plan:
I will be at a conference in Hawaii all next week.  If you need
to see me, contact Jenny Chen, x1693.
```

Figure 3-12   finger II: lists details about one user

w: Lists Users on the System

The w utility displays a list of the users who are logged in. As discussed in the section on who, the information that w displays is useful when you want to communicate with someone at your installation.

In Figure 3-13 the first column w displays shows that Alex, Jenny, and Scott are logged in. The second column shows the designation of the terminal that each person is using. The third column shows the time each person logged in. The fourth column indicates how long each person has been idle (how much time has elapsed since a key on the keyboard was pressed or the mouse was moved). The next two columns give measures of how much computer processor time each person has used during this login session and on the task that is running. The last column shows the command each person is running.

The first line that the w utility displays includes the time of day, how long the computer has been running (in days, hours, and minutes), how many users are logged in, and how busy the system is (load average). The three load average numbers represent the number of jobs waiting to run, averaged over the past 1, 5, and 15 minutes.

```
$ w
  8:20am  up 4 days,  2:28,  3 users,  load average: 0.04, 0.04, 0.00
USER     TTY      FROM           LOGIN@   IDLE    JCPU    PCPU  WHAT
alex     pts/4    :0             5:55am   13:45   0.15s   0.07s  w
alex     pts/5    :0             5:55am      27   2:55    1:01   -ksh
jenny    pts/7    bravo          5:56am   13:44   0.51s    30s   vi 3.txt
scott    pts/12   bravo          7:17pm           1.00s   0:14s  run_bdgt
```

Figure 3-13   The w utility

Comparison of w, who, and finger			‖ table 3-1
Information Displayed	**w**	**who**	**finger**
User login name	X	X	X
Terminal-line identification (tty)	X	X	X
Login day and time	X		X
Login date and time		X	
Idle time	X		X
What program the user is executing	X		
Where the user logged in from			X
CPU time used		X	
Full name (or other information from **/etc/passwd**)			X
User-supplied vanity information			X
System up time and load average—use **up-time** for this information only	X		

Communicating with Other Users

The utilities discussed in this section exchange messages and files with other users either interactively or through e-mail.

write: Sends a Message

The write utility sends a message to another user who is logged in. When you and another user use write to send messages to each other, you establish two-way communication. Initially a write command (Figure 3-14) displays a banner on the other user's terminal, saying that you are about to send a message.

The syntax of a write command line is

write **destination-user** *[terminal]*

```
$ write alex
Hi Alex, are you there? o
```

Figure 3-14   The write utility I

The *destination-user* is the login name of the user you want to communicate with. The *terminal* is the optional terminal name. You can display the login and terminal names of the users who are logged in on your system by using who, w, or finger.

To establish two-way communication with another user, you and the other user must each execute write, specifying the other's login name as the *destination-user.* The write utility then copies text, line by line, from one keyboard/display to the other (Figure 3-15). Sometimes it helps to establish a convention, such as typing o (for over) when you are ready for the other person to type and typing oo (for over and out) when you are ready to end the conversation. When you want to stop communicating with the other user, press CONTROL-D at the beginning of a line. Pressing CONTROL-D tells write to quit, displays EOF (end of file) on the other user's terminal, and returns you to the shell. The other user must do the same.

If the Message from ... banner appears on your screen and obscures something you are working on, press CONTROL-L or CONTROL-R to refresh the screen and remove the banner. Then you can clean up, exit from your work, and respond to the person who is writing you. You just have to remember who is writing you, as the banner will no longer be on your screen.

Refer to "Write Daemon" on page 331.

talk: Communicates with Another User

You can use the talk utility to carry on a two-way conversation with another person who is logged in on your system. If your system is connected to a network, you can also use talk to communicate with someone on a different computer. The talk utility splits your screen into two sections; once you establish contact with the other person, the messages that you type appear in the top half of your screen, and the messages from the other person are displayed in the bottom half. Each keystroke appears as you type it. In this example Alex needs some information from Jenny:

```
$ talk jenny
```

```
$ write Alex
Hi Alex are you there? o
        Message from alex@bravo.tcorp.com on pts/0 at 16:23 ...
Yes Jenny, I'm here. o
```

Figure 3-15   The write utility II

Alex's display is immediately split into two sections, and the following message appears at the top of his screen:

```
[Waiting for your party to respond]
```

Meanwhile, the following message appears on Jenny's screen and she responds. If she was unable to respond immediately, she could use CONTROL-L or CONTROL-R to refresh her screen and remove the banner (see the preceding discussion of talk):

```
Message from Talk_Daemon@bravo.tcorp.com at 9:22 ...
talk: connection requested by alex@bravo.
talk: respond with: talk alex@bravo
$ talk alex@bravo
```

Alex and Jenny are both using a computer named **bravo; alex@bravo** is Alex's network address, which is described in more detail in Chapter 7. Figure 3-16 shows what Jenny's and Alex's screens look like as they type their messages.

To end the talk session, one person interrupts by pressing CONTROL-C, and the following message appears before a new shell prompt is displayed:

```
[Connection closing. Exiting]
```

The other user must also press CONTROL-C to display a shell prompt. If you see the following message when you try to use talk to reach someone, the mesg command (see the next section) has been used to block interruptions:

```
[Your party is refusing messages]
```

Before the talk utility was available, people used the write command to interact with each other on the same computer. The talk utility has a few advantages over write: With talk the other person's messages appear on your screen, letter by letter, as

Alex's screen:

```
[Connection established]
Did you finish the slides
for the 9:30 meeting today?
Sounds good, see you in a few
minutes!

-----------------------------------
Hi, Alex, what's up?
Yes, they're all set.  Should
I just meet you in the conference
room?
Bye.
```

Jenny's screen:

```
[Connection established]
Hi, Alex, what's up?
Yes, they're all set.  Should
I just meet you in the conference
room?
Bye.

-----------------------------------
Did you finish the slides
for the 9:30 meeting today?
Sounds good, see you in a few
minutes!
```

Figure 3-16   talk communicates with another user

they are typed; write, on the other hand, sends only a whole line at a time. If you use write, sometimes you are not sure whether the person at the other end is discon- nected or just a slow typist. Also, unlike write, talk has been extended to support communication over the network.

KDE has enhanced talk so that it has an answering machine and forwarding ca- pability. Refer to "Talk Configuration" on page 1011 for setup information.

mesg: Denies or Accepts Messages

Give the following command when you do not wish to receive messages from an- other user:

```
$ mesg n
```

If Alex had given this command before Jenny tried to send him a message, she would have seen the following:

```
$ write alex
Permission denied
```

You can allow messages again by entering **mesg y**. Give the command **mesg** by itself to display is y (for yes, messages are allowed) or is n (for no, messages are *not* allowed).

E-Mail

E-mail, or *electronic mail,* is similar to post office mail but is usually much quicker and does not involve any paper, stamps, or human intervention at various points along the way. You can use e-mail to send and receive letters, memos, reminders, in- vitations, and even junk mail (unfortunately). E-mail can also transmit binary data, such as pictures or compiled code, as attachments. An *attachment* is a file that is at- tached to, but is not part of, a piece of e-mail. Attachments are frequently opened by programs, including your Internet browser, that are called by your mail program, so you may not be aware that they are not an integral part of an e-mail message.

You can use e-mail to communicate with users on your system and, if your in- stallation is part of a network, other users on the network. If you are connected to the Internet, you can communicate electronically with users around the world.

The e-mail utilities differ from write and talk in that they send a message to a user whether or not that user is logged in on the system. The e-mail utilities can also send the same message to more than one user at a time.

Many are mail programs are available for GNU/Linux, including the original character-based mail program, Netscape/Mozilla mail, pine, mail through emacs,

Kmail, evolution, and exmh which are supplied with Red Hat. Another popular graphical mail program is sylpheed (sylpheed.good-day.net). The next section describes pine, which works from a character-based terminal.

You can use two programs to make any mail program easier to use and more secure. The procmail program (www.procmail.org) creates and maintains mail servers and mailing lists; preprocesses mail by sorting it into appropriate files and directories; starts various programs, depending on the characteristics of incoming mail; forwards mail; and so on. The GNU Privacy Guard (gpg or GNUpg, pages 1030 and 1410) encrypts and decrypts e-mail and makes it almost impossible for anyone else to read.

Tutorial: Using pine to Send and Receive E-Mail

In 1989 a group at the University of Washington decided to write a UNIX mailer that was easy to learn and use, especially for beginners. The group wanted to provide administrative staff at the university with a mail utility that had a clean and friendly interface and that encouraged use without the risk of making serious and confusing errors. The group named the mailer pine (Program for Internet News and E-mail). The popularity of pine quickly extended beyond the boundaries of the university, and capabilities were added to meet the needs of the growing community of pine users. Since that time, a number of advanced features have been added to pine, including a mechanism for transmitting files containing any kind of data, and ways to tailor pine's behavior to the individual user. The pine utility runs on many versions of UNIX/Linux and MS Windows. Although still easy to use, pine is no longer geared to the beginner. Refer to page 1278 in Part III for more information on pine.

Getting Started

Try out the various features of pine until you are comfortable with them. To assist you in this process, help text is available for every screen. To start, give the following command at the shell prompt from either a terminal emulator window or a character terminal:

```
$ pine
```

You will see a welcome screen the first time you run pine. After that, pine displays the Main menu (Figure 3-17) which offers a choice of seven general pine commands in the middle portion of the screen. A letter representing each command appears to its left. The pine mailer also displays a status line at the top of the screen and two more complete lines of commands at the bottom. The third line from the bottom is the message line; pine uses this line to display messages and prompt you for input. The status line displays the version of pine you are using, the name of the

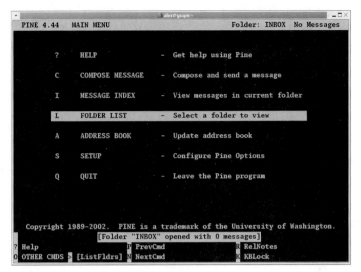

Figure 3-17 The pine Main menu

currently active screen (Main menu), and some additional information about the program. The bottom two lines of the screen list all the commands defined for the Main menu, including the general pine commands. On the bottom two lines, each command is represented by a single highlighted character, displayed to the left of the command's name.

You can execute a pine command in two ways. You can always press the key corresponding to the character to the left of the command you want to execute. For the general commands appearing in the middle of the screen, you can also use the ARROW keys (or **N** for next and **P** for previous) to position the cursor over the command you want and then press RETURN to execute the command.

Because the Main menu has too many commands to fit in the display at the bottom of the screen, the **O** (other) command provides a way to view the additional ones. Enter **O** to view another two-line display. These two two-line displays comprise the full set of commands that are active for the Main menu; the next **O** command also takes you back to the original two-line display.

The basic format of the Main menu appears throughout the many pine screens: a status line at the top and a two-line display at the bottom of the screen. The **O** command is available, if necessary, to view additional commands, and help text is available at strategic points along the way. In most screens the **M** command puts you back in the Main menu, and **Q** closes (quits) pine.

To learn more about pine, you can display the Help screen for the Main menu by entering a question mark (**?**). The Help screen displays general information about pine and a description of the commands available in the Main menu. As in all pine screens, the two-line display at the bottom of the Help screen tells you what commands are active.

Another way to view help text from the Main menu is to highlight the general pine command Help, using **N** and **P** or the arrow keys, and then press RETURN. Selecting highlighted items with RETURN is a shortcut available in most of the pine screens; you will find it useful as you become proficient in the use of pine.

When you start running pine, the general pine command Folder List is highlighted. Entering the command **N** or pressing the DOWN ARROW key highlights the next general pine command, and entering **P** or pressing the UP ARROW key highlights the previous one.

To get back to the shell prompt, enter **Q**. You are asked to confirm that you want to quit pine, at which point entering **Y** causes pine to quit and returns you to the shell.

Sending Mail

To learn about pine, send mail to yourself. Use the following example as a guide, replacing **alex** with your login name.

To send mail to himself, Alex types **pine** to bring up the Main menu. He then chooses the general pine command Compose Message and presses RETURN (he could also have entered **C**) to put himself in the message composer. The name of the current screen, Compose Message, is shown at the top of Figure 3-18. The line beginning with the To: prompt is highlighted. The mail header consists of the To: prompt and the next three lines.

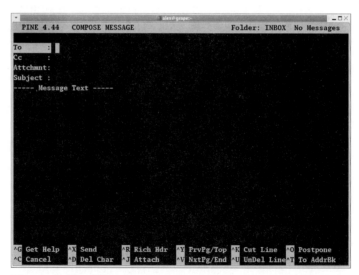

Figure 3-18   The pine Compose Message screen

The display at the bottom of the screen shows that all the commands require you to use the CONTROL key; the command Get Help, for instance, is CONTROL-G. Using CONTROL keys for commands allows pine to distinguish commands from text that you type to fill in the header fields and the mail message itself. There are a few other places in pine where commands are control characters, such as when you edit the address book (see the Main menu Help screen).

Because Alex is sending mail to himself, he types his login name after the To: prompt, followed by RETURN:

To: **alex**

As soon as Alex presses RETURN, pine replaces his login name with his full name and his e-mail address, inside angle brackets:

To: Alex Watson <alex@grape>

Alex's e-mail address allows others to send him e-mail. Alex can send mail to any user on his system by using that user's login name, but to send mail to users on other systems requires more complex addresses. If you press CONTROL-G when the To: prompt is highlighted, pine gives you help on addresses.

You can use the next line of the header, the Cc: line, to send copies of a message to other users. In response to this prompt, you can enter the login names of users to receive copies of the message. Separate the names in the list with commas and terminate the list by pressing RETURN or DOWN ARROW. Because Alex wants to send mail only to himself, he presses RETURN to highlight the next line of the header.

The third line displays the Attchmnt: (Attachment) prompt. In response to this prompt, you can give the name of a file or files (either text or binary) that you want attached to the mail message. Alex skips this line by pressing RETURN.

The last line of the header contains the Subject: prompt. Alex types in the subject of his message and presses RETURN:

Subject: **Test Message**

After typing in the subject, Alex types in a short message, ending each line with RETURN:

This is a test message that I am sending myself.
I am using Pine to write it and will use Pine to read it.

When he is finished typing his message, Alex presses CONTROL-X to send it. As with many pine commands, Alex is prompted to confirm his intention. After entering **y** for yes (or just pressing RETURN—yes is already highlighted), pine sends his message. Alex may remain in the mailer, perhaps to compose a message to someone else or to select another command from the Main menu. Because Alex is done for now, he enters **Q** to return to the shell.

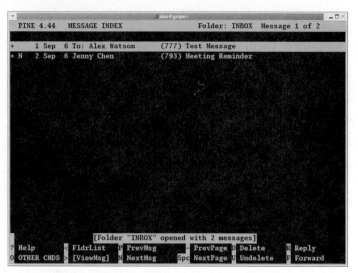

Figure 3-19   The pine Message Index screen

Entering **pine** followed by an e-mail address is a shortcut to the message composer. For example, Alex could have entered the message composer directly from the shell by using the following command:

```
$ pine alex
```

After sending a message by using this shortcut, Alex would have been returned directly to the shell without having to enter **Q**.

Receiving Mail

In order to read his mail, Alex starts pine by giving the following command to enter the Main menu:

```
$ pine
```

He selects the highlighted item Folder List for viewing a list of his message folders—files that pine uses to store mail messages. Alex gets a screen containing a list of three message folders with the first highlighted.

INBOX   sent-mail   saved-messages

The first time you run pine, the utility creates folders named **INBOX, sent-mail,** and **saved-messages. INBOX** stores messages before you read them and messages that you have read but have not removed. The **sent-mail** folder stores copies of all mail that you send to others, and the **saved-messages** folder by default stores messages that you want to save. You can also use pine to create and delete folders, transfer messages from one folder to another, and organize folders into collections of folders.

Figure 3-20   Alex's message to himself

Because Alex wants to read his new mail messages, he presses RETURN and sees
the screen shown in Figure 3-19. It contains a list of messages waiting for him in his
INBOX. The list includes a header for each message, consisting of codes on the left,
a message number, the name of the person who sent it, the date it was sent, its
length in bytes (characters), and the subject of the message.

The code **+** means that the message was sent directly to Alex, not as part of a
Cc:, for instance. The code N says that the message is new. Another common code is
D, which means that the message has been marked for deletion.

Alex has two messages: the one he just sent and one from Jenny. The current
message, the one he sent to himself, is highlighted. Alex presses RETURN to read the
highlighted message, shown in Figure 3-20. The first four lines of the message are
header lines listing the date, the sender, the receiver, and the subject of the message.
Alex has set up his signature to be automatically included in each message he sends.

Alex has many choices at this point: He can enter **R** to reply to the message, **F**
to forward the message to another person, **S** to save the message in a message folder,
and **D** to mark the message for deletion. These commands and others are listed at
the bottom of the screen. (Use the **O** command to display the **S** command.) Alex enters **D** to mark the message for deletion.

As soon as he presses **D**, pine displays the next message, the one from Jenny
(Figure 3-21). After reading this message (the :-) is a *smiley* [page 1492]), Alex
presses **M** to return to the Main menu. The message remains in **INBOX**.

When Alex quits, pine asks whether he wants to expunge the message marked
for deletion from the message folder. The deletion of a mail message is a two-step
process in pine: marking the message for deletion and expunging it from the message folder. This gives you an opportunity to change your mind about deleting a

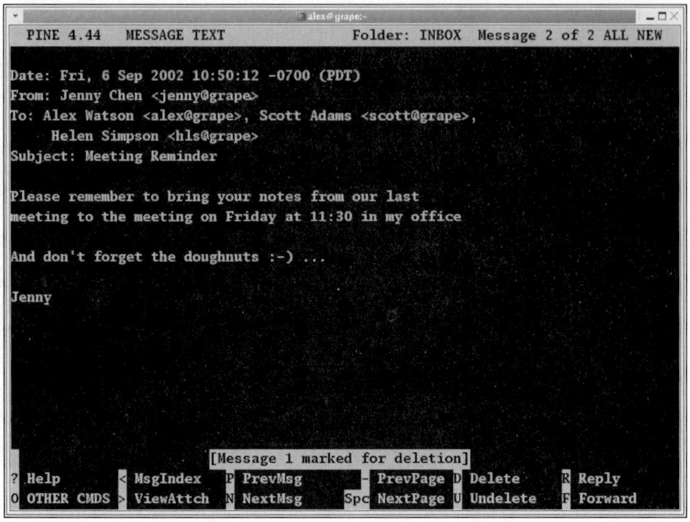

Figure 3-21   Receiving mail that was sent to more than one person

message and also prevents you from inadvertently deleting a message. Alex enters **Y** and is returned to the shell.

Like composing mail messages, reading mail is such a common use of pine that there is a shortcut to enter the Message Index screen from the command line:

```
$ pine -i
```

This command puts you directly into the Message Index screen, where pine displays the list of messages in your default folder (**INBOX**). If you are already in the mailer and want to read the messages in your default folder, you can bypass the Folder List screen by selecting Message Index from the Main menu.

Sending Mail to More Than One Person

You can send mail to more than one person at a time. Figure 3-21 shows a reminder that Jenny sent to Alex, Scott, and hls (Helen's login name). To access the message composer directly, Jenny types the following command at the shell prompt:

```
$ pine alex scott hls
```

From within the message composer, Jenny could have entered the three names in response to the To: prompt.

Network Addresses

If your system is part of a LAN you can generally send mail to and receive mail from users on other systems on the LAN by using their login names. Someone sending Alex e-mail on the Internet would need to specify his domain name (page 388) along with his login name. Use this address to send the author e-mail: mark@sobell.com.

Chapter Summary

The utilities introduced in this chapter and the previous one are a small but powerful subset of the utilities available on a Red Hat Linux system. Because you will use them frequently and because they are integral to the following chapters, it is important that you become comfortable using them.

This chapter introduces some general file manipulation utilities that compress files and file archives, identify or locate utilities on the system, obtain information about other users, and communicate electronically with others.

File Utilities

cp	Copies one or more files (page 61)
diff	Displays the differences between two files (page 67)
file	Displays information about the contents of a file (page 68)
grep	Searches a file for a string (page 64)
head	Displays the lines at the beginning of a file (page 65)
lpq	Displays a list of jobs in the print queue (page 64)
lpr	Places file(s) in the print queue (page 63)
lprm	Removes a job from the print queue (page 64)
mv	Renames file(s) or moves file(s) to another directory (page 63)
sort	Puts a file in order by lines (page 66)
tail	Displays the lines at the end of a file (page 66)
uniq	Displays the contents of a file, skipping successive duplicate lines (page 66)

(De)Compression Utilities

To reduce the amount of disk space a file occupies, you can compress it with the gzip utility. The compression works especially well on files that contain patterns, as do most text files, but reduces the size of almost all files. The inverse of gzip—gunzip—restores a file to its original, decompressed form.

compress	Compresses a file (not as well as gzip) (page 73)
gunzip	Returns a gzipped or compressed file to its original size and format (page 74)
gzip	Compresses a file (page 73)
zcat	Displays a compressed file (page 74)
bzip2, bunzip2, and bzcat	Compresses/decompresses/displays a file (better than gzip) (page 74)

Archive Utility

An archive is a file, usually compressed, that contains a group of smaller, related files. The tar utility packs and unpacks archives. The filename extensions .tar.gz and .tgz identify compressed tar archive files and are often seen on software packages obtained over the Internet.

tar	Creates or extracts files from an archive file (page 75)

Location Utilities

These utilities determine the location of a utility on your system. For example, they can display the pathname of a utility or a list of C++ compilers available on your system.

apropos	Searches the man page one-line descriptions for a keyword (page 79)
whereis	Displays the full pathnames of a utility, source code, or man page (page 78)

| which | Displays the full pathname of a command you can run (page 78) |

User and System Information Utilities

These utilities display information about other users. You can easily learn a user's full name, whether the user is logged in, the login shell of the user, and other items of information maintained by the system.

finger	Displays detailed information about users who are logged in, including full names (page 81)
w	Displays detailed information about users who are logged in (page 83)
who	Displays information about users who are logged in (page 80)

User Communication Utilities

mesg	Permits or denies messages sent by **write** or **talk** (page 87)
pine	Sends and receives e-mail (page 88)
talk	Sets up two-way communication with a local or remote user (page 85)
write	Sends a message to another user who is logged in (page 84)

Miscellaneous Utilities

| date | Displays the current date and time (page 70) |
| echo | Copies its *arguments* (page 1454) to the terminal (page 70) |

Exercises

1. What commands can you use to determine who is logged in on a specific terminal?

2. How can you keep other users from using write to communicate with you? Why would you want to?

3. What command sends the files **chapter1**, **chapter2**, and **chapter3** to the printer?

4. List some differences between talk and write. Why are three different communications utilities (talk, write, pine) useful? Describe a situation in which it makes sense to use

   a. pine instead of talk or write

   b. talk instead of write

   c. write instead of talk

5. Show how to use pine to send a single mail message to **agnes** on the system named **cougar** and to **jim** on the system named **ucsf**. Assume that your computer has network links to **cougar** and **ucsf**.

6. What happens when you give the following commands if the file named **done** already exists?

   ```
   $ cp to_do done
   $ mv to_do done
   ```

7. How can you find out which utilities are available on your system for editing files? What utilities are there for editing on your system?

8. How can you find the phone number for Ace Electronics in a file named **phone** that contains a list of names and phone numbers? What command can you use to display the entire file in alphabetical order? How can you remove adjacent duplicate lines from the file?

9. What happens when you use diff to compare two binary files that are not identical? (You can use gzip to create the binary files.) Explain why the diff output for binary files is different from the diff output for ASCII files.

10. Create a **.plan** file in your home directory. Does finger on your system display the contents of your **.plan** file?

11. What is the result of giving the which utility the name of a command that resides in a directory that is *not* in your search path?

12. Are any of the utilities discussed in this chapter located in more than one directory on your system? If so, which ones?

13. Experiment by calling the file utility with names of files in **/usr/bin**. How many different types of files are there?

14. What command can you use to look at the first few lines of a file named **status.report**? What command can you use to look at the end of the file?

Advanced Exercises

15. Recreate the **colors.1** and **colors.2** files used in Figure 3-7 on page 68. Test your files by running **diff –u** on them, and see whether you get the same results as in the figure.

16. Use the pine mailer to create a new folder named **tmp-mail**. Then describe how to move a message from the folder **sent-mail** to the folder **tmp-mail**.

17. Try giving these two commands:

    ```
    $ echo cat
    $ cat echo
    ```

    Explain the differences between them.

18. Repeat exercise 8 using the file **phone.gz**, a compressed version of the list of names and phone numbers. Try to consider more than one approach to each question, and explain how you chose your answer.

19. Find existing files or create files that

    a. gzip compresses by more than 80 percent

    b. gzip compresses by less than 10 percent

    c. get larger when compressed with gzip

    Use **ls –l** to determine the sizes of the files in question. Can you characterize the files in a, b, and c?

20. Some mailers, particularly older ones, are not able to handle binary files. Suppose that you are mailing someone a file that has been compressed with gzip, which produces a binary file, and you do not know what mailer the recipient is using. Refer to the man page on uuencode, which converts a binary file to ASCII. Learn about the utility and how to use it.

    a. Convert a compressed file to ASCII, using uuencode. Is the encoded file bigger or smaller than the compressed file? Explain.

    b. Would it ever make sense to use uuencode on a file before compressing it? Explain.

IN THIS CHAPTER

The GNU/Linux Filesystem

4

A *filesystem* is a *data structure* (page 1463) that usually resides on part of a disk. This chapter discusses the organization and terminology of the GNU/Linux filesystem, defines ordinary and directory files, and explains the rules for naming them. The chapter shows how to create and delete directories, move through the filesystem, and use pathnames to access files in various directories. This chapter also covers file access permissions which allow you to share selected files with other users. The final section describes links, which can make a single file appear in more than one directory.

The Hierarchical Filesystem

A *hierarchical* (page 1471) structure frequently takes the shape of a pyramid. One example of this type of structure is found by tracing a family's lineage: A couple has a child who may have several children, each of whom may have more children. This hierarchical structure shown in Figure 4-1 is called a *family tree*.

Like the family tree it resembles, the GNU/Linux filesystem is also called a *tree*. It is composed of a set of connected files. This structure allows you to organize files so you can easily find any particular one. On a standard GNU/Linux system, each user starts with one directory. You can make as many subdirectories as you like from your single directory, dividing subdirectories into additional subdirectories. In this manner you can continue expanding the structure to any level, according to your needs.

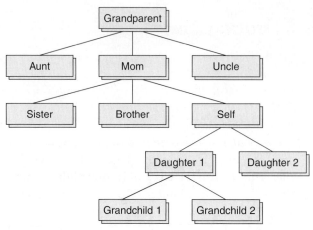

Figure 4-1   A family tree

Typically each subdirectory is dedicated to a single subject, such as a person, project, or event. The subject dictates whether a subdirectory should be subdivided further. For instance, Figure 4-2 shows a secretary's subdirectory named **correspond**. This directory contains three subdirectories: **business, memos,** and **personal.** The **business** directory contains files that store each letter the secretary types. If you expect many letters to go to one client, as is the case with **milk_co,** you can dedicate a subdirectory to that client.

One of the strengths of the GNU/Linux filesystem is its ability to adapt to users' needs. You can take advantage of this strength by strategically organizing your files so they are most convenient and useful for you.

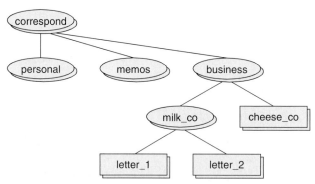

Figure 4-2   A secretary's directories

Directory and Ordinary Files

Like a family tree, the tree representing the filesystem is usually pictured upside down, with its *root* at the top. Figures 4-2 and 4-3 show that the tree "grows" downward from the root, with paths connecting the root to each of the other files. At the end of each path is either an ordinary file or a directory file. *Ordinary files*, frequently just called *files*, are at the ends of paths that cannot support other paths. *Directory files*, usually referred to as *directories* or *folders*, are the points that other paths *can* branch off from. (Figures 4-2 and 4-3 show some empty directories.) When you refer to the tree, *up* is toward the root and *down* is away from the root. Directories directly connected by a path are called *parents* (closer to the root) and *children* (farther from the root). A *pathname* is a series of names that trace a path along branches from one file to another.

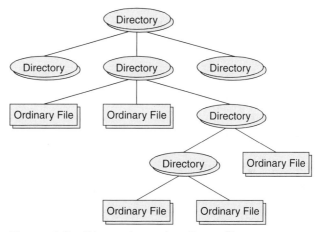

Figure 4-3   Directories and ordinary files

Filenames

Every file has a *filename*. The maximum length of a filename varies with the type of filesystem; GNU/Linux includes support for various types of filesystems. On most filesystems you can create files with names up to 255 characters long, but some filesystems may restrict you to 14-character names. Although you can use almost any character in a filename, you will avoid confusion if you choose characters from the following list:

- Uppercase letters (A–Z)

- Lowercase letters (a–z)

- Numbers (0–9)

- Underscore (_)

- Period (.)

- Comma (,)

The **root** directory is always named **/** (slash) and referred to by this single character. No other file can use this name or have a **/** in its name. However, in a pathname, which is a string of filenames, including directory names, the slash *separates* filenames (page 110).

Like children of one parent, no two files in the same directory can have the same name. (Parents give their children different names because it makes good sense, but GNU/Linux requires it.) Files in different directories, like children of different parents, can have the same name.

The filenames you choose should mean something. Too often a directory is filled with important files with such names as **hold1**, **wombat**, and **junk**, not to mention **foo** and **foobar**. Such names are poor choices because they do not help you recall what you stored in a file. The following filenames conform to the suggested syntax *and* convey information about the contents of the file:

- **correspond**

- **january**

- **davis**

- **reports**

- **2001**

- **acct_payable**

When you share your files with users on other systems, you may need to make long filenames differ within the first 14 characters. If you keep the filenames short, they are easy to type; later you can add extensions to them without exceeding the 14-character limit imposed by some filesystems. The disadvantage of short filenames is that they are typically less descriptive than long filenames. When you share files with systems running DOS or older versions of MS Windows, you must respect the 8-character filename body length and 3-character filename extension length imposed by those systems.

Long filenames enable you to assign descriptive names to files. To help you select among files without typing entire filenames, shells support filename completion. See the "Filename Completion" tip on page 54.

You can use upper- and/or lowercase letters within filenames. GNU/Linux is case sensitive; thus files named **JANUARY**, **January**, and **january** represent three distinct files.

Do Not Use SPACEs within Filenames || caution

Although you can use SPACEs within filenames, it is a poor idea. Because a SPACE is a special character, you must quote it on a command line. Quoting a character on a command line can be difficult for a novice user and cumbersome for an experienced user. Use periods, underscores, or hyphens instead of SPACEs: joe.02.04.26, for–sam, new_stuff.

Filename Extensions

In the filenames listed in Table 4-1, *filename extensions* help describe the contents of the file. A filename extension is the part of the filename following an embedded period. Some programs, such as the C programming language compiler, depend on specific filename extensions, but in most cases filename extensions are optional. Use extensions freely to make filenames easy to understand. If you like, you can use several periods within the same filename: for example, **notes.4.10.01** or **files.tar.gz**.

Filename || table 4-1

compute.c	A C programming language source file
compute.o	The object code for the program
compute	The same program as an executable file
memo.0410	A text file
memo.pdf	A PDF file; view with **xpdf**
memo.ps	A postscript file; view with **gs**
memo.Z	A file compressed with **compress** (page 73); use **uncompress** (or **gunzip**—page 74) to decompress
memo.tar.Z	A **tar** (page 75) archive of files compressed with **compress** (page 73)
memo.gz	A file compressed with **gzip** (page 73); view with **zcat** or decompress with **gunzip** (both on page 74)

Filename (Continued)	‖ table 4-1
memo.bz2	A file compressed with bzip2 (page 74); view with bzcat or decompress with bunzip2
memo.tgz or **memo.tar.gz**	A tar archive of files compressed with gzip (page 73)
memo.tbz2 or memo.**tar.bz2**	A tar archive of files compressed with bzip2 (page 74)
memo.html	A file meant to be viewed using a Web browser, such as Mozilla
photo.jpg or **photo.gif**	A file containing graphical information, such as a picture (also .jpeg)

Invisible Filenames

A filename that begins with a period is called an *invisible filename* (or *invisible file* or sometimes *hidden file*) because ls does not normally display it. The command **ls –a** displays *all* filenames, even invisible ones. Startup files (page 109) are usually invisible so that they do not clutter a directory. The **.plan** file (page 82) is also invisible. Two special invisible entries—a single and double period (**.** and **..**)—appear in every directory (page 112).

mkdir: Creates a Directory

The mkdir utility creates a directory. The *argument* (page 1454) to mkdir becomes the pathname of the new directory. The following examples develop the directory structure shown in Figure 4-4. The directories that are added are lighter than the others and connected by dashes.

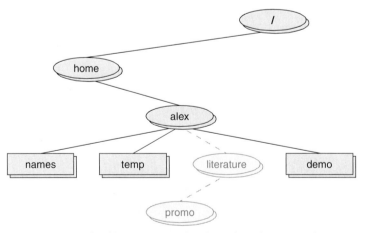

Figure 4-4   The file structure developed in the examples

```
$ ls
demo   names   temp
$ mkdir /home/alex/literature
$ ls
demo   literature   names   temp
$ ls -F
demo   literature/   names   temp
$ ls literature
$
```

Figure 4-5   The mkdir utility

In Figure 4-5 ls shows the names of the files Alex has been working with in his home directory: **demo, names,** and **temp**. Next, using mkdir, Alex creates a directory named **literature** as a child of the **/home/alex** directory. When you use mkdir, enter the pathname of *your* home directory in place of **/home/alex**. The second ls verifies the presence of the new directory.

You can use the −F option with ls to display a slash after the name of each directory and an asterisk after each executable file (utility or program). When you call it with an argument that is the name of a directory, ls lists the contents of the directory. If no files are in the directory, ls does not display anything.

The Working Directory

While you are logged in on a character-based interface to a GNU/Linux system, you are always associated with one directory or another. The directory you are associated with, or are working in, is called the *working directory*, or *current directory*. Sometimes this association is referred to in a physical sense: "You are *in* (or *working in*) the **jenny** directory." The pwd command displays the pathname of the working directory.

To access any file in the working directory, you do not need a pathname but rather only a simple filename. To access a file in another directory, you *must* use a pathname.

Significance of the Working Directory

Typing a long pathname is tedious and increases the chance of making a mistake. This is less true under a GUI, where you click filenames or icons. You can choose a working directory for any particular task to reduce the need for long pathnames. Your choice of a working directory does not allow you to do anything you could not do otherwise but simply makes some operations easier.

Refer to Figure 4-6 as you read this paragraph. Files that are children of the working directory can be referenced by simple filenames. Grandchildren of the

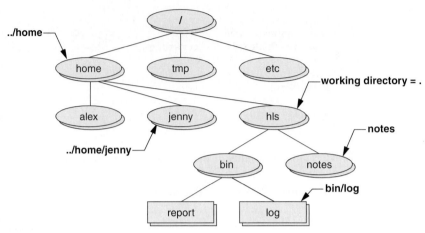

Figure 4-6   Relative pathnames

working directory can be referenced by short relative pathnames: two filenames separated by a slash. When you manipulate files in a large directory structure, short relative pathnames can save time and aggravation. If you choose a working directory that contains the files used most for a particular task, you need to use fewer long, cumbersome pathnames.

Home Directory

When you first log in on a GNU/Linux system, your working directory is your *home directory*. To display the absolute pathname of your home directory, use pwd just after you log in (Figure 4-7).

Without any arguments, the ls utility displays a list of the files in the working directory. Because your home directory has been the only working directory you have used so far, ls has always displayed a list of files in your home directory. (All the files you have created up to now were created in your home directory.)

cd: Changes to Another Working Directory

The cd (change directory) utility makes another directory the working directory but does *not* change the contents of the working directory. The first cd command in Figure 4-8 makes the **/home/alex/literature** directory the working directory, as verified by pwd.

```
login: alex
Password:
Last login: Wed Oct 20 11:14:21 from zach
$ pwd
/home/alex
```

Figure 4-7   Log in

```
$ cd /home/alex/literature
$ pwd
/home/alex/literature
$ cd
$ pwd
/home/alex
```

Figure 4-8   cd changes your working directory

Without an argument, cd makes your home directory the working directory, as it was when you first logged in. The second command in Figure 4-8 does not have an argument and makes Alex's home directory the working directory.

The Working Directory versus Your Home Directory || tip

The working directory is not the same as your home directory. Your home directory remains the same for the duration of your session and usually from session to session. Each time you log in, you are working in the same directory: your home directory.

Unlike your home directory, your working directory can change as often as you like. You have no set working directory. That is why some people refer to it as the *current directory*. When you log in and until you change directories by using cd, your home directory is your working directory. If you were to change directories to Scott's home directory, then Scott's home directory would be your working directory.

Startup Files

Important files that appear in your home directory are *startup files*. They give the shell and other programs information about you and your preferences. Frequently one of these files tells the shell what kind of terminal you are using (page 1402) and executes the stty (set terminal) utility (page 1335) to establish your line kill and erase keys.

Either you or the system administrator can put a shell startup file, containing shell commands, in your home directory. The shell executes the commands in this file each time you log in. With the bash shell, the filename is **.bash_profile** (page 565); with zsh, it is **.zprofile** (page 737); with tcsh, it is **.login** (page 684). Because the startup files have invisible filenames, you must use the **ls –a** command to see whether one of these files is in your home directory. A GUI has many startup files. Usually you do not have to work with these files directly but can control startup sequences by using icons on your desktop.

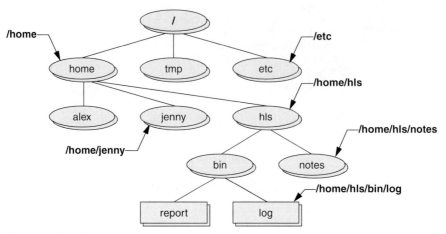

Figure 4-9   Absolute pathnames

Absolute Pathnames

Every file has a pathname. Figure 4-9 shows the pathnames of directories and ordinary files in part of a filesystem hierarchy.

An absolute pathname always starts with a slash (/), the name of the root directory. You can build the absolute pathname of a file by tracing a path from the root directory through all the intermediate directories to the file. String all the filenames in the path together, separating each from the next with a slash (/) and preceding the group of filenames with a slash (/).

This path of filenames is called an *absolute pathname* because it locates a file absolutely, by tracing a path from the root directory to the file. The part of a pathname following the final slash is called a *simple filename*, or *filename*.

Another form of absolute pathname begins with a tilde (~), which represents a home directory. For more information, refer to "Special Pathnames" on page 116.

Relative Pathnames

A *relative pathname* traces a path from the working directory to a file. The pathname is *relative* to the working directory. Any pathname that does not begin with the root directory (/) or a tilde (~) is a relative pathname. Like absolute pathnames, relative pathnames can describe a path through many directories.

Alex could have created the **literature** directory in Figure 4-5 more easily by using a relative pathname.

```
$ pwd
/home/alex
$ mkdir literature
```

The pwd command shows that Alex's home directory (**/home/alex**) is the working directory. The mkdir utility displays an error message if a directory or file named **literature** exists: You cannot have two files or directories with the same name in one directory. The pathname used in this example is a simple filename. A simple filename is a kind of relative pathname that specifies a file in the working directory.

When Using a Relative Pathname, Know Which Is Your Working Directory   ‖ caution

The location of the file that you are accessing with a relative pathname is dependent on (relative to) the working directory. Always make sure you know which is the working directory before using a relative pathname. Use **pwd** to verify the directory: If you are using **mkdir** and you are not where you think you are in the file hierarchy, the new directory will end up in an unexpected location.

It does not matter which directory is the working directory when you use an absolute pathname.

The following commands show two ways to create the **promo** directory as a child of the newly created **literature** directory. The first way assumes that **/home/alex** is the working directory and uses a relative pathname:

```
$ pwd
/home/alex
$ mkdir literature/promo
```

the second way uses an absolute pathname:

```
$ mkdir /home/alex/literature/promo
```

Use the **−t** option to mkdir to create both the **literature** and **promo** directories with one command:

```
$ pwd
/home/alex
$ ls
demo  names  temp
$ mkdir -t literature/promo
```

or

```
$ mkdir -t /home/alex/literature/promo
```

The . and .. Directory Entries

The mkdir utility automatically puts two entries in every directory you create: a single period and a double period, representing the directory itself and the parent directory, respectively. These entries are invisible because each of their filenames begins with a period.

Because mkdir automatically places these entries in every directory, you can rely on their presence. The . is synonymous with the pathname of the working directory and can be used in its place; .. is synonymous with the pathname of the parent of the working directory.

The following example uses .. to copy **temp** to the parent directory (**/home/alex**) and then lists the contents of the **/home/alex** directory from **/home/alex/literature**, again to represent the parent directory:

```
$ pwd
/home/alex/literature
$ ls ..
demo   literature   names   temp
$ cp temp ..
$ ls ..
demo   temp   literature   names   temp
```

While working in his **promo** directory, Alex can use the following relative pathname to edit a file in his home directory. Before calling the editor, Alex checks which directory he is in:

```
$ pwd
/home/alex/literature/promo
$ vi ../../names
```

Virtually anywhere that a utility program requires a filename or pathname, you can use an absolute or relative pathname or a simple filename. This holds true for ls, vi, mkdir, rm, and most other GNU/Linux utilities.

Important Standard Directories and Files

Originally files on a GNU/Linux system were not located in standard places. That made it difficult to document and maintain a GNU/Linux system and just about impossible for someone to release a software package that would compile and run on various GNU/Linux systems. The first version of the first standard for the GNU/Linux filesystem, the FSSTND (Linux Filesystem Standard), was released on February 14, 1994. In early 1995 work was started on a broader standard covering many UNIX-like systems: FHS (Linux Filesystem Hierarchy Standard—www.pathname.com/fhs). More recently FHS has been incorporated in LSB (Linux Standard Base—www.linuxbase.org), a workgroup of FSG (Free Standards

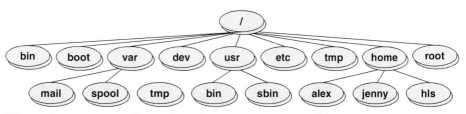

Figure 4-10   A typical FHS-based GNU/Linux system file structure

Group—www.freestandards.org). Figure 4-10 shows the locations of some important directories and files, as specified by FHS. The significance of many of these directories will become clear as you continue reading.

The following list describes the directories shown in Figure 4-10, along with some of the directories described by FHS and some others. Red Hat Linux does not use all the directories specified by FHS. You cannot always determine the function of a directory by its name: Although **/opt** stores add-on software, **/etc/opt** stores configuration files for the software in **/opt**. See also "Important Files and Directories" on page 956.

/ **Root**   The root directory, present in all GNU/Linux system file structures, is the ancestor of all files in the filesystem.

/bin **Essential command binaries**   This directory holds the files needed to bring the system up and run it when it first comes up in single-user mode (page 949).

/boot **Static files of the boot loader**   This directory contains most of the files needed to boot the system.

/dev **Device files**   This directory contains all files that represent peripheral devices, such as disk drives, terminals, and printers.

/etc **Machine–local system configuration**   Administrative, configuration, and other system files are kept here. One of the most important is the **/etc/passwd** file, which contains a list of all users who have permission to use the system. See Chapter 17 for more information about the administrative uses of the **/etc** directory.

/etc/X11 **Machine–local configuration for the X Window System**

/etc/opt **Configuration files for add-on software packages kept in /opt**

/home **User home directories**   Each user's home directory is typically one of many subdirectories of the **/home** directory. As an example, assuming that users' directories are under **/home**, the absolute pathname of Jenny's home directory is **/home/jenny**. On some systems the users' directories may not be under **/home** but instead might all be under **/inhouse**; some might be under **/inhouse** and others under **/clients**.

/lib **Shared libraries and kernel modules**

/lib/modules   Loadable kernel modules

/mnt   Mount point for temporary mounting of filesystems

/opt   Add-on software packages (optional packages)

/proc   Kernel and process information virtual filesystem

/root   Home directory for root

/sbin   **Essential system binaries**   Utilities used for system administration are stored in **/sbin** and **/usr/sbin**. The **/sbin** directory includes utilities needed during the booting process, and **/usr/sbin** holds those utilities that are most useful after the system is up and running. In older versions of GNU/Linux, many system administration utilities were scattered through several directories that often included other system files (/etc, /usr/bin, /usr/adm, /usr/include).

/tmp   **Temporary files**   Many programs use this directory to hold temporary files.

/usr   **Second major hierarchy**   This directory traditionally includes subdirectories that contain information used by the system. Files in **/usr** subdirectories do not change often and may be shared by multiple systems.

/usr/bin   **Most user commands**   This directory contains the standard GNU/Linux utility programs: binaries that are not needed in single-user mode (page 949).

/usr/bin/X11   Symbolic link to /usr/X11R6/bin

/usr/games   Games and educational programs

/usr/include   Header files included by C programs

/usr/include/X11   Symbolic link to /usr/X11R6/include/X11

/usr/lib   Libraries

/usr/lib/X11   Symbolic link to /usr/X11R6/lib/X11

/usr/local   **Local hierarchy**   This directory holds locally important files and directories that are often added to Red Hat. Subdirectories of **/usr/local** include **bin, games, include, lib, sbin, share,** and **src.**

/usr/man   Online manuals

/usr/sbin   Nonvital system administration binaries   See **/sbin.**

/usr/share   **Architecture-independent data**   Subdirectories of **/usr/share** include **dict, doc, games, info, locale, man, misc, terminfo,** and **zoneinfo.**

/usr/share/doc   Miscellaneous documentation

/usr/share/info   GNU info system's primary directory

/usr/src   Source code

/usr/X11R6 X Window System, version 11 release 6.

/var **Variable data** Files with contents that vary as the system runs are found in subdirectories under **/var**. The most common examples are temporary files, system log files, spooled files, and user mailbox files. Subdirectories of **/var** include **cache, lib, lock, log, opt, run, spool, tmp,** and **yp**. Older versions of GNU/Linux scattered such files through several subdirectories of **/usr** (**/usr/adm, /usr/mail, /usr/spool, /usr/tmp**).

/var/log **Log files** This directory contains **lastlog** (record of the last login of each user), **messages** (system messages from **syslogd**), and **wtmp** (record of all logins/logouts).

/var/spool **Spooled application data** This directory contains **anacron, at, cron, lpd, mail, mqueue, news, samba,** and **uucp**. The file **/var/spool/mail** has a symbolic link in **/var**.

Working with Directories

This section covers deleting directories, copying and moving files between directories, and moving directories. It also describes how to use pathnames to make your work with GNU/Linux easier.

rmdir: Deletes a Directory

The rmdir (remove directory) utility deletes a directory. You cannot delete the working directory or a directory that contains other than . and .. entries. If you need to delete a directory with files in it, first use rm to delete the files and then delete the directory. You do not have to delete the . and .. entries; rmdir removes them automatically. The following command deletes the directory that was created in Figure 4-5:

```
$ rmdir /home/alex/literature
```

The rm utility has a **–r** option (**rm –r** *filename*) that recursively deletes files, including directories, within a directory and also deletes the directory itself.

Use rm –r Carefully, if at All || caution

Although rm –r is a handy command, you must use it carefully. Do not use it with an ambiguous file reference such as *. It is quite easy to wipe out your entire home directory with a single short command.

Pathnames

In the following example **/home/alex** is the working directory. The example uses a relative pathname to copy the file **letter** to the **/home/alex/literature/promo** directory . The copy of the file has the simple filename **letter.0610**:

```
$ pwd
/home/alex
$ cp letter literature/promo/letter.0610
```

Use a text editor to create a file named **letter** if you want to experiment with the examples that follow.

Assuming that Alex has not changed to another directory, the following command allows him to edit the copy of the file he just made:

```
$ vi literature/promo/letter.0610
.
.
.
```

If Alex does not want to use a long pathname to specify the file, he can use cd to make the **promo** directory the working directory before using vi.

```
$ cd literature/promo
$ pwd
/home/alex/literature/promo
$ vi letter.0610
.
.
.
```

If Alex wants to make the parent of the working directory (named **/home/alex/literature**) the new working directory, he can give the following command, which takes advantage of the **..** directory entry:

```
$ cd ..
$ pwd
/home/alex/literature
```

Optional

Special Pathnames

To save typing, the shells and some utilities, such as vi, recognize a few shortcuts in pathnames. The shell expands the characters **~/** (a tilde followed by a slash) at the start of a pathname into the pathname of your home directory. Using this shortcut, you can examine your **.login** file with the following command no matter which directory is your working directory:

```
$ less ~/.login
```

A tilde quickly references paths that start with your or someone else's home directory. The shell expands a tilde followed by a login name at the beginning of a pathname into the pathname of that user's home directory. Assuming he has permission to do so, Alex can examine Scott's **.login** file with

```
$ less ~scott/.login
```

Refer to "~   Tilde Expansion" on page 609 for a discussion of this topic.

mv, cp: Moves or Copies a File

Chapter 3 discussed the use of mv to rename files. However, mv is more general than that: You can use mv to move files from one directory to another (change the pathname of a file) and to change a simple filename.

When used to move one or more files to a new directory, the syntax of the mv command is

> *mv existing-file-list directory*

If the working directory is **/home/alex**, Alex can use the following command to move the files **names** and **temp** from the working directory to the **literature** directory:

```
$ mv names temp literature
```

This command changes the absolute pathnames of the **names** and **temp** files from **/home/alex/names** and **/home/alex/temp** to **/home/alex/literature/names** and **/home/alex/literature/temp** (Figure 4-11). As with most GNU/Linux commands, mv accepts either absolute or relative pathnames.

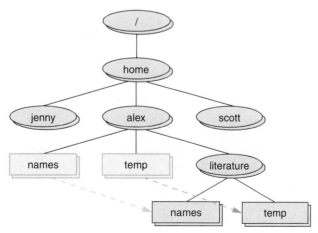

Figure 4-11   Directories and ordinary files

As you work with GNU/Linux and create more and more files, you will need to create directories, using mkdir, to keep the files organized. The mv utility is a useful tool for moving files from one directory to another as you develop your directory hierarchy. The cp utility works the same way that mv does but makes copies of the *existing-file-list* in the specified *directory*.

mv: Moves a Directory

Just as it moves ordinary files from one directory to another, mv can also move directories. The syntax is similar except that you specify one or more directories, not ordinary files, to move:

> *mv existing-directory-list new-directory*

If **new-directory** does not exist, the **existing-directory-list** must contain just one directory name, which mv changes to **new-directory** (mv renames the directory). Although directories can be renamed using mv, their contents cannot be copied with cp unless you use the **−r** option (page 1122). Refer to tar and cpio in Part III for other ways to copy/move directories.

Access Permissions

Three types of users can access a file: the owner of the file (*owner*), a member of a group to which the owner belongs (*group;* see page 959 for more information on groups), and everyone else (*other*). A user can attempt to access an ordinary file in three ways: by trying to *read from, write to,* or *execute* it. Three types of users, each able to access a file in three ways, equal a total of nine possible ways to access an ordinary file.

ls −l: Displays Permissions

When you call ls with the **−l** option and the name of an ordinary file, ls displays a line of information about the file. The following example displays information for two files. The file **letter.0610** contains the text of a letter, and **check_spell** contains a shell script, a program written in a high-level shell programming language:

```
$ ls -l letter.0610 check_spell
-rw-r--r-- 1 alex   pubs   3355  May   2 10:52 letter.0610
-rwxr-xr-x 2 alex   pubs    852  May   5 14:03 check_spell
```

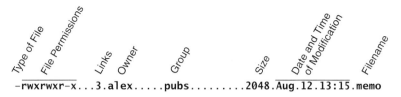

Figure 4-12   The columns displayed by the ls –l command

From left to right, the lines contain the following information (refer also to Figure 4-12):

- The type of file (first character)
- The file's access permissions (the next nine characters)
- The number of links to the file (see page 123)
- The name of the owner of the file (usually the person who created the file)
- The name of the group that has group access to the file
- The size of the file in characters (bytes)
- The date and time the file was created or last modified
- The name of the file

The type of file (first column) for **letter.0610** is a hyphen (-) because it is an ordinary file (directory files have a d in this column).

The next three characters represent the access permissions for the *owner* of the file: r indicates read permission and w indicates write permission. The – in the next column indicates that the owner does *not* have execute permission; otherwise you would see an x here.

In a similar manner the next three characters represent permissions for the *group,* and the final three characters represent permissions for *other* (everyone else). In the preceding example the owner of the file **letter.0610** can read from and write to it, whereas group and others can only read from the file, and no one is allowed to execute it. Although execute permission can be allowed for any file, it does not make sense to assign execute permission to a file that contains a document, such as a letter. The **check_spell** file is an executable shell script, and execute permission is appropriate. (The owner, group, and others have execute access permission.)

chmod: Changes Access Permissions

The owner of a file controls which users have permission to access the file and how they can access it. When you own a file, you can use the chmod (change mode) utility to change access permissions for that file. In the following example chmod adds (**+**) read and write permission (**rw**) for all (**a**) users:

You Must Have Read Permission to Execute a Shell Script   ‖ tip

Because a shell needs to read a shell script (an ASCII file containing shell commands) before it can execute the commands within the script, you must have read permission to the file containing the script in
order to execute it. You also need execute permission to execute a shell script directly on the command
line. Binary (program) files do not need to be read; they are executed directly. You need only execute
permission to run a binary (nonshell) program.

```
$ chmod a+rw letter.0610
$ ls -l letter.0610
-rw-rw-rw- 1 alex  pubs   3355  May  2 10:52 letter.0610
```

In the next example chmod removes (–) read and execute (**rx**) permissions for
users other (**o**) than the owner of the file (Alex) and members of the group associated with the file (**pubs** group):

```
$ chmod o-rx check_spell
$ ls -l check_spell
-rwxr-x--- 2 alex  pubs    852  May  5 14:03 check_spell
```

In addition to **a** (for *all*) and **o** (for *other*), you can use **g** (for *group*) and **u** (for
user, although user refers to the owner of the file, who may or may not be the user
of the file at any given time) in the argument to chmod. Refer to pages 545 and 1103
for more information on chmod.

The GNU/Linux file access permission scheme lets you give other users access
to the files you want to share and keep your private files confidential. You can allow
other users to read from *and* write to a file (you may be one of several people working on a joint project). You can allow others to only read from a file (perhaps a
project specification you are proposing). Or you can allow others to only write to a
file (similar to an in-basket or mailbox, where you want others to be able to send
you mail but do not want them to read your mail). Similarly, you can protect entire
directories from being scanned (covered shortly).

There is an exception to the access permissions just described. Anyone who
knows the **root** password can log in as Superuser (page 896) and have full access to
all files, regardless of owner or access permissions.

chmod: **o** for Other, **u** for Owner   ‖ tip

When using **chmod**, many people assume that the **o** stands for *owner;* it does not. The **o** stands for
other, whereas **u** stands for *owner* (*user*).

Minimize Use of Setuid and Setgid Programs Owned by root || security

Executable files that are setuid and owned by **root** have Superuser privileges when they are run even if they are not run by **root**. This type of program is very powerful because it can do anything that Superuser can do (that the program is designed to do). Similarly, executable files that are setgid and belong to the group **root** have extensive privileges.

Because of the power they hold and the potential destruction they can do, avoid creating and using setuid and setgid programs owned by or belonging to the group **root** indiscriminately. Because of the inherent dangers, many sites do not allow these programs on their machines at all. See page 898 for information on setuid and Superuser.

Setuid and Setgid Permissions

When you execute a file that has setuid (set user ID) permission, the process executing the file takes on the privileges of the owner of the file. For example, if you run a setuid program that removes all the files in a directory, you can remove files in any of the file owner's directories even if you do not normally have permission to do so. In a similar manner setgid (set group ID) permission means that the process executing the file takes on the privileges of the group the file is associated with. The ls utility shows setuid permission as an s in the owner's executable position and setgid as an s in the group's executable position:

```
$ ls -l program1
-rwxr-xr-x    1 alex      pubs       15828 Nov  5 06:28 program1
$ chmod u+s program1
$ ls -l program1
-rwsr-xr-x    1 alex      pubs       15828 Nov  5 06:28 program1
$ chmod g+s program1
$ ls -l program1
-rwsr-sr-x    1 alex      pubs       15828 Nov  5 06:28 program1
```

Do Not Write Setuid Shell Scripts || security

Never write shell scripts that are setuid. Several techniques for subverting them are well known.

Directory Access Permissions

Access permissions have slightly different meanings when used with directories. Although the three types of users can read from or write to a directory, the directory cannot be executed. Execute access permission is redefined for a directory: It means that you can cd into the directory and/or examine files that you have permission to read from in the directory. It has nothing to do with executing a file.

When you have only execute permission for a directory, you can use ls to list a file in the directory if you know its name. You cannot use ls without an argument to list the contents of the directory. In the following exchange Jenny first verifies that she is logged on as herself. Then she checks the permissions on Alex's **info** directory and cds into it. (You can view the access permissions associated with a directory by running ls with the –d [directory] and –l [long] options. The d at the left end of the line that ls displays indicates that **/home/alex/info** is a directory.) Because Jenny does not have read permission for the directory, the **ls –l** command without any arguments returns an error. The period (.) in the error message represents the working directory:

```
$ who am i
jenny       pts/7   Aug 21 10:02
$ ls -ld /home/alex/info
drwx-----x   2 alex       pubs              512 Aug 21 09:31 /home/alex/info
$ cd /home/alex/info
$ ls -l
.: Permission denied
total 2
```

When Jenny specifies the names of the files she wants information about, she is not reading new directory information, just searching for specific information, which she is allowed to do with execute access to the directory. She cannot display **financial**, because she does not have read access to it. She does have read access to **notes**, so she has no problem using cat to display the file.

```
$ ls -l memo.1 memo.2 financial notes summary
-rw-------   1 alex       pubs         34 Aug 21 09:31 financial
-rw-r--r--   1 alex       pubs         21 Aug 21 09:31 memo.1
-rw-r--r--   1 alex       pubs         21 Aug 21 09:32 memo.2
-rw-r--r--   1 alex       pubs         30 Aug 21 09:32 notes
-rw-r--r--   1 alex       pubs         32 Aug 21 09:32 summary
$ cat financial
cat: cannot open financial
$ cat notes
This is the file named notes.
```

Next, Alex uses the following command to give everyone read access to his **info** directory:

```
$ chmod o+r /home/alex/info
```

Now when Jenny checks access permissions on **info**, she finds that she has both read and execute access to the directory. Now **ls –l** works just fine without arguments, but she still cannot read **financial**. (This is an issue of file permissions, not directory permissions.) Finally, she tries to create a file named **newfile** by redirecting output from cat (page 145). If Alex were to give her write permission to the **info** directory, she would be able to create new files in it:

```
$ ls -ld /home/alex/info
drwx---r-x    2 alex      pubs            512 Aug 21 09:31 /home/alex/info
$ ls -l
total 10
-rw-------    1 alex      pubs             34 Aug 21 09:31 financial
-rw-r--r--    1 alex      pubs             21 Aug 21 09:31 memo.1
-rw-r--r--    1 alex      pubs             21 Aug 21 09:32 memo.2
-rw-r--r--    1 alex      pubs             30 Aug 21 09:32 notes
-rw-r--r--    1 alex      pubs             32 Aug 21 09:32 summary
$ cat financial
cat: financial: Permission denied
$ cat > newfile
bash: newfile: Permission denied
```

Links

A *link* is a pointer to a file. Every time you create a file using vi or cp or by any other means, you are putting a pointer in a directory. This pointer associates a filename with a place on the disk. When you specify a filename in a command, you are indirectly pointing to the place on the disk where the information that you want is located.

Sharing files can be useful when two or more people are working on a project and need to share some information. You can make it easy for other users to access one of your files by creating additional links to the file.

To share a file with another user, first give the user permission to read from and write to the file. (In addition, you may have to change the access permission of the parent directory of the file to give the user read, write, and/or execute permission.) Once the permissions are appropriately set, the user can create a link to the file so that each of you can access the file from your separate directory hierarchies.

A link can also be useful to a single user with a large directory hierarchy. You can create links to cross-classify files in your directory hierarchy, using different classifications for different tasks. For example, if your directory hierarchy is the one depicted in Figure 4-2, you might have a file named **to_do** in each of the subdirectories of the **correspond** directory—that is, in **personal**, **memos**, and **business**. Then if you find it difficult to keep track of everything you need to do, you can create a separate directory, named **to_do** in the **correspond** directory, and link each to-do list into that directory. You could link the file named **to_do** in the **memos** directory to a file named **memos** in the **to_do** directory. This set of links is shown in Figure 4-13.

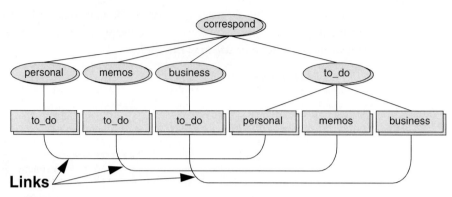

Links

Figure 4-13   Using links to cross-classify files

Although this may sound complicated, this technique keeps all your to-do lists conveniently in one place. The appropriate list is also easily accessible in the task-related directory when you are busy composing letters, writing memos, or handling personal business.

About the Discussion of Hard Links   ‖ tip

There are two kinds of links: hard links and symbolic, or soft, links. Hard links, discussed first, are older and becoming dated. The section on hard links is marked optional; you can skip it, although it discusses inodes and gives you insight into how the filesystem is structured.

Optional

Hard Links

The ln (link) utility (without the **–s** or **––symbolic** option) creates an additional hard link to an existing file. The new link appears as another file in the file structure. If the file appears in the same directory as the one the file is linked with, the links must have different filenames. This restriction does not apply if the linked file is in another directory. The syntax for ln is

ln existing-file new-link

The following command makes the link shown in Figure 4-14 by creating a new link named **/home/alex/letter** to an existing file named **draft** in Jenny's home directory:

```
$ pwd
/home/jenny
$ ln draft /home/alex/letter
```

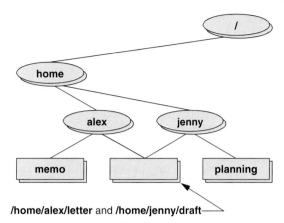

Figure 4-14   Two links to the same file: **/home/alex/letter** and **/home/jenny/draft**

The new link appears in the **/home/alex** directory with the filename **letter**. In practice it may be necessary for Alex to change directory and file permissions as shown in the previous section in order to give Jenny the necessary permissions. Even though **/home/alex/letter** appears in Alex's directory, Jenny is the owner of the file.

The ln utility creates an additional pointer to an existing file but does *not* make another copy of the file. Because there is only one file, the file status information, such as access permissions, owner, and the time the file was last modified, is the same for all links. Only the filenames differ. When Jenny modifies **/home/jenny/draft**, Alex sees the changes in **/home/alex/letter**.

cp versus ln

The following commands verify that ln does not make an additional copy of a file. Create a file, use ln to make an additional link to the file, change the contents of the file through one link, and verify the change through the other link:

```
$ cat file_a
This is file A.
$ ln file_a file_b
$ cat file_b
This is file A.
$ vi file_b
.
.
.
$ cat file_b
This is file B after the change.
$ cat file_a
This is file B after the change.
```

If you try the same experiment using cp instead of ln and make a change to a *copy* of the file, the difference between the two utilities will become clearer. Once you change a *copy* of a file, the two files are different:

```
$ cat file_c
This is file C.
$ cp file_c file_d
$ cat file_d
This is file C.
$ vi file_d
.
.
.
$ cat file_d
This is file D after the change.
$ cat file_c
This is file C.
```

You can also use ls with the –l option, followed by the names of the files you want to compare, to see that the status information is the same for two links to a file and is different for files that are not linked. In the following example the **2** in the links field (just to the left of **alex**) shows there are two links to **file_a** and **file_b**:

```
$ ls -l file_a file_b file_c file_d
-rw-r--r-- 2 alex pubs 33  May 24 10:52 file_a
-rw-r--r-- 2 alex pubs 33  May 24 10:52 file_b
-rw-r--r-- 1 alex pubs 16  May 24 10:55 file_c
-rw-r--r-- 1 alex pubs 33  May 24 10:57 file_d
```

Although it is easy to guess which files are linked to one another in this example, ls does not explicitly tell you.

Use ls with the –i option to determine without a doubt which files are linked. The –i option lists the *inode number* for each file. An *inode* is the control structure for a file. If the two filenames have the same inode number, they share the control structure and are links to the same file. Conversely, when two filenames have different inode numbers, they are different files. The following example shows that **file_a** and **file_b** have the same inode number and that **file_c** and **file_d** have different inode numbers:

```
$ ls -i file_a file_b file_c file_d
3534 file_a    3534 file_b    5800 file_c    7328 file_d
```

All links to a file are of equal value: The operating system cannot distinguish the order in which multiple links were made. When a file has two links, you can remove either one and still access the file through the remaining link. You can remove the link used to create the file and, as long as there is a remaining link, still access the file through that link.

Symbolic Links

The links that are described in the preceding, optional section are *hard links*. In addition to hard links, GNU/Linux supports links called *symbolic links, soft links,* or *symlinks.* A hard link is a pointer to a file (directory entry → inode), whereas a symbolic link is an *indirect* pointer to a file. A symbolic link is a directory entry that contains the pathname of the pointed-to file (a pointer to the hard link to the file).

Symbolic links were developed because of the limitations of hard links. No one can create a hard link to a directory; anyone can create a symbolic link to a directory. Also, a symbolic link can point to any file, regardless of where it is located in the file structure, but a hard link to a file must be in the same filesystem as the other hard link(s) to the file.

Often the GNU/Linux file hierarchy is composed of several filesystems. Because each filesystem keeps separate control information (that is, separate inode tables) for the files it contains, it is not possible to create hard links between files in different filesystems. When you create links only among files in your own directories, you will not notice these limitations.

One of its big advantages over a hard link is that a symbolic link can point to a nonexistent file. This ability is useful if you need a link to a file that periodically gets removed and recreated. A hard link would keep pointing to the removed file, which the hard link would keep alive because of its being a hard link, even after a new file was created. A symbolic link would always point to the newly created file and not interfere with deleting the old file. For example, a symbolic link could point to a file that gets checked in and out under the Source Code Control System, a .o file that is recreated by the C compiler each time you run make, or a log file that is periodically archived.

Although they are more general than hard links, symbolic links have some disadvantages. Whereas all hard links to a file have equal status, symbolic links do not have the same status as hard links. When a file has multiple hard links, it is like a person having multiple full legal names, as many married women do. In contrast, symbolic links are like nicknames. Anyone can have one or more nicknames, but nicknames have a lesser status than legal names. Some of the peculiarities of symbolic links are described in the following sections.

ln: Creates a Symbolic Link

Use ln with the --symbolic (or -s) option to create a symbolic link. The following example creates a symbolic link, /tmp/s3, to the file sum in Alex's home directory. When you use the ls -l command to look at the symbolic link, ls displays the name of the link and the name of the file it points to. The first character of the listing is l (for link):

```
$ ln --symbolic /home/alex/sum /tmp/s3
$ ls -l /home/alex/sum /tmp/s3
-rw-rw-r--   1 alex     alex               38 Jun 12 09:51 /home/alex/sum
lrwxrwxrwx   1 alex     alex               14 Jun 12 10:09 /tmp/s3 ->
/home/alex/sum
$ cat /tmp/s3
This is sum.
```

Use Absolute Pathnames with Symbolic Links || tip

Symbolic links are literal and are not aware of directories: A link that points to a relative pathname, which includes simple filenames, assumes that the relative pathname is relative to the directory that the link was created *in* (and not the directory the link was created *from*). In the following example the link points to the file named **sum** in the **/tmp** directory. Because there is no such file, **cat** gives an error message:

```
$ pwd
/home/alex
$ ln --symbolic sum /tmp/s3
$ ls -l sum /tmp/s3
lrwxrwxrwx   1 alex      alex            3 Jun 12 10:13 /tmp/s3 -> sum
-rw-rw-r--   1 alex      alex           38 Jun 12 09:51 sum
$ cat /tmp/s3
cat: /tmp/s3: No such file or directory
```

The sizes and times of the last modification of the two files are different. Unlike a hard link, a symbolic link to a file does not have the same status information as the file itself.

Similarly, you can use **ln** to create a symbolic link to a directory. When you use the **––symbolic** option, **ln** does not care whether the file you are creating a link to is a regular file or a directory.

Optional

cd and Symbolic Links

When you use a symbolic link as an argument to **cd** to change directories, the results can be confusing, particularly if you did not realize that you were using a symbolic link. Adding to the confusion is the fact that the **bash**, **tcsh**, and **zsh** shells handle symbolically linked directories differently when using **cd**.

Symbolically Linked Directories under bash

If you use **cd** to change to a directory that is represented by a symbolic link, the **pwd** builtin lists the name of the symbolic link. The **pwd** utility (**/bin/pwd**) lists the name of the linked-to directory, not the link, regardless of how you got there:

```
$ ln -s /home/alex/grades /tmp/grades.old
$ pwd
/home/alex
$ cd /tmp/grades.old
$ pwd
/tmp/grades.old
$ /bin/pwd
$/home/alex/grades
```

When you change directories back to the parent, you end up in the directory holding the symbolic link:

```
$ cd ..
$ pwd
/tmp
$ /bin/pwd
/tmp
```

Symbolically Linked Directories under *tcsh*

When you perform the same exercise under the TC Shell, pwd and **/bin/pwd** show the name of the original directory, not the link:

```
> cd /tmp/grades.old
> pwd
/home/alex/grades
> /bin/pwd
/home/alex/grades
```

Because pwd does not identify the symbolic link, tcsh provides a variable named **cwd** (current working directory) that contains the name of the symbolic link. To display the value of **cwd**, use echo, SPACE, and the variable name, preceded by a dollar sign:

```
> echo $cwd
/tmp/grades.old
```

Shell variables and the use of the dollar sign are explained in Chapters 12 through 15.

With the TC Shell, changing directories to the parent directory that you accessed through a symbolic link leaves you in the parent of the linked-to directory:

```
> cd ..
> pwd
/home/alex
```

Symbolically Linked Directories under *zsh*

The Z Shell keeps track of the symbolic links when using cd to move into a symbolically linked directory and when moving back to the parent of that directory:

```
% cd /tmp/grades.old
% pwd
/tmp/grades.old
% /bin/pwd
/home/alex/grades
% cd ..
% pwd
/tmp
```

rm: Removes a Link

When you create a file, there is one hard link to it. You can delete the file or, using GNU/Linux terminology, remove the link with the rm utility. When you remove the last hard link to a file, you can no longer access the information stored in the file, and the operating system releases the space the file occupied on the disk for use by other files.[1] The space is released even if symbolic links remain. When there is more than one hard link to a file, you can remove a hard link and still access the file from any remaining link.

When you remove all the hard links to a file, you will not be able to access the file through a symbolic link. In the following example cat reports that the file **total** does not exist, because it is a symbolic link to a file that has been removed:

```
$ ls -l sum
-rw-r--r-- 1 alex pubs 981  May 24 11:05 sum
$ ln -s sum total
$ rm sum
$ cat total
cat: total: No such file or directory
$ ls -l total
lrwxrwxrwx 1 alex pubs 6  May 24 11:09 total -> sum
```

When you remove a file, be sure to remove all symbolic links to it. Remove a symbolic link in the same way you remove other files:

```
$ rm total
```

Chapter Summary

GNU/Linux has a hierarchical, or treelike, file structure that makes it possible to organize files so that you can find them quickly and easily. The file structure contains directory files and ordinary files. Directories contain other files, including other directories, whereas ordinary files generally contain text, programs, or images. The ancestor of all files is the root directory named /.

Most GNU/Linux filesystems support 255-character filenames. Nonetheless, it is a good idea to keep filenames simple and intuitive. Filename extensions can help make filenames more meaningful.

An absolute pathname starts with the root directory and contains all the filenames that trace a path to a given file. Such a pathname starts with a slash representing the root directory and contains additional slashes between the other filenames in the path.

---

1. Unlike DOS/MS Windows, there is no easy way to undelete a file once you have removed it. A skilled hacker can, in some cases, piece the file together with time and effort.

A relative pathname is similar to an absolute pathname, but starts the path tracing from the working directory. A simple filename is the last element of a pathname and is a form of a relative pathname.

When you are logged in, you are always associated with a working directory. Your home directory is your working directory from the time you first log in until you use cd to change directories.

A GNU/Linux filesystem contains many important directories including **/usr/bin**, which stores most of the GNU/Linux utility commands, and **/dev**, which stores device files, many of which represent a physical piece of hardware. An important standard file is **/etc/passwd**; it contains information about users, such as the user ID and full name.

Among the attributes associated with each file are access permissions. These determine who can access the file and the manner in which the file may be accessed. Three groups of user(s) can access the file: the owner, members of a group, and all other users. A regular file can be accessed in three ways: read, write, and execute. The ls utility with the –l option displays these permissions. For directories, execute access is redefined to mean that the directory can be searched, meaning that it can be used as part of a pathname.

The owner of a file or Superuser can use the chmod utility to change the access permissions of a file at any time. This utility defines read, write, and execute permissions for the owner, the file's group, and all other users on the system.

A link is a pointer to a file. You can have several links to a single file, so that you can share the file with other users or have the file appear in more than one directory. Because there is only one copy of a file with multiple links, changing the file through any one link causes the changes to appear in all the links. Hard links cannot link directories or span filesystems, whereas symbolic links can.

Utilities Introduced in This Chapter

cd	Associates you with another working directory (page 108)
chmod	Changes the access permissions on a file (page 119)
ln	Makes a link to an existing file (page 124)
mkdir	Creates a directory (page 106)
pwd	Displays the pathname of the working directory (page 107)
rmdir	Deletes a directory (page 115)

Exercises

1. Is each of the following an absolute pathname, a relative pathname, or a simple filename?

   a. **milk_co**

   b. **correspond/business/milk_co**

   c. **/home/alex**

   d. **/home/alex/literature/promo**

   e. **..**

   f. **letter.0610**

2. List the commands you can use to

   a. Make your home directory the working directory

   b. Identify the working directory

3. If your working directory is **/home/alex** with a subdirectory named **literature,** give three sets of commands that you can use to create a subdirectory named **classics** under **literature**. Also give several sets of commands that you can use to remove the **classics** directory and its contents.

4. The df utility displays all mounted filesystems along with information about each. Use the df utility with the **–h** (humanly readable) option to answer the following questions.

   a. How many filesystems are on your GNU/Linux system?

   b. Which filesystem stores your home directory?

   c. Assuming that your answer to part 4a is two or greater, attempt to create a hard link to a file on another filesystem. What error message do you get? What happens when you attempt to create a symbolic link to the file instead?

5. Suppose that you have a file that is linked to a file owned by another user. What can you do so that changes to the file are no longer shared?

6. You should have read permission for the **/etc/passwd** file. To answer the following questions, use cat or less to display **/etc/passwd**. Look at the fields of information in **/etc/passwd** for the users on your system.

   a. What character is used to separate fields in **/etc/passwd**?

   b. How many fields are used to describe each user?

   c. How many users are on your system?

   d. How many different login shells are in use on your system? (*Hint:* Look at the last field.)

   e. The second field of **/etc/passwd** stores user passwords in encoded form. If the password field contains an x, your system uses shadow passwords and stores the encoded passwords elsewhere. Does your system use shadow passwords?

7. If **/home/jenny/draft** and **/home/alex/letter** are links to the same file and the following sequence of events occurs, what will be the date in the opening of the letter?

   a. Alex gives the command **vi letter**.

   b. Jenny gives the command **vi draft**.

   c. Jenny changes the date in the opening of the letter to January 31, 2003, writes the file, and exits from vi.

   d. Alex changes the date to February 1, 2003, writes the file, and exits from vi.

8. Suppose that a user belongs to a group that has all permissions on a file named **jobs_list**, but the user, as the owner of the file, has no permissions. Describe what operations, if any, the user can perform on **jobs_list**. What command that the user can give will grant the user all permissions on the file?

9. Does the root directory have any subdirectories that you cannot search? Does the root directory have any subdirectories that you cannot read? Explain.

10. Assume that you are given the directory structure shown in Figure 4-2 and the following directory permissions:

```
d--x--x---   3 jenny    pubs           512 Mar 10 15:16 business
drwxr-xr-x   2 jenny    pubs           512 Mar 10 15:16 business/milk_co
```

For each category of permissions—owner, group, and other—what
happens when you run each of the following commands? Assume that the
working directory is the parent of **correspond** and that the file **cheese_co** is
readable by everyone.

a. **cd correspond/business/milk_co**

b. **ls –l correspond/business**

c. **cat correspond/business/cheese_co**

Advanced Exercises

11. Create a file named **–x** in an empty directory. Explain what happens when
    you try to rename it. How can you rename it?

12. Suppose that the working directory contains a single file named **andor**.
    What error message do you get when you run the following command
    line?

    ```
    $ mv andor and\/or
    ```

    Under what circumstances is it possible to run the command without
    producing an error?

13. The **ls –i** command displays a filename preceded by the inode number of
    the file (page 126). Write a command to output inode/filename pairs for
    the files in the working directory, sorted by inode number. (*Hint:* Use a
    pipe.)

14. Do you think that the system administrator has access to a program to
    decode user passwords? Why or why not (see exercise 6)?

15. Is it possible to distinguish a file from a hard link to a file? That is, given a
    filename, can you tell whether it was created using an **ln** command?
    Explain.

16. Explain the error messages displayed in the following sequence of commands:

```
$ ls -l
total 1
drwxrwxr-x    2 alex        bravo          1024 Mar  2 17:57 dirtmp
$ ls dirtmp
$ rmdir dirtmp
rmdir: dirtmp: Directory not empty
$ rm dirtmp/*
rm: No match.
```

17. How can you create a file named –i? Which techniques do not work, and why do they not work?

18. How can you remove a file named –i? Which techniques do not work, and why do they not work?

IN THIS CHAPTER

The Shell I

5

This chapter takes a close look at the shell and explains how to use some of its features. The chapter discusses command line syntax and how the shell processes a command line and initiates execution of a program. The chapter shows how to redirect input to and output from a command, construct pipes and filters on the command line, and run a command as a background task. The final section covers filename expansion and explains how you can use this feature in your everyday work. Except as noted, everything in this chapter applies to the Bourne Again, TC, and Z Shells. However, this chapter uses the Bourne Again Shell for most examples; if you use another shell, the exact format or wording of the shell output may differ from what you see here. Refer to Chapters 12 through 15 for shell-specific information and more on writing and executing shell scripts.

The Command Line

The shell executes a program when you give it a command in response to its prompt. For example, when you give the ls command, the shell executes the utility program named ls. You can cause the shell to execute other types of programs—such as shell scripts, application programs, and programs you have written—in the same way. The line that contains the command, including any arguments, is called the *command line*. In this book the term *command* refers to the characters you type on the command line as well, as to the program that action invokes.

Syntax

Command line syntax dictates the ordering and separation of the elements on a command line. When you press the RETURN key after entering a command, the shell scans the command line for proper syntax. The syntax for a basic command line is

command [arg1] [arg2] ... [argn] RETURN

One or more SPACEs must appear between elements on the command line. The *command* is the command name, *arg1* through *argn* are arguments, and RETURN is the keystroke that terminates all command lines. The arguments in the command line syntax are enclosed in brackets to show that they are optional. Not all commands require arguments: Some commands do not allow arguments; other commands allow a variable number of arguments; and others require a specific number of arguments. Options, a special kind of argument, are usually preceded by a hyphen (also called a dash or minus sign: –). (No *smiley* [page 1492] intended.)

Command Name

Some useful GNU/Linux command lines consist of only the name of the command without any arguments. For example, ls by itself lists the contents of the working directory. Most commands accept one or more arguments. Commands that require arguments typically give a short error message, called a *usage message,* when you use them without arguments, with incorrect arguments, or with the wrong number of arguments.

Arguments

On the command line each sequence of nonblank characters is called a *token,* or *word.* An *argument* is a token, such as a filename, string of text, number, or other object that a command acts on. For example, the argument to a vi or emacs command is the name of the file you want to edit.

The following command line shows cp copying the file named **temp** to **tempcopy**:

```
$ cp temp tempcopy
```

Arguments are numbered starting with the command itself as argument zero. In this example **cp** is argument zero, **temp** is argument one, and **tempcopy** is argument two. The cp utility requires two arguments on the command line. (The utility can take more but not fewer: see Part III.) Argument one is the name of an existing file, and argument two is the name of the file that cp is creating or overwriting. Here the arguments are not optional; both arguments must be present for the command to work. When you do not supply the right number or kind of arguments, cp displays a usage message. Try typing **cp** and then pressing RETURN.

Options

An *option* is an argument that modifies the effects of a command. You can frequently specify more than one option, modifying the command in several different ways. Options are specific to and interpreted by the program that the command line calls.

By convention, options are separate arguments that follow the name of the command. Most utilities require you to prefix options with a hyphen. However, this requirement is specific to the utility and not to the shell. GNU program options are frequently preceded by two hyphens in a row, with – –**help** generating a (sometimes extensive) usage message.

Figure 5-1 first shows what happens when you give an ls command without any options. By default, ls lists the contents of the working directory in alphabetical order, vertically sorted in columns. Next, you see that the –**r** (reverse order; because this is a GNU utility, you can also use – –**reverse**) option causes the ls utility to display the list of files in reverse alphabetical order, still sorted in columns. The –**x** option causes ls to display the list of files in horizontally sorted rows.

When you need to use several options, you can usually group multiple single-letter options into one argument that starts with a single hyphen; do not put SPACEs between the options. You cannot combine options that are preceded by two hyphens this way. Specific rules for combining options depend on the program you are running. Figure 5-1 shows both the –**r** and –**x** options with the ls utility. Together these options generate a list of filenames in horizontally sorted columns, in reverse alphabetical order. Most utilities allow you to list options in any order; **ls –xr** produces the same results as **ls –rx**. The command **ls –x –r** also generates the same list. For more information, refer to "Option Processing" on page 771.

```
$ ls
alex   house   mark    office     personal  test
hold   jenny   names   oldstuff   temp
$ ls -r
test   personal  office  mark   house  alex
temp   oldstuff  names   jenny  hold
$ ls -x
alex     hold      house      jenny  mark  names
office   oldstuff  personal   temp   test
$ ls -rx
test   temp    personal  oldstuff  office  names
mark   jenny   house     hold      alex
```

Figure 5-1   Using options

> ### The Human Readable Option || caution
>
> Most utilities that report on file sizes tell you the size of a file in bytes. That is all right when you are
> dealing with smaller files, but the numbers can get difficult to read when you are working with file sizes
> that are measured in megabytes or gigabytes. Give the command **df**, which reports on the space avail-
> able on your system (and possibly on other systems). Look at the **Used** and **Avail** columns. Now
> give the command **df –h** or **df ––human-readable**. See the difference? Many utilities that report on
> file sizes, including **ls** with the **–l** option, have this option.

Processing the Command Line

As you enter a command line, the Linux tty device driver (part of the Linux operating
system kernel) examines each character to see whether it must take immediate action. When you press CONTROL-H (to erase a character) or CONTROL-U (to kill a line), the
device driver immediately adjusts the command line as required; the shell never sees
the character you erased or the line you killed. Often a similar adjustment occurs
when you press CONTROL-W (to erase a word). When the character does not require immediate action, the device driver stores the character in a buffer and waits until it
receives additional characters. When you press RETURN, the device driver passes the
command line to the shell for processing.

When it processes a command line, the shell looks at the line as a whole and
parses (breaks) it into its component parts (Figure 5-2). Next, the shell looks for the
name of the command. Usually[1] the name of the command is the first thing on the
command line after the prompt (argument zero), so the shell takes the first characters on the command line, up to the first blank (TAB or SPACE), and looks for a command with that name. The command name (the first token) can be specified on the
command line either as a simple filename or as a pathname. For example, you can
call the ls command in either of the following ways:

```
$ ls
```

or

```
$ /bin/ls
```

---

1. The shell does not require that the name of the program appear as the first argument on the command
line. You *can* structure a command line as follows:

```
$ >bb <aa cat
```

When the shell sees the redirect symbols (page 145), it recognizes and processes them and their arguments
before finding the name of the program that the command line is calling. This is a properly structured,
although uncommon, command line.

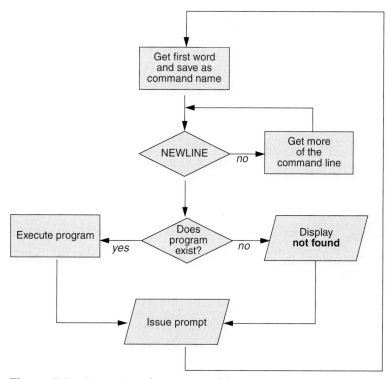

Figure 5-2   Processing the command line

When you give an absolute pathname on the command line or a relative pathname that is not a simple filename (that is, any pathname that includes at least one slash), the shell looks in the specified directory (**/bin** in this case) for a file that has the name **ls** and that you have permission to execute. When you give a simple filename, the shell searches through a list of directories for a filename that matches the name that you specified and that you have execute permission for. The shell does not look through all directories but rather only the ones specified by the *shell variable* named **PATH**. Refer to page 577 or page 708 for more information on **PATH**. Also refer to the discussion of which and whereis on page 78.

When it cannot find the executable file,[2] the Bourne Again Shell displays a message such as the following:

---

2. One reason the shell may not be able to find the executable file is that it is not in a directory in your **PATH**. Under bash the following command adds the working directory (.) to your **PATH** temporarily:

    $ PATH=$PATH:.

For reasons of security, you may not want to add the working directory to your **PATH** permanently; see the tip "**PATH** and Security" on page 578.

```
$ abc
bash: abc: command not found
```

When the shell [bash tcsh zsh][3] finds the program but cannot execute it (you do not have execute access to the file that contains the program), you see a message similar to

```
$ def
bash: ./def: Permission denied.
```

Executing the Command Line

If it finds an executable file with the same name as the command, the shell starts a new process. A *process* is the execution of a program (page 560). The shell makes each command line argument, including options and the name of the command, available to the called program. While the command is executing, the shell waits, inactive, for the process to finish. The shell is in a state called *sleep*. When the program finishes execution, the shell returns to an active state (wakes up), issues a prompt, and waits for another command.

Because the shell does not process command line arguments but only hands them to the called program, the shell has no way of knowing whether a particular option or other argument is valid for a given program. Any error or usage messages about options or arguments come from the program itself. Some utilities ignore bad options.

Standard Input and Standard Output

The *standard output* is a place that a program can send information, such as text. The command (program) never "knows" where the information it sends to standard output is going (Figure 5-3). The information can go to a printer, an ordinary file, or your screen. The following sections show that, by default, the shell directs standard output from a command to the screen[4] and describe how you can cause the shell to redirect this output to another file. Standard input is a place that a program gets information from. As with standard output, the command never "knows" where the information came from. The following sections also explain how to redirect *standard input* to a command so that it comes from an ordinary file instead of from the keyboard (the default).

---

3. Refer to "Shell Specifier" on page 26 for an explanation of the [bash tcsh zsh] symbol.

4. The term *screen* is used throughout to mean screen, terminal emulator window, and workstation: *Screen* refers to the device that you see the prompt and messages displayed on.

Figure 5-3   The command does not know where standard input comes from or where standard output and standard error go.

In addition to standard input and standard output, a running program normally has a place to send error messages: *standard error*. Refer to pages 552, 691, and 781 for more information on handling standard error under the various shells.

---

chsh: **Changes Your Login Shell**   ‖ tip

The person who sets up your account determines which shell you will use when you first log in on the system or when you open a terminal emulator window in a GUI environment. You can run any shell you like once you are logged in. Enter the name of the shell you want to use (**bash**, **tcsh**, or **zsh**) and press RETURN; the next prompt will be that of the new shell. Experiment with the shell as you like and give an **exit** command to return to your previous shell. Because shells you call in this manner are nested (one runs on top of the other), you will be able to log out only from your original shell. When you have nested several shells, keep giving **exit** commands until you are back to your original shell. Then you will be able to log out.

Use the **chsh** utility when you want to change your login shell permanently: Give the command **chsh**. Then, in response to the prompts, enter your password and the absolute pathname of the shell you want to use (**/bin/bash**, **/bin/tcsh**, or **/bin/zsh**).

The Screen as a File

Chapter 4 introduced ordinary files, directory files, and hard and soft links. GNU/Linux has an additional type of file: a *device file*. A device file resides in the GNU/Linux file structure, usually in the **/dev** directory, and represents a peripheral device, such as a terminal emulator window, screen, printer, or disk drive.

The device name that the who utility displays after your login name is the filename of your screen/window. When who displays the device name **pts/4**, the pathname of your screen/window is **/dev/pts/4**. When you work with multiple windows, each one has its own device name. You can also use the tty utility to display the name of the screen that you give the command from. Although you would not normally have occasion, you can read from and write to this file as though it were a text file. Writing to it displays what you wrote on the screen; reading from it reads what you entered on the keyboard.

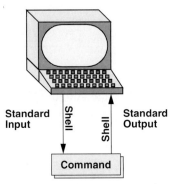

Figure 5-4   By default, standard input comes from the keyboard, and standard output goes to the screen/window.

The Screen/Keyboard as Standard Input and Standard Output

When you first log in, the shell directs standard output of your commands to the device file that represents your window/screen (Figure 5-4). Directing output in this manner causes it to appear on your screen. The shell also directs standard input to come from the same file, so that your commands receive anything you type on your keyboard as input.

The cat utility provides a good example of the way the screen/keyboard functions as standard input and standard output. When you use cat, it copies a file to standard output. Because the shell directs standard output to the screen, cat displays the file on the screen.

Up to this point cat has taken its input from the filename (argument) you specified on the command line. When you do not give cat an argument (that is, when you give the command cat followed immediately by a RETURN), cat takes input from standard input. The cat utility can now be described as a utility that, when called without an argument, copies standard input to standard output, one line at a time.

To see how cat works, type **cat** and press RETURN in response to the shell prompt. Nothing happens. Enter a line of text and press RETURN. The same line appears just under the one you entered. The cat utility is working. When you type a line of text using the keyboard, the shell associates that line with cat's standard input. Then cat copies your line of text to standard output, which the shell associated with the screen. This exchange is shown in Figure 5-5.

The cat utility keeps copying until you enter CONTROL-D on a line by itself. Pressing CONTROL-D sends an EOF (end of file) signal to cat to indicate that it has reached the end of standard input and that there is no more text for it to copy. When you enter CONTROL-D, cat finishes execution and returns control to the shell, which gives you a prompt.

```
$ cat
This is a line of text.
This is a line of text.
Cat keeps copying lines of text
Cat keeps copying lines of text
until you press CONTROL-D at the beginning
until you press CONTROL-D at the beginning
of a line.
of a line.
CONTROL-D
$
```

Figure 5-5   The cat utility copies standard input to standard output.

Redirection

The term *redirection* encompasses the various ways you can cause the shell to alter where standard input of a command comes from and where standard output goes. As the previous section demonstrated, by default the shell associates standard input and standard output of a command with the window/screen and keyboard. You can cause the shell to redirect standard input and/or standard output of any command by associating the input or output with a command or file other than the device file representing the screen/keyboard. This section demonstrates how to redirect output to and input from ordinary text files and utilities.

Redirecting Standard Output

The *redirect output symbol* (>) instructs the shell to redirect the output of a command to the specified file instead of to the screen (Figure 5-6). The format of a command line that redirects output is

> *command [arguments] > filename*

where **command** is any executable program (such as an application program or a utility), **arguments** are optional arguments, and **filename** is the name of the ordinary file the shell redirects the output to.

In Figure 5-7 cat demonstrates output redirection. This figure contrasts with Figure 5-3 on page 143, where both standard input *and* standard output are associated with the screen and keyboard. In Figure 5-7 only the input comes from the screen. The redirect output symbol on the command line causes the shell to associate cat's standard output with the file specified on the command line: **sample.txt**.

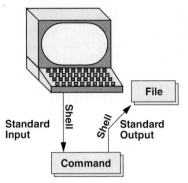

Figure 5-6   Redirecting standard output

Now the file **sample.txt** contains the text you entered. You can use cat with an argument of **sample.txt** to display the file. The next section shows another way to use cat to display the file.

Redirecting Output Can Destroy a File I   ‖ caution

Use caution when you redirect output to a file. If the file exists, the shell overwrites it and destroys its contents. For more information see the caution named "Redirecting Output Can Destroy a File II" on page 149.

Figure 5-7 shows that redirecting the output from cat is a handy way to make a file without using an editor. The drawback is that once you enter a line and press RE-TURN, you cannot edit the text. While you are entering a line, the erase and kill keys work to delete text. This procedure is useful for making short, simple files.

```
$ cat > sample.txt
This text is being entered at the keyboard.
Cat is copying it to a file.
Press CONTROL-D to indicate the
End of File.
CONTROL-D
$
```

Figure 5-7   cat with its output redirected

Figure 5-8 shows how to use cat and the redirect output symbol to *catenate* (join one after the other: the derivation of the name of the cat utility) several files into one larger file. The first three commands display the contents of three files:

```
$ cat stationery
2000 sheets letterhead ordered:     10/7/02
$ cat tape
1 box masking tape ordered:         10/14/02
5 boxes filament tape ordered:      10/28/02
$ cat pens
12 doz. black pens ordered:         10/4/02
$ cat stationery tape pens > supply_orders
$ cat supply_orders
2000 sheets letterhead ordered:     10/7/02
1 box masking tape ordered:         10/14/02
5 boxes filament tape ordered:      10/28/02
12 doz. black pens ordered:         10/4/02
$
```

Figure 5-8   Using cat to catenate files

stationery, **tape**, and **pens**. The next command shows cat with three filenames as arguments. When you call it with more than one filename, cat copies the files, one at a time, to standard output. In this case standard output is redirected to the file **supply_orders**. The final cat command shows that **supply_orders** contains the contents of all three files.

Redirecting Standard Input

Just as you can redirect standard output, you can redirect standard input. The *redirect input symbol* (<) instructs the shell to redirect a command's input from the specified file instead of the keyboard (Figure 5-9). The format of a command line that redirects input is

command [arguments] < filename

where **command** is any executable program (such as an application program or a utility), **arguments** are optional arguments, and **filename** is the name of the ordinary file the shell redirects the input from.

Figure 5-10 shows cat with its input redirected from the **supply_orders** file that was created in Figure 5-8 and standard output going to the screen. This setup causes cat to display the sample file on the screen. The system automatically supplies an EOF (end of file) signal at the end of an ordinary file, so no CONTROL-D is necessary.

Giving a cat command with input redirected from a file yields the same result as giving a cat command with the filename as an argument. The cat utility is a member

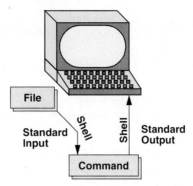

Figure 5-9   Redirecting standard input

of a class of GNU/Linux utilities that function in this manner. Some of the other members of this class of utilities are lp, sort, and grep. These utilities first examine the command line that you use to call them. If you include a filename on the command line, the utility takes its input from the file you specify. If you do not specify a filename, the utility takes its input from standard input. It is the utility or program, not the shell or the operating system, that functions in this manner.

```
$ cat < supply_orders
2000 sheets letterhead ordered:    10/7/02
1 box masking tape ordered:        10/14/02
5 boxes filament tape ordered:     10/28/02
12 doz. black pens ordered:        10/4/02
```

Figure 5-10   cat with its input redirected

The shell provides a feature called **noclobber** (page 554) that stops you from inadvertently overwriting an existing file using redirection. When you enable this feature by setting the **noclobber** variable and you attempt to redirect output to an existing file, the shell presents an error message and does not execute the command. If the preceding examples result in one of the following messages, the **noclobber** feature is in effect. The following examples set **noclobber**, attempt to redirect the output from echo into an existing file, and then unset **noclobber** in each of the major shells:

bash
```
bash $ set -o noclobber
bash $ echo "hi there" > tmp
bash: tmp: Cannot overwrite existing file
bash $ set +o noclobber
```

Redirecting Output Can Destroy a File II || caution

Depending on which shell you are using and how your environment has been set up, a command such as the following may give you undesired results:

```
$ cat orange pear > orange
cat: orange: input file is output file
```

Although **cat** displays an error message, the shell goes ahead and destroys the contents of the existing **orange** file. If you give the preceding command, the new **orange** file will have the same contents as **pear** because the first action the shell takes when it sees the redirection symbol (>) is to remove the contents of the original **orange** file. If you want to catenate two files into one, use **cat** to put the two files into a third, temporary file, and then use **mv** to rename the third file as you desire:

```
$ cat orange pear > temp
$ mv temp orange
```

What happens with the typo in the next example can be even worse. The user giving the command wants to search through files **a**, **b**, and **c** for the word **apple** and redirect the output from **grep** (page 64) to the file **a.output**. Instead, the user enters the filename as **a output**, omitting the period and leaving a SPACE in its place:

```
$ grep apple a b c > a output
grep: output: No such file or directory
```

The shell obediently removes the contents of **a** and then calls **grep**. The error message takes a moment to appear, giving you a sense that the command is running correctly. Even after you see the error message, it may take a while to realize that you destroyed the contents of **a**.

---

tcsh
```
tcsh $ set noclobber
tcsh $ echo "hi there" > tmp
tmp: File exists.
tcsh $ unset noclobber
```

zsh
```
zsh % set -o noclobber
zsh % echo "hi there" > tmp
zsh: file exists: tmp
zsh % set +o noclobber
```

Appending Standard Output to a File

The *append output symbol* (**>>**) causes the shell to add new information to the end of a file, leaving intact any information that was there. This symbol provides a convenient way of catenating two files into one. The following commands demonstrate the action of the append output symbol. The second command accomplishes the catenation described in the preceding caution box:

```
$ cat orange
this is orange
$ cat pear >> orange
$ cat orange
this is orange
this is pear
```

You first see the contents of the **orange** file. Next, the contents of the **pear** file is added on to the end of (catenated with) the **orange** file. The final cat shows the result.

Do Not Trust noclobber || caution

This technique is simpler to use than the two-step procedure just described, but you must be careful to include both greater than signs. If you accidentally use only one and the noclobber feature is not on, you will overwrite the orange file. Even if you have the noclobber feature turned on, it is a good idea to keep backup copies of files you are manipulating in these ways, in case you make a mistake.

Although it protects you from making an erroneous redirection, noclobber cannot stop you from overwriting an existing file using cp or mv. These utilities include the –i (interactive) option that protects you from this type of mistake by verifying your intentions when you try to overwrite a file. For more information see the Tip titled "cp Can Destroy a File" on page 62.

Figure 5-11 shows how to create a file that contains the date and time (the output from date), followed by a list of who is logged in (the output from who). The first line in Figure 5-11 redirects the output from date to the file named **whoson**. Then cat displays the file. Next, the example appends the output from who to the **whoson** file. Finally, cat displays the file containing the output of both utilities.

/dev/null: Data Sink

The **/dev/null** device is a *data sink*, commonly referred to as a *bit bucket*. You can redirect output that you do not want to keep or see to **/dev/null**. The output disappears without a trace:

```
$ echo "hi there" > /dev/null
$
```

When you read from **/dev/null**, you get a null string. Give the following cat command to truncate a file named **messages** to zero length while preserving the ownership and permissions of the file:

```
$ ls -l messages
-rw-r--r--   1 alex      pubs          25315 Oct 24 10:55 messages
$ cat /dev/null > messages
$ ls -l messages
-rw-r--r--   1 alex      pubs              0 Oct 24 11:02 messages
```

```
$ date >whoson
$ cat whoson
Thu Mar 27 14:31:18 PST 2003
$ who >>whoson
$ cat whoson
Thu Mar 27 14:31:18 PST 2003
root          console        Mar 27 05:00(:0)
alex          pts/4          Mar 27 12:23(:0.0)
alex          pts/5          Mar 27 12:33(:0.0)
jenny         pts/7          Mar 26 08:45 (bravo.tcorp.com)
```

Figure 5-11   Redirecting and appending output

Pipes

The shell uses a *pipe* to connect standard output of one command directly to standard input of another command. A pipe (sometimes referred to as a *pipeline*) has the same effect as redirecting standard output of one command to a file and then using that file as standard input to another command. A pipe does away with separate commands and the intermediate file. The symbol for a pipe is a vertical bar (|). The syntax of a command line using a pipe is

>   *command_a [arguments] | command_b [arguments]*

This command line uses a pipe to generate the same result as the following group of command lines:

>   *command_a [arguments] > temp*
>   *command_b [arguments] < temp*
>   *rm temp*

In the preceding sequence of commands, the first line redirects standard output from *command_a* to an intermediate file named *temp*. The second line redirects standard input for *command_b* to come from *temp*. The final line deletes *temp*. The command using a pipe is not only easier to type, it is generally more efficient because it does not create a temporary file.

You can use a pipe with a member of the class of GNU/Linux utilities that accepts input either from a file specified on the command line or from standard input. You can also use pipes with commands that accept input only from standard input. For example, the tr (translate) utility (page 1362 in Part III) takes its input from standard input only. In its simplest usage tr has the following format:

>   *tr string1 string2*

```
$ ls > temp
$ lpr temp
$ rm temp

or

$ ls | lpr
$
```

Figure 5-12   A pipe

The tr utility accepts input from standard input and looks for characters that match one of the characters in *string1*. Finding a match, tr translates the matched character in *string1* to the corresponding character in *string2*. (The first character in *string1* translates into the first character in *string2*, and so forth.) In the following examples tr displays the contents of the **abstract** file with the letters **a, b,** and **c** translated into **A, B,** and **C,** respectively:

```
$ cat abstract | tr abc ABC
```

or

```
$ tr abc ABC < abstract
```

The tr utility does not change the contents of the original file.

The lpr (line printer) utility is among the utilities that accept input from either a file or standard input. When you type the name of a file following lpr on the command line, it places that file in the print queue. When you do not specify a filename on the command line, lpr takes input from standard input. This feature enables you to use a pipe to redirect input to lpr. The first set of commands in Figure 5-12 shows how you can use ls and lpr, with an intermediate file (**temp**), to send a list of the files in the working directory to the printer. If the **temp** file exists, the first command overwrites its contents. The second set of commands sends the same list (with the exception of **temp**) to the printer, using a pipe.

The commands in Figure 5-13 redirect the output from the who utility to **temp** and then display this file in sorted order. The sort utility (page 66) takes its input

```
$ who > temp
$ sort < temp
alex        pts/4        Mar 27 12:23
alex        pts/5        Mar 27 12:33
jenny       pts/7        Mar 26 08:45
root        console      Mar 27 05:00
$ rm temp
```

Figure 5-13   Using a temporary file to store intermediate results

```
$ who | sort
alex        pts/4         Mar 27 12:23
alex        pts/5         Mar 27 12:33
jenny       pts/7         Mar 26 08:45
root        console       Mar 27 05:00
```

Figure 5-14   A pipe doing the work of a temporary file

from the file specified on the command line or, when a file is not specified, from standard input and sends its output to standard output. The sort command line in Figure 5-13 takes its input from standard input, which is redirected (<) to come from **temp**. The output that sort sends to the screen lists the users in sorted (alphabetical) order.

Because sort can take its input from standard input or from a filename on the command line, you can omit the < symbol from Figure 5-13 to yield the same results.

Figure 5-14 achieves the same result without creating the **temp** file. Using a pipe, the shell redirects the output from who to the input of sort. The sort utility takes input from standard input because no filename follows it on the command line.

When a lot of people are using the system and you want information about only one of them, you can send the output from who to grep (page 64), using a pipe. The grep utility displays the line containing the string you specify—root in the following example:

```
$ who | grep 'root'
root        console       Mar 27 05:00
```

Another way of handling output that is too long to fit on the screen, such as a list of files in a crowded directory, is to use a pipe to send the output through less or more (both on page 54).

```
$ ls | less
```

The less utility displays text a screen at a time.[5] To view another screen, press the SPACE bar. To view one more line, press RETURN. Press **h** for help and **q** to quit.

Filters

A *filter* is a command that processes an input stream of data to produce an output stream of data. A command line that includes a filter uses a pipe to connect standard

---

5. Some utilities change the format of their output when you redirect it. Compare the output of ls by itself and when you send it through a pipe to less.

output of one command to the filter's standard input. Another pipe connects the filter's standard output to standard input of another command. Not all utilities can be used as filters.

In the following example sort is a filter, taking standard input from standard output of who and using a pipe to redirect standard output to standard input of lpr. The command line sends the sorted output of who to the printer:

```
$ who | sort | lpr
```

This example demonstrates the power of the shell combined with the versatility of GNU/Linux utilities. The three utilities who, sort, and lpr were not specifically designed to work with each other, but they all use standard input and standard output in the conventional way. By using the shell to handle input and output, you can piece standard utilities together on the command line to achieve the results you want.

tee: Sends Output in Two Directions

In a pipe the tee utility sends the output of a command to a file and also to standard output. The utility is aptly named: It takes a single input and sends the output in two directions. In Figure 5-15 the output of who is sent via a pipe to standard input of tee. The tee utility saves a copy of standard input in a file named **who.out** and also sends a copy to standard output. Standard output of tee goes via a pipe to standard input of grep, which displays lines containing the string root.

```
$ who | tee who.out | grep root
root       console     Mar 27 05:00
$ cat who.out
root       console     Mar 27 05:00
alex       pts/4       Mar 27 12:23
alex       pts/5       Mar 27 12:33
jenny      pts/7       Mar 26 08:45
```

Figure 5-15   Using tee

Running a Program in the Background

In all the examples so far in this book, commands were run in the *foreground*. When you run a command in the foreground, the shell waits for it to finish before giving you another prompt and allowing you to continue. When you run a command in the *background,* you do not have to wait for the command to finish before you start running another command.

A *job* is a series of one or more commands connected by one or more pipes. You can have only one foreground job in a window or on a screen, but you can have many background jobs. By running more than one job at a time, you are using one of GNU/Linux's important features: multitasking. running a command in the background can be useful when the command will be running for a long time and does not need supervision. The window/screen is free so that you can use it for other work. Of course, when you are using a GUI, you can simply open another window to run another job.

To run a command in the background, type an ampersand (&) just before the RETURN that ends the command line. The shell assigns a small number to the job and displays this *job number* between brackets. Following the job number, the shell displays the *process identification* (PID) number—a bigger number assigned by the operating system. Each of these numbers identifies the command running in the background. Then the shell gives you another prompt so you can enter another command. When the background job finishes running, the shell displays a message giving both the job number and the command line used to run the command.

The following examples use the Bourne Again Shell. The TC and Z Shells produce almost identical results. The next example runs in the background and sends its output through a pipe to lpr, which sends it to the printer.

```
bash $ ls -l | lpr &
[1] 22092
bash $
```

The [1] following the command line indicates that the shell has assigned job number 1 to this job. The 22092 is the PID number of the first command in the job. (The TC Shell shows PID numbers for all commands in the job.) When this background job completes execution, you see the message

```
[1]+ Done            ls -l | lpr
```

You can stop a foreground job from running by pressing the suspend key, usually CONTROL-Z. The shell stops the process and disconnects standard input from the screen keyboard. You can put a job in the background and start it running by using the bg command, followed by a percent sign and the job number. You do not need to use the job number when you have only one stopped job.

Only the foreground job can take input from the keyboard. To connect the keyboard to the program running in the background, you must bring it into the foreground: Type **fg** without any arguments when only one job is in the background.

When more than one job is in the background, type **fg** (optional) followed by a percent sign and the job number of the job you want to bring into the foreground. The shell displays the command you used to start the job, and you can enter any input the program requires to continue:

```
bash $ fg %1
[1] promptme
```

Redirect the output of a job you run in the background to keep it from interfering with whatever you are doing on the screen. Refer to "Separating and Grouping Commands" on page 547 for more detail about background tasks.

The interrupt key (usually CONTROL-C) cannot abort a process you are running in the background; you must use kill (page 901) for this purpose. Follow **kill** on the command line with either the PID number of the process you want to abort or a percent sign (%) followed by the job number.

If you forget the PID number, you can use the ps (process status [page 561]) utility to display it. Using the TC Shell, the following example runs a **tail –f outfile** command (the **–f** option causes tail to watch **outfile** and display any new lines that are written to it) as a background job, uses ps to display the PID number of the process, and aborts the job with kill. So that it does not interfere with anything on the screen, the message saying that the job is terminated does not appear until you press RETURN after the RETURN that ends the kill command:

```
tcsh $ tail -f outfile &
[1] 22170
tcsh $ ps | grep tail
22170 pts/7     0:00 tail
tcsh $ kill 22170
tcsh $ RETURN
[1]    Terminated              tail -f outfile
tcsh $
```

If you forget the job number, you can use the jobs command to display a list of job numbers. The following example is similar to the previous one but uses the job number in place of the PID number to kill the job:

```
tcsh $ tail -f outfile &
[1] 3339
tcsh $ bigjob &
[2] 3340
tcsh $ jobs
[1]  - Running                tail -f outfile
[2]  + Running                bigjob
tcsh $ kill %1
tcsh $RETURN
[1]    Terminated              tail -f outfile
tcsh $
```

Filename Generation/Pathname Expansion

When you give the shell abbreviated filenames that contain special characters, also called *metacharacters,* the shell can generate filenames that match the names of existing files. These special characters are also referred to as *wildcards* because they act as the jokers do in a deck of cards. When one of these special characters appears in an argument on the command line, the shell expands that argument in sorted order (refer to "LC_COLLATE" on page 1431) into a list of filenames and passes the list to the program that the command line calls. Filenames that contain these special characters are called *ambiguous file references* because they do not refer to any one specific file. The process that the shell performs on these filenames is called *pathname expansion,* or *globbing.*

Ambiguous file references refer to a group of files with similar names quickly, saving you the effort of typing the names individually, as well as a file whose name you do not remember in its entirety. If no filename matches the ambiguous file reference, the shell generally passes the unexpanded reference, special characters and all, to the command.

The ? Special Character

The question mark (?) is a special character that causes the shell to generate filenames. The question mark matches any single character in the name of an existing file. The following command uses this special character in an argument to the lpr utility:

```
$ lpr memo?
```

The shell expands the **memo?** argument and generates a list of files in the working directory that have names composed of **memo** followed by any single character. The shell passes this list to lpr. The lpr utility never "knows" that the shell generated the filenames it was called with. If no filename matches the ambiguous file reference, the shell `bash tcsh zsh` passes the string itself (**memo?**) to lpr or, if it is set up to do so, displays an error message `bash tcsh zsh`.

The following example uses ls first to display the names of all of the files in the working directory and then to display the filenames that memo? matches:

```
$ ls
mem     memo12  memo9  memoalex   newmemo5
memo    memo5   memoa  memos
$ ls memo?
memo5   memo9   memoa  memos
```

The **memo?** ambiguous file reference does not match **mem, memo, memo12, memoalex,** or **newmemo5.** You can also use a question mark in the middle of an ambiguous file reference:

```
$ ls
7may4report   may4report      mayqreport   may_report
may14report   may4report.79   mayreport    may.report
$ ls may?report
may.report   may4report   may_report   mayqreport
```

To practice generating filenames, you can use echo and ls; echo displays the arguments that the shell passes to it:

```
$ echo may?report
may.report   may4report   may_report   mayqreport
```

The shell expands the ambiguous file reference into a list of all files in the working directory that match the string may?report and passes this list to echo, as though you had entered the list of filenames as arguments to echo. The echo utility responds by displaying the list of filenames. A question mark does not match a leading period (one that indicates an invisible filename). When you want to match filenames that begin with a period, you must explicitly include the period in the ambiguous file reference.

The * Special Character

The asterisk (*) performs a function similar to that of the question mark but matches any number of characters, *including zero characters,* in a filename. The following example shows all the files in the working directory and then shows three commands that display all the filenames that begin with the string **memo**, end with the string **mo**, and contain the string **alx**:

```
$ ls
amemo    memo         memoalx.0620   memosally   user.memo
mem      memo.0612    memoalx.keep   sallymemo
memalx   memoa        memorandum     typescript
$ echo memo*
memo memo.0612 memoa memoalx.0620 memoalx.keep memorandum memosally
$ echo *mo
amemo memo sallymemo user.memo
$ echo *alx*
memalx memoalx.0620 memoalx.keep
```

The ambiguous file reference **memo*** does not match **amemo, mem, sallymemo,** or **user.memo.** As with the question mark, an asterisk does not match a leading period in a filename.

The **–a** option causes ls to display invisible filenames. The command **echo *** does not display **.** (the working directory), **..** (the parent of the working directory), **.aaa,** or **.profile.** The command **echo .*** displays only those four names:

```
$ ls
aaa memo.0612 memo.sally report sally.0612 saturday thurs
$ ls -a
.     aaa      memo.0612    .profile   sally.0612   thurs
..    .aaa     memo.sally   report     saturday

$ echo *
aaa memo.0612 memo.sally report sally.0612 saturday thurs
$ echo .*
. .. .aaa .profile
```

In the following example .p* does not match **memo.0612, private, reminder,** or
report. Following that, the ls .* command causes ls to list **.private** and **.profile** in
addition to the entire contents of the . directory (the working directory) and the ..
directory (the parent of the working directory). With the same argument, echo displays only the filenames from the working directory that begin with a dot (.):

```
$ ls -a
.        .private   memo.0612   reminder
..       .profile   private     report
$ echo .p*
.private .profile
$ ls .*
.private .profile

.:
memo.0612  private    reminder   report

..:
.

.

$ echo .*
.private .profile
```

When you establish conventions for naming files, you can take advantage of
ambiguous file references. For example, when you end all text filenames with **.txt,**
you can reference that group of files with *.txt. Following this convention, the next
command sends all the text files in the working directory to the printer. The ampersand causes lpr to run in the background.

```
$ lpr *.txt &
```

The [ ] Special Characters

A pair of brackets surrounding a list of characters causes the shell to match filenames containing the individual characters. Whereas memo? matches **memo** followed by any character, memo[17a] is more restrictive, matching only **memo1,
memo7,** and **memoa.** The brackets define a *character class* that includes all the
characters within the brackets. The shell expands an argument that includes a character-class definition, substituting each member of the character class, *one at a time,*

in place of the brackets and their contents. The shell passes the list of matching file-names to the program it is calling.

Each character-class definition can replace only a single character within a file-name. The brackets and their contents are like a question mark that substitutes only the members of the character class.

The first of the following commands lists the names of all the files in the work-ing directory that begin with a, e, i, o, or u. The second command displays the con-tents of the files named **page2.txt**, **page4.txt**, **page6.txt**, and **page8.txt**:

```
$ echo [aeiou]*
. . .
$ less page[2468].txt
. . .
```

A hyphen within brackets defines a range of characters within a character-class definition. For example, [6–9] represents [6789], [a–z] represents all lowercase let-ters in English, and [a–zA–Z] represents all letters, upper- and lowercase, in English.

The following command lines show three ways to print the files named **part0**, **part1**, **part2**, **part3**, and **part5**. Each of the command lines causes the shell to call lpr with five filenames:

```
$ lpr part0 part1 part2 part3 part5

$ lpr part[01235]

$ lpr part[0-35]
```

The first command line explicitly specifies the five filenames. The second and third command lines use ambiguous file references, incorporating character-class defini-tions. The shell expands the argument on the second command line to include all files that have names beginning with **part** and ending with any of the characters in the character class. The character class is explicitly defined as 0, 1, 2, 3, and 5. The third command line also uses a character-class definition but defines the character class to be all characters in the range 0–3 and 5.

The following command line prints 39 files, **part0** through **part38**:

```
$ lpr part[0-9] part[12][0-9] part3[0-8]
```

The following two examples list the names of some of the files in the working directory. The first lists the files whose names start with **a** through **m**. The second lists files whose names end with **x**, **y**, or **z**:

```
$ echo [a-m]*
.
.
.
$ echo *[x-z]
.
.
.
```

Optional

When an exclamation point (!) or a caret (^) immediately follows the opening bracket ([), the string enclosed by the brackets matches any character not between the brackets, so that [^ab]* matches any filename that does not begin with **a** or **b**. You can match a hyphen (–) or a closing bracket (]) by placing it immediately before the final closing bracket.

The Shell Expands Ambiguous File References   ‖ tip

The shell does the expansion when it processes an ambiguous file reference, not the program that the shell runs. In the examples in this section, *the utilities* (ls, cat, echo, lpr) *never see the ambiguous file references.* The shell expands the ambiguous file references and passes the utility a list of ordinary filenames. In the previous examples echo shows this to be true because all it does is display its arguments and never displays the ambiguous file reference.

The following example demonstrates that the ls utility has no ability to interpret ambiguous file references. First, ls is called with an argument of ?old. The shell expands ?old into a matching filename, **hold**, and passes that name to ls. The second command is the same as the first, except the ? is quoted (refer to "Special Characters" on page 55), so the shell does not recognize it as a special character and passes it on to ls. The ls utility generates an error message saying that it cannot find a file named ?old (because there is no file named **?old**):

```
$ ls ?old
hold
$ ls \?old
?old: No such file or directory
```

As with most utilities and programs, ls cannot interpret ambiguous file references; that work is left to the shell.

Builtins

A *builtin* is a utility (also called a *command*) that is built into a shell. Each of the three major shells—the Bourne Again, TC, and Z—has its own set of builtins. When it runs a builtin, the shell does not fork a new process. Consequently, builtins run more quickly and can affect the environment of the current shell. Because builtins are used in the same way as utilities, you will not typically be aware of whether a utility is built into the shell or is a stand-alone utility.

The echo ▣ utility is a shell builtin. The shell always executes a shell builtin before trying to find a command/utility with the same name. Refer to "which, whereis, and Builtin Commands" on page 79 for information on using which and whereis to locate echo and other builtin commands. See page 670 for bash builtins, page 724 for tcsh builtins, and page 767 for zsh builtins.

To get a complete list of bash builtins, give the command **help | less** from a bash shell prompt. You can also give the command **info bash** to display the top level info page on bash.[6] Next, give the command **m builtin** to display a menu of bash builtin commands. Use the DOWN ARROW key to move the cursor to the line that lists the builtin you are interested in. Press **m** RETURN to display the corresponding info page. Alternatively, after typing **info bash**, give the command **/builtin**, which searches the bash documentation for the string builtin. The cursor will rest on the word Builtin in a menu; press **m** RETURN to display a menu on builtins. For tcsh, give the command **man tcsh** to display the tcsh man page, and then search for the second occurrence of Builtin commands with the following two commands: **/Builtin commands** (search for the string) and **n** (search for the next occurrence of the string). Give the command **man zshbuiltins** for a list of zsh builtins.

Chapter Summary

The shell is the GNU/Linux command interpreter. It scans the command line for proper syntax, picking out the command name and any arguments. The first argument is referred to as argument one, the second as argument two, and so on. The name of the command itself is sometimes referred to as argument zero. Many programs use options to modify the effects of a command. Most GNU/Linux utilities identify an option by its leading one or two hyphens.

When you give it a command, the shell tries to find an executable program with the same name as the command. When it does, the shell executes the program. When it does not, the shell tells you that it cannot find or execute the program. If the command is expressed as a simple filename, the shell searches the directories given in the variable **PATH** in an attempt to locate the command.

When it executes a command, the shell assigns a file to the command's standard input and standard output. By default, the shell causes a command's standard input to come from the keyboard and standard output to go to the screen. You can instruct the shell to redirect a command's standard input from or standard output to any reasonable file or device. You can also connect standard output of one command to standard input of another using a pipe. A filter is a command that reads its standard input from standard output of one command and writes its standard output to standard input of another command.

---

6. Because bash was written by GNU, the info page has better information than does the man page.

When a command runs in the foreground, the shell waits for it to finish before it gives you another prompt and allows you to continue. When you put an ampersand (&) at the end of a command line, the shell executes the command in the background and gives you another prompt immediately. Put a command in the background when you think it may not execute quickly and you want to enter other commands at the shell prompt. The jobs builtin displays a list of background jobs and includes the job number of each.

The shell interprets shell special characters on a command line for filename generation: A question mark represents any single character, and an asterisk represents zero or more characters. A single character may also be represented by a character class: a list of characters within brackets. A reference that uses special characters (wildcards) to abbreviate a list of one or more filenames is called an ambiguous file reference.

Utilities Introduced in This Chapter

tr	Maps one string of characters into another (page 151)
tee	Sends standard input to both a file and to standard output (page 154)
bg	Moves a process to the background (page 155)
fg	Moves a process to the foreground (page 155)
jobs	Displays a list of currently running jobs (page 156)

Exercises

1. What does the shell ordinarily do while a command is executing? What should you do if you do not want to wait for a command to finish before running another command?

2. Using sort as a filter, rewrite the following sequence of commands:

   ```
   $ sort list > temp
   $ lpr temp
   $ rm temp
   ```

3. What is a PID number? Why are they useful when you run processes in the background?

4. Assume that the following files are in the working directory:

```
$ ls
intro       notesb      ref2        section1    section3    section4b
notesa      ref1        ref3        section2    section4a   sentrev
```

Give commands for each of the following, using wildcards to express filenames with as few characters as possible.

a. List all files that begin with section.

b. List the **section1**, **section2**, and **section3** files only.

c. List the **intro** file only.

d. List the **section1**, **section3**, **ref1**, and **ref3** files.

5. Refer to the documentation of utilities in Part III or the man pages to determine what commands will

a. Output the number of lines in the standard input that contain the *word* a or A.

b. Output only the names of the files in the working directory that contain the pattern $(.   *nema*   *on*   *words*

c. List the files in the working directory in their reverse alphabetical order.

d. Send a list of files in the working directory to the printer, sorted by size.

6. Give a command to

a. Redirect the standard output from a sort command into a file named **phone_list**. Assume that the input file is named **numbers**.

b. Translate all occurrences of characters [and { to the character (, and all occurrences of the characters] and } to the character) in the file **permdemos.c**. (*Hint:* Refer to tr on page 1362 in Part III.)

c. Create a file named **book** that contains the contents of two others files: **part1** and **part2**.

7. The lpr and sort utilities accept input from either a file named on the command line or from standard input.

a. Name two other utilities that function in a similar manner.

b. Name a utility that accepts its input only from standard input.

8. Give an example of a command that uses grep

a. With both input and output redirected.

b. With only input redirected.

c. With only output redirected.

d. Within a pipe.

In which of the preceding is grep used as a filter?

9. Explain the following error message. What filenames would a subsequent ls display?

```
$ ls
abc   abd   abe   abf   abg   abh
$ rm abc ab*
rm: cannot remove 'abc': No such file or directory
```

Advanced Exercises

10. When you use the redirect output symbol (>) with a command, the shell creates the output file immediately, before the command is executed. Demonstrate that this is true.

11. In experimenting with shell variables, Alex accidentally deletes his **PATH** variable. He decides that he does not need the **PATH** variable. Discuss some of the problems he may soon encounter, and explain the reasons for these problems. How could he *easily* return **PATH** to its original value?

12. Assume that your permissions allow you to write to a file but not to delete it.

a. Give a command to empty the file without invoking an editor.

b. Explain how you might have permission to modify a file that you cannot delete.

13. If you accidentally create a filename with a nonprinting character, such as a CONTROL character in it, how can you rename the file?

14. Why can the **noclobber** variable *not* protect you from overwriting an existing file with cp or mv?

15. Why do command names and filenames usually not have embedded SPACEs? How would you create a filename containing a SPACE? How would you remove it? (This is a thought exercise, not a recommended practice. If you want to experiment, create and work in a directory with nothing but your experimental file in it.)

16. Create a file named **answers** and give the following command:

```
$ > answers.0102 < answers cat
```

Explain what the command does and why. What is a more conventional way of expressing this command?

PART II

Intermediate/Advanced GNU/Linux

IN THIS CHAPTER

X Window System and Graphical User Interface

6

Over the past two decades, it has become the norm to use a GUI (Graphical User Interface) to interact with a computer system. It is difficult to imagine using a GNU/Linux system (other than a server) that is not configured to take full advantage of the graphical displays and pointing devices that have become standard equipment.[1]

This chapter begins with a short background on the X Window System and how it works with GNU/Linux. The chapter builds a foundation for Chapters 7 (GNOME Desktop Manager) and 8 (KDE Desktop Environment) by describing the attributes that are common to most GUIs, including the GNOME and KDE desktop environments, and concludes with a section that covers X in more depth, showing you how to customize X for use with a desktop manager. Although you can configure X and the interfaces in complex ways, this chapter acquaints you with the basic terminology and operations. For clarity this chapter focuses on examples that are straightforward; it does not describe every method or shortcut available in X.

---

1. Some claim, and rightfully so, that they can be more efficient working with a command line interface and such tools as emacs (Chapter 11), lynx, and others. The emacs "editor" is so comprehensive that some programmers spend all their time working from within it, receiving their mail, browsing the Web, and doing other tasks.

X and GUI: Desktop, Window, and Mouse

A user interface is the connection between the user and, in this case, the computer system (Figure 6-1). The user interface controls how the user interacts with the system. In addition to using a GUI, some readers may want to use the command line interface. A terminal emulator window enables you to use a command line interface from within a GUI. Using a GUI doesn't mean giving up the command line interface but rather having more choices about how to perform a task.

Which Mouse Button?　‖ tip

In general, the left mouse button selects and drags, whereas the right mouse button displays a context menu, and the middle button (or both buttons together on a two-button mouse) pastes previously selected text. When this book does not specify which mouse button to click or drag, always use the left button. When you need to use the right or middle button, this book says so explicitly.

Be Careful What You Paste　‖ tip

Be careful when copying and pasting text. When you paste text in a window running a shell (a terminal emulator window), any text you have copied is sent to the shell just as if you had typed it. This can produce exciting results, as the shell tries to interpret the pasted text as commands.

X Window System

The X Window System (www.x.org) was created in 1984 at the Massachusetts Institute of Technology (MIT) by researchers working on a distributed computing project at the Laboratory for Computer Science and on a campuswide distributed environment, Project Athena, with support from Digital Equipment Corporation (DEC) and International Business Machines (IBM). This system was not the first windowing software to run on a UNIX system, but it was the first to become widely available. In 1985 MIT released X (version 9) to the public, license free. Three years later a group of vendors formed the X Consortium to support the continued development of X, under the leadership of MIT. By 1998 the X Consortium had become part of the Open Group, which in 2001 released version 11, release 6.6 (commonly called X11R6.6). This release includes a few extensions and enhancements and is fully compatible with X11R6.

Figure 6-1 KDE desktop environment under Red Hat

X was inspired by the ideas and features found in earlier proprietary window systems but is written to be portable and flexible. X is designed to run on a workstation, typically attached to a LAN. The designers built X with the network in mind. If you can communicate with a remote computer over a network, running an X application on that computer and sending the results to your local display are straightforward. The X Window System includes the X Toolkit, a library of powerful routines that handle common graphics operations. As a result, programmers need to know little about the low-level graphical display details and can develop portable applications more quickly.

Often developers provide collections of routines with more powerful interface components than found in the X Toolkit. These *widget sets* let application programmers quickly build sophisticated interfaces to their programs and enforce a uniform look-and-feel to all parts of the GUI. The X Window System comes with Athena, a simple widget set. Other popular widget sets available for use with GNU/Linux include an enhanced version of the Athena widget set that provides a three-dimensional (3D) appearance and the Motif and Tk widget sets. The Tk widget set was made to resemble the popular Motif widget set; they both give a similar look-and-feel to applications.

The popularity of X has extended outside the UNIX community and beyond the workstation class of computers it was conceived for. X is available for Macintosh computers, as well as for PCs running MS Windows. It is also available on a special kind of display terminal, known as an X *terminal*, developed specifically to run X.

X Window System and GNU/Linux

Computer networks are central to the design of X. It is possible to run an application on one computer and display the results on a screen attached to a different computer; the ease with which this can be done distinguishes X from other window systems available today. Because X has this capability, a scientist can run a program on a powerful supercomputer in another building or another country and view the results on a personal workstation or laptop computer. For more information, refer to "Remote Computing and Local Displays" on page 193.

When you start an X Window System session, you set up a *client/server environment*. One process, called the *X server*, displays desktops/windows under X. Each application program and utility that makes a request of the X server is a *client* of that server. Examples of X clients are xterm, Sawfish, kwin, xclock, and such general applications as word processing and spreadsheet programs. A typical request from a client is to display an image or open a window.

The server also monitors keyboard and mouse actions (*events*) and passes them on to the appropriate clients. For example, when you click the border of a window, this event is sent by the server to the window manager client. Characters typed into a terminal emulation window are sent to that terminal emulation client. The client takes appropriate action on receiving an event: In the preceding examples, that is making a window active or displaying the typed character.

Where Are the X Utilities?   ‖ tip

Many tools are not listed in KDE and GNOME's menus. You will find X utilities and application programs in many locations on a GNU/Linux system. Some of the most popular are in /usr/X11R6/bin (and /usr/bin/X11, which is a link to /usr/X11R6/bin); look on your system to familiarize yourself with the tools that are available. Read the manual pages for the tools you are not familiar with or just experiment with them. Some of the most useful X utilities are listed in Table 6-2 on page 197.

Separating the physical control of the display (the server) from the processes needing access to the display (the client) makes it possible to run the server on one computer and the client(s) on other(s). The following sections discuss running the X server and client applications on a single machine. Refer to "Remote Computing and Local Displays" on page 193 for more information about using X in a distributed environment.

You can run xev (X event) by giving the command **/usr/bin/X11/xev** from a terminal emulation window and watch the information flow from the client to the server and back again. This utility opens a window with a box in it and asks the X server to send it events each time anything happens, such as moving the mouse, clicking a mouse button, moving into the box, typing, resizing. Then xev displays information about each event in the window it opens. You can use xev as an educational tool: Start it and see how much information is being processed each time you move the mouse. Use CONTROL-C to exit from xev.

Starting X from a Character-Based Display

Once you have logged in on a virtual console (refer to "Character-Based Interface" on page 29), you can start an X Window System server by using startx. The X server displays an X screen, using one of the available virtual consoles. The following command causes startx to run in the background so that you can switch back to this virtual console and give other commands to this shell:.

```
$ startx &
```

Changing to a Different Desktop Manager

The easiest way to change your desktop manager is to run switchdesk either from a character-based command line or from a terminal emulator. From a terminal emulator switchdesk without an argument brings up the Desktop Switcher window, which presents a choice of desktops. After making your choice, exit from the GUI (log out or press CONTROL-ALT-BACKSPACE for a quick exit). From a character-based display other than a terminal emulator, give the command **switchdesk** followed by **KDE** or **GNOME**. In either case, the next time you start X (bring up your desktop environment), you will be running the manager you selected. The following example selects KDE as your desktop manager the next time and subsequent times you start X.

```
[alex@kudos examples]$ switchdesk KDE
Red Hat Linux switchdesk 3.9
Copyright (C) 1999-2001 Red Hat, Inc
Redistributable under the terms of the GNU General Public License
Desktop now set up to run KDE.
For system defaults, remove /home/alex/.Xclients
[alex@kudos examples]$
```

Substitute GNOME (upper- or lowercase letters work) for KDE when you want to run GNOME. This utility works by creating or modifying two files in your home directory: **.Xclients** and **.Xclients-default**. Setting these two files overrides any systemwide desktop setup. As the switchdesk message indicates, you can delete **~/.Xclients** to use the system's default desktop manager. Refer to "Setting Up the Default Desktop Manager" on page 923 for information about changing the system-wide default desktop manager.

Desktop

A *desktop* gets its name from a traditional desktop that has all the tools you need to work laid out in front of you in a defined area. A desktop (see the tip following this paragraph) is a collection of windows, toolbars, and icons/buttons, some or all of which appear on your display. Sometimes a desktop has a name. When you are working in a complex environment and using many windows to run a variety of programs simultaneously, it is convenient to divide your desktop into several areas, each *appearing* as a desktop unto itself and occupying your entire display. These areas are virtual extensions to a single desktop. The workspace is what is currently on the screen: buttons/icons, toolbars/panels, windows, and the *root window* (the unoccupied workspace). You can also have multiple desktops, each with its own set of workspaces. Typically GNOME and KDE set you up with a single desktop with four workspaces. For more information, refer to "Workspace Switcher/Window List" on page 179.

Is It a Desktop, a Workspace, or What?   ‖ tip

Confusion reigns over naming the subcomponents, or divisions, of a desktop. This book, in conformance with the GNOME 2 documentation, refers to everything that usually occupies your display monitor, or screen, as a *workspace; desktop* refers to the sum of your workspaces. Or, put another way, the desktop is divided into workspaces. Infrequently, you may have more than one desktop, each with its own set of workspaces.

KDE documentation uses the term *desktop* and Metacity uses the term *virtual desktop* in place of *workspace* as just defined.

Other terms you may see in place of workspace are: desktop area, viewport, virtual console, virtual terminal, or virtual screen.

Desktop Layout

You can arrange the windows on your desktop in many ways. Just as you might stack or overlap pieces of paper on your desk, you can position one window on top of another (as in Figure 6-1). The topmost window is fully visible, covering up pieces of the windows below. If you choose to overlap windows, it is a good idea not to cover the lower windows completely. It is easier to *raise* a window (bring it to the top of the stack) when you can position the mouse pointer somewhere on its border.

Another approach is to set up your windows so that there is no overlap, like floor tiles (called *tiling*). This arrangement is useful if you need to see the full contents of all of your windows at the same time.

Unfortunately, the space on your desktop is limited; one of the disadvantages of tiling is that when you need more than a few windows, you need to make each one quite small. To give yourself more room on a workspace you can iconify (turn into an icon) or shade (page 185) windows that you are not using so they do not take up much space.

Desktop Theme

In a GUI a *theme* is a recurring pattern and overall look that (ideally) pleases the eye and is easy to interpret and use. Go to www.themes.org/themes to view a wide variety of themes. You can control the appearance of KDE, GNOME, and most other desktop managers by using themes.

Desktop Manager

A *desktop manager* is a picture-oriented user interface to system services (commands). It allows you to run application programs and use the filesystem (copy, move, and delete files) by manipulating icons and using menus instead of typing the corresponding commands to a shell.

People who are unaccustomed to working with computers or with a GNU/Linux system often feel more comfortable working with a desktop manager. KDE (Figure 6-1, page 171) and GNOME (Figure 7-1, page 205) are desktop managers available for GNU/Linux. Each of these user-friendly desktop managers provides several advantages over other desktop managers and command line interfaces:

- Simplifies the GNU/Linux command line interface.
- Provides a set of tools and conventions that enable applications to work together and to present users with a uniform look-and-feel.
- Gives a standardized look-and-feel to all desktop elements.
- Makes use of desktop integration services: common interface for multiple applications running on local or remote machines, cut and paste between applications, communication with other applications, and more.

- Allows for personal preferences and cultural differences (fonts, colors, keyboard and mouse bindings, and locale-specific configuration files, including language and numeric representation). Each desktop manager is available in more than 38 languages.

- Provides a configurable user interface that you can set up to look, feel, and function the way you want.

- Provides panels that you can use to start applications and a desktop to hold your data and applications.

- A *session manager* that remembers how your desktop was set up the last time you logged out and attempts to set it up the same way next time you log in.

- Network transparency, which allows you to manipulate files located on remote servers in the same way as files on the local system, without special treatment.

- Integrated help systems.

- A standard, devised by the KDE and GNOME teams, among others, specifying implementation details for window managers. Each desktop manager works with an integrated but separable window manager (kwin and Metacity).

- Powerful universal browser/file manager (Nautilus and Konqueror).

- Suites of applications with a consistent look-and-feel including graphical, office, utilities, multimedia, game, administration, and network applications with more under development.

GNOME/KDE (Main) Menu

The main menu hierarchy consists of entries, submenus with entries, and more submenus. Under KDE this menu is called the K menu, and under GNOME it is called the GNOME menu. The main menu gives you access to many of the programs you can run. You can modify the main menu to make it suit your needs. By default you can open the main menu by clicking a button on a panel with an icon of a red hat (both GNOME and KDE, as released by Red Hat).

Desktop Menu

You can open a window or perform a task by making a selection from the Desktop menu. This menu gives you a choice of tasks that you can perform. Figure 6-2 shows the KDE Desktop menu (right click with the mouse pointer on the root window). KDE displays the Window List menu when you click the middle mouse

Figure 6-2   The KDE Desktop menu

button while the mouse pointer is over the root window. GNOME uses the same buttons to provide similar menus.

Terminal Emulator/Shell

A terminal emulator is a window that functions as a character-based terminal (page 35). You can run character-based programs that would normally run on a terminal in it. You can also start graphical programs, such as xclock, from it. A graphical program will open its own window. When you run a program from GNOME or KDE, you will frequently be asked whether you want to run the program in a terminal. When you say **yes**, the program starts running in a terminal emulator window (Figure 6-3).

A terminal emulator is a useful transition tool, easing the move from character-based to graphics-based computing. You do not give up any of your tools when you move to a GUI but do get a new set of tools to work with.

When you open a terminal emulator you start a shell whose standard input comes from your keyboard and whose standard output and standard error go to

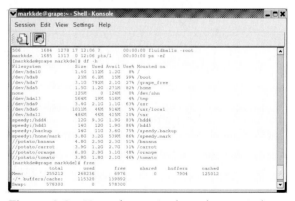

Figure 6-3   Konsole terminal emulator window

the terminal emulator screen in the window. Because you are already logged in and are creating a subshell under a desktop manager, you do not need to log in again. To start a terminal emulator under KDE or GNOME, click the red hat/file folder at the lower left of the screen to display the K or GNOME menu and select System Tools ⇨ Terminal.

File Manager

A file manager displays, creates, finds, uses, deletes, and manipulates files, folders, URLs, and applications. For example, a file manager can open, move, copy, or delete a file. File managers try to identify the type of a file before they open it so that they can use the proper tool to open it: a browser to open an HTML file, an editor to open a text file, a package manager to open an RPM file, and so on. When it cannot determine the type of a file, a file manager asks you which program to use to open the file.

MIME Types

MIME (Multipurpose Internet Mail Extension) types were originally used to describe how specific types of files that were attached to e-mail were to be handled. Today MIME types describe how many types of files are to be handled, based on their filename extensions. Both GNOME and KDE use MIME types to figure out which program to use to open a file. An example of a MIME *type* is **audio/x-mp3**. The MIME *group* is **audio** and the MIME *subtype* is **x-mp3**. (There are seven MIME groups: application, audio, image, inode, message, text, and video.)

KDE associates **audio/x-mp3** with ✳.mp3 and ✳.MP3, and both of these are associated with the KDE Media Player. When you click a file whose name is **bigtime.mp3**, KDE opens the file with its Media Player program, which plays the file. Other techniques, such as examining a file's *magic number* (page 1478), are used when a file has a nonstandard filename extension.

Panel

A *panel* is a narrow strip that appears somewhere on the workspace and holds objects. A main panel is typically positioned along the bottom of the desktop, as shown in Figure 6-1 on page 171. You can create additional general and special-purpose panels. Panels generally hold buttons that display *icons* (page 1472) for

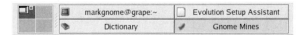

Figure 6-4   GNOME Workspace Switcher/Window List

identification. When you click a button, you start an action: displaying a menu, starting a program, opening a window, or something similar. Some icons, such as a clock, display information. You move a GNOME or KDE panel out of sight when you click an arrow at one end of the panel. A panel does not allow you to do anything you could not do otherwise; it simply collects things in one place and makes your work with the system easier.

Workspace Switcher/Window List

Two panel tools can help you work with multiple tasks on multiple workspaces and desktops. GNOME calls these tools *Workspace Switcher* (smaller boxes to the left in Figure 6-4) and *Window List* (rectangles to the right). KDE calls them *Pager* and *Taskbar*. These tools switch between different tasks running in different windows on different desktops and workspaces.

A system administrator, for example, might be working on several distinct activities, each of which involves more than one window. One workspace might consist of a series of windows set up to edit, compile, and debug software. On another workspace the task might be to locate and restore some lost files. A third workspace might be dedicated to reading mail and news. The advantage of these tools is the ease of switching between sets of tasks without having to fuss with minimized or overlapping windows.

You can move around on the whole desktop, controlling which portion of it is visible in full size on your physical display. Metacity, Sawfish and kwin implement a workspace using a Workspace Switcher/Pager (Figure 6-4) that is divided into a grid. Each rectangle in the grid represents a workspace. The size of the grid is based on the number of workspaces you have set up and their arrangement (2x2, 2x3, 2x4, 3x3, and so on). Click one of the rectangles to display the corresponding workspace.

Windows

On a display screen a *window* is a region that runs, or is controlled by, a particular program (Figure 6-5). This section covers working with windows, window tools, and window menus.

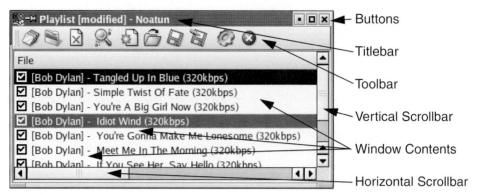

Figure 6-5   A typical window

Window Manager

A *window manager,* the program that controls the look-and-feel of the basic GUI, runs on top of a desktop manager and controls all aspects of the windows in the X Window System environment. The window manager defines the appearance of the windows on your desktop, as well as how you operate and position them: open, close, move, resize, iconify, and so on. The window manager may also handle some session management functions, such as how to pause, resume, restart, or end a windowing session (page 185).

A window manager controls window decorations: the titlebar and border of a window. Aside from the aesthetic aspects of changing window decoration, you can alter the functionality by modifying the number and placement of buttons on the titlebar.

The window manager takes care of window manipulation so that the client programs do not need to. This setup is very different from that of many other operating systems, and the way that GNOME and KDE deal with window managers is different from other desktop environments. Window managers do more than manage windows by providing a useful, good-looking, graphical shell to work from. Their open design allows users to define their own policy down to the fine details.

GNOME and KDE are not dependent on any particular window manager and can work with several different window managers. Because of their flexibility, you will not see major parts of your desktop environment change when you switch from one window manager to another. These desktop managers work with a window manager to make your work environment intuitive and easy to use. The desktop manager does not control window placement but does get information from the window manager about window placement.

Red Hat Window Managers

Many window managers are available for use with the X Window System, each with different characteristics. Choosing a window manager is largely a matter of individual taste; all window managers perform the basic operations described in this chapter, but how you perform them differs. You should be able to run any X application under any window manager. Although most window managers will run under most desktop managers, all window managers are not completely compliant with all desktop managers. When you run a noncompliant window manager, you may run into problems, such as drag-and-drop not working between windows.

Red Hat Linux ships with the Metacity, Sawfish, kwin, twm (Tab), and other window managers. Metacity, the default window manager for GNOME, provides window management and starts many components through GNOME panel commands. It also communicates with and facilitates access to other components in the environment. The kwin window manager is the default window manager for KDE.

Using the standard X libraries, individual programmers have created such window managers as vtwm (Virtual Tab Window Manager), gwm (GNU Window Manager), afterstep (a NeXTStep clone), and fvwm2 (originally Feeble Virtual Window Manager). These window managers are readily available and are free of charge.

Optional

Window Manager without a Desktop Manager

It is interesting to see exactly where the line between a window manager and a desktop manager falls. Toward this end you can run Metacity without GNOME. Create the following **.xinitrc** file in your home directory:

```
$ cat .xinitrc
xterm &
metacity
```

Next, give the command **startx**. You should see a black screen with a fully decorated window running xterm. You can give commands from this window to open other windows. Try xeyes, xterm, and xclock. Use CONTROL-ALT-BACKSPACE to exit from Metacity.

Titlebar

A titlebar appears at the top of most windows and in many ways controls the window it belongs to. By changing the window decoration, you can change the appearance and function of a titlebar, but at least you will usually have the functionality of the buttons shown in Figure 6-6.

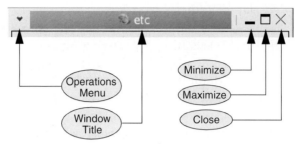

Figure 6-6   A Metacity titlebar

The minimize button makes the window appear as an icon on the panel; click the icon to restore the window. Maximize expands the window so that it occupies the whole workspace; click the same button which now appears with a double-window icon to restore the window. Close closes the window and terminates the program that was running in the window. Click Operations menu to see a menu of window operations. Right click the titlebar and drag the window to reposition it.

Tooltips

Tooltips, available from both GNOME and KDE, is a minicontext help system that you activate by moving your mouse pointer over a button, icon, window border, or applet (such as those on a panel) and leaving it there for a moment (called *hovering*). When you do this, GNOME and KDE display a brief explanation of the object your mouse pointer is hovering over (Figure 6-7).

Changing the Input Focus

When you type on the keyboard, the window manager directs the characters you are typing somewhere, usually to a window. The *active window* (the window accepting input from the keyboard) is said to have the *input focus*. You can use the mouse in four ways to change the input focus. (You can also use the keyboard; see the next section, "Window Cycling.")

• **click-to-focus** (*explicit focus*)   Gives the input focus to a window when you click the window; that window continues to accept input from your keyboard regardless of the position of the mouse pointer. The window loses the focus when you click another window. Although clicking the middle or the right mouse button also activates a window, use only the left mouse button for this purpose; other buttons may have unexpected effects when you use them to activate a window.

Figure 6-7   Tooltip

- **focus-follows-mouse** (*sloppy focus, point to give focus*, or *enter-only*)   Gives the input focus to a window when you move the mouse pointer onto the window. That window maintains the input focus until you move the mouse pointer onto another window, at which point the new window gets the focus. Specifically, when you move the mouse pointer off a window and onto the root window, the window that had the focus does not lose it.

- **focus-under-mouse**   Same as focus-follows-mouse (KDE).

- **focus-strictly-under-mouse** (*enter-exit*)   Gives the input focus to a window when you move the mouse pointer onto the window. That window maintains the input focus until you move the mouse pointer off the window with the focus, at which point no window has the focus. Specifically, when you move the mouse pointer off a window and onto the root window, the window that had the focus loses it, and any input from the keyboard is lost.

Under GNOME, use Main menu: Preferences⇨Window Focus to change the focus policy; under KDE, use Main menu: Preferences⇨Look & Feel⇨Window Behavior⇨Focus (page 323).

To determine which window has the input focus compare the window borders; the border color of the active window is different from the others or is darker on a monochrome display. Another indication that a window is active is that the keyboard cursor is a solid rectangle; in windows that are not active, it is an outline of a rectangle.

Which keyboard focus method are you using? If you position the mouse pointer in a window and that window does not get the input focus, your window manager is configured to use the click-to-focus method. If the border of the window changes, you are using the focus-follows-mouse/focus-under-mouse or focus-strictly-under-mouse method. To determine which of these methods you are using, start typing something, with the mouse pointer on a window, and then move the mouse pointer over the root window and continue typing. If characters continue to appear within the window, you are using focus-follows-mouse/focus-under-mouse. Otherwise, you are using focus-strictly-under-mouse.

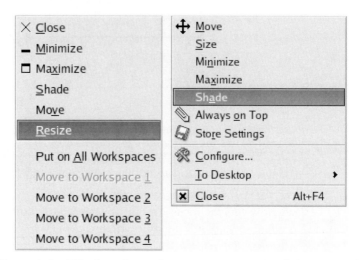

Figure 6-8   Window Operations menus: Metacity, left; kwin, right

Window Cycling

You can also change which window has the input focus by using the keyboard; this process is called *window cycling*. When you press ALT-TAB, the input focus moves to the window that was active just before the currently active window, making it easy to switch back and forth between two windows. When you hold ALT and press TAB multiple times, the focus moves from window to window, and you see in the center of the desktop a box that displays the *titlebar* (page 181) information from the window that currently has the input focus. Under KDE you can hold ALT and SHIFT and repeatedly press TAB to cycle in the other direction. For window-cycling options under KDE, refer to the entry "Walk through windows mode" in the table on page 323; for options under GNOME refer to "Window Cycling" on page 261.

Window Operations Menu

The Window Operations menu (Figure 6-8) contains most of the common operations that you need to perform on any window. You can access this menu by clicking the left mouse button while the mouse pointer is positioned on the Window Operations menu button (typically the button at the left top of a window, a check mark in the default Red Hat setup under both GNOME and KDE) or by pressing the right mouse button while the mouse pointer is over the titlebar.

Context Menu

A context menu is one that applies specifically to the window you click. Frequently a right click brings up a context menu. For example, right click the GNOME terminal emulator to display the context menu for the terminal emulator. This menu includes selections that start another terminal emulator, change your preferences for the terminal emulator, and determine whether the terminal emulator menubar is displayed. Try right clicking with the mouse pointer in different places: You will find some interesting menus.

Shading a Window

When you double-click the titlebar (page 181) or click Shade in the Window Operations menu, the window rolls up like a window shade, with only the titlebar visible. Double-click the titlebar or click Shade in the Window Operations menu again to restore the window.

KDE offers shade-hover mode which keeps shaded any windows that you want shaded unless the mouse pointer is over that window. In this mode few windows clutter your desktop; there are just shaded windows. When the mouse pointer hovers over the titlebar of a shaded window for a short time, such as one-quarter second, the window unshades. When you move the mouse pointer off the window, it immediately shades again. In order for you to put a window in shade-hover mode, you must shade it once manually. After that, the shading and unshading are automatic. This mode is controlled by K Menu: Preferences⇨Look & Feel⇨Window Behavior⇨Advanced⇨ Shading⇨Enable Hover (page 325).

Session Manager

A session starts when you log in and ends when you log out or reset the session. With a fully compliant GNOME or KDE application, these desktop managers can *session manage* your data. When you run a managed session, the desktop looks pretty much the same when you log in as it did when you logged out the previous time. The data in this case includes not only the data that the application manipulates but also all the information about the state of the application when you end your session: what windows were open and where they were located, what each of the applications was doing, and so forth.

If you want to start an application each time you log in, regardless of whether it was running when you logged out, refer to "Autostart" on page 346 (KDE).

X Window System

Before the convenience of GUI utilities enabled you to set up a mouse for a left-handed person, set up your desktop the way you want it, perform system administration tasks with the click of a mouse, and so forth, people used files, including many shell scripts, to set things up. Most of the files are still there with a graphical interface, but you do not see them unless you go looking. You never *have* to use them. If these files interest you, read on. This section explains how to customize applications, set X resources, remap mouse buttons and discusses remote computing.

Customizing X Applications from the Command Line

The possibilities for customizing your environment can seem daunting. Before you try to customize a particular application, get some experience with its default performance. After you are familiar with an application, it is easier to read the manual page and explore the details of its features and how to use and change them. This section describes some of the basic methods that enable you to set up your X environment by using nongraphical tools. You can accomplish many of the same changes by using a GUI, as explained in Chapters 7 (GNOME Desktop Manager) and 8 (KDE Desktop Environment).

Each X client (application) understands certain attributes, or *resources,* such as typeface, size, and color. You can change resources to match your preferences in several ways. One method is to specify options on the command line when you start an application. The following example turns on the scrolling feature in xterm, using the **–sb** (scrollbar) option (this is the default), and saves the specified number of lines that have scrolled off the top of the screen, using the **–sl** (save lines) option; if you do not change xterm's default characteristics, it starts up with a scrollbar and saves 64 lines. The following example saves 200 lines:

```
$ xterm -sb -sl 200 &
```

When you are working at a color display, the following example starts a terminal window titled Hard to Read that presents characters in yellow (foreground) on a green background:

```
$ xterm -bg green -fg yellow -title "Hard to Read" &
```

You can also control the placement and size of X application windows with the **–geometry** option. The default size of an xterm window includes 24 lines of 80 characters each. The following command creates an xterm window that has 30 lines of 132 characters:

```
$ xterm -geometry 132x30 &
```

For most X applications the **–geometry** option recognizes pixels as the unit of size; for some applications, such as a terminal emulator, it is more natural to think in terms of rows and columns, and the application is designed to interpret the values

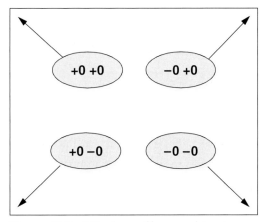

Figure 6-9 Window offset combinations

accordingly. The following command starts an xclock that is 200 pixels wide by 200 high (larger than the default):

```
$ xclock -geometry 200x200 &
```

To place a window in a particular location on the screen, specify *x*- and *y*-axis offset values, where distance is measured in pixels. The following command places a terminal window 25 pixels in from the left edge of the screen and 15 pixels down from the top edge:

```
$ xterm -geometry +25+15 &
```

Positive offset values refer to the distance from the upper-left corner of the screen; negative values refer to the distance from the lower-right corner. Figure 6-9 summarizes the effects of the four possible window offset combinations. You can specify both the size and location of a window with one **–geometry** specification. The following command places a long terminal window toward the bottom right of the screen:

```
$ xterm -geometry 80x35-10-10 &
```

Although you may find it awkward to estimate pixel offsets to place windows on your screen, you begin to develop a feeling for these values as you work with the window manager. When you move a window on your screen, the window manager may display a box that reports the offset values, updating them as you drag the window around the screen. You can also use xwininfo (run it from a terminal emulator) to display properties associated with a particular window, including the offset values (to the right of the line that starts with –geometry). Table 6-1 lists some of the common options that enable you to change the way an X application looks.

X Options

|| table 6-1

−bg **color** −background **color**	Sets the background color to *color.*
−fg **color** −foreground **color**	Sets the foreground color to *color.*
−rv −reverse	Reverses fore- and background colors.
−bd **color** −bordercolor **color**	Sets the border color to *color.*
−bw **num** −borderwidth **num**	Sets the border width to *num* pixels.
−display **display**	Specifies the display for the program output. Refer to "Remote Computing and Local Displays" on page 193.
−fn **name** −font **name**	Sets the font to *name.* Use **xfontsel** or **xlsfonts** to determine which fonts are available to you.
−geometry **wxh1±h2±v**	Specifies the size and location of a window, where *w* is the width and *h1* is the height of the window (both generally measured in pixels); *h2* is the horizontal position and *v* is the vertical position of the window (in pixels). Refer to "Customizing X Applications from the Command Line" on page 186.
−iconic	Minimizes the application when it starts.

Setting X Resources

This section explains how to use the **.xinitrc** or **.xsession** file to start programs automatically and customize the look of your desktop each time you start X.

switchdesk Moves ~/.xinitrc and Creates ~/.Xdefaults

The **switchdesk** utility moves ~/.xinitrc to ~/.xinitrc.switchdesk so that it is no longer functional. You can rename it with its original name but make sure to remove ~/.Xdefaults if you want ~/.xinitrc to work. Create ~/.Xdefaults at any time by running **switchdesk**.

.xinitrc

The ~/.xinitrc file is a user's X initialization file. The xinit utility starts the X Window System server and an initial client. When X starts, it locates a blank virtual console, switches the display to that console, and then executes the commands in the user's .xinitrc (if there is one). If your system is configured to use xdm to manage X sessions, use .xsession instead of .xinitrc to customize your X environment. Set up .xsession just as you would .xinitrc. By default Red Hat uses xinit.

When you do not specify a client and do not have a .xinitrc file, xinit brings up xterm.[2] Because you are running without a window manager, you cannot move or resize xterm, the mouse buttons have no effect outside of xterm, and there is no decoration around xterm. If you create another instance of xterm by giving an **xterm** command from the first xterm, the new xterm appears on top of the first. Because you cannot move the xterm, you cannot use the first xterm until you exit from the second by giving an **exit** command. After giving an **xinit** command, you will have an instance of xterm on a plain screen.

If a **.xinitrc** file is present in your home directory, X reads commands from that file. This makes **.xinitrc** a convenient place to start commonly used applications and the window manager of your choice. For example, if you use KDE and want a clock and a terminal window present on your screen whenever you start X, you could use the following **.xinitrc** file:

```
$ cat .xinitrc
/usr/bin/X11/xclock &
/usr/bin/X11/xterm &
/usr/bin/startkde
```

The commands in **.xinitrc** are executed sequentially. Leaving the ampersand (&) off the xclock line would prevent the initialization of your X session from continuing past that point and xterm, and KDE would not start until you exited from xclock, which you cannot do because the window manager is not running. For the same reason, it is necessary to run xterm in the background.

The last command is left as a foreground job because X quits and returns you to the virtual console when it has finished executing all the commands in **.xinitrc**. Usually, you put the command for starting your window manager last. In the example the **startkde** shell script starts KDE, the kwin window manager, and many other programs. Take a look at it in **/usr/bin/startkde**.

You can customize how individual applications start up by specifying appropriate options on each command line in **.xinitrc**. The following **.xinitrc** file paints the root window, or background, a solid steel blue. This command completes so quickly

---

2. Although this may be considered to be an xterm *window*, it is not referred to as such here because it has none of the characteristics that you normally associate with a window: no border (decoration) and no controls (Window Operations menu).

that it does not need to be run in the background. The second line starts xterm as an icon, which by default has a scrollbar; when you need it, you can "restore" it to full size by clicking its icon. The third line starts another xterm, with a red background. The next lines start Nautilus, Metacity, and the GNOME panel.

```
$ cat .xinitrc
xsetroot -solid SteelBlue
xterm -iconic &
xterm -bg red &
nautilus &
metacity &
gnome-panel
```

If you prefer to display a picture in your background window, you can use the xv program (which you will probably need to load) to load an image as follows:

```
xv -root Images/lighthouse.gif -max -quit &
```

This command line instructs xv to load the root window with the file **lighthouse.gif** from the directory **~/Images**, expanding the image to the maximum size allowed by the display (to fill the display), and then to quit, leaving the image displayed on the root window.

In addition to using **.xinitrc** to start applications, you can use it to customize your X work environment. See "Remapping Mouse Buttons" on page 196 for information on xmodmap.

A Bad .xinitrc or .xsession File Can Hang Your System || caution

Be careful when experimenting with your .xinitrc or .xsession file; if the file contains an error (for example, leaving the & off a command line), the X server may not start up properly. If this happens, terminate the X server by pressing CONTROL-ALT-BACKSPACE, and fix the problem.

.Xdefaults

Although it is convenient to specify command line attributes for a few applications in a **.xinitrc** or **.xsession** file, it is awkward to type complicated option specifications on a command line each time you start a new application during the course of your session. You may also find that you always want to run certain applications with the same options such as xterm without a scrollbar. To run utilities/programs with the same options consistently, you can store your preferences in your **~/.Xdefaults**[3] file. The format of each line of **.Xdefaults** is

name-of-application ❋ name-of-resource: value

---

3. If you are running KDE and your **.Xdefaults** file does not have any effect, remove **.Xclients** and **.Xclients-default,** and try again. These files are replaced each time you run switchdesk.

The systemwide application defaults are controlled by files in the **/usr/lib/X11/app-defaults** directory. Any settings in your **~/.Xdefaults** file override the system values. If you specify different options on the command line when you start an application, those values override the settings in your **.Xdefaults** file.

The following entries in a **.Xdefaults** file start all xterm windows with red characters on a blue background (run xterm from a terminal emulator):

```
XTerm*background:    blue
XTerm*foreground:    red
```

When you omit the name of the application, the resources and values you list are used by all applications that recognize them. For example, the following entries cause all windows to have a blue background, with the exception of xclock, which has a turquoise background:

```
*background:         blue
XClock*background:   turquoise
```

The asterisk is a pattern that matches only the whole name of an application or resource component. The specification **XT*background** would apply to an application named **XT**, if one existed, and would have no effect on other applications with names that start with the letters **XT**, such as xterm. The following example includes some useful entries to guide you in setting up your own **.Xdefaults** file. You can include comments in the file by starting a line with an exclamation point (**!**).

```
$ cat ~/.Xdefaults
! Resources for Xterm:
!
! Turn on the scrollbar.
XTerm*scrollBar:        True
! Use large font (10 pixels wide, 20 pixels high).
XTerm*Font:             10x20
! Retain more lines to scroll through.
XTerm*saveLines:        150
!
! Resources for the calculator
!
XCalc*Background:           slategray
XCalc*Foreground:           white
XCalc*screen.LCD.Background:  lightgray
XCalc*screen.LCD.Foreground:  black
!
! Set up Netscape resources
!
Netscape*Foreground:    White
Netscape*Background:    #B2B2B2
!
! Some defaults for all windows (including XTerms)
!
*highlight:             black
*borderColor:           black
*Foreground:            black
*Background:            bisque
```

When the X server starts, it gathers information from many sources to create a resource database in the X server process. After merging system default information, the server typically merges information from your ~/.Xdefaults file, if it exists. These resources are application dependent and are usually listed under RESOURCES in the man and info pages for the application.

When you have accounts on multiple computers with different home directories, you can customize the resources for any application on a per host basis. For example, if you set XTerm*background: blue in your .Xdefaults file on **bravo** and XTerm*background: black on **kudos**, the background color of the xterm windows on your screen varies, depending on whether you run xterm on **bravo** or on **kudos**. If your home directory is shared by many machines over a network filesystem, you can achieve the same effect by creating multiple .Xdefaults files in your home directory, each including the name of the host where it is recognized. To extend the preceding example, files named **.Xdefaults-bravo** and **.Xdefaults-kudos** set the resources for applications started on those particular hosts.

You can apply resources consistently across multiple hosts by loading the configuration directly into the X server. Resources loaded into the server are typically stored in **~/.Xresources** and take precedence over those specified in **.Xdefaults**. When you change your **.Xresources** file after starting the X Window System, you can load the new specifications immediately with the following command:

```
$ xrdb -load ~/.Xresources
```

Changing the Resolution of the Display

The X server starts at a specific display resolution and color depth. Although you can change the color depth only when you start an X server, you can switch a running X server between different resolutions. The number of resolutions available depends both on your display hardware and on how X has been configured on your system (see Chapter 17 for details). Many users prefer to do most of their work at a higher resolution but might want to switch to a lower resolution for some tasks. Many games, such as DOOM, work better at lower resolutions. You can move between different display resolutions by pressing either CONTROL-ALT-KEYPAD-+ or CONTROL-ALT-KEYPAD--, using the + and − on the keyboard's numeric keypad.

Optional

The X Server's Virtual Display

The GUI you see on the physical display is a representation of a display that is kept in display memory. When you change the display resolution as described in the previous section, the display memory is not changed; what changes is how the contents of that memory are mapped to the physical display. When you switch to a lower resolution, the pixels in the display memory are mapped to larger pixels on the screen.

The representation of your display in display memory is called the *virtual display,* as only a portion of it might be visible on the physical display at once.

If the resolution of the virtual display is greater than the resolution of the physical display, you can see different parts of the virtual display by moving the mouse pointer up against the edges of the physical display. The X server adjusts the physical display to show more of the virtual display in that direction. If the virtual and physical displays are the same size, moving the mouse pointer against an edge of the display has no effect as far as the X server is concerned. However, when you move the mouse pointer against an edge of the display, the window manager may respond by moving you to a different workspace or even a different desktop.

Changing to a lower resolution has the effect of zooming in on your display, so you may no longer be able to view the entire workspace at once. If you are using a scrollbar and it is moved off the screen by lowering the resolution, you will not be able to scroll the display until you change back to a higher resolution.

Virtual Consoles

When you move between the virtual consoles (page 36), you will notice that some consoles display login messages, whereas others may be blank, based on the **/etc/inittab** file (page 960). The blank consoles are used by X servers as they are started. Having more than one blank virtual console means that more than one X server can run simultaneously. For example, you might want to have one X server running at high resolution (say, 1280x1024 pixels) with 8-bit color and another running at a lower resolution (perhaps 800x600 pixels) with 24-bit color. You can then switch between these displays by switching between the virtual consoles they are running on.

To bring up a particular virtual console, hold the CONTROL and ALT keys down and press the function key with a number corresponding to the number of the virtual console you want to view. For example, to bring up virtual console one, press CONTROL-ALT-F1. Because X brings up its display on a blank (unused) virtual console, X is not running on virtual console one, even though you logged in and started X on that virtual console. Depending on how many ttys are set up in **/etc/inittab**, your X display can use any virtual console. In fact, **inittab** is frequently set up with six or seven ttys so that the X display comes up on screen 7 or 8. Press CONTROL-ALT-F7 to display virtual console seven.

Remote Computing and Local Displays

There are two ways to identify the display that an X application should use. The most common method is to use the **DISPLAY** environment variable, which is a locally unique identification string that is automatically set by xinit when it starts the X server.

The **DISPLAY** shell environment variable contains the screen number of a display:

```
$ echo $DISPLAY
:0
```

The format of the complete (globally unique) ID string for a display is

hostname:X-server:screen-number

where *hostname* is the name of the machine running the X server, *X-server* is the X server number and is 0 unless you are using virtual servers, and *screen-number* is 0 unless you have multiple displays. When you are working with a single physical screen, you can shorten the identification string. For example, you can use **bravo:0.0** or **bravo:0** to identify the only physical display on the machine named **bravo**. When the X server and the X clients are running on the same machine, you can shorten this identification string even further to **:0.0** or even **:0**.

If **DISPLAY** is empty or not set, the local computer is not using an X display screen. An application (the X client) uses the value of the **DISPLAY** variable to determine which display, keyboard, and mouse (all together, the X server) to use. One way to run an X application, such as xman, on your local computer but have it use the X Window System display on a remote computer is to change the value of the **DISPLAY** variable on your local computer to identify the remote X server:[4]

```
$ export DISPLAY=bravo:0.0
$ xman &
```

The preceding example starts xman with the default X server running on the computer **bravo**. After giving **DISPLAY** the ID of the **bravo** server, all X programs you start have their displays on **bravo**. If this is not what you want, you can also specify the display you want to use on the command line:

```
$ xman -display bravo:0.0
```

Many X programs use the **–display** option, which affects only the one command you use it with. All other X-related commands will have their displays on the display whose ID is contained in the **DISPLAY** variable.

When You Change the Value of DISPLAY || tip

Remember that when you change the value of the DISPLAY variable, all X programs send their output to the display named by $DISPLAY.

You can start multiple X servers, but you must give each one a different ID string. The following command starts a second X server:

```
$ startx -- :1
```

---

4. If you get a refused/not authorized error, refer to the tip "xhost Grants Access to a Display" on page 195.

The −− option (the − option but preceded by −, as are most options) to startx separates options to the startx command itself from options to be passed on to the X server. Any options that appear before the −− option are treated as options to startx, which passes options after −− to the X server.

The most common reason for starting a second X server is to have a second display with a different number of bits allocated to each screen pixel. (Refer to "Virtual Consoles" on page 193 for more information on how to switch to a virtual console for a second server.) Having more bits per pixel means that you can display more colors simultaneously. Most X servers available for GNU/Linux default to 8 bits per pixel, which permits the use of any combination of 256 colors simultaneously. Starting an X server with 16 bits per pixel permits the use of any combination of 65,536 colors at the same time. The number of bits per pixels you can use depends on your computer graphics hardware and your X server. The most common values that are allowed are 8, 16, 24, and 32 bits per pixel. The following command starts a second X server running at 16 bits per pixel.

```
$ startx -- -depth 16 :1 &
```

Of course, you can use 16 bits per pixel with your first X server as well:

```
$ startx -- -depth 16 &
```

---

xhost Grants Access to a Display   ‖ tip

If you get an error message when you try to open a window on a remote display, you need to have the remote user run **xhost** to grant you access to the display. For example, if you are logged in on a system named **kudos** and you want to create a window on Alex's display, Alex needs to run the following command:

```
$ xhost +kudos
```

If Alex wants to allow anyone to create windows on his display, the following command line grants access to all hosts:

```
$ xhost +
```

If you frequently work with others over a network, you may find it convenient to add an **xhost** line to your .profile or .login file. Be selective about granting access to your X display with **xhost**; if you allow another machine to access your display, you may find that your work is often interrupted by others.

Stopping the X Server

When you set up your **.xinitrc** file as described, terminating your window manager causes the X server to quit. How you terminate your window manager depends on which window manager you are running and how it is configured. When X does not respond, log in from another terminal or a remote system, or use telnet to gain access to the system. Then kill the process running X. Refer to "kill: Aborts a Process" on page 788. You can also press CONTROL-ALT-BACKSPACE to quit the X server. This method may not shut down the X session cleanly; use it only as a fail-safe way to stop X.

Security and xhost | security

Allowing a remote machine access to your display using xhost means that any user on the remote computer can watch everything you type in a terminal emulation window, including passwords. For this reason some software packages, such as the Tcl/Tk development system (tcl.sourceforge.net), restrict their own capabilities when xhost is used. If you are concerned about security or want to take full advantage of systems such as Tcl/Tk, you should use a safer means of granting remote access to your X session. See the xauth man page for information about a more secure replacement for xhost.

Remapping Mouse Buttons

Throughout this chapter each description of a mouse click has referred to the button by its position (left, middle, or right) because the position of a mouse button is more intuitive than an arbitrary name or number. In X terminology the leftmost mouse button is button 1, the middle one is button 2, and the right one is button 3.

If you are right-handed, you can conveniently press the left mouse button with your index finger; X programs take advantage of this by relying on button 1 for the most common operations. If you are left-handed, your index finger rests most conveniently on button 3 (the right button).

When you are running GNOME, use the GNOME menu: Preferences⇨Mouse⇨Buttons (page 241) to change to a left- or right-handed mouse. From KDE choose K menu: Preferences⇨Peripherals⇨Mouse⇨General⇨Button Mapping (page 327).

You can also change how X interprets the mouse buttons by using xmodmap. If you are left-handed, the following command causes X to interpret the right mouse button as button 1 and the left mouse button as button 3:

```
$ xmodmap -e 'pointer = 3 2 1'
```

Or with a two-button mouse:

```
$ xmodmap -e 'pointer = 2 1'
```

When you remap the mouse buttons, remember to reinterpret the descriptions in this chapter accordingly. When this chapter refers to the left button, use the right button instead.

X Applications

When you use X on your GNU/Linux system, you can use many applications from a variety of sources: tools that are part of the standard distribution from the X Consortium (www.x.org), tools provided by your X server developer (www.xfree86.org), software added by your GNU/Linux distributor (www.redhat.com), other tools purchased from third-party suppliers, free applications that are publicly available, and perhaps some applications created locally. Table 6-2 lists a few of the tools often used with X on GNU/Linux. For detailed information about the tools that are available on your system, consult the online man and info pages and other documentation supplied with your system. For more information about tools that are not available on your system, visit the Internet sites that support GNU/Linux and the X Window System. These sites also contain information about many more X applications that you might find useful. See Appendix B for more information.

Several word processing systems are available when you are using X with GNU/Linux. Commercial systems include the WordPerfect system familiar to many MS Windows users, Applixware, and others. In addition to these commercial systems, free software packages offer word processing support. These include Koffice (includes KWord, KSpread, KPresenter, and more), Sun's StarOffice (includes a word processor, spreadsheet, presentation tool, and more, all of which Sun claims are compatible with Microsoft Office), and LyX, which provides a powerful GUI-based text-processing front end to the LaTeX document formatting system.

Utility	‖ table 6-2
appres	Lists resource values that apply to particular tools
bitmap	Builds small black-and-white bitmaps
gimp	GNU Image Manipulation Program, painting and markup suite
gs	GNU PostScript imaging engine, required by **ghostview** and **gv**
gv	Updated and enhanced version of **ghostview**
oclock	Displays a round (analog) clock
rxvt	A color terminal emulator that is smaller than **xterm**
showrgb	Shows all the color names available with X
ups	A powerful GUI-only debugger

Utility (Continued) || table 6-2

wish	Tcl/Tk interactive windowing shell
xcalc	Emulates a handheld calculator
xclipboard	Stores and displays text cut or copied from other applications
xclock	Displays a running time-of-day clock
xdpyinfo	Lists information about an X server
xfontsel	Displays available fonts and font names
xhost	Controls access to an X display
xload	Displays a running graph of how busy the system is
xlock	Keeps others from using your keyboard and display
xlsfonts	Lists names of available fonts
xmag	Displays a magnified image of part of the screen
xman	Browser interface to the online manual pages
xmodmap	Remaps mouse buttons and keyboard keys
xpaint	Paints images on the X display
xpdf	Viewer for Portable Document Format (PDF or Acrobat) files
xprop	Shows window and font properties
xrdb	Loads resource settings into the active X server database
xset	Sets user preferences (display, keyboard, and mouse)
xsetroot	Changes appearance of the root window
xterm	Emulates a character terminal
xv	Grabs, displays, and manipulates picture images
xwd	Stores a screen image (window dump) in a file
xwininfo	Displays information about a particular window
xwud	Displays an image created by xwd

Chapter Summary

One of the powerful features of the X Window System is that applications are independent of window managers; a window manager, such as Metacity, is just another application. As a result, you can run any X application with any window manager. An application does not inherit properties from the window manager. For example, the Athena scrollbar used by xterm appears and operates the same way under all window managers; it does not turn into a KDE style scrollbar when you invoke xterm while running KDE.

You can use a GUI to interact conveniently with many different applications and utilities by opening multiple windows, each capable of running a different program. A GUI also provides a way for you to work with pictures of objects and to select options from menus, an approach that many novice users prefer to the less intuitive command line interface of traditional shells. Most GUIs run on bit-mapped displays and respond to input from a mouse. In addition to the various menu types, GUIs typically provide you with graphical aids, such as scrollbars, buttons, tooltips, and dialog boxes, each of which enables you to use the mouse to control an aspect of the application.

The X Window System GUI is portable and flexible and makes it easy to write applications that work on many different types of systems without having to know low-level details about the individual systems. It can operate in a networked environment, allowing a user to run a program on a remote system and send the results to a local display. The concept of client and server is integral to the operation of the X Window System, with the X server responsible for fulfilling requests made of the X Window System applications or clients. Hundreds of clients run under X, and programmers can also write their own clients, using tools such as the Qt and KDE libraries to write KDE programs and the GTK+ and GTK+2 GNOME libraries to write GNOME programs.

The look-and-feel of an X GUI is determined by the window manager. Window managers control the appearance and operation of windows, such as how to open, resize, move, and close them. Although the many X Window System managers that have been written offer different styles of interaction, they have many features in common. Several window managers are available for GNU/Linux systems, including kwin, Metacity, and Sawfish. They are popular because they are easy to use and support the features that most people need, without requiring extensive customization.

The window managers, and virtually all X applications, are designed to permit users to tailor their work environments in simple or complex ways. You can designate applications that start automatically, set such attributes as colors and fonts, and even alter the way keyboard strokes and mouse clicks are interpreted. There are many ways to customize your work environment; you can specify desired attributes in your **.xinitrc** or **.xsession** file (run by the X server when it starts up), give options that control attributes on the command line that starts an application, use the GUI to configure your window manager, and so on.

Exercises

1. What is a window manager? Name two X Window System managers, and describe how they differ.

2. What happens when you position the mouse pointer in an xterm window's scrollbar and click the middle button? The right button? The left button? Do these techniques work for all scrollbars?

3. Describe three ways to

   a. Change the size of a window.

   b. Delete a window.

   c. Uncover a small window that is completely obscured by another, larger window.

4. When the characters you type do not appear on the screen, what might be wrong? How can you fix it?

5. Given two computer systems, **bravo** and **kudos,** that can communicate over a network, explain what the following command line does:

   ```
   bravo% xterm -sb -title bravo -display kudos:0.0 &
   ```

6. Many X applications use the **–fn** option to specify a font. The following **.Xdefaults** entries exist on the system named **bravo** but not on **kudos:**

   ```
   XTerm*saveLines: 100
   *Font: 10x20
   XTe*title: Terminal Emulator
   ```

   Describe fully the characteristics of the xterm window that is opened on **bravo** by each of the following:

   a. Using the Xterm entry on the Utilities menu to open a new xterm window

   b. Giving the command **xterm –sb &**

   c. Giving the command **xterm –fn 5x8 &**

   d. Giving the command **xterm –display kudos:0.0 &**

   On **kudos,** what is the effect of the following command line:

   ```
   $ xterm -display bravo:0.0 &
   ```

7. List at least three ways that a window manager differs from a desktop manager.

8. What is the main function of the main menu? What is this menu called under KDE? GNOME?

9. Explain the purpose of MIME. How does it facilitate your use of a GUI?

10. What is a terminal emulator? What does it allow you to do from a GUI that you would not be able to do without one?

11. Can you use Metacity under KDE? Explain why or why not.

12. What is input focus? When no window has the input focus, what happens to the letters you type on the keyboard? Which type of input focus do you think you would like to work with? Why?

13. What are the functions of a Window Operations menu? How do you display this menu?

Advanced Exercises

14. Try the experiment described in "Window Manager without a Desktop Manager" on page 181. What is missing from the screen? Based only on what you see, describe what a window manager provides. How does a desktop manager make it easier to work with a GUI?

15. Add the following customization: When you position the mouse pointer anywhere on the border of a window and press the middle mouse button, that window drops below any of the windows that overlap it.

16. How can you run pico (page 49) on a remote display or workstation?

17. Write an xeyes command to display a window that is 600 pixels wide and 400 pixels tall, is located 200 pixels from the right edge of the screen and 300 pixels from the top of the screen, and contains orange eyes outlined in blue with red pupils. (*Hint:* Refer to the xeyes man page.)

18. Try the experiment described in the optional box on page 173. You may want to redirect the output to a file so that you can review it at your leisure. Name five events and explain what you did to generate the event. Make sure to include a mouse, focus, and key event.

    a. Why would you use tee instead of a > symbol to redirect the output?

    b. What problem does using tee create?

    c. Use grep to filter out all but the first line of motion event reports. Does this make it easier to understand the output?

    d. Can you think of other ways that would make the output easier to understand?

19. What is the relationship between the X Window System, a window manager, and an application program. Are applications window-manager specific? Do applications inherit properties from a window manager?

20. What parts of a window are controlled by the window manger? By the application that is running in the window?

IN THIS CHAPTER

GNOME Desktop Manager

7

GNOME (www.gnome.org), a product of the GNU project (page 6), is the user-friendly default desktop manager under Red Hat Linux. The first part of this chapter explains how to use GNOME as it comes to you, covering the desktop, menus, the Nautilus File Manager, and GNOME utilities. Beginning with the section "Customizing GNOME," the chapter presents information on how to personalize GNOME to meet your needs better: using Start-Here/Preferences (Control Center), panels, and menus. The final major section, "The Sawfish Window Manager" (page 254), describes the features of and explains how to customize this powerful window manager.

Figure 7-1 shows a typical GNOME workspace, including the Main panel (the horizontal bar at the bottom), four windows—a game, a clock, the Mozilla browser, and Nautilus displaying the contents of a directory—and icons along the upper-left of the workspace (on the root window). Because you can so easily configure the GNOME desktop environment and the window managers it works with, your desktop may look like you are running NextStep, MS Windows, MacOS, or any other system; your desktop may look quite different from the one shown in Figure 7-1.

Choosing Your Window Manager

Through Red Hat version 7.3, Sawfish was the default window manager under GNOME. Starting with version 8.0, Red Hat uses Metacity as the default window manager under GNOME. Version 8.0 includes Sawfish, although you must install it, so you can use either Metacity or Sawfish.

You can use either window manager as it comes out of the box with equal ease. If you don't want to get involved with your window manager, are content to accept someone else's ideas of how things should be set up, and do not want to make a lot of changes to the way it works, Metacity is for you. From the Metacity **README** file:

> Metacity is not a meta-City as in an urban center, but rather Metaness as in the state of being meta. That is, metacity:meta as opacity:opaque. Also, it may have something to do with the Meta key on UNIX keyboards.

Sawfish, on the other hand, has been around for a while. It is well tested and can be customized to your pleasure. It offers several ways to do many things.

You control most aspects of Sawfish configuration with the Sawfish configurator (page 258). Metacity has fewer configuration options, and those it has are integrated with the GNOME controls: You never see the word Metacity on any menus or icons. For example, GNOME menu: Preferences⇨Menus & Toolbars controls Metacity menu and toolbar preferences.

You do not have to change anything to run Metacity with GNOME under Red Hat. Just bring up GNOME as described in Chapter 2. Refer to "Bringing Up Sawfish" on page 254 for instructions on using Sawfish.

Getting Started

Once you have logged in (page 29) and have a GNOME desktop to work with, you can get started. This section covers how to get help while using GNOME, the Main panel, the desktop, window managers, input focus, and menus.

Click On the Red Hat to Display the GNOME menu ‖ tip

Red Hat has replaced the GNOME foot icon with a red hat. Click on either one to display the GNOME menu. The red hat appears at the lower-left corner of Figure 7-1.

Help

This section lists various ways to get help while you are working with GNOME. Refer to page 182 for an explanation of tooltips.

Help Contents

Select GNOME menu: Help to display the GNOME Help Contents (Figure 7-2). Click Core Desktop, and the yelp (yes, this is the name of the utility) help browser displays a list of GNOME documents; click the section you are interested in.

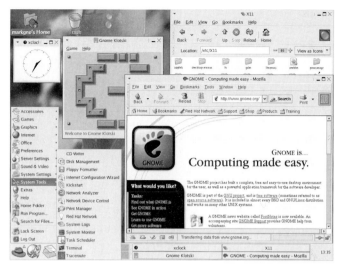

Figure 7-1   A GNOME workspace

Help Menu/Toolbar Selection

Windows, toolbars, and menus have varying degrees of help. Click a Help button or Help menu selection to get help with a specific program or tool. For example, you can read documentation on Nautilus by clicking Help on the Nautilus menubar.

Tooltips

Tooltips are described on page 182. Metacity always provides tooltips only on buttons. Sawfish controls tooltips that appear when the mouse pointer hovers over some part of a window border, including the titlebar. Refer to the entry "Tooltips" in the table on page 262.

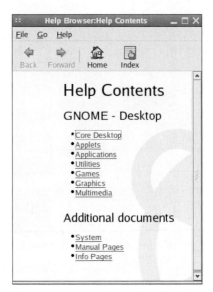

Figure 7-2   The GNOME Help Index displayed by Nautilus

Context Menus

Try right clicking within a window and other places on the desktop; the program that opened the window or Metacity frequently displays a context menu (page 184).

Different Clicks for Different Frame Styles   ‖ tip

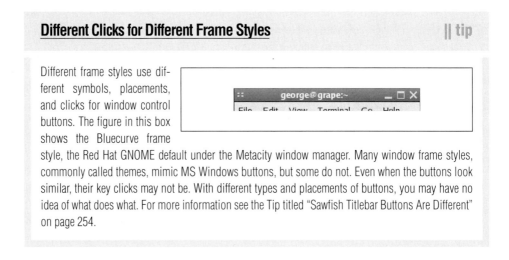

Different frame styles use different symbols, placements, and clicks for window control buttons. The figure in this box shows the Bluecurve frame style, the Red Hat GNOME default under the Metacity window manager. Many window frame styles, commonly called themes, mimic MS Windows buttons, but some do not. Even when the buttons look similar, their key clicks may not be. With different types and placements of buttons, you may have no idea of what does what. For more information see the Tip titled "Sawfish Titlebar Buttons Are Different" on page 254.

Windows and Mouse Clicks

It is important to know where to position the mouse pointer and which mouse buttons to use to accomplish various tasks. Table 7-1 describes the default values for selected mouse clicks under the Metacity window manager with the Bluecurve frame style (both are defaults under GNOME as shipped by Red Hat).

Mouse Clicks and Results	‖ table 7-1
The symbol [M] indicates that the feature is available only in Metacity; [S] indicates Sawfish. The absence of a symbol indicates that the feature is available from both window managers. Under Metacity, right clicks not listed display the Window Operations menu.	
Titlebar	See page 181.
Left double-click	Toggles window shaded/unshaded (page 185).
Left drag	Moves window interactively.
Middle drag [S]	Resizes the vertical aspect of the window interactively.
Right click [S]	Toggles raise/lower window.
Right click [M]	Displays the Window Operations menu.
Titlebar button	See **Window** button, following.
Border and corners	
Left drag	Resizes the vertical (bottom border) or horizontal (left and right sides) aspect of the window interactively. Left drag on a corner resizes in both directions.
Middle drag [S]	Moves window interactively.
Right click [S]	Raises window.
Within the window	
Right click	Sometimes displays a context menu. Depending on the program running in the window, this menu gives you different choices.

Mouse Clicks and Results (Continued) || table 7-1

Window button	Frequently the leftmost button on titlebar; the button that is not the **minimize**, **maximize**, or **close** button. [M] An outlined or filled triangle pointing down.
Left click	Displays the Window Operations menu (page 256).
Right click [S]	Closes the window.
Minimize Button	
Left click	Iconifies the window.
Right click	Displays the Window Operations menu (page 256).
Maximize Button	Any mouse button restores any maximized window.
Left click	Toggles maximize window horizontally and vertically.
Middle click [S]	Toggles maximize window vertically.
Right click [S]	Toggles maximize window horizontally.
Close Button	
Left click	Closes window.
Shift Left click [S]	Closes all windows in the group that the window belongs to.
Right click	Displays the Window Operations menu (page 256).
Root Window	On the desktop click anywhere that is not occupied by a window or other object.
Middle click [S]	Displays the Sawfish menu (page 258).
Right click	Displays the Desktop menu (page 212)

GNOME Menu

Display the GNOME menu by left clicking the GNOME menu button (either a stylized foot or the red hat shown in Figure 7-3) on the panel.

Because you can modify the GNOME menu, your menu may be different from that shown in the figure. There are many entries to choose from: System tools in-

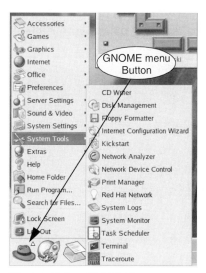

Figure 7-3   GNOME menu

cludes Terminal, a terminal emulator, Disk Management, and access to System Logs. Preferences opens the Control Center menu (page 237) where you can choose Control Center to display the Preferences (Control Center) window, or choose one of the Control Center's entries directly. Extras displays a menu similar to the GNOME menu but with additional entries. Table 7-2 lists some of the entries in the GNOME menu.

GNOME Menu (Partial List)	‖ table 7-2
Games	Displays a long list of games to keep you entertained.
Home Folder	Opens a Nautilus window displaying your home directory.
Lock Screen	Displays a screensaver until you click a button at which time it displays a window showing your login name and a place to enter your password. When you enter your password and press RETURN, your GNOME work area reappears.
Log Out	Displays a dialog box that lets you choose among logging out, halting the system, or rebooting the system (assuming you have permission to do so). When you click Save current setup, GNOME manages your session (does its best to save all your windows and running programs as they are and to restore your work areas next time you log in).

GNOME Menu (Partial List) (Continued)	‖ table 7-2
Preferences	Select Control Center to choose among all items or select the item you want to work with. Refer to "Start Here: Preferences/Control Center" on page 237.
Run Program	Brings up a Run dialog so that you can enter a command line, with options/arguments, that runs a program. You have the option of running the program within a terminal emulator (for non-GUI programs, such as a shell or the vi editor). Refer to "Run Program Window" on page 231.
System Settings	Duplicates Start Here: System Settings. Refer to Table 17-9 on page 985 for more information.
System Tools	Lists tools such as a CD Writer, Floppy Formatter, Hardware Browser, Red Hat Network interface, System Monitor, Terminal, and Task Scheduler.

Main Panel

When you log in, GNOME typically displays a workspace that includes the GNOME Main panel, the key to getting your work done easily and efficiently. Because the Main panel is easy to configure, you can set it up to hold the tools you use frequently, arranged the way you want: application launchers (such as the Terminal, Start Here, and Calendar buttons), menus (including the GNOME menu), *applets* (applications that are small enough to be executed within a panel), drawers (that can hold anything the panel can), and special objects (such as the Logout button). You can create multiple panels to hold different groups of tools.

A few icons are usually on the Main panel so that you can start programs quickly and easily. A few of the more common ones are shown in Figure 7-4. This section discusses the GNOME menu, Window List, Workspace Switcher, and how to hide the Main panel. Refer to "Panels" on page 246 for more information on the Main panel and how to configure it.

To copy an icon from the GNOME menu to a panel, left drag the item from the GNOME menu to a panel. When you want to remove an icon from a panel, right click the icon and choose Remove From Panel from the pop-up menu.

Icons/Buttons

The buttons on a panel have icons on them and are referred to as either *buttons* or *icons*. The Web Browser button displays a Web browser, Mozilla by default. The

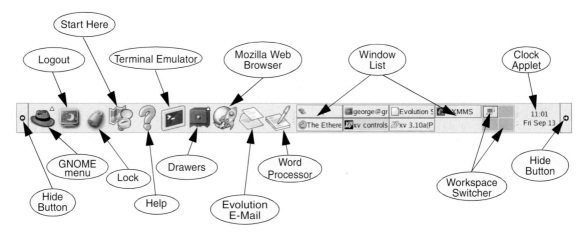

Figure 7-4   A customized GNOME Main panel

Email button starts Evolution, an e-mail and calendaring application. The Terminal Emulator button brings up a terminal emulator window where you can run character-based programs (page 233). The Logout button closes GNOME. See Figure 7-4. Almost anything on the system can be started using a button on a panel.

Window List and Workspace Switcher Applets

The GNOME Window List and Workspace Switcher applets (Figure 7-4), formerly called the Pager, help you go to a specific workspace or window/program on your desktop. The Workspace Switcher displays your desktop as a grid, with each section of the grid representing a workspace. The workspace you are using is shaded. Click a section of the grid to display the corresponding workspace.

By default the Window List lists each of the programs running on the displayed workspace. Click any of these to give the window that is running the application the input focus (GNOME first restores the window if it is iconified).

When you right click on the bumpy bar to the left of the Window List and select Preferences, GNOME displays the Window List Preferences window which controls the appearance and functioning of the Window List applet.

Hide Buttons

When you click one of the Hide buttons[1] (at either end of a panel, see Figure 7-4), the panel slides off the workspace in the direction of the closest edge of the desktop, leaving only the other Hide button showing. Click the visible Hide button to make

---

1. The Hide buttons may not have arrows on them.

the panel reappear. When the Hide buttons are not present, refer to the entry "Show hide buttons" in the table on page 251. When you want to make a panel disappear automatically when you are not using it, refer to the entry "Autohide" in the table on page 251.

Panel Icon Menus

The two types of icon menus are Panel Icon menus and Generic Icon menus. Display a Panel Icon menu by right clicking almost any object on a panel.

The Panel Icon menu contains the Panel menu (page 250) and selections that remove the icon from the panel, move the icon within the panel (page 252), and view and change the icon's properties. Some icons have additional context-based selections whereas some applets have a different menu.

Desktop

Icons on the root window respond appropriately to a double-click: A program starts running, a data file (such as a letter, calendar, or URL) runs the program that created it (with the data file loaded or, in the case of a URL, with the browser displaying the appropriate Web page), and a directory brings up the Nautilus File Manager (page 214). Within Nautilus you can move a file/directory by dragging and dropping it, copy a file by right dragging it and selecting Copy here from the resulting pop-up menu, and run or edit a file by double-clicking it. Right click an icon that is not in a panel to display the Generic Icon menu (following).

Desktop Menu

Right click the root window to display the Desktop menu. You can open a window or perform another task by making a selection from the Desktop menu. Table 7-3 lists the menu items on a typical Desktop menu:

Generic Icon Menus

Display a Generic Icon menu by right clicking an icon that is not on a panel. See the earlier discussion of Panel Icon menus.

The Generic Icon menu comes in handy when you are working with Nautilus as a file manager. This menu contains many of the same selections as Nautilus menubar: File. It is the only way to perform some operations with icons on the root window. Refer to "File" on page 220 and "Edit" on page 221.

Desktop Menu || table 7-3

New Window	Opens a Nautilus window displaying your home directory.
New Folder	Creates a new, empty directory on your workspace. The directory is located in ~/.gnome-desktop and is named **untitled folder**.*
New Launcher	Opens the Create Launcher window (page 247).
New Terminal	Opens a terminal emulator window (page 177) with your home directory as its working directory.
Scripts	Lists all executable files in ~/.gnome2/nautilus-scripts. Select one of these files to execute it, or click **Open Scripts Folder** to display the ~/.gnome2/nautilus-scripts directory.
Clean Up by Name	Refer to the entry "Clean Up by Name" in the table on page 222.
Cut/Copy/Paste File	Operate on files that you have selected on the desktop. Cut removes the original file once you have pasted it somewhere else (not on the desktop; a cut from and paste to the desktop does not change anything).
Disks	Mounts a floppy disk or a CD-ROM.
Use Default Background	Changes the desktop background to the default of the frame style that you are using.
Change Desktop Background	Displays the Background window, which you can use to change the desktop background.

* When you are working with a command line interface, you should avoid putting SPACEs within filenames because the SPACEs are difficult to work with. GNOME encourages the use of SPACEs, however, because they make filenames more readable.

Change Input Focus

You can change the input focus (page 182) by clicking a window in various ways, depending on how the window manager is set up (page 207). To make each window on the workspace active in turn, hold the ALT key down while repeatedly pressing TAB. As you hold ALT down, by default see in the center of the desktop a box that shows the contents of the titlebar (page 181) of the window that is active and will be moved to the top of the stack of windows if you release the ALT key at that point.

Menus

GNOME has many menus. Table 7-4 lists all the common menus and where to find information on each.

Menus	|| table 7-4
Context	Refer to "Context Menu" on page 184.
Desktop	Refer to "Desktop Menu" on page 212.
Generic Icon	Right click any icon that is *not* on a panel (page 212).
Help	Refer to "Help Menu/Toolbar Selection" on page 205.
Main	Refer to "GNOME Menu" on page 208.
Menu	Refer to "Menu Menu" on page 253.
Menu panel	Refer to "Menu Panel" on page 246.
Nautilus menubar	Refer to "Menubar" on page 220.
Panel	Refer to "Panel Menu" on page 250.
Panel Icon	Right click any object on a panel. (page 212)
Sawfish	Refer to "Sawfish Menu" on page 258.
Window List	Refer to "Window List and Workspace Switcher Applets" on page 211.
Window Operations	Refer to "Window Operations Menu" on page 256.

Nautilus: File Manager

Nautilus is many things.[2] This section discusses Nautilus the file manager. When Nautilus is not open, double-click the Home icon in the upper-left of the workspace or choose

---

2. As of the release of Red Hat version 8.0, Mozilla had not been ported to GTK 2, so Mozilla could not be linked with Nautilus, depriving Nautilus of most Web browsing capabilities. Open the Side Pane while browsing Web sites; Nautilus gives you the option of opening the URL in another browser.

GNOME menu: Home Folder to open a Nautilus window displaying the contents of your home directory (Figure 7-6, page 217), using icons (by default) to represent files.

URI

URI is an acronym for Uniform Resource Identifier. The format of a URI is familiar because URLs (page 407), such as **http:** and **ftp:**, are a subset of URIs. Nautilus uses URIs to specify special locations. The part of a URI preceding the colon is called a scheme and is handled by the **gnome-vfs** (virtual filesystem) module. The way **gnome-vfs** works, each scheme can have its own code to handle it. Standard code handles standard URI schemes, such as **http:** and **ftp:**. Special code, much of it introduced by Red Hat, handles nonstandard URIs.

When you log in, many systems display a Nautilus window showing the Start Here URI (**start-here:**). Following are the locations for the entries that Start Here displays:

- start-here: /etc/X11/starthere
- server-settings: /etc/X11/serverconfig
- system-settings: /etc/X11/sysconfig

All the files in **/etc/X11/starthere** are Desktop files. Along with other information, each of these files contains a line that begins with URL (URI):

```
$ cd /etc/X11/starthere; grep URL *
applications.desktop:URL=applications:///
preferences.desktop:URL=preferences:///
serverconfig.desktop:URL=server-settings:///
sysconfig.desktop:URL=system-settings:///
```

Each of these URIs points somewhere; the preceding list tells you where. In general, there is no correspondence between URIs and filesystem locations.

Desktop Files

Files with a **.desktop** filename extension store information about how they should be displayed and what they point to. The following, abbreviated file displays the red system_settings icon (Icon=system_settings.png) in the Start Here window. It is a link (Type=Link) to preferences: (URL=preferences:) which is called Preferences by default (Name=Preferences). The Italian name is Preferenze (Name[it]=Preferenze). The comment also has default and Italian values. When you look at the file on your system, you will see that many more languages are included in the file.

```
$ cat /etc/X11/starthere/sysconfig.desktop
Type=Link
Name=System Settings
Name[it]=Impostazioni di sistema
...
Comment=Change systemwide settings (affects all users)
Comment[it]=Modifica impostazioni generali del sistema (per tutti gli utenti)
...
Icon=redhat-system_settings.png
Terminal=0
Encoding=UTF-8

Terminal=0
URL=system-settings:///
```

Figure 7-5   Start Here icon and label

Start Here

When you log in on a Red Hat system, many systems display a Nautilus window showing the Start Here special location. You can also display Start Here by double-clicking the Start Here icon (Figure 7-5) on the root window, clicking the same icon on a panel once, or entering **start-here:** in the Nautilus location bar. Nautilus displays Start Here as a series of directories. Although Start Here is not strictly a menu, it is the root of a virtual directory structure that can help you in your day-to-day work on your system. In many areas Start Here functions overlap those of the GNOME menu. The Preferences folder, a subdirectory of Start Here, duplicates exactly the Preferences item on the GNOME menu. Look around and experiment; you will not be allowed to do anything harmful to the system unless you are logged in as **root**. Refer to "Start Here" on page 236 for more information.

GNOME Desktop and Nautilus   ‖ tip

The GNOME Desktop is run from a backend process that runs as part of Nautilus. If that process stops running, it will usually start up again automatically. If it does not, start Nautilus by giving the command **nautilus** to restore your desktop. You do not have to keep the Nautilus window open to keep the desktop alive.

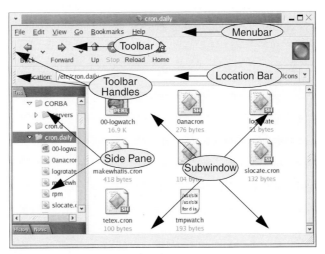

Figure 7-6   Nautilus displaying icons

Display

Nautilus displays a subwindow and, optionally, a side pane (Figure 7-6). The side pane, to the left of the subwindow, has three possible tabs—History, Notes, and Tree[3]—each of which changes what appears in the side pane. The figure shows part of the directory structure as a tree on its side (the Tree tab). The subwindow shows the contents of the directory that is highlighted in the tree view. Click a directory in the side pane to display its contents in the subwindow.

To the left of directories in the side pane are little triangles/arrows that point either right or down. Click a right arrow to expand the associated directory one level. Click a down arrow to close the directory.

Three control bars are usually at the top of the Nautilus window (Figure 7-6): a menubar, a toolbar, and a location bar. Table 7-6 on page 220 describes the dropdown menus presented by the menubar. The toolbar holds navigational tools and content specifiers (page 225). The location bar shows the name of the directory you are viewing and accepts the name of a directory that you want to view (page 224). Refer to Table 7-11 on page 244 for information about customizing Nautilus.

You can display icons or a list of filenames in the subwindow. Choose which you prefer by making a selection from the drop-down list that appears on the right end of the location bar. View as Icons is shown in Figure 7-6 and View as List is shown in Figure 7-7. At the left end of the toolbar are icons for Back, Forward, Up, Refresh, Home, Web Search, and Stop.

You can perform many operations in Nautilus using only the mouse. Table 7-5 shows what effects the mouse has within the Nautilus window.

---

3. Tree appears when you check the Nautilus menubar: Edit⇔Preferences⇔Side Panes⇔Tabs⇔Tree box.

Nautilus Mouse Action

|| table 7-5

Select an icon	Click the icon or drag a box around a portion of the icon. The name of the selected icon is highlighted. When your system is set up for single-click open, you must use the drag method. Refer to "Click Behavior" on page 245.
Select multiple icons	Select the first icon (its name is highlighted). Hold the CONTROL key down while you select additional icons. Each name is highlighted in addition to those already highlighted as you click each icon. Or drag a box around the icons you want to select. Each icon's name is highlighted as you drag/expand the box over it. You can also use a combination of these techniques.
Getting help	Choose **Nautilus menubar: Help⇨Contents** to display the Nautilus File Manager documentation.
Drag and drop	Drag the icon to its new location in this or another window, including the root window. To cancel a drag, press ESCAPE before you release the mouse button. Common drag-and-drop tasks are: • Drag a file onto a folder icon or within an open folder's window (moves the file). • Drag a file onto the root window (copies the file). • Drag a file onto the Printer control on a panel (prints the file). • Drag a file or folder onto the trash can on the workspace (moves the file to the **Trash** directory in preparation to delete the file). • Perform a right drag to display a menu that gives you a choice of moving, copying, or linking the file you are dragging.
View a folder	There are two ways to open a folder icon so you can view its contents. • Double-click the folder icon. (See footnote 4 on page 219.) • Right click a folder icon and choose **Open** from the pop-up menu.
View home folder	Click the **Home** button on the Nautilus toolbar.

Nautilus Mouse Action (Continued)	‖ table 7-5
View parent folder	Click the **Up arrow** on the Nautilus toolbar.
Open object	Refer to "Opening Files," following.

Figure 7-7   Nautilus displaying a list view with
the toolbar at the bottom of the window

Opening Files

You can double-click[4] a file or icon to open it, or you can right click the file and choose Open from the pop-up menu. When you open a file, Nautilus tries to figure out which tool to use to open it, using MIME (page 178) to associate the filename extension with a MIME type and a program. When you open a file with a filename extension of **ps** Nautilus calls **gs** (ghostscript), which displays the PostScript file in a readable format. When you open an executable file such as Mozilla, Nautilus runs the executable. When you open a text file, Nautilus opens a text editor that displays and allows you to edit the file. When you open a directory, Nautilus displays its contents. When Nautilus does not know which tool to use to open a file, it asks you. Refer to "File Types and Programs (MIME Types)" on page 232. for information on customization.

Control Bars

This section discusses the three control bars—the menubar (Figure 7-8), toolbar, and location bar—that initially appear at the top of a Nautilus window.

---

4. If your system is set up for single-click open, you open with a single click. Refer to "Click Behavior" on page 245.

Figure 7-8   Nautilus menubar

Menubar

The menubar presents a drop-down menu when you click one of its selections. Table 7-6 shows the menu selections and describes each of the choices within each selection. Nautilus varies its menu selections, depending on what it is displaying in its subwindow.

Nautilus Menubar	‖ table 7-6
File	You can right-click on a file to get a slightly different File menu.
New Window	Creates another Nautilus window that duplicates the window you are working on.
New Folder	Creates a folder in the working directory (shown on the location bar). Change the name from **untitled folder** by typing over this name. Right click the folder and choose **Rename** if the first method fails.
Open	Opens the selected icon/file, based on its filetype.
Open In New Window	Same as Open, except that where appropriate, the opened object appears in a new window.
Open With	Gives you a choice of applications and/or viewers to open the selected icon/file.
Scripts (list of scripts)	A list of executable files in ~/.gnome2/nautilus-scripts. Select one of these files to execute it. Nautilus uses as an argument the name of a file selected in the subwindow.
Open Scripts Folder	Displays the contents of ~/.gnome2/nautilus-scripts.
Properties	Opens a Properties window for the selected object (page 226).
Empty Trash	Permanently removes all of the objects from the trashcan.
Close All Windows	Closes the Nautilus window you are working with and all windows that were opened from that window.
Close Window	Closes the Nautilus window you are working with.

Nautilus Menubar (Continued) || table 7-6

Edit	
Cut File	Moves the selected object to the clipboard so that you can use it with **Paste**. The object is removed from the window.
Copy File	Copies the selected object to the clipboard so that you can use it with **Paste**. The object remains in the window.
Paste Files	Copies the object on the clipboard to the window with the input focus. You cannot paste all objects in all windows.
Clear Text	Deletes selected, editable text, such as in the side pane **Notes** tab, the edit box that appears when you are renaming a file, or the location bar.
Select All Files	Selects all the files in the window you are working in.
Duplicate	Makes a copy of the selected object. Execute permission is not set on a copy of an executable file.
Make Link	Makes a symbolic link to the selected object. The link appears in the same directory as the object.
Rename	Renames the selected object.
Move to Trash	Moves the selected object to the trashcan (~/.**Trash**).
Remove Custom Icon	Restores the original icon when you have specified a custom icon with **Generic Icon menu: Show Properties⇨Basic⇨ Select Custom Icon** (only on icons you have permission to change).
Backgrounds and Emblems	Choose **Patterns**, **Colors**, or **Emblems** and drag them to various parts of the Nautilus or root window.
Patterns	Drag a pattern to the root window, the main Nautilus window, or the side pane. Drag the **reset** object to reset the color to its default.
Colors	Works the same way as **Patterns**.
Emblems	Drag an emblem so that it is on top of an icon on the root window, an object in the main Nautilus window, or in the side pane. The emblem appears next to the object. Refer to "Emblems" on page 226.

Nautilus Menubar (Continued) || table 7-6

Preferences	Displays the Nautilus Preferences window. Refer to "Nautilus Menubar: Edit⇨Preferences" on page 244.
View	
Stop	Stops loading information. Generally used to stop downloading a Web page.
Reload	Redraw everything in the Nautilus side pane and subwindow. The refresh reflects changes in any of the underlying data (for example, a new file in a directory that is displayed). Also available as a button on the Nautilus toolbar.
Side Pane Toolbar Location Bar Status Bar	A check mark appears to the left of each control bar that is displayed. Click a choice to change the state of the corresponding control bar.
Reset View to Defaults	Resets Default View, Icon View Defaults, and List View Defaults as defined in **Nautilus menubar: Edit⇨Preferences⇨Views** (page 244).
Arrange Items	Gives you a choice of ways to lay out objects in the Nautilus subwindow. **Manually** enables you to drag and place objects as you please within the subwindow. **Name**, **Size**, **Type**, **Modification Date**, and **Emblems** (page 226) sort the objects accordingly. **Tighter Layout** brings the objects closer together whereas **Reversed Order** reverses the order you selected to lay out the objects with (for example, when you select **By Name** and **Reversed Order** the objects appear by name in reverse alphabetical order).
Clean Up by Name	Same as **Arrange Items⇨By Name** when you have previously selected **Arrange Items⇨Manually**.
Zoom In Zoom Out Normal Size	Adjusts the magnification of the objects in the Nautilus subwindow. Also available by clicking the plus (+), minus (−), or number in the middle of the magnifying glass on the location bar.
View as Icons View as List View as Music	Specifies the way you want to view the contents of the Nautilus subwindow. Also available from the pop-up menu at the right end of the location bar.
View as	Brings up the Open with Other Viewer window.

Nautilus Menubar (Continued) || table 7-6

Choose a view for "*viewname*"	Specifies the name of the view that this window is working with (Start Here, Desktop, the name of your home directory, and so on). The list displays the possible views and the status of each. Highlight the view you want to work with.
View as *viewtype*	The *viewtype* corresponds to the highlighted view in the preceding list: **Icons**, **List**, or **Music**. Click **Modify** to display the Modify window for the highlighted view.
Modify	Displays the Modify window. The titlebar of the Modify window (such as, View as Icons) specifies the view you are working with.
Include in the menu for "folder" items	Includes this view as a selection in the **Nautilus menubar: View** and in the pop-up menu at the right end of the location bar for all directories. This menu entry is always present unless you select **Don't include**.
Use as default for "folder" items	Specifies *viewtype* as the default view for all directories.
Include in the menu just for "*viewname*"	Includes *viewtype* in **Nautilus menubar: View** and in the pop-up menu at the right end of the location bar for *viewname* only. This menu entry is always present unless you select **Don't include**.
Use as default just for "*viewname*"	Specifies that *viewtype* is the default view for this *viewname* only.
Don't include in the menu for "folder" items	Do not include *viewname* in **Nautilus menubar: View** and in the pop-up menu at the right end of the location bar for any directory.
File Types and Programs	Refer to "File Types and Programs (MIME Types)" on page 232.
Go There	Closes the Open with Other Viewer window and displays the Edit File Type window.
Choose	Implements the changes you have made.
Go	
Back/Forward/Up/Home	Navigates among the objects you have viewed in the Nautilus subwindow. **Home** displays the contents of your home directory.

Nautilus Menubar (Continued)	|| table 7-6
Start Here	Refer to "Start Here" on page 216.
Trash	Displays the contents of the trashcan (~/.Trash).
Location	Highlights the text field in the location bar so that you can enter a pathname or URL. Press RETURN to display the location you enter.
Clear History	Removes the history list, which is visible below this selection and on the **History** selection from the side pane. Making this selection means that you are not able to use the **Back** arrow on the toolbar or **Nautilus toolbar: Back** to visit any of the locations that you have visited previously.
(history list)	A list of previously visited locations. Click a location to display it in the Nautilus subwindow. Also available from the **History** tab on the side pane.
Bookmarks	
Add Bookmark	Add the location displayed in the Nautilus subwindow to the list of bookmarks.
Edit Bookmarks	Changes the name or location of a bookmark or removes it.
(list of bookmarks)	A list of bookmarks and/or directories of bookmarks that you or Red Hat has created. Click a bookmark to display it in the Nautilus sub-window.

Toolbar

The Nautilus toolbar (Figure 7-9) holds navigation tools. Table 7-7 describes each of the buttons.

Location Bar

The location bar (Figure 7-10) text box displays the pathname of the directory that is displayed in the subwindow and highlighted in the Tree tab (when it is displayed). You can also use the location bar text box to specify a local or remote directory or

Figure 7-9   Nautilus toolbar

Nautilus Toolbar ‖ table 7-7

Back	Similar to the browser button with the same name: It redisplays the previous subwindow.
Forward	Similar to the browser button with the same name: It redisplays the subwindow that you just backed up from.
Up	Displays the contents of the parent directory. The location bar shows the name of the working directory. This icon is grayed out when there is no parent directory.
Stop	Stops whatever Nautilus is doing. Commonly used to stop a Web page from downloading.
Reload	Redisplays the subwindow to reflect any changes to its contents.
Home	Displays the contents of your home directory in the subwindow.

URL (FTP, HTTP, and so on) site that you want to display in the subwindow: Enter the absolute pathname of the directory or URL (an FTP address must be in the form **ftp://***address*) and press RETURN. Nautilus displays the contents of the directory or URL. However, see footnote 2 on page 214.

The location bar holds two tools in addition to the location bar text box: the magnification selector and the View as drop-down menu. To change the magnification of the display in the subwindow, click the plus or minus sign on either side of the magnifying glass; click the magnifying glass itself to return to 100% magnification. Click anywhere on the View as menu (to the right of the magnifying glass) to display the choices.

Tear-Away Bars

One handy feature of Nautilus is the ability to reposition, or tear away, the toolbar or the location bar. You can move either control bar onto the root window or position it at the top or bottom of the Nautilus window. You can also move the toolbar so that it is vertical on either side of the Nautilus window. Drag the striped vertical bar (marked *Toolbar Handles* in Figure 7-6 on page 217) at the left or top end of one of the control bars, and you will drag the bar. To position the toolbar on one of the vertical sides of the window, drag the toolbar handle toward the middle of the

Figure 7-10   Nautilus Location bar

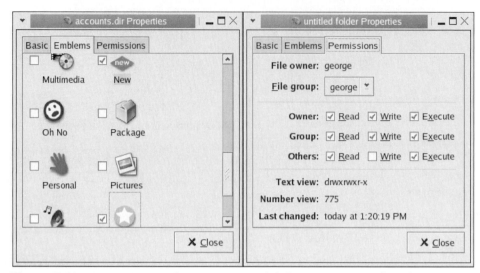

Figure 7-11   Properties window: Emblems tab left; Permissions tab right

side you want it on, and it snaps into place. Once the toolbar is vertical, you can move it to the root window and it will remain vertical. Figure 7-7 shows the toolbar at the bottom of the Nautilus window. To return a bar to the window, drag it back and it snaps into place.

Properties

You can view information about a file, such as ownership, permission, size, and so on, by right clicking any filename or icon (except icons on a panel; see page 247 for those) and selecting Properties from the drop-down menu. The Properties window initially displays some basic information; click the tabs at the top of the window to see additional information. Different types of files display different sets of tabs, depending on what is appropriate to the file (context menu). You can modify settings in this window only if you have permission to do so.

Basic

The Basic tab displays information about the file and enables you to select a custom icon for the file or change its name. To change the name of the file, make your changes in the text box and press RETURN.

Emblems

The Emblems tab (Figure 7-11, left) allows you to add or remove emblems associated with the file by placing/removing a check mark next to an emblem in the Emblems

Figure 7-12   Emblems

tab. Figure 7-12 shows what the Important, New, and Special emblems (Figure 7-11) look like when they are displayed along with the file icon. Nautilus displays emblems in both its icon view and list view.

Permissions

The Permissions tab (Figure 7-11, right) allows you to change file permissions (page 118). When the Read button in the Owner row (*User* elsewhere, see the tip "chmod: o for Other, u for Owner" on page 120) has a check mark in it, the owner has permission to read from the file. When you click all the buttons in the Owner row so that they all contain check marks, the owner has read, write, and execute permission. The owner of a file can change the group that the file is associated with to any other group the owner is associated with. When you run as Superuser, you can change the name of the user who owns the file and the group associated with the file. Directory permissions work as explained on page 121.

GNOME Utilities

GNOME comes with many utilities that make your work on the desktop easier and more productive. This section covers several of the tools that are integral to the use of GNOME.

Search Tool

Display the GNOME Search tool (gnome-search-tool) by selecting GNOME menu: Search for Files (Figure 7-13). This tool is a front end for the find, grep, and locate utilities. The Simple tab is generally associated with locate; the Advanced tab with find. You can display the command either query generates by selecting from the menu bar Search: Show Command after you have filled out the text boxes.

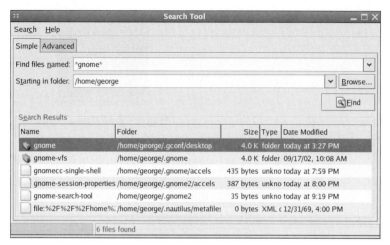

Figure 7-13   GNOME Search tool, Simple tab

Simple Search

Enter a filename in the Find files named text box, Enter an absolute pathname of a folder in the Starting in folder text box, and click Find. A string with no wildcard characters matches that string anywhere in the absolute pathname of a file. A string that includes a wildcard character must match the absolute pathname of a file.

Although locate is usually executed, **/usr/bin/locate** is a link to slocate, a secure version of locate. Because it searches a prebuilt, compressed database of filenames, the slocate utility performs more quickly than find. By default the updatedb command in

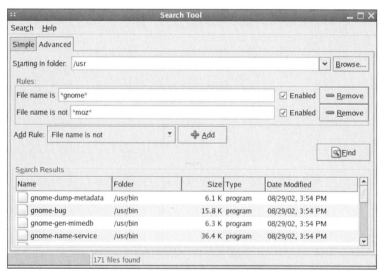

Figure 7-14   GNOME Search tool, Advanced tab

/etc/cron.daily/slocate.cron recreates this database every night so that a Simple search frequently does not find files that were created during the day, since the last run of updatedb. If updatedb is not run regularly, Simple search will not work properly.

Advanced Search

A minimal Advanced Search command requires the name of a directory that you want to start the search from (the root of the search) and a filename to search for. Figure 7-14 shows the Start in directory as **/usr**; the Advanced Search tool enters your home directory in this location by default. Change the Start in folder as you like, and enter a filename in the Find files named text box (you can use wildcard characters). You can click Find at this point, and the results of your search will be appended to any existing results in the Search Results window, which opens automatically if it is not already open.

You can add search criteria to a basic search by clicking the pop-up menu at Add Rule, selecting a criterion, and clicking Add. A new criterion line appears. Fill in text boxes on the new criterion line as appropriate (just as you entered the name of the file to search for in the File name is text box), and, if necessary, click the Enable box so that a check mark appears. Turn off a criterion line by removing the Enable check mark; remove a criterion line by clicking the associated Remove button. Each of the criteria that you specify is ANDed with the next so that a file must meet all criteria to appear in the Search Results window. Refer to find on page 1165 for more information on search criteria and how find works.

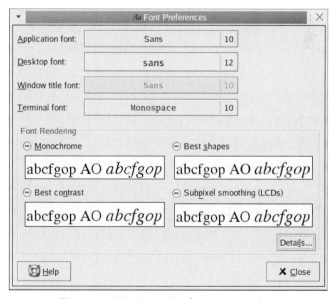

Figure 7-15   Font Preferences window

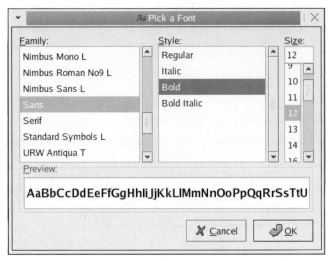

Figure 7-16   Pick a Font window

Font Preferences

Display the GNOME Font Preferences window (gnome-font-properties) by selecting GNOME menu: Preferences⇨Font (Figure 7-15). Click one of the four font bars at the top of the window to display the Pick a Font window (next section), and change the font that GNOME uses for applications, the desktop, window title, or terminal.

Look at the four boxes in the Font Rendering frame and select the one that looks best to you. Subpixel smoothing is usually best for LCD monitors. Click Details to refine the font rendering further. Again, pick the box in each of the frames that looks best to you.

Pick a Font Window

The Pick a Font window (Figure 7-16) appears when you need to choose a font, such as when you select GNOME menu: Preferences⇨Font⇨Application font to choose a font for applications that you run. Select a font family, a style, and a size that you want to use. A preview appears in the Preview frame under the columns. Click OK when you are satisfied with your choice.

Pick a Color Window

The Pick a color window (Figure 7-17) appears when you need to choose a color, such as when you choose Desktop menu: Change Desktop Background and click the

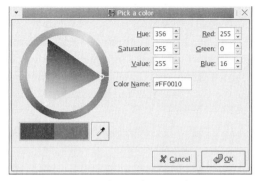

Figure 7-17   Pick a color window

box to the right of Top Color. When the window opens, the bar below the color circle displays the existing color. Click the color you want from the outer ring, and click/drag the lightness of that color in the triangle. As you change the color, the right end of the bar displays the color you selected, and the left end keeps on displaying the existing color. Use the eyedropper to pick up a color from the workspace: Click the eyedropper, and then click the resulting crosshairs on the color you want. The color will be displayed in the Pick a color window.

Run Program Window

The Run Program window (Figure 7-18) enables you to run a program with options as though you had run it from the command line; for character-based programs it in-

Figure 7-18   Run Program window

cludes the option of running the program within a terminal emulator. The window can also display a list of programs that you can choose from. Display the Run Program window by selecting Run Program from the GNOME menu. Figure 7-18 displays the list of Known Applications, shows xboard (a GNOME chess application interface) selected from the list, and includes the command line in the text box at the top of the window. You can also enter a command manually in the text box. Click Append File to select a filename to use as an argument to the command in the text box. Click Run in terminal to run text-based applications in a terminal emulator window.

File Types and Programs (MIME Types)

The File Types and Programs window (Figure 7-19) displays and enables you to modify MIME types and their association to filename extensions (page 178). Display this window with GNOME menu: Preferences⇨File Types and Programs. Add a MIME type by clicking Add file type and filling out the Add File Type window. Delete or modify a MIME type by selecting the MIME type/filename extension combination you want to work with from the scroll list and clicking Delete or Edit. The Add/Edit File Type windows are very similar. Enter or edit values in the text boxes as appropriate, change the icon by clicking the icon box at the top of the window, and change the default action by working with the items in the Actions frame.

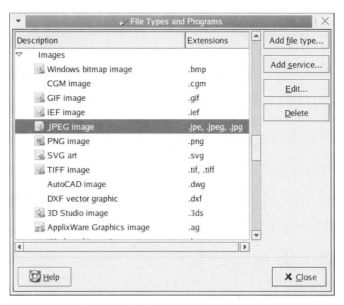

Figure 7-19   File Types and Programs window

GNOME Terminal Emulator/Shell

The GNOME terminal emulator (gnome-terminal) displays a window that mimics a character-based terminal (page 177). Bring up the terminal emulator by either clicking the Terminal Emulator button on a panel (Figure 7-4, page 211) or by selecting GNOME menu: System Tools⇨Terminal. When the GNOME terminal emulator is already displayed, you can select GNOME Terminal menubar: File⇨New Window⇨Default to display another terminal emulator window.

The gnome-terminal utility uses *profiles* in place of *preferences* because you can set up more than one set of preferences; each set is called a profile.

The choices under the Settings entry on the menubar change the appearance and functionality of the terminal emulator. In particular, look at the GNOME Terminal menubar: Edit⇨Current Profile window, which controls most aspects of the terminal emulator. Table 7-8 explains the choices in this window.

GNOME Terminal Emulator Menubar: Edit⇨Current Profile	table 7-8
General	
Profile name	Specifies a name for a terminal configuration. Although you can enter a new name here, doing so will change the name of an existing profile. To create a new profile select New in the Edit Profiles window. Then edit the new profile to set it up the way you want. Before you create any new profiles, **Default** is the default profile.
Use the same font as other applications	Specifies that **gnome-terminal** is to use the GNOME default monospaced font. Uncheck this box and click the wide box below it to specify another font. Select a font, font style, and size from the Choose a terminal font window, and click **OK**.
Profile icon	Displays the icon for this profile. Click the icon to choose another one.
Allow bold text	Enables bold text within the terminal emulator window.
Cursor blinks	Causes the cursor to blink.
Show menubar by default in new terminals	Causes the menubar to be displayed when you open a gnome-terminal window.
Terminal bell	Turns on the terminal bell.

GNOME Terminal Emulator Menubar: Edit⇨ Current Profile (Continued) table 7-8

Select-by-word characters	When you double-click a string within the terminal emulator to highlight a word, the characters that are in this text-entry box are included. The highlight does not include any characters not in this box. The most obvious character that is missing is a SPACE, a typical word delimiter.
Title and Command	
Title	
Initial title	Specifies the name displayed in the terminal window titlebar when it first appears. You can change this value.
Dynamically-set title	Specifies what happens to the title when a command running in the terminal emulator attempts to change the title. Choose a value from this pop-up list.
Command	
When command exits	Specifies whether to close the terminal emulator or to restart the command when the command running in the terminal emulator terminates.
Run command as a login shell	Refer to "Startup Files" on page 565 for a description of a login shell.
Update utmp/wtmp records when command is launched	Records all logins/logouts.
Run a custom command instead of my shell	When the terminal-emulator opens, runs the command that you specify in the **Custom command** text box instead of your default shell.
Colors	
Foreground and Background	
Use colors from system theme	Specifies that **gnome-terminal** is to use the same colors as the window manager theme.

GNOME Terminal Emulator Menubar: Edit⇨ Current Profile (Continued) table 7-8

Built-in schemes	Selects one of three predefined color schemes or a custom color scheme that you define. The color scheme that you specify translates a color request from a program into a specific color/shade that appears on the terminal emulator.
Text color	When you select **Built-in schemes⇨Custom**, click this box to open the Pick a color window. Choose the foreground color (the color of the type) from this window.
Background color	Same as the **Text color** but specifies the background color (the color of the window overall).
Palette	Specifies the colors that each of the Built-in and the Custom schemes uses. Click on a color to modify it.
Effects	Controls the background image for the terminal emulator.
Background	
None (use solid color)	Uses no image; color is as specified in the **Colors** tab.
Background image	Specifies that the file named in the Image file text box be used as the background of the terminal emulator.
Background image scrolls	Specifies that the background image scrolls with the text.
Transparent background	Causes the terminal emulator background to match the root window.
Shade transparent or image background	Dims the background image as specified by the slider.
Scrolling	
Scrollbar is	Specifies that the scrollbar appear on the left or right of the terminal emulator window or that it not appear at all (**disabled**).
Scrollback	
lines	Specifies the number of lines that the terminal emulator keeps in memory (that you can scroll back through).

GNOME Terminal Emulator Menubar: Edit⇨ Current Profile (Continued)   table 7-8

kilobytes	Specifies the maximum amount of memory that the terminal uses to store the scrollback lines.
Scroll on keystroke	Scrolls to the end of the display when you press a key.
Scroll on output	Scrolls to the end of the display when output is sent to the terminal emulator.
Compatibility	Changes the ASCII sequence the BACKSPACE or DELETE keys generate. Change these values only when a program expects other than the default ASCII sequences from these keys as these changes may have undesirable side effects.

Customizing GNOME

This section covers four ways of changing the way your GNOME desktop looks and works: start-here: Preferences⇨Control Center (following), panels (page 246), menus (page 253), and the Sawfish window manager (page 254) which you can use in place of Metacity. Much of the customization information is stored in files in your **~/.gnome-desktop** directory. Table 7-9 lists the top-level choices available from Start Here.

Start Here || table 7-9

Applications	Displays several directory objects, each containing programs. This directory matches the menu items in the GNOME menu (page 209).
Preferences	Displays the same pseudodirectory as **GNOME menu: Preferences⇨Control Center**. Refer to "Start Here: Preferences/Control Center" following this table.
Server Settings	Displays programs that configure the installed servers. The most common server is the Apache Web server, called HTTP Server. This selection displays the same pseudodirectory as **GNOME menu: Server Settings**.

Start Here	|| table 7-9
System Settings	Contains several property, configuration, and wizard programs. Depending on your situation and experience, you may want to work with **Date & Time** to set the system time and date; **Display** to configure your display monitor; and **Printing** to help you set up printers. Refer to Table 17-9 on page 985 for more information. This selection displays the same pseudodirectory as **GNOME menu: Server Settings**.

Start Here: Preferences/Control Center

You can configure many aspects of the user interface of the GNOME desktop manager and the Metacity window manager by using GNOME menu: Preferences⇨Control Center or start-here: Preferences. You can also type **preferences:** in the Nautilus location text box or select the aspect of the Control Center that you want from GNOME menu: Preferences. These entries to the GNOME Control Center present identical information (Figure 7-20) and enable you to set up a screensaver; establish or modify keyboard shortcuts; modify keyboard, mouse, CD-ROM, and dialog properties, and so on, using small programs called applets to do the work. (An *applet* is a small portable program written in Java; Control Center applets are sometimes called capplets.) Table 7-10 describes in detail each of the selections you can make from this window.

Figure 7-20   Preferences (Control Center) window.

GNOME Preferences/Control Center
|| table 7-10

About Myself	Specifies your login shell and display information stored in /etc/passwd. Refer to "/etc/passwd" on page 962 for more information about the passwd file.
Accessibility	The choices offered by the Keyboard Accessibility Configuration tool, also called AccessX, make it easier for some people to use GNOME. Refer to the *Linux Accessibility HOWTO* for more information.
General	
Enable keyboard accessibility	Toggles all the features in the Keyboard Accessibility Configuration window: Without a check mark in this box, none of the features in this window will work.
Beep when ending/disabling keyboard accessibility features	Causes the system to beep when you change the setting in one of the Enable boxes that follow.
Disable if unused for __ seconds	Disables keyboard accessibility when one of its features has not been used for the number of seconds specified in the spin box.
Enable Mouse Keys	All *Mouse Keys are on the numeric pad* **of the keyboard.** Specifies that you can use the keys on the numeric pad of the keyboard to perform functions otherwise performed using the mouse. Use the sliders in this tab to adjust how the ARROW keys move the mouse pointer. • ARROW keys on the *numeric pad* move the mouse pointer. • Press RETURN to click. • DEL + 0 (zero) selects item mouse pointer is over. • DEL then opens the selected item. • Or ARROW keys drag the selected item. • After dragging DEL drops the item with choice of **Copy**, **Move**, or **Link**. • ESCAPE cancels the drag.
Enable Bounce Keys	Does not accept a second keystroke until the amount of delay time specified by the slider has elapsed.
Toggle and Repeat Keys	Beeps once when a keyboard LED is turned on and twice when it is turned off. Click **Repeat Key Preferences** to set key repeat, cursor blink, and keyboard bell features, refer to the entry "Keyboard" in the table on page 241.
Enable Slow Keys	Does not accept a keystroke until you hold the key down for at least the amount of delay time specified by the slider.

GNOME Preferences/Control Center (Continued) || table 7-10

Enable Sticky Keys	Specifies that pressing a modifier key (SHIFT, ALT, or CONTROL) and then another key sequentially performs the same function as depressing and holding the modifier key while you press the other key. Allows you to press CONTROL and release it before pressing c instead of pressing and holding CONTROL while you press c.
Testing Area	An area for you to test and adjust the settings in this window.
Background	
Select picture	Specifies an image to display on the root window (desktop). Click within the **Select picture** box to select an picture that must be an image file, such as **jpg** or **png**.
Picture Options	Select how you want the image displayed: **Wallpaper** (several copies of the image laid down on the workspace as tiles), **Centered** (one image in the center of the workspace), **Scaled** (keeps the proportions, or aspects, of the enlarged image the same as the original), **Stretched** (makes the image as large as possible without regard to maintaining proportion), or **No Picture**.
Background Style	Specifies a background of one or two colors. Choose **Solid color** to use a single color. To use two colors, select **Horizontal gradient** or **Vertical gradient**, depending on which way you want one color to flow into the other.
Left/Right, Top/Bottom, or just plain Color	Specifies a background color. Click one of the color boxes to display the Pick a color window (page 230).
CD Properties	Specifies what you want GNOME to do when you insert a data CD-ROM, a music CD-ROM, or a video DVD.
Extras	Displays tools that were left off the GNOME menu.
CDDB	Controls the CDDB server you access and the information you use to log in on it. CDDB is Gracenote's CD-ROM database, which lets you look up title and track information for a CD-ROM: www.cddb.com. This information prevents you from having to enter title, track, and artist information manually when you are storing or copying an audio CD-ROM.
Desktop Switching Tool	Opens a graphical interface to **switchdesk**, which can change your default desktop manager. The change does not take place until you restart your desktop manager. Refer to "Changing to a Different Desktop Manager" on page 173.
HTML Viewer	Establishes **Fonts, Keyboard Shortcuts, Behavior**, and **Spell Checking** parameters for the **gtkhtml** viewer.
Panel	Controls whether panel drawers close automatically and panel animation speed, such as when you hide a panel.

GNOME Preferences/Control Center (Continued) || table 7-10

Preferred Applications	Specifies your default **Web Browser**, **Text Editor**, and **Terminal**.
Sawfish window manager	Refer to "Customizing Sawfish: The Sawfish Configurator" on page 258. Has no effect when you are running Metacity.
Sessions	
Session Options	
Show splash screen on login	The splash screen is the window that identifies GNOME and lists each of the parts of GNOME as it starts up. It appears when you start GNOME unless you raise this button.
Prompt on logout	Specifies whether you are prompted when you attempt to log out (**Really log out?**).
Automatically save changes to session	Specifies whether GNOME saves your GNOME session as it is when you log out. When you do not choose to have GNOME automatically save sessions, you can still save them with a button on the logout window, assuming that you have chosen to be prompted. For more information, refer to "Session Manager" on page 185.
Sessions	The bottom portion of this window **Add**s, **Delete**s, and renames (**Edit**) sessions.
Current Session	Works with the highlighted, session-managed program in your current session. Refer to "Method 2" on page 255 for a discussion of using this tab to kill the window manager.
Order	Specifies the order in which the session manager starts the program. The default value is 50.
Style	• **Normal** Starts when GNOME starts. Kill with **kill**. • **Respawn** Starts when GNOME starts. Restarts when the program gets **kill**ed or otherwise dies. Kill with **Remove** button in this window. • **Trash** Does not start when GNOME starts. • **Settings** Starts when GNOME starts. Usually stores configuration settings and has a low Order number.
Remove	Kills the highlighted program.
Apply	Applies the changes you have made.
Startup Programs	The GNOME Session Manager can control only GNOME-compliant programs. This frame specifies programs that are not controlled by the Session Manager and that you want to start each time you bring GNOME up. Use the **Add**, **Edit**, and **Delete** buttons to work with Startup Programs. The **Priority** controls which programs start first: Specify a priority of 50 unless you have a reason to do otherwise.
File Types and Programs	Refer to "File Types and Programs (MIME Types)" on page 232.

GNOME Preferences/Control Center (Continued) || table 7-10

Font	Refer to "Font Preferences" on page 230.
Keyboard	
Keyboard	Controls the keyboard.
Repeat Keys	Turns autorepeat on/off, sets the delay before autorepeat takes effect, and sets the repeat rate.
Cursor Blinks	Turns a blinking cursor on/off and controls the rate of the blinks.
Sound	Turns the keyboard bell on/off.
Keyboard Shortcuts	
Text editing shortcuts	Specifies the type of shortcut you want to use: emacs or GNOME Default.
Desktop shortcuts	The scrolling text box displays a list of each of the commands that has/could have a key bound to it. Click the action/shortcut you want to change; the shortcut changes to Type a new accelerator. Press the key or key combination you want to use as a shortcut. Press BACKSPACE to disable a shortcut.
Login Photo	Sets up an identification photo that you can click on, instead of typing your name, to log in on the system. GDM (GNOME Display Manager) must be set up in order to use this option.
Menus & Toolbars	
Toolbar	Specifies whether to display text, icons, or both in Toolbars, and where to place the text when you choose to have text. A sample toolbar displays the result of your choice. Also specifies whether Toolbars can be detached. Refer to "Tear-Away Bars" on page 225.
Menus	Specifies whether to show icons in menus.
Mouse	
Buttons	Specifies a mouse for a left-handed person and adjusts the double-click delay. You can test the delay by double-clicking the light bulb to the right.
Cursors	Specifies a mouse pointer style. Log out and back on to cause a new pointer style to take effect. Put a check mark in the Show position of cursor when the Control key is pressed box to help you find the mouse pointer when you press the CONTROL key.
Motion	Sets the speed and acceleration of the mouse pointer as well as the distance you need to move the mouse pointer before it starts to drag an item.
Network Proxy	Specifies HTTP proxy information. Refer to "Proxy Server" on page 397.

GNOME Preferences/Control Center (Continued)

|| table 7-10

Password	Changes your login password.
Pilot/Handspring Tool	Initially brings up the GNOME-Pilot wizard to help you get your Pilot/Handspring PDA sync'd. Subsequently displays the Pilot Conduits window which you can use to maintain the settings.
Screensaver	Specifies a screensaver and when to turn off the monitor.
Display Modes	
Mode	Select a screensaver mode of operation; **Disable**, **Blank**, **One**, or **Random** from the pop-up menu. Select none, one, or many screensavers that you want to see from the scroll list, as appropriate; it is displayed in the small preview frame to the right. Click the up or down arrow below the scroll list to display on the full screen the screen saver above or below the selected one.
	The BSOD (Blue Screen of Death, a reference to a common failure display of a popular operating system) screen saver is off by default. Highlight it in the scroll list and click **Settings** when you have a few minutes to spare.
Blank After __ minutes	Blanks the screen and turns on the screensaver, as specified by **Mode**, after the specified time.
Cycle After __ minutes	When you specify **Mode** as **Random**, changes screensavers after the specified time.
Lock Screen After __ minutes	Locks screen after the specified time. Refer to the entry "Lock Screen" in the table on page 209.
Preview	Displays a full-screen preview of the screen saver shown in the small frame on the right. Click anywhere to close the full-screen preview.
Settings	Controls available settings for the screen saver shown in the small frame.
Advanced	
Image Manipulation	Specifies where screensavers that manipulate images should get their images from.
Diagnostics	Specifies various levels of diagnostic messages.
Display Power Management	For Energy Star Compliant monitors. Put a check mark next to **Power Management Enabled** to turn on power management. Specifies how long before GNOME puts the monitor in a **Standby** (minimum energy savings and a quick return to an active state), **Suspend** (large energy savings and a slow return to an active state), or **Power Off** (maximum energy savings and the slowest return to an active state) state. The time you specify starts at the last use of the keyboard or mouse. GNOME activates the monitor when you use the mouse or keyboard again; use the mouse or a key that will not have any effect, such as the CONTROL key.

GNOME Preferences/Control Center (Continued) || table 7-10

Colormaps	Controls the installation of a colormap and whether the screen fades to/from a screensaver or changes images immediately.
Sound	To adjust the volume and balance of the sound, choose **GNOME menu: Sound & Video⇨Volume Control** (or run **gnome-volume-control** from a command line).
General	
Enable sound server startup	Starts the sound server when the system starts.
Sound for events	Turns on sounds for such window events as shading/unshading a window or maximizing/unmaximizing a window. The **Enable sound server startup** box must be checked in order to change the setting of this button.
Sound Events	This tab is grayed out (unusable) when the **Sound for events** box is not checked. View events and the sound files that are associated with each event in the large scrollable list. Click the **down** arrow next to the **Browse** button to view and choose sounds from the small drop-down menu. Click the **Browse** button to look through the filesystem for sounds. Select **Play** to play the sound listed in the text box to its right.
Theme	
Application	Specifies a theme for windows, but not their decoration. The default Red Hat theme is Bluecurve. Select a theme from the list of installed themes and GNOME displays it on your workspace. Click **Install new theme** to install a new theme, Go to theme folder to open ~/.themes, and **Close** to keep the theme you selected. Search for **gnome themes** on the Web to find additional themes.
Window Border	Specifies a window decoration theme. Window decoration comprises the titlebar and border of a window. Aside from the aesthetic aspects of changing window decoration, you can alter the functionality by choosing a theme that has a different number and/or placement of buttons on the titlebar.
Window Focus	Specifies the focus policy. Refer to "Changing the Input Focus" on page 182

Nautilus Menubar: Edit⇨Preferences

When you select Edit Preferences from the Preferences selection on the Nautilus menubar, Nautilus displays the Preferences window, which you can use to change many of the aspects of how Nautilus appears and functions (Table 7-11).

Nautilus Menubar: Edit⇨Preferences || table 7-11

Views	
Default View	
View new folders using	Specifies what appears by default in the Nautilus subwindow: icons (**Icon View**) or a text list (**List View**). The next two frames specify the default appearance for each of these types.
Icon View Defaults	Specifies the default arrangement, size, and layout for **Icon View**.
List View Defaults	Specifies the default arrangement and size for **List View**.
Appearance	
Themes	Lists themes you can choose from. This choice has no effect unless **Use Nautilus to draw the desktop** is selected. Click **Add Theme** to add a new theme (go to www.themes.com to download themes).
Windows	
New Window Behavior	
Open each file or folder in a new window	Causes each file you open to appear in a new window. Otherwise, the new file replaces what appears in the current Nautilus subwindow.
New Window Display	Specifies which bars you want to appear in a new Nautilus window.
Desktop & Trash	
Desktop	
Use Nautilus to draw the desktop	As an integral part of your desktop manager, Nautilus is normally responsible for taking care of the details of your desktop, such as which icons appear on it and its appearance (fonts, themes, and so on). Turn off this option to take that responsibility away from Nautilus.
Use your home folder as the desktop	Displays all the folders and files in your home directory on the desktop. Works only if you choose **Use Nautilus**.
Trash Behavior	
Ask before emptying Trash or deleting files	Prompts before permanently deleting a file.

Nautilus Menubar: Edit⇨Preferences (Continued) || table 7-11

Include a Delete command that bypasses Trash	Includes a **Delete** command on the Generic Icon menu (page 212). Clicking **Trash** moves the file to the Trash file; clicking **Delete** permanently removes the file from the system.

Icon & List Views

Click Behavior

Activate items with a single/double click	Specifies whether a single- or double-click is required to open an object. When you choose single-click, you can no longer select an object with a single click. You can drag the mouse pointer onto the object to select it.
Executable Text Files	Specifies what Nautilus does when you click or otherwise open a text file that you have execute permission for. Choose **Execute**, **Display**, or **Ask each time**.

Show Options

Hidden files (filenames start with ".")	Displays hidden files in the Nautilus subwindow.
Backup files (filenames end with "~")	Displays files with names that end in tilde (~) in the Nautilus subwindow.
Special flags in Properties dialog	Causes the property window for a file to show when the setuid, setgid, or Sticky bits are set.

Sort

Folders before files	Causes all directories to be listed in the Nautilus subwindow before any ordinary files. Any layout that you specify (page 222) is performed separately within the directories and ordinary files.

Icon Captions	Nautilus always displays below the icon the name of the file that an icon represents. More information is displayed as you zoom in on the icon. This choice specifies the additional information that appears and in what order. There are three drop-down lists: The top one specifies what information appears when you zoom in a little bit, the middle one appears when you zoom in a little more, and the bottom one when you fully zoom in.

Side Panes

Tabs	Controls which tabs you see in the side pane.
Tree Show folders only	Causes ordinary files not to be displayed under the **Tree** tab in the side pane. Only directories are displayed.

Nautilus Menubar: Edit⇨Preferences (Continued) || table 7-11

Performance	Select **Always**, **Local Files Only**, or **Never** for each of the following situations. **Never** is fastest, but **Local Files Only** does not use a lot of computer resources. **Always** includes remote files and uses the greatest amount of computer resources. Adjust these according to your needs/desires and the power/use of your machine and others on your network.
Show Text in Icons	Displays a small portion of the contents of a text file within the icon for the file.
Show Number of Items in Folders	Displays the number of items in a folder below the icon for that folder.
Show Thumbnails for Image Files	Displays a small portion of an image file within the icon for that file. Specifies the largest file that you want to see thumbnails for. Files over this size do not display thumbnails.
Preview Sound Files	Plays part of a sound file when you select the icon for the file.

Panels

You can modify many aspects of the look and function of panels. This section discusses types of panels, the objects on a panel, and how to work with panels and the Panel menu.

Types of Panels

There are five types of panels: Menu, edge, corner, sliding, and floating. You can fully configure each of them except for the Menu panel. The Main panel that appears by default when you start GNOME is an edge panel.

Menu Panel

The Menu panel is similar to a menubar positioned at the top of the workspace. You cannot move the Menu panel, and it lacks some of the other functionality that other panels have. The submenus on the Menu panel mostly duplicate submenus available from the GNOME menu.

Edge Panel

An edge panel stretches the height or width of the workspace and is positioned along one of its four sides.

Corner Panel

A corner panel is similar to the edge panel but is short and stretches only to accommodate icons you put in it. You can position it at any corner or at the middle of one of the sides of the workspace. When it is positioned in a corner and you click the hide button that points to the far corner, the corner panel jumps to the far corner. You need to click the same button again to make the panel disappear.

Sliding Panel

A sliding panel is similar to a corner panel, with two differences. You can position a sliding panel anywhere along the edge of the workspace, and the hide buttons always hide the panel.

Floating Panel

A floating panel is similar to a sliding panel but can be positioned anywhere on the workspace.

Panel Objects

A panel can contain five types of objects: applets, menus, application launchers, drawers, and special objects.

Applets

Many applets are represented by buttons on a panel. Most of these applets launch programs, some display menus, and others give status information. Left click an applet to execute it if it is executable (the clock is not), or right click to display a context menu for that applet. The choices on an applet context menu usually include Remove From Panel (delete applet from a panel), Move (move applet within a panel), and Properties (for this applet).

Menus

You can display several menus from a panel, including the GNOME menu and the Add to Panel menu (right click on any empty place on a panel and select Add to Panel—page 250). You can identify a menu button by a small triangle above and to the right of the icon. Drawers (page 249) also have this triangle because they too give you additional selections when you click them.

Application Launchers

Any of the buttons that start a program running are *application launchers*, usually referred to as *launchers*. The Terminal Emulator and the Start Here buttons are two examples.

Figure 7-21   Launcher properties window

To modify an existing launcher, select Panel Icon menu: Properties from the icon you want to modify. (Display the Panel Icon menu by right clicking the icon and selecting Properties from the resulting pop-up menu): GNOME displays the Launcher Properties window (Figure 7-21).

To create a new launcher, select Panel menu: Add to panel⇨Launcher from the panel you want the launcher to appear on. GNOME displays the Create launcher applet window. The Create launcher applet and Launcher Properties windows are the same except for the buttons at the bottom of the windows. Table 7-12 describes the text boxes that appear in these windows.

Launcher Properties/Create Launcher Windows	‖ table 7-12
Basic	
Name	Name of the launcher, used when you put the launcher on the desktop or on a menu.
Generic name	An optional name that you can use to specify the type of program, such as `terminal emulator`.
Comment	Tooltip that you see when the mouse pointer hovers over the launcher when it is on a panel.

Launcher Properties/Create Launcher Windows (Continued) || table 7-12

Command	The command line that starts the application when you click the launcher. This is the only mandatory field.
Type	Type of launcher. Usually Application.
Icon	Icon that appears on the panel or menu. Click the icon (or where it says **No icon**) to display the Browse icons window.
Run in Terminal	Check this box if **Command** runs a nongraphical (character-based) program.
Advanced	
Try this before using	When GNOME cannot execute the command entered in this text box, this launcher/menu item does not appear on the panel/menu.
Documentation	Name of the documentation file for the program.
Name/Comment translations	Specifies the country, language, and character set you want to use. When you want to add a language for which there is a translation, see www.gnome.org/i18n, i18n.kde.org, and the *KDE Translation HOWTO*. Once installed, the language should appear in this section of the Control Center when you restart it. Text boxes below the small window add, modify, or remove lines from the small window.

Drawers

A drawer behaves very similarly to a panel except that you can close a drawer but not close a panel, although you can make it disappear. Frequently drawer buttons display a wooden file cabinet icon with a small triangle above and to the right of the icon (Figure 7-22). You can change a drawer icon to any icon you like. A drawer holds a secondary panel that extends perpendicular to the Main panel. In Figure 7-22 the main panel is horizontal at the bottom of the workspace, and the open drawer extends vertically from the drawer icon. You can store several items in a drawer so they take up less space on the panel and are grouped together. To open a drawer, click the drawer icon. To close a drawer, click either the drawer icon or the tab at the unattached end of the drawer.

When you create a drawer, it is empty. You can put applets into it the same way that you put applets into a panel (page 252). Open the GNOME menu and drag objects into the drawer; you can to drop the objects on top of other applets, as the drawer will make space for the new objects. You can also right click the tab at the

Figure 7-22   An Opened drawer

unattached end of the drawer, select Add to Panel, and make a choice from the re-sulting menu.

Special Objects

Special objects do not behave like other objects. The special objects are the logout and lock buttons (Figure 7-4, page 211), as well as the run button.

Panel Menu

Selections on the Panel menu create, move, remove, maintain, and change the prop-erties of panels. See Table 7-13. Display the Panel menu by right clicking an empty place on the panel or one of the Hide tabs. When you have multiple panels, the choices you make from a Panel menu affect only the panel that you clicked on to bring up the menu.

Panel Menu	‖ table 7-13
Add to panel	
Accessories, Amusements, Internet, Multimedia, Utility	Gives you a large selection of applets to choose from in a two-tiered menu. Select an applet, and it appears on the panel.
Launcher	Refer to "Application Launchers" on page 247.

Panel Menu (Continued)

|| table 7-13

Launcher from menu	Adds a program from the GNOME menu to a panel.
GNOME Menu	Adds the GNOME menu applet to a panel.
Drawer	Refer to "Drawers" on page 249.
Log Out Button	Adds a button that closes the GNOME desktop manager.
Lock button	Refer to the entry "Lock Screen" in the table on page 209.
Delete This Panel	Deletes the panel and everything on it. Use with caution.
Properties	Displays the Panel Properties window.
Edge Panel	This section describes the Edge Panel Properties window, the Properties windows for other types of panels are similar.
Position	Positions the panel on one of the four sides of the workspace when you click one of the thin rectangles that represent the sides of the workspace.
Size	Specifies a panel size from **XX Small** to **XX Large**.
Autohide	Causes the panel to hide automatically when you are not using it. Moves the mouse pointer to the edge of the workspace where the panel normally appears to make the panel reappear.
Show hide buttons	Displays Hide buttons at the ends of the panel.
Arrows on hide buttons	Places arrows on the Hide buttons. **Show hide buttons** must have a check mark for this check box to be active.
Background	Controls the background of the panel.
Background type	Specifies one of three types of backgrounds: **Default**, **Color**, or **Image**.
Background color	When you specify a **Background type** of Color, click the small colored rectangle to display the Pick a color window (page 230) that you can choose a color from.
Image	When you specify a **Background type** of Image, choose an image by clicking **Browse** or entering the pathname of the image file in the text box under the space for the image.

Panel Menu (Continued)

|| table 7-13

Do not scale image to fit	Displays as much of the full-size image as will fit on the panel and repeats it as necessary to occupy the entire panel.
Scale image	Adjusts the image so that the whole image fits vertically (on a horizontal panel) or horizontally (on a vertical panel) on the panel and repeats the image to occupy the entire panel.
Stretch image	Takes the entire image and stretches it to fit on the panel without repeating.
Rotate image for vertical panels	Changes the aspect of the image by 90° on a vertical panel.
New panel	Creates one of the five types of panels that GNOME offers: Menu, edge, corner, sliding, and floating. Refer to "Types of Panels" on page 246.

Working with Panel Objects

A panel object is anything that appears on a panel. This section discusses adding, moving, and deleting panel objects, as well as swallowed applications.

Adding an Object to a Panel

The easiest way to add an applet to a panel or workspace is to drag it from the GNOME menu to a panel or the root window. You can add applets that are not on the GNOME menu by using the Panel menu. Refer to the entry "Add to panel" in the table on page 250.

Another way to add an object from the GNOME menu to a panel is to bring up the GNOME menu and position the mouse pointer over the item that you want to copy to the panel. Right click and choose Add this launcher to panel, and GNOME copies the launcher to the panel.

Removing an Object from a Panel

Select Panel Icon menu: Remove From Panel.

Moving Objects within a Panel

You can move most objects within a panel by dragging them, using the middle mouse button. Or you can right click an object on the panel and select Move from the Panel

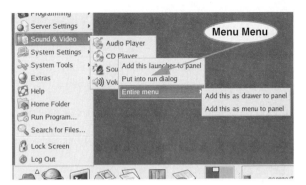

Figure 7-23 Menu menu

Icon menu: The mouse pointer turns into cross-hairs. Using the cross-hairs/mouse pointer (do not click), move the object to the desired location on the panel. Click a mouse button once the object is positioned where you want it.

Menus

Menus are central to using the desktop. They display other menus and hold menu entries or selections that start programs and open windows. Internally GNOME does not distinguish between a menu entry and a launcher: They both do the same thing. (You have seen how to copy a menu entry so that it appears on a panel as a launcher.) This section covers several of the important menus on the GNOME desktop.

Menu Menu

The Menu menu (Figure 7-23) copies menus and menu items from the GNOME menu to the Main panel. When you want a menu or menu item on a panel other than the Main panel, first copy the menu or item to the Main panel, and then drag it to another panel. Selections on the Menu menu that you do not have permission to use or that do not make sense to use are grayed out.

To copy a menu, display the submenu of the GNOME menu that is the menu, or contains the entry, that you want to copy. Right click the entry you want to copy, and choose what you want to do from the Menu menu. When you choose Entire menu it does not matter which entry in the Menu menu you click on. Entire menu is selected in Figure 7-23. Table 7-14 explains the entries on the Menu menu.

Menu Menu	table 7-14
Add this launcher to panel	Adds the menu item that you selected to the Main panel as a launcher button.
Put into run dialog	Copies the command line that a menu item would execute into a run dialog (page 210) so that you can modify the command with arguments and options.
Entire menu	
Add this as drawer to panel	Add the submenu that you selected so that each menu item is an object in a drawer in the Main panel.
Add this as menu to panel	Add the submenu that you selected as a menu on the Main panel. Click the menu object to display the menu.

The Sawfish Window Manager

Sawfish (formerly Sawmill, sawmill.sourceforge.net) is a GNOME-compliant extensible window manager. All its high-level functions are written in LISP so that they can be extended or redefined, and the user interface policy is controlled through a LISP scripting language. Sawfish gives you control over window decoration, key bindings in many contexts when the input focus changes, window placement, workspaces, and more. Sawfish gives you intuitive window management that is easy to work with. Refer to "Customizing Sawfish: The Sawfish Configurator" on page 258 for information on changing the way Sawfish looks and works.

Sawfish Titlebar Buttons Are Different	tip
Refer to Figure 7-24. The close window button is on the left, the minimize button is at the left end of the group on the right, maximize is in the middle, and a new button, shade, is at the right end. These functions assume a left click. Allow the mouse pointer to hover over the buttons and the tool tips will tell you about the button's other functions.	

Bringing Up Sawfish

Before starting, give the command **sawfish**. If you see command not found, Sawfish is not installed. See page 930 for instructions on installing the sawfish rpm. There are two ways to bring up Sawfish. The first method is simpler; the second method gives

Figure 7-24   The default Sawfish titlebar

you experience with the gnome-session-properties utility which is available as Start Here: Preferences⇨Extras⇨Sessions⇨Current Session. You can use either method to switch back to Metacity by substituting metacity for sawfish in the relevant steps of the method. Give the command **rpm –q sawfish** to make sure that Sawfish is installed on your system before proceeding.

- **Method 1**

  a. Give the following command from a terminal emulator or text-based command line to remove your **session** file:

     ```
     $ rm ~/.gnome2/session
     ```

  b. Add the following line to your **~/.bashrc** file to set the **WINDOW_MANAGER** variable:

     ```
     export WINDOW_MANAGER=sawfish
     ```

  c. If you are using a command-line interface, give the following command to execute the command you just put into **~/.bashrc**:

     ```
     $ source ~/.bashrc
     ```

  d. Bring up GNOME. You are now running Sawfish under GNOME.

  e. Verify that you are running Sawfish by giving the command:

     ```
     $ ps -e | grep saw
     ```

- **Method 2**

  a. Bring up GNOME.

  b. To open the Sessions window, select GNOME menu: Run Program and enter

     ```
     gnome-session-properties
     ```

  c. Click the Current Session tab in the Sessions window.

  d. Click metacity in the Program column to highlight the row that holds metacity.

  e. Click the Remove button near the top of the window.

  f. Click the Apply button near the top of the window. You are no longer running with a window manager; all the decoration is gone from your windows.

g. If you cannot type anything in either Run Program or a terminal emulator, click GNOME menu: Logout, check Save current setup, and click OK to log out. If you can type, go to step i.

h. Bring up GNOME.

i. From Run Program give the command **sawfish,** or from a terminal emulator, run **sawfish &.** Watch the window decorations appear. You are now running Sawfish under GNOME.

j. Verify that you are running Sawfish by giving the command:

```
$ ps -e | grep saw
```

The Language of Sawfish Window Border Tooltips   ‖ tip

Sawfish, which displays the tooltips that you see when your mouse pointer hovers over a window border or titlebar, (page 181) uses special words to keep tooltips short.

- **Button 1** is the left mouse button, and **Button 3** is the right one, unless you have set the mouse up as a left-handed mouse, in which case the right is 3 and the left is 1. **Button 2** is always the middle button and sometimes the right and left buttons together on a two-button mouse.

- **Button1-Move** means left drag.

- **Button1-Click2** means double-click the left button.

- **Button3-Off** means the moment at which you release the right button after having previously pressed it.

- **S** means hold the SHIFT key.

Working with Sawfish

This section covers the two menus that control Sawfish: the Window Operations menu, which controls only the window that you open it from, and the Sawfish menu, which gives you global control over Sawfish.

Window Operations Menu

The Window Operations menu (Table 7-15) gives you many options: from simple minimizing/maximizing to changing the layout and style of the window you call it from. Display the Window Operations menu by clicking the button at the left end of the titlebar. The default Red Hat frame style requires a right click; others require a left click. Sometimes the "wrong one" closes the window; turn on tooltips to figure out which is which (page 205).

Window Operations Menu

|| table 7-15

Minimize/Maximize/Close	Performs as you might expect.
Toggle	
Sticky	Makes the window appear in the same position in all workspaces, as though it were stuck to the glass on the screen.
Shaded	Causes the window to be shaded.
Ignored	Causes the window to be an *ignored window* (page 1472).
Focusable	Makes the window able to get the input focus. Without this button depressed the window can never have the input focus.
Cyclable	Makes this window one that you can cycle through (page 261).
In window list	Causes this window to appear in **Sawfish menu: Windows** (page 258).
In group	Changes the group a window belongs to. When you create a new group, it takes on the local address of your home page (for example, **alex@kudos:~**). Typically all windows from a given application belong to the same group.
Send window to	Moves or copies the window you are working with to another workspace, using **Next** or **Previous**.
Stacking	Windows are grouped into two layers: upper and lower. Windows in the lower layer never appear on top of windows in the upper layer, even when you raise them. This selection specifies a layer for a window and raises or lowers the window.
Frame type	Specifies which parts of the frame Sawfish displays. The frame comprises the titlebar (the top border) and the borders on the three other sides. **Top-border** and **Border-only** remove buttons from the titlebar that **Title-only** displays.
Frame style	Specifies which frame style to use for this window.

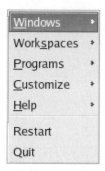

Figure 7-25   Sawfish menu

Sawfish Menu

One of the keys to working with Sawfish is the Sawfish menu (Figure 7-25); middle click the root window to display it. From this menu you can give a window the keyboard focus by selecting it from the Windows submenu; select, add, and merge with the Workspace submenu; run a program by selecting it from the Program submenu; or customize Sawfish from the Customize submenu.

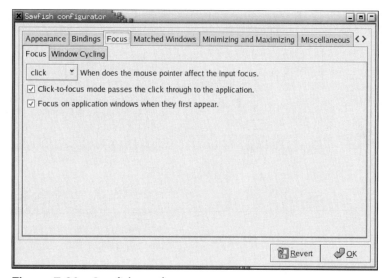

Figure 7-26   Sawfish configurator

Customizing Sawfish: The Sawfish Configurator

The Sawfish configurator and Sawfish window manager window customize many aspects of the way Sawfish looks and works. These two windows bring up the same configuration windows but have different ways of getting to them. The configurator has a row of tabs on the top and a display area on the bottom. Pick the item you want from the tabs and work with the choices on the bottom. The window manager displays a number of icons that correspond to the tabs in the configurator. For simplicity this section explains the Sawfish configurator only. You can follow this section by using either method to customize Sawfish.

Display the Sawfish configurator by selecting Sawfish menu (middle click root window): Customize⇨All settings. You will see a window similar to the one shown in Figure 7-26 when you click Workspaces in the tree menu. Display the Sawfish window manager window by selecting start-here: Preferences⇨Extras⇨Sawfish window manager.

To use Sawfish configurator, choose the item you want to work with from the tabs at the top of the window (Table 7-16). The changes you make are reflected immediately in all the windows displayed on the workspace. Click Revert if you do not want to keep the changes. Click OK when you are done using the configurator.

Sawfish Configurator ‖ table 7-16

Appearance	When you use the tools in this tab to change your default frame style, you may need to exit from the Sawfish configurator and start it again to see the subtab that corresponds to the new style.
Appearance	Displays the comments of the author of the style.
Default frame style	Scrolls to display all the available frame styles. Choose one to see what it looks like; click **Revert** if you do not want to use it.
Default font	Click **Browse** to display the Select font window.
Crux Theme	When you choose **Crux** as the **Default frame style** under the **Appearance** tab, the following choices appear in the Crux Theme subtab and control the appearance of the windows.
Accent color for focused windows	Specifies the color that distinguishes the active window from others. This color appears on the titlebar and part of the window border. When there is no check mark in this box Sawfish uses the GTK+ selection color.
Display the window's icon in its menu button	Displays a small icon on the button at the upper-left corner of the window.
Display title buttons to mimic ___	Changes the style, placement, and function of the buttons that appear on titlebars. Choose between Default, MacOS Platinum, MacOS X, MS Windows, or NeXTSTEP.
CoolClean Settings	When you choose **CoolClean** as the **Default frame style** under the **Appearance** tab, the **CoolClean Settings** tab appears (you may have to restart Sawfish configurator). Under Control Center you may need to click **OK** and return to **Appearance** to see the tab.
___ Direction of gradient	Specifies the direction of the color gradient in the titlebar.

Sawfish Configurator (Continued) || table 7-16

Use solid colors instead of gradients (Uses 'From' colors).	Makes the titlebar the solid color specified as the **From** colors following.
'From' color of inactive frames	For a window without the input focus, specifies the color at one end of the gradient in the titlebar.
'To' color of inactive frames	For a window without the input focus, specifies the color at the other end of the gradient in the titlebar.
'From' color of active frames	For a window with the input focus, specifies the color at one end of the gradient in the titlebar.
'To' color of active frames	For a window with the input focus, specifies the color at the other end of the gradient in the titlebar.
Title text color of inactive frames	For a window without the input focus, specifies the color of the text in the titlebar.
Title text color of active frames	For a window with the input focus, specifies the color of the text in the titlebar.
Font for window titles	Specifies the titlebar text font. Click **Browse** to open the Select font window (page 230).
Simple Theme	When you choose **simple** as the **Default frame style** under the **Appearance** tab, the **Simple Customization** subtab appears. Under Control Center you may need to click **OK** and return to **Appearance** to see the tab.
Color of inactive frames in 'simple' frame style	For windows that do not have the input focus, specifies the color of the titlebar and the bottom border.
Color of active frames in 'simple' frame style	For a window with the input focus, specifies the color of the titlebar and the bottom border.
Bindings	(This option appears only on the Sawfish Configurator; use **Shortcuts** from the Sawfish window manager.)
Context	Selects the context (such as **Global**, **Root window**, **Border**, **Close** button) for which you want to define or change key bindings.
(subwindow)	Shows the **Key** and the **Command** that it is bound to. Highlight one and click **Add**, **Edit**, or **Delete**. **Add** and **Edit** display the **Edit binding** window, which specifies a **Key** and a **Command**. The bottom frame within the **Edit binding** window defines the highlighted **Command**. The **Grab** button allows you to press the key you want to specify instead of entering it manually. See the next cell for an explanation of **W-TAB**.

Sawfish Configurator (Continued)

|| table 7-16

Modifier key(s) used for default window manager shortcuts	The W- in the Key column of the subwindow is the *Window Manager Modifier*, a virtual modifier that is controlled from this text box. Whatever appears in this text box replaces the W- in the subwindow above it. For example, when control appears in the this text box, W-TAB in the key column of the subwindow means that you press CONTROL-TAB to issue the command in the Command column. Some modifier keys may not work.
Focus	Refer to "Changing the Input Focus" on page 182 for more information.
Focus	
When does the mouse pointer affect the input focus	Specifies when the input focus is taken away from one window and given to another. Refer to "Changing the Input Focus" on page 182.
Click-to-focus mode passes the click through to the application	Specifies that when you specify click in the preceding cell and click a window that does not have the focus, the click is passed through to the window (and the application it is running) once the window has the input focus.
Focus on application windows when they first appear	Moves the focus to any new window running an application or utility.
Window Cycling	Controls which windows and which *workspaces* (page 1502) are included while cycling through windows (page 184) and how the information box and windows are displayed.
Matched Windows	Specifies windows that match certain criteria and automatically takes specified actions (placement, appearance, and so on) on those windows when they appear.
Minimizing and Maximizing	
Minimizing a window also removes its _____	When you iconify a window, Sawfish iconifies these related windows. Refer to *transient window* (page 1498) and *group (of windows)* (page 1469).
Unminimizing a window also restores its _____	When you uniconify a window, Sawfish uniconifies these related windows. Refer to *transient window* (page 1498) and *group (of windows)* (page 1469).
Unshade selected windows	Sawfish unshades a window when it becomes active.
Lock position and size while windows are maximized	Sets the position and size of a maximized window so that you cannot move or resize the window. Once you unmaximize the window, you can once again move or resize it.

Sawfish Configurator (Continued) || table 7-16

Miscellaneous	
Miscellaneous	
Automatically reload themes when they are updated	Reloads a theme that is in use when the file that specifies that theme is modified.
Stacking	
Keep transient windows stacked above __	Makes sure that dialog boxes are visible above all windows or their parent window. You can also choose not to raise dialog boxes.
When raising a window, also raise its __	When you raise a window, also raise its *transient windows* (page 1498) or other windows in its *group (of windows)* (page 1469). You can also choose not to raise any other windows.
Tooltips	Controls tooltips other than those on window borders (page 205).
Display tooltips for window frames	Displays tooltips when the mouse pointer hovers over the titlebar or border of a window.
Show full documentation in tooltips	Causes tooltips to display more complete documentation.
Error Handling	
Beep when errors occur	Causes errors to generate an audible beep.
Display error messages to __	Specifies whether to display error messages **nowhere** or on the **screen** or to send them to **standard error**.
Move and Resize	
Show current position of windows while moving	Displays in the center of the workspace a small window that shows the position of the upper-left corner of the window relative to the upper-left corner of the workspace as you move it.
Show current dimensions of windows while resizing	Displays in the center of the workspace a small window that shows the size of the window as you resize it.
Distance in pixels before window edges align with each other	Specifies the distance, in pixels, between two windows before the one you are moving snaps next to the adjacent window. See *snap (windows)* on page 1493.

Sawfish Configurator (Continued)

|| table 7-16

Placement	
Method of placing windows	Specifies where Sawfish should place new windows.
Method of placing dialog windows	Specifies where Sawfish should place dialog boxes.
Sound	Use the subwindow to add, modify, and delete sounds for window events (only when following box is checked).
Play sound effects for window events	Turns on sounds for window events, such as shading/unshading a window or maximizing/unmaximizing a window.
Workspaces	
Workspace names	Click **Add** to specify a name that is assigned to a desktop. **Edit** or **Delete** names as you desire. These names are visible in **Sawfish menu: Workspaces** (page 258).

Chapter Summary

Built on top of the X Window System, GNOME is a desktop manager that you can use as is or customize. It is a graphical user interface to system services (commands), the filesystem, applications, and more. Although not part of it, the Metacity window manager works closely with GNOME and is the default window manager for GNOME on Red Hat systems. The window manager controls all aspects of the windows: placement, decoration, grouping, minimizing and maximizing, sizing, moving, and so on. Many aspects of GNOME and Metacity are controlled through the Start Here directory/menu system.

The most important object on a GNOME desktop is the Main panel (kicker), which holds application launchers, menus, drawers, special objects, applets, and the GNOME menu. Applets are small programs that run on the panel and display clocks, control audio CD-ROM players, hold iconified windows, display and move between workspaces, display menus, and so forth. The GNOME menu starts programs, displays other menus, configures the panel, logs you out, and more. In addition to the Main panel, you can create Menu, edge, aligned, sliding, and floating panels.

Nautilus, the GNOME file manager, is network transparent, meaning that it displays a local filesystem, a remote FTP site, and a local or remote Web page the same way. You can split the Nautilus window in two, have one subwindow show your local filesystem and the other a remote FTP site, and drag files between the two.

GNOME also provides many graphical utilities that customize your desktop (pick a font, pick a color) and work with it (search tool, run a program, terminal emulator). GNOME also supports MIME extensions so that when you click on an icon, it generally knows which tool to use to open whatever is represented by the icon.

You can customize all facets of GNOME, including Nautilus, panels, and menus. Nautilus has so many options that a thick book could be written on Nautilus alone. The Panel menu enables you to create and add objects to a panel, as well as to customize panel properties: type, hiding policy, size, background of the panels, and more. The Menu menu gives you the ability to copy items or entire menus from the GNOME menu to a panel or drawer on a panel.

You can replace Metacity with the Sawfish window manager. Sawfish is more configurable than Metacity and also more complex. The Sawfish Window Operations menu enables you to control many aspects of a specific window, including its decoration, which group it belongs to, what history it remembers, and what parts of the frame are displayed. Overall customization is done using the Sawfish configurator. The configurator tree menu gives you the option of modifying most aspects of the Sawfish window manager.

In sum, GNOME is a powerful desktop manager that can make your job easier and more fun. (Try playing with the desktop background, including multiple colors, gradients, and wallpaper.)

Exercises

1. Where is the GNOME menu button, and what does it look like? Why is it an important tool?

2. What is the Main panel? What does your Main panel show you, and what can you do with it? Discuss the Window List and Workspace Switcher applets.

3. What is a URI? A desktop file?

4. What happens when you click a Start-Here button? How is this useful?

5. What are tooltips? How are they useful? How can you turn them off in Metacity?

6. What is Nautilus?

    a. List two ways that you can you open a file using Nautilus.

    b. How does Nautilus "know" what tool to use to open different types of files?

    c. Which are the three common Nautilus toolbars? What kinds of tools do you find on each?

    d. Discuss the use of the Nautilus Location bar.

7. List the steps you would take to cause GNOME to lock the screen after you had not used it for 15 minutes.

8. How would you turn the monitor off after you had not used the system for 30 minutes?

9. Create a new application launcher on the Main panel that displays a clock when you click it. Choose an icon that you like. What steps did you take to set up the launcher?

Advanced Exercises

10. What is the MIME type for a *.mp3 file? What is the filename extension for an application launcher? What is the corresponding MIME type?

11. How would you set up a shortcut that would display workspace 2 when you pressed CONTROL-F6?

12. What steps would you take to set up the screensaver so that it cycled through two or three screensavers, one every two minutes, and went blank after 10 minutes.

13. What happens when you run vim from the Run Program window without specifying that it be run in a terminal? Where does the output go?

14. Bring up Sawfish under GNOME. How would you start the CoolClean theme with red text in inactive frames and white text in active frames? Describe any issues that slowed you down.

15. Explain how you would

    a. Add a drawer containing the entire Games menu to the Main panel.

    b. Add a drawer to the Main panel that has the Games menu as a button/icon in the drawer so that the games menu opened parallel to the Main panel.

IN THIS CHAPTER

KDE Desktop Environment

8

KDE (K Desktop Environment),[1] written in C++, is an open-source, easy-to-use interactive/integrated desktop environment for UNIX and UNIX-like systems, including GNU/Linux. KDE terminology is slightly different from that of GNOME. This chapter covers KDE release 3.

Because KDE has so many features, associated utilities, and programs, including a complete office suite (Koffice), this chapter cannot cover them all but rather attempts to familiarize you with the content and style of KDE. It is up to you to explore and find out more. One of the best ways to learn about KDE is to go through the online documentation and experiment. You can also browse www.kde.org. For more information refer to "Help" on page 268.

As with GNOME, you can use almost any window manager you like with KDE. The KDE window manager (kwin) is tightly integrated with the desktop as a whole and is well covered in the documentation. This integration keeps life simple for the user who sticks with kwin, and there are good reasons to do so, primarily because kwin works well with KDE. This book follows KDE's lead and does not separate the functions of kwin from those of KDE in general. When you want to use a different window manager, see "Specifying a Window Manager" on page 345.

---

1. The *K* does not stand for anything in particular.

Figure 8-1   Typical KDE workspace

What Is a Desktop? || tip

In KDE documentation the term *desktop* refers to a single division of a larger area. This book, in conformance with the GNOME 2 documentation, refers to everything that usually occupies your display monitor as a *workspace*. A *desktop* is divided into workspaces.

Getting Started

This section gives you a quick overview of the desktop: help and where to get it; the K menu, from which you can start almost any program (analogous to the GNOME menu); the title and scrollbars and how they differ from others; mouse clicks and which do what; the input focus and different ways of changing it; the Main panel, which is the key to the desktop; and menus. Figure 8-1 shows a KDE workspace.

Help

This section discusses the several kinds of help that KDE offers, from instant on-the-screen assistance to finding a subject in a manual.

Click On the Red Hat to Display the K Menu || tip

Red Hat has replaced the K-in-a-gear icon with a red hat. Click on either one to display the K menu. The red hat appears at the lower-left of Figure 8-1.

Figure 8-2   KDE HelpCenter

KDE Control Center Is Different from GNOME Control Center   ‖ tip

KDE and GNOME share the same **Start Here** icon and Preferences window. Under GNOME the Preferences window is also called the Control Center (**GNOME menu: Preferences⇨Control Center**). The KDE Control Center is different; display it by going to **K menu: Control Center** (page 314).

What's This?

The Help selection on the menubar of some windows provides contextual help: Click Help and a drop-down menu appears; click What's This? from the Help menu, and the mouse pointer turns into a question mark. Move the question mark until it is over the item you have a question about, and click again; you will see information about that item.[2] You can also position the mouse over the item you have a question about and press SHIFT-F1.

KDE HelpCenter

Click the Help button on the K menu to display KDE HelpCenter (Figure 8-2). From here you can read the introductory material on the right portion of the window and follow the links in it, or you can select information that you want to review from

---

2. This help feature is implemented in the Control Center window (page 314); experiment with it there.

the left side. Click KDE user's manual to display the *KDE Desktop Environment manual* with a hypertext-linked table of contents. Click an item from the table of contents—an underline will probably appear when the mouse pointer hovers over it—and KDE HelpCenter displays that item. You can use the three navigation arrows on the toolbar to move between the pages you view.

On the toolbar click the Find icon (the magnifying glass with paw prints around it), enter a keyword or words that you want to look up, and click the Find button. The KDE HelpCenter displays a match in the table of contents of the *KDE User's Guide*; the match is a link to the source document.

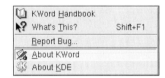

Figure 8-3   Typical menubar Help menu

Help Menubar Selection

When you click the Help selection on a menubar, a drop-down menu similar to the one shown in Figure 8-3 appears. Different application windows show different menus. Typically, a Contents selection displays the manual for the application or utility that you are running. The What's This? selection is explained on page 269. The KWord Help menu (Figure 8-3) also gives you the options of reporting a bug or getting version information and more about KWord or KDE.

Tooltips

Refer to page 182 for an explanation of tooltips and the "Tooltips Not Working?" tip to turn them on.

Tooltips Not Working? || tip

When tooltips that should appear on objects on panels do not appear, make sure that K menu: Control Center⇨Look & Feel⇨Panel⇨Look & Feel⇨General⇨Show tooltips (page 320) has a check mark in it.

Context Menus

Try right clicking on a window's titlebar and other places on the workspace; the program that opened the window or kwin frequently displays a context menu (page 184).

Windows and Mouse Clicks

A KDE window running under kwin looks and behaves a little differently from its GNOME counterpart running under either Metacity or Sawfish. The titlebar has different symbols with different functions in different windows. Scrollbars work differently, as explained on page 273.

Table 8-1 describes the default values for selected mouse clicks. You can change the results of some of the actions by using K menu:Control Center (refer to "Actions" on page 324).

Mouse Click and Result	‖ table 8-1
Titlebar or Border	
Left double-click	Raises window to top of stack and shades (page 185).
Middle double-click	Lowers window to bottom of stack and shades (page 185).
Left click	Raises window to top of stack and makes it active.
Middle click	Lowers window to bottom of stack.
Right click	If window is active, displays the Operations menu; otherwise, makes window active.
ALT + Left drag	Moves window.
ALT + Middle click	Raises or lowers window.
ALT + Right drag	Resizes the window. Depending on where the mouse pointer was when you clicked the mouse, you can resize the window horizontally (pointer close to one of the sides of the window), vertically (pointer close to the top or bottom of the window), or in both directions (pointer near a corner).
Border and Corners	
Drag	Resizes the window. Left/right borders resize horizontally; top/bottom borders resize vertically; corners resize in both directions at once.
Titlebar	
Drag	Moves window.

Mouse Click and Result (Continued) || table 8-1

Operations Menu: Left, Middle, Right click	Displays Operations menu (Figure 8-4 on page 273 and page 312).
Help (?)	For more information refer to "What's This?" on page 269.
Minimize Left, Middle, Right click	Minimizes window so that it appears as an icon and title in the Taskbar on a panel.
Maximize	When the window is not maximized, the mouse buttons have the following effects when you click the maximize button. When the window is maximized, any mouse button restores the window.
Left click	Maximizes window horizontally and vertically.
Middle click	Maximizes window vertically.
Right click	Maximizes window horizontally.
Close Left, Middle, Right click	Closes window.
Inside the Window	
Right click	Context menu: Displays different menus in different windows.
Root Window	On the workspace, click anywhere that is not occupied by a window or other object.
Middle click	Window List menu (page 312)
Right click	Pop-up Desktop menu (page 308)

Toolbars

A toolbar (usually a rectangular area) appears on your workspace or within a window and contains displays, icons, text, applets, menus, and more that you can work with. There are many kinds of toolbars; see Table 8-23 on page 340. One type of toolbar has no name other than *toolbar*. Figure 8-2 on page 269 shows the KDE Helpcenter window toolbar: the bar that has left and right arrows at its left end, toward the top of the window. Above the toolbar is a menubar, another type of toolbar. The titlebar, because it is not part of the window, is not a toolbar. Rather, a titlebar is part of the window decoration and is placed there by the window manager.

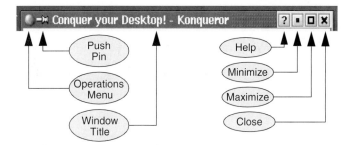

Figure 8-4   KDE titlebar with KDE2 decoration

Titlebar

A titlebar (Figures 6-6 and 8-4) appears at the top of most windows and in many ways controls the window it is attached to. By changing the window decoration (page 325), you can change the appearance and function of a titlebar, but you will usually have at least the functionality of the buttons shown in Figure 6-6. Titlebars under the default Red Hat Bluecurve theme look the same under KDE and GNOME (Figure 6-6). Figure 8-4 shows a titlebar with KDE2 decoration (K menu: Control Center⇨Look & Feel⇨Window Decoration⇨General⇨Window Decoration).

Push Pin

The Push Pin (Figure 8-4) "sticks" the window you are working with to the glass of your monitor: The window appears in the same position, no matter which workspace you view. Use the Push Pin to place a clock on every window area you work with. The Push Pin is also a convenient way to move a window from one workspace to another: Click the Push Pin to stick the window and change workspaces; click the Push Pin again to unstick the window in the new workspace.

Scrollbar

When you are *not* using Bluecurve window decoration (page 325), the KDE scrollbar (Figure 8-5) has one more button than most. At the bottom—or right if it is horizontal—of the scrollbar is the typical down/right button that scrolls the display forward or left: moves the image up/left on the screen. Just above this button is an extra up/left button. This button performs the same function as the up/left button at the top/left of the scrollbar—scrolls the display backward/right—but keeps you from having to move the mouse pointer the height/width of the image to move between the up and down buttons. It takes a little getting used to but is very efficient. The slider is standard, with its height proportional to the amount of text or other material in the buffer.

Figure 8-5   Native KDE scrollbar (Bluecurve decoration makes it look different)

Changing the Input Focus

To make each window on the workspace active in turn, hold the ALT key down while repeatedly pressing TAB. As long as you hold ALT down, by default you see in the center of the workspace a box that shows you which window will be active if you release the ALT key. To display each workspace in turn, repeatedly press CONTROL-TAB. For information on changing the focus policy, refer to the entry "Focus policy" in the table on page 323.

K Menu (Application Starter)

The K menu (red hat) button usually appears at the left end of the Main panel and is perhaps the most important button on the KDE workspace. You can run many of the applications on a GNU/Linux system from this menu and most of the KDE-specific ones. You can display the K menu by pressing ALT-F1 or clicking the K menu icon. The K menu has many submenus; Figure 8-6 shows the main K menu (left) and the Sound & Video submenu (right).

By default the top section of this menu displays the programs you have run from the K menu most recently: Noatun in Figure 8-6. Run Command (ALT-F2) opens a dialog box that accepts a command line for execution (page 282). Lock Screen prevents anyone from using your keyboard or seeing what is on your desktop until you type your password (page 309). Logout ends your KDE session.

Quick Browser

K menu: Quick Browser brings up any file on the system quickly and easily, based on its location in the directory structure (Figure 8-7). If Quick Browser is not on your K Menu (it should be near the bottom), turn it on by putting a check mark

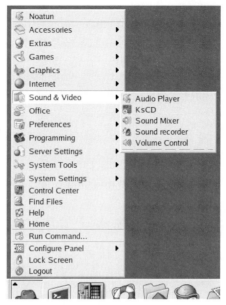

Figure 8-6   K (red hat) menu

in K menu: Preferences⇨ Look & Feel⇨Panel⇨Menus⇨Show "Quick Browser" submenu. Quick Browser opens a file using its default MIME associated application (refer to page 178 and "General" on page 315). The first submenu gives you the choice of looking at your home directory, the root directory, or the system configuration

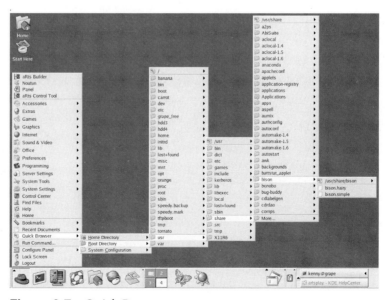

Figure 8-7   Quick Browser

directory (/etc). From one of these directories you can go to any level of subdirectory and display, edit, or execute any file that you have permission to work with. Figure 8-7 shows the K menu and a series of submenus leading to the /usr/share directory. The /usr/share directory is so large that Quick Browser first displays a single column of files with the word More at the bottom. Click More to see the second column, which also has the word More at the bottom, and so on.

Other Menus

KDE abounds with menus. Table 8-2 lists all the common menus, their basic functions, and where to find information on each.

KDE Menus	|| table 8-2
(Window) Operations menu	Works with the window you click on: moves, resizes, shades (page 185), changes decoration (page 325), moves to another workspace, and more. Right click any titlebar (page 273).
Desktop menu	Two Desktop menus (page 308) create new files, directories, and links; works with bookmarks, icons, and desktop configuration; locks the screen; and logs you out.
Panel menu	Allows you to add items to a panel, change the size or settings of a panel, get help, or edit the K menu. Right click an applet handle or a button, including a **Hide** button, or click an empty space on a panel and select **Panel** (page 339).
Toolbar menu	Allows you to change the properties of the toolbar. Right click almost anywhere on a toolbar that has handles (page 342).
Window List menu	Makes any workspace or window active. Click the **Window List** button on the Taskbar on a panel, or middle click the root window (page 312).
Window menubar	A menubar found in most windows. Refer to "Terminal Emulator (konsole) Menubar" on page 279, "Menubar" on page 293, and "Desktop Menus" on page 308.

kicker: Main Panel

The Main panel, also referred to as kicker (the name of the program that displays the Main panel), is a bar that usually appears at the bottom of the workspace. You can create additional panels, technically called *extensions*, or *extension panels*, because

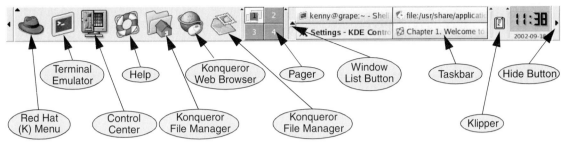

Figure 8-8   kicker

they are extensions of kicker. This chapter uses the term *panel* to refer to both kicker and extension panels. The default kicker displays a row of buttons with an icon on each; a small group of numbered squares representing the workspaces (the pager); a group of rectangles, each listing the name of a program that is running on the displayed workspace (the taskbar); and perhaps the Clipboard tool, Kandalf (useful tips); and a clock. At one or both ends may be an arrow that you can use to move kicker out of sight toward that end, except for a little arrow that it leaves in place so you can recall kicker when you want to. Refer to page 338 for more information on panels.

Figure 8-8 and Table 8-3 gives more information on some of the more common buttons/icons, applets, and other items on kicker and extension panels. Buttons and applets are of two types: ones that execute a program and ones that display a menu of programs. You can tell which ones display a menu by the little black triangle pointing up at the upper left of the button. The most important and most used menu is the K menu, which is discussed on page 274.

Common Panel Buttons and Applets

|| table 8-3

K menu (red hat)	Refer to "K Menu (Application Starter)" on page 274.
Show Desktop	Toggles the windows on the workspace between minimized and restored. Windows that were minimized before you click this button are not restored by it. (Not shown in Figure 8-8.)
Terminal Emulator/Shell	Opens a terminal emulator window (page 177).
Konqueror File Manager (Home Directory)	Refer to "File Manager" on page 288
Konqueror Web Browser	Refer to "Web Browser" on page 290

Common Panel Buttons and Applets (Continued)	‖ table 8-3
Help	Refer to "KDE HelpCenter" on page 269
Hide Button	Refer to the next section. The arrows at either end of kicker in Figure 8-8 are **Hide** buttons.
Mozilla Web Browser	Opens the Mozilla Web browser.
Taskbar	Refer to "Taskbar" on page 311.
Window List	Refer to "Window List Menu" on page 312.
Pager	Click one of these boxes to display a workspace. Refer to Figure 8-8.

If you are not sure what one of the buttons or applets on kicker does, allow the mouse pointer to remain motionless for a moment. When the mouse pointer hovers over the object, a tooltip appears. See the tip on page 270 if the tooltip does not appear.

Hide Button

Hide buttons are located at one or both ends of kicker or an extension (Figure 8-8). Arrows on the buttons show which way the panel slides off the screen and disappears when you click one of them. When a panel disappears, it leaves the Hide button from the other end showing. Click the exposed Hide button, and the panel reappears. You can make a a panel disappear automatically when you are not using it: Refer to "Automatic Hide" (page 319) for kicker and "Extensions" (page 321) for extension panels.

KDE Utilities

KDE has many utilities available from the K menu and more on its Web site. You can also use utilities that were not specifically designed with KDE in mind. This section lists a few of the most commonly used utilities.

konsole: Terminal Emulator

The KDE terminal emulator (konsole) displays a window that mimics a character-based terminal (page 177). Bring up the terminal emulator by clicking the Terminal

Emulator button on a panel (Figure 8-8, page 277) or by selecting K menu: System Tools⇨Terminal.

You can have multiple terminal sessions within a single Terminal window. With a KDE terminal emulator displayed, make a selection from KDE Terminal menubar: Session or click the New icon (on the toolbar, usually at the bottom of the window) to display another terminal emulator in place of the first. Click and hold the New icon for a few moments to display the session menu giving you a choice of sessions to start. Refer to "Session" on page 331 when you want to modify this list. Switch between terminals by clicking the terminal icons, also on the toolbar, or by holding SHIFT and pressing the right or LEFT ARROW key.

Although it starts at the bottom of the window, you can move the toolbar to any of the sides of the window or onto the root window. Refer to "Toolbar Handles" on page 342.

Table 8-4 explains the choices on the konsole menubar.

Terminal Emulator (konsole) Menubar || table 8-4

Sessions	
New Shell	Opens a new session with a terminal shell.
New Linux Console	Opens a new session with a shell that emulates a GNU/Linux console with **Settings** (below) appropriate to a GNU/Linux console. Similar to **New Shell** but with different **Settings**.
New Midnight Commander	Opens a shell that runs Midnight Commander, a pseudographical file manager. Go to www.gnome.org/projects/mc for more information.
New Screen Session	Opens a new session running **screen**, a virtual terminal manager. For more information, see the **screen man** page or go to www.gnu.org/software/screen/screen.html.
New Root Console	Opens a **New Linux Console** with root privileges.
New Root Midnight Commander	Opens a **New Midnight Commander** with root privileges.
Close Session	Closes the currently displayed session. Terminates konsole when only one session remains.
Quit	Terminates konsole, warning you of open sessions.

Terminal Emulator (konsole) Menubar (Continued) || table 8-4

Edit	
Paste	Pastes text from the clipboard buffer at the current location of the cursor.
Send Signal	Sends the specified signal to the displayed shell. For a discussion of common signals, refer to Table 13-5 on page 667.
Find in History	Locates and highlights the most recent occurrence in the current session's history of the string you specify.
Save History As	Saves the current session's history to a text file.
Clear History	Removes the current session's history.
Clear All Histories	Removes the history of all sessions.
View	
Rename Session	Changes the name of the current session displayed on the window's toolbar.
Monitor for Activity	Displays a lighted light bulb on the toolbar when there is activity on the current session. Allows you to track activity on a session other than the current one.
Monitor for Silence	Displays a dark light bulb on the toolbar when there is not activity on the current session for 10 seconds.
Send Input to All Sessions	Causes whatever you type in the current session to be typed in all sessions. The icon on the toolbar becomes a small radio to indicate which sessions are broadcasting.
Move Session Left	Makes the session that is to the left of the current one on the toolbar the current session.
Move Session Right	Makes the session that is to the right of the current one on the toolbar the current session.
[list of sessions]	Lists all the sessions. Click a session on the list to make that the current session.
Settings	You can display part of this submenu by right clicking anywhere within the window.

Terminal Emulator (konsole) Menubar (Continued) || table 8-4

Show Menubar	Toggles the menubar. When the menubar is not displayed you can turn it on again by right clicking the window and choosing **Show Menubar**.
Show Toolbar	Toggles the toolbar.
Scrollbar	Specifies that the scrollbar appear on the **Left** or **Right** of the window or that it be **Hidden**.
Full-Screen	Maximizes the window. To return the window to its previous size right click the window, select **Settings**, and then select **Full-Screen**.
Bell	Sets the system bell to **None**, **System Notification**, or **Visible Bell**.
Font	Specifies a type size from **Tiny** to **Huge**. Click **Custom** to display the Select Font window.
Keyboard	Specifies a keyboard/keymapping.
Schema	Specifies the foreground and background colors for the window. **Transparent** means that the root window appears as the background color.
Size	Specifies the size of the window in columns (characters) and rows (lines).
History	Enables/disables history and specifies the number of lines saved.
Save Settings	Saves the settings of the displayed shell as the default.
Configure Konsole	Opens **K menu: Control Center**⇨**Personalization**⇨ **Konsole** (page 330).

kcolorchooser: Selects a Color

The Select Color window (kcolorchooser, Figure 8-9) appears when you click a color bar, such as the two in the Background window (right click the root window, select Configure Desktop, then click Background). The square centered on top of the line above the buttons always displays the selected color. When you click the OK button, this color is returned to the color bar that you initially clicked on.

There are several ways to select a color:

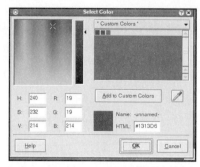

Figure 8-9   Select Color window

- Click the color/shade you want on the multicolored box at the upper-left corner of the window.

- Click the eyedropper to the right of the Add to Custom Colors button. The mouse pointer turns into a cross-hairs. Position the cross-hairs over the color you want, anywhere on the workspace, and click. The color you click on becomes the selected color.

- Choose a line from the combo box at the upper-right corner of the window. You have a choice of several groups of colors, including Recent Colors (an automatically generated list of colors you have selected) and Custom Colors (colors you have added to the list of custom colors by selecting and then clicking the Add to Custom Colors button). Then click a color in the area below the combo box.

- Enter the HTML specification for the color you want.

- Enter the appropriate numbers in the H, S, and V (hue, saturation, value) column of text boxes or in the R, G, and B (red, green, blue) column.

After you select a color you can adjust its brightness by clicking the vertical bar to the right of the multicolor box or by dragging the pointer on the right side of this bar up or down. Click OK when you have selected the color you want.

Run Command

To run a character-based program display the Run Command window by selecting Run Command from the K menu or from any of several other menus or by pressing ALT-F2. Enter the name of the program in the Command text box, click Options, put a check mark in the Run in terminal box, and click Run. KDE runs the program in a Terminal Emulator window. When you run telnet in this manner, you see the telnet> prompt in a new window. Enter **quit**, telnet finishes, and the window closes.

When you run who in this manner, you see a window flash on the screen for a moment and disappear. KDE ran who in a terminal emulator window, who finished, and KDE closed the window. When you want to run who, you need to open a terminal emulator window (page 278) and give the command from the resulting window. When you call the terminal emulator in this manner, it runs a shell that persists between commands so that you can see the output of who. Alternatively you can give the command **bash –c 'who;read'** from the Run Command window. The **–c** option causes bash to execute the string that follows the option. After it executes who, it executes read, which waits for you to enter something at the keyboard, leaving the output of who visible until you press a key.

Cut and Paste

Two simple cut-and-paste tools are built in to KDE: left mouse button/middle mouse button and CONTROL-C/CONTROL-V. For both of these techniques, you start by selecting the object (text, figure, and so on) by left dragging over the object(s) you want to select. You can also double-click to select a word or triple-click to select a line. Paste the selected object by positioning the mouse pointer where you want to put the object and pressing the middle mouse button. You can give other commands after selecting the object and before you paste it, as long as you do not deselect the object.

By default CONTROL-C[3] copies the selected text or figure, and CONTROL-V pastes the copied object at the location of the mouse pointer. You can give as many commands as you like between the CONTROL-C and the CONTROL-V, as long as you do not use another CONTROL-C. For more information, refer to "Shortcuts" on page 302. Use K menu: Applications⇨AbiWord or K menu: Editors⇨Kate to experiment with these controls.

klipper: Clipboard Utility

The klipper utility is a sophisticated multiple-buffer cut-and-paste utility. In addition to cutting and pasting from multiple buffers, klipper can execute a command based on the contents of a buffer. To start klipper, choose K-menu: Run Command, enter **klipper**, and click Run. The klipper utility does not start a second occurrence of itself when it is already running. The klipper icon (bottom of Figure 8-10) appears in the Main panel.

Each time you highlight text, klipper copies it into its buffer. Click the klipper icon or press ALT-CONTROL-V to display the klipper pop-up menu (Figure 8-10). The top

---

3. CONTROL-C does not copy text in a terminal emulator window because the shell running in the window intercepts the control character before KDE receives it. You must either use the mouse to cut and paste in this environment or change your shortcut/key binding (page 302).

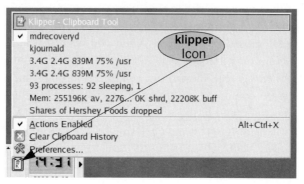

Figure 8-10   klipper pop-up menu with icon below

part of this menu lists the text that klipper has in its buffers. When the lines are too long to fit in the width of the window, klipper uses ellipses (...) to indicate missing material. To paste the text from a buffer into your document, display the klipper pop-up menu and click the line you want to paste; the pop-up menu closes. Move the mouse pointer to the location you want to paste the text and middle click. In a terminal emulator window, the text is always pasted at the location of the text cursor.

Preferences

Below the list of buffers in the klipper pop-up menu are three other choices: Actions Enabled (see the next section for a discussion of actions); Clear Clipboard History, which clears all the buffers and empties the upper part of this menu; and Preferences. When you click Preferences, klipper displays the Klipper Preferences window (Table 8-5).

Klipper Preferences Window	‖ table 8-5
General	
Popup menu at mouse-cursor position	Specifies that when you click the **klipper** icon or press CONTROL-ALT-V, the **klipper** pop-up menu appears next to the mouse pointer. When you do not check this box, the menu appears in the lower-right corner of the workspace.
Save clipboard contents on exit	Specifies that **klipper** is to save the contents of its buffers when you quit using it or close X (log out or go back to the command line prompt).

Klipper Preferences Window (Continued)	‖ table 8-5
Replay actions on an item selected from history	Plays the appropriate action when you select a buffer from the pop-up menu. See "Actions," next section.
Prevent empty clipboard	Keeps at least the most recent item from the clipboard in the clipboard history.
Timeout for Action popups	Specifies the number of seconds that the choice of actions window remains visible. Refer to "Actions," following this table.
Clipboard history size	Specifies the number of lines of buffers that appear on the pop-up menu.
Actions	Refer to "Actions," following this table.
Shortcuts	Allows you to change three shortcuts, two of which have to do with actions. This tab works the same way as the Configure Shortcuts window, which is explained on page 302. The tab allows you to change three shortcuts: **Enable/Disable Clipboard Actions** (turns on/off the action feature of **klipper**—refer to the pop-up menu to see whether they are enabled), **Manually Invoke Action on Current Clipboard** (runs the action associated with the current buffer), and **Show Klipper Popup-Menu** (displays the pop-up menu).

Actions

The klipper utility has the ability to execute a command when you select (fill a buffer with) text that matches a specified regular expression. The regular expressions are specified under the Actions tab of the Klipper Preferences window.[4] For example, look at the Web-URL regular expression ^https?://—the description is in the right column, which may not be visible unless you scroll right. This regular expression defines a string that begins with http, optionally followed by an s, which is followed by a colon and two forward slashes. The caret (^) matches the beginning of a line or string, the http matches itself, the s? matches zero or one occurrence of s, and the two forward slashes (//)match themselves. Refer to Appendix A for more information on regular expressions.

---

4. The Actions tab presents a portion of a wide frame, with a scrollbar at the bottom. To make your work with this frame easier, widen the Preferences window until the bottom scrollbar disappears. Alternatively you can scroll to the right until you see the Description heading, and drag the vertical line to the left of the word Description to make the frame narrower so that the bottom scrollbar disappears.

The Action list reveals the actions that klipper can take in a tree view; click the plus sign in the box to the left of an action to expand the listing. Each command line has options that are appropriate to the way it is used. Under Web-URL are two lines for kmail: one to send the URL and one to send the page that the URL points to.

When you highlight a URL, such as http://www.kde.org, and press CONTROL-ALT-R,[5] klipper displays a dialog box that allows you to choose which command you want to run on the selected text. This box closes when you click a choice or in Timeout for Action popups seconds (see Table 8-5 on page 284), whichever occurs first.

---

klipper **and** kmail ‖ tip

Many of the default actions provided with **klipper** send objects using **kmail**. These actions will not work properly unless you are running **kmail** at the time you give the command for **klipper** to take the action. You can view the error messages on the system console (typically CONTROL-ALT-F1)

Konqueror Browser/File Manager

Even though Konqueror is much more than a Web browser, its name takes its place in the evolution of browsers: Navigator, Explorer, and now Konqueror, spelled with a K because it is part of KDE (Figure 8-11).

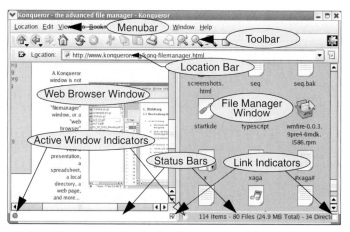

Figure 8-11   Konqueror displaying browser and file manager windows

---

5. If CONTROL-ALT-R does not bring up the klipper dialog box, try changing the Manually Invoke Action on Current Clipboard shortcut to ALT-R using the Shortcuts tab in the klipper Preferences window.

Konqueror easily morphs among a file manager, browser, and executor of many programs, both within and outside the borders of its window. Konqueror provides network transparent access, which means that it is as easy to work with files on your system as it is to work with files on remote systems, and you can copy files from/to a remote system, using the same techniques you use for copying files locally.

Because it opens an application within itself, Konqueror makes the process of clicking and viewing almost any type of file transparent to the user. Click a **pdf** (Acrobat) file/icon within Konqueror, and it opens the file within the Konqueror window, using xpdf. You see the file that you clicked open within the Konqueror window.

Getting Started

You can bring up Konqueror as a browser or a file manager, and you can switch from one to the other while you are working with it. Select K Menu: Home to open Konqueror the file manager. Alternatively, you can click the Home icon on the workspace. Once Konqueror is open, enter a URL, such as www.redhat.com, in the location bar and press RETURN to switch Konqueror to browser mode. You can remove the Navigation Panel (the narrow subwindow on the left), if it is present, by pressing F9 or selecting Konqueror menubar: Window⇨Show Navigation Panel.

You can change the appearance and functionality of Konqueror very easily. What your system displays may not match what is shown and described in these pages.

Konqueror works with different kinds of targets: plain (including executable) files, directory files, and URLs, including HTTP and FTP addresses. You specify the target by clicking the target's icon within a Konqueror *view* (subwindow) or entering its pathname/address in the location bar. Konqueror takes action based on the kind of target it finds:

- **Plain file** (local or remote): Is the file executable? If yes, run it. If no, figure out what utility (builtin or external) to open it with. (First try to figure out the MIME type; if that doesn't work, use file (page 1163) to determine the file type.) Execute the utility to open the file within the Konqueror window.

- **Directory file:** Displays the contents of the directory in a Konqueror File Manager view.

- **HTTP address:** Opens the URL in the HTML viewer, which has been loaded and embedded within the Konqueror window.

- **FTP address:** Treats a file obtained by ftp just as it would treat a plain or directory file.

Running a Program

In the Konqueror location bar, enter **/usr/X11R6/bin/xclock** RETURN, an executable file that runs under X. After checking that you really want to run it, Konqueror runs xclock. When you want to run a character-based (text mode) program, use Konqueror menubar: Tools⇨Run Command. Refer to "Run Command" on page 282.

Views I

Choose Konqueror menubar: Window to add and remove views (subwindows) from the Konqueror display. The choices in this menu always work on the *active view*, the one with a green dot at the lower left (or the only view). For more information refer to "Window" on page 297. Also refer to "Views II" on page 300.

Toolbar

The Konqueror toolbar (the toolbar with the icons in Figure 8-12) is straightforward. A right arrow at the right end of the toolbar indicates that not all the icons would fit in the width of the window. Click the arrow to display (and choose from) the remaining icons.

File Manager

Konqueror can manipulate files in many ways. Table 8-6 shows what effects various actions have within the active Konqueror File Manager view.

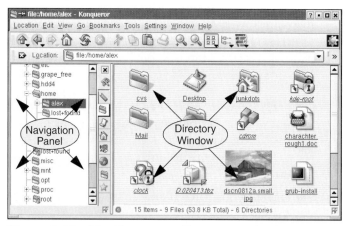

Figure 8-12   The Konqueror file manager displaying icons

Konqueror Left Mouse Button Commands

|| table 8-6

Select one or more icons	Click or drag a box around an icon. You can drag a box around more than one icon to select several icons at once. When you select icons, Konqueror highlights them. CONTROL+left click acts as a toggle, deselecting selected icons and selecting those that are not selected. SHIFT+left click selects all the icons between the icon you clicked and the previous icon you clicked. If the two icons are not in a row, Konqueror selects all the icons within the rectangle that has the two icons as opposite corners.
Get help	Choose **Konqueror menubar: Help** (or press F1) to display the Konqueror Help menu. For more information, refer to "Help" on page 268.
Drag and drop	There are many ways to copy and move files. An easy way is to left drag an icon to its new location outside of its current view (subwindow). When you release the mouse button, Konqueror displays a menu: **Copy Here**, **Move Here**, and **Link Here**. Choose one, or press ESCAPE to cancel the operation. You can move icons (files or directories) within a single Konqueror view (just repositions the icon within the view), between multiple Konqueror views within the same or different instances of Konqueror, or from/to the root window. Whenever you use multiple views, make sure that they are not linked, by making sure that the little square at the lower right of each view is empty (click it if it is not). You can also right click an icon and select **Cut** (to move the file) or **Copy** (to copy the file) and right click the new location and select **Paste**. Common drag-and-drop tasks are to • Drag a file onto a folder or within an open folder's view (copies, moves, or links the file). • Drag a file onto the root window (copies, moves, or links the file on the workspace). • Drag an object into a panel (places the object on the panel). • Drag a file onto the **Printer** icon on the workspace (prints the file). • Drag a file or folder onto the trashcan on the workspace (moves the file to the **Trash** directory for later deletion).
View a directory	Double click the folder icon.
View your home directory	Click the **Home** button on the toolbar.
View the parent directory	Click the **Up** arrow on the toolbar.

Konqueror Left Mouse Button Commands (Continued) || table 8-6

Open object/Launch application	There are three ways to open an object icon so you can view its contents or run it: • Double left click the object icon. This method uses Konqueror's "intelligence" to determine which utility to open the file with. When you open an executable file, such as Mozilla, Konqueror runs the executable. When you open a text file, a text editor displays and allows you to edit the file. When you open a directory, Konqueror displays its contents. • CONTROL+middle click does the same thing as double-left click but in a new window. • Right click an object icon and choose **Open With** from the pop-up menu. Click the program type (**Editors**, **Graphics**, and so on), and select a specific program to use. After you have used **Open With** one or more times, you will see at the bottom of the menu a list of the programs that you have used, and you can quickly select from that menu.
Find (search)	Select **Tools** from the Konqueror menubar and then **Find file** from the drop-down menu. Refer to "**kfind**: Finds Files" on page 298.
Rename	Right click an icon and select **Rename**. Enter/edit the name of the icon in the filename box next to the icon.
File Properties	Right click an icon and select **Properties**. From the **General** tab you can change the filename. When you look at a directory, you can click **Refresh** to reread it. From the **Permissions** tab you can graphically set the file's permissions bits (pages 118 and 1103) and, if you wish, cause the changes to propagate to all the file's subdirectories and the files within those subdirectories.

Web Browser

Konqueror is a versatile Web browser (Figure 8-13). Display a Web page by entering a URL in the location bar or clicking a URL button. The most important feature of the Web browser, the file manager, and the other faces of Konqueror is that each of these separate tools is seamlessly integrated into the same window and shares appearance, tools (such as bookmarks), menu system, icons, and functional characteristics. You can browse from a Web site to an FTP site, copy a file from the FTP site to your local filesystem or workspace as though you were copying it locally, and run, edit, or display the file within the Konqueror window or in another window.

Enhanced Browsing

Enhanced browsing enables you to search for a keyword rapidly, using a default or specified search engine. You specify a search engine by using a shortcut. "Search

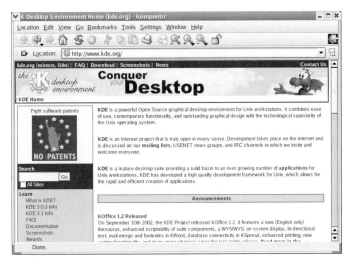

Figure 8-13   Konqueror the Web browser

engines" can include dictionaries, bug-tracking systems, classic search engines, and more. For example, to look up the word *colocation* in the Free Online Dictionary of Computing, enter the shortcut **foldoc:colocation** in the location bar. To search for discussions about Samba on Google Groups, enter **groups:samba**. Other abbreviations that you may find useful are **gg** for Google (standard search), **webster** (Merriam-Webster Dictionary), and **fm** for Freshmeat. You can perform the same searches by entering the same search parameters in the Konqueror menubar: Tools⇨Run Command dialog box (page 282). When you enter **porcupine** on the location bar without specifying a search engine, Konqueror looks it up by using your default search engine. For more information refer to "Enhanced Browsing" on page 335.

Bookmarks

As with any browser, bookmarks give a name to a URL or local pathname and allow you to return to the bookmarked location by selecting the name from a menu. Figure 8-14 shows the Konqueror Bookmarks menu. Konqueror displays the bookmarks list below the standard entries in the Bookmarks menu (Add, Edit, and New Folder in Figure 8-14). Click the bookmark name that represents the location you want to visit, and Konqueror displays that location. In the figure the Personal bookmark/menu choice is a folder that contains other bookmarks. You can nest bookmark folders.

Choose Konqueror menubar: Bookmarks⇨Add Bookmark (or press CONTROL-B) to add to your bookmarks list whatever is displayed in the active view. Select

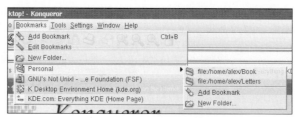

Figure 8-14   Konqueror Bookmarks menu

Konqueror menubar: Bookmarks⇨Edit Bookmarks to bring up the Bookmark Editor, which displays an editable list of your bookmarks. To edit the name of or location associated with a bookmark, click it once to highlight it, pause, and click again (this is not a double-click) on either the name or the URL, depending on which you want to edit. Select Edit⇨Change Icon to change the icon associated with the bookmark. You can also change the order of the bookmarks by using the Bookmark Editor. Use the mouse to drag the highlighted bookmark where you want it to appear in the list or use the up/down arrow keys to move the highlighted bookmark. The right/left arrow keys open/close directories/folders of bookmarks. New Folder inserts a new folder below the highlighted bookmark.

Netscape Bookmarks displays your Netscape bookmarks so that you can use them from Konqueror. This choice appears automatically when you have installed and run Netscape.

Optional

Kparts

By itself Konqueror has very little functionality; it is an application that uses other applications to do all its work. Konqueror takes advantage of KDE *i/o slaves* and *components* (KParts). The i/o slaves accept or gather input and change it to a standard format that a component can display. When you open Konqueror to view your home directory, Konqueror calls the File i/o slave, which gathers information about the filesystem and uses the Icon View component (Konqueror menubar: View⇨View Mode⇨Icon View) or the Text View component (Konqueror menubar: View⇨View Mode⇨Text View) to display the information it got from the File i/o slave.

The i/o slaves are discrete modules; it is relatively easy to write a new one. Konqueror uses an i/o slave automatically when you put it in the directory structure (**$KDEDIR/lib/kde2/kio_***protocol*.✳ and **$KDEDIR/share/services/***protocol*.**desktop**). $KDEDIR is **/usr** by default, and *protocol* is the name of the protocol. Some examples of i/o slaves and their output format are FTP (virtual filesystem), POP3 (each retrieved piece of e-mail appears as a file), and the audio CD-ROM browser (**kio_audiocd**, each track appears as a file).

The components display the information they receive from the i/o slaves. One i/o slave can feed several different components, and one component can receive input from several different i/o slaves. There must be both an i/o slave *and* a component pair to display information within a Konqueror view.

Toolbars

Konqueror has five toolbars that you can turn on and off from Settings on the Konqueror menubar: menubar, toolbar, extra toolbar, location bar, and bookmark toolbar. Except for the menubar, each of these toolbars has a toolbar handle (Figure 8-29, page 342) that you can use to move the toolbar. Right click almost anywhere on a toolbar that has a handle to display the toolbar menu (page 311).

Menubar

The menus on the menubar change, depending on what Konqueror is displaying. A selection from the menubar produces a drop-down menu when you click it. Table 8-7 covers many of these selections.

Konqueror Menubar	‖ table 8-7
In this table [fm] indicates a choice that is available for a file manager view, [web] means that the choice is available for a Web view, and [sv] is a choice that is available only when more than one view is displayed (split view).	
Location	Open a new or duplicate view or a location you specify as local or remote (HTTP, FTP, or a file of almost any type). Print the contents of, send as a link or file, the active view, or **Quit** Konqueror. Other choices depend on the context or the type of file or Web site that is displayed.
Edit	Perform typical editing functions, such as undo, cut, copy, paste, rename, delete, and so on. **Shred** overwrites the file many times with different bit patterns so it is difficult to undelete. **Shred** is not a secure method for removing the information contained in a file. Other choices depend on context.
View	These choices act on the active window.
View Mode [fm]	Choose between having the Directory Window display icons, multiple columns of icons, a tree view, a detailed view with small icons, or a text view that is very similar to the detailed view except without icons. You can choose Cervisia to view a CVS (page 879) directory.
Use index.html [fm]	When you open a directory that contains an **index.html** file, Konqueror displays that file and not the contents of the directory.

Konqueror Menubar (Continued) || table 8-7

Lock to current location [sv]	Ensures that the currently active view will not change even if you click a new location. For more information refer to "Lock to Current Location/Unlock View" on page 301. See also the tutorial on page 303.
Unlock view [sv]	File Manager: Unlocks a lock created with **Lock to current location** (page 301).
Link view [sv]	Same as clicking the Link Indicator (page 301). See also the tutorial on page 303.
Reload	Rereads the location displayed in the active window.
Stop	Browser: Stops searching/downloading.
View Document Source [web]	Displays the source of the document in ASCII, including all embedded codes.
View Frame Source [web]	Displays the source of a frame within a document in ASCII, including all embedded codes.
Security [web]	Displays a dialog box that tells you whether the active browser connection is secured with SSL and gives you the option of opening **K menu: Control Center**⇨**Personalization**⇨**Crypto**⇨**SSL** (page 329) to configure cryptography settings.
Set Encoding [web]	Establishes the character encoding used to display HTML pages.
Use Stylesheet [web]	Specifies a stylesheet to use.
Icon Size [fm]	Specifies the size of the icons in Icon View mode.
Sort [fm]	Specifies several ways of sorting files in the Directory window. Each of these ways can be modified by specifying **Descending** and/or **Directories** first.
Preview [fm]	File Manager in Icon View: Displays an icon that shows a little picture of what is in the file (images, PostScript, PDF, text, and HTML). A sound file is played when the mouse pointer hovers over the icon representing the file.
Show Hidden Files [fm]	File Manager: Displays files and directories whose names begin with a period.
Background Color [fm]	File Manager: Chooses a background color for the File Manager.
Background Image [fm]	File Manager: Choose a background image for the File Manager. You can use your own image or choose one supplied by Konqueror.
Go	
[navigation]	The basic navigation tools are displayed at the top of this menu.

Konqueror Menubar (Continued) || table 8-7

Applications	Displays the contents of $KDEHOME/.kde/share/applnk-redhat, which contains Desktop files (page 345). The value of **KDEHOME** defaults to ~/.kde when the variable is not set.
Trash	Displays your trash directory (~/**Desktop/Trash**) in a separate window.
Templates	A template (/usr/share/templates by default) stores information about the file type, including the name and comment (in many languages) that Konqueror displays when you get information on the file. It also holds the name of the file (in /usr/share/templates/.source by default) that a KDE editor copies when you open a new file of that type.
Autostart	Refer to "Autostart" on page 346.
Most Often Visited	Displays a list of the Web sites you have visited the most.
[history list]	The last few lines of the Go menu list the locations/files that you have visited with Konqueror most recently. This is a quick-reference version of **History** on the Navigation panel.
Bookmarks	Refer to "Bookmarks" on page 291.
Add Bookmark	Adds the location currently displayed by Konqueror to your of bookmarks.
Edit Bookmarks	Displays your bookmarks for editing. Bookmarks are stored in ~/.kde/share/apps/konqueror/bookmarks.xml.
New Folder	Creates a new bookmark folder entry in ~/.kde/share/apps/konqueror/bookmarks.xml.
Netscape Bookmarks	Displays bookmarks created in or transferred to Netscape. Appears only after you have run Netscape.
(history list)	The last few lines of the Bookmarks menu list the bookmarked locations that you have visited with Konqueror most recently.
Tools	Different choices are available, based on what type of page the active view is displaying.
Run Command	Displays a dialog box that you can enter a command in (page 282).
Open Terminal	Opens a **konsole** terminal emulator (page 278) by default in a separate window with the directory shown in the location bar as its working directory (if possible).
Find File	Embeds **kfind** as part of the Konqueror window (page 298).
View Filter [fm]	This drop-down menu presents a list of all the types of files in the active view and allows you to specify which you want to see. **Show Count** displays the number of files of each type in the menu.

Konqueror Menubar (Continued) || table 8-7

Create Image Gallery [fm]	Generates an HTML page showing images from the active view.
Execute Shell Command [fm]	Opens a dialog box for you to enter a command executed in the directory displayed by the active view.
HTML Settings [web]	Presents some of the basic choices from **K menu: Control Center**⇨**Web Browsing**⇨**Konqueror Browser**⇨**HTML** (page 335).
Translate Web Page [web]	Displays a translation of the active Web page.
Show DOM tree [web]	An API for accessing the contents of HTML and XML documents. See *DOM* on page 1465.
Validate Web Page [web]	Validates the HTML or CSS of the active Web page, using predefined Web-based tools. You can change the tools by choosing **Configure Validator**.
Archive Web Page [web]	Creates a *.war (Web archive) file, which you can subsequently open with Konqueror or another browser.
Change Browser Identification [web]	Presents some of the basic choices from **K menu: Control Center**⇨**Web Browsing**⇨**User Agent** (page 338).

Settings

Show Menubar	Turns the menubar (displaying this menu entry, page 293) off. Right click within a view, and select **Show Menubar** to turn it back on.
Show Toolbar	Toggles the toolbar on and off (page 298).
Show Extra Toolbar	Toggles the Extra Window toolbar on and off (page 298).
Show Location Toolbar	Toggles the location bar on and off (page 298).
Show Bookmark Toolbar	Toggles the Bookmark toolbar on and off (page 298).
View Properties Saved in Directory [fm]	Determines whether Konqueror saves the properties of the current view in the **.directory** file in the directory named in the location bar. [Konqueror does not display the **.directory** file even when you turn on **Show Hidden Files** (page 294)]. When you do not check this choice, Konqueror does not modify the **.directory** file when you make a change in how you view the directory (refer to "View Mode [fm]" on page 293).

Konqueror Menubar (Continued)

|| table 8-7

Remove Directory Properties [fm]	Removes the view properties saved in the **.directory** file in the directory named in the location bar. Other information, such as the name of the icon that Konqueror uses to show the directory, remains.
Configure Shortcuts	Opens the Configure Shortcuts window, which allows you to add and change shortcut key combinations, such as CONTROL-C for copy and CONTROL-V for paste. Refer to "Shortcuts" on page 302.
Configure Toolbars	Refer to "Configure Toolbars [Konqueror only]" on page 312.
Configure Konqueror	Opens **Settings** in a separate window that duplicates parts of the **K menu: Control Center** menu (page 314) in a different order.
Window	These commands work on the active view.
Split View Left/Right	Creates a new view that duplicates the active view. The new view is placed next to the active view.
Split View Top/Bottom	Creates a new view that duplicates the active view. The new view is placed below the active view.
Remove Active View [sv]	Removes the active view.
Show Terminal Emulator	Displays a terminal emulator view across the bottom of the Konqueror window (page 301).
Show Navigation Panel	Displays the Navigation panel (page 306).
Save View Profile "*xxx*"	Saves the profile necessary to reproduce the current Konqueror view under the name *xxx*. KDE saves profiles in the **~/.kde/share/apps/konqueror/profiles** directory.
Configure View Profile	Saves the profile for the current Konqueror setup under a new or existing name. Also deletes or renames an existing profile. Two check boxes allow you to save URLs and window-size information in the profile. See the end of the tutorial that starts on page 303.
Load View Profile	Loads the profile that you specify on the submenu.
Full-Screen Mode	Maximizes Konqueror, removing the titlebar and menubar in the process. To restore (unmaximize) Konqueror, click the **Exit Full-Screen Mode** icon on the toolbar or right click in one of the views to display a menu from which you can choose **Exit Full-Screen Mode**.

Toolbar

The Konqueror toolbar typically has a left and right arrow that take you linearly through what you have viewed with Konqueror. The up arrow takes you up in a directory hierarchy. Clicking the house displays your home directory; reload (the arrows going in a circle) reloads an image (typically used to reload a Web image that may be changing) or file structure (in case it has changed). Stop (the red X) halts the search for or loading of a Web page, and Print sends the image in the active view to the printer. Cervisia displays a CVS (page 879) directory.

Extra Window Toolbar

Choose Konqueror menubar:⇨Settings⇨Show Extra Toolbar to display the extra toolbar. Use Konqueror menubar:⇨Settings⇨Configure Toolbars selection to change the icons that appear on this toolbar.

Location Bar

The location bar has two items you can work with: the text box and the Clear button. The Clear button (the reversed-out X at the left end of the toolbar) clears whatever is in the text box. You can enter a local or remote filename/URL or modify whatever is in the text box. The up and down arrows scroll through the list of entries that have been in the text box. You can also click the down arrow at the right of this box and choose from the display of other locations you have visited with Konqueror.

Bookmark Toolbar

The bookmark toolbar gives you quick access to bookmarks. Display the Bookmark toolbar with Konqueror: Settings⇨Show Bookmark Toolbar. Nothing will be in it unless you set one of your bookmark folders as a toolbar folder, which you can do from the Bookmark editor (Konqueror: Bookmarks⇨Edit Bookmarks). Create a new directory or choose an existing one, click it to highlight it, and then, from the right-click menu, select Set as Toolbar Folder.

kfind: Finds Files

Of the many ways to start kfind, the easiest is to click Konqueror menubar: Tools⇨Find file. Konqueror opens a new view that has three tabs: Name/Location, Date Range, and Advanced. The view opens to the Name/Location tab with a default filename to search for—*[6] (matches all filenames, *including* those that begin with a

---

6. Or the previous name you searched for, if you have used kfind previously.

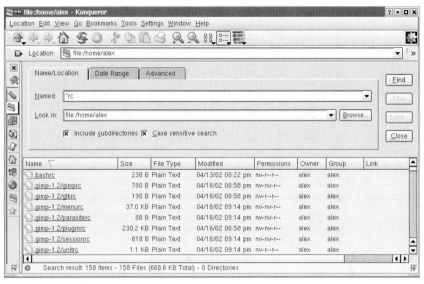

Figure 8-15   Find File window

period)—and your home directory as the place to start the search. Put in the Named text box the name of the file you want to search for (you can include wildcard characters) and in the Look in text box the directory that you want to start the search in. The Browse button helps you find the directory you want to start in. Put a check mark in the Include subdirectories box when you want to search through subdirectories. Click Find to start the search. The part of the window with the fields you just filled in dims as the results are tabulated at the bottom of the window and displayed in the lower half of the window. You can do whatever you want with the found files: copy, move, delete, edit, display, and so on.

Figure 8-15 shows a case-sensitive (page 1459) search for all files whose names end with **rc** (*rc) in Alex's home directory and all subdirectories. Here the asterisk matches filenames that begin with a period.

In addition to or in place of filling in the Name/Location tab, you can click the Date Range tab to specify a single day or a range of dates that the file was created or modified on. The default is All files. Put a check mark in the Find all files created or modified text box to specify a range of dates. In order to be found when you specify a range, the file must match the Name/Location criteria *and* the Date Range criteria.

In addition, you can use the Advanced tab to specify the file type, text within the file, and the relative size of the file. Click Case Sensitive when you want kfind to perform a case-sensitive search for the text you put in the Containing Text field.

You can save the results of your search to a file by clicking Save, two buttons below Find on the right side of the window. You will be given a choice of filename, location, and type of file (text or HTML) you want to save.

Views II

Views, or subwindows, are key to taking advantage of Konqueror's power. This section covers some of the buttons, indicators, and menu choices that work with views.

Two indicators are important when you work with more than one view: the Active View indicator and the Link indicator.

Figure 8-16 shows two side-by-side views with a terminal emulator below. The toolbar and location bar are side-by-side.

Active View Indicator

A small circle at the lower-left of each view (Figure 8-16) is green on the active view and white on all others. The active view has the input focus and is the object of all Konqueror menu commands. The location bar displays the location of the file displayed in the active view. Click within a view to make it the active view.

Konqueror Terminology: View versus Window   ‖ tip

The Konqueror window is the entire window with four sides adjacent to the root window, the edge of the workspace, or other windows, usually with a menubar, location bar, and toolbar. The Konqueror window can house multiple views, the term used to describe subwindows within the Konqueror window. In addition to views, Konqueror can have a Navigation panel and a terminal emulator subwindow. Figure 8-16 shows a Konqueror window with two views and a terminal emulator subwindow.

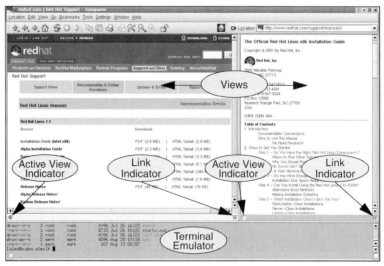

Figure 8-16   Konqueror showing two views and a terminal emulator

Link Indicator

A small rectangle at the lower-right corner of each view (Figure 8-16) has a small piece of a chain link fence in it in all views that are linked. Two linked views always show the same thing, with a very useful exception, which is covered in the next paragraph. Although linked views display the same information, each may display it differently. For example, one may have an icon view, and the other a detailed list view.

Lock to Current Location/Unlock View

Choose Konqueror menubar: View⇨Lock to current location to cause the contents of the active view to remain constant, regardless of what links (URLs) you click. With a normal (not locked) view, you click a link, and the view is replaced by the contents of that link. When you have two linked views, neither of which is locked, and you click a link in one, both views change to reflect the contents of the link. When a locked view is linked to an unlocked view and you click a link in the locked view, the contents of the link appears in the unlocked view. Click Unlock view to return the view to its normal, unlocked state. Refer to the tutorial on page 303.

Terminal Emulator

When you work locally, a linked terminal emulator (Window⇨Show Terminal Emulator) displays the appropriate cd command each time you change directories graphically in a linked view, helping you to alternate between the graphical interface and the character-based one within a single window.

Table 8-8 shows what to expect when you link various combinations of views, the Navigation panel, and the terminal emulator.

Links in Views, Navigation Panel, and Terminal Emulator	table 8-8
View and View	
No link, no lock	Each view displays whatever you click or enter in the location bar while it is the active view.
Link, no lock	Both views display the same thing: whatever you click or enter in the location bar while either window is active.
Link, lock	The unlocked view displays whatever you click in the locked or unlocked view or enter in the location bar while it is the active view. The locked view always displays the view that it displayed when you locked it.

Links in Views, Navigation Panel, and Terminal Emulator (Continued)   table 8-8

Navigation Panel and View	
No link, no lock	Navigation panel always displays the Navigation panel. The view displays whatever you click in the view or enter in the location bar (it is always the active view).
Link, no lock	Navigation panel always displays the Navigation panel. The view displays whatever you click in the Navigation panel or the view or enter in the location bar (it is always the active view).
Link, lock	Not very useful. The Navigation panel always displays the Navigation panel; when you lock the view, it always displays the view that it displayed when you locked it.
View and Terminal Emulator	
No link, no lock	No connection. The view and terminal emulator work independently.
Link, no lock	As long as you are working locally, the working directory of the terminal emulator is always the directory that the view displays.
Link, lock	Not very useful. When you lock the view, it always displays the same thing.

Shortcuts

A *shortcut*, called a key binding in earlier versions of KDE, is the connection between a key or keys (CONTROL-C, for example) that you hold/press at one time and an action that the system performs when you do so. Figure 8-17 shows the Konqueror menubar: Settings⇨Configure Shortcuts window with the action Copy at the top showing that CONTROL-C (Ctrl+C) is a shortcut for *copy* and that CONTROL-Insert is an alternate shortcut. The action Find file is highlighted in the figure with a shortcut of CONTROL-F. The bottom portion of the window shows that CONTROL-F is a Custom shortcut. When you highlight Copy, you see that CONTROL-C is a Default shortcut.

You can highlight any action and remove a shortcut by selecting None or revert to the default shortcut (if there is one) by selecting Default. Assign or change a custom binding by clicking the keycap button (the button with Ctrl+F in it in Figure 8-17) or the Custom radio button. The Define Shortcut window appears. To specify a

Figure 8-17   Configure Shortcuts window

single-key shortcut (clear the Multi-Key check box if it has a check mark in it) and press the key that you want to use for the shortcut. For a multiple-key shortcut put a check mark in the Multi-Key check box, press the key combination you want to use for the shortcut, and click OK. The names of the keys that are now bound to the highlighted action appear on the keycap button.

The shortcuts that you set in the Configure Shortcuts window apply to anything you do within Konqueror. You can set global and application shortcuts (page 321) in a similar manner. The bindings you establish in the Konqueror Configure Shortcuts window take precedence over other bindings that you set up.

Tutorial: Active, Linked, and Locked Views

Open Konqueror, enter www.redhat.com/docs in the location bar, and press RETURN. You may see a Cookie Alert; accept or reject *cookies* (page 1462) as you please. You should see a single Konqueror view similar to the one shown in Figure 8-18. Because there is only a single view, there are no Active View indicator and no Link indicator. You may want to make the window a little larger by dragging one of the corners.

Choose Red Hat Linux Manuals from the Software drop down menu and click Go. Click x86 Installation Guide. You should now see the table of contents for the current Installation Guide.[7] Open a second view by selecting Konqueror menubar: Window⇨Split View Left/Right. You should have two views, each showing the same page.

---

7. As Red Hat changes its Web site, the steps to display this page may change. If this procedure does not work, try going to www.redhat.com/docs/manuals/linux and selecting the x86 Installation Guide from there.

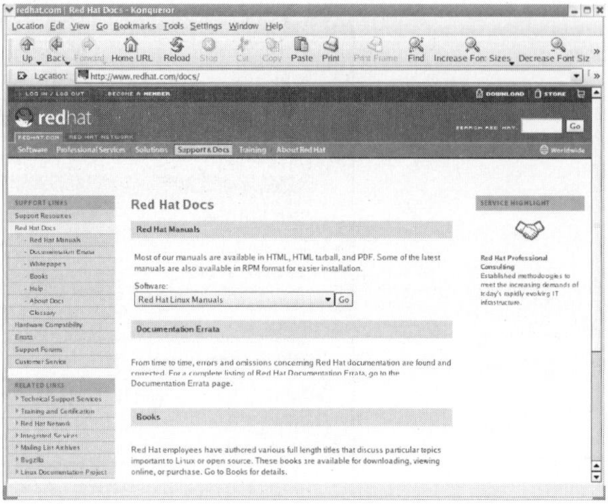

Figure 8-18   The Konqueror browser displaying the Red Hat **docs** page

If the two views are not already linked, click one of the view's square Link indicator until the small piece of a chain link fence appears in both views. In the left view scroll down (the right view will not move), and click the name of the section you want to look at. This tutorial uses *No boxed Set? No Problem!* in Chapter 1 of the Installation Guide. The manual appears in both views: not too useful. Click the left (Back) arrow on the toolbar to redisplay the previous views.

Now lock the left view by clicking within the left view to make it active (do not click a link) and selecting Konqueror menubar: View⇨Lock to current location. Locking prevents this view from changing, preventing the view from displaying the manual page when you click a link.

Now click the manual link in the left window again. What happens this time? The left view is forced to stay the same, but the (linked) right view changes to display the manual page (Figure 8-19). Now you can search the table of contents for the Installation Guide in the left view; and when you want to view another section, you simply click it in the left view. This type of link is useful in many situations. You can work with your Web site by bringing up the directory structure, via ftp, in the locked view while the Web pages are displayed in the other view.

When you get Konqueror set up the way you want for a particular purpose, you can put an icon on a panel that will open Konqueror that way.

1. Click Window⇨Configure View Profiles and enter the name of your profile following Enter Profile Name to save the setup. For this tutorial enter the name **newprofile**. Make sure that Save URLs in profile and Save window size in profile both have check marks next to them. Click Save.

2. Attach this new profile name to a panel icon: Drag the Home icon from the K menu to a clear space on the panel. If there is no clear space, see page 339. The dragged icon is a copy; the original icon is still on the K menu.

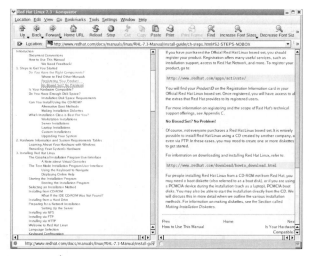

Figure 8-19   Konqueror: Two linked views with the left one locked

3. Right click the new button to display the Icon menu, and select Preferences. Click the icon under the General tab if you want to change the icon on the new Web button on the panel. Click the Execute tab, and change the word following `kfmclient openProfile` on the command line to the name of your profile (**newprofile** in this tutorial) so that the command line looks like this:

```
kfmclient openProfile newprofile
```

Click OK.

4. Click the new button to open the Konqueror views you designed.

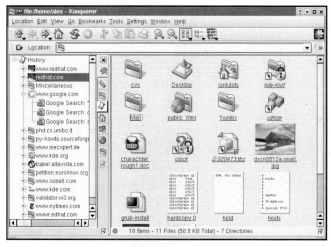

Figure 8-20   Konqueror Navigation panel is on the left

Close Navigation Panel

Navigation Panel Menu

Bookmarks

History

Home Directory

Sidebar media Player

Network

root Directory

Services

Figure 8-21   Navigation panel icons

Navigation Panel

The Konqueror Navigation panel (Figure 8-20) displays an expandable list of directories and pseudodirectories, similar to a tree view. Next to this list is a column of icons (Figure 8-21) that control what the list displays.

Turn the Navigation panel on and off by using Konqueror menubar: Window⇨Show Navigation panel (page 297). Although the Navigation panel is a view, it has a different background from other views and cannot be active. When the Navigation panel is linked to a view and you click an entry in the Navigation panel, Konqueror opens, in the linked view, the file/directory pointed to by the URL property of that entry.

The icons in the column of icons represent Desktop files (page 345) that are stored in **$KDEHOME/share/apps/konqsidebartng/entries**. Initially you see the icons shown in Figure 8-21. Click one of the icons to display a list of directories and files that correspond to the icon. In the list click a plus sign in a small box to expand a directory and see what is in it; click a minus sign in a box to collapse a directory. When you see an entry without a box next to it, click that entry to have Konqueror display it. When you click a directory in this manner, Konqueror displays a filemanager view of the directory. When you click a URL of a Web site, Konqueror displays the Web site.

Each of the initial icons in the Navigation panel gives you a different perspective on your system and what you have been doing with it (Table 8-9). You can modify, delete, and add to some of these icons by right clicking an icon (Table 8-10).

Navigation Panel Icons

|| table 8-9

Close Navigation panel	Closes the Navigation panel, including the menu.
Navigation Panel menu	The menu of icons shown in Figure 8-21.
Bookmarks	Displays a list of your bookmarks just as Bookmarks on the menu-bar does.
History	Lists the URLs of the sites you have visited recently.
Home directory	Lists the contents of your home directory.
Sidebar Media player	Plays different types of media when you drop a file on it.
Network	Lists some of the locations you can reach by using your network.
root directory	Lists the contents of the root (/) directory.
Services	Lists some of the services available on your system.

Navigation Panel Icon (Right Click) Menu

|| table 8-10

URL	Changes what the icon points to. Enter a local pathname or a URL of a Web or FTP site.
Icon	Opens the Select Icon window, which allows you to chose an icon.
Remove	Removes the icon from the list of icons.
Configure Navigation Panel	You can also display this menu by clicking the hammer-and-wrench icon or right clicking an empty part of the Icon menu.
Add New	After you add a new icon, you can subsequently change what it points to (**URL**) and what it looks like (**Icon**).
Folder/Directory	Gives you a choice of adding a bookmark, directory, or history icon to the list of Panel icons.
Sidebar Media Player	Adds a sidebar media player to the list of Panel icons.
Multiple Views	Enables the Navigation panel to display multiple views when you click more than one icon. Without this choice enabled, the Navigation panel replaces the existing view with a new one when you click an icon.

Navigation Panel Icon (Right Click) Menu (Continued)	‖ table 8-10
Show Tabs Left	Moves the list of icons to the left of the Navigation panel.
Show Extra Buttons	Displays the X (close Navigation panel) and hammer-and-wrench (configure Navigation panel) icons.
Close Navigation Panel	

Menus

This section describes the Desktop menus, Taskbar, Toolbar menu, Window List menu, and Operations menu in detail. Table 8-2 on page 276 lists all the common menus, their basic functions, and where to find information on each.

Desktop Menus

There are two Desktop menus.

- The Desktop menu that appears when you right click the root window is a pop-up menu that is displayed on the root window. This book refers to this menu as the *Pop-up Desktop menu* (Figure 8-22).

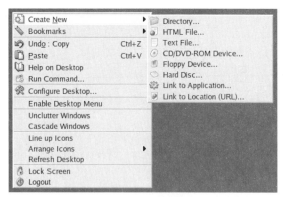

Figure 8-22   The Pop-up Desktop menu with the Create New submenu to the right

Figure 8-23 The Menubar Desktop menu displaying the New submenu

- The other Desktop menu appears at the top of the workspace when you choose Enable Desktop Menu from the Pop-up Desktop menu. This book refers to this menu as the *Menubar Desktop menu* (Figure 8-23).

  Unlike other desktop environments that have a menubar for each window, KDE has a single, optional menubar for all windows. The Menubar Desktop menu is always associated with the window that has the input focus; it is similar to other menubars but there is only one and it is not attached to any window. Table 8-11 describes the selections in both Desktop menus.

You can open a window or perform a task by making a selection from either Desktop menu. The Create New submenu of the Pop-up Desktop menu shown in Figure 8-22 is the same as the New submenu of the Menubar Desktop menu shown in Figure 8-23. Because these menus are so similar, Table 8-11 describes the selections of both menus.

Desktop Menus || table 8-11

In this table [pm] stands for the Pop-up Desktop menu and [mm] stands for the Menubar Desktop menu.	
File [mm]	Menu available on [mm] only; entries available on [pm].
Run Command	A top-level selection on [pm]. Refer to "Run Command" on page 282.
Lock Screen	A top-level selection on [pm]. Displays a screensaver and locks your keyboard. Move the mouse or press a key to display a password dialog box. When you enter your password and press RETURN, KDE unlocks the keyboard, removes the screensaver, and restores your workspace.

Desktop Menus (Continued) || table 8-11

Logout	A top-level selection on [pm]. Displays a dialog box that lets you end your KDE session. If you click **Restore session**, KDE saves all your KDE- and XSM- (X Session Manager) compliant windows and running programs as they are and restores your work areas next time you log in. See Autostart (page 346) to bring up noncompliant programs automatically when you start KDE.
New [mm] Create New [pm]	Creates new icons and files, links, and devices on your workspace (~/**Desktop** directory).
Bookmarks	
Edit Bookmarks	Opens the KDE Bookmark Editor (**keditbookmarks**).
[list of recent bookmarks]	Chooses one of these bookmarks to open it.
Undo [pm]	Undoes the last action on the workspace, such as copying, creating, or deleting an icon/file/pointer.
Paste [pm]	Pastes whatever is on the clipboard.
Desktop	Menu available on [mm] only; entries available on [pm].
Unclutter Windows	A top-level selection on [pm]. Calculates the best arrangement of windows on the workspace so that the greatest area of each window is visible and places the window in that arrangement.
Cascade Windows	A top-level selection on [pm]. Places windows on the workspace so that the upper-left corner of each is visible.
Line up Icons	A top-level selection on [pm]. Positions icons on the workspace so that they line up horizontally and vertically.
Arrange Icons	A top-level selection on [pm]. Specifies several ways of sorting files in the Directory window. Same as **Konqueror menubar: View⇨Sort**.
Refresh Desktop	A top-level selection on [pm]. Redraws the workspace.
Configure Desktop	A top-level selection on [pm]. Opens **K menu: Control Center⇨ Look & Feel⇨Desktop** (page 317).

Desktop Menus (Continued)	|| table 8-11
Enable/Disable Desktop Menu	A top-level selection on [pm]. Displays/removes the Menubar Desktop menu (page 308).
Windows [mm]	Displays the Window List menu (page 312). You can middle click on the root window to get the same menu.
Help Help on Desktop	Opens the KDE HelpCenter. Same as clicking the **help** button on a panel.

Taskbar

Each rectangle within the Taskbar displays the title of the window it represents (Figure 8-24). Click one of the rectangles to make the corresponding window active if it is not already active. Click the Taskbar rectangle corresponding to an active or iconified window to toggle the window between iconified and displayed (restored). Right click to display a menu with these choices: Minimize, Maximize, Restore, Shade (page 185), Always on Top (always visible on top of other windows), Close, and To Desktop (move the window to another workspace), To Current Desktop (move a window from another workspace to the displayed workspace. You can configure the Taskbar to represent the windows on all workspaces or just the windows on the displayed workspace (default).

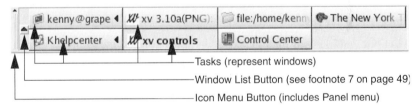

Figure 8-24   Taskbar

Toolbar Menu

Right click almost anywhere on a toolbar that has a handle to display the Toolbar menu (Table 8-12) which positions the toolbar within the window (Orientation); displays text, icons, or both on the toolbar (Text position); specifies the size of the icons on the toolbar (Icon size); or configures any of the toolbars (Configure Toolbars).

Toolbar Menu || table 8-12

Orientation	
Top, Left, Right, Bottom	Positions the toolbar along one of the sides of the window. You can also left click and drag the toolbar to where you want.
Flat	Closes the toolbar so that only the lined toolbar handle (page 342) is visible and rotates a vertical handle so that it is horizontal. Use the flat handle to access the toolbar menu or reopen the toolbar.
Text position	
Icons only	Displays only icons on the toolbar.
Text only	Displays only text on the toolbar.
Text aside icons	Displays text to the side of icons on the toolbar.
Text under icons	Displays text under icons on the toolbar.
Icon size	Selects the size that you would like the icons to appear on the toolbar.
Configure Toolbars [Konqueror only]	Refer to "Configure Konqueror Toolbar" on page 341.

Window List Menu

When you middle click the root window or click the Window List button on the Taskbar on a panel (Table 8-24),[8] KDE displays the Window List menu (Figure 8-25 left, and Table 8-13). For instructions on how to turn it off and on (default), refer to the entry "Show window list button" in the table on page 322. The Window List menu lists the workspaces and the windows open on each. Click one of the programs to display the workspace that contains the window for that program.

(Window) Operations Menu

The (window) Window Operations menu (Figure 8-25 right, right click a titlebar) has five basic choices: Move, Size, Minimize, Maximize, and Shade (page 185). Always On Top keeps the window visible on a stack of windows. Configure displays the

---

8. Put a check mark in K menu: Control Center⇨Look & Feel⇨Taskbar⇨Show window list button to display the Window List button on the Taskbar.

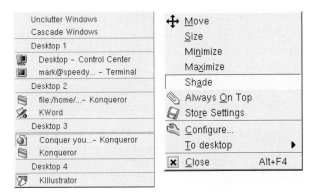

Figure 8-25   Window List menu (left), Operations menu (right)

Window Behavior (page 323) and Window Decoration (page 325) portions of the Control Center. To Desktop moves the window to another workspace or to all of them, and Close closes the window.

Window List Menu		‖ table 8-13
Unclutter Windows	Calculates the best arrangement of windows on the workspace so that the greatest area of each window is visible and places the window in that arrangement.	
Cascade Windows	Places windows on the workspace so that the upper-left corner of each is visible.	
Desktop 1	Lists all the windows open on the first workspace. Click a window in the list to switch to the workspace it is open on and make it the active window.	
Desktop 2	Lists all the windows open on the second workspace. Click a window in the list to switch to the workspace it is open on and make it the active window.	
[and so on. . .]		

Customizing KDE

Customizing a KDE desktop is not difficult; it is just another step in learning about KDE. You can customize many features with a few keystrokes and mouse clicks. Other features, such as designing and installing themes (page 323), are more difficult. The value of **KDEHOME** defaults to **~/.kde** when the variable is not set.

Control Center

The KDE Control Center allows you to get information on and control many aspects of your desktop: the K Desktop Environment and the kwin window manager. Bring up the Control Center window by clicking the Control Center icon on a panel (Figure 8-26) or choosing Control Center from the K menu. Tables 8-14 through 8-21 describe a basic set of Control Center menus; your menus may differ.

Make it Stick || tip

At the bottom of each Control Center window is an **Apply** button. Before you leave a window that you have made a change in, click **Apply** to keep the change. If you do not apply the change, you will lose it. (The Control Center does gracefully remind you when you forget.)

Figure 8-26   Control Center icon

About Myself

Displays the User Information window which can modify your entry in the **/etc/passwd** file; also can change your login shell.

File Browsing

In addition to file browsing, the Control Center offers control over LAN browsing (page 992) and Web browsing (page 334). The File Browsing section (Table 8-14) controls file associations (MIME types, page 178), File Manager behavior and appearance, and kuick, the Quick Copy and Move plugin.

KDE Control Center⇨File Browsing || table 8-14

File Associations	View and change file-type associations and MIME types (page 178).
Find filename pattern	Finds the file type associated with a filename pattern (usually a filename extension). Enter a pattern (such as **mp3**) in this text box and descriptive information appears to the right. Alternatively, you can use the **Known Types** frame, following.

KDE Control Center⇨ File Browsing (Continued)

|| table 8-14

Known Types	Finds a file type by presenting you with a tree view of all file types. For example, the MIME group **audio** appears under Known Types. Double-click **audio**, then click **x-mp3** (the MIME subgroup); descriptive information appears to the right. Alternatively, you can use the Find filename pattern text box, preceding.
General	Allows you to change which filename patterns are associated with which programs. For example, the image type **jpeg**, with a Description of JPEG image, is associated with the filename extensions (MIME types, page 178) **jpeg**, **jpg**, and **JPG**. The Application Preference Order specifies the programs that KDE uses to open this type of file in the order it tries the programs (not all may be installed on your system). Select an application from the list, and you can change its order (**Move Up** or **Move Down**), **Edit**, or **Remove** it. You can also add new applications.
Embedding	
Left click action	Choose how you want Konqueror to display a file: in an embedded viewer (in a view within the Konqueror window), in a separate/external viewer, or using the MIME-type specifications for the group the file's file type belongs to.
Services Preference Order	When the names of one or more tools appear in this box and you right click in Konqueror a file that matches one of the Filename Patterns specified under the **General** tab, **Preview in** appears in the menu that Konqueror displays. Click **Preview in**, and you will see the programs that are listed in this box. When nothing is in this box, the **Preview in** selection does not appear. Use the buttons on the side to change the order the programs are listed in and/or add or delete programs.
File Manager	When you click the file manager button on a panel or on the Konqueror toolbar (both have little houses) or on a directory, Konqueror displays the Konqueror file manager (page 288). This module sets the Konqueror options specific to file management.
Behavior	
Open directories in separate windows	When Open directories in separate windows is not checked (default) and you click a directory within the File Manager, Konqueror replaces the active view with the contents of the directory that you clicked on. When you check this box, the File Manager opens a new window to display each directory you click.
Show network operations in a single window	Displays information on all concurrent downloads in a single Collected Download Dialog box as opposed to information on each download appearing in an Individual Download Dialog box.
Show file tips	Displays information about a file when you move the mouse pointer over the file. **Number of file tip entries** specifies how many pieces of information are shown for each file.

KDE Control Center⇨File Browsing (Continued)   ‖ table 8-14

Home URL	The Home URL is the address of the directory or URL that Konqueror displays when you click the **home** icon (house and file folder), frequently your home directory (~).
Minimize memory usage	Controls when Konqueror tries to conserve memory. When you have enough memory, conserving memory slows Konqueror down. When you do not have enough memory, it can speed things up. When you are working with the File Manager aspects of Konqueror, **For local browsing** is the recommended choice; **Always** is not recommended unless you have very little memory.
Appearance	Specifies the font family, size, and color for the file manager. You can also specify that you want the text under the icons to be word-wrapped (it is truncated if you do not check this box) and that you want the filenames underlined (may make them more readable). **Display file sizes in bytes** affects the nonicon views of Konqueror the File Manager.
Trash	Specifies whether you have to confirm when you move a file to the trash, delete a file, or shred a file.
Previews	Replaces desktop icons for HTML, image, PostScript/PDF, text, and many other types of files, with small preview images showing the contents of the file. The sound file is played when the mouse pointer hovers over the icon representing a sound file. Select the types of files (protocols) that you want to see previews for. Set the Maximum file size to the largest size file that you want to see a preview for. Files over this size will not display previews.
Quick Copy & Move Plugin	Configures **kuick**, the Quickcopy and Move plugin for Konqueror. These frames affect the Copy To and Move To submenus that are displayed when you right click an icon in a Konqueror window and some icons in the root window. After making a change here, you must bring up a new Konqueror window to see the results.

Information

The Information section of the Control Center (Table 8-15) displays information about system components.

KDE Control Center⇨Information   ‖ table 8-15

There are many entries under Information; this section covers just a few.	
Block Devices	Displays a graphical version of **df**, with bar charts indicating the amount of each device in use and icons that you can click to mount devices (if you have permission).
Memory	Displays a graph of memory usage (may not be accurate).
Processor	Displays information about the CPU(s) in your system.

Login Photo

The Login Photo section of the Control Center sets up an identification photo that you can click on, instead of typing your name, to log in on the system. GDM (GNOME Display Manager) must be set up in order to use this option.

Look & Feel

The Look & Feel section of the Control Center (Table 8-16) controls how information is presented to the user, including all the elements on the desktop.

KDE Control Center⇨Look & Feel	‖ table 8-16
Background	Sets up one background for all workspaces or a different background for each. You can specify a **Mode** (flat, pattern, vertical gradient, and so on) and **Color 1**. Refer to "kcolorchooser: Selects a Color" on page 281 for help with the Select Color window. When you specify a **Mode** with a **Gradient**, you can choose **Color 2**. The **Wallpaper** tab allows you to specify one or more wallpapers, each remaining on the window for a period of time; the **Advanced** tab lets you specify the balance and blending of wallpapers. You can specify a maximum amount of memory (cache) that KDE will use to store the image.
Colors	Specifies a color scheme for the windows and desktop. Click one of the **Color Schemes** and see it rendered at the top of the window. You can modify the displayed color scheme by working with the Widget color frame: Select the component as labeled at the top of the window and specify a color for that component by clicking the color bar. When you click the color bar Konqueror displays the Select Color window (page 281). Click a color and then click **OK**. Save scheme in the **Color Scheme** tab to give the scheme a name. You can delete only schemes that you have created.
Desktop	
Desktop	
Enable Desktop Menu	Displays the Menubar Desktop menu along the top of the workspace (page 308).
Enable Icons on Desktop	Permits icons to appear on the workspace.
Align Icons Vertically on Desktop	Displays icons vertically along the left side of the workspace starting at the top. By default they are displayed horizontally across the top.
Show Hidden Files on Desktop	Displays icons on the workspace for files whose names begin with a period.
Programs in Desktop Window	Enables X programs, such as **xsnow**, that display on the root window. This option may disable some X programs.
Show Previews for	Displays a subset of the choices in the **Previews** frame. See "Previews" on page 316.

KDE Control Center⇨Look & Feel (Continued) || table 8-16

<u>Clicks on the desktop</u>	Specifies what happens when you click each of the mouse buttons on the root window.
Appearance	Controls the workspace font color and size. Text Background Color controls the color of the box around the icon labels on the workspace. If you do not check this box, there will be no text background so you will see the wallpaper or color. If you choose to underline filenames, readability may be improved.
Number of Desktops	Use the slider to specify the number of workspaces you want. Change the workspace names in the text boxes.
Paths	Specifies where files that control KDE are located. Be careful: Changing these files can cause your desktop to stop working. You can change the **Desktop path** (where desktop information is stored), **Trash path**, **Autostart path** (page 346), and the **Documents path** (where you keep your documents). When you change one of these paths KDE, moves the files in the old directory to the new one.
Fonts	Controls the size and style of fonts that KDE uses for various tasks. Click **Use Anti-Aliasing for fonts** to turn on *antialiasing* (page 1454).
Icons	
Theme	Allows you to install a new theme, remove an existing one, or select a theme from the window. Click each selection, and watch the icons at the top of the window change. Additional themes available at www.kde-look.org. The default theme under Red Hat is Bluecurve.
Advanced	Specifies configuration for icons that are used for different purposes. Select from the Use of Icon list, and then specify how these icons are to appear in the rest of this tab. To the right of this list, you can specify the size of the icons in pixels: double-sized pixels for larger, blocky icons, and Blend alpha channel for smoother transitions between icons and their backgrounds. Blend alpha channel can make icons flicker, so you may not want to use it. The lower portion of the **Advanced** tab controls how the icons appear in their default, active (when the mouse pointer is over them), and disabled states. Click the **Set Effect** button that appears below the state you want to change.
Launch Feedback	
Busy Cursor	Displays a cursor showing some action when you start a program. It is easy to see this cursor when you start KDE. You can choose to have the cursor blink. Because some programs may not recognize the busy cursor, Startup indication timeout specifies the number of seconds before the busy cursor is turned off.

KDE Control Center⇨Look & Feel (Continued) || table 8-16

Taskbar Notification	Displays an hourglass in motion on the Taskbar when you start a program. Because some programs may not recognize the Taskbar notification, Startup indication timeout specifies the number of seconds before the busy cursor is turned off.
Panel	You can also display this section by choosing **Panel menu: Preferences**.
Position	*This tab refers to kicker (the Main panel) only.* Refer to "Extensions" on page 321 for information on changing extension panels. See page 338 for a discussion of panels.
Location	Specifies the side of the workspace that you want **kicker** to appear: **Left**, **Right**, **Top**, or **Bottom**. You can also change the position of **kicker** by clicking and dragging a **Hide** button (page 278) or any blank place on **kicker**.
Alignment	Specifies whether **kicker** is to be aligned with the right or left edge of the workspace or centered.
Size	Specifies the size of **kicker** from **Tiny** through **Large** or **Custom**.
Length	Specifies the percent of the height or width of the workspace that **kicker** is to occupy. When you select the **Expand to fit required size** option, **kicker** expands beyond the percentage that you specify, if necessary, to fit all the objects it is displaying.
Hiding	
Hide Buttons	Displays **Hide** buttons at none, one, or both ends of **kicker** (page 278).
Hide Button Size	Use the slider to specify the size of the **Hide** buttons.
Manual Hide Animation	Causes **kicker** to flow gently off the workspace when you click a **Hide** button (page 278) instead of disappearing all at once. Use the slider to specify how quickly **kicker** disappears.
Automatic Hide	**Enable Automatic Hide** causes **kicker** to disappear from the workspace automatically once you have moved the mouse pointer off it. It appears again when you move the mouse pointer to the edge of the workspace that it disappeared from. Use the slider to specify the number of seconds that **kicker** remains visible after you move the mouse pointer off it. **Show panel when switching desktop** displays **kicker** when you move from one workspace to another, as when you press CONTROL-TAB.
Automatic Hide Animation	Causes **kicker** to flow gently off the workspace when it is time for it to disappear automatically instead of disappearing all at once (only when you **Enable automatic hide**). Use the slider to choose how quickly **kicker** disappears.

KDE Control Center⇨Look & Feel (Continued) || table 8-16

Look & Feel	
General	
Enable background tiles	Turns on background tiles and allows you to make selections from the other frames in this tab.
Enable icon zooming	Causes tiny, small, and medium panel buttons to expand when the mouse pointer passes over them. Refer to "Size" on page 319.
Show tooltips	Displays tooltips on objects on panels (page 270).
K-Menu Tiles	Enables and specifies background tiles for panel buttons. A background tile is a colored and sometimes textured rectangle that appears behind a button. You can specify a different color/texture for each of six types of tiles: K-Menu, Application Launcher, Window List, Quickbrowser, Legacy Application Launcher, and Desktop Access Tiles.
Background Image	Just as you can choose an image for the root window, you can choose one for kicker. Check the box and specify the absolute pathname of the image file you want to use.
Menus	This tab controls various aspects of the K menu.
K menu Layout	This frame specifies whether the following submenus appear on the K menu.
Show side image	Displays a decorative image along the side of the K menu.
Show "Recent Documents" submenu	Displays a submenu that lists the documents you have used so that you can edit them again quickly and easily. Also refer to Quick Start.
Detailed menu entries	Adds parenthetical comments after program names in K menu submenus.
Show "Bookmarks" submenu	Displays a submenu that allows you to browse and edit your list(s) of bookmarks (page 300).
Show "Quick Browser" submenu	Displays a submenu that gives you quick access to files in commonly used directories (page 274).
Available/Selected Menus	Lists the K menu plugins on your system and allows you to activate/deactivate them.
Browser menus	
Show hidden files in browser menus	Displays files whose names begin with a period in the K menu⇨Quick Browser (page 274).

KDE Control Center⇨Look & Feel (Continued) || table 8-16

Maximum browser menu entries	Determines how many entries appear in the K menu⇨Quick Browser (page 274). The smaller your workspace and the lower the resolution, the fewer the entries that will fit on the workspace at one time.
Max number of "Quick Start" entries	The Quick Start entries appear at the top of the K menu and quickly start programs you have run before. See also **"Quick Start" section contains** (following).
"Quick Start" section contains	Specifies whether the **Most recently used items** or **Most frequently used items** appear at the top of the **K menu**.
Extensions	Controls panel extensions. **Panel Location**, **Automatic Hide**, **Hide Buttons**, and **Hide Button Size** work the same way as their counterparts do for **kicker**. Refer to "Position" on page 319 and "Hiding" on page 319. Select the extension you want to work with from the **Extensions** column, and make the changes you want to the right. Click **Apply**, and then work with another extension, if appropriate. The Extensions column displays only extensions that appear on your workspace. You cannot add extensions using this tab; use **Panel menu: Add⇨Extension** (page 340) to add an extension.
Screensaver	Allows you to specify a screensaver (**Random** gives you a taste of each), test it, specify its priority, and specify how long it takes after your last keystroke before it starts. You can also require a password for making changes to the settings.
Shortcuts	
Shortcut Schemes	Works the way that Konqueror shortcuts work (refer to "Shortcuts" on page 302), but you can choose from different **Schemes** at the top of the window. The tabs allow you to choose among working with **Global shortcuts** (non-application-specific bindings), **Shortcut Sequences** (moving windows to different workspaces and switching workspaces), and **Application shortcuts** (bindings normally used within an application). Make the changes you want and click **Save**. Because **konsole** runs a shell, the CONTROL-C (for copy) and other bindings do not work within a **konsole** window.
Modifier Keys	Displays the modifier keys (SHIFT, CONTROL, and so on) and their X-11 mappings. This tab allows you to specify a Macintosh keyboard and to cause KDE to behave more like the MacOS.
Style	Specifies how KDE draws widgets (buttons, menus, scrollbars, and so on).
Style	
Widget style	Choose from a predefined style. The lower frame displays a sample of the selected style.

KDE Control Center⇨Look & Feel (Continued) || table 8-16

Effects	These choices turn on various subtle effects for combo boxes (drop-down menus), tooltips, and menus. Fade effects cause menus and tooltips to appear gradually, and animate effects cause menus to slide in or drop down more slowly than otherwise. In order to keep the effects from being tedious, they do not work on the K menu, only on the first appearance of one of its submenus.
Miscellaneous	
Misc Toolbar Settings	
Highlight buttons under mouse	Causes buttons to change color or otherwise let you know when the mouse pointer passes over them.
Transparent Toolbars when moving	Causes a toolbar to turn into an outline while you drag it, putting less of a load on your computer.
Toolbar Icons	Specifies whether to display icons or text only or a combination of the two in toolbars.
Visual Appearance	
Show Icons on buttons	Displays icons on buttons.
Enable Tooltips	Displays tooltips on application toolbars (page 270).
Menubar on top of the screen in the style of MacOS	Displays the menubar at the top of the screen.
Taskbar	Refer to "Taskbar" on page 311. You can also display this section by choosing **Panel menu: Preferences⇨Taskbar**.
Taskbar	
Show windows from all desktops	Displays all windows in the Taskbar, not just those on the current workspace.
Show window list button	Displays the **Window List** button (Figure 8-24, page 311).
Group similar tasks	Saves space on the taskbar by displaying a single icon/name for multiple, like windows. For example, when you have three terminal emulators running, you see a single terminal emulator on the taskbar. Click the icon/name, and the taskbar displays the names of each instance of the program for you to choose from.

KDE Control Center⇨Look & Feel (Continued) || table 8-16

Sort tasks by virtual desktop	Places the icons/names from the first workspace at the left/top of the taskbar, those from the second workspace next to the first, and so on.
Show application icons	Displays application icons in the taskbar. Disable this option to save space on the taskbar.
Actions	Specifies what action KDE takes when you click each of the mouse buttons while the mouse pointer is over a taskbar.
Theme Manager	Specifies a desktop theme (page 175) or creates a new one. For additional themes go to www.themes.org/themes/kde.
Window Behavior	*This section applies only when you use the KDE Window Manager,* kwin.
Focus	
Focus policy	Determines when window focus changes (when an active window becomes inactive or an inactive window becomes active). See "Changing the Input Focus" on page 182 for details.
Click to focus	Specifies that you must click within a window to make it the active window.
Focus follows mouse	Specifies that the window under the mouse pointer is the active window and remains active until the mouse pointer is over another window. When the mouse pointer is over the root window, the input focus remains with the last window that had the input focus.
Focus under mouse	Same as **Focus follows mouse**.
Focus strictly under mouse	Similar to **Focus under mouse**, but when you move the mouse off a window and onto the root window, the window becomes unfocused so that there is no input focus.
Auto Raise	Causes the active window to appear on top of (not be covered by) other windows automatically. Useful with all focus/mouse policies; automatic with **Click to focus**.
Click Raise	Causes a window to be raised only when you click it.
Keyboard	
Walk through windows mode	Specifies how window cycling works. In **KDE** mode window cycling works as described on page 184. In **CDE** mode there is no box, and the order of windows is not determined by their activity.
Traverse windows on all desktops	Specifies that ALT-TAB and ALT-SHIFT-TAB move through all windows, not just those on the current workspace.

KDE Control Center⇨Look & Feel (Continued) || table 8-16

Actions	Sets up what happens when you click different parts of active and inactive windows. Refer to "Mouse Click and Result" on page 271. KDE displays the **Operations menu** when you right click the titlebar (page 273); **Nothing** means that the click does nothing, and **pass click** means that when you click an inactive window and it has been made active (given the input focus), your mouse click is passed to the now active window.
Titlebar double-click	Specifies what happens when you double-click on a window's titlebar.
Titlebar and frame	Specifies results of clicking the titlebar or frame of an active or inactive window with each mouse button.
Inactive inner window	Specifies results of clicking the inner part of an inactive window with each mouse button.
Inner window, titlebar and frame	Specifies what happens when you hold the ALT or META key (as specified by **Modifier Key**) and click any part of an active or inactive window with each of the mouse buttons.
Moving	
Windows	The first three of these choices use more computer power when checked. Leave the boxes unchecked on lower-powered machines or when KDE is not very responsive during the action.
Display content in moving windows	Displays the contents of a window as you drag it.
Display content in resizing windows	Displays the contents of a window as you resize it.
Animate Minimize and Restore	Shrinks window into and expands it out of the taskbar on a panel instead of disappearing and appearing all at once. Use the slider to control the speed of the animation.
Allow Moving and Resizing of maximized windows	Makes the borders and titlebar of a maximized window active so that you can move and re-size it. When not checked, you cannot perform these operations on a maximized window.
Placement	Determines how KDE places a new window on the workspace. **Smart** means place the window so that it overlaps the least existing window area possible. **Cascade** means that the windows are overlapping. **Random** means place the windows randomly.
Snap Zones	
Border snap zone	Specifies how close, in pixels, to the edge of the workspace you must drag a window before it will snap to the workspace edge.
Window snap zone	Specifies how close, in pixels, two windows must be before the moving window snaps to the other.

KDE Control Center⇨Look & Feel (Continued) || table 8-16

Snap windows only when overlapping	Causes windows to snap only when they overlap another window or the edge of the workspace.
Advanced	
Shading	Refer to "Shading a Window" on page 185.
Animate	Rolls window up slowly into titlebar instead of disappearing all at once.
Enable Hover	Refer to "Shading a Window" on page 185. The Delay specifies the amount of time that the mouse pointer must remain over the titlebar before the window unshades.
Xinerama	Allows window managers (and applications) to use two or more physical displays as one large virtual display. Xinerama is an extension of XFree86 Release 6 Version 4.0 (X4.0). Refer to sourceforge.net/projects/xinerama and to the *Xinerama-HOWTO*.
Active Desktop Borders	Enables you to move windows or the mouse pointer from one workspace to an adjacent workspace by holding the window or cursor against the edge of a workspace for the amount of time specified by the slider. Makes it difficult to raise the panel when it is set to automatic hide.
Window Decoration	Window decorations comprise the titlebar and border of a window. Aside from the aesthetic aspects of changing window decoration, you can alter the functionality by modifying the number and placement of buttons on the titlebar.
General	
Window Decoration	Choose a decoration from this frame, and click **Apply** to see what it looks like. Select the previous decoration if you do not like it.
General Options (if available)	
Use custom titlebar positions	Enables the **Buttons** tab.
Show window button tooltips	Displays tooltips when the mouse pointer hovers over a window button.
Buttons	Allows you to reposition and remove buttons on the titlebar. You can also add buttons that you previously removed. Drag the buttons on the preview titlebar to reposition them; drag them to the available items list (below **Spacer**) to remove them; and drag them from the available items list to the preview titlebar to add them. You can drag as many spacers as you want to position buttons exactly where you want.
Configure [...]	Holds material generated by the selected decoration: as simple as a check box (ModSystem) or more complex (IceWM). Follow your intuition and the instructions in this tab.

Network

Refer to "KDE Control Center: Network Module" on page 992.

Password

Allows you to change your password.

Peripherals

The Peripherals section of the Control Center (Table 8-17) controls an optional digital camera, the system keyboard, and the system mouse.

KDE Control Center⇨Peripherals   ‖ table 8-17

Digital Camera	Allows you to work with a digital camera from within Konqueror or other KDE applications. Click the icon of the camera, and set it up as required. Go to camera:/ in Konqueror to view and download pictures. This is an interface to **gphoto2** (www.gphoto.org).
Keyboard	
Layout	
Enable keyboard layouts	Turns on the **Configuration** frame so that you can configure your keyboard layout.
Configuration	
Keyboard Model	Specifies the physical model of the keyboard you are using.
Primary Layout	Specifies which keys generate which characters, based on the language you are working in.
Primary Variant	Further defines the keyboard.
Additional layouts	Specifies one or more additional layouts. You can choose from among these layouts or make further changes to the list of layouts by right clicking the flag icon in the system tray (in the panel).
Options	
Switching Policy	Specifies whether the keyboard layout switches on a **Global**, **Window Class**, or **Window** basis.
Xkb Options	Specifies various options about the X keyboard.
Advanced	
Keyboard repeat	Allows you to hold a key down for a period of time instead of repeatedly pressing the key to generate multiple keystrokes.

KDE Control Center⇨Peripherals (Continued)

|| table 8-17

Key click volume	Controls the loudness of the simulated key clicks. Set to zero to turn off key clicks.
NumLock on KDE startup	Specifies whether NumLock is turned on, off, or remains unchanged when KDE starts up.
Mouse	
General	
Button Mapping	Select **Right** or **Left** handed to switch the functions of the right and left mouse buttons. Does not affect the function of the middle mouse button. This book assumes a right-handed mouse. When you change to a left-handed mouse, you need to switch each of the right/left click instructions in this book.
Icons	
Single-click to open files and folders	Requires a single click to activate an icon. Selected by default. Select an icon without open-ing it by dragging a box around it or holding down the CONTROL key when you click it.
Change pointer shape over icons	Causes the mouse pointer to change from an arrow to a hand over an icon.
Automatically select icons	Causes an icon to be selected when the mouse pointer is on top of it. Use the slider to change the amount of time that the pointer must remain over the icon for it to be selected.
Double-click to open files and folders (select icons on first click)	Requires a double-click to activate an icon (a single click selects it).
Visual feedback on activation	Causes a dashed box to appear briefly and expand around an icon when you activate it. Does not affect the icon appearing to be pressed when you activate it. Turn off to improve slightly the speed of navigating between directories in Konqueror while reducing visual feedback.
Large Cursor	Doubles the size of the mouse pointer to make it more visible. Restart KDE for this selec-tion to take effect.
Advanced	
Pointer Acceleration Pointer Threshold	When you first move the mouse, the mouse pointer moves on the workspace at the same speed that you move the mouse (the pointer moves 1x the speed of the mouse). After you move it over the number of pixels specified by Pointer Threshold, the mouse pointer can move a number of times faster than you move the mouse, as specified by the Pointer Ac-celeration. The faster you make the Pointer Acceleration, the larger you should make the Pointer Threshold.
Double Click Interval	The longest time between two clicks in order for KDE to consider them a double-click. If the time is longer, KDE considers them as two single clicks.

KDE Control Center⇨Peripherals (Continued) || table 8-17

Drag Start Time Drag Start Distance	Time/distance after you start dragging an object before the object starts to move. These delays help prevent you from dragging objects when you do not mean to. They are not used together; rather some applications use one and some use the other.
Mouse Wheel Scrolls By	Specifies the number of lines that one step or click of the mouse wheel scrolls.

Personalization

The Personalization section of the Control Center (Table 8-18) controls accessibility for disabled users; country and language specific settings; cryptography, Konsole, spell checking, and password set up; and session manager configuration.

KDE Control Center⇨Personalization || table 8-18

Accessibility	These choices make it easier for some people to use KDE. Refer to the *Linux Accessibility HOWTO* for more information.
Bell	
Audible bell	
Use System bell	Uses the computer's internal speaker to emit a beep when a bell is called for.
Use customized bell	Uses the computer's soundcard to play the sound file that you specify in Sound to play when a bell is called for.
Visible bell	The colors on the screen are inverted, or a color is flashed on the screen when a bell is called for. Specify the color by clicking the button to the right of the words Flash screen. Specify the duration of the inversion or the color by using the slider labeled Duration.
Keyboard	
Sticky Keys Use sticky keys	Specifies that pressing a modifier key (SHIFT, ALT, or CONTROL) and then another key sequentially performs the same function as depressing and holding the modifier key while you press the other key. Allows you to press CONTROL and release it before pressing C instead of pressing and holding CONTROL while you press C.
Lock sticky keys	Similar to sticky keys but when you press the modifier key twice, it stays activated until you press it again. Thus SHIFT SHIFT nnn would yield NNN.
Slow Keys	Does not accept a keystroke unless you hold the key down for at least the amount of delay time specified by the slider.

KDE Control Center⇨Personalization (Continued) || table 8-18

Bounce Keys	Does not accept a second keystroke until the amount of delay time specified by the slider has elapsed.
Mouse	Select **Move mouse with keyboard (using the Num pad)** to use the keys on the *numeric pad* of the keyboard to perform functions otherwise performed using the mouse. Use the sliders in this tab to adjust how the ARROW keys move the mouse pointer. • ARROW keys on the *numeric pad* move the mouse pointer. • Press RETURN to click. • DEL + 0 (zero) selects item the mouse pointer is over. • DEL then opens the selected item. • Or ARROW keys drag the selected item. • After dragging DEL drops the item with choice of **Copy**, **Move**, or **Link**. • ESCAPE cancels the drag.
Country & Language	Experiment with the Numbers, Money, Time & Dates settings, and see the results immediately in the box at the bottom of the window.
Locale	Specifies the country and language you want to use. To add a language that there is a translation for, download the **kde-i18n** package from an ftp.kde.org mirror and install it. The language should appear in this section of the Control Center once you restart it. At the bottom of this tab is a listing of how everything that you can set in the remaining tabs in this section looks.
Numbers	Specifies the characters to use for the decimal symbol, thousands separator, and the positive and negative signs when the system displays a number.
Money	Specifies the characters to use for the currency symbol, decimal symbol, thousands separator, and the number of fractional digits (for example, cents would occupy two fractional digits) when the system displays a monetary amount. Also specifies, for both positive and negative money amounts, whether to use a currency symbol and where to place it.
Time & Dates	Specifies the Date, Short date, and Time formats. When you do not put a check mark in Start week on Monday, the week starts on Sunday.
Other	Specifies the **Paper Format** and the **Measure System** (**Imperial** or **Metric**).
Crypto	*Experts only:* Controls the way applications running under KDE exchange encrypted information using files and/or networks. Three check boxes near the bottom of the **SSL** tab control whether you are warned as you enter and exit SSL mode and when you send unencrypted data. Everything else controls which encryption methods are used. Make changes here only if you know what you are doing.

KDE Control Center⇨Personalization (Continued)   ‖ table 8-18

Konsole	
General	
Default Terminal Application Use Konsole as default terminal application	Specifies that **konsole** is called as the default terminal application, as when you click the **terminal** icon on the control panel. When you want to use another program, remove the mark from this check box, and put the name of the program that you want to use in the Default Terminal text box.
Misc	
Show Terminal Size when Resizing	Displays a small rectangle that shows the dimension, in columns and rows, of the terminal window as you resize it.
Show Frame	Displays an inner frame (line) around the inside of the Konsole window.
Warn for Open Sessions on Quit	Displays a warning dialog box when you attempt to quit Konsole while you have more than one open session (other shells, consoles, and so on).
Blinking Cursor	Causes the Konsole cursor to blink.
Require Ctrl key for drag and drop	Prevents normal drag-and-drop of text unless you hold the CONTROL key down during the action.
Line Spacing	Specifies the spacing between lines of text on Konsole. **Normal** and **1** show single spacing (no blank lines).
Double Click	Double-clicking text highlights a word. The characters in the text box are considered part of that word.
Schema	Specifies what the Konsole window looks like. You can choose any of the schemata in the Schema frame from any Konsole window (**Konsole menubar: Settings⇨Schema**). When you want Konsole windows to come up with a specific schema automatically, you must specify that schema as the default schema in the Schema frame.
Title	Displays the title of the schema you are working with as shown in the Schema frame. Enter a new title in this text box when you want to create a new schema.
Colors	Specifies the colors that the schema named in Title uses.
Schema	Chooses an existing schema to work with. Changes the name in the Title text box.
Set as default schema	Sets the highlighted schema as the default schema.
Save Schema	Saves the highlighted schema under the name in the Title text box.

KDE Control Center⇨Personalization (Continued) || table 8-18

Remove Schema	Removes the highlighted schema .
Background	Specifies an image to use as the background and the transparency of the Konsole window.
Session	Specifies the names and properties of Konsole sessions that you can select when you click and hold the **New** button on the Konsole toolbar (page 278). You can add and remove sessions as you please.
Write Daemon Start write daemon on KDE startup	Starts the daemon that allows you to use **write** (page 84) under KDE on your machine.
Passwords	Controls how **kdesu**, the program that puts up the dialog box asking you for the **root** password works. The first frame controls how the password you enter is echoed: **1 star** echoes one ✳ for each character you enter, **3 stars** echo ✳ ✳ ✳ for each character you enter, and **no echo** echoes nothing. Check Remember passwords to cause **kdesu** to remember and not ask you for the **root** password for the number of minutes you specify on the spinner.
Session Manager	
General	Specifies whether to display the End session dialog box to confirm a command to log out and whether the Save sessions for future logins box in the same dialog box has a check mark in it. Refer to "Session Manager" on page 185 for more information on session management.
Default action after logout	Specifies what action KDE should take after you log out.
Spell Checking	Sets **aspell** options for KDE applications. (The **ispell** utility is no longer used; the file with that name is now a brief shell script that translates **ispell** command line options into **aspell** options.) Refer to /usr/share/doc/aspell-✳/man-html/index.html for more information. Look for **aspell** to merge with **pspell** (see pspell.sourceforge.net).

Pilot/Handspring Tool

The Pilot/Handspring Tool section of the Control Center establishes a connection with your Pilot or Handspring PDA and allows you to work with the device.

Power Control

The Power Control section of the Control Center (Table 8-19) controls battery operation and monitoring for battery-powered computers and energy conservation settings for the monitor.

KDE Control Center⇨Power Control || table 8-19

Battery Monitor	For computers that run on batteries. Displays the Battery Monitor and specifies how often to check (poll) the battery and which icons to display in the Battery Monitor.
Energy	For Energy Star Compliant monitors. Specifies how long before KDE puts the monitor in a Standby (minimum energy savings and a quick return to an active state), Suspend (large energy savings and a slow return to an active state), or Power Off (maximum energy savings and the slowest return to an active state) state. The time you specify starts at the last use of the keyboard or mouse. KDE activates the monitor when you use the mouse or keyboard again; use a key that will not have any effect, such as the CONTROL key.
Laptop & Low Battery	Specifies what happens when as the battery on a laptop runs down.

Sound

The Sound section of the Control Center (Table 8-20) controls various aspects of system sound including the system bell and system notifications.

KDE Control Center⇨Sound || table 8-20

Audio CD IO-Slave	Allows you to change settings for audio CD-ROMs. Each of the tabs covers device, encoding, or information-lookup settings: CDDA (CD-ROM digital audio), Ogg Vorbis (a format for encoding audio files, similar to MP3 but free with smaller file sizes and better fidelity, www.vorbis.com), MP3, and CDDB (Gracenote's CD-ROM database, which lets you look up title and track information for a CD-ROM you are playing: www.cddb.com).
Midi	Specifies the MIDI device that KDE uses. When you want a MIDI Mapper, check the Use Midi Mapper box and specify the program to use.
Mixer	Configures basic options of the KDE mixer, kmix. You can save the current volumes as the defaults, restore the default volumes, and specify that KDE load the default volumes when you log in. Maximum number of probed mixers specifies the number of sound cards in the system. The kmix mixer stops looking after it finds this many sound cards. Maximum number of probed devices per mixer specifies how many devices kmix should look for on each soundcard. Increase this number if kmix does not find all your devices.
Sound Server	Refer to "Sound" on page 346 for information on aRts as you read this section.
General	

KDE Control Center⇨Sound (Continued) | table 8-20

Start aRts soundserver on KDE startup	Starts the aRts sound server when KDE starts up. You may still be able to hear system sounds even when the aRts soundserver is not running because a separate sound program is used as a fallback. KDE-based multimedia applications, such as **noatun**, require the aRts soundserver to be running.
Enable network transparency	*For advanced users:* Allows aRts to enable one computer to send audio over the network and have it played on another.
Exchange security and reference info over the X11 server	*For advanced users:* Enables a secure method of communication between aRts servers.
Run soundserver with realtime priority	Refer to "Sound" on page 346.
Autosuspend if idle for *n* seconds	Allows non-aRts-enabled programs to use the sound device when aRts is idle. Also, because aRts uses CPU time even if it not playing sounds, you may find that your system is more responsive if you allow aRts to suspend itself when it is idle when you are using aRts to play only system sounds.
Display messages using	Specifies how aRts should communicate to you: for example, when it cannot find the soundcard. There is usually no reason to change the default.
Message Display	Specifies which messages you want to see.
Sound I/O	
Sound I/O method	The aRts soundserver can output audio, using various methods. Which methods are available depends on which packages are installed on your system. The usual method is by using the OSS (Open Sound System), which is the standard GNU/Linux audio output system, and is automatically detected (**Autodetect**). Change this option only if you understand what the other output methods are.
Enable full duplex operation	Enables simultaneous recording and playing of audio. Usually, aRts configures a soundcard to allow only input *or* output but not both at the same time. Some soundcards do not work properly with full duplex enabled.
Use custom sound device	*For advanced users:* Passes the option to the GNU/Linux sound system.

KDE Control Center ⇨ Sound (Continued) || table 8-20

Use custom sampling rate	Changes the sampling rate. The *sampling rate* is the amount of audio data passed to the soundcard during a period of time. Most soundcards work well at a sampling rate of 44,100Hz (44,100 samples per second.) Some soundcards work best with a different sampling rate.
Other custom options	*For advanced users:* Refer to the aRts project page (www.arts-project.org) for information on available options.
Sound quality	Most soundcards work well with 16-bit audio (CD quality), but some older soundcards can play only 8-bit audio (telephone quality). **Autodetect** usually picks the right quality.
Audio buffer size (response time)	Determines how quickly aRts gets audio from a program to the soundcard. A larger buffer size (slider toward the right) is appropriate for casual listening and system sounds.
System Bell	By default KDE uses System Notifications to alert you to important events. System Notifications can be whatever you want: playing a sound, displaying a message box, and so on. Check Use System Bell instead of System Notification to revert to the system beep method of notification. After you check this box, you can control the **Volume**, **Pitch**, and **Duration** of the system bell by using the sliders. See also "Bell" on page 328.
System Notifications	Allows you to specify whether and how you want to be notified when various events occur. Expand the tree menu to see the events. For each event, you can specify zero to four notification options: **Log to file**, **Play sound**, **Show messagebox**, and **Standard error output**. For the first two you specify a log file or sound file.

System

Refer to "KDE Control Center: System Module" on page 988 in Chapter 17.

Web Browsing

The Web Browsing section of the Control Center (Table 8-21) controls the use of cache, cookies, proxies, stylesheets, and the user agent and enhanced browsing and other Konqueror-specific settings.

KDE Control Center ⇨ Web Browsing || table 8-21

Cache	Stores recently downloaded Web pages in memory for faster repeat access. This section defines *cache* (page 1459) policy and size.
Use Cache	*Enables the rest of this tab.* Causes the Konqueror Web browser to use cache.

KDE Control Center⇨Web Browsing (Continued) || table 8-21

Policy	Specifies how aggressively Konqueror keeps the cache current. **Keep Cache in sync** causes Konqueror to check cache and, if the page is not there, to download it to cache and then display it from cache. **Use Cache if possible** causes Konqueror to check cache for the requested page and download and display if it is not there. **Offline Browsing Mode** causes Konqueror to check cache and give up if the requested page is not there.
Disk Cache Size	Specifies the average amount of memory the cache is to occupy.
Clear Cache	Clears cache memory.Refer to "KDE Control Center: System Module" on page 988
Cookies	These settings apply to the Konqueror browser only. Other browsers (Netscape, Mozilla, and so on) have their own ways for you to deal with *cookies* (page 1462).
Policy	
Enable Cookies	Enables the browser to use cookies. Leave blank if you do not want to use cookies at all.
Default Policy	Specifies the default policy for cookies. You can override this policy in the next frame.
Domain specific policy	Adds/deletes hosts with specific cookie policies. Specify a policy of **Accept**, **Reject**, or **Ask** for each host.
Management	Displays cookies grouped by domain in a tree view. Expand a domain to see the individual cookies. Highlight a cookie in the Host column to see the details in the Cookie Details frame. Delete cookies as you desire.
Enhanced Browsing Keywords	*Applies to the Konqueror browser only:* Displays and allows you to manipulate a list of Web Shortcuts. Refer to "Enhanced Browsing" on page 290.
Enable Internet Keywords	Enables Internet keyword searches without Web shortcuts. Uses the search engine you specify in Fallback Search Engine.
Fallback Search Engine	Specifies the search engine that Konqueror uses when you do not specify one.
Enable Web Shortcuts	Enables Web shortcuts in Internet keyword searches and allows you to add, delete, or change shortcuts (page 290).
Konqueror Browser	*Applies to Konqueror only:* Changes are made the next time you open Konqueror.
HTML	

KDE Control Center ⇨ Web Browsing (Continued) || table 8-21

Form Completion Enable completion of forms	Enables Konqueror to fill out Web forms for you. Maximum completions specifies the maximum number of fields that you want Konqueror to fill in.
Change cursor over links	Causes the mouse pointer to change to a hand when it is over a link.
Right click goes back in history	Causes a right click to display the previously displayed Web page.
Automatically load images	Causes images to be loaded when a page is loaded (default). For a slow connection, do not check this box, and load images manually by clicking the box that appears in place of the image.
Allow automatic delayed reloading / redirecting	Allows Konqueror to process requests from a server to reload a page or redirect you to another page.
Underline Links	Specifies whether links in the browser are underlined or whether they are underlined only when the mouse pointer is hovering over the link.
Animations	Specifies how/whether you want to view those annoying little moving things on Web pages.
Appearance Font Size	
Minimum Font Size	Absolute minimum font size; cannot be overridden.
Medium Font Size	Specifies the default and base font size; used when a Web page does not specify a size and as a base size for HTML smaller and larger instructions.
Standard/Fixed/Serif ... Font	Specify the fonts you want to use for the HTML font encodings
Font size adjustment for this encoding	Adjusts font size when the font you have chosen is too large or too small.
Default Encoding	The fallback character set for use when a Web page does not specify one. Normally set to **Use language encoding**.
Java	Controls Konqueror's execution of Java, which allows Web sites to download and run programs on your machine.
Global Settings: Enable Java globally	*Enables the rest of this tab.* Allows Java to be used globally except for hosts/domains specified in the following frame. Use with caution, as Java from a remote site can jeopardize system security.

KDE Control Center ⇨ Web Browsing (Continued) || table 8-21

Domain-specific	Use this frame to specify domain-specific exceptions to the global Java policy.
Java Runtime Settings	Specifies settings to **Show Java Console**, **Use Security Manager**, and **Shutdown Applet Server when inactive**. Also specifies a nonstandard path for the Java program and additional arguments to appear on the Java command line.
JavaScript	Controls Konqueror's execution of JavaScript.
Global Settings: Enable JavaScript globally	Allows JavaScript to be used globally except for hosts/domains specified in the following frame.
Domain-specific	Use this frame to specify domain specific exceptions to the global JavaScript policy.
JavaScript web popups policy	Controls the ability of Web sites you visit to open new windows on your workspace. It can be annoying to have a remote Web site open a window that you have no interest in.
Plugins Global Settings: Enable Plugins globally	Permits Konqueror to use Netscape plugins.
Netscape Plugins	Konqueror can use Netscape plugins (for example, Flash and RealAudio)
Scan	Controls the search for Netscape plugins. You can ask KDE to scan the specified directories immediately and/or each time it starts The Scan Directories frame specifies which directories are to be searched.
Plugins	Lists the Netscape plugins that are in use.
Proxy	Controls the use of *proxies* (pages 397 and 1016). Select **Use Proxy** to enable the rest of this tab. Specifies Automatic, semiautomatic, or manual configuration and authorization.
Stylesheets	The term *stylesheet* (page 1495) is short for Cascading Stylesheets (CSS), which control the way a Web page appears in a browser. This section affects KDE applications that use the **khtml** renderer, such as Kmail, KDE HelpCenter, and Konqueror.
General Stylesheets	Specifies whether to use the default stylesheet, one you have defined in a file, or one you define in the **Customize** tab.
Customize	Selecting **Use accessibility stylesheet defined in "Customize"-tab** from the **General** tab *enables the selections in this tab*. The choices in this tab can help people with reading disabilities see pages more clearly and easily. It is designed to override styles specified by Web pages that may make pages more difficult to read.

KDE Control Center ⇨ Web Browsing (Continued) || table 8-21

Font family	Specifies the font family to use. **Use same family for all text** puts headlines in an easy-to-read font.
Font size	Specifies the base font size. Specific HTML instructions for larger and smaller base their changes on this size. **Use same size for all elements** causes all type, including very large and very small, to appear at the specified size.
Colors	Specifies a color scheme.
Images	Suppress (background) images causes images not to be loaded with a page. Click the box where the image would be to load the image.
Preview	Displays a window with a few headlines and a short paragraph, all based on your choices on this tab.
User Agent	When Konqueror connects to a remote Web site, by default it sends a user agent header that describes itself, for example, `Mozilla/5.0 (compatible; Konqueror/3; Linux)` Some Web sites do not accept a connection unless your browser says it is a specific browser. This section can make Konqueror report that it is anything you want.
Send browser identification	*Enables the rest of this tab.* Causes Konqueror to send a user agent header when it contacts a Web site.
Customize default identification	The line at the top of this frame is the user agent header. As you select options in this frame, this header changes to reflect your selections. Click **Apply** when you are satisfied with the header.
Site/domain specific identification	Specifies sites or domains that you want to send nondefault user agent headers to and the header that you want to send. Click **New** to display the Add Identification window: Specify a site or domain name (**sobell.com** matches all hosts in the **sobell.com** domain), and select an identity (user agent header); Control Center fills in the Alias text box for you. Click **OK** to save the information.

Panels

The KDE Main panel (kicker) and extension panels were introduced on page 276. A panel (Main or extension) houses buttons (icons with no handles) and applets (with handles). Left click a button to start the program associated with it. Right click a button to bring up a menu that includes the Panel menu (following) and other choices. Left click an applet to initiate whatever action the applet performs. Right click an applet to bring up a context menu. You can control many aspects of a

Handles

Figure 8-27 Panel applet handles

panel, including position and hiding methods, from the Panel menu or K menu: Control Center⇨Look & Feel⇨Panel (page 319).

Applet Handles

Each applet on kicker has a handle composed of several faint, diagonal lines on a narrow bar (Figure 8-27). These bars appear to the left of or above the objects, depending on the orientation of kicker. The kicker handles behave differently from the handles described under "Toolbars" on page 293.

Right click a handle to bring up a menu that typically includes Panel and Move, Remove, and sometimes Preferences choices. Use Preferences to alter the applet's appearance or the way it works.

Move Buttons/Applets

To move an applet/button within a panel, right click the applet handle or button and select Move; the mouse pointer turns into a cross with arrows at each end. Move the applet/button by moving the mouse pointer in a direction parallel to the length of the panel *without pressing a mouse button.* The cross does not have to be over the object you are moving: It is similar to controlling a marionette. You can drag an applet/button through other applets/buttons on a panel, but you cannot move it past the end of a panel.

When there is space in the direction you are moving the applet/button it moves through the space. When there is another applet/button in the direction you are moving the applet/button, the object you are moving exchanges places (moves through) the object that is in the way.

To make more room on a panel, you can squeeze the taskbar on a horizontal panel. Click and hold the taskbar handle, and the taskbar contracts to its smallest size to show you how much space you have to work with. When you release the mouse button, the taskbar grows to occupy the space to its right. When a vertical panel has insufficient room, make the panel and the buttons smaller (refer to "Size" on page 319).

Panel Menu

Right click an applet handle, a button, including a Hide button, or an empty space on a panel, and select Panel to display the Panel menu (Table 8-22).

Panel Menu | table 8-22

Add	
Applet	Adds an applet to the panel.
Button	Selects a program from the same list as the K menu to add to the panel.
Extension	You can have only one Dock Application bar, one KasBar, and one External taskbar. Create them through the following menu selections. When a menu selection is grayed out, you already have the corresponding toolbar on your workspaces (each appears on all workspaces). Right click on an extension **Hide** button, and select **Remove** to get rid of the extension.
Child Panel	Refer to "Child Panel" on page 343.
Dock Application Bar	Refer to "Dock Application Bar" on page 343.
External Taskbar	Refer to "External Taskbar" on page 343.
KasBar	Refer to "KasBar" on page 343.
Special Button	Adds an icon with a special meaning to the panel.
Size	Select the size of a panel from **Tiny** to **Large** or **Custom**. The smaller a panel, the more buttons/applets fit on it.
Preferences	Displays K menu: Control Center⇨Look & Feel⇨Panel (page 319) and **Control Center: Look & Feel**⇨Taskbar (page 322).
Help	Displays the *Kicker Handbook*.

Toolbars

Table 8-23 lists all of the standard KDE toolbars and where to find information about each.

Toolbars | table 8-23

Child panel	Refer to "Child Panel" on page 343.
Dock Application bar	Refer to "Dock Application Bar" on page 343.

Toolbars (Continued)

|| table 8-23

KasBar	Refer to "KasBar" on page 343.
External taskbar	Refer to "External Taskbar" on page 343.
Bookmark toolbar	Refer to "Bookmark Toolbar" on page 298.
Extra Window toolbar	Refer to "Extra Window Toolbar" on page 298.
Desktop files	Refer to "Desktop Files" on page 345.
Location bar	Refer to "Location Bar" on page 298.
Toolbar	Refer to "Toolbar" on page 298.
Navigation panel	Refer to "Navigation Panel" on page 306.
kicker or Main panel	Refer to "kicker: Main Panel" on page 276.
Menubar	Refer to "Menubar" on page 293.

Configure Konqueror Toolbar

Right click the Konqueror toolbar to display the Toolbar menu. Click Toolbar menu: Configure Toolbars, to open the Configure Toolbars window (Figure 8-28), which allows you to add/delete buttons to/from Konqueror toolbars. Select the toolbar you want to work on from the scrolling window under the word Toolbar. Click an action from the Available actions column, and click the right arrow between the columns to add it to the Current actions column, which contains the buttons that appear on the toolbar. Highlight one of the current actions, and click the up and down arrows to move its location on the toolbar. Click the left arrow to remove it from the toolbar.

A <Merge> action is replaced by the actions of a Konqueror component ("Kparts" on page 292). When you are viewing your home directory as icons (click Home on the toolbar), select a file, and click Print; Konqueror displays the Print actions (Print frame, Find, and so on) in place of the <Merge> action on the toolbar.

An ActionList, such as viewmode_toolbar, is a predefined set of actions. Specifically, viewmode_toolbar equates to Konqueror⇨View⇨View Mode (Icon View, MultiColumn View, and so on). Konqueror replaces ActionList: action_name in the Current actions column with its equivalent.

When present in the list of Current actions, the Animated Logo always appears at the right end of the toolbar.

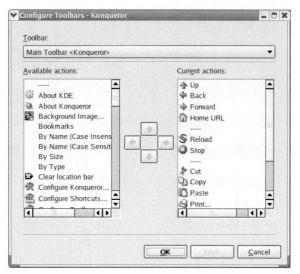

Figure 8-28   Konqueror Configure Toolbars window

Toolbar Handles

A toolbar handle appears as several faint, diagonal lines on a narrow bar (Figure 8-29). The handle is positioned either at the top or left end of a toolbar or panel applet, depending on its orientation. Right click a toolbar handle to bring up the Toolbar menu (page 311), or left drag a toolbar handle to move the toolbar. In addition to moving the toolbar to one of the sides of its window, in most cases you can move it anywhere on the workspace. Return a toolbar to its window by dragging it back into the window close to one of the sides and releasing it. The toolbar snaps into place.

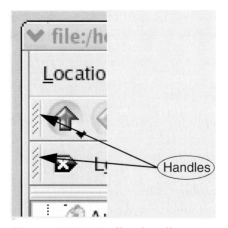

Figure 8-29   Toolbar handles

Child Panel

A Child panel is a small extension panel that works similarly to kicker. Drag this panel using a Hide button. Right click an applet/button on a Child panel and select Panel (page 339) to display the Panel menu. As with kicker, you cannot flatten a Child panel. You can create as many Child panels as you like.

Dock Application Bar

The Dock Application bar swallows WindowMaker (www.windowmaker.org) applets. For example, install wmfire (RPM files are available), start a Dock Application bar, and run wmfire. The wmfire applet takes up residence in the Dock Application bar.

External Taskbar

The External taskbar is identical to the kicker taskbar (page 311) but does not reside in kicker and provides its own panel. At the top/left end, click the arrow that points perpendicular to the External taskbar (next to the Hide button if there is one), to display the Window List menu (page 312). Right click the same arrow to display the External taskbar menu, which removes the External taskbar or opens the Preferences window. This window is the same one that controls kicker, so any changes you make here also apply to kicker. You can control some aspects of the External taskbar separately from other panels/extensions by using K menu: Control Center⇨Look & Feel⇨ Panel⇨Extensions (page 321).

KasBar

The principles of operation of the KasBar (page 311) are identical to those of the taskbar; however, the two bars look different, and you interact with them differently. The KasBar contains a column or row of boxes, each representing a program that is running on the workspace. Each box has as much of the program name as fits, the program icon, and the number of the workspace that the program is running on. Click in the box to make the application window the active window (and change the displayed workspace, if necessary), click a second time to iconify the program window, and click again to restore the program window. These functions do not work while the KasBar Preferences window is displayed. A square at the lower-right corner of the box indicates that the program window is visible; a triangle indicates that it is minimized. A nontransparent background indicates that the window is the active window. When the mouse pointer hovers over a box, the KasBar displays a thumbnail of the window that the box represents. You can control the size of the thumbnails to be larger, readable representations of windows.

Display the KasBar Preferences window by right clicking a Hide button and selecting Preferences. Refer to "Extensions" on page 321 if you need to add a Hide button.

Miscellaneous

This section covers working with the K menu editor, using Desktop files, starting applications automatically when you bring up KDE, reporting bugs, and using KDE's sound features.

kmenuedit: Edits the K Menu

The K menu editor (Figure 8-30) allows you to alter the K menu (page 274) by adding/removing/modifying submenus and individual menu selections. Right click the K menu icon (or red hat) and select Menu Editor to display the Edit K Menu window. Expand the tree view (left side) as necessary, and click the selection you want to change, delete, move, or copy or the section below which you would like to insert a new selection. Change the subwindow on the right as you desire, or click the appropriate icon on the toolbar. After you create a new submenu, you will need to create a new item within that submenu.

The subwindow (right side) describes the program you want the menu selection to execute. The only entry you must fill out is the Command text box, which holds the command line that you want to execute when the selection is chosen from the K menu. The Name is the name of the selection within the K menu. The Comment is a comment. The Type, which describes the type of program, is almost always Application and is filled in by the K menu editor. When you want to assign an icon or change an existing one, click the icon to the right of the Work Path text box. The Work Path is the absolute pathname of the directory that the program is started in.

Figure 8-30   Edit K Menu window

When you are specifying a character-based program, you must run it in a terminal emulator; put a check mark in the box next to Run in terminal, and specify any command line options in Terminal Options. When you have permission, you can run the program as a different user. The Current key line specifies the shortcut key(s) that execute the command. Click on the keycap at the right of this frame to change which keys execute the command. Refer to "Shortcuts" on page 302 for an explanation of how to change keys.

Desktop Files

Desktop files have a **.desktop** filename extension, store information about how they should be displayed, and have a URL that specifies what they point to. The URL can be a local file or directory, an Internet URL, or an FTP address. The following abbreviated file named **home.desktop**, resides in **$KDEHOME/share/apps/konqsidebartng/entries**, displays in the Konqueror Navigation panel toolbar as a house icon, and links to the **$HOME** directory:

```
$ cat home.desktop
[Desktop Entry]
Encoding=UTF-8
Type=Link
URL=file:$HOME
Icon=folder_home
Name=Home Directory
Name[af]=huis gids
Comment=This folder contains your personal files
Comment[af]=hierdie kabinet bevat jou persoonlike lêers
Open=false
X-KDE-TreeModule=Directory
X-KDE-KonqSidebarModule=konqsidebar_tree
```

Look at some of the other Desktop files in the same directory to see what a complete Desktop file looks like. See also "Navigation Panel" on page 306 and "Show Navigation Panel" on page 297.

Specifying a Window Manager

Almost at the end of the **/usr/bin/startkde** file is a line that could specify the window manager KDE is to work with. Because it does not specify a window manager KDE defaults to kwin:[9]

```
kwrapper ksmserver --restore || \
```

---

9. The line that follows is a continuation of this one: Make sure that a backslash is the last character on your new line.

To specify the Sawfish window manager, work as root to change the preceding line to

```
kwrapper ksmserver --restore --windowmanager sawfish || \
```

Autostart

When you start KDE, it automatically starts the programs in the global autostart directory (**$KDEDIR/share/autostart**, where the value of **$KDEDIR** defaults to **/usr** when the variable is not set) and then the ones in your **Autostart** directory (**$KDE-HOME/Autostart**). Although KDE can use its session management capability (page 185) to restart KDE-compliant windows and running programs when you close KDE and bring them up again when you restart KDE, you must place noncompliant programs in your **Autostart** directory to have them restart automatically. Drag and copy or link noncompliant programs you want to start automatically into the **Autostart** directory.

Reporting a Bug

Select K menu: Extras⇨Programing⇨Bug Report Tool to open the Bug Buddy window which facilitates sending a bug report to the KDE group. Follow the instructions in the window to submit a bug report.

Sound

Sound is controlled by K menu: Control Center⇨Sound. By default KDE runs the aRts (analog real-time synthesizer, www.arts-project.org) sound server in the background. Without a sound server, a program that needs to play a sound asks the system for control of the sound device (the soundcard) before continuing. The aRts server provides above the sound device a layer that allows programs to output sound without waiting for the device to become available. The aRts server mixes sounds. If you are playing music (with, for example, noatun, a media player for KDE) and another application plays a sound, aRts plays this sound alongside the music without interrupting it.

The aRts server is a professional soundserver; it provides the advanced features required by professional music composition software. Because GNU/Linux was not designed with professional (real-time) multimedia in mind, you have to choose between (1) highest-quality sound that uses many system resources and CPU cycles and (2) lower-quality sound for casual listening that uses fewer resources and CPU cycles. For improved performance, when you select K menu: Control Center⇨Sound⇨Sound Server⇨Run soundserver with realtime priority, you may want to investigate the Linux kernel low-latency patch (people.redhat.com/mingo/lowlatency-patches).

Chapter Summary

The KDE desktop environment presents an extensive array of tools, including multiple help systems; a flexible file manager and browser; an office package that includes word processing, spreadsheet, presentation, charting, and e-mail packages; numerous panels and menus that you can configure in many ways; and enough options to please the most critical user.

The help system includes What's This?, KDE HelpCenter, and the Help menubar selection in many windows. The K menu application starter and kicker, the Main panel, make KDE comfortable to drive. You can customize tools in many ways to make the desktop suit any environment and user.

Konqueror, the KDE file manager and browser, has very little functionality of its own. It is dependent on other programs to do its work. Konqueror opens these programs within its own window, giving the impression that it is very capable. It is a good example of seamless program integration. When you ask Konqueror to open a file (which can be a local or remote text, music, picture, or even an HTML file), it needs to figure out what kind of file it is and then which program to use to open/display it. Konqueror takes advantage of MIME, which uses a file's three- or four-letter filename extension to determine the type of file.

Panels and menus, which are closely related, give you the opportunity to select an object (which can be just about anything on the system) from a list. On a panel you generally click an icon from a box of icons (the panel), whereas on a menu you typically click text in a list.

The Control Center provides a way of setting/changing many characteristics of KDE and kwin, the KDE window manager. Using the Control Center, you can control Web and file browsing with Konqueror, the look-and-feel of your desktop, the sound component of the system, network aspects of the desktop, and personalization of the desktop, including options that make it easier for people with special needs to use. For Superuser the Control Center contains a module on system administration.

As implemented by Red Hat, the KDE desktop appears very similar to the GNOME desktop. Underneath the veneer are two desktop managers that perform many of the same functions, yet work very differently.

The KDE environment provides the casual user, office worker, power user, and programmer/system designer a space to work in and a set of tools to work with. KDE also provides off-the-shelf productivity and almost limitless ways to customize its look, feel, and response.

Exercises

1. What is a context menu? How does a context menu differ from other menus?

2. What happens when you ALT + right drag within a window? What difference does it make where the mouse pointer is within the window (top, side, and so on) when you start to drag?

3. What happens when you right click the root window? How can you use this?

4. How does the KDE scrollbar differ from most other scrollbars? Why is this useful?

5. Regarding kicker,

   a. What is another name for kicker?

   b. How can you cause kicker to hide automatically when you are not using it?

   c. How can you make kicker disappear slowly?

6. What is klipper? How do you use it to cut and paste text?

7. Regarding Konqueror the file manager,

   a. What is Konqueror?

   b. List four things that you can use it for.

   c. How do you use Konqueror to search for a file?

8. Regarding Konqueror the Web browser,

   a. What is enhanced browsing and how do you use it?

   b. How would you use Konqueror to transfer local files to a remote FTP site? Describe how you would do this using a Konqueror window with two views.

9. Establish a desktop background that uses wallpaper and two colors (Mode is not Flat) that you select using the Select Color window. Experiment until you have a background that you like. Which are your favorite tools/effects? What does *maxpect* mean? Use ksnapshot to take a picture of the background you designed and print it or display it in some manner.

10. List at least four things you can do from the Taskbar.

11. What are file tips? How do you turn on file tips? Set a maximum of four tips?

Advanced Exercises

12. Discuss Konqueror's lack of functionality and how it performs so many tasks. What is a Kpart?

13. Bring up the Metacity window manager under KDE. How did you do it? Did you run into any problems? What did you observe?

14. Write and demonstrate a klipper action that runs xeyes when you highlight the word xeyes and press the Manually Invoke Action on Current Clipboard shortcut keys (CONTROL-ALT-R by default, but see footnote 5 on page 286).

IN THIS CHAPTER

Networking and the Internet

9

The communications facilities linking computers are continually improving, allowing faster and more economical connections. The earliest computers were unconnected stand-alone machines. To transfer information from one system to another, you had to store it in some form (usually magnetic tape, paper tape, or punch cards—called IBM or Hollerith cards), carry it to a compatible system, and read it back in. A notable advance occurred when computers began to exchange data over serial lines, although the transfer rate was slow (hundreds of bits per second). People quickly invented new ways to take advantage of this computing power, such as e-mail, news retrieval, and bulletin board services. With the speed of today's networks, it is normal for a piece of e-mail to cross the country or even travel halfway around the world in a few seconds.

It would be difficult to find a computer facility that does not include a LAN to link the systems. GNU/Linux systems are typically attached to an *Ethernet* (page 1466) network. Wireless networks are becoming prevalent as well. Large computer facilities usually maintain several networks, often of different types, and almost certainly have connections to larger networks (company- or campuswide and beyond).

The Internet is a loosely administered network of networks (an *internetwork*) that links computers on diverse LANs around the globe. An internet (small *i*) is a generic network of networks that may share some parts in common with the public Internet. It is the Internet that makes it possible to send an e-mail message to a colleague thousands of miles away and receive a reply within minutes. A related term, *intranet,* refers to the networking infrastructure within a company or other institution. Intranets are usually private; access to them from external networks may be limited and carefully controlled, typically using firewalls (page 358).

Over the past decade many network services have emerged and become standard. On GNU/Linux systems, as on UNIX computers, special processes called *daemons* (page 1463) support such services by exchanging specialized messages with other systems over the network. Several software systems have been created to allow computers to share their filesystems with one another, making it appear as though remote files are stored on local disks. Sharing remote filesystems allows users to share information without knowing where the files physically reside, without making unnecessary copies, and without learning a new set of utilities to manipulate them. Because the files appear to be stored locally, you can use standard utilities (such as cat, vi, lpr, mv, or their graphical counterparts) to work with them.

Developers have been creating new tools and extending existing ones to take advantage of higher network speeds and work within more crowded networks. The rlogin, rsh, and telnet utilities, designed long ago, have largely been supplanted by ssh (secure shell—page 374). The ssh utility allows a user to log in on or execute commands securely on a remote computer. Users rely on such utilities as scp and ftp to transfer files from one system to another across the network. Communication utilities, including e-mail utilities, and chat programs, such as talk, Internet Relay Chat (IRC), ICQ, and AOL Instant Messenger (AIM), have become so prevalent that many people with very little computer experience use them on a daily basis to keep in touch with friends and family.

An *intranet* is a network that connects computing resources at a school, company, or other organization but, unlike the Internet, typically restricts access to internal users. An intranet is very similar to a LAN but is based on Internet technology. An intranet can provide database, e-mail, and Web page access to a limited group of people, regardless of their geographic location.

The fact that an intranet is able to connect dissimilar machines is one of its strengths. Think of all the machines that are on the Internet: Macs, PCs running different versions of MS Windows, various machines running UNIX and GNU/Linux, and so on. Each of these machines can communicate via IP (page 360), a common protocol. So it is with an intranet: Different machines can all talk to one another.

Another key difference between the Internet and an intranet is that the Internet will transmit only one protocol suite: the IP protocol suite. An intranet can be set up to use a number of protocols, such as IP, IPX, Appletalk, DECnet, XNS, or various other protocols developed by vendors over the years. Although these protocols cannot be transmitted directly over the Internet, you can set up special gateway boxes at remote sites that tunnel or encapsulate these protocols into IP packets in order to use the Internet to pass them.

You can use an *extranet* (or *partner net*) to improve your security. A closely related term is virtual private network (VPN). These terms describe ways to connect remote sites securely to a local site, typically by using the public Internet as a carrier and using encryption as a means of protecting data in transit.

As with the Internet, the communications potential of intranets is boundless. You can set up a private chat between people at remote locations, access a company database, see what is new at school, or read about the new university president. Companies that developed products for use on the Internet are investing more and more time and money developing intranet software applications as the intranet market explodes. Following are some words you may want to become familiar with before you read the rest of this chapter. Refer to the Appendix G on page 1453 for definitions.

ASP	bridge	extranet	firewall	gateway
hub	internet	Internet	intranet	ISP
packet	router	sneakernet	switch	VPN

Types of Networks and How They Work

Computers communicate over networks by using unique addresses assigned by system software. A computer message, called a *packet, frame,* or *datagram,* includes the address of the destination computer and the sender's return address. The three most common types of networks are *broadcast, point-to-point,* and *switched.* Once popular token-based networks (such as FDDI and Token Ring) are rarely seen anymore.

Speed is important to the proper functioning of the Internet. Newer specifications (cat 6 and cat 7) are being standardized for 1000BaseT (10 gigabits per second, called gigabit Ethernet, or GIG-E) and faster networking. Some of the networks that form the backbone of the Internet run at speeds up to almost 10 gi-ga*bytes* per second (OC192) to accommodate the ever-increasing demand for network services. Table 9-1 lists some of the common specifications in use today.

Specification	‖ table 9-1
DS0	64 kilobits per second
ISDN	Two DS0 lines plus signaling (16 kilobits per second) or 128 kilobits per second

Specification (Continued)	‖ table 9-1
T-1	1.544 megabits per second (24 DS0 lines)
T-3	43.232 megabits per second (28 T-1s)
OC3	155 megabits per second (100 T-1s)
OC12	622 megabits per second (4 OC3s)
OC48	2.5 gigabits per seconds (4 OC12s)
OC192	9.6 gigabits per second (4 OC48s)

Broadcast

On a *broadcast network*, such as Ethernet, any of the many systems attached to the network cable can send a message at any time; each system examines the address in each message and responds only to messages addressed to it. A problem occurs on a broadcast network when multiple systems send data at the same time, resulting in a collision of the messages on the cable. When messages collide, they can become garbled. The sending system notices the garbled message and resends it after waiting a short but random amount of time. Waiting a random amount of time helps prevent those same systems from resending the data at the same moment and experiencing another collision. The extra traffic that results from collisions can put quite a load on the network; if the collision rate gets too high, the retransmissions result in more collisions, and the network becomes unusable.

Point-to-Point

A point-to-point link does not seem like much of a network at all because only two endpoints are involved. However, most connections to WANs are through point-to-point links, using wire cable, radio, or satellite links. The advantage of a point-to-point link is that because only two systems are involved, the traffic on the link is limited and well understood. A disadvantage is that each system can typically be equipped for a small number of such links, and it is impractical and costly to establish point-to-point links that connect each computer to all the rest.

Point-to-point links often use serial lines and modems but can use personal computer parallel ports for faster links between GNU/Linux systems. The use of a modem with a point-to-point link allows an isolated system to connect inexpensively into a larger network.

The most common types of point-to-point links are the ones used to connect to the Internet. When you use DSL[1] (digital subscriber line), you are using a point-to-point link to connect to the Internet. Serial lines, such as T-1, T-3, ATM links, and ISDN, are all point to point. Although it might seem like a point-to-point link, a cable modem is based on broadcast technology and in that way is similar to Ethernet.

Switched

A *switch* is a device that establishes a virtual path between source and destination hosts such that each path appears to be a point-to-point link, much like a railroad roundhouse. The telephone network is a giant switched network. The switch brings up and tears down virtual paths as hosts need to communicate with each other. Each host thinks that it has a direct point-to-point path to the host it is talking to. Contrast this with a broadcast network, where each host also sees traffic bound for other hosts. The advantage of a switched network over a pure point-to-point network is that each host requires only one connection: the connection to the switch. Using pure point-to-point connections, each host must have a connection to every other host. Scalability is provided by further linking switches.

LAN: Local Area Network

Local area networks (LANs) are confined to a relatively small area—a single computer facility, building, or campus. Today most LANs run over copper or fiberoptic cable, but other, wireless technologies, such as infrared (similar to most television remote control devices) and radio wave, are becoming more popular.

If its destination address is not on the local network, a packet must be passed on to another network by a router (page 357). A router may be a general-purpose computer or a special-purpose device attached to multiple networks to act as a gateway among them.

Ethernet

A GNU/Linux system connected to a LAN usually connects to the network by using Ethernet. A typical Ethernet connection can support data transfer rates from 10 megabits per second to 1 gigabit per second, with speed enhancements planned.

---

1. The term DSL incorporates the xDSL suite of technologies, including ADSL, XDSL, SDSL, and HDSL.

Owing to computer load, competing network traffic, and network overhead, file transfer rates on an Ethernet are always slower than the maximum, theoretical transfer rate.

An Ethernet network transfers data by using copper or fiberoptic (glass) cable or wireless transmitters and receivers. Originally each computer was attached to a thick coaxial cable (called *thicknet*) at tap points spaced at six-foot intervals along the cable. The thick cable was awkward to deal with, so other solutions, including a thinner coaxial cable known as *thinnet*, or 10Base2,[2] were developed. Today most Ethernet connections are either wireless or made over unshielded twisted pair (referred to as UTP, Category 3 (cat 3), Category 5 (cat 5), Category 5e (cat 5e) 10BaseT, or 100BaseT) wire—similar to the type of wire used for telephone lines and serial data communications.

A *switched Ethernet* network is a special case of a broadcast network that works with a *network switch*, or just *switch*, which is a special class of hub that has intelligence. Instead of having a dumb repeater (hub) that broadcasts every packet it receives out of every port, a switch learns which devices are connected to which of its ports. A switch sorts packets so that it sends traffic to only the machine the traffic is intended for. A switch also has buffers for holding and queuing packets.

Some Ethernet switches have enough bandwidth to communicate simultaneously, in full-duplex mode, with all the devices that are connected to it. A nonswitched (hub-based) broadcast network can run in only half-duplex mode. Full-duplex Ethernet further improves things by eliminating collisions. Each host can transmit and receive simultaneously at 10/100/1000 megabits per second for an effective bandwidth between hosts of 20/200/2000 megabits per second, depending on the capacity of the switch.

Wireless

Wireless networks are becoming increasingly common. They are used in offices, homes, and public places, such as universities and airports. Wireless access points provide functionality similar to an Ethernet hub. They allow multiple users to interact, using a common radio frequency spectrum. A wireless, point-to-point connection allows you to wander about your home or office with your laptop, using an antenna to link to a LAN or to the Internet via an in-house base station. GNU/Linux has drivers for many of the common wireless boards. A wireless access point connects a wireless network to a wired network so that no special protocol is required for a wireless connection. Refer to the *Linux Wireless LAN HOWTO* and www.hpl.hp.com/personal/Jean_Tourrilhes/Linux.

---

2. Ethernet cables are classified as **XbaseY**, where **X** is the data rate in megabits per second, **base** means baseband (as opposed to radio frequency), and **Y** is the category of cabling.

WAN: Wide Area Network

A wide area network (WAN) covers a large geographic area. The technologies (such as Ethernet) used for LANs were designed to work over limited distances and for a certain number of host connections. A WAN may span long distances over dedicated data lines (leased from a telephone company) or radio or satellite links. WANs are often used to interconnect LANs. Major Internet service providers rely on WANs to connect to customers within a country and around the globe.

Some networks do not fit into either the LAN or the WAN designation: A MAN (metropolitan area network) is one that is contained in a smaller geographic area, such as a city. Like WANs, MANs are typically used to interconnect LANs.

Internetworking through Gateways and Routers

A LAN connects to a WAN through a *gateway,* a generic term for a computer or a special device with multiple network connections that passes data from one network to another. The purpose of the gateway is to convert the data traffic from the format used on the LAN to that used on the WAN. Data that crosses the country from one Ethernet to another over a WAN, for example, is repackaged from the Ethernet format to a different format that can be processed by the communications equipment that makes up the WAN backbone. When it reaches the end of its journey over the WAN, the data is converted by another gateway to the format appropriate for the receiving network. For the most part these details are of concern only to the network administrators; the end user does not need to know anything about how the data transfer is carried out.

A *router* is the most common form of a gateway. Routers play an important role in internetworking. Just as you might study a map to plan your route when you need to drive to an unfamiliar place, a computer needs to know how to deliver a message to a system attached to a distant network by passing through intermediary systems and networks along the way. You can imagine using a giant network road map to choose the route that your data should follow, but a static map of computer routes is usually a poor choice for a large data network. Computers and networks along the route you choose may be overloaded or down, without providing a detour for your message.

Routers communicate with one another dynamically, keeping one another informed about which routes are open for use. To extend the analogy, this would be like heading out on a car trip without consulting a map to find a route to your destination; instead you head for a nearby gas station and ask directions. Throughout the journey, you would continue to stop at one gas station after another, getting directions at each to find the next one. Although it would take a while to make the stops, each gas station would advise you of bad traffic, closed roads, alternative routes, and shortcuts.

The stops the data makes are much quicker than those you would make in your car, but each message leaves each router on a path chosen based on the most current information. Think of it as a GPS (global positioning system) setup that automatically gets updates at each intersection and tells you where to go next, based on traffic and highway conditions.

Figure 9-1 shows an example of how LANs might be set up at three sites interconnected by a WAN (the Internet). In network diagrams such as this, Ethernet LANs are drawn as straight lines, with devices attached at right angles; WANs are represented as clouds, indicating that the details have been left out; wireless connections are drawn as zigzag lines with breaks, indicating that the connection may be intermittent.

In Figure 9-1 a gateway or a router relays messages between each LAN and the Internet. Three of the routers in the Internet are shown (for example, the one closest to each site). Site A has a server, a workstation, a network computer, and a PC sharing a single Ethernet LAN. Site B has an Ethernet LAN that serves a printer and four GNU/Linux workstations. A firewall permits only certain traffic between the Internet router and the site's local router. Site C has three LANs linked by a single router, perhaps to reduce the traffic load that would result if they were combined or to keep workgroups or locations on separate networks. Site C includes a wireless access point that enables wireless communication with nearby computers.

Firewall

A firewall in a car separates the engine compartment from the passenger compartment, protecting the driver and passengers from engine fires, noise, and fumes. Computer firewalls separate computers from malicious and unwanted users.

A *firewall* prevents certain types of traffic from entering or leaving a network. A firewall might prevent traffic from your IP address from leaving the network and prevent anyone except users from select domains from using ftp to retrieve data from the network. The implementations of firewalls vary widely, from GNU/Linux machines with two *interfaces* (page 1473) running custom software to a *router* (page 1490) with simple access lists to esoteric, vendor-supplied firewall appliances. Most larger installations have at least one kind of firewall in place. A firewall is often accompanied by a proxy server/gateway (page 397) to provide an intermediate point between you and the host you are communicating with.

In addition to those found in multipurpose computers, firewalls are becoming increasingly common in consumer appliances. Firewalls are built into cable modems, wireless gateways, routers, and stand-alone devices.

When your need for privacy is critical, you can meet with a consulting firm that will discuss your security needs, devise a strategy, produce a written implementation

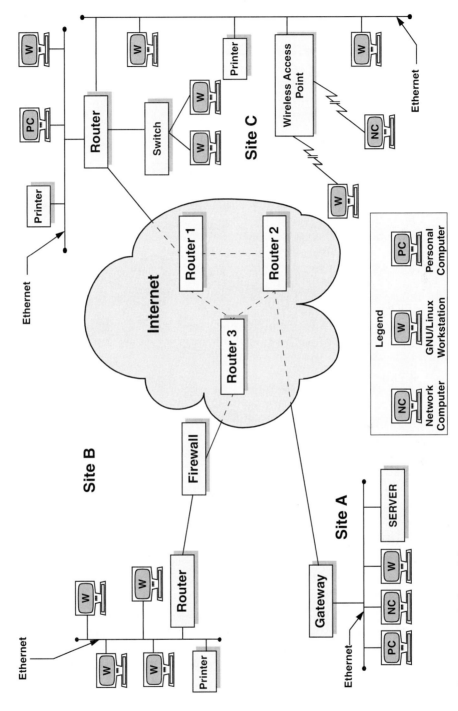

Figure 9-1   A slice of the Internet

policy, and design a firewall for you from scratch. Typically a single GNU/Linux machine can include a minimal firewall. A small group of GNU/Linux machines may have a cheap, slow GNU/Linux machine with two network interfaces and packet-filtering software functioning as a dedicated firewall. One of the interfaces connects to the Internet, modems, and other outside data sources, whereas the other connects, normally through a hub or switch, to the local network's machines. Refer to page 924 for information on setting up a firewall and to Appendix C for a discussion of security.

Network Protocols

To exchange information over a network, computers must communicate using a common language, or *protocol* (page 1486). The protocol determines the format of the message packets. The predominant network protocols used by GNU/Linux systems are TCP and IP, referred to as TCP/IP[3] (Transmission Control Protocol and Internet Protocol). Network services that need highly reliable connections, such as ssh and scp, tend to use TCP/IP. Another protocol used for some system services is UDP (User Datagram Protocol). Network services that do not require guaranteed delivery, such as RealAudio and RealVideo, operate satisfactorily with the simpler UDP.[4]

IP: Internet Protocol

Layering was introduced to facilitate protocol design: Layers distinguish functional differences between adjacent protocols. A grouping of layers can be standardized into a protocol model. IP is a protocol and has a corresponding model for what distinguishes protocol layers. The IP model differs from the ISO seven-layer protocol model (also called the OSI model) often illustrated in networking textbooks. IP uses a simplified five-layer model.

1. The first layer, called the *physical layer,* describes the physical medium (copper, fiber, wireless) and the data encoding used to transmit signals on that medium (pulses of light, electrical waves, or radio waves, for instance).

2. The second layer, called the *data link layer,* covers media access by network devices and describes how to put data into packets, transmit the data, and check it for errors. Ethernet is at this layer, as is 802.11 wireless.

---

3. All references to IP imply *IPv4* (page 1474).

4. Voice and video protocols are delay sensitive, not integrity sensitive. The human ear and eye accept and interpolate loss in an audio stream but cannot deal with variable delay. The guaranteed delivery that TCP provides introduces delay on a busy network when packets get retransmitted. This delay is not acceptable for video and audio transmissions, whereas less than 100 percent integrity is acceptable.

3. The third layer, called the *network layer*, frequently uses IP and addresses and routes packets.

4. The fourth layer, called the *transport layer*, is where TCP and UDP exist. This layer provides a means for applications to communicate with each other. Common functions of the transport layer include guaranteed delivery, delivery of packets in the order of transmission, flow control, error detection, and error correction. The transport layer is responsible for dividing data streams into packets. This layer also performs port addressing, which allows it to distinguish among different services using the same transport protocol. Port addressing keeps the data from multiple applications using the same protocol (for example TCP) separate.

5. Anything above the transport layer is the domain of the application and is part of the fifth layer. Unlike the ISO model, the Internet model does not distinguish among application, presentation, and session layers. All the upper-layer characteristics, such as character encoding, encryption, GUI, and so on, are part of the application. Applications choose the transport characteristics they require and choose the corresponding transport layer protocol to send and receive data.

TCP: Transmission Control Protocol

TCP is most frequently run on top of IP in a combination referred to as TCP/IP. TCP provides error recovery and guaranteed delivery in packet transmission order and works with multiple ports so that it can handle more than one application. TCP is a *connection-oriented protocol* (page 1461), also known as a streams-based protocol. Once established, a TCP connection looks like a stream of data, not individual IP packets. The connection is assumed to remain up and be uniquely addressable. Every piece of information you write to the connection always goes to the same destination and arrives in the order it was sent. Because TCP is connection oriented and establishes what you can think of as a *virtual circuit* between two machines, TCP is not suitable for one-to-many transmissions (see UDP, following). TCP has builtin mechanisms for dealing with congestion (or flow) control over busy networks and throttles back (slows the speed of data flow) when it has to retransmit dropped packets. TCP can also deal with acknowledgments, wide area links, high delay links, and other situations.

UDP: User Datagram Protocol

UDP runs at layer 4 of the IP stack, just as TCP does, but is much simpler. Like TCP, UDP works with multiple ports/multiple applications and has checksums for error detection but does not automatically retransmit packets that fail the checksum. UDP is a packet- (or datagram-) oriented protocol: Each packet must carry its own address and port information. Each router along the way examines each packet to determine the destination one hop at a time. You can broadcast or multicast UDP packets to many destinations at the same time by using special addresses.

PPP: Point-to-Point Protocol

PPP provides serial line point-to-point connections that support IP. PPP compresses data to make the most of the limited bandwidth available on serial connections. PPP, which replaces SLIP (Serial Line IP), acts as a point-to-point layer 2/3 transport that many other types of protocols can ride on. PPP is used mostly for IP-based services and connections, such as TCP or UDP.[5] For more information, refer to "Internet Configuration Wizard" on page 1023.

Xremote and LBX

Two protocols that speed up work over serial lines are Xremote and LBX. Xremote compresses the X Window System protocol so that it is more efficient over slower serial lines. LBX (low-bandwidth X) is based on the Xremote technology and is a part of the X Window System release X11R6.

Host Address

Each computer interface is identified by a unique address, or host number, on its network. A system that is attached to more than one network has multiple interfaces, one for each network and each with a unique address.

Each packet of information that is broadcast over the network has a destination address. All hosts on the network must process each broadcast packet to see whether it is addressed to that host.[6] If the packet is addressed to a given host, that host continues to process it. If not, the host ignores it.

The network address of a machine is an IP address, which is represented as one number broken into four segments separated by periods (for example, 192.168.184.5). Domain names and IP addresses are assigned through a highly distributed system coordinated by ICANN (Internet Corporation for Assigned Names and Numbers—www.icann.org) via many registrars (see www.internic.net). ICANN is funded by the various domain name registries and registrars and IP address registries, which supply globally unique identifiers for hosts and services on the Internet. Although you may not deal with any of these agencies directly, your Internet service provider does.

---

5. SLIP was one of the first serial line implementations of IP and has slightly less overhead than PPP, but PPP supports multiple protocols (such as Appletalk and IPX), whereas SLIP supports only IP.

6. Contrast broadcast packets with unicast packets: Ethernet hardware on a computer filters out unicast packets that are not addressed to that machine; the operating system on that machine never sees them.

How a company uses IP addresses is determined by the system or network administrator. For example, the leftmost two sets of numbers in an IP address might represent a large network (campus- or companywide); the third set might specify a subnetwork (perhaps a department or single floor in a building); and the rightmost number, an individual computer. The operating system uses the address in a different, lower-level form, converting it to its binary equivalent, a series of 1s and 0s. See the following Optional section for more information. Refer to "private address space" on page 1486 in the Glossary for information about addresses you can use on your LAN without registering them.

Static versus Dynamic IP addresses

A static IP address is one that remains the same. A dynamic IP address is one that can change each time you connect to your ISP. A dynamic address remains the same during a single login session. Any server (mail, Web, and so on) must have a static address so that clients can find the machine that is the server. End user machines usually work well with dynamic addresses. During a given login session, they can function as a client (your Web browser, for example) because they have a constant IP address. When you log out and log in again, it does not matter that you have a new IP address, because your computer, acting as a client, establishes a new connection with a server. The advantage of dynamic addressing is that it allows inactive addresses to be reused, reducing the total number of IP addresses needed. Refer to "DHCP Client" on page 1028 for more information about dynamic IP addressing.

Optional

IP Classes

To facilitate routing on the Internet, IP addresses are divided into *classes*. Classes, labeled *class A* through *class E,* allow the Internet address space to be broken into blocks of small, medium, and large networks that are designed to be assigned based on the number of hosts within a network.

When you need to send a message to an address outside your network, your system looks up the address block/class in its routing table and sends the message to the next router on the way to the final destination. Every router along the way does a similar lookup to forward the message. At the destination, local routers direct the message to the specific address. Without classes and blocks, your host would have to know every network and subnetwork address on the Internet before it could send a message. This would be impractical because of the number of addresses on the Internet.

IP Classes

|| table 9-2

Class	Start Bits	Address Range	All Bits (including start bits)			
			0–7	8–15	16–23	24–31
Class A	0	001.000.000.000-126.000.000.000	0--netid--	==========hostid==========		
Class B	10	129.000.000.000-191.255.000.000	10-------netid------	======hostid=====		
Class C	110	192.000.000.000-223.255.255.000	110----------netid------------	=hostid==		
Class D (Multicast)	1110	224.000.000.000-239.255.255.000	1110			
Class E (Reserved)	11110	240.000.000.000-255.255.255.000	11110			

Each of the four numbers in the IP address is in the range of 0–255 because each segment of the IP address is represented by 8 bits (an *octet*), each bit capable of taking on two values; the total number of values is $2^8 = 256$. When you start counting at 0, 1–256 becomes 0–255.[7] Each IP address is divided into a net address (*netid*) portion (which is part of the class) and a host address (*hostid*) portion. See Table 9-2.

The first set of addresses, defining class A networks, is for extremely large corporations, such as General Electric (3.0.0.0) and Hewlett-Packard (15.0.0.0), or for ISPs. One start bit (0) in the first position designates a class A network, 7 bits hold the network portion of the address (netid), and 24 bits hold the host portion of the address (hostid, Table 9-2). This means that GE can have 2^{24}, or approximately 16 million hosts on its network. Unused address space and *subnets* (page 1495) lower this number quite a bit. The 127.0.0.0 subnet is reserved (page 368), as are 128.0.0.0 and several others.

Two start bits (10) in the first two positions designate a class B network, 14 bits hold the network portion of the address (**netid**), and 16 bits hold the host portion of the address, for a potential total of 65,534 hosts.[8] A class C network uses 3 start bits (100), 21 netid bits (2 million networks), and 8 hostid bits (254 hosts). Today a new large customer will not receive a class A or B network but is likely to receive a class C or several (usually contiguous) class C networks, if merited.

Several other classes of networks exist. Class D networks are reserved for *multicast* (page 1480) networks. When you run **netstat –nr** on your GNU/Linux system, you can see whether your machine is a member of a multicast network. A 224.0.0.0 in the Destination column that netstat displays indicates a class D, multicast address

---

7. Internally, the IP address is represented as a set of four unsigned 8-bit fields, or a 32-bit unsigned number, depending on how programs are using it. The most common format in C is to represent it as a union of an unsigned 32-bit long integer, four unsigned chars, and two unsigned short integers.

(Table 9-2). A multicast is like a broadcast, but only hosts that subscribe to the multicast group receive the message. To use Web terminology, a broadcast is like a push. A host pushes a broadcast on the network, and every host on the network must check each packet to see whether it contains relevant data. A multicast is like a pull. A host will see a multicast only if it registers itself as subscribed to a multicast group or service and pulls the appropriate packets from the network.

Table 9-3 shows some of the computations for IP address 131.204.027.027. Each address is shown in decimal, hexadecimal, and binary. Binary is the easiest to work with for bitwise, (binary) computations. The first three lines show the IP address. The next three lines show the *subnet mask* (page 1495) in three bases. Next, the IP address and the subnet mask are ANDed together bitwise to yield the *subnet number* (page 1495), which is shown in three bases. The last three lines show the *broadcast address* (page 1458), which is computed by taking the subnet number and turning the hostid bits to 1s. The subnet number is the name/number of your local network. The subnet number and the subnet mask determine what range the IP address of your machine must be in. They are also used by routers to segment traffic; see *network segment* (page 1482). A broadcast on this network goes to all hosts in the range 131.204.27.1 through 131.204.27.254 but will be acted on only by hosts that have a use for it.

Subnets

Each host on a network must process each broadcast to determine whether the information in the broadcast packet is useful to that host. If a lot of hosts are on a network, each host must process many packets. To maintain efficiency, most networks, particularly shared media networks, such as Ethernet, need to be split into subnetworks, or *subnets*.[9] The more hosts on a network, the more dramatically network performance is impacted. Organizations use router and switch technology called VLANs (virtual local area network) to group similar hosts into broadcast domains (subnets) based on function. It's not uncommon to see a switch with different ports being part of different subnets.

---

8. A 16-bit (class B) address can address $2^{16} = 65,536$ hosts, yet the potential number of hosts is two less than that because the first and last addresses on any network are reserved. In a similar manner an 8-bit (class C) address can address only 254 hosts ($2^8 - 2 = 254$). The 0 host address (for example, 194.16.100.0 for a class C or 131.204.0.0 for a class B) is reserved as a designator for the network itself. Several older operating systems use this as a broadcast address. The 255 host address (for example, 194.16.100.255 for a class C or 131.204.255.255 for a class B) is reserved as the IP broadcast address. An IP packet (datagram) that is sent to this address is broadcast to all hosts on the network.

The **netid** portion of a subnet does not have the same limitations. Often you are given the choice of reserving the first and last networks in a range as you would a **hostid**, but now this is rarely done in practice. More often, the first and last network in the netid range are used to provide more usable address space. Refer to "Subnets" on this page.

9. This is also an issue with other protocols, particularly Appletalk.

Computations for IP address 131.204.027.027 || table 9-3

	--------------Class B--------------		netid	hostid	
IP Address	131	.204	.027	.027	decimal
	8C	CC	1B	1B	hexadecimal
	1000 1100	1100 1100	0001 1011	0001 1011	binary
Subnet Mask	255	.255	.255	.000	decimal
	FF	FF	FF	00	hexadecimal
	1111 1111	1111 1111	1111 1111	0000 0000	binary
IP Address bitwise AND	1000 1100	1100 1100	0001 1011	0001 1011	decimal
Subnet Mask	1111 1111	1111 1111	1111 1111	0000 0000	hexadecimal
= Subnet Number	1000 1100	1100 1100	0001 1011	0000 0000	binary
Subnet Number	131	.204	.027	.000	decimal
	83	CC	1B	00	hexadecimal
	1000 1100	1100 1100	0001 1011	0000 0000	binary
Broadcast Address (Set host bits to 1)	131	.204	.27	.255	decimal
	83	CC	1B	FF	hexadecimal
	1000 0011	1100 1100	0001 1011	1111 1111	binary

A *subnet mask* (or *address mask*) is a bit mask that identifies which parts of an IP address correspond to the network address and subnet portion of the address. This mask has 1s in positions corresponding to the network and subnet numbers and 0s in the host number positions. When you perform a bitwise AND on an IP address and a subnet mask (Table 9-3), the result is an address that contains everything but the host address (**hostid**) portion.

There are several ways to represent a subnet mask: A network could have a subnet mask of 255.255.255.0 (decimal), FFFFFF00 (hexadecimal), or /24 (the number of bits used for the subnet mask). If it were a class B network (of which 16 bits are already fixed), this yields 2^8 (24 total bits – 16 fixed bits = 8 bits, 2^8 = 256) networks[10] with $2^8 - 2$ (256 – 2 = 254) hosts[11] on each network. If you do use a subnet mask, use netconfig to let the system know about it.

For example, when you divide the class C address 192.25.4.0 into eight subnets, you get a subnet mask of 255.255.255.224, FFFFFFE0, or /27 (27 1s). The eight resultant networks are 192.25.4.0, 192.25.4.32, 192.25.4.64, 192.25.4.96, 192.25.4.128, 192.25.4.160, 192.25.4.192, and 192.25.4.224. You can use a Web-based subnet mask calculator to calculate subnet masks (page 1401). To use this calculator to determine the preceding subnet mask, use an IP host address of 192.25.4.0. Go to www.telusplanet.net/public/sparkman/netcalc.htm for a nice subnet calculator.

CIDR: Classless Inter-Domain Routing

CIDR (pronounced *cider*) allows groups of addresses that are smaller than a class C block to be assigned to an organization or ISP and further subdivided and parceled out. In addition, it helps to alleviate the potential problem of routing tables on major Internet backbone and peering devices becoming too large to manage.

The pool of available IPv4 addresses has been depleted to the point that no one gets a class A address anymore. The trend is to reclaim these huge address blocks, if possible, and recycle them into groups of smaller addresses. Also, as more class C addresses are assigned, routing tables on the Internet are filling up and causing memory overflows. The solution is to aggregate[12] groups of addresses into blocks and allocate them to ISPs which in turn subdivide these blocks and allocate them to customers. The address class designations (A, B, and C) described in the previous section are used less today, although subnets are still used. When you request an address block, your ISP usually gives as many addresses as you need and no more. The ISP aggregates several contiguous smaller blocks and routes them to your location. This aggregation is CIDR. Without CIDR, the Internet as we know it would not function.

For example, you might be allocated the 192.168.5.0/22 IP address block, which could support 2^{10} hosts (32 – 22 = 10). Your ISP would set its routers so that any packets going to an address in that block would be sent to your network. Internally,

---

10. The first and last networks are reserved in a manner similar to the first and last host, although the standard is flexible. You can configure your router(s) to reclaim the first and last networks in a subnet. Different routers have different techniques for reclaiming these networks.

11. Subtract 2 because the first and last host addresses on every network are reserved.

12. *Aggregate* means to join. In CIDR the aggregate of 208.178.99.124 and 208.178.99.125 is 208.178.99.124/23 (the aggregation of two class Cs).

your own routers might further subdivide this block of 1024 potential hosts into subnets, perhaps into four networks. Four networks require an additional two bits of addressing (2^2 = 4). You could set up your router to have four networks with this allocation: 192.168.5.0/24, 192.168.6.0/24, 192.168.7.0/24, and 192.168.8.0/24. Each of these networks could have 254 hosts. CIDR lets you arbitrarily divide networks and subnetworks into ever smaller blocks along the way. Each router has enough memory to keep track of the addresses it needs to direct and aggregates the rest. This scheme uses memory and address space efficiently. You could take 192.168.8.0/24 and further divided it into 16 networks with 14 hosts each. The 16 networks require four more bits (2^4 = 16), so you'd have 192.168.8.0/28, 192.168.8.16/28, 192.168.8.32/28, and so on to the last subnet of 192.168.8.240/16, which would have the hosts 192.168.8.241 through 192.168.8.254.

Hostnames

People generally find it easier to work with symbolic names than with numbers, and GNU/Linux provides several ways to associate hostnames with IP addresses. The oldest method is to consult a list of names and addresses that are stored in the **/etc/hosts** file:

```
$ cat /etc/hosts
127.0.0.1       localhost
130.128.52.1  gw-tcorp.tcorp.com    gw-tcorp
130.128.52.2  bravo.tcorp.com       bravo
130.128.52.3  hurrah.tcorp.com      hurrah
130.128.52.4  kudos.tcorp.com       kudos
```

The address 127.0.0.1 is reserved for the special hostname **localhost**, which serves as a hook for the system's networking software to operate on the local machine without going out onto a physical network. The names of the other systems are shown in two forms: in a *fully qualified domain* (FQDN) format that is meant to be unique and as a nickname that is unique locally but usually not unique over all the systems attached to the Internet.

As more hosts joined networks, storing these name-to-address mappings in a regular text file proved to be inefficient and inconvenient. The file grew ever larger and impossible to keep up-to-date. GNU/Linux supports NIS (Network Information Service, page 390) and NIS+, which were developed for use on Sun computers. Each of these network services stores information in a database. These solutions make it easier to find a specific address but are useful only for host information within a single administrative domain. Hosts outside the domain cannot access the information.

The solution is DNS (Domain Name Service, page 388). DNS effectively addresses the efficiency and update issues by arranging the entire network naming space as a hierarchy. Each domain in the DNS manages its own name space (addressing and name resolution), and each domain can easily query for any host or IP address by following the tree up or down the name space until the appropriate domain is found. By providing a hierarchical naming structure, DNS distributes name administration across the entire Internet.

IPv6

The explosive growth of the Internet has uncovered deficiencies in the design of the current address plan, most notably lack of addresses. Over the next few years, a revised protocol, named IPng (IP Next Generation), or IPv6 (IP version 6),[13] will be phased in (it may take longer; the phase-in is going quite slowly). This new scheme is designed to overcome the major limitations of the current approach and can be phased in gradually because it is compatible with the existing address usage. IPv6 makes it possible to assign many more unique Internet addresses (2^{128}, or 340 *undecillion* [10^{36}]) and offers support for security and performance control features.

IPv6

- Enables autoconfiguration. With IPv4 autoconfiguration is available via optional DHCP. With IPv6 autoconfiguration is mandatory, making it easy for hosts to configure their IP addresses automatically.

- Reserves 24 bits in the header for advanced services, such as resource reservation protocols, better backbone routing, and improved traffic engineering.

- Makes multicast protocols mandatory and uses them extensively. In IPv4 multicast, which improves scalability, is optional.

- Aggregates address blocks more efficiently because of the huge address space. This aggregation obsoletes *NAT* (page 1481), which decreased scalability and introduced protocol issues.

- Provides a simplified packet header that allows hardware accelerators to work better.

A sample IPv6 address is fe80::a00:20ff:feff:5be2/10. Each group of four hexadecimal digits is equivalent to a number between 0 and 65536 (16^4). A pair of adjacent colons indicates a hex value of 0x0000, and leading 0s need not be shown.

---

13. IPv5 referred to an experimental real-time stream protocol named ST; thus the jump from IPv4 to IPv6.

With eight sets of hexadecimal groupings, you have $65,536^8 = 2^{128}$ possible addresses. In an IPv6 address on a host with the default autoconfiguration, the first characters in the address are always fe80. The last 64 bits hold an interface ID designation which is often the *MAC address* (page 1478) of the Ethernet controller on the system.

Communicate over a Network

Many commands that you can use to communicate with other users on a single computer system have been extended to work over a network. Three examples of extended utilities, all of which were introduced in Chapter 3, are electronic mail programs (such as pine), information-gathering utilities (such as finger), and communications utilities (such as talk). These utilities are examples of the UNIX philosophy: Instead of creating a new, special-purpose tool, modify an existing one.

Many utilities understand a convention for the format of network addresses: **user@host** (spoken as *user at host*). When you use an @ sign in an argument to one of these utilities, the utility interprets the text that follows as the name of a remote host. When it does not include an @ sign, a utility assumes that you are requesting information from or corresponding with someone on your LAN.

The prompts shown in the examples in this chapter include the hostname of the machine you are using. When you frequently use more than one system over a network, you may find it difficult to keep track of which system you are using at any particular moment. If you set your prompt to include the hostname of the current system, it will always be clear which system you are using. To identify the computer you are using, run hostname or **uname –n**:

```
$ hostname
kudos
```

See pages 579 [bash tcsh] and 749 [zsh] for information on how you can change your prompt.

finger: Displays Information about Remote Users

The finger utility displays information about one or more users on a system. This utility was designed for local use, but when networks became popular, it was obvious that finger should be enhanced to reach out and collect information remotely. In the following examples, finger displays information about all the users logged in on the system named **bravo**:

```
[kudos]$ finger @bravo
[bravo.tcorp.com]
Login     Name            Tty   Idle  Login Time   Office      Office Phone
root      root            *1    1:35  Oct 22  5:00
alex      Alex Watson     4           Oct 22 12:23 (kudos)
alex      Alex Watson     5      19   Oct 22 12:33 (:0)
jenny     Jenny Chen      7     2:24  Oct 22  8:45 (:0)
hls       Helen Simpson   11     2d   Oct 20 12:23 (:0)
```

A user's login name in front of the @ sign causes finger to display information from the remote system for the specified user only. If there are multiple matches for that name on the remote system, finger displays the results for all of them.

```
[kudos]$ finger alex@bravo
[bravo.tcorp.com]
Login     Name            Tty   Idle  Login Time   Office      Office Phone
alex      Alex Watson     4           Oct 22 12:23 (kudos)
alex      Alex Watson     5      19   Oct 22 12:33 (:0)
```

The finger utility works by querying a standard network service, the **fingerd** daemon, that runs on the system being queried. Although this service is supplied with Red Hat Linux, some sites choose not to run it to minimize the load on their systems, reduce security risks, or maintain privacy. When you use finger to obtain information about someone at such a site, you will see an error message or nothing at all. It is the remote **fingerd** daemon that determines how much information to share with your system and in what format. As a result, the report displayed for any given system may differ from the preceding examples.

The fingerd Daemon   ‖ security

The finger daemon (fingerd) gives away system account information that can aid a malicious user. Some sites disable finger or randomize user account IDs to make a malicious user's job more difficult. Disable finger by giving the following command as root: chkconfig finger off.

The information for remote finger looks much the same as it does when finger runs on your local system, with one difference: Before displaying the results, finger reports the name of the remote system that answered the query (**bravo**, as shown in brackets in the preceding example). The name of the host that answers may be different from the system name you specified on the command line, depending on how the finger daemon service is configured at the remote end. In some cases several hostnames may be listed if one finger daemon contacts another to retrieve the information.

Sending Mail to a Remote User

Given a user's login name on a remote system and the name of the remote system or its domain, you can use an e-mail program, such as pine (page 87), to send a message over the network or the Internet, using the @ form of an address:

```
jenny@bravo
```

or

```
jenny@tcorp.com
```

Although the @ form of a network address is recognized by many GNU/Linux utilities, you may find that you can reach more remote computers with e-mail than with the other networking utilities described in this chapter. The reason for this disparity is that the mail system can deliver a message to a host that does not run IP, even though it appears to have an Internet address. The message may be routed over the network, for example, until it reaches a remote system that has a point-to-point, dial-up connection to the destination system. Other utilities, such as talk, rely on IP and operate only between networked hosts.

Mailing List Servers

A mailing list server (listserv[14]) allows you to create, manage, and administrate an e-mail list. An electronic mailing list provides a means for people interested in a topic to participate in an electronic discussion and for a person to disseminate information periodically to a potentially large mailing list. One of the most powerful features of most list servers is the ability to archive e-mail postings to the list, create an archive index, and allow users to retrieve postings from the archive based on keywords or discussion threads. Typically you can subscribe and unsubscribe from the list with or without human intervention. The owner of the list can restrict who can subscribe, unsubscribe, and post messages to the list. Popular list servers include LISTSERV (www.lsoft.com), Lyris (www.lyris.com), Majordomo (www.greatcircle.com/majordomo), Mailman (www.list.org), and ListProc (www.listproc.net). Red Hat maintains several mailing lists (https://listman.redhat.com) and list archives (www.redhat.com/mailing-lists). Use a browser to search on linux mailing list to find (many) other lists.

---

14. Although the term *listserv* is sometimes used generically to include many different list server programs, it is a specific product and a registered trademark of L-soft International, Inc.: LISTSERV (www.l-soft.com).

Network Utilities

To make use of a networked environment, it made sense to extend certain tools, some of which have already been described. Networks also created a need for new utilities to control and monitor them; this led to ideas for new tools that took advantage of network speed and connectivity. This section describes concepts and utilities for systems attached to a network; without a network connection, they are of little use.

Trusted Hosts

Some commands, including rcp and rsh, work only if the remote system trusts your local computer (that is, the remote system knows your local computer and believes that it is not pretending to be a system that it is not). The **/etc/hosts.equiv** file lists trusted systems. For reasons of security, Superuser account does not rely on this file to identify trusted Superusers from other systems.

Host-based trust is largely obsolete. The rcp, rlogin, and rsh commands[15] are deprecated in favor of ssh (page 374) and scp (page 376). Because there are many ways to subvert trusted host security, including subverting DNS systems and *IP spoofing* (page 1474), authentication based on IP address is widely regarded as insecure and obsolete. In a small homogeneous network of machines with local DNS control, it can be "good enough." The ease of use in these situations may outweigh the security concerns.

Do Not Share Your Login Account || security

You can use a .rhosts file to allow another user to log in as you from a remote system without knowing your password. *This setup is not recommended.* Do not compromise the security of your files or the entire system by sharing your login account. Use **ssh** and **scp** instead of **rsh** and **rcp** whenever possible.

---

15. The daemons necessary to set up a trusted host server are not included in default configurations of recent Red Hat releases, but the programs needed to access such a server are. This allows backward compatibility without propagating old technology. The **rsh-server*.rpm** package provides the **rlogind** and **rshd** daemons as well as files necessary to set up an rcp, rlogin, and/or rsh server.

ssh: Logs in or Runs a Command on a Remote Computer

You can use the secure ssh utility to log in on a remote system over the network. You might choose to use a remote system to access a special-purpose application, use a device that is available only on that system, or because you know that the remote system is faster or not as busy as your local computer. While traveling, many people use ssh on a laptop to log in on a system at headquarters. From a GUI you are able to use many systems simultaneously by logging in on each, using a different terminal emulator window.

You can log in on a remote machine that is running the **sshd** daemon and that you have an account on. For information on configuring ssh, see page 1029. All communication under ssh, including your name and password, is encrypted. When your login name is the same on the local and remote machines, give the command **ssh** *hostname*, where *hostname* is the name of the machine that you want to log in on:

```
[bravo]$ ssh kudos
alex@kudos's password:
Last login: Sat Sep 14 06:51:59 from bravo
Have a lot of fun...
You have new mail.
[kudos]$
...
[kudos]$ logout
Connection to kudos closed.
[bravo]$
```

After you supply your password, you are running a shell on the remote machine. When you log out, the connection is broken, and you resume using your local computer. To log in with a user name different from the one you are using on the local machine, give the command **ssh** *user@hostname*, where *user* is your login name on the remote machine named *hostname*:[16]

```
[bravo]$ ssh watson@kudos
watson@kudos's password:
...
[kudos]$
```

The ssh utility also allows you to run a command on a remote system without logging in on that system. When you need to run more than one command, it is usually easier to log in and run the commands on the remote machine. The next example runs ls on the **memos** directory on the remote system **kudos**. The example assumes that the user running the command has a login on **kudos** and that **memos** is in the user's home directory on **kudos**:

---

16. The –l (ell) option performs the same function: **ssh –l watson kudos**.

```
[bravo]$ ssh kudos ls memos
alex@kudos's password:
memo.0921
memo.draft
[bravo]$
```

Suppose that a file named **memo.new** is on your local machine and that you cannot remember whether it contains certain changes or whether you made these changes to the file named **memo.draft** on the system named **kudos**. You could copy **memo.draft** to your local system and run diff (page 67) on the two files, but then you would have three similar copies of the file spread across two systems. If you are not careful about removing the old copies when you are done, you may be confused again in a few days. Instead of copying the file, you can use ssh:

```
[bravo]$ ssh kudos cat memos/memo.draft | diff memos.new -
```

When you run ssh, standard output of the command run on the remote machine is passed to the local shell as though the command had been run in place on the local machine. Unless you quote characters that have special meaning to the shell, they are interpreted by the local machine. In the preceding example the output of the cat command on **kudos** is sent through a pipe on **bravo** to diff (running on **bravo**), which compares the local file **memos.new** to standard input (–). The following command line has the same effect but causes diff to run on the remote system:

```
[bravo]$ cat memos.new | ssh kudos diff - memos/memo.draft
```

Standard output from diff on the remote system is sent to the local shell, which displays it on the screen (because it is not redirected). Refer to page 1321 in Part III for more information on ssh.

Optional

The ssh utility can tunnel other protocols. You can secure protocols including POP, X, IMAP, and WWW using ssh as a virtual private network (VPN) between the two systems. Assume that you have a POP client on your local machine, the POP server is on a remote network that is protected by a firewall, and that you can access the remote network only using ssh. You can tunnel the POP protocol, which uses port 110, through an ssh tunnel. In this example, **kudos** is the firewall gateway machine, **pophost** is the POP server, and 1550 is a local port that you selected to use on your end of the tunnel.

```
$ ssh -N -L 1550:pophost:110 kudos
```

The **–N** option causes ssh not to execute any remote commands: ssh works only as a private network to forward ports. You can forward ports in either direction and in combination by using the **–L** and **–R** flags. See the ssh man page for details.

Once you are authenticated, you can set your POP client so that the POP server is **localhost** and the POP port is 1550. Then, when the client fetches e-mail, it makes a connection to port 1550 on the local machine which is forwarded through the ssh tunnel to **kudos** and then to **pophost** port 110 where the real daemon is running.

scp: Copies a file from/to a Remote Computer

The scp (secure copy) utility copies a file from one computer to another on a network. Using ssh to transfer files, scp uses the same authentication mechanism as ssh and therefore provides the same security. The scp utility asks you for a password when it is needed for security. The format of an scp command is

scp [fromhost:]source-file [tohost:][destination-file]

You can copy from or to your local machine or between two remote machines. When you specify a simple, or relative, filename, it is assumed to be relative to your home directory on a remote machine and relative to your working directory on your local machine. An absolute pathname describes a path from the root directory on any machine. Make sure that you have read permission to the file you are copying and write permission for the directory you are copying it into. In the following example, Alex uses scp to copy **rain.jpg** from his working directory on **bravo** (which happens to be his home directory) to his home directory on **kudos**:

```
[alex@bravo alex]$ scp rain.jpg kudos:
alex@kudos's password:
rain.jpg          100% |*************************| 30161    00:00
```

As the transfer progresses, the percent and number of bytes transferred increase and the time remaining decreases. The asterisks provide a visual representation of the progress of the transfer.

Use the **–r** option to copy a directory recursively. See the scp man page for more information.

telnet: Logs in on a Remote Computer

You can use the TELNET protocol to interact with a remote computer. The telnet utility, a user interface to this protocol, is older than ssh and is not secure but may work where ssh is not available (there is more non-UNIX support for TELNET access than there is for ssh access). In addition, many legacy devices, such as terminal servers and network devices, do not support ssh.

```
[bravo]$ telnet kudos
Trying 130.128.52.2...
Connected to kudos.tcorp.com
Escape character is '^]'.

Welcome to SuSE Linux 7.3 (i386) - Kernel 2.4.10-4GB (2).
kudos login: watson
Password:
You have old mail in /var/mail/watson.
Last login: Mon Feb 25 14:46:55 from bravo.tcorp.com
watson@kudos:~>
.
.
.
watson@kudos:~> logout
Connection closed by foreign host.
[bravo]$
```

When you connect to a remote UNIX or GNU/Linux system through telnet, you are presented with a regular login: prompt. Unless you specify differently, the ssh utility assumes that your login name on the remote system matches that on the local system. Because telnet is designed to work with non-UNIX/Linux systems, it makes no such assumptions.

telnet Is Not Secure || security

Whenever you enter sensitive information, such as your password, while you are using telnet, it is transmitted in cleartext and can be read by someone who is listening in on the session.

Another difference between these two utilities is that telnet allows you to configure many special parameters, such as how RETURNs or interrupts are processed. When using telnet between two UNIX/Linux systems, you rarely need to change any parameters.

When you do not specify the name of a remote host on the command line, telnet runs in an interactive mode. The following example is equivalent to the previous telnet example:

```
[bravo]$ telnet
telnet> open kudos
Trying 130.128.52.2...
Connected to kudos.tcorp.com
Escape character is '^]'.
...
```

Before connecting you to a remote system, telnet tells you what your *escape character* is; in most cases it is ^] (the ^ represents the CONTROL key on your keyboard). When you press CONTROL-], you escape to telnet's interactive mode. Continuing the preceding example:

```
[kudos]$ CONTROL-]
telnet> ?
```

(displays help information)

```
telnet> close
Connection closed.
[bravo]$
```

When you enter a question mark in response to the telnet> prompt, telnet displays a list of its commands. The **close** command ends the current telnet session, returning you to your local system. To get out of telnet's interactive mode and resume communication with the remote system, press RETURN in response to a prompt.

It has been possible to use telnet to access special remote services at sites that have chosen to make such services available. However, many of these services, such as the U.S. Library of Congress Information System (LOCIS), have moved to the Web, so you can now obtain the same information by using a Web browser.

ftp: Transfers Files over a Network

You can use the ftp[17] (file transfer protocol) utility to transfer files between systems on a network. This interactive utility allows you to browse through a directory on the remote system to identify files you may want to transfer:

```
[kudos]$ ftp bravo
Connected to bravo.tcorp.com.
220 bravo.tcorp.com FTP server (Version wu-2.6.1-20) ready.
Name (bravo:alex): watson
331 Password required for watson.
Password:
230 User watson logged in.
Remote system type is UNIX.
Using binary mode to transfer files.
ftp> bin
200 Type set to I.
ftp> cd memos
250 CWD command successful.
```

---

17. The sftp (secure file transfer program) utility, which is included with Red Hat Linux, is similar to ftp but works over an encrypted ssh connection. See the sftp man page for more information.

```
ftp> put memo.921
local: memo.921 remote: memo.921
200 PORT command successful.
227 Entering Passive Mode (192,168,0,1,225,45)
150 Opening BINARY mode data connection for memo.921. (8401 bytes)
100% |***************************| 8401   3.38 KB/s   00:00 ETA
226 Transfer complete.
8401 bytes received in 00:02 (3.38 KB/s)
ftp> quit
221-You have transferred 56064 bytes in 1 files.
221-Total traffic for this session was 56485 bytes in 1 transfers.
221-Thank you for using the FTP service on bravo.tcorp.com.
221 Goodbye.
[kudos]$
```

The remote system prompts you for a login name and password. By default the system expects that your login name is the same on both systems; just press RETURN if it is. In this case it is not, so Alex enters **watson** before pressing RETURN. Then he enters his password.

Although it is not necessary in this case, Alex gives a **bin** (binary) command as a matter of habit; he always establishes binary transfer mode as soon as he logs in.[18] With ftp in binary mode, you can transfer ASCII and binary files. ASCII mode can guarantee the successful transfer of ASCII files only.

Binary mode transfers an exact, byte-for-byte image of a file. ASCII mode performs end-of-line conversions between different systems and is consequently slower than binary mode. DOS/MS Windows, Macintosh, and UNIX/Linux each use different characters to indicate the end of a line of text. For example, Microsoft operating systems use a RETURN (CONTROL-M) followed by a NEWLINE (CONTROL-J) to mark the end of a line, whereas UNIX/Linux uses a NEWLINE by itself. Use ASCII mode to transfer plain text files (sometimes indicated by a **.txt** filename extension) only. Transfer Microsoft Word and other word processing documents in binary mode, as they are not plain text files. Unless you specifically need to convert the end-of-line characters, use binary mode.

Before transferring the file, Alex uses ftp's **cd** command to change directories *on the remote system* (use **lcd** to change directories on the local system). Then the **put** command, followed by the filename, transfers the file to the remote system in the remote working directory (**memos**).

The ftp utility makes no assumptions about filesystem structure, because you can use ftp to exchange files with non-UNIX/Linux systems (whose filenaming conventions may be different).

---

18. The ncftp utility, which is included with Red Hat Linux, takes care of the binary issue and others automatically. It is a front end for standard ftp that runs in place of ftp. See the ncftp man page for more information.

Anonymous FTP

Systems often provide ftp access to anyone on a network by providing a special lo-gin: **anonymous** (you can usually use the login name **ftp** in place of **anonymous**). The anonymous FTP user is usually restricted to a portion of a filesystem that has been set aside to hold files that are to be shared with remote users. Traditionally any password is acceptable for anonymous FTP; by convention you are expected to give your e-mail address. Some sites reject your connection if they cannot iden-tify the name of your computer or if you supply a password that doesn't match the name of your site. Alex can enter **alex@tcorp.com** in response to the password prompt.

While using ftp, you can type **help** at any ftp> prompt to see a list of com-mands. For using Mozilla to perform an anonymous FTP transfer, see "Down-loading a File" on page 408. Refer to page 1180 in Part III for more information on ftp.

ping: Tests a Network Connection

The ping[19] utility (http://ftp.arl.mil/~mike/ping.html) sends an ECHO_REQUEST packet to a remote computer. This packet causes the remote system to send back a reply. This is a quick way to verify that a remote system is available, as well as to check how well the network is operating, such as how fast it is or whether it is dropping data packets. The protocol ping uses is ICMP (Internet Control Message Protocol). Without any options ping tests the connection once per second until you abort the execution with CONTROL-C.

```
[kudos]$ ping tsx-11.mit.edu
PING tsx-11.mit.edu (18.86.0.44) from 10.0.1.5 : 56(84) bytes of data.
64 bytes from TSX-11.MIT.EDU (18.86.0.44): icmp_seq=0 ttl=48 time=500.199 msec
64 bytes from TSX-11.MIT.EDU (18.86.0.44): icmp_seq=1 ttl=48 time=518.703 msec
64 bytes from TSX-11.MIT.EDU (18.86.0.44): icmp_seq=2 ttl=48 time=516.304 msec
64 bytes from TSX-11.MIT.EDU (18.86.0.44): icmp_seq=3 ttl=48 time=95.807 msec
CONTROL-C

--- tsx-11.mit.edu ping statistics ---
4 packets transmitted, 4 packets received, 0% packet loss
round-trip min/avg/max/mdev = 95.807/407.753/518.703/180.243 ms
```

In this example the remote system named **tsx-11.mit.edu** is up and available to you over the network.

---

19. The name ping mimics the sound of a sonar burst used by submarines to identify and communicate with each other. The word ping also expands to Packet Internet Groper.

By default ping sends packets containing 64 bytes (56 data bytes and 8 bytes of protocol header information). In the preceding example four packets were sent to the system **tsx-11.mit.edu** before the user interrupted ping by pressing CONTROL-C. The four-part number in parentheses on each line is the remote system's IP address. A packet sequence number (called **icmp_seq**) is also given. If a packet is dropped, a gap occurs in the sequence numbers. The round-trip time is listed last, in microseconds; this represents the time that elapsed from when the packet was sent from the local system to the remote system until the reply from the remote system was received by the local system. This time is affected by the distance between the two systems, as well as by network traffic and the load on both computers. Before it terminates, ping summarizes the results, indicating how many packets were sent and received, as well as the minimum, average, maximum, and mean deviation round-trip times it measured.

When ping **Cannot Connect** ‖ tip

If unable to contact the remote system, **ping** continues trying until you interrupt it with CONTROL-C. There may be several reasons why a system does not answer: The remote computer may be down, the network interface or some part of the network between the systems may be broken, there may be a software failure, or the remote machine may be set up, for reasons of security, not to return **ping**s (try pinging www.microsoft.com or www.ibm.com).

---

traceroute: Traces a Route over the Internet

The traceroute utility, supplied with Red Hat Linux, traces the route an IP packet follows, including all the intermediary points traversed (called *network hops*), to its destination (the argument to traceroute—an Internet host). It displays a numbered list of host names, if available, and IP addresses, together with the round-trip time it took for a packet to get to each router along the way and an acknowledgment to get back. You can put this information to good use when you are trying to determine where a network bottleneck is.

The traceroute utility has no concept of the path from one host to the next; it simply sends out packets with increasing *TTL* values. TTL is an IP header field that indicates how many more hops the packet should be allowed to make before being discarded or returned. In the case of a traceroute packet, the packet is returned by the host that has the packet when the TTL value is zero. The result is a list of hosts that the packet travels through to get to its destination.

The traceroute utility can help you solve routing configuration problems and routing path failures. When you cannot reach a host, use traceroute to see what path the packet follows, how far it gets, and what the delay is.

The next example is the output of traceroute following a route from a local computer to **www.linux.org**. The first line tells you the IP address of the target, the maximum number of hops that will be traced, and the size of the packets that will be used. Each numbered line contains the name and IP address of the intermediate destination, followed by the time it takes a packet to make a round-trip to that destination and back. The traceroute utility sends three packets to each destination; thus there are three times on each line. Line 1 shows the statistics when a packet is sent to the local gateway (under 3 ms). Lines 4–6 show it bouncing around Mountain View (California) before it goes to San Jose. Between hops 13 and 14 the packet travels across the United States (San Francisco to somewhere in the East). By hop 18 the packet has found **www.linux.org**. The traceroute utility displays asterisks when it does not receive a response. Each asterisk indicates that traceroute has waited three seconds.

```
$ /usr/sbin/traceroute www.linux.org
traceroute to www.linux.org (198.182.196.56), 30 hops max, 38 byte packets
 1  gw.localco.com. (204.94.139.65)  2.904 ms   2.425 ms   2.783 ms
 2  covad-gw2.meer.net (209.157.140.1)  19.727 ms   23.287 ms   24.783 ms
 3  gw-mv1.meer.net (140.174.164.1)  18.795 ms   24.973 ms   19.207 ms
 4  d1-4-2.a02.mtvwca01.us.ra.verio.net (206.184.210.241)  59.091 ms d1-10-0-0-200.a03.
     mtvwca01.us.ra.verio.net (206.86.28.5)  54.948 ms   39.485 ms
 5  fa-11-0-0.a01.mtvwca01.us.ra.verio.net (206.184.188.1)  40.182 ms   44.405 ms 49.362 ms
 6  p1-1-0-0.a09.mtvwca01.us.ra.verio.net (205.149.170.66)  78.688 ms   66.266 ms 28.003 ms
 7  p1-12-0-0.a01.snjsca01.us.ra.verio.net (209.157.181.166) 32.424 ms 94.337 ms 54.946 ms
 8  f4-1-0.sjc0.verio.net (129.250.31.81)  38.952 ms   63.111 ms   49.083 ms
 9  sjc0.nuq0.verio.net (129.250.3.98)  45.031 ms   43.496 ms   44.925 ms
10  mae-west1.US.CRL.NET (198.32.136.10)  48.525 ms   66.296 ms   38.996 ms
11  t3-ames.3.sfo.us.crl.net (165.113.0.249)  138.808 ms   78.579 ms   68.699 ms
12  E0-CRL-SFO-02-E0X0.US.CRL.NET (165.113.55.2)  43.023 ms   51.910 ms   42.967 ms
13  sfo2-vva1.ATM.us.crl.net (165.113.0.254)  135.551 ms   154.606 ms   178.632 ms
14  mae-east-02.ix.ai.net (192.41.177.202)  158.351 ms   201.811 ms   204.560 ms
15  oc12-3-0-0.mae-east.ix.ai.net (205.134.161.2)  202.851 ms   155.667 ms   219.116 ms
16  border-ai.invlogic.com (205.134.175.254)  214.622 ms  *  190.423 ms
17  router.invlogic.com (198.182.196.1)  224.378 ms   235.427 ms   228.856 ms
18  www.linux.org (198.182.196.56)  207.964 ms   178.683 ms   179.483 ms
```

host and dig: Queries Internet Name Servers

The host utility looks up an IP address given a name or vice versa. This utility is easy to use and replaces nslookup in its simplest case. The following example shows how to use host to look up the domain name of a machine, given an IP address:

```
$ host 140.174.164.2
2.164.174.140.in-addr.arpa. domain name pointer ns.meer.net.
```

You can also use host to determine the IP address of a domain name:

```
$ host ns.meer.net
ns.meer.net. has address 140.174.164.2
```

The dig (domain information groper) utility queries DNS servers and individual machines for information about a domain. A powerful utility, dig has many features that you may never use. It is more involved than host and replaces nslookup in its complex cases. The following dig command uses the keyword **any** to get any available information about the **upstate.edu** domain.

```
# dig any upstate.edu
; <<>> DiG 9.1.3 <<>> any upstate.edu
;; global options:  printcmd
;; Got answer:
;; ->>HEADER<<- opcode: QUERY, status: NOERROR, id: 30224;; flags: qr rd ra; QUERY: 1,
ANSWER: 11, AUTHORITY: 5, ADDITIONAL: 7

;; QUESTION SECTION:
;upstate.edu.                    IN      ANY

;; ANSWER SECTION:
upstate.edu.            74567   IN      NS      dns.duc.upstate.edu.
upstate.edu.            74567   IN      NS      dns.eng.upstate.edu.
upstate.edu.            74567   IN      NS      dns.acesag.upstate.edu.
upstate.edu.            74567   IN      NS      dns.upstate.edu.
upstate.edu.            74567   IN      NS      nr01.netmgt.upstate.edu.
upstate.edu.            83413   IN      SOA     dns.upstate.edu. bailebn.noc.upstate.edu.
2002022106 3600 900 259200 86400
upstate.edu.            83438   IN      MX      10 ducserv6.duc.upstate.edu.
upstate.edu.            83438   IN      MX      10 ducserv3c.duc.upstate.edu.
upstate.edu.            83438   IN      MX      10 ducserv6b.duc.upstate.edu.
upstate.edu.            83438   IN      MX      20 ducserv3.duc.upstate.edu.
upstate.edu.            83438   IN      MX      20 ducserv3b.duc.upstate.edu.

;; AUTHORITY SECTION:
upstate.edu.            74567   IN      NS      dns.duc.upstate.edu.
upstate.edu.            74567   IN      NS      dns.eng.upstate.edu.
upstate.edu.            74567   IN      NS      dns.acesag.upstate.edu.
upstate.edu.            74567   IN      NS      dns.upstate.edu.
upstate.edu.            74567   IN      NS      nr01.netmgt.upstate.edu.

;; ADDITIONAL SECTION:
dns.duc.upstate.edu.      2867   IN      A       192.168.2.10
dns.eng.upstate.edu.     68182   IN      A       192.168.10.13
dns.acesag.upstate.edu. 132867   IN      A       192.168.46.50
dns.upstate.edu.        160958   IN      A       192.168.41.3

nr01.netmgt.upstate.edu. 74567   IN      A       192.168.253.191ducserv6.duc.upstate.edu.
83438   IN      A       192.168.2.27
ducserv3c.duc.upstate.edu. 83438 IN      A       192.168.2.148

;; Query time: 29 msec
;; SERVER: 140.174.164.2#53(140.174.164.2)
;; WHEN: Thu Feb 28 15:54:33 2002
;; MSG SIZE  rcvd: 499
```

The dig utility displays a lot of information.

- The Authority Section specifies the primary name servers, and the Additional Section specifies the IP addresses that correspond to the names in the Authority Section.

- The SERVER line (toward the end) specifies the name and IP address of the DNS server that the local system uses: This is where dig gets its information.

- The second column specifies the *TTL* (page 1499) in seconds.

- IN in the third column is the query class and indicates that this is an Internet class query.

- NS, SOA, MX, NS, or A in the fourth column specifies the type of information (DNS query type) that the row holds:

  - The NS (name server) record(s) specify name servers that **upstate.edu** uses. An NS record is meaningful only when you query a domain.

  - The MX (mail exchanger) record(s) specify a mail server for the domain you are querying. The **upstate.edu** domain has several mail servers. The lower the preference value (the number before the mail server domain in the right column), the higher the priority (**ducserv6b** is always tried before **ducserv3**).

  - There is one SOA (start or zone of authority) for a given domain. The SOA

    - Is the authoritative primary DNS for the domain.

    - Defines who the point of contact is for the domain.

    - Controls the TTL for records from the DNS.

    - Controls how often another name server will retry the domain's name server.

    - Controls when another name server will timeout when trying to contact the domain's name server.

  - The A (network Address) record specifies in the last column the IP address that corresponds to the domain name in the first column.

The dig utility has many query types. The **any** type is used in the preceding example. You can also use **mx, ns, soa,** and others. Refer to the dig man page for more details.

whois: Looks Up Information about an Internet Site

The whois utility queries a whois server for information about an Internet site. This utility returns site contact and InterNIC or other registry information that can help you track down the person responsible for a site: Perhaps that person is sending you or your company *spam* (page 1493). Many sites on the Internet are easier to use and faster than whois. Use a browser to search on whois or go to www.netsol.com/cgi-bin/whois/whois or www.ripe.net/perl/whois to get started.

When you search by name, whois may return more than one entry. In the following example, whois returns SOBELL.NET and SOBELL.COM when queried for sobell:

```
$ whois sobell
[whois.crsnic.net]

Whois Server Version 1.3

Domain names in the .com, .net, and .org domains can now be registered
with many different competing registrars. Go to http://www.internic.net
for detailed information.

SOBELL.NET
SOBELL.COM

To single out one record, look it up with "xxx", where xxx is one of the
of the records displayed above. If the records are the same, look them up
with "=xxx" to receive a full display for each record.

>>> Last update of whois database: Tue, 26 Feb 2002 05:22:08 EST <<<

The Registry database contains ONLY .COM, .NET, .ORG, .EDU domains and
Registrars.
```

When you do not specify a whois server, whois defaults to **whois.crsnic.net**. Set the **NICNAMESERVER** or **WHOISSERVER** shell variables, or use the **–h** option to whois to specify a different whois server.

To obtain information on a domain name, specify the complete domain name as in the following example:

```
$ whois sobell.com
[whois.crsnic.net]

Whois Server Version 1.3

Domain names in the .com, .net, and .org domains can now be registered
with many different competing registrars. Go to http://www.internic.net
for detailed information.

   Domain Name: SOBELL.COM
   Registrar: NETWORK SOLUTIONS, INC.
   Whois Server: whois.networksolutions.com
   Referral URL: http://www.networksolutions.com
   Name Server: NS.MEER.NET
   Name Server: NS2.MEER.NET
   Updated Date: 05-nov-2001
```

```
>>> Last update of whois database: Tue, 26 Feb 2002 05:22:08 EST <<<

The Registry database contains ONLY .COM, .NET, .ORG, .EDU domains and
Registrars.

Registrant:
Sobell Associates Inc (SOBELL-DOM)
    PO Box 1089
    Menlo Park, CA 94026
    US

    Domain Name: SOBELL.COM

    Administrative Contact, Billing Contact:
        Sobell, Mark  (MS989)  sobell@MEER.NET
        Sobell Associates Inc
        PO Box 1089
        Menlo Park, CA 94026
[No phone]
    Technical Contact:
        meer.net hostmaster  (MN85-ORG)  hostmaster@MEER.NET
        meer.net
        po box 390804
        Mountain View, CA 94039
        US
        +1.888.844.6337
        Fax- +1.888.844.6337

    Record last updated on 09-Apr-2000.
    Record expires on 08-Apr-2004.
    Record created on 07-Apr-1995.
    Database last updated on 26-Feb-2002 01:57:00 EST.

    Domain servers in listed order:

    NS.MEER.NET                    140.174.164.2
    NS2.MEER.NET                   216.206.136.2
```

Several top-level registries serve various regions of the world. The ones you are most likely to use are

- North American Registry: **whois.arin.net**

- European Registry: **www.ripe.net**

- Asia-Pacific Registry: **www.apnic.net**

- American Military: **whois.nic.mil**

- American Government: **www.nic.gov**

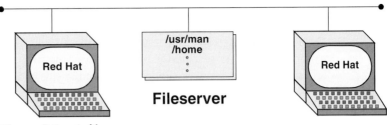

Figure 9-2   A fileserver

Distributed Computing

When many similar systems are on a network, it is often desirable to share common files and utilities among them. For example, a system administrator might choose to keep a copy of the system documentation on one computer's disk and to make those files available for all remote systems. In this case the system administrator configures the files so that users who need to access the online documentation are not aware that the files are stored on a remote system. This type of setup, which is an example of *distributed computing,* not only conserves disk space but also allows you to update one central copy of the documentation rather than tracking down and updating copies scattered throughout the network on many different systems.

Figure 9-2 illustrates a *fileserver* that stores the system manual pages and users' home directories. With this arrangement, a user's files are always available to that user—no matter which system the user is on. Each system's disk might contain a directory to hold temporary files, as well as a copy of the operating system. For more information refer to "**exportfs**: Stores Permissions to Mount Local Filesystems" on page 1018 and "**autofs**: Automatically Mounts Filesystems" on page 979.

The Client/Server Model

Although there are many ways to distribute computing tasks on hosts attached to a network, the client/server model dominates UNIX and GNU/Linux system networking. A server system offers services to its clients and is usually a central resource. In Figure 9-2 the system that acts as the documentation repository is a server, and all the systems that contact it to display information are clients. Some servers are designed to interact with specific utilities, such as Web servers and browser clients. Other servers, such as those supporting DNS, communicate with one another in addition to answering queries from a variety of clients; in other words, a server can act as a client when it queries another server.

The client/server terminology also applies to processes that may be running on one or more systems. A server process may control a central database while client processes send queries to the server and collect replies. In this case the client and server processes may be running on the same computer. The client/server model underlies most of the network services described in this chapter.

DNS: Domain Name Service

DNS is a distributed service: Name servers on thousands of machines around the world cooperate to keep the database up-to-date. The database itself, which contains the information that maps hundreds of thousands of alphanumeric hostnames into numeric IP addresses, does not exist in one place. That is, no system has a complete copy of the database. Instead each system that runs DNS knows about the hosts that are local to that site and how to contact other name servers to learn about other, nonlocal hosts.

Like the GNU/Linux filesystem, DNS is organized hierarchically. Each country has an ISO (International Standards Organization) country code designation as its domain name, (For example, AU represents Australia, IL is Israel, and JP is Japan; see www.iana.org/cctld/cctld.htm for a complete list.) Although the United States is represented in the same way (US) and uses the standard two-letter Postal Service abbreviations to identify the next level of the domain, only governments and a few organization use these codes. Schools in the US domain are represented by a third- (and sometimes second-) level domain: k12. For example, the domain name for Myschool in New York state could be www.myschool.k12.ny.us.

Following is a list of the six original, common, top-level domains. These domains are used extensively within the United States and, to a lesser degree, by users in other countries:

- COM   Commercial enterprises
- EDU   Educational institutions
- GOV   Nonmilitary government agencies
- MIL   Military government agencies
- NET   Networking organizations
- ORG   Other (often nonprofit) organizations

As this book was being written, the following additional top-level domains had been approved for use:

- AERO   Air-transport industry
- BIZ   Business
- COOP   Cooperatives
- INFO   Unrestricted use
- MUSEUM Museums
- NAME Name registries

As with Internet addresses, domain names used to be assigned by the Network Information Center (NIC [page 362]). Now they are assigned by several companies. A system's full name, referred to as its *fully qualified domain name* (FQDN), is unambiguous in the way that a simple hostname cannot be. The system **okeeffe.berkeley.edu** at the University of California, Berkeley (Figure 9-3) is not the same as one named **okeeffe.moma.org**, which might represent a host at the Museum of Modern Art. The domain name not only tells you something about where the system is located but also adds enough diversity to the name space to avoid confusion when different sites choose similar names for their systems.

Unlike the filesystem hierarchy, the top-level domain name in the United States appears last (reading from left to right). Also, domain names are not case sensitive. The names **okeeffe.berkeley.edu**, **okeeffe.Berkeley.edu**, and **okeeffe.Berkeley.EDU** refer to the same computer. Once a domain has been assigned, the local site is free to extend the hierarchy to meet local needs.

With DNS, mail addressed to **user@tcorp.com** can be delivered to the **tcorp.com** computer that handles the corporate mail and knows how to forward messages to user mailboxes on individual machines. As the company grows, the site administrator might decide to create organizational or geographical subdomains. The name **tcorp.ca.tcorp.com** might refer to a system that supports California offices, with **alpha.co.tcorp.com** dedicated to Colorado. Functional subdomains might be another choice, with **tcorp.sales.tcorp.com** and **alpha.dev.tcorp.com** representing the sales and development divisions, respectively.

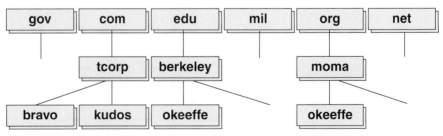

Figure 9-3   United States top-level domains

On GNU/Linux systems the most common interface to the DNS is BIND (Berkeley Internet Name Domain) software. BIND follows the client/server model. On any given local network, one or more systems may be running a name server, supporting all the local hosts as clients. When it wants to send a message to another host, a system queries the nearest name server to learn the remote host's IP address. The client, called a *resolver,* may be a process running on the same computer as the name server, or it may pass the request over the network to reach a server. To reduce network traffic and accelerate name lookups, the local name server has some knowledge of distant hosts. If the local server has to contact a remote server to pick up an address, when the answer comes back, the local server adds that to its internal table and reuses it for a while. The name server deletes the nonlocal information before it can become outdated. Refer to "TTL" on page 1499.

How the system translates symbolic hostnames into addresses is transparent to most users; only the system administrator of a networked system needs to be concerned with the details of name resolution. Systems that use DNS for name resolution are generally capable of communicating with the greatest number of hosts—more than would be practical to maintain in an **/etc/hosts** file or private NIS database.

Four common sources are used for host name resolution: NIS, NIS+, DNS, and system files (such as **/etc/hosts**). GNU/Linux does not ask you to choose among these sources; rather, the **nsswitch.conf** file (page 962) allows you to choose any of these sources, in any combination, and in any order.

NIS: Network Information Service

NIS is another example of the client/server paradigm. Sun Microsystems developed NIS to simplify the administration of certain common administrative files by maintaining them in a central database and having clients contact the database server to retrieve information. Just as the DNS addresses the problem of keeping multiple copies of the **hosts** file up-to-date, NIS keeps system-independent configuration files (such as **/etc/passwd**) current. Most networks today are *heterogeneous* (page 1470), and even though they run different varieties of UNIX or GNU/Linux, they have certain common attributes (such as the **passwd** file).

NIS was formerly named the *Yellow Pages,* and people still refer to it by this name. Sun renamed the service because another corporation holds the trademark to that name. The names of NIS utilities, however, are still reminiscent of the old name: ypcat displays an NIS database, ypmatch searches, and so on.

Consider the **/etc/group** file, which maps symbolic names to group ID numbers. If NIS is administering this configuration file on your system, you might see the following single entry instead of a list of group names and numbers:

```
$ cat /etc/group
+:*:*
...
```

When it needs to map a number to the corresponding group name, a utility encounters the plus sign (+) and knows to query the NIS server at that point for the answer. You can display the **group** database with the ypcat utility:

```
$ ypcat group
pubs::141:alex,jenny,scott,hls,barbara
...
```

Or you can search for a particular group name by using ypmatch:

```
$ ypmatch pubs group
pubs::141:alex,jenny,scott,hls,barbara
```

You can retrieve the same information by filtering the output of ypcat through grep, but ypmatch is more efficient because it searches the database directly, using a single process. The database name is not the full pathname of the file it replaces; the NIS database name is the same as the simple filename (**group**, not **/etc/group**). The ypmatch utility works only on the key for the table (the group name in the case of groups). When you want to match members of the group, the group number, or other fields of a map (such as the full name in the **passwd** map), you need to use ypcat with grep.

As with DNS, ordinary users need not be aware that NIS is managing system configuration files. Setting up and maintaining the NIS databases is a task for the system administrator; individual users and users on single-user GNU/Linux systems rarely need to work directly with NIS.

NFS: Network Filesystem

NFS lets you can work locally with files that are stored on a remote computer's disks. These files appear as if they are present on the local computer. The remote system is the fileserver (server); the local system is the client. The client makes requests of the server.

Unfortunately NFS is based on the trusted-host paradigm (page 373) and therefore has all the security shortcomings that plague services based on this paradigm.

NFS is configured by the person responsible for the system. When you work with a file, you may not be aware of where the file is physically stored. In many computer facilities today, user files are commonly stored on a central fileserver equipped with many large-capacity disk drives and devices that quickly and easily make backup copies of the data. A GNU/Linux system may be *diskless*, where a floppy disk (or CD-ROM) is used to start GNU/Linux and load system software from another machine on the network. The Linux Terminal Server Project (LTSP.org) Web site says it all: "Linux makes a great platform for deploying diskless workstations that boot from a network server. The LTSP is all about running thin client computers in a GNU/Linux environment." Because a diskless workstation does not require a lot of computing power, you can give older, retired computers a second life by using them as diskless systems.

Another type of GNU/Linux system is the *dataless* system, in which the client has a disk but stores no user data (only GNU/Linux and the applications are kept on the disk). Setting up this type of system is a matter of choosing which filesystems are mounted remotely.

You can even *netboot* (page 1481) some machines. Red Hat includes the PXE (Preboot Execution Environment) server package for netbooting Intel machines. Older machines with netcard-mounted boot ROMs sometimes use tftp (trivial file transfer protocol) for netbooting. Non-Intel architectures have historically included netboot capabilities that Red Hat Linux supports. The Linux kernel contains the capability to be built to mount **root** (*/*), using NFS.

Of the many ways to set up your system, the one you choose depends on what you want to do. Setting up these specialized boot configurations is not a trivial task. See the *Remote-boot mini HOWTO* for more information.

The df utility displays a list of the filesystems available on your system, along with the amount of disk space, free and used, on each. Filesystem names that are prepended with **hostname:** are available to you through NFS.

```
[bravo]$ pwd
/kudos/home/jenny
[bravo]$ df
Filesystem          1k-blocks      Used Available Use% Mounted on
/dev/sda1              311027    189038    105926  64% /
...
/dev/sdc3             1336804        13   1267712   0% /c3
zach:/c              2096160   1896704    199456  90% /zach_c
zach:/d              2096450   1865761    230689  89% /zach_d
panda:/c             1542016    433568   1108448  28% /panda_c
panda:/d             1542208   1189026    353182  77% /panda_d
kudos:/home           198275     68408    119612  36% /kudos/home
```

In this example Jenny's home directory is stored on the remote system **kudos**. The **/home** filesystem on **kudos** is mounted on **bravo**, using NFS; as a reminder of its physical location, the system administrator has made it available using a pathname that includes the remote server's name. Filesystems on **zach** and **panda** are also available on **bravo**: These are the C: and D: drives on two MS Windows machines. Use the **–h** (human) option to df to make the output more intelligible. Refer to page 1147 in Part III for more information on df.

The physical location of your files should not matter to you; all the standard GNU/Linux utilities work with NFS-remote files the same way as they operate with local files. At times, however, you may lose access to your remote files: Your computer may be up and running, but a network problem or a remote system crash may make these files temporarily unavailable: When you try to access a remote file, you get an error message, such as NFS server kudos not responding. When your system can contact the remote server again, you see a message, such as NFS server kudos OK.

automount: Mounts Filesystems Automatically

With distributed computing you can log in on any machine on the network, and all your files, including startup scripts, will be easily available. A distributed computing environment commonly has all machines able to mount all filesystems on all servers: Whichever machine you log in on, your home directory will be waiting for you.

Having all machines mount all servers all the time can be problematic. Suppose that machine A mounts some filesystems from machine B and machine B mounts some from machine A. What happens when you bring one of these machines down for maintenance or it crashes? In what order do you reboot them when they depend on each other to be up? In a large network you can have one machine mounting disks from tens or hundreds of others for software files and home directories.

One way around this problem is to mount filesystems only on demand. On GNU/Linux machines demand mounting is handled by the autofs system (using the **automount** daemon), which is replacing the older, less efficient **amd** (automounting daemon). Because autofs runs in kernel space (**amd** runs in user space), you need to have support for it in the kernel (Filesystems/Kernel automounter support). For example, when you issue the command **ls /home/alex**, autofs goes to work: It looks in the **/etc/auto.home** map, finds that **alex** is a key that says to mount **franklin:/export/homes/alex**, and mounts the remote filesystem.

Once the filesystem is mounted, ls displays the list of files you want to see. If after this mounting sequence you give the command **ls /home**, ls shows that **alex** is present within the **/home** directory. The df utility shows that **alex** is mounted from **franklin**. By default the **automount** daemon automatically unmounts this filesystem after five minutes of inactivity.

Automounting filesystems is similar in concept to MS Windows 9x network neighborhood. When you know there are NFS servers named **franklin, adams,** and **madison,** you can see all the filesystems that are exported by each by using ls to display (for example) **/net/franklin, /net/adams,** and **/net/madison.** Once these filesystems are mounted, you can browse through them if you have permission.

The GNU/Linux automount facility is flexible and powerful. Refer to "autofs: Automatically Mounts Filesystems" on page 979 and the automount man page for more information.

Optional

Internet Services

GNU/Linux Internet services are provided by daemons that run continuously or by a daemon that is started automatically by the **xinetd** daemon (page 397) when a service request comes in. The **/etc/services** file lists network services (for example **telnet, ftp, ssh**) and their associated numbers. Any service that uses TCP/IP or UDP/IP uses an entry in this file. IANA (Internet Assigned Numbers Authority) maintains a database of all permanent, registered services. The **/etc/services** file usually lists a small, commonly used subset of services. Go to www.rfc.net/rfc1700.html for more information and a complete list of registered services.

Most of the daemons (the executable files) are stored in **/usr/sbin**. By convention the names of many daemons end with the letter **d** to distinguish them from utilities.[20] The prefix **in.** or **rpc.** is often used for daemon names. Look at **/usr/sbin/*d** to see a list of many of the daemon programs on your system. Refer to "rc Scripts: Start and Stop System Services" on page 944 and service: Configures Services I on page 945 for information about starting and stopping these daemons.

For example, when you run ssh, your local system contacts the ssh daemon (**sshd**) on the remote system to establish the connection. The two systems negotiate the connection according to a fixed protocol. Each system identifies itself to the other, and then they take turns asking each other specific questions and waiting for valid replies. Each network service follows its own protocol.

In addition to the daemons that support the utilities described up to this point, many other daemons support system-level network services that you will not typically interact with. Some of these daemons are listed in Table 9-4.

Daemon	Used For or By	Function || table 9-4
apmd	Advanced power management	Reports and takes action on specified changes in system power, including shutdowns. Very useful with machines, such as laptops, that run on batteries.
atd	at	Executes a command once at a specific time and date. See **crond** for periodic execution of a command.
automount	Automatic mounting	Automatically mounts filesystems when they are accessed. Automatic mounting is a way of demand-mounting remote directories without having to hard-configure them into /etc/fstab.

20. One common daemon whose name does not end in d is **sendmail**.

Daemon	Used For or By	Function (Continued)	‖ table 9-4
comsat	Notifies users of new mail	Used by **biff**, a utility that notifies users of incoming mail. If the user is logged on and has run **biff y**, **comsat** sends a message to the user's shell, saying that there is new mail (at an appropriate time). Security-conscious sites may want to disable this service, as it has a history of security holes. Launched by **xinetd**.	
crond	cron	Used for periodic execution of tasks, this daemon looks in the /var/spool/cron/ directory for files that have filenames that correspond to users' login names. It also looks at the /etc/crontab file and at files in the /etc/cron.d directory. When a task comes up for execution, **crond** executes it as the user who owns the file that describes the task.	
dhcpcd	DHCP	Client daemon. Refer to "DHCP Client" on page 1028.	
dhcpd	DHCP	Assigns Internet address, subnet mask, default gateway, DNS, and other information to hosts. This protocol answers DHCP requests and, optionally, BOOTP requests. See *DHCP* on page 1465.	
fingerd	finger	Handles requests for user information from the **finger** utility. Launched by **xinetd**.	
ftpd	FTP	Handles FTP requests. Refer to "**ftp**: Transfers Files over a Network" on page 378. Launched by **xinetd**.	
gpm	General-purpose mouse or GNU paste manager	Allows you to use a mouse to cut and paste text on console applications.	
httpd	HTTP	A Web server daemon. See *HTTP* on page 1472.	
inetd		Deprecated in favor of **xinetd**.	
lpd	line printer spooler daemon	Launched by **xinetd** when printing requests come to the machine.	
named	DNS	Supports *DNS* (page 1465), which has replaced the use of the /etc/hosts table for hostname-to-IP address mapping on most networked UNIX/Linux systems.	
nfsd, statd, lockd, mountd, rquotad	NFS	These five daemons operate together to handle *NFS* (page 1482) operations. The **nfsd** daemon handles file and directory requests. The **statd** and **lockd** daemons implement network file and record locking. The **mountd** daemon takes care of converting a filesystem name request from the **mount** utility into an NFS handle and checks access permissions. Finally, if disk quotas are enabled, **rquotad** handles those.	

Daemon	Used For or By	Function (Continued) || table 9-4
ntpd	NTP	Synchronizes time on network computers. Requires a /etc/ntp.conf file. For more information go to www.eecis.udel.edu/~mills/ntp/servers.htm and www.eecis.udel.edu/~ntp.
portmap	RPC	Maps incoming requests for RPC service numbers to a TCP or UDP port numbers on the local machine. Refer to "RPC Network Services" on page 398.
pppd	PPP	For a modem this protocol controls the pseudointerface represented by the IP connection between your computer and a remote computer. Refer to "PPP: Point-to-Point Protocol" on page 362.
rexecd	rexec	Allows a remote user with a valid username and password to run programs on a machine. Its use is generally deprecated because of security, but certain programs, such as PC-based X servers, may still have it as an option. Launched by **xinetd**.
routed	Routing tables	Manages the routing tables so that your system knows where to send messages that are destined for remote networks. If your system does not have a /etc/defaultrouter file, **routed** is started automatically to listen to incoming routing messages and to advertise outgoing routes to other systems on your network. A newer daemon, the Gateway daemon (**gated**), offers enhanced configurability and support for more routing protocols and is proportionally more complex.
sendmail	Mail programs	The **sendmail** daemon came from Berkeley and has been available for a long time. The de facto mail transfer program on the Internet, the **sendmail** daemon always listens on port 25 for incoming mail connections and then calls a local delivery agent, such as /bin/mail. Mail user agents, such as **pine** and Mozilla mail, typically use **sendmail** to deliver mail messages.
smbd, nmbd	Samba	Allow MS Windows PCs to share files and printers with UNIX/Linux computers.
sshd	ssh, scp	Enables secure logins between remote machines (page 374).
syslogd	System log	Transcribes important system events and stores them in files and/or forwards them to users or another host running the **syslogd** daemon. This daemon is configured with /etc/syslog.conf and used with the **syslog** utility.
talkd	talk	Allows you to have a conversation with another user on the same or a remote machine. The **talkd** daemon handles the connections between the machines. The **talk** utility on each machine contacts the **talkd** daemon on the other machine for a bidirectional conversation. Launched by **xinetd**.

Daemon	Used For or By	Function (Continued)	|| table 9-4
telnetd	TELNET	One of the original Internet remote access protocols (page 376). Launched by **xinetd**.	
tftpd	TFTP	Used to boot a system or get information from a network. Examples include network computers, routers, and some printers. Launched by **xinetd**.	
timed	Time server	On a LAN synchronizes time with other computers that are also running **timed**.	
xinetd	Internet *Superserver*	Listens for service requests on network connections and starts up the appropriate daemon to respond to any particular request. Because of **xinetd**, your system does not need to have all the daemons running all the time in order to handle various network requests. The configuration file for **xinetd** is /etc/xinetd.conf, which frequently includes all the files in the /etc/xinetd.d directory with the line	

```
includedir /etc/xinetd.d
```

Each of the files in **xinetd.d** is named after a service that it controls. Each file contains a line that starts with `disable =` and finishes with `yes` or `no`. This line determines whether the service can run.

Proxy Server

A *proxy* is a network service that is authorized to act for a system while not being part of that system. A proxy server or proxy gateway provides proxy services; it is a transparent intermediary, relaying communications back and forth between an application, such as a browser and a server, usually outside of your LAN and frequently on the Internet. When more than one process uses the proxy gateway/server, it must keep track of which processes are connecting to which hosts/servers so that it can route the return messages to the proper process. The most common proxies that a user encounters are e-mail and Web proxies.

A proxy server/gateway insulates the local computer from all other computers or from specified domains by using at least two IP addresses: one to communicate with your local computer and one to communicate with a server. The proxy server/gateway examines and changes the header information on all packets it handles so that it can encode, route, and decode them properly. The difference between a proxy gateway and a proxy server is that the proxy server usually includes *cache* (page 1459) to store frequently used Web pages so that the next request for that page is available locally and quickly whereas a proxy gateway usually does not use cache. The terms proxy server and proxy gateway are frequently interchanged.

Proxy servers/gateways are available for such common Internet services as HTTP, HTTPS, FTP, SMTP, and SNMP. When an HTTP proxy sends queries from local machines, it presents a single organization-wide IP address (the external IP address of the proxy server/gateway) to all servers. It funnels all user requests to servers and keeps track of them. When the responses come back, it fans them out to the appropriate applications, using each machine's unique IP address, protecting local addresses from remote/specified servers. Proxy servers/gateways are generally just one part of an overall firewall strategy to prevent intruders from stealing information or damaging an internal network. Other functions, which can be combined with or be separate from the proxy server/gateway, are packet filtering, which blocks traffic based on origin and type, and user activity reporting, which helps management learn how the Internet is being used.

Refer to "Proxies" on page 1016 for practical information on setting up a proxy.

RPC Network Services

An RPC (remote procedure call) is a call to a *procedure* (page 1486) that acts transparently across a network. The procedure itself is responsible for accessing and using the network. The RPC libraries make sure that network access is transparent to the application. RPC runs on top of TCP/IP or UDP/IP.

The **/etc/rpc** file lists servers for RPCs.[21] This file has three columns: the name of the server for the RPC program, the RPC program number, and the names of programs that use the RPC program.

When an RPC server is initialized, it picks an arbitrary *port* (page 1485) that it communicates over. The server then registers this port with the RPC portmapper on the same machine, using the portmap utility. The portmap utility always listens on port 111 for both TCP and UDP.

When it wishes to execute an RPC against an RPC server, a client contacts portmap on the remote machine and asks which port the RPC server (for example **rpc.rstatd**) is listening on. The portmapper looks in its tables and returns a UDP or TCP port number. The client then contacts the server on that port.

The client sends arguments, just as a local function call or procedure would; the RPC libraries take care of transmission; the remote procedure executes with the arguments and generates a result; the RPC libraries encode the result and return it over the network to the client.

---

21. These are Sun-style RPCs, ONC or Open Network Computing RPC, as opposed to Microsoft RPCs, which are something different.

Usenet

One of the earliest information services available on the Internet, Usenet is an electronic bulletin board that allows users with common interests to exchange information. Usenet is an informal, loosely connected network of systems that exchange e-mail and news items (commonly referred to as *netnews*). Usenet was formed in 1979 when a few sites decided to share some software and information on topics of common interest. They agreed to contact one another and to pass the information along over dial-up telephone lines (at that time running at 1200 baud at best), using UNIX's uucp utility (UNIX-to-UNIX copy program).

The popularity of Usenet led to major changes in uucp to handle the ever-escalating volume of messages and sites. Today much of the news flows over network links using a sophisticated protocol designed especially for this purpose: NNTP (Network News Transfer Protocol). The news messages are stored in a standard format, and the many public domain programs available let you read them. An old, simple interface is named readnews. Others, such as rn, its X Window System cousin xrn, tin, nn, and xvnews have many features that help you browse through and reply to the articles that are available or create articles of your own. In addition, Netscape and Mozilla include an interface that you can use to read news (Netscape/Mozilla News) as part of its Web browser. The program you select to read netnews is largely a matter of personal taste.

Because programs to read netnews articles have been ported to non-UNIX/Linux systems, the community of netnews users has diversified. In the UNIX tradition categories of netnews groups are structured hierarchically. The top level includes such designations as **comp** (computer-related), **misc** (miscellaneous), **rec** (recreation), **sci** (science), **soc** (social issues), and **talk** (ongoing discussions). Usually at least one regional category is at the top level, such as **ba** (San Francisco Bay Area), and includes information about local events. Many new categories are continually being added to the more than 30,000 newsgroups. The names of newsgroups resemble domain names but are read from left to right (like GNU/Linux filenames): **comp.os.UNIX.misc, comp.lang.c, misc.jobs.offered, rec.skiing, sci.med, soc.singles, talk.politics**. The following article appeared in **linux.redhat.install**:

```
> I have just installed linux redhat 7.2 and when i try to start X i get the
> following error message:
>
> Fatal Server Error.
> no screens found
>
> XIO: Fatal IO err 104 (connection reset by peer) on X server ",0.0" after
> 0 requests (0 known processed) with 0 events remaining.
>
> How can i solve this problem?
>
> Thanks,
> Fred
```

```
Fred,

It would appear that your X configuration is incorrect or missing.  You
should run XConfigurator and set up the configuration for your video card
and monitor.  You may also have to run mouseconfig to set it up.

Carl
```

A great deal of useful information is available on Usenet, but you need patience and perseverance to find what you are looking for. You can ask a question, as the user did in the previous example, and someone from halfway around the world may answer it. Before posing such a simple question and causing it to appear on thousands of systems around the world, ask yourself whether you can get help in a less invasive way.

- Refer to the man pages and info.

- Look through the files in **/usr/share/doc**.

- Ask your system administrator or another user for help.

- All the popular newsgroups have FAQs (lists of frequently asked questions). Consult these lists and see whether your question has been answered. FAQs are periodically posted to the newsgroups; in addition, all the FAQs are archived at sites around the Internet, including ftp://ftp.uu.net, ftp://rtfm.mit.edu/pub/usenet-by-hierarchy,[22] and the Usenet newsgroup **comp.answers**.

- Because someone has probably asked the same question before you, search the netnews archives for an answer: Try looking at groups.google.com, which has a complete netnews archive.

- Use a search engine to find an answer. One good way to get help is to search on an error message.

- Review support documents at **www.redhat.com**.

- Contact a Red Hat Linux user's group.

Use the worldwide Usenet community as a last resort. If you are stuck on a GNU/Linux question and cannot find any other help, try submitting it to one of these newsgroups:

---

22. Also see ftp://rtfm.mit.edu/pub for other Usenet archives and miscellaneous interesting information.

- linux.redhat.development
- linux.redhat.install
- linux.redhat.misc

For more generic questions try these lists:

- comp.os.linux.misc
- comp.os.linux.networking
- comp.os.linux.security
- comp.os.linux.setup
- linux.dev.newbie
- linux.redhat.rpm

One way to find out about new tools and services is to read Usenet news. The **comp.os.linux** hierarchy is of particular interest to GNU/Linux users; for example, news about newly released software for GNU/Linux is posted to **comp.os.linux.announce**. People often announce the availability of free software there, along with instructions on how to get a copy for your own use using anonymous FTP (page 380). Other tools to help you find resources, both old and new, exist on the network; see Appendix B.

Tutorial: Using **pine** as a Newsreader

The *pine* news interface resembles the *pine* mail interface (page 88), with as much consistency among commands, screen displays, and folder organization as possible. This consistency makes it easier for those used to the *pine* mailer to use *pine* as a newsreader. If you are using Mozilla, you may prefer to use Mozilla News (page 405).

In order to use any newsreader, you must have access to Usenet news. Ask your ISP or system administrator for the address of your news server. If your site has no news server, you will not be able to read news.

Start *pine* and select SETUP from the MAIN MENU. Enter **c** (Config) on the initial SETUP screen to display the SETUP CONFIGURATION screen, where you can view and modify many configurable aspects of *pine*'s behavior (Figure 9-4). Highlight the *pine* variable **nntp-server**, select **a** (Add Value), and enter the URL of your news server.

In most cases this is all you need to do to start using *pine* as a newsreader. The next time you run *pine*, it will contact the news server on your behalf as you give commands to read and post news.

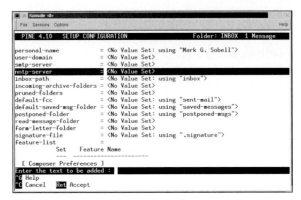

Figure 9-4   pine's Setup/Configuration screen

If you use pine for mail, you are probably accustomed to seeing the FOLDER LIST screen containing the mail folders INBOX, sent-mail, and saved-messages, and any other mail folders you have created. If this group, or *collection*, of folders is the only one defined, pine displays the individual folders within the collection when you select FOLDER LIST. Once you set up news, an additional collection—News—is automatically defined, and the FOLDER LIST screen becomes the COLLECTION LIST screen and displays a list of the two folder collections instead: Mail and News. Highlight the line for the News and press RETURN to use the news feature (Figure 9-5). The pine program displays the FOLDER LIST for news groups.

The news groups FOLDER LIST screen displays folders, each corresponding to a single newsgroup that you have subscribed to. To start, no folders are displayed. You can move among the newsgroups, or folders, by using the ARROW keys; select any newsgroup by pressing RETURN.

Figure 9-5   pine's Folder List screen

Figure 9-6   Partial results of a query for newsgroups containing Linux in their titles

Subscribing to Newsgroups

The *news subscription file*, **.newsrc** in your home directory, is used by pine to keep track of your news subscriptions. It is in a standard format that can be used by most newsreaders. You may find this file in your home directory, initialized with a list of newsgroups deemed to be of general interest. If not, pine will create the file for you the first time you subscribe to a newsgroup.

A newsgroup that might be useful at this point is **comp.mail.pine**. To subscribe to this newsgroup, while still in the FOLDER LIST for news groups screen, enter **a** (Add) followed by **comp.mail.pine** at the prompt and press RETURN. After a while pine displays Subscribed to "comp.mail.pine" on the message line and adds the new newsgroup to the list of newsgroups displayed on the FOLDER LIST screen. Each step involved in subscribing to a news group may take a while, depending on your environment.

To display all the newsgroups that include Linux in their titles, enter **linux** in response to the prompt you get when you give an **a** (Add) command. (Figure 9-6 shows partial results of this query.) Press RETURN immediately after you give an **a** command to display a list of all newsgroups (the list is long and takes a while to display).

Reading News

Use the ARROW keys to highlight one of the newsgroups that is displayed on the FOLDER LIST screen, and then press RETURN to display the Message Index screen. If you see the message Group now downloading, please check back later, press < to go back to the FOLDER LIST screen, and return to the MESSAGE INDEX screen for that newsgroup later.

Most aspects of reading mail apply to reading news: When you view the MESSAGE INDEX screen, you see a numbered list of messages (*posts*) identified with dates, sender names, and subject lines. Highlight the line that interests you, and press RETURN to view the message.

Using pine, you can select messages that interest you, mark messages for deletion, export messages to files, and so on. When viewing a news message, you will see headers that resemble the headers used in pine mail messages. The fields Date:, From:, and Subject: appear in the four-line header, with similar meanings. To emphasize that recipients of news messages are newsgroups, the To: field is replaced with the Newsgroups: field. This field lists one or more newsgroups that are receiving the post.

Unlike other newsreaders, pine does not automatically delete the news messages that you have read; you must explicitly mark news messages for deletion, using the **d** command, as you do for pine mail messages. Because pine remembers which messages you have deleted between pine sessions, you can pick up where you left off the next time you run pine to read news.

Posting News

The commands to post news in pine are nearly identical to those to send pine mail. The main difference is that the list of recipients comprises newsgroup names, not the addresses of individual users. As with mail messages, news messages can be sent to multiple recipients.

Use R With Care ‖ caution

When you enter **r** (Reply) to reply to a news post, you will be asked whether you want to include the original message in your reply; answer as you wish. Next, you will be given the following choices:

- Follow-up to news groups (F)
- Reply via email to author (R)
- Both (B)

Enter **F** or **B** only with the greatest caution; your message will reach thousands of people. Unless you want your message to go to *all* the subscribers of *all* the newsgroups listed in the Newsgroups: field of the header, enter **R** at this prompt. **R** causes your reply to be sent as an e-mail message only to the individual who posted the original message.

Unsubscribing from a Newsgroup

When you decide that you do not wish to belong to a newsgroup, you can unsubscribe from it. You will probably want to unsubscribe from many newsgroups if your **.newsrc** file was initialized for you; the list of such newsgroups is likely to be long and diverse.

To unsubscribe from a newsgroup, select News from the COLLECTION LIST screen, press RETURN to display the news group FOLDER LIST screen, highlight the newsgroup you want to unsubscribe from, and press **d** (Delete). Unsubscribing from a newsgroup does not remove the newsgroup from the **.newsrc** file; it simply tells pine not to include that newsgroup in the FOLDER LIST display. If you decide to subscribe to the same newsgroup again, pine remembers what messages you deleted, and you can resume reading the posts where you left off.

Netnews with Mozilla

You can also use Mozilla to read netnews. Use the Account Wizard to set up Mozilla to read and post netnews. How you display the Account Wizard depends on whether you already have a mail and/or newsgroup account set up with Mozilla. In either case select Mozilla menubar: Tasks⇨Mail & Newsgroups. If Mozilla displays the Account Wizard, you are set. When Mozilla displays the message center window,[23] select message center menubar: Edit⇨Mail & Newsgroups Account Settings to see the Mail & Newsgroups Account Settings window. Click Add Account and Mozilla displays the Account Wizard window.

From the Account Wizard window click Newsgroup account and then Next. Follow the prompts in the next windows, verify the information you entered on the final window, and click Finish to close the Account Wizard window. Click OK to close the Account Settings window.

If the message center window is not already displayed, select Mozilla menubar: Tasks⇨Mail & Newsgroups to display it. The news folder is generally at the bottom of the tree list on the left, labeled with the name of your news server. To add newsgroups, right click the news folder and click Subscribe from the pop-up menu. To see individual newsgroups, expand a news directory by clicking the plus sign (+) to the left of the news directory's name. Enter or pick the groups you want to subscribe to by double-clicking the name of the newsgroup. Click OK when you are done subscribing to newsgroups. Mozilla returns you to the message center window. Double-click the newsgroup you want to visit, and Mozilla displays items from the newsgroup.

---

23. The message center window displays the name of the highlighted folder on its titlebar.

The upper portion of the right side of the window lists the postings (the newsgroup items), including the name of the sender and the subject. Click a posting that interests you; after a moment the item appears in the lower portion of the screen. You can read and reply to postings from this window. For more information on Mozilla News, refer to the online Mozilla documentation by selecting Help at the right end of the menubar.

WWW: World Wide Web

The World Wide Web (WWW, W3, or the Web) provides a unified, interconnected interface to the vast amount of information stored on computers around the world. The idea that created the World Wide Web came from the mind of Tim Berners-Lee of the European Particle Physics Laboratory (CERN) in response to a need to improve communications throughout the High Energy Physics community. The first generation was a notebook program named Enquire, short for "Enquire Within Upon Everything" (the name of a book from his childhood), that he created in 1980 and that provided for links to be made between named nodes. It was not until 1989 that the concept was proposed as a global hypertext project to be known as the World Wide Web. In 1990 Berners-Lee wrote a proposal for a HyperText project, which eventually produced HTML, HyperText Markup Language, the common language of the Web. The World Wide Web program became available on the Internet in the summer of 1991. By designing the tools to work with existing protocols, such as FTP and gopher, the researchers who created the Web created a system that is generally useful for many types of information and across various types of hardware and operating systems.

The WWW is another example of the client/server paradigm. You use a WWW client application, or *browser,* to retrieve/display information stored on a server that may be located anywhere on your local network or the Internet. WWW clients can interact with many types of servers; for example, you can use a WWW client to contact a remote FTP server (page 408) and display the list of files it offers for anonymous FTP (page 380). Most commonly you use a WWW client to contact a WWW server, which offers support for the special features of the World Wide Web that are described in the remainder of this chapter.

The power of the Web is in its use of *hypertext,* a way to navigate through information by following cross-references (called *links*) from one piece of information to another. To use the Web effectively, you need to be able to run interactive network applications. The first GUI for browsing the Web was a tool named Mosaic, released in February 1993. It was designed at the National Center for Supercomputer Applications at the University of Illinois and sparked a dramatic increase in the number of users of the World Wide Web. Marc Andreessen, who participated in the Mosaic project at the University of Illinois, later cofounded Netscape Communications with the founder of Silicon Graphics, Jim Clark. They created Netscape Navigator, a Web client program that was designed to perform better and support more features than the Mosaic browser. Netscape Navigator has enjoyed immense success and has become a popular choice for users exploring the World Wide Web. Important for GNU/Linux users is fact that from the beginning, Netscape has provided versions of its tools that run on GNU/Linux. Also, Netscape created Mozilla (mozilla.org) as an open-source browser project.

Mozilla and the Netscape Navigator[24] provide GUIs that allow you to listen to sounds, watch Web events or live news reports, and display pictures as well as text, giving you access to *hypermedia*. A picture on your screen may be a link to more detailed, nonverbal information, such as a copy of the same picture at a higher resolution or a short animation. When you run Mozilla or Netscape on a system that is equipped for audio, you can to listen to audio clips that have been linked to from a document.

URL: Uniform Resource Locator

Consider the URL http://www.w3.org/pub/WWW. The first component in the URL indicates the type of resource, in this case, **http** (HTTP—HyperText Transfer Protocol). Other valid resource names, such as **https** (HTTPS—secure HTTP), and **ftp** (FTP—File Transfer Protocol), represent information available on the Web, using other protocols. Next comes a colon and double slash (**://**). Frequently the `http://` string is omitted from a URL in print, as you seldom need to enter them to get to the URL. Following this is the full name of the host that acts as the server for the information (**www.w3.org**). The rest of the URL is a relative pathname to the file that contains the information (**pub/WWW**). Enter a URL in the location bar text box of a Web browser, and the Web server returns the page, frequently an *HTML* (page 1472) file, pointed to by this URL.

By convention many sites identify their WWW servers by prefixing a host or domain name with **www**. For example, you can reach the Web server at the New Jersey Institute of Technology at www.njit.edu. When you use a browser to explore the World Wide Web, you may never need to use a URL directly. However, as more information is published in hypertext form, you cannot help but find URLs everywhere—not just online in mail messages and Usenet articles but also in newspapers, advertisements, and product labels.

---

24. Netscape runs only on a GUI. If you are working on a character-based terminal or emulator, use lynx or links to access the Internet.

Browsers

You might want to consider using Web browsers other than Netscape with your GNU/Linux system. If you do not use the X Window System, try a text browser, such as lynx or links. Mozilla (www.mozilla.org) is the open-source counterpart to Netscape. Mozilla was first released in March 1998 and was based on Netscape 4 code. Since that time Mozilla has been under development by employees of Netscape (now a division of AOL), Red Hat, other companies, and contributors from the community and has released its version 1.0. KDE offers Konqueror, an all-purpose file manager and Web browser (page 286). Other browsers include Galeon (galeon.sourceforge.net), Opera (www.opera.com), BrowseX (browsex.com), and SkipStone (muhri.net/skipstone). Although each Web browser is unique, they all allow you to move about the Internet, viewing HTML documents, listening to sounds, and retrieving files.

Search Engine

Search engine is a name that applies to a group of hardware and software tools that help you find World Wide Web sites that have the specific information you are looking for. A search engine relies on a database of information collected by a *Web crawler*, a program that regularly looks through the millions of pages that make up the World Wide Web. A search engine must also have a way of collating the information the Web crawler collects so that you can access it quickly, easily, and in a manner that makes it most useful to you. This part of the search engine, called an *index*, allows you to search for a word, a group of words, or a concept and returns the URLs of Web pages that pertain to what you are searching for.

Many different types of search engines are on the Internet. Each type of search engine has its own set of strengths and weaknesses. You can obtain a partial list of search engines by going to home.netscape.com/escapes/internet_search.html or by clicking the Search button on the Netscape or Mozilla menubar.

Downloading a File

You can use Mozilla, Netscape, or another browser to look at and download a file from an FTP or HTML site. Suppose you enter ftp://ibiblio.org/Linux in the text box of the location bar and press RETURN. After seeing the initial set of directories, click **pub** (many sites give their public directory this name). You can then click any of the directories (try **Linux**) to view the available files. Following this example you will find directories named with the classifications of software, documentation, distributions, and more. Each contains a wealth of directories with more directories and files that you can download. You will also find **html** files that display a graphical interface to the directories. When you click a file that is intended to be downloaded, Mozilla or Netscape opens a window asking you where to put the file on your system. Refer to "Installing and Removing Software" on page 926 for information about unpacking and installing the software that you download.

When a File is Downloaded to Your Screen (and You See Garbage) || tip

If garbage appears on your screen, the file is being downloaded to your screen. Click **Stop** and then **Back**: You should be back where you started. This time hold the SHIFT key down while you click the file you want: This tells Mozilla/Netscape to download the file instead of trying to display it.

Chapter Summary

A GNU/Linux system attached to a network is probably communicating on an Ethernet, which may be linked to other local area networks (LANs) and wide area networks (WANs). Communication between LANs and WANs requires the use of gateways and routers. Gateways translate the local data to a format suitable for the wide area network, and routers make decisions about optimal routing of the data along the way. The most widely used network, by far, is the Internet.

Basic networking tools allow GNU/Linux users to log in and run commands on remote systems (ssh, telnet) and copy files quickly from one system to another (scp, ftp/sftp). Many tools that were originally designed to support communication on a single-host computer (for example, finger, talk, pine) have been extended to recognize network addresses, thus allowing users on different systems to interact with one another. Other features, such as the Network Filesystem (NFS), were created to extend the basic UNIX model and to simplify information sharing.

Concern is growing for the security and privacy of machines connected to networks and of data transmitted over networks. Toward this end many new tools and protocols have been created: ssh, scp, HTTPS, IPv6, firewall hardware and software, VPN, and so on. Many of these tools take advantage of newer, more impenetrable encryption techniques. In addition, some concepts, such as that of trusted hosts, and some tools, such as finger and rwho, are being discarded in the name of security.

Two major advantages of computer networks over other ways of connecting computers are that they enable systems to communicate at high speeds and require few physical interconnections (typically one per system, often on a shared cable). The Internet Protocol (IP), the universal language of the Internet, has made it possible for dissimilar computer systems around the world to communicate easily with one another. Technological advances continue to improve the performance of computer systems and the networks that link them.

One way to gather information on the Internet is Usenet news (netnews). Many GNU/Linux users routinely read Usenet news to learn about the latest resources available for their systems. Usenet news is organized into newsgroups that cover a wide range of topics, computer-related and otherwise. To read Usenet news, you need to have access to a news server and the appropriate client software. Many modern mailers, such as pine, Mozilla, and Netscape, are capable of reading netnews.

The rapid increase of network communication speeds in recent years has encouraged the development of many new applications and services. The World Wide Web provides access to vast information stores on the Internet and is noted for its extensive use of hypertext links to promote efficient searching through related documents. The World Wide Web adheres to the client/server model so pervasive in networking; typically the WWW client is local to a site or is made available through an Internet service provider. WWW servers are responsible for providing the information requested by their many clients.

Netscape Navigator is a WWW client program that has enormous popular appeal. Netscape and Mozilla use a GUI to give you access to text, picture, and audio information: Making extensive use of these hypermedia simplifies access to and enhances the presentation of information.

Exercises

1. Describe the similarities and differences among these utilities:

   a. scp and ftp

   b. ssh and telnet

   c. rsh and ssh

2. Assuming that rwho is disabled on the systems on your LAN, describe two ways to find out who is logged in on some of the other machines attached to your network.

3. Explain the client/server model, and give three examples of services that take advantage of this model on GNU/Linux systems.

4. What is the difference between a diskless and a dataless workstation? Name some advantages and disadvantages of each.

5. A software implementation of chess was developed by GNU and is free software. How can you use the Internet to find a copy and download it to your system?

6. What is the difference between the World Wide Web and the Internet?

7. If you have access to the World Wide Web, answer the following:

    a. What browser do you use?

    b. What is the URL of the author of this book's home page? How many links does it have?

    c. Does your browser allow you to create bookmarks? If so, how do you create a bookmark? How can you delete one?

8. Explain what happens if you transfer a binary file while running ftp in ASCII mode. What happens if you transfer an ASCII file in binary mode?

9. Give one advantage and two disadvantages of using a wireless network.

Advanced Exercises

10. Suppose that the link between routers 1 and 2 is down in the Internet shown in Figure 9-1 on page 359. What happens if someone at Site C sends a message to a user on a workstation attached to the Ethernet cable at Site A? What happens if the router at Site A is down? What does this tell you about designing network configurations?

11. If you have a class B network and want to divide it into subnets, each with 126 hosts, what subnet mask should you use? How many networks will be available? What are the four addresses (broadcast and network number) for the network starting at 131.204.18?

12. Suppose that you have 300 hosts and want to have no more than about 50 hosts per subnet. What size address block should you request from your ISP? How many class C-equivalent addresses would you need? How many subnets would you have left over from your allocation?

13. On your machine find two daemons running that are not listed in this chapter, and explain what purpose they serve.

14. Review what services/daemons are automatically started on your system, and consider which you might turn off. Are there any services/daemons in the list that starts on page 394 that you would consider adding?

IN THIS CHAPTER

The vim Editor

This chapter begins with a history and description of vi, the original, powerful, sometimes cryptic, interactive, visually oriented text editor. The chapter continues with a tutorial that shows you how to use vim (a vi clone supplied with Red Hat Linux) to create and edit a file. Following the tutorial, the chapter delves into the details of many vim commands and explains the use of parameters for customizing vim to meet your needs. The chapter concludes with a quick reference/summary of vim commands.

History

Before vi was developed, the standard UNIX system editor was ed (available on your Red Hat system), a line-oriented editor that made it difficult to see the context of your editing. Next came ex,[1] a superset of ed. The most notable advantage that ex has over ed is a display-editing facility that allows you to work with a full screen of text instead of just a line. While using ex, you can bring up the display-editing facility by giving a vi (Visual mode) command. People used the display-editing facility of ex so extensively that the developers of ex made it possible to start the editor with the display-editing facility already running, without having to start ex and give the vi command. Appropriately, they named the program vi. You can call the Visual

---

1. The ex program under Red Hat is a link to **/bin/vi**, which is a version of vim.

mode from ex, and you can go back to ex while you are using vi. Start by running ex; give ex a **vi** command to switch to Visual mode, and give a **Q** command while in Visual mode to use ex.

GNU/Linux offers a number of versions, or *clones,* of vi. The most popular vi clones found on GNU/Linux are elvis, ni, nvi,[2] and vim. Each clone offers additional features beyond those provided with the original vi.

The examples in this book are based on vim. Red Hat supports two versions of vim. The version in **/bin/vi** is a minimal build of vim: compact and faster to load but with fewer features. The version in **/usr/bin/vim** is a full-featured version of vim. If you use one of the other clones, you may notice slight differences from the examples presented in this chapter. The vim (vi improved) editor is compatible with almost all vi commands and runs on many platforms, including MS Windows, MacOS, and GNU/Linux. Refer to the vim home page (www.vim.org) for more information.

The vim editor is not a text formatting program. It does not justify margins or provide the output formatting features of a sophisticated word processing system. Rather, vim is a sophisticated text editor meant to be used to write code (C, HTML, Java, and so on), short notes, and input to a text formatting system, such as groff or troff.

Because vim is so large and powerful, only some of its features are described here. Nonetheless, if vim is completely new to you, you may find even the limited set of commands described in this chapter overwhelming. The vim editor provides a variety of ways to accomplish any specified editing task. A useful strategy for learning vim is to begin by learning a subset of commands to accomplish basic editing tasks. Then, as you become more comfortable with the editor, you can learn other commands that enable you to do things more quickly and efficiently. The following tutorial section introduces a basic but useful set of vim commands and features that create and edit a file.

Tutorial: Creating and Editing a File with vim

This section explains how to start vim, enter text, move the cursor, correct text, save the file to the disk, and exit from vim. The tutorial discusses two of the modes of operation of vim and how to go from one mode to the other. It also covers commands you can use to create a file and store it on disk. Try the program named vimtutor: Give its name as a command to run it.

---

2. The true vi is hiding out as nvi, which you can download: See bostic.com/vi and download the source and build as explained in "GNU Configure and Build System" on page 931.

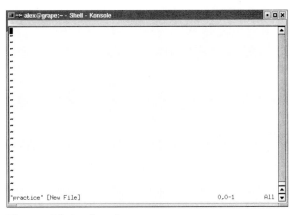

Figure 10-1   Starting vim

Specifying a Terminal

Because vim takes advantage of features that are specific to various kinds of terminals, you must tell it what type of terminal or terminal emulator you are using. On many systems your terminal type is set for you automatically. If you need to specify your terminal type, refer to "Specifying Your Terminal" on page 1402.

Starting vim

Start vim with the following command line to create and edit a file named **practice**:

```
$ vim practice
```

When you press RETURN, the command line disappears, and the terminal screen looks similar to the one shown in Figure 10-1.

The tildes (~) at the left of the screen indicate that the file is empty. They go away as you add lines of text to the file. If your screen looks like a distorted version of the one shown, your terminal type is probably not set correctly.

If you start vim with a terminal type that is not in the **terminfo** database, the following message is displayed for a few of seconds, and the terminal type defaults to **ansi**, which works on many terminals. In the following examples, the user mistyped **vt100** and set the terminal type to **vg100**:

```
Terminal entry not found in terminfo
'vg100' not known. Available builtin terminals are:
    builtin_riscos
    builtin_amiga
    builtin_beos-ansi
    builtin_ansi
    builtin_pcansi
    builtin_win32
```

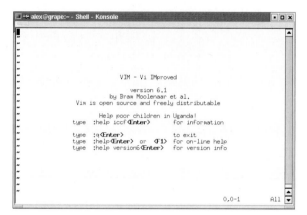

Figure 10-2   Starting vim without a filename

```
        builtin_vt320
        builtin_vt52
        builtin_xterm
        builtin_iris-ansi
        builtin_debug
        builtin_dumb
defaulting to 'ansi'
```

If you want to reset your terminal type, press ESCAPE, and then give the following command to exit from vim and get the shell prompt back:

:q!

When you enter the colon (:), vim moves the cursor to the bottom line of the screen. The characters q! tell vim to quit without saving your work. (You will not ordinarily exit from vim this way because you typically want to save your work.) You must press RETURN after you give this command. Once you get the shell prompt back, refer to "Specifying Your Terminal" on page 1402, and then start vim again.

If you start it without a filename, vim assumes that you are a novice and tells you how to get started (Figure 10-2).

Continuing with the **practice** file example: The **practice** file is new, so it contains no text. The vim editor displays a message similar to the one shown in Figure 10-1 on the status (bottom) line of the terminal to show that you are creating and editing a new file. Your version of vim may display a different message. When you edit an existing file, vim displays the first few lines of the file and gives status information about the file on the status (bottom) line.

Command and Input Modes

Two of the vim editor's modes of operation are *Command mode* and *Input mode* (Figure 10-3). While vim is in Command mode, you can give vim commands. For example, in Command mode you can delete text or exit from vim. You can also

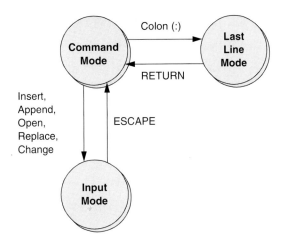

Figure 10-3   Modes in vim

command vim to enter Input mode. In Input mode vim accepts anything you enter as text and displays it on the screen. Press ESCAPE to return vim to Command mode.

By default the vim editor keeps you informed about which mode it is in: You will see --INSERT-- at the lower-left corner of the window while you are in Insert mode. The following command causes vim not to display the mode it is in while you are entering text:

    :set noshowmode

The colon (:) in this command puts vim into another mode, *Last Line mode*. While in this mode, vim keeps the cursor on the bottom line of the screen. When you finish the command by pressing RETURN, vim restores the cursor to its place in the text. Input modes are Open, Insert, and Append. Refer to "Show mode" on page 453. Refer to page 422 for an explanation of Change and Replace.

When you give vim a command, remember that the editor is case sensitive. The vim editor interprets the same letter as two different commands, depending on whether you enter an upper- or lowercase character. Beware of the key that causes your keyboard to send only uppercase characters; it is typically labeled CAPS LOCK or SHIFTLOCK. If you set this key to enter uppercase text while you are in Input mode and then exit to Command mode, vim interprets your commands as uppercase letters. It can be very confusing when this happens because vim does not appear to be following the commands you are giving it.

Entering Text

When you start a new session with vim, you must put it in Input mode before you can enter text. To put vim in Input mode, press the **i** key (insert before the cursor) or the **a** key (append after the cursor).

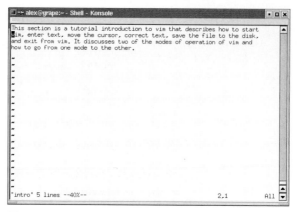

Figure 10-4   Entering text with vim

If you are not sure whether vim is in Input mode, press the ESCAPE key; vim returns to Command mode if it was in Input mode or beeps/flashes if it is already in Command mode. You can put vim back in Input mode by pressing the i key again.

While vim is in Input mode, you can enter text by typing on the terminal. If the text does not appear on the screen as you type, you are not in Input mode.

Enter the sample paragraph shown in Figure 10-4, pressing the RETURN key to end each line. If you do not press RETURN before the cursor reaches the right side of the screen or window, vim will wrap the text so that it appears to start a new line: Physical lines will not correspond to programmatic lines, and editing will become more difficult.

While you are using vim, you can always correct any typing mistakes you make. If you notice a mistake on the line you are entering, you can correct it before you continue. Refer to "Getting Help" (following). You can correct other mistakes later. When you finish entering the paragraph, press ESCAPE to return vim to Command mode.

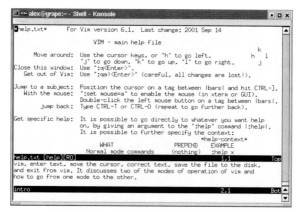

Figure 10-5   The main help file

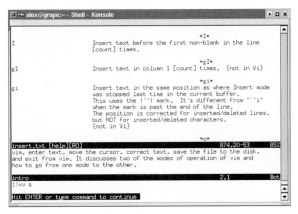

Figure 10-6   Help with insert

Getting Help

You can get help while you are using vim by typing **:help** [*feature*] followed by RETURN (you must be in Command mode). As before, the colon puts the cursor on the last line of the window. If you type **:help**, vim displays an introduction to vim Help (Figure 10-5). Each dark band near the bottom of the window names the file that is displayed above it. The **help.txt** file occupies most of the window while only one line of the file that was being edited (**memo.txt**) is displayed. Give the command **:q!** to close the Help window.

Read through the introduction to Help by scrolling the Help window as you read. Pressing **j** or the DOWN ARROW key moves the cursor down one line at a time whereas pressing CONTROL-D and CONTROL-U scroll the cursor down/up half a screen at a time. You can get help with the insert commands by giving the command **:help insert** while you are using vim in Command mode (Figure 10-6).

Correcting Text as You Insert It

The keys that back up and correct a shell command line serve the same functions when vim is in Input mode. These keys include the erase, line kill, and word kill keys (usually CONTROL-H, CONTROL-U, and CONTROL-W). Although vim may not remove deleted text from the screen as you back up over it, vim removes it when you type over it or press RETURN.

Moving the Cursor

When you are using vim, you need to move the cursor on the screen so that you can delete, insert, and correct text. While vim is in Command mode, you can use the RE-TURN key, the SPACE bar, and the ARROW keys to move the cursor. If you prefer to keep your hand closer to the center of the keyboard, if your terminal does not have ARROW keys, or if the emulator you are using does not support them, you can use the **h, j, k,** and **l** (ell) keys to move the cursor left, down, up, and right, respectively.

Deleting Text

You can delete a single character by moving the cursor until it is over the character you want to delete and then giving the command **x**. You can delete a word by positioning the cursor on the first letter of the word and giving the command **dw** (delete word). You can delete a line of text by moving the cursor until it is anywhere on the line you want to delete and then giving the command **dd**.

Undoing Mistakes

If you delete a character, line, or word by mistake or give any command you want to undo, give the command **u** (undo) immediately after you give the command you want to undo; vim restores the text to the way it was before you gave the last command. If you give the **u** command again, vim undoes the command you gave before the one it just undid. You can use this technique to back up over many of your actions.

    If you undo a command you did not mean to undo, give a redo command: Either CONTROL-R or **:red**, and vim will redo the undone command. As with undo, you can give this command many times in a row.

Inserting Additional Text

When you want to insert new text within text that you have already entered, move the cursor so that it is on the character that follows the new text you plan to enter. Then give the **i** (insert) command to put vim in Input mode, enter the new text, and press ESCAPE to return vim to Command mode. Or position the cursor on the character that precedes the new text, and use the **a** (append) command.

    To enter one or more lines, position the cursor on the line above where you want the new text to go. Give the command **o** (open). The vim editor opens a blank line, puts the cursor on it, and goes into Input mode. Enter the new text, ending each line with a RETURN. When you are finished entering text, press ESCAPE to return vim to Command mode.

Correcting Text

To correct text, use **dd, dw,** or **x** to remove the incorrect text. Then use **i** or **o** to insert the correct text.

    For example, one way to change the word tutorial to section in Figure 10-4 is to use the ARROW keys to move the cursor until it is on top of the t in tutorial. Then give the command **dw** to delete the word tutorial. Put vim in Input mode by giving an **i** command, enter the word section followed by a SPACE, and press ESCAPE.

The word is changed, and vim is in Command mode, waiting for another command. A shorthand for the two commands **dw** followed by the **i** command is **cw** (change word). The command **cw** automatically puts vim into Input mode.

Page Breaks for the Printer   ‖ tip

A CONTROL-L is a signal to a printer to skip to the top of the next page. You can enter this character anywhere in a document by simply pressing CONTROL-L. If a ^L does not appear, press CONTROL-V before CONTROL-L.

Ending the Editing Session

While you are editing, vim keeps the edited text in an area named the *Work buffer*. When you finish editing, you must write out the contents of the Work buffer to a disk file so that the edited text is saved and available when you next want it.

Make sure that vim is in Command mode, and use the **ZZ** command (you must use uppercase **Z**s) to write your newly entered text to the disk and end the editing session. After you give the **ZZ** command, vim returns control to the shell. You can exit with **:q!** if you do not want to save your work. Refer to page 463 for a summary of vim commands.

Do Not Confuse ZZ **with** CONTROL-Z   ‖ caution

When you exit from **vim** with ZZ, make sure that you use ZZ and not CONTROL-Z (typically the suspend key). When you press CONTROL-Z, **vim** disappears from your screen, almost as though you had exited from it. But **vim** will be running in the background with your file unsaved. Refer to "Job Control" on page 554. If you try to start editing the same file with a new **vim** command, **vim** displays a message about a swap file; refer to "File Locks" on page 425.

Introduction to vim Features

This section covers modes of operation, online help, the Work buffer, emergency procedures, and other vim features. To see the features that are incorporated in a build, give a **vim** command followed by the **--version** option (substitute the path and/or name of your vim program).

Online Help

As covered briefly earlier, vim provides help while you are using it. Give the command **:help** *feature* to display information about *feature*. Some common features of interest are insert, delete, and opening-window. As you scroll through the various help texts, you will see words with an asterisk on either side. You can use these words in place of *feature*. Although *opening-window* is not intuitive, you will get to know the *features* as you spend more time with vim. You can also give the command **:help doc-file-list** to view a complete list of all the help files. Although vim is a free program, the author requests that you donate the money you would have spent on similar software to help the kids in Uganda (**:help uganda** for more information).

Modes of Operation

The vim editor is a part of the ex editor, which has five modes of operation:

- ex Command mode
- ex Input mode
- vim Command mode
- vim Input mode
- vim Last Line mode

While you are using vim, you use mostly vim Command and Input modes. On occasion you use Last Line mode (as with the **:help** commands). While in Command mode, vim accepts keystrokes as commands, responding to each command as you enter it. In Command mode vim does not display the characters you type. In Input mode vim accepts keystrokes as text that it eventually puts into the file you are editing and displays the text as you enter it. All commands that start with a colon (:) put vim in Last Line mode. The colon moves the cursor to the bottom line of the screen, where you enter the rest of the command.

In addition to the position of the cursor, there is another important difference between Last Line mode and Command mode. When you give a command in Command mode, you do not terminate the command with a RETURN. However, you must terminate all Last Line mode commands with a RETURN.

You do not normally use the ex modes. When this chapter refers to Input and Command modes, it means the vim modes, not the ex modes.

At the start of an editing session, vim is in Command mode. Several commands, such as Insert and Append, put vim in Input mode. When you press the ESCAPE key, vim always reverts to Command mode.

The Change and Replace commands combine Command and Input modes. The Change command deletes the text you want to change and puts vim in Input mode so you can insert new text. The Replace command deletes the character(s) you over-write and inserts the new one(s) you enter. Figure 10-3 on page 417 shows the modes and the methods for changing between them.

Watch the CAPS LOCK Key and What Mode You Are In || tip

Almost anything you type in Command mode means something to vim. If you think that vim is in Input mode when it is in Command mode, the result of typing in text can be very confusing. When learning vim, you may want to set the **showmode** parameter (page 453) to help remind you which mode you are using. If you want to put vim in "beginner mode," set the **showmode** parameter (page 453) and turn off the **magic** parameter (page 454).

Also keep your eye on the CAPS LOCK key. In Command mode the effects of uppercase letters are different from those of lowercase ones. It can be disorienting to give commands and have vim give the "wrong" responses.

The Display

The vim editor uses the status line and several special symbols to give information about what is happening during an editing session.

Status Line

The vim editor displays status information on the bottom line of the display area. This information includes error messages, information about the deletion or addition of blocks of text, and file status information. In addition, vim displays Last Line mode commands on the status line.

Redrawing the Screen

Sometimes the screen becomes garbled or overwritten. When vim puts characters on the screen, it sometimes leaves @ on a line instead of deleting the line. When your screen is overwritten by another user, the other user's message becomes intermixed with the display of the Work buffer, and things can get confusing. The other user's message *does not* become part of the Work buffer but affects only the display. If this happens when you are in Input mode, press ESCAPE to get into Command mode, and then press CONTROL-L to redraw (refresh) the screen.

Be sure to read the other user's message before redrawing the screen, because redrawing the screen causes the message to disappear. You can write back to the other user while in vim (page 458), quit vim and use the write utility from the shell, or open another window on a GUI.

Tilde (~) Symbol

If the end of the file is displayed on the screen, vim marks lines that would appear past the end of the file with a tilde (~) at the left of the screen. When you start editing a new file, the vim editor marks every line on the screen, except for the first line, with these symbols.

Correcting Text as You Insert It

While vim is in Input mode, you can use the erase and line kill keys to back up over text that you are inserting so you can correct it. You can also use CONTROL-W to back up to the beginning of the word you are entering. Using these techniques, you cannot back up past the beginning of the line you are working on or past the beginning of the text you entered since you most recently put vim into Input mode.

Work Buffer

The vim editor does all its work in the Work buffer. At the start of an editing session, vim reads the file you are editing from the disk into the Work buffer. During the editing session, vim makes all changes to this copy of the file but does not change the disk file until you write the contents of the Work buffer back to the disk. Normally when you end an editing session, you command vim to write out the contents of the Work buffer, which makes the changes to the text final. When you edit a new file, vim creates the file when it writes the contents of the Work buffer to the disk, usually at the end of the editing session.

Storing the text you are editing in the Work buffer has advantages and disadvantages. If you accidentally end an editing session without writing out the contents of the Work buffer, all your work is lost. However, if you unintentionally make some major changes (such as deleting the entire contents of the Work buffer), you can end the editing session without implementing the changes. The vim editor leaves the file as it was when you last wrote it.

If you want to use vim to look at a file but not to change it, you can use the view utility:

```
$ view filename
```

Calling the view utility is the same as calling the vim editor with the **–R** (readonly) option. Once you have invoked the editor in this way, you cannot write the contents of the Work buffer back to the file whose name appeared on the command line. You can always write the Work buffer out to a file with a different name.

Line Length and File Size

The vim editor operates on any format file, provided the length of a single "line" (that is, the characters between two NEWLINE characters) can fit into available memory. The total length of the file is limited only by available disk space and memory.

Windows

The vim editor allows you to open, close, and hide multiple windows each editing a different file. Most of the window commands are CONTROL-W followed by another letter. For example, CONTROL-W **s** opens a second window (splits the screen) editing the same file. CONTROL-W **n** opens a second window that is editing an empty file. CONTROL-W **w** moves the cursor between windows, and CONTROL-W **q** (or **:q**) quits (closes) a window. If you give a Quit command and have not written out the text you have entered/changed, vim will prompt you to do so. Give the command **:help windows** for a complete list of windows commands.

File Locks

When you edit an existing file, vim displays the first few lines of the file, gives status information about the file on the status line, and locks the file. A user attempting to edit the same file at the same time as you (assuming proper permissions) will see a message similar to the one shown in Figure 10-7.

Although it is advisable to follow the instructions that vim displays, the second user can edit the file and write it out with a different filename. Refer to the next section.

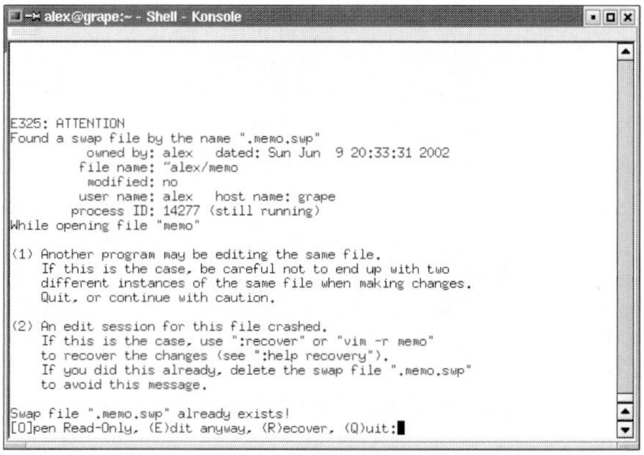

Figure 10-7   Attempting to open a locked file

Abnormal Termination of an Editing Session

You can end an editing session in one of two ways: Either vim saves the changes you made during the editing session, or it does not save them. You can use the **ZZ** or **:wq** command from Command mode to save your changes and exit from vim (page 421).

You can end an editing session without writing out the contents of the Work buffer by giving the following command:

    :q!

When you use this command to end an editing session, vim does not preserve the contents of the Work buffer; you lose all the work you did since the last time you wrote the Work buffer to disk. The next time you edit or use the file, it appears as it did the last time you wrote the Work buffer to disk. Use the **:q!** command cautiously.

When You Cannot Write Out a File   ‖ tip

It may be necessary to write a file using *:w filename*, if you do not have write permission for the file you are editing. If you give the ZZ command and see the message `File is read only`, you do not have write permission for the file. Use the Write command with a temporary filename to write the file to disk under a different filename. If you do not have write permission to the working directory, **vim** may still not be able to write your file to the disk. Give the command again, using an absolute pathname of a dummy (nonexistent) file in your home directory in place of the filename. (For example, Alex might give the command :w /home/alex/temp or :w ~/temp.)

If vim reports `File exists`, you will need to use :w! filename to overwrite the existing file (make sure that this is what you want to do). Refer to page 450.

Sometimes you may find that you created or edited a file, and vim will not let you exit. For example, if you forgot to specify a filename when you first called vim, you get a message that the file cannot be written when you give the **ZZ** command. If vim does not let you exit normally, you can use the Write command (**:w**) to name the file and write it to disk before you quit using vim. To write the file, give the following command, substituting the name of the file in place of *filename* (remember to follow the command with a RETURN):

:w filename

After you give the Write command, you can use **:q** to quit using vim. You do not need to use the exclamation point (as in **q!**), because the exclamation point is necessary only when you have made changes since the last time you wrote the Work buffer to disk. Refer to page 449 for more information about the Write command.

Recovering Text after a Crash

The vim editor temporarily stores the file you are working on in a *swap file*. If the system crashes while you are editing a file with vim, you can often recover text (from the swap file) that would otherwise be lost. In the next example, Alex checks whether the swap file exists for a file named **memo**, which he was editing when the system went down.

```
$ vim -r
Swap files found:
   In current directory:
1.    .memo.swp
            dated: Mon Jun 10 13:16:06 2002
          owned by: alex
         file name: ~alex/memo
         host name: bravo.tcorp.com
         user name: alex
        process ID: 19786
   In directory ~/tmp:
      -- none --
   In directory /var/tmp:
      -- none --
   In directory /tmp:
      -- none --
```

You will see a list of any swap files that vim has saved (some may be old). If your work was saved, give the same command followed by a SPACE and the name of your file. After giving the command, you will be editing a recent copy of your Work buffer. Use :w *filename* immediately to save the salvaged copy of the Work buffer to disk under a name different from the original file. Then check the recovered file to make sure it is OK. Following is Alex's exchange with vim as he recovers **memo**:

```
$ vim -r memo
Using swap file ".memo.swp"
Original file "~/memo"
Recovery completed. You should check if everything is OK.
(You might want to write out this file under another name
and run diff with the original file to check for changes)
Delete the .swp file afterwards.

Press RETURN or enter command to continue
:w memo2
:q
```

Command Mode: Moving the Cursor

While vim is in Command mode, you can position the cursor over any character on the screen. You can also display a different portion of the Work buffer on the screen. By manipulating the screen and cursor position, you can place the cursor on any character in the Work buffer.

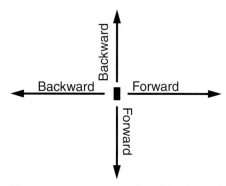

Figure 10-8   Forward and backward

You can move the cursor forward or backward through the text. As illustrated in Figure 10-8, *forward* always means toward the bottom of the screen and the end of the file. *Backward* means toward the top of the screen and the beginning of the file. When you use a command that moves the cursor forward past the end (right) of a line, the cursor generally moves to the beginning (left) of the next line. When you move it backward past the beginning of a line, the cursor moves to the end of the previous line.

The length of a line in the Work buffer may be too long to appear as a single line of the display area. When this happens, vim will wrap the current line onto the next line.

You can move the cursor through the text by any *Unit of Measure* (that is, character, word, line, sentence, paragraph, or screen). If you precede a cursor-movement command with a number, called a *Repeat Factor,* the cursor moves that number of units through the text. Refer to pages 460 and 463 at the end of this chapter for more precise definitions of these terms.

Moving the Cursor by Characters

The SPACE bar moves the cursor forward, one character at a time, toward the right side of the screen. The l (ell) key and the RIGHT ARROW key (Figure 10-9) do the same thing. The command 7 SPACE or 7l moves the cursor seven characters to the right. These keys *cannot* move the cursor past the end of the current line to the beginning of the next. The **h** and LEFT ARROW keys are similar to the l key but work in the opposite direction.

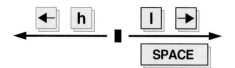

Figure 10-9   Moving the cursor by characters

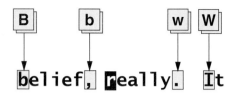

Figure 10-10 Moving the cursor by words

Moving the Cursor to a Specific Character

You can also move the cursor to the next occurrence of a specified character on the current line by using the Find command. For example, the following command moves the cursor from the current position to the next occurrence of the character **a**, if one appears on the same line:

    fa

You can also find the previous occurrence by using a capital **F**, so the following command moves the cursor to the position of the closest previous **a** in the current line:

    Fa

A semicolon (;) repeats the last Find command.

Moving the Cursor by Words

The **w** (word) key moves the cursor forward to the first letter of the next word (Figure 10-10). Groups of punctuation count as words. This command goes to the next line if that is where the next word is. The command **15w** moves the cursor to the first character of the fifteenth subsequent word.

The **W** key is similar to the **w** key but moves the cursor by blank-delimited words, including punctuation, as it skips forward. (Refer to "Blank-Delimited Word" on page 461.)

The **b** (back) key moves the cursor backward to the first letter of the previous word. The **B** key moves the cursor backward by blank-delimited words. Similarly, the **e** key moves the cursor to the end of the next word; **E** moves it to the end of the next blank-delimited word.

Moving the Cursor by Lines

The RETURN key moves the cursor to the beginning of the next line (Figure 10-11), and the **j** and DOWN ARROW keys move it down one line to the character just below the

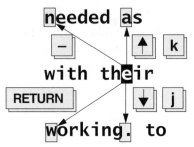

Figure 10-11   Moving the cursor by lines

current character. If no character is immediately below the current character, the cursor moves to the end of the next line. The cursor will not move past the last line of text in the work buffer.

The **k** and UP ARROW keys are similar to the **j** key but work in the opposite direction. Also, the minus (−) key is similar to the RETURN key but works in the opposite direction.

Moving the Cursor by Sentences and Paragraphs

The **)** and **}** keys move the cursor forward to the beginning of the next sentence or paragraph, respectively (Figure 10-12). The **(** and **{** keys move the cursor backward to the beginning of the current sentence or paragraph. Refer to pages 461 and 462 for more about sentences and paragraphs in vim.

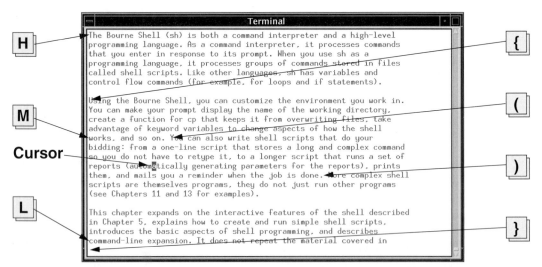

Figure 10-12   Moving the cursor by sentences, paragraphs, H, M, and L

Moving the Cursor within the Screen

The **H** (home) key positions the cursor at the left end of the top line of the screen. The **M** (middle) key moves the cursor to the middle line, and **L** (lower) moves it to the bottom line (Figure 10-12).

Viewing Different Parts of the Work Buffer

The screen displays a portion of the text that is in the Work buffer. You can display the text preceding or following the text on the screen by *scrolling* the display. You can also display a portion of the Work buffer based on a line number.

Press CONTROL-D to scroll the screen down (forward) through the file so that vim displays half a screen of new text. Use CONTROL-U to scroll the screen up (backward) the same amount. If you precede either of these commands with a number, vim will scroll that number of lines each time you use CONTROL-D or CONTROL-U for the rest of the session (unless you change the number of lines to scroll again). The CONTROL-F (forward) or CONTROL-B (backward) keys display almost a *whole* screen of new text, leaving a couple of lines from the previous screen for continuity.

When you enter a line number followed by **G** (goto), vim positions the cursor on that line in the Work buffer. If you press **G** without a number, vim positions the cursor on the last line in the Work buffer. Line numbers are implicit; your file does not need to have actual line numbers for you to use this command. Refer to "Line numbers" on page 453 if you want vim to display line numbers.

Input Mode

The Insert, Append, Open, Change, and Replace commands put vim in Input mode. While vim is in Input mode, you can put new text into the Work buffer. Always press the ESCAPE key to return vim to Command mode when you finish entering text. Refer to "Show mode" on page 453 if you want vim to remind you when it is in Input mode.

Inserting Text

The **i** (insert) command puts vim in Input mode and places the text you enter *before* the character the cursor is on (the *current character*). The **I** command places text at the beginning of the current line (Figure 10-13). Although **i** and **I** commands sometimes overwrite text on the screen, the characters in the Work buffer are not

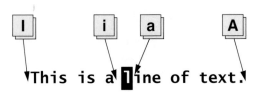

Figure 10-13   The I, i, a, and A commands

changed; only the display is affected. The overwritten text is redisplayed when you press ESCAPE and vim returns to Command mode. Use **i** or **I** to insert a few characters or words into existing text or to insert text in a new file.

Appending Text

The **a** (append) command is similar to the **i** command, except that it places the text you enter *after* the current character (Figure 10-13). The **A** command places the text *after* the last character on the current line.

Opening a Line for Text

The **o** (open) and **O** commands open a blank line within existing text, place the cursor at the beginning of the new (blank) line, and put vim in Input mode. The **O** command opens a line *above* the current line; **o** opens one below. Use the Open commands when entering several new lines within existing text.

Replacing Text

The **R** (replace) and **r** commands cause the new text you enter to overwrite (replace) existing text. The single character you enter following an **r** command overwrites the current character. After you enter that character, vim automatically returns to Command mode. You do not need to press the ESCAPE key.

The **R** command causes *all* subsequent characters to overwrite existing text until you press ESCAPE to return vim to Command mode.

Replacing TABS || caution

These commands may appear to behave strangely if you replace TAB characters. TAB characters can appear as several SPACES—until you try to replace them. They are actually only one character and are replaced by a single character. Refer to "Invisible Characters" on page 454 for information on how to display TABS as visible characters.

Quoting Special Characters

While you are in Input mode, you can use the Quote command, CONTROL-V, to enter any characters into your text, including characters that normally have special meaning to vim. Among these characters are CONTROL-L (or CONTROL-R), which redraws the screen; CONTROL-W, which backs the cursor up a word to the left; and ESCAPE, which ends Input mode.

To insert one of these characters into your text, type CONTROL-V and then the character. CONTROL-V quotes the single character that follows it. For example, to insert the sequence ESCAPE[2J into a file you are creating in vim, you type the character sequence CONTROL-V ESCAPE[2J. This is the character sequence that clears the screen of a DEC VT-100 and other similar terminals. Although you would not ordinarily want to type this sequence into a document, you might want to use it or another ESCAPE sequence in a shell script you are creating in vim. Refer to Chapters 13 through 15 for information about writing shell scripts.

Command Mode: Deleting and Changing Text

This section describes the commands to delete and replace, or change, text in the document you are editing. The Undo command is also covered because it allows you to restore deleted or changed text.

Undoing Changes

The Undo command, **u**, restores text that you just deleted or changed by mistake. A single Undo command restores only the most recently deleted text. If you delete a line and then change a word, the first Undo restores only the changed word; you have to give a second Undo command to restore the deleted line. The U command restores the last line you changed to the way it was before you started changing it, even after several changes.

Deleting Characters

The **x** command deletes the current character. You can precede the **x** command by a Repeat Factor (page 463) to delete several characters on the current line, starting with the current character. The **X** command deletes characters to the left of the cursor.

Deleting Text

The **d** command removes text from the Work buffer. The amount of text that **d** removes depends on the Repeat Factor and the Unit of Measure (page 460) you enter after the **d**. After the text is deleted, vim is still in Command mode.

Use dd to Delete a Single Line || tip

The command **d** RETURN deletes two lines: the current line and the following one. Use the **dd** command to delete just the current line, or precede **dd** by a Repeat Factor (page 463) to delete several lines.

You can delete from the current cursor position up to a specific character on the same line. To delete up to the next semicolon (;), give the command **dt;**. If you want to delete the remainder of the current line, use **D** or **d$**. Table 10-1 lists some Delete commands. Each command, except the last group that starts with **dd**, deletes *from* the current character.

Delete Command Examples || table 10-1

dl	Deletes current character (same as the **x** command)
d0	Deletes to beginning of line
d^	Deletes to the first character of the line (not including spaces or tabs)
dw	Deletes to end of word
d3w	Deletes to end of third word
db	Deletes to beginning of word
dW	Deletes to end of blank-delimited word
dB	Deletes to beginning of blank-delimited word
d7B	Deletes to seventh previous beginning of blank-delimited word
d)	Deletes to end of sentence

Delete Command Examples (Continued) || table 10-1

d4)	Deletes to end of fourth sentence
d(	Deletes to beginning of sentence
d}	Deletes to end of paragraph
d{	Deletes to beginning of paragraph
d7{	Deletes to seventh paragraph preceding beginning of paragraph
dd	Deletes the current line
d/*text*	Deletes forward in text up to but not including the next occurrence of word *text*
df*c*	Deletes forward on current line up to and including next occurrence of character *c*
dt*c*	Deletes on current line up to the next occurrence of *c*
D	Deletes to the end of line
d$	Deletes to the end of line
5dd	Deletes five lines starting with the current line
dL	Deletes through last line on screen
dH	Deletes through first line on screen
dG	Deletes through end of Work buffer
d1G	Deletes through beginning of Work buffer

Exchange Characters and Lines || tip

If two characters are out of order, position the cursor on the first character, and give the commands **xp**.
If two lines are out of order, position the cursor on the first line, and give the commands **ddp**.

Changing Text

The **c** command replaces existing text with new text. The new text does not have to occupy the same space as the existing text. You can change a word to several words, a line to several lines, or a paragraph to a single character. The **C** command replaces the text from the cursor position to the end of the line.

The Change command deletes the amount of text specified by the Unit of Measure (page 460) that follows it and puts vim in Input mode. When you finish entering the new text and press ESCAPE, the old word, line, sentence, or paragraph is changed to the new one. Pressing ESCAPE without entering new text has the effect of deleting the specified text.

When you change less than a line of text, vim does not delete the text immediately. Instead, the **c** command places a dollar sign at the end of the text that is to be changed and leaves vim in Input mode. You may appear to overwrite text, but only the text that precedes the dollar sign changes in the Work buffer. Other text remains in the Work buffer and is redisplayed when you press ESCAPE. When you change one or more lines, vim deletes the lines as soon as you give the Change command.

Table 10-2 lists some Change commands. Except for the last two, each command changes text *from* the current character.

dw Works Differently From cw || tip

The **dw** command deletes all the characters through (including) the SPACE at the end of a word, whereas the **cw** command changes only the characters in the word, leaving the trailing SPACE intact.

Change Command Examples || table 10-2

cl	Changes the current character
cw	Changes to end of word
c3w	Changes to end of third word
cb	Changes to beginning of word
cW	Changes to end of blank-delimited word
cB	Changes to beginning of blank-delimited word
c7B	Changes to beginning of seventh previous blank-delimited word

Change Command Examples (Continued) || table 10-2

c$	Changes to the beginning of the line
c0	Changes to the end of the line
c)	Changes to end of sentence
c4)	Changes to end of fourth sentence
c(	Changes to beginning of sentence
c}	Changes to end of paragraph
c{	Changes to beginning of paragraph
c7{	Changes to beginning of seventh preceding paragraph
ct*c*	Changes on current line up to the next occurrence of *c*
C	Changes to end of line
cc	Changes the current line
5cc	Changes five lines starting with the current line

Replacing Text

The s and S commands also replace existing text with new text (Table 10-3). The s command, which deletes the character the cursor is on and puts vim into Input mode, has the effect of replacing the single character that the cursor is on with whatever you type until you press ESCAPE. The S command has the same effect as the cc command from the previous section. The s command will replace characters only on the current line. If you specify a Repeat Factor before an s command and this action would replace more characters than exist on the current line, s changes characters only to the end of the line (same as C, preceding).

Changing Case

The tilde (~) character changes the case of the character under the cursor from upper- to lowercase or vice versa. You can precede the tilde with a number to specify the number of characters you want the command to affect. For example, 5~ will transpose the next five characters, starting with the character under the cursor.

Substitute Command Examples	‖ table 10-3
s	Substitutes one or more characters for the current character
S	Substitutes one or more characters for current line
5s	Substitutes one or more characters for five characters, starting with the current character

Searching and Substituting

Searching for and replacing a character, a string of text, or a string that is matched by a regular expression is a key feature of any editor. The vim editor provides simple commands for searching for a character on the current line. It also provides more complex commands for searching for and optionally substituting for single and multiple occurrences of strings or regular expressions anywhere in the Work buffer.

Searching for a Character

You can search for and move the cursor to the next occurrence of a specified character on the current line by using the Find command. Refer to "Moving the Cursor to a Specific Character" on page 429.

The next two commands are used in the same manner as the Find command. The **t** command places the cursor on the character before the next occurrence of the specified character, whereas the **T** command places it on the character after the previous occurrence of the specified character.

A semicolon (;) repeats the last **f, F, t,** or **T** command.

You can combine these search commands with other commands. For example, the command **d2fq** deletes the text from the location of the cursor to the second occurrence of the letter q on the current line.

Searching for a String

The forward and backward search commands just discussed are restricted to searches within the current line. The vim editor can also search backward or forward through the Work buffer to find a specific string of text or a string that matches a regular expression (see Appendix A). To find the next occurrence of a string (forward), press the forward slash (/) key, enter the text you want to find (called the *search string*), and press RETURN. When you press the slash key, vim displays a slash on the status line. As you enter the string of text, it too is displayed on the status line. When you press RETURN, vim searches for the string. If it finds the string, vim positions the cursor on the first character of the string. If you use a question mark (?) in place of the forward slash, vim searches for the previous occurrence of the string. If you need to include a forward slash in a forward search or a question mark in a backward search, you must quote it by preceding it with a backslash (\).

The **N** and **n** keys repeat the last search without the need for you to enter the search string again. The **n** key repeats the original search exactly, and the **N** key repeats the search in the opposite direction of the original search.

Normally, if you are searching forward and vim does not find the search string before it gets to the end of the Work buffer, vim *wraps around* and continues the search at the beginning of the Work buffer. During a backward search, vim wraps around from the beginning of the Work buffer to the end. Also, vim normally performs case-sensitive searches. Refer to "Wrap Scan" (page 454) and "Ignore case in searches" (page 454) for information about how to change these search parameters.

Special Characters in Search Strings

Because the search string is a regular expression, some characters take on a special meaning within the search string. The following paragraphs list some of these characters. The first two (^ and $) always have their special meanings within a search string unless you quote them (page 433), and the rest can have their special meanings within a search string turned off by a single command. Refer to "Allow special characters in searches" on page 454.

^ *(Beginning-of-Line Indicator)*

When the first character in a search string is a caret, or circumflex, it matches the beginning of a line. The command **/^the** finds the next line that begins with the string **the**.

$ *(End-of-Line Indicator)*

Similarly, a dollar sign matches the end of a line. The command **/!$** finds the next line that ends with an exclamation point.

. *(Any-Character Indicator)*

A period matches *any* character, anywhere in the search string. The command **/l..e** finds **line, followed, like, included, all memory,** or any other word or character string that contains an l followed by any two characters and an e. To search for a period, use a backslash to quote the period (\.).

\>   (End-of-Word Indicator)

This pair of characters matches the end of a word. The command **/s\>** finds the next word that ends with an s. Whereas a backslash (\) is typically used to *turn off* the special meaning of a character, the character sequence \> has a special meaning, and > alone does not.

\<   (Beginning-of-Word Indicator)

This pair of characters matches the beginning of a word. The command **/\<The** finds the next word that begins with The. The beginning-of-word indicator uses the backslash in the same, atypical way as the end-of-word indicator.

\(...\)   (Save Pattern)

These delimiters save whatever is between them into a special holding buffer. This buffer can then be referenced to call back up to nine previously saved patterns by using a backslash followed by a number (\1 through \9).

*   (Zero or More Occurrences)

This character is a modifier that will match zero or more occurrences of the character immediately preceding it. The command **/dis*m** will match the string di followed by zero or more s characters followed by an m. Examples of successful matches would include dim or dism or dissm.

[ ]   (Character-Class Definition)

Brackets surrounding two or more characters match any *single* character located between the brackets. The command **/dis[ck]** finds the next occurrence of *either* disk or disc.

There are two special characters you can use within a character-class definition. A caret (^) as the first character following the left bracket defines the character class to be *any but the following characters*. A hyphen between two characters indicates a range of characters. Refer to the examples in Table 10-4.

Substituting One String for Another

A Substitute command, a combination of a Search command and a Change command, searches for a string just as the **/** command does, allowing the same special characters that the previous section discussed. When it finds a string, the Substitute command changes it. The syntax of the Substitute command is

> *:[g][address]s/**search-string**/**replacement-string**[/option]*

As with all commands that begin with a colon, vim executes a Substitute command from the status line.

Search Examples

|| table 10-4

/and	Finds the next occurrence of the string **and** Examples: s and and standard s l ander andi ron
\<and\>	Finds the next occurrence of the word **and** Example: and
/^The	Finds the next line that starts with **The** Examples: The... There...
/^[0-9][0-9])	Finds the next line that starts with a two-digit number followed by a right parenthesis Examples: 77)... 01)... 15)...
\<[adr]	Finds the next word that starts with an **a**, **d**, or **r** Examples: apple drive road argument right
/^[A-Za-z]	Finds the next line that starts with an upper- or lowercase letter Examples: Will not find a line starting with the number 7... Dear Mr. Jones ... in the middle of a sentence like this ...

The Substitute Address

If you do not specify an *address,* Substitute searches only the current line. If you use a single line number as the *address,* Substitute searches that line. If the *address* is two line numbers separated by a comma, Substitute searches those lines and the lines between. Refer to "Line numbers" on page 453 if you want vim to display line numbers. Any place a line number is allowed in the address, you may also use an *address*-string enclosed between slashes. The vim editor operates on the next line that the *address*-string matches. When you precede the first slash of the *address*-string with the letter **g** (for global), vim operates on all lines in the file that the *address*-string matches. (This **g** is not the same as the one that goes at the end of the Substitute command to cause multiple replacements on a single line; see "Searching for and Replacing Strings" following).

Within the *address,* a period represents the current line, a dollar sign represents the last line in the Work buffer, and a percent sign represents the entire Work buffer.

You can perform *address* arithmetic using plus and minus signs. Some examples of *address*es are shown in Table 10-5.

Address	Portion of Work Buffer Addressed	|| table 10-5
5	Line 5	
77,100	Lines 77 through 100 inclusive	
1,.	Beginning of Work buffer through current line	
.,$	Current line through end of Work buffer	
1,$	Entire Work buffer	
%	Entire Work buffer	
/pine/	The line containing the next occurrence of the word `pine`	
g/pine/	All lines containing the word `pine`	
.,.+10	Current line through tenth following line (11 lines in all)	

Searching for and Replacing Strings

An **s** comes after the *address*, indicating that a Substitute command follows. A delimiter follows the **s**, marking the beginning of the *search-string*. Although the examples in this book use a forward slash, you can use as a delimiter any character that is not a letter, number, blank, or backslash. You must use the same delimiter at the end of the *search-string*.

Next comes the *search-string*. It has the same format as the search string in the / command and can include the same special characters. (The *search-string* is a regular expression; refer to Appendix A for more information.) Another delimiter marks the end of the *search-string* and the beginning of the *replace-string*.

The *replace-string* is the string that replaces the text matched by the *search-string*. The *replace-string* should be followed by the delimiter character. Some versions of vim allow you to omit the last delimiter when no option follows the *replace-string*; it is always required if an option is present. Several characters have special meaning in the *search-string*, and other characters have special meaning in the *replace-string*. For example, an ampersand (&) in the *replace-string* represents the text that was matched by the *search-string*. A backslash in the *replace-string* quotes the character that follows it. Refer to Table 10-6 and Appendix A.

Search and Replace Examples

|| table 10-6

:s/bigger/biggest/	Replaces the string `bigger` on the current line with `biggest` **Example:** `bigger` → `biggest`

:1,.s/Ch 1/Ch 2/g	Replaces every occurrence of the string `Ch 1`, before or on the current line, with the string `Ch 2`
	Examples:
	`Ch 1` → `Ch 2`
	`Ch 12` → `Ch 22`

:1,$s/ten/10/g	Replaces every occurrence of the string `ten` by the string `10`
	Examples:
	`ten` → `10`
	`often` → `of10`
	`tenant` → `10ant`

:g/chapter/s/ten/10/	Replaces the first occurrence of the string `ten` with the string `10` on all lines containing the word `chapter`
	Examples:
	`chapter ten` → `chapter 10`
	`chapters will often` → `chapters will of10`

:s/\(first\)\(last\)/\2\1/	Uses the pattern-holding buffers to swap `first` and `last` on the current line **Example:** `firstlast` → `lastfirst`
:%s/\<ten\>/10/g	Replaces every occurrence of the word `ten` by the string `10` **Example:** `ten` → `10`

:.,.+10s/every/each/g	Replaces every occurrence of the string `every` by the string `each` on the current line through the tenth following line
	Examples:
	`every` → `each`
	`everything` → `eachthing`

:s/\<short\>/"&"/	Replaces the word `short` on the current line with `"short"` (enclosed within quotation marks) **Example:** `the shortest of the short` → `the shortest of the "short"`

Normally, the Substitute command replaces only the first occurrence of any text that matches the *search-string* on a line. If you want a global substitution—that is, if you want to replace all matching occurrences of text on a line—append the g (global) option after the delimiter that ends the *replace-string*. Another useful option is c (check). This option causes vim to ask whether you would like to make the change each time it finds text that matches the *search-string*. Pressing y replaces the *search-string*, pressing q terminates the command, and pressing any other character simply continues the search without making that replacement.

The *address*-string need not be the same as the *search-string*. For example,

```
:/candle/s/wick/flame/
```

will substitute wick for the first occurrence of flame on the next line that contains the string candle, Similarly,

```
:g/candle/s/wick/flame/
```

will perform the same substitution on the first occurrence on each line of the file containing the string candle.

If the *search-string* is the same as the *address*-string, you can leave the *search-string* blank. For example, the command :/candle/s//lamp/ is equivalent to :/candle/s/candle/lamp/.

Using the following fraction of a poem,[3] you will see what damage the Substitute command can do:

```
$ tail -20 walrus
"But wait a bit," the Oysters cried,
"Before we have our chat;
For some of us are out of breath,
And all of us are fat!"
"No hurry!" said the Carpenter.
They thanked him much for that.

"A loaf of bread," the Walrus said,
"Is what we chiefly need:
Pepper and vinegar besides
Are very good indeed--
Now if you're ready, Oysters dear,
We can begin to feed."

"But not on us!" the Oysters cried,
Turning a little blue.
"After such kindness, that would be
A dismal thing to do!"
"The night is fine," the Walrus said.
"Do you admire the view?"
```

---

3. With apologies to Lewis Carroll, from *Through the Looking-Glass and What Alice Found There*, 1872.

Suppose that you give the following Substitute commands while editing this file:

```
%s/Walrus/Penguin/g
%s/Oysters/Goldfish/g
```

You will end up with a file that looks like this:

```
$ tail -20 walrus
"But wait a bit," the Goldfish cried,
"Before we have our chat;
For some of us are out of breath,
And all of us are fat!"
"No hurry!" said the Carpenter.
They thanked him much for that.

"A loaf of bread," the Penguin said,
"Is what we chiefly need:
Pepper and vinegar besides
Are very good indeed--
Now if you're ready, Goldfish dear,
We can begin to feed."

"But not on us!" the Goldfish cried,
Turning a little blue.
"After such kindness, that would be
A dismal thing to do!"
"The night is fine," the Penguin said.
"Do you admire the view?"
```

Miscellaneous Commands

Table 10-7 lists three commands that do not fit naturally into any other groups.

Miscellaneous Commands	|| table 10-7
Join	The Join command, J, joins the line below the current line to the end of the current line, inserting a SPACE between what was previously two lines and leaving the cursor on this SPACE. If the current line ends with a period, vim inserts two SPACEs. You can always "unjoin" (break) a line into two lines by replacing the SPACE or SPACEs where you want to break the line with a RETURN.
Status	The Status command, CONTROL-G, displays the name of the file you are editing, whether the file has been modified and/or locked, the line number of the current line, the total number of lines in the Work buffer, and the percent of the Work buffer preceding the current line.

Miscellaneous Commands (Continued)	‖ table 10-7
. (period)	The **.** (period) command repeats the most recent command that made a change. If, for example, you had just given a **d2w** command (delete the next two words), the **.** command deletes the next two words. If you had just inserted text, the **.** command would repeat the insertion of the same text. This command is useful if you want to change some occurrences of a word or phrase in the Work buffer. Search for the first occurrence of the word (use **/**), and then make the change you want (use **cw**). Following these two commands, you can use **n** to search for the next occurrence of the word and **.** to make the same change to it. If you do not want to make the change, use **n** again to find the next occurrence.

Yank, Put, and Delete Commands

The vim editor has a General-Purpose buffer and 26 Named buffers that can hold text during an editing session. These buffers are useful if you want to move or copy a portion of text to another location in the Work buffer. A combination of the Delete and Put commands removes text from one location in the Work buffer and places it in another. The Yank and Put commands copy text to another location in the Work buffer, without changing the original text.

The General-Purpose Buffer

The vim editor stores the text that you most recently changed, deleted, or yanked in the General-Purpose buffer. The Undo command retrieves text from the General-Purpose buffer when it restores text.

Copying Text to the Buffer

The Yank command (**y**) is identical to the Delete (**d**) command but does not delete text from the Work buffer. The vim editor places a *copy* of the yanked text in the General-Purpose buffer, so that you can use Put (see following) to place another copy of it elsewhere in the Work buffer. Use the Yank command just as you use **d**, the Delete command. The uppercase **Y** command yanks an entire line into the General-Purpose buffer.

Use yy to Yank One Line || tip

Just as **d** RETURN deletes two lines, **y** RETURN yanks two lines. Use the **yy** command to yank and **dd** to delete the current line.

D Works Differently From Y || tip

The **D** command (page 434) does not work in the same manner as the **Y** command: Whereas **D** deletes to the end of the line, **Y** yanks the entire line, regardless of the cursor position.

Copying Text from the Buffer

The Put commands, **P** and **p**, copy text from the General-Purpose buffer into the Work buffer. If you delete or yank characters or words into the General-Purpose buffer, **P** inserts them before the current *character,* and **p** inserts them after. If you delete or yank lines, sentences, or paragraphs, **P** inserts the contents of the General-Purpose buffer before the *line* the cursor is on, and **p** inserts them after.

Put commands do not destroy the contents of the General-Purpose buffer, so it is possible to place the same text at several points within the file by using one Delete or Yank command and several Put commands.

Because vim has only one General-Purpose buffer and vim changes the contents of this buffer each time you give a Change, Delete, or Yank command, *you can use only cursor-movement commands between a Delete or Yank command and the corresponding Put command.* Any other commands change the contents of the General-Purpose buffer and therefore change the results of the Put command. If you do not plan to use the Put command immediately after a Delete or Yank, use a Named buffer rather than the General-Purpose buffer.

Deleting Text Copies it into the Buffer

Any of the Delete commands described earlier in this chapter (page 433) automatically place the deleted text in the General-Purpose buffer. Just as you can use the Undo command to put the deleted text back where it came from, you can use a Put command to put the deleted text at another location in the Work buffer.

For example, if you delete a word from the middle of a sentence by using the **dw** command and then move the cursor to a SPACE between two words and give a **p** command, vim places the word you just deleted at the new location. Or if you delete a line by using the **dd** command and then move the cursor to the line *below* the line where you want the deleted line to appear and give a **P** command, vim places the line at the new location.

Named Buffers

You can use a Named buffer with any of the Delete, Yank, or Put commands. Each of the 26 Named buffers is named by a letter of the alphabet. Each Named buffer can store a different block of text so that you can recall each block as needed. Unlike the General-Purpose buffer, vim does not change the contents of a Named buffer unless you use a command that specifically overwrites that buffer. The vim editor maintains the contents of the Named buffers throughout an editing session.

The vim editor stores text in a Named buffer if you precede a Delete or Yank command with a double quotation mark (") and a buffer name (for example "**kyy** yanks a copy of the current line into buffer **k**). You can use a Named buffer in two ways. If you give the name of the buffer as a lowercase letter, vim overwrites the contents of the buffer when it deletes or yanks text into the buffer. If you use an uppercase letter, vim appends the newly deleted or yanked text to the end of the buffer. This feature enables you to collect blocks of text from various sections of a file and then deposit them at one place in the file with a single command. Named buffers are also useful when you are moving a section of a file and do not want to use Put immediately after the corresponding Delete and when you want to insert a paragraph, sentence, or phrase repeatedly in a document.

If you have one sentence that you use throughout a document, you can yank the sentence into a Named buffer and put it wherever you need it by using the following procedure. After entering the first occurrence of the sentence and pressing ESCAPE to return to Command mode, leave the cursor on the line containing the sentence. (The sentence must appear on a line or lines by itself for this procedure to work.) Then yank the sentence into Named buffer **a** by giving the "**ayy** command (or "**a2yy** if the sentence takes up two lines). Now any time you need the sentence, you can return to Command mode and give the command "**ap** to put a copy of the sentence below the line the cursor is on.

This technique provides a quick and easy way to insert text that you use frequently in a document. For example, if you were editing a legal document, you might use a Named buffer to store the phrase The Plaintiff alleges that the Defendant to save yourself the trouble of typing it every time you want to use it. Similarly, if you were creating a letter that frequently used a long company name, such as National Standards Institute, you might put it into a Named buffer.

Numbered Buffers

In addition to 26 Named buffers and 1 General-Purpose buffer, there are 9 Numbered buffers. These are, in one sense, readonly buffers. The vim editor automatically fills them with the nine most recently deleted chunks of text that are at least one line long. The most recently deleted pattern is held in " **1**, the next most recent in " **2**, and so on. If you delete a block of text and then give other vim commands so you cannot reclaim the deleted text with Undo, use " **1p** to paste the most recently deleted chunk of text below the location of the cursor. If you have deleted several blocks of text and want to reclaim a specific one, proceed as follows: Paste the contents of the first buffer with " **1p**. If the first buffer does not have the text you are looking for, undo the paste with **u**, and then give the period (.) command to repeat the previous command. The Numbered buffers work in a unique way with the period command: Instead of pasting the contents of buffer " **1**, the period command will paste the contents of the next buffer (" **2**). Another **u** and period replace the contents of buffer " **2** with that of buffer " **3**, and so on through the nine buffers.

Reading and Writing Files

The vim editor reads a disk file into the Work buffer when you call vim from the shell. The **ZZ** command that terminates the editing session writes the contents of the Work buffer back to the disk file. This section discusses other ways of reading text into the Work buffer and writing it out.

Reading Files

The Read command reads a file into the Work buffer. The new file does not overwrite any text in the Work buffer but is positioned following the single address you specify (or the current line if you do not specify an address). You can use an address of 0 to read the file into the beginning of the Work buffer. The format of the Read command is

:[address]r [filename]

As with other commands that begin with a colon, when you enter the colon, it appears on the status line. The *filename* is the pathname of the file that you want to read and must be terminated by RETURN. If you omit the *filename*, vim reads the file you are editing from the disk.

Writing Files

The Write command writes part or all of the Work buffer to a file. You can use an address to write out part of the Work buffer and a filename to specify a file to receive the text. If you do not use an address or filename, vim writes the entire contents of the Work buffer to the file you are editing, updating the file on the disk.

During a long editing session, it is a good idea to use the Write command occasionally. Then if a problem develops, a recent copy of the Work buffer is safe on the disk. If you use a :q! command to exit from vim, the disk file reflects the version of the Work buffer at the time you last used the Write command. The formats of the Write command are

> :*[address]w[!] [filename]*
> :*[address]w>> filename*

You can use the second format of the Write command to append text to an existing file. The following list covers the components of the Write command.

address If you use an *address*, it specifies the portion of the Work buffer that you want vim to write to the disk. The *address* follows the form of the *address* that the Substitute command uses. If you do not use an *address*, vim writes out the entire contents of the Work buffer.

w! Because Write can quickly destroy a large amount of work, vim demands that you enter an exclamation point following the **w** as a safeguard against accidentally overwriting a file. The only times you do not need an exclamation point are when you are writing out the entire contents of the Work buffer to the file being edited (using no *address* and no filename) and when you are writing part or all of the Work buffer to a new file. When you are writing part of the file to the file being edited or when you are overwriting another file, you must use an exclamation point.

filename The optional *filename* is the pathname of the file you are writing to. If you do not specify a *filename*, vim writes to the file you are editing.

Identifying the Current File

The File command provides the same information as the Status command (CONTROL-G); it displays the name of the file you are editing, whether the file has been modified and/or locked, the line number of the current line, the total number of lines in the Work buffer, and the percent of the Work buffer preceding the current line. The filename the File command displays is the one the Write command uses if you give a **:w** command (rather than **:w filename**). The File command is

> :f

An example of the display produced by the File command is

```
"practice" [Modified] line 11 of 35 --31%--
```

Setting Parameters

You can adapt vim to your needs and habits by setting vim parameters. These parameters perform such functions as displaying line numbers, automatically inserting RETURNs for you, and establishing nonstandard searches.

You can set parameters in several ways. You can set them while you are using vim to establish the environment for the current editing session. Alternatively, you can set the parameters in your **.profile** ^{bash zsh} or **.login** ^{tcsh} file or in a startup file that vim uses, **.vimrc**. When you set the parameters in any of those files, each time you use vim, the environment has been established, and you can begin editing immediately.

Setting Parameters from within vim

To set a parameter while you are using vim, enter a colon (:), the word **set**, a SPACE, and the parameter (refer to "Parameters" on page 452). The command appears on the status line as you type it and takes effect when you press RETURN.

Setting Parameters in a Startup File

If you are using bash or zsh, you can put the following lines in the **.profile** file in your home directory:

> *EXINIT='set param1 param2 . . .'*
> *export EXINIT*

Replace *param1* and *param2* with parameters selected from the list in the next section. **EXINIT** is a shell variable that vim reads. Following is a statement that ignores the case of characters in searches, displays line numbers, uses the TC Shell to execute GNU/Linux commands, and wraps text 15 characters from the right edge of the screen looks:

```
EXINIT='set autoindent numbers shell=/bin/tcsh wrapmargin=15'
export EXINIT
```

Or, if you use the parameter abbreviations, it looks like this:

```
EXINIT='set ai nu sh=/usr/bin/csh wm=15'
export EXINIT
```

If you are using tcsh, put the following line in the **.login** file in your home directory:

setenv EXINIT 'set param1 param2 . . .'

Again, replace *param1* and *param2* with parameters from the following section. The values between the single quotation marks are the same as shown in the preceding example.

The .vimrc Startup File

Instead of setting vim parameters in your **.login** or **.profile** file, you can create a **.vimrc** file and set them there. If you set the parameters in a **.vimrc** file, use the following format:

set param1 param2 . . .

Following are examples of **.vimrc** files that perform the same function as **EXINIT** described previously:

```
$ cat .vimrc
set ignorecase
set number
set shell=/bin/tcsh
set wrapmargin=15

$ cat .vimrc
set ic
set nu
set sh=/bin/tcsh
set wm=15
```

When you start, vim looks for a **.vimrc** file that you own in your home directory and in your working directory. If it finds such a file, vim uses the values that it contains. If you set parameters in your **.profile** or **.login** file, as well as in **.vimrc**, the parameters in **.vimrc** take precedence because **.vimrc** is executed later than **.profile** and **.login**. Parameters set in **.vimrc** also take precedence over those from the **EXINIT** shell variable.

Parameters

Table 10-8 lists some of the most useful vim parameters. The vim editor displays a complete list of parameters and how they are currently set when you give the command **:set all** followed by a RETURN while using vim. There are two classes of parameters: those that contain an equal sign (and can take on a value) and those optionally prefixed with **no** (switches that are on or off). You can change the sense of a switch parameter by giving the command **:set [no]***param*. For example, give the command **:set number** or **:set nonumber** to turn on/off line numbering (Table 10-8). To change the value of a parameter that takes on a value (and uses an equal sign), give a command such as **:set shiftwidth=15**. Most parameters have abbreviations that you can use in their place (**nu** for number and **nonu** for no number, **sw** for shiftwidth; the abbreviations are listed in the left column of Table 10-8.

Parameters   ‖ table 10-8

Line numbers number, nu	The **vim** editor does not normally display the line number associated with each line. To display line numbers, set the parameter **number**. To cause line numbers not to be displayed, set the parameter **nonumber**. Line numbers, whether displayed or not, are not part of the file, are not stored with the file, and are not displayed when the file is printed. They appear on the screen only while you are using **vim**.
Line wrap margin wrapmargin, wm	The line wrap margin causes **vim** to break the text that you are inserting at approximately the specified number of characters from the right margin. The **vim** editor breaks the text by inserting a NEWLINE character at the closest blank-delimited word boundary. Setting the line wrap margin is handy if you want all your text lines to be about the same length. It relieves you of having to remember to press RETURN to end each line of input. Set the parameter **wrapmargin=nn**, where **nn** is the number of characters *from the right side of the screen* where you want **vim** to break the text. This number is not the column width of the text but the distance from the end of the text to the right edge of the screen. Setting the wrap margin to 0 (zero) turns this feature off. By default, **vim** sets the wrap margin to 0.
Shell shell, sh	While you are using **vim**, you can cause it to spawn a new shell. You can either create an interactive shell (if you want to run several commands) or run a single command. The **shell** parameter determines what shell **vim** invokes. By default **vim** sets the **shell** parameter to your login shell. To change it, set the parameter **shell=pathname**, where **pathname** is the full pathname of the shell you want to use.
Show mode showmode, smd	The **vim** editor does not normally give you a visual cue to let you know when it is in Input mode. On some versions of **vim**, however, you can set the parameter **showmode** to display the mode in the lower-right corner of the screen when **vim** is in Input or Command mode. Three types of Input mode are Open, Insert, and Append. Set **noshowmode** to cause **vim** not to display the message.

Parameters (Continued) || table 10-8

Flash flash, fl	The **vim** editor normally causes the terminal to beep when you give an invalid command or press ESCAPE when you are in Command mode. Setting the parameter **flash** causes the terminal to flash instead of beep. Set **noflash** to cause it to beep. Not all terminals/emulators support this parameter.
Ignore case in searches ignorecase (ic/noic)	The **vim** editor normally performs case-sensitive searches, differentiating between upper- and lowercase letters. It performs case-insensitive searches when you set the **ignorecase** parameter. Set **noignorecase** to restore case-sensitive searches.

Allow special characters in searches
magic
	Refer to "Special Characters in Search Strings" on page 439. The following characters have special meanings when used in a search string:
	
	   . [ ] *
	
	When you set the **nomagic** parameter, these characters no longer have special meanings. The **magic** parameter gives them back their special meanings.
	    The ^ and $ characters always have a special meaning within search strings, regardless of how you set this parameter.

Invisible Characters list	To cause **vim** to display each TAB as ^I and to mark the end of each line with a $, set the **list** parameter. To display TABS as whitespace and not mark ends of lines, set **nolist**.
Wrap Scan wrapscan, ws	Normally when a search for the next occurrence of a search string reaches the end of the Work buffer, **vim** continues the search at the beginning of the Work buffer. The reverse is true of a search for the previous occurrence of a search string. The **nowrapscan** parameter stops the search at either end of the Work buffer. Set the **wrapscan** parameter if you want searches to wrap once again around the ends of the Work buffer.
Automatic Indention autoindent, ai	The automatic indention feature works with the **shiftwidth** parameter to provide a regular set of indentions for programs or tabular material. This feature is normally off. You can turn it on by setting **autoindent** and turn it off by setting **noautoindent**. When automatic indention is on and **vim** is in Input mode, CONTROL-T moves the cursor from the left margin (or an indention) to the next indention position, RETURN moves the cursor to the left side of the next line under the first character of the previous line, and CONTROL-D backs up over indention positions. The CONTROL-T and CONTROL-D keys work only before text is placed on a line.

Parameters (Continued)	|| table 10-8
Automatic Write autowrite, aw	By default **vim** asks you before writing out the Work buffer when you have not explicitly told it to do so (as when you give a :n command to edit the next file). The **autowrite** option causes **vim** to write the Work buffer automatically when you use commands, such as :n, to edit to another file. You can disable this parameter by setting the **noautowrite** or **noaw** option.
Show Match showmatch, sm	This parameter is useful for programmers working in languages that use braces ({}) or parentheses as expression delimiters (Lisp, C, Tcl, and so on). When **showmatch** is set and you are entering code (in Input mode) and type a closing brace or parenthesis, the cursor will jump briefly to the matching opening brace or parenthesis (that is, the preceding corresponding element at the same nesting level). After it highlights the matching element, the cursor resumes its previous position. When you type a right brace or parenthesis that does not have a match, **vim** beeps. Use **noshowmatch** to turn off automatic matching.
Report report	Causes **vim** to display a report on the status line whenever you make a change that affects at least *n* lines (**set report=***n*). For example, if **report** is set to 5 and you delete five lines, you will see the message 5 lines deleted. When you delete four or fewer lines, **vim** does not display a message. The default for **report** is 5.
Shift Width shiftwidth, sw	Controls the functioning of CONTROL-T and CONTROL-D in Input mode when automatic indention is on. Set the parameter **shiftwidth=nn**, where **nn** is the spacing of the indention positions. Setting the shift width is similar to setting the TAB stops on a typewriter; with **shiftwidth**, however, the distance between TAB stops is always constant.

Advanced Editing Techniques

This section presents several commands that you may find useful once you have become comfortable using vim. While you are using vim, you can set and use markers to make addressing more convenient. Set a marker by giving the command **m***c*, where *c* is any character. (Letters are preferred because some characters, such as a single quotation mark, have special meanings when used as markers.)

Optional

Using Markers

Once you have set a marker, you can use it in a manner similar to a line number. The vim editor does not preserve markers when you stop editing a file.

You can move the cursor to the beginning of a line that contains a marker by preceding the marker name with a single quotation mark. For example, to set marker **t**, position the cursor on the line you want to mark, and give the command **mt**. During this editing session, unless you reset marker **t** or delete the line it marks, you can return to the beginning of the line you marked with the command **'t**.

You can delete all text from the current line through the line containing marker **r** with the following command:

```
d'r
```

You can use a grave accent (`‘`—also called a grave mark, back tick, or reverse single quotation mark) to go to the exact position of the mark on the line. After setting marker **t**, you can move the cursor to the location of this marker (not the beginning of the line containing the marker) with the command **`t**. The following command deletes all the text from the current line up to the character where the mark **r** was placed; the rest of the line containing the marker remains intact:

```
d`r
```

You can use markers in addresses of commands in place of line numbers. The following command replaces all occurrences of The with THE on all lines from marker **m** to the current line (marker **m** must precede the current line):

```
:'m,.s/The/THE/g
```

Editing Other Files

The following command causes vim to edit the file you specify with *filename*:

:e[!] [filename]

If you want to save the contents of the Work buffer, you must write it out (using **:w**) before you give this command. If you do not want to save the contents of the Work buffer, vim insists that you use an exclamation point to show that you know that you will lose the work you did since the last time you wrote out the Work buffer. If you do not supply a *filename*, vim edits the same file you are currently working on.

You can give the command **:e!** to start an editing session over again. This command returns the Work buffer to the state it was in the last time you wrote it out or, if you have not written it out, the state it was in when you started editing the file. This is useful when you make mistakes editing a file and decide that it would be easier to start over than to fix the mistakes.

Because this command does not destroy the contents of the Named buffers, you can store text from one file in a Named buffer, use a **:e** command to edit a second file, and put text from the Named buffer in the second file. A **:e** command does destroy the contents of the General-Purpose buffer and any markers you have set.

The command **:e#** attempts to close the current file and open the last file you were editing, placing the cursor on the line that it was on when you last closed the file. If you do not save the file you are working on before you give this command, vim will prompt you, reminding you to save the file you are closing. Setting the **autowrite** parameter (page 455) will not stop vim from prompting you.

The **:e#** command can help you copy blocks of text from one file to another. Call vim with the names of several files as arguments. You can use **:n** to edit the next file, **:e#** to edit the file you just edited, and **:rew** to rewind the sequence of files so that you are editing the first file again. As you move between files, you can copy text from one file (into a Named buffer [page 448]) and paste it into another. You can use **:n!** to force vim to close a file without writing out changes before it opens the next file.

Macros and Shortcuts

The vim editor allows you to create your own macros and shortcuts. The **:map** command defines a key or sequence of keys that perform some action in Command mode. The following command maps CONTROL-X to the commands that will find the next left bracket on the line the cursor is on (**f[**), delete all characters from that bracket to the next right bracket (**f]**) on the same line, delete the next character (**x**), move the cursor down two lines (**2j**), and, finally, move the cursor to the beginning of the line (**0**):

```
:map ^X f[df]x2j0
```

You can use ESCAPE and CONTROL sequences, but try to avoid remapping characters or sequences that are vim commands. Type **:map** by itself to see a list of the current mappings.

The **:abbrev** command is similar to **:map** but creates abbreviations you can use while in Input mode. When you are in Input mode and type a command you have defined with **:abbrev**, followed by a SPACE, vim replaces the command and the SPACE with the characters you specified when you defined the command. For ease of use, do not use common sequences of characters when creating abbreviations. The following command defines **ZZ** as an abbreviation for Mark G. Sobell. Even though **ZZ** is a vim command, it is used only in Command mode. It has no special meaning in Input mode, where you use abbreviations:

```
:abbrev ZZ Mark G. Sobell
```

Executing Shell Commands from within vim

You can execute shell commands in several ways while you are using vim. You can create a new interactive shell by giving the following command and pressing RETURN:

> :sh

The vim **shell** parameter determines what kind of shell is created (usually bash, tcsh, or zsh). By default **shell** is the same as your login shell.

After you have done what you want to do in the shell, you can return to vim by exiting from the shell (press CONTROL-D or give the command **exit**).

If :sh Does Not Work Correctly || tip

It is possible for the :sh command to behave strangely, depending on how your shell has been configured. You may get warnings with the :sh command, or it may even hang. Experiment with the :sh command to be sure it works with your configuration. If it does not, then you might want to try using a different shell by setting the vim shell parameter to another shell before using :sh. For example, the following command causes vim to use zsh with the :sh command:

> :set shell=/bin/zsh

You may need to change the SHELL environment variable after starting :sh to show the correct shell.

Edit Only One Copy of a File || caution

When you create a new shell by using :sh, you must remember that you are still using vim. A common mistake is to try to start editing the same file from the new shell, forgetting that vim is already editing the file from a different shell. Because you can lose information by editing the same file from two instances of an editor, vim warns you when you start to edit a file that is already being edited. Refer to "File Locks" on page 425 to see an example of the message that vim displays.

You can execute a shell command line from vim by giving the following command, replacing *command* with the command line you want to execute. Terminate the command with a RETURN:

> :!*command*

The vim editor spawns a new shell that executes the ***command***. When the command runs to completion, the newly spawned shell returns control to the editor.

Users frequently use this feature to carry on a dialog with the write utility. If Alex gets a message from Jenny while he is using vim, he can use the following command to write back to Jenny. After giving the command, Alex can carry on a dialog with Jenny in the same way he would if he had invoked write from the shell:

```
:!write jenny
```

If Alex has modified the Work buffer since he last wrote the file to disk, vim displays the following message before starting the write command:

```
[No write since last change]
```

When Alex finishes his dialog with Jenny, he presses CONTROL-D to terminate the write command. Then vim displays the following message:

```
Press RETURN or enter command to continue
```

When Alex presses RETURN, he can continue his editing session in vim.

You can execute a command from vim and have it replace the current line with the output from the command. If you do not want to replace any text, put the cursor on a blank line before giving the following command:

!!command

Nothing happens when you enter the first exclamation point. When you enter the second one, vim moves the cursor to the status line and allows you to enter the command you want to execute. Because this command puts vim in Last Line mode, you must end the command with a RETURN.

Finally, you can execute a command from vim with standard input to the command coming from all or part of the file you are editing and standard output from the command replacing the input in the file you are editing. You can use this type of command to sort a list in place in a file you are working on.

To specify the block of text that is to become standard input for the command, move the cursor to one end of the block of text. Then enter an exclamation point followed by a command that would normally move the cursor to the other end of the block of text. For example, if the cursor is at the beginning of the file and you want to specify the whole file, give the command !G. If you want to specify the part of the file between the cursor and marker **b**, give the command ! ' b. After you give the cursor-movement command, vim displays an exclamation point on the status line and allows you to give a command.

For example, to sort a list of names in a file, move the cursor to the beginning of the list and set marker **q** with an **mq** command. Then move the cursor to the end of the list and give the following command:

```
! ' qsort
```

Press RETURN and wait. After a few seconds, you see the sorted list replace the original list on the screen. If the command did not do what you expected, you can usually undo the change with a **u** command.

> ### ! Can Destroy Your File || caution
>
> If you enter the wrong command or mistype a command, you can destroy your file (for example, if the command hangs, or stops **vim** from working). For this reason it is a good idea to save your file before using this command. The Undo command (page 433) can be a lifesaver. A **:e!** command (page 456) will get rid of your changes, bringing the buffer back to the state it was in last time you saved it.
>
> Also, as with the **:sh** command, your default shell may not work properly with the ! command. You may want to test your shell with a simple test file before relying on the use of the ! command. If your usual shell doesn't work properly, change the **shell** parameter.

Units of Measure

Many vim commands operate on a block of text—from one character to many paragraphs. You can specify the size of a block of text with a *Unit of Measure*. You can specify multiple Units of Measure by preceding a Unit of Measure with a Repeat Factor (page 463). This section defines the various Units of Measure.

Character

A character is one character, visible or not, printable or not, including SPACEs and TABs. Some examples of characters are

        a q A . 5 R — > TAB SPACE

Word

A word, similar to an ordinary word in the English language, is a string of one or more characters bounded on both sides by any combination of one or more of the following elements: a punctuation mark, SPACE, TAB, numeral, or NEWLINE. In addition, vim considers each group of punctuation marks to be a word (Table 10-9).

Word Count	Text || table 10-9
1	pear
2	pear!
2	pear!)
3	pear!) The
4	pear!) "The
11	This is a short, concise line (no frills).

Blank-Delimited Word

A blank-delimited word is the same as a word but includes adjacent punctuation. Blank-delimited words are separated by one or more of the following elements: a SPACE, TAB, or NEWLINE (Table 10-10).

Blank-Delimited Word Count	‖ table 10-10
1	pear
1	pear!
1	pear!)
2	pear!) The
2	pear!) "The
8	This is a short, concise line (no frills).

Line

A line is a string of characters bounded by NEWLINEs and is not necessarily a single physical line on the terminal. You can enter a very long single (logical) line that wraps around (continues on the next physical line) several times or disappears off the right edge of the display. It is a good idea, however, to avoid long logical lines by terminating lines with a RETURN before they reach the right side of the screen. Terminating lines in this manner ensures that each physical line contains one logical line and avoids confusion when you edit and format text. Some commands do not *appear* to work properly on physical lines that are longer than the width of the screen. For example, with the cursor on a long logical line that wraps around several physical lines, pressing RETURN once appears to move the cursor down more than one line.

Sentence

A sentence is an English sentence or the equivalent. A sentence starts at the end of the previous sentence and ends with a period, exclamation point, or question mark, followed by two SPACES or a NEWLINE (Table 10-11).

Sentence Count	‖ table 10-11
One: only one SPACE after the first period and a NEWLINE after the second period	That's it. This is one sentence.

Sentence Count (Continued)	‖ table 10-11
Two: two SPACES after the first period and a NEWLINE after the second period	`That's it. This is two sentences.`
Three: two SPACES after the first two question marks and a NEWLINE after the exclamation point	`What? Three sentences? One line!`

One: NEWLINE after the period	`This sentence takes`
	`up a total of`
	`three lines.`

Paragraph

A paragraph is preceded and followed by one or more blank lines. A blank line is composed of two NEWLINE characters in a row (Table 10-12).

Paragraph Count	‖ table 10-12
One: blank line before and after text	`One paragraph`

One: blank line before and after text	`        This may appear to be`
	`more than one paragraph.`
	`        Just because there are`
	`two indentions does not mean`
	`it qualifies as two paragraphs.`

Three: three blocks of text separated by blank lines	`Even though in`
	
	`English this is only`
	`one sentence,`
	
	`vim considers it to be`
	`three paragraphs.`

Screen

The terminal screen is a window that opens onto part of the Work buffer. You can position this window so that it shows different portions of the Work buffer.

Repeat Factor

A number that precedes a Unit of Measure (page 460) is a Repeat Factor. Just as the 5 in *5 inches* causes you to consider *5 inches* as a single Unit of Measure, a Repeat Factor causes vim to group more than one Unit of Measure and consider it as a single Unit of Measure. For example, the command **w** moves the cursor forward 1 word. The command **5w** moves the cursor forward 5 words, and **250w** moves it forward 250 words. If you do not specify a Repeat Factor, vim assumes that you mean one Unit of Measure. If the Repeat Factor would move the cursor past the end of the file, it is left at the end of the file.

Chapter Summary

This summary of vim includes all the commands covered in this chapter, plus a few more.

Starting vim

vim *filename*	Edits *filename* starting at line1
vim +*n filename*	Edits *filename* starting at line *n*
vim + *filename*	Edits *filename* starting at the last line
vim +/*pattern filename*	Edits *filename* starting at the first line containing *pattern*
vim −r *filename*	Recovers *filename* after a system crash
vim −R *filename*	Edits *filename* readonly

Moving the Cursor by Units of Measure

You must be in Command mode to use commands that move the cursor by Units of Measure. They are the Units of Measure that you can use in Change, Delete, and Yank commands. Each of these commands can be preceded by a Repeat Factor.

SPACE, l, *or* RIGHT ARROW	Space to the right
h *or* LEFT ARROW	Space to the left
w	Word to the right
W	Blank-delimited word to the right
b	Word to the left
B	Blank-delimited word to the left
$	End of line
e	End of word to the right
E	End of blank-delimited word to the right
0	Beginning of line (cannot be used with a Repeat Factor)
RETURN	Beginning of next line
j *or* DOWN ARROW	Down one line
–	Beginning of previous line
k *or* UP ARROW	Up one line
)	End of sentence
(	Beginning of sentence
}	End of paragraph
{	Beginning of paragraph
%	Move to matching brace of same type at same nesting level

Viewing Different Parts of the Work Buffer

CONTROL-D	Forward one-half screen
CONTROL-U	Backward one-half screen
CONTROL-F	Forward one screen

CONTROL-B	Backward one screen
*n*G	To line *n* (without *n*, to the last line)
H	To top of screen
M	To middle of screen
L	To bottom of screen

Adding Text

The commands in this section (except r) leave vim in Input mode. You must press ES-CAPE to return to Command mode.

i	Before cursor
I	Before first nonblank character on line
a	After cursor
A	At end of line
o	Open a line below current line
O	Open a line above current line
r	Replace current character (no ESCAPE needed)
R	Replace characters, starting with current character (overwrite until ESCAPE)

Deleting and Changing Text

In the following list M is a Unit of Measure that you can precede with a Repeat Factor, *n* is an optional Repeat Factor, and *c* is any character.

*n*x	Deletes the number of characters specified by *n*, starting with the current character
*n*X	Deletes *n* characters before the current character, starting with the character preceding the current character
d*M*	Deletes text specified by *M*

*n*dd	Deletes the number of lines specified by *n*
dt*c*	Deletes to the next character *c* on the current line
D	Deletes to end of the line
n~	Change case of the next *n* characters
The following commands leave **vim** in Input mode. You must press ESCAPE to return to Command mode.	
*n*s	Substitutes the number of characters specified by *n*
S	Substitutes for entire line
c*M*	Changes text specified by *M*
*n*cc	Changes the number of lines specified by *n*
ct*c*	Changes to the next character *c* on the current line
C	Changes to end of line

Searching for a String

In the following list *rexp* is a regular expression that can be a simple string of characters.

/*rexp*RETURN	Searches forward for *rexp*
?*rexp* RETURN	Searches backward for *rexp*
n	Repeats original search exactly
N	Repeats original search, opposite direction
/RETURN	Repeats original search forward
?RETURN	Repeats original search backward
f*c*	Positions the cursor on the next character *c* on the current line
F*c*	Positions the cursor on the previous character *c* on the current line

t*c*	Positions the cursor on the character before (to the left of) the next character *c* on the current line
T*c*	Positions the cursor on the character after (to the right of) the previous character *c* on the current line
;	Repeats the last f, F, t, or T command

Substituting for a String

The format of a Substitute command is

:[address]s/search-string/replacement-string[/g]

address	A search string, one line number, or two line numbers separated by a comma. A . represents the current line, $ represents the last line, and % represents the entire file. You can use a marker or a search string in place of a line number.
search-string	A regular expression that can be a simple string of characters.
replacement-string	The replacement string.
g	Indicates a global replacement (more than one replacement per line).

Miscellaneous Commands

J	Joins the current line and the following line
.	Repeats the most recent command that made a change
:w *filename*	Writes contents of Work buffer to *filename* (or to current file if there is no *filename*)
:q	Quits vim
ZZ	Writes contents of Work buffer to the current file and quits vim

:f *or* CONTROL-G	Displays the filename, status, current line number, number of lines in the Work buffer, and percent of the Work buffer preceding the current line
CONTROL-V	Inserts the next character literally even if it is a vim command (use in Input mode)

Yanking and Putting Text

In the following list *M* is a Unit of Measure that you can precede with a Repeat Factor, and *n* is a Repeat Factor. You can precede any of these commands with the name of a buffer in the form of "*x* where *x* is the name of the buffer (*a–z*).

y*M*	Yanks text specified by *M*
*n*yy	Yanks the number of lines specified by *n*
Y	Yanks to end of line
P	Puts text before or above
p	Puts text after or below

Advanced Commands

m*x*	Sets marker *x*, where *x* is a letter from a to z.
' ' (two single quotation marks)	Moves cursor back to its previous location.
'*x*	Moves cursor to line with marker *x*.
`*x*	Moves cursor to character with marker *x*.
:e *filename*	Edits *filename*, requiring you to write out changes to the current file (with :w or autowrite) before editing the new file. Use :e! *filename* to discard changes to current file. Use :e! without a filename to discard changes to the current file and start editing the saved version of the current file.

:n	Edits the next file when vim is started with multiple file-name arguments. It requires you to write out changes to the current file (with :w or autowrite) before editing the next file. Use :n! to discard changes to current file and edit the next file.
:rew	Rewinds the filename list when vim is started with multiple filename arguments and starts editing with the first file. It requires you to write out changes to the current file (with :w or autowrite) before editing the first file. Use :rew! to discard changes to current file and edit the first file.
:sh	Starts a shell.
:!*command*	Starts a shell and executes *command*.
!!*command*	Starts a shell, executes *command*, places output in file replacing the current line.

Exercises

1. How can you cause vim to enter Input mode? How can you make vim revert to Command mode?

2. What is the Work buffer? Name two ways of writing the contents of the Work buffer to the disk.

3. Suppose that you are editing a file that contains the following paragraph and the cursor is on the second tilde (~):

   ```
   The vim editor has a command, tilde (~),
   that changes lowercase letters to
   uppercase and vice versa.
   The ~ command works with a Unit of Measure or
   a Repeat Factor, so you can change
   the case of more one character at a time.
   ```

   How can you

   a. Move the cursor to the end of the paragraph?

   b. Move the cursor to the beginning of the word Unit?

   c. Change the word character to letter?

4. In vim, with the cursor positioned on the first letter of a word, give the command **x** followed by **p.** Explain what happens.

5. What are the differences between the following commands?

   a. **i** and **I**

   b. **a** and **A**

   c. **o** and **O**

   d. **r** and **R**

   e. **u** and **U**

6. What command would you use to search backward through the Work buffer for lines that start with the word `it`?

7. What command substitutes all occurrences of the phrase `this week` with the phrase `next week`?

8. Consider the following scenario: You start vim to edit an existing file. You make many changes to the file and then realize that you deleted a critical section of the file early in your editing session. You want to get that section back but do not want to lose all the other changes you made. What would you do?

9. Consider the following scenario: Alex puts the following line in his **.login** file:

   ```
   setenv EXINIT 'set number wrapmargin=10 showmode'
   ```

   Then Alex creates a **.vimrc** file in the directory **/home/alex/literature** with the following line in it:

   ```
   set nonumber
   ```

   What will the parameter settings be when Alex runs vim while the working directory is **/home/alex/bin**? What will they be when he runs vim from the directory **/home/alex/literature**? What will they be when he edits the file **/home/alex/literature/promo**?

10. Use vim to create the **letter_e** file of e's used on page 73. Use as few vim commands as possible. What vim commands did you use?

Advanced Exercises

11. What commands can you use to take a paragraph from one file and insert it in a second file?

12. Create a file that contains the following list, and then execute commands from within vim to sort the list and display it in two columns. (*Hint:* Refer to page 1286 in Part III for more information on pr.)

```
Command mode
Input mode
Last Line mode
Work buffer
General-Purpose buffer
Named buffer
Regular Expression
Search String
Replacement String
Startup File
Repeat Factor
```

13. How do the Named buffers differ from the General-Purpose buffer?

14. Assuming that your version of vim does not support multiple Undo commands, if you delete a line of text and then delete another line and then a third line, what commands would you use to recover the first two lines that you deleted?

15. What command would you use to swap the words hither and yon on any line with any number of words between them? (You need not worry about special punctuation, just upper- and lowercase letters and spaces.)

IN THIS CHAPTER

The **emacs** Editor

11

In 1956 the Lisp (List processing) language was developed at MIT by John McCarthy. In its original conception, Lisp had only a few scalar (called *atomic*) data types and only one *data structure* (page 1463): a list. Lists could contain atomic data or perhaps other lists. Lisp supported recursion and nonnumeric data (exciting concepts in those FORTRAN and COBOL days) and, in the Cambridge culture at least, was once the favored implementation language. Richard Stallman and Guy Steele were part of this MIT Lisp culture, and in 1975 they collaborated on emacs, which was maintained by Stallman himself for a long time. This chapter discusses the emacs editor as implemented by the Free Software Foundation (GNU) and provided with Red Hat Linux.

History

Initially emacs was prototyped as a series of editor commands or macros for the late 1960s text editor TECO (Text Editor and COrrector). The acronymic name, Editor MACroS, reflects these beginnings, although there have been many humorous reinterpretations, including ESCAPE META ALT CONTROL SHIFT, Emacs Makes All Computing Simple, and the unkind translation Eight Megabytes And Constantly Swapping.

Evolution

Since then, emacs has grown and evolved through more than 20 major revisions to the mainstream GNU version alone. The emacs editor, coded in C, contains a complete Lisp interpreter and fully supports the X Window System and mouse interaction. The original TECO macros are long gone, and emacs is a work still very much in progress. The Free Software Foundation has announced plans to add capabilities to emacs. There are plans to support variable-width fonts, wide character sets, and the world's major languages, as well as to move emacs in the direction of a WYSIWYG (what you see is what you get) word processor and make it easier for beginners to use.

The emacs editor has always been considerably more than a text editor. Not having been developed originally in a UNIX environment, emacs does not adhere to the UNIX/Linux philosophy. Whereas a UNIX/Linux utility is typically designed to do one thing and to be used in conjunction with other utilities, emacs is designed to "do it all." Because a programming language (Lisp) underlies it, emacs users tend to customize and extend the editor rather than to use existing utilities or create new general-purpose tools. Instead they share their **.emacs** (customization) files.

Well before the X Window System, Stallman put a great deal of thought and effort into designing a window-oriented work environment, and he used emacs as his research vehicle. Over time he built facilities within emacs for reading and composing e-mail messages, reading and posting netnews, giving shell commands, compiling programs and analyzing error messages, running and debugging these programs, and playing games. Eventually it became possible to enter the emacs environment and not come out all day, switching from window to window and from file to file. If you had only an ordinary serial, character-based terminal, emacs gave you tremendous leverage.

In an X Window System environment, emacs does not need to control the whole display, usually operating only one or two windows. However, part or all of the original work environment is still available for those who want to use it.

As a *language-sensitive* editor, emacs has special features that you can turn on to help edit text, nroff, TeX, Lisp, C, Fortran, and so on. These feature sets are called *modes*, but they are not related in any way to the Command mode and Input mode found in vi and other editors. Because you never need to switch emacs between Input and Command modes, emacs is called a *modeless* editor.

emacs versus vi

Like vi, emacs is a display editor: It displays on the screen the text you are editing and changes the display as you type each command or insert new text. Unlike vi, emacs does not require you to keep track of whether you are in Command mode or

Insert mode: Commands always use a CONTROL or other special key. The emacs editor always inserts ordinary characters, another trait of modeless editing. For many people this is convenient and natural.

As in vi, you edit a file in a work area, or *buffer,* and have the option of writing this buffer back to the file on the disk when you are finished. With emacs, however, you can have many work buffers, changing among them without having to write out and read back in. Furthermore, you can display multiple buffers at one time, each in its own window. This is often helpful in cut-and-paste operations or to keep C declarations in one window while editing related code in another part of the file in another window.

Like vi, emacs has a rich, extensive command set for moving about in the buffer and altering text, but in emacs this command set is not "cast in concrete." You can change or customize commands at any time. Literally any key can be coupled, or *bound,* to any command, to match a particular keyboard better or just to fulfill a personal whim. Usually key bindings are set in the .emacs startup file, but they can also be changed interactively during a session. All the key bindings described in this chapter are standard on current GNU emacs versions, which also support many visual, mouse-oriented capabilities that are not covered here.

Too Many Key Bindings || caution

If you change too many key bindings, you can easily produce a command set that you will not remember or that will make it impossible for you to get back to the standard bindings again in the same session.

Finally, and *very* unlike vi, emacs allows you to use Lisp to write new commands or override old ones. Stallman calls this feature *online extensibility,* but it would take a gutsy Lisp guru to write and debug a new command while editing live text. It is much more common to add a few extra debugged commands to the .emacs file, where they are loaded automatically when emacs starts up.

Tutorial: Getting Started with emacs

The emacs editor has many, many features, and there are many ways to use it. Its complete manual has more than 35 chapters. However, you can do a considerable amount of meaningful work with a relatively small subset of the commands. This section describes a simple editing session, explaining how to start and exit from emacs and how to move the cursor and delete text. Some issues are postponed or simplified in the interest of clarity. If you are using emacs in an X Window System environment, refer to "emacs and the X Window System" on page 520 as you read this section.

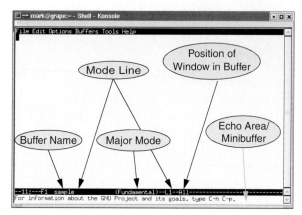

Figure 11-1   The emacs welcome screen

Starting emacs

To edit a file named **sample** as a text-based editor (without a GUI), enter the following command:

```
$ emacs -q -nw sample
```

This command starts emacs, reads the file named **sample** into a buffer, and displays its contents on the screen or window. If no file has this name, emacs displays a blank screen with New File at the bottom. If the file exists, emacs displays another message (Figure 11-1). The **–q** option tells emacs *not* to read the **.emacs** startup file from your home directory. This guarantees that you get standard, uncustomized behavior and is sometimes useful for beginners or for other users wanting to bypass a **.emacs** file.

The screen starts with a single window. At the bottom of this window is a reverse-video titlebar called the *Mode Line*. At a minimum, the Mode Line shows the name of the buffer that the window is viewing, whether the buffer has been changed, what major and minor modes are in effect, and how far down the buffer the window is currently positioned. When you have more than one window, one Mode Line is in each window. At the bottom of the screen, emacs leaves a single line open. This *Echo Area*, or *Minibuffer*, line is for short messages and special one-line commands.

A cursor is in the window, or Minibuffer. All the input and nearly all the editing takes place at the cursor. As you type ordinary characters, emacs inserts them at the cursor position. If characters are under the cursor or to its right, they get pushed over as you type, so no characters are lost.

Stopping emacs

The command to exit from emacs is the two-key sequence CONTROL-X CONTROL-C. You can give this command at almost any time (in some modes you may have to press CONTROL-G first). It stops emacs gracefully, asking you to confirm changes if you made any during the editing session.

If you want to cancel a half-typed command or stop a running command before it is done, you can quit by pressing CONTROL-G. The emacs editor displays Quit in the Echo Area and waits for your next command.

Inserting Text

Typing an ordinary (printing) character pushes the cursor and any characters to the right of the cursor one position to the right and inserts the new character in the position just opened. Backspacing pulls the cursor and any characters to the right of the cursor one position to the left, erasing the character that was there before.

Deleting Characters

Depending on your keyboard and emacs startup files, different keys may delete characters in different ways. CONTROL-D typically deletes the character that the cursor is on top of, as does DELETE and DEL. BACKSPACE typically deletes the character to the left of the cursor. Try each of these keys and see what it does.

> ### More about Deleting Characters | tip
>
> If what is described in this section does not work for you, read the emacs info section on deletion: Give this command from a shell prompt:
>
> $ info emacs
>
> Once info is up, give the command m deletion to display a document that describes in detail how to delete small amounts of text. Use the SPACE bar to scroll through the document.

Start emacs and type a few lines of text. If you make a mistake, use the deletion characters discussed previously. The RETURN key inserts an invisible end-of-line character in the buffer and returns the cursor to the left margin, one line down. It is possible to back up past the start of a line and up to the end of the line just above. Figure 11-2 shows a sample buffer.

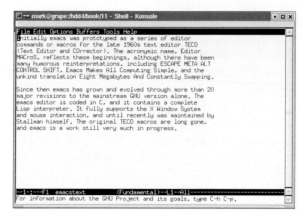

Figure 11-2   Sample buffer

Moving the Cursor

You can position the cursor over any character in the emacs window and move the window so it displays any portion of the buffer. You can move the cursor forward or backward through the text (see Figure 10-8 on page 428) by various textual units (for example, characters, words, sentences, lines, paragraphs). Any of the cursor-movement commands can be preceded by a repetition count (CONTROL-U followed by a numeric argument), which causes the cursor to move that number of textual units through the text. Refer to page 484 for further discussion of numeric arguments.

Moving the Cursor by Characters

Pressing CONTROL-F moves the cursor forward one character. If the cursor is at the end of a line, this command wraps it to the beginning of the next line. The command CONTROL-U 7 CONTROL-F moves the cursor seven characters forward (to the right).

Pressing CONTROL-B moves the cursor backward one character. The command CONTROL-U 7 CONTROL-B moves the cursor seven characters backward (to the left). CONTROL-B works in a manner similar to CONTROL-F (Figure 11-3).

Moving the Cursor by Words

Pressing META-f moves the cursor forward one word. To press META-f hold down the META or ALT key while you press f; if you do not have either of these keys, press ESCAPE, re-

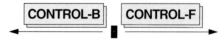

Figure 11-3   Moving the cursor by characters

Figure 11-4   Moving the cursor by words

lease it, and then press **f**. It leaves the cursor on the first character that is not part of the word the cursor started on. The command CONTROL-U **4** META-f moves the cursor forward one space past the end of the fourth word. See page 482 for more about keys. Pressing META-b moves the cursor backward one word so the cursor is on the first letter of the word it started on. It works in a manner similar to META-f (Figure 11-4).

Moving the Cursor by Lines

Pressing CONTROL-A moves the cursor to the beginning of the line it is on; CONTROL-E moves it to the end. Pressing CONTROL-P moves the cursor up one line to the position directly above where the cursor started; CONTROL-N moves it down. As with the other cursor-movement keys, you can precede CONTROL-P and CONTROL-N with CONTROL-U and a numeric argument to move up or down multiple lines. You can use pairs of these commands to move the cursor up to the beginning of the previous line, down to the end of the following line, and so on (Figure 11-5).

Moving the Cursor by Sentences, Paragraphs, and Window Position

Pressing META-a moves the cursor to the beginning of the sentence the cursor is on; META-e moves the cursor to the end. META-{ moves the cursor to the beginning of the paragraph the cursor is on; META-} moves it to the end. You can precede any of these commands by a repetition count (CONTROL-U and a numeric argument) to move the cursor that many sentences or paragraphs.

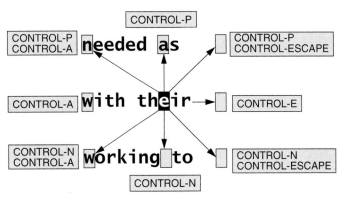

Figure 11-5   Moving the cursor by lines

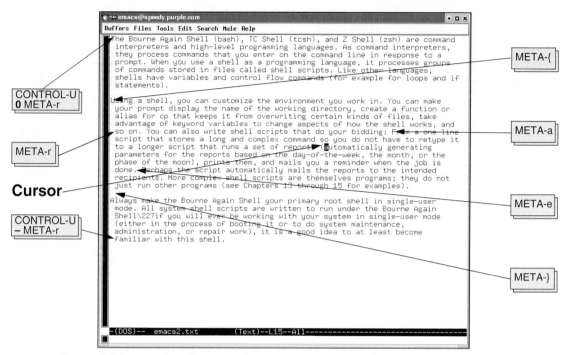

Figure 11-6   Moving the cursor by sentences, paragraphs, and window position

Pressing META-r moves the cursor to the beginning of the middle line of the window. You can precede this command with a CONTROL-U and a line number (here CONTROL-U does not indicate a repetition count but a screen line number). The command CONTROL-U 0 META-r moves the cursor to the beginning of the top line (line zero) in the window. You can replace zero with the line number of the line you want to move the cursor to or a minus sign (–), in which case the cursor moves to the beginning of the last line of the window (Figure 11-6).

Editing at the Cursor Position

You can type in new text and push the existing text to the right. Entering new text requires no special commands once the cursor is positioned. If you type in so much that the text in a line goes past the right edge of the window, emacs puts a backslash (\) in column 80 and then wraps the remainder of the text to the next line. The backslash appears on the screen but is never printed out. Although you can create an arbitrarily long line, some UNIX tools have problems with text files containing these very long lines. You can split a line at any point by positioning the cursor and pressing RETURN.

Pressing DELETE removes characters to the left of the cursor. The cursor and the remainder of the text on this line both move to the left each time you press DELETE. To join a line with the line above it, position the cursor on the first character of the second line and press DELETE.

Press CONTROL-D to delete the character under the cursor. The cursor remains stationary, and the remainder of the text on this line moves left to replace the deleted character. See the tip "More about Deleting Characters" on page 477 if either of these keys does not work as described.

Saving and Retrieving the Buffer

No matter what happens to a buffer during an emacs session, the associated file is not changed until you save the buffer. If you leave emacs without saving the buffer (this *is* possible if you are insistent enough), the file is not changed, and the session's work is discarded.

As mentioned previously, emacs prompts you about unsaved changes to the buffer contents. As it writes a buffer's edited contents back out to the file, emacs may optionally first make a backup of the original file contents. You can choose among no backups, one level (default), or an arbitrary number of levels. The one-level backup filenames are formed by appending the ~ character to the original filename. The multilevel backups append .~n~ to the filename where **n** is the sequential backup number, starting with 1.

The command CONTROL-X CONTROL-S saves the current buffer in its associated file. The emacs editor confirms a successful save with a message in the Echo Area.

If you are already editing a file with emacs and wish to begin editing another file (also called *visiting* a file), you can copy the new file into a new emacs buffer by giving the command CONTROL-X CONTROL-F. The emacs editor prompts you for a filename, reads that file into a new buffer, and displays that buffer in the current window. Having two files open in one editing session is more convenient than exiting from emacs, returning to the shell, and then starting a new copy of emacs to edit a second file.

Basic Editing Commands

This section takes a more detailed look at the fundamental emacs editing commands. It covers straightforward editing of a single file in a single window.

> **Visiting a File with** CONTROL-X CONTROL-F || tip
>
> When using CONTROL-X CONTROL-F, emacs partially completes the path to the filename you are to enter. Normally this is the path to the working directory, but in some situations emacs may display a different path, such as the path to your home directory. You can edit this already displayed path if it is not pointing to the directory you want.

Keys: Notation and Use

Mainstream emacs uses 128-character ASCII codes. ASCII keyboards have a typewriter-style SHIFT key and a CONTROL key. Some keyboards also have a META (diamond or ALT) key that controls the eighth bit. It takes seven bits to describe an ASCII character; the eighth bit of an eight-bit byte can be used to communicate other information. Because so much of the emacs command set is in the non-printing CONTROL or META case, Stallman was one of the first to confront the problem of developing a notation for writing about keystrokes.

His solution, although not popular outside the emacs community, is clear and unambiguous (see Table 11-1). It uses the capital letters **C** and **M** to denote holding down the CONTROL and META keys, respectively, and a few simple acronyms for the most common special characters, such as RET (this book uses RETURN), LFD (LINEFEED), DEL (DELETE), ESC (ESCAPE), SPC (SPACE), and TAB. Most emacs documentation, including the online help, uses this notation.

Character	**Classic emacs Notation** || table 11-1
(lowercase) **a**	a
(uppercase) SHIFT-a	A
CONTROL-a	C-a
CONTROL-A	C-a (do *not* use SHIFT), equivalent to CONTROL-a
META-a	M-a
META-A	M-A (*do* use SHIFT)
CONTROL-META-a	C-M-a
META-CONTROL-a	M-C-a (not used frequently)

This use of keys had some problems. Many keyboards had no META key, and some operating systems discarded the META bit. The emacs character set clashes with XON-XOFF flow control, which also uses CONTROL-S and CONTROL-Q and continues to do so today.

Although the flow-control problem still exists, the META key issue was resolved by making it an optional two-key sequence starting with ESCAPE. For instance, you can type ESCAPE-a in place of META-a or ESCAPE CONTROL-A to get CONTROL-META-a. If your keyboard does not have a META or ALT key, you can use the two-key ESCAPE sequence by pressing the ESCAPE key, releasing it, and then pressing the key following the META key in this book. For example, when this book says to press META-r you can either press the META or ALT key while you press **r** or press and release ESCAPE and then press **r**.

An aside on notation: This book uses an uppercase letter following the CONTROL key and a lowercase letter following the META key. In either case you *do not ever have to hold down the* SHIFT *key while entering a* CONTROL *or* META *character*. Although the META uppercase character (that is, META-A) is a different character, it is usually set up to cause no action or the same effect as its lowercase counterpart.

Key Sequences and Commands

In emacs the relationship between key sequences (one or more keys that are pressed together or in sequence to issue an emacs command) and commands is very flexible, and there is considerable opportunity for exercising your personal preference. You can translate and remap key sequences to other commands and replace or reprogram commands themselves.

Although most emacs documentation glosses over all the details and talks about keystrokes as though they were the commands, it is important to know that the underlying machinery is separate from the key sequences and to understand that the behavior of the key sequences and the commands can be changed (page 515).

META-x: Running a Command without a Key Binding

The emacs keymaps (the tables, or vectors, that emacs uses to translate key sequences to commands [page 517]) are very crowded, and often it is not possible to bind every single command to a key sequence. You can execute any command by name by preceding it with META-x. The emacs editor prompts you for a command in the Echo Area and executes the command after you enter the command name and press the RETURN key.

Sometimes, when a command has no common key sequence, it is described as META-x ***command-name***. The emacs editor has a *smart completion* for most prompted answers, using SPACE or TAB to complete, if possible, to the end of the current word or the whole command, respectively. Forcing a completion past the last unambiguous point or typing ? displays a list of alternatives. You can find more details on smart completion in the online emacs manual.

Numeric Arguments

Some of the emacs editing commands take a numeric argument and interpret it as a repetition count. The argument immediately prefixes the key sequence for the command, and the most common case of no argument is almost always interpreted as a count of 1. Even an ordinary alphabetic character can have a numeric argument, which means "insert this many times." To give a command a numeric argument, you can do either of the following:

- Press META with each digit (0–9) or the minus sign (–) (for example, to insert 10 z characters, type META-1 META-0 z).
- Use CONTROL-U to begin a string of digits, including the minus sign (for example, to move the cursor forward 20 words, type CONTROL-U 20 META-f).

For convenience CONTROL-U defaults to *multiply by 4* when you do not follow it with a string of one or more digits. For example, entering CONTROL-U **r** means insert **rrrr** (4 * 1), whereas CONTROL-U CONTROL-U **r** means insert **rrrrrrrrrrrrrrrr** (4 * 4 * 1). For quick partial scrolling of a tall window, you may find it convenient to use repeated sequences of CONTROL-U CONTROL-V to scroll down four lines, CONTROL-U META-v to scroll up four lines, CONTROL-U CONTROL-U CONTROL-V to scroll down 16 lines, or CONTROL-U CONTROL-U META-v to scroll up 16 lines.

Point and the Cursor

Point is the place in a buffer where editing takes place, and this is where the cursor is positioned. Strictly speaking, Point is the left edge of the cursor—it is thought of as always lying *between* two characters.

Each window has its own Point, but there is only one cursor. When the cursor is in a window, moving the cursor also moves Point. Switching the cursor out of a window does not change that window's Point; it is in the same place when you switch the cursor back to that window.

All the cursor-movement commands previously described also move Point. In addition, you can move the cursor to the beginning of the buffer with META-< or to the end of the buffer with META->.

Scrolling through a Buffer

A buffer is likely to be much larger than the window through which it is viewed, so there has to be a way of moving the display of the buffer contents up or down to put the interesting part in the window. *Scrolling forward* refers to moving the text upward, with new lines entering at the bottom of the window. Use CONTROL-V to scroll forward one window (minus two lines for context). *Scrolling backward* refers to moving the text downward, with new lines entering at the top of the window. Use META-v to scroll backward one window (again leaving two lines for context). Pressing CONTROL-L clears the screen and repaints it, moving the current line to the center of the window. This command is useful if the screen display becomes garbled.

A numeric argument to CONTROL-V or META-v means "scroll that many lines"; thus CONTROL-U 10 CONTROL-V means scroll forward ten lines. A numeric argument to CONTROL-L means "scroll the text so the cursor is on that line of the window," where 0 means the top line and –1 means the bottom, just above the Mode Line. Scrolling occurs automatically if you exceed the window limits with CONTROL-P or CONTROL-N.

Erasing Text

When text is erased, it can be discarded, or it can be moved into a holding area and optionally brought back later. The term *delete* means *permanent discard,* and the term *kill* means *move to a holding area.* The holding area, called the *Kill Ring,* can hold several pieces of killed text. You can use the text in the Kill Ring in many ways (refer to "Cut and Paste: Yanking Killed Text" on page 494).

The META-d command kills from the cursor forward to the end of the current word. CONTROL-K kills forward to the end of the current line. It does *not* delete the line-ending LINEFEED character unless Point and the cursor are just to the left of the LINEFEED. This allows you to get to the left end of a line with CONTROL-A, kill the whole line with CONTROL-K, and then immediately type a replacement line without having to reopen a hole for the new line. Another consequence is that, from the beginning of the line, it takes CONTROL-K CONTROL-K (or CONTROL-U 2 CONTROL-K) to kill the text and close the hole.

Searching

The emacs editor has several types of search commands. You can search in the following ways:

- Incrementally for a character string
- Incrementally for a regular expression (possible but very uncommon)
- For a complete character string
- For a complete full regular expression (Appendix A)

You can run each of the four subsequent searches either forward or backward in the buffer.

The *complete* string searches behave in the same manner as a search on other editors. Searching begins only when the search string is complete. In contrast, an *incremental* search begins as you type the first character of the search string and keeps going as you enter additional characters. Initially this sounds confusing, but it is surprisingly useful and is the preferred search technique in emacs.

Incremental Searches

A single command selects the direction of and starts an incremental search. CONTROL-S starts a forward incremental search, and CONTROL-R starts a reverse incremental search.

When you start an incremental search, emacs starts a special one-line dialog in the Echo Area. You are prompted with I-search: to enter some characters. When you enter a character, emacs begins searching for that character in the buffer. If it finds that character, emacs moves Point and cursor to that position so you can see the search progress.

After you enter each character of the search string, you can take any one of several actions.

- The search reaches your target in the buffer, and the cursor is positioned just to its right. In this case exit from the search, and leave the cursor in its new position by entering RETURN. (Any emacs command not related to searching also takes you out, but remembering exactly which ones can be difficult. For a new user RETURN is safer.)

- The search reaches the current search string, but it's not yet at the target you want. Now you can refine the search string by adding another letter, reiterate your CONTROL-R or CONTROL-S to look for the next occurrence of this search string, or enter RETURN to stop the search and leave the cursor at its current position.

- The search hits the beginning or end of the buffer and reports Failing I-Search. You can proceed in several ways at this point.

  - If you mistyped the search string or reiterated CONTROL-S too often, press BACKSPACE to back out some of the wrong characters or search reiterations. The text and cursor in the window jump backward in step with you.

  - If you want to wrap past the beginning or end of the buffer and continue searching, you can force a wrap by entering CONTROL-R or CONTROL-S again.

- If the search has not found what you want but you want to stay at the current position, press RETURN to stop the search at that point.

- If the search has gone wrong and you just want to get back to where you started, press CONTROL-G (the quit character). From an unsuccessful search a single CONTROL-G backs out all the characters in the search string that could not be found. If this takes you back to a place you wish to continue searching from, you can add characters to the search string again. If you do not want to continue the search from here, a second CONTROL-G ends the search and leaves the cursor where it was to begin with.

Nonincremental Searches

If you prefer that your searches succeed or fail without showing all the intermediate results, you can give the nonincremental commands CONTROL-S RETURN to search forward or CONTROL-R RETURN to search backward. Searching does not begin until you enter a search string in response to the emacs prompt and press RETURN again. Neither of these commands wraps past the end of the buffer.

Regular Expression Searches

You can perform both incremental and nonincremental regular expression searching in emacs. To begin a regular expression search, you can use the commands listed in Table 11-2.

Searching for Regular Expressions	**‖ table 11-2**
META-CONTROL-X	Incrementally searches forward for regular expression; prompts for a regular expression one character at a time
META-x isearch-backward-regexp	Incrementally searches backward for regular expression; prompts for a regular expression one character at a time
META-CONTROL-S RETURN	Prompts for and then searches forward for a complete regular expression
META-x isearch-backward-regexp RETURN	Prompts for and then searches backward for a complete regular expression

Online Help

The emacs help system is always available. With the default key bindings, you can start it with CONTROL-H. The help system then prompts you for a one-letter help command. If you do not know which help command you want, type **?** or CONTROL-H. This switches the current window to a list of help commands, each of them with a one-line description, and again requests a one-letter help command. If, while still being prompted about what help you want, you decide you do not want help after all, you can type CONTROL-G to cancel your help request and get back to your former buffer.

If the help output is only a single line, it appears in the Echo Area. If it is more, the output appears in its own window. To scroll this output you can use SPACE to scroll forward and DELETE to scroll backward. When you are done with the help window, you can delete it by typing **q**. See page 501 for a discussion on working with multiple windows.

Some help commands, such as **news** (CONTROL-H **n** for recent emacs changes) and tutorial (CONTROL-H **t**), have so much output that they give you a whole window right away. When you are done with this help window, you can delete it with CONTROL-X **k**, which deletes the emacs buffer holding the information. See page 500 for more information on using buffers.

On many terminals the BACKSPACE or LEFT ARROW key generates CONTROL-H. If you forget that you are using emacs and try to back over a few characters, you may find yourself in the help system unintentionally. There is no danger to the buffer you are editing, but it can be unsettling to lose the window contents and not have a clear picture of how to restore it. In this case type CONTROL-G to return to editing the buffer. Some users elect to put help on a different key (page 517). Table 11-3 lists some of the help commands.

Help Commands ‖ table 11-3

CONTROL-H a	Prompts for *string* and then shows a list of commands whose names contain *string*.
CONTROL-H b	Shows a table (it is long) of all the key bindings now in effect.
CONTROL-H c ***key-sequence***	Prints the name of the command bound to *key-sequence*. Multiple key sequences are allowed; however, for a long key sequence where only the first part is recognized, the command describes the first part and quietly inserts the unrecognized part into your buffer. This can happen with three-character function keys (F1, F2, and so on, on the keyboard) that generate such character sequences as ESCAPE [SHIFT.

Help Commands (Continued)

|| table 11-3

CONTROL-H k *key-sequence*	Prints the name and documentation of the command bound to *key-sequence*. (See the notes on the preceding command.)
CONTROL-H f	Prompts for the name of a Lisp function and prints the documentation for it. Because commands are Lisp functions, you can use a command name with this command.
CONTROL-H i	Takes you to the top menu of **info**, a documentation browser. Generally a complete **info** manual and **emacs** manual are kept online, and other GNU packages may have manuals here too. The **info** utility has its own help system. Type **?** for a summary or **h** for a tutorial.
CONTROL-H l (lowercase "ell")	Shows the last 100 characters typed. The record is kept *after* the first-stage keyboard translation. If you have customized the keyboard translation table, you must make a mental reverse translation.
CONTROL-H m	Shows the documentation and special key bindings for the current Major mode (that is, Text, C, Fundamental, and so on).
CONTROL-H n	Shows the **emacs** news file (new changes made to **emacs**, ordered with most recent first).
CONTROL-H t	Runs an **emacs** tutorial session. When you are finished with the tutorial, you can reselect your original buffer with CONTROL-X b or kill the help buffer with CONTROL-X k (page 500).
CONTROL-H v	Prompts for a Lisp variable name and gives the documentation for that variable.
CONTROL-H w	Prompts for a command name and gives the key sequence, if any, bound to that command. Multiple key sequences are allowed. However, for a long key sequence in which only the first part is recognized, the command describes the first part and quietly inserts the unrecognized part into your buffer. This can happen with three-character function keys (F1, F2, and so on, on the keyboard) that generate character sequences, such as ESCAPE [SHIFT.

Even in this abridged presentation, it is clear that you can use the help system to browse through the emacs internal Lisp system. For the curious here is Stallman's suggested list of strings that match many names in the Lisp system:

backward	beginning	buffer	case	change
char	defun	delete	describe	dir
down	end	file	fill	find
forward	goto	indent	insert	kill
line	list	mark	mode	next
page	paragraph	previous	region	register
screen	search	sentence	set	sexp
up	view	what	window	word
yank				

To get a view of the internal functionality of emacs, you can use any of the preceding strings with the commands in Table 11-4.

Commands to View emacs Internals	‖ table 11-4
CONTROL-H a	This command is part of the help system and prompts for a string and then displays the commands whose names contain that string.
META-x apropos	Prompts for a string and shows all the Lisp commands and variables whose names contain that string.

Advanced Editing Topics

The basic emacs commands are sufficient for many editing tasks, but the serious user quickly finds the need for more power. This section presents some of the more advanced emacs capabilities.

Undoing Changes

An editing session begins when you read a file into an emacs buffer. At that point the buffer content matches the file exactly. As you insert text and give editing commands, the buffer content becomes more and more different from the file. If you are satisfied with the changes, you write the altered buffer back out to the file and end the session.

A window's Mode Line has an indicator immediately to the left of emacs: that shows the modification state of the buffer in the window. Its three states are -- (not modified), ** (modified), and %% (readonly).

The emacs editor keeps a record of all the keys you have pressed (text and commands) since the beginning of the editing session, up to a limit currently set at 20,000 characters. If you are within the limit, it is possible to undo the entire session for this buffer, one change at a time. If you have multiple buffers (page 500), each buffer has its own undo record.

Undoing is considered so important that it is given a backup key sequence, just in case some keyboards cannot easily handle the primary sequence. The two sequences are CONTROL-_ (underscore, which on old ASR-33 TTY keyboards was LEFT ARROW) and CONTROL-X u. When you type CONTROL-_, emacs undoes the last command and moves the cursor to that position in the buffer, so you can see what happened. If you type CONTROL-_ a second time, the next to the last command is undone, and so on. If you keep on typing CONTROL-_, eventually you get the buffer back to its original unmodified state, and the ** Mode Line indicator changes to --. This is in contrast to the original vi, where undo works only on the most recent commands.

When you break the string of Undo commands with *anything* (text or any command except Undo), all the reverse changes you made during the string of undos become a part of the change record and can themselves be undone. This offers a way to redo some or all the undos. If you decide you backed up too far, type a command (something innocuous, such as CONTROL-F, that does not change the buffer), and begin undoing in reverse. Table 11-5 lists some examples.

Commands | table 11-5

Commands	
CONTROL-_	Undoes the last change
CONTROL-_ CONTROL-F CONTROL-_	Undoes the last change and changes it back again
CONTROL-_ CONTROL-_	Undoes the last two changes
CONTROL-_ CONTROL-_ CONTROL-F CONTROL-_ CONTROL-_	Undoes two changes and changes them both back again
CONTROL-_ CONTROL-_ CONTROL-F CONTROL-_	Undoes two changes and changes one of them back again

If you do not remember the last change you made, you can type CONTROL-_ and undo it. If it was a change that you wanted to make, type CONTROL-F CONTROL-_ and make it again. If you modified a buffer by accident, you can keep typing CONTROL-_ until the Mode Line indicator shows -- once more.

If the buffer is completely ruined and you want to start over, issue the command META-x **revert-buffer** to discard the current buffer contents and reread from the associated file; emacs will ask you to confirm your command.

Mark and Region

In a buffer, Point is the current editing position, which you can move anywhere in the buffer by moving the cursor. It is also possible to set a Mark in the buffer. The contiguous characters between Point and Mark (either one may come first) are called the *Region*. Many commands operate on a buffer's current Region, not just on the characters near Point.

Mark is not as easy to move as Point. Once set, Mark can be moved only by setting it somewhere else. Each buffer has only one Mark. The CONTROL-@ command explicitly sets the Mark at the current cursor (and Point) position. Some keyboards generate CONTROL-@ when you type CONTROL-Q. Although this is not really a backup key binding, it is occasionally a convenient alternative. You can use CONTROL-X CONTROL-X to exchange Point and Mark.

To establish a Region, you usually position Point at one end of the desired Region, set Mark with CONTROL-@, and then move Point to the other end of the Region. If you forget where you left the Mark, you can move the cursor back to it again with CONTROL-X CONTROL-X or hop back and forth with repeated CONTROL-X CONTROL-X to show the Region more clearly.

If one Region boundary or the other is not to your liking, swap Point and Mark with CONTROL-X CONTROL-X to move the cursor from one end of the Region to the other, and move Point. Continue until you are satisfied with the Region.

There are many possibilities for operating on a Region. Some examples are listed in Table 11-6.

Operating on a Region	‖ table 11-6
META-w	Copies the Region between Point and Mark nondestructively (without killing it) to the Kill Ring
CONTROL-W	Kills the Region
META-x **print-region**	Sends the Region between Point and Mark to the print spooler

Operating on a Region (Continued) || table 11-6

META-x append-to-buffer	Prompts for a buffer and appends Region between Point and Mark to that buffer
META-x append-to-file	Prompts for a filename and appends Region between Point and Mark to that file
CONTROL-X CONTROL-U	Converts Region between Point and Mark to uppercase
CONTROL-X CONTROL-L	Converts Region between Point and Mark to lowercase

Each time you set the Mark in a buffer, you are also pushing the Mark's former location onto the buffer's *Mark Ring*. The Mark Ring is organized as a FIFO (first-in-first-out) list and holds the 16 most recent locations where the Mark was set. Each buffer has its own Mark Ring. This record of recent Mark history is useful because it often holds locations that you want to jump back to quickly. Jumping to a location pointed to by the Mark Ring can be faster and easier than scrolling or searching your way through the buffer to find the site of a previous change.

To work your way backward along the trail of former Mark locations, give the command CONTROL-U CONTROL-@ one or more times. Each time you give the command, emacs

- Moves Point (and the cursor) to the current Mark location

- Saves the current Mark location at the *oldest* end of the Mark Ring

- Pops off the *youngest* (most recent) Mark Ring entry and sets Mark

Each additional CONTROL-U CONTROL-@ command causes emacs to move Point and the cursor to the previous entry on the Mark Ring.

Although this process may seem complex, it is really just a safe jump to a previous Mark location. It is safe because each jump's starting point is recirculated back through the Mark Ring, where it is easy to find again. You can jump to all the previous locations on the Mark Ring (it may be fewer than 16) by giving the command CONTROL-U CONTROL-@ again and again. You can go around the ring as many times as you like and stop whenever you want to.

Some commands set Mark automatically: The idea is to leave a bookmark before moving Point a long distance. One example is META->, which sets Mark before jumping to the end of the buffer. You can then go back to your starting position with CONTROL-U CONTROL-@. Searches behave similarly. To avoid surprises the message Mark Set appears in the Echo Area whenever Mark is set, either explicitly or implicitly.

Cut and Paste: Yanking Killed Text

Recall that killed text is not discarded but rather is kept in the Kill Ring. The Kill Ring holds the last 30 pieces of killed text and is visible from all buffers.

Retrieving text from the Kill Ring is called *yanking*. This terminology is opposite from vi's: In vi *yanking* pulls text from the buffer, and *putting* puts text into the buffer. Killing and yanking, roughly analogous to cutting and pasting, are emacs's primary mechanisms for moving and copying text. Table 11-7 lists the most common kill and yank commands.

Common Kill and Yank Commands	‖ table 11-7
META-d	Kills forward to the end of the current word
META-D	Kills backward to the beginning of the previous word
CONTROL-K	Kills to the end of the line, not including LINEFEED
CONTROL-U **1** CONTROL-K	Kills to the end of the line, including LINEFEED
CONTROL-U **0** CONTROL-K	Kills back to beginning of current line
META-w	Copies Region between Point and Mark to Kill Ring but does *not* erase from the buffer
CONTROL-W	Kills Region from Point to Mark
META-z *char*	Kills up to but not including the next occurrence of *char*
CONTROL-Y	Yanks the most recently killed text into the current buffer at Point, sets Mark at the beginning of this text, and positions Point and cursor at the end
META-y	Erases the just-yanked text, rotates the Kill Ring, and yanks the next item (only after CONTROL-Y or META-y)

To move two lines of text, move Point to the beginning of the first line, and enter CONTROL-U **2** CONTROL-K to kill two lines. Then move Point to the destination position, and enter CONTROL-Y.

To copy two lines of text, move Point to the beginning of the first line, and CONTROL-U **2** CONTROL-K CONTROL-Y to kill and then yank back immediately. Then move Point to the destination position and type CONTROL-Y.

To copy a larger piece, set the Region to cover this piece, and then type CONTROL-W CONTROL-Y to kill and yank back at once. Then move Point to the destination, and type

CONTROL-Y. You can also set the Region and use META-w to copy the Region to the Kill Ring.

The Kill Ring is organized as a fixed-length FIFO list, with each new entry causing the eldest to be discarded (once you build up to 30 entries in the Kill Ring). Simple cut-and-paste operations generally use only the newest entry. The older entries are kept to give you time to change your mind about a deletion. If you do change your mind, it is possible to "mine" the Kill Ring like an archaeological dig, working backward through time and down through the strata of killed material to copy a specific item back into your buffer.

To view every entry in the Kill Ring, begin a yanking session with CONTROL-Y. This copies the youngest entry to your buffer at the current cursor position. If this is not the item you want, continue the yanking session by typing META-y. This erases the previous yank and copies the next youngest entry to the buffer at the current cursor position. If this still is not the item you wanted back, type META-y again to erase it and retrieve a copy of the next entry, and so on. You can continue this all the way back to the very oldest entry. If you continue to type META-y, you wrap back to the youngest again. In this manner you can examine each entry as many times as you wish.

The sequence is CONTROL-Y followed by any mixture of CONTROL-Y and META-y. If you type any other command after META-y, the sequence is broken, and you must give the CONTROL-Y command again to start another yank session.

As you work backward in the Kill Ring, it is useful to think of advancing a Last Yank pointer back through history to older and older entries. This pointer is *not* reset to the youngest entry until you give a new kill command. Using this technique, you can work backward part way through the Kill Ring with CONTROL-Y and a few META-y's, give some commands that do not kill, and then pick up where you left off with another CONTROL-Y and a succession of META-y's.

It is also possible to position the Last Yank pointer with positive or negative numeric arguments to META-y. Refer to the online documentation for more information.

Inserting Special Characters

As stated earlier, emacs inserts everything that is not a command into the buffer at the current cursor position. To insert characters that would ordinarily be emacs commands, you can use the emacs escape character, CONTROL-Q. There are two ways of using this escape character.

- CONTROL-Q followed by any other character inserts that character in the buffer, no matter what command interpretation it was supposed to have.

- CONTROL-Q followed by three octal digits inserts a byte with that value in the buffer.

> ### CONTROL-Q || caution
>
> Depending on the way your terminal is set up, CONTROL-Q may clash with software flow control. If CONTROL-Q seems to have no effect, it is most likely being used for flow control. In that case you must bind another key to insert special characters (page 517).

Global Buffer Commands

The vi editor and its predecessors have global commands for bufferwide search and replacement. Their default operating Region was the entire buffer. The emacs editor has a similar family of commands. Their operating Region begins at Point and extends to the end of the buffer. If you wish to operate on the complete buffer, use META-< to set Point at the beginning of the buffer before issuing the command.

Line-Oriented Operations

The commands listed in Table 11-8 take a regular expression and apply it to the lines between Point and the end of the buffer.

Line-Oriented Operations	|| table 11-8
META-x occur	Prompts for a regular expression and lists each line with a match for the expression in a buffer named *Occur*
META-x delete-matching-lines	Prompts for a regular expression and then deletes each line with a match for the expression
META-x delete-non-matching-lines	Prompts for a regular expression and deletes each line that does *not* have a match for that expression

The META-x **occur** command puts its output in a special buffer named *Occur*, which you can peruse and discard or use as a jump menu to reach each line quickly. To use the *Occur* buffer as a jump menu, switch to it (page 500), get the cursor on the copy of the desired destination line, and type CONTROL-C CONTROL-C. This switches to the buffer that was searched and positions the cursor on the line that the regular expression originally matched.

As with any buffer change, you can undo the deletion commands.

Unconditional and Interactive Replacement

The commands listed in Table 11-9 operate on the characters between Point and the end of the buffer, changing every string match or regular expression match. An unconditional replacement makes all replacements without question. An interactive replacement gives you the opportunity to see and approve each replacement before it is made.

Replacement || table 11-9

META-x replace-string	Prompts for *string* and *newstring* and then replaces every instance of *string* with *newstring*. Point is left at the site of the last replacement, but Mark is automatically set when you give the command, so you can return to it with CONTROL-U CONTROL-@.
META-x replace-regexp	Prompts for *regexp* and *newstring* and then replaces every instance of *regexp* with *newstring*. Point is left at the site of the last replacement, but Mark is automatically set when you give the command, so you can return to it with CONTROL-U CONTROL-@.
META-% *string* or META-x query-replace	First form uses *string* whereas the second form prompts for *string*. Both forms prompt for *newstring* and then replace each instance of *string* with *newstring*. Point is left at the site of the last replacement, but Mark is automatically set when you give the command, so you can return to it with CONTROL-U CONTROL-@.
META-x query-replace-regexp	Prompts for *regexp* and *newstring* and then queries each instance of *regexp* and, depending you your response, replaces it with *newstring*. Point is left at the site of the last replacement, but Mark is automatically set when you give the command, so you can return to it with CONTROL-U CONTROL-@.

If you perform an interactive replacement, emacs displays each instance of *string* or match of *regexp* and prompts you for an action to take. Table 11-10 lists some of the possible responses.

Responses to Interactive Replacement Prompts || table 11-10

RETURN	Do not do any more replacements; quit now.
SPACE	Make this replacement and go on.

Responses to Interactive Replacement Prompts (Continued) || table 11-10

DELETE	Do *not* make this replacement. Skip over it and go on.
, (comma)	Make this replacement, display the result, and ask for another command. Any command is legal except DELETE is treated like SPACE and does not undo the change.
. (period)	Make this replacement and quit searching.
! (exclamation point)	Replace this and all remaining instances without asking any more questions.

Files

When you *visit* (emacs terminology for calling up) a file, emacs reads it into an internal buffer (page 500), edits the buffer contents, and eventually saves the buffer back to the file. The commands discussed here relate to visiting and saving files.

Each emacs buffer keeps a record of its default directory (the directory the file was read from or the working directory, if it is a new file) that is prepended to any relative pathname you give it. This is a convenience to save some typing. Enter META-x **pwd** to print the default directory for the current buffer or META-x **cd** to prompt for a new default directory and assign it to this buffer.

Visiting Files

The emacs editor deals well with visiting a file that has already been called up and whose image is now in a buffer. After a check of modification time to be sure the file has not been changed since it was last called up, emacs simply switches you to that buffer. Refer to Table 11-11 for a list of commands used to visit files.

Visiting Files || table 11-11

CONTROL-X CONTROL-F	Prompts for a filename and reads its contents into a freshly created buffer. Assigns the file's final pathname component as the buffer name. Other buffers are unaffected. It is common and often useful to have several files simultaneously open for editing.
CONTROL-X CONTROL-V	Prompts for a filename and replaces the current buffer with a buffer containing the contents of the requested file. The current buffer is destroyed.

Visiting Files || table 11-11

CONTROL-X **4** CONTROL-F	Prompts for a filename and reads its contents into a freshly created buffer. Assigns the file's final pathname component as the buffer name. Creates a new window for this buffer and selects that window. The window selected before the command still shows the buffer it was showing before, although the new window may cover up part of the old window.

To create a nonexistent file, simply call it up. An empty buffer is created and properly named, so you can eventually save it. The message (New File) appears in the Echo Area, reflecting emacs's understanding of the situation. Of course, if this "new file" grew out of a typographical error, you probably want to issue CONTROL-X CONTROL-V with the correct name.

Saving Files

You save a buffer by copying its contents back to the original file you called up. The relevant commands are listed in Table 11-12.

Saving Files || table 11-12

CONTROL-X CONTROL-S	This is the workhorse file-saving command. It saves the current buffer into its original file. If the current buffer is not modified, you get the message (No changes need to be saved).
CONTROL-X **S**	For each modified buffer, you are asked whether you wish to save it. Answer y or n. This command is given automatically as you exit emacs, to save any buffers that have been modified but not yet written out. However, if you want to save intermediate copies of your work, you can give this command at any time.
META-x set-visited-file-name	Prompts for a filename and sets this name as the current buffer's "original" name.
CONTROL-X CONTROL-W	Prompts for a filename, sets this name as the "original" file for the current buffer, and saves the current buffer into that file. This is equivalent to META-x *set-visited-file-name* followed by CONTROL-X CONTROL-S.
META-~ (tilde)	Clears modified flag from the current buffer. If you have mistakenly typed META-~ against a buffer with changes you want to keep, you need to make sure that the modified condition and its ✷ ✷ indicator are turned back on before leaving emacs, or all the changes will be lost. One easy way to do this is to insert a SPACE into the buffer and then remove it again with DELETE.

Did You Modify a Buffer by Mistake? || caution

It is usually during CONTROL-X s that you discover files whose buffers were modified by mistake, and now emacs wants to save the wrong changes back to the file. *Do not* answer y if you are not sure. First get done with the CONTROL-X s dialog by typing n to any saves you are not clear about. Then you have several options.

- Save the suspicious buffer into a temporary file with CONTROL-X CONTROL-W, and analyze it later.
- Undo the changes with a string of CONTROL-_ until the ** indicator disappears from the buffer's Mode Line.
- If you are sure that all the changes are wrong, use META-x **revert-buffer** to get a fresh copy of the file.
- Kill the buffer outright. Because it is modified, you are asked whether you are sure.
- Give the META-~ (tilde) command to clear the modified condition and ** indicator. A subsequent CONTROL-X s then believes that the buffer does not need to be written.

You Can Exit without First Getting a Warning || caution

Clearing the modified flag (META-~) allows you to exit without saving a modified buffer with no warning. Be careful if you choose to use this technique.

Buffers

An emacs buffer is a storage object that you can edit. It often holds the contents of a file but can also exist without being associated with any file. You can select only one buffer at a time, designated as the *current buffer*. Most commands operate only on the current buffer, even when multiple windows show two or more buffers on the screen. For the most part each buffer is its own world: It has its own name, its own modes, its own file associations, its own modified state, and may even have its own special key bindings. You can use the commands shown in Table 11-13 to create, select, list, and manipulate buffers.

Work with Buffers || table 11-13

CONTROL-X **b**	Prompts for a buffer name and selects it. If it does not exist, this command creates it first.

Work with Buffers (Continued) || table 11-13

CONTROL-X **4 b**	Prompts for a buffer name and selects it in another window. The existing window is not disturbed, although the new window may overlap it.
CONTROL-X CONTROL-B	Creates a buffer named *Buffer List* and displays it in another window. The existing window is not disturbed, although the new window may overlap it. The new buffer is not selected. In the *Buffer List* buffer, each buffer's data is shown, with name, size, mode(s), and original filename. A % appears for a readonly buffer, a * indicates a modified buffer, and **.** appears for the selected buffer.
META-x rename-buffer	Prompts for a new buffer name and gives this new name to the current buffer.
CONTROL-X CONTROL-Q	Toggles the current buffer's readonly status and the associated %% Mode Line indicator. This can be useful to prevent accidental buffer modification or to allow modification of a buffer when visiting a readonly file.
META-x append-to-buffer	Prompts for a buffer name and appends the current Region between Point and Mark to the end of that buffer.
META-x prepend-to-buffer	Prompts for a buffer name and appends the current Region between Point and Mark to the beginning of that buffer.
META-x copy-to-buffer	Prompts for a buffer name and deletes the contents of the buffer before copying the current Region between Point and Mark into that buffer.
META-x insert-buffer	Prompts for a buffer name and inserts the entire contents of that buffer into the current buffer at Point.
CONTROL-X **k**	Prompts for a buffer name and deletes that buffer. If the buffer is modified but unsaved, you are asked to confirm.
META-x kill-some-buffers	Goes through the entire buffer list and offers the chance to delete each buffer. As with CONTROL-X k, you are asked to confirm the kill order if a modified buffer is not yet saved.

Windows

An emacs *window* is a viewport that looks into a buffer. The emacs screen begins by displaying a single window, but this screen space can later be divided among two or more windows. On the screen the *current window* holds the cursor and views the *current buffer*.

A window views one buffer at a time. You can switch the buffer that a window views by giving the command CONTROL-X b *buffer-name* in the current window. Multiple windows can view one buffer; each window may view different parts of the same buffer, and each window carries its own value of Point. Any change to a buffer is reflected in all the windows viewing that buffer. Also, a buffer can exist without a window open on it.

Splitting a Window

One way to divide the screen is to split the starting window explicitly into two or more pieces. The command CONTROL-X 2 splits the current window in two, with one new window above the other. A numeric argument is taken as the size of the upper window in lines. The command CONTROL-X 3 splits the current window in two, with the new windows arranged side by side (Figure 11-7). A numeric argument is taken as the number of columns to give the left window. For example, CONTROL-U CONTROL-X 2 splits the current window in two, and because of the special "times 4" interpretation of CONTROL-U standing alone, the upper window is to be given four lines (barely enough to be useful).

Figure 11-7   Splitting a window vertically

Although these commands split the current window, both windows continue to view the same buffer. You can select a new buffer in either or both new windows, or you can scale each window to show different positions in the same buffer.

Manipulating Windows

You can use CONTROL-X o (the letter "oh") to select the other window. If more than two windows are on the screen, a sequence of CONTROL-X o commands cycles through them in top-to-bottom, left-to-right order. The META-CONTROL-V command scrolls the other window. If there are more than two, the command scrolls the window that CONTROL-X o would select next. You may use a positive or negative scrolling argument, just as with CONTROL-V scrolling in the current window.

Other-Window Display

In normal emacs operation, explicit window splitting is not nearly so common as the implicit splitting done by the family of CONTROL-X **4** commands. One of these commands is CONTROL-X **4b,** which prompts for a *buffer name* and selects it in the other window. If there is no other window, the command begins with a half-and-half split that arranges the windows one above the other. Another command, CONTROL-X **4f,** prompts for a *filename,* calls it up in the other window, and selects the other window. If there is no other window, the command begins with a half-and-half split that arranges the windows one above the other.

Adjusting and Deleting Windows

Windows may be destroyed when they get in the way; no data is lost in the window's associated buffer, and you can make another window anytime you like. The CONTROL-X **0** (zero) command deletes the current window and gives its space to its neighbors, whereas CONTROL-X **1** deletes all windows except the current window.

It is also possible to adjust the dimensions of the current window, once again at the expense of its neighbors. You can make a window shorter with META-x **shrink-window.** Use CONTROL-X ^ to increase the height of a window, CONTROL-X } to make the window wider (Figure 11-7), and CONTROL-X { to make the window narrower. Each of these commands adds or subtracts one line or column to or from the window, unless you precede the command with a numeric argument.

The emacs editor has its own guidelines for a window's minimum useful size and may destroy a window before you force one of its dimensions to zero. Although the window is gone, the buffer remains intact.

Foreground Shell Commands

The emacs editor can run a subshell (a shell that is a child of the shell that is running emacs—refer to "Job Control" on page 554) to execute a single command line, optionally with input from a Region of the current buffer and optionally with command output replacing the Region contents (Table 11-14). This is analogous to executing a shell command from the vi editor and having the input come from the file you are editing and having the output go back into the same file (page 459). As with vi, how well this works depends in part on the capabilities of your shell.

Foreground Shell Commands | table 11-14

META-! (exclamation point)	Prompts for a shell command, executes it, and displays the output
CONTROL-U META-! (exclamation point)	Prompts for a shell command, executes it, and inserts the output at Point
META-| (vertical bar)	Prompts for a shell command, gives the Region contents as input, filters it through the command, and displays the output
CONTROL-U META-| (vertical bar)	Prompts for a shell command, gives the Region contents as input, filters it through the command, deletes the old Region contents, and inserts the output in that position

The emacs editor can also start an interactive subshell, running continuously in its own buffer. See "Shell Mode" on page 514 for more information.

Background Shell Commands

The emacs editor can run processes in the background, with output fed into a growing emacs buffer that does not have to remain in view. You can continue editing while the background process runs and look at its output later. Any shell command can be run, without any restrictions.

The growing output buffer is always named *compilation*, and you can read it, copy from it, or edit it in any way, without waiting for the background process to finish. Most commonly this buffer is used to see the output of program compilation and then to correct any syntax errors found by the compiler.

To run a process in the background, give the command META-x **compile** to prompt for a shell command and begin executing it as a background process. The screen splits in half to show the *compilation* buffer.

You can switch to the *compilation* buffer and watch the execution, if you wish. To make the display scroll as you watch, position the cursor at the very end of the text with a META-> command. If you are not interested, just remove the window (with CONTROL-X 0 if you are in it or CONTROL-X 1 otherwise) and keep working. You can switch back to the *compilation* buffer later with CONTROL-X b.

You can kill the background process with META-x **kill-compilation**. The emacs editor asks for confirmation and then kills the background process.

If standard format error messages appear in *compilation*, you can automatically visit the line in the file where each error occurred. You can give the command CONTROL-X ` (backquote or accent grave) to split the screen into two windows and visit the file and line of the next error message. Scroll the *compilation* buffer so that this error message appears at the top of its window. Use CONTROL-U CONTROL-X ` to start over with the first error message and visit that file and line.

Language-Sensitive Editing

The emacs editor has a large collection of feature sets specific to a certain variety of text. The feature sets are called *Major modes,* and a buffer may have only one Major mode at a time.

A buffer's Major mode is private to the buffer and does not affect editing in any other buffer. If you switch to a new buffer having a different mode, rules for the new mode are immediately in effect. To avoid confusion, the name of a buffer's Major mode appears in the mode Line of any window viewing that buffer.

The three classes of Major modes are for

- Editing human languages (for example, text, nroff, TeX)
- Editing programming languages (for example, C, Fortran, Lisp)
- Special purposes (for example, shell, mail, dired, ftp)

In addition, one Major mode—Fundamental—does nothing special at all. A Major mode usually sets up the following:

- Special commands unique to the mode, possibly with their own key bindings. There may be just a few for languages, but special-purpose modes may have dozens.
- Mode-specific character syntax and regular expressions defining word constituent characters, delimiters, comments, whitespace, and so on. This conditions the behavior of commands oriented to syntactic units, such as words, sentences, comments, or parenthesized expressions.

Selecting a Major Mode

The emacs editor chooses and sets a mode when a file is called up by matching the filename against a set of regular expression patterns describing the filename and filename extension. The explicit command to enter a Major mode is META-x **mode-name-mode.** This command is rarely used except to correct wrong guesses.

A file can define its own mode by having the text **– ✳ – modename – ✳ –** somewhere in the first nonblank line, possibly buried inside a comment suitable for that programming language.

Human-Language Modes

A *human* language is meant eventually to be used by humans, possibly after being formatted by some text-formatting program. Human languages share many conventions about the structure of words, sentences, and paragraphs; with regard to these textual units, the major human language modes all behave the same.

Beyond the common region, each mode offers additional functionality oriented to a specific text formatter, such as TeX, LaTeX, or nroff. Text-formatter extensions are beyond the scope of this presentation; the focus here is on the commands relating to human textual units (for example, words, sentences, and paragraphs).

Words

As a mnemonic aid, the bindings are defined parallel to the character-oriented bindings CONTROL-F, CONTROL-B, CONTROL-D, DELETE, and CONTROL-T.

Just as CONTROL-F and CONTROL-B move forward and backward over characters, META-f and META-b move forward and backward over words. They may start from a position inside or outside the word to be traversed, but in all cases Point finishes just beyond the word, adjacent to the last character skipped over. They accept a numeric argument specifying the number of words to be traversed.

Just as CONTROL-D and DELETE delete characters forward and backward, the keys META-d and META-DELETE kill words forward and backward. They leave Point in exactly the same finishing position as META-f and META-b, but they kill the words they pass over. They also accept a numeric argument.

META-t transposes the word before Point with the word after Point.

Sentences

As a mnemonic aid, three of the bindings are defined parallel to the line-oriented bindings: CONTROL-A, CONTROL-E, and CONTROL-K. As discussed earlier, META-a moves back to the beginning of a sentence, and META-e moves forward to the end. In addition, CONTROL-X DELETE kills backward to the beginning of a sentence whereas META-k kills forward to the end of a sentence.

The emacs editor recognizes sentence ends with a regular expression kept in a variable named **sentence-end**. (If you are curious, give the command CONTROL-H **v sentence-end** RETURN to view this variable.) Briefly, it looks for the characters ., ?, or ! followed by two SPACEs or an end-of-line marker, possibly with close quotation marks or close braces.

The META-a and META-e commands leave Point adjacent to the first or last nonblank character in the sentence. They accept a numeric argument specifying the number of sentences to traverse; a negative argument runs them in reverse.

The META-k and CONTROL-X DELETE commands kill sentences forward and backward, in a manner analogous to CONTROL-K line kill. They leave Point in exactly the same finishing position as META-a and META-e but kill the sentences they pass over. They too accept a numeric argument. CONTROL-X DELETE is useful for quickly backing out of a half-finished sentence.

Paragraphs

As discussed earlier, META-{ moves back to the most recent paragraph beginning, and META-} moves forward to the next paragraph ending. The META-h command marks the paragraph (that is, puts Point at the beginning and Mark at the end) that the cursor is currently on, or the next paragraph if it is in between.

The META-} and META-{ commands leave Point at the beginning of a line, adjacent to the first character or last character of the paragraph. They accept a numeric argument specifying the number of paragraphs to traverse and run in reverse if given a negative argument.

In human-language modes, paragraphs are separated by blank lines and text-formatter command lines, and an indented line starts a paragraph. Recognition is based on the regular expressions stored in the variables **paragraph-separate** and **paragraph-start**. A paragraph is composed of complete lines, including the final line terminator. If a paragraph starts following one or more blank lines, the last blank line before the paragraph belongs to the paragraph.

Fill

The emacs editor can *fill* a paragraph to fit a specified width, breaking lines and rearranging them as necessary. Breaking takes place only between words, and there is no hyphenation. Filling can be done automatically as you type or in response to your explicit command.

META-x **auto-fill-mode** turns Auto Fill mode on or off. Turn it off or on by giving the same command again. When Auto Fill mode is on, emacs automatically breaks lines when you type SPACE or RETURN and are currently beyond the specified line width. This feature is useful when you are entering new text.

Auto Fill mode does not automatically refill the entire paragraph you are currently working on. If you add new text in the middle of a paragraph, Auto Fill mode breaks your new text as you type but does not refill the complete paragraph. To refill a complete paragraph or Region of paragraphs, use either META-q to refill the current paragraph or META-x *fill-region* to refill each paragraph in the Region between Point and Mark.

As before, paragraph boundaries are defined by the regular expressions stored in the **paragraph-separate** and **paragraph-start** variables.

You can change the filling width from its default value of 70 by setting the **fill-column** variable with either CONTROL-X f to set fill-column to the current cursor position or CONTROL-U *nnn* CONTROL-X f to set fill-column to *nnn*, where 0 is the left margin.

Case Conversion

The emacs editor can force words or Regions to all uppercase, all lowercase, or initial caps (the first letter of each word uppercase, the rest lowercase). Refer to Table 11-15.

Case Conversion	table 11-15
META-l (lowercase "ell")	Converts word to the right of Point to lowercase
META-u	Converts word to the right of Point to uppercase
META-c	Converts word to the right of Point to initial caps
CONTROL-X CONTROL-L	Converts Region between Point and Mark to lowercase
CONTROL-X CONTROL-U	Converts Region between Point and Mark to uppercase

The word-oriented conversions move Point over the word just converted, the same as META-f, allowing you to walk through text, converting each word with META-l, META-u, or META-c, and skipping over words to be left alone with META-f. A positive numeric argument converts that many words to the right of Point, moving Point as it goes. A negative numeric argument converts that many words to the left of Point but leaves Point stationary. This is useful for quickly changing the case of words you have just typed. Some examples appear in Table 11-16.

Characters and Commands	Results	table 11-16
HELLOMETA—META-l (lowercase "ell")	hello	
helloMETA—META-u	HELLO	
helloMETA—META-c	Hello	

The word conversions are not picky about beginning in the middle of a word. In all cases, they consider the first word-constituent character to the right of Point as the beginning of the word to be converted.

Text Mode

With very few exceptions, the commands for human-language text units, such as words and sentences, are always turned on and available, even in the programming language modes. Text mode adds very little to these basic commands but is still worth turning on just to get the TAB key. Use the command META-x **text-mode**.

In Text mode TAB runs the function **tab-to-tab-stop**. By default TAB stops are set every eight columns. You can adjust them with META-x **edit-tab-stops**, which switches to a special ✳**Tab Stops**✳ buffer, where the current stops are laid out on a scale for you to edit. The new stops are installed when/if you type CONTROL-C CONTROL-C, but you are free to kill this buffer (CONTROL-X **k**) or switch away from it (CONTROL-X **b**) without ever changing the stops.

The tab stops you set here affect *only* the interpretation of TAB characters arriving from the keyboard. The emacs editor automatically inserts enough spaces to reach the TAB stop. This does *not* affect the interpretation of TAB characters already in the buffer or the underlying file. If you edit the TAB stops and then use them, you can still print your file, and the hard copy will look the same as the text on the screen.

C Mode

Programming languages are read by humans but are interpreted by machines. Besides continuing to handle some of the human-language text units (for example, words and sentences), the major programming language modes address the additional problems of dealing with

- "Balanced expressions" enclosed by parentheses, brackets, or braces as textual units
- Comments as textual units
- Indention

In emacs there are Major modes to support C, Fortran, and several variants of Lisp. In addition, many users have contributed modes for their favorite languages. In these modes the commands for human textual units are still available, with occasional redefinitions: For example, a paragraph is bounded only by blank lines, and indention does not signal a paragraph start. In addition, each mode has custom coding to handle the language-specific conventions for balanced expressions, comments, and indention. This presentation discusses only C mode.

Expressions

The emacs Major modes are limited to lexical analysis. They can recognize most tokens (for example, symbols, strings, numbers) and all matched sets of parentheses, brackets, and braces. This is enough for Lisp but not for C. The C mode lacks a full-function syntax analyzer and is not prepared to recognize all of C's possible expressions.[1]

---

1. In the emacs documentation the recurring term *sexp* refers to the historic Lisp term *S-expression*. Unfortunately, it is sometimes used interchangeably with *expression*, even though the language might not be Lisp at all.

Table 11-17 lists the emacs editor commands applicable to parenthesized expressions and some tokens. By design the bindings run parallel to the CONTROL commands for characters and the META commands for words. All these commands accept a numeric argument and run in reverse if that argument is negative.

Commands for Expressions and Tokens || table 11-17

CONTROL-META-f	Moves forward over an expression. The exact behavior for CONTROL-META-f depends on what character lies to the right of Point (or left of Point, depending on which direction you are moving Point): • If the first nonwhitespace is an opening delimiter (parenthesis, bracket, or brace), Point is moved just past the matching closing delimiter. • If the first nonwhitespace is a token, Point is moved just past the end of this token.
CONTROL-META-b	Moves backward over an expression.
CONTROL-META-k	Kills an expression forward. It leaves Point at the same finishing position as CONTROL-META-f but kills the expression it traverses.
CONTROL-META-@	Sets Mark at the position CONTROL-META-f would move to but does not change Point. To see the marked region clearly, you can look at both ends with a pair of CONTROL-X CONTROL-X commands to interchange Point and Mark.

Function Definitions

In emacs a balanced expression at the outermost level is considered to be a function definition and is often called a *defun,* even though that term is specific to Lisp alone. Most generally, it is understood to be a function definition in the language at hand.

In C mode a function definition is understood to include the return data type, the function name, and the argument declarations appearing before the { character. Table 11-18 shows the commands for operating on function definitions.

Function Definitions || table 11-18

CONTROL-META-a	Moves to the beginning of the most recent function definition. Use this command to scan backward through a buffer one function at a time.
CONTROL-META-e	Moves to the end of the next function definition. You can use this command to scan forward through a buffer one function at a time.

Function Definitions (Continued) || table 11-18

CONTROL-META-h	Puts Point at the beginning and Mark at the end of the current (or next, if between) function definition. This command sets up an entire function definition for a Region-oriented operation such as kill.

Function Indention Style || caution

The **emacs** editor now believes that an opening brace at the left margin is part of a function definition. This is a heuristic to speed up the reverse scan for a definition's leading edge. If your code has an indention style that puts that opening brace elsewhere, you may get unexpected results.

Indention

The **emacs** C mode has extensive logic to control the indention of C programs. Furthermore, you can adjust the logic for many different styles of C indention (Table 11-19).

Indention Commands || table 11-19

TAB	Adjusts the indention of the current line. TAB inserts or deletes whitespace at the beginning of the line until the indention conforms to the current context and rules in effect. Point is not moved at all unless it lies in the whitespace area; in that case, it is moved to the end of that whitespace. TAB does not insert anything except leading whitespace, so you can hit it at any time and at any position in the line. If you really want to insert a tab in the text, you can use META-i or CONTROL-Q TAB.
LINEFEED	Shorthand for RETURN followed by TAB. The LINEFEED key is a convenience for entering new code, giving you an autoindent as you begin each line. The following two commands each indent multiple lines with a single command.
CONTROL-META-q	Reindents all the lines inside the next pair of matched braces. CONTROL-META-q assumes that the left brace is correctly indented and drives the indention from there. If the left brace itself needs help, type TAB on its line before giving this command. All the lines up to the matching brace are indented as if you had typed TAB on each one.

Indention Commands (Continued)	‖ table 11-19
CONTROL-META-\	Reindents all the lines in the current Region between Point and Mark. Put Point just to the left of a left brace and then give the command. All the lines up to the matching brace are indented as if you had typed TAB on each one.

Customizing Indention

Many styles of C programming have evolved, and emacs does its best to support automatic indention for all of them. The indention coding was completely rewritten for emacs version 19; it supports C, C++, Objective-C, and Java. The emacs syntactic analysis is much more precise and is able to classify each syntactic element of each line of program text into a single syntactic category (out of about 50), such as *statement, string, else-clause,* and so on. With that analysis in hand, emacs goes to an offset table named **c-offsets-alist** and looks up how much this line should be indented from the preceding line.

In order to customize indention, you have to change the offset table. It is possible to define a completely new offset table for each customized style but much more convenient to feed in a short list of exceptions to the standard rules. Each mainstream style (GNU, K&R [Kernighan and Ritchie], BSD, and so on) has such an exception list; all are collected in **c-style-alist**. Here is one entry from **c-style-alist**:

```
("gnu"
(c-basic-offset . 2)
(c-comment-only-line-offset . (0 . 0))
(c-offsets-alist . ((statement-block-intro . +)
    (knr-argdecl-intro . 5)
    (substatement-open . +)
    (label . 0)
    (statement-case-open . +)
    (statement-cont . +)
    (arglist-intro . c-lineup-arglist-intro-after-paren)
    (arglist-close . c-lineup-arglist)
    ))
)
```

Constructing one's own custom style is beyond the scope of this book; if you are curious, the long story is available in emacs online info, beginning at "Customizing C Indentation." The sample .emacs file adds a very simple custom style and arranges to use it on every .c file that is edited.

Comments

Each buffer has its own **comment-column** variable, which you can view with the CONTROL-H **v** **comment-column** RETURN help command. The commands listed in Table 11-20 facilitate working with comments.

Comments	‖ table 11-20
META-; (semicolon)	Inserts a comment on this line or aligns an existing comment. Its behavior differs according to the current situation on this line. • If no comment is on this line, an empty one is created at the value of **comment-column**. • If text already on this line overlaps the position of **comment-column**, a comment is placed one SPACE after the end of the text. • If a comment is already on this line but not at the current value of **comment-column**, the command realigns the comment at that column. If text is in the way, the command places the comment one SPACE after the end of the text. Once an aligned (possibly empty) comment exists on the line, Point moves to the start of the comment text.
CONTROL-X ;	Sets **comment-column** to the column after Point. The left margin is column 0.
CONTROL-U – CONTROL-X ;	Kills the comment on the current line. This command sets **comment-column** from the first comment found above this line and then performs a META-; command to insert or align a comment at that position.
CONTROL-U CONTROL-X ;	Sets **comment-column** to the position of the first comment found above this line and then executes a META-; command to insert or align a comment on this line.

Special-Purpose Modes

The emacs editor has a third family of Major modes that are not oriented toward a particular language or even toward ordinary editing. Instead they perform some special function. These modes, which may define their own key bindings and commands to accomplish that function, are

- Rmail: reads, archives, and composes e-mail
- Dired: moves around in an **ls –l** display and operates on files
- VIP: simulates a complete vi environment
- Shell: runs an interactive subshell from inside an emacs buffer

This book discusses only Shell mode.

Shell Mode

One-time shell commands and Region filtering were discussed earlier. Refer to "Foreground Shell Commands" on page 503. In Shell mode, however, each emacs buffer has an underlying interactive shell permanently associated with it. This shell takes its input from the last line of the buffer and sends its output back to the buffer, advancing Point as it goes. The buffer, if not edited, is a record of the complete shell session.

The shell runs asynchronously, whether or not you have its buffer in view. The emacs editor uses idle time to read the shell's output and add it to the buffer.

Type META-x **shell** to create a buffer named ✳**shell**✳ and start a subshell. If a buffer named ✳**shell**✳ exists already, emacs just switches to that buffer.

The shell name to run is taken from one of the following sources:

- The Lisp variable **explicit-shell-file-name**
- The environment variable **ESHELL**
- The environment variable **SHELL**

If you really want to start a second shell, first use META-x **rename-buffer** to change the name of the existing shell's buffer. This process can be continued to create as many subshells and buffers as you want, all running in parallel.

In Shell mode a special set of commands is defined (Table 11-21). They are bound mostly to two-key sequences starting with CONTROL-C. Each sequence is meant to be similar to the ordinary control characters found in UNIX but with a leading CONTROL-C.

Shell Mode	‖ table 11-21
RETURN	If Point is at the end of the buffer, emacs inserts the RETURN and sends this (the last) line to the shell. If Point is elsewhere, it copies this line to the end of the buffer, peeling off the old shell prompt (see the regular expression **shell-prompt-pattern**), if one existed. Then this copied line, now the last in the buffer, is sent to the shell.

Shell Mode || table 11-21

CONTROL-C CONTROL-D	Sends CONTROL-D to the shell or its subshell.
CONTROL-C CONTROL-C	Sends CONTROL-C to the shell or its subshell.
CONTROL-C CONTROL-\	Sends quit signal to the shell or its subshell.
CONTROL-C CONTROL-U	Kills the text on the current line not yet completed.
CONTROL-C CONTROL-R	Scrolls back to the beginning of the last shell output, putting the first line of output at the top of the window.
CONTROL-CCONTROL-O	Deletes the last batch of shell output.

Optional

Customizing emacs

At the heart of emacs is a Lisp interpreter written in C. This version of Lisp is significantly extended with many special commands specifically oriented to editing. The interpreter's main task is to execute the Lisp-coded system that implements the look-and-feel of emacs.

Reduced to essentials, this system implements a continuous loop that watches keystrokes arrive, parses them into commands, executes those commands, and updates the screen. This behavior can be customized in a number of ways.

- As single keystrokes come in, they are mapped immediately through a keyboard translation table. By changing the entries in this table, it is possible to swap keys. If you are used to vi, you can swap DELETE and CONTROL-H. Then CONTROL-H backspaces as it does in vi, and DELETE, which is not used by vi, is the help key. Of course, if you use DELETE as an interrupt key, you may want to choose another key to swap with CONTROL-H.

- The mapped keystrokes are then gathered into small groups called *key sequences*. A key sequence may be only a single key, such as CONTROL-N, or may have two or more keys, such as CONTROL-X CONTROL-F. Once gathered, the key sequences are used to select a particular procedure to be executed. The rules for gathering each key sequence and the specific procedure name to be executed when that sequence comes in are all codified in a series of tables called *keymaps*. By altering the keymaps, you can change the gathering rules or change which procedure is associated with which sequence. If you are used to vi's use of CONTROL-W to back up over the word you are entering, you may want to change emacs CONTROL-W binding from its standard **kill-region** to **delete-word-backward**.

- The command behavior is often conditioned by one or more global variables or options. It may be possible to get the behavior you want by setting some of these variables.

- The command itself is usually a Lisp program that can be reprogrammed to make it behave as desired. Although this is not for beginners, the Lisp source to nearly all commands is available, and the internal Lisp system is fully documented. As mentioned before, it is common to load customized Lisp code at startup time, even if you did not write it yourself.

Most emacs documentation glosses over all the translation, gathering, and procedure selection and talks about keystrokes as though they were the commands. However, it is still important to know that the underlying machinery exists and to understand that its behavior can be changed.

The .emacs Startup File

Each time you start emacs, it loads the file of Lisp code named ~/.emacs. Using this file is the most common way to customize emacs for yourself. Two command line options control the use of the ~/.emacs file. The **–q** option ignores the .emacs file so that emacs starts up without it; this is one way to get past a bad .emacs file. The **–u** *user* option uses the *~user/*.emacs file (the .emacs file from the home directory of *user*).

The **.emacs** startup file is generally concerned only with key bindings and option settings; it is possible to write the Lisp statements for this file in a straightforward style. Each parenthesized Lisp statement is a Lisp function call. Inside the parentheses the first symbol is the function name, and the rest of the SPACE-separated tokens are arguments to that function. The most common function in the .emacs file, **setq**, is a simple assignment to a global variable. The first argument is the name of a variable to be set, and the second argument is its value. The following example sets the variable named **c-indent-level** to 8:

```
(setq c-indent-level 8)
```

Set the default value for a variable that is buffer-private, using the function name **setq-default**. To set a specific element of a vector, use the function name **aset**. The first argument is the name of the vector, the second is the target offset, and the third is the value of the target entry. In the startup file the new values are usually constants. The formats of these constants are shown in Table 11-22.

Formats of Constants in .emacs	**‖ table 11-22**
Numbers	Decimal integers, with an optional minus sign
Strings	Similar to C strings but with extensions for CONTROL and META characters: \C-s yields CONTROL-S, \M-s yields META-s, and \M-\C-s yields CONTROL-META-s
Characters	*Not* like C characters; start with ? and continue with a printing character or with a BACKSLASH escape sequence (for example ?a, ?\C-i, ?\033)
Booleans	*Not* 1 and 0; use instead t for *true* and nil for *false*
Other Lisp objects	Begin with a single quotation mark, and continue with the object's name

Remapping Keys

The emacs command loop begins each cycle by translating incoming keystrokes into the name of the command to be executed. The basic translation operation uses the ASCII value of the current incoming character to index a 128-element vector called a *keymap*.

Sometimes a character's eighth bit is interpreted as the META *case*, but this cannot always be relied on. At the point of translation, all META characters appear with the ESCAPE prefix, whether or not they were actually typed that way.

Each position in this vector is one of the following:

- Not defined at all. No translation possible in this map.

- The name of another keymap—switches to that keymap and waits for the next character to arrive.

- The name of a Lisp function to be called. Translation process is done; call this command.

Because keymaps can reference other keymaps, an arbitrarily complex recognition tree can be set up. However, the mainstream emacs bindings use at most three keys, with a very small group of well-known *prefix keys*, each with its well-known keymap name.

Each buffer can have a *local keymap* that, if present, is used first for any keystrokes arriving while a window into that buffer is selected. This allows the regular mapping to be extended or overridden on a per buffer basis and is most often used to add bindings for a Major mode.

The basic translation flow runs as follows:

- Map the first character through the buffer's local keymap; if it is defined as a Lisp function name, translation is done, and emacs executes that function. If not defined, use this same character to index the global top-level keymap.

- Map the first character through the top-level global keymap **global-map**. At this and each following stage, the following conditions hold:

  - If the entry for this character is not defined, it is an error. Send a bell to the terminal and discard all the characters entered in this key sequence.

  - If the entry for this character is defined as a Lisp function name, translation is done and the function is executed.

  - If the entry for this character is defined as the name of another keymap, switch to that keymap and wait for another character to select one of its elements.

Everything must be a command or an error. Ordinary characters that are to be inserted in the buffer are usually bound to the command **self-insert-command**. The well-known prefix characters are each associated with a keymap (Table 11-23).

Keymaps   ‖ table 11-23

ctl-x-map	For characters following CONTROL-X
ctl-x-4-map	For characters following CONTROL-X 4
help-map	For characters following CONTROL-H
esc-map	For characters following ESCAPE (including META characters)
mode-specific-map	For characters following CONTROL-C

To see the current state of the keymaps, type CONTROL-H **b**. They appear in the following order: local, global, and then the shorter maps for each prefix key. Each line has the name of the Lisp function to be called; the documentation for that function can be retrieved with the commands CONTROL-H **f function-name** or CONTROL-H **k key-sequence**.

The most common sort of keymap customization is making small changes to the global command assignments without creating any new keymaps or commands. This is most easily done in the **.emacs** file, using the Lisp function **define-key**. The **define-key** takes three arguments:

- Keymap name
- Single character defining a position in that map
- Command to be executed when this character appears

For instance, to bind the command **backward-kill-word** to CONTROL-W, use the statement

```
(define-key global-map "\C-w" 'backward-kill-word)
```

To bind the command **kill-region** to CONTROL-X CONTROL-K, use the statement

```
(define-key ctl-x-map "\C-k" 'kill-region)
```

The \ character causes C-w to be interpreted as CONTROL-W instead of three letters (equivalent to \^w also). The unmatched single quotation mark in front of the command name is correct. It is a Lisp escape character to keep the name from being evaluated too soon.

A Sample .emacs File

The following **.emacs** file produces a plain editing environment that minimizes surprises for vi users. Of course, if any section or any line is inapplicable or not to your liking, you can edit it out or comment it with one or more ; comment characters, beginning in column 1.

```
;;; Preference Variables

(setq make-backup-files nil)           ;Do not make backup files
(setq backup-by-copying t)             ;If you do, at least do not destroy links
(setq delete-auto-save-files t)        ;Delete autosave files when writing orig
(setq blink-matching-paren nil)        ;Do not blink opening delim
(setq-default case-fold-search nil)    ;Do not fold cases in search
(setq require-final-newline 'ask)      ;Ask about missing final newline

;; Reverse mappings for C-h and DEL.
(keyboard-translate ?\C-h ?\177)
(keyboard-translate ?\177 ?\C-h)


;; reassigning C-w to keep on deleting words backward

;; C-w is supposed to be kill-region, but it's a great burden for vi-trained fingers.
;; Bind it instead to backward-kill-word for more familiar, friendly behavior.
(define-key global-map "\^w" 'backward-kill-word)

;; for kill-region use a two-key sequence c-x c-k.
(define-key ctl-x-map "\^k" 'kill-region)
```

```
;; C mode customization: set vanilla (8-space bsd) indention style

(require 'cc-mode)                              ;kiss: be sure it's here

(c-add-style                                    ;add indentation style
 "bsd8"                                         ;old bsd (8 spaces)
 '((c-basic-offset . 8)
   (c-hanging-comment-ender-p . nil)    ;isolated "*/" ends blk comments
   (c-comment-only-line-offset . 0)
   (c-offsets-alist . ((statement-block-intro . +)
                       (knr-argdecl-intro . +)
                       (substatement-open . 0)
                       (label . 0)
                       (statement-cont . +)
                       ))
  ))
(add-hook                                       ;this is our default style,
 'c-mode-hook                                   ;set it always in c-mode-hook.
 (function
  (lambda ()
    (c-set-style "bsd8")))))

;; end of c mode style setup
```

emacs and the X Window System

With Version 19, GNU emacs fully embraced the X Window System environment and can manage multiple X-level windows (called *frames* to avoid confusion with emacs windows). Each frame can contain multiple emacs windows, as well as a menubar. See Figure 11-8.

Start emacs on X || tip

Start the graphical version of emacs under a GUI by giving the command emacs from a terminal emulator or by selecting **Run Command** from a menu and entering emacs.

  The graphical version of emacs is *not* xemacs (www.xemacs.org). The xemacs program is not a GNU project.

The usual mouse-oriented actions, including cut and paste with other X clients, are supported. Besides selecting a frame, the mouse can select, split, expand, or delete emacs windows within a frame. Each window can have its own scrollbar.

Mouse events have a notation similar to keyboard events—that is, M-Mouse-1 (META-Mouse-1 in this book) means hold the META key while giving a single click of the

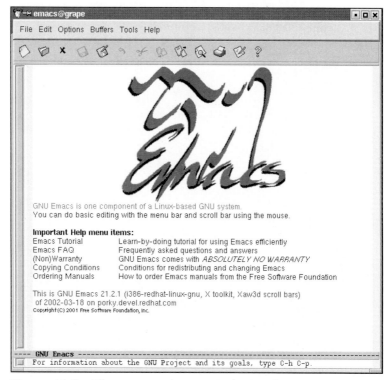

Figure 11-8   The emacs welcome window under X

leftmost mouse button. As with keys, you can rebind mouse clicks to customize the look-and-feel of emacs.

You can select type fonts and foreground and background colors for each screen region.

Mouse Commands for Cut and Paste

The cut-and-paste scheme that emacs uses works much like the scheme that mainstream X applications use, most notably xterm. You are assumed to be using a three-button mouse, but as usual on a two-button mouse, the center button may be simulated by pressing the left and right buttons at the same time. The emacs documentation numbers these buttons from left to right and calls them Mouse-1, Mouse-2, and Mouse-3.

As with xterm, regions are defined by dragging the left mouse button (Drag-Mouse-1) or by marking the endpoints with single clicks of Mouse-1 and Mouse-3. Once defined, a region is pasted in emacs or another X application with a single click of Mouse-2. See Table 11-24 for details.

Cut-and-Paste Mouse Commands

|| table 11-24

Mouse-1	Selects the emacs window where the mouse is currently positioned and moves Point to that window at the location of the mouse pointer. This is the basic mouse-oriented technique for selecting an emacs frame and an emacs window within that frame. Within a specific window it is also the way to move Point without keyboard commands.
Drag-Mouse-1	First performs the Mouse-1 action to select frame, window, and initial Point and then sets Mark to the same position. Point follows the mouse as you drag, but Mark remains at the initial position. The region between Point and Mark will be highlighted and also added to the emacs Kill Ring just as though you had typed META-w. However, the region is not deleted and is made known to the X server (both as the primary selection and in the cut buffer) so that you can paste the highlighted region to other X applications.
Mouse-2	First performs the Mouse-1 action to select frame, window, and Point, then yanks the Kill Ring's most recent entry just as though you had typed CONTROL-Y. Point is left at the end of the yanked material.
Mouse-3	Like emacs, Mouse-3 is powerful and confusing, and its behavior depends on the current state of emacs. If no region is currently highlighted, Mouse-3 leaves Mark at the current Point and moves Point to the clicked position. The region between Point and Mark is highlighted, and its contents are added to the emacs Kill Ring. The net effect is precisely equivalent to Drag-Mouse-1. This is most often useful when you wish to define a large region that does not fit in one emacs window. If a region is currently highlighted, emacs extends or contracts the nearest boundary of the region so the clicked position becomes an edge. The region's Kill Ring entry and X definition are also extended or contracted so the contents remain in step. If a highlighted region exists and you have just clicked Mouse-3, a second consecutive click of Mouse-3 at the same position will kill this region from the buffer. It is already on the Kill Ring, so emacs does not put it there a second time.
Double-Mouse-1	Selects and highlights a region around the clicked-on syntax unit specific to the current mode. (In text double-click inside a word to mark that word; in C double-click a double quotation to mark a string, and so on). Mouse-3 region adjustments will be made in syntax-unit granules.

Cut-and-Paste Mouse Commands (Continued) || table 11-24

Double-Drag-Mouse-1 ("dit-dahhhh")	Selects and highlights a contiguous region of syntax units for this mode.
Triple-Mouse-1	Selects and highlights the region around the clicked-on line. Mouse-3 region adjustments will be made in line granules.
Triple-Drag-Mouse-1 ("dit-dit-dahhhh")	Selects and highlights a contiguous region of complete lines.

Table 11-25 shows the suggested mouse-oriented methods (by no means the only methods) to accomplish some common editing actions.

Edit with a Mouse || table 11-25

Killing text	Click Mouse-1 at one end, Double-Mouse-3 at the other. To see the doomed region clearly, give just one Mouse-3, and the area will be highlighted. Then you can give a second Mouse-3 (don't move the mouse between clicks), and the highlighted area will disappear. The killed text can be pasted elsewhere in emacs with CONTROL-Y or Mouse-2 or possibly in another X application (often, not always, using Mouse-2 at that end).
Marking a region	Use Drag-Mouse-1 if the desired region is onscreen; otherwise, use Mouse-1 and Mouse-3. The highlighted region is on the Kill Ring, just as though you had put it there with META-w, and it can be copied elsewhere in emacs with CONTROL-Y or Mouse-2 or into another X application. This region is delimited by Point and Mark and is therefore accessible to all the region-oriented emacs commands.
Importing text	Cut the text in another X application, and switch to an emacs frame and window. CONTROL-Y or Mouse-2 will insert the cut text at Point.

Mouse-2 Selections

Yanking text is not common or even meaningful in every buffer (for example, dired, info, compilation), and for these buffers highlighting and Mouse-2 are often managed differently in a mode-sensitive manner. Usually the scheme is to highlight some of the buffer objects by positioning the mouse over them and then to operate on the object by clicking Mouse-2. The "operation" is package-specific; for dired, the file is visited; for a compilation error message, the source-code file is visited; and for an info menu, that frame is visited.

Except in the compilation buffer, where each line is hot, you can nearly always spot objects that are Mouse-2-able. They will highlight as you move the mouse over them.

Scrollbars

The emacs editor implements optional scrollbars for each window; the scrolling scheme follows mainstream X applications, in particular xterm. The scrollbar appears at the right of each window, with a familiar rectangular box representing the window's current viewing position in the emacs buffer. Refer to Table 11-26 for a list of commands that are active within the scrollbar region.

Scrollbar Commands	table 11-26
Mouse-2	Position (jump) the window to this point in the buffer.
Drag-Mouse-2	(On the rectangular box) scroll the window to follow the mouse.
Mouse-1	Scroll the window contents upward toward end of file, moving the line at the clicked position up to the top of the screen. Often remembered as "here to top." In this scheme it's irrelevant whether you are above or below the rectangular box.
Mouse-3	Scroll the window contents downward toward start of file, moving the line at the top of the screen down to the clicked position. Often remembered as "top to here."
CONTROL-Mouse-2	Split this window vertically, with the boundary at the clicked position.

Manipulating Windows with the Mouse

The emacs editor accepts mouse commands to adjust window boundaries and size. Within a window's mode line, the commands shown in Table 11-27 are active.

Window Mode Line Commands	table 11-27
Mouse-1	Select this window without moving Point.
Drag-Mouse-1	Adjust this window boundary upward or downward.

Window Mode Line Commands (Continued) || table 11-27

Mouse-2	Expand this window to fill the frame.
Mouse-3	Delete this window.
CONTROL-Mouse-2	Split this window into two side-by-side windows, with the boundary at the clicked position.

Frame Management

A single instantiation of emacs can drive any reasonable number of frames on the X display. Each frame has its own emacs window configuration. With a very few exceptions, each frame is independent of the others. Often it is convenient to open a new frame, perhaps for reading mail or news, without disturbing the emacs window configuration in the current frame.

An emacs frame is simply an X window and can be given input focus, resized, manipulated, killed, iconified, or restored with whatever mouse commands your window manager defines. The emacs editor defines a family of keyboard commands for frame management (Table 11-28), somewhat parallel to the commands for emacs window management. They mostly begin with CONTROL-X 5, whereas the emacs window-oriented commands begin with CONTROL-X 4.

Frames || table 11-28

CONTROL-X **5 o** (lowercase "oh")	Selects the next frame and raises it to the top if necessary. Repeated use will cycle through all the frames of this **emacs** instantiation.
CONTROL-X **5 0** (number zero)	Deletes the currently selected frame unless it is the only frame. You cannot delete your only **emacs** frame this way. (Of course, you are always free to exit completely with CONTROL-x CONTROL-c.)
CONTROL-Z	Iconifies the currently selected frame. This command will also restore an **emacs** icon. This command suspends a non-X **emacs**.
CONTROL-X CONTROL-C	Exits from **emacs** and kills all the frames, including the current one. This is usually the command that reminds you the hard way that frames are not fully independent and is mentioned here only as a cautionary note. There is no standard command to "kill all the frames except this one."

Just as with a window, you can create a frame that does not exist and select a frame that does exist (Table 11-29).

Frame Creation ‖ table 11-29

CONTROL-X **5 2**	Unconditionally creates a new frame that is a copy of the current frame. Each window in the new frame is viewing the same position in the same buffer as its counterpart, and editing changes to one will appear in the other. This is fun to look at for a few seconds; but, of course, you will probably select some other files and buffers for the second frame to view.
CONTROL-X **5b buffername** RETURN	Prompts for a buffer name, and either creates a new frame for it or selects an existing frame with a window open on that buffer.
CONTROL-X **5f filename** RETURN	Prompts for a filename and visits it in another frame. Creates a new frame for the visit if needed.

Menubars

Any emacs command may be executed explicitly with META-x *command* RETURN or bound to a specific key sequence. Menubars offer a third, mouse-oriented possibility. By default emacs places a menubar at the top of each frame, just below the window manager's titlebar. Most commonly the bar holds the following menu headings:

```
File Edit Options Buffers Tools Help
```

With the mouse pointer positioned on one of these headings, the mouse command Down-Mouse-1 (press and hold the left mouse button) pulls down a menu. You select a menu item by dragging the mouse pointer to that item. As the mouse points to each item, it is highlighted. Releasing Mouse-1 erases the menu and either selects the highlighted item or selects nothing when no item was highlighted.

A menu item may be a buffer to switch to (in the Buffers menu) or perhaps an emacs command to execute. When a command is bound to a key sequence, that sequence is also shown in the menu item.

Some menu items bring up a submenu when selected; this secondary menu stays put even after you release Mouse-1. You select an item by highlighting it and clicking Mouse-1. To get out of the menu without doing anything, click Mouse-1 while nothing is highlighted.

Menubar usage is optional. If you prefer not to use it, you can free up the menu line so you can display more buffer text. To turn menubars on or off, execute the command

META-x **menu-bar-mode**

Resources for **emacs**

A lot of emacs documentation is available in both paper and electronic form. This section lists some of the sources.

The emacs Web Ring

The emacs *Web ring* (page 1501) has its home at www.gnusoftware.com/WebRing. It provides a wide variety of information, including a site for programmers who "are being forced to learn how to use the emacs editor after years of using the UNIX standard vi editor" (grok2.tripod.com).

Usenet emacs FAQ (Frequently Asked Questions)

If you have access to Usenet, many newsgroups now maintain a file of frequently asked questions (FAQ) and their answers. An excellent emacs FAQ file that addresses more than 125 common questions is available; copies of it can be found in the newsgroups **gnu.emacs.help**, **comp.emacs**, and **news.answers**. It has the most up-to-date information and is strongly recommended as a starting point.

Access to emacs

The emacs editor is part of the Red Hat distribution. If you have access to the Internet, you can use anonymous FTP to copy the current distribution from the host named prep.ai.mit.edu. There is no charge. First **cd** to the **/gnu/emacs/** directory, and then get the latest **emacs-2x.x.tar.gz** file. You will need to compile this source code. Refer to "Installing Non-rpm Software" on page 931. To make things easier, you can get an emacs rpm file from rpmfind (page 1401) and use rpm to install it. Refer to "rpm: Red Hat Package Manager" on page 928.

If you have no electronic access to the Internet, you can order emacs on tape directly from the Free Software Foundation for about $200. Many different media and tape formats are available, and you can also buy typeset copies of the emacs User Manual, the emacs Lisp Manual, and an emacs Reference Card.

The Free Software Foundation can be reached at these addresses:

Mail: Free Software Foundation, Inc.
59 Temple Place, Suite 330
Boston, MA 02111-1307, USA

E-mail: gnu@gnu.org

Phone: 1-617-542-5942

Chapter Summary

You can precede many of the commands in the following tables with a numeric argument to make the command repeat the number of times specified by the argument. Precede a numeric argument with CONTROL-U to keep emacs from entering the argument as text.

Moving the Cursor

CONTROL-F	Forward by characters
CONTROL-B	Backward by characters
META-f	Forward by words
META-b	Backward by words
META-e	To end of sentence
META-a	To beginning of sentence
META-{	To end of paragraph
META-}	To beginning of paragraph
META->	Forward to end of buffer
META-<	Backward to beginning of buffer
CONTROL-ESCAPE	To end of line
CONTROL-A	To beginning of line
CONTROL-N	Down by lines
CONTROL-P	Up by lines
CONTROL-V	Forward (scroll) by windows
META-v	Backward (scroll) by windows
CONTROL-L	Clear and repaint screen, and scroll current line to center of window
META-r	To beginning of middle line
CONTROL-U *num* META-r	To beginning of line number *num* (0 = top, − = bottom)

Killing and Deleting

CONTROL-DELETE	Deletes characters under cursor
DELETE	Deletes characters to the left of cursor
META-d	Kills from cursor forward to the end of current word
META-DELETE	Kills from cursor backward to beginning of previous word
META-k	Kills forward to end of a sentence
CONTROL-X DELETE	Kills backward to beginning of a sentence
CONTROL-K	Kills text from cursor forward to, but not including, the line ending LINEFEED and if there is no text between the cursor and the LINEFEED, kills the LINEFEED itself
CONTROL-U **1** CONTROL-K	Kills from cursor forward to and including LINEFEED
CONTROL-U **0** CONTROL-K	Kills from cursor backward to beginning of this line
META-z *char*	Kills up to, but not including, next occurrence of *char*
META-w	Copies Region to Kill Ring; does not erase from buffer
CONTROL-W	Kills Region
CONTROL-Y	Yanks most recently killed text into current buffer at Point; sets Mark at beginning of this text, with Point and cursor at the end
META-y	Erases just-yanked text, rotates Kill Ring, and yanks next item (only after CONTROL-Y or META-y)

Searching

CONTROL-S	Incrementally prompts for a string and searches forward for a match
CONTROL-S RETURN	Prompts for a complete string and searches forward for a match
CONTROL-R	Incrementally prompts for a string and searches backward for a match
CONTROL-R RETURN	Prompts for a complete string and searches backward for a match

META-CONTROL-S	Incrementally prompts for a regular expression and searches forward for a match
META---CONTROL-S RETURN	Prompts for a complete regular expression and searches forward for a match
META-x **isearch-backward-regexp**	Incrementally prompts for a regular expression and searches backward for a match
META-x **isearch-backward-regexp** RETURN	Prompts for a complete regular expression and searches backward for a match

Online Help

CONTROL-H **a**	Prompts for *string* and then shows a list of commands whose names contain *string*
CONTROL-H **b**	Shows a table (it is long) of all the key bindings now in effect
CONTROL-H **c** *key-sequence*	Prints the name of the command bound to this *key-sequence*
CONTROL-H **k** *key-sequence*	Prints the name and documentation of the command bound to this *key-sequence*
CONTROL-H **f**	Prompts for the name of a Lisp function and prints the documentation for that function
CONTROL-H **i** (lowercase "eye")	Takes you to the top menu of **info**, a documentation browser
CONTROL-H **l** (lowercase "ell")	Shows the last 100 characters typed
CONTROL-H **m**	Shows the documentation and special key bindings for the current Major mode
CONTROL-H **n**	Shows the **emacs** news file
CONTROL-H **t**	Runs an **emacs** tutorial session
CONTROL-H **v**	Prompts for a Lisp variable name and gives the documentation for that variable
CONTROL-H **w**	Prompts for a command name and gives the key sequence, if any, bound to that command

Region

META-W	Copies the Region nondestructively to the Kill Ring
CONTROL-W	Kills the Region
META-x **print-region**	Sends the Region to the print spooler
META-x **append-to-buffer**	Prompts for buffer name and appends Region to that buffer
META-x **append-to-file**	Prompts for filename and appends region to that file
CONTROL-X CONTROL-U	Converts Region to uppercase
CONTROL-X CONTROL-L	Converts Region to lowercase

Lines

META-x **occur**	Prompts for a regular expression and lists each line with a match for the expression in a buffer named ✷Occur✷
META-x **delete-matching-lines**	Prompts for a regular expression and deletes each line with a match for that expression
META-x **delete-nonmatching-lines**	Prompts for a regular expression and deletes each line that does *not* match that expression

Replacement: Unconditional and Interactive

META-x **replace-string**	Prompts for a string and new string, replaces every instance of the string with the new string, and sets Mark at the start of the command
META-% *or* META-x **query-replace**	As above but queries for replacement of each instance of *string*
META-x **replace**-regexp	Prompts for a regular expression and new string, replaces every instance of the regular expression with the new string, and sets Mark at the start of the command
META-x **query-replace-regexp**	As above but queries for replacement of each instance of the regular expression

Replacement Query Responses

RETURN	Does not do any more replacements; quits now
SPACE	Makes this replacement and goes on
DELETE	Does *not* make this replacement; skips over it and goes on
, (comma)	Makes this replacement, displays the result, and asks for another command
. (period)	Makes this replacement and quits searching
! (exclamation point)	Replaces this and all remaining instances without asking any more questions

Windows

CONTROL-X **b**	Switches buffer that window views
CONTROL-X **2**	Splits current window vertically into two
CONTROL-X **3**	Splits current window horizontally into two
CONTROL-X **o** (lowercase "oh")	Selects other window
META-CONTROL-V	Scrolls other window
CONTROL-X **4b**	Prompts for buffer name and selects it in other window
CONTROL-X **4f**	Prompts for filename and selects it in other window
CONTROL-X **0** (zero)	Deletes current window
CONTROL-X **1**	Deletes all but current window
META-x **shrink-window**	Makes current window one line shorter
CONTROL-X **^**	Makes current window one line taller
CONTROL-X **}**	Makes current window one character wider
CONTROL-X **{**	Makes current window one character narrower

Files

CONTROL-X CONTROL-F	Prompts for a filename and reads its contents into a freshly created buffer; assigns the file's simple filename as the buffer name.
CONTROL-X CONTROL-V	Prompts for a filename and reads its contents into the current buffer (overwriting the contents of the current buffer).
CONTROL-X **4** CONTROL-F	Prompts for a filename and reads its contents into a freshly created buffer. Assigns the file's simple filename as the buffer name. Creates a new window for this buffer and selects that window. This command splits the screen in half if you begin with only one window.
CONTROL-X CONTROL-S	Saves the current buffer to the original file.
CONTROL-X **S**	Prompts for whether to save each modified buffer (y/n).
META-x **set-visited-file-name**	Prompts for a filename and sets this name as the current buffer's "original" name.
CONTROL-X CONTROL-W	Prompts for a filename, sets this name as the "original" file for the current buffer, and saves the current buffer into that file.
META-~ (tilde)	Clears modified flag from the current buffer. Use with caution.

Buffers

CONTROL-X CONTROL-S	Saves the current buffer into its associated file.
CONTROL-X CONTROL-F	Prompts for a filename and visits that file.
CONTROL-X **b**	Prompts for a buffer name and selects it. If it does not exist, creates it first.
CONTROL-X **4b**	Prompts for a buffer name and selects it in another window. The existing window is not disturbed, although the new window may overlap it.
CONTROL-X CONTROL-B	Creates a buffer named ☀Buffer List☀ and displays it in another window. The existing window is not disturbed, although the new window may overlap it. The new buffer is not selected. In the ☀Buffer List☀ buffer, each buffer's data is shown with name, size, mode(s), and original filename.

META-x **rename-buffer**	Prompts for a new buffer name and gives this new name to the current buffer.
CONTROL-X CONTROL-Q	Toggles the current buffer's readonly status and the associated %% Mode Line indicator.
META-x **append-to-buffer**	Prompts for buffer name and appends the current Region to the end of that buffer.
META-x **prepend-to-buffer**	Prompts for buffer name and appends the current Region to the end of that buffer.
META-x **copy-to-buffer**	Prompts for buffer name and deletes the contents of the buffer before copying the current Region into that buffer.
META-x **insert-buffer**	Prompts for buffer name and inserts the entire contents of that buffer into the current buffer at Point.
CONTROL-X **k**	Prompts for buffer name and deletes that buffer.
META-x **kill-some-buffers**	Goes through the entire buffer list and offers the chance to delete each buffer.

Shell Commands: Foreground

These commands may not work with all shells.	
META-! (exclamation point)	Prompts for a shell command, executes it, and displays the output
CONTROL-U META-! (exclamation point)	Prompts for a shell command, executes it, and inserts the output at Point
META-| (vertical bar)	Prompts for a shell command, gives the Region contents as input, filters it through the command, and displays the output
CONTROL-U META-| (vertical bar)	Prompts for a shell command, gives the Region contents as input, filters it through the command, deletes the old Region contents, and inserts the output in that position

Shell Commands: Background

META-x **compile**	Prompts for a shell command and runs it in the background, with output going to a buffer named ✻compilation✻
META-x **kill-compilation**	Kills the background process

Case Conversion

META-l (lowercase "ell")	Converts word to the right of Point to lowercase
META-u	Converts word to the right of Point to uppercase
META-c	Converts word to the right of Point to initial caps
CONTROL-X CONTROL-L	Converts Region between Point and Mark to lowercase
CONTROL-X CONTROL-U	Converts Region between Point and Mark to uppercase

C Mode

CONTROL-META-f	Moves forward over an expression.
CONTROL-META-b	Moves backward over an expression.
CONTROL-META-k	Kills an expression forward. It leaves Point at the same finishing position as CONTROL-Z f, but kills the expression it traverses.
CONTROL-META-@	Sets Mark at the position CONTROL-Z f would move to, without changing Point.
CONTROL-META-a	Moves to the beginning of the most recent function definition.
CONTROL-META-e	Moves to the end of the next function definition.
CONTROL-META-h	Puts Point at the beginning and Mark at the end of the current (or next, if between) function definition.

Shell Mode

RETURN	Sends the current line to the shell
CONTROL-C CONTROL-D	Sends CONTROL-D to shell or its subshell
CONTROL-C CONTROL-C	Sends CONTROL-C to shell or its subshell
CONTROL-C CONTROL-\	Sends quit signal to shell or its subshell
CONTROL-C CONTROL-Ux	Kills the text on the current line not yet completed
CONTROL-C CONTROL-R	Scrolls back to beginning of last shell output, putting the first line of output at the top of the window
CONTROL-C CONTROL-O	Deletes the last batch of shell output

Exercises

1. Given a buffer full of English text, answer the following questions:

   a. How would you change every instance of his to hers?

   b. How would you do this only in the final paragraph?

   c. Is there a way to look at every usage in context before changing it?

   d. How would you deal with the possibility that His might begin a sentence?

2. What command moves the cursor to the end of the current paragraph? Can you use this command to skip through the buffer in one-paragraph steps?

3. Suppose that you get lost in the middle of typing a long sentence.

   a. Is there an easy way to kill the botched sentence and start over?

   b. What if only one word is incorrect? Is there an alternative to backspacing one letter at a time?

4. After you have been working on a paragraph for a while, most likely some lines will have become too short and others too long. Is there a command to "neaten up" the paragraph without rebreaking all the lines by hand?

5. Is there a way to change the whole buffer to capital letters? Can you think of a way to change just one paragraph?

6. How would you reverse the order of two paragraphs?

7. How would you reverse two words?

8. Imagine that you saw a Usenet posting with something particularly funny in it and saved the posting to a file. How would you incorporate this file into your own buffer? What if you wanted only a couple of paragraphs? How would you add > to the beginning of each included line?

9. On the keyboard alone emacs has always offered a full set of editing possibilities. For any editing task there are generally several techniques that will accomplish the same goal. In the X environment the choice is enlarged still further with a new group of mouse-oriented visual alternatives. From these options you must select the way that you like to solve a given editing puzzle best.

   Consider this Shakespeare fragment:

   ```
    1. Full fathom five thy father lies;
    2.    Of his bones are coral made;
    3. Those are pearls that were his eyes:
    4.    Nothing of him that doth fade,
    5. But doth suffer a sea-change
    6. Into something rich and strange.
    7. Sea-nymphs hourly ring his knell:
    8.              Ding-dong.
    9. Hark! now I hear them--
   10.      Ding-dong, bell!
   ```

   That fragment has been typed with some errors:

   ```
    1. Full fathiom five tyy father lies;
    2. These are pearls that were his eyes:
    3.    Of his bones are coral made;
    4.    Nothin of him that doth fade,
    5. But doth susffer a sea-change
    6. Into something rich and strange.
    7. Sea-nymphs hourly ring his knell:
    8.              Ding=dong.
    9. Hard! now I hear them--
   10.      Ding-dong, bell!
   ```

   Use only the keyboard to answer the following:

   a. How many ways can you think of to move the cursor to the spelling errors?

   b. Once the cursor is on or near the errors, how many ways can you think of to fix them?

c. Are there ways to fix errors without explicitly navigating to/searching for them? How many can you think of?

d. Lines 2 and 3 are transposed. How many ways can you think of to correct this situation?

Use the mouse to answer the following:

e. How do you navigate the cursor to a spelling error?

f. Once the cursor is on or near the errors, how many ways can you think of to fix them?

g. Lines 2 and 3 are transposed. Is there a visually oriented way to fix them?

h. Is there a visual way to correct multiple errors (similar to META-%)?

Advanced Exercises

10. Assume that your buffer contains the C code shown here, with the Major mode set for C and the cursor positioned at the end of the **while** line as shown by the black square:

```
/*
 * Copy string s2 to s1.   s1 must be large enough
 * return s1
 */
char *
strcpy(s1, s2)
register char *s1, *s2;
{
      register char *os1;

      os1 = s1;
      while (*s1++ = *s2++)
        ;
return(os1);
}

/* Copy source into dest, stopping after '\0' is copied, and
     return a pointer to the '\0' at the end of dest.   Then our caller
     can concatenate to the dest string without another strlen call. */
char *
stpcpy (dest, source)
     char *dest;
     char *source;
{
```

```
    while ((*dest++ = *source++) != '\0') ■
        ; /* void loop body */
    return (dest - 1);
}
```

a. What command moves the cursor to the opening brace of **strcpy**? What command moves the cursor past the closing brace? Can you use these commands to skip through the buffer in one-procedure steps?

b. Assume the cursor is just past the closing parenthesis of the **while** condition. How do you move to the matching opening parenthesis? How do you move back to the matching close parenthesis again? Does the same command set work for matched [] and {}? How does this differ from the vi % command?

c. One procedure is indented in the Berkeley indention style; the other is indented in the GNU style. What command reindents a line in accordance with the current indention style you have set up? How would you reindent an entire procedure?

d. Suppose that you want to write five string procedures and intend to use **strcpy** as a starting point for further editing. How would you make five duplicate copies of the **strcpy** procedure?

e. How would you compile the code without leaving emacs?

IN THIS CHAPTER

The Shell II: The Bourne Again Shell

12

Although it focuses on the Bourne Again Shell, much of this chapter also applies to the Z Shell. The chapter notes where the zsh or tcsh implementation of a feature differs from that of bash; if appropriate, you are directed to the place in this book where the alternative implementation is discussed. Chapter 13 explores control flow commands and more advanced aspects of Bourne Again and Z Shell programming in detail.

The Bourne Again Shell (bash), TC Shell (tcsh), and Z Shell (zsh) are command interpreters and high-level programming languages. As command interpreters, these shells process commands that you enter on the command line in response to a prompt. When you use it as a programming language, a shell processes groups of commands stored in files called *shell scripts*. Like other languages, shells have variables and control flow commands (for example, **for** loops and **if** statements).

Using a shell, you can customize the environment you work in. You can make your prompt display the name of the working directory, create a function or alias for cp that keeps it from overwriting certain kinds of files, take advantage of keyword variables to change aspects of how the shell works, and so on. You can also write shell scripts that do your bidding (from a one-line script that stores a long and complex command so you do not have to retype it to a longer script that runs a set of reports, automatically generating parameters for the reports based on the day of the week, the month, or the phase of the moon), print them, and mail you a reminder when the job is done. Perhaps the script automatically mails the reports to the intended recipients. More complex shell scripts are themselves programs; they do not just run other programs (see Chapters 13 through 15 for examples).

Always make the Bourne Again Shell your primary root shell in single-user mode. All system shell scripts are written to run under the Bourne Again Shell; if you will ever be working in single-user mode as when you boot your system or do system maintenance, administration, or repair work, it is a good idea at least to become familiar with this shell.

Without repeating the material in "Filename Generation/Pathname Expansion" on page 157 of Chapter 5, this chapter expands on the interactive features of the shell described in Chapter 5, explains how to create and run simple shell scripts, introduces the basic aspects of shell programming, and describes command line expansion. Chapter 14 covers interactive use of the TC Shell and TC Shell programming, and Chapter 15 explores some of the Z Shell features that are absent from the Bourne Again Shell and presents some more challenging shell programming problems.

All the advanced shell chapters (12–15) discuss each of the shells as appropriate, giving page references for more details of a topic within a specific shell. The [1] symbol indicates which shells a particular utility, builtin, or variable is a part of.

Background

The Bourne Again Shell is based on the Bourne Shell (an early UNIX shell that this book refers to as the *original Bourne Shell* to avoid confusion), which was written

---

1. Refer to "Shell Specifier" on page 26 for an explanation of the symbol.

Shell Programming || tip

Because many users prefer the Bourne Again Shell's programming language to that of the TC Shell and because it shares many common features with the Z Shell programming language, this and the following chapter describe **bash** (and **zsh**) programming in detail.

by Steve Bourne of AT&T's Bell Laboratories. Over the years the original Bourne Shell has been expanded and is still the basic shell provided with many commercial versions of UNIX.

Because of its long and successful history, the Bourne Shell has been used to write many of the shell scripts that help manage UNIX systems. Some of these scripts appear in GNU/Linux as Bourne Again Shell scripts. Although **bash** includes many extensions and features not found in the Bourne Shell, **bash** maintains compatibility with the Bourne Shell so you can run Bourne Shell scripts under **bash**. Traditionally, the Bourne Shell is named **sh**. On GNU/Linux systems **sh** is a symbolic link to **bash** so that scripts that require the presence of the Bourne Shell still run.

System V UNIX introduced the Korn Shell (**ksh**), written by David Korn. This shell extended many features of the Bourne Shell and then added many new features. Some of the features of the Bourne Again Shell, such as command aliases and command line editing, are based on similar features found in the Korn Shell. If you are familiar with the Korn Shell, you may prefer to use the Z Shell, discussed in Chapter 15, because it more closely resembles the Korn Shell.

The POSIX standardization group has defined a standard for shell functionality (POSIX 1003.2). The Bourne Again Shell provides the features that match the requirements of this POSIX standard. Efforts are under way to make the Bourne Again Shell fully comply with the POSIX standard. In the meantime, if you invoke **bash** with the **––posix** option, the behavior of the Bourne Again Shell will more closely match the POSIX requirements.

Shell Basics

This section covers variables and assignment statements and how to write a simple shell script and make it executable.

Assignment Statements

The Bourne Again, TC, and Z Shells allow you to create and use variables. The rules for naming and referring to variables are similar in all three shells (page 566).

You assign values to variables in the Bourne Again and Z Shells with the following syntax:

VARIABLE=value

There can be no whitespace on either side of the equal (=) sign. If you want to include SPACEs in the value of the variable, put quotation marks around the value or quote the SPACEs.

In all three shells you reference the value of a variable by preceding the variable name with a dollar sign and enclosing it in braces, as in ${VARIABLE}. The braces are optional unless the name of the variable is followed by a letter, digit, or underscore. Also, the Bourne Again Shell refers to the arguments on its command line by position, using the special variables $1, $2, $3, and so forth up to $9. If you wish to refer to arguments past the ninth, you must use braces, as in ${10}. The name of the command is held in $0.

You can unset (remove the variable's value and attributes) one or more variables with the unset builtin `bash tcsh zsh`:[2]

```
$ unset PREF SUFF
```

The Bourne Again Shell permits you to put variable assignments on a command line. These assignments are local to the command shell, that is, they apply to the command only. The following command runs **my_script** with the value of **TEMPDIR** set to ~/temp:

```
$ TEMPDIR=~/temp my_script
```

The **TEMPDIR** variable is set only in the shell that is spawned to execute **my_script**. It is not set, or if it is already set, it is not changed, in the interactive shell you are executing the script from.

Under bash you can place the assignments anywhere on the command line. (The Z Shell requires you to place assignments at the beginning of the line.)

Writing a Simple Shell Script

A *shell script* is a file that contains commands that the shell can execute. The commands in a shell script can be any commands you can enter in response to a shell prompt. For example, a command in a shell script might run a GNU/Linux utility, a compiled program you have written, or another shell script. As with commands you give on the command line, a command in a shell script can use ambiguous file

---

2. A *builtin* (page 161) is a command that is built into and is part of the shells named within the shaded rectangle following its name (`bash tcsh zsh` [page 26]). Give the command **help | less** to see a list of bash builtins.

references and can have its input or output redirected from/to a file or sent through a pipe (page 151). You can also use pipes and redirection with the input and output of the script itself.

In addition to the commands you would ordinarily use on the command line, *control flow* commands (also called *control structures*) find most of their use in shell scripts. This group of commands enables you to alter the order of execution of commands in a script as you would alter the order of execution of statements using a typical structured programming language. Refer to "Control Structures" on page 626 `bash`, page 714 `tcsh`, and page 768 `zsh` for specifics.

The easiest way to run a shell script is to give its filename on the command line. The shell then interprets and executes the commands in the script, one after another. By using a shell script, you can simply and quickly initiate a complex series of tasks or a repetitive procedure.

chmod: Makes a File Executable

To execute a shell script by giving its name as a command, you must have permission to read and execute the file that contains the script (refer to "Access Permissions" on page 118). Execute permission tells the shell and the system that the owner, group, or public has permission to execute the file; it implies that the content of the file is executable.

When you create a shell script using an editor, the file does not typically have its execute permission set. The following example shows a file, **whoson**, that is a shell script containing three command lines:

```
$ cat whoson
date
echo Users Currently Logged In
who

$ whoson
bash: ./whoson: Permission denied
```

Command Not Found?   ‖ tip

When you type **whoson** in response to a shell prompt and get an error message saying `bash: whoson: command not found`, your login shell is not set up to search for executable files in the working directory. Give this command:

```
$ ./whoson
```

The `./` explicitly tells the shell to look for an executable file in the working directory. To change your environment so that the shell searches the working directory automatically, refer to the **PATH** variable on page 577.

```
$ ls -l whoson
-rw-rw-r--   1 alex     group                40 May 24 11:30 whoson

$ chmod u+x whoson
$ ls -l whoson
-rwxrw-r--   1 alex       group                40 May 24 11:30 whoson

$ whoson
Sat May 24 11:40:49 PST 2003
Users Currently Logged In
jenny    pts/7    May 23 18:17
hls      pts/1    May 24 09:59
scott    pts/12   May 24 06:29 (bravo.tcorp.com)
alex     pts/4    May 24 09:08
```

Figure 12-1   Using chmod to make a shell script executable

When you create a file such as **whoson**, you cannot execute it by giving its name as a command because you do not have execute permission for the file.

The shell does not recognize **whoson** as an executable file and issues an error message when you try to execute it. You can execute it by giving the filename as an argument to bash (**bash whoson**). When you do this, bash takes the argument to be a shell script and executes it. In this case bash is executable, and **whoson** is an argument that bash executes so you do not need to have permission to execute **whoson**. You can do the same with tcsh and zsh.

You can use chmod (pages 119 and 1103) to change the access privileges associated with a file. Figure 12-1 shows ls with the –l option displaying the access privileges of **whoson** before and after chmod gives the owner execute permission.

The first ls displays a hyphen (–) as the fourth character, indicating that the owner does not have permission to execute the file. Then chmod uses an argument to give the owner execute permission. The **u+x** causes chmod to add (**+**) execute permission (**x**) for the owner (**u**). (The **u** stands for *user*, although it means the owner of the file who may be the user of the file at any given time.) The second argument is the name of the file. The second ls shows an **x** in the fourth position, indicating that the owner now has execute permission.

If other users are going to execute the file, you must also change group and/or public access privileges. Any user must have execute access to a file to use the file's name as a command. If the file is a shell script (a shell command file), the user trying to execute the file must also have read access to the file. You do not need read access to execute a binary executable (compiled program). Finally, the shell executes the file when its name is given as a command. For more information refer to "Access Permissions" (page 118) and to ls and chmod in Part III.

Now you know how to write and execute simple shell scripts. The sections "Separating and Grouping Commands" (following) and "Redirecting Standard Error" (page 552) describe features that are useful when you are running commands either on a command line or from within a script. The section "Job Control" (page 554) explains the relationships between commands and GNU/Linux system processes.

Separating and Grouping Commands

This section applies to the Bourne Again, TC, and Z Shells. Whether you give the shell commands interactively or write a shell script, you must separate commands from one another. This section reviews the ways to do this that were covered in Chapter 5 and introduces a few new ones.

; and NEWLINE   Separate Commands

The NEWLINE character is a unique command separator because it initiates execution of the command preceding it. You have seen this throughout this book each time you press the RETURN key at the end of a command line.

The semicolon (;) is a command separator that *does not* initiate execution of a command and *does not* change any aspect of how the command functions. You can execute a series of commands sequentially by entering them on a single command line and separating them with a semicolon (;). You initiate execution of the sequence of commands by pressing RETURN:

```
$ x ; y ; z
```

If **x**, **y**, and **z** are commands, the preceding command line yields the same results as the next three commands. The difference is that in the next example, the shell issues a prompt after each of the commands (**x**, **y**, and **z**) finishes executing, whereas the preceding command line causes the shell to issue a prompt only after **z** is complete:

```
$ x
$ y
$ z
```

Although the whitespace around the semicolons in the earlier example makes the command line easier to read, it is not necessary. None of the command separators needs to be surrounded by SPACEs or TABs.

\   Continues a Command

When you enter a long command line and the cursor reaches the right side of your screen or window, you can use a backslash (\) character to continue the command on the next line. The backslash quotes, or escapes, the NEWLINE character that follows it so that the shell does not treat it as the command terminator (page 55).

| and &   Separate Commands and Do Something Else

Other command separators are the pipe symbol (|) and the background task symbol (&). These command separators *do not* start execution of a command but *do* change some aspect of how the command functions. The pipe symbol alters the source of standard input or the destination of standard output, and the background task symbol causes the shell to execute the task in the background so you get a prompt back right away and can continue working on other things.

Each of the following command lines initiates a single job comprising three tasks:

```
$ x | y | z
$ ls -l | grep tmp | less
```

In the first job, the shell directs the output from task **x** to task **y** and directs **y**'s output to **z**. Because the shell runs the entire job in the foreground, you do not get a prompt back until task **z** runs to completion: Task **z** does not finish until task **y** finishes, and task **y** does not finish until task **x** finishes. In the second job, task **x** is an **ls –l** command, task **y** is **grep tmp**, and task **z** is the pager, **less**. You end up with a long (wide) listing of the filenames of all the files in the working directory that contain the string tmp, piped through less.

The next command line executes tasks **d** and **e** in the background and task **f** in the foreground:

```
$ d & e & f
[1] 14271
[2] 14272
```

The shell displays the job number between brackets [bash tcsh zsh] and the PID (process identification) number for each process running in the background. You get a prompt back as soon as **f** finishes.

Before displaying a prompt for a new command, the shell checks whether any background jobs have completed. For each job that has completed, the shell [bash tcsh zsh] displays its job number, the word Done, and the command line that invoked the job; then the shell displays the prompt. When the job numbers are listed, the number of the last job started is followed by a + character, and the job number of the previous job is followed by a – character. Any other jobs listed show a SPACE character. After running the last command, the shell displays the following before issuing a prompt:

```
[1]-  Done                    d
[2]+  Done                    e
```

The following command line executes all three tasks as background jobs. You get a shell prompt immediately:

```
$ d & e & f &
[1] 14290
[2] 14291
[3] 14292
```

You can use pipes to send the output from one task to the next and an ampersand (&) to run the whole job as a background task. Again the prompt comes back
immediately. The shell regards the commands joined by a pipe as a single job. The
shell treats all pipes as single jobs, no matter how many tasks are connected with
the pipe (l) symbol or how complex they are. The TC Shell shows three processes
(all belonging to job 1) placed in the background. The Bourne Again and Z Shells
show only one process:

```
% x | y | z &
[1] 14302 14304 14306
%
```

Optional

Multitasking Demonstration

You can demonstrate sequential and concurrent processes running in both the foreground and the background. Create executable files named **a**, **b**, and **c**, and have
each file echo [bash tcsh zsh] its name over and over as file **a** does.

```
$ cat a
echo "aaaaaaaaaaaaaaaaaaaaaaaaaa"
echo "aaaaaaaaaaaaaaaaaaaaaaaaaa"
echo "aaaaaaaaaaaaaaaaaaaaaaaaaa"
echo "aaaaaaaaaaaaaaaaaaaaaaaaaa"
echo "aaaaaaaaaaaaaaaaaaaaaaaaaa"
```

Execute the files sequentially and concurrently, using the example command
lines from this section. When you execute two of these shell scripts sequentially, the
output of the second file follows the output of the first file. When you execute the
two files concurrently, their output is interspersed as control is passed back and
forth between the tasks (multitasking).[3] The results are not always identical because
GNU/Linux schedules jobs slightly differently each time they run. Concurrent execution does not guarantee faster completion than sequential execution, and all
background execution guarantees is a faster return of the prompt. Two sample runs
are shown here:

---

3. With faster computers and short programs, there may be no change of control back and forth: Each
program may finish before it is time to change control. Try a similar script, with 1,000 or more echo
commands, to see the switch. The command (a&b&c&) > **hold** redirects the output to the file named **hold**
for easier viewing. See the next section for information about parentheses on the command line.

```
$ a & b & c &
[1] 14717
[2] 14718
[3] 14719
$ aaaaaaaaaaaaaaaaaaaaaaaaaaa
aaaaaaaaaaaaaaaaaaaaaaaaaaaa
aaaaaaaaaaaaaaaaaaaaaaaaaaaa
aaaaaaaaaaaaaaaaaaaaaaaaaaaa
bbbbbbbbbbbbbbbbbbbbbbbbbbbb
cccccccccccccccccccccccccccc
aaaaaaaaaaaaaaaaaaaaaaaaaaaa
bbbbbbbbbbbbbbbbbbbbbbbbbbbb
bbbbbbbbbbbbbbbbbbbbbbbbbbbb
bbbbbbbbbbbbbbbbbbbbbbbbbbbb
bbbbbbbbbbbbbbbbbbbbbbbbbbbb
cccccccccccccccccccccccccccc
cccccccccccccccccccccccccccc
cccccccccccccccccccccccccccc
cccccccccccccccccccccccccccc

$ a & b & c &
[1] 14738
[2] 14739
[3] 14740
$ aaaaaaaaaaaaaaaaaaaaaaaaaaa
bbbbbbbbbbbbbbbbbbbbbbbbbbbb
cccccccccccccccccccccccccccc
bbbbbbbbbbbbbbbbbbbbbbbbbbbb
bbbbbbbbbbbbbbbbbbbbbbbbbbbb
bbbbbbbbbbbbbbbbbbbbbbbbbbbb
cccccccccccccccccccccccccccc
cccccccccccccccccccccccccccc
cccccccccccccccccccccccccccc
cccccccccccccccccccccccccccc
aaaaaaaaaaaaaaaaaaaaaaaaaaaa
aaaaaaaaaaaaaaaaaaaaaaaaaaaa
aaaaaaaaaaaaaaaaaaaaaaaaaaaa
aaaaaaaaaaaaaaaaaaaaaaaaaaaa
bbbbbbbbbbbbbbbbbbbbbbbbbbbb
```

( ) Groups Commands

You can use parentheses to group commands. The shell creates a copy of itself, called a *subshell*, for each group, treating each group of commands as a job and creating a new process to execute each of the commands (refer to "Process Structure" on page 560 for more information on creating subshells). Each subshell (job) has its own environment; among other things, this means that it has its own set of variables with values that can be different from those of other subshells.

The following command line executes commands **a** and **b** sequentially in the background while also executing **c** in the background. The shell prompt returns immediately:

```
$ (a ; b) & c &
15007
```

This example differs from the earlier example **a** & **b** & **c** & because tasks **a** and **b** are initiated sequentially, not concurrently.

Similarly, the following command line executes **a** and **b** sequentially in the background and, at the same time, executes **c** and **d** sequentially in the background. The subshell running **a** and **b** and the subshell running **c** and **d** run concurrently. The prompt returns immediately:

```
$ (a ; b) & (c ; d) &
15020
15021
$
```

In the following shell script, the second pair of parentheses creates a subshell to run the commands following the pipe. Because of these parentheses, the output of the first **tar** command is available for the second **tar** command, despite the intervening **cd** command. Without the parentheses, the output of the first **tar** command would be sent to **cd** and lost because **cd** does not process input from standard input. The **$1** and **$2** are shell variables that represent the first and second command line arguments (page 582). The first pair of parentheses, which creates a subshell to run the first two commands, is necessary so that users can call **cpdir** with relative pathnames. Without these parentheses, the first **cd** command would change the working directory of the script (and, consequently, the working directory of the second **cd** command); with the parentheses, only the working directory of the subshell is changed:

```
$ cat cpdir
(cd $1 ; tar -cf - . ) | (cd $2 ; tar -xvf - )
$ cpdir /home/alex/sources /home/alex/memo/biblio
```

This command line copies the files and subdirectories included in the **/home/alex/sources** directory to the directory named **/home/alex/memo/biblio**. This shell script is almost the same as using **cp** with the **–r** option. See "Process Structure" on page 560 for more information on creating subshells. Refer to Part III for more information on **cp** (page 1122) and **tar** (page 1343).

Redirecting Standard Error

Chapter 5 covered the concept of standard output and explained how to redirect a command's standard output. In addition to standard output, commands can send their output to another place: *standard error*. A command can send error messages to standard error to keep them from getting mixed up with the information it sends to standard output. Just as it does with standard output, the shell sends a command's standard error to the screen/window unless you redirect it. Unless you redirect one or the other, you may not know the difference between the output a command sends to standard output and the output it sends to standard error. This section covers the syntax used by the Bourne Again and Z Shells. See page 691 if you are using the TC Shell.

When you execute a program, the process running the program opens three *file descriptors*, which are places the program sends its output to and gets its input from: 0 (standard input), 1 (standard output), and 2 (standard error). The redirect output symbol (> [page 145]) is shorthand for **1>**, which tells the shell to redirect standard output. Similarly, **<** (page 147) is short for **<0**, which redirects standard input. The symbols **2>** redirect standard error. The program does not "know" where its input comes from nor where its output goes to; the shell takes care of that. For more information refer to "File Descriptors" on page 781.

The following examples demonstrate how to redirect standard output and standard error to different files and to the same file. When you run cat with the name of a file that does not exist and the name of a file that does exist, cat sends an error message to standard error and copies the file that does exist to standard output. Unless you redirect them, both messages appear on the screen/window:

```
$ cat y
This is y.
$ cat x y
cat: x: No such file or directory
This is y.
```

When you redirect standard output of a command by using the greater than (>) symbol, output sent to standard error is not affected and still appears on the screen:

```
$ cat x y > hold
cat: x: No such file or directory
$ cat hold
This is y.
```

Similarly, when you send standard output through a pipe, standard error is not affected. The following example sends standard output of cat through a pipe to tr (translate), which in this example converts lowercase characters to uppercase. The text that cat sends to standard error is not translated because it goes directly to the screen/window rather than through the pipe:

```
$ cat x y | tr "[a-z]" "[A-Z]"
cat: x: No such file or directory
THIS IS Y.
```

The following example redirects standard output and standard error to different files. The notation **2>** tells the shell where to redirect standard error (file descriptor 2). The **1>** tells the shell where to redirect standard output (file descriptor 1). You can use **>** in place of **1>**:

```
$ cat x y 1> hold1 2> hold2
$ cat hold1
This is y.
$ cat hold2
cat: x: No such file or directory
```

In the next example **1>** redirects standard output to **hold**. Then **2>&1** declares file descriptor 2 to be a duplicate of file descriptor 1. The result is that both standard output and standard error are redirected to **hold**:

```
$ cat x y 1> hold 2>&1
$ cat hold
cat: x: No such file or directory
This is y.
```

In the preceding example **1> hold** precedes **2>&1**. If they had been listed in the opposite order, standard error would have been redirected to be a duplicate of standard output before standard output was redirected to **hold**. In that case only standard output would have been redirected to the file **hold**.

The next example declares file descriptor 2 to be a duplicate of file descriptor 1 and sends the output for file descriptor 1 through a pipe to the tr command:

```
$ cat x y 2>&1 | tr "[a-z]" "[A-Z]"
CAT: X: NO SUCH FILE OR DIRECTORY
THIS IS Y.
```

You can also use **1>&2** to redirect standard output of a command to standard error. This technique is often used in shell scripts to send the output of echo to standard error. In the following script, standard output of the first echo is redirected to standard error:

```
$ cat message_demo
echo This is an error message. 1>&2
echo This is not an error message.
```

If you redirect standard output of **message_demo**, error messages such as the one produced by the first echo still go to the screen/window because you have not redirected standard error. Because standard output of a shell script is typically redirected to another file, this technique is often used so that error messages generated by the script are displayed on the screen. The **lnks** script (page 635) and several other scripts in the next chapter use this technique. You can also use the exec *builtin* to create additional file descriptors and to redirect standard input, standard output, and standard error of a shell script from within the script (page 665).

noclobber: Avoids Overwriting Files

Setting the **noclobber** variable prevents you from accidentally overwriting a file when you redirect output to the file. To override **noclobber**, put a pipe symbol after the symbol you use for redirecting or appending output (for example >| and >>|).

In the following example the user creates or overwrites a file named **a** by redirecting the output of date to the file. Next, the user sets the **noclobber** variable and tries redirecting output to **a** again. The shell returns an error message. Then the user tries the same thing but using a pipe symbol after the redirect symbol: The shell allows the user to overwrite the file. Finally, the user unsets **noclobber** (using a plus sign in place of the dash) and verifies that it is no longer set:

```
$ date > a
$ set -o noclobber
$ date > a
bash: a: Cannot overwrite existing file
$ date >| a
$ set +o noclobber
$ date > a
```

For more information on **noclobber,** refer to page 713 (tcsh) and page 824 (zsh).

Job Control

A job is a command pipeline. You run a simple job whenever you give GNU/Linux a command (for example, type **date** on the command line and press RETURN: You have run a job). You can also create several jobs with multiple commands on a single command line:

```
$ find . -print | sort | lpr & grep -l alex /tmp/* > alexfiles &
[1] 18839
[2] 18876
```

The portion of the command line up to the first **&** is one job, consisting of three processes: (find [page 1165], sort [page 66], and lpr [page 63]) connected by pipes. The second job is a single process running grep. Both jobs have been put into the background by the trailing **&** characters, so bash does not wait for them to complete before giving you a prompt. Before the prompt, the shell displays information about each background job: its job number in brackets followed by the PID of the last process in the job.

Using job control, you can move commands from the foreground to the background and vice versa, stop commands temporarily, and get a list of the commands that are currently running or stopped.

jobs: Lists Jobs

The jobs builtin `bash tcsh zsh` lists all background jobs. The following sequence demonstrates what happens when you give the command **jobs** from the Bourne Again Shell. In the following example the sleep command run in the background creates a background job that jobs can report on, and jobs builtin displays job information:

```
$ sleep 60 &
[1] 7809
$ jobs
[1] + Running                    sleep 60&
```

fg: Brings a Job to the Foreground

The shell assigns a job number to commands that you run in the background (page 548). In the following example several jobs are started in the background. For each the Shell lists the job number and PID number immediately, just before it issues a prompt.

```
$ xman &
[1] 1246
$ date &
[2] 1247
$ Sun Dec 7 11:44:40 PST 2003
[2]+ Done            date
$ find /usr -name ace -print > findout &
[2] 1269
$ jobs
[1]- Running        xman &
[2]+ Running        find /usr -name ace -print > findout &
```

The jobs command lists the first job, xman, as job 1. The date command does not appear in the jobs list because it completed before jobs was run. Because the date command completed before find was run, the find command became job 2.[4]

---

4. Job numbers are discarded when a job is finished and can be reused. When you start or put a job in the background, the shell assigns the lowest number that is not in use and is not less than a job number that is currently in use.

To move a background job into the foreground, use the fg builtin [bash tcsh zsh] with a per-cent sign (%) followed by the job number as an argument. The following example moves job 2 into the foreground:

```
$ fg %2
```

You can also refer to a job by following the percent sign with a string that uniquely identifies the beginning of the command line used to start the job. Instead of the preceding command, for example, you could have used **fg %find** or **fg %f**, because either one uniquely identifies job 2. If you follow the percent sign with a question mark and a string, the string matches itself anywhere on the command line. In the preceding example, **%?ace** also refers to job 2.

Often the job you wish to bring into the foreground is the only job running in the background or is the job that jobs lists with a plus (+). In these cases you can use fg without any arguments.

bg: Sends a Job to the Background

To put the foreground job into the background, you must first suspend the job by pressing the suspend key (usually CONTROL-Z). Pressing the suspend key stops the job immediately. Once the job is suspended, use the bg builtin [bash tcsh zsh] to resume execution of the job, putting it in the background:

```
$ bg
```

If a background job attempts to read from the terminal, the shell stops it (puts it to sleep [pages 142 and 562]) and notifies you that the job has been stopped and is waiting for input. When this happens, you must move the job into the foreground so that it can read from the terminal. The shell displays the command line as it moves the job into the foreground:

```
$ (sleep 5; cat > mytext) &
[1] 1343
$ date
Sun Dec 7 11:58:20 PST 2003
[1]+ Stopped (tty input)    ( sleep 5; cat >mytext )
$ fg
( sleep 5; cat >mytext )
Remember to let the cat out!
CONTROL-D
```

In this example, the shell displays the job number and PID number of the background job as soon as it starts, followed by a prompt. At this point the user enters date, and its output appears on the screen. The shell waits until just before it issues a prompt (after date has finished) to notify you that job 1 is waiting for input. The reason for this delay is so that the notice does not disrupt your work: the default behavior of the shell. After the shell puts the job in the foreground, you can enter the input that the command was waiting for. Terminate the input with a CONTROL-D to signify EOF (end of file), and the shell displays another prompt.

The shell keeps you informed about changes in the status of a job, notifying you when a background job starts, completes, or is waiting for input from the terminal. The shell also lets you know when a foreground job is suspended. Because notices about a job being run in the background can disrupt your work, the shell delays these notices until it is ready to display a prompt.

If you try to leave a shell while jobs are stopped, the shell gives you a warning and does not allow you to exit. If, after the warning, you use jobs to review the list of jobs or you immediately try to leave the shell again, the shell allows you to leave and terminates your stopped jobs. Jobs that are running (not stopped) in the background continue to run. In the following example, find (job 1) continues to run after the second exit terminates the shell, but cat (job 2) is terminated:

```
$ find / -size +100k > $HOME/bigfiles 2>&1 &
[1] 1426
$ cat > mytest &
[2] 1428
$ exit
exit
There are stopped jobs.

[2]+ Stopped (tty input)    cat > mytext
$ exit

login:
```

Manipulating the Directory Stack

Using a shell ^{bash tcsh zsh}, you can store a list of directories you are working with, enabling you to move easily among them. The list is referred to as a *stack*. You can think of it as a stack of dinner plates; you typically add plates to and remove plates from the top of the stack: a first-in last-out, or *FILO*, stack.

dirs: Displays the Stack

The dirs builtin ^{bash tcsh zsh} displays the contents of the directory stack. If you call dirs when the directory stack is empty, it displays the name of the working directory:

```
$ dirs
~/literature
```

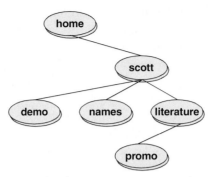

Figure 12-2 The directory structure in the examples

The dirs builtin uses a tilde (~) to represent the name of the user's home directory. The examples in the next several sections assume that you are referring to the directory structure shown in Figure 12-2.

pushd: Pushes a Directory on the Stack

To change directories and at the same time add a new directory to the top of the stack, use the pushd (push directory) builtin bash tcsh zsh. In addition to changing directories, the pushd builtin displays the contents of the stack. The following example is illustrated in Figure 12-3:

```
$ pushd ../demo
~/demo ~/literature
$ pwd
/home/scott/demo
$ pushd ../names
~/names ~/demo ~/literature
$ pwd
/home/scott/names
```

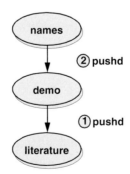

Figure 12-3 Creating a directory stack

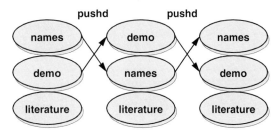

Figure 12-4   Using pushd to change working directories

When you use pushd without an argument, it swaps the top two directories on the stack and makes the new top directory (which was the second directory) the new working directory (Figure 12-4):

```
$ pushd
~/demo ~/names ~/literature
$ pwd
/home/scott/demo
```

Using pushd in this way, you can easily move back and forth between two directories. To access another directory in the stack, call pushd with a numeric argument preceded by a plus sign. The directories in the stack are numbered starting with the top directory, which is number 0. The following pushd command changes the working directory to **literature** and moves it to the top of the stack:

```
$ pushd +2
~/literature ~/demo ~/names
$ pwd
/home/scott/literature
```

popd: Pops a Directory off the Stack

To remove a directory from the stack, use the popd (pop directory) builtin `bash tcsh zsh`. As Figure 12-5 shows, without an argument popd removes the top directory from the stack and changes the working directory to the new top directory:

```
$ popd
~/demo ~/names
$ pwd
/home/scott/demo
```

To remove a directory other than the top one from the stack, use popd with a numeric argument preceded by a plus sign:

```
$ popd +1
~/demo
$ pwd
/home/scott/demo
```

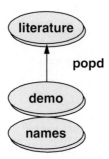

Figure 12-5   Using popd to remove a directory from the stack

If you remove a directory other than directory number 0 on the stack, this command does not change the working directory.

Processes

A *process* is the execution of a command by GNU/Linux. The shell that starts up when you log in is a command, or a process, like any other. Whenever you give the name of a GNU/Linux utility on the command line, you initiate a process. When you run a shell script, another shell process is started, and additional processes are created for each command in the script. Depending on how you invoke the shell script, the script is run either by a new shell or by a subshell of the current shell. A process is not started when you run a shell builtin, such as cd ^{bash tcsh zsh}, from the command line or within a script. The information in this section pertains to the Bourne Again, TC, and Z Shells.

Process Structure

Like the file structure, the process structure is hierarchical, with parents, children, and even a *root*. A parent process *forks*[5] a child process, which in turn can fork other processes. (You can also use the term *spawn;* the words are interchangeable.) The operating system routine, or *system call,* that creates a new process is named **fork**. One of the first things GNU/Linux does to begin execution when a machine is started up is to start init, a single process, called a *spontaneous process,* with PID number 1. This process holds the same position in the process structure as the root directory does in the file structure: It is the ancestor of all processes that each user

---

5. The term *fork* is used to convey that, as with a fork in the road, one process turns into two. Initially the two forks are identical except that one is identified as the parent and one as the child.

works with. When the system is in multiuser mode, init runs getty or mingetty processes, which display login: prompts on the virtual consoles. When someone responds to the prompt and presses RETURN, getty hands control over to a utility named login, which checks the user's name and password combination. After the user logs in, the login process becomes the user's shell process.

Process Identification

GNU/Linux assigns a unique PID number at the inception of each process. As long as a process exists, it keeps the same PID number. During one session, the same process is always executing the login shell. When you fork a new process—for example when you use an editor—the PID number of the new (child) process is different from that of its parent process. When you return to the login shell, you will find that it is still being executed by the same process and has the same PID number as when you logged in.

The following interaction shows that the process running the shell forked (is the parent of) the process running ps (page 156). When you call it with the –l option, ps displays a long listing of information about each process. The line of the ps display with bash in the CMD column refers to the process running the shell. The column headed by PID lists the PID number. The column headed PPID lists the PID number of the *parent* of each of the processes. From the PID and PPID columns, you can see that the process running the shell (PID 2168) is the parent of the process running sleep (PID 2191). The parent PID number of sleep is the same as the PID number of the shell (2168):

```
$ sleep 10 &
[1] 2891
$ ps -l
  F S   UID   PID  PPID  C PRI  NI ADDR     SZ WCHAN  TTY          TIME CMD
100 S   500  2168  2167  0  72   0    -     454 wait4  pts/1    00:00:00 bash
000 S   500  2891  2168  0  63   0    -     286 nanosl pts/1    00:00:00 sleep
000 R   500  2892  2168  0  76   0    -     628 -      pts/1    00:00:00 ps
```

Refer to page 1288 in Part III for more information on ps and all the columns it displays with the –l option. When you give another **ps –l** command, you can see that the shell is still being run by the same process but that it forked another process to run sleep:

```
$ sleep 10 &
[1] 2893
$ ps -l
  F S   UID   PID  PPID  C PRI  NI ADDR     SZ WCHAN  TTY          TIME CMD
100 S   500  2168  2167  0  71   0    -     454 wait4  pts/1    00:00:00 bash
000 S   500  2893  2168  0  63   0    -     286 nanosl pts/1    00:00:00 sleep
000 R   500  2894  2168  0  75   0    -     628 -      pts/1    00:00:00 ps
```

You can also use pstree to see the parent/child relationship of processes. The next example shows the **–p** option to pstree, which causes it to display PID numbers:

```
$ pstree -p
init(1)-+-adsl-connect(1591)---pppd(1619)---pppoe(1620)
        |-apmd(832)
        |-atd(1148)
        |-crond(1089)
        |-gpm(1047)
        |-httpd(1070)-+-httpd(1088)
        |                     '-httpd(1538)
        .
        .
        .
        |-nfsd(1000)
        |-nfsd(1001)
        |-nmbd(1112)
        |-ntpd(852)
        |-portmap(686)
        |-rhnsd(1170)
        |-rpc.mountd(989)
        |-rpc.rquotad(984)
        |-rpc.statd(714)
        |-rpciod(805)
        |-sendmail(1028)
        |-smbd(1107)---smbd(2118)
        |-sshd(909)
        |-syslogd(663)
        '-xinetd(942)
```

See the list starting on page 394 for information on some of the daemons listed by pstree. See "$$ PID Number" on page 586 for a description of how to instruct the shell to report on PID numbers.

Executing a Command

When you give it a command, the shell usually forks (spawns) a child process to execute the command. While the child process is executing the command, the parent process *sleeps*. While a process is sleeping, it does not use any computer time but remains inactive, waiting to wake up. When the child process finishes executing the command, it tells its parent of its success or failure via the exit status and dies. The parent process (which is running the shell) wakes up and prompts you for another command.

When you request that the shell run a process in the background by ending a command with an ampersand (**&**), the shell forks a child process without going to sleep and without waiting for the child process to run to completion. The parent process, executing the shell, reports the job number and PID number of the child and prompts you for another command. The child process runs in the background, independent of its parent.

Although the shell forks a process to run most of the commands you give it, some commands are built into the shell. The shell does not need to fork a process to run builtins. Each of the shell's info/man pages contains a list of builtin commands (page 161).

Within a given process, such as your login shell or a subshell, you can declare, initialize, read, and change variables. By default, however, a variable is local to a process. When a process forks a child process, the parent does not pass the value of a variable to the child. You can make the value of a variable available to child processes by using the export [bash zsh] builtin (page 571).

Running a Shell Script

Whenever you give it a command on the command line, the shell **fork**s a new process, creating a duplicate of the shell process (a subshell). The new process attempts to **exec**, or execute, the command. Like **fork**, the **exec** routine is executed by the operating system (a system call). If the command is an executable program, such as a compiled C program, **exec** succeeds, and the system overlays the newly created subshell with the executable program. If the command is a shell script, **exec** fails. When **exec** fails, the command is assumed to be a shell script, and the subshell runs the commands in the script. Unlike your login shell, which expects input from the command line, the subshell takes its input from a file: the shell script.

As discussed earlier, if you have a shell script in a file that you do not have execute permission for, you can run the commands in the script by using a bash command to **exec** a shell to run the script directly. In the following example, bash creates a new shell that takes its input from the file named **whoson**:

```
$ bash whoson
```

Because the bash command expects to read a file containing commands, you do not need execute permission for **whoson**. (However, you do need read permission.) Although bash reads and executes the commands in the file **whoson**, standard input, standard output, and standard error are still connected to the terminal. You can run tcsh and zsh scripts in the same manner.

Although you can use bash to execute a shell script, this technique causes the script to run more slowly than giving yourself execute permission and directly invoking the script. Users typically prefer to make the file executable and run the script by typing its name on the command line. It is also easier simply to type the name, and it is consistent with the way other kinds of programs are invoked (so you do not need to know whether you are running a shell script or another kind of program). However, if bash is not your interactive shell or if you want to see how the script runs with different shells, you should give the bash (or the name of another shell) command, followed by the name of the file containing the script, as shown earlier.

sh Does Not Call the Original Bourne Shell || caution

The original Bourne Shell was invoked with the command sh. Although you can call bash with an sh command, it is not the original Bourne Shell. It is a symbolic link to /bin/bash, so it is simply another name for the bash command. When you call bash using the command sh, bash tries to mimic the behavior of the original Bourne Shell as closely as possible. It does not always succeed.

#!   Specifies a Shell

You can also put a special sequence of characters on the first line of a shell script to indicate to the operating system that it is a script or another type of file. Because the operating system checks the initial characters of a program before attempting to **exec** it, these characters save the system from making an unsuccessful attempt and also tell the system which utility to use (usually bash, tcsh, or zsh). If #! are the first two characters of a script, the system interprets the characters that follow as the absolute pathname of the program that should execute the script. This can be the pathname of any program, not just a shell. The following example specifies that the current script should be run by bash:

```
$ cat sh_script
#!/bin/bash
echo "This is a Bourne Again Shell script."
```

This feature is also useful if you have a script intended to be run with a shell other than bash. The following example shows a script that is intended to be executed by tcsh:

```
$ cat tcsh_script
#!/usr/bin/tcsh
echo "This is a tcsh script."
set person = jenny
echo "person is $person"
```

The script can be run from any shell, but tcsh must execute it. Because of the #! line, the operating system sees to it that tcsh executes it no matter which shell you run it from.

Following is a demonstration program that displays the name of the shell it was run under:

```
$ cat whichshell
#!/bin/tcsh
ps -f | grep $0
$ whichshell
zach      5141   2168   0 14:36 pts/1     00:00:00 tcsh ./whichshell
zach      5143   5141   0 14:36 pts/1     00:00:00 grep ./whichshell
```

The –f option causes ps to display the full command line, which includes the name of the shell running the script. The $0 variable [bash tcsh zsh] holds the name of the calling program, so grep looks through the lines output by ps –f for the name of the program. It displays two lines: one for tcsh and the other for grep, which is running under tcsh.

If you do not follow the #! with the name of an executable program, the shell reports that it cannot find the command that you asked it to run. You can optionally follow #! with SPACEs. If you omit the #! line and try to run, for example, a tcsh script from bash, the shell generates error messages, or the script may just not run properly.

Begins a Comment

Comments make shell scripts and all code easier to read and maintain by you or by others. The comment syntax is common to the Bourne Again, TC, and Z Shells.

If a pound sign (#) in the first character position of the first line of a script is not immediately followed by an exclamation point (!) or if a pound sign occurs in any other location in a script, the shell interprets it as the beginning of a comment and ignores everything between the pound sign and the end of the line (the next NEWLINE character).

Startup Files

When a shell starts, it runs certain startup files (scripts) with commands in them to initialize itself. Which files the shell runs depends on whether it is a login shell, an interactive shell that is not a login shell, or a noninteractive shell—one used to execute shell scripts.

When bash is started as a login shell or if you use the **–login** option when starting a bash shell, bash first reads **/etc/profile** for commands. Then a bash login shell looks in your home directory for **.bash_profile** and executes it. Otherwise, it executes **.bash_login**. If neither of these files exists, bash executes **.profile** file. When you log out, this same shell reads and executes commands from the **.bash_logout** file in your home directory, if it exists (Table 12-1).

When bash is started as a nonlogin interactive shell (such as you get by giving the command **bash**), bash reads only the **.bashrc** file. However, this shell inherits any environment (exported) variables from the parent shell, so environment variables set in **/etc/profile** and **.bash_profile** are passed to the nonlogin shell.

Finally, nonlogin, noninteractive shells (shells that have standard input and standard output not connected to your terminal) look for the environment variable **BASH_ENV** and then **ENV**, if BASH_ENV does not exist. If either of these environment variables has a filename as a value, the shell reads and executes commands from this file.

Order of Execution of bash Startup Files || table 12-1

File	Interactive (Login) Shell	Noninteractive (Nonlogin) Shell
/etc/profile	First	Not executed, but the shell inherits from the parent shell variables that were originally set by these files.
.bash_profile	Second	
.bash_login	Second if no .bash_profile	
.profile	Second if no .bash_profile or .bash_login	
.bashrc	Executed only by interactive, nonlogin shells	Not executed.
BASH_ENV or ENV	Not executed	Execute the commands listed in the file named by one of these variables. When the shell is started in POSIX mode, the file named by ENV is executed using source. Otherwise, the file named by BASH_ENV is executed.
.bash_logout	Executed on logout	Not executed.

Although the numbers of shell types and initialization files might seem confusing, many bash users have only **.bash_profile** and **.bashrc** in their home directories. Most of the commands that they want all instances of bash to execute are placed into **.bashrc**, whereas **.bash_profile** includes a command to load and run commands from **.bashrc**, as well as an assignment of the string ~/.bashrc to the **ENV** variable. This way, **.bashrc** is executed, no matter how the shell gets started. You can put the following commands into **.bash_profile** to get this effect:

```
export ENV=~/.bashrc
if [ -f ~/.bashrc ]; then source ~/.bashrc; fi
```

Parameters and Variables

Within the shell, a *shell parameter* is associated with a value that is accessible to the user. There are several kinds of *shell parameters*. Parameters whose names consist of letters, digits, and underscores are often referred to as *shell variables,* or simply *variables.* A variable name must start with a letter or underscore, not with a number. Thus **A76, MY_CAT,** and **___X___** are valid variable names, whereas **69TH_STREET** (starts with a digit) and **MY-NAME** (contains a hyphen) are not. Shell variables that you can name and assign values to are *user-created variables.* One convention is to use only uppercase letters for names of global variables (*environment variables*) and to use mixed-case or lowercase letters for other variables. You can change the values of user-created variables at any time, and you can make them *readonly* so that their value cannot be changed. You can also make user-created variables global. A global variable is available to all shells and other programs you fork from the original shell.

When you want to assign a value to a variable in the Bourne Again and Z Shells, use its name with no SPACEs on either side of the equal sign:

```
$ myvar=abc
```

Refer to the beginning of Chapter 14 (page 681) if you are using tcsh.

When you want to use the value of a variable ^{bash} ^{tcsh} ^{zsh}, use its name preceded by a dollar sign (**$**):

```
$ echo $myvar
abc
```

Variables that have special meaning to the shell are called *keyword shell variables* (or simply *keyword variables*) and usually have short, mnemonic names. When you start a shell (by logging in, for example), the shell inherits several keyword variables from the environment. Among these variables are **HOME,** which identifies your home directory, and **PATH,** which determines what directories the shell searches and in what order to locate a command that you give the shell. The shell creates and initializes (with default values) other keyword variables when you start it; still other variables do not exist until you set them.

You can change the values of most of the keyword shell variables at any time, although it is usually not necessary to change the values of keyword variables initialized in **/etc/profile.** If you need to change the value of a variable, do so in one of the files in your home directory listed in the Interactive column of Table 12-1 on page 566 ^{bash} ^{zsh}. For more information see "Startup Files" on page 684 ^{tcsh}. Just as you can make user-created variables global, you can make keyword variables global; this is often done automatically when the shell starts. You can also make a keyword variable readonly.

The names of one group of parameters do not resemble variable names. Most of these parameters have one-character names (for example, **1, ?,** and **#**) and are referenced (as are all variables) by preceding the name with a dollar sign (for example, **$1, $?,** and **$#**). The values of these parameters reflect different aspects of your ongoing interaction with the shell. For example, whenever you give a command on the command line, each argument on the command line becomes the value of a *positional parameter*. Positional parameters enable you to access command line arguments, a capability that you will often require when you write sophisticated shell scripts. Other frequently needed shell script values, such as the name of the last command executed, the number of command line arguments, and the status of the most recently executed command, are available as *special parameters*. With the exception of the set builtin (page 584), you cannot assign values to positional and special parameters.

User-Created Variables

As described earlier, you can declare any sequence of letters, digits, and underscores as the name of a variable, as long as the first character is not a number. The first line in the following example declares the variable named **person** and initializes it with the value alex (use **set person = alex** in tcsh):

```
$ person=alex
$ echo person
person
$ echo $person
alex
```

When you assign a value to a variable in bash and zsh, *you must not precede or follow the equal sign with a* SPACE *or* TAB. Because the echo builtin `bash tcsh zsh` copies its arguments to standard output, you can use it to display the values of variables.

The second line shows that **person** does not represent alex. The string person is echoed as person. The shell substitutes the value of a variable only when you precede the name of the variable with a dollar sign ($). The command **echo $person** displays the value of the variable **person** but does not display $person because the shell does not pass $person to echo as an argument. Because of the leading $, the shell recognizes that $person is the name of a variable, *substitutes* the value of the variable, and passes that value to echo. The echo builtin displays the value of the variable, not its name, never knowing that you called it with a variable. The final command in the preceding example displays the value of the variable **person**.

You can prevent the shell from substituting the value of a variable by quoting the leading **$**:

```
$ echo $person
alex
$ echo "$person"
alex
$ echo '$person'
$person
$ echo \$person
$person
```

Double quotation marks do not prevent the substitution; single quotation marks or a backslash (\) does.

Because they do not prevent variable substitution but do turn off the special meanings of most other characters, double quotation marks are useful when you assign values to variables and when you use those values. To assign a value that contains SPACEs or TABs to a variable, use double quotation marks around the value. Although double quotation marks may not be required, it is a good idea to place them around variables whose values you are using, as you can see from the second following example:

```
$ person="alex and jenny"
$ echo $person
alex and jenny
```

When you reference a variable that contains TABs or multiple adjacent SPACEs, you need to use quotation marks to preserve the spacing. If you do not quote the variable, echo collapses each string of nonblank characters into a single SPACE when it copies them to standard output:

```
$ person="alex    and    jenny"
$ echo $person
alex and jenny
$ echo "$person"
alex    and    jenny
```

When you execute a command with a variable as an argument, the shell replaces the name of the variable with the value of the variable and passes that value to the program being executed. If the value of the variable contains a special character, such as * or ?, the shell *may* expand that variable.

The first line in the following sequence of commands assigns the string alex* to the variable **memo**. The Bourne Again Shell does *not expand the string*, because bash does not perform pathname expansion (page 157) when assigning a value to a variable. All shells process a command line in a specific order. Within this order the Bourne Again Shell (but not tcsh) expands variables before it interprets commands. In the following echo command line, the double quotation marks quote the asterisk (*) and prevent the Bourne Again Shell from expanding the **memo** variable before passing its value to the echo command:

```
$ memo=alex*
$ echo "$memo"
alex*
```

All shells interpret special characters as special when you reference a variable containing a special character that is not quoted. In the following example the shell expands the value of the **memo** variable because it is not quoted:

```
$ ls
alex.report
alex.summary
$ echo $memo
alex.report alex.summary
```

The preceding example shows that when you do not quote **memo**, the shell matches the value `alex*` to two files in the working directory: **alex.report** and **alex.summary**.

unset: Removes a Variable

Unless you remove a variable, it exists as long as the shell in which it was created exists. To remove the *value* of a variable but not the variable itself, set the value to null (use **set person =** in tcsh):

```
$ person=
$ echo $person

$
```

You can remove a variable with the unset builtin ░. To remove the variable **person**, give the following command:

```
$ unset person
```

readonly: Makes a Variable Permanent

You can use the readonly builtin ░ to ensure that the value of a variable cannot be changed. The next example declares the variable **person** to be readonly. You must assign a value to a variable *before* you declare it to be readonly; you cannot change its value after the declaration. When you attempt to change the value of a readonly variable, the shell displays an error message:

```
$ person=jenny
$ echo $person
jenny
$ readonly person
$ person=helen
bash: person: readonly variable
```

If you use the readonly builtin without an argument, it displays a list of all read-only shell variables. This list includes keyword variables that are automatically readonly, as well as any keyword or user-created variables that you have declared as readonly.

export: Makes a Variable Global

Variables are ordinarily local to the process in which they are declared: A shell script does not have access to variables declared in your login shell unless you explicitly make the variables available (global). You can use export ^{bash}_{zsh} to make a variable available to a child process. Use setenv ^{bash}_{tcsh} from the TC Shell to replace the assignment *and* the exporting required by bash (page 699). The examples in this section work with all shells if you use the proper syntax for assigning values to variables and for making them global.

Once you use the export builtin with a variable name as an argument, the shell places the value of the variable in the calling environment of child processes. This *call by value* gives each child process a copy of the variable for its own use.

The following **extest1** shell script assigns a value of american to the variable named **cheese** and then displays its filename (**extest1**) and the value of **cheese**. The **extest1** script then calls **subtest**, which attempts to display the same information. Then **subtest** declares a **cheese** variable and displays its value. When **subtest** finishes, it returns control to the parent process, which is executing **extest1**. Then **extest1** again displays the value of the original **cheese** variable.

```
$ cat extest1
cheese=american
echo "extest1 1: $cheese"
subtest
echo "extest1 2: $cheese"
$ cat subtest
echo "subtest 1: $cheese"
cheese=swiss
echo "subtest 2: $cheese"
$ extest1
extest1 1: american
subtest 1:
subtest 2: swiss
extest1 2: american
```

The **subtest** script never receives the value of **cheese** from **extest1**, and **extest1** never loses the value. Contrary to life, a child can never impact its parent's attributes. When it attempts to display the value of a variable that has not been declared, as is the case with **subtest**, a process displays nothing; the value of an undeclared variable is that of a null string.

The following script, **extest2**, is the same as **extest1** but uses export[6] to make **cheese** available to the **subtest** script:

---

6. Although it is rarely done, you can export a variable before you assign a value to it. Also, you do not need to export a variable a second time after you change its value.

```
$ cat extest2
export cheese
cheese=american
echo "extest2 1: $cheese"
subtest
echo "extest2 2: $cheese"
$ extest2
extest2 1: american
subtest 1: american
subtest 2: swiss
extest2 2: american
```

Here the child process inherits the value of **cheese** as american and, after displaying this value, changes *its copy* to swiss. When control is returned to the parent, the parent's copy of **cheese** still retains its original value: american.

declare: Sets Attributes and Values for a Shell Variable

The declare (same as typeset) builtin ^{bash}_{zsh} allows you to set attributes and values for shell variables. You can associate several attributes with a variable by using declare; five of these follow:

1. The –a option declares a variable as an array.

2. The –f option makes a variable a function name (functions are discussed on page 672).

3. The –i option marks a variable so that integer values are stored efficiently (this speeds up shell arithmetic involving the variable).

4. The –r option makes a variable readonly.

5. The –x option marks a variable for export.

The following commands declare several variables and set some attributes. The first line declares **person1** and assigns it a value of alex:

```
$ declare person1=alex
$ declare -r person2=jenny
$ declare -rx person3=helen
$ declare -x person4
```

The readonly and export builtins are synonyms for the commands **declare –r** and **declare –x**, respectively. It is legal to declare a variable without assigning a value to it, as the preceding declaration of the variable **person4** illustrates. This declaration makes **person4** available to all subshells and, until an assignment is made to the variable, it has a null value whenever it is referenced.

You can list the options to declare separately in any order. The following is equivalent to the declaration of **person3**:

```
$ declare -x -r person3=helen
```

Also, you can use the + character in place of – if you want to remove an attribute from a variable. After the following command is given, making an assignment to the variable **person3** does not result in an error:

```
$ declare +r person3
```

If the declare builtin is given with options but no variable names as arguments, the command lists all shell variables that have the indicated attributes set. For example, the option **–r** with declare gives a list of all readonly shell variables. After the declarations in the preceding example have been given, the results are as follows:

```
$ declare -r
declare -ar BASH_VERSINFO='([0]="2" [1]="05b" [2]="0" [3]="1" ... )'
declare -ir EUID="500"
declare -ir PPID="936"
declare -r SHELLOPTS="braceexpand:emacs:hashall:histexpand:history:..."
declare -ir UID="500"
declare -r person2="jenny"
declare -rx person3="helen"
```

The first five entries are keyword variables that are automatically declared as readonly. Some of these variables are also stored as integers, as the option **–i** indicates. The **–a** option indicates that **BASH_VERSINFO** is stored as an array variable; the value of each element of the array is listed to the right of the equal sign. If you had used readonly to make a keyword variable readonly, the keyword variable would also appear in the list. Another way to get the same list of shell readonly variables is by using readonly with no arguments.

Without any arguments or options, the declare builtin lists all the shell variables. The same list is output when you run set (page 584) without any arguments. Another name for declare is typeset. You may see it often in shell scripts, including complex scripts that come with the GNU/Linux system.

read: Accepts User Input

As you begin writing shell scripts, you soon realize that one of the most common uses of user-created variables is storing information a user enters in response to a prompt. Using read ^bash _zsh , your scripts can accept input from the user and store the input in variables that you create. (See page 706 for tcsh.) The read builtin reads one line from standard input and assigns the line to one or more variables:

```
$ cat read1
echo -n "Go ahead: "
read firstline
echo "You entered: $firstline"
$ read1
Go ahead: This is a line.
You entered: This is a line.
```

The first line of the **read1** script uses echo to prompt the user to enter a line of text. The **–n** option suppresses the following NEWLINE, allowing you to enter a line of text on the same line as the prompt. The second line in **read1** reads the text into the variable **firstline**. The third line verifies the action of read by displaying the value of **firstline**. The variable is quoted (along with the text string) in this example because you, as the scriptwriter, cannot anticipate what characters the user might enter in response to the prompt. Consider what would happen if the variable were not quoted and the user entered * in response to the prompt:

```
$ cat read1_no_quote
echo -n "Go ahead: "
read firstline
echo You entered: $firstline
$ read1_no_quote
Go ahead: *
You entered: read1 read1_no_quote script.1
$ ls
read1    read1_no_quote    script.1
```

The ls command lists the same words as the script, demonstrating that the shell expands the asterisk into a list of all the files in the working directory. When the variable **$firstline** is surrounded by double quotation marks, the shell does not expand the asterisk. Thus the **read1** script behaves correctly:

```
$ read1
Go ahead: *
You entered: *
```

If you want the shell to interpret the special meanings of special characters, do not use quotation marks.

The **read2** script prompts for a command line and reads it into the variable **command**. The script then executes the command line by placing $command on a line by itself. When it executes the script, the shell replaces the variable with its value and executes the command line as part of the script:

```
$ cat read2
echo -n "Enter a command: "
read command
$command
echo Thanks
```

In the following example **read2** reads a command line that calls the echo builtin. The shell executes the command and then displays Thanks. Next, **read2** reads a command line that executes the who utility:

```
$ read2
Enter a command: echo Please display this message.
Please display this message.
Thanks
$ read2
Enter a command: who
alex      pts/4        Jun 17 07:50  (:0.0)
scott     pts/12       Jun 17 11:54  (bravo.tcorp.com)
Thanks
```

The following **read3** script reads values into three variables. The read builtin assigns one word (a sequence of nonblank characters) to each variable:

```
$ cat read3
echo -n "Enter something: "
read word1 word2 word3
echo "Word 1 is: $word1"
echo "Word 2 is: $word2"
echo "Word 3 is: $word3"
$ read3
Enter something: this is something
Word 1 is: this
Word 2 is: is
Word 3 is: something
```

When you enter more words than read has variables, read assigns one word to each variable, with all the leftover words going to the last variable. In fact, both **read1** and **read2** assigned the first word and all the leftover words to the one variable they each had to work with. In the following example, read accepts five words into three variables, assigning the first word to the first variable, the second word to the second variable, and the third through fifth words to the third variable:

```
$ read3
Enter something: this is something else, really.
Word 1 is:  this
Word 2 is:  is
Word 3 is:  something else, really.
```

$(...) or `...`   Command Substitution

Command substitution replaces a command with the output of the command. You can use command substitution to produce arguments for another command or assignment statement. Place a dollar sign and an open parenthesis before and a close parenthesis after the command whose output you want to use. This is the preferred method under bash and zsh. Alternatively, you can enclose the command you want to substitute for between two backquotes, or grave accent marks [bash tcsh zsh]. Thus **$(pwd)** is equivalent to `pwd`. For more information refer to "Command Substitution" on page 803. The next chapter contains several scripts that use command substitution to assign values to variables (pages 635, 655, and 669).

Following, the shell executes pwd and substitutes the output of the command for the command and surrounding punctuation. Then the shell passes the output of the command, which is now an argument, to echo, which displays it as follows:

```
$ echo $(pwd)
/home/alex
```

The next shell script assigns the output of the pwd utility to the variable **where** and displays a message containing the value of this variable:

```
$ cat where
where=$(pwd)
echo "You are using the $where directory."
$ where
You are using the /home/jenny directory.
```

Although it illustrates how to assign the output of a command to a variable, this example is not realistic. You can more directly display the output of pwd without using a variable:

```
$ cat where2
echo "You are using the $(pwd) directory."
$ where2
You are using the /home/jenny directory.
```

Keyword Variables

Most keyword variables are either inherited or declared and initialized by the shell when it starts. You can assign values to these variables from the command line or from the **.bash_profile** [bash zsh], **.profile** [bash zsh], **.tcshrc** [tcsh], or **.login** [tcsh] file in your home directory. Typically users want these variables to apply to any shells or subshells that they create, as well as to their login shell. Consequently, for those variables not automatically exported by the shell, you must use export [bash zsh] or setenv [tcsh] to make them available to descendants.

HOME: Your Home Directory

By default your home directory is your working directory when you log in. Your home directory is determined when you establish your account and is stored in the **/etc/passwd** file. When you log in, the shell inherits the pathname of your home directory and assigns it to the variable **HOME** [bash tcsh zsh].

When you give a **cd** command without an argument, cd makes the directory whose name is stored in **HOME** the working directory:

```
$ pwd
/home/alex/laptop
$ echo $HOME
/home/alex
$ cd
$ pwd
/home/alex
```

This example shows the value of the **HOME** variable and the effect of the cd utility. After you execute cd without an argument, the pathname of the working directory is the same as the value of **HOME** (your home directory).

In a similar manner the shell uses **HOME** to expand pathnames that use the shorthand tilde (~) notation to denote a user's home directory. The following example illustrates the use of this shortcut, with ls listing the files in Alex's **laptop** directory:

```
$ ls ~/laptop
tester      count       lineup
```

PATH: Where the Shell Looks for Programs

When you give the shell an absolute or relative pathname rather than a simple file-name as a command, it looks in the specified directory for an executable file with the appropriate filename. If the executable file does not have the exact pathname that you specify, the shell reports that it cannot find (or execute) the program. Alter-natively, if you give it a simple filename as a command, the shell searches through certain directories for the program you want to execute. The shell looks in several directories for a file that has the same name as the command and that you have ex-ecute permission for (a compiled program) or read and execute permission for (a shell script). The **PATH** bash/tcsh/zsh shell variable controls this search.

When you log in, the shell assigns a default value to the **PATH** variable. The shell gets this value from the **/etc/profile** bash/zsh, **/etc/csh.cshrc** tcsh, or **/etc/csh.login** tcsh file. Normally, the default specifies that the shell search your working directory and several system directories used to hold common commands. These system directo-ries include **/bin** and **/usr/bin** and other directories that might be appropriate for your system. When you give a command, if the shell does not find the executable file named by the command in any of the directories listed in your **PATH** variable, the shell reports that it cannot find (or execute) the program.

The **PATH** variable specifies the directories in the order the shell is to search them. Each must be separated from the next by a colon. The following command sets **PATH** so that a search for an executable file starts with the **/usr/local/bin** direc-tory. If it does not find the file in this directory, the shell looks in **/bin**, followed by **/usr/bin**. If the search in those directories also fails, the shell looks in **/home/alex/bin** and in the working directory last. A null value in the string indicates the working directory. There is a null value (nothing between the colon and the end of the line) as the last element of the string. The working directory is represented by a leading colon (not recommended; see the following security box), a trailing colon (as in the example), or two colons next to each other anywhere in the string. You can also represent the working directory explicitly with a period (.). The following command assigns a value to and exports the **PATH** variable. Exporting **PATH** makes its new value accessible to subshells that may be invoked during the login session:

```
$ export PATH=/usr/local/bin:/bin:/usr/bin:/home/alex/bin:
```

See "PATH" in the list on page 708 for a tcsh example. Because GNU/Linux stores many executable files in directories named **bin** (*binary*), users also typically put their executable files in their own **~/bin** directories. If you put your own **bin** directory at the end of your **PATH** as Alex has, the shell looks there for any commands that it cannot find in directories listed earlier in **PATH**.

PATH and Security || security

Do not put the working directory first in your **PATH** when security is a concern. For example, most people type **ls** as the first command when entering a directory. If the owner of the directory has an executable file named **ls** in this directory, this file is executed instead of the system command **ls**, possibly with undesirable results. If you are running as Superuser, you should *never* put the working directory first in your **PATH**. In fact, it is common for Superuser **PATH** to omit the working directory entirely. You can always execute a file in the working directory by prepending a ./ to the name, as in ./ls.

If you want to add directories to your **PATH**, you can reference the old value of the **PATH** variable while you are setting **PATH** to a new value. The following command adds **/usr/X11R6/bin** to the front of the current **PATH** and **/usr/bin** to the end:

```
$ PATH=/usr/X11R6/bin:$PATH:/usr/bin:
```

MAIL: Where Your Mail Is Kept

The **MAIL** variable [bash tcsh zsh] contains the pathname of the file that your mail is stored in (your *mailbox*, usually **/var/spool/mail/***name*, where ***name*** is your login name).

The **MAILPATH** variable [bash zsh] contains a list of filenames separated by colons. If this variable is set, the shell informs you when any one of the files is modified (for example, when mail arrives). You can follow any of the filenames in the list with a percent sign (%), followed by a message. The message replaces the you have mail message when you get mail while you are logged in.

The **MAILCHECK** variable [bash zsh] specifies how often, in seconds, the shell checks for new mail. The default is 60 seconds. If you set this variable to zero, the shell checks before each prompt. If you unset **MAILCHECK** as follows, the shell does not check for mail at all:

```
$ unset MAILCHECK
```

PS1: User Prompt (Primary)

The **PS1** [bash zsh] or **prompt** [tcsh] (page 708) variable holds the prompt that the shell uses to let you know that it is waiting for a command. The bash prompt used in the examples throughout this chapter is a **$** followed by a SPACE; your prompt may differ. When you change the value of **PS1** or **prompt**, you change the appearance of your prompt.

If you are working on more than one machine, it can be helpful to incorporate a machine name into your prompt. The following example shows how to change the prompt to the name of the machine you are using, followed by a colon and a SPACE (a SPACE at the end of the prompt makes the commands that you enter following the prompt easier to read):

```
$ PS1="`hostname`: "
bravo.tcorp.com: echo test
test
bravo.tcorp.com:
```

The preceding command works under both bash and tcsh. The preferred construct under bash is

```
$ PS1="$(hostname): "
```

PS2: User Prompt (Secondary)

Prompt String 2 is a secondary prompt that the shell stores in **PS2** [bash zsh]. On the first line of the following example, an unclosed quoted string follows echo. The shell assumes that the command is not finished and, on the second line, gives the default secondary prompt (>). This prompt indicates that the shell is waiting for the user to continue the command line. The shell waits until it receives the quotation mark that closes the string and then executes the command:

```
$ echo "demonstration of prompt string
> 2"
demonstration of prompt string
2
$ PS2="secondary prompt: "
$ echo "this demonstrates
secondary prompt: prompt string 2"
this demonstrates
prompt string 2
```

The second command changes the secondary prompt to `secondary prompt:` followed by a SPACE. A multiline `echo` demonstrates the new prompt.

IFS: Separates Input Fields

The **IFS** variable `bash zsh` holds the internal field separators. Refer to "Word Splitting" on page 612.

CDPATH: Broadens the Scope of cd

The **CDPATH** `bash zsh` and **cdpath** `tcsh` variables allow you to use a simple filename as an argument to `cd` to change your working directory to one that is not a child of your working directory. If you have several directories you like to work out of, this variable can speed things up and save you the tedium of using `cd` with longer pathnames to switch among them.

When **CDPATH** or **cdpath** is not set and you specify a simple filename as an argument to `cd`, `cd` searches the working directory for a subdirectory with the same name as the argument. If the subdirectory does not exist, `cd` issues an error message. When **CDPATH** or **cdpath** is set, `cd` searches for an appropriately named subdirectory in the directories in the **CDPATH** list. If `cd` finds one, that directory becomes the working directory. With **CDPATH** or **cdpath** set, you can use `cd` and a simple filename to change your working directory to a child of any of the directories listed in **CDPATH** or **cdpath**.

The **CDPATH** or **cdpath** variable takes on the value of a colon-separated list of directory pathnames (similar to the **PATH** variable) and is usually set in the .bash_profile `bash zsh`, .profile `bash zsh`, .tcshrc `tcsh`, or .login `tcsh` file in your home directory with a command line such as one of the following. For bash and zsh:

```
export CDPATH=$HOME:$HOME/literature
```

For tcsh:

```
setenv CDPATH $HOME\:$HOME/literature
```

This setup causes `cd` to search your home directory, the **literature** directory, and then your working directory when you give a `cd` command.[7] If you do not include your working directory in **CDPATH** or **cdpath**, `cd` searches the working directory after the search of all the other directories in **CDPATH** or **cdpath** fails. If you want `cd` to search the working directory first (which you should never do when you are logged in as **root**—refer to the tip "PATH and Security" on page 578), include a null string, represented by two colons (::), as the first entry in **CDPATH**:

```
export CDPATH=::$HOME:$HOME/literature
```

---

7. The tcsh shell interprets the colon (:) as a special character and will give you an error message if you do not quote the colon.

If the argument to the cd builtin **bash tcsh zsh** is an absolute filename—one starting with a slash (/)—the shell does not consult **CDPATH** or **cdpath**.

Running a Startup File with the . (Dot) or source Builtin

After you edit your startup file (such as **.bash_profile** **bash zsh** or **.tcshrc** **tcsh**) to change the values of keyword shell variables, you do not have to wait until the next time you log in to put the changes into effect. You can run the startup file using the . (dot) **bash zsh** or source builtin **tcsh** (page 728). As with all other commands, the . must be followed by a SPACE on the command line. Using the . or source builtin is similar to running a shell script, except that these commands run the script as part of the current process. Consequently, when you use . or source to run a script from your login shell, changes you make to the variables from within the script affect the login shell. You can use the . or source command to run any shell script, not simply a startup file, but undesirable side effects (such as having the value of shell variables you rely on changed) may occur. If you ran a startup file as a regular shell script and did not use the . or source builtin, the new variables would be in effect only in the subshell running the script. Refer to "export: Makes a Variable Global" on page 571.

In the following example **.bash_profile** sets several variables and sets **PS1** to the machine name. The . builtin puts the new values into effect:

```
cat .bash_profile
TERM=vt100
PATH=/bin:/usr/bin:/usr/sbin:/home/alex/bin
export PS1="$(hostname -f): "
export CDPATH=:$HOME
stty kill '^u'
$ . .bash_profile
bravo.tcorp.com: $
```

Positional Parameters

When you call a shell script, the command name and arguments are the positional parameters. They are called positional because within a shell script, you refer to them by their position on the command line. Although you can reference them, only the set builtin **bash tcsh zsh** [8] allows you to change the values of positional parameters (page 584).

$0: Name of the Calling Program

The shell stores the name of the command you used to call a program in parameter $0 **bash tcsh zsh** . It is parameter number zero because it appears before the first argument on the command line:

---

8. Although it is a tcsh builtin, set cannot change the values of the positional parameters.

```
$ cat abc
echo The name of the command used
echo to execute this shell script was $0
$ abc
The name of the command used
to execute this shell script was abc
```

This shell script uses echo to verify the name of the script you are executing.

$1–$n: Command Line Arguments

The first argument on the command line is represented by the parameter $1 `bash tcsh zsh` , the second argument by the parameter $2 `bash tcsh zsh` , and so on up to $x `bash tcsh zsh` . The following script displays positional parameters that hold command line arguments:

```
$ cat display_5args
echo The first five command line
echo arguments are $1 $2 $3 $4 $5
$ display_5args jenny alex helen
The first five command line
arguments are jenny alex helen
```

The **display_5args** script displays the first five command line arguments. The shell assigns a null value to each of the parameters that represents an argument that is not present on the command line. The **$4** and **$5** variables have a null value.

The **$*** variable `bash tcsh zsh` represents all the command line arguments, as the **display_all** program demonstrates:

```
$ cat display_all
echo All the command line arguments are:
echo $*
$ display_all a b c d e f g h i j k l m n o p
All the command line arguments are:
a b c d e f g h i j k l m n o p
```

When you refer to a positional parameter, enclose the reference between double quotation marks. The quotation marks are particularly important when using positional parameters as arguments to commands; without double quotation marks, a positional parameter with a null value disappears:

```
$ cat showargs
echo "I was called with $# arguments, the first is :$1:."
$ showargs a b c
echo I was called with 3 arguments, the first is :a:.
$ echo $3

$ showargs $3 a b c
echo I was called with 3 arguments, the first is :a:.
$ showargs "$3" a b c
echo I was called with 4 arguments, the first is ::.
```

The preceding example first calls **showargs** with three simple arguments. The **showargs** script displays the number of arguments and the value of the first argument enclosed between colons. The shell stores the number of arguments passed to it in the $# special parameter `bash tcsh zsh`. (Refer to "$* and $@ Value of Command Line Arguments" on page 586 for more information.) The echo command demonstrates that the third positional parameter of the current shell ($3) has no value. In the final two calls to **showargs**, the first argument is $3. Because there is no value for this positional parameter, the shell replaces it with a null value. In the first case the command line becomes showargs a b c; the shell passes **showargs** three arguments. In the second case the command line becomes showargs "" a b c, which results in calling **showargs** with four arguments. The difference in the two calls to **showargs** illustrates a subtle potential problem that you must keep in mind when using positional parameters.

shift: Promotes Command Line Arguments

The shift builtin `bash tcsh zsh` promotes each of the command line arguments. The first argument (which was $1) is discarded. The second argument (which was $2) becomes the first (now $1), the third becomes the second, the fourth becomes the third, and so on.

Using the command line variables ($1–$9),[9] you can access only the first nine command line arguments from a shell script. The shift builtin gives you access to the tenth command line argument by making it the ninth. Successive shift commands make additional arguments available. The original first argument is discarded. Because there is no "unshift" command, it is not possible to bring back arguments that have been discarded.

The following **demo_shift** program is called with three arguments. Double quotation marks around the arguments to echo preserve the spacing of the output display. The program displays the arguments and shifts them repeatedly until there are no more arguments to shift:

```
$ cat demo_shift
echo "arg1= $1     arg2= $2     arg3= $3"
shift
echo "arg1= $1     arg2= $2     arg3= $3"
shift
echo "arg1= $1     arg2= $2     arg3= $3"
shift
echo "arg1= $1     arg2= $2     arg3= $3"
shift
$ demo_shift alice helen jenny
arg1= alice    arg2= helen    arg3= jenny
arg1= helen    arg2= jenny    arg3=
arg1= jenny    arg2=          arg3=
arg1=          arg2=          arg3=
```

---

9. tcsh and zsh: When you enclose the number in braces, you can address command line arguments greater than nine. For example, ${16} represents the sixteenth command line argument.

In the original Bourne Shell, the positional parameters were limited to **$1–$9**, so shell scripts that accepted more than nine arguments were forced to use shift to get to later arguments. The Bourne Again Shell has no limit on the number of positional parameters, so this use of shift has declined. However, repeatedly using shift is a convenient way to loop over all the command line arguments in shell scripts that expect an arbitrary number of arguments. See page 632 for a sample shell program that uses this technique.

set: Initializes Command Line Arguments

When you call the set builtin bash tcsh zsh with one or more arguments, it uses the arguments as values for positional parameters, starting with **$1** (for tcsh, see footnote 8 on page 581). The following script uses set to assign values to the positional parameters **$1, $2**, and **$3**:

```
$ cat set_it
set this is it
echo $3 $2 $1
$ set_it
it is this
```

Combining the use of command substitution (page 575) with the set builtin is a convenient way to get standard output of a command in a form that can be easily manipulated in a shell script. The following script shows how to use date and set to provide the date in a useful format. The first command shows the output of date. Then cat displays the contents of the **dataset** script. The first command in the script uses command substitution to set the positional parameters to the output of the date utility. The next command, **echo $***, displays all the positional parameters resulting from the previous set. Subsequent commands display the values of parameters **$1, $2, $3**, and **$4**. The final command displays the date in a format you can use in a letter or report:

```
$ date
Tue Apr 30 08:46:39 PDT 2002
$ cat dataset
set $(date)
echo $*
echo
echo "Argument 1: $1"
echo "Argument 2: $2"
echo "Argument 3: $3"
echo "Argument 6: $6"
echo
echo "$2 $3, $6"
```

```
$ dateset
Tue Apr 30 08:46:42 PDT 2002

Argument 1: Tue
Argument 2: Apr
Argument 3: 30
Argument 6: 2002

Apr 30, 2002
```

You can also use the **format** argument to date to modify the format of its output. Refer to page 1141 in Part III for more information on date.

Without any arguments, set displays a list of the shell variables that are set `bash tcsh zsh`, including user-created variables and keyword variables. This is the same output that declare gives when invoked without any arguments.

The set builtin also accepts a number of options that let you customize the behavior of the shell `bash zsh`. When you replace the hyphen with a plus sign before one of these options, set turns off the option. The value of many of these options should be clear now; others are explained in the remainder of this chapter. Some of the more useful options and their effects are listed in Table 12-2. These options are not available with the TC Shell version of set.

set Options `bash zsh` || table 12-2

Option	Effect
–a (allexport)	Marks variables that you create or modify for automatic export.
–f (noglob)	Stops **bash** from doing filename expansion (globbing).
–n (noexec)	Causes **bash** to read and perform expansions on commands but not to execute them. This option is useful if you want to check a shell script for syntax errors; it is ignored for interactive shells.
–t (exit)	Reads and executes a single command and then quits.
–u (nounset `bash`)	Returns an error when you try to expand a variable that is not set. When this option is not set, **bash** expands variables that have not been set to a null string. When this option is set, shell scripts terminate when the shell attempts to expand an unset variable; interactive shells display **unbound variable** and do not execute the current command.

Special Parameters

Special parameters make it possible to access useful values pertaining to command line arguments and the execution of shell commands. You reference a shell special parameter by preceding a special character with a dollar sign (**$**). As with positional parameters, it is not possible to modify the value of a special parameter.

$∗ and $@   Value of Command Line Arguments

The **$∗** parameter `bash tcsh zsh` represents all the command line arguments, as the **display_all** script on page 582 demonstrates. The **$@** `bash tcsh zsh` and **$∗** parameters are the same except when they are enclosed within double quotation marks. Using **"$∗"** yields a single argument (with SPACES between the positional parameters), whereas **"$@"** produces a list wherein each positional parameter is a separate argument. This difference makes **$@** more useful than **$∗** in shell scripts, as the **whos** script on page 642 demonstrates.

$#   Number of Command Line Arguments

As the **showargs** script on page 582 and the following example demonstrate, the **$#** parameter contains the number of arguments on the command line. This string parameter represents a decimal number.

```
$ cat num_args
echo "This shell script was called
with $# arguments."
$ num_args helen alex jenny
This shell script was called
with 3 arguments.
```

You can use **test** `bash zsh` to perform logical tests on this number (for more information on **test**, see page 627 and page 1352 in Part III; for tcsh refer to "Numeric Variables" on page 701).

The **echo** builtin in the preceding example displays a quoted string that spans two lines. Because the NEWLINE is quoted, the shell passes the entire string that is between the quotation marks, including the NEWLINE, to **echo** as an argument.

$$ PID Number

The shell stores in the **$$** parameter `bash tcsh zsh` the PID number of the process that is executing it. In the following interaction **echo** displays the value of this variable, and the **ps** utility confirms its value (ps lists a lot more processes if you are running X). Both commands show that the shell has a PID number of 5209:

```
$ echo $$
5209
$ ps
  PID TTY          TIME CMD
 5209 pts/1    00:00:00 bash
 6015 pts/1    00:00:00 ps
```

The echo **bash tcsh zsh** builtin keeps the shell from having to create another process when you give an echo command. However, the results are the same whether echo is a builtin or not, because the shell substitutes the value of $$ *before* it forks a new process to run a command. In the following example, the shell substitutes the value of $$ and passes that value to cp as a prefix for a new filename:

```
$ echo $$
8232
$ cp memo $$.memo
$ ls
8232.memo memo
```

This technique is useful for creating unique filenames when the meanings of the names do not matter; it is often used in shell scripts for creating names of temporary files. When two people are running the same shell script, these unique filenames keep them from inadvertently sharing the same temporary file.

The following example demonstrates that the shell creates a new shell process when it runs a shell script. The **id2** script displays the PID numbers of the process running it (not the process that called it; the substitution for $$ is performed by the shell that is forked to run **id2**):

```
$ cat id2
echo "$0 PID= $$"
$ echo $$
8232
$ id2
id2 PID= 8362
$ echo $$
8232
```

The first echo in the preceding example displays the PID number of the login shell. Then **id2** displays its name ($0) and the PID of the subshell that it is running in. The last echo shows that the current process is the login shell again.

The Bourne Again and Z Shells store the value of the PID number of the last process that you ran in the background in $! **bash zsh** . The following example executes sleep as a background task and then uses echo to display the value of $!:

```
$ sleep 60 &
8376
$ echo $!
8376
```

$? Exit Status

When a process stops executing for any reason, it returns an *exit status* to its parent process. The exit status is also referred to as a *condition code,* or *return code.* The $? `bash` `zsh` or $status `tcsh` variable stores the exit status of the last command.

By convention a nonzero exit status represents a *false* value and means that the command failed. A zero is *true* and means that the command was successful. In the following example the first ls command succeeds, whereas the second fails:

```
$ ls es
es
$ echo $?
0
$ ls xxx
ls: xxx: No such file or directory
$ echo $?
2
```

You can specify the exit status that a shell script returns by using the exit builtin `bash` `tcsh` `zsh`, followed by a number, to terminate the script. If you do not use exit with a number to terminate a script, the exit status of the script is that of the last command the script ran. The following example shows that the number following the word exit specifies the exit status:

```
$ cat es
echo This program returns an exit status of 7.
exit 7
$ es
This program returns an exit status of 7.
$ echo $?
7
$ echo $?
0
```

The es shell script displays a message and then terminates execution with an exit command that returns an exit status of 7, which is the user-defined exit status in this script. Then echo displays the value of the exit status of es. The second echo displays the value of the exit status of the first echo. The value is zero because the first echo was successful.

History

The history mechanism, a feature adapted from the C Shell, maintains a list of recently issued command lines, also called *events,* providing a shorthand way for re-executing any of the events in the list. This mechanism also enables you to execute variations of previous commands and to reuse arguments from them. You can replicate complicated commands and arguments that you used earlier in this login session or in a previous one and enter a series of commands that differ from one another in minor ways. The history list is also useful as a record of what you have done. It can be helpful when you have made a mistake and are not sure what you did or when you want to keep a record of a procedure that involved a series of commands. The history builtin `bash tcsh zsh` displays your history list. If it does not, read on; you need to set some variables.

The TC Shell and the Z Shell's history mechanisms are similar to bash's but have some important differences. In addition to the following sections, see page 686 `tcsh` and page 795 `zsh`.

history Can Help Track Down Mistakes || tip

When you have made a command line mistake (not an error within a script or program) and are not sure what you did wrong, you can look at the history list to review your recent commands. Sometimes this list can help you figure out what went wrong and how to fix things.

The value of the **HISTSIZE** `bash zsh` variable determines the number of events preserved in the history list during a session. Although the default value for **HISTSIZE** is 500, you may want to set it to a more convenient value, such as 100.

When you exit from the shell, the most recently executed commands are saved in the file given by the **HISTFILE** `bash zsh` variable (the default is **.bash_history** `bash` in your home directory). The next time you start up the shell, this file initializes the history list. The value of the **HISTFILESIZE** `bash` variable (default 500) determines the number of lines of history saved in **HISTFILE** (not necessarily the same as **HISTSIZE**). **HISTSIZE** holds the number of events remembered during a session, **HISTFILESIZE** holds the number remembered between sessions, and file designated by **HISTFILE** holds the name of the file that holds the history list. See Table 12-3

History Variables || table 12-3

Function	Variable	Default
Maximum number of events saved during a session	HISTSIZE	500 events
Location of the history file	HISTFILE	~/.bash_history
Maximum number of events saved between sessions	HISTFILESIZE	500 events

The Bourne Again Shell assigns a sequential *event number* to each of your command lines. You can display this event number as part of the bash prompt (refer to "PS1: User Prompt (Primary)" on page 579). Examples in this section show numbered prompts when they help to illustrate the behavior of a command or group of commands.

Give the following command manually, or place it in your **.bash_profile** ^{bash} _{zsh} or **.profile** ^{bash} _{zsh} startup file (to affect all future sessions) to establish a history list of the 100 most recent events:

```
$ HISTSIZE=100
```

The following command causes bash to save the 100 most recent events across login sessions:

```
$ HISTFILESIZE=100
```

After you set **HISTFILESIZE**, you can log out and log in again, and the 100 most recent events from the previous login session appear in your history list.

Give the command **history** to display the events in the history list. The list of events is ordered from oldest events at the top of the list to the most recent at the bottom. The last event in the history list is the **history** command that displayed the list. The following history list includes a command to modify the bash prompt to display the history event number as well as the command number.[10] To simplify the example, **HISTSIZE** has been set to the value 10 and **HISTFILESIZE** to 20. (The event number is 20 greater than the command number because the list of events includes those events that were saved from the last login session—20 in this case.)

```
32 $ history
   23  PS1="\! \# bash\$ "
   24  ls -l
   25  cat temp
   26  rm temp
   27  vi memo
   28  lpr memo
   29  vi memo
   30  lpr memo
   31  rm memo
   32  history
```

As you run commands and your history list becomes longer, it runs off the top of the screen when you use the history builtin. Pipe the output of history through less (page 54 and Part II) to browse through it, or give the command **history 10** to look at the last ten commands the shell executed.

---

10. The tcsh history builtin includes the time the command was executed between the event number and the event text.

Editing the Command Line

You can reexecute any event in the history list. This feature can save you time, effort, and aggravation. Not having to reenter long command lines allows you to reexecute events more easily, quickly, and accurately than you could if you had to retype the entire command line. You can recall, modify, and reexecute previously executed events in three ways: You can use the fc builtin (covered next); the Readline Library, which uses a one-line vi- or emacs-like editor to edit and execute events (page 598); or the TC Shell commands (page 594). If you are more familiar with vi or emacs and less familiar with the TC Shell, use fc or the Readline Library. If you are more familiar with the TC Shell and less familiar with vi and emacs, use the TC Shell commands. If it is a toss-up, try the Readline Library; it will benefit you in other areas of GNU/Linux more than learning the TC Shell commands will.

fc: Displays, Edits, and Reexecutes Commands

The fc (fix command) builtin `bash zsh` enables you to display the history file and to edit and reexecute previous commands. It provides many of the same capabilities as the command line editors.

Viewing the History List

When you call it with the −l option, fc displays commands from the history file on standard output. Without any arguments, **fc −l** lists the 16 most recent commands in a numbered list. The list of events is ordered from the oldest events at the top of the list to the most recent at the bottom:

```
$ fc -l
190   lpr memor.0795
191   lpr memo.0795
192   mv memo.0795 memo.071195
193   cd
194   view calendar
195   cd Work
196   vi letter.adams01
197   aspell -c letter.adams01
198   nroff letter.admas01 > adams.out
199   nroff letter.adams01 > adams.out
200   less adams.out
201   lpr adams.out
202   rm adams.out
203   cd ../memos
204   ls
205   rm *0486
```

The fc builtin can take zero, one, or two arguments with the –l option. The arguments specify a part of the history list to be displayed. The syntax is

fc –l [first [last]]

The fc builtin lists commands beginning with the most recent event that matches the first argument. The argument can be the number of the event, the first few characters of the command line, or a negative number, which is taken to be the *n*th previous command. If you provide a second argument, fc displays all commands from the most recent event that matches the first argument through the most recent event that matches the second. The next command displays the history list from event 197 through event 205:

```
$ fc -l 197 205
197   aspell -c letter.adams01
198   nroff letter.admas01 > adams.out
199   nroff letter.adams01 > adams.out
200   less adams.out
201   lpr adams.out
202   rm adams.out
203   cd ../memos
204   ls
205   rm *0486
```

The following command lists the most recent event that begins with the string view through the most recent command line that begins with the letters asp:

```
$ fc -l view asp
194   view calendar
195   cd Work
196   vi letter.adams01
197   aspell -c letter.adams01
```

To list a single command from the history file, use the same identifier for the first and second arguments. The following command lists event 197:

```
$ fc -l 197 197
197   aspell -c letter.adams01
```

Editing and Reexecuting Previous Commands

You can use fc to edit and reexecute previous commands.

fc [–e editor] [first [last]]

When you call fc with the –e option followed by the name of an editor, fc calls the editor with event(s) in the Work Buffer. Without *first* and *last*, fc defaults to the most recent command. The next example invokes the vi editor to edit the most recent command:

```
$ fc -e vi
```

The fc builtin uses the stand-alone vi editor. If you set the **FCEDIT** variable, you do not need to use the −e option to specify an editor on the command line. Because the value of **FCEDIT** has been changed to /usr/bin/pico and fc has no arguments, the following command edits the most recent command with the pico editor (page 49).

```
$ export FCEDIT=/usr/bin/pico
$ fc
```

If you call it with a single argument, fc invokes the editor on the specified command. The following example starts the editor with event 21 in the Work Buffer. When you exit from the editor, the shell automatically executes the command:

```
$ fc 21
```

Again, you can identify commands with numbers or by specifying the first few characters of the command name. The following example calls the editor to work on events from the most recent event that begins with the letters vi through event number 206:

```
$ fc vi 206
```

Clean Up the fc Buffer || caution

When you execute an fc command, the shell executes whatever you leave in the editor buffer, possibly with unwanted results. If you decide you do not want to execute a command, delete everything from the buffer before you leave the editor.

Reexecuting Commands without Calling the Editor

You can reexecute previous commands without going into an editor. If you call fc with the −s option, it skips the editing phase and reexecutes the command. The following example reexecutes event 201:

```
$ fc -s 201
lpr adams.out
```

The next example reexecutes the previous command:

```
$ fc -s
```

When you reexecute a command, such as lpr in the previous example, you can tell fc to substitute one string for another. The next example substitutes the string john for the string adams in event 201 and executes the modified event:

```
$ fc -s adams=john 201
lpr john.out
```

Reexecuting an Event with the C Shell History Mechanism

The C Shell history mechanism, available under bash, tcsh, and zsh, is frequently more cumbersome to use than fc but has some features you may want to use. For example, the !! command reexecutes the previous event, and the !$ token represents the last word on the previous command line.

You can reference an event using C Shell commands in three ways: by its absolute event number, by its number relative to the current event, or by the text it contains. All references to events begin with an exclamation point (!). One or more characters follow the exclamation point to specify an event.

!!   Reexecutes the Previous Event

You can always reexecute the previous event by giving the !! command. In the following example event 45 reexecutes event 44:

```
44 $ ls -l text
-rw-rw-r--   1 alex      group             45 Apr 30 14:53 text
45 $ !!
ls -l text
-rw-rw-r--   1 alex      group             45 Apr 30 14:53 text
```

This works whether or not your prompt displays an event number. As this example shows, when you use the history mechanism to reexecute an event, the shell displays the command it is reexecuting.

!n   Event Number

A number following an exclamation point refers to an event. If that event is in the history list, the shell executes it. If it is not in the history list, the shell gives you an error message. A negative number following an exclamation point references an event relative to the current event. The command !-3 refers to the third preceding event. After you issue a command, the relative event number of a given event changes (event -3 becomes event -4). Both of the following commands reexecute event 44:

```
51 $ !44
ls -l text
-rw-rw-r--   1 alex      group             45 Nov 30 14:53 text
52 $ !-8
ls -l text
-rw-rw-r--   1 alex      group             45 Nov 30 14:53 text
```

!string Event Text

When a string of text follows an exclamation point, the shell searches for and executes the most recent event that *began* with that string. If you enclose the string between question marks, the shell executes the most recent event that *contained* that string. The final question mark is optional if a RETURN would immediately follow it:

```
68 $ history
  59  ls -l text*    60  tail text5
  61  cat text1 text5 > letter
  62  vi letter
  63  cat letter
  64  cat memo
  65  lp memo
  66  pine jenny
  67  ls -l
  68  history
69 $ !l
ls -l
.
.
.
70 $ !lp
lp memo
request id is printer_1-1016 (1 file)
71 $ !?letter?
cat letter
.
.
.
```

Optional

!n:w Word within an Event

You can select any word or series of words from an event. The words are numbered starting with 0, representing the first word (usually the command) on the line, and continuing with 1, representing the first word following the command, through *n*, representing the last word on the line.

To specify a particular word from a previous event, follow the event designator (such as !14) with a colon and the number of the word in the previous event (for example, use !14:3 to specify the third word following the command from event 14). You can specify a range of words by separating two word designators with a hyphen. The first word following the command (word number 1) can be specified by a caret (^) and the last word by a dollar sign ($):

```
72 $ echo apple grape orange pear
apple grape orange pear
73 $ echo !72:2
echo grape
grape
74 $ echo !72:^
echo apple
apple
75 $ !72:0 !72:$
echo pear
pear
76 $ echo !72:2-4
echo grape orange pear
grape orange pear
77 $ !72:0-$
echo apple grape orange pear
apple grape orange pear
```

As the next example shows, **!$** refers to the last word of the previous event. You can use this shorthand to edit, for example, a file you just displayed with cat:

```
$ cat report.718
...
$ vi !$
vi report.718
...
```

If an event contains a single command, the word numbers correspond to the argument numbers. If an event contains more than one command, this correspondence is not true for commands after the first. Event 78, following, contains two commands separated by a semicolon so that the shell executes them sequentially; the semicolon is word number 5.

```
78 $ !72 ; echo helen jenny barbara
echo apple grape orange pear ; echo helen jenny barbara
apple grape orange pear
helen jenny barbara
79 $ echo !78:7
echo helen
helen
80 $ echo !78:4-7
echo pear ; echo helen
pear
helen
```

!!:s/new/old   Modifies the Previous Event

On occasion you may want to change an aspect of an event you are reexecuting. Perhaps you entered a complex command line with a typo or incorrect pathname. Or you may want to specify a different argument in the reexecuted command. You can modify an event or a word of an event by following the event or word specifier with a colon and a modifier. The following example shows the substitute modifier correcting a typo in the previous event:

```
$ car /home/jenny/memo.0507 /home/alex/letter.0507
bash: car: command not found
$ !!:s/car/cat
cat /home/jenny/memo.0507 /home/alex/letter.0507
.
.
.
```

^old^new   Performs a Quick Substitution

An abbreviated form of the substitute modifier is the *quick substitution*. Use it to reexecute the most recent event while changing some of the event text. The quick substitution character is the caret (^). For example, this command

```
$ ^old^new^
```

produces the same results as

```
$ !!:s/old/new/
```

Thus substituting cat for car in the previous event could have been entered as

```
$ ^car^cat
cat /home/jenny/memo.0507 /home/alex/letter.0507
.
.
.
```

As with other command line substitutions, the shell displays the command line as it appears after the substitution. You can omit the final caret if it would be followed immediately by a RETURN. See Table 12-4 for a list of event modifiers and their effects.

Event Modifier || table 12-4

h	Removes the last element of a pathname
r (root)	Removes the filename extension
e (extension)	Removes all but the filename extension
t (tail)	Removes all elements of a pathname except the last
p (print)	Does not execute the modified event, just prints it
[g]s/*old*/*new*/ (substitute)	Substitutes *new* for the first occurrence of *old;* with the g option, substitute all occurrences*

*The **s** modifier substitutes the *first* occurrence of the old string with the new one. Placing a **g** before the **s** (as in **gs/***old***/***new***/**) causes a global substitution, replacing *all* occurrences of the old string. The **/** is the delimiter in these examples; you can use any character that is not in either the old or the new string. The final delimiter is optional if a RETURN would immediately follow it. Like the vi Substitute command, the history mechanism replaces an ampersand (**&**) in the new string with the old string. The shell replaces a null old string (**s//***new***/**) with the previous old string or string within a command that you searched for with **?***string***?**.

The Readline Library

The Bourne Again Shell's command line editing has been implemented through a package developed by the Free Software Foundation: the *Readline Library* (named after the bash readline function). This library is available to application writers using the C programming language for use in their applications. Any application that uses the Readline Library supports line editing consistent with that provided in bash.

You can choose one of two basic modes when using this type of command line editing in bash: emacs or vi. Both modes provide you with many of the commands available in these editors. The default mode is emacs, but you can switch to vi mode interactively in bash with the command

```
$ set -o vi
```

To switch back to emacs mode, give the command

```
$ set -o emacs
```

Familiarity with emacs makes it easy to use the emacs-like editing keystrokes, and the notation used in the documentation is similar. There is also the familiar concepts of a kill ring and yanking to reinsert text, both of which are present in emacs.

Your keyboard keys have been bound to the commands available for command line editing. You can change these bindings in the **.inputrc** file in your home directory. Any application that uses the Readline Library first reads **.inputrc**, if it exists, to set the initial command bindings and any special configuration settings. See page 600 more information about using **.inputrc**.

Use **bind –v** to see what key bindings are in effect. This command displays a list of all the available commands and, if a command has been bound to a sequence of keystrokes, it also displays this sequence. The emacs mode is used in this discussion.

Basic Readline Commands

A number of categories of commands match those needed for general text editing:

- Moving back and forth in a command line
- Moving up and down through the history list
- Changing, deleting, and replacing text
- Undoing and redoing changes

Most of the commonly used emacs (or vi) commands for these operations are available, and you should experiment with those you have used to see how they work. You can also use the ARROW keys to move around. Up and down movements move you backward and forward through your history list. Refer to pages 463 and 409 for command summaries for vi and emacs.

Completion

You can use the TAB key to complete words you are entering on the command line. This facility is called *completion* and is similar to that found in tcsh and zsh. The type of completion depends on what you are typing.

If you are typing the name of a command (the first word on the command line), pressing TAB results in *command completion*; bash looks for a command whose name starts with the part of the word you have typed. If there is one, bash completes the rest of the command name for you. If there is more than one choice, bash beeps. Pressing TAB a second time causes bash to display a list of commands whose names start with the prefix you have typed and allows you to finish typing the command name.

If you are typing a filename, using TAB performs *filename completion*. If it can determine unambiguously what the name is, bash types the rest of the filename for you. As with command completion, you can use a second TAB to list alternatives. When typing in a variable name, pressing TAB results in *variable completion*, where bash tries to complete the name of the variable for you.

If you want to see a list of the possible completions at any time while you are entering a command, press ESCAPE ?.

Miscellaneous Commands

Table 12-5 lists some other useful Readline commands.

Miscellaneous Readline Commands	‖ table 12-5
ESCAPE ~	The tilde-expand command tries to expand the current word into the name of a user that starts with that prefix. For example, typing scTAB would result in scott if that is the only username that starts with sc on your system.
ESCAPE ^	The history-expand-line command performs history expansion on all history events in the current line.
ESCAPE-CONTROL-e	The shell-expand-line command does a full expansion on the current line, just as bash does when preparing to execute a command. The shell even performs alias and history expansions.

.inputrc

The Bourne Again Shell and other programs that use the Readline Library read .inputrc from your home directory for initialization information. This file is the default used if the INPUTRC environment variable is not set. If INPUTRC is set, its value is used as the name of the initialization file.

You can set variables in .inputrc to control the behavior of the Readline Library, using the following syntax:

set *variable value*

Choose *variable* from the (partial) list in Table 12-6.

In addition to setting variables, you can specify bindings that map keystroke sequences to Readline commands, allowing you to change or extend the default bindings. As with emacs, Readline includes many commands that start with no binding to any keystroke sequence. To use any of these unbound commands, you must give a mapping, using one of the following two forms:

keyname: command_name
" *keystroke_sequence* ": *command_name*

In the first form, spell out the name for a single key. For example, CONTROL-u would be written as control-u. This form is useful for binding commands to single keys.

Readline Variables
|| table 12-6

editing-mode	Set to **vi** to start Readline in **vi** mode. Setting it to **emacs** starts Readline in **emacs** mode, which is the default.
expand-tilde	Set to **on** to cause Readline to perform tilde expansion whenever it tries to complete a word. Normally it is **off**.
horizontal-scroll-mode	Set to **on** to cause long lines to extend off the edge of the display area. Moving the cursor to the right when you are at the edge shifts the line to the left so you can see more of the line. You can shift the line back by moving the cursor back past the left edge. The default value is **off**, which causes long lines to be wrapped onto multiple lines of the display.
mark-modified-lines	Set to **on** to cause Readline to precede modified history lines with an asterisk. The default value is **off**.

In the second form, you can give a string that describes a sequence of keys that are to be bound to the command. You can use the emacs-style escape sequences to represent the special keys CONTROL (**\C**), META (**\M**), and ESCAPE (**\e**). A backslash can be used by escaping it with another backslash, as in ****. Similarly, a double or single quotation mark can be escaped with a backslash, as in **\"** or **\'** .

Give the following command to bind the kill-whole-line command, which by default is unbound, to the keystroke sequence ESCAPE [11~:

```
"\e[11~": kill-whole-line
```

Because F1 (function key 1) generates this keystroke sequence (on the console running as terminal type **linux**), this binding turns F1 into a line-kill command key.

You can also bind text by enclosing it within double quotation marks:

```
"\e[12~": "The GNU/Linux Operating System"
```

This command inserts the string The GNU/Linux Operating System (without surrounding quotation marks) whenever you press F2.

Lines of **.inputrc** that are blank or that start with a pound sign (#) are treated as comments and ignored.

Finally, you can conditionally select parts of the **.inputrc** file by using the **$if** directive. You can supply a test with this directive; the lines following the directive are used if the test is true. Otherwise, these lines, up to a **$else** or **$endif**, are ignored. The **$else** directive works as you might expect: If the test used with the previous **$if** directive is false, the lines following the **$else** (up to a **$endif**) are used; otherwise, these lines are ignored.

The power of the **$if** directive lies in the three types of tests it can perform.

1. You can test to see which mode is currently set.

   ```
   $if mode=vi
   ```

   is *true* if the current Readline mode is vi and *false* otherwise.

2. You can test the type of terminal.

   ```
   $if term=xterm
   ```

   is *true* if you are using an xterm window.

3. You can test the application name.

   ```
   $if bash
   ```

   is *true* when you are running bash and not another program that uses the Readline Library.

All uses of **$if** should end with the **$endif** directive. These tests can customize the Readline Library based on the current mode, the type of terminal, and the application you are using. This gives you a great deal of power and flexibility when using the Readline Library with bash and with other programs.

Alias

The alias mechanism allows you to define new commands by letting you substitute any string for any command. The syntax of the alias builtin is

> *alias [name[=value]]*   `bash` `zsh`

or

> *alias [name[value]]*   `tcsh`

There are no SPACEs around the equal sign `bash zsh`. If *value* contains SPACEs or TABs, you must enclose *value* between quotation marks. The alias mechanism is disabled for noninteractive shells (that is, shell scripts).

An alias cannot be recursive: The *name* of the alias may not appear within the *value* of the alias you are defining. You can nest aliases. To see a list of the current aliases, give the command **alias**. To view the alias for a particular name, use alias followed by the name and nothing else.

Quotation Marks: Single versus Double

Use of either double or single quotation marks is significant in the alias syntax. If you enclose *value* within double quotation marks, any variables that appear in *value* are expanded when the alias is created. If you enclose *value* within single quotation marks, variables are not expanded until the alias is used. The following example shows the difference:

```
$ alias p1="echo my prompt is $PS1"
$ alias p2='echo my prompt is $PS1'
$ PS1=">>>>>>>>>>>>>> "
>>>>>>>>>>>>>> p1
my prompt is $
>>>>>>>>>>>>>> p2
my prompt is >>>>>>>>>>>>>>
>>>>>>>>>>>>>>
```

Examples

You can use alias to create short names for commands that you use often. For example, the following alias allows you to type **r** to repeat the previous command or **r abc** to repeat the last command line that began with abc:

```
$ alias r='fc -s'
```

Prevent the Shell from Invoking an Alias   ‖ tip

The shell checks only simple, unquoted commands to see if they are aliases. Commands given as relative or absolute pathnames and quoted commands are not checked. When you want to give a command that has an alias but do not want to use the alias, precede the command with a backslash, specify the command's absolute pathname, or give the command as *./command.*

If you use the command **ls –ltr** frequently, you can use the alias builtin to substitute ls -ltr when you give the command **l**:

```
$ alias l='ls -ltr'
$ l
total 41
-rw-r--r--  1 alex    group     30015 Mar  1 2002 flute.ps
-rw-r-----  1 alex    group      3089 Feb 11 2003 XTerm.ad
-rw-r--r--  1 alex    group       641 Apr  1 2003 fixtax.icn
-rw-r--r--  1 alex    group       484 Apr  9 2003 maptax.icn
drwxrwxr-x  2 alex    group      1024 Aug  9 17:41 Tiger/
drwxrwxr-x  2 alex    group      1024 Sep 10 11:32 testdir/
-rwxr-xr-x  1 alex    group       485 Oct 21 08:03 floor*
drwxrwxr-x  2 alex    group      1024 Oct 27 20:19 Test_Emacs/
```

Another common use of the alias mechanism is to protect yourself from mistakes. The following example uses an alias to substitute the interactive version of the rm utility when you give the command **zap**:

```
$ alias zap='rm -i'
$ zap f*
rm: remove `fixtax.icn'? n
rm: remove `flute.ps'? n
rm: remove `floor'? n
```

The **–i** option causes rm to ask you to verify each file that would be deleted, to protect you from accidentally deleting the wrong file.

In the next example, alias causes the shell to substitute ls –l every time you give an **ll** command and ls –F when you use **ls:**

```
$ ls
Test_Emacs XTerm.ad  flute.ps   testdir
Tiger      fixtax.icn maptax.icn
$ alias ls='ls -F'
$ alias ll='ls -l'
$ ll
total 41
drwxrwxr-x  2 alex    group      1024 Oct 27 20:19 Test_Emacs/
drwxrwxr-x  2 alex    group      1024 Aug 9 17:41 Tiger/
-rw-r-----  1 alex    group      3089 Feb 11 2003 XTerm.ad
-rw-r--r--  1 alex    group       641 Apr 1 2003 fixtax.icn
-rw-r--r--  1 alex    group     30015 Mar 1 2002 flute.ps
-rwxr-xr-x  1 alex    group       485 Oct 21 08:03 floor*
-rw-r--r--  1 alex    group       484 Apr 9 2003 maptax.icn
drwxrwxr-x  2 alex    group      1024 Sep 10 11:32 testdir/
```

The **–F** option causes ls to print a slash (/) at the end of directory names and an asterisk (*) at the end of the names of executable files. In this example the string that replaces the alias **ll**, ls –l, itself contains an alias, **ls**. When it replaces an alias with its value, the shell looks at the first word of the replacement string to see whether it is an alias. In the preceding example, the replacement string contains the alias **ls**, so a second substitution occurs to produce the final command ls –F –l.

(To avoid a *recursive plunge*, the ls in the replacement text, although an alias, is not expanded a second time.)

When given a list of aliases without the *=value* or *value* field, the alias builtin responds by displaying the value of each defined alias. The alias builtin reports an error if an alias has not been defined:

```
$ alias ll ls wx
alias ll='ls -l'
alias ls='ls -F'
alias: 'wx' not found
```

When you give an alias builtin without any arguments, the shell displays a list of all the defined aliases:

```
$ alias
alias ll='ls -l'
alias l='ls -ltr'
alias ls='ls -F'
alias zap='rm -i'
```

You can avoid alias substitution by preceding the aliased command with a backslash (\):

```
$ \ls
Test_Emacs XTerm.ad  flute.ps  maptax.icn
Tiger      fixtax.icn floor     testdir
```

Because the replacement of an alias name with the alias value does not change the rest of the command line, any arguments are still received by the command that gets executed:

```
$ ll f*
-rw-r--r--  1 alex   group      641 Apr  1 2003 fixtax.icn
-rw-r--r--  1 alex   group    30015 Mar  1 2002 flute.ps
-rwxr-xr-x  1 alex   group      485 Oct 21 08:03 floor*
```

You can remove an alias with the unalias builtin `bash tcsh zsh`. When the **zap** alias is removed, it is no longer displayed with the alias builtin, and its subsequent use results in an error message:

```
$ unalias zap
$ alias
alias ll='ls -l'
alias l='ls -ltr'
alias ls='ls -F'
$ zap maptax.icn
bash: zap: command not found
```

Command Line Expansion

Before passing the command line to the program being called, the shell transforms the command line by using *command line expansion*. The shell also expands each line of a shell script as the shell executes the script. You can use any of the shells without knowing much about command line expansion, but you can make much better use of what they have to offer with an understanding of this topic.

Chapter 5 discussed one aspect of command line expansion in "Filename Generation/Pathname Expansion" on page 157. TC Shell command line expansion is covered starting on page 693, and Z Shell coverage of this topic begins on page 797. The following sections review several types of command line expansion you may be familiar with and introduce some new ones that bash uses. These sections also discuss the order in which the shell performs the various expansions and provide some examples. (Although bash provides history (page 588) and alias (page 602) expansion, they are not included in the following discussion, because they are available only in interactive shells and therefore cannot be used in shell scripts.)

When the shell processes a command, it does not execute the command immediately. One of the first things the shell does is to *parse* (isolate strings of characters in) the command line into tokens or words. The shell then proceeds to scan each token for special characters and patterns that instruct the shell to take certain actions. These actions often involve substituting one word or words for another. When the shell parses the following command line, it breaks it into three tokens (cp, ~/letter, and .):

```
$ cp ~/letter .
```

After separating tokens and before executing the command, the shell scans the tokens and performs *command line expansion*. You have seen many examples of command line expansion in this and previous chapters; a frequent one is the substitution of a list of filenames for an ambiguous file reference that includes any of the characters *, ?, [, and].

Order of Expansion

The Bourne Again Shell scans each token for the various types of expansion in the following order:

1. Brace expansion (page 607)

2. Tilde expansion (page 609)

3. Parameter expansion (page 609)

4. Variable expansion (page 610)

5. Command substitution (page 611)

6. Arithmetic expansion (page 611)

7. Word splitting (page 612)

8. Pathname expansion (page 614)

The order in which the various expansions take place is important; if the shell performed the expansions in a different order, a dramatically different result could occur. In the following example, if pathname expansion occurred prior to variable expansion, the asterisk (*) would not be treated specially; after expansion, the argument given to echo would be tmp*, and that would be the output of echo:

```
$ ls
tmp1 tmp2 tmp3
$ var=tmp*
$ echo $var
tmp1 tmp2 tmp3
```

It is important to keep in mind that double and single quotation marks cause the shell to behave differently when performing expansions (page 568). Double quotation marks permit parameter and variable expansion but suppress other types of expansion. Single quotation marks suppress all types of expansion.

{}   Brace Expansion

Brace expansion ^{bash}_{zsh}, which originated in the original C Shell, provides a convenient way to specify filenames when pathname expansion does not apply. Although brace expansion is almost always used to specify filenames, the mechanism can be used to generate arbitrary strings; the shell does not attempt to match the brace notation with a list of the names of existing files. The following example illustrates the way that brace expansion works:

```
$ ls
$ echo chap_{one,two,three}.txt
chap_one.txt chap_two.txt chap_three.txt
```

The ls command shows that no files are in the working directory. The shell expands the comma-separated strings inside the braces into a SPACE-separated list of strings. Each string from the list is prepended with the string chap_, called the *preamble*, and appended with the string .txt, called the *postamble*. Both preamble and postamble are optional, and the left-to-right order of the strings within the braces is preserved in the expansion. For the shell to treat the left and right braces specially and for brace expansion to occur, at least one comma must be inside the braces with no unquoted whitespace characters. Brace expansions may be nested.

Brace expansion is useful when there is a long preamble or postamble. The following example copies the four files **main.c**, **f1.c**, **f2.c**, and **tmp.c**, located in the **/usr/local/src/C** directory, to the working directory:

```
$ cp /usr/local/src/C/{main,f1,f2,tmp}.c .
```

Brace expansion can also create directories with related names. Because the directories do not already exist, pathname expansion does not work in this case:

```
$ ls -l
total 3
-rw-rw-r-- 1 alex     group         14 Jan 22 08:54 file1
-rw-rw-r-- 1 alex     group         14 Jan 22 08:54 file2
-rw-rw-r-- 1 alex     group         14 Jan 22 08:55 file3
$ mkdir version{A,B,C,D,E}
$ ls -l
total 8
-rw-rw-r-- 1 alex     group         14 Jan 22 08:54 file1
-rw-rw-r-- 1 alex     group         14 Jan 22 08:54 file2
-rw-rw-r-- 1 alex     group         14 Jan 22 08:55 file3
drwxrwxr-x 2 alex     group       1024 Jan 25 13:27 versionA
drwxrwxr-x 2 alex     group       1024 Jan 25 13:27 versionB
drwxrwxr-x 2 alex     group       1024 Jan 25 13:27 versionC
drwxrwxr-x 2 alex     group       1024 Jan 25 13:27 versionD
drwxrwxr-x 2 alex     group       1024 Jan 25 13:27 versionE
```

If ambiguous file reference notation had been used to specify the directories instead of the preceding notation, the result would be very different (and not what was desired).

```
$ ls -l
total 3
-rw-rw-r-- 1 alex     group         14 Jan 22 08:54 file1
-rw-rw-r-- 1 alex     group         14 Jan 22 08:54 file2
-rw-rw-r-- 1 alex     group         14 Jan 22 08:55 file3
$ mkdir version[A-E]
$ ls -l
total 4
-rw-rw-r-- 1 alex     group         14 Jan 22 08:54 file1
-rw-rw-r-- 1 alex     group         14 Jan 22 08:54 file2
-rw-rw-r-- 1 alex     group         14 Jan 22 08:55 file3
drwxrwxr-x 2 alex     group       1024 Jan 25 13:38 version[A-E]
```

Because it found no filenames matching version[A-E], the shell passed that string to mkdir, which created a directory with that name.

Braces are also useful to distinguish a variable from surrounding text without the use of a separator (for example, a SPACE):

```
$ prefix=Alex
$ echo $prefix is short for ${prefix}ander.
Alex is short for Alexander.
```

Without braces **prefix** would have to be separated from **ander** with a SPACE so that the shell would recognize **prefix** as a variable. This change would cause Alexander to become Alex ander.

~   Tilde Expansion

Chapter 4 showed a shorthand notation to specify your home directory or the home directory of another user (page 116). This section provides a more detailed explanation of *tilde expansion* bash tcsh zsh.

The tilde (~) is a special character when it appears at the start of a token on a command line. When it sees this type of tilde, the shell looks at the following string of characters—up to the first slash (/) or to the end of the word if there is no slash—as a possible login name. If this possible login name is null (that is, if the tilde appeared as a word by itself or if it was immediately followed by a slash), the shell substitutes the value of the **HOME** variable for the tilde. In other words the shell expands the tilde into the value of **HOME**. The following example demonstrates this substitution or expansion, with the last command copying the file named **letter** from Alex's home directory to the working directory.

```
$ echo $HOME
/home/alex
$ echo ~
/home/alex
$ echo ~/letter
/home/alex/letter
$ cp ~/letter .
```

If a string of characters forms a valid login name, the shell substitutes the path of the home directory associated with that login name for the tilde and name. If it is not null and not a valid login name, the shell does not make any substitution:

```
$ echo ~jenny
/home/jenny
$ echo ~root
/root
$ echo ~xx
~xx
```

$n   Parameter Expansion

Parameter expansion bash tcsh zsh occurs when the shell replaces a dollar sign followed by a one or more digits with the value of the positional parameter corresponding to the digits in the token.[11] Another type of parameter expansion occurs when a special character follows a dollar sign, in which case an aspect of the command or its arguments is substituted for the token (page 586).

$VARIABLE   Variable Expansion

Variable expansion [bash tcsh zsh] takes place when the shell processes a token consisting of a dollar sign ($) followed by a variable name (user-defined or keyword), as in *$VARIABLE*, the token, where VARIABLE is the name of a variable that the shell replaces with the value of the variable.

Optional

The **$VARIABLE** syntax is a special case of the more general syntax **${VARIABLE}**, in which the variable name is enclosed by **${}** [bash tcsh zsh]. The braces insulate the variable name from what surrounds it. Braces are necessary when catenating a variable value with a string:

```
$ PREF=counter
$ WAY=$PREFclockwise
$ FAKE=$PREFfeit
$ echo $WAY $FAKE

$
```

The preceding example does not work as planned. Only a blank line is output. The reason is that the symbols **PREFclockwise** and **PREFfeit** are valid variable names, but they are not set. By default the shell evaluates an unset variable as an empty (null) string and displays this value [bash zsh] or else generates an error message [tcsh]. To achieve the intent of these statements, refer to the **PREF** variable using braces:

```
$ PREF=counter
$ WAY=${PREF}clockwise
$ FAKE=${PREF}feit
$ echo $WAY $FAKE
counterclockwise counterfeit
```

---

11. In bash when you reference parameters greater than 9, the integer must be enclosed in braces, as in $(14).

$(...) Command Substitution

Command substitution bash tcsh zsh (page 575) allows you to use standard output of a command in-line within a shell script. (Another way of using standard output is to send it to a file and read it back in.) Command substitution is another type of command line expansion that occurs after the tokens on the command line have been identified. The preferred syntax bash zsh for command substitution is

$(command)

This notation instructs the shell to replace the token with standard output of **command**. To use standard output of **command**, the shell must first run *command* successfully. The TC Shell supports the `command` format of command substitution only.

Arithmetic Expansion

The shell performs *arithmetic expansion* by evaluating an arithmetic expression and then replacing it with the result. Arithmetic expansion is different for each of the three shells. Refer to "Numeric Variables" on page 701 tcsh and "Arithmetic Expansion" on page 804 zsh. Under bash the syntax for arithmetic expansion is

$[expression]

The rules for forming an expression are the same as those found in the C programming language; all standard C arithmetic operators are available. Arithmetic in bash is done using integers, although often the shell must convert string-valued variables to integers for the purpose of the arithmetic evaluation.

The following example uses arithmetic expansion and command substitution to estimate the number of pages required to print the contents of the file **letter.txt**. The dollar sign and parentheses instruct the shell to perform command substitution; the dollar sign and brackets indicate arithmetic expansion:

```
$ echo $[$(wc -l letter.txt | cut -c1-7)/66 + 1]
6
```

The output of the wc utility with the –l option is the number of lines in the file, in columns 1 through 7, followed by a SPACE and the name of the file (the first command in the following example). The cut utility with the –c option extracts the first seven columns (the second command). Arithmetic expansion is then used to divide this count by 66, the number of lines in a page. A 1 is added at the end because the integer division results in any remainder being discarded (preceding example):

```
$ wc -l letter.txt
    351 letter.txt
```

```
$ wc -l letter.txt | cut -c1-7
   351
```

Refer to Part III for more information on cut (page 1132) and wc (page 1372).

Another way to get the same result without using cut is to redirect the input to wc instead of having wc get its input from a file you name on the command line. When you redirect the input, wc does not display the name of the file.

```
$ wc -l < letter.txt
   351
```

It is common to assign the result of arithmetic expansion to a variable, as in

```
$ numpages=$[ $(wc -l < letter.txt)/66 + 1]
```

The let builtin ^{bash}_{zsh} allows you to evaluate arithmetic expressions without using arithmetic expansion, evaluating each argument you give it as an arithmetic expression. Thus the following is equivalent to the preceding expression:

```
$ let "numpages=$(wc -l < letter.txt)/66 + 1"
```

The double quotation marks keep the SPACEs (both those you can see and those that result from the command substitution) from separating the expression into separate arguments to let. The value of the last expression determines the exit status of let: If the *value* of the last expression is 0, the exit status of let is 1; otherwise, the exit status is 0.

You can give let multiple arguments on a single command line:

```
$ let a=5+3 b=7+2
$ echo $a $b
8 9
```

When you refer to variables when doing arithmetic expansion with either let or *$(expression)*, the shell does not require you to begin the variable name with a dollar sign ($), although it is a good practice to do so, as in most places you must. The following two expressions assign the same value to **numpages**:

```
$ let numpages=numpages+1
$ let numpages=$numpages+1
```

Word Splitting

The **IFS** (Internal Field Separators) shell variable ^{bash} specifies the characters that you can use to separate arguments on a command line and has the default value of SPACE

TAB NEWLINE. Regardless of what **IFS** is set to, you can always use one or more SPACE or TAB characters to separate arguments on the command line, provided that these characters are not quoted or escaped. When you assign **IFS** the value of characters, these characters can also separate fields, but only in the event that they undergo expansion. This type of interpretation of the command line is called *word splitting*. The following example demonstrates how setting **IFS** can affect the interpretation of a command line:

```
$ a=w:x:y:z
$ cat $a
cat: w:x:y:z: No such file or directory
$ IFS=":"
$ cat $a
cat: w: No such file or directory
cat: x: No such file or directory
cat: y: No such file or directory
cat: z: No such file or directory
```

The first time cat is called, the shell expands the variable a, interpreting the string w:x:y:z as a single token to be used as the argument to cat. The cat utility cannot find a file named **w:x:y:z** and reports an error for that filename. After **IFS** is set to a colon (:), the shell expands the variable **a** into four words as separate arguments to cat. This causes the cat utility to report an error on four separate files: **w, x, y,** and **z**. Word splitting based on the colon (:) takes place only *after* the variable **a** is expanded.

The shell splits all *expanded* words on a command line according to the separating characters found in **IFS**. When there is no expansion, there is no splitting. Consider the following commands:

```
$ IFS="p"
$ export IFS
```

Although IFS is set to p, nothing was expanded on the **export** command line, so the word export was not split. The following example uses variable expansion to produce the **export** command:

```
$ IFS=p
$ aa=export
$ $aa IFS
2 files to edit
ort: 2 files to edit: new file: line 1
:q
1 more files to edit
:q
$
```

This time there was expansion, and the character p in the token export was interpreted as a separator, so the effect of the command line is to start the ex editor with two filenames: **ort** and **IFS**.

Be Careful When Changing IFS   ‖ caution

Although sequences of SPACE or TAB characters are treated as single separators, *each occurrence* of another field-separator character acts as a separator.

Changing **IFS** has a variety of side effects so change it cautiously. You may find it useful to first save the value of **IFS** before changing it; that way you can easily restore it if you get unexpected results. Or you can fork a new shell with a **bash** or **zsh** command before experimenting with **IFS**; if you get into trouble, you can **exit** back to your old shell, where **IFS** is working properly. You can also set **IFS** to its default value with the following command:

```
$ IFS=$' \t\n'
```

Pathname Expansion

Pathname expansion (page 157) is the process of interpreting ambiguous file references and substituting the appropriate list of filenames. The shell performs this function when it encounters an ambiguous file reference—a token containing any of the characters *, ?, [, or]. If the shell is unable to locate any files that match the specified pattern, the token with the ambiguous file reference is left alone. The shell does not delete the token or replace it with a null string but passes it on to the program as is. An error message is generated by tcsh. In the first echo command in the following example, the shell expands the ambiguous file reference tmp* and passes three tokens (tmp1, tmp2, and tmp3) to echo, which displays the three filenames it was passed by the shell. After rm removes the three tmp* files, the shell finds no filenames that match tmp* when it tries to expand it and so passes the unexpanded string to the echo builtin, which displays the string it was passed. By default the same command causes the TC Shell to display an error message (see "**noglob**" in the list on page 713):

```
$ ls
tmp1 tmp2 tmp3
$ echo tmp*
tmp1 tmp2 tmp3
$ rm tmp*
$ echo tmp*
tmp*
$ tcsh
% echo tmp*
echo: No match
```

Putting double quotation marks around an argument causes the shell to suppress pathname and all other expansion except parameter and variable expansion. Putting single quotation marks around an argument suppresses all types of expansion. In the following example the variable **$alex** is between double quotation marks, which allow parameter expansion, so the shell expands the variable to its value: sonar. This expansion does not occur when single quotation marks are used. Because neither single nor double quotation marks allow pathname expansion, the last two commands display the unexpanded argument tmp*:

```
$ echo tmp* $alex
tmp1 tmp2 tmp3 sonar
$ echo "tmp* $alex"
tmp* sonar
$ echo 'tmp* $alex'
tmp* $alex
```

The shell distinguishes between the value of a variable and a reference to the variable and does not expand ambiguous file references if they occur in the value of a variable. This makes it possible for you to assign to a variable a value that includes special characters, such as an asterisk (*).

In the next example the working directory has three files whose names begin with tmp. When you assign the value tmp* to the variable **var**, the shell does not expand the ambiguous file reference, because it occurs in the value of a variable (in the assignment statement for the variable). No quotation marks are around the string tmp*. Context alone prevents the expansion. After the assignment, the set builtin (with the help of grep) shows the value of **var** to be tmp*.

The three **echo** commands demonstrate three levels of expansion. When **$var** is quoted with single quotation marks, the shell performs no expansion and passes echo the character string $var, which echo displays. When you use double quotation marks, the shell performs variable expansion only and substitutes the value of the **var** variable for its name, preceded by a dollar sign. There is no filename expansion on this command because double quotation marks suppress it. In the final command, the shell, without the limitations of quotation marks, performs variable substitution and then pathname expansion before passing the arguments on to echo:

```
$ ls tmp*
tmp1   tmp2   tmp3
$ var=tmp*
$ set | grep var
var=tmp*
$ echo '$var'
$var
$ echo "$var"
tmp*
$ echo $var
tmp1 tmp2 tmp3
```

Chapter Summary

The shell is both a command interpreter and a programming language. As a command interpreter, the shell executes commands you enter in response to its prompt. When you use it as a programming language, the shell executes commands from files called shell scripts.

You typically run a shell script by giving its name on the command line. To run a script in this manner, you must have execute permission for the file holding the script. Otherwise the shell does not know that the script is executable. Alternatively, you can execute the script by entering **bash**, **tcsh**, or **zsh** followed by the name of the file on the command line. Either way you need to have read permission for the file.

Job control is not part of the Bourne Again Shell but is included in the Job Shell, which is identical to the Bourne Again Shell in all other respects. A job is one or more commands connected by pipes. You can bring a job running in the background into the foreground with the fg builtin ^{bash tcsh zsh}. A foreground job can be put into the background with the bg builtin ^{bash tcsh zsh}, provided that it is first suspended by pressing the suspend key.

Each process has a unique identification, or PID, number and is the execution of a single GNU/Linux command. When you give it a command, the shell forks a new (child) process to execute the command, unless the command is built into the shell (see page 670 for a partial list of builtins). While the child process is running, the shell is in a state called sleep. By ending a command line with an ampersand (**&**), you can run a child process in the background and bypass the sleep state so that the shell prompt returns immediately after you press RETURN. Each command in a shell script forks a separate process, each of which may fork other processes. When a process terminates, it returns its exit status to its parent process: Zero signifies success, and nonzero signifies failure.

The shell allows you to define variables. You can declare and initialize a variable by assigning a value to it; you can remove a variable declaration by using unset. Variables are usually local to a process and must be exported by using the export ^{bash zsh} or setenv ^{tcsh} builtin to make them available to child processes. The shell also defines some variables and parameters. The positional and special parameters are preceded with dollar signs in the following table to reflect the only manner in which you can reference them. Unlike shell variables, you cannot assign values to them.

When it processes a command line, the Bourne Again Shell may replace some words with expanded text. Most of the various types of command line expansion are invoked by the appearance of a special character within a word (for example, a leading dollar sign denotes a variable). See the "Special Characters" table on page 618. The expansions take place in a specific order. The common expansions, in the order in which they occur, are parameter expansion, variable expansion, command substitution, and pathname expansion. Surrounding a word with double quotation marks suppresses all but parameter and variable expansion. Single quotation marks suppress all types of expansion, as does quoting (escaping) a special character by preceding it with a backslash.

Shell Variables/ Parameters

CDPATH `bash` `zsh` cdpath `tcsh`	List of directories for the shell to check when you give a **cd** builtin `bash` `tcsh` `zsh` (page 580).
HISTFILE `bash` `zsh` histfile `tcsh`	Name of the file in which history events are saved between login sessions (page 588).
HISTFILESIZE `bash`	Maximum number of lines saved in HISTFILE (page 589).
HISTSIZE `bash` `zsh`	Number of commands to remember in a given login session (number of commands that are displayed with the history builtin) (page 589).
HOME `bash` `tcsh` `zsh`	Pathname of your home directory (page 576).
IFS `bash`	Internal Field Separators (page 580).
MAIL `bash` `tcsh`	Name of the file where the system stores your mail (page 578).
MAILCHECK `bash`	How often (in seconds) the shell checks your mailbox for new mail (page 579).
MAILPATH `bash`	List of other potential mailboxes (page 578).
PATH `bash` `tcsh` `zsh`	Search path for commands (page 577).
prompt `tcsh` `zsh`	TC Shell Prompt String (page 708).
PS1 `bash`	Bourne Again and Z Shell Prompt String 1 (page 579).
PS2 `bash`	Bourne Again and Z Shell Prompt String 2 (page 579).
savehist `tcsh`	Maximum number of lines saved in **.history**. The presence of this variable turns on saving the history at the end of a session and reading it at the beginning. Assign a value in **~/.tcshrc**.

SHELL [bash tcsh zsh] shell [tcsh]	Pathname of the invoked shell.
status [tcsh zsh]	Exit status of the last task executed by the shell (page 588).
$0 [bash tcsh zsh]	Name of the calling program (page 581).
$n [bash tcsh zsh]	Value of the nth command line argument (can be changed by **set**) (page 582).
$* [bash tcsh zsh]	All command line arguments (can be changed by **set** in **bash** and **tcsh**) (page 586).
$@ [bash tcsh zsh]	All command line arguments (can be changed by **set** in **bash** and **tcsh**) (page 586).
$# [bash tcsh zsh]	Count of the command line arguments (page 582).
$$ [bash tcsh zsh]	PID number of the current process (page 586).
$! [bash tcsh zsh]	PID number of the most recent background task (page 586).
$? [bash tcsh zsh]	Exit status of the last task executed by the Bourne Again or Z Shell (page 588).

Special Characters ([bash tcsh zsh] Unless Noted)

NEWLINE	Initiates execution of a command (page 547)
;	Separates commands (page 547)
( )	Groups commands for execution by a subshell or identifies a function (page 550)
&	Executes a command in the background (pages 154 and 547)
|	Pipe (page 547)
>	Redirects standard output (page 145)
>>	Appends standard output (page 149)

<	Redirects standard input (page 147)
<<	Here document (page 659)
*	Any string of characters in an ambiguous file reference (pages 158 and 547)
?	Any single character in an ambiguous file reference (page 157)
\	Quotes the following character (page 55)
'	Quotes a string, preventing all substitutions (page 55)
"	Quotes a string, allowing only variable and command substitution (pages 55 and 568)
`...`	Performs command substitution (page 611)
[ ]	Character class in an ambiguous file reference (page 159)
$	References a variable (page 566)
. (dot builtin)	Executes a command (only at the beginning of a line) (page 581)
#	Begins a comment (page 636)
{ }	Command grouping (used to surround the contents of a function) (page 672)
: (null builtin)	Returns *true* exit status (page 669)
&& (Boolean AND)	Executes command on right only if command on left succeeds (returns a zero exit status [pages 719 and 764])
|| (Boolean OR)	Boolean OR: executes command on right only if command on left fails (returns a nonzero exit status [page 765])
! (Boolean NOT)	Boolean NOT: reverses exit status of command
$() **bash zsh**	Performs command substitution (preferred form) (page 575)
[ ]	Evaluates arithmetic expression (page 611)

620 Chapter 12 The Shell II: The Bourne Again Shell

Exercises

1. The following shell script adds entries to a file named **journal-file** in your home directory. The script can help you keep track of phone conversations and meetings:

```
$ cat journal
# journal: add journal entries to the file
# $HOME/journal-file

file=$HOME/journal-file
date >> $file
echo -n "Enter name of person or group: "
read name
echo "$name" >> $file
echo >> $file
cat >> $file
echo "--------------------------------------------------------------" >> $file
echo >> $file
```

   a. What do you have to do to the script in order to be able to execute it?

   b. Why does it use the read builtin the first time it accepts input from the terminal and the cat utility the second time?

2. What are two ways you can execute a shell script when you do not have execute access permission to the file containing the script? Can you execute a shell script if you do not have read access permission?

3. What is the purpose of the **PATH** variable?

   a. Set up your **PATH** variable so that it causes the shell to search the following directories in order:

   • /usr/local/bin

   • /usr/bin/X11

   • /usr/bin

   • /bin

   • /usr/openwin/bin

- Your own **bin** directory (usually **bin** or **.bin** in your home directory)

- The working directory

b. If a file named **whereis** is in **/usr/bin** and also in your **~/bin**, which one does **whereis** indicate will be executed? (Assume that you have execute permission for both of the files.)

c. If your **PATH** variable is not set to search the working directory, how can you execute a program located there?

d. What command can you use to add the directory **/usr/games** to the end of the list of directories in **PATH**?

4. Assume that you have made the following assignment:

```
$ person=jenny
```

Give the output of each of the following commands:

a. echo $person

b. echo ' $person '

c. echo "$person"

5. Explain the unexpected following result:

```
$ whereis date
date: /bin/date
$ echo $PATH
.:/usr/local/bin:/usr/bin:/bin
$ cat > date
echo "This is my own version of date."
$ date
Wed Mar 12 09:11:54 MST 2003
```

6. Assume that the **/home/jenny/grants/biblios** and **/home/jenny/biblios** directories exist. For both (a) and (b), give Jenny's working directory after she executes the sequence of commands given. Explain.

a.

```
$ pwd
/home/jenny/grants
CDPATH=$(pwd)
$ cd
$ cd biblios
```

b.

```
$ pwd
/home/jenny/grants
CDPATH=$(pwd)
$ cd $HOME/biblios
```

7. Name two ways you can identify the PID of your login shell.

8. Try giving the following command:

```
$ sleep 30 | cat /etc/motd
```

Is there any output from sleep? Where does cat get its input from? What has to happen before you get a prompt back?

Advanced Exercises

9. Write a sequence of commands or a script that demonstrates that parameter expansion occurs before variable expansion and that variable expansion occurs before pathname expansion.

10. Write a shell script that outputs the name of the shell that is executing it.

11. Type in the following shell scripts and run them:

```
$ cat report_dir
old_dir=$(pwd)
echo "Current working directory:  " $old_dir
go_home
echo "Current working directory:  " $(pwd)

$ cat go_home
cd
echo "New working directory:  " $(pwd)
echo "Last working directory: " $old_dir
```

What is wrong? Change them so that they work correctly.

12. The following is a modified version of the **read2** script from page 574. Explain why it behaves differently. For what type of input does it produce the same output of the original **read2** script?

```
$ cat read2
echo -n "Enter a command: "
read command
"$command"
echo "Thanks"
```

13. Explain the behavior of the following shell script:

```
$ cat quote_demo
twoliner="This is line 1.
This is line 2."
echo "$twoliner"
echo $twoliner
```

a. How many arguments does each echo command see in this script? Explain.

b. Redefine the **IFS** shell variable so that the output of the second echo is the same as the first.

IN THIS CHAPTER

Programming the Bourne Again Shell

13

Chapter 12 explained more about the shells, particularly the Bourne Again Shell. This chapter introduces additional commands, builtins, and concepts that carry shell programming to a point where it can be useful. The first programming constructs covered are control structures, or control flow constructs. These structures allow you to write scripts that can loop over command line arguments, make decisions based on the value of a variable, set up menus, and more. The Bourne Again Shell uses the same constructs found in such high-level programming languages as C.

This chapter goes on to explain how the Here document `bash tcsh zsh` makes it possible for you to redirect input to a script to come from the script itself, as opposed to the terminal or other file. The section titled "Expanding Null or Unset Variables" (page 661) shows you various ways to set default values for a variable. The section on the exec builtin `bash tcsh zsh` demonstrates how it provides an efficient way to execute a command by replacing a process and how you can use it to redirect input and output from within a script. The next section covers the trap builtin `bash zsh`, which provides a way to detect and respond to operating system signals (or interrupts, such as when you press CONTROL-C). Finally, the section on functions `bash zsh` gives you a clean way to execute code similar to scripts much more quickly and efficiently.

This chapter contains many examples of shell programs. Although they illustrate certain concepts, most use information from earlier examples as well. This overlap not only reinforces your overall knowledge of shell programming but also demonstrates how commands can be combined to solve complex tasks. Running, modifying, and experimenting with the examples is a good way to become comfortable with the underlying concepts.

Do Not Name Your Shell Script test   ‖ tip

You can create a problem for yourself if you give a shell script the name **test**. A GNU/Linux utility has the same name. Depending on how you have your **PATH** variable set up and how you call the program, you may run your script or the utility, leading to confusing results.

This chapter illustrates concepts with simple examples followed by more complicated examples in sections marked "Optional." The more complex scripts illustrate traditional shell programming practices and introduce some GNU/Linux utilities often used in scripts. You can skip these sections without loss of continuity the first time you read the chapter. Return to them later when you feel comfortable with the basic concepts.

Control Structures

The *control flow* commands alter the order of execution of commands within a shell script. The Bourne Again and Z Shells share a common syntax, whereas the TC Shell uses a different syntax (page 714). Control structures include the **if...then**, **for...in**, **while**, **until**, and **case** statements. In addition, the **break** and **continue** statements work in conjunction with the control flow structures to alter the order of execution of commands within a script.

if...then

The syntax of the **if...then** ^{bash zsh} control structure is

    *if **test-command***
       then
           commands
    fi

The *bold* words in the syntax description are the items you supply to cause the structure to have the desired effect. The *nonbold* words are the keywords the shell uses to identify the control structure.

Figure 13-1 shows that the **if** statement tests the status returned by the *test-command* and transfers control based on this status. The end of the **if** structure is marked by a **fi** statement, which is *if* spelled backward. The following script prompts you for two words, reads them in, and then uses an **if** structure to evaluate the result returned by the test builtin ^{bash zsh} when it compares the two words.

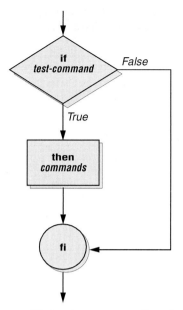

Figure 13-1   An **if...then** flowchart

The test builtin returns a status of *true* if the two words are the same and *false* if they are not. Double quotation marks around **$word1** and **$word2** make sure that test works properly if you enter a string that contains a SPACE or other special character:

```
$ cat if1
echo -n "word 1: "
read word1
echo -n "word 2: "
read word2

if test "$word1" = "$word2"
    then
        echo "Match"
fi
echo "End of program."
$ if1
word 1: peach
word 2: peach
Match
End of program.
```

In the preceding example the *test-command* is test "$word1" = "$word2". The test builtin returns a *true* status if its first and third arguments have the relationship specified by its second argument. If this command returns a *true* status (= 0), the shell executes the commands between the **then** and **fi** statements. If the command returns a *false* status (not = 0), the shell passes control to the statement after **fi** without executing the statements between **then** and **fi**. The effect of this **if** statement is to display Match if the two words match. The script always displays End of program.

In the Bourne Again and Z Shells, test is a builtin—part of the shell. It is also a stand-alone utility kept in **/usr/bin/test**. This chapter discusses and demonstrates many Bourne Again Shell builtins. Each bash builtin may or may not be a builtin in tcsh or zsh. You usually use the builtin version if it is available and the utility if it is not. Each version of a command may vary slightly from one shell to the next and from the utility to any of the shell builtins. To locate documentation, first determine whether you are using a builtin or a stand-alone utility. Use the type builtin [bash zsh] for this purpose:

```
$ type test cat echo who if
test is a shell builtin
cat is hashed (/bin/cat)
echo is a shell builtin
who is /usr/bin/who
if is a shell keyword
```

To get more information on a stand-alone utility, use the man or info command followed by the name of the utility. Refer to "Builtins" on page 161 for instructions on how to find information on a builtin command. You can also refer to the utilities and builtins covered in Part III of this book.

The next program uses an **if** structure at the beginning of a script to check that you supplied at least one argument on the command line. The **–eq** test operator compares two integers. This structure displays a message and exits from the script if you do not supply an argument:

```
$ cat chkargs
if test $# -eq 0
    then
        echo "You must supply at least one argument."
        exit 1
fi
echo "Program running."
$ chkargs
You must supply at least one argument.
$ chkargs abc
Program running.
```

A test like the one in shown in **chkargs** is a key component of any script that requires arguments. To prevent the user from receiving meaningless or confusing information from the script, the script needs to check whether the user has supplied the appropriate arguments. Sometimes the script simply tests whether arguments exist (as in **chkargs**). Other scripts test for a specific number or specific kinds of arguments.

You can use test to ask a question about the status of a file argument or the relationship between two file arguments. After verifying that at least one argument has been given on the command line, the following script tests whether the argument is the name of a regular file (not a directory or other type of file) in the working directory. The test builtin with the −f option and the first command line argument ($1) check the file:

```
$ cat is_regfile
if test $# -eq 0
    then
        echo "You must supply at least one argument."
        exit 1
fi
if test -f "$1"
    then
        echo "$1 is a regular file in the working directory"
    else
        echo "$1 is NOT a regular file in the working directory"
fi
```

You can test many other characteristics of a file with test and various options. Some of the options are listed in Table 13-1

Option	Test Performed on File	‖ table 13-1
−d	Exists and is a directory file	
−e	Exists	
−f	Exists and is a regular file	
−r	Exists and is readable	
−s	Exists and has a length greater than 0	
−w	Exists and is writable	
−x	Exists and is executable	

Other test options provide a way to test for a relationship between two files, such as whether one file is newer than another. Refer to later examples in this chapter, as well as to test in Part III for more detailed information. (Although test is a builtin in bash and zsh, the test utility described in Part III on page 1352 functions similarly.)

Always Test the Arguments || tip

To keep the examples in this and subsequent chapters short and focused on specific concepts, the code to verify arguments is often omitted or abbreviated. It is a good practice to include tests for argument verification in your own shell programs. Doing so will result in scripts that are easier to run and debug.

The following example, another version of **chkargs**, checks for arguments in a way that is more traditional for GNU/Linux shell scripts. The example uses the bracket ([]) synonym for test. Rather than using the word test in scripts, you can surround the arguments to test with brackets, as shown. The brackets must be surrounded by whitespace (SPACES or TABS).

```
$ cat chkargs
if [ $# -eq 0 ]
    then
        echo "Usage: chkargs argument..." 1>&2
        exit 1
fi
echo "Program running."
exit 0
$ chkargs
Usage: chkargs arguments
$ chkargs abc
Program running.
```

The error message that **chkargs** displays is called a *usage message* and uses the 1>&2 notation to redirect its output to standard error (page 552). After issuing the usage message, **chkargs** exits with an exit status of 1, indicating that an error has occurred. The **exit 0** command at the end of the script causes **chkargs** to exit with a 0 status after the program runs without an error.

The usage message is a common notation to specify the type and number of arguments the script takes. Many GNU/Linux utilities provide usage messages similar to the one in **chkargs**. When you call a utility or other program with the wrong number or kind of arguments, you often see a usage message. Following is the usage message that cp displays when you call it without any arguments:

```
$ cp
cp: missing file arguments
Try `cp --help' for more information.
```

if...then...else

The introduction of the **else** statement turns the **if** structure into the two-way branch shown in Figure 13-2. The syntax of the **if...then...else** ^bash ^zsh control structure is

*if **test-command***
> *then*
>> *commands*
> *else*
>> *commands*

fi

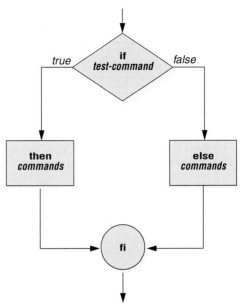

Figure 13-2   An **if…then…else** flowchart

Because a semicolon (;) ends a command just as a NEWLINE does, you can place **then** on the same line as **if** by preceding it with a semicolon. (Because **if** and **then** are separate builtins, they require a command separator between them; a semicolon and NEWLINE work equally well.) Some people prefer this notation for aesthetic reasons; others, because it saves space:

*if **test-command**; then*
>> *commands*
> *else*
>> *commands*

fi

If the ***test-command*** returns a *true* status, the **if** structure executes the commands between the **then** and **else** statements and then diverts control to the statement following **fi**. If the ***test-command*** returns a *false* status, the **if** structure executes the commands following the **else** statement.

The next script builds on **chkargs**. When you run **out** with arguments that are filenames, it displays the files on the terminal. If the first argument is a –v (called an option in this case), **out** uses less (page 54) to display the files one page at a time. After determining that it was called with at least one argument, **out** tests its first argument to see whether it is –v. If the result of the test is *true* (if the first argument is –v), **out** shifts the arguments to get rid of the –v and displays the files using less. If the result of the test is *false* (if the first argument is *not* –v), the script uses cat to display the files:

```
$ cat out
if [ $# -eq 0 ]
    then
        echo "Usage: out [-v] filenames..." 1>&2
        exit 1
fi
if [ "$1" = "-v" ]
    then
        shift
        less -- "$@"
    else
        cat -- "$@"
fi
```

Optional

In **out** the –– argument to cat and less tells the utility that no more options follow on the command line and not to consider leading hyphens (–) in the following list as indicating options. Thus –– allows you to view a file with a name that starts with a hyphen. Although not common, filenames beginning with a hyphen do occasionally occur. (One way to create such a file is to use the command **cat > –fname.**) The –– argument works with all GNU/Linux utilities that use the getopts (page 772) function to parse their options. It does not work with all GNU/Linux utilities (for example, more). It is particularly useful with rm to remove a file whose name starts with a hyphen (**rm –– –fname**), including any that you create while experimenting with the –– argument.

if...then...elif

The format of the **if...then...elif** ^bash_zsh control structure, shown in Figure 13-3, is as follows:

if **test-command**
       then
              commands
       elif **test-command**
              then
                     commands
.
.
       else
              commands
fi

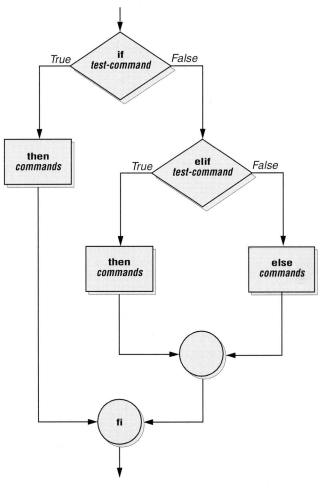

Figure 13-3   An **if...then...elif** flowchart

The **elif** statement combines the **else** statement and the **if** statement and allows you to construct a nested set of **if...then...else** structures (Figure 13-3). The difference between the **else** statement and the **elif** statement is that each **else** statement must be paired with a **fi** statement, whereas multiple nested **elif** statements require only a single closing **fi** statement.

The following example shows an **if...then...elif** control structure. This shell script compares three words that the user enters. The first **if** statement uses the AND operator (–a) as an argument to test. The test builtin returns a *true* status only if the first and the second logical comparisons are true (that is, if **word1** matches **word2** and **word2** matches **word3**). If **test** returns a *true* status, the program executes the command following the next **then** statement and passes control to the **fi** statement, and the script terminates:

```
$ cat if3
echo -n "word 1: "
read word1
echo -n "word 2: "
read word2
echo -n "word 3: "
read word3
if [ "$word1" = "$word2" -a "$word2" = "$word3" ]
    then
        echo "Match: words 1, 2, & 3"
    elif [ "$word1" = "$word2" ]
    then
        echo "Match: words 1 & 2"
    elif [ "$word1" = "$word3" ]
    then
        echo "Match: words 1 & 3"
    elif [ "$word2" = "$word3" ]
    then
        echo "Match: words 2 & 3"
    else
        echo "No match"
fi

$ if3
word 1: apple
word 2: orange
word 3: pear
No match
$ if3
word 1: apple
word 2: orange
word 3: apple
Match: words 1 & 3
$ if3
word 1: apple
word 2: apple
word 3: apple
Match: words 1, 2, & 3
```

If the three words are not the same, the structure passes control to the first **elif**, which begins a series of tests to see if any pair of words is the same. As the nesting continues, if any one of the **if** statements is satisfied, the structure passes control to the next **then** statement and subsequently to the statement after **fi**. Each time an **elif** statement is not satisfied, the structure passes control to the next **elif** statement. In the if3 script the double quotation marks around the arguments to echo that contain ampersands (&) prevent the shell from interpreting the ampersands as special characters.

Optional

The lnks Script

The following script, **lnks**, demonstrates the **if...then** and **if...then...elif** control structures. This script finds hard links to its first argument, a filename. If you provide a name of a directory as the second argument, **lnks** searches for links in that directory and all subdirectories. If you do not specify a directory, **lnks** searches the working directory and its subdirectories.

```
$ cat lnks
#!/bin/bash
# Identify links to a file
# Usage: lnks file [directory]

if [ $# -eq 0 -o $# -gt 2 ]; then
    echo "Usage: lnks file [directory]" 1>&2
    exit 1
fi
if [ -d "$1" ]; then
    echo "First argument cannot be a directory." 1>&2
    echo "Usage: lnks file [directory]" 1>&2
    exit 1
else
    file="$1"
fi
if [ $# -eq 1 ]; then
    directory="."
elif [ -d "$2" ]; then
    directory="$2"
else
    echo "Optional second argument must be a directory." 1>&2
    echo "Usage: lnks file [directory]" 1>&2
    exit 1
fi
```

```
# Check to make sure file exists and is a regular file:
if [ ! -e "$file" ]; then
    echo "lnks: $file not found or special file" 1>&2
    exit 1
fi
# Check link count on file
set -- $(ls -l "$file")

linkcnt=$2
if [ "$linkcnt" -eq 1 ]; then
    echo "lnks: no other link to $file" 1>&2
    exit 0
fi

# Get the inode of the given file
set $(ls -i "$file")

inode=$1

# Find and print the files with that inode number
echo "lnks: using find to search for links..." 1>&2
find "$directory" -xdev -inum $inode -print
```

In the following example Alex uses **lnks** while he is in his home directory to search for links to a file named **letter** in the working directory. The **lnks** script reports that **/home/alex/letter** and **/home/jenny/draft** are links to the same file:

```
$ lnks letter /home
lnks: using find to search for links...
/home/alex/letter
/home/jenny/draft
```

In addition to the **if...then...elif** control structure, **lnks** introduces other features that are commonly used in shell programs. The following discussion describes **lnks** section by section.

The first line of the **lnks** script specifies the shell to execute the script (refer to "#!   Specifies a Shell" on page 564):

```
#!/bin/bash
```

In this chapter the **#!** notation appears only in more complex examples. It ensures that the proper shell executes the script, even if the user is currently running a different shell. It also works correctly if invoked within another shell script.

The second and third lines of **lnks** are comments; the shell ignores the text that follows pound signs up to the next NEWLINE character. These comments in **lnks** briefly identify what the file does and how to use it.

```
# Identify links to a file
# Usage: lnks file [directory]
```

The first **if** statement in **lnks** tests whether **lnks** was called with zero arguments or more than two arguments:

```
if [ $# -eq 0 -o $# -gt 2 ]; then
    echo "Usage: lnks file [directory]" 1>&2
    exit 1
fi
```

If either of these conditions is true, **lnks** sends a usage message to standard error and exits with a status of 1. The double quotation marks around the usage message prevent the shell from interpreting the brackets as special characters. The brackets in the usage message indicate to the user that the **directory** argument is optional.

The second **if** statement tests to see whether **$1** is a directory (the **–d** argument to test returns a *true* value if the file exists and is a directory):

```
if [ -d "$1" ]; then
    echo "First argument cannot be a directory." 1>&2
    echo "Usage: lnks file [directory]" 1>&2
    exit 1
else
    file="$1"
fi
```

If it is a directory, **lnks** presents a usage message and exits. If it is not a directory, **lnks** saves the value of **$1** in the **file** variable because later in the script **set** resets the command line arguments. If the value of **$1** is not saved before the **set** command is issued, its value is lost.

The next section of **lnks** is an **if...then...elif** statement:

```
if [ $# -eq 1 ]; then
    directory="."
elif [ -d "$2" ]; then
    directory="$2"
else
    echo "Optional second argument must be a directory." 1>&2
    echo "Usage: lnks file [directory]" 1>&2
    exit 1
fi
```

The first *test-command* determines whether the user specified a single argument on the command line. If the *test-command* returns 0 (*true*), the user-created variable named **directory** is assigned the value of the working directory (.). If the *test-command* returns a *false* value, the **elif** statement tests whether the second argument is a directory. If it is a directory, the **directory** variable is set equal to the second command line argument, **$2**. If **$2** is not a directory, **lnks** sends a usage message to standard error and exits with a status of 1.

The next **if** statement in **lnks** tests whether **$file** does not exist. This is an important inquiry because it would be pointless for **lnks** to spend time looking for links to a nonexistent file.

The test builtin with the three arguments **!**, **–f**, and **$file** evaluates to *true* if the file **$file** does *not* exist:

```
[ ! -f "$file" ]
```

The **!** operator preceding the **–f** argument to test negates its result, yielding *false* if the file **$file** *does* exist and is a regular file.

Next, **lnks** uses set and **ls –l** to check the number of links **$file** has:

```
# Check link count on file
set -- $(ls -l "$file")
linkcnt=$2
if [ "$linkcnt" -eq 1 ]; then
    echo "lnks: no other links to $file" 1>&2
    exit 0
fi
```

The set builtin `bash lcsh zsh` uses command substitution (page 575) to set the positional parameters to the output of **ls –l**. In the output of **ls –l**, the second field is the link count, so the user-created variable **linkcnt** is set equal to **$2**. The **––** used with set prevents set from interpreting as an option the first argument **ls –l** produces (the first argument is the access permissions for the file, and it is likely to begin with **–**). The **if** statement checks whether **$linkcnt** is equal to 1; if it is, **lnks** displays a message and exits. Although this message is not truly an error message, it is redirected to standard error. The way **lnks** has been written, all informational messages are sent to standard error. Only the final product of lnks—the pathnames of links to the specified file—is sent to standard output, so you can redirect the output as you please.

If the link count is greater than one, **lnks** goes on to identify the inode (page 968) for **$file**. As explained in Chapter 4 (page 126), comparing the inodes associated with filenames is a good way to determine whether the filenames are links to the same file. The **lnks** script uses set again to set the positional parameters to the output of **ls –i**. The first argument to set is the inode number for the file, so the user-created variable named **inode** is set to the value of **$1**:

```
# Get the inode of the given file
set $(ls -i "$file")
inode=$1
```

Finally, **lnks** uses the find utility to search for filenames having inodes that match **$inode**.

```
# Find and print the files with that inode number
echo "lnks: using find to search for links..." 1>&2
find "$directory" -xdev -inum $inode -print
```

The find utility searches for files that meet the criteria specified by its arguments, beginning its search with the directory specified by its first argument (**$directory** in this case) and searching all subdirectories. The last three arguments to find specify that the filenames of files having inodes matching **$inode** should be sent to standard output. Because files in different filesystems can have the same inode number and not be linked, find must search only directories in the same filesystem as **$file** for accurate results. The **–xdev** argument to find prevents the search of subdirectories on other filesystems. Refer to page 123 and page 968 for more information about filesystems and links. Refer to page 1165 in Part III for more information on find.

The echo above the find command in **lnks**, which tells the user that find is running, is included because find frequently takes a long time to run. Because **lnks** does not include a final exit statement, the exit status of **lnks** is that of the last command it runs, find.

Debugging Shell Scripts

When you are writing a script such as **lnks**, it is easy to make mistakes. While you are debugging a script, you can use the shell's **–x** option `bash` `tcsh` `zsh`, which causes the shell to display each command before it runs the command. This trace of a script's execution can give you a lot of information about where the problem is.

Suppose that Alex wants to run **lnks** as in the previous example, while displaying each command before it is executed. He can either set the **–x** option for the current shell (**set –x**) so that all scripts display commands as they are run or use the **–x** option to affect only the script he is currently executing:

```
$ bash -x lnks letter /home
```

Each command that the script executes is preceded by a plus sign (**+**) so that you can distinguish the output of the trace from any output that your script produces. You can also set the **–x** option of the shell running the script by putting the following set command at the top of the script:

```
set -x
```

Turn off the debug option with a plus sign:

```
set +x
```

for...in

The **for...in** structure has the following format:

> *for loop-index in argument-list*
> *do*
>   *commands*
> *done*

This structure (Figure 13-4) assigns the value of the first argument in the *argument-list* to the *loop-index* and executes the *commands* between the **do** and **done** statements. The **do** and **done** statements mark the beginning and end of the **for** loop.

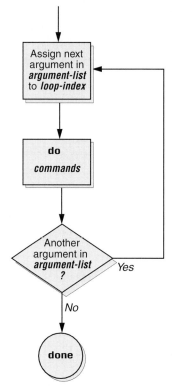

Figure 13-4   A **for...in** flowchart

After it passes control to the **done** statement, the structure assigns the value of the second argument in the *argument-list* to the *loop-index* and repeats the *commands*. The structure repeats the *commands* between the **do** and **done** statements: once for each argument in the *argument-list*. When the structure exhausts the *argument-list*, it passes control to the statement following **done**.

The following **for...in** structure assigns `apples` to the user-created variable **fruit** and then displays the value of **fruit**, which is `apples`. Next the structure assigns oranges to **fruit** and repeats the process. When it exhausts the argument list, the structure transfers control to the statement following **done**, which displays a message:

```
$ cat fruit
for fruit in apples oranges pears bananas
do
    echo "$fruit"
done
echo "Task complete."

$ fruit
apples
oranges
pears
bananas
Task complete.
```

The next script lists the names of the directory files in the working directory by looping over all the files, using test to determine which are directory files:

```
$ cat dirfiles
for i in *
do
    if [ -d "$i" ]
        then
            echo "$i"
    fi
done
```

The ambiguous file reference character * stands for all files (except invisible files) in the working directory. Prior to executing the **for** loop, the shell expands the * and uses the resulting list to assign successive values to the index variable i.

for

The **for** ^{bash zsh} control structure has the following format:

> *for loop-index*
> *do*
> > *commands*
> *done*

In the **for** structure the *loop-index* automatically takes on the value of each of the command line arguments, one at a time. It performs a sequence of commands, usually involving each argument in turn.

The following shell script shows a **for** structure displaying each of the command line arguments. The first line of the shell script, **for arg**, implies **for arg in "$@"**, where the shell expands **"$@"** into a list of quoted command line arguments **"$1"** **"$2"** **"$3"**.... The balance of the script corresponds to the **for...in** structure:

```
$ cat for_test
for arg
do
    echo "$arg"
done
$ for_test candy gum chocolate
candy
gum
chocolate
```

Optional

The whos Script

The following script, **whos**, demonstrates the usefulness of the implied **"$@"** in the **for** structure. You give **whos** one or more **ids** for users as arguments (for example, a user's name or login name), and **whos** displays information about the users. The **whos** script gets the information it displays from the first and fifth fields in the **/etc/passwd** file. The first field always contains a user's login name, and the fifth field typically contains the user's name. You can use a login name as an argument to **whos** to iden-tify the user's name or use a name as an argument to identify the login name. The **whos** script is similar to the finger utility, although **whos** provides less information:

```
$ cat whos
#!/bin/bash
# adapted from finger.sh by Lee Sailer
# UNIX/WORLD, III:11, p. 67, Fig. 2

if [ $# -eq 0 ]
    then
        echo "Usage: whos id..." 1>&2
        exit 1
fi
for i
do
    gawk -F: '{print $1, $5}' /etc/passwd |
    grep -i "$i"
done
```

In the following script **whos** identifies the user whose login is chas and the user whose name is Marilou Smith:

```
$ whos chas "Marilou Smith"
chas Charles Casey
msmith Marilou Smith
```

The **whos** script uses a **for** statement to loop through the command line arguments. In this script the implied use of "$@" in the **for** loop is particularly useful because it causes the **for** loop to treat as a single argument an argument containing a SPACE. In this example the user quotes Marilou Smith, which causes the shell to pass it to the script as a single argument. Then the implied "$@" in the **for** statement causes the shell to regenerate the quoted argument Marilou Smith so that it is again treated as a single argument.

For each command line argument, **whos** searches for **id** in the /etc/passwd file. Inside the **for** loop gawk extracts the first (**$1**) and fifth (**$5**) fields from the lines in /etc/passwd (which contain the user's login name and information about the user, respectively). The **$1** and **$5** are arguments that the gawk command sets and uses; they are included within single quotation marks and are not interpreted by the shell. (Do not confuse them with the positional parameters, which correspond to the command line arguments.) The first and fifth fields are sent, via a pipe, to grep. The grep utility searches for **$i** (which has taken on the value of a command line argument) in its input. The –i option causes grep to ignore case as it searches for and displays each line in its input that contains **$i**.

An interesting syntactical exception that the shells [bash zsh] give the pipe symbol (|) is shown on the line with the gawk command. You do not have to quote a NEWLINE that immediately follows a pipe symbol (that is, a pipe symbol that is the last thing on a line) to keep the NEWLINE from executing a command. You can see this if you give the command **who |** and press RETURN. The shell [bash zsh] displays a secondary prompt. If you then enter **sort** followed by another RETURN, you see a sorted who list. The pipe works even though a NEWLINE follows the pipe symbol.

Because it gets its information from the /etc/passwd file, information the **whos** script displays is only as informative and accurate as the information in /etc/passwd. See page 962 for more information about /etc/passwd. Refer to Part III for more information on gawk (page 1185) and grep (page 1215).

while

The **while** control structure [bash zsh] (Figure 13-5) has the following syntax:

*while **test-command***
do
        commands
done

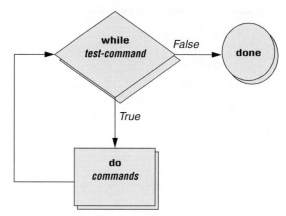

Figure 13-5   A **while** flowchart

As long as the *test-command* returns a *true* exit status, the structure continues to execute the series of *commands* delimited by the **do** and **done** statements. Before each loop through the *commands*, the structure executes the *test-command*. When the exit status of the *test-command* is *false*, the structure passes control to the statement after the **done** statement.

The following shell script first initializes the **number** variable to a value of zero. The test builtin then determines whether the value of **number** is less than 10. The script uses test with the –lt argument to perform a numerical test. For numerical comparisons, you must use **–ne** (not equal), **–eq** (equal), **–gt** (greater than), **–ge** (greater than or equal to), **–lt** (less than), or **–le** (less than or equal to); for string comparisons, = (equal) or != (not equal) when you are working with test. The test builtin has an exit status of 0 (*true*) as long as **number** is less than 10. As long as test returns *true*, the structure executes the commands between the **do** and **done** statements:

```
$ cat count
#!/bin/bash
number=0
while [ "$number" -lt 10 ]
    do
        echo -n "$number"
        number=$(expr $number + 1)
    done
echo
$ count
0123456789
$
```

The first command following **do** displays the string represented by **number**. The next command uses the expr utility to increment the value of **number** by one. Here expr converts its arguments to numbers, adds them, converts the result to characters, and sends them to standard output. The $(...) causes the enclosed command to be replaced by the output of the command (command substitution). This value is assigned to the variable **number**. The first time through the loop, number has a value of zero, so expr converts the strings 0 and 1 to numbers, adds them, and converts the result back to a string (1). The shell then assigns this value to the variable **number**. The **done** statement closes the loop and returns control to the **while** statement to start the loop over again. The final echo causes **count** to send a NEWLINE character to standard output, so that the next prompt occurs in the leftmost column on the display (rather than immediately following 9).

Optional

The spell_check Script

The aspell utility checks the words in a file against a dictionary of correctly spelled words. With the –l option, aspell runs in list mode: Input comes from standard input, and aspell displays each potentially misspelled word on standard output. The following command produces a list of possible misspellings in the file **letter.txt**:

```
$ aspell -l < letter.txt
```

The next shell script, spell_check, shows another use of a **while** structure. To find the incorrect spellings in a file, you can use **spell_check**, which uses aspell to check your file against a system dictionary but goes a step further: It enables you to specify your own list of correct words and removes these words from the output of aspell. This script is useful for removing words that you use frequently, such as names and technical terms, that are not in a standard dictionary.

Although you can duplicate the functionality of **spell_check** using aspell, **spell_check** is included here for its instructive value.

The **spell_check** script requires two filename arguments: The first file contains your list of correctly spelled words, and the second file is the one you want to check. The first **if** statement verifies that the user specified two arguments, and the next two **if** statements verify that both arguments are readable files. (The exclamation point negates the sense of the following operator; the –r operator causes test to determine whether a file is readable. The result is a test that determines whether a file is *not readable*.)

```
$ cat spell_check
#!/bin/bash
# remove correct spellings from aspell output

if [ $# -ne 2 ]
    then
        echo "Usage: spell_check file1 file2" 1>&2
        echo "file1: list of correct spellings" 1>&2
        echo "file2: file to be checked" 1>&2
        exit 1
fi

if [ ! -r "$1" ]
    then
        echo "spell_check: $1 is not readable" 1>&2
        exit 1
fi

if [ ! -r "$2" ]
    then
        echo "spell_check: $2 is not readable" 1>&2
        exit 1
fi

aspell -l < "$2" |
while read line
do
    if grep -v "^$line$" "$1" > /dev/null
        then
            echo $line
    fi
done
```

The **spell_check** script sends the output from aspell (with the **–l** option so that it produces a list of misspelled words on standard output) through a pipe to standard input of a **while** structure, which reads one line at a time (each line has one word on it in this case) from standard input. The *test-command* (that is, **read line**) returns a *true* exit status as long as it receives a line from standard input. Inside the **while** loop an **if** statement[1] monitors the return value of grep, which determines whether the line that was read is in the user's list of correctly spelled words. The pattern that grep searches for (the value of **$line**) is preceded and followed by special characters that specify the beginning and end of a line (^ and $, respectively). These special characters are used so that grep finds a match only if the **$line** variable matches an entire line in the file of correctly spelled words. (Otherwise, grep would match a

---

1. This **if** statement can also be written as

   ```
   if ! grep -qw "$line" "$1"
   ```

   The **–q** option suppresses the output from grep so only an exit code is returned, and the **–w** option causes grep to match only a whole word.

string, such as paul, in the output of aspell if the file of correctly spelled words contained the word paulson.) These special characters, together with the value of the $line variable, form a regular expression (page 1383). The output of grep is redirected to **/dev/null** (page 150) because the output is not needed; only the exit code is important. The **if** statement checks the negated exit status of grep (the leading exclamation point negates or changes the sense of the exit status—*true* becomes *false* and vice versa), which is 0 or *true* (*false* when negated) only if a matching line was found. If the exit status is *not* 0 or *false* (*true* when negated), the word was *not* in the file of correctly spelled words. The echo builtin [bash tcsh zsh] displays a list of words that are not in the file of correctly spelled words on standard output. Once it detects the EOF (end of file), the read builtin returns a *false* exit status, control is passed out of the **while** structure, and the script terminates.

Before you use **spell_check**, create a file of correct spellings containing words that you use frequently but that are not in a standard dictionary. For example, if you work for a company named Blankenship and Klimowski, Attorneys, you would put Blankenship and Klimowski into the file. The following example shows how **spell_check** checks the spelling in a file named **memo** and removes Blankenship and Klimowski from the output list of incorrectly spelled words:

```
$ aspell -l < memo
Blankenship
Klimowski
targat
hte
$ cat word_list
Blankenship
Klimowski
$ spell_check word_list memo
targat
hte
```

Refer to page 1089 for more information on aspell.

until

The **until** [bash zsh] and **while** structures are very similar, differing only in the sense of the test at the top of the loop. Figure 13-6 shows that **until** continues to loop *until* the *test-command* returns a *true* exit status. The **while** structure loops *while* the *test-command* continues to return a *true* or nonerror condition. The **until** structure is as follows:

*until **test-command***
do
        commands
done

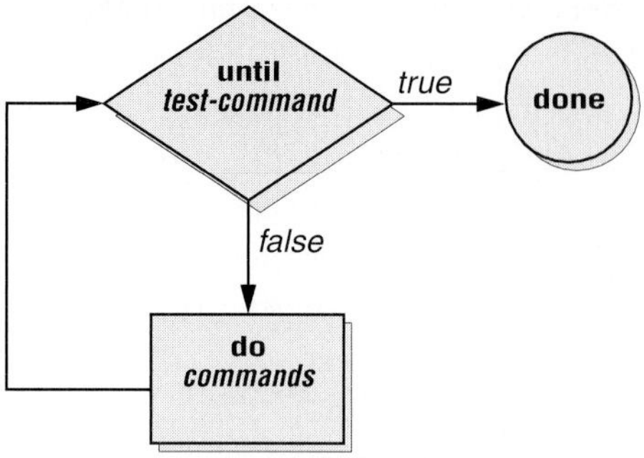

Figure 13-6   An **until** flowchart

The following script demonstrates an **until** structure that includes read. When the user enters the correct string of characters, the *test-command* is satisfied, and the structure passes control out of the loop:

```
$ cat until1
secretname=jenny
name=noname
echo "Try to guess the secret name!"
echo
until [ "$name" = "$secretname" ]
do
    echo -n "Your guess: "
    read name
done
echo "Very good."

$ until1
Try to guess the secret name!

Your guess: helen
Your guess: barbara
Your guess: rachael
Your guess: jenny
Very good
```

The following **locktty** script is similar to the lock command on Berkeley UNIX and the Lock Screen menu selection in GNOME. The script prompts the user for a key (password) and uses an **until** control structure to "lock" the terminal. The **until** statement causes the system to ignore any characters typed at the keyboard until the user types in the key on a line by itself, which unlocks the terminal. The **locktty** script can keep people from using your terminal while you are away from it for short periods of time. It saves you from having to log out if you are concerned about other users using your login:

```
$ cat locktty
#! /bin/bash
# UNIX/WORLD, III:4

trap '' 1 2 3 18
stty -echo
echo -n "Key: "
read key_1
echo
echo -n "Again: "
read key_2
echo
key_3=
if [ "$key_1" = "$key_2" ]
    then
        tput clear
        until [ "$key_3" = "$key_2" ]
        do
            read key_3
        done
    else
        echo "locktty: keys do not match" 1>&2
fi
stty echo
```

Forget Your Password?   ‖ tip

If you forget your key (password), you will need to log in from another (virtual) terminal and kill the process running **locktty**.

The trap builtin [bash zsh] (page 667) at the beginning of the **locktty** script stops a user from being able to terminate the script by sending it a signal (for example, by pressing the interrupt key). Trapping signal 18 means that no one can use CONTROL-Z (job control, a stop from a tty) to defeat the lock. See Table 13-5 on page 667 for a list of signals. The **stty –echo** command (page 1335) causes the terminal not to display characters typed at the keyboard. This prevents the key that the user enters from appearing on the screen. After turning off echo, the script prompts the user for a key, reads it into the user-created variable **key_1**, and then prompts the user to enter the same key again and saves it in the user-created variable **key_2**. The statement **key_3=** creates a variable with a NULL value. If **key_1** and **key_2** match, **locktty** clears the screen (with the tput command) and starts an **until** loop. The **until** loop keeps attempting to read from the terminal and assigning the input to the **key_3** variable. Once the user types in a string that matches one of the original keys (**key_2**), the **until** loop terminates, and echo is turned back on.

break and continue

You can interrupt a **for, while,** or **until** loop with a **break** [bash zsh] or **continue** [bash zsh] statement. The **break** statement transfers control to the statement after the **done** statement, terminating execution of the loop. The **continue** command transfers control to the **done** statement, which continues execution of the loop.

The following script demonstrates the use of these two statements. The **for...in** structure loops through the values 1–10. The first **if** statement executes its commands when the value of the index is less than or equal to 3 ($index –le 3). The second **if** statement executes its commands when the value of the index is greater than or equal to 8 ($index –ge 8). In between the two **if**s, echo displays the value of the index. For all values up to and including 3, the first **if** displays continue and executes a **continue** statement that skips echo $index and the second **if** and continues with the next **for**. For the value of 8, the second **if** displays break and executes a **break** that exits from the **for** loop. The echo builtin displays the values of **index:**

```
$ cat brk
for index in 1 2 3 4 5 6 7 8 9 10
    do
        if [ $index –le 3 ] ; then
            echo "continue"
            continue
        fi
#
    echo $index
#
    if [ $index –ge 8 ] ; then
        echo "break"
        break
    fi
done

$ brk
continue
continue
continue
4
5
6
7
8
break
```

case

Figure 13-7 shows the **case** structure, a multiple-branch decision mechanism. The path taken through the structure depends on a match or lack of a match between the *test-string* and one of the *patterns*.

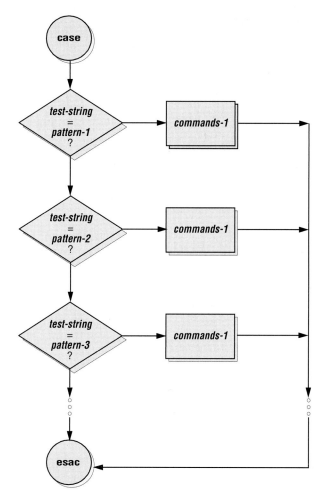

Figure 13-7   A **case** flowchart

The **case** structure bash zsh is

*case **test-string** in*
      pattern-1)
         commands-1
         ;;
      pattern-2)
         commands-2
         ;;
      pattern-3)
         commands-3
         ;;
...
esac

The following **case** structure uses the character that the user enters as the *test-string*. This value is held in the variable **letter**. If the *test-string* has a value of A, the structure executes the command following the *pattern* A. The right parenthesis is part of the **case** control structure, not part of the *pattern*. If the *test-string* has a value of B or C, the structure executes the command following the matching *pattern*. The asterisk (*) indicates *any string of characters* and serves as a catchall in case there is no match. If no *pattern* matches the *test-string* and if there is no catchall (*) *pattern*, control passes to the command following the **esac** statement, without the **case** structure taking any action. The second sample execution of **case1** shows the user entering a lowercase **b**. Because the *test-string* b does not match the uppercase B *pattern* (or any other *pattern* in the **case** statement), the program executes the commands following the catchall *pattern* and displays a message:

```
$ cat case1
echo -n "Enter A, B, or C: "
read letter
case "$letter" in
    A)
        echo "You entered A"
        ;;
    B)
        echo "You entered B"
        ;;
    C)
        echo "You entered C"
        ;;
    *)
        echo "You did not enter A, B, or C"
        ;;
esac

$ case1
Enter A, B, or C: B
You entered B
$ case1
Enter A, B, or C: b
You did not enter A, B, or C
```

The *pattern* in the **case** structure is analogous to that of an ambiguous file reference. The *pattern* can include any of the special characters and strings shown in Table 13-2.

Pattern	‖ table 13-2
*	Matches any string of characters. Use it for the default case.
?	Matches any single character.

Pattern (Continued)		table 13-2
[...]		Defines a character class. Any characters enclosed within brackets are tried, one at a time, in an attempt to match a single character. A hyphen between two characters specifies a range of characters.
|		Separates alternative choices that satisfy a particular branch of the **case** structure.

The next script accepts upper- and lowercase letters:

```
$ cat case2
echo -n "Enter A, B, or C: "
read letter
case "$letter" in
    a|A)
        echo "You entered A"
        ;;
    b|B)
        echo "You entered B"
        ;;
    c|C)
        echo "You entered C"
        ;;
    *)
        echo "You did not enter A, B, or C"
        ;;
esac

$ case2
Enter A, B, or C: b
You entered B
$
```

Optional

The following example shows how you can use the **case** structure to create a simple menu.[2] The **command_menu** script uses echo to present menu items and prompt the user for a selection. The **case** structure executes the appropriate utility, depending on the user's selection:

---

2. The Bourne Again and Z Shells have a menu control structure that automatically takes care of a lot of the work that this program does. See **select** on page 658.

```
$ cat command_menu
#!/bin/bash
# menu interface to simple commands

echo -e "\n         COMMAND MENU\n"
echo "  a.   Current date and time"
echo "  b.   Users currently logged in"
echo "  c.   Name of the working directory"
echo -e "  d.   Contents of the working directory\n"
echo -n "Enter a, b, c, or d: "
read answer
echo
case "$answer" in
    a)
        date
        ;;
    b)
        who
        ;;
    c)
        pwd
        ;;
    d)
        ls
        ;;
    *)
        echo "There is no selection: $answer"
        ;;
esac
```

```
$ command_menu

         COMMAND MENU

  a.   Current date and time
  b.   Users currently logged in
  c.   Name of the working directory
  d.   Contents of the working directory

Enter a, b, c, or d: a

Thu May  2 11:17:50 PDT 2002
```

The –e option causes echo to interpret the \ns (toward the beginning of **command_menu**) as NEWLINE characters. If you do not include this option, echo does not output the extra blank lines that make the menu easy to read but instead outputs the (literal) two-character sequence \n. The –e option causes echo to interpret several other backslash-quoted characters as well (Table 13-3). Remember to quote (with double quotation marks around the string) the backslash-quoted character so that the shell does not interpret it but passes the backslash and the character on to echo.

Quoted Character	echo Displays	‖ table 13-3
\a	Alert (bell).	
\b	BACKSPACE.	
\c	Suppress trailing NEWLINE.	
\f	FORMFEED.	
\n	NEWLINE.	
\r	RETURN.	
\t	Horizontal TAB.	
\v	Vertical TAB.	
\\	Backslash.	
\nnn	The character with the ASCII octal code *nnn*. If *nnn* is not valid, echo displays the string literally.	

You can also use the **case** control structure to take various actions in a script, depending on how many arguments the script is called with. The following script, **safedit**, uses a **case** structure that branches based on the number of command line arguments (**$#**). The **safedit** script saves a backup copy of a file you are editing with vi:

```
$ cat safedit
#!/bin/bash
# UNIX/WORLD, IV:11

PATH=/bin:/usr/bin
script=$(basename $0)
case $# in

    0)
        vi
        exit 0
        ;;

    1)
        if [ ! -f "$1" ]
            then
                vi "$1"
                exit 0
            fi
```

```
        if [ ! -r "$1" -o ! -w "$1" ]
            then
                echo "$script: check permissions on $1" 1>&2
                exit 1
            else
                editfile=$1
            fi
        if [ ! -w "." ]
            then
                echo "$script: backup cannot be " \
                    "created in the working directory" 1>&2
                exit 1
            fi
        ;;
    *)
        echo "Usage: $script [file-to-edit]" 1>&2
        exit 1
        ;;
esac
tempfile=/tmp/$$.$script
cp $editfile $tempfile
if vi $editfile
    then
        mv $tempfile bak.$(basename $editfile)
        echo "$script: backup file created"
    else
        mv $tempfile editerr
        echo "$script: edit error--copy of " \
            "original file is in editerr" 1>&2
fi
```

If you call **safedit** without any arguments, the **case** structure executes its first branch and calls vi without a filename argument. Because an existing file is not being edited, **safedit** does not create a backup file. (See the **:w** command on page 426 for an explanation of how to exit from vi when you have called it without a filename.) If the user calls **safedit** with one argument, **safedit** runs the commands in the second branch of the **case** structure and verifies that the file specified by **$1** does not yet exist or is the name of a file for which the user has read and write permission. The **safedit** script also verifies that the user has write permission for the working directory. If the user calls **safedit** with more than one argument, the third branch of the **case** structure presents a usage message and exits with a status of 1.

In addition to the use of a **case** structure for branching based on the number of command line arguments, the **safedit** script introduces several other features. First, at the beginning of the script, the **PATH** variable is set to search **/bin** and **/usr/bin**. This ensures that the commands executed by the script are standard utilities, which are kept in those directories. By setting **PATH** inside a script, you can avoid the problems that might occur if users have set up **PATH** to search their own directories first and have scripts or programs with the same names as utilities the script uses.

Second, the following line creates a variable named **script** and assigns the simple filename of the script to it:

```
script=$(basename $0)
```

The basename utility sends the simple filename component of its argument to standard output, which is assigned to the **script** variable, using command substitution. No matter which of the following commands the user calls the script with, the output of basename is the simple filename **safedit**:

```
$ /home/alex/bin/safedit memo
$ ./safedit memo
$ safedit memo
```

After the **script** variable is set, it is used in place of the filename of the script in usage and error messages. By using a variable that is derived from the command that invoked the script rather than a filename that is hardcoded (typed directly) into the script, you can create links to the script or rename it, and the usage and error messages will still provide accurate information.

A third significant feature of **safedit** is the use of the **$$** variable in the name of a temporary file. The statement below the **esac** statement creates and assigns a value to the **tempfile** variable. This variable contains the name of a temporary file that is stored in the **/tmp** directory, as are many temporary files. The temporary filename begins with the PID number of the current shell and ends with the name of the script. The PID number is used because it ensures that the filename is unique, and **safedit** will not attempt to overwrite an existing file, as might happen if two people were using **safedit** at the same time and not using unique filenames. The name of the script is appended so that, should the file be left in **/tmp** for some reason, you can figure out where it came from.

The PID is used in front of rather than after **$script** in the filename because of the 14-character limit on filenames on some filesystems on older versions of UNIX. GNU/Linux systems do not have this limitation. Because the PID ensures the uniqueness of the filename, it is placed first so that it cannot be truncated. (If the **$script** component is truncated, the filename is still unique.) For the same reason, when a backup file is created inside the **if** control structure a few lines down in the script, the filename is composed of the string **bak.** followed by the name of the file being edited. On an older system, if **bak** were used as a suffix rather than a prefix and the original filename were 14 characters, **.bak** might be lost, and the original file would be overwritten. The basename utility extracts the simple filename of **$editfile** before it is prefixed with **bak.**.

Fourth, **safedit** uses an unusual *test-command* in the **if** structure: vi $editfile. The *test-command* calls vi to edit $editfile. When you finish editing the file and exit from vi, vi returns an exit code that is the basis for branching by the **if** control structure. If the editing session completed successfully, vi returns a 0, and the statements following the **then** statement are executed. If vi does not terminate normally (as would occur if the user killed [page 1224] the vi process), vi returns a nonzero exit status, and the script executes the statements following **else**.

select

The Bourne Again Shell's **select** [bash zsh] control structure, based on the one found in the Korn Shell and corresponding to the **select** control structure in zsh, displays a menu, assigns a value to a variable based on the user's choice of items, and executes a series of commands. The syntax of a **select** structure is

> select *varname [in arg ...]*
> *do*
> > *commands*
>
> *done*

First, **select** generates and displays a menu of the *arg* items. The menu is formatted with numbers before each item. For example, a **select** structure that begins with

```
select fruit in apple banana blueberry kiwi orange watermelon STOP
```

displays the following menu:

```
1) apple       3) blueberry   5) orange       7) STOP
2) banana      4) kiwi        6) watermelon
```

You can have many items in the list of **args**. The **select** structure uses the values of the **LINES** and **COLUMNS** variables to determine the size of the display. (**LINES** has a default value of 24; **COLUMNS**, a default of 80.) With **COLUMNS** set to 20, the menu looks like this:

```
1) apple
2) banana
3) blueberry
4) kiwi
5) orange
6) watermelon
7) STOP
```

After displaying the menu, **select** displays the value of **PS3**, the special **select** prompt. The default value of **PS3** is the characters ?#, but typically you would set **PS3** to a more meaningful value.

If in the preceding menu you enter a valid number (one in the menu range), **select** sets the value of *varname* to the argument corresponding to the number entered and executes the commands between **do** and **done**. The **select** structure then reissues the **PS3** prompt and waits for another entry, doing this repeatedly until something causes it to exit from the statements between **do** and **done**, typically a **break**, **return**, or **exit** statement. The **break** statement exits from the loop. From within a function **return** returns control to the program that called the function. The **exit** statement exits from the current shell. The following script illustrates the use of **select**:

```
$ cat fruit
#!/bin/bash
PS3="Choose your favorite fruit from these possibilities: "
select FRUIT in apple banana blueberry kiwi orange watermelon STOP
do
if [ $FRUIT = STOP ]; then

echo "Thanks for playing!"
break
fi
echo "You chose $FRUIT as your favorite."
echo "That is choice number $REPLY."
echo
done

$ fruit
1) apple       3) blueberry   5) orange      7) STOP
2) banana      4) kiwi        6) watermelon

Choose your favorite fruit from these possibilities: 3
You chose blueberry as your favorite.
That is choice number 3.

Choose your favorite fruit from these possibilities:
```

An invalid menu choice causes zsh to assign a null string to **varname** and to execute the *commands* between **do** and **done**. If the user presses RETURN without entering a choice, the Z Shell redisplays the menu and the **PS3** prompt. The Z Shell stores the user's response in the keyword variable **REPLY**.

As the syntax indicates, you can omit the keyword **in** and the list of arguments. If you do, **select** uses the current values of the positional parameters **$@**.

Here Document

A Here document[3] `bash tcsh zsh` allows you to redirect input to a shell script from within the shell script itself. A Here document is so called because it is *here,* immediately accessible in the shell script, instead of *there,* perhaps in another file.

The following script, **birthday,** contains a Here document. The two less than (<<) symbols in the first line indicate to the shell that a Here document follows. One or more characters that delimit the Here document follow the less than symbols— this example uses plus signs. Whereas the opening delimiter can occur adjacent to the less than symbols, the closing delimiter must occur on a line by itself. The shell sends everything between the two delimiters to the process as standard input. In the following example it is as though you had redirected standard input to grep from a file, except that the file is embedded in the shell script:

---

3. The term *Here document* is not used in the zsh man pages; you must search for << instead.

```
$ cat birthday
grep -i "$1" <<+
Alex    June 22
Barbara February 3
Darlene May 8
Helen   March 13
Jenny   January 23
Nancy   June 26
+
$ birthday Jenny
Jenny   January 23
$ birthday June
Alex    June 22
Nancy   June 26
```

When you run **birthday**, it lists all the Here document lines that contain the argument you called it with. In the preceding example the first time **birthday** is run, it displays Jenny's birthday because it is called with an argument of **Jenny**. The second run displays all the birthdays in June.

Optional

The next script, **bundle**, includes a clever use of a Here document. The **bundle**[4] script is an elegant example of a script that creates a shell archive (or **shar**) file. The **bundle** program creates a file that is itself a shell script containing several other files as well as the code to recreate the original files.

Just as the shell does not treat special characters that occur in standard input of a shell script as special, the shell does not treat the special characters that occur between the delimiters in a Here document as special:

```
$ cat bundle
#!/bin/bash
# bundle:  group files into distribution package

echo "# To unbundle, bash this file"
for i
do
    echo "echo $i 1>&2"
    echo "cat >$i <<'End of $i'"
    cat $i
    echo "End of $i"
done
```

---

4. Brian W. Kernighan and Rob Pike, *The Unix Programming Environment* (Englewood Cliffs, N.J.: Prentice-Hall, 1984), 98. Reprinted with permission.

As the following example shows, the output that **bundle** creates is a shell script, which is redirected to a file named **bothfiles**. It contains the contents of each file given as an argument to **bundle** (**file1** and **file2** in this case) inside a Here document. To extract the original files from **bothfiles**, the user simply runs it. Before each Here document is a cat command that causes the Here document to be written to a new file when **bothfiles** is run:

```
$ cat file1
This is a file.
It contains two lines.
$ cat file2
This is another file.
It contains
three lines.
$ bundle file1 file2 > bothfiles
$ cat bothfiles
# To unbundle, bash this file
echo file1 1>&2
cat >file1 <<'End of file1'
This is a file.
It contains two lines.
End of file1
echo file2 1>&2
cat >file2 <<'End of file2'
This is another file.
It contains
three lines.
End of file2
```

Following, **file1** and **file2** are removed before **bothfiles** is run. The **bothfiles** script echoes the names of the files it creates as it creates them. Finally, the ls command shows that **bothfiles** has recreated **file1** and **file2**:

```
$ rm file1 file2
$ bash bothfiles
file1
file2
$ ls
bothfiles
file1
file2
```

Expanding Null or Unset Variables

The expression ${name} (or just $name if it is not ambiguous) expands to the value of the **name** variable (page 610). If **name** is null or not set, the shell **bash zsh** expands

${Name} to a null string. The shell ^{bash}_{zsh} provides the following alternatives to accepting the expanded null string as the value of the variable.

- Use a default value for the variable.
- Use a default value and assign that value to the variable.
- Display an error.

You can choose one of these alternatives by using a modifier with the variable name.

:‒   Uses a Default Value

The :‒ modifier ^{bash}_{zsh} uses a default value in place of a null or unset variable while allowing a nonnull variable to represent itself:

${name:‒default}

The shell interprets the :‒ as: "If *name* is null or unset, expand *default* and use the expanded value in place of *name*; else use *name*." The following command lists the contents of the directory named by the **LIT** variable; if **LIT** is null or unset, it lists the contents of **/home/alex/literature**:

```
$ ls ${LIT:-/home/alex/literature}
```

The default can itself have variable references that are expanded:

```
$ ls ${LIT:-$HOME/literature}
```

You can supply defaults for unset variables but leave null variables unchanged by omitting the colon:

```
$ ls ${LIT-$HOME/literature}
```

:=   Assigns a Default Value

The :‒ modifier ^{bash}_{zsh} does not change the value of a variable. You may want to change the value of a null or unset variable to its default in a script. You can do this with the := modifier:

${name:=default}

The shell expands the expression **${name:=default}** in the same manner as it expands **${name:‒default}** but also sets the value of *name* to the expanded value of *default.* When you omit the : from the :=, bash assigns a value to an unset variable but not a null one. If your script contains a line such as the following and **LIT** is unset or null at the point where this line is executed, it is assigned the value **/home/alex/literature**:

```
$ ls ${LIT:=/home/alex/literature}
```

Shell scripts frequently start with the : (colon) builtin followed on the same line by the := expansion modifier in order to set any variables that may be null or unset. The : builtin evaluates each token in the remainder of the command line but does not execute any commands. Without the leading colon (:), the shell evaluates and attempts to execute the "command" that results from the evaluation. The order of evaluation is such that if a variable is a command and you name that variable, it is executed. If it is not a valid command, the shell displays an error.

Use the following syntax to set a default for a null or unset variable in a shell script (there is a SPACE following the colon):

```
:   ${name:=default}
```

When your script needs a directory for temporary files and uses the value of **TEMPDIR** for the name of this directory, the following line makes **TEMPDIR** default to **/tmp**:

```
:   ${TEMPDIR:=/tmp}
```

:?   Displays an Error Message

Sometimes a script needs the value of a variable, and there is no reasonable default that you can supply at the time you write the script. If the variable is null or unset, you can cause the script to display an error message and terminate with an exit status of 1. The modifier for this purpose is :? bash zsh :

```
${name:?message}
```

If **TESTDIR** in the following command is null or unset, the shell displays the expanded value of **mesg3** on standard error and terminates the script:

```
$ cd ${TESTDIR:?mesg3}
```

You must quote **message** if it contains SPACEs. If you omit **mesg**, the shell displays the default error message (`parameter not set`). If you omit the colon (:), an error occurs only if the variable is unset; a null variable remains null. Interactive shells do not exit when you use **:?**.

String Pattern Matching

The shell ^{bash zsh} provides a powerful set of string pattern-matching operators that manipulate pathnames and other strings. These operators can delete from strings prefixes or suffixes that match patterns. The four operators are listed in Table 13-4.

String Operator	|| table 13-4
#	Removes minimal matching prefixes
##	Removes maximal matching prefixes
%	Removes minimal matching suffixes
%%	Removes maximal matching suffixes

The syntax for these operators is

${varname op pattern}

In this syntax *op* is one of the operators listed in Table 13-4, and *pattern* is a match pattern similar to that used for filename generation. These operators are commonly used to manipulate pathnames to extract or remove components or to change suffixes:

```
$ SOURCEFILE=/usr/local/src/prog.c
$ echo ${SOURCEFILE#/*/}
local/src/prog.c
$ echo ${SOURCEFILE##/*/}
prog.c
$ echo ${SOURCEFILE%/*}
/usr/local/src
$ echo ${SOURCEFILE%%/*}

$ echo ${SOURCEFILE%.c}
/usr/local/src/prog
$ CHOPFIRST=${SOURCEFILE#/*/}
$ echo $CHOPFIRST
local/src/prog.c
$ NEXT=${CHOPFIRST%%/*}
$ echo $NEXT
local
```

Filename Generation

An important feature of most shells is the ability to refer to files by giving a pattern that describes one or more filenames. For example, all the shells discussed in this book use *.c as a pattern describing all filenames that end in .c. The shells expand this pattern into a list of filenames that match the pattern. This process of matching filenames to a pattern is called *globbing*. Globbing is useful for specifying many files with a single pattern and long filenames with a short string.

Setting the **noglob** (**set –o noglob**) option turns off all pattern matching so that you will have to give filenames exactly: ***.c** will refer only to a file whose name consists of the three-character sequence *****, **.**, and **c**. See "Filename Generation/Pathname Expansion" on page 157.

Builtins

Commands that are built into a shell do not fork a new process when you execute them. The following sections discuss the exec and trap builtins and are followed by Table 13-6 on page 670, which lists many of the shell builtins.

exec: Executes a Command

The exec builtin ^{bash zsh} has two primary purposes: to run a command without creating a new process and to redirect standard input, output, or error of a shell script from within the script. When the shell executes a command that is not built into the shell, it typically creates a new process. The new process inherits environment (global or exported) variables from its parent but does not inherit variables that are not exported by the parent. Refer to "export: Makes a Variable Global" (page 571). In contrast, exec executes a command in place of (overlays) the current process.

Insofar as exec runs a command in the environment of the original process, it is similar to the . (dot) command (page 581). However, unlike the . command, which can run only scripts, exec can run both scripts and compiled programs. Also, whereas the . command returns control to the original script when it finishes running, exec does not. Finally, whereas the . command gives the new program access to local variables, exec does not. The syntax of the exec builtin is

exec command arguments

Because the shell does not create a new process when you use exec, the command runs more quickly. However, because exec does not return control to the original program, the exec builtin can be used only with the last command that you want to run in a script. The following script shows that control is not returned to the script:

```
$ cat exec_demo
who
exec date
echo This echo builtin is never executed.
$ exec_demo
jenny    pts/7    May 30   7:05 (bravo.tcorp.com)
hls      pts/1    May 30   6:59 (:0.0)
Thu May 30 11:42:56 PDT 2002
```

The next example, a modified version of the **out** script (page 632), uses exec to execute the final command the script runs. Because **out** runs either cat or less and then terminates, the new version, **out2**, uses exec with both cat and less:

```
$ cat out2
if [ $# -eq 0 ]
    then
        echo "Usage: out2 [-v] filenames" 1>&2
        exit 1
fi
if [ "$1" = "-v" ]
    then
        shift
        exec less "$@"
    else
        exec cat -- "$@"

fi
```

The second major use of exec is to redirect standard input, output, or error from within a script. Following the next command in a script, all the input to the script is redirected to come from the file named **infile**:

```
exec < infile
```

Similarly, the following command redirects standard output and error to **outfile** and **errfile**, respectively:

```
exec > outfile 2> errfile
```

When you use cxcc in this manner, the current process is not replaced with a new process, and exec can be followed by other commands in the script. When a script prompts the user for input, it is useful to redirect the output from within the script to go to the terminal. This redirection ensures that your prompt appears on the user's terminal, even if the user has redirected the output from the script. When redirecting the output in a script, you can use **/dev/tty** as a synonym for the user's terminal. The **/dev/tty** device is a pseudonym the system maintains for the terminal or window the user is using. This pseudonym enables you to refer to the user's terminal without knowing which device it is.[5] By redirecting the output from a script to **/dev/tty**, you ensure that prompts go to the user's terminal, regardless of which terminal the user is logged in on. The following command redirects the output from a script to the terminal the user is on:

```
exec > /dev/tty
```

Using exec to redirect the output to **/dev/tty** has one disadvantage: All subsequent output is redirected unless you use exec again in the script. If you do not want

---

5. The actual device appears in the second column of the output of who am i but lacks the leading **/dev/**. The tty utility returns the name of the screen/window device you are using.

to redirect the output from all subsequent commands in a script, you can redirect the individual echo commands that display prompts:

```
echo -n "Please enter your name: " > /dev/tty
```

You can also redirect the input to read to come from **/dev/tty**:

```
read name < /dev/tty
```

trap: Catches a Signal

A *signal* is a report to a process about a condition. GNU/Linux uses signals to report interrupts generated by the user (for example, by pressing the interrupt key) as well as bad system calls, broken pipes, illegal instructions, and other conditions. The trap builtin ^{bash zsh} catches, or traps, one or more signals, allowing you to direct the actions a script takes when it receives a specified signal.

This discussion covers the six signals that are significant when you work with shell scripts. Table 13-5 lists the signals, the signal numbers that systems often ascribe to them, and the conditions that usually generate each signal.

Signals*			‖ table 13-5
Type	**Name**	**Number**	**Generating Condition**
Not a real signal		0	Exit because of exit command or reaching the end of the program (not an actual signal but useful in trap).
Hang up	SIGHUP	1	Disconnect line.
Terminal interrupt	SIGINT	2	Press the interrupt key (usually CONTROL-C).
Quit	SIGQUIT	3	Press the quit key (usually CONTROL-SHIFT-| or CONTROL-SHIFT-\).
Kill	SIGKILL	9	The **kill** command with the −9 option (cannot be trapped, use only as a last resort).
Software termination	SIGTERM	15	Default of the kill command.
Stop	SIGTSTP	20	Press the suspend key (usually CONTROL-Z).

* Give the command **kill −l** for a list of signal names; for a complete list of signal names and numbers, see **/usr/include/bits/signum.h**.

When it traps a signal, a script takes whatever action you specify: remove files or finish any other processing as needed, display a message, terminate execution immediately, or ignore the signal. If you do not use trap in a script, any of the six signals in Table 13-5 terminates the script while it is running in the foreground. Because a process cannot trap the KILL signal, you can use **kill –KILL** (or **kill –9**) as a last resort to terminate a script or any other process. Refer to page 1224 in Part III for more information on kill. The format of trap is

trap ['commands'] [signal-numbers]

The trap builtin does not require the single quotation marks shown, but it is a good practice to use them. The single quotation marks cause shell variables within the *commands* to be expanded when the signal occurs, not when the shell evaluates the arguments to trap. Even if you do not use any shell variables in the *commands*, you need to enclose any command that takes arguments within either single or double quotation marks. Quoting the *commands* causes the shell to pass trap the entire command as a single argument.

The *signal-numbers* are the numbers of the signals that trap catches. The *commands* part is optional. If it is not present, trap resets the trap to its initial condition, which is usually to exit from the script. If the *commands* part is present, the shell executes the *commands* when it catches one of the specified signals. After executing the *commands*, the shell resumes executing the script where it left off. If you want trap to prevent a script from exiting when it receives a signal but not to run any commands explicitly, you can use trap with a null (empty) builtin, as shown in the **locktty** script (page 649). The following command traps signal number 15, and the script continues:

```
trap '' 15
```

If you call trap without any arguments, the command displays a list of commands associated with each signal. The following script demonstrates how the trap builtin can catch the terminal interrupt signal (2). You can use SIGINT, INT, or 2 to specify the signal. The script returns an exit status of 1:

```
$ cat inter
#!/bin/bash
trap 'echo PROGRAM INTERRUPTED; exit 1' INT
while true
do
    echo "Program running."
    sleep 1
done
$ inter
Program running.
Program running.
Program running.
CONTROL-C
PROGRAM INTERRUPTED
$
```

The second line of **inter** sets up a trap for the terminal interrupt signal, using INT. When trap catches the signal, the shell executes the two commands between the single quotation marks in the trap command. The echo builtin displays the message PROGRAM INTERRUPTED. Then the exit builtin [bash tcsh zsh] terminates the shell running the script, and the parent shell displays a prompt. If exit were not there, the shell would return control to the **while** loop after displaying the message. The **while** loop repeats continuously until the script receives a signal because the true utility always returns a *true* exit status. In place of true you can use the null builtin, which is written as a colon (:) and always returns a 0, or *true*, status. The **while** statement would then be **while :** instead of **while true**.

The trap builtin frequently removes temporary files when a script is terminated prematurely. Thus the files are not left around, cluttering up the filesystem.

The following shell script, **addbanner**, uses two traps to remove a temporary file when the script terminates normally or owing to a hangup, software interrupt, quit, or software termination signal:

```
$ cat addbanner
#!/bin/bash
script=`basename $0`

if [ ! -r "$HOME/banner" ]
    then
        echo "$script: need readable $HOME/banner file" 1>&2
        exit 1
fi

trap 'exit 1' 1 2 3 15
trap 'rm /tmp/$$.$script 2> /dev/null' 0

for file
do
    if [ -r "$file" -a -w "$file" ]
        then
            cat $HOME/banner $file > /tmp/$$.$script
            cp /tmp/$$.$script $file
            echo "$script: banner added to $file" 1>&2
        else
            echo "$script: need read and write permission for $file" 1>&2
        fi
done
```

When called with one or more filename arguments, **addbanner** loops through the files, adding a header to the top of each. This script is useful when you use a standard format at the top of your documents, such as a standard layout for memos, or when you want to add a standard header to shell scripts. The header is kept in a file named **banner** in the user's home directory. The **HOME** variable contains the pathname of the user's home directory, so that **addbanner** can be used by several users without modification. If Alex had written the script with

/home/alex in place of $HOME and then given the script to Jenny, either she would have had to change it, or **addbanner** would have used Alex's **banner** file when Jenny ran it.

The first trap in **addbanner** causes it to exit with a status of 1 when it receives a hangup, software interrupt (terminal interrupt or quit signal), or software termination signal. The second trap uses a 0 in place of **signal-number,** which causes trap to execute its command argument *whenever* the script exits because of an exit command or reaching its end. Together these traps remove a temporary file whether the script terminates normally or prematurely. Standard error of the second trap is sent to **/dev/null** for cases in which trap attempts to remove a nonexistent temporary file. In those cases rm sends an error message to standard error. Because the standard error is redirected to **/dev/null**, the user does see the message.

A Partial List of Builtins

Table 13-6 lists some of the shell builtins. See "Builtins" on page 161 for instructions on how to find complete lists of builtins for each of the shells.

Builtin	‖ table 13-6
. `bash tcsh zsh`	Returns 0 or *true.* (The **null** builtin, page 669)
. `bash zsh`	Executes a program or shell script as part of the current process (page 581)
bg `bash tcsh zsh`	Puts a job in the background (page 556)
break `bash tcsh zsh`	Exits from **for, while**, or **until** loop (page 650)
cd `bash tcsh zsh`	Changes to another working directory (page 108)
continue `bash tcsh zsh`	Starts with next iteration of **for, while**, or **until** loop (page 650)
echo `bash tcsh .zsh`	Displays arguments (page 70)
eval `bash tcsh zsh`	Scans and evaluates the command line (page 674)
exec `bash tcsh zsh`	Executes a program in place of the current process (page 665)

Builtin

|| table 13-6

Builtin	Description
exit `bash` `tcsh` `zsh`	Exits from the current shell (usually the same as CONTROL-D) (page 588)
export `bash` `zsh`	Places the value of a variable in the calling environment (makes it global) (page 571)
fg `bash` `tcsh` `zsh`	Brings a job into the foreground (page 555)
getopts `bash` `zsh`	Parses arguments to a shell script (page 772)
jobs `bash` `tcsh` `zsh`	Displays list of current jobs in the foreground and background (page 555)
kill `bash` `tcsh` `zsh`	Sends a signal to a process or job (page 1224)
pwd `bash` `tcsh` `zsh`	Prints the name of the working directory (page 107)
read `bash` `zsh`	Reads a line from standard input (page 573)
readonly `bash` `zsh`	Declares a variable to be readonly (page 570)
set `bash` `tcsh` `zsh`	Sets shell flags or command line argument variables; with no argument **set** lists all variables (pages 584 and 699)
shift `bash` `tcsh` `zsh`	Promotes each command line argument (page 583)
test `bash` `zsh`	Compares arguments (pages 627, 1352, and 701)
times `bash` `zsh`	Displays total times for the current shell and its children (**times man** page)
trap `bash` `zsh`	Traps a signal (page 667)
type `bash` `zsh`	Displays how each argument would be interpreted as a command (page 628)
umask `bash` `tcsh` `zsh`	Returns the value of the file-creation mask (page 1366)
unset `bash` `tcsh` `zsh`	Removes a variable or function (page 570)
wait `bash` `tcsh` `zsh`	Waits for a background process to terminate (page 729)

Functions

A shell function ^{bash}_{zsh} is similar to a shell script, storing a series of commands for execution at a later time. However, because the shell stores a function in the computer's main memory (RAM) instead of in a file on the disk, you can access it more quickly than you can access a script. Also, the shell preprocesses (parses) a function so that it starts up more quickly than a script. Finally, the shell executes a shell function in the same shell that called it.

You can declare a shell function in your **.bash_profile** file, in the script that uses it, or directly from the command line. You can remove functions with the **unset** builtin ^{bash}_{zsh}. The shell does not keep functions once you log out.

Removing Variables and Functions || tip

If you have a shell variable and a function with the same name, using **unset** removes the shell variable. If you then use **unset** again with the same name, it removes the function.

The syntax that declares a shell function is

function-name *()*
{
        commands
}

The *function-name* is the name you use to call the function. The *commands* comprise the list of commands the function executes when you call it. These *commands* can be anything you would include in a shell script, including calls to functions.

The next example shows how to create a simple function that displays the date, a header, and a list of the people who are using the system. This function runs the same commands as the **whoson** script described on page 545:

```
$ whoson ()
{
    date
    echo "Users Currently Logged On"
    who
}
```

```
$ whoson
Fri Aug  8 15:44:58 PDT 2003
Users Currently Logged On
hls        console      Aug  6 08:59  (:0)
alex       pts/4        Aug  6 09:33  (0.0)
jenny      pts/7        Aug  6 09:23  (bravo.tcorp.com)
```

If you want to have the **whoson** function always available without having to enter it each time you log in, put its definition in your *.bash_profile* (page 109) file. After adding **whoson** to your *.bash_profile* file, run *.bash_profile*, using the **.** (dot) command to put the changes into effect immediately:

```
$ cat .bash_profile
TERM=vt100
export TERM
stty kill '^u'
whoson ()
{
    date
    echo "Users Currently Logged On"
    who
}
$ . .bash_profile
```

You can specify arguments when you call a function. Within the function these arguments are available as positional parameters. The following example shows the **arg1** function entered from the keyboard. In this sequence the two greater–than (**>**) signs are secondary shell prompts (**PS2**); do not enter them.

```
$ arg1( ) {
> echo "$1"
> }
$ arg1 my_first_arg
my_first_arg
```

Optional

The following function allows you to export variables, using the syntax provided by the TC Shell under the Bourne Again and Z Shells. The **set** builtin lists all environment variables and their values and verifies that **setenv** has worked correctly:

```
$ cat .bash_profile
.
.
# setenv - keep csh users happy
setenv()
{
    if [ $# -eq 2 ]
        then
                eval $1=$2
                export $1
        else
                echo "Usage: setenv NAME VALUE" 1>&2
    fi
}
$ . .bash_profile
$ setenv TCL_LIBRARY /usr/local/lib/tcl
$ set | grep TCL_LIBRARY
TCL_LIBRARY=/usr/local/lib/tcl
```

This function uses the eval builtin `bash tcsh zsh` to force bash to scan the command **$1=$2** *twice.* Because **$1=$2** begins with a dollar sign (**$**), the shell treats the entire string as a single token—a command. With variable substitution performed, the command name becomes **TCL_LIBRARY=/usr/local/lib/tcl**, which results in an error. Using eval, a second scanning, which splits the string into the three desired tokens, is done, and the correct assignment occurs.

Chapter Summary

The shell is a programming language. Programs written in this language are called shell scripts, or simply scripts. Shell scripts provide the decision and looping control structures present in high-level programming languages while allowing easy access to system utilities and user programs. Shell scripts can also use functions to modularize and simplify complex tasks.

The Bourne Again and Z Shell control structures that use decisions to select alternatives are **if...then, if...then...else,** and **if...then...elif.** The **case** control structure provides a multiway branch and can be used when you want to express alternatives, using a simple pattern-matching syntax.

The test builtin can evaluate an expression in a shell script. The expression is often a comparison of two quantities or files or an inquiry about the status of a file. As with all decisions within GNU/Linux shell scripts, a *true* status is represented by the value zero; *false*, by any nonzero value.

The looping control structures available in the Bourne Again Shell and Z Shell are **for...in**, **for**, **until**, and **while**. These structures perform one or more tasks repetitively.

The **break** and **continue** control structures alter control within loops; **break** transfers control out of a loop, and **continue** transfers control immediately to the top of a loop.

The trap builtin `bash zsh` catches a signal sent by GNU/Linux to the process running the script and allows you to specify actions to be taken on receipt of one or more signals. The trap builtin might be used, for instance, to ignore the signal sent when the user presses the interrupt key.

The exec builtin `bash tcsh zsh` executes a command without creating a new process. The new command overlays the current process, assuming the same environment and PID number of that process. This builtin executes user programs and other GNU/Linux commands, when it is *not* necessary to return control to the calling process.

The Here document allows input to a command in a shell script to come from within the script itself.

A shell function is a series of commands that, unlike a shell script, are parsed prior to being stored in main memory. Shell scripts are parsed at run time and are stored on disk. Shell functions run faster than shell scripts and can be used repeatedly. A function can be defined on the command line or within a shell script; if you want the function definition to remain in effect across login sessions, you can define it in your .bash_profile file. Like the functions of a programming language, a shell function is called by giving its name along with any arguments.

In addition to the use of control structures, builtins, functions, and the like, useful shell scripts generally use GNU/Linux utilities. The find utility, for instance, is commonplace in shell scripts that involve a search for files in the system hierarchy and can perform a vast range of tasks, from simple to complex.

A well-written shell script adheres to the use of standard techniques, such as specifying the shell to execute the script on the first line of the script, verifying the number and type of arguments that the script is called with, displaying a standard usage message to report command line errors, and redirecting all informational messages to standard error.

Exercises

1. Rewrite the **journal** script of Chapter 12 (example 1, page 620) by adding commands to verify that the user has write permission for a file named **journal-file** in the user's home directory, if such a file exists. The script should take appropriate actions if **journal-file** exists and the user does not have write permission to the file. Verify that the modified script works.

2. The special parameter **$@** is referenced twice in the **out** script (page 632). Explain what would be different if the parameter **$*** were used in its place.

3. Write a filter that takes a list of files as input and outputs the basename (page 657) of each file in the list.

4. Write a function that takes a single filename as an argument and adds execute permission to the file for the user.

   a. When might such a function be useful?

   b. Revise the script so that it takes one or more filenames as arguments and adds execute permission for the user for each file argument.

   c. What can you do to make the function available every time you log in?

   d. What if, in addition to having the function available on subsequent login sessions, you want to make the function available now in your current shell?

5. When might it be necessary or advisable to write a shell script instead of a shell function? Give as many reasons as you can think of.

6. Write a shell script that will display the names of all directory files, but no other types of files, in the working directory.

7. If your GNU/Linux system runs the X Window System, open a small window on your screen, and write a script to display the time in that window every 15 seconds. Read about the date utility (page 1141) and display the time, using the **%r** field descriptor. Clear the window (using the clear command) each time before you display the time.

8. Enter the following script named **savefiles**, and give yourself execute permission to the file:

```
$ cat $HOME/bin/savefiles
#! /bin/bash
echo "Saving files in current directory in file savethem."
exec > savethem
for i in *
do
echo "========================================================="
echo "File: $i"
echo "========================================================="
cat "$i"
done
```

   a. What error message do you get when you execute this script? Rewrite the script so that the error does not occur, making sure the output still goes to **savethem**.

   b. What might be a problem with running this script twice in the same directory? Discuss a solution to this problem.

9. Read the bash info page, try some examples, and then describe

   a. How to export a function.

   b. What the hash builtin does.

   c. What happens if the argument to exec is not executable.

10. Using the find utility (page 1165), perform the following steps:

   a. List all files in the working directory that have been modified within the last day.

   b. List all files on the system that are bigger than 1 megabyte.

   c. Remove all files named **core** from the directory structure rooted at your home directory.

   d. List the inode numbers of all files in the working directory whose filenames end in **.c**.

   e. List all files on the root filesystem that have been modified in the last month.

11. Write a short script that tells you whether the permissions for two files, whose names are given as arguments to the script, are identical. If the permissions for the two files are identical, output the common permission

field. Otherwise, output each filename, followed by its permission field. (*Hint:* Try using the cut utility [page 1132].)

12. Write a script that takes the name of a directory as an argument and searches the file hierarchy rooted at that directory for zero-length files. Write the names of all zero-length files to standard output. If there is no option on the command line, have the script delete the file after displaying its name, asking the user for confirmation, and receiving positive confirmation. A –f option on the command line indicates that the script should display the filename but not ask for confirmation before deleting the file.

Advanced Exercises

13. Write a function that takes a colon-separated list of items and outputs the items, one per line, to standard output (without the colons).

14. Generalize the function written in exercise 13 so that the character separating the list items is given as an argument to the function. If this argument is absent, the separator should default to a colon.

15. Write a function named **funload** that takes as its single argument the name of a file containing other functions. The purpose of **funload** is to make all functions in the named file available in the current shell; that is, **funload** loads the functions from the named file. To locate the file, **funload** searches the colon-separated list of directories given by the environment variable **FUNPATH**. Assume that the format of **FUNPATH** is the same as **PATH** and that searching **FUNPATH** is similar to the shell's search of the **PATH** variable.

16. If your GNU/Linux system runs X Windows, write a script that turns the root window a different color when the amount of free disk space in any filesystem reaches a certain threshold. (*Hint:* See df on page 1147 in Part III.) Both the threshold and the color should be specified as arguments. Check disk usage every 30 minutes. Start the script executing when your X Windows session starts.

17. Enhance the **spell_check** script (page 646) to accept an optional third argument. If given, this argument specifies a list of words to be added to the output of **spell_check**. You can use a list of words like this to cull

usages you do not want in your documents. For example, if you decide that you want to use disk rather than disc in your documents, you can add disc to the list of words, and **spell_check** will complain if you use disc in a document. Make sure that you include appropriate error checks and usage messages.

18. Rewrite **bundle** so that the script it creates takes an optional list of filenames as arguments. If one or more filenames are given on the command line, only those files should be recreated; otherwise, all files in the shell archive should be recreated. For example, suppose that all files with the filename extension **.c** are bundled into an archive named **srcshell** and you want to unbundle just the files **test1.c** and **test2.c**. The following command will unbundle just these two files:

```
$ bash srcshell test1.c test2.c
```

19. Using a single command line (pipes are all right), find all the unique shells in the **/etc/passwd** file, and

   a. Print out two columns listing each shell followed by the username for every user who logs into that shell.

   b. Sort the columns by shell and then by username. (*Hint:* use gawk.)

20. What kind of links will the **lnks** script (page 635) not find? Why?

IN THIS CHAPTER

The TC Shell

14

The TC Shell (tcsh) performs the same function as the Bourne Again Shell, the Z Shell, and other shells: It provides an interface between you and the GNU/Linux operating system. The TC Shell is an interactive command interpreter as well as a high-level programming language. Although you use only one shell at any given time, you should be able to switch back and forth comfortably between them as the need arises (you may want to run different shells in different windows). Because many of the concepts covered in Chapters 12 and 13 apply to tcsh as well as to bash and zsh, those chapters provide a good background for this chapter, as well as for shell use in general. This chapter highlights facets of tcsh that differ from those of bash, are absent from bash altogether, or are traditional tcsh features that have not taken a strong hold in bash.

The TC Shell is an expanded version of the C Shell (csh), which originated on Berkeley UNIX and is now included with System V UNIX. The T in TC Shell comes from the names of the TENEX and TOPS-20 operating systems, which inspired the command completion (and other) features in the TC Shell.[1] The TC Shell comes with Red Hat Linux. A number of features not found in csh are present in tcsh, including file and user name completion, command line editing, and spelling correction. As with csh, you can customize tcsh to make it more tolerant of mistakes and easier to use. By setting the proper shell variables, you can have tcsh warn you when you appear to be accidentally logging out or overwriting a file. Many popular features of

---

1. For a more complete explanation, search for THE T IN TCSH in the tcsh man page.

the original C Shell are now shared by bash, zsh, and tcsh. The tcsh home page is www.tcsh.org/Home.

Although some of the functionality of tcsh is present in bash and zsh, there are differences in the syntax of some commands. For example, the tcsh assignment statement has the following syntax:

set variable = value

Having SPACEs on either side of the equal sign, though illegal in bash, is optional in tcsh. By convention, shell variables in tcsh are generally named with lowercase letters, not uppercase (you can use either). If you reference an undeclared variable (one that has had no value assigned to it), tcsh will give you an error message, whereas bash and zsh will not. Finally, the default tcsh prompt is a greater than sign (>), but Red Hat sets it to a single $ character followed by a SPACE. The examples in this chapter use a prompt of tcsh $ to avoid confusion with the bash prompt.

Do Not Use tcsh as a Programming Language   ‖ tip

If you have used UNIX and are comfortable with the C or TC Shell, you may want to use **tcsh** as your login shell. However, you may find that the TC Shell is not as good a programming language as **bash** or **zsh**. If you are going to learn only one shell programming language, learn **bash**. The Bourne Again Shell is used throughout GNU/Linux to program many system administration scripts, including all the scripts in /etc/rc❖.

Shell Scripts

With tcsh you can execute files containing TC Shell commands, just as bash and zsh can execute files containing Bourne Again and Z Shell commands. The concepts of writing and executing scripts in the two shells are similar. However, the methods of declaring and assigning values to variables and the syntax of control structures are different.

You can run bash, tcsh, and zsh scripts while using any one of the shells as a command interpreter. Various methods exist for selecting the shell that runs a script. Refer to "#! Specifies a Shell" on page 564 for more information.

If the first character of a shell script is a pound sign (#) and the following character is not an exclamation point (!), the TC Shell executes the script under tcsh. If the first character is anything other than #, tcsh calls bash to execute the script.

Shell Game || tip

When you are working with an interactive TC Shell, if you run a script in which # is *not* the first character of the script and you call the script *directly* (without preceding its name with tcsh), tcsh calls bash to run the script. Things may look pretty strange. The first of the following examples (from "Reading User Input" on page 706) issues a prompt but does not wait for you to respond. Although both examples are run from tcsh, the second one calls tcsh explicitly to run the script:

```
tcsh $ cat user_in
echo -n "Enter input: "
set input_line = "$<"
echo $input_line
tcsh $ user_in
-n Enter input:

tcsh $ tcsh user_in
Enter input: here is some input
here is some input
```

echo: Getting Rid of the RETURN || tip

The tcsh echo builtin accepts either a –n option or a trailing \c to get rid of the RETURN that echo normally displays at the end of a line. The zsh echo works the same way, whereas the bash echo builtin accepts only the –n option (refer to "read: Accepts User Input" on page 573).

Entering and Leaving the TC Shell

You can execute tcsh by giving the command tcsh. If you are not sure which shell you are using, use the ps utility to find out. It shows whether you are running tcsh, zsh, bash, sh (linked to bash), or possibly another shell. The finger command followed by your login name also displays the name of your login shell, which is stored in the /etc/passwd file. If you want to use tcsh as a matter of course, you can use the chsh (change shell) utility to change your login shell:

```
bash$ chsh
Changing shell for sam.
Password:
New shell [/bin/bash]: /bin/tcsh
Shell changed.
bash$
```

The shell you specify is in effect for your next login and all subsequent logins until you specify a different login shell. The name of the login shell is stored in the **/etc/passwd** file.

You can leave tcsh in several ways. The way you choose depends on two factors: whether the shell variable **ignoreeof** tcsh is set and whether you are using the shell that you logged in on (your login shell) or another shell that you created after you logged in. If you are not sure how to exit from tcsh, press CONTROL-D on a line by itself, with no leading SPACEs, just as you would to terminate standard input to another program. You will either exit or receive instructions on how to exit. If you have not set **ignoreeof** (page 712) and it has not been set for you in one of your startup files (see the next section), you can exit from any shell by using CONTROL-D (the same procedure you use to exit from the Bourne Again and Z Shells).

When **ignoreeof** is set, CONTROL-D does not work. The **ignoreeof** variable causes the shell to display a message telling you how to exit. You can always exit from tcsh by giving an **exit** command. A **logout** command allows you to exit only from your login shell.

Startup Files

When you log in on the TC Shell, it automatically executes various startup files. They are normally executed in the order shown, but you can compile tcsh to use a different order.

/etc/csh.login and **/etc/csh.cshrc**   These files contain systemwide configuration information, such as the default **path**, check for mail, and so on.

~/.tcshrc (or if it does not exist, **~/.cshrc**)   This file runs each time a tcsh process starts up (the ~/ indicates that the file is located in your home directory). You can use the **.tcshrc** file to establish variables and parameters that are local to a shell: Each time you create a new shell, tcsh reinitializes these variables for the new shell. In the following sample **.tcshrc** file, the tilde (~) represents the pathname of your home directory (refer to "~   Tilde Expansion" on page 609):

```
tcsh $ cat ~/.tcshrc
set noclobber
set dunique
set ignoreeof
set history=256
set path = (~/bin $path /usr/games)
alias h history
alias ll ls -l
```

This **.tcshrc** file sets several shell variables, establishes two aliases (page 689), and adds two new directories to **path**: one at the start of the list and one at the end.

~/.history Login shells rebuild the history list (next section) from the contents of this file. If the **histfile** variable exists, tcsh uses in place of **.history** the file that **histfile** points to.

~/.login This file reads and executes the commands in this file (login shells only). It contains commands that you want to execute once, at the beginning of each session. You can use setenv (page 699) to declare environment variables here. You can also declare the type of terminal that you are using and set some terminal characteristics in your **.login** file. A sample follows:

```
tcsh $ cat ~/.login
setenv history 20
setenv MAIL /var/spool/mail/$user
if ( -z $DISPLAY ) then
    setenv TERM vt100
else
    setenv TERM xterm
endif
stty erase '^h' kill '^u' -lcase tab3
date '+Login on %A %B %d at %I:%M %p'
```

This file establishes the type of terminal that you are using by setting the **TERM** variable (the **if** statement [page 714] tries to figure out whether you are using X and therefore what value should be assigned to **TERM**). The sample **.login** then runs stty (page 1335) to set terminal characteristics and date to display the time you logged in.

/etc/csh.logout
and ~/.logout This file runs when you exit from your login shell. The following sample **.logout** file uses date to display the time you logged out. The sleep command ensures that echo has time to display the message before the system logs you out. This is useful for dial-up lines that may take some time to display the message.

```
tcsh $ cat ~/.logout
date '+Logout on %A %B %d at %I:%M %p'
sleep 5
```

Features Common to the Bourne Again and TC Shells

Most of the features common to both bash and tcsh are derived from the original C Shell. These features include

- History
- Aliases
- Job control
- Filename substitution

Because the chapters on bash discuss these features in detail, this section focuses on the differences between the bash and tcsh versions.

History

The use of history in tcsh is similar to its use in bash. (See page 588 for a complete description of the history mechanism.) The same event and word designators work in both shells. For example, !! refers to the previous event in tcsh, just as it does in bash. The command !328 means to execute event number 328 and !?txt? means to execute the most recent event containing the string txt. Table 14-1 lists the few extra word modifiers in tcsh not found in zsh or bash.

Word Modifiers || table 14-1

u	Converts the first lowercase letter into uppercase
l	Converts the first uppercase letter into lowercase
a	Applies the next modifier globally within a single word

It is possible to use more than one word modifier in a command. For instance, the **a** modifier, in combination with the **u** or **l** modifier, is handy for changing the case of an entire word.

```
tcsh $ echo $VERSION
VERSION: Undefined variable.
tcsh $ echo !!:1:al
echo $version
tcsh 6.12.00 (Astron) 2002-07-23 (i386-intel-linux) options 8b,nls,...
```

The variables that you set to control history in tcsh are different from those in bash. Where bash uses **HISTSIZE** and **HISTFILESIZE** to determine the number of events that are preserved during and between sessions (page 590), tcsh uses **history** and **savehist** (Table 14-2).

History Variables || table 14-2

Function	Variable	Default
Maximum number of events saved during a session	history	100 events
Location of the history file	histfile	~/.history
Maximum number of events saved between sessions	savehist	

When you exit from the shell, the most recently executed commands are saved in the ~/.history file. Next time you start the shell, this file initializes the history list. The value of the **savehist** variable **tcsh** determines the number of lines of history saved in the ~/.history file (not necessarily the same as the **history** variable). The **history** variable holds the number of events remembered during a session, the **savehist** variable holds the number remembered between sessions. See Table 14-2.

The TC Shell assigns a sequential *event number* to each command line. You can display this event number as part of the tcsh prompt (see "prompt" in the list on page 708). Examples in this section show numbered prompts when they help to illustrate the behavior of a command or group of commands.

If you set the value of **history** too high, it can use too much memory. If it is unset or set to zero, the shell does not save any commands. To establish a history list of the 100 most recent events, give the following command manually, or place it in your .tcshrc startup file:

```
tcsh $ set history = 100
```

The following command causes tcsh to save the 100 most recent events across login sessions:

```
tcsh $ set savehist = 50
```

You can make multiple assignments within a single command. Combining the two preceding assignments gives the same result. (The SPACEs or absence thereof around the equal signs is not significant.)

```
tcsh $ set history=100 savehist=50
```

After you set **savehist**, you can log out and log in again, and the 50 most recent events from the previous login sessions appear in your history list. Set **savehist** in your .tcshrc file if you want to maintain your event list from login to login.

If set, the variable **histlit** (history literal) displays the commands in the history list exactly as they were typed in, without any shell interpretation. The following example shows the effect of this variable (compare the lines numbered 32) and of the –T option, which causes history to display timestamps for each command:

```
tcsh $ cat /etc/csh.cshrc
. . .
tcsh $ cp !!:1 ~
cp /etc/csh.cshrc ~
tcsh $ set histlit
tcsh $ history -T
. . .
    31  9:35      cat /etc/csh.cshrc
    32  9:35      cp !!:1 ~
    33  9:35      set histlit
    34  9:35      history -T
```

```
tcsh $ unset histlit
tcsh $ history -T
. . .
    31  9:35     cat /etc/csh.cshrc
    32  9:35     cp /etc/csh.cshrc ~
    33  9:35     set histlit
    34  9:35     history -T
    35  9:35     unset histlit
    36  9:36     history -T
```

Use the history builtin to display the events in your history list. The list of events is ordered with the oldest events at the top. The last event in the history list is the **history** command that displayed the list. The following history list includes a command to modify the tcsh prompt to display the history event number and the command number. To simplify the example, **history** has been set to 10 and **savehist** to 20. (The event number is 20 greater than the command number because the list of events includes those events that were saved from the last login session—20 in this case.)

```
32 12 $ history
    23   set prompt = "! $ "
    24   ls -l
    25   cat temp
    26   rm temp
    27   vi memo
    28   lp memo
    29   vi memo
    30   lp memo
    31   rm memo
    32   history
```

As you run commands and your history list becomes longer, history produces a list that runs off the top of the screen. Use a pipe to send the output of history through less (page 54) to browse through it or give the command **history 10** to look at your ten most recent commands.

You can change the name of the history file (normally **.history**) by changing the value of the **histfile** variable:

```
tcsh $ set histfile = "~/.tcsh_dir/history"
```

The **histfile** variable is not present in the TC Shell.

In addition to using event designators to access the history list, you can use the command line editor to access, modify, and execute previous commands (page 696).

Optional

There is a difference in how bash and tcsh expand history event designators. If you give the command **!250w**, bash replaces it with the command number 250 with a character w appended to it. In contrast, tcsh looks back through your history list for an event that begins with the string 250w to execute. The reason for the difference is that bash interprets the first three characters of 250w as the number of a command, whereas tcsh interprets them as part of the search string, 250w. (Of course, if the 250 stands alone, tcsh treats it as a command number.)

If you want to append a w to command number 250, you can insulate the event number from the w by surrounding it with braces:

```
!{250}w
```

Alias

The alias/unalias feature in tcsh closely resembles its counterpart in bash (page 602). The alias builtin itself, however, has a slightly different format. In bash you can create an alias for ls with the following command:

```
bash $ alias ls="ls -lF"
```

In tcsh you can create the same alias by replacing the equal sign with a SPACE:

```
tcsh $ alias ls "ls -lF"
```

Some alias names, called *special aliases* (Table 14-3), have special meaning to tcsh. If you define an alias with one of these names, it executes automatically at certain points in your interaction with the shell. Initially all the special aliases are undefined.

Special Alias	Executed	‖ table 14-3
beepcmd	Whenever the shell would normally ring the terminal bell. This gives you a way to have other visual or audio effects take place at those times.	
cwdcmd	Whenever you change to another working directory.	
periodic	Periodically, as determined by the number of minutes in the **tperiod** variable. If **tperiod** is unset or has the value 0, you cannot set **periodic**.	
precmd	Just before the shell displays a prompt.	
shell	Gives the name of the interpreter that you want to use on scripts that do not start with #! (page 564). The first word of the alias must be the full pathname of the interpreter to be used.	

To see a list of the current aliases, give the command **alias**. To view the alias for a particular name, give the command **alias** followed by the name.

Differences between the tcsh and bash alias Mechanisms

The alias builtin and substitution used in bash are patterned after the alias builtin found in the Z Shell. It is slightly different from the alias builtin used in tcsh, which is patterned after the alias builtin found in the TC Shell. The syntax of the version used by tcsh is

alias name value

The tcsh version of alias (next section) lets you substitute the command arguments. To do something similar in bash, you have to use a shell function (page 672).

History Substitution in an Alias

You can substitute command line arguments by using the history mechanism, with a single exclamation point representing the input line containing the alias. Modifiers are the same as those used by history (page 686). The exclamation points are quoted in the following example so that the shell does not interpret them when building the aliases (which would produce incorrect results):

```
21% alias last echo \!:$
22% last this is just a test
test
23% alias fn2 echo \!:2:t
24% fn2 /home/jenny/test /home/alex/temp /home/barbara/new
temp
```

Event 21 defines for **last** an alias that displays the last argument. Event 23 defines for **fn2** an alias that displays the simple filename, or tail, of the second argument on the command line.

Job Control

Job control in bash (page 554) and in tcsh is similar. You can move commands between the foreground and background, suspend jobs temporarily, and get a list of the current jobs. The % character references a job when followed by a job number or a string prefix that uniquely identifies the job. You will see a minor difference when you run a multiple-process command line in the background. Whereas bash displays only the PID number of the last background process in each job, tcsh displays the numbers for all the processes belonging to a job. The example from page 554 looks like this under tcsh:

```
tcsh $ find . -print | sort | lpr & grep -l alex /tmp/* > alexfiles &
[1] 18839   18840   18841
[2] 18876
```

Filename Substitution

The TC Shell expands the characters *, ?, and [] in a pathname just as bash does (page 157). The * matches any string of zero or more characters, ? matches any single character, and [] defines a character class, used to match single characters appearing within a pair of brackets.

The TC Shell expands command line arguments that start with a tilde (~) into filenames in much the same way that bash does (page 694), with the ~ standing for the user's home directory or the home directory of the user whose name follows the tilde. (The special expansions ~+ and ~- are not available in tcsh.)

Brace expansion is available in tcsh and, like tilde expansion, is regarded as an aspect of filename substitution. This is true even though brace expansion can generate strings that are not the names of actual files.

In tcsh and its predecessor, csh, the process of using patterns to match filenames is referred to as *globbing*, and the pattern itself is called a *globbing pattern*. If tcsh is unable to produce a list of one or more files that match a globbing pattern, it reports an error (unless the pattern contains a brace). Setting the shell variable **noglob** suppresses filename substitution, including both tilde and brace interpretation.

Manipulating the Directory Stack

Directory stack manipulation in bash (page 557) and in tcsh does not differ much. The dirs builtin displays the contents of the stack, and the pushd and popd builtins push directories onto and pop directories off the stack.

Command Substitution

The $(...) format for command substitution is *not* available in tcsh. In its place you must use the original `...` format. Otherwise, the implementation in bash and tcsh is identical. Refer to (page 575) for more info on command substitution.

Redirecting Standard Error

All three major shells use a greater than symbol (>) to redirect standard output. However, the Bourne Again and Z Shells' syntax to combine and redirect standard output and standard error (page 552) differs from that in the TC Shell, which uses a greater than symbol followed by an ampersand (>&). The following examples, like the bash example (page 552), reference the file **x**, which does not exist, and the file **y**, which contains a single line:

```
tcsh $ cat x
cat: x: No such file or directory
tcsh $ cat y
This is y.
tcsh $ cat x y >& hold
tcsh $ cat hold
cat: x: No such file or directory
This is y.
```

Unlike both bash and zsh, tcsh does not provide a simple way to redirect standard error separately from standard output. A workaround frequently provides a reasonable solution. With an argument of y in the preceding example, cat sends a string to standard output, whereas an argument of x causes cat to send an error message to standard error. A subshell runs cat with both arguments and redirects standard output to a file named **outfile**. Output sent to standard error is not touched by the subshell and is sent to the parent shell, where both it and standard output are combined and sent to **errfile**. Because standard output has already been redirected, **errfile** contains only output sent to standard error:

```
tcsh $ (cat x y > outfile) >& errfile
tcsh $ cat outfile
This is y.
tcsh $ cat errfile
cat: x: No such file or directory
```

It is useful to combine and redirect output when you want to run a slow command in the background and do not want its output cluttering up your terminal screen. For example, because the find utility often takes a while to complete, it is a good idea to run it in the background.

The next command finds in the filesystem hierarchy all the files that are named **bibliography**. The command runs in the background and sends its output to a file named **findout**. Because the find utility sends to standard error a report of directories that you do not have permission to search, you have a record in the **findout** file of any files named **bibliography** that are found, as well as a record of the directories that could not be searched. The find utility does not require **–print** in the following command; it is implied by the lack of an action:

```
tcsh $ find / –name bibliography –print >& findout &
```

In this example, if you did not combine standard error with standard output and redirected only standard output, the error messages would appear on your screen, and **findout** would contain only the list of files that were found.

While you are running in the background a command that has its output redirected to a file, you can look at the output by using tail with the –f option. The –f option causes tail to display new lines as they are written to the file:

```
tcsh $ tail -f findout
```

To terminate the tail command, press the interrupt key (usually CONTROL-C). Refer to Part III for more information on find (page 1165) and tail (page 1340).

Command Line Expansion

Various types of command line expansions are present in some or all the shells. Some are specific to a single shell. Refer to "Command Line Expansion" on page 606 for an introduction to command line expansion in the Bourne Again Shell. See "Processing a Command" on page 797 for information on the Z Shell. The following sections review several types of command line expansion you may be familiar with and introduce some new ones that are used by the TC Shell. These sections also discuss the order in which the shell performs the various expansions and provides some examples. As with the bash coverage, the history (page 686) and alias (page 689) expansions are not included in the following discussion because they cannot be used in a shell script.

The TC Shell scans each token for the various types of expansion in the following order:

1. History substitution (page 686)
2. Alias substitution (page 689)
3. Variable substitution (page 699)
4. Command substitution (page 691)
5. Filename substitution (page 691)
6. Directory stack substitution (page 691)

Word Completion

The TC Shell completes filenames, commands, and variable names on the command line when you prompt it to do so. The generic term used to refer to all these completions under tcsh is *word completion*.

Filename Completion

The TC Shell can complete filenames after you specify unique prefixes. Filename completion is similar to filename generation, but the goal of filename completion is always to select a single file. Together, they make it practical to use long, descriptive filenames.

To use filename completion when you are entering a filename on the command line, type enough of the name to identify the file in the directory uniquely and then press TAB; tcsh fills in the name and adds a SPACE, leaving the cursor so that you can enter additional arguments or press RETURN. The following example shows the user typing the command **cat trig1A** and pressing TAB; the system fills in the rest of the filename that begins with **trig1A**:

```
42 $ cat trig1A →TAB → cat trig1A.302488 ■
```

If two or more filenames match the prefix that you have typed, tcsh cannot complete the filename without more information from you. The shell attempts to maximize the length of the prefix by adding characters, if possible, and then beeps to signify that additional input is needed to resolve the ambiguity:

```
43 $ ls h*
help.hist    help.text    help.trig01
44 $ cat h → TAB → cat help. (BEEP)
```

You can fill in enough characters to resolve the ambiguity and then press TAB again. Alternatively, you can press CONTROL-D, and tcsh presents a list of matching filenames:

```
45 $ cat help. → CONTROL-D → cat help.
help.hist         help.trig01 help.txt
```

Then tcsh redraws the command line you have typed so that you can disambiguate the filename (and press TAB again) or finish typing the rest of the name.

Tilde Completion

The TC Shell parses a tilde (~) appearing as the first character of a word and attempts to expand it to a user name when you enter a TAB:

```
tcsh $ cd ~al → TAB → cd ~alex/RETURN
tcsh $ pwd
/home/alex
```

By appending a slash (/), tcsh lets you know that the completed word is a directory. The slash also makes it easy to continue specifying the pathname.

Command and Variable Completion

You can use the same mechanism that you use to complete and list filenames with command and variable names. Unless you give a full pathname, the shell uses the variable **path** in an attempt to complete a command name; the choices listed are likely to be located in different directories:

```
tcsh $ up → TAB → up(BEEP) → CONTROL-D
up2date             up2date-nox           update_scrshot_page
up2date-config      updatedb              uptime
tcsh $ upt → TAB → uptime RETURN
9:59am up 31 days, 15:11, 7 users, load average: 0.03, 0.02, 0.00
```

If you set the **autolist** variable as in the following example, the shell lists choices automatically when you invoke completion by pressing TAB; you do not have to press CONTROL-D:

```
tcsh $ set autolist
tcsh $ up → TAB(BEEP)
up2date             up2date-nox           update_scrshot_page
up2date-config      updatedb              uptime
tcsh $ upt → TAB → uptimeRETURN
10:01am up 31 days, 15:14, 7 users, load average: 0.20, 0.06, 0.02
```

If you set **autolist** to ambiguous, the shell lists the choices when you press TAB *only* if the word you enter is the longest prefix of a set of commands. Otherwise, pressing TAB causes the shell to add one or more characters to the word until it is the longest prefix; pressing TAB again then lists the choices:

```
tcsh $ set autolist=ambiguous
tcsh $ echo $h → TAB(BEEP)
histfile history home
tcsh $ echo $hi → TAB → echo $histTAB
histfile history
tcsh $ echo $histo → TAB → echo $history RETURN
1000
```

The shell must rely on the context of the word within the input line to determine whether it is a filename, a user name, a command, or a variable name. If a word is the first on an input line, it is assumed to be a command name; if it begins with the special character $, it is viewed as a variable name, and so on. In the following example the second which command does not work properly, because the context of the word up makes it look like a filename prefix to tcsh, not a command name prefix. The TC Shell supplies which with an argument of **updates**, a nonexecutable file; which displays an error message:

```
tcsh $ ls up*
updates
tcsh $ which updatedb ups uptime
/usr/bin/updatedb
/usr/local/bin/ups
/usr/bin/uptime
tcsh $ which up → TAB → which updates
updates: Command not found.
```

Editing the Command Line

The tcsh command line editing feature is similar to that of bash (and zsh, as you will see in the next chapter). You can use either GNU emacs-style commands or vi-style commands. The default is emacs, but you can change this easily with the bindkey builtin. If you are using emacs-style bindings, you can change to the vi commands with **bindkey –v**. Similarly, if you are using vi-style bindings, you can change to emacs with **bindkey –e**. The ARROW keys are bound to the obvious motion commands, so you can move back and forth (up and down) through your history list as well as left and right in the current command.

The bindkey builtin, without an argument, displays the current mappings between editor commands and the key sequences you can enter at the keyboard:

```
tcsh $ bindkey | less
```

The less utility is handy here because it lets you move and search back and forth through this long list as you read it. If you are familiar with emacs or vi, you will recognize some of the commands listed by bindkey.

Correcting Spelling

You can have tcsh attempt to do spelling correction on command names, filenames, and variables (but only using emacs-style key bindings). Spelling correction can take place only at two times: before and after you press RETURN.

Before You Press RETURN

In order for tcsh to correct a word or line before you press RETURN, you must give it an indication that you want to do so. The two functions for this purpose are **spell-word** and **spell-line**. Each of these functions is bound to a key sequence: META-s and META-$, respectively. To correct the spelling of the word to the left of the cursor, enter META-s.[2] Entering META-$ invokes the **spell-line** function, which attempts to correct all words on a command line. The following command lines illustrate the use of these functions:

---

2. On many keyboards the ALT key replaces the META key: Use ALT-S in place of META-S and ALT-$ for META-$. If these substitutions do not work, try pressing ESCAPE followed by s in place of META-S and ESCAPE $ in place of META-$. See "Moving the Cursor by Words" on page 478 for more information on the META key.

```
tcsh $ ls
bigfile.gz
tcsh $ gunzipp → META-s → gunzip bigfele.gz → META-s → gunzip bigfile.gz
tcsh $ gunzip bigfele.gz → META-$ → gunzip bigfile.gz
tcsh $ ecno $usfr → META-$ → echo $user
```

After You Press RETURN

The variable named **correct** controls what tcsh attempts to correct or complete *after* you press RETURN. Set **correct** to cmd to correct only commands; all to correct commands, variables, and filenames; or complete to complete commands. If you do not set **correct**, tcsh will not correct anything:

```
tcsh $ unset correct
tcsh $ ls morning
morning
tcsh $ ecno $usfr morbing
usfr: Undefined variable.³

tcsh $ set correct = cmd
tcsh $ ecno $usfr morbing

CORRECT>echo $usfr morbing (y|n|e|a)? yes
usfr: Undefined variable.

tcsh $ set correct = all
tcsh $ echo $usfr morbing

CORRECT>echo $user morning (y|n|e|a)? yes
alex morning
```

The preceding sequence of commands first makes sure that **correct** is not set and establishes the presence of the file named **morning**. After that it gives the same command three times, each with a different setting of **correct**: one with **correct** not set; one with **correct** set to cmd, showing the command name being corrected from ecno to echo; and the last with **correct** set to all, showing the command, variable, and filename being corrected.

Automatic spell checking displays a special prompt that lets you enter **y** to accept the command line, **n** to reject it, **e** to edit it, or **a** to abort the command. Refer to "prompt3" on page 709 for a discussion of the special prompt used in spelling correction.

---

3. The reason that the shell reports the error in the variable name and not the command name is that it expands variables before it executes the command (page 693). When you give a bad command name without any arguments, the shell reports on the bad command name.

In the next example, after setting the **correct** variable, you mistype the name of the ls command, and tcsh prompts for a correct command name. Because the command that tcsh has offered as a replacement is not ls, you choose to edit the command line and fix the mistake:

```
tcsh $ set correct=cmd
tcsh $ 1x -1
CORRECT>1ex -1 (y|n|e|a)? edit
tcsh $ 1x -1■
```

If you assign the value `complete` to the variable **correct**, tcsh attempts command name completion in the same manner as filename completion (page 693). Following, after setting **correct**, the user enters the command **up**. The shell responds with `Ambiguous command` because several commands start with these two letters but differ in the third letter. Then the user enters **upt** and the shell completes the command because these three letters are unique to the uptime utility:

```
tcsh $ set correct = complete
tcsh $ upRETURN
Ambiguous command
tcsh $ uptRETURN → uptime
4:45pm  up 5 days,  9:54,  5 users,  load average: 1.62, 0.83, 0.33
tcsh $ ec "hi there"
Ambiguous command
tcsh $ echo■"hi there"RETURN
hi there
```

The preceding final two commands show that completion works with arguments. The command **ec** is ambiguous, but both commands start with echo, so the shell gives you a message and displays the command line with as much of the command as is common to them. (The utilities are echo and echotc, so echo is common to them.) The shell places the prompt so that you can complete the command if you want to. In this case the user wanted to use echo and simply pressed RETURN.

Variables

Although tcsh stores variable values as strings, you can work with these variables as numbers. Expressions in tcsh can use arithmetic, logical, and conditional operators. The @ builtin can also evaluate arithmetic expressions but can work only with integers.

This section uses the term *numeric variable* to describe a string variable that contains a number that tcsh uses in arithmetic or logical arithmetic computations. However, no true numeric variables exist in tcsh.

A tcsh variable name consists of 1 to 20 characters, which can be letters, digits, and underscores (_). The first character cannot be a digit but can be an underscore.

Variable Substitution

Three builtins declare, display, and assign values to variables: set ^{tcsh}, @ ^{tcsh}, and setenv ^{tcsh}. The set and setenv builtins both assume nonnumeric string variables. The @ builtin works only with numeric variables. Both set and @ declare local variables. The setenv builtin declares a variable *and* places it in the calling environment of all child processes. Using setenv is similar to assigning a value to a variable and then using export in the Bourne Again Shell. See "export: Makes a Variable Global" on page 571 for a discussion of local and environment variables.

Once the value—or merely the existence—of a variable has been established, tcsh substitutes the value of that variable when the variable is on a command line or in a shell script. As with bash and zsh, tcsh recognizes as a variable a word that begins with a dollar sign. If you quote the dollar sign by preceding it with a backslash (\$), the shell does not perform the substitution. When a variable is within double quotation marks, the substitution occurs even if you quote the dollar sign. If the variable is within single quotation marks, the substitution does not occur, regardless of whether you quote the dollar sign.

String Variables

The TC Shell treats string variables similarly to the way the Bourne Again and Z Shells do. The major difference is in their declaration and assignment: tcsh uses an explicit command, set (or setenv), to declare and/or assign a value to a string variable.

```
tcsh $ set name = fred
tcsh $ echo $name
fred
tcsh $ set
argv    ()
cwd     /home/alex
home    /home/alex
name    fred
path    (/usr/local/bin /bin /usr/bin /usr/X11R6/bin)
prompt  $
shell   /bin/tcsh
status  0
term    vt100
user    alex
```

The first line in the example declares the variable **name** and assigns the string fred to it. (Unlike bash and zsh, tcsh allows but does not demand SPACEs around the equal sign.) The next line displays this value. When you give a set command without any arguments, it displays a list of all the local shell variables and their values (your list will be longer than the one in the example). Referring to the first two lines of the following example, you see that when you give a set command with the name of a variable and no value, the command sets the value of the variable to a null string. The next two lines show that the unset builtin removes a variable from the list of declared variables:

```
4 $ set name
5 $ echo $name
6 $ unset name
7 $ set
argv    ()
cwd     /home/alex
home    /home/alex
path    (/usr/local/bin /bin /usr/bin /usr/X11R6/bin)
prompt  $
shell   /bin/tcsh
status  0
term    vt100
user    alex
```

When using setenv instead of set, the variable name is separated from the string being assigned to it by one or more SPACEs, and *no* equal sign. The **tcsh** command creates a subshell, echo shows that the variable and its value are known to the subshell, and exit returns you to the original shell. Try this example, using set in place of setenv:

```
tcsh $ setenv SCRDIR /usr/local/src
tcsh $ tcsh
tcsh $ echo $SCRDIR
/usr/local/src
tcsh $ exit
```

If you use setenv with no arguments, it displays a list of the environment variables—variables that are passed to any child processes of the shell. By convention, environment variables are given uppercase names.

As with set, giving setenv a variable name without a value sets the value of the variable to a null string. Although you can use unset to remove environment and local variables, unsetenv can remove *only* environment variables.

Arrays of String Variables

An *array* tcsh is a collection of strings, each of which is identified by its index (1, 2, 3, and so on). Before you can access individual elements of an array, you must declare the entire array by assigning a value to each element of the array. The list of values must be enclosed in parentheses and separated by SPACEs:

```
8 $ set colors = (red green blue orange yellow)
9 $ echo $colors
red green blue orange yellow
```

```
10 $ echo $colors[3]
blue
11 $ echo $colors[2-4]
green blue orange
12 $ set shapes = ('' '' '' '' '')
13 $ echo $shapes
14 $ set shapes[4] = square
15 $ echo $shapes[4]
square
```

Event 8 declares the array of string variables named **colors** to have five elements and assigns values to each of them. If you do not know the values of the elements at the time you declare an array, you can declare an array containing the necessary number of null elements (event 12).

You can reference an entire array by preceding its name with a dollar sign (event 9). A number in brackets following a reference to the array refers to an element of the array (events 10, 14, and 15). Two numbers in brackets, separated by a hyphen, refer to two or more adjacent elements of the array (event 11). Refer to "Special Variable Forms" on page 706 for more information on arrays.

Numeric Variables

The **@** builtin assigns the result of a numeric calculation to a numeric variable (as described under "Variables" [page 698], tcsh has no true numeric variables). You can declare single numeric variables with **@**, just as you can use **set** to declare non-numeric variables. However, if you give it a nonnumeric argument, **@** displays an error message. Just as **set** does, the **@** command without any arguments gives you a list of all shell variables.

Many of the expressions that the **@** builtin can evaluate and the operators it recognizes are derived from the C programming language. The following format shows a declaration or assignment using **@**. The SPACE after the **@** is required:

@ *variable-name operator expression*

The *variable-name* is the name of the variable that you are assigning a value to. The *operator* is one of the C assignment operators: **=, +=, −=, *=, /=,** or **%=.** (See page 1190 for an explanation of these operators.) The *expression* is an arithmetic expression that can include most C operators; refer to "Expressions," following. You can use parentheses within the expression for clarity or to change the order of evaluation. Parentheses must surround parts of the expression that contain any of the following characters: **<, >, &,** or **l.**

Do Not Use a $ When Assigning a Value to a Variable || tip

As with the other shells, variables having a value assigned to them (those on the left of the operator) must not be preceded by a dollar sign ($). Thus

```
tcsh $ @ $answer = 5 + 5
```

will yield

```
answer: Undefined variable.
```

or

```
@: Variable name must begin with a letter.
```

whereas

```
tcsh $ @ answer = 5 + 5
```

assigns the value 10 to the variable answer

Expressions

An expression is composed of constants, variables, and the operators from Table 14-4 (listed in order of decreasing precedence [priority of evaluation]). Expressions that involve files rather than numeric variables or strings are described on page 715.

Operator || table 14-4

Parentheses		
	()	Change the order of evaluation
Unary Operators		
	−	Unary minus
	~	One's complement
	!	Logical negation
	++	Postfix increment
	−−	Postfix decrement

Operator (Continued)

|| table 14-4

Arithmetic Operators	
%	Remainder
/	Divide
*	Multiply
−	Subtract
+	Add
Shift Operators	
>>	Right shift
<<	Left shift
Relational Operators	
>	Greater than
<	Less than
>=	Greater than or equal to
<=	Less than or equal to
!=	Not equal to (compare strings)
==	Equal to (compare strings)
Bitwise Operators	
&	AND
^	Exclusive OR
|	Inclusive OR
Boolean Operators	
&&	AND
||	OR

Expressions follow these rules:

1. The shell evaluates a missing or null argument as 0.

2. All results are decimal numbers.

3. Except for != and ==, the operators act on numeric arguments.

4. You must separate each element of an expression from adjacent elements by a SPACE, unless the adjacent element is &, |, <, >, (, or).

Following are some examples that use @:

```
216 $ @ count = 0
217 $ echo $count
0
218 $ @ count = ( 10 + 4 ) / 2
219 $ echo $count
7
220 $ @ result = ( $count < 5 )
221 $ echo $result
0
222 $ @ count += 5
223 $ echo $count
12
224 $ @ count++
225 $ echo $count
13
```

Event 216 declares the variable **count** and assigns a value of 0 to it. Event 218 shows the result of an arithmetic operation being assigned to a variable. Event 220 uses @ to assign the result of a logical operation involving a constant and a variable to **result**. The value of the operation is *false* (= 0) because the variable **count** is not less than 5. Event 222 is a compressed form of the following assignment statement:

```
tcsh $ @ count = $count + 5
```

Event 224 uses a postfix operator to increment **count** by 1.

You can use the postfix increment (**++**) and decrement (**−−**) operators only in expressions containing a single variable name, as shown in the following example:

```
tcsh $ @ count = 0
tcsh $ @ count++
tcsh $ echo $count
1
tcsh $ @ next = $count++
@: Badly formed number.
```

Unlike in the C programming language, expressions in tcsh cannot use prefix increment and decrement operators.

Arrays of Numeric Variables

You must use the set builtin to declare an array of numeric variables before you can use @ to assign values to the elements of the array. The set builtin can assign any values to the elements of a numeric array, including zeros, other numbers, and null strings.

Assigning a value to an element of a numeric array is similar to assigning a value to a simple numeric variable. The only difference is that you must specify the element, or index, of the array. The format is

@ *variable-name[index] operator expression*

The *index* specifies the element of the array that is being addressed. The first element has an index of 1. The *index* cannot be an expression but rather must be either a numeric constant or a variable. In the preceding syntax the brackets around *index* are part of the syntax and do not indicate that *index* is optional. If you specify an *index* that is too large for the array you declared with set, tcsh displays @: Subscript out of range.

```
226 $ set ages = (0 0 0 0 0)
227 $ @ ages[2] = 15
228 $ @ ages[3] = ($ages[2] + 4)
229 $ echo $ages[3]
19
230 $ echo $ages
0 15 19 0 0
231 $ set index = 3
232 $ echo $ages[$index]
19
233 $ echo $ages[6]
ages: Subscript out of range.
```

Elements of a numeric array behave as though they were simple numeric variables. The difference is that you must use set to declare a numeric array. Event 226 in the preceding example declares an array with five elements, each having a value of 0. Events 227 and 228 assign values to elements of the array, and event 229 displays the value of one of the elements. Event 230 displays all the elements of the array, 232 specifies an element by using a variable, and 233 demonstrates the out-of-range error message.

Braces

As with bash and zsh, tcsh allows you to use braces to distinguish a variable from surrounding text without the use of a separator. For more information, refer to "{} Brace Expansion" on page 607.

Special Variable Forms

The special variable with the following syntax has the value of the number of elements in the *variable-name* array:

> $#*variable-name*

You can determine whether *variable-name* has been set by looking at the value of the variable with the following syntax:

> $?*variable-name*

This variable has a value of 1 if *variable-name* has been set and 0 otherwise:

```
tcsh $ set days = (mon tues wed thurs fri)
tcsh $ echo $#days
5
tcsh $ echo $?days
1
tcsh $ unset days
tcsh $ echo $?days
0
```

Reading User Input

Within a tcsh shell script, you can use the set builtin [tcsh] to read a line from the terminal and assign it to a variable. The following portion of a shell script prompts the user and reads a line of input into the variable **input_line**:

```
echo -n "Enter input: "
set input_line = "$<"
```

The value of the shell variable $< is a line from standard input. The quotation marks around it are necessary to keep the shell from assigning only the first word of the line of input to the variable **input_line**.

Shell Variables

This section lists some of the TC Shell variables that are set by the shell, inherited by the shell from the environment, or set by the user and used by the shell. Some variables take on significant values (for example the PID number of a background process). Other variables act as switches: *on* if they are declared and *off* if they are not. Many of the shell variables are often set from within one of tcsh's two startup files: **.login** and **.tcshrc** (page 684).

All the Variables in the Following List are Available in tcsh.   ‖ tip

The variables in the following list are all available in **tcsh**. Variables that are also available in other shells are marked with a shell box, such as [bash].

Shell Variables That Take on Values

argv This array contains the command line arguments (positional parameters) from the command line that invoked the shell. The array is indexed starting at 1, so that **argv[1]** contains the first command line argument. You can change any element of this array, use **argv[*]** to reference all the arguments together, and abbreviate references to **argv** as $* (short for $**argv[*]**) and $*n* (short for $**argv[*n*]**). Refer to "Positional Parameters" on page 581, but note that bash does not use the **argv** form, only the abbreviated form. Use $0 to reference the name of the calling program.

$#argv *or* **$#** Holds the number of elements in the **argv** array. Refer to "Special Variable Forms" on page 706.

autolist Controls command and variable completion (page 694).

autologout Enables tcsh's automatic logout facility, which logs you out if you leave the shell idle for too long. The value of the variable is the number of minutes of inactivity that tcsh waits before logging you out. The default is 60 minutes if you are Superuser; otherwise, this variable is initially unset.

cdpath Affects the operation of cd in the same way as the **CDPATH** ^{bash zsh} variable does (page 580). It takes on an array of absolute pathnames (see **path**, following) and is usually set in the **.login** file with a command line such as:

```
tcsh $ set cdpath = (/home/scott /home/scott/letters)
```

When you call cd with a simple filename, it searches the working directory for a subdirectory with that name. If one is not found, cd searches the directories listed in **cdpath** for the file.

correct Set to cmd for automatic spelling correction of command names, to all to correct the entire command line, and to complete for automatic completion of command names. Works on corrections that are made after you press RETURN. Refer to "After You Press RETURN" on page 697.

cwd The shell sets this variable to the name of the working directory. When you access a directory through a symbolic link, tcsh sets **cwd** to the name of the symbolic link. Refer to "Symbolic Links" on page 126.

dirstack The shell keeps the stack of directories used with the pushd, popd, and dirs builtins in this variable.

fignore You can set this variable to an array of suffixes that should be ignored during filename completion.

gid The shell sets this variable to your group ID.

histfile Gives the full pathname of the file to be used to save the history list between login sessions. If not set, the default file, **~/.history**, is used.

history   Controls the size of your history list. As a rule of thumb, its value should be kept around 100. Refer to "History" on page 686.

home *and* **HOME**   The **HOME** environment variable is part of the shell's environment when it starts and is used to initialize the **home** local variable. **HOME** has the value of the pathname of the home directory of the user. The cd builtin refers to this variable, as does the filename substitution of ~. Refer to "~   Tilde Expansion" on page 609.

owd   The shell keeps your previous (old) working directory in this variable. This is equivalent to ~– in bash and zsh.

path *and* **PATH**   The **PATH** environment variable is part of the shell's environment when the shell is started. The **path** local variable is an array set by the shell from the value of **PATH** (or to a default value if **PATH** is not set). The directories in the **path** array are searched for executable commands. If **path** is empty or unset, you can execute commands only by giving their full pathnames. You can set your **path** variable directly with a command such as the following:

```
tcsh $ set path = ( /usr/bin /bin /usr/local/bin /usr/bin/X11 ~/bin . )
```

Refer to "PATH: Where the Shell Looks for Programs" on page 577.

prompt   Holds the primary prompt, similar to the **PS1** variable (page 579); if it is not set, the prompt is **>**, or **#** for **root** (Superuser). The shell expands an exclamation point in the prompt string to the current event number. (Just as the shell replaces a variable in a shell script with its value, the shell replaces an exclamation point in the prompt string with the current event number.) The following is a typical line from a **.tcshrc** file that sets the value of **prompt**:

```
set prompt = '! $ '
```

Table 14-5 lists a number of special formatting sequences you can place into your prompt string for special effects.

Special Symbols	Display in Prompt	‖ table 14-5
%/	The value of **cwd** (your current working directory)	
%~	The same as the preceding, but the path of the user's home directory is replaced with a tilde when needed	
%! *or* %h *or* !	The current event number	
%m	The hostname without the domain	

Special Symbols	Display in Prompt (Continued)	‖ table 14-5
%M	The full hostname, including the domain	
%n	Your login name	
%t	The time of day through the current minute	
%p	The time of day through the current second	
%d	The day of the week	
%D	The day of the month	
%W	The month as mm	
%y	The year as yy	
%Y	The year as yyyy	
%#	A greater than sign (>) if you are not Superuser; a pound sign (#) if you are	
%?	The result returned by the preceding command	

prompt2 Holds the prompt used in **foreach** and **while** control structures (pages 720 and 722). The default value is '%R? ', where the R is replaced by the word while if you are inside a **while** structure and foreach if you are inside a **foreach** structure.

prompt3 Holds the prompt used during automatic spelling correction. The default value is 'CORRECT>%R (y|n|e|a)', where the R is replaced by the corrected string.

savehist Specifies the number of commands saved from the history list when you log out. These events are saved in a file named **.history** in your home directory. The shell uses them as the initial history list when you log in again, causing your history list to continue across login sessions.

shell Holds the pathname of the shell you are using.

shlvl This variable gets incriminated each time you start a subshell and decremented each time you exit a subshell. The value is set to 1 for login shells.

status Contains the exit status returned by the last command.

tcsh Holds the version number of tcsh that you are running. See the **version** variable (page 711) for more detail.

time This variable provides two functions: automatic timing of commands using the time builtin and the format used by time. You can set this variable to either a single numeric value or an array holding a numeric value and a string. The numeric value is used to control automatic timing; any command that takes more than that number of CPU seconds to run has time display the command statistics when it finishes execution. A value of 0 results in statistics being displayed after every command. The string is used to control the formatting of the statistics, using special formatting sequences, including those in Table 14-6.

Formatting Sequence ‖ table 14-6

%U	Time spent by the command running user code, in CPU seconds (user mode)
%S	Time spent by the command running system (kernel) code, in CPU seconds (kernel mode)
%E	Wall clock time (total elapsed) taken by the command
%P	Percent of time the CPU spent on this task during this period, computed as (%U+%S)/%E
%W	Number of times the command's processes were swapped out to disk
%X	Average amount of shared code memory used by the command, in kilobytes
%D	Average amount of data memory used by the command, in kilobytes
%K	Total memory used by the command (as %X+%D), in kilobytes
%M	Maximum amount of memory used by the command, in kilobytes
%F	Number of major page faults (pages of memory that had to be read from the disk)
%I	Number of input operations
%O	Number of output operations

By default the time builtin uses the string "%Uu %Ss %E %P%   %X+%Dk %I+%Oio %Fpf+%Ww", which generates output in the following format:

```
tcsh $ time
0.200u 0.340s 17:32:33.27 0.0%      0+0k 0+0io 1165pf+0w
```

You can time commands when you are concerned about system performance. If many of your commands show a lot of page faults and swaps, your system is probably memory starved, and you should consider adding more memory to the system. You can use the information that time reports to compare performances of various system configurations and program algorithms.

tperiod Set this variable to control how often, in minutes, the shell executes the special **periodic** alias (page 689).

user The shell sets this variable to your login name.

version The shell sets this variable to contain detailed information about the version of tcsh that you are using. See the **tcsh** variable (page 709) for less detail.

watch Set this to an array of user and terminal pairs to watch for logins and logouts. The word **any** means any user or any terminal, so (**any any**) monitors all logins and logouts on all terminals, and (**scott ttyS1 any console $user any**) watches for **scott** on **ttyS1,** any user who accesses the system console, and any logins and logouts that use your account (presumably to catch intruders). By default, logins and logouts are checked once every 10 minutes, but you can change this by beginning the array with a numeric value giving the number of minutes between checks. If you set **watch** to (**1 any console**), logins and logouts by any user will be checked once a minute. Reports are displayed only just before a new shell prompt is issued. Also, the log builtin forces an immediate check whenever it is executed. You can control the format of the **watch** messages; see **who.**

who Controls the format of the information displayed in **watch** messages. The formatting sequences listed in Table 14-7 are available.

Formatting Sequence	‖ table 14-7
%n	The name of the user
%a	The action taken by that user
%l	The terminal on which that action took place
%M	The full hostname of any remote host (or **local** if none) from which the action took place
$m	The hostname without the domain

The default string used for watch messages when **who** is unset is "%n has %a %l from %m", which generates the following line:

```
jenny has logged on tty2 from local
```

$ [bash tcsh zsh]   As in bash and zsh, this variable contains the PID number of the current shell.

All the Variables in the Following List Are Available in tcsh.   ‖ tip

The variables in the following list are all available in tcsh. Variables that are also available in other shells are marked with a shell box, such as [bash].

Shell Variables That Act as Switches

The following shell variables act as switches; their values are not significant. If the variable has been declared, the shell takes the specified action. If not, the action is not taken or is negated. You can set these variables in your **.tcshrc** file, in a shell script, or from the command line.

autocorrect   When set, the shell attempts spelling correction automatically, just before each attempt at completion.

dunique   Normally pushd blindly pushes the new working directory onto the directory stack. This means that you can end up with many duplicated entries on this stack. If the **dunique** variable is set, the shell looks for and deletes any entries that duplicate the one it is about to push.

echo   When you call tcsh with the **–x** option, it sets the **echo** variable. You can also set **echo** using set. In either case, when you declare **echo**, tcsh displays each command before it executes that command.

filec   The **filec** variable enables the filename completion feature when running tcsh as csh (and csh is linked to tcsh). Filename completion is always enabled when directly running tcsh. Filename completion is a tcsh feature that complements the filename generation facility. When **filec** is set, you can a enter a partial filename on the command line and press TAB to cause the shell to complete it, or you can press CONTROL-D to list all the filenames that match the prefix you entered. Refer to "Filename Substitution" on page 691.

histlit   When set, the commands in the history list are displayed exactly as entered, without interpretation by the shell.

ignoreeof   When set, you cannot use CONTROL-D to exit from the shell, so you cannot accidentally log out. When this variable is declared, you must use **exit** or **logout** to leave a shell.

listjobs   When set, the shell lists all jobs whenever a job is suspended.

listlinks   When set, the ls–F builtin shows the type of file each symbolic link points to instead of marking the symbolic link with an @ symbol.

loginsh   Set by the shell if the current shell is running as a login shell.

nobeep   Disables all beeping by the shell.

noclobber   Prevents you from accidentally overwriting a file when you redirect output and prevents you from creating a file when you attempt to append output to a nonexistent file (Table 14-8). To override **noclobber**, add an exclamation point to the symbol you use for redirecting or appending output (for example, **>!** and **>>!**). For more information on **noclobber**, refer to page 554 [bash] and page 824 [zsh].

How noclobber Works || table 14-8

Command Line	noclobber Not Declared	noclobber Declared
x > *fileout*	Redirects standard output from process x to *fileout*. Overwrites *fileout* if it exists.	Redirects standard output from process x to *fileout*. The shell displays an error message if *fileout* exists and does not overwrite the file.
x >> *fileout*	Redirects standard output from process x to *fileout*. Appends new output to the end of *fileout* if it exists. Creates *fileout* if it does not exist.	Redirects standard output from process x to *fileout*. Appends new output to the end of *fileout* if it exists. The shell displays an error message if *fileout* does not exist. It does not create the file.

noglob   When you declare **noglob**, tcsh does not expand ambiguous filenames. You can use *, ?, ~, and [] on the command line or in a shell script without quoting them. Refer to "Z Shell Options" on page 824 for information on the equivalent zsh option.

nonomatch   When set, tcsh passes an ambiguous file reference that does not match a filename to the command that is being called. The shell does not expand the file reference. When you do not set **nonomatch**, tcsh generates a No match error message and does not execute the command.

```
tcsh $ cat questions?
cat: No match
tcsh $ set nonomatch
tcsh $ cat questions?
cat: questions?: No such file or directory
```

notify   When set, tcsh sends a message to your terminal whenever one of your background jobs completes. Ordinarily tcsh notifies you about a job completion immediately before the next prompt. Refer to "Job Control" on page 554.

pushdtohome   When set, calling pushd without any arguments moves you to your home directory. This is equivalent to **pushd –**.

pushdsilent   When set, neither pushd or popd prints the directory stack.

rmstar   When set, the shell warns you and requests confirmation whenever you execute **rm** ✻.

verbose   The TC Shell declares this variable when you call it with the **–v** option. You can also declare it using set. In either case, **verbose** causes tcsh to display each command after a history substitution. Refer to "History" on page 686.

visiblebell   When set, causes audible beeps to be replaced by flashing the screen.

Control Structures

The TC Shell uses many of the same control structures as the Bourne Again Shell. In each case the syntax is different, but the effects are the same. This section summarizes the differences between the control structures in the two shells. For more information, refer to "Control Structures" on page 626.

if

The syntax of the **if** control structure `tcsh` is

> *if (expression) simple-command*

The **if** control structure works only with simple commands, not with pipes or lists of commands. You can use the **if...then** control structure (page 718) to execute more complex commands, such as the following:

```
tcsh $ cat if_1
#!/bin/tcsh
# Routine to show the use of a simple if
# control structure.
#
if ( $#argv == 0 ) echo "if_1: there are no arguments"
```

This program checks whether it was called without any arguments. If the expression (enclosed in parentheses) evaluates to *true*—that is, if zero arguments were on the command line—the **if** structure displays a message to that effect.

In addition to the logical expressions described on page 702, you can use expressions that return a value based on the status of a file. The syntax for this type of expression is

> *–n filename*

where *n* is from the list in Table 14-9.

Value of *n*

|| table 14-9

b	The file is a block special file.
c	The file is a character special file.
d	The file is a directory file.
e	The file exists.
f	The file is an ordinary file.
g	The file has the set-group-ID bit set.
k	The file has the sticky bit set.
l	The file is a symbolic link.
o	The user owns the file.
p	The file is a named pipe (FIFO).
r	The user has read access to the file.
s	The file is not empty (has nonzero size).
S	The file is a socket special file.
t	The file descriptor (a single digit) is open and connected to a terminal.
u	The file has the set-user-ID bit set.
w	The user has write access to the file.
x	The user has execute access to the file.
X	The file is either a builtin or an executable found by searching the directories in $path.
z	The file is 0 bytes long.

If the specified file does not exist or is not accessible, tcsh evaluates the expression as 0. If the result of the test is *true*, the expression has a value of 1; if it is *false*, the expression has a value of 0. The following example checks whether the file specified on the command line is an ordinary file:

```
tcsh $ cat if_2
#!/bin/tcsh
if -f $1 echo "Ordinary file"
```

You can combine operators where it makes sense. For example, **–ox filename** is *true* if you own and have execute permission for the file. This is equivalent to **–o filename && –x filename**.

Some operators return useful information about a file other than reporting *true* or *false*. They use the same *–n filename* format, where *n* is one of the values shown in Table 14-10.

Value of *n*	|| table 14-10
A	The last time the file was accessed, measured in seconds from the *epoch* (usually the start of January 1, 1970).
A:	The last access time as in **A** preceding, but in a human-readable format showing the day, date, time, and year.
M	The last time the file was modified, in seconds from the epoch (see **A** preceding).
M:	The last time the file was modified, in a human-readable format.
C	The last time that information about the file (that is, the information stored in the file's inode) was modified, measured in seconds since the epoch (see **A** preceding).
C:	The last time the inode was modified, in a human readable format.
D	The device number for the file. This is a number that uniquely identifies the device (disk partition, for example) on which the file resides.
I	The inode number for the file. The inode number uniquely identifies a file on a particular device (that is, another file on a different device may have the same inode number).
F	A string of the form **device:inode**. This string uniquely identifies a file anywhere on the system.
N	The number of hard (not symbolic) links connected to the file.
P	Shows the file's permissions, in octal, without a leading 0.
U	The numeric user ID of the file's owner.
U:	The username of the file's owner.

Value of *n* (Continued)	‖ table 14-10
G	The numeric group ID of the file's group.
G:	The groupname of the file's group.
Z	The number of bytes in the file.

You can use only one of these operators in a given test, and it must appear as the last operator in a multiple-operator sequence. Because 0 can be a valid response from some of these operators (for instance, the number of bytes in a file might be 0), most return −1 on failure instead of the 0 that the logical operators return on failure. The one exception is F, which returns a colon if it cannot determine the device and inode for the file.

When you want to use one of these operators outside of a control structure expression, you can use the filetest builtin to evaluate a file test and report the result:

```
tcsh $ filetest -z if_1
0
tcsh $ filetest -F if_1
2051:12694
tcsh $ filetest -Z if_1
131
```

goto

The syntax of a **goto** statement [tcsh] is

goto label

A **goto** builtin transfers control to the statement beginning with *label:*. The following program fragment demonstrates the use of **goto**:

```
tcsh $ cat goto_1
#!/bin/tcsh
#
# test for 2 arguments
#
if ($#argv == 2) goto goodargs
echo "Usage: goto_1 arg1 arg2"
exit 1
goodargs:
.
.
```

The **goto_1** script displays a standard usage message. Refer to page 630 for more information about usage messages.

Interrupt Handling

The **onintr** statement tcsh transfers control when you interrupt a shell script. The format of an **onintr** statement is

*onintr **label***

When you press the interrupt key during execution of a shell script, the shell transfers control to the statement beginning with ***label:***.

This statement allows you to terminate a script gracefully when it is interrupted. You can use it to ensure that when you interrupt a shell script, the script removes temporary files before returning control to the parent shell.

The following script demonstrates **onintr**. It loops continuously until you press the interrupt key, at which time it displays a message and returns control to the shell:

```
tcsh $ cat onintr_1
#!/bin/tcsh
# demonstration of onintr
onintr close
while ( 1 )
    echo "Program is running."
    sleep 2
end
close:
echo "End of program."
```

If a script creates temporary files, you can use **onintr** to remove them.

```
close:
rm -f /tmp/$$*
```

The ambiguous file reference **/tmp/$$*** matches all files in **/tmp** that begin with the PID of the current shell. Refer to page 586 for a description of this technique for naming temporary files.

if...then...else

The **if...then...else** tcsh control structure has three forms. The first form, an extension of the simple **if** structure, executes more complex ***commands*** or a series of ***commands*** if the ***expression*** is *true*. This form is still a one-way branch.

*if (**expression**) then*
   commands
endif

The second form is a two-way branch. If the *expression* is true, the first set of *commands* is executed. If it is *false,* the set of *commands* following **else** is executed.

> *if (**expression**) then*
> > *commands*
>
> *else*
> > *commands*
>
> *endif*

The third form is similar to the **if...then...elif** structure bash (page 632). It performs tests until it finds an *expression* that is *true* and then executes the corresponding *commands.*

> *if (**expression**) then*
> > *commands*
>
> *else if (**expression**) then*
> > *commands*
>
> .
>
> .
>
> *else*
> > *commands*
>
> *endif*

The following program assigns a value of 0, 1, 2, or 3 to the variable **class**, based on the value of the first command line argument. The program declares the variable **class** at the beginning for clarity; you do not need to declare it before its first use. Again, for clarity, the script assigns the value of the first command line argument to **number.**

```
tcsh $ cat if_else_1
#!/bin/tcsh
# routine to categorize the first
# command line argument
set class
set number = $argv[1]
#
if ($number < 0) then
    @ class = 0
else if (0 <= $number && $number < 100) then
    @ class = 1
else if (100 <= $number && $number < 200) then
    @ class = 2
else
    @ class = 3
endif
#
echo "The number $number is in class ${class}."
```

The first **if** statement tests whether **number** is less than 0. If it is, the script assigns 0 to **class**. If it is not, the second **if** tests whether the number is between 0 and 100. The **&&** is the Boolean AND operator, yielding a value of *true* if the expression on each side is true. If the number is between 0 and 100, 1 is assigned to **class**. A similar test determines whether the number is between 100 and 200. If it is not, the final **else** assigns 3 to **class**. The **endif** closes the **if** control structure. The final statement uses braces ({}) to isolate the variable **class** from the following period. Again, the braces isolate the period for clarity; the shell does not consider a punctuation mark as part of a variable name. The braces would be required if you wanted other characters to follow immediately after the variable.

foreach

The **foreach** builtin ^{tcsh} parallels the **for...in** structure ^{bash} (page 640). The syntax is

> *foreach* **loop-index** *(argument-list)*
>   *commands*
> *end*

This structure loops through the *commands*. The first time through the loop, the structure assigns the value of the first argument in the *argument-list* to the *loop-index*. When control reaches the **end** statement, the shell assigns the value of the next argument from the *argument-list* to the *loop-index* and executes the commands again. The shell repeats this procedure until it exhausts the *argument-list*.

The following tcsh script uses a **foreach** structure to loop through the files in the working directory containing a specified string of characters in their filename and to change the string. For example, you can use it to change the string **memo** in filenames to **letter**. The filenames **memo.1**, **dailymemo**, and **memories** would be changed to **letter.1**, **dailyletter**, and **letterries**.

This script requires two arguments: the string to be changed (the old string) and the new string. The *argument-list* of the **foreach** structure uses an ambiguous file reference to loop through all filenames that contain the first argument. For each filename that matches the regular expression, the mv utility changes the filename. The echo and sed commands appear within backprimes (` ) that indicate command substitution: The result of executing the commands within the backprimes replaces the backprimes and everything between them. Refer to "$(...) or `...`   Command Substitution" on page 575 for more information (the $(...) form of command substitution does not work in tcsh). The sed utility substitutes the first argument for the second argument in the filename. The **$1** and **$2** are abbreviated forms of **$argv[1]** and **$argv[2]**. Refer to page 1310 in Part III for more information on sed.

```
tcsh $ cat ren
#!/bin/tcsh
# Usage:      ren arg1 arg2
#             changes the string arg1 in the names of files
#             in the working directory into the string arg2
```

```
if ($#argv != 2) goto usage
foreach i ( *$1* )
    mv $i `echo $i | sed -n s/$1/$2/p`
end
exit 0

usage:
echo "Usage: ren arg1 arg2"
exit 1
```

Optional

The next script uses a **foreach** loop to assign the command line arguments to the elements of an array named **buffer**:

```
tcsh $ cat foreach_1
#!/bin/tcsh
# routine to zero-fill argv to 20 arguments
#
set buffer = (0 0 0 0 0 0 0 0 0 0 0 0 0 0 0 0 0 0 0 0)
set count = 1
#
if ($#argv > 20) goto toomany
#
foreach argument ($argv[*])
    set buffer[$count] = $argument
    @ count++
end
# REPLACE command ON THE NEXT LINE WITH THE PROGRAM
#    YOU WANT TO CALL.
exec command $buffer[*]
#
toomany:
echo "Too many arguments given."
echo "Usage: foreach_1 [up to 20 arguments]"
exit 1
```

This script calls another program named **command** with a command line guaranteed to contain 20 arguments. If **foreach_1** is called with fewer than 20 arguments, it fills the command line with zeros to complete the 20 arguments for **command**. More than 20 arguments cause it to display a usage message and exit with an error status.

The **foreach** structure loops through the commands one time for each of the command line arguments. Each time through the loop, **foreach** assigns the value of the next argument from the command line to the variable **argument**. Then the script assigns each of these values to an element of the array **buffer**. The variable **count** maintains the index for the **buffer** array. A postfix operator increments **count**, using @ (@ **count++**). The **exec** builtin ^{bash tcsh zsh} (page 665) calls **program** so that a new process is not initiated. (Once **program** is called, the process running this routine is no longer needed, so there is no need for a new process.)

while

The syntax of the **while** builtin `tcsh` is

while (expression)
        commands
end

This structure continues to loop through the *commands while* the *expression* is true. If the *expression* is false the first time it is evaluated, the structure never executes the *commands*:

```
tcsh $ cat while_1
#!/bin/tcsh
# Demonstration of a While control structure.
# This routine sums the numbers between 1 and
# n, n being the first argument on the command
# line.
#
set limit = $argv[1]
set index = 1
set sum = 0
#
while ($index <= $limit)
    @ sum += $index
    @ index++
end
#
echo "The sum is $sum"
```

This program computes the sum of all the integers up to and including *n*, where *n* is the first argument on the command line. The **+=** operator assigns the value of **sum + index** to **sum**.

break and continue

You can interrupt a **foreach** or **while** structure with a **break** `tcsh` or **continue** `tcsh` statement. These statements execute the remaining commands on the line before they transfer control. The **break** statement transfers control to the statement after the **end** statement, terminating execution of the loop. The **continue** statement transfers control to the **end** statement, which continues execution of the loop.

switch

The **switch** structure `tcsh` is analogous to the **case** structure `bash` (page 650):

switch (test-string)

case pattern:
　　　commands
breaksw

case pattern:
　　　commands
breaksw
　　　·
　　　·
default:
　　　commands
breaksw

endsw

The **breaksw** statement causes execution to continue after the **endsw** statement. If you omit a **breaksw**, control falls through to the next command. See Table 13-2 on page 652 for a list of special characters you can use within the *patterns*.

```tcsh
tcsh $ cat switch_1
#!/bin/tcsh
# Demonstration of a switch control structure.
# This routine tests the first command line argument
# for yes or no in any combination of upper- and
# lowercase letters.
#
# test that argv[1] exists
if ($#argv != 1) then
    echo "Usage: switch_1 [yes|no]"
    exit 1
else
# argv[1] exists, set up switch based on its value
    switch ($argv[1])
    # case of YES
        case [yY][eE][sS]:
        echo "Argument one is yes."
        breaksw
    #
    # case of NO
        case [nN][oO]:
        echo "Argument one is no."
    breaksw
    #
    # default case
        default:
        echo "Argument one is neither yes nor no."
        breaksw
    endsw
endif
```

Builtins

Builtins are commands that are part of (built into) the shell. When you give a simple filename as a command, the shell first checks whether it is the name of a builtin. If it is, the shell executes it as part of the calling process; the shell does not fork a new process to execute the builtin. The shell does not need to search the directory structure for builtin programs because they are immediately available to the shell.

If the simple filename is not a builtin, the shell searches the directory structure for the program you want, using the **PATH** variable as a guide. When it finds the program, the shell forks a new process to execute the program.

Although they are not listed in Table 14-11, all the control structure keywords (**if**, **foreach**, **endsw**, and so on) are builtins. The table describes many of the tcsh builtins, some of which are also built into other shells.

Builtins	**‖ table 14-11**
% *job* `bash tcsh zsh`	A synonym for the **fg** builtin. The *job* is the job number of the job you want to bring to the foreground (page 555).
% *job* & `bash tcsh zsh`	A synonym for the **bg** builtin, where *job* is the number of the job you want to put in the background (page 556).
@ `tcsh`	Similar to the **set** builtin but evaluates numeric expressions. Refer to "Numeric Variables" on page 701.
alias `tcsh zsh`	Creates and displays aliases. Refer to "Alias" on page 689.
alloc `tcsh`	Displays a report of the amount of free and used memory.
bg `bash tcsh zsh`	Moves a suspended job into the background (page 556).
bindkey `tcsh zsh`	Controls the mapping of keys to the **tcsh** command line editor commands. Under **zsh** **bindkey** works similarly. The most common uses follow.
bindkey	Without any arguments, **bindkey** lists all key bindings.
bindkey –l	Lists all the available editor commands and gives a short description of each.
bindkey –e	Causes the editor to use GNU **emacs**-like key bindings.
bindkey –v	Causes the editor to use **vi**-like key bindings.

Builtins (Continued)

|| table 14-11

bindkey *key command*	Attaches the editor command *command* to the key *key*.
bindkey –b *key command*	Similar to the previous form but allows you to give control keys by using the form C–x (where x is the character you type while you press the CONTROL key), give meta key sequences as M–x (on most keyboards used with GNU/Linux, the ALT key is the meta key), and give function keys as F-x.
bindkey –c *key command*	Binds the key *key* to the command *command*. Here the *command* is not an editor command but either a shell builtin or an executable program.
bindkey –s *key string*	Whenever you type *key*, *string* is substituted.
builtins **tcsh**	Displays a list of all the builtins.
cd **bash tcsh zsh** or chdir **tcsh zsh**	Changes working directories. Refer to "**cd**: Changes to Another Working Directory" on page 108.
dirs **bash tcsh zsh**	Displays the directory stack. Refer to "Manipulating the Directory Stack" on page 557.
echo **bash tcsh zsh**	Displays its arguments. You prevent a RETURN after echo displays a line by using a **–n** option **tcsh** (see "Reading User Input" on page 706) or by using a trailing \c **bash zsh** (see "**read**: Accepts User Input" on page 573). Refer to page 1157 in Part III for more information on **echo**.
eval **bash tcsh zsh**	Scans and evaluates the command line. When you put **eval** in front of a command, the command is scanned twice by the shell before it is executed. This is useful when you have a command that is generated as a result of command or variable substitution. Because of the order in which the shell processes a command line, it is sometimes necessary to repeat the scan in order to achieve the desired result (page 674).
exec **bash tcsh zsh**	Overlays the program currently being executed with another program in the same shell. The original program is lost. Refer to "**exec**: Executes a Command" on page 665 for more information; also refer to **source** (page 728).
exit **bash tcsh zsh**	Exit from a TC Shell. When you follow it with an argument that is a number, the number is the exit status that the shell returns to its parent process. For more information refer to "status" on page 709.

Builtins (Continued)

|| table 14-11

fg `bash tcsh zsh`	Moves a job into the foreground. Refer to "Job Control" on page 554.
filetest `tcsh`	Takes one of the file inquiry operators, followed by one or more filenames, and applies the operator to each filename. Returns the results as a space-separated list (page 717).
glob `tcsh`	Like **echo**, but does not display SPACEs between its arguments and does not follow its display with a NEWLINE.
hashstat `tcsh`	Reports on the efficiency of **tcsh**'s hash mechanism. The hash mechanism speeds the process of searching through the directories in your search path. See also **rehash** (page 727) and **unhash** (page 729).
history `tcsh`	Displays a list of recent commands. Refer to "History" on page 686.
jobs `bash tcsh zsh`	Identifies the current jobs, or commands running in the background. Refer to "Job Control" on page 554.
kill `bash tcsh zsh`	Terminates a job or process. Refer to "**kill**: Aborts a Process" on page 788.
limit `tcsh`	Limits the computer resources that the current process and any processes it creates can use. You can put limits on the number of seconds of CPU time the process can use, the size of files that the process can create, and so forth.
log `tcsh`	Immediately produces the report that the **watch** shell variable (page 711) would normally produce every 10 minutes (unless you have changed the default).
login `bash tcsh zsh`	Logs in a user. Can be followed by a username.
logout `bash tcsh zsh`	Ends a session if you are using your original (login) shell.
ls–F `tcsh`	Similar to **ls –F** but faster. (This builtin is the characters 1s–F in sequence without an intervening SPACE. The command it is similar to is the **ls** utility with the **–F** option.)

Builtins (Continued)

|| table 14-11

nice `tcsh`	Lowers the processing priority of a command or a shell. It is useful if you want to run a command that makes large demands on the central processing unit and you do not need the output right away. If you are Superuser, you can use **nice** to raise the processing priority of a command. Refer to "Notes" on page 1263 for more information on the **nice** builtin `tcsh` and to the same page in general for more information about the **nice** utility, which is available from **bash** and **zsh**.
nohup `tcsh`	Allows you to log out without terminating processes running in the background. Some systems are set up to do this automatically. Refer to **nohup** on page 1264 in Part III for information on both the **nohup** builtin `tcsh` and the **nohup** utility, which is available from **bash** and **zsh**.
notify `tcsh`	Causes the shell to notify you immediately when the status of one of your jobs changes. Refer to "Job Control" on page 554.
onintr `tcsh`	Controls what action an interrupt causes for a specific script. Refer to "Interrupt Handling" on page 718. Also refer to "**trap**: Catches a Signal" on page 667 for information on an equivalent command in **bash** and **zsh**.
popd `tcsh`	Removes a directory from the directory stack. Refer to "Manipulating the Directory Stack" on page 557.
printenv `tcsh`	Displays all the environment variable names and values.
pushd `tcsh`	Changes the working directory and places the new directory at the top of the directory stack. Refer to "Manipulating the Directory Stack" on page 557.
rehash `tcsh`	Recreates the internal tables used by the hash mechanism `tcsh`. Whenever a new instance of **tcsh** is invoked, the hash mechanism creates a sorted list of all commands available to the user, based on the value of **path**. After you add a command to one of the directories in **path**, use **rehash** to recreate the sorted list of commands. If you do not, **tcsh** may not be able to find the new command. Also refer to the **hashstat** (page 726) and **unhash** (page 729) builtins.

Builtins (Continued)

|| table 14-11

repeat `tcsh`	Takes two arguments—a count and simple command (no pipes or lists of commands)—and repeats the command the number of times specified by the count.
sched `tcsh`	Allows you to execute commands at scheduled times. For example, the following command causes the shell to print the message Dental appointment. at 10 AM: `tcsh $ sched 10:00 echo "Dental appointment."` If you call **sched** without any arguments, it prints the list of scheduled commands. When the time to execute a scheduled command arrives, **tcsh** executes the command just before it displays a prompt.
set `bash tcsh zsh`	Declares, initializes, and displays the values of local variables. Refer to "Variables" on page 698.
setenv `tcsh`	Declares and initializes the values of environment variables. Refer to "Variables" on page 698.
shift `bash tcsh zsh`	Analogous to the **shift** builtin `bash zsh` (page 583). Without an argument **shift** promotes the indexes of the **argv** array. You can use it with an argument to perform the same operation on another array.
source `tcsh`	Executes the shell script given as its argument: **source** does not fork another process. It is similar to the . (dot) builtin `bash` (page 581). The **source** builtin expects a TC Shell script, so no leading pound sign is required in the script. The current shell executes **source** so that the script can contain commands, such as **set**, that affect the current shell. After you make changes to your .tcshrc or .login file, you can use **source** to execute it from within the login shell in order to put the changes into effect without logging off and back on again. You can nest **source** builtins.
stop `bash tcsh zsh`	Stops a job or process that is running in the background. The **stop** builtin accepts multiple arguments.
suspend `bash tcsh zsh`	Stops the current shell and puts it in the background. It is similar to the suspend key, which stops jobs running in the foreground.

Builtins (Continued)

|| table 14-11

time `tcsh`	Executes the command that you give it as an argument. It displays a summary of time-related information about the executed command, according to the **time** shell variable (page 710). Without an argument **time** displays the times for the current shell and all its children.
umask `bash tcsh zsh`	Identifies or changes the access permissions that are assigned to files you create. Refer to page 1366 in Part III for more information on **umask**.
unalias `tcsh zsh`	Removes an alias. Refer to "Alias" on page 689.
unhash `tcsh`	Turns off the hash mechanism. See also **hashstat** (page 726) and **rehash** (page 727).
unlimit `tcsh`	Removes limits on the current process. Refer to the entry "limit" in the table on page 726.
unset `bash tcsh zsh`	Removes a variable declaration. Refer to "Variables" on page 698.
unsetenv `tcsh`	Removes an environment variable declaration. Refer to "Variables" on page 698.
wait `bash tcsh zsh`	Causes the shell to wait for all child processes to terminate. When you give a **wait** command in response to a TC Shell prompt, **tcsh** does not display a prompt and does not accept a command until all background processes have finished execution. If you interrupt it with the interrupt key, **wait** displays a list of outstanding processes before returning control of the shell to you.
where `tcsh zsh`	When given the name of a command as an argument, the **where** builtin locates all occurrences of the command and, for each, tells you whether it is an alias, a builtin, or an executable program in your path.
which `tcsh zsh`	Similar to **where** but reports only on the command that would be executed, not all occurrences. This builtin is much faster than the GNU/Linux **which** utility and knows about aliases and builtins.

Chapter Summary

Like the Bourne Again and Z Shells, the TC Shell is both a command interpreter and a programming language. Developed at the University of California at Berkeley, the TC Shell has popular features, such as history, alias, and job control, that have been adopted by other shells.

You may prefer to use tcsh as a command interpreter, especially if you are used to the TC Shell. In that case, if your default login shell is bash or zsh, you can ask the system administrator to change your login shell to tcsh. The administrator will make the change in the **/etc/passwd** file, so the shell you requested remains in effect across login sessions. However, this does *not* cause tcsh to run your shell scripts; they will continue to be run by bash unless you explicitly specify another shell on the first line of the script or invoke one on the command line. Specifying the shell on the first line of your shell scripts ensures the behavior you expect.

If you are used to bash, you will notice some differences between the two shells right away. For instance, the syntax you use to assign a value to a variable differs, and the SPACEs around the equal sign are optional. Both numeric and nonnumeric variables are created and given values using the set builtin. The @ builtin can evaluate numeric expressions for assignment to existing numeric variables.

Because there is no export builtin in tcsh, you must use the setenv builtin to create an environment variable. You can also assign a value to the variable with the setenv command. The command unset removes both local and environment variables, whereas the command unsetenv removes only environment variables.

The syntax of the tcsh alias builtin is slightly different from alias in bash. Unlike bash the tcsh alias feature permits you to substitute command line arguments, using the syntax available with the history mechanism.

Most other tcsh features, such as history, word completion, and command line editing, closely resemble their bash and zsh counterparts. The syntax of the tcsh control structures is slightly different but provides functionality equivalent to that found in bash and zsh.

The term *globbing*, a carryover from the Bourne Again Shell, refers to the matching of names containing special characters (such as * and ?) to filenames. If tcsh is unable to generate a list of filenames matching a globbing pattern, it displays an error message. This is in contrast to bash, which simply leaves the pattern alone.

Standard input and standard output can be redirected in tcsh, but there is no straightforward way to redirect them independently. To do so requires the creation of a subshell that redirects standard output to a file while making standard error available to the parent process.

Exercises

1. Assume that you are working with the following history list:

```
37  pine alex
38  cd /home/jenny/correspondence/business/cheese_co
39  less letter.0321
40  vi letter.0321
41  cp letter.0321 letter.0325
42  grep hansen letter.0325
43  vi letter.0325
44  lp letter*
45  cd ../milk_co
46  pwd
47  vi wilson.0321 wilson.0329
```

   Using the history mechanism, give commands to

   a. Send mail to Alex.

   b. Use vi to edit a file named **wilson.0329**.

   c. Send **wilson.0329** to the printer.

   d. Send both **wilson.0321** and **wilson.0329** to the printer.

2. How can you identify all the aliases currently in effect? Write an alias named **homedots** that lists the names (only) of all invisible files in your home directory.

3. How can you prevent a command from sending output to the terminal when you start it in the background? What can you do if you start a command in the foreground and later decide that it should run in the background?

4. What statement can you put in your **.tcshrc** file to prevent yourself from accidentally overwriting a file when you redirect output? How can you override this feature?

5. Assume that the working directory contains the following files:

```
adams.ltr.03
adams.brief
adams.ltr.07
abelson.09
abelson.brief
anthony.073
anthony.brief
azevedo.99
```

What happens if you press TAB after typing the following commands?

a. **less adams.l**

b. **cat a**

c. **ls ant**

d. **file az**

What happens if you press CONTROL-D after typing these commands?

e. **ls ab**

f. **less a**

6. Write an alias named **backup** that takes a filename as an argument and creates a copy of that file with the same name and a filename extension of **.bak**.

7. Write an alias named **qmake** (quiet **make**) that runs make with both standard output and standard error redirected to the file named **make.log**. The command **qmake** should accept the same options and arguments as make.

8. How can you make tcsh always display the pathname of the working directory as part of its prompt?

Advanced Exercises

9. What lines do you need to change in the Bourne Again Shell script **command_menu** (page 654) to make it a TC Shell script? Make the changes and verify that it works.

10. Users often find rm (and even **rm −i**) too unforgiving because it removes files irrevocably. Create an alias named **delete** that moves files specified by its argument(s) into the **~/.trash** directory. Create a second alias, named **undelete**, that moves a file from the **~/.trash** directory into the working directory. Finally, put the following line in your **.logout** file to remove any files that you deleted during the login session:

```
/bin/rm -f $HOME/.trash/* >& /dev/null
```

Explain what could be different if the following line were put in your **.logout** file instead:

```
rm $HOME/.trash/*
```

11. Modify the **foreach_1** program (page 721) so that it takes the command to exec as an argument.

12. Rewrite the program **while_1** (page 722) so that it runs faster. Use the time builtin to verify the improvement in execution time.

13. Write your own version of find named **myfind** that writes output to the file **findout** but without the clutter of error messages, such as when you do not have permission to search a directory. The **myfind** command should accept the same options and arguments as find. Can you think of a situation in which **myfind** does not work as desired?

14. When the **foreach_1** script (page 721) is supplied with 20 or fewer arguments, why are the commands following toomany: not executed? (Why is there no exit command?)

IN THIS CHAPTER

The Z Shell and Advanced Shell Programming

15

The Z Shell (zsh) combines many features of the Bourne Again, TC, and C Shells. In addition, zsh incorporates a number of new features. Because of the large number of features and configuration options available in zsh, this chapter concentrates on the most common ones and skips some of the more obscure ones. This chapter also explains how to customize zsh to meet your needs. If you have used csh or tcsh before, you can configure zsh to behave much the same way as csh and tcsh. If you have used the Korn Shell, setting up zsh to work like ksh may be useful to you.

This chapter builds on the material presented in the earlier chapters on shells and shell programming. If you read Chapters 12 through 14, you will recognize many of the features presented in this chapter. You may find it useful to refer back to these chapters while reading this chapter. For a complete description of the Z Shell, refer to the zsh man pages (give the command **man zsh** to see a list of sections; because the man page is so long, it has been broken into sections).

After an introduction, this chapter starts with a discussion of variables and shell builtins. Next is a discussion of command line editing, followed by a section on command processing that describes the various steps the shell takes when processing a command line. Then an extensive section on shell programming discusses recursion and guides you through the construction of two longer shell programs. This chapter ends with a list of Z Shell options.

> ## The Z Shell Is Not Automatically Installed with Red Hat ‖ tip
>
> The complete set of Red Hat disks includes the **zsh rpm** file (page 928). You can also download it from Red Hat's Web site or www.rpmfind.net.

The Z Shell, Korn Shell, and Pd-ksh

Although a complete version of the Korn Shell is now available as a commercial product for use with GNU/Linux, most users of the Korn Shell have relied on a public domain implementation named Pd-ksh (for Public Domain ksh; the name of the program is pdksh). Although pdksh (www.cs.mun.ca/~michael/pdksh) provides most of the basic features of the Korn Shell, it is missing some of the more advanced features that make the Korn Shell a powerful language for writing shell scripts. Most of these features (and then some) are present in zsh. In fact, if the Z Shell is linked to the filename **/bin/ksh**, running **/bin/ksh** results in the Z Shell starting with a default configuration that closely resembles the Korn Shell.

Z Shell Basics

If you want to use the Z Shell as your login shell, run chsh and specify the path **/bin/zsh** as described in "Entering and Leaving the TC Shell" (page 683). Alternatively, Superuser can set up the **/etc/passwd** file toward the same end.

The basic behavior of the Z Shell mimics that of the other shells: You type a command that names an executable program or script, optionally followed by arguments that are interpreted by the command. You can correct mistakes as described on page 37 before you press the RETURN key. You can also use the Z Shell's powerful command line editing (page 791) and history editing (page 795) facilities to create and modify command lines.

Like bash and tcsh, zsh evaluates variables, searches for aliases and functions, expands ambiguous file references, and handles redirection before executing a command. It is important to understand the precise sequence in which these steps are carried out because it affects the meaning of a command line. Before describing the steps in command line processing in detail, this chapter describes other aspects of the shell. Refer to "Processing a Command" on page 797.

Running Scripts

To execute a Z Shell script, use the script name as an argument to zsh:

```
zsh % zsh script_name
```

The preceding command calls zsh regardless of which shell you are working with. If you have execute permission for the file that contains the script, you can use the filename as a command:

```
zsh % script_name
```

When you start the first line of the script with #!/bin/zsh, the Z Shell runs the script, regardless of what shell you call the script from (page 564).

Startup Files

The Z Shell uses many of the same environment variables as bash and adds a few others. You can set these variables, along with commands that establish other characteristics of the Z Shell environment, in one of the Z Shell startup files (Table 15-1). All startup files with names that begin with a period reside in your home directory.

Startup Files	‖ table 15-1
/etc/zshenv	This file is created by Superuser to establish systemwide default characteristics for zsh. It is the first and only file that zsh *always* reads when it starts.
~/.zshenv	You create this file in your home directory. This file, the preferred location to set variables that override those set in /etc/zshenv, is the second file to be read.
/etc/zprofile	This file is created by Superuser to establish systemwide default characteristics for zsh login shells. It is read when a login shell starts up (or when zsh is called with the –l option) but not when you use the –f option. It is the preferred file for setting systemwide characteristics for users desiring a bash- or ksh-like shell.
~/.zprofile	You create this file in your home directory. This file is the preferred location to set variables that override those set in /etc/zprofile and read when a login shell starts up (or when zsh is called with the –l option) but not when the –f option is used. This file is preferred for setting personal characteristics for a bash- or ksh-like shell.

Startup Files (Continued)	‖ table 15-1
/etc/zshrc	This file is created by Superuser to establish systemwide default characteristics for **zsh** interactive shells (where standard input and standard output are both connected to a terminal). This file is not read when **zsh** is called with the **–f** option.
~/.zshrc	You create this file in your home directory. This file is read only by interactive shells (where standard input and standard output are both connected to a terminal) and is not read when **zsh** if called with the **–f** option.
/etc/zlogin	This file is created by Superuser to establish systemwide default characteristics for **zsh** login shells. This file is read when a login shell starts up (or when **zsh** is called with the **–l** option) but not when the **–f** option is used. It is the preferred file for setting system-wide characteristics for users desiring a C- or TC-like shell.
~/.zlogin	You create this file in your home directory. This file is the preferred location to set variables that override those set in **/etc/zlogin** and is read when a login shell starts up (or when **zsh** is called with the **–l** option) but not when the **–f** option is used. It is the preferred file for setting characteristics for users desiring a C- or TC-like shell.

Because **.zshenv** is the only user file that is always used for zsh initialization (except when you use **–f**), you can place all your variable initializations and option setups in this file. How you use the other startup files depends on how you use zsh: Is the invocation of zsh a login shell and/or an interactive shell?

Sample **.zshenv**, **.zprofile**, and **.zshrc** files follow. Some of the commands used in these files are not covered until later in this chapter. In any of the startup files, you must export variables and functions that you want to be available to child processes:

```
zsh % cat .zshenv
MAIL=/usr/spool/mail/${LOGNAME:?}
MANPATH=/usr/man:/usr/X11R6/man:/usr/local/man
PATH=$HOME/bin:/usr/local/bin:/usr/bin/X11:/usr/bin:/bin:
export MAIL MANPATH PATH
umask 002

zsh % cat .zprofile
FCEDIT=/usr/bin/vim
PS1='$ '
PS2='    >'
HISTSIZE=256
stty kill '^u' erase '^h' intr '^c'¦ quit '^\'
export FCEDIT PS1 PS2 HISTSIZE
```

```
zsh % cat .zshrc
set -a      # export all parameters defined herein
alias h='fc -l'
alias r='fc -e -'
alias a='alias'
alias e='fc'
alias pg='less'
alias vi='/usr/bin/vim -C'

#(name) X- start up X-windows
X() {
    startx >.startx.out 2>&1 &
    }

#(name) X16- start up 16-bit deep X-windows
X16() {
    startx -- -depth 16 >.startx.out 2>&1 &
    }
#(name) setenv- keep Cshellers happy
setenv() {
    if [ $# -eq 2 ]; then
        eval $1=$2
        export $1
    else
        echo "Usage: setenv NAME VALUE" >&2
    fi
    }
```

Commands That Are Symbols

The Z Shell uses the symbols (,), [,], and $ in various ways to identify builtin commands. To minimize confusion Table 15-2 lists the most common use of each of these commands, even though some of them are not introduced until later in the chapter.

Builtin	|| table 15-2
( )	Subshell (page 550)
$( )	Command substitution (page 803)
(( ))	Assignment operator (use when the enclosed value contains an equal sign [page 761])
$(( ))	Expression evaluation (not for use with an enclosed equal sign [page 762])

Builtin (Continued) || table 15-2

[ ]	The **test** command (see the **chkargs** script on page 628)
[[ ]]	Similar to [ ] but adds string comparisons (page 756)

The Z Shell supports the redirection operators shown in (Table 15-3).

Redirection Operators || table 15-3

< *filename*	Redirects standard input from *filename*.
<> *filename*	Redirects standard input from and standard output to *filename*. If NOCLOBBER is unset (that is, if CLOBBER is set), this redirection creates *filename* if it does not exist.
> *filename*	Redirects standard output to *filename*. If NOCLOBBER is unset (that is, if CLOBBER is set), this redirection creates *filename* if it does not exist.
>| *filename* or >! *filename*	Redirects standard output to *filename*, even if the file exists and the NOCLOBBER option (page 825) is set (that is, if CLOBBER is not set).
>> *filename*	Redirects and appends standard output to *filename*. If NOCLOBBER is unset (that is, if CLOBBER is set), this redirection creates *filename* if it does not exist.
<&*n*	Duplicates standard input from file descriptor *n*.
>&*n*	Duplicates standard output from file descriptor *n*.
[n]<&–	Closes standard input or file descriptor *n* if specified.
[n]>&–	Closes standard output or file descriptor *n* if specified.
[n]<&p	Transfers the input from the coprocess (page 806) to standard input or file descriptor *n* if specified.
[n]>&p	Transfers the output to the coprocess (page 806) to standard output or file descriptor *n* if specified.

Variables

Like bash and tcsh, zsh allows you to create and use variables. The rules for naming and referring to variables are similar in all three shells (page 566). As in the Bourne Again Shell, you assign values to variables with the following syntax:

VARIABLE=value

There can be no whitespace on either side of the equal (=) sign. If you want to include SPACEs in the value of the variable, put quotation marks around the value or quote the SPACEs.

In zsh, as in bash and tcsh, you reference the value of a variable by preceding the variable name with a dollar sign and enclosing it in braces, as in ${**VARIABLE**}. The braces are optional unless the name of the variable is followed by a letter, digit, or underscore. Also, the Z Shell refers to the arguments on its command line by position, using the special variables **$1**, **$2**, **$3**, and so forth up to **$9**. If you wish to refer to arguments past the ninth, you must use braces, as in **${10}**. The name of the command is held in **$0**.

You can unset one or more variables with the unset builtin bash tcsh zsh :[1]

```
zsh % unset PREF SUFF
```

This removes the variable's value and attributes.

Variable Attributes

In the Z Shell, as in the Bourne Again Shell, you can set a variable's attributes that control the values it can take on. The typeset builtin zsh sets attributes. The following example assigns the uppercase (**–u**) attribute to the variable **NAME**. A variable with this attribute translates all letters in its value to uppercase:

```
zsh % typeset –u NAME
zsh % NAME="Barbara Jackson"
zsh % echo $NAME
BARBARA JACKSON
```

Similarly, you can assign a variable the lowercase attribute with **typeset –l**.

The integer attribute is very useful. By default the values of Z Shell variables are stored as strings. However, if you want to do arithmetic on a variable, the string

---

1. A *builtin* (page 161) is a command that is built into a shell. Give the command **man zshbuiltins** to see a list of zsh builtins.

variable is internally converted into a number, manipulated, and then converted back to a string. A variable with the integer attribute is stored as an integer. This makes arithmetic much faster. Assign the integer attribute as follows:

```
zsh % typeset –i COUNT
```

The integer builtin ▨ zsh is almost identical to **typeset –i**, so the preceding example is the same as

```
zsh % integer COUNT
```

You can assign a base other than 10 to an integer variable. The Z Shell then uses this base to display the variable. The syntax is

typeset -i base variable

where *base* is the base you want to use to display the value. If the base is not 10, the value is displayed as *base#value* (in base 2 the value 20 is written as 10100):

```
zsh % COUNT=20
zsh % typeset –i2 BCOUNT
zsh % BCOUNT=$COUNT
zsh % echo $COUNT $BCOUNT
20 2#10100
```

The **export** attribute is similar to the export builtin ▨ bash zsh (page 571). If a variable has this attribute, a copy of it is inherited by all child processes. The Z Shell supports the export builtin and also provides **typeset –x** to set the **export** attribute. You can set the export attribute for functions as well as for variables; an exported function is available in all subshells.

The Z Shell supports several variable attributes that are useful for formatting output. You can assign a particular width (number of columns) to a variable and specify that it be left- or right-justified within that width. Leading zeros can be added or suppressed. Table 15-4 shows the corresponding options to the typeset builtin.

typeset Options   ‖ table 15-4

–L *width*	Left-justifies within a width of *width*
–R *width*	Right-justifies (blank filled) within a width of *width*
–Z *width*	Right-justifies (zero filled if digits) within a width of *width*

If you omit *width*, zsh uses the width of the first value assigned to the variable. See the last few lines of the following example, where **MONTH** is first assigned a value of 11 without specifying a width (establishing a width of two characters) and then assigned a value of 8, which is displayed in a two-character field with a trailing blank:

```
zsh % typeset -L8 FRUIT1 FRUIT2
zsh % FRUIT1=apple
zsh % FRUIT2=watermelon
zsh % echo $FRUIT1$FRUIT2
apple   watermel
zsh % echo $FRUIT2$FRUIT1
watermelapple
zsh % typeset -Z2 DAY
zsh % DAY=4; echo $DAY
04
zsh % typeset -L MONTH
zsh % MONTH=11; echo $MONTH/$DAY/02
11/04/02
zsh % MONTH=8; echo $MONTH/$DAY/02
8 /04/02
```

You can give the **readonly** attribute to a variable to prevent its value from being changed. You must assign values to **readonly** variables before you give them this attribute:

```
zsh % PATH=/usr/ucb:/usr/bin:/usr/local/bin:/usr/games
zsh % typeset -r PATH
zsh % PATH=/usr/bin:/usr/ucb:/usr/local/bin:/usr/games
zsh: read-only variable: PATH
```

You can use the readonly builtin [bash zsh] in place of **typeset –r**:

```
zsh % readonly TMP=/tmp
```

Without any arguments typeset displays a list of variables with their attributes and values. To see the value of a variable, use **typeset** *name*:

```
zsh % typeset DAY
DAY=2
```

Use typeset followed by an option to see which variables have a certain attribute set:

```
zsh % typeset -Z
DAY=2
```

Locality of Variables

By default, Z Shell variables that you create and use in a shell script are *global*: They are recognized throughout the current shell session and all subshells. You can also create variables that are *local* to a function. A variable that is local to a function is recognized only within that function. If a function has a local variable with the same name as a global variable, all references to that variable within the function refer to the local variable, whereas all references outside the function refer to the global variable.

Local variables are helpful in a function written for general use. Because the function is called by many scripts, perhaps written by different programmers, you need to make sure that names of the variables within the function do not interact with variables of the same name in the programs that call the function. Local variables eliminate this problem.

One of the uses of the typeset builtin is to declare a variable to be local to the function it is defined in (unless ALL_EXPORT [page 825] is set):

typeset **varname**

The next example shows the use of a local variable in an interactive session. This is a function, not a shell script; if you put the function in a file, do not attempt to execute it. If you save this function in a file named **countd**, you can place it in your environment with the . (dot) builtin (for example, . **countd**). Refer to "Running a Startup File with the . (Dot) or **source** Builtin" on page 581.

This example uses two variables named **count**. The first is declared and assigned a value of 10 in the login shell. Its value never changes, as is verified by echo before and after running **count_down**. The other **count** is declared, via typeset, to be local to the function. Its value, which is unknown outside the function, ranges from 6 to 1, as the echo command within the function confirms.

The example shows the function being entered from the keyboard. Once you start entering the function, zsh prompts you with function> to remind you that you are entering a function. While you are typing in the **while** loop, zsh prompts you with function while>:

```
zsh % count=10
zsh % function count_down {
function> typeset count
function> count=$1
function> while [ count -gt 0 ] ; do
function while> echo "$count..."
function while> ((count=count-1))
function while> sleep 1
function while> done
function> echo "Blast Off\!"
function> return
function> }
zsh % echo $count
10
zsh % count_down 6
6...
5...
```

```
4...
3...
2...
1...
Blast Off!
zsh % echo $count
10
```

The `((count=count-1))` assignment is enclosed between double parentheses, which cause the shell to perform the enclosed assignment (page 761). Within the double parentheses you can reference shell variables without the leading dollar sign ($). This feature is not found in bash.

Keyword Variables

The Z Shell automatically inherits and defines a number of variables, including most of the keyword shell variables from bash (page 576), when you start a session. Some have values that are set and changed during your session. Others are variables that you can assign values to and that have special meaning for the shell. Some are readonly variables that you cannot assign values to. See Table 15-5.

Keyword Variables || table 15-5

# bash tcsh zsh	$# The number of command line arguments (page 586).
* bash tcsh zsh	$* All the command line arguments as a single argument (page 586).
@ bash tcsh zsh	$@ All the command line arguments as individual arguments (page 586).

_ bash zsh	$_ The last argument of the previous simple command in the current instance of the shell. This is similar but not identical to !$ bash tcsh zsh :
	
	 `zsh % cat file1 file2 file3 > all3files`
	`zsh % echo $_`
	`file3`
	
	 If you had issued these commands using !$ from bash, tcsh, or zsh instead of $_ from zsh, the output would have been all3files. The Z Shell underscore argument specifically refers to arguments, not arbitrary symbols on the command line. Use !$ bash tcsh zsh to refer to the last symbol on the command line.

Keyword Variables (Continued) || table 15-5

CDPATH `bash` `zsh`	The list of absolute pathnames of directories searched by **cd** for subdirectories (page 580).
FCEDIT `bash` `zsh`	The name of the editor that the **fc** builtin uses (page 796).
FPATH `zsh` or fpath `zsh`	Contains a list of files that contain shell functions. See the discussion of shell functions and the **autoload** builtin `zsh` on page 786.
HISTFILE `bash` `zsh`	The name of the file that stores your history list (page 795).
HISTFILESIZE `bash` `zsh`	The number of lines of history stored in **HISTFILE** (page 795).
HISTSIZE `bash` `zsh`	The number of events stored in the history list during a session (page 795).
HOME `bash` `tcsh` `zsh`	The pathname of your home directory (page 576).
IFS `bash` `zsh`	The Internal Field Separator (page 612).

LINENO `bash` `zsh`	Before the shell executes a command from a script or function, it sets the value of **LINENO** to the line number of the command it is about to execute. The following script begins with the line #!/bin/zsh to ensure that the script runs under **zsh**:
	
	 ```zsh % cat showline```
	 ```#!/bin/zsh```
	 ```date```
	 ```echo "Script $0: at line $LINENO"```
	 ```echo "Script $0: at line $LINENO"```
	 ```echo "Script $0: at line $LINENO"```
	 ```zsh % showline```
	 ```Fri May 3 11:08:39 PDT 2002```
	 ```Script showline: at line 3```
	 ```Script showline: at line 4```
	 ```Script showline: at line 5```

LINES `bash` `zsh` and COLUMNS `bash` `zsh` and PS3 `bash` `zsh`	Controls the format of output generated by shell scripts using the **select** command `bash` `zsh` (page 770). Refer to page 658 for more information on **LINES** and **COLUMNS**.
MAIL `bash` `zsh`	The file where your mail is stored (page 578).

Keyword Variables (Continued) || table 15-5

OLDPWD `bash` `tcsh` `zsh` and PWD `bash` `tcsh` `zsh`	The shell stores the absolute pathname of the working directory, as set by the most recent **cd** command, in **PWD**, and the pathname of the previous working directory in **OLDPWD**. You can toggle between directories by giving the command **cd $OLDPWD**.

The value of **PWD** is not necessarily the same as the value returned by the **/bin/pwd** command, because the **PWD** variable keeps track of not only where you are, but also how you got there.

```
zsh % cd
zsh % mkdir -p top/level2/level3
zsh % ln -s top/level2 symdir
zsh % cd symdir
zsh % /bin/pwd
/home/alex/top/level2
zsh % echo $PWD
/home/alex/symdir
zsh % pwd
/home/alex/symdir
```

The **–p** option to **mkdir** causes the command to create any missing intermediate directories (in this case **top** and **level2**) when creating the target directory. The Z Shell **pwd** builtin `zsh` keeps track of symbolic links; the TC and Bourne Again Shell **pwd** builtins `bash` `tcsh` do not (page 128). The **pwd** utility (/bin/pwd) simply tells you the name of the directory you are in, regardless of how you got there.

OPTARG `bash` `zsh` and OPTIND `bash` `zsh`	These variables are set by the **getopts** builtin. Refer to "Builtins" on page 767.
PATH `bash` `tcsh` `zsh`	The list of directories that the shell searches for commands (page 577).
PPID `bash` `zsh`	The value of the PID of the parent process (the process running the process that is evaluating this variable). This value does not change throughout the lifetime of a shell session.
PS1 `bash` `zsh`	The shell prompt string (page 579).
PS2 `bash` `zsh`	The shell secondary prompt string (page 579).

Keyword Variables (Continued) || table 15-5

PS4 `bash` `zsh`	The prompt string used in debugging mode. When you turn on the trace facility with **set −x**, the shell precedes each line of trace output by **PS4**, which is + by default. For example, ``` zsh % MYNAME=alex zsh % set −x zsh % echo $MYNAME +zsh:137> echo alex alex zsh % PS4='DBG: ' +zsh:138> PS4=DBG: zsh % echo $MYNAME DBG: echo alex alex ```
RANDOM `bash` `zsh`	Each time this variable is referenced, it is assigned a random integer value between 0 and 32,767, inclusive. It is useful in several programming contexts, including test programs, generating dummy data, quizzes, and games.

SECONDS `bash` `zsh`	The number of seconds that have elapsed since the start of the shell session. You can include this variable in your prompt, but it is more useful for timing events in scripts:
	
	``
	zsh % cat quiz_short
	#!/bin/zsh
	echo "What is the smallest prime number that
	is larger than 50? \c"
	START=$SECONDS
	read ANSWER
	FINISH=$SECONDS
	echo "You took $(($FINISH - $START)) seconds
	to answer"
	if [$ANSWER -ne 53]; then
	    echo " and you were incorrect; the
	answer is 53."
	fi
	``
	
	The expression **$((FINISH − START))** is an example of the Z Shell's built-in arithmetic capability (dollar signs are not required within the double parentheses [page 761]).

TMOUT `bash` `zsh`	If set and if **TMOUT** seconds elapse after a prompt is issued with no input, the shell exits. This automatic logout feature helps prevent someone who is not known to the system from coming up to an idle terminal, giving commands, and compromising system security. This variable is usually set as a **readonly** variable in a global startup file. If it is not **readonly**, you can set it to 0 to disable it.

Controlling the Prompt

The default Z Shell prompt is your system hostname followed by a percent sign (%) or, when you are running as Superuser, a pound sign (#). When you run zsh as your root shell, which you normally do not, you may have a different prompt. To change your prompt, set the **PS1** variable as in the Bourne Again Shell. The first example that follows changes the prompt to the default prompt, adding a SPACE between the hostname and the percent or pound sign. The second example changes the prompt to the time followed by the name of the user. The third example changes the prompt to the one used in this chapter:

```
% PS1='%m %# '
bravo % PS1='%t %n: '
10:24PM alex: PS1='zsh %# '
zsh %
```

Table 15-6 describes the symbols used in these examples. Search for PROMPT EX-PANSION in the **zshmisc** man page for a complete (and lengthy) list of symbols.

Symbol	Display in Prompt	‖ table 15-6
%#	A # if this is a Superuser shell; otherwise, a %.	
%%	Always a %.	
%~	Pathname of the working directory.	
%.	Working directory tail (no pathname).	
%!	Current event number, as in tcsh.	
%b	Stop printing in boldface.	
%B	Start printing in boldface.	
%D	Date in yy-mm-dd format.	
%m	Machine hostname, without the domain.	
%M	Full machine hostname, including the domain.	
%n	Value of USERNAME variable.	
%n(x.true-text.false-text)	The *n* is a number (default is zero). The *x* is a test character from the following list. If *x* and *n* relate as *true*, replace this entire special symbol with *true-text;* otherwise, replace it with *false-text*. See the following examples.	

Symbol	Display in Prompt (Continued)	‖ table 15-6
Test Character	**Value** (one of the following)	
w	*True* if the day of the week is equal to *n*, where Sunday is 0. The *n* is an integer value (zero if omitted) that the value of the test character is compared to.	
d	*True* if the day of the month is equal to *n*.	
D	*True* if the month is equal to *n*, where January is 0.	
?	*True* if the exit status of the last command was *n* (0=*true*).	
n#	*True* if the user ID is *n*, so that %(#.#.%%) is the same as %#.	
C	*True* if the absolute pathname of the working directory has at least *n* elements.	
%t	Current time of day, in 12-hour, AM/PM format.	
%T	Current time of day in 24-hour format.	
%W	Date in mm/dd/yy format.	

The next example shows a prompt that displays the value returned by the previous command. The *n* is missing, so it defaults to 0. The ? returns 0, or *true*, if the previous command returned a value of 0 (*true*); otherwise, it returns *false* (see the following list). So the ? equals **n** (0), and the *true-text* (True:) is the prompt when the previous command returns a *true* exit status. This command uses slashes (/) in place of the periods shown in the table; you can use any character:

```
zsh % PS1='%(?/True: /False: )'
True: echo hi
hi
True: abcdef
zsh: command not found: abcdef
False:
```

Both the **true-text** and **false-text** sections may contain other special symbols, including repeated applications of **%(tc.true-text.false-text)**. Some of the *n*'s you can use are shown in the preceding table.

Expanding Shell Variables

Chapter 13 (page 661) discussed several alternatives to accepting a null value from an unset or null variable. The Z Shell incorporates the expansions that bash uses and adds a few of its own.

String Pattern Matching

The Z Shell provides a powerful set of string pattern–matching operators that manipulate pathnames and other strings. These operators can delete prefixes or suffixes that match patterns from strings. The four operators are listed in Table 15-7.

String Operator	|| table 15-7
#	Removes minimal matching prefixes
##	Removes maximal matching prefixes
%	Removes minimal matching suffixes
%%	Removes maximal matching suffixes

The syntax for these operators is

${varname op pattern}

In this syntax, *op* is one of the operators listed in the preceding table, and **pattern** is a match pattern similar to that used for filename generation. These operators are most commonly used to manipulate pathnames to extract or remove components or to change suffixes:

```
zsh % SOURCEFILE=/usr/local/src/prog.c
zsh % echo ${SOURCEFILE#/*/}
local/src/prog.c
zsh % echo ${SOURCEFILE##/*/}
prog.c
zsh % echo ${SOURCEFILE%/*}
/usr/local/src
zsh % echo ${SOURCEFILE%%/*}
```

```
zsh % echo ${SOURCEFILE%.c}
/usr/local/src/prog
zsh % CHOPFIRST=${SOURCEFILE#/*/}
zsh % echo $CHOPFIRST
local/src/prog.c
zsh % NEXT=${CHOPFIRST%%/*}
zsh % echo $NEXT
local
```

Other Operators

Some other operators provide special actions. The most useful of these operators are presented here.

The operation ${+name} [bash] [zsh] returns 0 if the variable name is unset. The operation returns 1 if it is set.

In bash, **IFS** expansion occurs whenever a variable is expanded to its value. This expansion does not occur unless the SH_WORD_SPLIT option [zsh] is set, or *on* (normally, SH_WORD_SPLIT is unset, or *off*). The **${=name}** operation sets SH_WORD_SPLIT for only this expansion and then lets SH_WORD_SPLIT revert to its previous value. When you use two equal signs, the shell unsets (turns *off*) this option for only this expansion. The change in the value of the option affects only the single expansion and does not apply to any other expansions on the command line:

```
zsh % IFS=:
zsh % a=a:b:c:d
zsh % cat $a
cat: a:b:c:d: No such file or directory
zsh % cat ${=a}
cat: a: No such file or directory
cat: b: No such file or directory
cat: c: No such file or directory
cat: d: No such file or directory
zsh % cat $a
cat: a:b:c:d: No such file or directory
```

The string-length operator, ${#name} [bash] [zsh], is replaced by the number of characters in the value of **name**:

```
zsh % echo $SOURCEFILE
/usr/local/src/Misc/viewfax-2.2/faxinput.c
zsh % echo ${#SOURCEFILE}
42
```

Parameter Expansion Flags

Finally, you can provide a list of special flag characters to any variable reference enclosed in braces. These flag characters specify actions to apply to the result of the variable expansion. You specify these flags by enclosing them within parentheses immediately following the opening brace. The Z Shell includes support for the flags listed in Table 15-8. For other flags, see the **zshexpn** man page.

Flag	table 15-8
o	Sorts the words resulting from the expansion in ascending order
O	Sorts the words resulting from the expansion in descending order
L	Converts all uppercase letters to lowercase
U	Converts all lowercase letters to uppercase
C	Capitalizes the first letter of each word
c	When used with $\{\#name\}$, counts the number of characters in the array, as if it were a string instead of an array
w	When used with $\{\#name\}$, counts the number of words in the value of **name**, whether this value is a string or an array (the current value of **IFS** is used to find word boundaries in strings)

The following example demonstrates most of these flags:

```
zsh % WORDS=(This is an array of words)
zsh % echo ${(o)WORDS}
an array is of This words
zsh % echo ${(O)WORDS}
words This of is array an
zsh % echo ${(L)WORDS}
this is an array of words
zsh % echo ${(U)WORDS}
THIS IS AN ARRAY OF WORDS
zsh % echo ${(C)WORDS}
This Is An Array Of Words
zsh % echo ${(c)WORDS}
This is an array of words
zsh % echo ${(c)#WORDS}
25
zsh % WORDS='This is a string of words'
zsh % echo ${(w)#WORDS}
6
```

Filename Generation

An important feature of most shells is the ability to refer to files by giving a pattern that describes one or more filenames. For example, all the shells discussed in this book use *.c as a pattern describing all filenames that end in .c. The shells expand this pattern into a list of filenames that match the pattern. This process of matching filenames to a pattern is called *globbing*. Globbing is useful for specifying many files with a single pattern, long filenames with a short string, and files with nonprinting characters in their names.

Globbing Terminology across the Shells || caution

Each of the shells uses its own terminology to describe globbing and related shell features. Although most of the terms are interchangeable most of the time, there are *some* differences in their use in the shells. Table 15-9 lists the terms used in the **man/info** pages for the shells.

Globbing Terms	bash	tcsh	zsh || table 15-9
globbing	Pathname expansion (page 614) or pattern expansion	Globbing pattern (page 691)	Filename generation (page 805) or pattern matching (page 751)
~ as the first character in a pathname	Tilde expansion (page 609)	Filename substitution (page 691)	Filename expansion (page 805)

The Z Shell has much more extensive support for filename generation than bash or tcsh, and you can use zsh options to control the level of support. For example, setting the NO_GLOB option turns off all pattern matching. If you have set the NO_GLOB option, you will have to give filenames exactly: *.c will refer only to a file whose name consists of the three character sequence *, ., and c. See "Filename Generation/Pathname Expansion" on page 157.

Table 15-10 describes the options that control filename pattern matching.

The characters that have special meaning when pattern matching (subject to the preceding restrictions and options) are listed in Table 15-11.

Setting and Unsetting Options

Set an option, such as NO_GLOB, by using the **set** builtin and preceding the option name with **-o**:

```
zsh % set -o NO_GLOB
```

The Z Shell strips out underscores when it processes a command like this; it also ignores case. The next command is equivalent to the previous one:

```
zsh % set -o noglob
```

Use a plus sign in place of the minus sign to unset an option:

```
zsh % set +o NO_GLOB
```

In addition, you can drop the **NO** so that **set +o glob** turns off globbing, and **set -o glob** turns it on (its initial state).

Another way of setting/unsetting options is with the **setopt/unsetopt** builtins. The following commands turn on globbing:

```
zsh % setopt glob
zsh % unsetopt noglob
```

These commands turn off globbing:

```
zsh % setopt noglob
zsh % unsetopt glob
```

Options That Control Filename Pattern Matching

|| table 15-10

NO_GLOB	Turns off all pattern matching; no characters have special meaning when specifying filenames to the shell. If NO_GLOB is not set, the characters *, |, <, and ? have special meaning when specifying filenames.
EXTENDED_GLOB	Adds the characters ^, ~, and # as special pattern-matching characters.
NULL_GLOB	Removes patterns from the command line if no filenames are found to match. If this option is not set, **zsh** displays an error message if no filenames match the pattern.
NO_NOMATCH	Causes **zsh** to leave the pattern intact on the command line, if no filenames match the pattern (for example, if no files match *.c, pass the string *.c to the command).

Options That Control Filename Pattern Matching (Continued) || table 15-10

GLOB_DOTS	Normally, to match a filename beginning with a period (.), you have to give the period explicitly in the pattern (none of the special characters match a leading period in a filename). Setting this option causes special characters to match leading periods. The filenames . and .. must always be given explicitly because no pattern ever matches them.

Pattern Matching Special Characters || table 15-11

*	Matches any string of characters, including the null string (for example, a string containing no characters at all).
?	Matches any single character.
[...]	Matches any one of the characters enclosed in the brackets (for example, [abc] matches either an a, b, or c). You can separate the first and last characters in a sequence with a hyphen (-), so [a-z] matches any lowercase letter, [0-9] matches any digit, and [A-Za-z] matches any upper- or lowercase letter. If the string within the brackets begins with a caret (^), the pattern matches any single character *except* those inside the brackets.
<x-y>	Matches any number from x through y (for example, <10-15> matches 10, 11, 12, 13, 14, and 15). As special cases <-y> matches any number less than y, <x-> matches any number greater than x, and <-> (or just <>) matches any number at all.
(x)	Any pattern x can be enclosed in parentheses for grouping.
^x	Matches any filename that is not matched by the pattern x (for example, ^*.c matches all filenames that do not end in .c). The Z Shell applies a ^ before matching a /, so ^top/level2 looks for files named **level2** in all the subdirectories of the working directory except for the subdirectory **top**.
x|y	Matches anything matched by pattern x or by pattern y, so *(tree|code).c matches all filenames ending in either tree.c or code.c. The | must always be enclosed in parentheses so that the shell does not treat it as a pipe symbol.

Pattern Matching Special Characters (Continued) || table 15-11

x#	Matches zero or more instances of whatever pattern x matches. Thus, (*/)#tree.c matches any pathname containing zero or more subdirectories and ending in the name **tree.c**. A useful shorthand is **/, which is equivalent to (*/)#. Neither (*/)# nor **/ follows any symbolic links, but the shorthand ***/ works similarly while following symbolic links.
x##	Matches one or more instances of whatever pattern x matches.
x~y	Matches any filename matched by x unless it also matches y. For example, *.h~system.h matches any filename ending in .h except for the filename **system.h**. The shell applies ~ before applying |, so (*.c)|(*.C)~main.C matches any filename ending in .c along with any filename ending in .C except for the filename **main.C**. You can use parentheses to override this behavior: ((*.c)|(*.C))~(main.*) matches all filenames ending in .c or .C unless it begins with main.

Glob Qualifiers

Finally, any pattern used for matching filenames can be followed by a list of qualifiers enclosed in parentheses. These flags restrict the list of filenames that are allowed to match the pattern. Some of the more useful flags are listed in Table 15-12.

Flag || table 15-12

/	Includes only directories
. (period)	Includes only plain files
@	Includes only symbolic links
r	Includes only files that are readable by the owner
w	Includes only files that are writable by the owner
x	Includes only files that are executable by the owner
R	Includes only files that are readable by everyone

Flag (Continued)	|| table 15-12
W	Includes only files that are writable by everyone
X	Includes only files that are executable by everyone

See the **zshexpn** man page more information about Z Shell pattern matching.

Array Variables

The Z Shell supports one-dimensional array variables. Subscripts are integers, with one-based subscripting (the first element of the array has the subscript 1). You declare and assign values to an array in one of two ways. The first way uses the set builtin and does not require parentheses (page 824):

set –A name element1 element2 ...

The following example demonstrates the use of an array variable (the brackets in the second echo command line are optional):

```
zsh % set -A NAMES alex helen jenny scott
zsh % echo $NAMES
alex helen jenny scott
zsh % echo ${NAMES[2]}
helen
```

As demonstrated earlier, you can also use an assignment statement with parentheses delimiting the array:

name=(element1 element2 ...)

The first line of the preceding example becomes

```
zsh % NAMES=(alex helen jenny scott)
```

You can display all the elements of the array by using an asterisk:

```
zsh % echo ${NAMES[*]}
alex helen jenny scott
```

You can extract sequential elements of an array by using two subscripts separated by a comma:

```
zsh % echo $NAMES[2,4]
helen jenny scott
```

A negative subscript counts from the right end of the array. The following example displays the array starting with the second element from the left side (specified by 2) through the second element from the right side (specified by –2):

```
zsh % echo $NAMES[2,-2]
helen jenny
```

There are some special, noninteger subscripts as well. The subscripts [*] and [@] both extract the entire array but work differently when used within double quotation marks. An @ produces an array that is a duplicate of the original array, whereas a * produces a single element of an array (or a plain variable) that holds all the elements of the array separated by the first character in **IFS** (normally a SPACE). In the following example the array **A** is filled with the elements of the **NAMES** variable, using a *, and B is filled using an @. The set builtin with the **–A** option and no arguments displays the values of all arrays:

```
zsh % set -A A "${NAMES[*]}"
zsh % set -A B "${NAMES[@]}"
zsh % set -A
. . .
A=('alex helen jenny scott')
B=(alex helen jenny scott)
NAMES=(alex helen jenny scott)
. . .
```

From the output of set, you can see that **NAMES** and B have multiple elements, whereas **A**, which was assigned its value with an @ sign within double quotation marks, has only one element: A has all its elements enclosed between single quotation marks. When echo tries to display elements 2 through 7 of array **A**, nothing is displayed because A has only one element (element number 1). When you attempt to display the same elements of array B, you see elements 2, 3, and 4. There are no elements numbered 5, 6, or 7:

```
zsh % echo $A[2,7]

zsh % echo $A[1]
alex helen jenny scott
zsh % echo $B[2,7]
helen jenny scott
zsh % echo $B[2]
helen
zsh % echo $A
alex helen jenny scott
```

Next, the $#*array* variable displays the number of elements in each array:

```
zsh % echo $#A
1
zsh % echo $#B
4
```

You can use subscripts on the left side of an assignment statement to replace selected elements of the array:

```
zsh % NAMES[4]=william
zsh % echo ${NAMES[*]}
alex helen jenny william
```

You can use subscripts with string (nonarray) values. If you use a subscript with a string variable, each character of the string is counted as though it were an element of an array:

```
zsh % C=$NAMES
zsh % echo $C[1]
a
zsh % echo $C[2,7]
lex he
```

In the preceding example $C[1] points to the first character of the value alex helen jenny scott, and $C[2,7] points to lex he. You can also use subscript strings on the left side of an assignment:

```
zsh % C[6,10]="alice"
zsh % echo $C
alex alice jenny william
```

It is possible to treat strings as though they were arrays. Use the **w** (word) and **s** (separator) flags, enclosed in parentheses, at the start of a subscript:

```
zsh % echo $#C
24
zsh % echo $C[2]
l
zsh % echo $C[(w)2]
alice
zsh % echo $C[(ws/l/)2]
ex a
```

In this example C holds a string of 22 characters. The second character in this string is the letter l, denoted by the subscript [2]. The (w) flag causes zsh to treat the value of C as an array, where SPACEs separate the elements. The subscript [(w)2] points to the second element in the array. The **s** flag changes the character used to separate elements, from SPACE to the specified character. In the preceding example **s/l/** changes it to the letter l, so the second element becomes the string of characters between the first and second l. You can use any other character in place of the slashes (/); for example, **s/:** uses a colon as the delimiter:

```
zsh % echo $PWD
/usr/local/bin
zsh % echo $PWD[(ws/:/)2]
local
```

You can apply the ${#name} operator [zsh] to array variables, returning the number of elements in the array. Another operator that works with array variables is ${^name} [zsh], where **name** has an array as its value. Like ${=name}, which turns on SH_WORD_SPLIT, ${^name} turns on RC_EXPAND_PARAM only for this evaluation. Use two carets (^^) to turn it off. When the option RC_EXPAND_PARAM is *on* and the value of **aa** is the array (1 2 3), the shell expands **side${aa}g** to side1g, side2g, side3g instead of side1 2 3g:

```
zsh % set -A SUFFIX c h o
zsh % echo ${#SUFFIX}
3
zsh % echo faxinput.${SUFFIX}
faxinput.c h o
zsh % echo faxinput.${^SUFFIX}
faxinput.c faxinput.h faxinput.o
```

Arithmetic

The Z Shell can perform assignments and evaluate many different types of arithmetic expressions. All arithmetic is done using integers, and you can represent numbers in any base from 2 to 36, using the *base#value* syntax (page 742).

Assignments

The shell can perform arithmetic assignments in a number of ways. One is with arguments of the let builtin [zsh]:

```
zsh % let "VALUE=VALUE * 10 + NEW"
```

In this example the variables **VALUE** and **NEW** contain integer values. Within a let statement, dollar signs ($) do not need to precede variable names. Double quotation marks enclose the arguments to prevent the shell from attempting to expand the asterisk as a file pattern-matching operator; arguments that contain SPACEs must be quoted. Because many expressions that are arguments to let need to be quoted, the Z Shell accepts ((expression)) as a synonym for let "expression", obviating the need for quotation marks and dollar signs ($):

```
zsh % ((VALUE=VALUE * 10 + NEW))
```

You can use either form any place a command is allowed. You can also get rid of SPACEs if you like. Each argument to let is evaluated as a separate expression, so you can assign values to more than one variable on a single line:

```
zsh % let COUNT=COUNT+1 "VALUE=VALUE*10+NEW"
```

Expressions

You can use an arithmetic expression as an argument to a command or in place of any numeric value. An arithmetic expression is enclosed between $((and))[2] and does not need to be enclosed within quotation marks, as the Z Shell does not perform filename expansion within the $((and)). This feature makes it easier for you to use an asterisk (*) for multiplication, as the following example shows:

```
zsh % echo There are $((60*60*24*365)) seconds in a non-leap year.
There are 31536000 seconds in a non-leap year.
```

You can use $[and] in place of $((and)):

```
zsh % echo There are $[60*60*24*366] seconds in a leap year.
There are 31622400 seconds in a leap year.
```

Fewer Dollar Signs ($) || tip

When you use variables within $((and)), the dollar signs that precede individual variable references are optional:

```
zsh % x=23 y=37
zsh % echo $((2*$x + 3*$y))
157
zsh % echo $((2*x + 3*y))
157
```

Optional

Operators

An arithmetic expression in the Z Shell uses the same syntax, precedence, and associativity of expressions as the C language. Table 15-13 lists all the operators you can use within arithmetic expressions in the Z Shell. The table is broken into groups of operators with equal precedence and includes some operators that are not available in C (for example, **).

Operator || table 15-13

+	Unary plus
–	Unary minus

---

2. This is expression substitution. Whereas ((...)) evaluates an expression and assigns the result to a variable, $((...)) evaluates an expression and replaces itself with the result [similar to $(...) command substitution].

Operator (Continued)

|| table 15-13

!	Boolean NOT
~	Complement
++	Preincrement and postincrement
––	Predecrement and postdecrement
&	Bitwise AND
^	Bitwise XOR
|	Bitwise OR
*	Multiplication
/	Division
%	Remainder
**	Exponentiation
+	Addition
–	Subtraction
<<	Left shift
>>	Right shift
<	Less than
>	Greater than
<=	Less than or equal
>=	Greater than or equal
==	Equality
!=	Inequality
&&	Boolean AND
^^	Boolean XOR
||	Boolean OR

Operator (Continued)	|| table 15-13
? :	Ternary operator
=, +=, −=, *=, /=, %=, &=, ^=, |=, <<=, >>=, &&=, ||=, ^^=, **=	Assignments
, (comma)	Comma operator

The preincrement, postincrement, predecrement, and postdecrement operators work with variables. The pre- operators, which appear in front of the variable name, as in **++COUNT** and **−−VALUE**, first change the value of variable (**++** adds one; **−−** subtracts one) and then provide the result for use in the expression. The post- operators appear after the variable name, as in **COUNT++** and **VALUE−−**, provide the unchanged value of the variable for use in the expression and then change the value of the variable:

```
zsh % ((N=10))
zsh % echo "$N"
10
zsh % echo "$((--N+3))"
12
zsh % echo "$N"
9
zsh % echo "$((N++ - 3))"
6
zsh % echo "$N"
10
```

The **&&** (AND) and **||** (OR) Boolean operators are called *short-circuiting* operators. If the result of using one of these operators can be decided by looking only at the left operand, the right operand is not evaluated. The **&&** operator causes the Z Shell to test the exit status of the command preceding it. If the command succeeds, zsh executes the next command; otherwise, it skips the remaining commands on the command line. You can use this construct to execute commands conditionally:

```
zsh % mkdir bkup && cp -r src bkup
```

This compound command creates the directory **bkup**. If mkdir succeeds, the contents of directory **src** is copied recursively to **bkup**.

The || separator also causes the Z Shell to test the exit status of the first command but has the opposite effect: The remaining command(s) are executed only if the first one failed (that is, exited with nonzero status):

```
zsh % mkdir bkup || echo "mkdir of bkup failed" >> /tmp/log
```

The exit status of a command list is the exit status of the last command executed. You can group lists with parentheses. For example, you could combine the previous two examples as

```
zsh % (mkdir bkup && cp -r src bkup) || echo "mkdir failed" >> /tmp/log
```

In the absence of parentheses, && and || have equal precedence and are grouped left to right. The following two commands yield an exit status of 1 (*false*):

```
zsh % true || false && false
zsh % echo $?
1
zsh % (true || false) && false
zsh % echo $?
1
```

Similarly the next two commands yield an exit status of 0 (*true*):

```
zsh % false && false || true
zsh % echo $?
0
zsh % (false && false) || true
zsh % echo $?
0
```

See page 588 for a description of the $? variable.

Because the expression on the right side of a short-circuiting operator may never get executed, you must be careful with assignment statements in that location. The following example demonstrates what can happen:

```
zsh % ((N=10))
zsh % ((Z=0))
zsh % echo $(( (N || ((Z+=1)) ))
1
zsh % echo $Z
0
```

Because the value of **N** is nonzero, the result of the || (OR) operation is 1 (*true*), no matter what the value of the right side is, so the ((**Z+=1**)) is never evaluated, and **Z** is not incremented.

The pipe symbol has highest precedence of all operators. You can use pipes anywhere in a command that you can use simple commands. The command line

```
zsh % cmd1 | cmd2 || cmd3 | cmd4 && cmd5 | cmd6
```

is interpreted as if you had typed

```
zsh % ((cmd1 | cmd2) || (cmd3 | cmd4)) && (cmd5 | cmd6)
```

The assignment operators, such as +=, are shorthand notations. For example, ((N+=3)) is the same as ((N=N+3)). The comma operator lets you put more than one sequence of operations into a single expression:

```
zsh % ((N=10,Z=0))
zsh % echo "$N and $Z"
10 and 0
```

The ternary operator, ? :, decides which of two expressions should be evaluated, based on the value returned from a third expression:

expression1 ? expression2 : expression3

If *expression1* produces a *false* (0) value, *expression3* is evaluated; otherwise, *expression2* is evaluated. The value of the entire expression is the value of *expresson2* or *expression3*, depending on which one is evaluated. If *expression1* is *true*, *expression3* is not evaluated. Similarly, if *expression1* is *false*, *expression2* is not evaluated:

```
zsh % ((N=10,Z=0,COUNT=1))
zsh % ((T=N>COUNT?++Z:--Z))
zsh % echo $T
1
zsh % echo $Z
1
```

The remainder operator (%) gives the remainder when its first operand is divided by its second. Thus the expression $((15%7)) has the value 1. The result of a Boolean operation is always either 0 (*false*) or 1 (*true*):

```
zsh % let "Var1=2#0101"
zsh % let "Var2=2#0110"
zsh % echo "$Var1 and $Var2"
5 and 6
zsh % echo $(( Var1 & Var2 ))
4
zsh % echo $(( Var1 && Var2 ))
1
zsh % echo $(( Var1 | Var2 ))
7
zsh % echo $(( Var1 || Var2 ))
1
zsh % echo $(( Var1 ^ Var2 ))
3
zsh % echo $(( !Var1 ))
0
zsh % echo $(( Var1 < Var2 ))
1
zsh % echo $(( Var1 > Var2 ))
0
```

The bitwise AND operator (&) selects the bits that are on in both 5 (0101 in binary) and 6 (0110 in binary); the result is binary 0100, which is 4 decimal. The Boolean AND operator (&&) produces a result of 1 if both of its operands are nonzero, and 0 otherwise. The bitwise inclusive OR operator (I) selects the bits that are on in either of 0101 and 0110, resulting in 0111, which is 7 decimal; it produces a result of 1 if either of its operands is nonzero, and 0 otherwise. The bitwise exclusive OR operator (^) selects the bits that are on in either, but not both, of the operands 0101 and 0110, giving 0011, which is 3 decimal. The Boolean NOT operator (!) produces a result of 1 if its operand is 0, and 0 otherwise. Because the exclamation point in $((!Var1)) is enclosed within double parentheses, it does not need to be escaped to prevent the Z Shell from interpreting the exclamation point as a history event (page 795). The comparison operators all produce a result of 1 if the comparison is *true,* and 0 otherwise.

Builtins

The Z Shell provides a much richer set of builtins—for option processing, I/O, control flow, and control of the user's environment—than either the Bourne Again or TC Shells. This section focuses on the builtins not covered previously.

Control Structures

Whereas this book refers to a *control structure* or *control flow command*, the Z Shell documentation refers to a *complex command*. This chapter will stay with the term *control structure* or *control flow command* for consistency with the rest of the book. The control flow commands are used primarily for shell programming, although they can also be useful in interactive work. The Z Shell control structures that control the process flow are **if...then, for...in, while, case, until, repeat,** and **select**. All these except **repeat** are also present in bash, although zsh provides several different syntactic forms for most of these commands (page 771).

The **if** (page 626), **while** (page 643), and **until** (page 647) structures have in common the use of a *test-command* (not the test builtin ^{bash}_{zsh}). You can use the same syntax for Z Shell *test-commands* that you use in the Bourne Again Shell. You can use the test builtin ^{bash}_{zsh}, the [[...]] builtin _{zsh}, or any other command as the *test-command*. The syntax of the [[...]] builtin is

[[conditions]]

The result of executing this builtin, like the test builtin, is a return status. The *conditions* allowed within the brackets are almost a superset of those accepted by test (page 1352). Where the test builtin uses –a as a Boolean AND operator, the Z Shell uses &&. Similarly, where test uses –o as a Boolean OR operator, the Z Shell uses ||. The Z Shell adds the tests listed in Table 15-14.

Test	table 15-14
–o *option*	*True* if the option named *option* is set
(*expression*)	*True* if *expression* is *true*
! *expression*	*True* if *expression* is *false*
expression1 && *expression2*	*True* if *expression1* and *expression2* are both *true*
expression1 || *expression2*	*True* if either *expression1* or *expression2* is *true*

You can use test's numeric relational operators –gt, –ge, –lt, –le, –eq, and –ne with [[...]]. The Z Shell allows you to use arithmetic expressions, not just constants, as the operands:

```
zsh % [[ $(( ${#HOME} + 14 )) -lt ${#PWD} ]]
zsh % echo $?
1
```

In this example the condition is *false* (1). The condition would be *true* (0) if the length of the string represented by the variable **HOME** plus 14 were less than the length of the string represented by **PWD**. See the **es** script on page 588 for more about **$?**.

Optional

The **test** builtin ^bash ^zsh tests whether strings are equal or unequal. The **[[...]]** builtin adds comparison tests for string operators: The **>** and **<** operators compare strings for order (so that, for example, "aa" < "bbb"). The **=** operator tests for pattern match, not just equality: *[[string = pattern]]* is *true* if **string** matches **pattern**. This operator is not symmetrical; the **pattern** must appear on the right side of the equal sign. For example, **[[artist = a*]]** is *true* (=0), whereas **[[a* = artist]]** is *false* (=1):

```
zsh % [[ artist = a* ]]
zsh % echo $?
0
zsh % [[ a* = artist ]]
zsh % echo $?
1
```

The next example has a command list that is started by a compound condition. The condition tests that the directory **bin** and the file **src/myscript.bash** exist. If this is true, **cp** copies **src/myscript.bash** to **bin/myscript**. If the copy succeeds, **chmod** makes **myscript** executable. If any of these steps fails, **echo** displays a message:

```
zsh % [[ -d bin && -f src/myscript.bash ]] && cp src/myscript.bash \
bin/myscript && chmod +x bin/myscript || echo "Cannot make \
executable version of myscript"
```

The **[[...]]** builtin is useful by itself, but you will probably use it most as the test command for control structures. This builtin also allows an arithmetic test. This test appears inside double parentheses (( )) instead of brackets. As shown in the next example, these double parentheses are not preceded by a **$**, and the value of this test is not a numeric value, only a *true* or *false* exit status:

```
zsh % a=45 b=20
zsh % ((a < b))
zsh % echo $?
1
zsh % ((a > b))
zsh % echo $?
0
```

You can use all the logical arithmetic operators shown on page 762. You can write one of the following:

```
if [[ $(( ${#HOME} + 14 )) -lt ${#PWD} ]]
then ...
```

or

```
if (( $(( ${#HOME} + 14 )) < ${#PWD} ))
then ...
```

or

```
if (( ${#HOME} + 14 < ${#PWD} ))
then ...
```

The last two commands use comparison operators that are similar to arithmetic and may be more natural for you to use.

The Z Shell recognizes the tokens [[and ((and treats them as special symbols, not commands. Thus you need not follow [[or ((with a SPACE.

select

The Z Shell's implementation of **select** _{bash zsh} is very similar to that of the Bourne Again Shell (page 658).

repeat

The **repeat** control structure _{zsh} allows you to specify how many times a sequence of commands is to be executed. The syntax of **repeat** is

> *repeat word*
> *do*
> > *commands*
> *done*

Here *word* is expanded and then evaluated as an arithmetic expression. The value of that expression determines how many times the *commands* are repeated.

```
zsh % repeat 3; do
repeat> echo "Bye"
repeat> done
Bye
Bye
Bye
zsh % read number
3
zsh % repeat $(($number + 2));do
repeat> echo Bye
repeat> done
Bye
Bye
Bye
Bye
Bye
```

Alternative Syntax for Control Structures

Unlike the other shells, the Z Shell provides several different syntaxes for many commands, often to provide a form similar to tcsh/csh. The forms of control structures that match the syntax of tcsh/csh follow.

The **for** structure has the following alternative syntaxes:

*foreach name (**word** ...)*
        commands
end

or

*for name (**word** ...){*
        commands
    }

The **while** structure can be written as follows:

*while (**command**) {*
        commands
}

Option Processing

The way that a utility interprets its command line is up to the specific utility. However, most GNU/Linux utilities conform to certain conventions. Refer to "The Command Line" on page 137. In particular, any option the utility takes is indicated by a letter preceded by a hyphen:

```
zsh % ls -l -r -t
```

(Refer to page 1235 in Part III for more information on ls.) The options usually must precede other arguments, such as filenames. Most utilities accept options that are combined behind a single hyphen. The previous command can also be written as

```
zsh % ls -lrt
```

Some utilities have options that themselves require arguments. The cc and gcc utilities have a −o option that must be followed by the name you want to give the executable file that is being generated. Typically, an argument to an option is separated from its option letter by a SPACE:

```
zsh % gcc -o prog prog.c
```

In the same manner the −o option to the set builtin takes an argument. The next command turns on the EXTENDED_GLOB option, which treats #, ~, and ^

as special characters that are added to the other special characters for filename generation:

```
zsh % set -o EXTENDED_GLOB
```

Another convention allows utilities to work with filenames that start with a hyphen. If you have a file whose name is –l, the following command is ambiguous:

```
zsh % ls -l
```

It could mean a long listing of all files in the working directory or a listing of the file named –l. It is interpreted as the former. Avoid creating files whose names begin with hyphens, but if you do create them, many utilities follow the convention that a –– argument (two consecutive hyphens) indicates the end of options (and the start of the arguments). To disambiguate the command, you can type

```
zsh % ls -- -l
```

or

```
zsh % ls ./-l
```

These are conventions, not hard-and-fast rules, and a number of utilities do not follow them (for example, find). Following such conventions is a good idea; it makes it much easier for users to learn to use your program. When you write shell programs that require options, follow the GNU/Linux option conventions.

GNU ––help Option   ‖ tip

A convention followed by most GNU utilities is to display a (sometimes extensive) help message when you call them with an argument of ––help:

```
zsh % gzip --help
gzip 1.2.4 (18 Aug 93)
usage: gzip [-cdfhlLnNrtvV19] [-S suffix] [file ...]
 -c --stdout      write on standard output, keep original ...
 -d --decompress  decompress
 -f --force       force overwrite of output file and ...
 -h --help        give this help
 -l --list        list compressed file contents
 -L --license     display software license
 ...
```

---

getopts: Parses Options

The getopts builtin ᵇᵃˢʰ/ᶻˢʰ makes it easier for you to write programs that follow the UNIX/Linux (including Red Hat) argument conventions. The syntax for getopts is

getopts optstring varname [arg ...]

The *opstring* is a list of the valid option letters. To indicate that an option takes an argument, follow the corresponding letter with a colon (:). The option string

dxo:1t:r indicates that getopts should search for –d, –x, –o, –l, –t, and –r options
and that the –o and –t options take arguments.

Using getopts as the *test-command* in a **while** control structure allows you to
loop over the options one at a time. The getopts builtin checks the option list for options that are in *optstring*. Each time through the loop, getopts stores the option letter it finds in *varname*. By default getopts uses the command line options. If you
supply a list of arguments (*arg*) after *varname*, it uses those instead.

The getopts builtin uses the OPTIND (option index) and OPTARG (option argument) variables to store option-related values. When a shell script starts, the
value of OPTIND is 1. Each time getopts locates an argument, it increments OPT-
IND to be the index of the next option to be processed. If the option takes an argument, zsh assigns the value of the argument to OPTARG.

Suppose that you want to write a program that can take three options.

1. A –b option indicates that your program should ignore whitespace at the
   start of input lines.

2. A –t option followed by the name of a directory indicates that your
   program should use that directory for temporary files. Otherwise, it
   should use **/tmp**.

3. A –u option indicates that your program should translate all its output to
   uppercase.

In addition, the program should ignore all other options and end option processing
when it encounters a ––.

The problem is to write the portion of the program that determines which options the user has supplied. The following solution does not use getopts:

```
SKIPBLANKS=
TMPDIR=/tmp
CASE=lower
while [[ "$1" = -* ]] # Remember, [[ = ]] does pattern match
do
    case $1 in
        -b)     SKIPBLANKS=TRUE ;;
        -t)     if [ -d "$2" ]
                    then
                        TMPDIR=$2
                        shift
                    else
                        print "$0: -t takes a directory argument." >&2
                        exit 1
                    fi ;;
        -u)     CASE=upper ;;
        --)     break     ;;      # Stop processing options
        *)      print "$0: Invalid option $1 ignored." >&2 ;;
    esac
    shift
done
```

This program fragment uses a loop to check and shift arguments while the argument is not two hyphens (--). As long as the argument is not two hyphens, the program continues to loop through a **case** statement that checks all the possible options. The -- **case** label breaks out of the **while** loop. The ❊ **case** label recognizes any option; it appears as the last **case** label to catch any unknown options, print an error message, and allow processing to continue. On each pass through the loop, the program does a shift to get to the next argument. If an option takes an argument, the program does an extra shift to get past that argument.

The following program fragment processes the same options, using getopts:

```
SKIPBLANKS=
TMPDIR=/tmp
CASE=lower

while getopts :bt:u arg
do
    case $arg in
        b)      SKIPBLANKS=TRUE ;;
        t)      if [ -d "$OPTARG" ]
                    then
                        TMPDIR=$OPTARG
                    else
                        print "$0: $OPTARG is not a directory." >&2
                        exit 1
                    fi ;;
        u)      CASE=upper ;;
        :)      print "$0: Must supply an argument to -$OPTARG." >&2
                exit 1 ;;
        \?)     print "Invalid option -$OPTARG ignored." >&2  ;;
    esac
done
shift $((OPTIND-1))
```

In this version of the code, the **while** structure evaluates the getopts builtin each time it comes to the top of the loop. The getopts builtin uses the **OPTIND** variable to keep track of the index of the argument it is to process the next time it is called. Thus the second example calls **shift** only once, at the end, whereas the first example uses **shift** to get each new argument. The getopts builtin returns a nonzero (*false*) status when it has handled all the arguments and control passes to the statement after **done**.

In the second example the **case** patterns do not start with a hyphen because the value of **arg** is just the option letter (getopts strips off the hyphen). Also, getopts recognizes -- as the end of the options, so you do not have to specify it explicitly in the **case** statement in the first example.

Because you tell getopts which options are valid and which require arguments, it can detect errors in the command line and can handle them in two ways. This example uses a leading colon in *optstring* to specify that you check for and handle errors in your code; when getopts finds an invalid option, it sets **varname** to ? and OPTARG to the option letter. When it finds an option that is missing an argument, getopts sets **varname** to : and OPTARG to the option lacking an argument.

The \? **case** pattern specifies the action to take when getopts detects an invalid option. The : **case** pattern specifies the action to take when getopts detects a missing option argument. In both cases getopts does not write any error message; it leaves that task to you.

If you omit the leading colon from **optstring**, both an invalid option and a missing option argument cause **varname** to be assigned the string ?. OPTARG is not set, and getopts writes its own diagnostic message to standard error. Generally this method is less desirable because you have less control over what the user sees when an error is made.

Using getopts will not necessarily make your programs shorter. Its principal advantages are that it provides a uniform programming interface and it enforces standard option handling.

Input and Output

A programming language needs commands for input and output. In the Z Shell, the input command is read, and the output command is print.

read: Accepts User Input

The syntax of read ^{bash zsh} is similar to the Bourne Again Shell's read (page 573), but the Z Shell read provides additional functionality:

> *read [–prs] [–un] [varname?prompt] [varname...]*

The variable names are optional. The following command is valid as it stands:

```
zsh % read
```

It reads an entire input line from standard input into the variable **REPLY**. When you supply arguments on the command line, read assumes that they are variable names and splits the input line (using the characters in **IFS** as word separators), assigning each word sequentially to a *varname* argument. If there are not enough variables, the last variable is assigned a string equal to the remainder of the input line. If there are not enough words, the leftover variables are set to null (page 575).

The Z Shell allows you to specify an input prompt by using the syntax *varname?prompt* for the first input variable name. The following example shows a read command and the prompt that it generates:

```
zsh % read MON\?"Enter month, day and year separated by spaces: " DAY YR
Enter month, day and year separated by spaces:
```

After the prompt, read pauses while you type an input line. If you type three values, they are assigned to **MON, DAY,** and **YR.** The question mark **(?)** is escaped to prevent the Z Shell from using it as a filename pattern-matching operator.

The read ▪zsh▪ builtin supports other options. Table 15-15 lists some of the more common ones.

read options || table 15-15

–A (array)	Breaks the input into words according to **IFS** and assigns the words as an array to the first variable name in the argument list.
–e (echo)	Displays the words that are typed in after the user presses RETURN but does not assign them to the variables named in the argument list.
–E (echo)	Displays the words that are typed in after the user presses RETURN.
–p (coprocess)	The command read –p... reads its input line from standard output of the coprocess. For more information, refer to "The Coprocess" on page 806.

–q (query)	Reads one character and returns. If the user enters a y or Y, **read** sets **varname** to y; otherwise, **varname** is set to n. The **read** builtin sets the return value to 0 if the user enters a y or Y. This makes it easier to prompt the user for simple yes/no responses, as in
	
	    if read –q ANSWER\?"Play a game (y/n)? "
	            then
	                . . . .
	        fi
	
	As soon as the user types a single character, **read** returns; there is no need to press RETURN.

–r (raw input)	Ordinarily if the input line ends in a backslash character (\), the backslash and the NEWLINE following it are discarded, and the next line is treated as a continuation of the same line of input. This option causes a trailing backslash to be treated as a regular character. One application is for reading an input file that is itself a shell script containing backslashes that you want to reproduce.

read options (Continued)

|| table 15-15

−u *n*	Uses the integer *n* as the file descriptor that **read** takes its input from.
	`read −u4 arg1 arg2`
	is equivalent to
	`read arg1 arg2 <&4`
	See "File Descriptors" (page 781) for a discussion of redirection and file descriptors.

The read builtin returns an exit status of 0 if it successfully reads any data. It has nonzero exit status when it reaches the EOF (end of file):

```
zsh % cat names
Alice Jones
Robert Smith
Alice Paulson
John Q. Public
zsh % while read First Rest
> do
>   print $Rest, $First
> done < names
Jones, Alice
Smith, Robert
Paulson, Alice
Q. Public, John
```

Optional

Each time you redirect input, the shell opens the input file and repositions the read pointer at the start of the file:

```
zsh % read line1 < names; print $line1; read line2 < names; print $line2
Alice Jones
Alice Jones
zsh % (read line1; print $line1; read line2; print $line2) < names
Alice Jones
Robert Smith
```

In the first example, each read opens **names** and starts at the beginning of the **names** file. In the second example, **names** is opened once, as standard input of the subshell created by the parentheses. Each read then reads successive lines of standard input.

Another way to get the same effect is to open the input file with exec and hold it open, as follows (refer to "File Descriptors" on page 781):

```
zsh % exec 3< names
zsh % read -u3 line1; print $line1; read -u3 line2; print $line2
Alice Jones
Robert Smith
zsh % exec 3<&-
```

Similar to the previous examples, the placement of the redirection symbol (<) for the **while** structure is critical. It is important that you place the redirection symbol only at the **done** statement and not at the call to read.

print: Displays Output

The syntax for the print builtin _{zsh}, which is a replacement for echo _{bash tcsh zsh}, is

print [–cDilnNoOpPrRs] [–un] [string...]

By default, print writes the strings to standard output and recognizes both syntaxes (\c at the end of a string and the –n option) for suppressing the trailing NEWLINE. You can embed escape sequences within *string* to display special characters (Table 15-16). Because each of these sequences starts with a backslash (\), which is a special character to the shell, you must quote each backslash, or escape it, within a print statement. Here is an example of the use of escape sequences within a print statement:

```
zsh % print "Columbus' ships:\n\tThe Nina\n\tThe Pinta\n\tIhe Santa Maria"
Columbus' ships:
    The Nina
    The Pinta
    The Santa Maria
```

Escape	table 15-16
\\	The backslash character
\0*nnn*	The ASCII character whose octal value is *nnn*—you can omit leading zeros
\a	The alert character (typically makes the display beep or flash)

Escape (Continued) || table 15-16

\b	The backspace character
\c	Suppresses a trailing NEWLINE
\e	ESCAPE character
\f	Form feed—puts a CONTROL-L character in the output stream
\n	NEWLINE—allows a single call to **print** to write multiple lines
\r	RETURN—puts a CONTROL-M character in the output stream
\t	TAB character
\v	The vertical tab character
\x*nnn*	The ASCII character whose hexadecimal value is *nnn*

Some of the options to print _{zsh} (Table 15-17) have the same meaning as the corresponding options to read _{zsh}.

print Options || table 15-17

−c (columns)	Displays output in columns.
−n (newline)	Suppresses trailing NEWLINES.
−o (output)	Sorts the arguments in ascending order before printing.
−O (output)	Sorts the arguments in descending order before printing.
−p	The command `    print −p...` directs its output line to standard input of the coprocess. Refer to "The Coprocess" (page 806).
−r (raw input)	Ignores the special meaning of the escapes; displays them as ordinary characters.

print Options (Continued) || table 15-17

–R (raw input)	Ignores the special meaning of the escapes; displays them as ordinary characters. Also treats any following fields as string arguments, even if they start with a hyphen (except for –n).
–D (directory)	Treats arguments as directory names. Replaces prefixes with ~ expressions where appropriate.
–i (insensitive)	Performs case-insensitive sorts. Use with the –o or –O option.
–l (line)	Outputs the arguments separated by NEWLINES instead of SPACES. Using the –l option, the example on page 778 can be written as zsh % **print –l "Columbus' ships:"** "\tThe Nina" \ "\tThe Pinta" "\tThe Santa Maria"
–N (null)	Outputs the arguments separated by null characters. Terminates the final argument with a null.
–P (prompt)	Allows you to use the escape sequences available when setting the PS1 prompt (page 749).
–s	Directs output to the history file.
–u *n*	Sends output to file descriptor *n*. For more information, refer to "File Descriptors" on page 781.

The following example demonstrates the effect of several print options:

```
zsh % print -R -n -p "NEWLINE \nwill not be recognized" ; echo " done"
-p NEWLINE \nwill not be recognized done
zsh % print "NEWLINE \nwill not be recognized" ; echo " done"
NEWLINE
will not be recognized
  done
```

You must (almost) always use double quotation marks around the arguments to print and echo. Without the quotation marks a \n would be displayed as n. In the preceding example the second command on the first command line displays done at the end of the output line to show that the –n option suppresses the trailing NEWLINE. The –R option causes the –p and the \n not to be interpreted as options or special characters. The second command line shows what happens without these options. Because the shell quickly erases the command line before displaying another prompt, you will never see the output from **print –n** if it is the only command on the command line.

Optional

Try the following command, which you might expect to display the word `hello` and, because of the `\c`, omit the trailing NEWLINE and display the next prompt on the same line as `hello`:

```
zsh % echo "hello \c"
zsh %
```

What happened? The next example gives you a clue:

```
zsh % echo "hello\ngoodby \c"
hello
zsh %
```

The reason you saw a prompt only in the first example and just the word `hello` followed on the next line by a prompt in the second example is that you cannot read quickly enough. When you use a `\c` or **–n** to suppress a trailing NEWLINE in an `echo` or print statement in the Z Shell, the shell does suppress the trailing NEWLINE. But then it backs the cursor over the whole line and issues a new prompt. The reason zsh does this is so that it can know exactly what column the cursor is in and properly drive the line editor. There is no reliable way to read the cursor column from the terminal; forcing the cursor to the beginning of a line is the most expedient way to know for sure where the cursor is.

Set the NO_PROMPT_CR option with the following command, and give the preceding commands again:

```
zsh % set -o NO_PROMPT_CR
zsh % echo "hello \c"
hello zsh $ echo "hello\ngoodby \c"
hello
goodby zsh %
```

There are the `hello`s and the prompts as you might expect.

Optional

File Descriptors

As discussed on page 553, before a process can read from or write to a file, it must open the file. When a process opens a file, GNU/Linux associates a number (called a *file descriptor*) with the file. Each process has its own set of open files and its own file descriptors. After opening a file, a process reads from and writes to that file by referring to it with the file descriptor. When it no longer needs the file, the process closes the file, freeing the file descriptor.

A typical GNU/Linux process starts with three open files: standard input (file descriptor 0), standard output (file descriptor 1), and standard error (file descriptor 2). Often those are all the files the process needs. The Z Shell allows you to redirect standard input, standard output, and standard error of all the commands you invoke, just as the Bourne Again Shell does. Recall that you can redirect standard output with the symbol > or the symbol 1> and that you redirect standard error with the symbol 2>. You can redirect other file descriptors, but because file descriptors other than 0, 1, and 2 do not have any special conventional meaning, it's rarely useful to do so. The exception is in programs that you write yourself, in which case you control the meaning of the file descriptors and can take advantage of redirection.

The Bourne Again and Z Shells open files using the **exec** builtin as follows:

```
zsh % exec 3> outfile
zsh % exec 4< infile
```

The first command opens **outfile** for output and holds it open, associating it with file descriptor 3. The second command opens **infile** for input, associating it with file descriptor 4.

The token **<&** duplicates both input and output file descriptors. You can duplicate a file descriptor by making it refer to the same file as another open file descriptor, such as standard input or output. The following command opens or redirects file descriptor *n* as a duplicate of file descriptor *m*:

```
zsh % exec n<&m
```

Once you have opened a file, you can use it for input and output in two different ways. First, you can use I/O redirection on any command line, redirecting standard output to a file descriptor with **>&***n* or redirecting standard input from a file descriptor with **<&***n*. Second, you can use the read (page 775) and print (page 778) builtins. If you invoke other commands, including functions (pages 672 and 784), they inherit these open files and file descriptors. When you have finished using a file, you can close it with

```
exec n<&-
```

When you invoke the next shell function with two arguments, it copies the file named by the first argument to the file named by the second argument: **mycp** copies **src** to **dest**. If you supply only one argument, the script interprets it as a source and copies **src** to standard output. If you invoke **mycp** with no arguments, it copies standard input to standard output:

```
function mycp
{
case $# in
0)      exec 3<&0 4<&1 ;;
1)      exec 3< $1 4<&1 ;;
2)      exec 3< $1 4> $2 ;;
*)      print "Usage: mycp [source [dest]]"
        exit 1 ;;
esac

cat <&3 >&4
exec 3<&- 4<&-
}
```

The real work of this function is done in the line that begins with cat. The rest of the script arranges for file descriptors 3 and 4, which are the input and output of the cat command, to be associated with the right file.

The next program takes two filenames on the command line and sorts both to temporary files. The program then merges the sorted files to standard output, preceding each line by a number that indicates which file it came from.

The Z Shell does not have *string* comparison operators for *less than or equal to* or *greater than or equal to*. You can use *not greater than*, as in this example ([[! "$Line1" > "$Line2"]] in the **if** statement), as an equivalent for *less than or equal to*:

```
zsh % cat sortmerge
#!/bin/zsh
usage ()
{
if [[ $# -ne 2 ]]
then
print -u2 "Usage: $0 file1 file2"
exit 1
fi
}
# Default temporary directory
: ${TEMPDIR:=/tmp}
# Check argument count
usage "$@"
# Set up temporary files for sorting
file1=$TEMPDIR/file1.$$
file2=$TEMPDIR/file2.$$
# Sort
sort $1 > $file1
sort $2 > $file2
# Open files $file1 and $file2 for reading. Use FD's 3 and 4.
exec 3<$file1
exec 4<$file2
# Read the first line of each file to figure out how to start.
read -u3 Line1
Status1=$?
read -u4 Line2
Status2=$?
```

```
# Strategy: while there is still input left in both files:
#        Output the lesser line.
#        Read a new line from the file that line came from.
while [[ $Status1 -eq 0 && $Status2 -eq 0 ]]
do
    if [[ ! "$Line1" > "$Line2" ]]
        then
        print "1.\t$Line1"
        read -u3 Line1
        Status1=$?
    else
        print "2.\t$Line2"
        read -u4 Line2
        Status2=$?
    fi
done
# Now one of the files is at end-of-file.
# Read from each file until the end.
# First file1:
while [[ $Status1 -eq 0 ]]
do
    print "1.\t$Line1"
    read -u3 Line1
    Status1=$?
done

# Next file2:
while [[ $Status2 -eq 0 ]]
do
    print "2.\t$Line2"
    read -u4 Line2
    Status2=$?
done
# Close and remove both input files
exec 3<&- 4<&-
rm -f $file1 $file2
exit 0
```

Functions

The syntax for a shell function has two formats (zsh accepts both formats, bash accepts only the first):

func_name()
{
commands
}

or

function *func_name*
{
commands
}

The first brace ({) can appear on the same line as the function name. If the function definition includes the names of aliases, they are expanded when the function is read, not when it is executed. You can use the **break** builtin inside a function to terminate its execution. The functions builtin _{zsh} lists all the defined functions.

Shell functions are useful as a shorthand as well as to define special commands. The following function starts a process named **process** in the background, with the output normally displayed by **process** saved in **.process.out**:

```
start_process() {
process > .process.out 2>&1 &
}
```

There is no setenv builtin in zsh. The following function mimics the behavior of this command, which is available in tcsh:

```
zsh % setenv() {
if [ $# -eq 2 ]; then
    export $1=$2
else
    echo "Usage: setenv NAME VALUE" >&2
fi
}
```

If there are two arguments, the setenv function assigns the value of the second argument to the name of the first and exports the first. (The Z Shell export builtin is identical to bash's [page 571]). If there are not two arguments, the function displays a usage message.

The unfunction builtin deletes a function definition:

unfunction *func_name*

The Z Shell stores functions in memory so that they run more efficiently than shell scripts. The source for the functions is loaded into memory each time a shell or subshell is started. If you define too many functions, the overhead of starting a subshell (as when you run a script) becomes unacceptable.

You can also store functions in files so that they are read into memory the first time they are called. The autoload builtin _{zsh} notifies zsh that a function is stored in a file. When autoload is executed (normally when you start a new shell), the shell does not load the function into memory but simply keeps track of its name (it declares it as an undefined function). When a script first calls an autoload function, zsh searches through the directories listed in **FPATH** for a file with the same name as the function. (The syntax of **FPATH** is identical to that of **PATH** [page 577]). When it finds the file, it loads the function into memory and leaves it there. The syntax for autoload is

*autoload **func_name** ...*

It is your responsibility to ensure that the function definition and the file it is stored in have the same name. Typically you have one directory with many small files, each containing a single function definition. If you are working on several projects that make use of different shell functions, you may have several such directories.

Special Functions

Table 15-18 lists names that, when used to define a function, are recognized as special by zsh and executed by zsh at specific times.

Special Functions	‖ table 15-18

chpwd	Runs when you change working directories. The following definition causes a message to be displayed when you change directories to your home directory:
	
	``zsh % chpwd () {
	        if ["$PWD" = "$HOME"] ; then
	                echo "Home at last\!"
	        fi
	}
	zsh % cd ..
	zsh % cd
	Home at last!
	zsh % cd Work
	zsh % cd ..
	Home at last!```

precmd	Runs just before the shell displays a prompt.

periodic	Runs every **PERIOD** seconds (only if **PERIOD** is defined) and only just before a prompt. The following example reminds you to perform an important chore, until you remove it with the **unfunction** builtin or **unset** the **PERIOD** variable:
	
	``zsh % PERIOD=300
	zsh % periodic( ) {
	echo "Call for dental appointment\!"
	}```

TRAP*xxx*	Runs whenever the shell receives a signal of type SIG*xxx*. The *xxx* is a signal name as given for the **kill** builtin (refer to "Job Control" on page 788.)

Special Functions (Continued)	table 15-18
TRAPZERR	Runs whenever a command returns a nonzero exit status.
TRAPDEBUG	Runs after every command.
TRAPEXIT	Runs when the shell or function it is defined in exits.

Builtin Commands

The Z Shell has many builtins (page 161). This section lists a few of the important ones. Refer to the **zshbuiltins** man page for a complete list.

alias: Shortcut for a Command

The zsh alias builtin is similar to the one in bash, with some added features. A zsh alias does not accept an argument (similar to bash—unlike tcsh). Use a zsh *function*—similar to bash functions (page 672)—when you need to use an argument. The syntax used to establish an alias is

> *alias [–grmL] [name[=value]]*

When you are creating an alias, the **–g** (global) option causes the shell to expand the alias no matter where it appears on a command line. Without this option, aliases are expanded only when they appear as the command name. Aliases are not saved from session to session, so users typically establish aliases in a startup file (page 737). Without any arguments the alias builtin lists active aliases. When you are listing aliases, the **–g** option lists global aliases, **–r** lists regular (nonglobal) aliases, **–m** lists all the aliases that have names matching a pattern that follows on the command line, and **–L** displays aliases so that they are in an appropriate format to enter into a startup file:

```
zsh % alias -m "p*"
pagef='less -f'
pd=_cd
page=less
pages='less -s'
```

You may need to enclose the pattern in single or double quotation marks to keep the shell from expanding it before running alias. Calling alias with an argument of an active alias displays the value of that alias:

```
zsh % alias pages
pages='less -s'
```

The next example creates and then uses a global alias:

```
zsh % alias -g n=alex
zsh % echo n
alex
```

To remove an alias, use unalias with an argument of the alias name. The following example removes the alias **delete**:

```
zsh % unalias delete
```

For more information refer to "Alias Substitution" on page 801.

kill: **Aborts a Process**

The kill builtin bash tcsh zsh sends a signal to a process or job, using the same syntax as bash. If you do not specify a signal, kill sends a TERM (software termination, number 15) signal. For more information on signal names and numbers, see Table 13-5 on page 667. In the following format the *n* is the signal number, and ***PID*** is the identification number of the process that is to receive the signal:

*kill –n **PID***

The shells also support named signals. To send a signal to a job, you can refer to the signal by name:

```
zsh % kill -TERM %1
```

This command sends the TERM signal to job number 1. Because TERM is the default signal for kill, you can also give the command as **kill %1**. Use the command **kill –l** to display a list of signal names.

Generally any of these signals terminates a process. A program that is interrupted often has things in an unpredictable state: Temporary files may be left behind (when they are normally removed), and permissions may be changed. A well-written application traps, or detects, the arrival of signals and cleans up before exiting. Most carefully written applications trap the INT, QUIT, and TERM signals. Try INT first (press CONTROL-C, if the job is in the foreground). Because an application can be written to ignore these signals, you may need to use the KILL signal, which cannot be trapped or ignored; it is a "sure kill." Refer to page 1224 in Part III for more information on kill.

Job Control

Job control under zsh is very similar to that of bash (page 554) and tcsh (page 690). The Z Shell follows tcsh in displaying all the PID numbers for multiple-process background jobs.

whence: Displays the Absolute Pathname of a Utility

The whence builtin _{zsh} is similar to the which builtin _{bash}, telling you the absolute pathname of a utility:

```
zsh % whence grep
/bin/grep
```

In this form whence reports only the name of an alias, function, or builtin. Use the **–v** option to report on the type of any command or reserved word that you can use in the Z Shell:

```
zsh % whence pwd
pwd
zsh % whence -v pwd
pwd is a shell builtin
zsh % whence -v myfunc
myfunc is a shell function
zsh % whence -v if
if is a reserved word
```

The type builtin _{bash zsh} is a synonym for **whence –v**.

trap: Catches a Signal

The trap builtin _{bash zsh} causes a shell script to execute a command when it receives an error or signal or when it exits from a function or script. The syntax of trap is similar to the Bourne Again Shell's trap (page 667), including the ability to use signal names in place of numbers:

   trap **'command'** *event*

Quote the **command**, because it must be passed to trap as a single argument. The *event* arguments are names of signals (for example INT, TERM), signal numbers, or one of those in Table 15-19.

Event	Occurrence ‖ table 15-19
DEBUG	Occurs after every simple command. The following command causes your script to append the line number of the script and the pathname of the working directory to /tmp/trace after each simple command: `trap 'echo $LINENO $PWD >> /tmp/trace' DEBUG`
EXIT or 0	Occurs whenever the script exits.

Event	**Occurrence (Continued)**	‖ table 15-19
HUP, INT, or any signal name without the SIG prefix	Occurs when the named signal is received. See Table 13-5 on page 667 for a list.	
ZERR	Occurs whenever a command completes with nonzero exit status. The following command causes your script to execute **cleanup** (a user-defined function) and then exit from the script with a status of 1: `trap 'cleanup ; exit 1' ZERR`	

If *command* is a null string, the corresponding signal or event is ignored. Any attempt to ignore or set a trap for the KILL (9) signal is ignored. If you have used trap to set the action for a signal or event and you want to reset it to its default behavior, use a hyphen (–) as the action. Without any arguments the trap builtin lists all current traps in a form that can be saved and reread later by the shell.

The following script, named **debug**, demonstrates how trap works. Modify the script and experiment with it to get a better feel for how to use trap: Look at the output in **trace**; ZERR is called when the script tries to run chpasswd (assuming you are not logged in as **root**); INT is called when you press CONTROL-C while the script is running. In addition, chpasswd displays its own error message:

```
zsh % cat debug
#!/bin/zsh
trap 'echo $LINENO $PWD >> trace' DEBUG
trap 'echo ERROR' ZERR:
trap 'echo INTERRUPT;exit' INT
trap 'echo EXIT' EXIT
count=4

while [ count -gt 0 ]
do
    echo "hi there"
    /usr/sbin/chpasswd
    sleep 1
    echo $count
    ((count = count - 1))
done
```

On the final pass through the **do** loop the expression ((**count = count - 1**)) yields a 0 and sets a return status of 1. (This expression returns a 0 if the result is not 0.) When control passes from this statement, ERR is set and displays ERROR.

By becoming familiar with the Z Shell's large collection of builtins, you can take advantage of those that will help you in your day-to-day work with GNU/Linux.

Even if you do not use zsh on a regular basis, you will be able to use it when another shell cannot help you solve the problem at hand as easily.

Command Line Editing

The Z Shell allows you to edit the current command line. If you make a mistake, you do not need to back up to the point of the mistake and reenter the command from there or press the line kill key and start over. You can use one of the command line editors to modify the command line. You can also access and edit previous command lines stored in your history file (page 796).

The Z Shell provides two command line editors: one similar to vim (Chapter 10), and the other similar to emacs (Chapter 11). Depending on how the Z Shell is set up on your system, you may be able to use one, both, or neither of the editors.

Use the following command to set up your environment so that you can use the vi command line editor:

```
zsh % bindkey -v
```

Use the next command to use the emacs command line editor:

```
zsh % bindkey -e
```

The vi Command Line Editor

When you are entering Z Shell commands with vi as your command line editor, you are in Input mode while you type commands. As you enter a command, if you discover an error before you press RETURN, you can press ESCAPE to switch to vi Command mode. This is different from the stand-alone vi editor's initial mode. You can then use many vi commands to edit the command line. It is as though you have a one-line window to edit the current command line as well as those for previous commands. You can use the vi cursor-positioning commands, such as **h** and **l**, or **w** and **b**, optionally preceded by a Repeat Factor (page 463). You can use the ARROW keys to position the cursor. You can also use the search-forward (**/**) or search-backward (**?**) commands. You can modify the command line by using vi Command mode editing commands, such as **x** (delete character), **r** (replace character), **~** (change case), and **.** (repeat last change). To change to Input mode, use an Insert (**i**, **I**), Append (**a**, **A**), Replace (**R**), or Change (**c**, **C**) command. You do not have to return to Command mode to run the command; simply press RETURN, even if you are in the middle of the command line.

The Stand-Alone Editor Starts in Command Mode || tip

The stand-alone editor starts in Command mode, whereas the command line editor starts in Input mode. If commands display characters and do not work properly, you are in Input mode: Press ESCAPE and enter the command again.

Pathname Operations

In Command mode you can also use several commands that are not included in the stand-alone vi editor. These commands manipulate filenames and are called *Pathname Listing*, *Pathname Completion*, and *Pathname Expansion*. These commands *will not work* unless you have set up your environment to use the vi command line editor (page 791).

Pathname Listing

While the cursor is on a word, enter Command mode (if you are not already in it), and type an equal sign (=). The vi command line editor responds by listing all the pathnames that would match the current word if an asterisk were appended to it. For example, suppose that the directory **films** contains the files **casablanca**, **city_lights**, **dark_passage**, **dark_victory**, and **modern_times**. You want to use cat to display one of the files, so you type

```
zsh % cat films/dar
```

At this point (before you have pressed RETURN), you realize that you are not sure what the full name of the file is. If you press ESCAPE and then =, the vi command line editor lists the files and then reechoes the partial command, including the prompt, like this:

```
dark_passage  dark_victory
zsh % cat films/dar
```

The cursor is on the letter r, where you left it, and you are in Command mode. To finish typing a pathname, you must first type **a** to append.

Pathname Completion

This facility allows you to type a portion of a pathname and have the vi command line editor supply the rest. You invoke Pathname Completion by pressing TAB. If the portion of the pathname that you have typed so far is sufficient to determine the entire pathname uniquely, that pathname is displayed.

If more than one pathname would match, the command line vi completes the pathname up to the point where there are choices and leaves you in Input mode to type more. If you enter

```
zsh % cat films/dar
```

and press TAB, the shell extends the command line as far as it can:

```
zsh % cat films/dark_
```

Because in the **films** directory every file that starts with **dar** has **k_** as the next characters, that's as far as zsh can extend the line without making a choice among files. You are left in Input mode, with the cursor just past the _ character. When you add enough information to distinguish between the two possible files, Pathname Completion will yield the entire filename. Suppose that you now enter **p** followed by TAB. (The emacs in-line editor also uses TAB for pathname completion.) The Z Shell completes the command line:

```
zsh % cat films/dark_passage
```

Because there is no further ambiguity, the shell appends a SPACE and leaves you in Input mode to finish typing the command line. You can press RETURN to complete the cat command. If the complete filename is that of a directory, zsh will append a slash (/) in place of a SPACE.

Pathname Expansion

This facility is an interactive version of ordinary filename generation. You invoke Pathname Expansion by typing a pattern followed by an asterisk (*) and a TAB, which causes the pattern to be replaced by all pathnames that match the pattern. If you enter

```
zsh % cat films/dar*
```

and then press TAB, the shell expands the command line to

```
zsh % cat films/dark_passage films/dark_victory
```

After it fills in the filenames, the vi command line editor leaves you in Input mode, with the cursor past the last character in the line. At this point you can continue to edit the line or press RETURN to execute the command. If no filenames match, the vi command line editor causes your terminal to beep. (Some displays flash instead.)

The vi command line editor commands are listed on page 829.

Pressing RETURN Executes the Command || caution

Remember that pressing RETURN causes the Z Shell to execute the command regardless of whether you are in Command mode or Input mode and regardless of where the cursor is on the command line. At the next prompt you are back in Input mode.

The emacs Command Line Editor

Unlike the vi editor, emacs is modeless: You do not switch between Command mode and Input mode. This modelessness is possible because most emacs commands are control characters, allowing emacs to distinguish between input and commands. The ESCAPE key also plays a special role in emacs, as do the erase and kill characters (page 482). As with vi, the emacs command line editor provides commands for moving around on the command line and through your command history and for modifying part or all the text. The emacs editor also supports the Pathname Listing, Pathname Completion, and Pathname Expansion commands. This discussion covers only Z Shell emacs command line editor commands, which differ, in a few cases, from the commands in the stand-alone emacs editor. The emacs command line editor commands are listed on page 832.

In emacs you perform cursor movement by using both CONTROL and ESCAPE commands. To move the cursor one character backward on the command line, press CONTROL-B. Pressing CONTROL-F moves it one character forward (page 478). As with vi, it is possible to precede these movements with counts. However, to use a count you must first press ESCAPE; otherwise, the numbers you type are entered on the command line.

Like vi, emacs also provides word motions and line motions. To move backward or forward one word in the command line, press ESCAPE b or ESCAPE f (page 478). To move several words use a count by pressing ESCAPE followed by the number and the appropriate ESCAPE sequence. To get to the beginning of the line, press CONTROL-A; to the end of the line, press CONTROL-E; and to the next instance of the character *c*, press CONTROL-X CONTROL-F followed by *c*.

You can add text to the command line by moving the cursor to the correct place and typing the desired text. To delete text, move the cursor just to the right of the characters that you want to delete, and then press the erase key once for each character you want to delete.

Using CONTROL-D   ‖ **tip**

If you want to delete the character directly under the cursor, press CONTROL–D. If you enter CONTROL–D on an empty line or at the beginning of the line, it may terminate your shell session.

If you want to delete the entire command line, type the line kill character. This has the usual effect, except that you can type it while the cursor is anywhere in the command line. If you want to delete from the cursor to the end of the line, use CONTROL-K.

Invoking the Pathname Listing, Completion, and Expansion commands using the emacs command line editor is similar to that when using the vi command line editor. With emacs, the sequence ESCAPE CONTROL-D performs Pathname Listing, the TAB key performs Pathname Completion, and the sequence CONTROL-X * expands any pattern-matching sequences in the preceding word (so **165*CONTROL-X*** would expand to all filenames that begin with 165).

History

The Z Shell keeps a history of recently executed commands in a file, which means that the history can persist from one shell session to the next. You can select, edit, and reexecute any command in the history list from the current or a previous login session. The shells' history mechanisms have an important difference. The Z Shell history remembers multiline commands in their entirety and allows you to edit them. In bash each line of a multiline command is treated as a separate command (unless you set the variable **command_oriented_history**—refer to the bash man page for more information), whereas tcsh remembers only the first line of multiline commands.

Although several of the history variables are the same as those used by bash (page 589), there are some important differences (Table 15-20). If it is set, the **HISTSIZE** variable determines the number of commands that are kept in the history list. If it is not set, only two commands are kept. The **HISTFILE** variable determines where the history list is saved when you exit from the Z Shell. If any commands are saved in **HISTFILE**, the Z Shell reads them in when the shell starts, so the commands become part of the history list for the current session. The **SAVEHIST** variable determines how much of the history gets saved to **HISTFILE**. If either **HISTFILE** or **SAVEHIST** is not set, the Z Shell does not save any commands when terminating. Refer to "History Expansion" on page 799.

Z Shell History Variables		table 15-20
Function	**Variable**	**Default**
Maximum number of events saved during a session	HISTSIZE	30
Location of the history file	HISTFILE	If not set, no history saved between sessions
Maximum number of events saved between sessions	SAVEHIST	Not set

To access and edit any of the commands in the history file, you can use the vi command line editor, the emacs command line editor, or the fc builtin ^{bash} ^{zsh} (see following).

Using the vi Command Line Editor on Previous Commands

When you are using the vi command line editor in Command mode (press ESCAPE to enter Command mode), you can access previous commands by using several vi commands that move the cursor up and down. It is as if you were using vi to edit a copy of the history file with a screen that has room for only one command on it. When you use the **k** command to move up one line, you access the previous command. If you then use the **j** command to move down one line, you will be back to the original command.

While in Command mode, press the question mark (?) key, followed by a search string to look *back* through your history list for the most recent command containing that string. If you have moved back in your history list, use a forward slash (/) instead of the question mark to search *forward* toward your most recent command. Unlike the search strings in the vi utility, these search strings cannot contain regular expressions, but you can start the search string with a caret (^) to force the Z Shell to locate commands that start with the search string. As in the vi utility, pressing **n** after a successful search continues the search for the next occurrence of the search string.

You can also access events in the history list by using the event numbers. While you are in Command mode, enter the event number, followed by a **G** to go directly to the command with that event number.

When you initially move to the command, you are in Command mode, not Input mode. Now you can edit the command as you like, or press RETURN to execute it.

fc: Displays, Edits, and Reexecutes Commands

The zsh version of the fc (fix command) builtin ^{zsh} is the almost the same as the bash version (page 591). The following paragraphs list the most important differences.

The Z Shell sets up an alias, history, for the **fc –l** command. So you can also use the history alias to display the history list.

When you use the editor to change a series of commands or when you call the editor to work on one command and then add other commands, the Z Shell treats the entire set of commands as one event. That is, if you edit a series of commands and execute them, they will be listed as a single new event in the history list. Following, 298 is a series of commands that were entered while fc was editing an event, and 301 is a semicolon-separated series of commands that were entered from the command line:

```
297    ls -l
298    ls
       who
       date
299    fc -l
300    history
301    who;date;ls
```

You can reexecute previous commands without going into an editor. If you call fc with the –e option and an argument of –, it skips the editing phase and reexecutes the command. The following example reexecutes event 201:

```
zsh % fc -e - 201
lpr adams.out
```

The next example reexecutes the previous command:

```
zsh % fc -e -
lpr adams.out
```

The r (repeat) builtin ▪, which does the same thing as fc –e –, is included for expediency. The next command does the same thing as the previous one:

```
zsh % r
lpr adams.out
```

When you reexecute a command, such as lpr in the previous example, you can tell fc to substitute one string for another. The next example substitutes the string john for the string adams in event 201:

```
zsh % fc -e - adams=john 201
lpr john.out
```

or

```
zsh % r adams=john 201
lpr john.out
```

Optional

Processing a Command

The Z Shell always reads at least one line before processing a command. Some of the Z Shell's builtins, such as **if** and **case**, span multiple lines. When the Z Shell recognizes a command that covers more than one line, it reads the entire command before processing it. Commands can include many lines. In interactive sessions the Z

Shell prompts you with relevant prompts after you have typed the first line of a multiline command until it recognizes the end of the command:

```
zsh % echo 'hi
quote> end'
hi
end
zsh % hello ()
function> echo hello there
zsh % hello there
hello
```

The Z Shell carries out the expansions and substitutions listed in Table 15-21 in five steps:[3]

Expansion and Substitution || table 15-21

History expansion	Allows you to use parts of previous commands in the command line you are constructing (page 799).
Alias expansion	Recognizes aliases and expands them (page 801).
Parsing the command line	The five following expansions and substitutions are included in parsing the command line and are performed in a single step, from left to right (page 801).
Process substitution	Replaces command arguments of the form <(command), >(command), and =(command) with pipes (in the first two cases) and a temporary filename (in the last case) (page 802).
Parameter expansion	Expands all variable expressions that are not quoted (page 803).
Command substitution	Evaluates commands within command substitution brackets [$()] or backquotes (` ... `) and replaces the commands with their standard output (page 803).
Arithmetic expansion	Replaces arithmetic expressions with the resulting values (page 804).
Brace expansion	Expands all expressions that involve braces ({}) (page 805).
Filename expansion	Replaces words that begin with ~ with their expanded values (page 805).

_____

3. In addition to reading the following pages, you can refer to the **zshexpn** man page for more information.

Expansion and Substitution (Continued)		**‖ table 15-21**
Filename generation	Replaces pathnames that contain filename-matching patterns with their expanded lists of pathnames (page 805).	

The order in which zsh carries out these steps affects the interpretation of the commands you enter. For example, if you set a variable to a value that looks like the instruction for output redirection and you enter a command using the variable's value to perform redirection, you might expect zsh to redirect the output:

```
zsh % SENDIT="> /tmp/saveit"
zsh % echo xxx $SENDIT
xxx > /tmp/saveit
zsh % cat /tmp/saveit
cat: /tmp/saveit: No such file or directory
```

This does not work. The Z Shell recognizes input and output redirection before it evaluates variables. When it executes the command line, the Z Shell checks for redirection and, finding none, goes on to evaluate the **SENDIT** variable. After replacing the variable with > /tmp/saveit, zsh passes the arguments to echo, which dutifully copies its arguments to standard output. No **/tmp/saveit** file is created.

The following sections provide more detailed descriptions of each of the steps involved in command processing.

History Expansion

The Z Shell provides a history mechanism similar to that found in tcsh. This mechanism allows you to refer to words found in previous commands without having to retype them. A use of the history mechanism is called a history *event* and always starts with an exclamation point (!). Table 15-22 gives the various types of history events that you can use with the Z Shell. You can put history events anywhere on a command line. To escape an exclamation point so it is treated literally instead of as the start of a history event, precede it with a backslash (\). Neither single nor double quotation marks prevent history substitution.

Event Specifier	**‖ table 15-22**
!	Starts a history event unless followed immediately by a SPACE, NEW-LINE, =, or (.

Event Specifier (Continued)   ‖ table 15-22

!!	The previous command.
!*n*	Command number *n* in the history list.
!–*n*	The *n*th command before the current command.
!*string*	The most recent command line that started with *string*.
!?*string*[?]	The most recent command that contained *string*. The last ? is optional.
!#	This is as much of the current command as you have typed so far.
!{...}	By enclosing the event in braces, you can embed the event in places where it can be difficult to determine the end of the event. So, !{–3}3 is the third most recently executed command line, followed in the current command line with a 3.

The event specifier identifies a specific command line in your history list. You can refer to words within that line by following the event specifier with a colon (:) followed by a *word designator* (Table 15-23). You can omit the colon separating the event from the word designator if the word designator starts with a comma, $, *, –, or %.

Word Designator   ‖ table 15-23

n	The nth word. Word 0 is normally the command name.
^	The first word (after the command name).
$	The last word.
m–n	All words from word number *m* through word number *n*. The *m* defaults to 0 if you omit it (0-*n*).
n∗	All words from word number *n* through the last word.
∗	All words except the command name. This is the same as 0∗.
%	The word matched by the most recent ?*string*? search.

Finally, you can end the event with zero or more *modifiers* (Table 15-24). Precede each modifier with a colon.

Modifier

|| table 15-24

& (again)	Repeats the last substitution.
e (everything)	Removes everything except the suffix that follows the period.
[g]s/*old*/*new*/	Replaces *old* (not a regular expression) with *new*. When you precede the **s** with **g** (with no colon between), all strings matching *old* are replaced. An ampersand (**&**) in *new* is replaced by *old* unless it is escaped with a backslash. Any character can be used in place of the slash to separate the parts of the modifier. A special form of history event has the form ^*old*^*new*, used by itself as a command. This repeats the previous command substituting *old* with *new*. (Refer to "^old^new For a Quick Substitution" on page 597.)
h (head)	Removes the last part of a pathname (**/home/alex/memos** becomes **/home/alex**).
p (print)	Prints the command, but does not execute it.
q (quote)	Quotes the substitution to prevent further substitutions on it.
r (remove)	Removes any suffix beginning with a period (for example, **do_report.c** becomes **do_report**).
x	Like **q** but quotes each word in the substitution individually.

Alias Substitution

Alias substitution determines whether the first token is an alias and replaces it if it is. It does not replace an alias while processing the same alias. This prevents infinite recursion in handling an alias such as the following:

```
zsh % alias ls='ls –F'
```

Parsing the Command Line

Next, the Z Shell *parses* the command line, splitting it into tokens (words or symbols). Then the shell performs process substitution, parameter expansion, command substitution, arithmetic expansion, and brace expansion on the command line in one pass, reading the command line from left to right.

Process Substitution

A special feature of the Z Shell is the ability to replace filename arguments with processes. An argument with the syntax <*(command)* causes *command* to be executed, writing to a named pipe (FIFO). The Z Shell replaces that argument with the name of the pipe. If that argument is then used as the name of an input file during processing, the output of *command* is read. Similarly, an argument with the syntax >*(command)* is replaced by the name of a pipe that *command* reads as standard input.

In the following example sort is used with the **–m** (merge) option to combine two word lists into a single list. Each word list is generated by a pipe that extracts words matching a pattern from a file and sorts the words in that list:

```
$ sort -m -f <(grep "[^A-Z]..$" memo1 | sort) <(grep ".*aba.*" memo2 |sort)
```

(The **–m** option to sort works correctly only if the input files are already sorted.)

Because process substitution passes the name of a pipe in place of a file on a disk, the command that uses this argument as a filename cannot do random access into the "file." If your command needs to be able to do random access on the input file named in the argument, you can still do process substitution by replacing the left angle bracket (<) with an equal sign (=). In this case the Z Shell runs the process argument to completion, putting any output into a temporary file. The name of this temporary file is used in place of the process argument. In the following example, **rline** produces a random line that starts with Alice from the file **names** (page 777):

```
zsh % cat rline
#!/bin/zsh
integer z
z=$(wc -l < $1)
sed -n "$[RANDOM % z + 1]p" $1
zsh % rline =(grep "Alice*" names)
Alice Jones
```

The second line of this script gives the variable **z** an integer attribute; the third line assigns it a value using command substitution. The arithmetic expression $[RANDOM % z + 1] produces a random number between 1 and the number of lines selected from the file (**z**). The zsh variable RANDOM produces a random number between 0 and 32,767 each time it is called. The rest of the expression, including the remainder operator (%), is identical to the C language expression for extracting a value between 1 and **z** from the value of RANDOM. The value that results from this expression is then passed to the sed utility as the line number of the line to print from the file. The **–n** instructs sed not to print any output unless explicitly requested to do so, and the **p** prints the line whose number precedes it.

Because the **rline** script needs to read the file twice—first to determine the number of lines and then to select one randomly—it does not work if given a named pipe. The **=(command)** form of process substitution allows you to use a command to produce the input data.

Parameter Expansion

The second step of parsing the command line is parameter expansion. Refer to "Expanding Shell Variables" on page 751. Variables are not expanded if they are enclosed within single quotation marks or if the leading dollar sign is escaped by preceding it with a backslash. If they are enclosed within double quotation marks, they are expanded, but the resulting text is not subject to filename generation (page 805).

Any string within double quotation marks is used as a single command line argument, so variables that are expanded within double quotation marks are still treated as part of a single argument. Outside of double quotation marks, the type of the variable helps determine what happens. For scalar variables, if the Z Shell option SH_WORD_SPLIT is set, the expanded value is split into individual arguments on the command line, using the first field separator in the **IFS** variable. Normally SH_WORD_SPLIT is left unset, so the result of expanding the scalar **$variable** is left as a single argument. Array variables are separated into individual arguments on the command line:

```
zsh % scalar="a b c d"
zsh % echo $scalar
a b c d
zsh % set $scalar
zsh % echo $1
a b c d
zsh % set -o SH_WORD_SPLIT
zsh % set $scalar
zsh % echo $1
a

zsh % array=(a b c d)
zsh % echo $array
a b c d
zsh % set $array
zsh % echo $1
a
zsh % set "$array"
zsh % echo $1
a b c d
```

Command Substitution

The third step of parsing the command line is command substitution. A command in the form **$(command)** is executed within a subshell, and the command, parentheses, and dollar sign are replaced by standard output of the command. The Z Shell also provides the older `command` syntax:

```
zsh % ls -l $(find . -name README -print)
```

This command uses find to find files under the working directory with the name **README**. The list of such files is standard output of find and becomes the list of arguments to ls. It is equivalent to

```
zsh % ls -l `find . -name README -print`
```

One advantage of the newer syntax is that it avoids the rather arcane rules for token handling, quotation mark handling, and escaped backquotes within the old syntax. Another advantage of the new syntax is that it can be nested, unlike the old syntax. For example, you can produce a long listing of all the **README** files whose size exceeds the size of **./README** with the following command:

```
zsh % ls -l $(find . -name README -size +$(echo $(cat ./README | wc -c)c ) -print )
```

Try giving this command after giving a **set –x** command to see how it is expanded. If there is no **README** file, you just get the output of ls –l.

$((versus $(‖ tip

The symbols **$((** constitute a separate token; they introduce an arithmetic expression, not a command substitution. Thus, if you want to use a parenthesized subshell within **$()**, you must have a space between the **$(** and the next **(**.

Arithmetic Expansion

The fourth step of parsing the command line is arithmetic expansion. The shell replaces an argument of the form **$((expression))** or **$[expression]** by evaluating the expression. Arithmetic expansion does not take place if the argument is enclosed within single quotation marks. Variable names within the expression do not need to be preceded by a dollar sign (**$**). In the following example an arithmetic expression determines how many years are left until age 60:

```
zsh % cat age_check
#!/bin/zsh
read age\?"How old are you? "
if ((30 < age && age < 60)); then
  echo "Wow, in $((60-age)) years, you'll be 60!"
fi
zsh % age_check
How old are you? 51
Wow, in 9 years, you'll be 60!
```

The preceding example would also work with $[60-age] in place of $((60-age)).

Brace Expansion

The fifth step of parsing the command line is brace expansion. Brace expansion can work in two ways (it is *not* part of filename generation [globbing]); the first is to expand a string that contains a pair of braces with a comma-separated list within:

```
zsh % echo b{a,e,i,o,u}t
bat bet bit bot but
```

The second way brace expansion works is

```
zsh % echo {1001..1010}
1001 1002 1003 1004 1005 1006 1007 1008 1009 1010
zsh % echo {15..01}
15 14 13 12 11 10 09 08 07 06 05 04 03 02 01
```

Filename Expansion

Filename expansion takes care of expanding tildes (~) on the command line (page 609). The Z Shell tilde (~) expansion feature replaces a ~ by itself on the command line with your home directory (**HOME**) and replaces a ~ followed by a user's login name with the home directory of that user. Tildes are also used in directory stack manipulation (page 557). Also, ~+ is a synonym for **PWD**, and ~– is a synonym for **OLDPWD**.

The Z Shell allows you to assign directory names to variables and then use a tilde to reference the directory name:

```
zsh % xbin=/usr/bin/X11
zsh % echo ~xbin
/usr/bin/X11
```

Any other token that starts with a tilde (~) is left unchanged.

If a word in a command line begins with an equal sign, that word is checked to see whether it is either a command or an alias. If it is a command, the word and equal sign are replaced by the full pathname of the command. If it is an alias, it is replaced by the text of the alias. If the word is both a command and an alias, the pathname of the command is used:

```
zsh % echo =ls
/usr/bin/ls
```

Filename Generation (Globbing)

If you have *not* set the NO_GLOB option, the shell uses patterns to generate filenames for use as arguments to the command (page 754). If no filenames match the pattern, the Z Shell displays an error message unless you have set the NULL_GLOB option. In that case the shell removes the unmatched pattern from the command line and continues processing. A period that either starts a pathname or follows a slash (/) in a pathname must be matched explicitly unless you have set the GLOB_DOTS option.

I/O Redirection

Except for the Z Shell's builtins, most commands you enter from the keyboard are executed in a new process. When an ordinary command is executed, any I/O redirection is performed on the new process before the command starts to run. If I/O redirection is applied to a builtin, the Z Shell arranges for the redirection to apply only to that command, even though it executes in the same process as the shell. Shell functions also execute in the current process, although they have private sets of positional parameters, traps, and options. For example, the command **set –x** within a function does not turn on the **xtrace** option for the parent shell.

The Coprocess

The Z Shell supports a feature known as the *coprocess,* which allows you to start a process that runs in the background and communicates directly with its parent shell (Figure 15-1). You invoke a process as the coprocess by beginning the command line with the word coproc, followed by the name of the file that holds the coprocess.

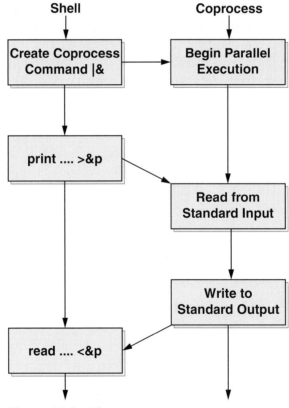

Figure 15-1   The coprocess

The coprocess command must be a filter (reads from standard input and writes to standard output), and it must flush its output whenever it has accumulated a line, rather than saving several lines for output at once. To invoke the command as the coprocess, it is connected via a two-way pipe to the current shell. You can read its standard output by using **<&p**. You can write to the coprocess's standard input with **>&p**.

The coprocess allows a process to exchange information with a background process. It can be useful when you are working in a client/server environment or setting up an *SQL* (page 1494) front end/back end. The coprocess also serves as a tool to put a new interface on an interactive program; you can easily construct shell scripts to do this.

```
zsh % cat to_upper
#!/bin/zsh
while read arg; do
echo "$arg" | tr '[a-z]' '[A-Z]'
done
```

The GNU/Linux tr utility does not flush its output after each line, but this "wrapper" script does. For each line read, it writes the line translated to uppercase to standard output. The following script invokes **to_upper** as the coprocess:

```
zsh % cat coproc_script
#!/bin/zsh
line_count=0
coproc to_upper
while read pathname; do
    ((line_count=line_count+1))
    print "$pathname" >&p
    read newpath <&p
    print $line_count: "$newpath" | tr '/' '\\'
done
zsh % echo /home/alex | coproc_script
1: \HOME\ALEX
```

The value of the coprocess is manifest when it is a frequently used tool and the invoking script transforms the tool's input or output.

Spelling Correction

If you set the CORRECT option, the Z Shell corrects the spelling of the command name just before executing the command. If the CORRECT_ALL option is set, spelling correction is attempted on every argument to the command:

```
zsh % set -o CORRECT
zsh % dor
zsh: correct `dor' to `dir' [nyae]? a
```

In this example the Z Shell does not find a command named **dor**, so it proposes a correction to dir and waits for your response. You can enter **n** for no change, which causes the shell to leave the line as entered; **y** for yes, change, which accepts the suggested correction; **a** for abort the command; or **e**, which allows you to edit the command line.

In the following example the CORRECT_ALL option is set, so zsh checks all the command arguments:

```
zsh % set -o CORRECT_ALL
zsh % vi ~/lok.icn
zsh: correct `~/lok.icn' to `/home/jenny/lock.icn' [nyae]? a
```

The Z Shell attempts to correct spelling only if it locates a *close* match. The rules for deciding what a close match is are not what you might expect. For example, if the misspelling of **lock.icn** had been **look.icn** instead of **lok.icn** in the previous example, the Z Shell would have executed the following command, using **look.icn** as the argument:

```
zsh % set -o CORRECT_ALL
zsh % ls look.icn
ls: look.icn: No such file or directory
```

Shell Programs

As an interactive shell, the Z Shell's great advantages lie in its aliasing capacity and its command line and history editing mechanisms. As a programming language, it has many features, some of which are not available in other shells:

- Powerful control structures: **for...in**, **if...then**, **while**, **case**, **select**, and **until**
- Recursive functions
- Local variables
- Built-in integer arithmetic and integer data types
- Extended trap handling
- Input (**read**) and output (**print**) facilities
- File control and I/O redirection for any file descriptor, including file descriptor duplication
- Coprocess implementation
- Array variables and string manipulation operators

Earlier sections of this chapter discussed most of these features, many of which are useful interactively as well as for shell programming. This section develops a complete shell program to show you how to combine some of these features effectively.

Program Structures

The structures that the Z Shell provides are not a random assortment. They have been carefully chosen to provide most of the structural features that are in other procedural languages, such as C or Pascal. A procedural language provides you with the ability to

- Declare, assign, and manipulate variables and constant data. The Z Shell provides string variables, together with powerful string operators, and integer variables, with a complete set of arithmetic operators.

- Break large problems into small ones by creating subprograms. The Z Shell allows you to create functions and call scripts from other scripts. Z Shell functions can be called recursively; that is, a Z Shell function can call itself. You may not need to use recursion often, but occasionally it allows you to solve apparently difficult problems with ease.

- Execute statements conditionally, using such statements as **if**.

- Execute statements iteratively, using such statements as **while** and **for**.

- Transfer data to and from the program, communicating both with data files and with users.

Programming languages implement these capabilities in different ways but with the same ideas in mind. When you want to solve a problem using a program, you must first figure out a procedure that leads you to a solution. Such a procedure is called an *algorithm*. Typically, you can implement the same algorithm in roughly the same way in different programming languages, using the same kinds of constructs in each language. Earlier in this chapter you saw examples of the use of all the Z Shell programming structures except recursion. An example of a recursive Z Shell function that proves useful is shown next.

Recursion

A recursive construct is one that is defined in terms of itself. This may seem circular, but it need not be. To avoid circularity a recursive definition must have a special case that is not self-referential. Recursive ideas occur in everyday life. For example, you can define an ancestor as your mother, your father, or one of their ancestors. This definition is not circular; it specifies unambiguously who your ancestors are:

your mother or your father or your mother's mother or father or your father's mother or father, and so on.

A number of GNU/Linux system utilities can operate recursively. See the **–R** option to the chmod (page 1103) and chown (page 1108) utilities in Part III for examples.

Solve the following problem by using a recursive shell function:

> Write a shell function named **makepath** that, given a pathname, creates all the components in that pathname as directories. For example, the command **makepath a/b/c/d** should create directories **a**, **a/b**, **a/b/c**, and **a/b/c/d**. (The mkdir utility supports a **–p** option that does exactly this. Solve the problem without using **mkdir –p**.)

One algorithm for a recursive solution follows.

1. Examine this path argument. If it is a null string or if it names an existing directory, do nothing and return.

2. If it is a simple path component, create it (using mkdir) and return.

3. Otherwise, call **makepath**, using the path prefix of the original argument. This eventually creates all the directories up to the last component, which you can then create with mkdir.

In general, a recursive function must invoke itself with a simpler version of the problem than it was given, until finally it gets called with a simple case that does not need to call itself. Here is one possible solution based on this algorithm:

```
# this is a function
# enter it at the keyboard, do not run it as a shell script
makepath()
{
    if [[ ${#1} -eq 0 || -d "$1" ]]
        then
            return 0        # Do nothing
    fi
    if [[ "${1%/*}" = "$1" ]]
        then
            mkdir $1
            return $?
    fi
    makepath ${1%/*} || return 1
    mkdir $1
    return $?
}
```

In the test for a simple component (the **if** statement in the middle of the function), the left expression is the argument after the shortest suffix that starts with a **/** character has been stripped away (page 751). If there is no such character (for example, if **$1** is a1ex), nothing gets stripped off, and the two sides are equal. If the argument is a simple filename preceded by a slash, such as **/usr**, the expression **${1%/*}** evaluates to a null string. To make the function work in this case, you must take two precautions: Put the left expression within quotation marks as shown, and ensure that your recursive function behaves sensibly when passed a null string as an argument. In general, good programs are robust: They are prepared for borderline, invalid, or meaningless input and behave appropriately.

By giving the following command from the shell you are working in, you turn on tracing so that you can watch the recursion work:

```
zsh % set -o xtrace
```

Give the same command, replacing the hyphen with a plus sign (**+**), to turn tracing off.

With debugging turned on, each line starts with a plus sign, the name of the function, a colon, the line number in the function (the opening brace is line 1), and a greater than symbol that ends the debugging comments. Then comes the line, totally expanded, as it was executed. Following, the line that starts with +zsh shows the shell calling **makepath**. You can see also that **makepath** is called with arguments of **a/b/c**, **a/b**, and finally **a**. All the work is done (using mkdir) as each call to **makepath** returns:

```
zsh % makepath a/b/c
+zsh:461> makepath a/b/c
+makepath:2> [[ 5 -eq 0 || -d a/b/c ]]
+makepath:6> [[ a/b == a/b/c ]]
+makepath:11> makepath a/b
+makepath:2> [[ 3 -eq 0 || -d a/b ]]
+makepath:6> [[ a == a/b ]]
+makepath:11> makepath a
+makepath:2> [[ 1 -eq 0 || -d a ]]
+makepath:6> [[ a == a ]]
+makepath:8> mkdir a
+makepath:9> return 0
+makepath:12> mkdir a/b
+makepath:13> return 0
+makepath:12> mkdir a/b/c
+makepath:13> return 00
```

You can see the function work its way down the recursive path and back up again. It is instructive to invoke **makepath** with an invalid path and see what happens. The following example, run with tracing on, shows what happens when you try to create the path **/a/b**, which requires that you create directory **a** in the root directory. Unless you have privileges, you are not permitted to do that:

```
zsh % makepath /a/b
+zsh:463> makepath /a/b
+makepath:2> [[ 4 -eq 0 || -d /a/b ]]
+makepath:6> [[ /a == /a/b ]]
+makepath:11> makepath /a
+makepath:2> [[ 2 -eq 0 || -d /a ]]
+makepath:6> [[  == /a ]]
+makepath:11> makepath
+makepath:2> [[ 0 -eq 0 ]]
makepath: return: too many arguments [4]
+makepath:6> [[  ==  ]]
+makepath:8> mkdir
mkdir: too few arguments
Try `mkdir --help' for more information.
+makepath:9> return 1
+makepath:11> return 1
+makepath:11> return 1
```

The recursion stops only when **makepath** is passed a null argument and the error return is passed all the way back, so the original **makepath** exits with nonzero status.

Use Local Variables with Recursive Functions   ‖ tip

The example has glossed over a potential problem that you may encounter when you use a recursive function. During the execution of a recursive function, many separate instances of that function may be simultaneously active. All but one of them are waiting for their child invocation to complete.

By default, Z Shell variables are global. When a recursive Z Shell function uses global variables, all instances of the function share a single copy of each variable. Sharing variables can give rise to side effects that are rarely what you want. As a rule, use **typeset** (page 743) to make local all the variables of a recursive function.

A Programming Problem: makercs

This section combines some of the Z Shell programming constructs into a complete program. The example uses ci, one of the Revision Control System (RCS) commands. If you are not familiar with RCS, refer to page 871 for a description. The example also makes use of find (page 1165). The specification for the program follows.

> Write a program, **makercs**, that takes two directory names as arguments: **source** and **target**. The program should create a copy of the hierarchy rooted at **source** in **target**, except that each regular file under **source** should be checked in to a corresponding RCS file under **target**, using the ci command. If **target** does not exist, create it. The program should ensure that the pathname **source** is not a prefix of the pathname **target**, and vice versa. The program should skip any file in **source** that is not a directory or regular file, such as a FIFO or socket.

The command

```
makercs srcdir rcsdir
```

should create under **rcsdir** a hierarchy identical to the hierarchy under **srcdir**, except that, if, for example, **srcdir/functions/func1.bash** is a regular file, the command should create **rcsdir/functions/s.func1.bash,v.**

There are as many ways to solve a problem like this as there are programmers, so your **makercs** program probably will not look like the one developed in this section. Here is an algorithm for solving the problem:

1. Check the command line for the correct number and type of arguments. If invalid, display usage message and exit.

2. Traverse the source tree, using the find command to produce pathnames. For each pathname that find returns:

   a. If the pathname refers to a directory, make the corresponding path under the target.

   b. If the pathname refers to a regular file,

      • Construct the name of the RCS file that would correspond to it.

      • Create that RCS file, using ci.

   c. If the pathname refers to any other type of file, write a message to a report file and skip the file.

   d. At each stage, if an error occurs, write an appropriate message to an error file.

A few functions to manipulate pathnames are useful in solving the problem. The GNU/Linux utility dirname, given a pathname, writes the path prefix to standard output. The basename utility does the opposite: The command **basename path** writes the last component of **path** to standard output.

If you have a file whose pathname is **a/b/c/d**, you want to create the pathname **a/b/c/d,v** as the corresponding RCS filename:

```
rcsname()
{
    echo ${1},v
}
```

The **rcsname** function appends **,v** to the filename. The answer is written to standard output to enable you to use **rcsname** inside a command substitution statement, such as

```
newname=$(rcsname oldname)
```

One function needs to check the command line arguments for validity. This function should ensure that exactly two arguments have been passed, that **$1** names an existing directory, that **$2** either does not exist or names an existing directory (not a plain file), and that neither argument is a prefix of the other:

```
checkargs()
{
    if [[ $# != 2 ]]
    then
        print -u2 "usage: makercs <source> <dest>"
        exit 1
    fi
    if [[ ! -d $1 ]]
    then
        print -u2 "$1: Not a directory"
        exit 1
    fi
    # Check second argument
    if [[ -a $2 && ! -d $2 ]]
    then
        print -u2 "$2: Not a directory"
        exit 1
    fi
    # Check that neither argument is a prefix of the other
    if [[ $1 = $2* || $2 = $1* ]]
    then
        print -u2 "Cannot create one hierarchy below or above the other"
        exit 1
    fi
    return 0
}
```

You can invoke this function with a command such as **checkargs "$@"**, which passes the command line arguments directly to **checkargs**.

The main part of the program uses find to locate the files and directories. The command **find $source –print** will write the pathname of each file in the hierarchy rooted at **$source**, one per line, to standard output. If it pipes this output into a loop and reads each pathname into a shell variable, the script can manipulate that variable as follows:

- Determine whether the pathname names a directory, a regular file, or something else.

- Construct a corresponding pathname rooted in the target directory.
- Use ci to create the RCS file at that pathname.

Thus the main body of the program can have the following structure:

find $source –print |
*while read **pathname***
do
        commands
done

The program has to deal sensibly with errors and special conditions. It opens two files: one file to report errors and another to log the names of files that were skipped.

With the various pieces put together and the missing ones filled in, here is a complete program to solve the problem:

```
zsh % cat makercs
#!/bin/zsh
#remove the # on the following line to turn on debugging
#set -o xtrace
makepath()
{
    if [[ ${#1} -eq 0 || -d $1 ]]
    then
        return 0
    fi
    if [[ "${1%/*}" = "$1" ]]
    then
        mkdir $1
        return $?
    fi
    makepath ${1%/*} || return 1
    mkdir $1
    return $?
}
rcsname()
{
    echo ${1},v
}
checkargs()
{
    if [[ $# != 2 ]]
    then
        print -u2 "usage: makercs <source> <dest>"
        exit 1
    fi
    if [[ ! -d $1 ]]
    then
        print -u2 "$1: Not a directory"
        exit 1
    fi
```

```
            # Check second argument
            if [[ -a $2 && ! -d $2 ]]
            then
                print -u2 "$2: Not a directory"
                exit 1
            fi
            # Check that neither argument is a prefix of the other
            if [[ $1 = $2* || $2 = $1* ]]
            then
                print -u2 "Cannot create one hierarchy below or above the other"
                exit 1
            fi
            return 0
    }
    ERRS=./err_file
    REPORT=./report
    checkargs "$@"
    # Open error and report files
    exec 3>$ERRS
    exec 4>$REPORT
    source=$1
    dest=$2
    find $source -print |
    while read pathname
    do
        target=$dest${pathname#$source}
        if [[ -d $pathname ]]
        then
            makepath $target || print -u3 "Cannot create $target"
        elif [[ -f $pathname ]]
        then
            target=$(rcsname $target)
            ci -l -q "-t-$pathname" "$pathname" "$target" >&4 2>&3 ||
                print -u3 "Cannot create $target"
        else
            print -u4 "$pathname not directory or regular file: skipped"
        fi
    done
    exec 3<&-
    exec 4<&-
    exit 0
```

There are a number of ways to improve this program. For example, its exit status does not always reflect what happened. The exercises at the end of this chapter ask you to modify the program in various ways.

Another Programming Problem: Quiz

Here is another problem that you can solve with a Z Shell program. This problem calls for interaction with the user, and consequently the solution will require different shell programming features. Following is the problem statement in general terms:

Write a generic multiple-choice quiz program. The program should get its questions from data files, present them to the user, and keep track of the number of correct and incorrect answers. The user must be able to exit the program at any time with a summary of results to that point.

The detailed design of this program and even the detailed description of the problem depend on a number of choices: How will the program know which subjects are available for quizzes? How will the user choose a subject? How will the program know when the quiz is over? Should the program present the same questions (for a given subject) in the same order each time, or should it scramble them?

Of course, you can make many perfectly good choices that implement the specification of the problem. The following details narrow the problem specification:

- Each subject will correspond to a subdirectory of a master quiz directory. This directory will be named in the environment variable **QUIZDIR**, whose default will be **/usr/lib/quiz**.

- Each question in a particular subject corresponds to a file in the subject directory.

- The representation of the question follows. The first line of the file is the text of the question. If it takes more than one line, you must escape the NEW-LINE with a backslash. (This choice makes it easy to read a single question with the built-in read command.) The second line of the file is an integer that is the number of choices. The next several lines are the choices themselves. The last line is the correct answer. For example, here is a sample question file:

```
Who discovered the principle of the lever?
4
Euclid
Archimedes
Thomas Edison
The Lever Brothers
Archimedes
```

- The program presents all the questions in a subject directory. At any point, the user can interrupt the quiz with CONTROL-C, whereupon the program will summarize the results so far and exit. If the user does not interrupt, the program summarizes the results and exits when it has asked all the questions.

- The program scrambles the questions in a subject before presenting them.

Following is a top-level design for this program:

1. Initialize. This involves a number of steps, such as setting counts of the number of questions asked so far, as well as the number correct and wrong, to zero.

2. Present the user with a choice of subject and get the user's response.

3. Change to the corresponding subject directory.

4. Determine the questions to be asked (that is, the filenames in that directory). Rearrange them in random order.

5. Repeatedly present questions and ask for answers until the quiz is over or is interrupted by the user.

6. Present the results and exit.

Clearly some of these steps (such as step 3) are simple, whereas others (such as step 4) are complex and worthy of analysis on their own. Use shell functions for any complex step, and use the trap builtin to handle a user interrupt.

Here is a skeleton version of the program, with empty shell functions:

```
function initialize
{
# To be filled in.
}
function choose_subj
{
# To be filled in. Will write choice to standard output.
}

function scramble
{
# To be filled in. Will store names of question files, scrambled,
# in an array variable named questions.
}

function ask
{
# To be filled in. Reads a question file, asks it, and checks the
# answer. Returns 1 if the answer was correct, 0 otherwise. If it
# encounters an invalid question file, exit with status 2.
}

function summarize
{
# To be filled in. Presents the user's score.
}

# Main program
initialize                        # Step 1 in top-level design
trap 'summarize ; exit 0' INT     # Handles user interrupts

subject=$(choose_subj)            # Step 2
[[ $? -eq 0 ]] || exit 2          # If no valid choice, exit
```

```
cd $subject || exit 2                 # Step 3

echo                                  # Skip a line
scramble                              # Step 4

for ques in ${questions[*]}           # Step 5
do
ask $ques
result=$?
((num_ques=num_ques+1))
if [[ $result == 1 ]]
then
((num_correct=num_correct+1))
fi
echo                                  # skip a line between questions
    sleep ${QUIZDELAY:=1}
done

summarize                             Step 6
exit 0
```

To make reading the results a bit easier for the user, there is a **sleep** call inside the question loop. It delays **$QUIZDELAY** seconds (default = 1) between questions.

Now the task is to fill in the missing pieces of the program. In a sense this program is being written backward. The details (the shell functions) come first in the file but come last in the development process. This common programming practice is called top-down design. Fill in the broad outline of the program first, and supply the details later. In this way you break the problem up into smaller problems, each of which you can work on independently. Shell functions are a great help in using the top-down approach.

One way to write the initialize function follows:

```
function initialize
{
num_ques=0                            # Number of questions asked so far
num_correct=0                         # Number answered correctly so far
first_time=true                       # true until first question is asked
cd ${QUIZDIR:=/usr/games/quiz} || exit 2
}
```

Although it is logically part of initialization, the trap statement belongs in the main program. In the Z Shell, a trap inside a function is local to that function (page 789). In this case, a trap statement in the initialize function would abort the program only if the user pressed CONTROL-C at the moment the initialize function was being executed.

The next function, **choose_subj,** is a bit more complicated and is implemented using a **select** statement:

```
function choose_subj
{
set -A subjects $(command ls)
PS3="Choose a subject for the quiz from the preceding list: "
select Subject in $subjects; do
    if [[ -z "$Subject" ]]; then
        print "No subject chosen.   Bye." >&2
        exit 1
    fi
    print $Subject
    return 0
done
}
```

The function starts by getting a list of subject directories, using the ls command. The call to ls is preceded by the reserved word **command** to ensure that if an alias or function is named ls, it will not be used. Next, the **select** structure (page 770) presents the user with a list of subjects (the directories found by ls) and places the chosen directory name in **Subject**. Finally the function writes the name of the subject directory to standard output. The main program uses command substitution to assign this value to the **subject** variable [subject=$(choose_subj)].

Be prepared for the cd command to fail. The directory may be unsearchable, or conceivably another user may have removed the directory in between the ls command and the cd command.

The **scramble** function presents a number of difficulties. In this solution it uses an array variable (**questions**) to hold the names of the questions and scrambles the various entries in an array by using the **RANDOM** variable ◼ zsh:

```
function scramble
{
typeset -i index quescount
set -A questions $(command ls)
quescount=${#questions}          # Number of elements
((index=quescount-1))
while [[ $index > 0 ]]; do
    ((target=RANDOM % index))
    exchange $target $index
    ((index -= 1))
done
```

This function initializes the array variable **questions** to the list of filenames (questions) in the working directory. The variable **quescount** is set to the number of such files. Then the following algorithm is used: Let the variable index count down from **quescount − 1** (the index of the last entry in the array variable). For each value of **index**, the function chooses a random value target between 0 and **index**, inclusive. The command

```
((target=RANDOM % index))
```

produces a random value between 0 and **index − 1** by taking the remainder (the %
operator) when **$RANDOM** is divided by **index**. The function then exchanges the
elements of **questions** at positions **target** and **index**. It is convenient to do this in another function, named **exchange**:

```
function exchange
{
temp_value=${questions[$1]}
questions[$1]=${questions[$2]}
questions[$2]=$temp_value
}
```

Function **ask** also uses the **select** structure. This function must read the question file named in its argument and use the contents of that file to present the question, accept the answer, and determine whether the answer is correct; see the code
that follows.

This function uses file descriptor 3 to read successive lines from the question
file, whose name was passed as an argument to the function. It reads the question
into the variable named **ques**. It constructs the variable **choices** by initializing it to
the null string, and then successively appending the next choice. Then it sets **PS3** to
the value of **ques** and uses the **select** structure, which prompts the user with **ques**.
The **select** structure places the user's answer in **answer**, and the function then
checks it against the correct answer from the file. If the user does not make a valid
choice, **select** continues to issue the prompt and wait for a response.

The construction of the **choices** variable is done with an eye to avoiding a potential problem. Suppose that one of the answers has some whitespace in it. Then it
might appear as two or more arguments in **choices**. To avoid this problem, make
sure that **choices** is an array variable. Be careful to remove the leading colon in
choices. The **select** statement's default feature of using the positional arguments
does the rest of the work:

```
zsh % cat quiz
#!/bin/zsh

#remove the # on the following line to turn on debugging
#set -o xtrace

#==================
function initialize
{
num_ques=0                          # Number of questions asked so far
num_correct=0                       # Number answered correctly so far
first_time=true                     # true until first question is asked
cd ${QUIZDIR:=/usr/games/quiz} || exit 2
}
```

```
#==================
function choose_subj
{
set -A subjects $(command ls)
PS3="Choose a subject for the quiz from the preceding list: "
select Subject in $subjects; do
    if [[ -z "$Subject" ]]; then
        print "No subject chosen.  Bye." >&2
        exit 1
    fi
    print $Subject
    return 0
done
}

#==================
function exchange
{
temp_value=${questions[$1]}
questions[$1]=${questions[$2]}
questions[$2]=$temp_value
}

#==================
function scramble
{
typeset -i index quescount
set -A questions $(command ls)
quescount=${#questions}        # Number of elements
((index=quescount-1))
while [[ $index > 0 ]]; do
    ((target=RANDOM % index))
    exchange $target $index
    ((index -= 1))
done
}

#==================
function ask
{
set -A choices
exec 3<$1
read -u3 ques || exit 2
read -u3 num_opts || exit 2

index=0
choices=""
while (( index < num_opts )); do
    read -u3 next_choice || exit 2
    choices=($choices $next_choice)
    ((index += 1))
done
read -u3 correct_answer || exit 2
exec 3<&-

if [[ $first_time = true ]]; then
    first_time=false
```

```
        print "You may press the Interrupt Key at any time to quit.\n"
fi

PS3=$ques"   "                          # Make $ques the prompt for select
                                        # and add some spaces for legibility.
select answer in $choices; do
    if [[ -z "$answer" ]]; then
        print  Not a valid choice. Please choose again.
            elif [[ "$answer" = "$correct_answer" ]]; then
        print "Correct!"
        return 1
            else
        print "No, the answer is $correct_answer."
        return 0
    fi
done
}


#==================
function summarize
{
if (( num_ques == 0 )); then
    print "You did not answer any questions"
    exit 0
fi

(( percent=num_correct*100/num_ques ))
print "You answered $num_correct questions correctly, out of \
$num_ques total questions."
print "Your score is $percent percent."
}


#==================
# Main program
initialize                          # Step 1 in top-level design
trap 'summarize ; exit 0' INT       # Handles user interrupts

subject=$(choose_subj)# Step 2
[[ $? -eq 0 ]] || exit 2            # If no valid choice, exit

cd $subject || exit 2               # Step 3
print                               # Skip a line
scramble                            # Step 4

for ques in ${questions}; do        # Step 5
    ask $ques
    result=$?
    (( num_ques=num_ques+1 ))
    if [[ $result == 1 ]]; then
        (( num_correct += 1 ))
    fi
    print                           # skip a line between questions
    sleep ${QUIZDELAY:=1}
done

summarize                           # Step 6
exit 0
```

Z Shell Options

The Z Shell has a number of options that you can use to alter the behavior of the shell. Table 15-25 describes many of the available options. Refer to the zsh options man page (**zshoptions**) for a complete list.

Z Shell option names are not case sensitive and ignore underscores. The following names refer to the same option: `ignoreeof`, `IGNOREEOF`, `Ignore_EOF`, `IGNORE_EOF`, `IgN___oRe_EoF`. (The last name would not be a good choice because it is difficult both to read and to type.) This book uses all uppercase letters to show option names.

The **set** builtin sets and unsets options. Use **set −o** to set, or turn on, an option and **set +o** to unset it, or turn it off.

```
zsh % set −o IGNORE_EOF
zsh % set +o MARK_DIRS
```

These commands turn on the IGNORE_EOF option and turn off the MARK_DIRS option. MARK_DIRS causes the shell to display a slash (**/**) following directory names generated by ambiguous file references.

You can also use the setopt and unsetopt builtins **zsh** as alternatives to **set −o** and **set +o**, respectively. The following commands perform the same functions as the preceding ones:

```
zsh % setopt IGNOREEOF
zsh % unsetopt MARKDIRS
```

You can determine whether an option is *on* or *off* with the [[...]] command **zsh** (refer to "Control Structures" on page 768). Because [[...]] generates only a return status, you must check the return status (**$?**) after you issue the command (0 = *true* and 1 = *false*). In the following example MARKDIRS is initially *off* (1), then is turned *on* (0), then is turned *off* again:

```
zsh % [[ −o MARKDIRS ]] ; echo $?
1
zsh % setopt MARKDIRS
zsh % [[ −o MARKDIRS ]] ; echo $?
0
zsh % unsetopt MARKDIRS
zsh % [[ −o MARKDIRS ]] ; echo $?
1
```

Some options have abbreviations that you can use to set or unset them quickly. The XTRACE option has an abbreviation of **x**, so that you can turn on XTRACE with the following command (do not use **±o** with an abbreviated option):

```
zsh % set −x
```

This command **bash zsh** turns on the debugging trace. You can set and unset several options with the same command. The following command turns on XTRACE (**−x**) while turning off IGNORE_EOF and NO_UNSET (**+u**):

```
zsh % set −x +o ignoreeof +u
```

In Table 15-25 the character in parentheses following some of the option names can be used to abbreviate the option.

Options | table 15-25

Options marked with an asterisk (*) are set by default in a login shell.

ALL_EXPORT (−a)	Causes all subsequently defined variables to be automatically exported.*
APPEND_HISTORY	Appends history lists to the history file instead of overwriting it.
AUTO_LIST (−9)	Automatically lists all choices when a completion attempt produces more than one alternative.
AUTO_PARAM_SLASH	Appends a slash (/) to directory filenames created by filename completion.
BAD_PATTERN (+2)	Displays an error message on badly formed file generation patterns. When unset, no error is displayed.
BANG_HIST (+K)	Allows history substitutions using !.
BEEP (+B)	Produces audible warnings (beeps) on errors in the Z Shell editors.
BG_NICE (−6)	Runs background jobs at a lower priority (default).*
BRACE_CCL	Permits brace expansion of the form {A-Za-z}. If this option is not set, {A-Z} is expanded, but {A-Za-z} is left as is.
BSD_ECHO	Causes the **echo** builtin to mimic the version of **echo** supplied with BSD UNIX. Setting this option disables escape sequences in the arguments to **echo** unless you give the −e option.
CLOBBER (+C)	Allows > to overwrite an existing file and >> to create a new file. If this option is not set, you must use >! and >>! instead. Frequently used as NO_CLOBBER.
CORRECT (− 0)	Attempts spelling correction on command names.
CORRECT_ALL (−O)	Attempts spelling correction on all the command line arguments.
ERR_EXIT (− e)	Executes the ZERR trap (if set) and exits from the shell if a command terminates with a nonzero exit status.
EXEC (+n)	Executes commands. When unset, the shell checks commands for errors but does not run them.

Options (Continued) || table 15-25

Options marked with an asterisk (*) are set by default in a login shell.

EXTENDED_GLOB	Turns on the special processing of #, ~, and ^ during filename generation. (A ~ at the beginning of a pathname is always expanded to a directory name, regardless of this option.)
GLOB (+F)	Allows filename generation.
GLOB_DOTS (−4)	Removes the restriction that leading periods (.) in filenames must be matched explicitly.
GLOB_SUBST	Examines the results of parameter and command substitution when doing filename expansion and generation.
HASH_CMDS	Looks for commands in the shell's fast-access hash table before looking through directories. Adds commands that are not found in the hash table. If this option is not set, the hash table is not used.*
HASH_DIRS	When a command is executed, hash all the directories in the path to the command. Has no effect unless the HASH_CMDS option is set.*
HASH_LIST_ALL	Before attempting command completion, hashes all the directories in the path to the command. Slows down the first completion but speeds up subsequent command executions.*
HIST_VERIFY	Does not execute commands containing history references. Performs history substitution and leaves the cursor on the resulting command line.
HUP	Sends the HUP signal to jobs that are running when the shell exits.
IGNORE_BRACES (−I)	Does not do any brace expansions.
IGNORE_EOF (7)	Ignores CONTROL-D and forces the user to use **exit** or **logout** (or an alias of one of these) to quit a shell.
INTERACTIVE (−i)	Makes the shell an interactive one; attaches standard input and standard output to the terminal. This option is set automatically in the login shell.*
INTERACTIVE_COMMENTS (−k)	Permits users to enter comments even when the interactive option is set.
LOGIN (−l)	Makes this a login shell and reads all the initialization files.*

Options (Continued)

|| table 15-25

Options marked with an asterisk (*) are set by default in a login shell.

MAIL_WARNING (–U)	Warns if any mail has arrived since the last time the shell checked. (Actually warns on any access of the mail file.)
MARK_DIRS (–8)	Appends a slash (/) to all directories resulting from filename generation.
MONITOR (–m)	Permits job control actions. Automatically set if the INTERACTIVE option is set.*
NOCLOBBER (–C)	See CLOBBER.
NOMATCH (+3)	Displays an error if there are no matches from filename generation or pattern matching. When this option is not set, errors are ignored and arguments are left unchanged. The inverse of this option is NO_NOMATCH.
NOTIFY (–5)	Notifies the user immediately when the status of a background job changes, instead of waiting until the next shell prompt. The inverse of this option is *not* TIFY.*
NULL_GLOB (–G)	Any pattern for filename generation that has no matches is silently dropped from the command line, overriding the NOMATCH option.
PROMPT_SUBST	Allows the use of the `${...}`, `$(...)`, `$[...]`, and `$((..))` expressions inside prompts.
RC_EXPAND_PARAM (–P)	If variable is an array variable, array expansions of the form x`${variable}`y are expanded, using each array element. So if the variable z is (0 1 2), x`${z}`y expands to x0y, x1y, and x2y. If this option is unset, the example would expand to x0 1 2y.
RC_QUOTES	Allows two successive single quotation marks to represent a single quotation mark within a singly quoted string.
RCS (+f)	Reads all shell initialization files. When unset, the shell reads /etc/zshenv and ignores all other initialization files.
RM_STAR_SILENT (–H)	Turns off the prompt asking the user to confirm an **rm *** or **rm path/*** command.
SHIN_STDIN (–s)	Reads commands from standard input; can be used only from the command line.*

Options (Continued) || table 15-25

Options marked with an asterisk (*) are set by default in a login shell.

UNSET (+u)	Treats unset parameters as empty and does not generate an error as would be the case if this option were not set.
VERBOSE (−v)	Displays each input line as the shell reads it.
XTRACE (−x)	Prints commands as they are executed. Does not print function calls or commands, such as ((and [[.
ZLE (−Z)	Enables the Z Shell line editor.*

Chapter Summary

The Z Shell implements nearly all the features of the Bourne Again Shell, as well as the most useful features of the TC Shell. You can customize the Z Shell to create a personal interactive environment by choosing settings for options and values for variables and by defining aliases and functions.

You assign attributes to Z Shell variables with the typeset builtin. The Z Shell provides operators to perform pattern matching on variables, provide default values for variables, and evaluate the length of the value of variables. The Z Shell supports array variables and local variables for functions and provides built-in integer arithmetic capability, using the let builtin and an expression syntax similar to the C programming language.

Condition testing is similar to that of the test utility, but the Z Shell provides more testing primitives, including string ordering and pattern matching. The Z Shell provides special syntax that uses arithmetic and logical expressions as conditions.

The Z Shell provides a rich set of control structures for conditional and iterative execution. The **select** control structure provides a simple method for creating menus in shell scripts and for repeatedly prompting the user for responses. The **while**, **until**, and **if...then** structures have the same syntax as their Bourne Again Shell counterparts but can take advantage of the Z Shell's more powerful logical and arithmetic condition testing. The **repeat** statement provides a convenient way to repeat a sequence of commands a number of times. Most Z Shell control structures are also available with a TC Shell syntax for users who are more familiar with the TC Shell.

The Z Shell provides the ability to manipulate file descriptors. Coupled with powerful read and print builtins, this allows shell scripts to have as much control over input and output as programs written in lower-level languages. The Z Shell provides all the I/O redirections of both bash and tcsh and more. A unique feature of the Z Shell is its ability to launch a coprocess: a process that executes in parallel with the parent shell and whose standard input and output are connected via a two-way pipe to the parent shell. From the parent shell you can read standard output of the coprocess, using **<&p**. You can write to standard input of the coprocess, using **>&p**.

Functions are a powerful feature of the Z Shell. You can call them from an interactive Z Shell or from a shell script. Because they do not require a new process when they are called, Z Shell functions are more efficient than shell scripts. As with functions in other modern programming languages, such as C, Z Shell functions may be recursive, which can lead to simpler solutions to some problems. The auto-load builtin can load a function only if it is actually used, making functions more efficient and programming easier. The Z Shell also provides some special functions that can be used to perform tasks periodically, to produce prompts that change dynamically, and to perform tasks when changing directories.

As with both the Bourne Again Shell and the TC Shell, the Z Shell includes the ability to start jobs as background tasks, to suspend jobs running in the foreground, and to move jobs between the background and foreground. Job control in the Z Shell more closely matches that of the TC Shell than the Bourne Again Shell.

Shell functions and the rich set of builtins and control structures are well suited to the use of the Z Shell for both interactive and scripting purposes. The complete set of command line substitutions and expansions are particularly useful during interactive use.

When using an interactive Z Shell, you can edit your command line and commands from the history file, using either of the Z Shell's command line editors (vi or emacs). If you use the vi command line editor, you start in Input mode, unlike the way you normally enter vi. You can switch between Command and Input mode. The emacs editor is modeless and distinguishes commands from editor input by recognizing control characters as commands.

Commands for the vi Command Line Editor

Not all the available vi command line editor commands are given here. See the zsh command line editor (**zshzle**) man page for a complete list.

Cursor-Movement Commands (vi)

In addition to the following commands, you may be able to use the ARROW keys to move about. The ARROW keys work regardless of mode.

| l (lowercase "ell") or SPACE | Moves one character to the right |
| h | Moves one character to the left |

w	Moves one word to the right
b	Moves one word to the left
W	Moves one space-delimited word to the right
B	Moves one space-delimited word to the left
0	Moves to beginning of line
$	Moves to end of line
e	Moves to end of word
E	Moves to end of space-delimited word
^	Moves to first nonblank position on line
f*x*	Moves to next (right) occurrence of *x*
F*x*	Moves to previous (left) occurrence of *x*
; (semicolon)	Repeats last f or F command
, (comma)	Repeats last f or F command but in opposite direction
*n*l	Moves to column *n*

Changing Text (vi)

i	Enters Insert mode before current character
a	Enters Insert mode after current character
I	Enters Insert mode before first nonblank character
A	Enters Insert mode at end of line
r*x*	Replaces current character with *x*
R	Overwrites, starting at current character, until ESCAPE
*n*x	Deletes *n* characters, starting at current character
*n*X	Deletes *n* characters, starting just past current character

D	Deletes from current character to end of line
dd	Deletes entire command
C	Changes from current character to end of line

History Editing Commands (vi)

j	Moves back one command in history
k	Moves forward one command in history
/*string* RETURN	Searches backward for command with *string* (not a regular expression except for ^ matching the start of a line)
?*string* RETURN	Searches forward for command with *string* (see previous entry)
n	Repeats previous search
N	Repeats previous search in opposite direction
*n*v	Enters full-screen vi to edit command number *n*, or current command if *n* is omitted
#	Inserts current command as a comment in history file

Miscellaneous Commands (vi)

ESCAPE =	Lists pathnames that match current word (pathname listing)
ESCAPE \	Completes current word to a unique or partial pathname (pathname completion)
ESCAPE *	Expands current word to all matching pathnames (pathname expansion)
u	Undoes previous change
~	Changes case of current character
n	Repeats, *n* times, the most recent command that caused a change; if *n* is omitted, it defaults to one

Commands for emacs Command Line Editor

Not all the emacs mode commands are given here. See the zsh command line editor (**zshzle**) man page for a complete list.

Cursor-Movement Commands (emacs)

In addition to the following commands, you may be able to use the ARROW keys to position the cursor.

CONTROL-F	Moves one character to the right
CONTROL-B	Moves one character to the left
ESCAPE f	Moves one word to the right
ESCAPE b	Moves one word to the left
CONTROL-A	Moves to beginning of line
CONTROL-E	Moves to end of line
CONTROL-] x	Moves to next instance of x

Changing Text (emacs)

Erase	Deletes character to the right of current character
CONTROL-D	Deletes current character
CONTROL-K	Deletes to end of line
Kill	Deletes entire line
CONTROL-T	Transposes current and previous (to left) characters
CONTROL-W	Deletes all characters from current character to Mark
ESCAPE D	Deletes one word to right
ESCAPE h	Deletes one word to left
ESCAPE l	Changes next word to all lowercase
ESCAPE c	Changes first letter of next word to uppercase

ESCAPE u	Changes next word to all uppercase
ESCAPE .	Inserts last word from previous command line before current character

History Editing Commands (emacs)

CONTROL-P	Moves to previous line in history file
CONTROL-N	Moves to next line in history file
ESCAPE <	Moves to first line in history file
ESCAPE >	Moves to last line in history file
CONTROL-R *string*	Search backward for *string*

Miscellaneous Commands (emacs)

ESCAPE =	Lists pathnames that match current word (pathname listing)
ESCAPE ESCAPE	Completes current word to a unique or partial pathname (pathname completion)
ESCAPE *	Expands current word to all matching pathnames (pathname expansion)
CONTROL-U	Repeats next command four times
CONTROL-V	Displays the current version of the Z Shell
CONTROL-L	Redisplays the current line

Exercises

1. The **dirname** utility treats its argument as a pathname and writes to standard output the path prefix, that is, everything up to but not including the last component. Thus

   ```
   dirname a/b/c/d
   ```

   writes a/b/c to standard output. If path is a simple filename (has no **/** characters), **dirname** writes a **.** to standard output.

Implement dirname as a Z Shell function. Make sure that it behaves sensibly when given such arguments as /.

2. Implement the basename utility, which writes the last component of its pathname argument to standard output, as a Z Shell function. For example,

```
zsh % basename a/b/c/d
```

writes d to standard output.

3. The GNU/Linux basename utility has an optional second argument. If you type

basename path suffix

basename removes the *suffix* from *path* after removing the prefix. For example,

```
zsh % basename src/shellfiles/prog.bash .bash
prog
zsh % basename src/shellfiles/prog.bash .c
prog.bash
```

Add this feature to the function you wrote for exercise 2.

4. Write a Z Shell function that takes a directory name as an argument and writes to standard output the maximum of the lengths of all filenames in that directory. If the function's argument is not a directory name, write an error message to standard output and exit with nonzero status.

5. Modify the function you wrote for exercise 4 to descend all subdirectories of the named directory recursively and to find the maximum length of any filename in that hierarchy.

6. Write a Z Shell function that lists the number of regular files, directories, block special files, character special files, FIFOs, and symbolic links in the working directory. Do this in two different ways:

a. Use the first letter of the output of **ls –l** to determine a file's type.

b. Use the file type condition tests of the [[builtin to determine a file's type.

7. The **makercs** program (page 812) depends on the fact that find writes the pathname of a directory before writing the pathname of any files in that directory. Suppose that this were not reliably true. Fix **makercs**.

8. Change **makercs** (page 812) so that if any call to ci fails, the program continues (as it does now) but eventually exits with nonzero status.

9. Modify the **quiz** program (page 816) so that the choices for a question are also randomly arranged.

Advanced Exercises

10. In the **makercs** (page 812) program, file descriptors 3 and 4 are opened; during the loop, output is directed to these descriptors. An alternative method would be simply to append the output each time it occurs, using, for example,

    ```
    print "Cannot create $target" >> $ERRS
    ```

    rather than

    ```
    print -u3 "Cannot create $target"
    ```

    What is the difference? Why does it matter?

11. The check in **makercs** (page 812) to prevent you from copying hierarchies on top of each other is simplistic. For example, if you are in your home directory, the call **makercs . ~/work/RCS** will not detect that the source and target directories lie on the same path. Fix this check.

12. In principle, recursion is never necessary. It can always be replaced by an iterative construct, such as **while** or **until**. Rewrite makepath (page 809) as a nonrecursive function. Which version do you prefer? Why?

13. Lists are commonly stored in environment variables by putting a colon (:) between each of the list elements. (The value of the **PATH** variable is a good example.) You can add an element to such a list by catenating the new element to the front of the list, as in

    ```
    PATH=/opt/bin:$PATH
    ```

    If the element you add is already in the list, you now have two copies of it in the list. Write a Z Shell function, **addenv** that takes two arguments: (1) the name of a shell variable and (2) a string to prepend to the list that is the value of the shell variable only if that string is not already an element of the list. For example, the call

    ```
    addenv PATH /opt/bin
    ```

    would add **/opt/bin** to **PATH** only if that pathname is not already in **PATH**. Be sure that your solution works, even if the shell variable starts out empty. Also make sure that you check the list elements carefully. If **/usr/opt/bin** is in **PATH** but **/opt/bin** is not, the example just given should still add **/opt/bin** to **PATH**. (*Hint:* You may find this easier to do if you first write a function **locate_field** that tells you whether a string is an element in the value of a variable.)

IN THIS CHAPTER

Programming Tools 16

With its rich set of languages and development tools, the GNU/Linux operating system provides an outstanding environment for programming. C is one of the most popular system programming languages to use with GNU/Linux, in part because the operating system itself is written mostly in C. Using C, programmers can easily access system services using function libraries and system calls. In addition, a variety of tools can make the development and maintenance of programs easier.

This chapter explains how to compile and link C programs. It introduces the GNU gdb debugger and tools that provide feedback about memory, disk, and CPU resources. It also covers some of the most useful software development tools: the make utility and two source code management systems, the Revision Control System (RCS) and the Concurrent Versions System (CVS). The make utility helps you keep track of which modules of a program have been updated and helps to ensure that when you compile a program, you use the latest versions of all program modules. Source code management systems track the versions of files involved in a project.

Programming in C

One of the main reasons the GNU/Linux system provides an excellent C programming environment is that C programs can easily access the services of the operating system. The system calls—the routines that make operating system services available to programmers—can be called from C programs. The system calls provide such services as creating files, reading from and writing to files, collecting information about files, and sending signals to processes. When you write a C program, you can use the system calls in the same way you use ordinary C program modules, or *functions*, that you have written. For more information, refer to "System Calls" on page 868.

A variety of *libraries* of functions have been developed to support programming in C. The libraries are collections of related functions that you can use just as you use your own functions and the system calls. Many of the library functions access basic operating system services through the system calls, providing the services in ways that are more suited to typical programming tasks. Other library functions, such as the math library functions, serve special purposes.

This chapter describes the processes of writing and compiling C programs. However, it will *not* teach you to program in C. If you want to learn C, the many excellent texts on the market will help you. You can also look for tutorials on the Internet.

Checking Your Compiler

Give the following command to see if you have access to the gcc compiler (www.gnu.org/software/gcc/gcc.html):[1]

```
$ gcc --version
bash: gcc: command not found
```

If you get a response other than version information, the compiler is not installed, or your **PATH** variable does not contain the necessary pathname (usually gcc is installed in **/usr/bin**). If you get version information from the gcc command, the GNU C compiler is installed.

Next, make sure that the compiler is functioning: As a simple test, create a file named **Makefile** with the following lines. The line that starts with gcc must be indented by using a TAB, not SPACEs:

```
$ cat Makefile
morning: morning.c
TAB gcc -o morning morning.c
```

Next, create a source file named **morning.c** with the lines

---

1. The C compiler in common use on GNU/Linux is GNU gcc, which comes as part of Red Hat. If it is not on your system, you need to install the **gcc** ∗ **.rpm** package.

```
$ cat morning.c
#include <stdio.h>
int main(int argc, char** argv) {
    printf("Good Morning\n");
    return 0;
}
```

Compile the file with the command **make morning**. When it compiles successfully, run the program by giving the command **morning** or **./morning**. When you get output from this program, you know that you have a working C compiler.

A C Programming Example

You must use an editor, such as pico, emacs, or vi, to create or change a C program. The name of the C program file must end in **.c**. Entering the source code for a program is similar to typing a memo or shell script. Although emacs and vim "know" that you are editing a C program, many editors do not know whether your file is a C program, a shell script, or an ordinary text document. You are responsible for making the contents of the file syntactically suitable for the C compiler to process.

Figure 16-1 illustrates the structure of a simple C program named **tabs.c**. The first two lines of the program are comments that describe what the program does. The string **/*** identifies the beginning of the comment, and the string ***/** identifies the end—the C compiler ignores all the characters between them. Because a comment can span two or more lines, the ***/** at the end of the first line and the **/*** at the beginning of the second are not necessary but are included for clarity. As the comment explains, the program reads standard input, converts TAB characters into the appropriate number of spaces, and writes the transformed input to standard output. Like many GNU/Linux utilities, this program is a filter.

Following the comments at the top of **tabs.c** are *preprocessor directives*, which are instructions for the C preprocessor. During the initial phase of compilation, the C preprocessor expands the directives, making the program ready for the later stages of the compilation process. Preprocessor directives begin with the pound sign (#) and may, optionally, be preceded by SPACE and TAB characters.

You can use the **#define** preprocessor directive to define symbolic constants and/or macros. *Symbolic constants* are names that you can use in your programs in place of constant values. For example, **tabs.c** uses a **#define** preprocessor directive to associate the symbolic constant **TABSIZE** with the constant 8. **TABSIZE** is used in the program in place of the constant 8 as the distance between TAB stops. By convention, the names of symbolic constants are composed of all uppercase letters.

By defining symbolic names for constant values, you can make your program easier to read and easier to modify. If you later decide to change a constant, you need to change only the preprocessor directive rather than the value everywhere it

```
 1   /* convert tabs in standard input to spaces in */
 2   /* standard output while maintaining columns */
 3
 4   #include        <stdio.h>
 5   #define         TABSIZE         8
 6
 7   /* prototype for function findstop */
 8   int findstop(int *);
 9
10   int main()
11   {
12   int c;          /* character read from stdin */
13   int posn = 0;   /* column position of character */
14   int inc;        /* column increment to tab stop */
15
16   while ((c = getchar()) != EOF)
17           switch(c)
18                   {
19                   case '\t':              /* c is a tab */
20                           inc = findstop(&posn);
21                           for( ; inc > 0; inc-- )
22                                   putchar(' ');
23                           break;
24                   case '\n':              /* c is a newline */
25                           putchar(c);
26                           posn = 0;
27                           break;
28                   default:                /* c is anything else */
29                           putchar(c);
30                           posn++;
31                           break;
32                   }
33   return 0;
34   }
35
36   /* compute size of increment to next tab stop */
37
38   int findstop(int *col)
39   {
40   int retval;
41   retval = (TABSIZE - (*col % TABSIZE));
42
43   /* increment argument (current column position) to next tabstop */
44   *col += retval;
45
46   return retval;          /* main gets how many blanks for filling */
47   }
```

Comments

Preprocessor Directives

Function Prototype

Main Function

Function

Figure 16-1   A simple C program (**tabs.c**—the line numbers are not part of the source code)

occurs in your program. If you replace the **#define** directive for **TABSIZE** in Figure 16-1 with the following directive, the program will place TAB stops every four columns rather than every eight:

```
#define     TABSIZE     4
```

Symbolic constants are one type of *macro*—the mapping of a symbolic name to *replacement text*. Macros are handy when the replacement text is needed at multiple points throughout the source code or when the definition of the macro is subject to frequent change. The process of substituting the replacement text for the symbolic name is called *macro expansion*.

You can also use **#define** directives to define macros with arguments. Use of such a macro resembles a function call. Unlike C functions, however, macros are replaced with C code prior to compilation into object files.

The following macro computes the distance to the next TAB stop, given the current column position, **curcol**:

```
#define NEXTTAB(curcol) (TABSIZE - ((curcol) % TABSIZE))
```

The definition of this macro uses the macro TABSIZE, whose definition must appear prior to NEXTTAB in the source code. The macro NEXTTAB could be used in **tabs.c** to assign a value to **retval** in the function **findstop**:

```
retval = NEXTTAB(*col);
```

When various modules of a program use several macro definitions, the definitions are typically collected together in a single file called a *header file,* or an *include file.* Although the C compiler does not put constraints on the names of header files, by convention they end in **.h**. The name of the header file is then listed in an **#include** preprocessor directive in each program source file that uses any of the macros. The program in Figure 16-1 uses **getchar** and **putchar**, which are macros defined in **stdio.h**. The **stdio.h** header file defines a variety of general-purpose macros and is used by many C library functions.

The angle brackets (**<** and **>**) that surround **stdio.h** in **tabs.c** instruct the C preprocessor to look for the header file in a standard list of directories (such as **/usr/include**). If you want to include a header file from another directory, you can enclose its pathname between double quotation marks. You can specify an absolute pathname within the double quotation marks, or you can give a relative pathname. If you give a relative pathname, searching begins with the working directory and is followed by the same directories that are searched when the header file is surrounded by angle brackets. By convention, header files that you supply are surrounded by double quotation marks.

Another way to specify directories to be searched for header files is to use the **–I** option to the C compiler. Assume that Alex wants to compile the program **deriv.c**, which contains the following preprocessor directive:

```
#include "eqns.h"
```

If the header file **eqns.h** is located in the subdirectory **myincludes**, Alex can compile **deriv.c** with the **–I** option to tell the C preprocessor to look for the file **eqns.h** there:

```
$ gcc -I./myincludes deriv.c
```

With this command, when the C preprocessor encounters the **#include** directive in the file **deriv.c** file, it look for **eqns.h** in the subdirectory **myincludes** of the working directory.

Use Relative Pathnames for Include Files || tip

Using absolute pathnames for include files does not work if the location of the header file within the filesystem changes. Using relative pathnames for header files works as long as the location of the header file relative to the working directory remains the same. Relative pathnames also work with the –I option on the gcc command line and allow header files to be moved.

Above the definition of the function **main** is a *function prototype*, a declaration that tells the compiler what type a function returns, how many arguments a function expects, and what the types of those arguments are. In **tabs.c** the prototype for the function **findstop** informs the compiler that **findstop** returns type *int* and that it expects a single argument of type *pointer to int*. Once the compiler has seen this declaration, it can detect and flag inconsistencies in the definition and uses of the function.

For example, suppose that the reference to **findstop** in **tabs.c** were replaced with the following statement:

```
inc = findstop();
```

The prototype for **findstop** would cause the compiler to detect a missing argument and issue an error message. The programmer could then easily fix the problem. When a function is present in a separate source file or is defined after it is referenced in a source file (as **findstop** is in the example), the function prototype helps the compiler check that the function is being called properly. Without the prototype, the compiler would not issue an error message, and the problem would manifest itself as unexpected behavior during execution. At this late point, finding the bug might be difficult and time-consuming.

Although you can call most C functions anything you want, each program must have exactly one function named **main**. The function **main** is the control module: Your program begins execution with the function **main**, which typically calls other functions in turn, which may call yet other functions, and so forth. By putting different operations into separate functions, you can make a program easier to read and maintain. The program in Figure 16-1 uses a function, **findstop**, to compute the distance to the next TAB stop. Although the few statements of **findstop** could easily have been included in the **main** function, isolating them in a separate function draws attention to a key computation.

Functions can make both development and maintenance of the program more efficient. By putting a frequently used code segment into a function, you avoid entering the same code into the program over and over again. Later when you want to make changes to the code, you need to change it only once.

If your program is long and involves several functions, you may want to split it into two or more files. Regardless of its size, you may want to place logically distinct parts of your program in separate files. A C program can be split into any number of different files; however, each function must be wholly contained within a single file.

Use a Header File for Multiple Source Files   ‖ tip

When you are creating a program that takes advantage of multiple source files, put #define preprocessor directives into a header file, and use an include statement with the name of the header file in any source file that uses the directives.

Compiling and Linking a C Program

To compile **tabs.c**, give the following command:

```
$ gcc tabs.c
```

The gcc utility calls the C preprocessor, the C compiler, the assembler, and the linker. The four components of the compilation process are shown in Figure 16-2. The C preprocessor expands macro definitions and also includes header files. The compilation phase creates assembly language code corresponding to the instructions in the source file. Then the assembler creates machine-readable object code. One object file is created for each source file. Each object file has the same name as the source file, except that the .c extension is replaced with a .o. The previous example creates a single object file, **tabs.o**. However, after successfully completing all phases of the compilation process for a program, the C compiler creates the executable file and then removes any .o files. If you successfully compile **tabs.c**, you will not see the .o file.

During the final phase of the compilation process, the linker searches specified libraries for functions your program uses and combines object modules for those functions with your program's object modules. By default, the C compiler links the standard C library, **libc.so** (usually found in **/lib**), which contains functions that handle input and output and provides many other general-purpose capabilities. If you want the linker to search other libraries, you must use the –l (ell) option to specify the libraries on the command line. Unlike most options to GNU/Linux system utilities, the **–l** option does not come before all filenames on the command line but usually comes after all the filenames of all modules that it applies to. In the next example, the C compiler searches the math library, **libm.so** (usually found in **/lib**):

```
$ gcc calc.c -lm
```

As you can see from the example, the **–l** option uses abbreviations for library names, appending the letter following **–l** to **lib** and adding a **.so** or **.a** extension. The **m** in the example stands for **libm.so**.

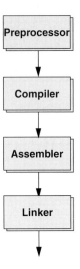

Figure 16-2   The compilation process

Using the same naming mechanism, you can have a graphics library named **libgraphics.a**, which could be linked on the command line with

```
$ gcc pgm.c -lgraphics
```

When this convention is used to name libraries, gcc knows to search for them in **/usr/lib** and **/lib**. You can have gcc also search other directories with the **–L** option:

```
$ gcc pgm.c -L. -L/usr/X11R6/lib -lgraphics
```

The preceding command causes gcc to search for the library file **libgraphics.a** in the working directory and in **/usr/X11R6/lib** before searching **/usr/lib** and **/lib**.

As the last step of the compilation process, the linker creates by default an executable file named **a.out**. Object files are deleted after the executable is created. In the next example, the **–O3** option causes gcc to use the C compiler *optimizer*. The optimizer makes object code more efficient so that the executable program runs more quickly. Optimization has many facets, including locating frequently used variables and taking advantage of processor-specific features. The number after the –O indicates the level of optimization: A higher number specifies more optimization. See the gcc info page for specifics. The following example also shows that the .o files are not present after **a.out** is created:

```
$ ls
acctspay.c  acctsrec.c  ledger.c
$ gcc -O3 ledger.c acctspay.c acctsrec.c
$ ls
a.out       acctspay.c  acctsrec.c  ledger.c
```

You can use the executable **a.out** in the same way you use shell scripts and other programs: by typing its name on the command line. The program in Figure 16-1 expects to read from standard input, so once you have created the executable, **a.out**, you can use a command such as the following to run it:

```
$ a.out < mymemo
```

If you want to save the **a.out** file, you should change the name to a more descriptive one. Otherwise, you might accidentally overwrite it during a later compilation:

```
$ mv a.out accounting
```

To save the trouble of renaming **a.out** files, you can specify the name of the executable file when you use gcc. The –o option causes the C compiler to give the executable the name of your choice rather than **a.out**. In the next example, the executable is named **accounting**:

```
$ gcc -o accounting ledger.c acctspay.c acctsrec.c
```

Assuming that **accounting** does not require arguments, you can run it with the following command:

```
$ accounting
```

You can suppress the linking phase of compilation by using the –c option with the gcc command. The –c option is useful because it does not treat unresolved external references as errors; this capability enables you to compile and debug the syntax of the modules of a program as you create them. Once you have compiled and debugged all the modules, you can run gcc again with the object files as arguments to produce an executable program. In the next example, gcc produces three object files but no executable:

```
$ gcc -c ledger.c acctspay.c acctsrec.c
$ ls
acctspay.c  acctspay.o  acctsrec.c  acctsrec.o  ledger.c   ledger.o
```

If you then run gcc again, naming the object files on the command line, gcc will produce the executable. Because it recognizes the filename extension .o, the C compiler knows that the files need only to be linked. You can also include both .c and .o files on a single command line, as in this example:

```
$ gcc -o accounting ledger.o acctspay.c acctsrec.o
```

The C compiler recognizes that the .c file needs to be preprocessed and compiled, whereas the .o files do not. The C compiler also accepts assembly language files ending in .s and treats them appropriately (that is, gcc assembles and links them). This feature makes it easy to modify and recompile a program. Refer to page 1210 in Part III for more information on gcc.

You can use separate files to divide a project into functional groups. You might put graphics routines in one file, string functions in another, and database calls in a third. Multiple files can enable several engineers to work on the same project concurrently and can speed up compilation. If all the functions are in one file and you make a change, the compiler must recompile all the functions in the file. That means that the entire program will be recompiled, which may take considerable time for a small change. When you use separate files, only the file that you make a change in must be recompiled. For large programs with many source files (for example, the C compiler or emacs), the time lost by recompiling one huge file for every small change would be enormous. For more information refer to "make: Keeps a Set of Programs Current" on page 849.

What Not to Name Your Program || tip

Do not name your program **test** or any other name of a builtin or other executable on your system. If you do, you will likely execute the builtin or other program in place of the program you intend to run. Use **which** (page 78) to determine which program you will run when you give a command.

Using Shared Libraries

Most modern operating systems use *shared* libraries, also called *dynamic* libraries, which are not linked into a program at compile time but rather are loaded when the program starts or later in some cases. The names of files housing shared libraries end with the filename extension .so (shared object). An example is **libc.so**. Usually **libaaa.so** is a symbolic link to **libaaa.so.x**, where x is a small number representing the version of the library. Many of these libraries are kept in **/usr/lib**: A typical GNU/Linux installation has more than 300 shared libraries in **/usr/lib** and more than

30 in **/usr/X11R6/lib**. Applications can have their own shared libraries; for example, the gcc compiler might keep its libraries in **/usr/lib/gcc-lib/i386-redhat-linux/3.2**.

Contrasted with shared libraries are the older, *statically linked* libraries (with a **.a** filename extension), also called *archived* libraries. Archive libraries are added to the executable file during the last (link) phase of compilation. This addition can make a program run slightly faster the first time it is run, at the expense of program maintainability and size. Together, the combined size of several executables that use a shared library and the size of the shared library is smaller than the combined size of the same executables with static libraries. Alternatively, when a running program has already loaded a dynamic library, a second program that requires the same dynamic library starts slightly faster.

Reducing memory usage and increasing maintainability are the primary reasons for using shared object libraries; they have largely replaced statically linked libraries as the library type of choice. Consider what happens when you discover an error in a library. If it is a static library, you need to relink every program that uses the library, once the library has been fixed and recompiled. With a dynamic library, you need to fix and recompile only the library itself.

Shared object libraries also make dynamic loading of program libraries on the fly possible (for example, perl, python, and/or tcl extensions and modules). The Apache (HTTP) Web server specifies modules in the **httpd.conf** file that it loads as needed.

The ldd (list dynamic dependencies) utility tells you which shared libraries a program needs. For example, the following shows that cp uses **libacl**,[2] the Access Control Lists library,[3] **libc**, the C library, **libattr**, the Extended Attributes library, and **ld-linux**, the runtime linker:

```
$ ldd /bin/cp
        libacl.so.1 => /lib/libacl.so.1 (0x40026000)
        libc.so.6 => /lib/i686/libc.so.6 (0x42000000)
        libattr.so.1 => /lib/libattr.so.1 (0x4002d000)
        /lib/ld-linux.so.2 => /lib/ld-linux.so.2 (0x40000000)
```

Running ldd on **/usr/bin/gnome-session** (a program that starts a GNOME session) lists 48 libraries from **/usr/lib**, **/usr/X11R6/lib**, and **/lib**.

The program that does the dynamic runtime linking, ld-linux.so, always looks in **/usr/lib** for libraries. The other directories that ld looks in varies, depending on how ld is set up. You can add directories for ld to look in by specifying a search path at compile (actually link) time, using the **–r** option followed by a colon-separated list of directories (do not put a SPACE after the **–r**). Use only absolute pathnames in the

---

2. Access Control Lists have not been fully implemented as of Red Hat 8.0.

3. Extended Attributes have not been fully implemented as of Red Hat 8.0.

search path. Although you use this option on the gcc command line, it is passed to the linker (ld). The gnome-session desktop manager was likely linked with a command such as the following:

>   *gcc **flags** –o gnome-session **objects** –r/lib:/usr/X11R6/lib **libraries***

This command line allows ld.so (and ldd) to search **/lib** and **/usr/X11R6/lib** in addition to the standard **/usr/lib** for the libraries the executable needs.

The compiler needs to see the shared libraries at link time to make sure that the needed functions and procedures are there as promised by the header (**.h**) files. Use the **–L** option to tell the compile-time linker to look in the directory **mylib** for shared or static libraries: **–L mylib**. Unlike the search path, **–L** can use relative pathnames, such as **–L ../lib**. This is handy when a program builds its own shared library. The library can be in one location at build time (**–L**) but in another location at runtime (after it is installed) (**–rpath**). (The SPACE after the **–L** is optional and is usually omitted. The **–r** must not be followed by a SPACE. You can repeat the **–L** and the **–r** options multiple times on the link line.)

Fixing Broken Binaries

The command line search path is a fairly new idea. The old way to create the search path was using the **LD_LIBRARY_PATH** and, more recently, **LD_RUN_PATH** environment variables. These variables have the same format as **PATH** (page 577). The directories in **LD_LIBRARY_PATH** are normally searched before the usual library locations. Newer GNU/Linux releases extend the function of **LD_LIBRARY_PATH** to specify directories to be searched either before or after the normal locations. See the ld man page for details. The **LD_RUN_PATH** variable behaves similarly to **LD_LIBRARY_PATH**, but if you use **–r**, **LD_LIBRARY_PATH** supersedes anything in **LD_RUN_PATH**.

The use of **LD_LIBRARY_PATH** has several problems. Because there is only one environment variable, it has to be shared among all programs. If two programs have the same name for a library or use different, incompatible versions of the same library, only the first will be found, and one of the programs will not run or, worse, will not run correctly.

LD_LIBRARY_PATH || security

Under certain circumstances a malicious user can create a Trojan horse named libc.so and place it in a directory that is searched before /usr/lib (any directory in LD_LIBRARY_PATH, which appears before /usr/lib). The fake libc will then be used instead of the real libc.

LD_LIBRARY_PATH still has its place in scripts, called *wrappers*, used to fix broken binaries. Suppose that the broken binary **bb** uses the shared library **libbb.so**, which you want to put in **/opt/bb/lib** and not **/usr/lib** as the bb programmer requested. The command **ldd bb** will tell you which libraries are missing. Not a problem; rename **bb** to **bb.broken** and create a **/bin/sh** wrapper named **bb**:

```
#!/bin/sh
LD_LIBRARY_PATH=/opt/bb/lib
export LD_LIBRARY_PATH
exec bb.broken "$@"
```

(The **$@** rather than **$*** preserves SPACEs in the parameters. See page 586.) This wrapper can also be used to install programs in arbitrary locations.

Creating Shared Libraries

Building a dynamically loadable shared library is not trivial: It involves using reentrant function calls, defining a library entrance routine, and performing other tasks. When you want to create a shared object library, you must, at a minimum, compile the source files with the **–fPIC** (position-independent code) option and link the resulting object files into the **lib*xx*.so** file, using the **–shared –x** options to the linker (for example, **ld –shared –x –o libmylib.so *.o**). The best resource for investigating shared library construction and usage is existing code on the Internet. You can start by looking at the source files for such programs as zlib (www.gzip.org/zlib).

C++ files have special needs, and libraries (shared or not) often have to be made by the compiler rather than ld or ar. Shared libraries can depend on other shared libraries and have their own search paths. If you set **LD_LIBRARY_PATH**, add the **–i** flag to the link phase when compiling to ignore the current **LD_LIBRARY_PATH**, or you may have unexpected results. Ideally you would not have **LD_LIBRARY_PATH** set at all on a global level but would use it only in wrappers as needed.

make: Keeps a Set of Programs Current

When you have a large program with many source and header files, the files typically depend on one another in complex ways. When you change a file that other files depend on, you *must* recompile all dependent files. For example, you might have several source files, all of which use a single header file. When you make a change to the header file, each of the source files must be recompiled. The header file might depend on other header files, and so forth. Figure 16-3 shows a simple example of dependency relationships. Each arrow in this figure points from a file to another file that depends on it. See also make on page 1247 in Part III.

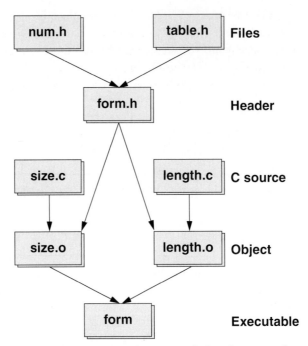

Figure 16-3   Dependency graph for the target **form**

When you are working on a large program, it can be difficult, time-consuming, and tedious to determine which modules need to be recompiled because of their dependency relationships. The make utility automates this process.

In its simplest use, make looks at *dependency lines* in a file named **Makefile** or **makefile** in the working directory. The dependency lines indicate relationships among files, specifying a *target file* that depends on one or more *prerequisite files*. If you have modified any of the prerequisite files more recently than their target file, make updates the target file based on construction commands that follow the dependency line. The make utility normally stops if it encounters an error during the construction process.

The file containing the updating information for the make utility is called a *makefile*. See page 838 for a trivial example. A simple makefile has the following syntax:

> *target: prerequisite-list*
> TAB *construction-commands*

The dependency line is composed of the **target** and the **prerequisite-list**, separated by a colon. Each **construction-commands** line (you may have more than one) must start with a TAB and must follow the dependency line. Long lines can be continued with a BACKSLASH (\) as the last character on the line.

The **target** is the name of the file that depends on the files in the **prerequisite-list**. The **construction-commands** are regular commands to the shell that construct (usually compile and/or link) the target file. The make utility executes the *construction-commands* when the modification time of one or more of the files in the *prerequisite-list* is more recent than that of the target file.

The following example shows the dependency line and construction commands for the file named **form** in Figure 16-3. The example depends on the prerequisites **size.o** and **length.o**. An appropriate gcc command constructs the **target**:

```
form: size.o length.o
TAB     gcc -o form size.o length.o
```

Each of the prerequisites on one dependency line can be a target on another dependency line. For example, both **size.o** and **length.o** are targets on other dependency lines. Although the example in Figure 16-3 is simple, the nesting of dependency specifications can create a complex hierarchy that specifies relationships among many files.

The following makefile (named **Makefile**) corresponds to the complete dependency graph shown in Figure 16-3. The executable file **form** depends on two object files, and the object files each depend on their respective source files and a header file, **form.h**. In turn, **form.h** depends on two other header files:

```
$ cat Makefile
form: size.o length.o
    gcc -o form size.o length.o
size.o: size.c form.h
    gcc -c size.c
length.o: length.c form.h
    gcc -c length.c
form.h: num.h table.h
    cat num.h table.h > form.h
```

Although the last line would not normally be seen in a makefile, it illustrates the fact that you can put any shell command on a construction line. Because makefiles are processed by the shell, the command line should be one that you could input in response to a shell prompt.

The following command builds the default target **form** if its prerequisites are more recent or if the target does not exist:

```
$ make
```

Thus, if the file **form** has been deleted, make will rebuild it, regardless of the modification dates of its prerequisite files. The first target in a makefile is the default and is built when you call make without any arguments.

If you want make to rebuild a target other than the first in the makefile, you must provide the target as an argument to make. The following command rebuilds only **form.h** if it does not exist or if its prerequisites are more recent:

```
$ make form.h
```

Implied Dependencies

You can rely on *implied* dependencies and construction commands to make your job of writing a makefile easier. For instance, if you do not include a dependency line for an object file, make assumes that it depends on a compiler or assembler source code file. Thus, if a prerequisite for a target file is **xxx.o** and there is no dependency line with **xxx.o** as a target, make looks at the extension to try to determine how to build the **.o** file. If it finds an appropriate source file, make provides a default construction command line that calls the proper compiler or the assembler to create the object file. Table 16-1 lists some of the filename extensions that make recognizes and the type of file that corresponds to the suffix.

Filename Extension	|| table 16-1
filename.c	C programming language source code
filename.C, filename.cc, filename.cxx, filename.c++, filename.cpp	C++ programming language source code
filename.f	FORTRAN programming language source code
filename.h	Header file
filename.l	flex, lex lexical analyzer generator source code
filename.o	Object module
filename.s	Assembler code
filename.sh	Shell scripts
filename.y	bison, yacc parser generator source code

C and C++ are traditional programming languages that are available with Red Hat. The bison and flex tools create command languages. The next example shows a makefile that keeps a file named **compute** up-to-date. The make utility ignores any line that begins with a pound sign (#). Thus the first three lines of the following makefile are comment lines. The first dependency line shows that **compute** depends on two object files: **compute.o** and **calc.o**. The corresponding construction line gives the command make needs to produce **compute**. The next dependency line shows that **compute.o** depends not only on its C source file but also on a header file, **compute.h**. The construction line for **compute.o** uses the C compiler optimizer (−O3 option). The third set of dependency and construction lines is not required.

In their absence make infers that **calc.o** depends on **calc.c** and produces the command line needed for the compilation:

```
$ cat Makefile
#
# Makefile for compute
#
compute: compute.o calc.o
        gcc -o compute compute.o calc.o

compute.o: compute.c compute.h
        gcc -c -03 compute.c

calc.o: calc.c
        gcc -c calc.c

clean:
    rm *.o *core* *~
```

There are no prerequisites for the last target, **clean,** in the preceding makefile. This target is commonly used to get rid of extraneous files that may be out of date or no longer needed, such as .o files.

Following are some sample executions of make, based on the previous makefile. As the ls command that follows shows, **compute.o, calc.o,** and **compute** are not up-to-date. Consequently, the make command runs the construction commands that recreate them.

```
$ ls -ltr
total 22
-rw-rw----  1 alex   pubs   311 Jun 21 15:56 makefile
-rw-rw----  1 alex   pubs   354 Jun 21 16:02 calc.o
-rwxrwx---  1 alex   pubs  6337 Jun 21 16:04 compute
-rw-rw----  1 alex   pubs    49 Jun 21 16:04 compute.h
-rw-rw----  1 alex   pubs   880 Jun 21 16:04 compute.o
-rw-rw----  1 alex   pubs   780 Jun 21 18:20 compute.c
-rw-rw----  1 alex   pubs   179 Jun 21 18:20 calc.c

$ make
gcc -c -03 compute.c
gcc -c calc.c
gcc -o compute compute.o calc.o
```

If you run make once and then run it again without making any changes to the prerequisite files, make indicates that the program is up-to-date and does not execute any commands.

```
$ make
make: 'compute' is up to date.
```

The following example uses the touch utility to change the modification time of a prerequisite file. This simulation shows what happens when you make a change to the file. The make utility executes only the commands necessary to make the out-of-date targets up-to-date:

```
$ touch calc.c
$ make
gcc -c calc.c
gcc -o compute compute.o calc.o
```

In the next example touch changes the modification time of **compute.h**. The make utility recreates **compute.o** because it depends on **compute.h** and recreates the executable because it depends on **compute.o**:

```
$ touch compute.h
$ make
gcc -c -O3 compute.c
gcc -o compute compute.o calc.o
```

As these examples illustrate, touch is useful when you want to fool make into recompiling programs or into *not* recompiling them. You can use touch to update the modification times of all the source files so that make considers that nothing is up-to-date. The make utility will then recompile everything. Alternatively, you can use touch or the **–t** option to make to touch all relevant files so that make considers everything to be up-to-date. This is useful if the modification times of files have changed yet the files are all up-to-date (as happens when you copy a set of files from one directory to another). If you want to see what make *would* do if you ran it, run make with the **–n** option. The **–n** option shows the commands that make would execute, but it does not execute them.

Once you are satisfied with the program you have created, you can use the makefile to clean out the files you no longer need. It is useful to keep intermediate files around while you are writing and debugging your program, so that you need rebuild only the ones that change. If you will not be working on the program again for a while, though, you should release the disk space. The advantage of using a **clean** target in your makefile is that you do not have to remember all the little pieces that can safely be deleted. The example that follows simply removes all the object (.o) files:

```
$ make clean
rm *.o
```

Optional

Macros

The make utility's macro facility enables you to create and use macros within a makefile. The syntax of a macro definition is

ID = list

Replace *ID* with an identifying name, and replace *list* with a list of filenames. After this macro definition, $(ID) represents *list* in the makefile.

You can use a macro so that you can compile a program with any of several C compilers, making only a minor change to the makefile. By using the **CC** macro and replacing all occurrences of gcc in the makefile on page 853 with $(CC), you need to assign a value only to **CC** to use the compiler of your choice.[4] (There are commercial, high-performance compilers available for GNU/Linux. The compiler from the Portland Group, pgcc, could be specified by replacing the CC=gcc assignment with CC=pgcc.)

```
$ cat Makefile
#
# Makefile for compute
#
CC=gcc
compute: compute.o calc.o
        $(CC) -o compute compute.o calc.o

compute.o: compute.c compute.h
        $(CC) -c -O3 compute.c

calc.o: calc.c
        $(CC) -c calc.c

clean:
        rm *.o
```

If you do not assign a value to the **CC** macro, it defaults to gcc under GNU/Linux. The **CC** macro invokes the C compiler with only the options that you specify.

Additional macro definitions are commonly used in programs. The **CFLAGS** macro sends arguments to the C compiler, **LDFLAGS** sends arguments to the linker (ld, or gcc –o), and **CPPFLAGS** sends arguments to the C preprocessor and programs that use it, including gcc. The **COMPILE.c** macro expands to $(CC) –c $(CFLAGS) $(CPPFLAGS), and **LINK.c** expands to $(CC) $(CFLAGS) $(CPP-FLAGS) $(LDFLAGS).

By default make invokes the C compiler without any options (except the –c option when it is appropriate to compile but not to link a file). You can use the **CFLAGS** macro definition, shown next, to cause make to call the C compiler with specific options. Replace *options* with the options you want to use:

CFLAGS = options

---

4. This example assumes that the compiler/loader flags are the same across compilers/loaders. In a more complex situation, you will need to create macros for these flags or stay with the default values.

The following makefile uses macros, as well as implied dependencies and constructions:

```
# makefile: report, print, printf, printh
#
CC=gcc
CFLAGS = -O3
# comment out the two lines above and uncomment the
# two below when you are using the Portland Group's compiler
#CC=pgcc
#CFLAGS = -fast
FILES = in.c out.c ratio.c process.c tally.c
OBJECTS = in.o out.o ratio.o process.o tally.o
HEADERS = names.h companies.h conventions.h

report: $(OBJECTS)
        $(LINK.c) -o report $(OBJECTS)

ratio.o: $(HEADERS)

process.o: $(HEADERS)

tally.o: $(HEADERS)

print:
    pr $(FILES) $(HEADERS) | lp

printf:
    pr $(FILES) | lp

printh:
    pr $(HEADERS) | lp
```

Following the comment lines, the makefile uses the **CFLAGS** macro to cause make always to use the optimizer (**–O3** option) when it invokes the C compiler as the result of an implied construction. (The **CC** and **CFLAGS** definitions for the pgcc C compiler perform the same functions when they are uncommented and you are using pgcc, except that you use **–fast** with pgcc in place of **–O3** with gcc.) Whenever you put a construction line in a makefile, the construction line overrides the corresponding implied construction line, if one exists. If you want to apply a macro to a construction command, you must include the macro in that command. This was done, for example, with **OBJECTS** in the construction command for the **report** target. Following **CFLAGS**, the makefile defines the **FILES**, **OBJECTS**, and **HEADERS** macros. Each of these macros defines a list of files.

The first dependency line shows that **report** depends on the list of files that **OBJECTS** defines. The corresponding construction line links the **OBJECTS** and creates an executable file named **report**.

The next three dependency lines show that three object files depend on the list of files that **HEADERS** defines. There are no construction lines, so when it is necessary, make looks for a source code file corresponding to each of the object files and compiles it. These three dependency lines ensure that the object files are recompiled if any of the header files is changed.

Finally, the **LINK.c** macro is invoked to link the executable file. If you specify any **LDFLAGS**, they are used in this step.

You can combine several targets on one dependency line, so these three dependency lines could have been combined into one line as follows:

```
ratio.o process.o tally.o: $(HEADERS)
```

The three final dependency lines send source and header files to the printer. They have nothing to do with compiling the **report** file. None of these targets (**print**, **printf**, and **printh**) depends on anything. When you call one of these targets from the command line, make executes the construction line following it. The following command prints all the source files that **FILES** defines:

```
$ make printf
```

You can override macros in a makefile by specifying them on the command line, causing debugging symbols to be added to all object files:

```
$ make CFLAGS=-g ...
```

Debugging C Programs

The C compiler is liberal about the kinds of constructs it allows in programs. In keeping with the UNIX philosophy that "no news is good news" and that the user knows what is best, gcc, like many other GNU/Linux utilities, accepts almost anything that is logically possible according to the definition of the language. Although this approach gives the programmer a great deal of flexibility and control, it can make debugging difficult.

Figure 16-4 shows **badtabs.c,** a flawed version of the **tabs.c** program discussed earlier. It contains some errors and does not run properly but illustrates some debugging techniques.

In the following example, **badtabs.c** is compiled and then run with input from the **testtabs** file. Inspection of the output shows that the TAB character has not been replaced with the proper number of SPACEs:

```
$ gcc -o badtabs badtabs.c
$ cat testtabs
abcTABxyz
$ badtabs < testtabs
abc    xyz
```

```
 1  /* convert tabs in standard input to spaces in */
 2  /* standard output while maintaining columns */
 3
 4  #include        <stdio.h>
 5  #define         TABSIZE         8
 6
 7  /* prototype for function findstop */
 8  int findstop(int *);
 9
10  main()
11  {
12  int c;          /* character read from stdin */
13  int posn = 0;   /* column position of character */
14  int inc;        /* column increment to tab stop */
15
16  while ((c = getchar()) != EOF)
17          switch(c)
18                  {
19                  case '\t':               /* c is a tab */
20                          inc = findstop(&posn);
21                          for( ; inc > 0; inc-- )
22                                  putchar(' ');
23                          break;
24                  case '\n':               /* c is a newline */
25                          putchar(c);
26                          posn = 0;
27                          break;
28                  default:                 /* c is anything else */
29                          putchar(c);
30                          posn++;
31                          break;
32                  }
33
34  }
35
36  /* compute size of increment to next tab stop */
37
38  int findstop(int *col)
39  {
40  int colindex, retval;
41  retval = (TABSIZE - (*col % TABSIZE));
42
43  /* increment argument (current column position) to next tabstop * /
44  *col += retval;
45
46  return retval;          /* main gets how many blanks for filling */
47  }
```

| Comments |
| Preprocessor Directives |
| Function Prototype |
| Main Function |
| Function |

Figure 16-4   The **badtabs.c** program (The line numbers are not part of the source code; the arrows point to errors in the program.)

One way to debug a C program is to insert **print** statements at critical points throughout the source code. To learn more about the behavior of **badtabs.c** when it runs, you can replace the contents of the **switch** statement with

```
case '\t':                /* c is a tab */
    fprintf(stderr, "before call to findstop, posn is %d\n", posn);
    inc = findstop(&posn);
    fprintf(stderr, "after call to findstop, posn is %d\n", posn);
    for( ; inc > 0; inc-- )
        putchar(' ');
    break;
```

```
case '\n':                 /* c is a newline */
    fprintf(stderr, "got a newline\n");
    putchar(c);
    posn = 0;
    break;
default:                    /* c is anything else */
    fprintf(stderr, "got another character\n");
    putchar(c);
    posn++;
    break;
```

The **fprintf** statements in this code send their messages to standard error, so if you redirect standard output of this program, it will not be interspersed with the output sent to standard error. Following is an example that demonstrates the operation of this program on the input file **testtabs**:

```
$ gcc -o badtabs badtabs.c
$ badtabs < testtabs > testspaces
got another character
got another character
got another character
before call to findstop, posn is 3
after call to findstop, posn is 3
got another character
got another character
got another character
got a newline
$ cat testspaces
abc    xyz
```

The **fprintf** statements provide additional information about the execution **of tabs.c,** especially that the value of the variable **posn** is not incremented in **findstop,** as it should be. This might be enough to lead you to the bug in the program. If not, you might attempt to "corner" the offending code by inserting **fprintf** statements in **findstop.**

For simple programs or when you have an idea of what is wrong with your program, adding **print** statements that trace the execution of the code can often help you solve the problem quickly. A better strategy may be to switch to one of the tools that GNU/Linux provides to help you debug programs.

gcc: Compiler Warning Options Find Errors in Programs

The gcc compiler has many of the features of lint, the classic C program verifier,[5] built into it and then some. This compiler is able to identify many C program constructs

---

5. Not available for Red Hat; use splint (secure programming lint, www.splint.org) instead.

that pose potential problems, even for programs that conform to the syntax rules of the language. For instance, if you request, the compiler can report whether a variable is declared but not used, a comment is not properly terminated, or a function returns a type not permitted in older versions of C. Options that enable this stricter compiler behavior all begin with the uppercase letter W (Warning).

Among the **−W** options is a class of warnings that typically result from programmer carelessness or inexperience. The constructs causing these warnings are generally easy to fix and easy to avoid. Table 16-2 lists some of these options.

−W Option	Reports These Errors	‖ table 16-2
−Wimplicit	When a function or parameter is not explicitly declared	
−Wreturn-type	When a function that is not void does not return a value, or when the type of a function defaults to **int**	
−Wunused	When a variable is declared but not used	
−Wcomment	When the characters /*, which normally begin a comment, are seen within a comment	
−Wformat	When certain input/output statements contain format specifications that do not match the arguments	

To get warnings about all the preceding errors, along with others in this class, use the **−Wall** option.

The program **badtabs.c** is syntactically correct (it compiles without generating an error). However, if you compile (**−c** causes gcc to compile but not to link) it with the **−Wall** option, you see several problems:[6]

```
$ gcc -c -Wall badtabs.c
badtabs.c:47: warning: '/*' within comment
badtabs.c:11: warning: return-type defaults to 'int'
badtabs.c: In function 'main':
badtabs.c:34: warning: control reaches end of non-void function
badtabs.c: In function 'findstop':
badtabs.c:40: warning: unused variable 'colindex'
badtabs.c:49: warning: control reaches end of non-void function
```

The first warning message references line 47. Inspection of the code for **badtabs.c** around that line reveals a comment that is not properly terminated. The compiler sees the string /* in the following line as the beginning of a comment:

---

6. Warning messages do not stop the program from compiling, whereas error messages do.

```
/* increment argument (current column position) to next tabstop * /
```

However, because the characters * and / at the end of the line are separated by a SPACE, they do not signify the end of the comment to the compiler. Instead the compiler interprets all the statements, including the statement that increments the argument, through the string */ at the very end of the **findstop** function as part of the comment.

Compiling with the **–Wall** option can be very helpful when debugging a program. By removing the SPACE between the characters * and /, **badtabs** produces the correct output.

The next few paragraphs discuss the remaining warning messages. Although most do not cause problems in the execution of **badtabs**, programs can generally be improved by rewriting parts of the code that produce warnings.

Because the definition of the function **main** does not include an explicit type, the compiler assumes type **int**, the default. This results in the warning message referencing line 11 in **badtabs.c**, the top of the function **main**. An additional warning is given when the compiler encounters the end of the function **main** (line 34) without seeing a value returned.

If a program runs successfully, it should, by convention, return a zero value; if no value is returned, the exit code is undefined. Although it is common to see C programs that do not return a value, the oversight can cause problems when the program is executed. When you add the following statement at the end of the function **main** in **badtabs.c**, the warning referencing line 34 disappears:

```
return 0;
```

Line 40 of **badtabs.c** contains the definition for the local variable **colindex** in the function **findstop**. The warning message referencing that line occurs because the **colindex** variable is never used. Removing its declaration gets rid of the warning message.

The final warning message, referencing line 49, results from the improperly terminated comment discussed earlier. The compiler issues the warning message because it never sees a return statement in **findstop**. (The compiler ignores commented text.) Because the function **findstop** returns type **int**, the compiler expects a return statement before reaching the end of the function. The warning disappears when the comment is properly terminated.

Many other **–W** options are available with the gcc compiler. The ones not covered in the **–Wall** class often involve portability differences; modifying the code causing these warnings may not be appropriate. The warnings usually result from programs written in different C dialects as well as from constructs that may not work well with other (especially older) C compilers. To learn more about these and other warning options, see gcc on page 1210 in Part III. Also refer to the gcc info page.

Symbolic Debugger

Many debuggers are available to tackle problems that evade the simpler methods involving print statements and compiler warning options. These debuggers include gdb, kdbg, and xxgdb (supplied with Red Hat) and mxgdb, ddd, and ups, which are available from the Web (refer to Appendix B). All are high-level symbolic debuggers, enabling you to analyze the execution of a program in terms of C language statements. The debuggers also provide a lower-level view for analyzing the execution of a program in terms of the machine instructions. Except for gdb, each of the debuggers mentioned in this paragraph provides a GUI.

A debugger enables you to monitor and control the execution of a program. You can step through a program line by line while you examine the state of the execution environment. A debugger also allows you to examine *core* files. (Core files are named **core**.) When a serious error occurs during the execution of a program, the operating system can create a core file containing information about the state of the program and the system when the error occurred. This file is a dump of the computer's memory (it used to be called *core memory*; thus the term *core dump*) that was being used by the program. To conserve disk space, your system may be set up so that core files are not saved. You can use the ulimit ^{bash}_{zsh} or limit ^{tcsh} builtin to enable core files to be saved. If you are running bash, the following command allows core files of unlimited size to be saved to disk:

```
$ ulimit -c unlimited
```

The operating system advises you when it dumps core. You can use a symbolic debugger to read information from the core file to identify the line in the program where the error occurred, to check the values of variables at that point, and so forth. Because core files tend to be large, be sure to remove them when you are done.

gdb: Symbolic Debugger

The following examples demonstrate the use of the GNU gdb debugger. Other symbolic debuggers offer a different interface but operate in a similar manner. To make full use of a symbolic debugger with a program, it is necessary to compile the program with the **–g** option. The **–g** option causes gcc to generate additional information that the debugger uses. This information includes a *symbol table*—a list of variable names used in the program and associated values. Without the symbol table information, the debugger is unable to display the values and types of variables. If a program is compiled without the **–g** option, gdb is unable to identify source code lines by number, as many gdb commands require. The following example uses the **–g** option when creating the executable file **tabs** from the C program **tabs.c**, discussed at the beginning of this chapter:

```
$ gcc -g tabs.c -o tabs
```

Input for **tabs** is contained in the file **testtabs**, which consists of a single line:

```
$ cat testtabs
xyzTABabc
```

Avoid Using Optimization Flags with the Debugger   ‖ tip

Limit the optimization flags to –O or –O2 when you compile a program for debugging. Because debugging and optimizing inherently have different goals, it may be best to avoid combining the two.

You cannot specify the input file to **tabs** when you first call the debugger. Specify the input file once you have called the debugger and started execution with the **run** command.

To run the debugger on the sample executable, give the name of the executable file on the command line when you run gdb. You will see some introductory statements about gdb, followed by the gdb prompt (gdb). The debugger is ready to accept commands. The **list** command displays the first ten lines of source code. A subsequent **list** command displays the next ten lines of source code:

```
$ gdb tabs
GNU gdb 4.18
Copyright 1998 Free Software Foundation, Inc.
GDB is free software, covered by the GNU General Public License,
and you are welcome to change it and/or distribute copies of it
under certain conditions.
Type "show copying" to see the conditions.
There is absolutely no warranty for GDB.  Type "show warranty" for details.
This GDB was configured as "i386-redhat-linux"
(gdb) list
4       #include        <stdio.h>
5       #define         TABSIZE         8
6
7       /* prototype for function findstop */
8       int findstop(int *);
9
10      int main()
11      {
12      int c;          /* character read from stdin */
13      int posn = 0;   /* column position of character */
(gdb) list
14      int inc;        /* column increment to tab stop */
15
16      while ((c = getchar()) != EOF)
17              switch(c)
18                      {
19                      case '\t':              /* c is a tab */
20                              inc = findstop(&posn);
21                              for( ; inc > 0; inc-- )
22                                      putchar(' ');
23                              break;
(gdb)
```

One of the most important features of a debugger is the ability to run a program in a controlled environment. You can stop the program from running whenever you want. While it is stopped, you can check on the state of an argument or variable. The **break** command can be given a source code line number, an actual memory address, or a function name as an argument. The following command tells gdb to stop the process whenever the function **findstop** is called:

```
(gdb) break findstop
Breakpoint 1 at 0x804849f: file tabs.c, line 41.
(gdb)
```

The debugger acknowledges the request by displaying the breakpoint number, the hexadecimal memory address of the breakpoint, and the corresponding source code line number (41). The debugger numbers breakpoints in ascending order as you create them, starting with 1.

Having set a breakpoint, you can issue a **run** command to start execution of **tabs** under the control of the debugger. The **run** command syntax allows you to use angle brackets to redirect input and output (just as the shells do). Following, the **testtabs** file is specified as input. When the process stops (at the breakpoint), you can use the **print** command to check the value of ∗**col**. The **backtrace** (or **bt**) command displays the function stack. The example shows that the currently active function has been assigned the number 0. The function that called **findstop** (**main**) has been assigned the number 1:

```
(gdb) run < testtabs
Starting program: /home/mark/book/14/tabs < testtabs

Breakpoint 1, findstop (col=0xbffffc70) at tabs.c:41
41      retval = (TABSIZE - (*col % TABSIZE));
(gdb) print *col
$1 = 3
(gdb) backtrace
#0  findstop (col=0xbffffc70) at tabs.c:41
#1  0x804843a in main () at tabs.c:20
(gdb)
```

You can examine anything in the current scope, including variables and arguments in the active function as well as globals. The following example shows that the request to examine the value of the variable **posn** at breakpoint 1 results in an error. The error results because the variable **posn** is defined locally in the function **main**, not in the function **findstop**:

```
(gdb) print posn
No symbol "posn" in current context.
```

The **up** command changes the active function to the caller of the currently active function. Because **main** calls the function **findstop**, the function **main** becomes the active function when the **up** command is given. (The **down** command does the inverse.) The **up** command may be given an integer argument specifying the number of levels in the function stack to backtrack, with **up 1** meaning the same as **up**. (You can use the **backtrace** command, if necessary, to determine the argument to use with **up**.)

```
(gdb) up
#1  0x804843a in main () at tabs.c:20
20                              inc = findstop(&posn);
(gdb) print posn
$2 = 3
(gdb) print *col
No symbol "col" in current context.
(gdb)
```

The **cont** (continue) command causes the process to continue running from where it left off. The **testtabs** file contains only one line; the process finishes executing, and the results appear on the screen. The debugger reports the exit code of the program. A **cont** command given after a program has finished executing reminds you that execution of the program has completed. Following, the debugging session is ended with a **quit** command:

```
(gdb) cont
Continuing.
abc     xyz

Program exited normally.
(gdb) cont
The program is not being run.
(gdb) quit
$
```

The **gdb** utility supports many commands that are designed to make debugging easier. Type **help** at the (gdb) prompt to get a list of the command classes available under **gdb**:

```
(gdb) help
List of classes of commands:

aliases -- Aliases of other commands
breakpoints -- Making program stop at certain points
data -- Examining data
files -- Specifying and examining files
internals -- Maintenance commands
obscure -- Obscure features
running -- Running the program
stack -- Examining the stack
status -- Status inquiries
support -- Support facilities
tracepoints -- Tracing of program execution without stopping the program
user-defined -- User-defined commands
```

```
Type "help" followed by a class name for a list of commands in that class.
Type "help" followed by command name for full documentation.
Command name abbreviations are allowed if unambiguous.
(gdb)
```

As given in the instructions following the list, entering **help** followed by the name of a command class or command name will give more information. The following lists the commands in the class **data:**

```
(gdb) help data
Examining data.

List of commands:

call -- Call a function in the program
delete display -- Cancel some expressions to be displayed when program stops
disable display -- Disable some expressions to be displayed when program stops
disassemble -- Disassemble a specified section of memory
display -- Print value of expression EXP each time the program stops
enable display -- Enable some expressions to be displayed when program stops
inspect -- Same as "print" command
output -- Like "print" but don't put in value history and don't print newline
print -- Print value of expression EXP
printf -- Printf "printf format string"
ptype -- Print definition of type TYPE
set -- Evaluate expression EXP and assign result to variable VAR
set variable -- Evaluate expression EXP and assign result to variable VAR
undisplay -- Cancel some expressions to be displayed when program stops
whatis -- Print data type of expression EXP
x -- Examine memory: x/FMT ADDRESS

Type "help" followed by command name for full documentation.
Command name abbreviations are allowed if unambiguous.
(gdb)
```

The following requests information on the command **whatis**, which takes a variable name or other expression as an argument:

```
(gdb) help whatis
Print data type of expression EXP.
```

Graphical Symbolic Debuggers

There are several GUIs to gdb. Two interfaces that are similar are xxgdb and mxgdb (a Motif-based interface that requires that you have Motif installed on your system). These graphical versions of gdb provide you with a number of windows, including a Source Listing window, a Command window that contains a set of commonly used commands, and a Display window for viewing the values of variables. The left mouse button selects commands from the Command window. You can click the desired line in the Source Listing window to set a breakpoint, and you can select variables by clicking them in the Source Listing window. Selecting a variable and clicking print in the Command window display the value of the variable in the Display window. You can view lines of source code by scrolling (and resizing) the Source Listing window.

The ddd debugger also provides a GUI to gdb. Unlike xxgdb and mxgdb, ddd can graphically display complex C structures and the links between them. This display makes it easier to see errors in these structures. Otherwise, the ddd interface is very similar to that of xxgdb and mxgdb.

Unlike xxgdb and mxgdb, ups was designed from the ground up to work as a debugger with a GUI; the graphical interface was not added on after the debugger was complete. The result is an interface that is simple yet powerful. For example, ups automatically displays the value of a variable when you click it and has a built-in C interpreter that allows you to attach C code to the program you are debugging. Because this attached code has access to the variables and values in the program, you can use it to perform sophisticated checks, such as following and displaying the links in a complex *data structure* (page 1463).

Threads

A *thread* is a single sequential flow of control within a process. Threads are the basis for multithreaded programs, which allow a single program to control concurrently running threads, each performing a different task. Multithreaded programs generally use *reentrant* code (code that multiple threads can use simultaneously) and are most valuable when run on multiple-CPU machines. Under GNU/Linux multithreaded servers, such as NFS, can provide a cleaner interface and may be easier to write than multiple server processes. When applied judiciously, multithreading can also serve as a lower-overhead replacement for the traditional fork-exec idiom for spawning processes. See the FAQ at tldp.org/FAQ/Threads-FAQ.

Multiple Threads Are Not Always Better || tip

If you write a multithreaded program with no clear goal or division of effort for a single CPU machine (for example, a parallel-server process), you are likely to end up with a program that runs more slowly than a nonthreaded program on the same machine.

System Calls

Three fundamental responsibilities of the Linux kernel are to control processes, manage the filesystem, and operate peripheral devices. As a programmer you have access to these kernel operations through system calls and library functions. This section discusses system calls at a general level; a detailed treatment is beyond the scope of this book.

As the name implies, a system call instructs the system (kernel) to perform some work directly on your behalf. The request is a message that tells the kernel what work needs to be done and includes the necessary arguments. For example, a system call to open a file includes the name of the file. A library routine is indirect; it issues system calls for you. The advantages of a library routine are that it may insulate you from the low-level details of kernel operations and that it has been written carefully to make sure that it performs efficiently.

For example, it is straightforward to use the standard I/O library function **fprintf( )** to send text to standard output or standard error. Without this function you would need to issue several system calls to achieve the same result. The calls to the library routines **putchar( )** and **getchar( )** in Figure 16-1 ultimately use the **write( )** and **read( )** system calls to perform the I/O operations.

strace: Traces System Calls

The strace utility is a debugging tool that prints out a trace of all the system calls made by a process or program. Because you do not need to recompile the program that you want to trace, you can use strace on binaries that you do not have source for.

System calls are events that take place at the interface (boundary) between user code and kernel code. Examining this boundary can help you isolate bugs, track down race conditions, and perform sanity checking. The Linux kernel does not fully cooperate with strace. See the strace home page (www.liacs.nl/~wichert/strace) for kernel patches that improve kernel cooperation with strace.

Controlling Processes

When you enter a command line at a shell prompt, the shell process calls the **fork** system call to create a copy of itself (spawn a child) and then uses an **exec** system call to overlay that copy in memory with a different program (the command you asked it to run). Table 16-3 lists system calls that affect processes.

System Call: Processes Control || table 16-3

fork()	Creates a copy of a process
exec()	Overlays a program in memory with another
getpid()	Returns the process ID of the calling process
wait()	Causes the parent process to wait for the child to finish running before it resumes execution
exit()	Causes a process to exit
nice()	Changes the priority of a process
kill()	Sends a signal to a process

Accessing the Filesystem

Many operations take place when a program reads from or writes to a file. The program needs to know where the file is located; the filename must be converted to an inode number on the correct filesystem. Your access permissions must be checked not only for the file itself but also for all the intervening directories in the path to the file. The file is not stored in one continuous piece on the disk; all the disk blocks that contain pieces of the file must be located. The appropriate kernel device driver must be called to control the operation of the disk. Finally, once the file has been found, the program may need to find a particular location within the file rather than working with it sequentially from beginning to end. Table 16-4 lists some of the most common system calls in filesystem operations.

System Call: Filesystem || table 16-4

stat()	Gets status information from an inode, such as the inode number, the device on which it is located, owner and group information, and the size of the file
lseek()	Moves to a position in the file
creat()	Creates a new file

System Call: Filesystem (Continued)	|| table 16-4
open( )	Opens an existing file
read( )	Reads a file
write( )	Writes a file
close( )	Closes a file
unlink( )	Unlinks a file (deletes a name reference to the inode)
chmod( )	Changes file access permissions
chown( )	Changes file ownership

Access to peripheral devices on a UNIX/Linux system is handled through the filesystem interface. Each peripheral device is represented by one or more special files, usually located under **/dev**. When you read or write to one of these special files, the kernel passes your requests to the appropriate kernel device driver. As a result, you can use the standard system calls and library routines to interact with these devices; you do not need to learn a new set of specialized functions. This is one of the most powerful features of a UNIX/Linux system because it allows users to use the same basic utilities on a wide range of devices.

The availability of standard system calls and library routines is the key to the portability of GNU/Linux tools. For example, as an applications programmer, you can rely on the read and write system calls working the same way on different versions of the GNU/Linux system and on different types of computers. The systems programmer who writes a device driver or ports the kernel to run on a new computer, however, must understand the details at their lowest level.

Source Code Management

When you work on a project involving many files that evolve over long periods of time, it can be difficult to keep track of the versions of the files, particularly if several people are updating the files. This problem frequently occurs in large software development projects. Source code and documentation files change frequently as you fix bugs, enhance programs, and release new versions of the software. It becomes even more complex when more than one version of each file is active. Frequently customers are using one version of a file while a newer version is being modified. You can easily lose track of the versions and accidentally undo changes or duplicate earlier work.

To help avoid these kinds of problems, GNU/Linux includes utilities for managing and tracking changes to files. These utilities comprise two source code management systems: RCS (Revision Control System, www.gnu.org/software/rcs) and CVS (Concurrent Versions System, www.cvshome.org), which is built on top of RCS. Although they can be used on any file, these tools are most often used to manage source code and software documentation. RCS is oriented toward managing version control over the files in a single directory, whereas CVS expands version control across a hierarchical set of directories. CVS is based on RCS and is designed to control the concurrent access and modification of source files by multiple users.

A graphical front end to CVS, tkCVS (www.twobarleycorns.net/tkcvs.html), simplifies the use of CVS, especially if you do not use it frequently enough to memorize its many commands and options. Another excellent front end is cervisia, which comes with Red Hat.

All three programs/interfaces control who is allowed to update files. For each update, the programs record who made the changes and include notes about why the changes were made. Because they store the most recent version of a file and the information needed to recreate all previous versions, it is possible to regenerate any version of a file.

A set of file versions for several files may be grouped together to form a *release*. An entire release can be recreated from the change information stored with each file. Saving the changes for a file rather than a complete copy of the file generally conserves a lot of disk space, well in excess of the space required to store each update in the RCS and CVS files themselves.

The following sections provide overviews of RCS, CVS, and tkCVS. Because CVS is built on RCS, these two systems function similarly; study the RCS sections even if you are planning on using CVS or tkCVS. As a general rule, you should pick one source code management system and use it for all your work. Which one you choose may depend on personal preference, the type of work put under source code management, and whether others are sharing the same files. See the *CVS-RCS-HOW-TO Document for Linux* for more information.

RCS: Revision Control System

When you change a file and record the changes using RCS, the set of changes is called a *revision*. The revision is stored in an *RCS file*, which includes any previous revisions of the file, descriptive text for each revision, and additional identifying information. RCS filenames always end with **,v** and are generally not edited. The file you are working with and possibly changing with an editor (for example, vi or emacs) is called the *working file* and has no special naming convention.

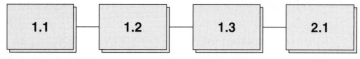

Figure 16-5   The evolution of an RCS file

When you *check out* a file, you retrieve, or extract, a working file from an RCS file. To update an RCS file from a working file, you *check in* the file. RCS automatically creates an RCS file the first time you check in a working file.

If two users edit two copies of the same file at the same time, after the first user checks in the file, that user's changes will be overwritten (and lost) when the second user checks in the file. To prevent this loss of data, RCS provides a locking mechanism for working files. If you are working with a locked copy of the working file, no other user can retrieve a locked copy of the same file. Also, no one can check in an unlocked file.

You can check out an RCS file (and create a working file) in two modes: locked or not locked. Unlocked revisions are retrieved as readonly files. There are no additional restrictions beyond GNU/Linux file permissions on unlocked working files. If you want to check out a locked working file from an RCS file, you must be authorized to do so. You are always authorized if you are the owner of the file or Superuser. Otherwise, you must appear on the list of users permitted to retrieve the file, if such a list exists. Refer to "The rlog Utility" on page 876.

The ci (check in) utility records the changes you have made to a locked working file. Because checking in a file alters the RCS file, you must be authorized to use the ci utility. This means that you must either appear on the access list for the file or be the owner of the file or Superuser. When you check in a file, RCS updates the matching RCS file with the changes and, unless you specify otherwise, removes the working file. Along with the changed text, RCS records the author, date, time, and a message summarizing the changes. Each revision is associated with a *revision number* consisting of an even number of integer fields separated by periods. By default RCS assigns the number 1.1 to the first revision of a file and increments the rightmost field of a revision number to get the next revision number. This results in the sequence 1.1, 1.2, 1.3, and so on, with a new revision number assigned each time you check in a file. The −r option to ci allows you to specify a revision number of your choice. It can be used to skip revision numbers, as shown in Figure 16-5, where revision number 1.3 is followed by the number 2.1. Refer to "Using the −r Option to Specify a Revision" on page 876.

Files usually undergo a sequential development, with each revision based on all previous revisions. This is the kind of development shown in Figure 16-5. Although both left and right fields in the revision numbers change, the numbers can still be arranged in a linear sequence. When changes occur to intermediate versions of a file,

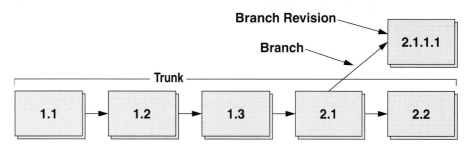

Figure 16-6   A branch in the evolution of an RCS file

it is more natural to represent the changes by using a tree structure. For example, if you are working on revision 2.2 of the file shown in Figure 16-6 and have to make a custom change to revision 2.1 to deliver to a customer, you will want to record a revision that reflects that customization but that excludes the changes involved in revision 2.2. For this customization, you can create a *branch revision* at revision 2.1. All branch revision numbers consist of an even number of four or more fields. Those revisions consisting of exactly two fields compose the *trunk*.

In Figure 16-6 revision 2.1 has a branch, branch 2.1.1, that has a single revision numbered 2.1.1.1. Successive revisions on that branch would be 2.1.1.2, 2.1.1.3, and so forth. The next branch at revision 2.1 would be 2.1.2.

With RCS you can merge two revisions to produce a new revision. The new revision can incorporate the changes made on a branch that split off at some earlier point. The merging of revisions is shown in Figure 16-7, where revision 2.1.1.1 and the working revision (revision 2.2) are merged. When the merged revision is checked in, it is given the number 2.3. See the rcsmerge man page for more information on merging file revisions.

The evolution of an RCS file can become complicated when there are many *branch revisions*. When you check in a file, try to keep the evolution of the versions as simple as possible. You should check in a revision to a file only when you are sure that the changes you have made are complete. For example, when you are fixing a

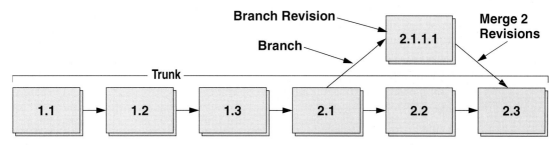

Figure 16-7   Merging two RCS files

group of bugs in a file, you should fix and test all of them before checking in the new revision. This technique saves you from having revisions that reflect incomplete, transitional stages in the history of a file.

The ci Utility

The ci (check in) utility creates or updates an RCS file. The syntax of ci is

> *ci [options] file-list*

For each file in *file-list,* ci creates or updates an RCS file. Because RCS files and working files are automatically paired, RCS utilities permit you to use either filename to stand for the other or to stand for the pair. The name of the working file is usually given in *file-list.*

In the following example the user checks in the file **xbuff.c** for the first time. Before the ci command is given, a listing of the working directory includes the working file **xbuff.c** as well as a subdirectory named RCS:

```
$ ls
RCS xbuff.c
$ ci xbuff.c
RCS/xbuff.c,v <-- xbuff.c
enter description, terminated with single '.' or end of file:
NOTE: This is NOT the log message!
>> This file contains functions to display a buffer in an X-window.
>> It can optionally print or save the buffer.
>> .
initial revision: 1.1
done
$ ls
RCS
$ ls RCS
xbuff.c,v
```

RCS generates the name of the RCS file for **xbuff.c** by adding the extension **,v,** yielding the name **xbuff.c,v.** RCS first checks whether a subdirectory named RCS is in the working file's directory—the working directory in this case. Finding a subdirectory with that name, RCS creates the RCS file there. Had it not found a subdirectory with that name, RCS would have created the RCS file in the working file's directory. Because it is the initial check in for **xbuff.c,** RCS asks for a description of the file **xbuff.c,** which must be terminated with a period or an end-of-file character (CONTROL-D) on a line by itself. Each subsequent revision of **xbuff.c** will require a brief log message prior to the insertion of the revision into the RCS file. Each log message is also terminated with a period or a CONTROL-D on a line by itself. When the ci command is completed, the working file **xbuff.c** no longer appears in a listing of the working directory.

If the **–l** (lock) option is used with the ci utility, the working file is not removed. This permits subsequent editing of the working file. The **–u** (unlock) option is similar but retains a readonly version of the file. These two options are often used with the ci utility and the co utility (discussed in the next section).

The co Utility

The co (check out) utility uses the RCS file to recreate a revision that it stores in the corresponding working file. The co utility in the following example specifies the working file **xbuff.c**; the latest revision on the trunk is checked out by default:

```
$ ls
RCS
$ co xbuff.c
RCS/xbuff.c,v --> xbuff.c
revision 1.1
done
$ ls
RCS xbuff.c
```

Checking out a revision in this way produces a working file with readonly permission: RCS assumes that you want to look only at the current revision and that you do not plan to produce a new revision. The readonly permission is established by the same locking mechanism that prevents more than one user from checking out, editing, and checking in a file.

While you have a revision locked, RCS prevents other users from locking it also. If you want to check out a revision so that you can make changes to it and produce a new revision, you must use the **–l** option to lock the RCS file to ensure that other users cannot make changes to the file and check them in while you are working on it:

```
$ co -l xbuff.c
RCS/xbuff.c,v --> xbuff.c
revision 1.1 (locked)
done
```

You can now edit **xbuff.c**. After making changes to **xbuff.c**, you can check in a new revision of the file. In the following example, the file is checked in for the second time; the new revision is assigned the number 1.2:

```
$ ci xbuff.c
RCS/xbuff.c,v <-- xbuff.c
new revision: 1.2; previous revision: 1.1
enter log message, terminated with single '.' or end of file:
>> Some unused functions have been removed.
>> .
done
```

The rlog Utility

With the rlog utility you can review the history of changes made to a working file at any time. The output of rlog includes a list of revisions, with the descriptive text, date, and author for each revision. You can also see what revisions currently have locks set and by whom:

```
$ rlog xbuff.c
RCS file: RCS/xbuff.c,v
Working file: xbuff.c
head: 1.2
branch:
locks: strict
        alex: 1.2
access list:
symbolic names:
comment leader: " * "
keyword substitution: kv
total revisions: 2; selected revisions: 2
description:
This file contains functions to display a buffer in an X-window.
It can optionally print or save the buffer.
----------------------------
revision 1.2 locked by: alex;
date: 2000/06/26 22:03:26; author: alex; state: Exp; lines: +0 -38
Some unused functions have been removed.
----------------------------
revision 1.1
date: 2000/06/26 22:01:16; author: alex; state: Exp;
Initial revision
=====================================================================
```

Other information at the top of the rlog output includes a list of users who are permitted to make changes to the RCS file. In the example just shown, the *access list* is empty, meaning that anyone can access the file. If the access list has one or more names in it, only the named users, the owner, and Superuser can access the RCS file. The *head*, or the last checked-in revision on the trunk, is given at the top of the rlog output, as well as the number of revisions and a description of the revisions contained within the RCS file.

Using the –r Option to Specify a Revision

Several RCS utilities use the **–r** option to allow you explicitly to specify a revision number on the command line. This option is helpful if you want to check out a revision other than the default (the latest revision on the trunk). In the following example, revision 1.1 of **xbuff.c** is checked out using the **–r** option:

```
$ co -r1.1 xbuff.c
RCS/xbuff.c,v --> xbuff.c
revision 1.1
done
```

Most of the utilities in the RCS system allow you to omit the **–r** option if you can specify the revision number with another option, such as **–l**. You can lock and check out version 1.1 of **xbuff.c** with the following command:

```
$ co -l1.1 xbuff.c
```

If you change revision 1.1 and check it in, RCS will create the branch 1.1.1 and assign the number 1.1.1.1 to the new revision. Often one line of development continues along a branch while another proceeds along the trunk. At a later point the branch may be merged into the trunk.

Changing Attributes of an RCS File

The rcs utility lets you make changes to the attributes of existing revisions stored in an RCS file. Following, rcs with the **–l** option locks revision 1.2 of **xbuff.c** after it is checked out without locking. (This might be done, for instance, to prevent others from checking out revision 1.2 while the revision is being examined.)

```
$ co xbuff.c
RCS/xbuff.c,v --> xbuff.c
revision 1.2
done
$ rcs -l xbuff.c
```

Other options to the rcs utility include **–u** to unlock a revision and **–o** (outdate) to remove a revision from an RCS file. The following example removes revision 1.1 from the RCS file for **xbuff.c**. Because you must unlock a revision before you can delete it from an RCS file, the example uses an **rcs –u** command before the **rcs –o** command:

```
$ rcs -u1.1 xbuff.c
RCS file: RCS/xbuff.c,v
1.1 unlocked
done
$ rcs -o1.1 xbuff.c
RCS file: RCS/xbuff.c,v deleting revision 1.1
done
```

Later revisions, such as 1.2, are *not* renumbered when an earlier revision is dropped. If the most recent revision is 1.2, the next ci utility sequence will create revision 1.3. When you delete a revision, the changes made to that revision are not discarded but are merged with the next release level, if there is one. However, you will not be able to go back to the deleted release. If there is not a higher release level, the changes are discarded.

Like the ci utility, the rcs utility alters the RCS file. Therefore, the same authorization criteria apply.

Checking Differences between RCS Files

You can use rcsdiff to compare two revisions of an RCS file or to compare a checked-in revision to the working file. The following example compares the most recent revision on the trunk with the working file **pi.c**—the default values for the two revisions undergoing the comparison. The familiar output of the comparison is from diff, which is invoked by rcsdiff:

```
$ rcsdiff pi.c
===================================================================
RCS file: RCS/pi.c,v
retrieving revision 1.3
diff -r1.3 pi.c
136c136
< submm(a,b,c) /* subtract big number b from big number a */
---
> void submm(a,b,c) /* subtract big number b from big number a */
157c157
< inform(a) /* display the result (given in big number a) */
---
> void inform(a) /* display the result (given in big number a) */
170c170
< outnum(a) /* print out the big number a */
---
> void outnum(a) /* print out the big number a */
$
```

You can use the **–r** option to specify one or both of the revisions to compare. The following rcsdiff compares the first two revisions of **pi.c**:

```
$ rcsdiff -r1.1 -r1.2 pi.c
===================================================================
RCS file: RCS/pi.c,v
retrieving revision 1.1
retrieving revision 1.2
diff -r1.1 -r1.2
15c15,19
< * (time to compute pi to 10000 places: <9 cpu hours on PDP-11/44,
---
> * (time to compute pi to 10000 places: <9 cpu hours on PDP-11/44,
> * 486dx2/66 [Linux 1.2.13]: 126 cpu seconds,
> * 486dx4/100 [Linux 1.2.13]: 92 cpu seconds)
>
> *
21c25
< #define MAXNUM 100000 /* largest allowable accuracy */
---
> #define MAXNUM 1000000 /* largest allowable accuracy */
$
```

If you specify only one revision with the **–r** option, rcsdiff compares the specified revision to the working file:

```
$ rcsdiff -r1.2 pi.c
===================================================================
RCS file: RCS/pi.c,v
retrieving revision 1.2
diff -r1.2 pi.c
80c80
< outnum(r); /* display the result */
---
> inform(r); /* display the result */
153a154,166
> }
>
>
> inform(a) /* display the result (given in big number a) */
> long a[];
> {
> printf("\n\n\n\tPI Calculation\n\n\n");
> printf("\t\t# of words/number\t= %d\n",nwd);
> printf("\t\t# of digits/word\t= %d\n",NDS);
> printf("\t\t# of accurate places\t= %d\n",places);
> printf("\t\t# Arithmetic base is %d\n",WDSZ);
> printf("\n\n\tPI is:\n\n");
> outnum(a);
$
```

CVS: Concurrent Versions System

Although it is easy to use, RCS has some weaknesses as a source code management system, including the following:

- A project can be organized only as a collection of individual files, not as a single, integrated unit. For example, if a project is large and involves several directories, RCS requires revision files to be associated with each directory. Multiple revision files can make it difficult to collect the files needed for a particular release and, if there are multiple developers, to keep track of the contributions of each.

- The locking mechanism that RCS uses to control access to RCS files makes it impossible for two or more people to make changes to a file at the same time, even if those changes involve different parts of the file. This type of locking can be useful for smaller-scale version control but tends to impede progress if a team of developers is working together on a large project.

CVS (Concurrent Versions System—www.cvshome.org) addresses these problems by treating whole collections of files as single units, making it easy to work on large projects and permitting multiple users to work on the same file. CVS also provides valuable self-documenting features for utilities in the CVS system.

Built-in CVS Help

Where RCS uses several different programs, CVS uses a single utility: cvs. To display the instructions for getting help, use the **--help** option:

```
$ cvs --help
Usage: cvs [cvs-options] command [command-options-and-arguments]
  where cvs-options are -q, -n, etc.
    (specify --help-options for a list of options)
  where command is add, admin, etc.
    (specify --help-commands for a list of commands
    or --help-synonyms for a list of command synonyms)
  where command-options-and-arguments depend on the specific command
    (specify -H followed by a command name for command-specific help)
  Specify --help to receive this message

The Concurrent Versions System (CVS) is a tool for version control.
For CVS updates and additional information, see
    the CVS home page at http://www.cvshome.org/ or Pascal Molli's CVS
    site at http://www.loria.fr/~molli/cvs-index.html
```

To get help with a cvs command, use the **--help** option followed by the name of the utility. The following example shows how to get help with the log command:

```
$ cvs --help log
Usage: cvs log [-lRhtNb] [-r[revisions]] [-d dates] [-s states]
    [-w[logins]] [files...]
        -l        Local directory only, no recursion.
        -R        Only print name of RCS file.
        -h        Only print header.
        -t        Only print header and descriptive text.
        -N        Do not list tags.
        -b        Only list revisions on the default branch.
        -r[revisions]    Specify revision(s)s to list.
          rev1:rev2    Between rev1 and rev2, including rev1 and rev2.
          rev1::rev2   Between rev1 and rev2, excluding rev1 and rev2.
          rev:         rev and following revisions on the same branch.
          rev::        After rev on the same branch.
          :rev         rev and previous revisions on the same branch.
          ::rev        Before rev on the same branch.
          rev          Just rev.
          branch       All revisions on the branch.
          branch.      The last revision on the branch.
        -d dates        Specify dates (D1<D2 for range, D for latest before).
        -s states        Only list revisions with specified states.
        -w[logins]        Only list revisions checked in by specified logins.
(Specify the --help global option for a list of other help options)
```

Options for individual cvs commands (command options) go to the *right* of the individual command names. However, options to the cvs utility itself, such as the **--help** option to the log command, go to the *left* of all the individual command names (that is, they follow the word cvs on the command line). The two types of options sometimes use the same letter yet may have an entirely different meaning.

How CVS Stores Revision Files

With CVS, revision files are kept in a common area called a *source repository*. This area is identified by the value of the environment variable **CVSROOT**, which holds the absolute pathname of the repository. Your system administrator can tell you what value of **CVSROOT** to use, or you can create your own private repository.

The source repository is organized as a hierarchical collection of files and directories. In CVS you are not limited to checking out one file at a time; you can check out an entire subdirectory containing many files—typically all the files for a particular project. A subdirectory of **CVSROOT** that can be checked out as a single unit is called a *module*. Several people can check out and simultaneously modify the files within a single module.

It is common practice for CVS users to store all the modules they are currently working on in a special directory. If you want to follow this practice, you must use cd to make that special directory your working directory before you check out a module. When you check out a module, *CVS replicates the module's tree structure in the working directory.* Multiple developers can check out and edit CVS files simultaneously because the originals are retained in the source repository; the files in the repository undergo relatively infrequent modification in a controlled manner.

Basic CVS Commands

Although there are many cvs commands, a handful of commands allows a software developer to use the CVS system and to contribute changes to a module. A discussion of some useful commands follows. All examples assume that the appropriate modules have been installed in the CVS source repository. "Adding a Module to the Repository" (page 885) explains how to install a module.

Of the commands discussed in this section, the cvs commit command is the only one that changes the source repository. The other commands affect only the files in the working directory.

To simplify examples in the following sections, the pathname of the working directory is given by the variable **CVSWORK**; all modules can be assumed to be subdirectories of **CVSWORK**. Although this variable has no special meaning to CVS, you may find it helpful to define such a variable for your own work.

Checking out Files from the Source Repository

To check out a module from the CVS source repository, use the cvs checkout command. The following example checks out the **Project2** module, which consists of four source files. First, use cd to change working directories to the directory you want the module copied into (**CVSWORK** in this case); cvs always copies into the working directory:

```
$ cd $CVSWORK
$ ls
Project1
$ cvs checkout Project2
cvs checkout: Updating Project2
U Project2/adata.h
U Project2/compute.c
U Project2/randomfile.h
U Project2/shuffle.c
$ ls
Project1 Project2
$ ls Project2
CVS adata.h compute.c randomfile.h shuffle.c
```

The name of the module, **Project2**, is given as an argument to **cvs checkout**. Because the **Project2** directory does not already exist, cvs creates it in the working directory and places copies of all source files for the **Project2** module into it: The name of the module and the name of the directory holding the module are the same. The checkout command preserves the tree structure of the cvs module, creating subdirectories as needed.

The second ls command after checkout reveals, in addition to the four source files for **Project2**, a directory named CVS. The CVS system uses this directory for administrative purposes; it is not normally accessed by the user.

Once you have your own copies of the source files, you can edit them as you see fit. You can makes changes to files within the module, even if other developers are making changes to the same files at the same time.

Making Your Changes Available to Others

To check in your changes so that others have access to them, you need to run the cvs commit command. When you give this command, cvs prompts you for a brief log message describing the changes, unless you use the –**m** option. With this option cvs uses the string following the option as the log message. The file or files that you want to commit follow the optional log message on the command line:

```
$ cvs commit -m "function shuffle inserted" compute.c
cvs commit: Up-to-date check failed for `compute.c'
cvs [commit aborted]: correct above errors first!
```

The cvs utility reports an error because the version of **compute.c** that you modified is not up-to-date. A newer version of **compute.c** has been committed by someone else since you last checked it out of the source repository. After informing you of the problem, cvs exits without storing your changes in the source repository.

To make your version of **compute.c** current, you need to run the update command (see the next section). A subsequent commit will then succeed, and your changes will apply to the latest revision in the source repository.

Updating Your Copies with Changes by Others

As the preceding example shows, CVS does not notify you when another developer checks in a new revision of a file since you checked out your working copy. You learn this only when you attempt to commit your changes to the source repository. To incorporate up-do-date revisions of a CVS source file, use the cvs update command:

```
$ cvs update compute.c
RCS file: /usr/local/src/master/Project2/compute.c,v
retrieving revision 1.9
retrieving revision 1.10
Merging differences between 1.9 and 1.10 into compute.c
M compute.c
```

The changes made to the working copy of **compute.c** remain intact because the update command merges the latest revision in the source repository with the version specified on the update command line. The result of the merge is not always perfect. The cvs update command will inform you if it detects overlapping changes.

Adding New Files to the Repository

You can use the cvs add command to schedule new files to be added to the source repository as part of the module you are working on. Once you have moved to the directory containing the files, give the cvs add command, listing the files you want to add as arguments:

```
$ cd $CVSWORK/Project2
$ ls
CVS compute.c shuffle.c tabout2.c
adata.h randomfile.h tabout1.c
$ cvs add tabout[1-2].c
cvs add: scheduling file 'tabout1.c' for addition
cvs add: scheduling file 'tabout2.c' for addition
cvs add: use 'cvs commit' to add these files permanently
```

The add command marks the files **tabout1.c** and **tabout2.c** for entry into the repository. The files will not be available for others until you give a commit command. This staging allows you to prepare several files before others incorporate the changes into their working copies with the cvs update command.

Removing Files from the Repository

The cvs remove command records the fact that you wish to remove a file from the source repository and, like the add command, does not affect the source repository. To delete a file from the repository, you must first delete your working copy of the file, as the following example shows:

```
$ cvs remove shuffle.c
cvs remove: file 'shuffle.c' still in working directory
cvs remove: 1 file exists; use 'rm' to remove it first
$ rm shuffle.c
$ cvs remove shuffle.c
cvs remove: scheduling 'shuffle.c' for removal
cvs remove: use 'cvs commit' to remove this file permanently
```

After using rm to remove the working copy of **shuffle.c**, invoke the cvs remove command. Again, you must give the commit command before the file is actually removed from the source repository.

Other CVS Commands

Although the commands given earlier are sufficient for most work on a module, you may find some other commands that are useful as well.

Tagging a Release

You can apply a common label, or *tag*, to the files in a module as they currently exist. Once you have tagged files of a module, you can recreate them in exactly the same form even if they have been modified, added, or deleted since that time. This enables you to *freeze* a release and still allows development to continue on the next release:

```
$ cvs rtag Release_1 Project1
cvs rtag: Tagging Project1
```

Here the **Project1** module has been tagged with the label **Release_1**. You can use this tag with the cvs export command (see the following) to extract the files; they were frozen at this time.

Extracting a Release

The cvs export command lets you extract files as they were frozen and tagged.

```
$ cvs export -r Release_1 -d R1 Project1
cvs export: Updating R1
U R1/scm.txt
```

This command works like the cvs checkout command but does not create the CVS support files. You must give either the **–r** option to identify the release (as shown) or a date with the **–D** option. The **–d R1** option instructs cvs to place the files for the module into the directory R1 instead of using the module name as the directory.

Removing Working Files

When you are finished making changes to the files you have checked out of the repository, you may decide to remove your copy of the module from your working directory. One simple method is to move into the working directory and recursively remove the module. For example, if you want to remove your working copy of **Project2**, you could use the following commands:

```
$ cd $CVSWORK
$ rm -rf Project2
```

The repository will not be affected. However, if you had made changes to the files but had not yet committed those changes, they would be lost if you use that approach. The cvs release command is helpful in this situation:

```
$ cd $CVSWORK
$ cvs release -d Project2
```

The release command also removes the working files but first checks each one to see whether it has been marked for addition into the repository but has not been committed. If that is the case, the release command warns you and asks you to verify your intention to delete the file. If you want, you can fix the problem at this point and redo the release command. The release command also warns you if the repository holds a newer version of the file than the one in your working directory. This gives you the opportunity to update and commit your file before deleting it. (Without the −d option, your working files will not be deleted, but the same sequence of warning messages will be given.)

Adding a Module to the Repository

The discussion of CVS to this point assumes that a module is already present in the CVS source repository. If you want to install a directory hierarchy as a new module in the repository or update an existing module with a new release that was developed elsewhere, go to the directory that holds the files for the project and run the cvs import command. The following example installs the files for **Project1** in the source repository:

```
$ cvs import -m "My first project" Project1 ventag reltag
```

The −m option allows you to enter a brief description of the module on the command line. Following the description is the directory or the pathname of the directory under **CVSROOT** that you want to hold the module. The last two fields are symbolic names for the vendor branch and the release. Although they are not significant here, they can be useful when releases of software are supplied by outside sources. You can now use the cvs checkout command to check out the **Project1** module:

```
$ cvs checkout Project1
```

CVS Administration

Before you install a CVS repository, think about how you would like to administer it. Many installations have a single repository where separate projects are kept as separate modules. You may choose to have more than one repository. The CVS system supports a single repository that is shared across several computer systems using NFS.

Inside a repository is a module, named CVSROOT, that contains administrative files (here CVSROOT is the name of a module and is different from the **CVSROOT** directory). Although the files in this module are not required to use CVS, they can simplify access to the repository.

Do not change any of the files in the CVSROOT module by editing them directly. Instead, check out the file you want to change, edit the checked-out copy, and then check it back in, just as you would with files in any other module in the repository. For example, to check out the **modules** file from the CVSROOT module, use the command

```
$ cvs checkout CVSROOT/modules
```

This command creates the directory **CVSROOT** in your working directory and places a checked out copy of **modules** into that directory. After checking it out, you can edit the **modules** file in the **CVSROOT** directory.

```
$ cd CVSROOT
$ vi modules
```

After you edit the **modules** file, check it back into the repository.

```
$ cd ..
$ cvs checkin CVSROOT/modules
```

Of the administrative files in the CVSROOT module, the **modules** file is the most important. You can use the **modules** file to attach symbolic names to modules in the repository, allow access to subdirectories of a module as if they were themselves modules, and specify actions to take when checking specific files in or out.

As an example, most repositories start with a **modules** file that allows you to check out the **modules** file with the following command, instead of the one shown earlier:

```
$ cvs checkout modules
```

Here CVS creates a subdirectory named **modules** within your working directory, instead of one named **CVSROOT**. The **modules** file is checked out into this directory.

The following is an example of a **modules** file (the lines that start with a # are comment lines and, along with blank lines, are ignored by CVS):

```
# The CVS modules file
#
# Three different line formats are valid:
#    key -a aliases...
#    key [options] directory
#    key [options] directory files...
#
# Where "options" are composed of:
#    -i prog      Run "prog" on "cvs commit" from top-level of module.
#    -o prog      Run "prog" on "cvs checkout" of module.
#    -t prog      Run "prog" on "cvs rtag" of module.
#    -u prog      Run "prog" on "cvs update" of module.
#    -d dir       Place module in directory "dir" instead of module name.
#    -l           Top-level directory only -- do not recurse.
#
# And "directory" is a path to a directory relative to $CVSROOT.
#
# The "-a" option specifies an alias.  An alias is interpreted as if
# everything on the right of the "-a" had been typed on the command line.
#
#
# You can encode a module within a module by using the special '&'
# character to interpose another module into the current module.  This
# can be useful for creating a module that consists of many directories
# spread out over the entire source repository.



# Convenient aliases
world       -a .

# CVSROOT support; run mkmodules whenever anything changes.
CVSROOT     -i mkmodules CVSROOT
modules     -i mkmodules CVSROOT modules
loginfo     -i mkmodules CVSROOT loginfo
commitinfo  -i mkmodules CVSROOT commitinfo
rcsinfo     -i mkmodules CVSROOT rcsinfo
editinfo    -i mkmodules CVSROOT editinfo


# Add other modules here...
testgen     testgen
testdata1   testdata1
testdata2   testdata2
testdata3   testdata3
testdata4   testdata4
testcode    testgen/_code
cvs         cvs
```

The lines after the comment and blank lines define symbolic names for many modules. For example, the following line defines the name **world** to be an alias for the root of the CVS repository:

```
world        -a .
```

You can use such names in CVS commands as the names of modules, so the following command checks out the entire repository (probably not a good idea):

```
$ cvs checkout world
```

In the sample **modules** file shown, the administrative files have been given definitions that attach both a symbolic name to the file and an action (**–i mkmodules**) to take when each file is checked into the repository. The **–i mkmodules** action causes CVS to run the mkmodules program when the file is checked in. This program ensures that a copy of the checked-in file exists in a location where CVS can locate it.

Following the action is the name of the subdirectory in **CVSROOT** where the file (or files) associated with the symbolic name are located. Any remaining arguments on the line are the names of specific files within that directory.

The following line identifies the name CVSROOT as the module name for the module in the directory **$CVSROOT/CVSROOT**; that is, all the administrative files for CVS:

```
CVSROOT     -i mkmodules CVSROOT
```

Similarly, the following line associates the module named **modules** with the **modules** file within the **CVSROOT** directory:

```
modules     -i mkmodules CVSROOT modules
```

This line that allows the following command to find and check out the **modules** file:

```
$ cvs checkout modules
```

The last set of lines in the sample **modules** file associate symbolic module names with directories and files in the repository.

Using tkcvs

The CVS utility is useful enough that an X Window System interface, tkcvs, has been written for it, using the Tk extension to the Tcl programming language (tcl.sourceforge.net). This utility provides a convenient point-and-click interface to CVS (Figure 16-8). After you have downloaded and installed tkcvs, start it by using cd to change to the directory you want to work in and entering the following command:

```
$ tkcvs &
```

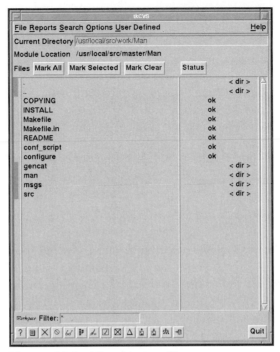

Figure 16-8   The **tkCVS** utility

All operations are available through the pull-down menus at the top of the window. Along the bottom are buttons for accessing the most common actions. Because the icons on the buttons may not make sense to you, a longer description of the action bound to a button appears when you position the mouse pointer on top of a button.

In the middle of the window is a *browse list*. Move into a subdirectory by double-clicking the left mouse button while the mouse pointer is on the directory name in the list. Edit a file by double-clicking the filename. To select more than one file, drag the mouse pointer across several names while holding down the left mouse button. Clicking the right mouse button will *mark* all selected files. Some of the operations (such as viewing the revision log messages) will work on all marked files.

The Help pull-down menu in the upper-right corner is an excellent way to learn how tkCVS works. For example, when you select the Help menu item CVS modules file..., an explanation of the lines that you can add to the CVS **modules** file to support the tkCVS utility better appears in a window. If you choose not to add these lines to the **modules** file, some of the tkCVS commands, such as browsing the repository, may not display all available modules.

Chapter Summary

The operating system interface to C programs and a variety of software development tools make the GNU/Linux system well suited to programming in C. The C libraries provide general-purpose C functions that make operating system services and other functionality available to C programmers. The standard C library, **libc,** is always accessible to C programs, and you can specify other libraries by using the **–l** option to the gcc compiler.

You can write a C program by using a text editor, such as pico, vi, or emacs. C programs always have a function named **main** and often have several other functions. Preprocessor directives define symbolic constants and macros and instruct the preprocessor to include header files.

When you use gcc, it calls the C preprocessor followed by the C compiler and the assembler. The compiler creates assembly language code, which the assembler uses to create object modules. Finally, the linker combines the object modules into an executable file. You can use the **–Wall** option to gcc to detect *risky* constructs—ones that are legal but suggest the possibility of later problems. Other options to gcc can help locate areas of your code that might not be portable.

Although using **printf** statements and the **–Wall** option can help in tracking program bugs, it is a good practice to compile C programs routinely with the **–g** option. This option causes information to be generated with your executable file that can be interpreted by gdb, a symbolic debugger. When you run your program under the control of gdb, you can specify points where you want gdb to pause your program, inquire about the values of variables, display the program stack, and use a wide range of debugger commands to learn about many other aspects of your program's behavior.

The make utility uses a file named **Makefile** (or **makefile**) that documents the relationships among files. It keeps track of which modules of a program are out-of-date and compiles files in order to keep all modules up-to-date. The dependency line, which specifies the exact dependency relationship between target and prerequisite files, is the key to the operation of a makefile. A dependency line not only specifies a relationship but also gives the construction commands that make the target up-to-date. Implied dependencies and construction commands, as well as the make macro facility, are available to simplify the writing of complex makefiles.

The GNU/Linux system includes utilities that assist in keeping track of groups of files that undergo multiple revisions, often by multiple developers. These source code management systems include RCS and CVS. RCS, the Revision Control System, consists of several separate utilities and is appropriate for small-scale projects involving a group of files that are not organized hierarchically. CVS, the Concurrent Versions System, is built on top of RCS but provides a much more extensive set of operations for managing directories of files that may be accessed and modified by many users. It is a better choice for large-scale projects and for maintaining software releases that are sent to and from other sites.

Exercises

1. What function does every C program have? Why should you split large programs into several functions?

2. What command could you use to compile **prog.c** and **func.c** into an executable named **cprog**?

3. Show two ways to instruct the C preprocessor to include the header file **/usr/include/math.h** in your C program. Assuming that the **declar.h** header file is located in the subdirectory named **headers** of your home directory, describe two ways to instruct the C preprocessor to include this header file in your C program.

4. Both C functions **getchar** and **putchar** appear in the standard C library **libc.so**. Show that **getchar** and **putchar** are also macros on your system. Can you think of more than one way to show this?

5. How are the names of system libraries abbreviated on the gcc command line? Where does gcc search for libraries named in this manner? Describe how to specify your own library on the gcc command line.

6. What command can you use to create an RCS file for a file named **answers**? What command can you use to retrieve an editable version of **answers**?

7. Write a **makefile** that reflects the following relationships.

   a. The C source files **transactions.c** and **reports.c** are compiled to produce an executable **accts**.

   b. Both **transactions.c** and **reports.c** include a header file **accts.h**.

   c. The header file **accts.h** is composed of two other header files: **trans.h** and **reps.h**.

8. How can you retrieve the RCS working file **answers** so that

   a. Only Barbara and hls can make changes?

   b. No one except the owner and Superuser can make changes to Release 2?

9. If you retrieve Version 4.1 of the file **answers** for editing and then attempt to retrieve the same version again, what will RCS do? Why is RCS set up this way?

10. Answer the questions from exercise 9 for CVS.

Advanced Exercises

11. What RCS commands modify the access list? Explain how to ensure that only the owner of a file or Superuser can check out a locked revision of an RCS file.

12. Modify the **tabs.c** program so that it exits cleanly (with a specific return value). Compile the program, and run it using the dbx or another debugger. What values does the debugger report when the program finishes executing?

13. For the following makefile, identify

    a. Targets

    b. Construction commands

    c. Prerequisites

    ```
    $ cat Makefile
    leads: menu.o users.o resellers.o prospects.o
                gcc -o leads menu.o users.o resellers.o prospects.o

    menu.o: menu.h dialog.h inquiry.h

    users.o: menu.h dialog.h

    prospects.o: dialog.h
    ```

14. Refer to **Makefile** in exercise 13 to answer the following questions:

    a. If the target **leads** is up-to-date and you then change **users.c**, what happens when you run make again? Be specific.

    b. Rewrite the makefile to include the following macros:

    ```
    OBJECTS = menu.o users.o resellers.o prospects.o
    HFILES = menu.h dialog.h
    ```

15. Read about make on page 1247 in Part III and the make man page to answer the following questions:

    a. What does the **–t** option do?

    b. If you have files in the working directory named **makefile** and **Makefile**, how can you instruct make to use **Makefile**?

    c. Give two ways to define a variable so that you can use it inside a makefile.

16. Suppose that the file named **synchr.c** has four revisions numbered 1.1 through 1.4. Show how to

a. Check out the latest revision for editing.

b. Check out the latest revision for compiling only.

c. Check in a new revision after editing the latest revision but allow editing of the working file to continue.

d. Check out revision 1.2 for editing.

e. Delete revision 1.2.

17. Read about the RCS system, or experiment with it to answer the following questions:

a. How do you assign a symbolic name to a revision?

b. How is a branch revision created?

c. What happens when you attempt to check in an editable revision that has not been modified?

d. How do you delete a revision? Can this cause other revisions to be renumbered?

18. Refer to the makefile for **compute** on page 853. Suppose that a file in the working directory is named **clean**. What is the effect of giving the following command. Explain.

```
$ make clean
```

The discussion of the makefile on page 851 states that the following command is not normally seen in makefiles:

```
cat num.h table.h > form.h
```

a. Discuss the effect of removing this construction command from the makefile while retaining the dependency line.

b. The preceding construction command works only because the file **form.h** is made up of **num.h** and **table.h**. More often **#include** directives in the target define the dependencies. Suggest a more general technique that updates **form.h** whenever **num.h** or **table.h** has a more recent modification date.

IN THIS CHAPTER

Red Hat Linux System Administration

17

The job of a system administrator is to keep one or more systems useful and convenient for the users. On a GNU/Linux system the administrator and user may both be you, with you and a single computer only a few feet apart. Or the system administrator may be half-way around the world, supporting a network of systems, with you simply one of thousands of users. A system administrator can be one person who works part time taking care of a system and perhaps is also a user of the system. Or the administrator can be several people, all working full time to keep many systems running.

A well-maintained system

- Runs quickly enough so that users do not get too frustrated waiting for the system to respond or complete a task.

- Has enough storage to accommodate users' reasonable needs.

- Provides a working environment appropriate to each user's abilities and requirements.

- Is secure from malicious and accidental acts altering its performance or compromising the security of the data it holds and exchanges with other systems.

- Is backed up regularly with recently backed-up files readily available to users.

- Has recent copies of the software that users need to get their jobs done.

- Is easier to administer than a poorly maintained system.

In addition, a system administrator should be available help users with all types of system-related problems: from logging in to obtaining and installing software updates to tracking down and fixing obscure network issues.

This chapter familiarizes you with the concepts you need to understand and the tools you need to use to maintain a Red Hat Linux system. Where it is not possible to go into depth about a subject, the chapter provides references to other sources.

GNU/Linux systems are getting increasingly easy to set up and maintain. If you are not running an installed copy of Red Hat Linux and need to install it yourself, the process is much easier than it used to be. Red Hat has done a lot to improve and simplify installation and maintenance. One tool that Red Hat developed is the rpm (Red Hat package manager) utility, which makes installing/upgrading system and application software much easier. Because Red Hat released it under the GNU GPL (page 7), rpm has been improved by engineers outside of Red Hat, and it appears in other distributions of GNU/Linux. A more recent development is RHN (Red Hat Network), which allows Red Hat to keep your system up-to-date with little or no user interaction.[1] With the Kickstart Configurator, you can design a simple script that allows you to install the same configuration of Red Hat Linux on multiple machines with very little effort. Finally, all these tools, as well as other administration utilities, are available with GUIs, making each easier to set up and use.

Because GNU/Linux is configurable and runs on various platforms (Sun SPARC, DEC/Compaq Alpha, Intel x86, AMD, PowerPC, and more), this chapter cannot discuss every system configuration or every action you will have to take as a system administrator. This chapter assumes that you are familiar with the following terms. Refer to the glossary (page 1453) for definitions.

block (device)	environment	mount (a device)	spawn
daemon	filesystem	process	system console
device	fork	root filesystem	X server
device filename	kernel	runlevel	
disk partition	login shell	signal	

System Administrator and Superuser

Much of what a system administrator does is work that ordinary users do not have permission to do. When doing one of these tasks the system administrator logs in as

---

1. There may be a charge for this service.

root (or uses another method; see the list starting on page 898) in order to have systemwide powers that are beyond those of ordinary users: A user with **root** privileges is referred to as *Superuser*. The login name is **root** by default and should not be changed. Although you can set up a GNU/Linux system with any name in place of **root**, it will break the system: Many programs depend on this name being **root**. Superuser has the following powers and more:

- Some commands, such as those that add new users, partition hard drives, and change system configuration, can be executed only by **root**.[2]

- Read, write, and execute file access and directory access permissions do not affect **root**: Superuser can read from, write to, and execute all files, as well as examine and work in all directories.

- Some restrictions and safeguards that are built into some commands do not apply to **root**. For example, **root** can change any user's password without knowing the old password.

When you are running with **root** (Superuser) privileges, the shell by convention displays a special prompt to remind you of your status. By default this prompt is or ends with a pound sign (#).

To lessen the chance that a user other than Superuser will try to use them by mistake, many of the commands that Superuser runs are kept in the **/sbin** and **/usr/sbin** directories, rather than in **/bin** and **/usr/bin**. (Many of these commands can be run by ordinary users.) You can execute these commands by giving their full pathnames on the command line (for example, **/sbin/runlevel**). When you log in as **root**, these directories are in your **PATH** by default.

Least Privilege || caution

When you are working on the computer, especially when you are working as the system administrator, perform any task by using the least privilege possible. When you can perform a task logged in as an ordinary user, do so. When you must be logged in as Superuser, do as much as you can as an ordinary user, log in or **su** so that you have **root** privileges, do as much of the task as has to be done as Superuser, and revert to being an ordinary user as soon as you can. Because you are more likely to make a mistake when you are rushing, this concept becomes more important when you have less time to apply it.

---

2. Superuser can use certain tools, such as sudo, which is covered shortly, to give specific users permission to perform tasks that are normally reserved for Superuser.

You can become Superuser in a number of ways.

1. When you bring the system up in single-user mode (page 949), you are Superuser.

2. Once the system is up and running in multiuser mode (page 950), you can log in as **root**: When you supply the proper password, you will be Superuser.

3. You can give an su (substitute user) command while you are logged in as yourself, and, with the proper password, you will have Superuser privileges. For more information refer to "su: Gives You Another User's Privileges" on page 900.

4. You can use sudo selectively to give users Superuser privileges for a limited amount of time on a per user and per command basis. The sudo utility is controlled by the **/etc/sudoers** file, which must be set up by **root**. Refer to the sudo man page for more information.

5. Any user can create a *setuid* (Set User ID) file (page 121). Setuid programs run on behalf of the owner of the file and have all the access privileges that the owner has. While you are running as Superuser, you can change the permissions of a file owned by **root** to setuid. When an ordinary user executes a file that is owned by **root** and has setuid permissions, the program has *full **root** privileges*. In other words, this program can do anything that **root** can do and that the program does or allows the user to do. The user's privileges do not change. When the program finishes running, all user privileges are back to the way they were before the program was started. Setuid programs that are owned by **root** are extremely powerful and also extremely dangerous to system security, which is why very few of them are on the system. Examples of setuid programs that are owned by **root** include passwd, at, and crontab. The following example shows two ways for Superuser to give a program setuid privileges:

```
# ls -l my*
-rwxr-xr-x   1 root      other      24152 Apr 29 16:30 myprog
-rwxr-xr-x   1 root      other      24152 Apr 29 16:31 myprog2
# chmod 4755 myprog
# chmod u+s myprog2
# ls -l my*
-rwsr-xr-x   1 root      other      24152 Apr 29 16:30 myprog
-rwsr-xr-x   1 root      other      24152 Apr 29 16:31 myprog2
```

Refer to chmod (page 1103) and ls ("Notes" on page 1237) in Part III for more details on creating and identifying programs that are setuid.

6. Some programs ask you for a password (either your password or the **root** password, depending on the particular command and the configuration of

the system) when they start. When you provide the **root** password, the program runs with Superuser privileges.

When a program requests the **root** password when it starts, you stop running as the privileged user when you quit using the program. This helps keep you from remaining logged in as Superuser when you do not need/intend to be. Refer to "**consolehelper**: Runs Programs as Root" on page 901.

Some techniques limit the number of ways to become Superuser. PAM controls over the who, when, and how of logging in (page 1043). The **/etc/securetty** file allows you to control which terminals (ttys) a user can log in from as **root**. The **/etc/security/access.conf**[3] file adds another dimension to login control.

root-Owned Setuid Programs Are Extremely Dangerous || security

Because a **root**-owned setuid program allows someone who does not know the **root** password to have the powers of Superuser, it is a tempting target for a malicious user. Your site should have as few of these programs as necessary. You can disable setuid programs at the filesystem level by mounting a filesystem with the **nosuid** option (page 976).

Do Not Allow root Access over the Internet || security

Prohibiting **root** access over a network is the default policy of Red Hat Linux and is implemented by PAM. The **/etc/security/access.conf** file must contain the names of all the users and terminals/workstations that you want a user to be able to log in from as **root**. If you need to have **root** access to a machine over a network, use **ssh** (page 1029). Initially, every line in **access.conf** is commented out.

System Administration Tools

Many tools can help you be an efficient and thorough system administrator. A few of these tools/utilities are described in the following sections. GUI tools are discussed starting on page 985, another group of administration utilities is described starting on page 1049, and many others are scattered throughout the chapter.

---

3. See this file for a description and examples of its use.

su: Gives You Another User's Privileges

The su (substitute user) utility can create a shell or execute a program with the identity and permissions of any user. Follow **su** on the command line with the name of a user; if you are **root** or if you know that user's password, you take on the identity of that user. When you give an su command without an argument, su defaults to Superuser so that you take on the identity of **root** (you have to know the **root** password).

To be sure that you are using the system's official version of su (and not one planted on your system by a malicious user), specify su's absolute pathname (**/bin/su**) when you use it.[4]

When you give an su command to become Superuser, you spawn a new shell, which displays the # prompt. You return to your normal status (and your former shell and prompt) by terminating this shell: Press CONTROL-D or give an exit command. Giving an su command by itself changes your user and group IDs but makes minimal changes to your environment. You still have the same **PATH** you did when you logged in as yourself. When you run a utility that is normally run by **root** (those in **/sbin** and **/usr/sbin**), you need to specify an absolute pathname for the utility (as in **/sbin/runlevel**). When you give the command **su –** (you can use –l or ––login in place of the dash), you get a **root** login shell: It is as though you logged in as **root**. Not only are your user and group IDs those of **root**, but your entire environment is that of **root**. The login shell executes the appropriate start-up scripts before giving you a prompt, and your **PATH** is set to what it would be if you had logged in as **root**, typically including **/sbin** and **/usr/sbin**.

You can see the changes in your user and group IDs and the groups you are associated with by giving the id command:

```
$ id
uid=500(alex) gid=500(alex) groups=500(alex)
$ su
Password:
# id
uid=0(root) gid=0(root) groups=0(root),1(bin),2(daemon),3(sys), ...
```

You can use su with the –c option to run a single command with **root** privileges, returning to your original shell when the command finishes executing. The following example first shows that a user is not permitted to kill a process. With the use of **su –c** and the **root** password, the user is permitted to kill the process. The quotation marks are necessary because **su –c** takes its command as a single argument.

```
$ kill -15 4982
-bash: kill: (4982) - Operation not permitted
```

---

4. Of course, if someone has compromised your system enough to have you run a fake su command, you are in serious trouble anyway, but using an absolute pathname for su is still a good idea.

```
$ su -c "kill -15 4982"
Password:
$
```

Superuser, PATH, and Security || security

The fewer directories you keep in your PATH when you are root, the less likely that you will execute an untrusted program as root. If possible, keep only the default directories, along with /sbin and /usr/sbin, in root's PATH. *Never include the working directory (as . or : : anywhere in PATH, or : as the last element of PATH).*

consolehelper: Runs Programs as Root

The consolehelper utility makes it easier for someone who is logged in on the system console but not logged in as **root** to run system programs that normally can be run only by **root**. PAM (page 1043) authenticates users and can be set to trust all console users or to require user passwords (not the **root** password) before granting trust. Thus Alex can log in on the console as himself and run halt without knowing the **root** password. The concept behind consolehelper is that anyone who has access to the console is trustworthy. You can turn this feature off if you need to. For more information refer to the discussion of consolehelper on page 954 and to the consolehelper man page.

kill: Sends a Signal to a Process

The kill builtin [bash tcsh zsh] sends a signal to a process. This signal may or may not terminate (kill) the process, depending on the signal sent and how the process is designed. Refer to "trap: Catches a Signal" on page 667 for a discussion of the various signals and how a process receives them. Running kill is not the first method a user or system administrator should try when a process needs to be aborted.

kill: Method of Last Resort || caution

Because of its inherent dangers, using kill is a method of last resort, especially when you are running as Superuser. One kill command issued by root can bring the system down without warning.

When you do need to use kill, send the termination signal (kill −TERM or kill −15) first. Only when that does not work should you attempt to use the kill signal (kill −KILL or kill −9).

Usually a user can kill a process from another window or by logging in on another terminal. Sometimes you may have to log in as **root** (or use su) to kill a process for a user. To kill a process, you need to know the PID of the process. The ps utility can give you this information once you know the name of the program the user is running and/or the login name of the user.

In the following example Alex complains that Netscape (www.netscape.com) is stuck and that he cannot do anything from the Netscape window, not even close it. A more experienced user could open another window and kill the process, but in this case you kill it for Alex. First, use ps with the **–u** option, followed by the name of the user and the **–f** (full/wide) option to view all the processes associated with that user:

```
$ ps -u alex -f
UID        PID  PPID  C STIME TTY       TIME CMD
alex      2841  2840  0 19:39 tty1    00:00:00 -bash
alex      2896  2841  0 19:40 tty1    00:00:00 /bin/sh /usr/X11R6/bin/startx
alex      2903  2896  0 19:40 tty1    00:00:00 xinit /etc/X11/xinit/xinitrc --
alex      2908  2903  0 19:40 tty1    00:00:00 /bin/bash /usr/bin/startkde
alex      2974     1  0 19:41 ?       00:00:00 kdeinit:dcopserver --nosid
alex      2977     1  0 19:41 ?       00:00:00 kdeinit:klauncher
alex      2980     1  0 19:41 ?       00:00:00 kdeinit:kded
alex      3002     1  0 19:41 ?       00:00:03 /usr/bin/artsd -F 10 -S 4096 -s 60
alex      3008     1  0 19:41 ?       00:00:00 kdeinit:knotify
alex      3009     1  0 19:41 ?       00:00:00 kdeinit:Running...
alex      3010  2908  0 19:41 tty1    00:00:00 ksmserver --restore
alex      3012  3009  0 19:41 ?       00:00:00 kdeinit:kwin
alex      3014     1  0 19:41 ?       00:00:00 kdeinit:kdesktop
alex      3019     1  0 19:41 ?       00:00:01 kdeinit:kicker
alex      3024     1  0 19:41 ?       00:00:00 kdeinit:klipper -icon klipper
alex      3028     1  0 19:41 ?       00:00:00 kdeinit:kwrited
alex      3029     1  0 19:41 ?       00:00:00 alarmd
alex      3030  3028  0 19:41 pts/2   00:00:00 /bin/cat
alex      3040  3009  0 19:41 ?       00:00:00 kdeinit:konsole -icon konsole
alex      3041  3040  0 19:41 pts/3   00:00:00 /bin/bash
alex      3069     1  0 19:41 ?       00:00:00 kdeinit:kcontrol -caption Control
alex      3074  3041  0 19:42 pts/3   00:00:03 /usr/lib/netscape/netscape-communi
alex      3101  3074  0 19:42 pts/3   00:00:00 (dns helper)
alex      3121  3014 33 19:49 ?       00:00:41 kscience.kss -window-id 4194310
```

This list is fairly short and the process running Netscape is easy to find. Another way to go about searching is to use ps to produce a long list of all the processes and then use grep to find all the processes running Netscape:

```
$ ps -ef | grep netscape
alex      3074     1  1 10:22 tty1    00:00:01 /usr/lib/netscape/netscape-commu
alex      3157  2573  0 10:25 pts/1   00:00:00 grep netscape
```

Many people may be running Netscape, and you may need to look in the left column to find the name of the user so that you can kill the right process. You can combine the two commands as **ps –u alex –f | grep netscape**.

Now that you know the PID (3074) of Alex's process running Netscape, you can use kill to terminate it. The safest way to do this is to log in as Alex (perhaps allow him to log in for you or su to alex [**su alex**] if you are logged in as **root**) and give the command

```
$ kill -TERM 3074
```

Only if this command fails should you send the kill signal as

```
$ kill -KILL 3074
```

The **–KILL** option instructs kill to send a **SIGKILL** signal, which the process cannot ignore. You can give the same command while you are logged in as **root**, but a typing mistake can have much more far-reaching consequences than when you make the mistake while you are logged in as an ordinary user. A user can kill only her or his own processes, whereas Superuser can kill any process, including system processes.

As a compromise between speed and safety, you can combine the su and kill utilities by using the **–c** option to su. The following command runs the part of the command line following the **–c** with the identity of Alex:

```
# su alex -c "kill -TERM 3074"
```

Refer to page 1224 in Part III for more information on kill. Two useful utilities that are related to kill are killall and pidof. The first is very similar to kill but uses a command name in place of a PID number. To kill all your processes that are running netscape or vi, you can give the command

```
$ killall netscape vi
```

When **root** gives this command, all processes that are running netscape or vi on the system are killed.

The pidof utility displays the PID number of each of the processes running the command you specify. Because this utility resides in **/sbin**, you must give the absolute pathname if you are not running as **root**:

```
$ /sbin/pidof httpd
567 566 565 564 563 562 561 560 553
```

If it is difficult to find the right process, try using top (page 1062). Refer to the man pages for each of these utilities for more information, including lists of available options.

Avoiding a Trojan Horse

A *Trojan horse* is a program that does something destructive or disruptive to your system while appearing to be benign. As an example, you could store the following script in an executable file named mkfs:

```
while true
    do
    echo 'Good Morning Mr. Jones. How are you? Ha Ha Ha.' > /dev/console
    done
```

If you are running as Superuser when you run this command, it would continuously write a message to the console. If the programmer were malicious, it could do worse. The only thing missing in this plot is access permissions.

A malicious user could implement this Trojan horse by changing Superuser's **PATH** variable to include a publicly writable directory at the start of the **PATH** string.[5] Then you would need to put the bogus mkfs program file in that directory. Because the fraudulent version appears in a directory mentioned earlier than the real one in **PATH**, the shell runs it. The next time Superuser tries to run mkfs, the fraudulent version would run.

Trojan horses that wait for and take advantage of the misspellings that most people make are one of the most insidious types. For example, you might type **sl** instead of **ls**. Because you do not regularly execute a utility named sl and you may not remember typing the command **sl**, it is more difficult to track down this type of Trojan horse than one that takes the name of a utility you are familiar with.

A good way to prevent executing a Trojan horse is to make sure that your **PATH** variable does not contain a single colon (:) at the beginning or end of the **PATH** string or a period (.) or double colon (::) anywhere in the **PATH** string. A common way to check for a Trojan horse is to examine the filesystem periodically for files with setuid (refer to item 5 on page 898). The following command lists these files:

```
# find / -perm -4000 -exec ls -lh {} \; 2> /dev/null
-rwsr-xr-x   1 root     root           19K 06-23 17:05 /usr/bin/rcp
-rwsr-xr-x   1 root     root           15K 06-23 17:05 /usr/bin/rlogin
-rwsr-xr-x   1 root     root           10K 06-23 17:05 /usr/bin/rsh
-rwsr-xr-x   1 root     root           33K 06-23 17:20 /usr/bin/chage
-rwsr-xr-x   1 root     root           34K 06-23 17:20 /usr/bin/gpasswd
-rwsr-xr-x   1 root     root           36K 06-23 07:09 /usr/bin/at
---s--x--x   1 root     root           83K 06-27 16:57 /usr/bin/sudo
-r-s--x--x   1 root     root           15K 05-28 10:52 /usr/bin/passwd
-rws--x--x   1 root     root           16K 06-28 09:28 /usr/bin/chfn
-rws--x--x   1 root     root           15K 06-28 09:28 /usr/bin/chsh
-rws--x--x   1 root     root          6.8K 06-28 09:28 /usr/bin/newgrp
-rwsr-xr-x   1 root     root           21K 06-23 18:19 /usr/bin/crontab
-rwsr-xr-x   1 root     root           18K 06-23 07:37 /usr/bin/lppasswd
-rwsr-xr-x   1 root     root          6.8K 06-27 03:50 /usr/bin/kcheckpass
-rws--x--x   1 root     root          159K 06-27 08:50 /usr/libexec/opens...
-rwsr-xr-x   1 root     root           32K 06-23 11:14 /usr/sbin/ping6
```

5. The catch is that you need to be able to write to **/etc/profile**—where the **PATH** variable is set for **root**—and only **root** can do that.

```
-rwsr-xr-x   1 root    root        13K 06-23 11:14 /usr/sbin/traceroute6
-rwsr-xr-x   1 root    root        31K 06-23 17:41 /usr/sbin/traceroute
-r-s--x---   1 root    apache      44K 06-26 08:00 /usr/sbin/suexec
...
```

This command uses find to locate all the files that have their setuid bits set (mode 4000). The hyphen preceding the mode causes find to report on any file that has this bit set, regardless of how the other bits are set. The output sent to standard error is redirected to **/dev/null** so that it does not clutter the screen.

You can also set up a program, such as tripwire, that will take a snapshot of your system and check it periodically as you specify. Red Hat Linux includes tripwire; see the man page and www.tripwire.com/downloads for more information.

Installing Red Hat Linux (Overview)

It is not difficult to install and bring up a GNU/Linux system, but the more you know about the process before you start, the easier it is. The installation software collects information about your system and can help you make decisions. However, your system will work better for you when you know how you want your disk partitioned rather than letting the install program partition it without your input. Your screen will be easier to use if you know what resolution you want. There are many details, and the more details you take control of, the happier you will be with the finished product. If you read this section in conjunction with the Red Hat installation manual, you will end up with a system that you understand and know how to change when you need to.

Finding the Installation Manual

The definitive resource for instructions on how to install Red Hat Linux is *The Official Red Hat Linux x86 Installation Guide* for the release you are installing (Red Hat also produces an installation guide for S/390 systems). You can find this document on the Red Hat Documentation CD-ROM (point your browser toward **index-en.html** at the top level of the CD-ROM, click HTML, then click the manual you want). You can also go to www.redhat.com/docs/manuals/linux and choose the manual you want. Finally, you can go to a Red Hat mirror[6] for a list of sites that mirror the Red Hat site, choose a URL from the column titled Red Hat Linux, and work your way down the file hierarchy of the FTP site from **redhat** through

---

6. A list of mirrors is at www.redhat.com/download/mirror.html. Make sure that you click the column you want: Red Hat Linux to download the whole release or a good portion of it; Updates to download updates; Contrib to download contributed software.

doc, where you can click **index-en.html** to view a document or go to **RH-DOCS** to download a document. A typical path you might follow to the **doc** directory of a mirror site is **ftp://ftp.gmd.de/mirrors/redhat.com/redhat/linux/8.0/en/doc/.**

Additional installation, setup, and troubleshooting resources are available from Red Hat: Go to the Red Hat home page, select Support and Docs, and then select a link on that page or one of the choices from the Support Links at the upper-left of the page. You can also search for a keyword or words by using the Search Red Hat box at the upper-right of most Red Hat pages.

Read the Instructions	**|| tip**
Find, print out if you like, read, and follow the installation instructions no matter if they are in printed manuals, in PostScript or plain text files, on a CD-ROM, or on the Internet. This section is simply an overview of some parts of the installation process and does not replace the instructions that are part of the Red Hat distribution you are installing.	

Downloading, Burning, and Installing a CD-ROM Set

You can download and burn your own Red Hat CD-ROMs. Although you will not get hard-copy manuals or free, limited customer support, you will not pay anything. One of the beauties of free software (Appendix E) is that it is always available for free. Red Hat makes it easy to obtain and use its GNU/Linux code by providing ISO images (refer to "ISO9660" on page 1475) of its CD-ROMs online. These files are large, about 650 megabytes, so they take days to download unless you have something faster than a 56K modem, in which case they can take hours.

Red Hat's FTP site and mirror sites maintain the ISO images you need (see footnote 6 on page 905). The pathnames in Table 17-1 outline the *usual* structure of the hierarchy that holds the Red Hat 8.0 release, code named Psyche. When you download a different release of Red Hat, you need to make appropriate changes to these pathnames, all of which are relative to ftp.redhat.com or the **redhat** directory of the mirror site.

Directory at ftp.redhat.com	**|| table 17-1**
pub/redhat/linux	Holds the various releases of Red Hat Linux.
pub/redhat/linux/8.0	Holds various language versions of Red Hat Linux.

Directory at ftp.redhat.com (Continued) | table 17-1

pub/redhat/linux/8.0/en	Holds the English-language components of Red Hat Linux.
pub/redhat/linux/8.0/en/doc	Holds the English-language documentation for Red Hat Linux.
pub/redhat/linux/8.0/en/iso	Holds the English-language CD-ROM images of Red Hat Linux.
pub/redhat/linux/8.0/en/os	Holds architecture-specific directories, such as **i386** for the Intel i386 architecture which includes Pentium processors. Each of these directories holds everything you need to install Red Hat Linux, including boot-disk image files, DOS utilities, and **rpm** packages; packages in RPMS are compiled, and packages in SRPMS (the first S stands for source) are in source form and must be compiled.

The following pathnames point to the files that you need to download in order to make CD-ROMs for installing a Red Hat system. Change the 8.0 and the word psyche as appropriate. These pathnames point to the three software CD-ROM ISO files and a short **MD5SUM** file that verifies that the files downloaded correctly. (See *MD5* on page 1478.) In the same directory are images of disks 4 and 5 that hold the source code in the form of SRPMS files, which you do not normally need to install Red Hat Linux:

```
pub/redhat/linux/8.0/en/iso/i386/MD5SUM
pub/redhat/linux/8.0/en/iso/i386/psyche-i386-disc1.iso
pub/redhat/linux/8.0/en/iso/i386/psyche-i386-disc2.iso
pub/redhat/linux/8.0/en/iso/i386/psyche-i386-disc3.iso
```

Rename the **MD5SUM** file to **MD5SUM.discs** so that when you download other **MD5SUM** files they do not overwrite this one.

Next, download the Red Hat Documentation CD-ROM ISO file along with its **MD5SUM** file which you can rename **MD5SUM.docs**. Finally, download the contents of the directory that holds the boot image files, one of which you will need if your computer cannot boot from a CD-ROM and you cannot copy the boot image off the CD-ROM, (refer to "Beginning Installation" on page 921):

```
pub/redhat/linux/8.0/en/iso/doc/psyche-docs.iso
pub/redhat/linux/8.0/en/os/i386/images/*
```

Run the following commands to check your **psyche-i386-disc1.iso** file:

```
$ md5sum *disc1.iso; grep disc1 MD5SUM
d7b16b081c20708dc0dd7d41793a4177  psyche-i386-disc1.iso
d7b16b081c20708dc0dd7d41793a4177  psyche-i386-disc1.iso
```

Computing an MD5 sum for a large file takes a while. The two long strings must be identical: If they are not, you must download the file again.

Burning an ISO file is not the same as burning other files on a CD-ROM. Refer to the instructions for burning ISO files for your CD-ROM drive. You can download and burn the CD-ROMs on any operating system that has the required software tools and hardware. Red Hat provides very detailed instructions (at www.redhat.com/download/howto_download.html) on downloading and using ISO files.

Types of Installations

There are several ways to install Red Hat Linux. You can choose a graphical installation, which displays graphics on the screen and allows you to use the mouse, window buttons, and scroll lists to choose how you want to configure the system. The Anaconda utility controls a graphical installation. If you have a smaller system with less memory or a system with an unsupported graphics board, you can use the text-mode installation. This mode performs the same functions as the graphical mode, but it uses plain text to prompt you with questions about how you want to configure the system.

In addition to graphical or text mode, you need to specify the source location of the programs you want to install. The most common location is a CD-ROM. In some cases you may have the programs on your hard disk. Each of these sources works in either graphics or text mode. You can also install the programs from a remote computer by using an FTP, NFS, or HTTP install.

Another choice you need to make is whether you want to use expert mode. Expert mode, which works in both graphic and text modes, requires you to answer more questions than normal mode. Use expert mode when default settings do not work and you have to work around a hardware problem. Some people use expert mode because it gives them more control over the installation.

Hardware

Most common Intel and AMD-based hardware run Red Hat. A searchable database of hardware that is supported by and compatible with various releases of Red Hat Linux is at hardware.redhat.com. There is also a *Linux Hardware Compatibility HOWTO*, and you can search for Linux hardware compatibility on the Internet to find more sites that cover this subject.

The most complex feat you will need to perform involving the hardware is partitioning the hard disk. Red Hat Linux gives you the option of automatically or semiautomatically doing this for you . When you choose to partition the disk yourself, you are given the choice of several tools to use. The classic and most common of these tools is fdisk (different from MSDOS fdisk). For more information refer to "fdisk: Reports on and Partitions a Disk" on page 914. Red Hat also offers another tool that is easier to use for partitioning your hard disk: Refer to "Disk Druid: Partitions a Disk" on page 918.

Red Hat runs on Intel, AMD, DEC/Compaq Alpha, IBM/S390, and Sun Sparc hardware. Most of this book applies to GNU/Linux running on all architectures. Some parts of the book and some commands pertain to the Intel/AMD architecture only. These commands are pointed out as such.

Classes of Installations

There are four classes of Red Hat Linux that you can install. You can also choose to upgrade an already installed version of Red Hat Linux (6.2 or later).

- **Personal Desktop**   Good for those who are new to GNU/Linux. This installation gives you a GUI and loads many of the programs you will likely need.

- **Workstation**   Good for software developers and system administrators. Gives you a GUI and loads many software development and system administration tools.

- **Server**   For those who want to deploy a GNU/Linux-based server without doing heavy customization. This installation has more services and fewer end user programs. Although you do not normally bring up a GUI on a server,[7] GNOME and KDE are available.

- **Custom** presents you with all the programs and services that Red Hat supports and lets you decide which you want to install. Only this installation gives you full control over which packages you install. This choice is recommended for experienced users only.

Regardless of the type of installation you choose, you can always add or remove programs once the system is up and running. For more information, refer to "redhat-config-packages: Adds and Removes Software Packages" on page 926.

---

7. On a server, you normally want to dedicate as many resources to the server and as few to anything that is not absolutely required by the server. For this reason you would not normally bring up a GUI, which requires a lot of resources, on a server.

Optional

Kickstart Configurator

GNOME	GNOME menu: System Tools⇨Kickstart
KDE	K menu: System Tools⇨Kickstart
Graphical	**redhat-config-kickstart**

Kickstart is Red Hat's program that completely or partially automates the same installation and postinstallation configuration on one or more machines. You create a single file that answers all the questions that are normally asked during an installation. Then the installation script refers to this file instead of asking you the questions. Using Kickstart, you can automate language selection, network configuration, keyboard selection, boot loader installation (grub or lilo), disk partitioning, mouse selection, and X Window System configuration.

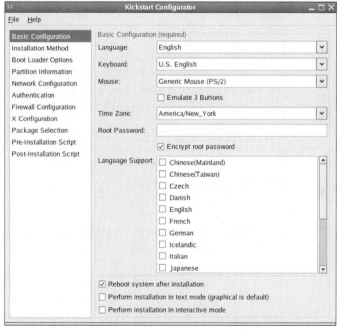

Figure 17-1   Kickstart Configurator

Figure 17-1 shows the first window that the Kickstart Configurator displays. The first text box, Language, is the language that will be used for installation. The Language Support box toward the bottom of the window, is the language that the new system will use after installation. In order to generate a Kickstart file (**ks.cfg** by default), you must go through each section of this window (along the left side) and fill in the answers and mark the appropriate boxes. Click the Help button for instructions on completing these tasks. When you are finished and click Save File, the Kickstart configurator gives you a chance to review the generated script before it saves the file. Refer to the *Red Hat Linux Customization Guide* for more information.

Preparing for Installation

You need to have information about your machine before you can install GNU/Linux. It is trivial to obtain some of the information: When the installation program asks you what kind of mouse you have, you can look at it, perhaps turn it over to read the label, and know what kind of mouse you have. And more and more, the installation software can probe the hardware and figure out what you have. Newer equipment is more likely to report on itself than older equipment is. Sometimes you just have to know. You might need to know what kind of video card or monitor you are using. When you are upgrading GNU/Linux from an earlier version, you definitely want to have a list of your partitions and where each is mounted so you don't overwrite your data. One thing that GNU/Linux can never figure out is all the relevant IP addresses (unless you are running DHCP, in which case most of the addresses are set up for you).

Following is a list of items you may need information about:

- Hard disks
- Memory (you don't need it for installation, but it is good to know)
- SCSI adapter board
- Network adapter board
- Video adapter board (including amount of video RAM/memory)
- Sound board and compatibility with standards, such as SoundBlaster
- Mouse
- Monitor
- Hostname for your computer (anything you like)
- IP address for your computer or just the fact that your IP address is dynamically assigned using DHCP (page 1028)

- IP address for the gateway system (your connecting point to the network/Internet) or a phone number when you use a dial-up connection

- IP address for your nameserver(s), also called DNS addresses

- Domain name (not required)

Get as much information on each item as you can: manufacturer, model number, size (megabytes, gigabytes, and so forth), number of buttons, chipset (boards), and so on. The IP addresses come from your system administrator or ISP.

A minimal custom installation requires about 0.35 gigabytes (350 megabytes). Installing all of the Red Hat packages takes up about 3.5 gigabytes. Your installation will probably fall somewhere in the middle: A graphical workstation with GNOME or KDE requires a minimum of 1.5 gigabytes; you need about 0.3 gigabytes more if you want both GNOME and KDE.

Partitioning a Disk

A *partition* (also called a *slice*, or *filesystem*) is a (hard) disk section that has a name so that you can address it separately from other sections. Under DOS/MS Windows, partitions (and sometimes whole disks) are labeled with **C:**, **D:**, and so on. This section discusses how to set up partitions under Red Hat Linux.

It can be difficult to plan your partition sizes appropriately if you are new to GNU/Linux. For this reason many people choose to have only two partitions. Partition 1 is reserved for the swap partition, which can be any size from 0 up to many hundreds of megabytes or, rarely, gigabytes. Partition 0 is designated as root and contains the remainder of the disk space. This makes managing space much easier. But if a program runs amok, the entire disk can fill up, and system accounting and logging information (which may contain data that can tell you what went wrong) may be lost.

As of Red Hat version 8.0, the Logical Volume Manager (LVM) allows you to change the size of logical volumes (LV, the LVM equivalent of partitions) on the fly: Using LVM, if you find you made a mistake in setting up your logical volumes or your needs change, you can make LVs smaller or larger easily and without affecting your data. You must choose to use LVM at the time you install the system or add a hard disk; you cannot retroactively apply it to a disk full of information. Refer to "LVM: Logical Volume Manager" on page 919.

Because it holds the bulk of system logs, package information, and accounting data, making **/var** a separate partition is a good idea. If a user runs a job that uses up all the disk space, the logs will not be affected. A good size for the **/var** partition is anything from about 500 megabytes up to several gigabytes for extremely active systems with many verbose daemons and a lot of printer activity (files in the print queue are stored on **/var**). Systems serving as license servers for licensed software often fall into the category of extremely active systems.

It is also common strategy to put user home directories into their own separate disk or partition. If you do not have a separate disk for the home directories, putting them in their own partition can avoid some problems. Common partition names are **/home** and **/usr/home**.

Using dump and restore to Manage Backups?   ‖ tip

Plan your partitions around what data you want to back up and how often you want to back it up. One very large partition can be more difficult to back up than several smaller ones.

Some sites choose to separate the root (**/**), **/boot**, and **/usr** partitions. This can be useful if you want to export **/usr** to another machine and want the extra security that a separate partition can give. By itself the root partition usually consumes less than 30 megabytes of disk space. On occasion you may install a special program that has many kernel drivers that consume a lot of space in the root partition. If you expect to run into this situation, you need to adjust the space allotted to the root partition accordingly. The size of **/usr** depends largely on the number of OS packages you install.

Where to Put the /boot Partition   ‖ tip

The /boot partition must reside *completely below cylinder 1,023* of the disk (except for some newer BIOSs). When you have more than one hard drive, the /boot partition must also reside on a drive on

- Multiple IDE or EIDE drives: the primary controller
- Multiple SCSI drives: ID 0 or ID 1
- Multiple IDE and SCSI drives: the primary IDE controller or SCSI ID 0

Finally, **/opt** and **/usr/local** are other candidates for separation. If you plan to install many software packages in addition to Red Hat, you may want to keep them on a separate partition. If you install the additional software in the same partition as the users, for example, it may start to encroach on the disk space allotted for the users' home directories. Many sites keep all the **/opt** or **/usr/local** software on one server and export it to others. If you choose to create a **/opt** or **/usr/local** partition, its size should be appropriate to the software you plan to install. Table 17-2 lists sample partition sizes for 4 and 20 gigabyte hard drives. You can extrapolate these values for larger drives.

Partition Name	Sample Partition Sizes in Kilobytes ‖ table 17-2	
	4 Gigabyte Drive	20 Gigabyte Drive
/ (root)	500	500
/boot	20	20
/home	1,080	10,000
/opt	350	2,980
(swap)	500	500
/tmp	250	500
/usr	1,000	2,500
/usr/local	n/a	2,000
/var	300	1,000
Total	4,000	20,000

fdisk: Reports on and Partitions a Disk

The fdisk utility can report on and change partitions on a disk. When you first install Red Hat or when you add a new disk drive to a Red Hat system, you can let
the installer partition the disk automatically, semiautomatically with your input, or
manually by running fdisk (or Disk Druid, page 918) to divide the disk into partitions and to identify the type of each partition. The system normally gets the disk
configuration information (number of cylinders, tracks, sectors/track, and more)
automatically by querying the disk.

Partitions can be of two types: primary and extended. A hard drive can have up
to four primary partitions or three primary partitions and an extended partition,
which can have any number of partitions encapsulated within it. MS Windows must
boot from a primary partition. GNU/Linux can boot from an extended partition by
using a boot loader (page 1039); however, the **/boot** partition must usually reside
completely below cylinder 1023 of the disk.

You can display the size (in 1024-byte blocks by default) of a hard disk by using
the fdisk with the –s option followed by the device name of the hard drive:

```
# fdisk -s /dev/hda
12714912
```

Typically IDE drives are named starting with **/dev/hda** (and continue with **hdb**, **hdc**, and so on), SCSI drives start with **/dev/sda**, PS2 ESDI drives start with **/dev/eda**, and hardware RAID devices start with **/dev/rd/c0d0** or **/dev/ida/c0d0**. Running fdisk with the **–l** option shows information about partitions.

```
# /sbin/fdisk -l /dev/hda

Disk /dev/hda: 255 heads, 63 sectors, 1582 cylinders
Units = cylinders of 16065 * 512 bytes

    Device Boot    Start      End    Blocks   Id  System
/dev/hda1    *         1        2     16033+   83  Linux
/dev/hda2              3     1582  12691350    5  Extended
/dev/hda5              3      512   4096543+   83  Linux
/dev/hda6            513      831   2562336    83  Linux
/dev/hda7            832      959   1028128+   83  Linux
/dev/hda8            960     1087   1028128+   83  Linux
/dev/hda9           1088     1215   1028128+   83  Linux
/dev/hda10          1216     1358   1148616    83  Linux
/dev/hda11          1359     1390    257008+   82  Linux swap
/dev/hda12          1391     1582   1542208+   83  Linux
```

In addition to reporting on the layout and size of a disk drive, you can use fdisk interactively to modify the layout. Be *extremely* careful when using fdisk in this manner, and always back up your system before starting. Changing the partition information (the *partition table*) on a disk destroys the information on the disk. Read the fdisk man page and the *Linux Partition mini-HOWTO* before modifying a partition table.

---

fdisk **Can Destroy Everything**   **|| caution**

Be as careful with **fdisk** as you would be with a utility that formats a hard drive. Changes you make with **fdisk** can easily result in the loss of large amounts of data. If you are using **fdisk** and have any question about what you are doing, back out with **q** (quit without saving changes)—your changes do not take effect until you leave **fdisk**.

To partition a disk, start fdisk without any options, and give an **m** command, which displays the following help message:[8]

---

8. You can safely ignore a warning message about the number of cylinders being too large.

```
# fdisk /dev/hda

Command (m for help): m
Command action
   a   toggle a bootable flag
   b   edit bsd disklabel
   c   toggle the dos compatibility flag
   d   delete a partition
   l   list known partition types
   m   print this menu
   n   add a new partition
   o   create a new empty DOS partition table
   p   print the partition table
   q   quit without saving changes
   s   create a new empty Sun disklabel
   t   change a partition's system id
   u   change display/entry units
   v   verify the partition table
   w   write table to disk and exit
   x   extra functionality (experts only)
```

When you choose **p** (print), fdisk displays the current partitions on your disk:

```
Command (m for help): p

Disk /dev/hda: 255 heads, 63 sectors, 1582 cylinders
Units = cylinders of 16065 * 512 bytes
   Device Boot    Start       End    Blocks   Id  System
/dev/hda1     *       1         2     16033+  83  Linux
/dev/hda2             3      1582  12691350    5  Extended
/dev/hda5             3       512   4096543+  83  Linux
/dev/hda6           513       831   2562336   83  Linux
/dev/hda7           832       959   1028128+  83  Linux
/dev/hda8           960      1087   1028128+  83  Linux
/dev/hda9          1088      1215   1028128+  83  Linux
/dev/hda10         1216      1358   1148616   83  Linux
/dev/hda11         1359      1390    257008+  82  Linux swap
/dev/hda12         1391      1582   1542208+  83  Linux
```

Each disk entry includes its filename within the **/dev** directory, the cylinder that the partition starts and ends on (use **u** to change the units to sectors), the number of 1024 (1 kilobyte) blocks, the ID number of the partition type (**l** to list the partition types), and the name corresponding to the partition type. Partitioning allows you to divide a disk into a maximum of eight separate *partitions,* or subdisks. You can use each partition independently for swap devices, filesystems, databases, other functions, and even other operating systems.

In the preceding example partition 2 defines an extended partition that includes almost the entire disk. You cannot make changes to this partition without affecting all the partitions within it. Following are guidelines to remember when defining a partition table for a disk. For more information, refer to "Partitioning a Disk" on page 912.

1. Do not modify the partition that defines the entire disk. This partition is called the **backup**, or **overlap**, partition.

2. Do not overlap partitions that contain data. If the first partition ends at cylinder 187, the second partition should begin at cylinder 188. If you overlap partitions, the filesystem will become corrupt as data for overlapping files is written to the disk. Because the overlap partition contains no data or filesystem, it is safe to have other partitions overlap it.

3. Older disks used a constant number of sectors per track. This made positioning the disk head easier but resulted in a lot of wasted space on the outer tracks. Newer disks use an encoding named ZBR (zone-bit recording): The sector size of the disk stays constant, which means that the outer cylinders have more sectors; consequently more information passes under the disk head per disk revolution, and data access is faster on these sectors. These outer cylinders correspond to the lower cylinder numbers (cylinders starting at zero). Put your speed-critical data on the lower-numbered cylinders.

4. Never put a raw partition on cylinder 0. A few sectors on cylinder 0 are reserved for such things as the disk label, bad blocks, and partition tables. A filesystem will preserve this information, but when you use cylinder 0 as part of a raw partition, this information is deleted, and the disk may become unusable. An example of a raw partition is a swap partition or raw database partition, as used for a Sybase or Oracle database. Start all raw partitions at cylinder 1 or greater. For more information, refer to "swap" on page 967.

5. It is a good to idea put **/boot** at the beginning of the drive (partition 1) so that there is no issue of GNU/Linux having to boot from a partition too far into the drive. When you can afford the disk space, it is desirable to put each major filesystem on a separate partition. Many people choose to combine root, **/var**, and **/usr** into a single partition, which generally results in less wasted space but can, on rare occasions, cause problems. You can also make the **boot** directory part of the root filesystem.

6. When using megabytes to specify the size of a partition, remember to check how many cylinders have been allocated so that you know where to begin the next partition.

7. Use tune2fs (page 982) to make all partitions except swap type **ext3** unless you have a reason not to.

Following is the sequence of commands necessary to define a 300 megabyte, bootable, GNU/Linux partition as partition 1 on a clean disk:

```
# /sbin/fdisk /dev/hda

Command (m for help): n                    (create new partition)
Command action
   l   logical (5 or over)
   p   primary partition (1-4)
p                                          (select primary partition)
Partition number (1-4): 1                  (select partition number 1)
First cylinder (1-1582, default 1):        (allow first cylinder to default to 1)
Using default value 1
Last cylinder or +size or +sizeM or +sizeK (1-2, default 2): +300M  (300 MB partition)
Command (m for help): t                    (set partition type)
Partition number (1-12): 1
Hex code (type L to list codes): 83        (83 is Linux, 82 is Linux swap, press L for a list)
Changed system type of partition 1 to 83  (Linux)

Command (m for help): a                    (specify a bootable partition)
Partition number (1-12): 1                 (specify partition 1 as bootable)
```

After defining a partition using **k** or **m** to specify kilobytes or megabytes, run **p** to check for the ending cylinder. Do this before defining the next contiguous partition so that you do not waste space or have any overlap. After setting up all the partitions and exiting from fdisk with a **w** command, make a filesystem (mkfs, page 1057) on each partition that is to hold a filesystem (not swap). Use mkswap to create a swap partition (page 967). You can use e2label to label partitions (page 1057).

Disk Druid: Partitions a Disk

Disk Druid, a graphical disk-partitioning program that can add, delete, and modify partitions on a hard drive, is part of the Red Hat installation system, so you can use Disk Druid only while you are installing a system: It cannot be run on its own. You must use fdisk to install or modify disks after you have installed Red Hat Linux.

When you want a basic set of partitions you can allow Disk Driud to partition the hard drive automatically. You can also use Disk Druid to partition the hard drive manually with steps that are similar to fdisk. Click Show Help to display instructions. Follow the instructions on the side panel as you proceed. Make your filesystems type **ext3** unless you have reason to do otherwise.

With the introduction of Red Hat version 8.0, Disk Druid includes Clone, a tool that copies the partitioning scheme from a single drive to as many other drives as needed. The Clone tool is useful for making multiple copies of a RAID drive when you are creating a large RAID array of identically partitioned drives. Click the RAID button to access the Clone tool, which is active only when at least one unallocated RAID partition exists.

LVM: Logical Volume Manager

New with Red Hat 8.0, the LVM (Logical Volume Manager) is a subsystem that manages online disk storage. It provides a high-level perspective of disk storage that releases the system administrator from the constraints imposed by viewing the storage devices physically. Instead, a system administrator can concentrate on user and application storage needs, allocating storage dynamically and letting LVM take care of the housekeeping. The LVM supports IDE and SCSI drives as well as multiple devices (RAID or MD).

The LVM groups disk components (hard disks or storage device arrays), called *physical volumes* (PVs), into a storage pool, or virtual disk, called a *volume group* (VG). See Figure 17-2. You allocate a portion of a VG to create a *logical volume* (LV).

An LV is similar in function to a traditional disk partition in that you can create a filesystem on an LV. It is much easier, however, to change and move LVs than partitions: When you run out of space on a filesystem on an LV, you can grow (expand) the LV, and its filesystem, into empty or new disk space, or you can move the filesystem to a larger LV. LVM's disk space manipulation is transparent to users; service is not interrupted.

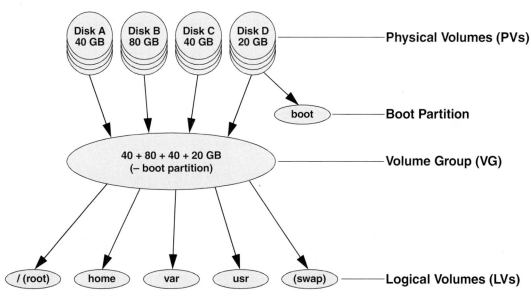

Figure 17-2   LVM: Logical Volume Manager

LVM also eases the burdens of storage migration. When you outgrow or need to upgrade PVs, LVM can move data to new PVs, again without interrupting users.

For specifics, refer to www.sistina.com/products_LVM_publications.htm, the *LVM HOWTO*, the **lvm** man page, and the "See also" man pages listed at the bottom of the **lvm** man page.

mkbootdisk: Creates a Rescue/Emergency/Boot Floppy Disk

A rescue disk, which is called by many names, including emergency boot floppy, contains a stripped-down version of GNU/Linux that you can use to boot your system when you cannot boot from the hard disk. You will rarely if ever need this disk, but when you do, you will really need it. Make a couple of rescue disks, make sure that they work by booting your system with each of them, and keep them in safe places. It is cheap insurance.

As an alternative you can boot using the first installation CD-ROM and enter **linux rescue** at the prompt. Although this technique does not bring up your kernel, it does mount your filesystems so that you can fix problems.

You have a chance to create a rescue disk while you are installing the system. You can also make a rescue disk anytime after the system is installed, using mkbootdisk. Before running mkbootdisk, determine the kernel version you are running by using the following command:

```
# uname -r
kernel-version
```

Then copy *kernel-version* (which will be something like 2.4.18-14) from the previous command into the following:

```
# /sbin/mkbootdisk kernel-version
```

or, perhaps simpler (refer to page 575 for additional information on command substitution):

```
# /sbin/mkbootdisk $(uname -r)
```

Finally, when you are not running as **root**, you can use

```
$ su -c "/sbin/mkbootdisk $(uname -r)"
```

Any of these commands produces an emergency boot floppy on the disk in your first floppy drive. Use the **--verbose** option to cause mkbootdisk to report on its progress as it writes to the disk. Additional rescue disks and programs are available at www.ibiblio.org/pub/Linux/system/recovery.

Test Each Rescue Disk after You Make It	**|| tip**

Always test a rescue disk after you create it. Do not wait until you need it to find out that it does not work.

Beginning Installation

Unless you are installing GNU/Linux from DOS, you generally start the installation by booting the Linux kernel from a floppy disk or a CD-ROM. Booting Linux directly from the CD-ROM or from a boot floppy does not require that you have DOS installed on your computer.[9] Most modern CD-ROM drives and BIOSs are capable of booting,[10] so if the source of your files is a CD-ROM, try this technique first: Reboot your machine without a floppy and with the Red Hat **disc1** CD-ROM in your machine. If you get a BOOT: prompt, this technique is working.

If the CD-ROM technique does not work, you need to boot from a floppy disk. Red Hat comes with one boot floppy. If this floppy does not have the correct boot image for you or if you do not have the floppy, use the Red Hat **disc1** CD-ROM, which has many floppy boot images, to create a boot disk. You can download these images if necessary. Some of the more common images are **boot.img** (CD-ROM and hard disk install), **bootnet.img** (network install), and **pcmcia.img** (laptop install). There are also several supplemental driver disk images, which you may need later in the installation: **drvblock.img** (block device drivers), **drvnet.img** (network drivers), **oldcdrom.img** (CD-ROM drivers), and **pcmciadd.img** (PCMCIA drivers).

When you have found the boot image you want to use and have copied it to your local machine, you need to copy it to a floppy disk. You can use dd to write the image file to a floppy when you are using a UNIX or GNU/Linux machine. From an MS Windows machine you need to use rawrite, which is in the **dosutils** directory on Red Hat **disc1** CD-ROM.

---

9. You will need access to a DOS/Windows system or another GNU/Linux or UNIX-like system to write a boot disk. All official releases of Red Hat come with a boot disk.

10. You may have to change your BIOS (page 1457) setup in order to boot from a CD-ROM: Watch the screen as you boot, and you will see a message telling you to press a key, such as F2 or DELETE, to enter setup. Setup is where you can change your BIOS settings. Press the key that is called for, and move the cursor to the screen and line that deals with booting the system. Generally there is a list of three or four devices that the system tries to boot from; failing the first, the system tries the second and so on. Manipulate the list so that the CD-ROM is the first choice, save your choices, and reboot. Refer to your hardware/BIOS manual for more information.

Put the boot floppy in the first drive (make sure that your BIOS is set up to boot from a floppy; see footnote 10 on page 921), and boot the computer. Look for the BOOT: prompt as your assurance that the boot is proceeding normally.

Continue the installation, following the instructions on the screen and the help they provide. Refer to the *Red Hat Linux x86 Installation Guide* as necessary.

redhat-config-xfree86: Sets Up X

GNOME	GNOME Menu: System Settings⇨Display
KDE	K Menu: System Settings⇨Display
graphical	**redhat-config-xfree86**
help	**redhat-config-xfree86 --help**

Formerly Xconfigurator, the redhat-config-xfree86 utility generates the file named **/etc/X11/XF86Config**,[11] which X (XFree86 version 4) uses to initialize itself. The redhat-config-xfree86 utility runs as part of the Red Hat Linux install, and you can run it by itself when you want to regenerate the **XF86Config** file (such as when you get a new monitor, want to add an additional screen resolution, and so on). It moves the existing configuration file to **XF86Config.backup** before generating a new one. You can also write or modify **XF86Config** with an editor. Always make a backup copy of a system file such as this one before you make changes to it. Even with a backup copy it is nice to comment out the code you want to remove and annotate the code you add so you can remember what you did when you come back to the file in the future.

The deeper the color (millions of colors, generated by a 24-bit color depth, is the deepest) and the higher the resolution (1600x1200 is the highest resolution of many monitors), the more resources the system uses displaying the video and the slower an older system will run. Video resource use versus system speed should not be an issue on a modern system.

Once X is running, you can switch between your choices by pressing CONTROL-ALT-+ or CONTROL-ALT-− (use the plus or minus on the numeric keypad).

The redhat-config-xfree86 utility can run from a command line; it opens a window if possible, even if you are not running a GUI. Use the **--help** option to display a list of options that it accepts. Table 17-3 describes the Display settings window that redhat-config-xfree86 brings up.

---

11. Prior to Red Hat version 8.0, Xconfigurator generated an **XF86Config-4** file for use with version 4 of XFree86. It also generated **XF86Config** for use with version 3 of XFree86. Red Hat versions 8.0 and higher generate only an **XF86Config** file, which is for use with version 4 of XFree86.

redhat-config-xfree86	‖ table 17-3
Display	The top part of this tab shows the relative display size with the name of the monitor and video card below.
Resolution	Sets the screen resolution.
Color Depth	Specifies the color depth. Using more colors requires more video memory.
Advanced	
Monitor	Specifies the type of monitor attached to the system. Click **Configure** to select from a list of monitors or to specify the characteristics of your monitor. From the Monitor Settings window, click **Probe Monitor** to have the system attempt to determine the type of monitor you are using.
Video Card	Specifies the type of video card in the system. Click **Configure** to select from a list of video cards. From the Video card settings window, click **Probe Videocard** to have the system attempt to determine the type of video card in your system.

Initializing Databases

After booting the system, log in as, or su to, **root** and run makewhatis to update the **whatis** database so that whatis (page 79) and apropos (page 79) work properly; then run updatedb to update the **slocate** database so that slocate[12] works properly. The best way to run these utilities is to run the cron scripts that run them daily. Working as **root**, give the following commands:

```
# /etc/cron.daily/makewhatis.cron
# /etc/cron.daily/slocate.cron
```

These utilities run for up to several minutes and may complain about not being able to find a file or two. When you get the prompt back, your **whatis** and **slocate** databases are up-to-date.

Setting Up the Default Desktop Manager

Red Hat introduced the Desktop Switcher scheme, which can replace the traditional scheme that uses the **~/.xinitrc** and **/etc/X11/xinit/xinitrc** files to select a desktop

---

12. The slocate (secure locate) utility allows you to index and search for files on your system quickly and securely.

manager. Refer to "Changing to a Different Desktop Manager" on page 173 for instructions on how to change a single user's default desktop manager by using the Desktop Switcher.

You can establish a default desktop manager by using the Desktop Switcher scheme. First, make sure that all users who want to use the default desktop manager do not have a ~/.Xclients file. Delete it if they do. Then place GNOME or KDE (upper- or lowercase) in the **/etc/sysconfig/desktop** file; any additional text, variables, or equations have no effect. When you (or the system) runs startx (the script that starts the X Window System), the **/etc/X11/xinit/Xclients** script uses **grep –i** to look for either GNOME or KDE in the **desktop** file.

On a single-user system it does not matter whether you change your personal file or the system file. On a multiple-user system the administrator should change the **/etc/sysconfig/desktop** file to accommodate the majority of the users, whereas the other users can run switchdesk to create/modify their ~/.Xclients file.

Starting a Program Automatically under X   ‖ tip

When it is run (to bring up the X Window System), startx runs the executable files in the /etc/X11/xinit/xinitrc.d directory. For example, you can put an xclock command in a file in this directory and make the file executable; X will display a clock every time it starts up. The only catch is that X displays nothing else until your command finishes execution. You must run all but the quickest of commands in the background.

---

redhat-config-securitylevel: Sets up a Firewall

A firewall helps protect your computer against malicious users (page 358). Depending on your needs, you can spend 15 minutes or 15 days setting up a firewall. This section describes the redhat-config-securitylevel graphical firewall creation tool. The gnome-lokkit wizard configures the same parameters as redhat-config-securitylevel but provides more help along the way.

These tools are for an average GNU/Linux user and do not configure arbitrary (custom) firewalls. You must use other tools and directly manipulate files to create complex firewalls. Refer to the *Red Hat Linux Security Guide* and *Red Hat Linux Reference Guide* for more information. You can also search on firewall from the Linux Documentation Project home page (www.tldp.org).

The redhat-config-securitylevel utility offers three levels of protection:

- **High Security:** Allows only DNS replies and DHCP (page 1028) network connections. Instant messaging services (IRC, IRQ, and so on) and Real-Audio require proxies (page 397).

- **Low Security:**   Disables remote X Window System sessions, remote NFS, FTP, SSH, TELNET, HTTP, and all connections to ports lower than 1023.

- **Disable Firewall:**   Creates no new security rules. This choice is not recommended for systems that are connected to remote systems (including the Internet) and that are not behind a firewall. This choice makes no changes to your system.

A Firewall Can Prevent Network Services from Working   ‖ tip

Depending on its level of protection and how you set it up, a firewall can prevent network services, such as NFS, from working. Test for this condition by turning the firewall off, running the service to see whether it works, and then resetting the firewall to the level and with the options you desire, and see whether the service still works.

After you choose a security level, you can stay with the default firewall rules applicable to the level you chose, or you can customize the rules. When you click Customize, the Trusted devices frame specifies which network interfaces you trust. When you are working with a system with a single network interface and that interface is connected to a machine or network that is not local/secure (including a cable or DSL modem), do not trust that interface. When the interface is connected to only local, trusted hosts, you can trust the interface. When you have more than one network interface, choose to trust or not trust each interface, based on the these rules. Put a check mark in each check box next to an interface you trust.

The Allow incoming frame specifies which protocols remote, untrusted machines can use to initiate connections to your machine:

- **WWW (HTTP):**   Permits a connection to a Web server on your machine

- **FTP:**   Permits someone to log in on your machine using FTP

- **SSH:**   Permits authorized, encrypted remote access to your machine (page 1029)

- **DHCP:**   Establishes an Internet connection (page 1028)

- **Mail (SMTP):**   Accepts incoming mail (not required for IMAP, POP3, or fetchmail)

- **TELNET:**   Permits authorized remote access to your machine (not secure; use ssh to log in on your machine remotely)

The Other ports frame specifies other port/protocol combinations that the firewall accepts. Refer to redhat-config-services: Configures Services II on page 946 to disable/enable other system services. Refer to "xinetd" on page 397 for information on the **xinetd** daemon, which is what redhat-config-services configures.

Installing and Removing Software

A software package is the collection of scripts, programs, files, and directories required to run a software application. Using packages makes it easier to transfer, install, and uninstall applications. A package contains either object (executable) files or source code files that you need to compile and install. Object files are precompiled for a specific processor and operating system[13] whereas source files need to be compiled but will run on a wide range of machines and operating systems.

Software for your system can come in different kinds of packages, such as rpm (page 928), the GNU Configure and Build System (page 931), tar, compressed tar, dpkg, slp, and others.[14] The most popular package is rpm. Other packages (such as tar), which were popular before the introduction of rpm, are used less now because they require more work on the part of the installer (you) and do not provide the depth of prerequisite and compatibility checking that rpm offers.

redhat-config-packages: Adds and Removes Software Packages

GNOME	GNOME Menu: System Settings⇨Packages Start Here: System Settings⇨Packages
KDE	K Menu: System Settings⇨Packages Start Here: System Settings⇨Packages
graphical	**redhat-config-packages**

Red Hat has made the process of adding and removing software packages that they supply very easy with the redhat-config-packages package management utility (Figure 17-3). This is the same tool that you use during installation when you choose to select packages manually.

The package manager divides software packages into categories: Desktops, Applications, Servers, Development, and System. Within each category are package groups. Figure 17-3 shows the Desktops category and part of the Applications category; three package groups are visible within each of these categories. The two numbers in brackets to the left of each of the Details buttons tell you how many packages are (to be) installed and how many are available. Before you make any

---

13. Some packages run under operating systems other than the one it was compiled under.

14. Alien (kitenet.net/programs/alien) is a program that converts among the rpm, Debian **dpkg**, Stampede **slp**, and Slackware **tgz** package formats. The Alien home page suggests that you *not use Alien to convert important system packages*, as different distributions frequently set up these packages differently and are not interchangeable.

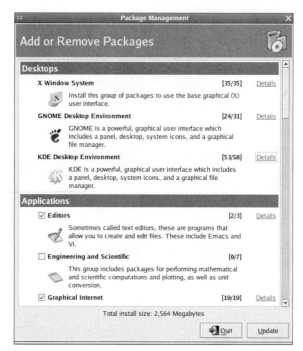

Figure 17-3   Red Hat Package Management window

changes, these numbers tell you how many packages are installed; after you make changes, they tell you how many packages will be installed after you click Update.

Boxes to the left of the names of the package groups indicate whether a group is selected (with check mark) or not (no check mark). Click a box to add or remove a package group.

The Desktop package groups cannot be removed (there are no boxes to the left of the group names); the Application package groups can be removed. In Figure 17-3 the Engineering and Scientific group is not installed or will be removed: There is no check mark in the box, and the numbers in brackets show that zero out of seven [0/7] packages are selected.

Once a package group is selected, you can click Details to display the Package Details window. Figure 17-4 shows the Details window for the KDE package group. Within a package group are two sets of packages: those that are standard when you select the group (Standard Packages) and those that are optional (Extra Packages). Click the triangle to the left of the name of the package set to hide or display the list of packages. Put a check mark in the boxes next to the names of the Extra Packages you want on your system. Remove check marks next to Extra Packages you do not want. Click Close to return to the Package Management window when you finish selecting packages. Click Update to install/remove packages as you specified. The package manager will ask you for the install disks it needs.

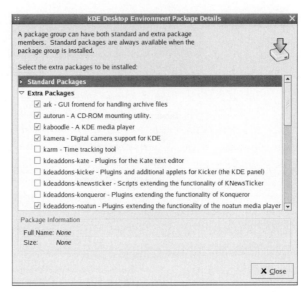

Figure 17-4   Red Hat Package Management Details window

rpm: **Red Hat Package Manager**

The rpm (Red Hat Package Manager) utility works only with software packages that have been built for processing by rpm; it installs, uninstalls, upgrades, queries, and verifies rpm packages. Because Red Hat released rpm under the GPL (page 7), rpm is used by several distributions. Together with information contained within software packages assembled for use with rpm (named ***.rpm**), the rpm utility keeps track of where software packages should be installed, the versions of the packages that you have installed, and the dependencies between the packages.

Source rpm packages are frequently found in a directory named **SRPMS** (source rpms), whereas object rpm packages are in **RPMS**. When you download object packages, make sure that they are relevant to your operating system (both distribution and release—for example, **redhat 7.2**) and were compiled on the appropriate architecture (**i386** covers all Intel- and most AMD-based systems, **i586** covers Pentium-class processors and above, **S390** is for IBM System/390, **ia64** is for the 64-bit Intel processor, **alpha** is for the DEC/Compaq Alpha chip, **athlon** denotes the AMD Athlon family, **ppc** is for the Power PC chip, and **sparc** covers the Sun Sparc processor).[15] The name of the rpm file contains almost all the necessary information. Each of the following lines from a search for sendmail on www.rpmfind.net gives you the information you need:

---

15. Many rpm packages run on releases and even distributions other than the ones they were compiled on/for.

```
sendmail-8.11.6-3.ia64.html ...     RedHat-7.2 for ia64        sendmail-8.11.6-3.ia64.rpm
sendmail-8.11.6-3.i386.html ...     RedHat-7.2 for i386        sendmail-8.11.6-3.i386.rpm
sendmail-8.11.6-2.7.1.src.html ...  Yellow Dog PPC             sendmail-8.11.6-2.7.1.src.rpm
sendmail-8.11.6-2.7.1.i386.html ... RedHat-7.1 Updates for i386 sendmail-8.11.6-2.7.1.i386.rpm
sendmail-8.11.6-2.7.1.ppc.html ...  Yellow Dog PPC             sendmail-8.11.6-2.7.1.ppc.rpm
sendmail-8.11.6-2.7.1.alpha.html ... RedHat-7.1 Updates for alpha sendmail-8.11.6-2.7.1.alpha.rpm
sendmail-8.11.6-2.7.0.i386.html ... RedHat-7.0 Updates for i386 sendmail-8.11.6-2.7.0.i386.rpm
sendmail-8.11.6-2.7.0.alpha.html ...  RedHat-7.0 Updates for alpha    sendmail-8.11.6-2.7.0.alpha.rpm
```

Click the **html** filename at the left to display all the information about the file. Click the **rpm** filename at the right to download the file. Both of these names tell you the name of the program, its version number, and its format (source or compiled for **i386, alpha, ia64,** and so on). The column to the left of the **rpm** filename tells you which distribution the file is from/for.

Querying Packages and Files

The rpm utility can be run from a command line. Use **rpm –qa** to get a list of one-line summaries of all the packages installed on your system (any user can run this utility). Use **rpm –q** followed by the name of the package to get more information about a particular package. For instance **rpm –q nis** will tell you whether NIS is installed and if so, what version. Use the **–ql** options to get a list of files in a package:

```
$ rpm -q nis
package nis is not installed
$ rpm -ql logrotate
/etc/logrotate.conf
/etc/logrotate.d
/usr/sbin/logrotate
/usr/share/doc/logrotate-3.5.9
/usr/share/doc/logrotate-3.5.9/CHANGES
/usr/share/man/man8/logrotate.8.gz
```

The **–qi** options give you quite a bit of information about a package:

```
$ rpm -qi logrotate
Name        : logrotate          Relocations: (not relocateable)
Version     : 3.5.9                    Vendor: Red Hat, Inc.
Release     : 1                    Build Date: Tue 04 Sep 2001 01:40:18 PM PDT
Install date: Wed 28 Nov 2001 02:14:06 PM PST    Build Host: porky.devel.redhat.com
Group       : System Environment/Base    Source RPM: logrotate-3.5.9-1.src.rpm
Size        : 40032                   License: GPL
Packager    : Red Hat, Inc. <http://bugzilla.redhat.com/bugzilla>
Summary     : Rotates, compresses, removes and mails system log files.
Description :
The logrotate utility is designed to simplify the administration of
log files on a system which generates a lot of log files. Logrotate
allows for the automatic rotation compression, removal, and mailing of
log files. Logrotate can be set to handle a log file daily, weekly,
monthly, or when the log file gets to a certain size. Normally,
logrotate runs as a daily cron job.
```

Installing, Upgrading, and Removing Packages

You can use rpm to install or upgrade a package. Log in as, or su to, **root**[16] and use the **–i** option, followed by the name of the file that contains the rpm version of the package you want to install. Add the **–v** (verbose) option to get a little more information about what is going on and the **–h** (or **––hash**) option to see hash marks as the package is unpacked and installed. For example, while logged in as **root**, use the following command to add samba to your system:

```
# rpm -ivh samba-2.2.1a-4.i386.rpm
```

Or usually the following will work:

```
# rpm -ivh samba*
```

When you install a package, your working directory must be the directory that contains the rpm file, or you must use a pathname that points to the file.

To remove the same package, give the following command:

```
# rpm -e samba
```

The rpm utility queries its database to find out the information it needs to uninstall the package and removes links, unloads device drivers, and stops daemons as necessary. Refer to the rpm man page for other rpm options.

up2date: Queries and Installs Packages

Refer to "up2date: RHN Update Agent" on page 939 for information about querying and installing software packages using Red Hat Network.

Installing a Linux Kernel Binary

Take the following steps to install a new Linux kernel binary. Refer to "Rebuilding the Linux Kernel" on page 1031 when you want to configure and rebuild a kernel, not install a new, prebuilt kernel binary. Rebuilding a kernel is more involved than installing a new one.

1. Run rpm with the **–i** option to install the new kernel. Do not use the **–U** option, as you are installing a new kernel that has a name different from the old kernel: You are not upgrading the existing kernel.

2. Add the new kernel information to **/etc/lilo.conf** (and run lilo) or **/etc/grub.conf**. There is no need to run grub after modifying **grub.conf**.

---

16. Although you can run rpm as a nonprivileged user, you will not have permission to write to the necessary directories during an install or uninstall, and the install/uninstall will fail. During a query, you do not need this permission, so you can (and should) work as a nonprivileged user.

3. Make sure that the new kernel works before you remove the old kernel. To verify that the new kernel works, reboot the system using the new kernel.

4. Remove the old kernel by removing the files that contain the release number (and EXTRAVERSION number [page 1036], if applicable) in their filenames from **/boot** or **/** (root). Remove information about the old kernel from **lilo.conf** or **grub.conf**. Remember to run lilo if you modify **lilo.conf**. You may want to wait a while before removing the old kernel to make sure that there are no problems with the new one.

Installing Non-rpm Software

Most software that does not come in rpm format comes with detailed instructions on how to configure, build (if necessary), and install it. Some binary distributions (those containing prebuilt executables that run on Red Hat) require you to unpack the software from the root directory of your system. Some newer application packages include scripts to install themselves automatically into a directory hierarchy under **/opt**, with files in a **/opt** subdirectory that is named after the package and executables in **/opt/bin** or **/opt/*package*/bin**. These scripts are relatively new additions to Red Hat but familiar ones to Sun Solaris users.

Other software packages allow you to choose where you unpack them. Because the software available for GNU/Linux is developed by many different people, there is no consistent method for doing installations. As you acquire local software, you should install it on your system in as consistent and predictable a manner as possible. The default Red Hat file structure has a directory tree under **/usr/local** for binaries (**/usr/local/bin**), manual pages (**/usr/local/man**), and so forth. To prevent confusion later and to avoid overwriting or losing the software when you install standard software upgrades in the future, avoid installing nonstandard software in standard system directories (such as **/usr/bin**). Make sure that the users on your system know where to find the local software, and remember to make an announcement whenever you install, change, or remove local tools.

GNU Configure and Build System

The GNU Configure and Build System makes it easy to build a program that is distributed as source code (see autoconf at developer.gnome.org/tools/build.html). This two-step process does not require special tools other than a shell, make, and gcc (GNU C compiler). You do not need to work with **root** privileges for either of these steps.

The following example assumes that you have downloaded GNU chess (www.gnu.org/software/chess/chess.html) in the working directory. First, you need to unpack and decompress it and cd to the new directory:

```
$ tar -xvzf chess*
gnuchess-5.03/
gnuchess-5.03/book/
gnuchess-5.03/book/README
...
$ cd gnuchess*
```

After reading the **README** and **INSTALL** files, proceed to the first of the two steps: Run the configure script, which finds out about your system and generates the **Makefile** file:

```
$ ./configure
checking for a BSD compatible install... /usr/bin/install -c
checking whether build environment is sane... yes
checking for mawk... mawk
checking whether make sets ${MAKE}... yes
checking for gcc... gcc
checking for C compiler default output... a.out
checking whether the C compiler works... yes
   .
   .
   .
checking for memset... yes
configure: creating ./config.status
config.status: creating Makefile
config.status: creating src/Makefile
config.status: creating src/config.h
```

Refer to page 1120 in Part III for more information on configure, specifically the **--prefix** option, which causes the install phase to place the software in a directory other than **/usr/local**. The second step is to run make.

```
$ make
Making all in src
make[1]: Entering directory '/hdd4/gnuchess-5.03/src'
cd .. \
&& CONFIG_FILES= CONFIG_HEADERS=src/config.h \
/bin/sh ./config.status
config.status: creating src/config.h
config.status: src/config.h is unchanged
make  all-am
make[2]: Entering directory '/hdd4/gnuchess-5.03/src'
source='atak.c' object='atak.o' libtool=no \
depfile='.deps/atak.Po' tmpdepfile='.deps/atak.TPo' \
depmode=gcc3 /bin/sh ../depcomp \
gcc -DHAVE_CONFIG_H -I. -I. -I.      -g -O2 -c 'test -f atak.c || echo './''atak.c
   .
   .
```

```
gcc  -g -O2   -o gnuchess  atak.o book.o cmd.o epd.o eval.o genmove.o hash.o hung.o init.o
iterate.o main.o move.o null.o output.o players.o pgn.o quiesce.o random.o repeat.o
search.o solve.o sort.o swap.o test.o ttable.o util.o version.o  -lreadline -lncurses -lm
make[2]: Leaving directory '/hdd4/gnuchess-5.03/src'
make[1]: Leaving directory '/hdd4/gnuchess-5.03/src'
make[1]: Entering directory '/hdd4/gnuchess-5.03'
make[1]: Nothing to be done for 'all-am'.
make[1]: Leaving directory '/hdd4/gnuchess-5.03'
$ ls src/gnuchess
src/gnuchess
```

After the second step, the gnuchess executable is in the **src** directory. If you want to install it, give the following command while running with **root** privileges:

```
# make install
Making install in src
make[1]: Entering directory '/hdd4/gnuchess-5.03/src'
make[2]: Entering directory '/hdd4/gnuchess-5.03/src'
/bin/sh ../mkinstalldirs /usr/local/bin
/usr/bin/install -c gnuchess /usr/local/bin/gnuchess
make[2]: Nothing to be done for 'install-data-am'.
...
```

You can run the two steps and install the software with this command line:

```
# ./configure && make && make install
```

The Boolean operator && (AND) allows the execution of the next step only if the previous step returned a successful exit status.

Keeping Software Up-to-Date

Of the many reasons to keep the software on your system up-to-date, one of the most important is security. Although you hear about software-based security breaches, you do not hear about the fixes that were available but never installed before the breach. Timely installation of software updates is critical to system security. GNU/Linux Open Source software is the ideal environment to find and fix bugs and make repaired software available quickly. When you keep your system and application software up-to-date, you keep abreast of bug fixes, new features, support for new hardware, speed enhancements, and more.

Bugs

A *bug* is an unwanted and unintended program property, especially one that causes the program to malfunction.[17] Bugs have been around forever, in many types of systems,

---

17. Courtesy of www.foldoc.org. Refer to the full definition of *bug* therein.

machinery, thinking, and so on. All sophisticated software contains bugs. Bugs in system software or application packages can crash the system or cause programs not to run correctly. Security holes (a type of bug) can compromise the security of the system, allowing malicious users to read and write files, send mail to your contacts in your name, or destroy all the data on the system, rendering the system useless. If the engineers fixed all the bugs, there would still be feature requests as long as anyone used the software. Bugs, feature requests, and security holes are here to stay and must be properly tracked if the developers are to fix the most dangerous/important bugs first, users are to research and report bugs in a logical manner, and users are to be able to apply the developer's fixes quickly and easily.

Early on, Netscape used an internal bug-tracking system named BugSplat. Later, after Netscape created Mozilla (mozilla.org) as an Open Source browser project, the Mozilla team decided that it needed its own bug-tracking system. Netscape's IS department wrote a very short-lived version of Bugzilla. Then Terry Weissman, who had been maintaining BugSplat, wrote a new, Open Source version of Bugzilla in Tcl, rewriting it in Perl a couple of months later.

Bugzilla belongs to a class of programs formally known as Defect Tracking Systems, of which Bugzilla is now preeminent. It is the tool that almost all GNU/Linux developers use to track problems with and enhancement requests for their software. Red Hat uses Bugzilla to track bugs and bug fixes for its GNU/Linux distribution; Red Hat Network takes advantage of Bugzilla to notify users of and distribute these fixes.

Errata: Security Alerts, Bugfixes, and Enhancements

In Red Hat's nomenclature, software enhancements and solutions or fixes to software bugs are referred to as *errata*. The enhancement requests and bugs are divided into three classes: *security, bugfixes,* and *enhancements.* To announce the availability of an erratum, Red Hat appends the term *alert* to its class: *Security Alerts, Bugfix Alerts,* and *Enhancement Alerts.* The easiest way to learn of new errata and to obtain and install them is to use Red Hat Network (page 936).

As the GNU/Linux community, including Red Hat, finds and fixes operating system and software package bugs, including security holes, Red Hat generates rpm files (page 928) that contain the code that fixes the problems. Installing a new version of a package is almost the same as installing the package in the first place. When running rpm, use –U (upgrade) in place of the –i option. The upgrade option is the same as the install option except that it removes the earlier version of the package.

Lists of errata for all recent releases of Red Hat Linux are available at www.redhat.com: Support and Docs⇨Errata. Click the release you are using and the package you are interested in to view a summary of errata. A lot of information is on this page, including Bug IDs that link to Red Hat's internal Bugzilla system, a list of architectures that this errata applies to, and a list of links to the appropriate rpm files for each of the applicable Red Hat releases. Under each heading that names a release of Red Hat Linux are subheadings, the first of which is SRPMS. The rpm files under this heading contain source files that you must compile; they work on any architecture that runs the corresponding version of Red Hat Linux. Next are the RPMS (binary) files; choose them with regard to the architecture you are running on. The subheads specify the architecture that the binary files within the rpm file were compiled on.

The rpm files are available via anonymous FTP from ftp://updates.redhat.com or from one of its mirrors (see footnote 6 on page 905). Log in on one of these FTP sites as **anonymous**, and give your e-mail address as your password (your browser may do this for you). When you are downloading updates, you will be presented with a list of release numbers. Choose the release number you are using, and follow the hierarchy until you find the rpm file you want. Your path will look similar to ftp://sunsite.ualberta.ca/pub/unix/linux/redhat/updates/8.0/en/os/i386. The part of the path preceding **redhat** varies from site to site, but the part to the right of **redhat** is always the same for a given file. When you select a site from the Update column of **mirror.html**, you start in the directory named **updates** and see the list of version numbers. When you are working from a browser, double-click the icon next to the file/version number that you want to look in or the file that you want to download. When you are running ftp from a command line, refer to "ftp: Transfers Files over a Network" on page 378. Red Hat Network (next) provides an automated way of keeping your system up-to-date.

While you are browsing, you may come across the directories in Table 17-4.

Directories in the Release Hierarchy || table 17-4

alpha	Binary code **rpm** files for DEC/Compaq Alpha-based machines
i386	Binary code **rpm** files for Intel x386–based machines
images	Various floppy disk boot images
ls–lR	A recursive listing of all the files below this directory
ls–lR.gz	A compressed, recursive listing of all the files below this directory
noarch	Non-architecture-specific **rpm** files—use on any platform that GNU/Linux runs on
sparc	Binary code **rpm** files for Sun Sparc–based machines
SRPMS	Source **rpm** files of source code that you need to compile

Red Hat Network

GNOME	GNOME menu: System Tools⇨Red Hat Network start-here: Applications⇨System Tools⇨Red Hat Network Red Hat Network Alert Notification Tool Icon (page 938)
KDE	K menu: System Tools⇨Red Hat Network Red Hat Network Alert Notification Tool Icon (page 938)
graphical	**up2date** page 939
character-based	**up2date-nox**
Help	www.redhat.com (RHN Home Page: log in and look around) www.redhat.com/docs/manuals/RHNetwork (RHN Manuals) rhn.redhat.com/help (Help Desk) rhn.redhat.com/network/quickstart.pxt (Quick Start Guide) up2date man page

Red Hat Network (RHN, rhn.redhat.com) is a service provided by Red Hat, an Internet-based system that can keep the software on one or more of your Red Hat machines up-to-date with minimal work on your part. You must subscribe to this service in order to use it. Red Hat uses the term *entitle* to indicate that a system is subscribed to RHN: Your system must be entitled before you can use RHN. To date, Red Hat allows each user to register one system for free. You can choose to make RHN more or less automated, giving you various degrees of control over the update process.

The systems that are entitled are the clients; Red Hat maintains the RHN server. The RHN Server is much more than a single server; it involves many systems and databases that are replicated and located in different areas. For the purpose of understanding how to use the client tools on your system, picture the RHN Server as a single server. For additional information refer to the *RHN User Reference Guide* (www.redhat.com/docs/manuals/RHNetwork).

Red Hat built RHN with security as a priority. Any time you allow a remote system to put a program on your system and run it, the setup must be very close to the theoretical ideal of absolute security. Toward this end RHN never initiates communication with your system. Once a program running on your system sends a message to the RHN server, the server can respond and your system can trust the response.

Subscribing to Red Hat Network

Perform the following tasks to start using RHN. Although you can perform the tasks in a different order, the following order is convenient, and it works.

- Set up your RHN system profile. When you do not have a profile, any call to up2date, the primary RHN tool on your system, opens the RHN Update Agent Configuration window, which starts the registration process.

  Left click the Red Hat Network Alert Notification Tool (a blue circle icon with a check mark or a red circle icon with an exclamation point on the panel), or select the K or GNOME menu: System Tools⇨Red Hat Network to open the configuration window. Refer to "up2date-config: Configures the RHN Update Agent" on page 940 for help with this window.

- When you close the configuration window, the Red Hat Update Agent window opens.

  - Read the information in the first window, and click Forward.

  - The Step 1: Review the Red Hat Privacy Statement window opens. If you are comfortable with the information in this window, click Forward.

  - The Step 2: Register or Update a User Account window opens. Fill in the information in the Required Information frame. RHN will recognize your information if you are already registered with RHN or will establish an account for you if you are not already registered. Fill in the Org Info frame only if you are registering as part of a registered organization. Click Forward.

  - The Step 3: Register a System Profile - Hardware window opens. This window establishes a profile name for your computer. The default name is your node (machine) name. You can put any information to help you identify this machine in this text box. The window also confirms that you want to include the hardware and network information in the profile information that you will send to RHN at the end of this process. When you click Forward, the program compiles a list of all the rpm packages that are installed on your machine.

  - The Step 3: Register a System Profile - Packages window opens (there are two Step 3 windows). This window confirms that you want to include your installed rpm packages as part of your system profile and gives you the option of removing packages from your profile so that they do not get updated. Click Forward.

  - Click Forward to send your profile to RHN, or click Cancel and nothing will be sent.

- Entitle your system. The error: `Service not enabled for server profile: "profilename"` means that your system is not entitled. If you get this message, go to rhn.redhat.com, and log in with the user name and password you set up in Step 2, preceding.

Click Your RHN, Entitlements, and then the Service Entitlements tab. You should see your *profilename* in the Name column toward the bottom of the frame. Use the drop down list in the Entitled column to select Basic for your system. Click Update Entitlements.

- Check for updates. Run up2date, or choose Red Hat Network Alert Notification Tool Icon menu: Check for updates (page 939) to see if the RHN server downloads files to or exchanges information with your system. You can also give the command **up2date --list** to see whether any packages are available for your system, thereby testing your connection with the RHN server.

You can start the flow of updates from your system or from the Web site. From your system, run up2date. From the Web site log in, click Systems⇨Systems List⇨Detailed View, click UPDATE NOW on the line with *profilename* on it, and click Confirm Update For This System. In either case the next time the **rhnsd** daemon on your system contacts the RHN server, you will get updates per the RHN system profile (installed or not, left on the system or not, source code or not, and so on).

Red Hat Network Alert Notification Tool

The Red Hat Network Alert Notification Tool can take care of everything you need to do from your system to set up, run, and administer your RHN account. The Red Hat Network Alert Notification Tool is represented by a round button on both the GNOME and KDE Main panel. It shows one of four icons:

- Blue with a check mark indicates that all is well: There are no pending downloads.

- Red with an exclamation point indicates that files need to be downloaded. Click the button.

- Green with half arrows pointing left and right indicates that the system is communicating with the RHN server.

- Grey with a question mark indicates that there has been an error. Click the icon to display the error message.

If the button is not on the Main panel, run rhn-applet-gui from Run Program on the GNOME menu or Run Command on the K menu to display it. Table 17-5 describes the selections on the Red Hat Network Alert Notification Tool panel icon menu (right click),

Red Hat Network Alert Notification Tool Icon Menu	**‖ table 17-5**
Check for updates	Runs **up2date** (page 939) in the background to check for updates. The green icon with arrows on the Red Hat Network Alert Notification button shows you that your system is communicating with the RHN server.
Launch up2date	Runs **up2date** (page 939) in the foreground, opening a series of windows that do not give you many options.
Configuration	Opens a series of windows that display the Terms of Service, allows you to configure a proxy, and checks for updates.

up2date: RHN Update Agent

The up2date utility is the workhorse at the client end of RHN: Its basic function is to download rpm packages from the RHN server. It works with many files and directories, in graphical and character-based modes, and has many options.

One of the most important options, −−**configure**, generates up2date's system profile file (**/etc/sysconfig/rhn/up2date**). The up2date-config utility (next section) is a link to up2date with the −−**configure** option. You do not normally use this option because up2date configures itself (creates the RHN system profile) when necessary. The −−**nox** option (also up2date-nox) runs up2date in noninteractive, character-based mode. Refer to the up2date man page for more information.

In addition to updating packages that are on your system, up2date can download and install Red Hat packages that are not on your system. Following, the user calls links, the character-based browser program, finds it is not on the system, and confirms that finding with whereis. Then, up2date, with the −−**whatprovides** option, queries RHN to find that the **elinks** package provides links. Finally, up2date, with an argument of the rpm package to be installed, downloads the **elinks** package from RHN. In this case up2date installs the package because that is what the system profile is set up to do. You must run up2date as Superuser to install or upgrade a package.

```
$ links
bash: links: command not found
$ whereis links
links:
$ up2date --whatprovides links
elinks-0.3.2-1
$ su
Password:
```

```
# up2date elinks

Fetching package list for channel: redhat-linux-i386-8.0...
######################################

Fetching Obsoletes list for channel: redhat-linux-i386-8.0...
######################################

Fetching rpm headers...

Testing package set / solving RPM inter-dependencies...
######################################
elinks-0.3.2-1.i386.rpm:  ######################### Done.
Preparing       ############################################[100%]

Installing...
1:elinks                 ######################################### [100%]
```

up2date-config: Configures the RHN Update Agent

The RHN Update Agent Configuration Tool, up2date-config,[18] sets some of the parameters in your RHN system profile. You can run up2date-config from a command line, but it is not usually required because up2date configures itself as necessary, usually the first time you run it. In a graphical environment, this tool displays a window with three tabs: General, Retrieval/Installation, and Package Exceptions (Table 17-6).

Red Hat Network Configuration Window	‖ table 17-6
General Network Settings	
Select a Red Hat Network Server to use	This text box is already filled in for you. Do not change it unless you have reason to do so.
If you need a HTTP proxy, enter it here in the format HOST:PORT e.g. squid.mysite.org:3128	
Enable HTTP Proxy	Enter your HTTP proxy server (page 397) in the required format if you need to use a proxy server.

---

18. The up2date-config command is a link to up2date. When called using this link, up2date determines it was called as up2date-config and takes the same actions as it would had it been called directly with the −−**configure** option.

Red Hat Network Configuration Window (Continued) || table 17-6

Use Authentication	Select **Use Authentication** and fill in the **Username** and **Password** text boxes when your proxy server requires authentication. These spaces are for the proxy server, *not for your RHN username and password*.
Retrieval/Installation	
Package Retrieval Options	
Do not install packages after retrieval	Download, but do not install packages. You will need to install the new packages manually.
Do not upgrade packages when local configuration file has been modified	Do not download or install packages that have been customized. This option is not necessary unless you are using other than the standard Red Hat packages.
Retrieve source RPM along with binary package	Download the source code (*.src.rpm) file in addition to the binary file (*.architecture.rpm) that is to be installed. RHN does nothing with the source file except download it.
Package Verification Options	
Use GPG to verify package integrity	Uses Red Hat's GPG (page 1030) signature to verify the authenticity of the files you are downloading. If you do not have Red Hat's signature on your machine, you will be asked if you want the system to download it for you. This is a critical link in the security of RHN, and it is a good idea to select this option.
Package Installation Options	
After installation, keep binary packages on disk	Normally the binary **rpm** files are removed once the files they contain have been installed on your system. Select this option if you want them left on your system in the **Package storage directory** (following).
Enable RPM rollbacks (allows "undo" but requires additional storage space)	By using extra disk space, RHN can store information so that it can uninstall a package that it has installed and reinstall the version of the package that was there previously.

Red Hat Network Configuration Window (Continued)	**‖ table 17-6**
Override version stored in System Profile	Downloads and installs packages for a version of Red Hat that you specify in the text box, overriding the version number that is stored in your system profile.
Package storage directory	Specifies a directory to store the downloaded files in. By default they are stored in /var/spool/up2date.
Package Exceptions	Specifies packages and files that you do not want to download. These names can include wildcard characters.
Package Names to Skip	By default kernel* appears in this list box, meaning that no **rpm** packages whose names begin with the letters **kernel** will be downloaded. Installing a new kernel is an important event, and Red Hat assumes that you do not want this to happen without your knowledge. Use the **Add**, **Edit**, and **Remove** buttons to adjust the list box to meet your requirements. Normally you do not have to make any changes here.
File Names to Skip	Similar to **Package Names to Skip** except you can specify filenames that you want to skip here.

rhnsd: RHN Daemon

The RHN daemon (**rhnsd**) is a background service that periodically queries the RHN server to find out whether any new packages need to be downloaded. This daemon is one of the keys to RHN security; it is the component that initiates contact with the RHN server so that the server never has to initiate contact with your system. Refer to service: Configures Services I on page 945 to start, stop, or display the status of **rhnsd** immediately and to redhat-config-services: Configures Services II on page 946 to start or stop **rhnsd** at specified runlevels.

System Operation

This section covers the basics of how the system functions and how you can make intelligent decisions as a system administrator. This section does not cover every aspect of system administration in the depth necessary to set up or modify all system functions. It provides a guide to bringing a system up and keeping it running from day to day. Subsequent sections of this chapter and Part III of this book describe many of the system administration files and utilities in detail.

Booting the System

Booting a system is the process of reading the Linux *kernel* (page 1475) into system memory and starting it running. Refer to "Boot Loader" on page 1039 for more information on the initial steps of bringing a system up.

As the last step of the boot procedure, GNU/Linux runs the init program as PID number 1. The init program is the first genuine process to run after booting and is the parent of all system processes.[19]

The **initdefault** entry in the **/etc/inittab** file (page 960) tells init what runlevel to bring the system to (Table 17-7).

Runlevels || table 17-7

Number	Name	Login	Network	Filesystems
0	Halt			
1*	Single user	Text	Down	Not mounted
2	Undefined			
3	Multiuser	Text	Up	Mounted
4	Undefined			
5	Multiuser with X	Graphics	Up	Mounted
6	Reboot			

*Do not use **S** or **s** in place of **1**, as they are not meant to be used directly. They are intended to be used from scripts.

List the Kernel Boot Messages || tip

To save a list of kernel boot messages, give the following command immediately after booting the system and logging in:

```
$ dmesg > dmesg.boot
```

This command saves the kernel messages in the **dmesg.boot** file. This list can be educational. It can also be useful when you are having a problem with the boot process.

---

19. That is why when you run as **root** and kill process **1**, the system dies.

rc Scripts: Start and Stop System Services

The first script that init runs is **/etc/rc.d/rc.sysinit**, which runs initlog to set up command logging for the duration of the boot process. The **rc.sysinit** script also performs basic system configuration, including setting the system clock, hostname, and keyboard mapping; setting up swap partitions; checking the filesystems for errors; and turning on quota management.

Next, the **/etc/rc.d/rc** script runs the scripts that handle the services that need to be started when you first bring the system up and to be started or stopped when the system goes from single-user to multiuser mode and back down again. Many of the **rc** (run command) scripts are shell scripts—located in the **/etc/rc.d/init.d** directory—run via symbolic links in the **/etc/rc.d/rc*n*.d** directory, where *n* is the runlevel the system is entering.

The **/etc/rc.d/rc*n*.d** directories contain scripts whose names begin with **K** (**K15httpd, K72autofs, K30sendmail,** and so on) and scripts whose names begin with **S** (**S05kudzu, S10network, S13portmap,** and so on). When entering a new runlevel, each of the **K** (kill) scripts is executed with an argument of **stop**, and then each of the **S** (start) scripts is executed with an argument of **start**. Each of the **K** files is run in numerical order. The **S** files are run similarly. This setup allows the person who sets up these files to control which services are stopped and which are started and in what order, whenever the system enters a given runlevel. Using scripts with **start** and **stop** arguments is flexible because it allows one script to both start and kill a process, depending on the argument it is called with.

To customize system initialization, you can add shell scripts to the **/etc/rc.d/init.d** directory and add links to the files in **init.d** from the **/etc/rc.d/rc*n*.d** directories. The following example shows several links to the **lpd** script. These links are called to start or stop the **lpd** daemon at various runlevels:

```
# pwd
/etc/rc.d
# ls -l */*lpd
-rwxr-xr-x   1 root      root           1176 Sep 10 14:40 init.d/lpd
lrwxrwxrwx   1 root      root             13 Nov  6 06:41 rc0.d/K60lpd -> ../init.d/lpd
lrwxrwxrwx   1 root      root             13 Nov  6 06:41 rc1.d/K60lpd -> ../init.d/lpd
lrwxrwxrwx   1 root      root             13 Nov  6 06:41 rc2.d/S60lpd -> ../init.d/lpd
lrwxrwxrwx   1 root      root             13 Nov  6 06:41 rc3.d/S60lpd -> ../init.d/lpd
lrwxrwxrwx   1 root      root             13 Nov  6 06:41 rc4.d/S60lpd -> ../init.d/lpd
lrwxrwxrwx   1 root      root             13 Nov  6 06:41 rc5.d/S60lpd -> ../init.d/lpd
lrwxrwxrwx   1 root      root             13 Nov  6 06:41 rc6.d/K60lpd -> ../init.d/lpd
```

Each link in **/etc/rc.d/rc*n*.d** should point to a file in **/etc/rc.d/init.d**. The file **/etc/rc.d/rc1.d/K60lpd** is a link to the file named **lpd** in **/etc/rc.d/init.d**.[20] The

---

20. The numbers that are part of the filenames of the links in the **/etc/rc.d/rc*n*.d** directories may change from one OS release to the next, but the scripts in **/etc/rc.d/init.d** always have the same names.

names of files in the **/etc/rc.d/init.d** directory are functional. When you want to turn NFS services on or off, use the **nfs** script. When you want to turn basic network services on or off, run the **network** script. The **lpd** script controls the printer daemon. Each of the scripts takes an argument of **stop** or **start**, depending on what you want to do. Some of the scripts also take arguments of **restart, reload, status,** and some others. Run a script without an argument to cause it to display a usage message telling you which arguments it accepts (a few do not).

Following are three examples of calls to these scripts:

```
# sh /etc/rc.d/init.d/nfs stop
# sh /etc/rc.d/init.d/network start
# sh /etc/rc.d/init.d/network restart
```

The first example stops all processes related to serving filesystems over the network, using NFS. The second example starts all processes related to basic network services. The third example stops and then starts these same processes.

Maintain the Links in the /etc/rc[0–6].d Hierarchy || tip

Refer to page 947 for information about using **chkconfig** to maintain the symbolic links in this hierarchy.

The **/etc/rc.d/rc.local** file is executed after all the other **rc** scripts. Put commands that customize the system in the **rc.local** file. Among other things, **rc.local** generally sets up the **/etc/issue** file and is frequently changed so that it adds a message to **/etc/motd**. You can add any commands you like to **rc.local**; however, it is best to run them in the background so that if they hang, they do not stop the boot process.

service: Configures Services I

Red Hat provides **service**, a handy character-based script that reports on or changes the status of any of the system services in **/etc/rc.d/init.d**. In place of the commands toward the end of the previous section, you can give the following commands from any directory:

```
# service nfs stop
# service network start
# service network restart
```

The command **service ––status–all** displays the status of all system services.

redhat-config-services: Configures Services II

GNOME	GNOME menu: Server Settings⇨Services start-here: Server Settings⇨Services
KDE	K menu: Server Settings⇨Services start-here: Server Settings⇨Services
graphical	**redhat-config-services**
character-based	Use ntsysv (page 948) or chkconfig (page 947) instead

Formerly serviceconf, redhat-config-services is a graphical utility that has two distinct functions: It turns system services on and off, and it controls which services are stopped and started at runlevels 3, 4 (not used), and 5. The line below the toolbar gives you two pieces of information: the current runlevel of the system and the runlevel that you will edit (the last entry in the following list). The redhat-config-services utility controls two groups of services: independent services listed in **/etc/rc.d/init.d** and those controlled by **xinetd** (page 397) and usually listed in **/etc/xinetd.d** (or as specified in **/etc/xinetd.conf**). Scroll to and highlight the service you are interested in; a short description appears in the bottom text box. When the description includes You must enable xinetd to use this service, the highlighted service is dependent on **xinetd**; otherwise, it is an independent service.

The **xinetd** superserver is an independent service. You must make sure that it is turned on for the runlevels at which you want to run services that are dependent on **xinetd**. It is usually on for runlevels 3, 4, and 5.

The redhat-config-services utility does the following:

- **Turns independent services on and off.** When you highlight an independent service, you can click the toolbar or make a selection from Actions in the menubar to stop, start, or restart (stop and start) the service. The system turns on/off the service immediately; the change does not affect whether the service will run the next time you bring up the system, enter another runlevel, or reenter the current runlevel.

- **Turns xinetd-controlled services on and off.** When you highlight a service that is controlled by **xinetd**, the Start, Stop, and Restart buttons on the toolbar are grayed out. Until you click the box to the left of the service, the Save and Cancel buttons are grayed out too. The only things you can do are to turn this service off or on. Click the small box, and click the Save button to change the state of the service. You are changing the yes/no parameter of the **disable** line discussed in xinetd on page 397. When you click Save, the system restarts **xinetd** with the service status change you requested.

This change affects all runlevels and will stay in effect through changes in runlevels and reboots unless you change it again.

- **Controls future execution of independent services in runlevels 3, 4, and 5.** Select the runlevel you want to affect, using the Edit Runlevel selection from the menubar. Highlight an independent service, and click the box next to it to indicate whether you want the service on or off at the runlevel you specified. Click the Save button. When you enter that runlevel in the future, the service will be on or off as you specified. The current state of the service is not changed. See the first item in this list when you want to change the current state of the service.

chkconfig: Configures Services III

The chkconfig character-based utility duplicates much of what redhat-config-services does: make it easier for a system administrator to maintain the **/etc/rc.d** directory hierarchy. This utility can add, remove, list start-up information, and check the state of system services. To see a list of all services, give the following command:

```
# chkconfig --list
dhcrelay        0:off   1:off   2:off   3:off   4:off   5:off   6:off
dhcpd           0:off   1:off   2:off   3:off   4:off   5:off   6:off
syslog          0:off   1:off   2:on    3:on    4:on    5:on    6:off
atd             0:off   1:off   2:off   3:on    4:on    5:on    6:off
gpm             0:off   1:off   2:on    3:on    4:on    5:on    6:off
. . .
xinetd based services:
        chargen-udp:    off
        rsync:  off
        chargen:        off
        daytime-udp:    off
        daytime:        off
. . .
```

All the services that run their own daemons are listed, one to a line, followed by their configured state for each runlevel. Following that list, chkconfig displays each of the **xinetd**-based services and their current status. You can check on a specific daemon by adding its name to the previous command:

```
# chkconfig --list sshd
sshd            0:off   1:off   2:on    3:on    4:on    5:on    6:off
```

In the next example, chkconfig configures the **/etc/rc.d** directory hierarchy so that **sshd** will be off in runlevels 2, 3, 4, and 5 and then confirms the change.

```
# chkconfig --level 2345 sshd off
# chkconfig --list sshd
sshd            0:off   1:off   2:off   3:off   4:off   5:off   6:off
```

But both ps and service confirm that even though chkconfig set things up so that **sshd** would be off in all runlevels, it is still running. The chkconfig utility did not shut down **sshd**. In the following example, the second command line shows that when you give a service command followed by the name of a daemon, you get the usage message for the daemon's script (in this case **/etc/rc.d/init.d/sshd**):

```
# ps -ef | grep sshd
root       697     1  0 Oct01 ?        00:00:00 /usr/sbin/sshd
root     17185 21650  0 15:15 pts/4    00:00:00 grep sshd
# service sshd
Usage: /etc/init.d/sshd {start|stop|restart|reload|condrestart|status}
# service sshd status
sshd (pid 697) is running...
```

When you reboot the machine, **sshd** will not start, but you can stop it more easily:

```
# service sshd stop
Stopping sshd:                                          [  OK  ]
# ps -ef | grep sshd
root     17209 21650  0 15:16 pts/4    00:00:00 grep sshd
# service sshd status
sshd is stopped
```

ntsysv: Configures Services IV

The ntsysv utility presents a character-based/pseudographical interface that allows you to configure which services run at which runlevels. This utility works with services at the current runlevel unless you use the --**level** option. Follow this option with the levels you want to affect, with no separators between them (--**level 345** affects levels 3, 4, and 5). Use the TAB key to move between sections of the ntsysv display and the up/down ARROW keys to scroll the list of services. Press the SPACEBAR to place an asterisk (*) in or remove it from the brackets on the highlighted line. An asterisk indicates that the service will run at the specified runlevel; the absence of an asterisk means that it will not run.

Emergency Mode

When you use lilo or grub to boot, you can set the emergency kernel flag that gets passed to init and causes init to run sulogin (single-user login). When you are bringing the machine up using lilo, you will see a Boot: prompt. Enter **linux emergency** and press RETURN.

When you are using grub, press e as soon as the grub screen appears to edit the boot commands. If grub displays multiple bootable kernels when it first appears, move the highlight to the one you want to boot before pressing e. Then, using the up/down ARROW keys, move the highlight to the line that starts with kernel. Press **e** to bring up the grub editor; the cursor will be at the end of the kernel command line. Type SPACE **emergency**, press RETURN to return to the previous grub screen, and then press **b** to boot the system.

With either grub or lilo, when the boot process hands control to init, init runs su-login, which displays the following message:

```
Give root password for system maintenance
(or type Control-D for normal startup):
```

Enter the **root** password, and you will see the **root** shell prompt. At this point the only mounted filesystems are root (/) and maybe **/proc** (page 966); root is mounted as a readonly filesystem (despite what the mount command says). If **/proc** is not mounted, give the command

```
# mount /proc
```

The ps, top, fsck, and other programs require the **/proc** filesystem. The –L and –U mount options, as well as the LABEL= and UUID= specifications in the **/etc/fstab** file (page 978), also require **/proc**.

Now you can safely use fsck to check the integrity of the root filesystem:

```
# fsck /
```

If you need to write any files to the root filesystem, you need to remount it in read-write mode:

```
# mount -n -o remount,rw /
```

The **–n** argument keeps mount from trying to write to the **/etc/mtab** file first. If it were to attempt to write to a readonly filesystem, mount would fail, and the filesystem would remain mounted in readonly mode.

When you are ready to bring the system up to multiuser mode, exit from the shell. GNU/Linux will either continue booting or reboot to the default runlevel.

Single-User Mode

When the system is in single-user mode, only the system console is enabled. You can run programs from the console in single-user mode as you would from any terminal in multiuser mode. The differences are that not all filesystems may be mounted, so you may not be able to access some files, and few of the system daemons will be running. The **root** filesystem is always mounted in single-user mode. The scripts in **/etc/rc.d/rc1.d** are run as part of single-user initialization.

With the system in single-user mode, you can perform system maintenance that requires filesystems unmounted or just a quiet system—no one except you using it, so that no user programs interfere with disk maintenance and backup programs. The classical UNIX term for this state is *quiescent*. See "Backing Up Files" on page 997 for a discussion of one of the most important and often neglected areas of system administration.

Going Multiuser

After you have determined that all is well with all filesystems, you can bring the operating system up to multiuser mode. When you exit from your single-user shell, init brings you to the default runlevel—usually 3 or 5 (see Table 17-7 on page 943). Or, the following command in response to the Superuser prompt brings the system to multiuser mode:

```
# telinit 3
```

The telinit utility tells init what runlevel to enter. The telinit executable is a symbolic link to the init executable, but by convention, running telinit is preferred to running init directly.

When it goes from single- to multiuser mode, the system executes the **K** (kill or stop) scripts and then the **S** (start) scripts in **/etc/rc.d/rc3.d**. For more information, refer to "rc Scripts: Start and Stop System Services" on page 944. Use chkconfig (page 947) when you want to stop one of these scripts from running.

Once a machine that is connected to a network is in multiuser mode and running NFS (runlevel 3), you should be able to share local filesystems with remote machines and remote filesystems with the local machine. Add scripts that start such processes as a Web server or a database to **/etc/rc3.d**. In general, runlevel 3 is used to provide services to other users on a network. Runlevel 2 is referred to as multiuser mode, and runlevel 3 is extended multiuser mode. But because runlevel 2 is rarely used, this chapter uses the term *multiuser* to refer to runlevel 3. Runlevel 4 is not used, and runlevel 5 is graphics or X11 mode.

Multiuser Mode

Multiuser mode is the normal state for a GNU/Linux system. All appropriate filesystems are mounted, and users can log in from all connected terminals, dial-in lines, and network connections. All support services and daemons are enabled and running. Once the system is in multiuser mode, you will see a login screen or prompt. Most systems are set up to boot directly to multiuser mode without stopping at single-user mode.

Logging In

The system uses init, mingetty, and login to allow a user to log in; login uses PAM modules (page 1043) to authenticate users. Once the system is in multiuser mode, init is responsible for spawning a mingetty process on each of the lines that a user can log in on.

When you enter your login name, mingetty establishes the characteristics of your terminal and then overlays itself with a login process and passes to the login process whatever you entered in response to the login: prompt. The login program consults the **/etc/passwd** file to see whether a username matches the login name you entered. This program then consults the **/etc/shadow** file to see whether a password is associated with the login name. If there is, login prompts you for a password; if not, it continues without requiring a password. When your login name requires a password, login verifies the password you enter by checking the **/etc/shadow** file again. If either your login name or password is not correct, login displays Login incorrect and prompts you to log in again.

All passwords in the **/etc/shadow** file are encrypted or hashed using *MD5* (page 1478). It is not possible to recover an encrypted password. When you log in, the login process encrypts/hashes the password you type in at the prompt and compares it to the encrypted/hashed password in **/etc/shadow**. If it matches, you are authenticated.

With NIS or NIS+, login compares your login name and password with the information in the appropriate naming service instead of (or in addition to) the **passwd** and **shadow** files. If your system is configured to use more than one of these methods (**/etc/passwd** or NIS, or NIS+), it checks the **/etc/nsswitch.conf** file to see what order to consult them in. For example, the following line in **/etc/nsswitch.conf** indicates that the system should check the **/etc/passwd** file first, followed by NIS and then NIS+ (page 390).

```
passwd:      files nis nisplus
```

For more information on the **/etc/nsswitch.conf** file and the services it affects, refer to page 1022 and the **nsswitch.conf** man page.

PAM, the Pluggable Authentication Module facility, allows you greater control over user logins than the **/etc/passwd** and **/etc/shadow** files do. Using PAM, you can specify multiple levels of authentication, mutually exclusive authentication methods, or parallel methods that are each in themselves sufficient to grant access to the system. For example, you can have a different authentication method for console logins and for TELNET logins. And you can require that modem users authenticate themselves via two or more methods (such as a smartcard or badge reader and a password). PAM modules also provide security technology vendors with a more convenient way to interface their hardware or software products with a system. The files in the **/etc/pam.d** directory configure these services. Refer to "PAM" on page 1043, and point a browser at **/usr/share/doc/pam-*/html/index.html** for more information.

When the login name and password are correct, login consults the appropriate services to initialize your user and group IDs, establish your home directory, and determine which shell you will be working with.

The login utility assigns values to the **HOME, PATH, LOGNAME, SHELL, TERM,** and **MAIL** variables. It looks in the **/etc/group** file to identify all the groups the user belongs to (page 959). When login has finished its work, it overlays itself with the login shell, which inherits the variables login has set.

The login shell assigns values to additional shell variables (Chapters 12 through 15 cover these variables) and then executes the commands in the system start-up shell script(s) **/etc/profile** and **/etc/bashrc** `bash`, **/etc/csh.cshrc** and **/etc/csh.login** `tcsh`, and **/etc/zshenv** `zsh`. Some systems have additional system start-up shell scripts. Exactly what these scripts do is system dependent, but they usually display the contents of the **/etc/motd** (message of the day) and **/etc/issue** files, let you know that you have mail, and set umask (page 1366), the file-creation mask.

After executing the system start-up commands, the shell `bash tcsh zsh` executes the commands from the personal start-up shell scripts in your home directory. For a list of these scripts refer to page 565 `bash`, page 684 `tcsh`, and page 737 `zsh`. Because the shell executes these scripts *after* the system script, a sophisticated user can override any variables or conventions that were established by the system, whereas a new user can remain uninvolved in these complications.

Running a Program and Logging Out

When you see a shell prompt, you can execute a program or exit from the shell. If you exit from a shell, the process running the shell dies and the parent process wakes up. When the shell is a child of another shell, the parent shell wakes up and displays a prompt. Exiting from a login shell causes the operating system to send init a signal that one of its children has died. Upon receiving this signal, init takes action based on the contents of the **/etc/inittab** file. In the case of a process controlling a line for a terminal, init informs mgetty that the line is free for another user.

When you are at runlevel 5 and exit from a GUI, the display manager (gdmlogin—the GNOME display manager, gdm, kdm—the KDE display manager, or on some older systems xdm) takes care of initiating a new login display.

Bringing the System Down

The shutdown and halt utilities perform all the tasks needed to bring the system down safely. These utilities can restart the system, prepare the system to be turned off, put the system in single-user mode, and on some hardware, power down the system. The poweroff and reboot utilities are linked to halt. When you call halt when the system is not shutting down (runlevel 0) or rebooting (runlevel 6), halt calls shutdown.[21]

You must tell shutdown when you would like to bring the system down. This can be expressed as an absolute time of day, as in 19:15, which causes the shutdown to occur at 7:15 P.M. Alternatively, you can give the number of minutes from the present time, as in +15, which stands for fifteen minutes from now. To bring the system down immediately (recommended only for emergency shutdowns or when you are the only user logged in), you can give the argument +0, or its synonym: **now**. For shutdown times longer than 5 minutes, all non-**root** logins are disabled for the last 5 minutes before shutdown.

Calling shutdown with the **–r** option causes the system to reboot (same as the reboot command except that reboot implies **now**). Adding the **–f** option forces a fast reboot, where filesystem checking is disabled (see the shutdown man page for details). Using **–h** instead of **–r** forces the system to halt (same as the halt command except that halt implies **now**). A message appears once the system has been safely halted: System halted.

Because GNU/Linux is a multiuser system, shutdown warns all users before taking any action. This gives users a chance to prepare for the shutdown, perhaps by writing out editor files or exiting from networking applications. You can replace the default shutdown message with one of your own by following the time specification on the command line with a message:

```
# /sbin/shutdown -h 09:30 Going down 9:30 to install disk, up by 10am.
```

Do Not Turn the Power Off before Bringing the System Down ‖ caution

Avoid rebooting your GNU/Linux system without first bringing it down as described here. GNU/Linux, like UNIX systems, speeds up disk access by keeping an in-memory collection of disk buffers that are written to the disk periodically or when system use is momentarily low. When you turn off or reset your computer without writing the contents of these disk buffers to the disk, you lose any information in the buffers. Running **shutdown** forces these buffers to be written. You can force the buffers to be written at any time by issuing a **sync** command. However, **sync** does not unmount filesystems, nor does it bring the system down.

CONTROL-ALT-DEL: Reboots the System

By default, the **/etc/inittab** file on an Intel-based computer has the entry

```
ca::ctrlaltdel:/sbin/shutdown -t3 -r now
```

---

21. When you are running as other than Superuser, the link is through consolehelper (page 901).

This entry allows any user[22] to reboot the computer safely by pressing the key sequence CONTROL-ALT-DEL on the console (also referred to as the *three-finger salute,* or the *Vulcan death grip*). Because of its hooks into the keyboard driver, this key sequence sends a SIGINT signal to the init process, which in response runs shutdown. Because it runs as **root**, init causes shutdown to run as **root** also, even if the key sequence is initiated by an ordinary user. You can disable CONTROL-ALT-DEL by deleting the preceding line from **/etc/inittab** (or putting a # at the left end of the line) and then sending init a HUP signal (**kill –HUP 1**), which causes it to reread the **/etc/inittab** file.

consolehelper: Allows an Ordinary User to Run a Privileged Command

As shown following, there are two executable **halt** files:

```
$ file /sbin/halt /usr/bin/halt
/sbin/halt:    ELF 32-bit LSB executable, Intel 80386, version 1 (SYSV)...
/usr/bin/halt: symbolic link to consolehelper
```

The one in **/sbin** runs the halt utility whereas the one in **/usr/bin** is a link to consolehelper (page 901). In **root**'s **PATH** variable **/sbin** normally precedes **/usr/bin** so that when someone running as **root** gives a halt command, the shell begins the execution of **/sbin/halt** (the halt utility). Normally **/sbin** does not appear in a regular user's **PATH**; when a regular user gives a halt command, the shell follows the link from **/usr/bin/halt** and begins execution of **/usr/bin/consolehelper**.

What consolehelper does depends on how PAM is set up (refer to **/etc/pam.d/halt** for the modules it calls and **/usr/share/doc/pam-*/txts/*** for descriptions of the modules). Refer to "PAM" on page 1043 for more information.

The consolehelper utility prompts for *your* password; when you supply it and are logged in on the console, consolehelper proceeds to shut the system down. While you are logged in as Superuser with the default **PATH**, typing **halt** runs **/sbin/halt**, which is the halt utility.

Going Single-user

Because going from multiuser to single-user mode can affect other users, you must be Superuser to make this change. Make sure that you give other users enough warning before going to single-user mode; otherwise, they may lose whatever they were working on.

Following is a method of manually bringing the system down to single-user mode—the point where it is safe to turn the power off. You must be running as Superuser to perform these tasks.

---

22. When you include the **–a** option in the shutdown command in **/etc/inittab** and the **/etc/shutdown.allow** file exists, one of the users whose name appears in this file (or **root**) must be logged in on one of the virtual consoles in order for a non-**root** user to run shutdown from a virtual console.

1. Use wall (write all) to warn everyone who is using the system to log out.

2. If you are sharing files via NFS, use **exportfs –ua** to disable network access to the shared filesystems. (Use **exportfs** without an argument to see what filesystems are being shared.)

3. Use **umount –a** to unmount all mounted devices. (Use **mount** without an argument to see what devices are mounted.)

4. Give the command **telinit 1** to bring the system down to single-user mode.

Turning the Power Off

Once the system is in single-user mode, shutting it down is quite straightforward. Give the command **telinit 0** (preferred) or **halt** to bring the system down. You can build a kernel with apm so that it turns the machine off at the appropriate time. If your machine is not set up this way, turn the power off when the appropriate prompt appears or the system starts rebooting.

Crash

A *crash* occurs when the system suddenly stops/fails when you do not intend it to. A crash may result from software or hardware problems or a loss of power. As a running system loses power, nothing is regular or predictable. In a fraction of a second, some components are supplied with enough voltage and others are not. Buffers are not flushed, corrupt data may be written to the hard disk, and so on. IDE drives do not behave as predictably as SCSI drives under these circumstances. After a crash, you must bring the operating system up carefully to minimize possible damage to the filesystems. Frequently there will be little or no damage.

Repairing a Filesystem

Although the filesystems are checked automatically during the boot process if needed, you will have to check them manually if a problem cannot be repaired automatically. To check the filesystems manually after a crash, boot the system up to emergency mode (page 948). *Do not* mount any devices other than root, which Linux mounts automatically. Run fsck on all the local filesystems that were mounted at the time of the crash, repairing them as needed. The **fsck.ext3** module of fsck handles **ext3** (journaled) filesystems. Depending on how your system is set up, when fsck cannot repair a filesystem automatically, the system enters single-user mode so you can run fsck manually (refer to "Single-User Mode" on page 949). Make note of any ordinary files or directories that you repair (and can identify), and inform their owners that they may not be complete or correct. Look in the **lost+found** directory *in each filesystem* for missing files. For more information, refer to "Notes" on page 1177. After successfully running fsck, type **exit** to exit from the single-user shell and resume booting.

If files are not correct or are missing altogether, you may have to recreate them from a backup copy of the filesystem. For more information, refer to "Backing Up Files" on page 997.

When the System Does Not Boot

When you cannot boot the computer from the hard drive, use your rescue floppy or the first of your installation CD-ROMs (refer to "mkbootdisk: Creates a Rescue/Emergency/Boot Floppy Disk" on page 920). If that works, run fsck on the root filesystem and try rebooting from the hard drive again.

When all else fails, perform an "upgrade" to your current version of Red Hat. Red Hat Linux can perform a nondestructive upgrade and can fix quite a bit in the process.

Optional

File, Directory, and Filesystem

Filesystems hold directories of files. These structures store your data and the system data that are the basis of your work on the system and the system's existence. This section discusses important files and directories, various types of files and how to work with them, and filesystems and their uses and maintenance.

Important Files and Directories

This section details the most common files used to administrate the system. Also refer to "Important Standard Directories and Files" on page 112.

~/.bash_profile Contains an individual user login shell `bash` initialization script. The shell executes the commands in this file in the same environment as the shell each time a user logs in. The file must be located in a user's home directory.

The **.bash_profile** file usually specifies a terminal type (for vi, terminal emulators, and other programs), runs stty to establish terminal characteristics desired by the user, and performs other housekeeping functions when a user logs in.

A typical **.bash_profile** file specifying a vt100 terminal and CONTROL-H as the erase key follows:

```
$ cat .bash_profile
export TERM=vt100
stty erase '^h'
```

When you log in from more than one type of terminal, you may want to construct a more elaborate routine, such as the following one, which asks you for the terminal type each time you log in:

```
$ cat .bash_profile
echo -n "Terminal type: "
read TERM
export TERM
stty erase '^h'
```

For more information, refer to "Startup Files" on page 565.

~/.bashrc Contains an individual user, interactive, nonlogin shell [bash] initialization script. The shell executes the commands in this file in the same environment as the (new) shell each time a user creates a new interactive shell. The **.bashrc** script differs from **.bash_profile** in that it is executed each time a new shell is spawned, not only when you log in. For more information, refer to "Startup Files" on page 565.

~/.login Performs the same function for tcsh as **.bash_profile** does for bash: It is the individual user login shell [tcsh] initialization script.

~/.tcshrc Performs the same function for tcsh as **.bashrc** does for bash: It is the individual user, interactive, nonlogin shell [tcsh] initialization script.

/dev/null Output sent to this file disappears; also called a *bit bucket*. The **/dev/null** file is a device file and must be created with mknod. Input that you redirect to come from this file appears as nulls, creating an empty file. You can create an empty file named **nothing** by giving the following command:

```
$ cat /dev/null > nothing
```

or

```
$ cp /dev/null nothing
```

or, without explicitly using **/dev/null**

```
$ > nothing
```

This last command redirects the output of a null command to the file with the same result as the previous commands.

You can use this technique to truncate an existing file to zero length without changing its permissions. See touch on pages 853 and 1359. You can also use **/dev/null** to get rid of output that you do not want:

```
$ grep portable * 2>/dev/null
```

The preceding command looks for the word portable in all files in the working directory. Any output to standard error (page 552), such as permission or directory errors, is discarded while output to standard output appears on the screen.

/dev/pts The /dev/pts pseudofilesystem, a hook into the Linux kernel, helps you visualize the open pseudoterminals—it is part of the pseudoterminal support. Pseudoterminals are used by remote login programs, such as ssh, telnet, and xterm. The following sequence of commands demonstrates that the user is logged in on **/dev/pts/1**. After using **who am i** to verify the line the user is logged in on and using ls to show that that line exists, the user redirects the output of an echo command to **/dev/pts/1**, whereupon the output appears on the user's screen:

```
$ who am i
bravo.tcorp.com!alex       pts/1    May 10 13:03
$ ls /dev/pts
0  1  2
$ echo Hi there > /dev/pts/1
Hi there
```

/dev/zero Input you take from this file contains an infinite string of zeros (nulls or numerical, not ASCII, zeros). You can fill a file (such as a swap file—page 967) or overwrite a file with zeros with a command such as the following. The od utility shows the contents of the new file:

```
$ dd if=/dev/zero of=zeros bs=1024 count=10
10+0 records in
10+0 records out
$ ls -l zeros
-rw-rw-r--    1 alex      alex          10240 Dec  3 20:26 zeros
$ od -c zeros
0000000  \0  \0  \0  \0  \0  \0  \0  \0  \0  \0  \0  \0  \0  \0  \0 \0
*
0024000
```

When you try to do with **/dev/zero** what you can do with **/dev/null**, you quickly fill the partition you are working in:

```
$ cp /dev/zero bigzero
cp: writing 'bigzero': No space left on device
$ rm bigzero
```

/etc/aliases Used by the mail delivery system (typically sendmail) to construct **aliases** for users. Edit this file to suit your local preferences. This file contains a number of good examples showing how you can create **aliases** for users, create mailing lists, and direct e-mail to files. After editing this file, run newaliases to rebuild the **aliases** database. Refer to "aliases: Setting up E-Mail Aliases" on page 1054.

/etc/at.allow, /etc/at.deny, /etc/cron.allow, and /etc/cron.deny	By default users can use the at and cron utilities. The **at.allow** file lists the users who are allowed to use at. The **cron.allow** file works in the same manner for cron. The **at.deny** and **cron.deny** files specify users who are not permitted to use the corresponding utilities. If you wish to allow everyone to use at, create an empty **at.deny** file; do not create an **at.allow** file. The cron utility works in the same manner with the **cron.allow** and **cron.deny** files. To prevent anyone except Superuser from using at, remove the **at.allow** and **at.deny** files. The cron utility works the same way with **cron.allow** and **cron.deny**. Refer to "cron and crontab: Schedule Routine Tasks" on page 1059 and to these utilities in Part III.

/etc/csh.cshrc   Contains a systemwide shell `tcsh` initialization script that is run each time an interactive shell starts; similar to **/etc/profile** (page 963).

/etc/csh.login   Contains a systemwide login shell `tcsh` initialization script that is run once when a user logs in on the system.

/etc/dumpdates   Contains information about the last execution of dump. For each filesystem, it stores the time of the last dump at a given dump level. The dump utility uses this information to determine which files to back up when executing at a particular dump level. Refer to "Backing Up Files" on page 997 or dump in Part III for more information. Following is a sample **/etc/dumpdates** file from a machine with four filesystems and a backup schedule that uses three dump levels:

```
/dev/hda1          5 Thu Apr 23 03:53:55 2002
/dev/hda8          2 Sun Apr 19 08:25:24 2002
/dev/hda9          2 Sun Apr 19 08:57:32 2002
/dev/hda10         2 Sun Apr 19 08:58:06 2002
/dev/hda1          2 Sun Apr 19 09:02:27 2002
/dev/hda1          0 Sun Mar 22 22:08:35 2002
/dev/hda8          0 Sun Mar 22 22:33:40 2002
/dev/hda9          0 Sun Mar 22 22:35:22 2002
/dev/hda10         0 Sun Mar 22 22:43:45 2002
```

The first column contains the raw device name of the dumped filesystem. The second column contains the dump level and the date of the dump.

/etc/fstab   **filesystem (mount) table**   Contains a list of all mountable devices as specified by the system administrator. Programs do not write to this file, but only read from it. Refer to "**fstab**: Keeps Track of Filesystems" on page 978.

/etc/group   Groups allow users to share files or programs without allowing all system users access to them. This scheme is useful if several users are working with files that are not public. The **/etc/group** file associates one or more user names with each group (number).

An entry in the **/etc/group** file has four fields in the following format:

group-name:password:group-ID:login-name-list

The *group-name* is the name of the group. The *password* is an optional encrypted password. This field is rarely used and frequently contains an x indicating that group passwords are not used. The **group-ID** is a number, with 1–499 reserved for system accounts. The *login-name-list* is a comma-separated list of users that belong to the group. If an entry is too long to fit on one line, end the line with a backslash (\), which quotes the following RETURN, and continue the entry on the next line. A sample entry in a **group** file follows. The group is named **pubs,** has no password, and has a group ID of 100:

```
pubs:x:100:alex,jenny,scott,hls,barbara
```

Each user has a primary group, which is the group that user is assigned in the **/etc/passwd** file. By default Red Hat Linux has user private groups: Each user's primary group has the same name as the user. In addition, a user can belong to other groups, depending on which *login-name-lists* the user appears on in the **/etc/group** file. In effect, you simultaneously belong to both your primary group and any groups you are assigned to in **/etc/group.** When you attempt to access a file you do not own, the operating system checks whether you are a member of the group that has access to the file. If you are, your access permissions are controlled by the group access permissions for the file. If you are not a member of the group that has access to the file and you do not own the file, you are subject to the public access permissions for the file.

When you create a new file, it is assigned to the group associated with the directory the file is being written into, assuming that you belong to the group. If you do not belong to the group that has access to the directory, the file is assigned to your primary group.

/etc/inittab   **initialization table**   Controls how the init process behaves. Each line in **inittab** has four colon-separated fields:

> *id:runlevel:action:process*

The *id* uniquely identifies an entry in the **inittab** file. The *runlevel* is the system runlevel(s) at which *process* is executed. The *runlevel(s)* are zero or more characters chosen from 0123456S. If more than one runlevel is listed, the associated *process* is executed at each of the specified runlevels. When you do not specify a runlevel, init executes *process* at all runlevels. When the system changes runlevels, the *processes* specified by all entries in **inittab** that do not include the new runlevel are sent the SIGTERM signal to allow them to terminate gracefully. After 5 seconds these *processes* are killed if they are still running. The *process* is any bash command line.

The *action* is one of the following keywords: **respawn, wait, once, boot, boot-wait, ondemand, powerfail, powerwait, powerokwait, powerfailnow, ctrlaltdel, kbrequest, off, ondemand, initdefault,** or **sysinit.** This keyword controls how the *process* is treated when it is executed. The most commonly used keywords are **wait** and **respawn.**

The **wait** keyword instructs init to start *process* and wait for it to terminate. All subsequent scans of **inittab** ignore this **wait** entry. Because a **wait** entry is started only once (on entering *runlevel*) and not executed again while the system remains at *runlevel,* it is often used to redirect init output to the console.

The **respawn** entry tells init to start *process* if it does not exist but not to wait for it to terminate. If *process* does exist, init goes on to the next entry in the **inittab.** The init utility continues to rescan **inittab,** looking for processes that have died. When a *process* dies, a **respawn** entry causes init to restart it.

The **initdfault** entry tells init what runlevel to bring the system to (see Table 17-7 on page 943). Without this information, init prompts for a runlevel on the system console. The value of the **initdefault** entry is set when you configure the system or when you edit **inittab** directly.[23]

Each virtual console (page 36) has in **inittab** a **mingetty** entry that includes a unique terminal identifier (such as **tty1,** which is short for **/dev/tty1**). Add or remove **mingetty** lines to add or remove virtual consoles. Remember to leave a virtual console for each X window that you want to run. Following is the **mingetty** entry for **/dev/tty2**:

```
2:2345:respawn:/sbin/mingetty tty2
```

The *id* on a **mingetty** line corresponds to the **tty** number.

All the *actions* are documented in the **inittab** man page. For more information, refer to "Booting the System" on page 943.

/etc/motd   Contains the message of the day, which is displayed each time someone logs in. This file typically contains site policy and legal information. The file should be kept short because users tend to see the message many times.

/etc/mtab   When you call mount without any arguments, it consults this file and displays a list of mounted devices. Each time you (or an **rc** script) call mount or umount, these utilities make the necessary changes to **mtab.** Although this is an ASCII text file, you should not edit it. See also **/etc/fstab.**

---

23. Be careful when you edit **inittab** by hand. Always make a backup copy in the same directory before you edit the file. If you make a mistake, you may not be able to boot the system. If this happens, refer to "Emergency Mode" on page 948.

Fixing mtab || tip

The operating system maintains its own internal mount table, which may occasionally differ from this file. Use **cat** to display the contents of **/proc/mounts** to see the internal mount table. To bring the **mtab** file in line with the operating system's mount table, you can reboot the system or replace **/etc/mtab** with a symbolic link to **/proc/mounts** (some information will be lost). Refer to "**mount**: Mounts a Filesystem" on page 974 for more information.

/etc/nsswitch.conf   See page 1022.

/etc/pam.d   Files in this directory specify the authentication methods used by PAM (Pluggable Authentication Module, page 1043) applications.

Be Cautious Changing PAM Files || caution

Unless you thoroughly understand how to configure PAM, avoid changing the files in **/etc/pam.d**. Mistakes in the configuration of PAM can make your system unusable.

/etc/passwd   Describes users to the system. Do not edit this file directly, but instead, use one of the utilities discussed in "Configuring User and Group Accounts" on page 992. Each line in **passwd** has seven colon-separated fields that describe one user:

login-name:dummy-password:user-ID:group-ID:info:directory:program

The *login-name* is the user's login name—the name that you enter in response to the `login:` prompt or GUI login screen. The value of the *dummy-password* is the character x. An encrypted/hashed password is stored in **/etc/shadow** (page 965). For security, every account should have a password. By convention, disabled accounts have an asterisk (*) in this field.

The *user-ID* is a number, with 0 indicating Superuser and 1–499 reserved for system accounts. The *group-ID* identifies the user as a member of a group. It is a number, with 0–499 reserved for system accounts. You can change these values and set maximum values in **/etc/login.defs**.

The *info* is information that various programs, such as accounting programs and e-mail, use to identify the user further. Normally it contains at least the first and last name of the user.

The *directory* is the absolute pathname of the user's home directory. The *program* is the program that runs once the user logs in. If *program* is not present,

/bin/bash is assumed. You can put **/bin/tcsh** here to log in using the TC Shell or **/bin/zsh** to log in using the Z Shell. The chsh utility (page 1056) changes this value.

The *program* specified in the right-hand field of each line in the **passwd** file is usually a shell but can be any program. The following line in the **passwd** file creates a "user" whose only purpose is to execute the who utility:

```
who:x:1000:1000:execute who:/usr:/usr/bin/who
```

Using **who** as a login name causes the system to log you in, execute the who utility, and log you out. The output of who flashes by in a hurry as the new login prompt clears the screen immediately after who finishes running. This entry in the **passwd** file does not provide a shell; there is no way for you to stay logged in after who finishes executing.

This technique is useful for providing special accounts that may do only one thing. For instance, sites may create an ftp (page 1180) account in order to enable anonymous FTP access to their systems. Because no one logs in on this account, set the shell to **/bin/false** (which returns a false exit status) or to **/sbin/nologin** (which does not permit the user to log in). When you put a message in **/etc/nologin.txt,** nologin displays that message (except it has the same problem as the output of who: It is removed so quickly that you cannot see it).

Do Not Replace a Login Shell with a Shell Script || security

Be careful when using special shells in place of login shells in /etc/passwd. Do not use shell scripts as replacements for shells. A user may be able to interrupt a shell script, giving him or her full shell access when you did not intend to do so. When installing a dummy shell, use a compiled program, not a shell script.

/etc/printcap The printer capability database. This file describes system printers and is derived from 4.3BSD UNIX. Refer to page 1012 and the **printcap** man page.

/etc/profile Contains a systemwide interactive shell ^{bash} initialization script for environment and start-up programs. When you log in, the first thing the shell does is to execute the commands in this file in the same environment as the shell. (For more information on executing a shell script in this manner, refer to the discussion of the **.** [dot] command on page 581.) This file allows the system administrator to establish systemwide environment parameters that individual users can override. Using this file, you can set shell variables, execute utilities, and take care of other housekeeping tasks. See also "~/.bash_profile" on page 956.

Following is an example of a **/etc/profile** file that displays the message of the day (the **/etc/motd** file), sets the file-creation mask (umask), and sets the interrupt character to CONTROL-C:

```
# cat /etc/profile
cat /etc/motd
umask 022
stty intr '^c'
```

Take a look at the **/etc/profile** file on your system as another example. Following is a more extensive **/etc/profile** file:

```
# cat /etc/profile
# /etc/profile

# System wide environment and startup programs
# Functions and aliases go in /etc/bashrc

PATH="$PATH:/usr/X11R6/bin"

PS1="[\u@\h \W]\\$ "

ulimit -c 1000000
if [ 'id -gn' = 'id -un' -a 'id -u' -gt 14 ]; then
    umask 002
else
    umask 022
fi

USER='id -un'
LOGNAME=$USER
MAIL="/var/spool/mail/$USER"

HOSTNAME='/bin/hostname'
HISTSIZE=1000
HISTFILESIZE=1000
LESSOPEN="|/usr/bin/lesspipe.sh %s"
export PATH PS1 HOSTNAME HISTSIZE HISTFILESIZE USER LOGNAME MAIL LESSOPEN
export LESS=-X
export HISTCONTROL=ignoredups
shopt -s cdspell

for i in /etc/profile.d/*.sh ; do
    if [ -x $i ]; then
        . $i
    fi
done
unset i
```

/etc/rc.d Holds the run command (rc) scripts. The init program executes several run command scripts each time it changes state or runlevel. The **/etc/rc.d/init.d** directory holds all the scripts. Each runlevel has a dedicated directory within **/etc/rc.d.** For example, runlevel **3** has the **/etc/rc.d/rc3.d** directory. The files in each of these directories are links to the files in **init.d.** The **rc** scripts perform such tasks as mounting filesystems (when the system goes multiuser), removing temporary files after the filesystems are mounted, and unmounting filesystems when the system is returned to single-user mode or brought down. For more information refer to "rc Scripts: Start and Stop System Services" on page 944.

/etc/shadow   Contains encrypted or *MD5* (page 1478) hashed user passwords. Each entry occupies one line composed of nine fields, separated by colons:

login-name:password:last-mod:min:max:warn:inactive:expire:flag

The *login-name* is the user's login name—the name that the user enters in response to the login: prompt or GUI login screen. The *password* is an encrypted or hashed password that passwd puts into this file. If unauthorized access is not a problem, the password field can initially be null (::). When logging in, the user first can run passwd to select a password. Otherwise, you can run passwd while you are Superuser to assign a password after setting up a new user.

The *last-mod* field indicates when the password was last modified. The *min* is the minimum number of days that must elapse before the password can be changed; *max* is the maximum number of days before the password must be changed. The *warn* specifies how much advance warning (in days) to give the user before the password expires. The account will be closed if the number of days between login sessions exceeds the number of days specified in the *inactive* field. The account will also be closed as of the date in the *expire* field. The last field in an entry, *flag*, is reserved for future use.

The **shadow** password file should be owned by **root** and not be publicly readable or writable, making it more difficult for someone to break into your system by identifying accounts without passwords or by using specialized programs that try to match hashed passwords.

A number of conventions exist for making special **shadow** entries. An entry of *LK* or NP in the *password* field indicates *locked* and *no password,* respectively. *No password* is different from an empty password, implying that this is an administrative account that nobody ever logs in on directly. Occasionally programs will run with the privileges of this account for system maintenance functions. These accounts are set up under the principle of least privilege.

Entries in the **shadow** file must appear in the same order as in the **passwd** file. There must be one and only one **shadow** entry for each **passwd** entry.

/etc/sysconfig   A directory containing a hierarchy of system configuration files. For more information refer to the **/usr/share/doc/initscripts**∗**/sysconfig.txt** file.

/etc/zshenv   Contains a systemwide login shell zsh initialization script; similar in function to **/etc/profile** (page 963).

/proc   The **/proc** pseudofilesystem provides a window into the Linux kernel. Through **/proc** you can obtain information on any process running on your computer, including its current state, memory usage, CPU usage, terminal, parent, group, and more. You can extract information directly from the files in **/proc**. An example follows:

```
$ sleep 10000 &
[1] 17924
$ cd /proc/17924
$ ls -l
total 0
-r--r--r--  1 alex     alex           0 Feb  2 17:13 cmdline
lrwx------  1 alex     alex           0 Feb  2 17:13 cwd -> /home/alex
-r--------  1 alex     alex           0 Feb  2 17:13 environ
lrwx------  1 alex     alex           0 Feb  2 17:13 exe -> /bin/sleep
dr-x------  2 alex     alex           0 Feb  2 17:13 fd
pr--r--r--  1 alex     alex           0 Feb  2 17:13 maps
-rw-------  1 alex     alex           0 Feb  2 17:13 mem
lrwx------  1 alex     alex           0 Feb  2 17:13 root -> /
-r--r--r--  1 alex     alex           0 Feb  2 17:13 stat
-r--r--r--  1 alex     alex           0 Feb  2 17:13 statm
-r--r--r--  1 alex     alex           0 Feb  2 17:13 status
$ cat < status
Name:   sleep
State:  S (sleeping)
Pid:    17924
PPid:   17909
TracerPid:      0
Uid:    0       0       0       0
Gid:    0       0       0       0
FDSize: 256
Groups: 0 1 2 3 4 6 10
VmSize:     1144 kB
VmLck:         0 kB
VmRSS:       420 kB
VmData:       20 kB
...
```

In this example bash creates a background process (PID 17924) for sleep. Next, the user changes directories to the directory in **/proc** that has the same name as the PID of the subject background process (**cd /proc/17924**). This directory holds information about the process for which it is named. In this case it holds information about the sleep process. The ls –l command shows that some of the entries in this directory are links (**cwd** is a link to the directory the process was started from, and **exe** is a link to the executable file that this process is running), and some appear to be regular files. All appear to be empty. When you attach one of these files (**status** in the example) to standard input of cat, you get the output shown earlier. Obviously this is not a regular file.

/sbin/shutdown A utility that brings the system down (see page 952).

swap Even though **swap** is not a file, swap space can be added and deleted from the system dynamically. Swap space is used by the virtual memory subsystem. When it runs low on real memory (RAM), your machine writes memory pages from RAM to the swap space on your disk. Which pages are written and when they are written are controlled by finely tuned algorithms in the Linux kernel. When needed by running programs, these pages are brought back into RAM. This technique is called *paging* (page 1484). When a system is running very short on memory, an entire process may be paged out to disk.

Running an application that requires a large amount of virtual memory may result in the need for additional swap space. If you run out of swap space, you can use mkswap to create a new swap file and swapon to enable it. Normally you use a disk partition as swap space, but you can also use a file.

If you are using a file as swap space, first use df to make sure that you have enough space in the partition for the file. In the following sequence of commands, the administrator first uses dd and **/dev/zero** (page 958) to create an empty file (do not use cp as you may create a file with holes, which may not work) in the working directory. Next, mkswap takes an argument of the name of the file created in the first step to set up the swap space. For security, change the file so that it cannot be read from or written to by anyone but **root**. Use swapon with the same argument to turn the swap file on, and then use **swapon –s** to confirm that the swap space is available. The final two commands turn off the swap file and remove it:

```
# dd if=/dev/zero of=swapfile bs=1024 count=65536
65536+0 records in
65536+0 records out
# mkswap swapfile
Setting up swapspace version 1, size = 67104768 bytes
# chmod 600 swapfile
# swapon swapfile
# swapon -s
Filename                     Type            Size      Used    Priority
/dev/hda12                   partition       265032    38216   -1
/var/swapfile                file            65528     0       -2
.
.
.
# swapoff swapfile
# rm swapfile
```

/usr/share/magic Most files begin with a unique identifier called a *magic number*. This file is a text database listing all known magic numbers on the system. When you use the file utility, it consults **/usr/share/magic** to determine the type of a file. Occasionally you will acquire a new tool that creates a new type of file that is unrecognized by the file command. When this happens, you need to update the **/usr/share/magic** file; refer to the **magic** man page for details. See also "magic number" on page 1478.

/var/log Holds system log files.

/var/log/messages Contains messages from daemons, the Linux kernel, and security programs. For example, you will find `filesystem full` warning messages, error messages from system daemons (NFS, syslog, printer daemons), SCSI and IDE disk error messages, messages from such security-related programs as su, and more in **messages**. Check **/var/log/messages** periodically to keep informed about important system events. Much of the information displayed on the system console is also sent to **messages**. If you have a system problem and do not have access to the console, check this file for messages about the problem.

Optional

File Types

Linux supports many types of files. The following sections discuss major and minor device numbers (page 971) and the following types of files:

- "Ordinary File, Directory, Link, and Inode"(following)
- "Symbolic Link" (page 969)
- "Special Files" (page 969)
- "FIFO Special File (Named Pipe)" (page 970)
- "Sockets" (page 971)
- "Block and Character Devices" (page 971)
- "Raw Devices" (page 972)

Ordinary File, Directory, Link, and Inode

An *ordinary* file stores user data, such as textual information, programs, or an image, such as a **jpeg** or **tiff** file. A *directory* is a standard-format disk file that stores information, including names, about ordinary files and other directory files.

A directory relates each of its filenames to a specific inode, which is identified by an inode number. An *inode* is a *data structure* (page 1463), stored on disk, that defines a file's existence. An inode contains critical information, such as the name of the owner of the file, where it is physically located on the disk, and how many links point to it.

When you move (mv) a file within a filesystem, you change the filename portion of the directory entry associated with the inode that describes the file. You do not create a new inode. If you move a file to another filesystem, mv first creates a new inode on the destination filesystem and then deletes the original inode. You can also use mv to move a directory recursively, in which case all the objects are copied and deleted.

When you make an additional hard link (ln) to a file, you create another reference (an additional filename) to the inode that describes the file. You do not create a new inode.

When you remove (rm) a file, you delete the directory entry that describes the file. When you remove the last link to a file, the operating system puts all the blocks the inode pointed to back in the *free list* (the list of blocks that are available for use on the disk) and frees the inode to be used again.

Every directory has at least two entries (. and ..). The . entry is a link to the directory itself. The .. entry is a link to the parent directory. In the case of the root directory, there is no parent, and the .. entry is a link to the root directory itself. It is not possible to create hard links to directories.

Symbolic Link

Because each filesystem has a separate set of inodes, you can create hard links to a file only from within the filesystem that holds that file. To get around this limitation, GNU/Linux provides symbolic links, which are files that point to other files. Files that are linked by a symbolic link do not share an inode: You can create a symbolic link to a file from any filesystem. You can also create a symbolic link to a directory, device, or other special file. For more information, refer to "Symbolic Links" on page 126.

Special Files

Special files represent Linux kernel routines that provide access to an operating system feature. FIFO (first in, first out) special files allow unrelated programs to exchange information. Sockets allow unrelated processes on the same or different computers to exchange information. One type of socket, the UNIX domain socket, is a special file. Symbolic links are another type of special file.

Device files, which include block and character special files, represent device drivers that let you communicate with peripheral devices, such as terminals, printers, and hard disks. By convention, device files appear in the **/dev** directory and its subdirectories. Each device file represents a device: You read from and write to the file to read from and write to the device it represents. Although you do not normally read directly from or write directly to device files, the Linux kernel and many system utilities do. The following example shows part of the output that an **ls –l** command produces for the **/dev** directory:

```
$ ls -l /dev
crw-------   1 root      sys         14,  4 Apr 17  2002 audio
crw-------   1 root      root         5,  1 Jan 22 08:31 console
crw-------   1 root      root         5, 64 May  5  2002 cua0
crw-------   1 root      root         5, 65 May  5  2002 cua1
brw-rw----   1 root      floppy       2,  0 May  5  2002 fd0
brw-rw----   1 root      floppy       2, 12 May  5  2002 fd0D360
brw-rw----   1 root      floppy       2, 16 May  5  2002 fd0D720
brw-rw----   1 root      floppy       2, 28 May  5  2002 fd0H1440
brw-rw----   1 root      floppy       2, 12 May  5  2002 fd0H360
brw-rw----   1 root      disk         3,  0 May  5  2002 hda
brw-rw----   1 root      disk         3,  1 May  5  2002 hda1
brw-rw----   1 root      disk         3,  2 May  5  2002 hda2
brw-rw----   1 root      disk         3,  3 May  5  2002 hda3
brw-rw----   1 root      disk         3,  4 May  5  2002 hda4
brw-rw----   1 root      disk         3,  5 May  5  2002 hda5
brw-rw----   1 root      disk         3,  6 May  5  2002 hda6
...
```

The first character of each line is always –, **b**, **c**, **d**, **l**, or **p** for ordinary (plain), block, character, directory, symbolic link, or named pipe (see the following section). The next nine characters represent the permissions for the file, followed by the number of hard links and the names of the owner and group. Where the number of bytes in a file would appear for an ordinary or directory file, a device file shows its *major* and *minor device numbers* separated by a comma. The rest of the line is the same as any other **ls –l** listing.

FIFO Special File (Named Pipe)

A *FIFO special* file, also called a *named pipe*, represents a pipe: You read from and write to the file to read from and write to the pipe. The term *FIFO* stands for *first in, first out*—the way any pipe works. The first information that you put in one end is the first information that comes out the other end. When you use a pipe on a command line to send the output of a program to the printer, the printer prints the information in the same order that the program produced it and sent it into the pipe.

Unless you are writing sophisticated programs, you will not be working with FIFO special files. However, many of the programs that you use on GNU/Linux, including the windowing system and file manager, use named pipes for interprocess communication. You can create a pipe such as the one used by the X Window System display by using mkfifo:

```
# mkfifo AA
# ls -l AA
prw-rw-r--   1 root      root              0 Apr 26 13:11 AA
```

The **p** at the left end of the output of **ls –l** indicates that the file is a pipe. Programs that are X clients, such as xterm, use files like this to communicate with the X server (your display).

The UNIX and GNU/Linux systems have had pipes for many generations. Without named pipes, only processes that were children of the same ancestor could use pipes to exchange information. Using named pipes, *any* two processes on a single machine can exchange information. One program writes to a FIFO special file. Another program reads from the same file. The programs do not have to run at the same time or be aware of each other's activity. The operating system handles all buffering and information storage. The term *asynchronous (async)* applies to this type of communication because the programs on the ends of the pipe do not have to be synchronized.

Sockets

Like a FIFO special file, a socket allows asynchronous processes that are not children of the same ancestor to exchange information. Sockets are the central mechanism of the interprocess communication that is the basis of the networking facility. When you use networking utilities, pairs of cooperating sockets manage the communication between the processes on your computer and the remote computer. Sockets form the basis of such utilities as ssh and scp.

Major and Minor Device Numbers

A *major device number* represents a class of hardware devices: a terminal, printer, tape drive, hard disk, and so on. In the preceding list of the **/dev** directory, all the hard disk partitions have a major device number of 3.

A *minor device number* represents a particular piece of hardware within a class. Although all the hard disk partitions are grouped together by their major device number, each has a different minor device number (**hda1** is 1, **hda2** is 2, and so on). This setup allows one piece of software (the device driver) to service all similar hardware and to be able to distinguish among different physical units.

Block and Character Devices

This section describes typical device drivers. Because device drivers can be changed to suit a particular purpose, the descriptions in this section may not pertain to every system.

A *block device* is an I/O (input/output) device that is characterized by

- Being able to perform random access reads.
- Having a specific block size.
- Handling only single blocks of data at a time.
- Accepting only transactions that involve whole blocks of data.
- Being able to have a filesystem mounted on it.
- Having the Linux kernel buffer its input and output.
- Appearing to the operating system as a series of blocks numbered from 0 through $n - 1$, where n is the number of blocks on the device.

The common block devices on a Linux system are hard and floppy disks and CD-ROMs.

A *character device* is any device that is not a block device. Some examples of character devices are printers, terminals, tape drives, and modems.

The device driver for a character device determines how a program reads from and writes to the device. For example, the device driver for a terminal allows a program to read the information you type on the terminal in two ways. A program can read single characters from a terminal in *raw* mode (that is, without the driver doing any interpretation of the characters). This mode has nothing to do with the *raw device* described in the following section. Alternatively, a program can read a line at a time. When a program reads a line at a time, the driver handles the erase and kill characters so that the program never sees corrected typing mistakes. In this case the program reads everything from the beginning of a line to the RETURN that ends a line; the number of characters in a line can vary.

Raw Devices

Device driver programs for block devices usually have two entry points so they can be used in two ways: as block devices *or* as character devices. The character device form of a block device is called a *raw* device. A raw device is characterized by

- Direct I/O (no buffering through the Linux kernel).
- A one-to-one correspondence between system calls and hardware requests.
- Device-dependent restrictions on I/O.

An example of a utility that uses a raw device is fsck. It is more efficient for fsck to operate on the disk as a raw device, not restricted by the fixed size of blocks in the block device interface. Because it has full knowledge of the underlying filesystem structure, fsck can operate on the raw device by using the largest possible units. When a filesystem is mounted, processes normally access the disk through the block device interface. This explains why it is important to allow fsck to modify only an unmounted filesystem. On a mounted filesystem there is the danger that, while fsck is rearranging the underlying structure through the raw device, another process would change a disk block using the block device, resulting in a corrupted filesystem.

Filesystems

Table 17-8 lists some of the types of filesystems available under GNU/Linux.

Filesystem || table 17-8

adfs	The Acorn Disc Filing System.
affs	The Amiga FFS filesystem.
autofs	Automounting filesystem.
coda	The CODA distributed filesystem (being developed at Carnegie-Mellon).
devpts	A pseudofilesystem for pseudoterminals (page 958).
ext2	A standard filesystem for Red Hat systems, usually with the **ext3** extension.
ext3	A journaling (page 1475) extension to the **ext2** filesystem; greatly improves recovery time from crashes (it takes a lot less time to run **fsck**), promoting increased availability. As with any filesystem, a journaling filesystem can lose data during a system crash or hardware failure.
hfs	Hierarchical Filesystem: used by all Macintoshes from the Mac Plus on.
hpfs	High Performance Filesystem: the native filesystem for IBM's OS/2.
iso9660	The standard filesystem for CD-ROMs.
minix	Very similar to Linux, the filesystem of a small operating system that was written for educational purposes by Prof. Andrew S. Tanenbaum (www.cs.vu.nl/~ast/minix.html).
msdos	The filesystem used by DOS and subsequent Microsoft operating systems.
ncpfs	Novell NetWare NCP Protocol Filesystem: used to mount remote filesystems under NetWare.
nfs	Network Filesystem: Developed by Sun Microsystems, a protocol that allows a computer to access remote files over a network as if they were local.
ntfs	NT Filesystem: the native filesystem of Windows NT.

Filesystem (Continued) || table 17-8

proc	An interface to several Linux kernel *data structures* (page 1463) that behaves like a filesystem (page 966).
qnx4	The QNX 4 Operating System filesystem.
reiserfs	A journaling (page 1475) filesystem, based on balanced-tree algorithms. See **ext3** for more on journaling filesystems.
romfs	A dumb, readonly filesystem used mainly for RAM disks (page 1488) during installation.
software RAID	RAID implemented in software (not hardware). Refer to "RAID Filesystem" on page 984.
smbfs	Samba Filesystem. Refer to "Samba/**swat**" on page 1025.
sysv	System V UNIX filesystem.
ufs	Default filesystem under Sun's Solaris Operating System and other UNIXs.
umsdos	A full-feature UNIX-like filesystem that runs on top of a DOS FAT filesystem.
vfat	Developed by Microsoft, a standard that allows long file names on FAT partitions.

mount: Mounts a Filesystem

The mount utility allows you to connect filesystems to your Linux file hierarchy. These filesystems can be on remote and local disk partitions, CD-ROMs, and floppy disks. Linux also allows you to mount *virtual filesystems* that have been built inside regular files, filesystems built for other operating systems, and the special **/proc** filesystem (page 966), which maps useful Linux kernel information into a directory-like structure.

The *mount point* for the filesystem that you are mounting is a directory in your local filesystem. The directory must exist before mounting; its contents disappear as long as a filesystem is mounted on it and reappear when you unmount the filesystem.

Without any arguments, mount lists all the currently mounted filesystems, showing the physical device holding the filesystem, the mount point, the type of filesystem, and any options set when each filesystem was mounted:

```
$ mount
/dev/hdb1 on / type ext2 (rw)
/dev/hdb4 on /tmp type ext2 (rw)
/dev/hda5 on /usr type ext3 (rw)
/dev/sda1 on /usr/X386 type ext2 (rw)
/dev/sda3 on /usr/local type ext2 (rw)
/dev/hdb3 on /home type ext3 (rw)
/dev/hda1 on /dos type msdos (rw,umask=000)
none on /proc type proc (rw)
/dev/scd0 on /mnt/cdrom type iso9660 (ro,noexec,nosuid,nodev)
```

The utility gets this information from the **/etc/mtab** file (page 961). This section covers mounting local filesystems; refer to page 1019 for information on using NFS to mount remote filesystems.

The first six entries in the preceding example show disk partitions holding standard Linux **ext2** and **ext3** filesystems. Disk partitions are on three disks: two IDE disks (**hda, hdb**) and one SCSI disk (**sda**). Disk partition **/dev/hda1** has a DOS (**msdos**) filesystem mounted at the directory **/dos** in the Linux filesystem. You can access the DOS files and directories on this partition as if they were Linux files and directories, using GNU/Linux utilities and applications. The line starting with **none** shows the special **/proc** filesystem (page 966). The last line shows that a CD-ROM has been mounted on a SCSI CD-ROM drive (**/dev/scd0**).

On occasion the list of files in **/etc/mtab** may not be synchronized with the partitions that are mounted. You can remedy this situation by rebooting the system, or you can refer to the contents of the **/proc/mounts** file, which may have slightly different information than **mtab** but is always correct. You can even replace **mtab** with a symbolic link to **/proc/mounts**:

```
# rm /etc/mtab
# ln -s /proc/mounts /etc/mtab
```

Do Not Mount Anything on Root (/) || caution

Always mount network filesystems and removable devices at least one level below the root level of the filesystem. The root filesystem is mounted on /; you cannot mount two filesystems in the same place. If you were to try to mount something on /, all the files, directories, and filesystems that were under root would no longer be available, and the system would crash.

When you add a line for a filesystem to the **/etc/fstab** file (page 959), Superuser can mount that filesystem by giving the associated mount point (or the device) as the argument to mount. For example, the SCSI CD-ROM listed earlier was mounted using the following command:

```
$ mount /mnt/cdrom
```

This command worked because **/etc/fstab** contains the additional information needed to mount the file:

```
/dev/scd0 /mnt/cdrom iso9660 user,noauto,ro
```

You can also mount filesystems that do not appear in **/etc/fstab**. For example, when you insert a floppy disk that holds a DOS filesystem into your floppy disk drive, you can mount that filesystem by using the command

```
# mount -t msdos /dev/fd0 /mnt/floppy
```

The **–t msdos** specifies a filesystem type of **msdos**. You can mount DOS filesystems only if you have configured your Linux kernel (page 1031) to accept DOS filesystems. You do not need to mount a DOS filesystem in order to read from and write to it. Refer to "Mtools" on page 1256. You do need to mount a DOS filesystem to use GNU/Linux commands (for example, vi) on files on the disk.

Mount Options

The mount utility takes many options which you can specify on the command line or in the **/etc/fstab** file (page 978). For a complete list of mount options for local filesystems, see the mount man page; for remote filesystems, the nfs man page.

The **noauto** option means that the filesystem will not be mounted automatically. The **nosuid** option forces mounted setuid executables to run with regular permissions (no effective user ID change) on the local system (the system that mounted the filesystem).

Unless you specify the **user, users,** or **owner** option, only Superuser can mount and unmount filesystems. The **user** option means that any user can mount the filesystem, but it must be unmounted by the same user who mounted it; **users** means that any user can mount and unmount the filesystem. These options are frequently used for CD-ROM and floppy drives. The **owner** option, used only under special circumstances, is similar to the **user** option except that the user mounting the device must own the device.

Mounting a Linux Floppy

Mounting a Linux floppy is similar to mounting a partition of a hard disk. Put an entry similar to the following in **/etc/fstab** for a disk in the first floppy drive.

```
/dev/fd0     /mnt/floppy     ext2     noauto,users          0 0
```

Create the **/mnt/floppy** directory if necessary. Insert a diskette and try to mount it. In the following examples, the error message following the first command usually indicates that no filesystem is on the diskette: Use mkfs (page 1057) to create a filesystem, but be careful, mkfs destroys the data on the disk:

```
# mount /dev/fd0
mount: wrong fs type, bad option, bad superblock on /dev/fd0,
       or too many mounted file systems
# mkfs /dev/fd0
mke2fs 1.17, 26-Oct-1999 for EXT2 FS 0.5b, 95/08/09
Filesystem label=
OS type: linux
Block size=1024 (log=0)
Fragment size=1024 (log=0)
184 inodes, 1440 blocks
72 blocks (5.00%) reserved for the super user
First data block=1
1 block group
8192 blocks per group, 8192 fragments per group
184 inodes per group

Writing inode tables: done
Writing superblocks and filesystem accounting information: done
```

Try the mount command again:

```
# mount /dev/fd0
# mount
...
/dev/fd0 on /mnt/floppy type ext2 (rw,nosuid,nodev)
```

```
# df /dev/fd0
Filesystem              1k-blocks      Used Available Use% Mounted on
/dev/fd0                     1412        13      1327   1% /mnt/floppy
```

The mount command without any arguments and **df /dev/fd0** show that the floppy is mounted and ready for use.

umount: Unmounts a Filesystem

The umount utility unmounts a filesystem as long as it does not house any files or directories that are in use (open). For example, a logged-in user's working directory must not be on the filesystem you want to unmount. The next command unmounts the CD-ROM shown earlier:

```
$ umount /mnt/cdrom
```

To unmount all filesystems except for the one mounted at **/**, which can never be unmounted, use

```
# umount -a
```

Unmount a floppy or a remote filesystem the same way you would unmount a partition of a hard drive.

The umount utility consults **/etc/fstab** to get the necessary information and then unmounts the appropriate filesystem from its server. When a process has a file open on the filesystem that you are trying to unmount, umount displays a message similar to

```
umount: /home: device is busy
```

When You Cannot Unmount a Device Because It Is in Use   ‖ tip

When a process has a file open on a device you need to unmount, use **fuser** to determine which process has the file opened and to kill it. For example, when you want to unmount the floppy, give the command **fuser –ki /mnt/floppy**, which, after checking with you, kills the process using the floppy.

You can unmount all filesystems by using the **–a** option to umount, and you can combine that option with the **–t** option to unmount filesystems of a given type (**ext3**, **nfs**, or others). For example, use the following command to unmount all mounted **nfs** filesystems that are not being used:

```
# umount -at nfs
```

fstab: Keeps Track of Filesystems

The system administrator maintains the **/etc/fstab** file, which lists local and remote filesystems, most of which the system mounts automatically when it boots. The **fstab** file has six columns; a dash keeps the place of a column that has no value. The six columns are

1. **Name:**   The name of the block device (page 971) or remote filesystem. A remote filesystem appears as *hostname:pathname*, where *hostname* is the name of the host that houses the filesystem, and *pathname* is the absolute pathname of the directory that is to be mounted. You can substitute the volume label of the filesystem by using the form **LABEL=**_xx_, where *xx* is the volume label. Refer to e2label on page 1057.

2. **Mount point:**   The name of a directory file that the remote filesystem is to be mounted over. If it does not exist, create this directory with mkdir.

3. **Type:**   The type of filesystem that is to be mounted. Local filesystems are generally **ext2** or **ext3**, and remote ones are **nfs**. See Table 17-8 on page 973 for a list of filesystem types.

4. **Mount options:**   A comma-separated list of mount options, such as whether the filesystem is mounted for reading and writing (**rw**, the default) or readonly (**ro**). Refer to the mount man page for a list of options.

5. **Dump:**   Used by dump to determine when to back up the filesystem (page 1002).

6. **Fsck:**   Determines which filesystem fsck should check first. Root (**/**) should have a **1** in this column, other filesystems that need to be checked should have a **2**, and filesystems that do not need to be checked (for example, a remotely mounted filesystem or a CD-ROM) should have a **0**.

The following example shows a typical **fstab** file:

```
# cat /etc/fstab
/dev/hda12      /               ext3    defaults            1 1
/dev/hda1       /boot           ext2    defaults            1 2
/dev/hda5       /home           ext3    defaults            1 2
/dev/cdrom      /mnt/cdrom      iso9660 noauto,owner,ro     0 0
/dev/hda7       /tmp            ext2    defaults            1 2
/dev/hda6       /usr            ext3    defaults            1 2
/dev/hda11      swap            swap    defaults            0 0
/dev/fd0        /mnt/floppy     ext2    noauto,owner        0 0
none            /proc           proc    defaults            0 0
none            /dev/pts        devpts  gid=5,mode=620      0 0
bravo:/home     /bravo_home     nfs     defaults            0 0
kudos:/home/alex /kudos_alex    nfs     defaults            0 0
```

Exporting Symbolic Links and Device Files   ‖ tip

When you export a symbolic link, make sure that the object of the link is available on the client (remote) machine. If the object of the link does not exist on a client machine, you must export and mount it along with the exported link; otherwise, it will not point to the file it points to on the server.

A device file refers to a Linux kernel interface. When you export a device file, you export that interface. If the client machine does not have the same type of device, the exported device will not work.

A mounted filesystem with a mount point within an exported filesystem will not be exported with the exported filesystem. You need to export each filesystem that you want exported, even if it resides within an already exported filesystem. When you have two filesystems, **/opt/apps** and **/opt/apps/oracle**, residing on two partitions to export, you must export each explicitly, even though **oracle** is a subdirectory of **apps**. Most other subdirectories and files are exported automatically.

autofs: Automatically Mounts Filesystems

An **autofs** filesystem is like any other filesystem but remains unmounted until it is needed, at which time the system mounts it automatically (*demand mounting*). The system unmounts an **autofs** filesystem when it is no longer needed. Automatically mounted filesystems are an important part of administrating a large collection of machines in a consistent way. The automount utility is particularly useful when there is a large number of servers or a large number of filesystems. It also helps to remove server-server dependencies. When you have two servers that each mount filesystems from the other and both machines are down, both may hang as they are brought up, as each tries to mount a filesystem from the other, using traditional **fstab**-based mounts. The automount facility gets around this by mounting a filesystem from another machine only when a process tries to access it.

The **automount** daemon is usually started by the **/etc/rc.d/init.d/autofs** script when the system enters runlevels 3 or 5. When a process attempts to access one of the directories within the unmounted **autofs** filesystem, the filesystem notifies **automount**, which mounts the **autofs** filesystem.

You have to give a command, such as **cd /home/alex**, that accesses the **autofs** mount point (in this case **/home/alex**) in order to create the demand that causes **automount** to mount the **autofs** filesystem so you can see it. Before you issue the **cd** command, **alex** does not appear to be in **/home**.

A Linux kernel must support **autofs** in order for you to use it. Red Hat includes the **autofs.o** kernel module. Use either of the following tests to see whether the **autofs.o** module is enabled:

```
# cat /proc/filesystems | grep autofs
nodev   autofs
```

or

```
# /sbin/lsmod | grep autofs
autofs                  9152      0      (unused)
```

When you do not see a line with the word autofs following either command, **autofs** is not enabled. Give the following command to enable it:

```
# /sbin/modprobe autofs
```

If you get an error message, you need to include CONFIG_EXPERIMENTAL=y and CONFIG_AUTO_FS=y and recompile the kernel (page 1031).

The main file that controls the behavior of automount is **/etc/auto.master**. A simple example follows:

```
# cat auto.master
/free1 /etc/auto.misc  --timeout 60
/free2 /etc/auto.misc2 --timeout 60
```

The **auto.master** file has three columns: The first column names the parent of the **autofs** *mount point*—the location where the **autofs** filesystem is to be mounted (**/free1** and **/free2** in the example are not mount points but will hold the mount points when the filesystems are mounted). Supplemental configuration information is stored in the files, called *map files,* named in the second column. The optional third column holds mount options for map entries that do not specify an option.

The map files can have any names, but one is traditionally named **auto.misc.** Following are the two map files specified in **auto.master:**

```
# cat auto.misc
sam                    -fstype=ext3             :/dev/hda8

# cat auto.misc2
helen                  -fstype=ext3             :/dev/hda9
```

The first column of a map file holds the relative **autofs** mount point (sam and helen). This mount point is prepended with the corresponding **autofs** mount point from column one of the **auto.master** file to create the absolute **autofs** mount point. In this example, **/free1** (from **auto.master**) is prepended to **sam** (from **auto.misc**) to make **/free1/sam.** The second column holds the options, and the third column shows the server and filesystem to be mounted. This example shows local drives; an NFS-mounted device would have the hostname of the remote machine before the colon (**bravo:/dev/hda3**).

Before the new setup can work, you have to create directories for the parents of the mount points (**/free1** and **/free2** in the preceding example) and start or restart the **automount** daemon using **autofs.** You can see what is going on with **autofs** with the following command:

```
# /sbin/service autofs status
```

Give the same command, replacing **status** with **stop** to stop **autofs** or with **start** to start it. Use the following **chkconfig** (page 947) command to start **autofs** each time the system enters runlevels 3 or 5:

```
# chkconfig --level 35 autofs on
```

Refer to the autofs, automount, **auto.master** man pages; a tutorial at www.linuxhq.com/lg/issue24/nielsen.html; and the *Automount mini-HOWTO* for more information.

fsck: Checks Filesystem Integrity

The fsck (filesystem check) utility verifies the integrity of filesystems and, if possible, repairs any problems it finds. Because many filesystem repairs can destroy data, particularly on a non*journaling filesystem* (page 1475), such as **ext2,** fsck asks you for confirmation, by default, before making each repair.

The following command checks all the filesystems that are marked to be checked in **/etc/fstab** (page 959) except for the root filesystem:

```
# fsck -AR
```

Do Not Run fsck on a Mounted Filesystem ‖ caution

Do not run **fsck** on a mounted filesystem (except **/**). When you attempt to check a mounted filesystem, **fsck** warns you and asks you whether you want to continue. Reply **no**. You can run **fsck** with the **−N** option on a mounted filesystem as it will not write to the filesystem, so no harm will come of running it.

The **−A** option causes **fsck** to check filesystems listed in **fstab**, and **−R** skips the **root** filesystem. You can check a specific filesystem with a command similar to one of the following:

```
# fsck /home
```

or

```
# fsck /dev/hda6
```

The **/etc/rc.d/rc.sysinit** start-up script looks for two flags in the root directory of each partition to help determine whether **fsck** needs to be run on that partition. The **.autofsck** flag (the *crash flag*) indicates that the user should be asked whether the partition should be checked. By default the person bringing up the machine has 5 seconds to respond to a prompt with a **y**, or the check is skipped. The other flag, **forcefsck**, is also in the root directory of a partition. When this flag is set, the user is given no choice; **fsck** is automatically run on the partition. These checks are in addition to those established by **tune2fs** (next section). The **.autofsck** flag is present while the system is running and is removed when the system is properly shut down. When the system crashes, the flag will be present when the system is brought up. The **forcefsck** flag is placed on the filesystem when a hard error is on the disk and the disk must be checked. Refer to page 1176 in Part III for more information on **fsck**.

tune2fs: Changes Filesystem Parameters

The **tune2fs** utility displays and modifies filesystem parameters on **ext2** filesystems and on **ext3** filesystems, as they are modified **ext2** filesystems. This utility can also set up journaling on an **ext2** filesystem so that it becomes an **ext3** filesystem. With more reliable hardware and software, it becomes more important to check filesystems regularly. By default **fsck** is run on each partition while the system is brought up, before the partition is mounted.[24] Depending on the flags, **fsck** may do nothing more than display a message saying that the filesystem is clean. The larger the

---

24. The checks scheduled by tune2fs are separate and scheduled differently from the checks that are done following a system crash or hard disk error (see the previous section).

partition, the more time it takes to check it, assuming a nonjournaling filesystem. These checks are frequently unnecessary. The tune2fs utility helps you to find a happy medium between checking filesystems each time you reboot the system and never checking them. It does this by scheduling when fsck checks a filesystem (these checks occur only when the system is booted).[25] You can use two scheduling patterns: time elapsed since the last check and number of mounts since the last check. The following command causes **/dev/hda6** to be checked when fsck runs after it has been mounted eight times or after 15 days have elapsed since its last check, whichever happens first:

```
# tune2fs -c 8 -i 15 /dev/hda6
tune2fs 1.27, (8-Mar-2002)
Setting maximal mount count to 8
Setting interval between check 1296000 seconds
```

The next tune2fs command is similar except that it works on a different partition and sets the current mount count to 4. When you do not specify a current mount count, as in the previous example, it is assumed to be zero:

```
# tune2fs -c 8 -i 15 -C 4 /dev/hda10
tune2fs 1.27, (8-Mar-2002)
Setting maximal mount count to 8
Setting current mount count to 4
Setting interval between check 1296000 seconds
```

The **–l** option displays a list of information about the partition. You can combine this option with others. Below the Maximum mount count is –1, which means that the mount count information is ignored by fsck and the kernel. A mount count of 0 works the same way:

```
# tune2fs -l /dev/hda5
tune2fs 1.27, (8-Mar-2002)
Filesystem volume name:    /free1
Last mounted on:           <not available>
Filesystem UUID:           f93d69a8-a419-11d4-944c-e77d13cd6039
Filesystem magic number:   0xEF53
Filesystem revision #:     1 (dynamic)
Filesystem features:       has_journal filetype needs_recovery sparse_super
Filesystem state:          clean
Errors behavior:           Continue
Filesystem OS type:        Linux
Inode count:               513024
Block count:               1024135
...
```

---

25. For systems whose purpose in life is to run continuously, this kind of scheduling does not work. You must come up with a schedule that is not based on system reboots but rather on a clock. Each filesystem must be unmounted periodically, checked with fsck (preceding section), and remounted.

```
Last mount time:          Thu Dec 20 20:59:51 2001
Last write time:          Thu Dec 20 20:59:51 2001
Mount count:              6
Maximum mount count:      -1
Last checked:             Thu Dec  6 09:23:23 2001
Check interval:           0 (<none>)
```

Set the filesystem parameters on your system so that they are appropriate to the way you use your computer. Using the **–C** option to stagger the checks ensures that all the checks do not occur at the same time. Always check new and upgraded filesystems to make sure that they have checks scheduled as you desire.

To change an **ext2** filesystem to an **ext3** filesystem, you must put a journal (page 1475) on the filesystem, and the kernel must support **ext3** filesystems. Use the **–j** option to set up a journal on an unmounted filesystem:

```
# tune2fs -j /dev/hdd3
tune2fs 1.27, (8-Mar-2002)
Creating journal inode: done
This filesystem will be automatically checked every -1 mounts or
0 days, whichever comes first.  Use tune2fs -c or -i to override.
```

Before you can use **fstab** (page 959) to mount the changed filesystem, you must modify its entry in the **fstab** file to reflect its new type. Change the third column to **ext3**.

This command changes an unmounted **ext3** filesystem to an **ext2** filesystem:

```
# tune2fs -O ^has_journal /dev/hdd3
tune2fs 1.27, (8-Mar-2002)
```

Refer to the tune2fs man page for more details.

RAID Filesystem

RAID (Redundant Arrays of Inexpensive[26] Disks) spreads information across several disks to combine several physical disks into one larger virtual device. RAID improves performance and creates redundancy. There are more than six types of RAID configurations. Using Red Hat tools, you can set up *software* RAID. *Hardware* RAID requires hardware that is designed to implement RAID and is not covered here.

Do Not Replace Backups with RAID   ‖ caution

Do not use RAID as a replacement for regular backups. If your system undergoes a catastrophic failure, RAID will be useless. Earthquake, fire, theft, and so on may leave your entire system inaccessible (if your hard drives are destroyed or missing). RAID does not take care of something as simple as deleting a file you need. In these cases a backup on removable media (that has been removed) is the only way you will be able to restore your filesystem.

---

26. As disk prices have dropped, the Inexpensive part no longer applies.

RAID can be an effective *addition* to a backup. Red Hat has robust RAID software that you can install when you install your Red Hat system or as an afterthought. The Linux kernel can automatically detect RAID disk partitions at boot time if the partition ID is set to 0xfd, which fdisk recognizes as Linux raid autodetect.

The kernel disk code implements software RAID so it is much cheaper than a hardware RAID. Not only does it avoid specialized RAID disk controllers, but it also works with both the less expensive IDE disks as well as SCSI disks. For more information refer to the *Software-RAID HOWTO*.

GUI System Administration Tools

In addition to the system administration tools available in a character-based environment, you have the option of using graphical tools in a GUI. Many of these tools are built specifically for the GNOME and KDE desktops.

GNOME System Settings Window/Menu

Display the System Settings window by double-clicking a Start Here icon (page 216) and clicking System Settings, or by entering **system-settings:** in a Nautilus Location bar. Double-clicking on any of the icons opens a window that enables you to work with the corresponding system settings. You can display the same windows from GNOME menu:System Settings. The Extras icon opens a window with additional choices; it is not available from the GNOME menu. Most of these tools require you to supply the **root** password when you are not running as Superuser. Table 17-9 lists the tools in this window. Refer to "Start Here" on page 236 for information on other items in the Start Here window.

GNOME System Settings Window	‖ table 17-9
Authentication	Specifies whether to **Cache User Information** and whether to use and configure NIS (page 1021), *hesiod* (page 1470), and *LDAP* (page 1476). A second tab specifies whether to use shadow passwords (page 965) and/or *MD5* (page 1478) passwords and whether to use and configure *Kerberos* (page 1475) and SMB (page 1025) authentication.
Date & Time	Runs **dateconfig**.
Date & Time	Sets the date and time. Use the Date and Time frames to set the system clock manually. Use 24-hour time to set the clock even when you want the system to display a 12-hour clock. Or use the Network Time Protocol frame to synchronize your computer to a remote time server.

GNOME System Settings Window (Continued) || table 17-9

Network Time Protocol	Refer to "NTP" on 1482 in the glossary.
Enable Network Time Protocol	Turns on NTP so that your computer sets its clock periodically by consulting the specified server.
Server	Specifies the time server that you want to use to set your system clock.
Time Zone	There are two ways to specify the time zone that you want to use: the map or the scroll list.
View	Move the mouse pointer until the green arrow points to a city that is in your time zone, and click. Check that the right city is highlighted in the scroll list.
System clock uses UTC	Check this box if you want the system clock to use UTC (see the —utc option to **date** on page 1143).
(scroll list)	You can use the scroll list manually. Scroll the list, and click a city that is in your time zone.
Display	Sets the physical display characteristics. Refer to "**redhat-config-xfree86**: Sets Up X" on page 922.
Extras	Not available from the GNOME menu. Displays additional tools.
Keyboard	Sets the language and style of keyboard you are using.
Language	Sets the language GNOME uses for titles, prompts, labels, and so forth. For more information, refer to "locale" on page 1477.
Login Screen	Runs **gdmsetup** which displays the GDM (GNOME Display Manager) Setup window. See **/etc/X11/gdm/gdm.conf** for additional parameters.
General	Use the **Automatic** and **Timed login** choices with caution as they allow a user who is not present to log in automatically on an unattended console.
Greeter	Specifies whether to use the Standard or Graphical greeter for Local and Remote logins. Refer to the next two tabs to set up these greeters.
Automatic login	Logs in the specified user automatically when the system is booted.
Timed login	A timed login is an **Automatic login** that displays the Login window for the number of seconds that you specify before logging in the user. This delay allows another user to log in.

GNOME System Settings Window (Continued) || table 17-9

Standard/Graphical greeter	Specifies the characteristics of these greeters. The Standard greeter **Show choosable user images (face browser)** selection allows the display of images (presumably of users) in the Login window (Figure 2-3, page 32). Each user can click his/her picture to enter his/her name in the login text box. After that the login proceeds as usual.
Security	These options control local, remote, and timed logins by **root** and other users. **Show system menu** displays the System menu on the Login window. This menu includes the shutdown, reboot, and configuration choices. The Retry delay is the number of seconds that a user must wait to log in after providing incorrect name/password information.
XDMCP	Controls the X Display Manager Control Protocol, which allows you to configure remote non-GNU/Linux systems with X Windows. Refer to the *Linux XDMCP HOWTO* for more information.
Mail Transport Agent Switcher	Changes the system's mail transport agent. You can choose between **sendmail** and **postfix**.
Mouse	Selects the type of mouse attached to the system and allows you to specify that simultaneously pressing the two buttons on a two-button mouse emulates pressing the middle button on a three-button mouse (**Emulate 3 button click**).
Network	Runs **neat**, a network configuration tool.
Active Profile	Network configuration profiles enable you to name profiles so that you can easily switch profiles as needed. This feature is useful on laptops that frequently change environments. This frame selects, renames, removes, and creates new profiles.
Devices	
Add	Displays the Add new Device Type window (refer to "Internet Configuration Wizard" on page 1023). In most situations you do not have to use this tab as the system sets up a network hardware device when you install the hardware.
Edit	Displays the configuration window appropriate to the hardware that is highlighted so that you can make changes.
Copy	Copies the highlighted device and gives it a nickname that ends in **Copy0**, **Copy1**, and so on.
Delete	Deletes the highlighted device. You must deactivate the device before you can delete it.
Activate	Activates the highlighted device.

GNOME System Settings Window (Continued) || table 17-9

Deactivate	Deactivates the highlighted device.
Hardware	
Add	Displays the Choose Hardware Type window. When you select a hardware type (**Ethernet**, **Modem**, **ISDN**, **Token Ring**) from the combo box, it displays the configuration window appropriate to the type of hardware. In most situations, you do not have to use this tab as the system sets up a network hardware device when it first sees it.
Edit	Displays the configuration window appropriate to the hardware that is highlighted so that you can make changes.
Delete	Deletes the highlighted hardware.
Hosts	
Hosts	Edits the **/etc/hosts** file (page 1017).
DNS	Edits the **/etc/resolv.conf** file; refer to "DNS: Domain Name Service" on page 1021 for an overview. Fill in the **Hostname** text box with your system's hostname. Fill in the three DNS text boxes with the domain name servers that your system uses. You do not need three, but it is a good idea to have at least two. Next is the DNS Search Path frame: Specify the domain names of systems you want in your search domain—a search list for hostname lookup that defaults to the local domain name.
Packages	Refer to "**redhat-config-packages**: Adds and Removes Software Packages" on page 926.
Printing	Refer to "**printconf-gui**: Configures and Manages LPRng Printers" on page 1006.
Root Password	Runs **redhat-config-rootpassword**, a utility that allows you to choose a new **root** password.
Security Level	Refer to "**redhat-config-securitylevel**: Sets up a Firewall" on page 924.
Soundcard Detection	Runs **redhat-config-soundcard**, which displays sound card information and allows you to test the sound system.
Users and Groups	Refer to "**redhat-config-users**: Manages User Accounts" on page 993.

KDE Control Center: System Module

Select this module from K menu: Control Center⇨System; you can select the individual functions from K menu: Preferences⇨System.

When you are not running as **root**, many of the items in the System section of the Control Center are grayed out, indicating that you cannot modify or use them. In each of the windows that contains grayed-out sections, clicking the Administrator Mode button at the lower-right corner of the window allows you to supply the **root** password to bring all the items in the window to life so that you can modify/use them (Table 17-10).

KDE Control Center: System Module || table 17-10

Alarm Daemon	Configures **kalarmd**, the alarm daemon, which monitors the **kalarm**, **korganizer**, and other applications' calendar files.
Boot Manager (LILO)	Sets up and modifies **lilo**. Click the **Expert** tab to display the **/etc/lilo.conf** file. Refer to "**lilo**: The Linux Loader" on page 1040.
Linux Kernel Configurator	Refer to "The KDE Linux Kernel Configurator" on page 1035.
Login Manager	Controls the appearance and functionality of the GUI Login window.
Appearance	
Appearance	
Greeting	The message you see on the GUI Login window.
Logo area	Determines what appears in the logo area of the GUI Login window. You can display nothing, a clock, or an image of your choice.
Logo	With **Show logo** selected in the Logo area, displays the logo that will be displayed. Double-click the logo to select a different logo.
Position	Specifies the location of the GUI Login window on the screen. Choose **Centered**, or click **Specify** and enter the X and Y coordinates in pixels.
GUI Style	Specifies the GUI style that the Login Manager will use.
Echo mode	Specifies what KDE displays as you enter your password.
Locale: Language	The language KDE uses for titles, prompts, labels, and so forth. For more information, refer to "locale" on page 1477.

KDE Control Center: System Module (Continued) || table 17-10

Font	Specifies the fonts used in the GUI Login window. Select **Greeting**, **Fail**, or **Standard** from the drop-down list, and specify the font you want to use by clicking **Change font**. The Example frame displays the font you choose. You can specify *antialiasing* (page 1454) if you like.
Background	These apply to the background visible while the login window is displayed.
Background	Choose a **Mode** of **Flat** for a single-color background; **Background Program** to run a program, specified in **Setup**, to generate the background; or one of the other selections for a two-color background. Click **Color 1** or **Color 2** to display the Select Color window. View the effect of your choice in the picture of a monitor near the top of the window.
Wallpaper	Choose a wallpaper from the Wallpaper drop-down list or by clicking the **Browse** button. Specify how you want the wallpaper displayed from the **Mode** drop-down list. View the effect of your choice in the picture of a monitor near the top of the window.
Sessions	
Allow shutdown	After you click **Shutdown** on the Login window, you are given the choice of shutting the system down or rebooting it.
Console	Specifies which users can shut down the system when they are logged in on the system console.
Remote	Specifies which users can shut down the system when they are logged in remotely.
Commands	Specifies which commands are used to halt and reboot the system when a user chooses **Power off** or **Restart Computer** in the login window (Figure 2-3, page 32).
Lilo	Displays boot options when the user reboots from the Login window.
Show boot options	Displays the options for the **lilo** boot manager when you boot/reboot the system. Each of the following two text boxes must be correct for this feature to work.
Lilo command	The command that runs **lilo**.
Lilo map file	The name of the **lilo**-maintained file that contains the name and location of the kernel(s) that **lilo** boots.
Session types	Defines which session types are available from the GUI Login window.

KDE Control Center: System Module (Continued) || table 17-10

New type	To add a new session, enter the name of the new session type, and click **Add new**.
Available types	Lists available session types. To remove a session type, highlight it, and click **Remove**.
Users	The GUI Login window presents a list of users for the convenience of the person logging in, who can click a user in the list to fill the **Login:** text box or can enter a login name directly into the text box. This tab divides the users into three groups: **Remaining users**, **Selected users**, and **No-show users**. Move the users between the boxes by highlighting a user and clicking the arrows between the boxes. The **Show users** frame specifies which users are presented in the GUI Login window: **No-show users** are never displayed, **Selected only** presents the **Selected users**, **All but no-show** presents the **Remaining users** and the **Selected users**, and **None** does not present any users. **Sort users** displays the users in alphabetical order. Highlight a user, and click the icon just above the **Show users** frame to change the icon that represents the user in the GUI Login window.
Convenience	*Use the items in this tab only on a home system that is not connected to a network. Anything you change compromises security in order to make it easier to log in.*
Automatic login	
Enable auto-login	Enables you to log in as the user specified in the **Preselect User** frame (following). Performs **Truly automatic login** when you kill the X server (CONTROL-ALT-BACKSPACE).
Truly automatic login	Logs in the specified user automatically each time the Login window is displayed.
Preselect User	Specifies a user name that automatically appears in the Login text box of the GUI Login window. You can specify that no name appear, that the name of the previous user who logged in appear, or that the user's name specified in the **User** drop-down menu appear. Checking **Focus password** causes the cursor to appear in the Password text box, ready for the preselected user to enter a password.
Password-less login	Enables users in the **Skip password check** column to log in without providing a password.
Miscellaneous	**Automatically log in again after X server crash** causes KDE to log you in again after the X server crashes and you bring it up again.
Printing Manager	Refer to "KDEPrint: Manages Printers" on page 1014.

KDE Control Center: Network Module

Select this module from K menu: Control Center⇨Network; you can select the individual functions from K menu: Preferences⇨Network. The Network module of the KDE Control Center mixes simple and complex tasks (Table 17-11). Set up basic e-mail and news ticker services here, or work on LAN browsing by setting up the LISa or ResLISa daemon.

KDE Control Center: Network Module	‖ table 17-11
Email	Sets up your e-mail information and specifies a default e-mail client.
Kisdndock	Automatically starts the KDE ISDN Dock, which allows you to connect/disconnect quickly to *ISDN* (page 1474) links when you start KDE. Run **redhat-config-network** to start the Network Configuration module (page 987), and run **internet-druid** to start the Internet Configuration Wizard (page 1023).
LAN Browsing	Sets up LISa (LAN Information Server, lisa-home.sourceforge.net) or ResLISa for browsing your LAN. Functioning similarly to MS Network Neighborhood, LISa relies solely on the TCP/IP stack and not on *SMB* (page 1492). The resLISa program is more secure than LISa; *The LISa Handbook* (docs.kde.org/2.2.2/kdenetwork/lisa/index.html) describes both. Using the *Guided LISa Setup* makes it easier to set up LISa.
Preferences	
Timeout Values	Specifies the length of time to wait for the specified network operation to complete. The default values usually work well; adjust them if your connection is very slow.
FTP Options	
Enable Passive Mode (PASV)	Enables *passive FTP* (page 1484) so that you can use **ftp** through a firewall.
Mark partially uploaded files	Uses a special filename for files as they are being uploaded and changes the name when the upload is complete.
SOCKS	Enables and sets up *SOCKS* (page 1493) support on the local system.

Configuring User and Group Accounts

More than a login name is required for a user to be able to log in and use the system. A user should have the necessary files, directories, permissions, and optionally a password in order to log in. Minimally a user must have an entry in the **/etc/passwd** and **/etc/shadow** files and a home directory. The following sections describe several ways you can work with user accounts. Refer to page 390 and the *NIS-HOWTO* when you want to run a Network Information Service (NIS or NIS+) to manage the **passwd** database.

redhat-config-users: **Manages User Accounts**

GNOME	GNOME menu: System Settings⇨Users and Groups start-here: System Settings⇨Users and Groups
KDE	K menu: System Settings⇨Users and Groups start-here: System Settings⇨Users and Groups
graphical	**redhat-config-users**

The Red Hat User Manager is a graphical tool that enables you to add, delete, and modify system users and groups.

The Search filter selects users or groups whose names match the string, which can include wildcards, that you enter in the Search filter text box. The string must match the beginning of a name. Characters in the name, following the match, are discounted. For example, ***nob** matches nobody and nfsnobody, whereas **nob** matches only nobody. After you enter the string, click Apply filter or press RETURN.

Red Hat User Manager: User and Group Properties || tip

The Red Hat User Manager window has two small tabs just above the display area of the window:

- Click the **Users** tab to display the list of users. Highlight a user, and click **Properties** on the toolbar to work with the properties of the highlighted user.

- Click the **Groups** tab to display the list of groups. Highlight a group, and click **Properties** on the toolbar to work with the properties of the highlighted group.

To create a new user or group, click the Add User or Add Group button on the toolbar. The User Manager displays the Create New User window, which is similar to the User Data tab of the User/Group Properties window (Table 17-12 and Table 17-13). Enter the information for the new user or group and close the window. Once the user or group exists, you can work with its properties to add/change/remove information. To modify a user or group, highlight the user or group, and click Properties on the toolbar.

Red Hat User Manager: Users || table 17-12

In this table [CNU] indicates an item that is present only in the Create New User window.

User Data	
User Name	The identification string (login name) that you use to log in on the system. Sometimes it resembles the user's name.
Full Name	The user's real name or how the user would like to be thought of. Can include other identifying text, such as a phone extension.
Password	The string that the user enters, after the User Name, to log in on the system. For more information, refer to "Keeping the System Secure" on page 1070.
Confirm Password	A repetition of the password to make sure that you got it right the first time.
Create home directory [CNU]	Causes the User Manager to create a home directory for the user.
Home Directory	By default the name of the new home directory is **/home/***username*, where *username* is the **User Name**. You can specify a different path and/or name.
Login Shell	The shell the user wants to log in on. Leave the default (**bash**) when you do not know or care.
Account Info	
Enable account expiration	Enables you to set a date when the account expires. This is different from the date the password expires; the user can do nothing about it.
Account expires on date	Sets the date when the account expires.
User account is locked	Sets an administrative lock that causes the user name and password not to work. Turn off the lock by clicking the check box to remove the check mark.
Password Info	For more information on passwords, see "Keeping the System Secure" on page 1070.
Enable password expiration	Enables you to set time periods within which the user must or must not change his or her password.

Red Hat User Manager: Users (Continued)   ‖ table 17-12

Days before change allowed	Specifies the number of days before the user is allowed to change his or her password.
Days before change required	Specifies the number of days before the user must change his or her password.
Days warning before change	Specifies the number of days warning the system gives before the user must change his or her password.
Days before account inactive	Specifies the number of days before the account becomes inactive.
Groups	Click to place a check mark in the box next to the name of a group that this user is to belong to.

Red Hat User Manager: Groups   ‖ table 17-13

Group Data	
Group Name	When you are creating a new group, enter the name of the group. When you want to change the name of a group, enter the new name.
Group Users	Click to place a check mark in the box next to the names of users who are to be in this group.

kuser: Manages User Accounts under KDE

The kuser user manager is easy to use yet handles most of the chores that you, a system administrator, are likely to encounter in your day-to-day work. Give the command **kuser** while you are logged in as **root** to display the kuser User Manager window. This window has two tabs (Users and Groups) and displays a list of users (from **/etc/passwd**) or groups (from **/etc/group**). In either case you can sort the list by clicking the label at the top of the column you want to sort by.

The toolbar has six icons: Add, Delete, and Edit, for both User and Group. Highlight the user/group that you want to work with, and click Delete to remove it or Edit to modify it. You can also double-click the user/group to modify it. When you choose Modify, kuser displays the User Properties window, which has three tabs:

User Info, Password Management, and Groups. The User Info tab allows you to change the user's name, password, login shell, and miscellaneous information that appears in the /etc/passwd file. Password Management lets you configure password and account expiration. Under the Groups tab you can specify which groups the user belongs to. When you click Add User on the toolbar, kuser asks you for the new user's name and displays the User/ Properties window so that you can set up the new user. Add Group asks for the new group's name.

For more information read the kuser handbook, available by clicking Kuser menubar: Help⇨Contents.

useradd: **Adds a User Account**

The useradd utility (and the link to it, named adduser) makes it easy to add new user accounts to your system. By default useradd assigns the next highest unused user ID to a new account and specifies the bash as the user's login shell. The following example creates the user's home directory (in /home), specifies the user's group ID, and puts the user's full name in the comment field:

```
# useradd -g 500 -c "Alex Watson" alex
```

Once you have added a user, use passwd to give the user a password. Based on the /etc/login.defs file, Red Hat systems create a home directory for the new user without the use of the –m option. When useradd creates a home directory, it copies the contents of /etc/skel to that directory. On Red Hat systems, this directory contains bash and other startup files. For more information on adding and modifying user information, see the useradd and usermod man pages.

userdel: **Removes a User Account**

If appropriate, make a backup copy of all the files belonging to the user before deleting them. The userdel utility makes it easy to delete old user accounts from your system. The following command removes alex's account, his home directory, and all his files:

```
# userdel -r alex
```

To turn off a user's account temporarily, you can use usermod to change the expiration date for the account. Because it specifies that his account expired in the past (December 31, 2001), the following command line prevents alex from logging in:

```
# usermod -e "12/31/01" alex
```

groupadd: Adds a Group

Just as useradd adds a new user to the system, groupadd adds a new group by adding an entry to **/etc/group**. The first example that follows demonstrates creating a new group, named **rtfm**, for users who are allowed to update the online manual pages:

```
# groupadd -g 1024 rtfm
```

Unless you use the **–g** option to assign a group ID, the system picks the next available sequential number greater than 500. The **–o** option allows the group ID to be nonunique if you want to have multiple names for the same group ID.

The analogue of userdel for groups is groupdel, which takes a group name as an argument. You can also use groupmod to change the name or group ID of a group, as in the following examples:

```
# groupmod -g 1025 rtfm
# groupmod -n manuals rtfm
```

The first example gives the previously created **rtfm** group a new group ID. The second example renames the **rtfm** group **manuals**.

Group ID Cautions   ‖ caution

The groupmod utility does not change group numbers in /etc/passwd when you renumber a group. You must edit /etc/passwd and change the entries yourself. If you change the number of a group, files that belonged to the group will no longer belong to the group. They may belong to no group or to another group with the old group ID.

Backing Up Files

One of the most neglected tasks of the system administrator is making backup copies of files on a regular basis. The backup copies are vital in three instances: when the system malfunctions and files are lost, when a catastrophic disaster (fire, earthquake, and so on) occurs, and when a user or the system administrator deletes or corrupts a file by accident. Even when you set up RAID striping with parity, or a mirror, you still need to maintain a backup. Although mirrors and RAID are useful for fault tolerance (disk failure), they will not help in a catastrophic disaster or when a file is accidentally removed or corrupted. It is a good idea to have a written backup policy and to keep copies of backups offsite (in another building, at home, or at a completely different facility or campus, if possible) in a fireproof vault or safe.

The time to start thinking about backups is when you partition your disk. Refer to "Partitioning a Disk" on page 912. Make sure that the capacity of your backup device and your partition sizes are in line. Although you can back up a partition onto multiple volumes, it is easier not to and much easier to restore from a single volume.

You must back up the filesystems on a regular basis. Backup files are usually kept on magnetic tape or other removable media. Exactly how often you should back up which files depends on your system and needs. The criterion is: If the system crashes, how much work are you willing to lose? Ideally you would back up all the files on the system every few minutes so that you would never lose more than a few minutes of work.

The tradeoff is, How often are you willing to back up the files? The backup procedure typically slows down the machine for other users, takes a certain amount of your time, and requires that you have and store the media (tape or disk) that you keep the backup on. Avoid backing up an active filesystem; the results may be inconsistent, and restoring from the backup may be impossible. This requirement is a function of the backup program and the filesystem you are backing up.

Another question is when to run the backup. Unless you kick the users off and bring the machine down to single-user mode (not a very user-friendly practice), you want to do it when the machine is at its quietest. Depending on the use of the machine, sometime in the middle of the night can work well. Then the backup is least likely to impact the users, and the files are not likely to change as they are being read for backup.

A *full* backup makes copies of all files, regardless of when they were created or accessed. An *incremental* backup makes copies of the files that have been created or modified since the last (usually full) backup.

The more people using the machine, the more often you should back up the filesystems. A common schedule might have you perform an incremental backup one or two times a day and a full backup one or two times a week.

Choosing a Backup Medium

Traditionally, personal computers used floppy diskettes for performing backups. However the large, hard disks now available for computers makes this impractical. If you have a ten gigabyte disk on your system, you would need more than 6,000 floppy diskettes to do a full backup. Even if files are compressed as you back them up, the number of diskettes required would be unmanageable. If your computer is connected to a network, you can write your backups to a tape drive on another system. This is often done with networked computers to avoid the cost of having a tape drive on each computer in the network and to simplify management of doing backups for many computers in a network. Most likely you want to use a tape system for backing up your computer. Because tape drives are available to hold many gigabytes of data, using tape simplifies the task of backing up your system, making it more likely that you regularly do this important task. Other options for holding backups are writable CD-ROMs, DVDs, and removable hard disks. These devices, although not as cost-effective or able to store as much information as tape systems, offer convenience and improved performance over using tapes.

Backup Utilities

A number of utilities help you back up your system, and most work with any media. Most GNU/Linux backup utilities are based on one of the archive programs—tar or cpio—and augment these basic programs with bookkeeping support for managing backups conveniently.

You can use any one of the tar, cpio, or dump/restore utilities to construct full or partial backups of your system. Each utility constructs a large file that contains, or archives, other files. In addition to file contents, an archive includes header information for each file inside it. This header information can be used when extracting files from the archive to restore file permissions and modification dates. An archive file can be saved to disk, written directly to tape, or shipped across the network while it is being created.

In addition to helping you back up your system, these programs are convenient for bundling files for distribution to other sites. The tar program is often used for this purpose, and some software packages available on the Internet are bundled as tar archive files.

The amanda (Advanced Maryland Automatic Network Disk Archiver—www.amanda.org) utility, one of the more popular backup systems, uses dump or tar and takes advantage of Samba to back up MS Windows systems. The amanda utility backs up a LAN of heterogeneous hosts to a single tape drive. It is available under Red Hat; refer to the amanda man page for details.

tar: Archives Files

The tar (tape archive) utility stores and retrieves files from an archive and can compress the archive to conserve space. You can specify an archive device with the –f option. If you do not specify an archive device, tar uses **/dev/rmt0** (which may not exist on your system). With the –f option, tar uses the argument to –f as the name of the archive device. You can use this option to refer to a device on another computer system on your network. Although a lot of options are available with tar, you need only a few in most situations. The following command displays a complete list of options:

```
# tar --help | less
```

Most options for tar can be given either in a short form (a single letter) or as a descriptive word. Descriptive-word options are preceded by two dashes, as in --help. Single-letter options can be combined into a single command line argument and do not need to be preceded by a dash (for consistency with other utilities, it is good practice to use the dash anyway).

Although the following two commands look quite different, they specify the same tar options in the same order. The first version combines single-letter options into a single command line argument, whereas the second version uses descriptive words for the same options:

```
# tar -ztvf /dev/st0
```

```
# tar --gzip --list --verbose --file /dev/st0
```

Both commands tell tar to generate a (**v**, **verbose**) table of contents (**t**, **list**) from the tape on /dev/st0 (**f**, **file**), using gzip (**z**, **gzip**) to decompress the files. Unlike the original UNIX tar, the GNU version strips the leading / from absolute pathnames.

The options in Table 17-14 tell the tar program what you want it to do. You must include exactly one of these options whenever you use tar.

tar Option   ‖ table 17-14

--append (–r)	Appends files to an archive
--catenate (–A)	Adds one or more archives to the end of an existing archive
--create (–c)	Creates a new archive
--delete	Deletes files in an archive (not on tapes)
--dereference (–h)	Follows symbolic links
--diff (–d)	Compares files in an archive with disk files
--extract (–x)	Extracts files from an archive
--help	Displays a help list of **tar** options
--list (–t)	Lists the files in an archive
--update (–u)	Like the –r option, but the file is not appended if a newer version is already in the archive

The −c, −t, and −x options are used most frequently. You can use many other options to change how tar operates. The −j option compresses/decompresses the file by filtering it through bzip2 (page 74). Refer to tar on page 1343 in Part III for a more complete list of options and additional examples of their use.

cpio: Archives Files

The cpio (copy in/out) program is similar to tar but can use archive files in a variety of formats, including the one used by tar. Normally cpio reads the names of the files to insert into the archive from standard input and produces the archive file as standard output. When extracting files from an archive, cpio reads the archive as standard input.

As with tar, some options can be given in both a short, single-letter form and a more descriptive word form. However, unlike tar, the syntax of the two forms differs when the option must be followed by additional information. In the short form you must use a SPACE between the option and the additional information; with the word form you must separate the two with an equal sign and no SPACES.

Running cpio with −−help displays a full list of options, although not as nice a list as tar. Refer to cpio on page 1124 in Part III for a more complete list of options and examples of their use.

Performing a Simple Backup

When you prepare to make a major change to your system, such as replacing a disk drive or updating the Linux kernel, it is a good idea to archive some or all of your files so you can restore any that are damaged if something goes wrong. For this type of backup, tar or cpio works well. For example, if you have a SCSI tape drive as device **/dev/st0** that is capable of holding all your files on a single tape, you can use the following commands to construct a backup tape of your entire system:

```
# cd /
# tar -cf /dev/st0 .
```

This command creates an archive (c) on the device **/dev/st0** (f). All the commands in this section start by using cd to change to the root directory so you are sure to back up the entire system. If you would like to compress the archive, replace the preceding tar command with the following command, which uses **j** to call bzip2:

```
# tar -cjf /dev/st0 .
```

You can back up your system with a combination of find and cpio.[27] The options create an output file and set the I/O block size to 5120 bytes (the default is 512 bytes):

---

27. When it creates a file, cpio may generate inode truncated error messages, which you can ignore.

```
# cd /
# find . -depth | cpio -oB > /dev/st0
```

The following command restores all the files in the **/home** directory from the preceding backup. The options extract files from an archive (–i) in verbose mode, keeping the modification times and creating directories as needed.

```
# cd /
# cpio -ivmd /home/\* < /dev/st0
```

Exclude Some Directories from a Backup || tip

In practice you exclude some directories from the backup process. For example, not backing up /tmp or /var/tmp (or its link, /usr/tmp) can save room in the archive. Also, do not back up the files in /proc. Because the /proc filesystem is not a disk filesystem but rather a way for the Linux kernel to provide you with information about the operating system and system memory, you need not back up /proc; you cannot restore it later. You do not need to back up filesystems that are mounted from disks on other computers in your network. Do not back up FIFOs; the results are unpredictable. If you plan on using a simple method, similar to those just shown, create a file naming the directories to exclude from the backup, and use the appropriate option with the archive program.

Although any of the archive programs works well for such simple backups, only amanda has the support to provide a sophisticated backup and restore system. For example, to determine whether a file is in an archive requires you to read the entire archive. If the archive is split across several tapes, this is particularly tiresome. More sophisticated utilities, including amanda, assist you in several ways, including keeping a table of contents of the files in a backup.

dump, restore: Back Up and Restore Filesystems

The dump utility, first seen in UNIX version 6, backs up an entire filesystem, or only those files that have changed since the last dump. The restore utility restores an entire filesystem, an individual file, or a piece of the filesystem hierarchy (a directory and its descendants). You will get the best results if you perform a backup on a quiescent system so that the files are not changing as you make the backup.

The following command performs a complete backup of all files (including directories and special files) on the **root** (/) partition onto SCSI tape 0:[28]

---

28. Frequently there is a link to the active tape drive, named **/dev/tape**, which you can use in place of the actual entry in the **/dev** directory.

```
# dump -0uf /dev/st0 /
```

The option specifies that the whole filesystem is to be backed up (a full backup). There are ten dump levels: 0–9. Zero is the highest (most complete) level and always backs up the entire filesystem. Each additional level is incremental with respect to the level above it. For example, 1 is incremental to 0 and backs up only files that have changed since the last level 0 dump. Level 2 is incremental to 1 and backs up only files that have changed since the last level 1 dump, and so on. You can construct a very flexible schedule by using this scheme. Also, you do not need to use sequential numbers for backup levels. You can perform a level 0 dump, followed by level 2 and 5 dumps.

The **u** option updates the **/etc/dumpdates** file (page 959) with filesystem, date, and dump level information for use by the next incremental dump. The **f** option and its argument (**/dev/st0**) write the backup to the file named **/dev/st0**.

The following command makes a partial backup containing all the files that have changed since the last level 0 dump. The first argument is a 1, specifying a level 1 dump.

```
# dump -1uf /dev/st0 /
```

To restore an entire filesystem from a tape, first restore the most recent complete (level 0) backup. Do this carefully, because restore can overwrite the existing filesystem. When you are logged in as Superuser, cd to the directory the filesystem is mounted on, and give the following command:

```
# restore -if /dev/st0
```

The **i** option invokes an interactive mode that allows you to choose which files and directories you would like to restore. As with dump, the **f** option specifies the name of the device that the backup tape is mounted on. When restore finishes, load the next lower-level (higher number) dump tape and issue the same restore command. If you have multiple incremental dumps at a particular level, always restore with the most recent one. You do not need to invoke restore with any special arguments to restore an incremental dump; it will restore whatever is on the tape.

You can also use restore to extract individual files from a tape by using the **x** option and specifying the filenames on the command line. Whenever you restore a file, the restored file will be in your working directory. Before restoring files, make sure that you are working in the right directory. The following commands restore the **etc/xinetd.conf** file from the tape in **/dev/st0**. The filename of the dumped file does not begin with a /, because all dumped pathnames are relative to the filesystem that you dumped—in this case /. Because the restore command is given from the / directory, the file will be restored to its original location: **/etc/xinetd.conf**:

```
# cd /
# restore -xf /dev/st0 etc/xinetd.conf
```

If you use the **x** option without specifying a file or directory name to extract, the entire dumped filesystem is extracted. Use the **r** option to restore an entire filesystem without having to go through the interactive interface. The following command restores the filesystem from the tape on **/dev/st0** into the working directory without interaction:

```
# restore -rf /dev/st0
```

You can also use dump and restore to access a tape drive on another system over the network (specify the file/directory as *host:file,* where *host* is the hostname of the machine that the tape drive is on and *file* is the file/directory you want to dump/restore).

Occasionally restore may prompt you with

```
You have not read any volumes yet.
Unless you know which volume your file(s) are on you should start
with the last volume and work towards the first.
Specify next volume #:
```

Enter **1** (one) in response to this prompt. If the filesystem spans more than one tape or disk, this prompt allows you to switch tapes.

At the end of the dump, you will receive another prompt:

```
set owner/mode for '.'? [yn]
```

Answer **y** to this prompt when restoring entire filesystems or files that have been accidentally removed. Doing so will restore the appropriate permissions to the files and directories being restored. Answer **n** if you are restoring a dump to a directory other than the one it was dumped from; the working directory permissions and owner will be set to those of the person doing the restore (typically **root**).

Various device names can access the **/dev/st0** device. Each name accesses a different minor device number that controls some aspect of how the tape drive is used. After you complete a dump when you use **/dev/st0**, the tape drive automatically rewinds the tape to the beginning. Use the nonrewinding SCSI tape device (**/dev/nst0**) to keep the tape from rewinding on completion. This feature allows you to back up multiple filesystems to one volume. Following is an example of backing up a system where the **/home, /usr,** and **/var** directories are on different filesystems:

```
# dump -0uf /dev/nst0 /home
# dump -0uf /dev/nst0 /usr
# dump -0uf /dev/st0 /var
```

The preceding example uses the nonrewinding device for the first two dumps. If you use the rewinding device, the tape rewinds after each dump, and you are left with only the last dump on the tape. For more information refer to the mt (magnetic tape) and st (SCSI tape) man pages.

You can use mt to manipulate files on a multivolume dump tape. The following mt command positions the tape (**fsf 2** instructs mt to skip forward *past* two files leaving the tape at the start of the third file). The restore command restores the **/var** filesystem from the previous example:

```
# mt -f /dev/st0 fsf 2
# restore rf /dev/st0
```

Printing

Unlike Microsoft operating systems, UNIX/Linux takes a simplistic approach to printers. You do not need to load special drivers to use a printer. Printers are simply attached to a serial or parallel port (or directly to the network). Applications are responsible for generating output that will properly drive the printer. This choice makes operating system support for printers very easy (at the expense of the application developer). The www./linuxprinting.org Web site, a good source of information on printers and printing under GNU/Linux, offers printer recommendations and hosts a support database with details about many printers, including notes and driver information. The site also has forums, articles, and a HOWTO on printing.

A *printing system* handles the tasks implicit in getting a print job from an application (or the command line) through the appropriate filters into a queue for a suitable printer and getting it printed. For example, some filter programs can convert PostScript files into files specific to a given model of printer by calling the ghostscript utility with the appropriate arguments. Some filters can automatically determine the type of input file and call the proper utility to convert it into the form needed by a certain printer. While handling a job, a printing system can also keep track of billing information so that the proper accounts can be charged for printer use. When a printer fails, the printing system can redirect jobs bound for that printer to other, similar printers.

UNIX has traditionally had two printing systems: the BSD Line Printer Daemon (**lpd**) and the AT&T Line Printer system (**lp**). GNU/Linux adapted those systems at first, and both UNIX and GNU/Linux have seen modifications to and replacements for these systems, notably LPRng. As of Red Hat 8.0, the default printing system is LPRng[29] running the Berkeley UNIX printer package (**lpd/lpr**). In addition, Red Hat supports several printing systems, including CUPS (page 1010).

---

29. Even though LPRng is the default printing system under Red Hat 8.0, Red Hat has deprecated LPRng and will remove it in a future release. CUPS (page 1010) is expected to become the new default.

printconf-gui: Configures and Manages LPRng Printers

GNOME	GNOME menu: System Settings⇨Printing
	start-here: System Settings⇨Printing
KDE	K menu: System Settings⇨Printing
	start-here: System Settings⇨Printing
graphical	printconf-gui

LPRng (www.lprng.com) implements Berkeley LPR functionality with added portability and features. It provides improved security checks and error messages, dynamic redirection of print queues, and non-suid permissions for client programs; and it enables multiple printers to serve a single print queue.

The printconf-gui utility adds, removes, and modifies print queues on your local system, including local queues that send their output to remote printers. This utility configures the **lpd** daemon and the LPRng printing system by modifying entries in the **/etc/printcap** file. (As of Red Hat 8.0 printconf-gui does not support CUPS.) Refer to Table 17-15 and the step-by-step instructions on page 1008 for more information. You can perform these functions manually as an exercise; see page 1011.

printconf-gui Toolbar || table 17-15

New	Displays the Add A New Print Queue window.
Add A New Print Queue	Introductory window; nothing to do. Click **Forward**.
Set the Print Queue Name and Type	Specifies the name and type of the new queue (Figure 17-6, page 1008). See the five choices that follow.
Local Printer	A local printer is one that is attached directly to your machine via a serial or parallel port. By the time you see this window, **printconf-gui** has had a chance to scan your printer's ports for printers. Click **Rescan Devices** if you just plugged the printer in or if there is another reason the program might not have detected the printer. Click **Custom Device** to specify manually the device the printer is attached to (such as **/dev/tty0**).
Unix Printer	A remote UNIX (**lpd**) queue is a UNIX printer attached to another UNIX/Linux machine that is running an **lpd** daemon. For this type of printer, you must specify the hostname of the remote machine and, optionally, the name of the print queue on the remote machine. The remote **/etc/hosts.lpd** usually controls access to the queue.

printconf-gui Toolbar (Continued) || table 17-15

Windows Printer	Use the Windows queue for a printer on another machine that is a Samba (SMB) or MS Windows server.
Novell Printer	The Novell (NetWare) printer works with a printer on an NCP server. This queue requires **nprint**, which you may need to install.
JetDirect Printer	Specifies the IP address and port for a JetDirect printer.
Configure a *Xxx* Printer	Specifies parameters pertaining to the type of printer you are installing (an *Xxx* printer).
Select a Print Driver	Presents a printer tree (click the triangles to expand or contract the tree) that goes down at least three levels (Figure 17-7, page 1009). Highlight the printer you are working with and click **Forward**. See www.linuxprinting.org/printer_list.cgi for more information about your specific printer.
Finish, and Create the New Print Queue	Presents a summary of the printer that you specified. Click **Apply** to install the queue.
Edit	Displays the Edit Queue window, which affects the highlighted queue.
Name and Aliases	Edits the name of the queue, and adds, edits, and deletes aliases for that name.
Queue Type	Changes the type of a queue (Queue Type at the top of the window), rescans devices, specifies a custom device, and autoselects a driver (sometimes).
Driver	The same as Select a Print Driver.
Driver Options	Gives you several driver-dependent options for the queue.
Delete	Deletes the highlighted queue.
Default	Specifies that the highlighted queue is the default queue.
Apply	Restarts the daemon that controls the highlighted queue.

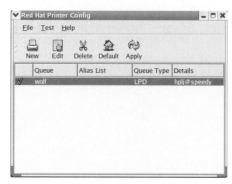

Figure 17-5   printconf-gui showing one print queue

Adding a Local Printer

Following is an example of how to use printconf-gui to install a local printer named **argon** attached to port **/dev/ttyS0** (the first serial port). When you start printconf-gui, it displays a window listing available print queues. Figure 17-5 shows that there is one queue.

Click the New button on the toolbar to bring up the Add a New Print Queue window, and then click Forward to display the Set the Print Queue Name and Type window (Figure 17-6). This window selects the type of printer you want to add. Choose Local Printer because **argon** is directly attached to the local system, and enter **argon** in the Queue Name text box. Click Forward to display the Configure a Local Printer window.

Highlight a device from the list in the Configure a Local Printer window, click Rescan Devices when a device is not listed, or click Custom Device to specify another device. For this example click /dev/ttyS0 if it is listed, or, if it is not listed, specify it as a custom device. Click Forward to display the Select a Print Driver window (Figure 17-7).

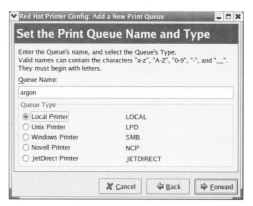

Figure 17-6   Set the Print Queue Name and Type window

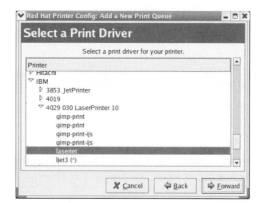

Figure 17-7   Select a Print Driver window

See whether your printer appears in the scrollable list: Find the printer brand, and click the triangle next to it. Then find the model from the sublist that appears, and click the triangle next to it. Keep finding and clicking until you get to a line that represents your printer and does not have a triangle. When your printer does not appear in the list, select one of the first three entries as appropriate: PostScript Printer, Text-Only Printer, or Raw Printer. Click to highlight this line, and click Forward to display the Finish and Create the New Print Queue window. Review the information there, and click Apply to create the print queue.

The original printconf-gui window is still on the workspace, showing a listing that includes the printer you just created. Close this window when you are finished working with printers.

Adding a UNIX (Network) Printer

Adding a network (possibly remote) printer is almost the same as adding a local printer except that you have to specify the remote host and queue in the Configure a Unix Print Queue window, which you get to from the Set the Print Queue Name and Type window (Figure 17-6). You must specify the name of the host, but you do not have to specify a queue. Make sure that the local system is specified in either **/etc/hosts.lpd** or **/etc/hosts.equiv** on the remote system, as discussed on page 1014.

Removing a Printer

Before physically removing a local printer from the system or turning off access to a remote printer, you need to remove the printer from service in order to prevent files from accumulating in the print queue and to keep the printer from consuming system resources. To remove either a local or remote printer from service, bring up printconf-gui, highlight the printer you want to remove, and click the Delete button. Click yes to the confirmation prompt that appears in a dialog box, and printconf-gui removes the printer. If you do not have access to printconf-gui, give the following commands, substituting the name of your printer for **argon**:

```
# lpc disable argon
Printer: argon@kudos
argon@kudos.com: disabled

# lpc stop argon
Printer: argon@kudos
argon@kudos.com: stopped
```

Then remove the spool directory. Although not necessary, you can delete the entry in **/etc/printcap** when the printer is removed permanently.

CUPS

browser	**localhost:631** (in the browser's location text box)
graphical or **character-based**	**cupsconfig** (opens Mozilla or links and points it to http://localhost:631)
help	www.cups.org www./linuxprinting.org "KDEPrint: Manages Printers" (page 1014)

You Must Start the cupsd Daemon before You Can Use CUPS || tip

If your system is running the **lpd** daemon (for LPRng), you need to stop **lpd** and start the **cupsd** daemon to work with CUPS:

```
# /usr/sbin/service lpd stop
# /usr/sbin/service cups start
```

With the **cupsd** daemon started, you can bring up the CUPS browser-based interface by entering **localhost:631** in a browser location text box. At this point, click **Administration**⇨**Add Printer** to get started. You may need to supply the **root** password.

CUPS, the Common UNIX Printing System, is a cross-platform printing system for UNIX/Linux systems (Figure 17-8). CUPS is based on the IPP (Internet Printing Protocol), provides System V and Berkeley command line interfaces, and supports **lpd**, **smb**, and JetDirect protocols with reduced functionality. CUPS has a clean, easy-to-use, browser-based interface that blends easily with its Web site (click Software from the CUPS interface).

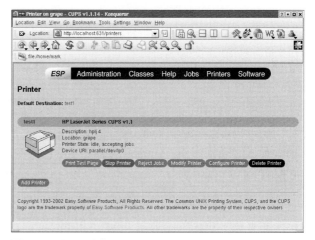

Figure 17-8   The CUPS Printer page

You can use the CUPS interface to set up and maintain printers while still using all the standard lpr commands followed by **.cups**:

lpr.cups	Sends a job to the printer
lpq.cups	Displays the print queue
lprm.cups	Removes a job from the print queue

Refer to lpr on page 1232 for information about the corresponding lpr commands.

Manually Adding a Local Printer

To add a local printer manually, you must perform these steps while you are working as **root**:

1. Name the printer.

2. Create a **printcap** entry.

3. Create a spool directory.

4. Turn on the print queue (spooler).

5. Start or restart the **lpd** daemon.

The following simple entry in **/etc/printcap** starts with the name of the printer (**fox**), followed by capabilities that you can set to a value. Each capability must be separated from the next with a colon; for clarity, the example uses two colons between the last entry on one physical line and the first on the next. The **printcap** entry must appear on one logical line: Each line in the example ends with a backslash that quotes the following NEWLINE.

```
# cat /etc/printcap
fox:\
        :sd=/var/spool/lpd/fox:\
        :mx#0:\
        :sh:\
        :lp=/dev/ttyS1:
```

After the name of the printer come entries that describe the printer. Refer to "**/etc/printcap**: Describes Printers," following.

Once you have set up the **printcap** entry, you need to create the spool directory that you named in the **printcap** entry. The following command creates the needed file for this example:

```
# mkdir /var/spool/lpd/fox
```

After you have manually added a printer, you need to tell the spooler that it can accept jobs for the printer. The lpc utility allows you to manipulate the printers and the print queues. The next command[30] uses lpc to enable spooling on the local print queue for the printer named **fox**:

```
# lpc enable fox
```

The following lpc command enables printing and starts a spooling daemon for **fox**:

```
# lpc start fox
```

The **lpc stop** command reverses the effect of the **lpc start** command, and **lpc disable** reverses **lpc enable**. Use **lpc clean**, followed by the name of a queue or the word **all**, to remove abandoned temporary and control files from the queue.

The final step is to start or restart the **lpd** daemon with the following command:

```
# service lpd start
```

This command generates warning and error messages when appropriate.

/etc/printcap: Describes Printers

Each entry in the **/etc/printcap** file describes a printer on the local system. Although it is convenient to think of each entry as a different physical printer, you can have several entries refer to the same printer but apply different filters. The following two entries allow users to send jobs to a single HP Deskjet printer; users can select one entry for color output or the other for black and white:

---

30. You can use lpc interactively by giving only its name on the command line. Enter a question mark in response to the lpc> prompt to display a list of commands.

```
# Default device. The dj-filter script handles postscript and
# other formats automatically in black and white.
lp|ps:lp=/dev/lp1:sd=/usr/spool/lp1:sh:mx#0:\
:if=/usr/bin/dj-filter:\
:lf=/var/log/lpd-errs:


# Color postscript
cps:lp=/dev/lp1:sd=/usr/spool/lp1:sh:mx#0:\
:if=/usr/local/bin/start-djcps:\
:lf=/var/log/lpd-errs:
```

The fields in each entry describe the printer for the **lpd** daemon. For example, the first field gives the names that can be used to reference that printer. You print color PostScript files by using lpr with the argument **–Pcps**, which tells **lpd** to use the second of these two entries. The first entry has two possible names: **lp** and **ps**. The **lp** name is special to **lpd** and identifies this as the default entry to use when lpr is called without the **–P** option. The remaining fields give the device (**/dev/lp1**), the directory to queue files in while waiting for the device to become available (**/usr/spool/lp1**), instructions to **lpd** not to print a banner page (**sh**), the maximum number of blocks to allow in a single print job (**mx#0**, where 0 means no limit), the input filter to apply to the job (the entries have different input filters), and the name of the log file for errors (**/var/log/lpd-errs**). More fields are possible; see the **printcap** man page for details.

Do Not Edit /etc/printcap by Hand || tip

Each time the **lpd** daemon starts, it recreates the **/etc/printcap** file, and you will lose any manual changes. Use printconf-gui to edit this file. You can manually add an entry to **/etc/printcap.local**. Although **printconf-gui** does not display entries in **/etc/printcap.local**, the **lpd** daemon reads it.

The **lpd** daemon can also forward print jobs to another computer. If you have a printer that you would like to share on a network, you need to have a **printcap** entry similar to those shown previously on the system that is directly connected to the printer. On other systems, you need **printcap** entries that identify the remote machine with the printer. For example, the following entry on a remote machine instructs **lpd** to send files for the printer named **hires** to **bravo** for printing:

```
# remote printer on bravo (600 dpi, postscript, and duplex)
hires:\
    :lp=:rm=bravo:sd=/usr/spool/lj4si:lf=/var/log/lpd-errs:
```

Use the **–Phires** argument to lpr on a remote machine to cause **lpd** to forward the print job to **bravo** for printing.

The **/etc/hosts.lpd** and/or the **/etc/hosts.equiv** files contain a list of remote systems that are allowed to send print requests to the local system. The **lpd** daemon rejects a print job from any machine not listed in one of these files.

Use hosts.lpd to Grant Permission to Print   ‖ security

The /etc/hosts.equiv file allows users from a remote machine to do a lot more than print. Put the name of the remote system in /etc/hosts.lpd if you want to grant permission only to print.

When the remote printer is not available, your print requests are queued on your machine until that printer becomes available. This is handy if you have a laptop computer, as print jobs are printed when you reconnect the laptop to the local network.

KDEPrint: Manages Printers

KDE	Control Center: System⇨Printing Manager K menu: Preferences⇨System⇨Printing Manager
graphical	**kcmshell printmgr** **kprinter** (functionality limited to printing a file)
(when you ask to print a file)	The system runs **kprinter** which has limited functionality.
help	KDEPrint Handbook: KDE HelpCenter: Glossary⇨K⇨KDEPrint Handbook (from Control Center only) Display Printing Manager window as above, click Help tab at top left, and click **here** at bottom of column under tabs.

The KDEPrint printing manager is not a stand-alone program and does not replace a printing system such as CUPS or LPRng/lpr. Rather, KDEPrint is an interface between an application or user submitting a print job and the printing system (Figure 17-9). With proper permissions KDEPrint

- **Starts print jobs.**   You can start a print job with KDEPrint, as well as from a command line or within an application.

- **Controls print jobs.**   The Print queue window (PrintJob viewer) displays information on each of your print jobs. It displays the same information as the Jobs tab in KDEPrint. From these windows you can cancel print jobs (even

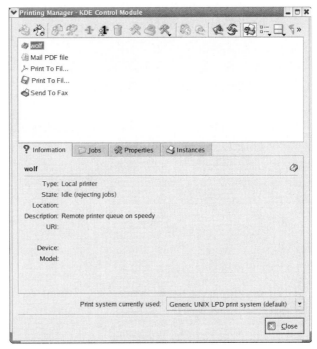

Figure 17-9 KDEPrint Printing Manager

when they have started printing), hold and release print jobs, and move print jobs to a different queue (as long as they have not started printing).

- **Works with printers.** You can add, remove, and modify printers and their properties.

- **Works with multiple printing systems.** KDEPrint works with CUPS, LPRng, RLPR, PDQ, and other printing systems.

- **Works with filters.** KDEPrint allows you to import existing printing filters or install new ones.

Refer to the *KDEPrint Handbook* (see "Help" in the table at the start of this section) for more information.

Configuring Network Services

A network can be as big as the Internet, connecting millions of machines with backbones running around the globe, or as small as a home network connecting two machines in the same room. The software to connect a machine to a network can be set up in three ways: at install time, by responding to prompts; after the system is up, by running a program and responding to prompts; and manually, by editing files.

sys-unconfig: **Reconfigures Network Services**

On an installed system the easiest way to (re)configure network services is to run the sys-unconfig utility, which first uses touch to create the file named **/.unconfigured** (this file is just a flag; its contents are not important) and then halts the system. When the system comes back up, **/etc/rc.d/rc.sysinit** runs passwd (for root), netconfig (to configure networking), timeconfig (to set the time zone), authconfig (to configure authentication), and ntsysv (to configure services). You can manually give the commands that sys-unconfig issues. The next sections discuss some of the network services and the files that control them.

Proxies

Typically the system administrator who maintains the proxy server/gateway (page 397) or the firewall should provide you with the proxy names and numbers you need to fill in the information that an application asks for. When you need to set up your own proxy, several toolkits and software packages can help: Refer to the *Firewall and Proxy Server HOWTO*, which covers some more theory and several tools you can use for building proxy servers/gateways. The squid program provides much more than an HTTP proxy and is included with Red Hat. Go to www.squid-cache.org for more information. Many firewall products, both Open Source and commercial, have proxies built in. You can use the Firewall Toolkit (www.fwtk.org), or FWTK for short, as a base to create a firewall, including proxies. You should be familiar with C programming and security to tackle FWTK, but in any event look at the Web site as it has a lot of information. *SOCKS* (page 1493) is the original proxy; it is a proxy at the application layer, meaning that the application you are using must have its code modified to support the SOCKS protocol. Unless you have an application that is set up for SOCKS, you probably do not want to use it (www.socks.nec.com; look at the FAQ).

Setting Up a Proxy Gateway/Server for Mozilla or Netscape

You are most likely to run into an HTTP (Web) proxy than any other kind of proxy. In Mozilla and Netscape >= 6,[31] select from the menubar Edit⇨Preferences. Netscape displays the Preferences window. Click the right-pointing triangle or plus sign just to the left of Advanced, and then click Proxies from the drop-down list. The Proxies frame displays three radio buttons: Direct connection to the Internet, Manual proxy configuration, and Automatic proxy configuration URL. The first choice is the default and means that Netscape does not use proxies.

---

31. For earlier versions of Netscape, you follow a similar procedure, but the choices are simpler and more constraining.

The second choice, Manual proxy configuration, allows you to specify the name or internal IP address of the proxy gateway/server and the *port* (page 1485) that the proxy service listens on for each of several types of proxies. You may need to set up only one or two of these, such as HTTP and FTP. Once you fill in the address and port for one or more of the services, click OK and that/those service(s) will send and receive data to/from the corresponding proxy. The final item in this list is SOCKS Host (which you need only if you are using SOCKS); below that are two radio buttons that specify the version of SOCKS you are using. At the bottom of this list, just below the two radio buttons, is the No Proxy For text box, in which you can enter a SPACE-separated list of domains that you want to communicate with directly (no proxy). Entries here are exceptions to the previous entries. Enter your domain name here so that you do not use a proxy when you communicate with local servers.

The third choice, Automatic proxy configuration URL, is the most flexible of the three proxy choices. The URL that you enter in the text box contains a JavaScript program that is executed when you attempt to connect to a Web site. This program can contain text matches and control statements that connect you to one proxy for one domain, another for another domain, and possibly a default or no proxy for all other domains. In the same manner, it can deal differently with different services. The URL with its script is usually provided by your firewall administrator.

hosts: Stores a List of Machines

The **/etc/hosts** file stores the name, IP address, and optional alias of the other machines that your machine knows about. At the very least, the file must have the hostname and IP address that you have chosen for your local machine and a special entry for **localhost**. This entry is for a *loopback service,* which allows the local machine to talk to itself (for example, for RPC services). The IP address of the loopback service is always 127.0.0.1. Following is a minimal **/etc/hosts** file for a machine named **achilles**:

```
# cat /etc/hosts
#
# Internet host table
#
127.0.0.1        localhost
10.0.1.5         achilles
```

If you are not using NIS, NIS+, or DNS to look up hostnames (called *hostname resolution*), you must include in **/etc/hosts** all the hosts that you want your machine to be able to contact. The order in which hostname resolution services are checked is controlled by the **hosts** entry in the **/etc/nsswitch.conf** file (page 1022).

NFS: Network Filesystem

The NFS (Network Filesystem, see page 391) protocol, developed by Sun Microsystems, allows you to share selected local files with remote machines and to access remote files from the local machine. Under NFS it is difficult to distinguish a remote file from a local one. NFS is a de facto standard and supports heterogeneous environments.[32]

The physical location of a file is irrelevant to a user under NFS. Traditionally one copy of an application program is stored on each machine. In order to upgrade the program, you need to upgrade it on each of the machines. With NFS you can store one copy of a program on one machine and give other users access to it over the network. This scenario uses storage more efficiently by reducing the number of locations that the same data needs to be stored. In addition to efficiency, NFS gives users on the network access to the same data (not just application programs), improving data consistency and reliability. By consolidating data, NFS reduces system administration and overhead and improves security.

Before you use NFS, make sure that the necessary daemons are running:

```
# service nfs status
...
```

or

```
# /etc/rc.d/init.d/nfs status
rpc.mountd (pid 15795) is running...
nfsd (pid 15813 15812 15811 15810 15809 15808 15807 15806) is running...
rpc.rquotad (pid 15784) is running...
```

When NFS is not running, you will see messages telling you that each of the daemons is stopped. To start the daemons give the command **service nfs start**. If you get no output, perhaps no entries are in **/etc/exports**.

exportfs: Stores Permissions to Mount Local Filesystems

The **/etc/exports** file controls which remote systems can access which directories. You can edit this file directly. The following simple **exports** file gives **bravo** read and write access to all the files in **/home** and gives **kudos** read access to **/home/alex**. In each case, access is implicitly granted for all subdirectories. Recent versions of exportfs (following) have changed the default commit process to conform to the NFS protocol[33] and to complain when you do not specify **sync** or **async**.

---

32. NFS runs on UNIX, MS-DOS/Windows, DEC/Compaq VMS, GNU/Linux (including Red Hat), and more.

33. In versions higher than 1.0.0, **sync** is the default.

```
# cat /etc/exports
/home bravo.tcorp.com(rw,sync)
/home/alex kudos.tcorp.com(ro,sync)
```

You can include more than one machine on a line. Refer to the **exports** man page for other options.

The exportfs utility maintains the record of NFS exported filesystems in **/var/lib/nfs/xtab**. Normally this file is initialized automatically from **/etc/exports** when the system is brought up and kept up-to-date as remote systems mount and unmount filesystems, using NFS. Without changing **/etc/exports**, the exportfs utility can add or delete individual filesystems from the list of filesystems that can be mounted.

The following command exports all the entries in **/etc/exports**:

```
# exportfs -a
```

Replace the **–a** with **–r** to reexport or synchronize the entries that the kernel watches in **/var/lib/nfs/xtab** with those in **/etc/exports**. Remove an exported directory with the **–u** option. Refer to the exportfs man page for details and other options.

mount: Mounts a Remote Filesystem

This section covers what needs to be done at the remote system. In order to use a remote filesystem on your local machine, it must be mounted. The following examples show two ways to mount a remote filesystem, assuming that a machine named **donald** is on the same network as the local machine and is sharing its **/export/home**, **/export/apps**, and **/export/apps/oracle** filesystems with the local machine. In either case, you use mkdir to make the directories that are the mount points:

```
# mkdir /myhome /apps
```

If you want to mount the filesystems one time, it is easy to use mount to mount the filesystems manually:

```
# mount donald:/export/home /myhome
# mount -o r,nosuid donald:/export/apps /apps
# mount -o r donald:/export/apps/oracle /apps/oracle
```

By default, filesystems are mounted read-write (assuming that the NFS server, **donald** in this case, is exporting with read-write permissions). The first preceding command line mounts the **/export/home** directory from the machine named **donald** on the local directory **/myhome**. The second and third mount lines use the **–o r** option to force a readonly mount. The second mount line also adds the **–o nosuid** option by using the multiple-option form of the **–o** option. The **nosuid** option forces mounted setuid executables to run with regular permissions on the local machine.

If you will be mounting the filesystems frequently, it is more convenient to edit the **/etc/fstab** file (page 978). The following **/etc/fstab** entries mount the same directories automatically whenever the machine is booted.

```
donald:/export/home        /myhome        nfs    -         0  0
donald:/export/apps        /apps          nfs    r,nosuid  0  0
donald:/export/apps/oracle /apps/oracle   nfs    r         0  0
```

Exporting Symbolic Links and Device Files   ‖ **tip**

When you export a symbolic link, make sure that the object of the link is available on the client (remote) machine. Either, the object of the link must exist on a client machine, or you must export and mount it along with the exported link, otherwise it will not point to the file it points to on the server.

A device file refers to a Linux kernel interface. When you export a device file, you export that interface. If the client machine does not have the same type of device, the exported device will not work.

A file that is mounted using NFS is always type **nfs** on the local machine, regardless of what it is on the remote machine. Typically you never run fsck on or back up an NFS filesystem. The entries in the third, fifth, and sixth columns of **fstab** are usually **nfs**, **0**, and **0**. Also, the options for mounting an NFS filesystem differ from those for an **ext2** or **ext3** filesystem. Refer to the mount and nfs man pages for details.

umount: Unmounts a Remote Filesystem

Use umount to unmount a remote filesystem the same way you unmount a local one (page 977).

showmount: Displays NFS Status Information

The showmount utility provides NFS status information. Call showmount with an argument of the hostname of the machine that you want information about. No argument or an argument of **localhost** causes showmount to report on your local machine. An argument of the name of a remote machine reports on that machine. Without any options, showmount displays a list of machines that are allowed to mount local directories. In the following example, **kudos** and **bravo** can mount local directories, but you do not know which ones:

```
# /usr/sbin/showmount localhost
Hosts on localhost:
kudos.tcorp.com
bravo.tcorp.com
```

The **–a** option tells you which directories are exported to which remote machines. This information is stored in **/etc/exports**. Although this example is trivial, remember that showmount can report the same information for remote machines that are NFS servers:

```
# /usr/sbin/showmount -a localhost
All mount points on localhost:
kudos.tcorp.com:/home
bravo.tcorp.com:/home
```

The same information from another vantage point: The local **/home** directory is exported (**–e**) to **kudos** and **bravo**:

```
# /usr/sbin/showmount -e
Export list for localhost:
/home kudos.tcorp.com,bravo.tcorp.com
```

NIS: Network Information Service

NIS (page 390) is the Sun Microsystems client/server protocol for distributing system configuration data, such as user and host names, passwords, groups, service names, aliases, automount maps, and a few other less frequently used tables between computers on a network. NIS allows you to add, delete, and relocate resources easily. Refer to the *NIS-HOWTO* for more information on setting up NIS.

DNS: Domain Name Service

DNS (page 388) is a database of domain names that is distributed over thousands of computers. To use DNS for hostname resolution, you need to create a file named **/etc/resolv.conf** (following) and edit **/etc/nsswitch.conf** (page 1022). Also refer to the *DNS-HOWTO*.

resolv.conf: Resolves Hostnames

The following example shows a resolver configuration file (**/etc/resolv.conf**) for the **tcorp.com** domain. A **resolv.conf** file usually has at least two lines: a domain line and a nameserver line:

```
# cat /etc/resolv.conf
domain tcorp.com
nameserver 10.0.0.50
nameserver 10.0.0.51
```

The first line (optional) specifies the domain name. Your **resolv.conf** file may have search in place of domain: In the simple case the two perform the same function. In either case, this domain name is appended to all hostnames that are not fully qualified. (See *FQDN* on page 1468.)

The **domain** keyword takes a single domain name as an argument: This name is appended to all DNS queries, shortening the time to query hosts at your site. When you put domain tcorp.com in **resolv.conf**, any reference to a host within the **tcorp.com** domain or a subdomain (such as **marketing.tcorp.com**) can use the abbreviated form of the host: Instead of **ping speedy.marketing.tcorp.com**, you can use **ping speedy.marketing.**

This search keyword is similar to domain but can contain multiple domain names. The domains are searched in order in the process of resolving a hostname. The following line in **resolv.conf** causes the **marketing** subdomain to be searched first, followed by **sales**, and finally the whole **tcorp.com** domain:

```
search marketing.tcorp.com sales.tcorp.com tcorp.com
```

Put the most frequently used domain names first to try to outguess possible conflicts. If both **speedy.marketing.tcorp.com** and a **speedy.tcorp.com** exist, the order of the search determines which one you get when you invoke DNS. Do not overuse this feature. The longer the search path (three or four names is typically enough), the more network DNS requests are generated, and the slower the response is.

The **nameserver** line(s) indicate which machines the local machine should query to resolve hostnames to IP addresses and vice versa. These machines are consulted in the order they appear with a 10-second timeout between queries. The preceding file causes this machine to query 10.0.0.50 followed by 10.0.0.51 when the first machine does not answer within 10 seconds. The **resolv.conf** file may be automatically updated when a PPP- (Point to Point Protocol) or DHCP (Dynamic Host Configuration Protocol)-controlled interface is activated. Refer to the **resolv.conf** and **resolver** man pages for more information.

nsswitch.conf: Specifies the Order in Which to Consult Name Services

GNU/Linux keeps databases containing information on, among others, hosts, networks, services, and users. The data to populate these databases can come from many sources. Hostnames and addresses can come from the local **/etc/hosts** and **/etc/passwd** files, DNS, NIS, NIS+, and more. The **/etc/nsswitch.conf** file controls the order in which the various sources are consulted to fulfill a request from the system. Each line in this file contains a database name followed by a colon, whitespace, and zero or more sources separated by SPACEs. A basic line from **nsswitch.conf** tells the system that all requests to the **hosts** database should be filled by local files, such as **/etc/hosts**:

```
hosts:     files
```

Options for sources are `files`, `nis`, and `dns`. To consult DNS when your request for a host is not resolved by local files, add `dns` to the **hosts** line as follows:

```
hosts:    files dns
```

The next line contains another example of how the **hosts** database can be configured:

```
hosts:    dns nis [NOTFOUND=return] files
```

The square brackets ([]) specify criteria that modify how the search is performed. This example first consults the `dns` source. If `dns` has the answer, no further searching takes place. If `dns` does not provide an answer, `nis` is checked. When `nis` returns `NOTFOUND` (indicating that it could not find an answer), the process stops (`[NOTFOUND=return]`), and no answer is returned. Only when `nis` does not return an answer *and* does not return `NOTFOUND` are the local files (**/etc/hosts**) consulted. In other words, NIS provides an authoritative answer; only when NIS is not available should the system consult local files. Refer to the **nsswitch.conf** man page, the *NIS-HOWTO*, and the *DNS-HOWTO* for more information.

Internet Configuration Wizard

GNOME	GNOME menu: System Tools⇨Internet Configuration Wizard start-here: Applications⇨System Tools⇨Internet Configuration Wizard
KDE	K menu: System Tools⇨Internet Configuration Wizard start-here: Applications⇨System Tools⇨Internet Configuration Wizard
graphical	**internet-druid**
help	pppd man page (PPP daemon) *PPP-HOWTO* ipppd man page (ISDN PPP daemon) *The Kppp Handbook* at KDE HelpCenter: Internet⇨Internet Dialer www./linuxtr.net (token ring) *Token-Ring mini-HOWTO* sites.inka.de/~bigred/devel/cipe.html (cipe) *The Linux Cipe+Masquerading mini-HOWTO*

Clicking Internet Configuration Wizard[34] opens the Add new Device Type window (Figure 17-10). Add new Device Type can set up seven types of connections:

---

34. Despite the name of this selection, none of the connections has to be to the Internet, although they frequently are.

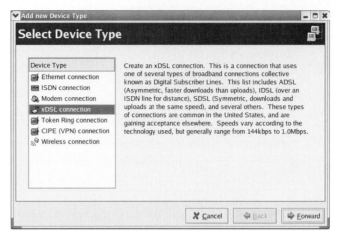

Figure 17-10   Add new Device Type window

Ethernet (page 355), *ISDN* (page 1474), modem, *xDSL* (page 1502), *token ring* (page 1498), *CIPE* (page 1460), and wireless. ISDN, modem, xDSL, CIPE, and wireless are PPP (Point-to-Point Protocol) connections: PPP is a serial line protocol that establishes a connection between two systems, putting them on the same network. PPP is capable of handling several protocols, the most common of which is TCP/IP, which provides compression for increased efficiency. The two machines can then run ssh, X, or any other network application between them. Ethernet and token ring connect to LANs.

Before you get started with the Add new Device Type window, make sure that you have the necessary information from your ISP (or other computer you are connecting to), including: the dial-in phone number (for ISDN and modem connections), your login name and password, one or more DNS addresses, and in some cases a gateway address. Choose the type of connection you want to establish from the Add new Device Type window, and click Forward. Some of the selections probe for information. You can accept entries in the text boxes that are already filled in on the following window. Fill in blank text boxes as appropriate. When you have finished setting up your device, the Add new Device Type window closes, and the Network Configuration window (page 987) opens, displaying the device you just added. Highlight the new device and click Activate to bring it on line. Modify the Hosts and DNS tabs as necessary.

The KDE kppp Internet dialer is an alternative if you are setting up a modem-based Internet connection. Both a dialer and front end for **pppd**, kppp helps you set up the initial connection with a script generator and maintains statistics on your calls, including phone costs.

Samba/swat

GNOME	GNOME menu: Extras⇨Server Settings⇨Samba Configuration start-here: Server Settings⇨Extras⇨Samba Configuration
KDE	K menu: Extras⇨Server Settings⇨Samba Configuration start-here: Server Settings⇨Extras⇨Samba Configuration
graphical	Point a browser on the local system to http://127.0.0.1:901
character-based	Point lynx or links on the local system to http://127.0.0.1:901
help	www.samba.org swat home page links to local documentation

Samba is a free suite of programs that implement the Server Message Block (SMB) protocol on several operating systems, including GNU/Linux. A Samba server shares files and printers on a host system with client systems. Systems that use the SMB protocol natively, and are thus potential clients, include MS Windows, Lan-Manager, and OS/2. The Common Internet Filesystem (CIFS), Microsoft Networking, and the NetBIOS protocol all use the SMB protocol.

The Samba suite includes many programs, each having many options, switches, modes, and so on, so that you can work with Samba on many different levels. This section gives you an introduction so that you can set up and use Samba in a minimal configuration; it also points you toward the documentation you will need to work with Samba at a higher level.

Before you start, make sure that you have all the necessary Samba packages installed:

```
$ rpm -qa | grep samba
samba-common-2.2.5-10
samba-2.2.5-10
samba-swat-2.2.5-10
```

The Samba Web Administration Tool (swat) is a browser-based utility that allows you to control Samba setup and administration graphically and gives you access to the Samba documentation. Before you can use swat, you must enable **xinetd** to launch swat and enable the **swat** daemon: Run Service Configuration (redhat-config-services: Configures Services II on page 946), and repeat the following for runlevels (on the menubar) 3 and 5:

- Click smb to put a check mark in the check box.
- Click Start (on the toolbar) to start the smb service.

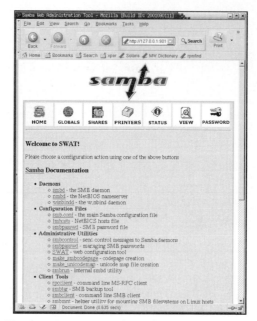

Figure 17-11   *Local* Samba/swat home page

- Click swat to put a check mark in the check box.
- Make sure that a check mark is in the box next to **xinetd**; click to highlight the **xinetd** line.
- Click Restart on the toolbar.
- Click Save on the toolbar.
- Click Exit on the toolbar.

Now you should be able to open a browser, enter **http://127.0.0.1:901** or **http://localhost:901** in the location bar, and give the username **root** and the root password in response to swat's request to display the local Samba/swat home page (Figure 17-11). This page has local links to Samba documentation and buttons that display other windows. You can access this page from other systems, but doing so means that your password is sent in cleartext over whatever connection you are using.

It is quite easy to establish a basic Samba setup so that you can see a partition from your GNU/Linux drive on an MS Windows machine (any version of Windows from 3.1 on). More work is required to set up a secure connection or one with special features. The following example uses swat to create a basic setup. Each of the options that you configure has the word Help next to it. Click Help, and a new browser window containing an explanation of the option appears. For this example do not click any of the Set Default buttons. Make sure to click Commit Changes after you finish making your changes in a window before you click a button at the top of the window; otherwise, swat will not keep your changes.

First, click GLOBALS at the top of the Samba/swat home page (Figure 17-11). Leave everything at its default setting except as indicated in Table 17-16.

Changes to Samba GLOBALS || table 17-16

Base Options		
	workgroup	Change to the name of your workgroup on the MS Windows system.
Security Options		
	hosts allow	Enter the hostname or IP address of the MS Windows machine.

Click Commit Changes when you are done with the GLOBALS window.

A *share* (or *window share*) is a directory and its children that you share with another system using Samba. Next, click the SHARES button. Three buttons and two text boxes appear. In the box adjacent to the Create Share button, enter the name you want to assign to this share. This name can be anything you want; it does not specify the directory that you are sharing. Click Create Share. When you want to modify an existing share, bring up the name of the share in the combo box, and click Choose Share. Either of these actions displays the complete Share Parameters window. Leave everything at its default setting except as indicated in Table 17-17.

Changes to Samba Shares || table 17-17

Base Options		
	comment	An optional comment about the purpose of this share and its location on the GNU/Linux system can be helpful.
	path	Change this to the absolute pathname of the share (directory) on the GNU/Linux system.
Security Options		
	hosts allow	Put the hostname or IP address of the MS Windows system.

Click Commit Changes when you are done with the SHARES window. If you want to see how many options there really are, click Advanced View.

When everything is set up correctly, you should be able to open an explorer window on the Windows machine, click Tools on the menubar, and select Map Network Drive, which opens the Map Network Drive window. Select an unused drive letter from the Drive combo box, and enter the (MS Windows) path to the share you just created. When you want to share **/home/jenny** on the machine named **bravo** and have named the share **bookkeeping** (in swat), enter **\\bravo\bookkeeping** in the Folder text box and click Finish. Assuming that you choose the drive letter **J**, you should be able to access the **/home/jenny** directory located on **bravo** as **J** (**bookkeeping**) on the MS Windows machine.

A lot of help is available from the local swat/Samba home page (Figure 17-11). In addition to local documentation, there is the Diagnostic Utilities section, which lists three useful utilities: smbstatus displays a report on open Samba connections, testparm checks the **/etc/samba/smb.conf** file and displays its contents (only a check for internal correctness, not for service availability or correct/expected operation), and testprns checks the validity of the name of a printer. When you click the word Samba (not the logo, but the one just before Documentation on the HOME window), swat displays the Samba man page, which defines each Samba program.

DHCP Client

DHCP (Dynamic Host Configuration Protocol) dynamically allocates IP addresses to computers on a LAN.[35] The administrator of the DHCP server provides a pool of IP addresses, and each client computer on the LAN has its TCP/IP software configured to request an IP address from the DHCP server.

When you are not assigned a specific IP address, your provider uses DHCP to assign a temporary IP address to your machine each time you establish a connection with your provider. The address remains the same as long as your machine is connected to the provider, but the address can be different each time you connect.

The client daemon, **dhcpcd**, communicates with the server daemon, **dhcpd**, to obtain the IP address, netmask, broadcast address, and so on, that it should use. DHCP is broadcast based, so the client and server must be on the same subnet (page 1495). To use DHCP as a client, start the **dhcpcd** daemon with redhat-config-services: Configures Services II on page 946 or chkconfig: Configures Services III on page 947. For more information refer to "Static versus Dynamic IP addresses" on page 363.

---

35. Under IPv4, autoconfiguration is optional and is performed by DHCP. With IPv6, autoconfiguration is mandatory, making it easy for hosts to configure their IP addresses automatically (page 369).

OpenSSH: Provides Secure Network Tools

character-based	ssh
home	www.openssh.com
help	www.openssh.com/portable.html
	secureshell@securityfocus.com (mailing list)
	comp.security.ssh (newsgroup)

OpenSSH is a free version of the SSH protocol suite and is the basis for many secure network tools. Whereas telnet and rlogin send all communications, including passwords, as cleartext, ssh (one of the openSSH tools) performs the same functions while encrypting everything, including passwords, that goes over the network. This encryption eliminates most evesdropping, connection hijacking, and other network attacks. The openSSH tools also provide secure tunneling capabilities (page 375) and several methods of authentication.

Both ssh (the client or the one who logs in on the server) and sshd (the server that the ssh client logs in on) are quite easy to set up. On the client side, give the command **ssh** *hostname* when you have the same login name on both machines or **ssh –l** *login-name hostname* to use *login-name* as your login name on the remote machine named *hostname.*

The client machine must have permission to connect to the remote machine, and the user must present a valid name and password to the remote machine. In addition, the server must positively identify itself to the client to prevent a person-in-the-middle attack (refer to footnote 3 on page 1410). The easiest way to give a client access to a host is to put the client's host (and domain) names in the **/etc/hosts.equiv** or **/etc/ssh/shosts.equiv** file on the server.

The **~/.ssh/known_hosts** file on the client machine contains electronic fingerprints of all the hosts you have connected to using openSSH tools. The openSSH tools use this file to identify a server positively. When you launch an ssh session, the client (local) machine verifies the fingerprint that the host returns against information stored in **known_hosts**. This process is normally transparent to you. However, the first time you attempt to connect to a server, your local machine cannot prove the identity of the server and displays a message such as the following:

```
$ ssh -l alex kudos
The authenticity of host 'kudos (192.168.0.1)' can't be established. RSA key
fingerprint is 4f:59:34:d0:92:47:84:5a:cd:60:cc:1c:19:60:aa:be.
Are you sure you want to continue connecting (yes/no)? yes
```

You must respond to this query with **yes** (*spelled out*) when you want to log in on the remote machine, **kudos**. Make sure that you are logging in on the correct machine. When you are not sure, a telephone call to someone who logs in on that machine locally can help verify that you are on the intended machine. When you answer **yes**, openSSH stores the server's fingerprint in **~/.ssh/known_hosts** (**ssh** protocol with *RSA* [page 1491]) or **~/.ssh/known_hosts2** (**ssh2** protocol with *DSA* [page 1465]) and associates it with the name of the machine that you are logging in on. When you attempt to use one of the openSSH tools to communicate with this machine again, the key that the machine returns must match the one that your local machine has stored.

The following message tells you that the locally stored fingerprint does not match the one returned by the server:

```
$ ssh -1 alex kudos
@@@@@@@@@@@@@@@@@@@@@@@@@@@@@@@@@@@@@@@@@@@@@@@@@@@@@@@@@@@@@
@    WARNING: REMOTE HOST IDENTIFICATION HAS CHANGED!    @
@@@@@@@@@@@@@@@@@@@@@@@@@@@@@@@@@@@@@@@@@@@@@@@@@@@@@@@@@@@@@
IT IS POSSIBLE THAT SOMEONE IS DOING SOMETHING NASTY!
Someone could be eavesdropping on you right now (man-in-the-middle attack)!
It is also possible that the RSA1 host key has just been changed.
The fingerprint for the RSA1 key sent by the remote host is
ad:96:ad:25:eb:cc:f5:df:0c:78:d0:92:8e:d0:b8:22.
Please contact your system administrator.
Add correct host key in /home/alex/.ssh/known_hosts to get rid of this message.
Offending key in /home/alex/.ssh/known_hosts: 1
RSA1 host key for kudos has changed and you have requested strict checking.
```

Despite its frightening appearance, this message frequently means only that the fingerprint of the server has changed as the result of an openSSH or server upgrade. Again use the telephone to verify the cause of the change. Assuming that it does turn out to be something innocuous, edit your **~/.ssh/known_hosts** (or **known_hosts2**) file, find the line with the hostname of the server you are trying to connect with, delete that line, and run ssh again. Now you get the first message preceding; proceed as though this were your first connection with this server, and answer **yes**.

Refer to pages 374 and 1321 for more information on how to use ssh. Refer to pages 376 and 1308 for information on using scp.

GnuPG: GNU Privacy Guard

character-based	gpg
home	www.gnupg.org
help	www.gnupg.org/docs.html *The GNU Privacy Handbook* *Gnu Privacy Guard (GnuPG) Mini Howto* gpg info page

The GnuPG system, whose main program is gpg, is a cryptographic tool that enables secure network communications and protects the integrity and privacy of data during storage. This system can encrypt and decrypt data, create and validate digital signatures, and manage keys. Refer to Appendix C for more information on security, keys, and GnuPG (page 1410).

It is not difficult to use gpg. The following line encrypts a message so that Alex can read it:

```
$ gpg -ear alex@tcorp.com < infile > outfile
```

This command encrypts the contents of **infile** and sends it to **outfile**, which you can attach to or put in-line in an e-mail message. You can sign the message by using the –s option.

Usually you do not use gpg from the command line. The program is intended to be called from utilities and applications (www.gnupg.org/frontends.html). You will see GnuPG incorporated into more and more programs, especially mail user agents (page 1050), as the word spreads and its popularity increases.

Rebuilding the Linux Kernel

Once you have installed Red Hat, you may want to reconfigure and rebuild the Linux kernel. Red Hat comes with a prebuilt kernel that simplifies the installation process. This kernel may not be properly configured for all your system's features, however. By reconfiguring and rebuilding the kernel, you can build one that is customized for your system and needs.

Maybe You Just Need to Install a New Linux Kernel Binary?	‖ tip

Refer to "Errata: Security Alerts, Bugfixes, and Enhancements" on page 934 when you want to install a Linux kernel binary that you do not need to configure or build.

Because recent releases of the Linux kernel are so modular, usually you do not need to rebuild them. You can dynamically change many things that used to require rebuilding the kernel. Two ways to make these changes are by using boot options (**append=***string*) in **/etc/lilo.conf** or by modifying **/etc/sysctl.conf**, which is used by sysctl[36] when the system is booted. If you are using grub, append *string* to the kernel line in **/boot/grub/grub.conf** or its symbolic link, **/etc/grub.conf**.

The **append** kernel configuration parameter in **lilo.conf** appends *string* to the parameter line that is passed to the kernel. You can use this parameter to specify parameters so that you do not have to rebuild the kernel, parameters that cannot be detected automatically, and parameters that you do not want to probe for. The following example turns off the Advanced Power Management BIOS:

```
append="apm=off"
```

The sysctl utility modifies kernel parameters while the system is running. This utility uses the facilities of **/proc/sys**, which is required in order for sysctl to work and defines the parameters that sysctl can modify.

You can get a complete list of sysctl parameters with a **sysctl –a** command. An example of displaying and changing the **domainname** kernel parameter follows. The quotation marks are not required in this example but will quote any characters that would otherwise be interpreted by the shell.

```
# /sbin/sysctl kernel.domainname
kernel.domainname = tcorp.com
# /sbin/sysctl -w kernel.domainname="testing.com"
kernel.domainname = testing.com
```

When you do not need a complete rebuild, you can use sys-unconfig (page 1016).

Have a Tested Rescue Disk at Hand When You Rebuild the Kernel ‖ caution

When you rebuild the Linux kernel to install a new version or to change the configuration of the existing version, make sure that you have a rescue disk handy. This disk allows you to reboot your computer even when you have destroyed your system software completely. Always follow these instructions; having a working rescue disk can make the difference between momentary panic and a full-scale nervous breakdown. Refer to "**mkbootdisk**: Creates a Rescue/Emergency/Boot Floppy Disk" on page 920 for instructions on how to make a rescue disk.

Fortunately, rebuilding a Linux kernel is fairly straightforward. When you do need to rebuild the kernel, perform the following steps.

Preparing Source Code

Before you can get started, you must locate/install and clean the source code and read the documentation that comes with the Linux kernel.

---

36. Prior to Red Hat 6.2, the files in the **/etc/sysconfig** directory were used.

Locating Source Code

When you have the kernel source on your system, the **/usr/src** directory will look something like the following:

```
$ ls -l /usr/src
total 8
lrwxrwxrwx   1 root     root             15 Oct  1 03:15 linux-2.4 -> linux-2.4.18-14
drwxr-xr-x  17 root     root           4096 Oct  1 03:14 linux-2.4.18-14
drwxr-xr-x   7 root     root           4096 Oct  1 02:38 redhat
```

The usual setup has a longer, descriptive name in the directory that contains the kernel source and a link with a shorter name that points to the directory with the longer name. In the preceding example the name **linux-2.4.18-14** means that the directory contains version 2.4 of the Linux kernel, release 18-14. The name **linux-2.4** always points to the version of the kernel that you are running or building. Before you start to work with a new release of the kernel, make sure that **/usr/src/linux-2.4** points to the new release. If the source code is present on your system, skip to "Cleaning the Source Tree" on page 1034.

Installing Source Code

When the source is not present on your system, you need to find it on the installation CD-ROM set or on the Red Hat Web site. You need **kernel-source✻.rpm**.[37] The kernel used in the examples came from **kernel-source-linux-2.4.18-14.i386.rpm**. You need to work as **root** to use rpm to install the kernel package.

Once you have located the **kernel-source** rpm package, give an rpm command to install it. The following command installs the **kernel-source** rpm package from the directory that contains the package (refer to "rpm: Red Hat Package Manager" on page 928 for more information on using rpm):

```
$ rpm -ivh kernel-source✻.rpm
```

Read the Documentation

The kernel package includes the latest documentation, some of which may not be available in other documents. Review the **README** file and the relevant files in the **Documentation** directory. Read the *Linux Kernel-HOWTO* for an excellent, detailed generic guide to installing and configuring the Linux kernel.

Always have *Appendix A: Building a Custom Kernel* of the *Red Hat Customization Guide* in front of you as you proceed (on the Red Hat documentation CD-ROM and at www.redhat.com/docs/manuals/linux).

---

37. With Red Hat version 7.2 and earlier, you must also install the **kernel-headers✻.rpm** file.

> ### Now the Working Directory Is /usr/src/linux-2.4   ‖ tip
>
> All commands in this section on building a kernel are given relative to the /usr/src/linux-2.4 directory.
> Make sure that /usr/src/linux-2.4 is your working directory before proceeding.

Configuring and Compiling the Linux Kernel and Modules

This section describes how to configure the kernel to meet your needs and how to compile it.

Cleaning the Source Tree

If you want to save your existing configuration file (**/usr/src/linux-2.4/.configure**), copy it to another directory (such as your home directory) before you proceed, as the following command removes it. Purge the source tree (all the subdirectories and files within **/usr/src/linux-2.4**) of all configuration and potentially stale ✳.o files by giving the following command:

```
$ make mrproper
```

Configuring the Linux Kernel

Before you can compile the code and create the Linux kernel, you must decide and specify what features you want the kernel to support. A kernel can support most features in two ways: by building the feature into the kernel or by specifying the feature as a loadable kernel module (page 1038), which is loaded into the kernel only as needed. Trade off the size of the kernel against the time it takes to load a module. Make the kernel as small as possible while minimizing the frequency of module loading. Do not make the SCSI driver modular unless you have reason to do so.

The **configs** directory has sample configuration files for various processors, multiple processors, and configurations. You may want to look at these before you get started or even use one of these as your start point. To use one, copy it from the **configs** directory to the **linux-2.4** (or other) directory and rename it **.config**. You must configure the Linux kernel after you copy a file from **configs**, otherwise make fails due to a missing file.

The three standard commands to configure the Linux kernel follow. Alternatively, you can use The KDE Linux Kernel Configurator (page 1035).

```
$ make config
```

```
$ make menuconfig
```

```
$ make xconfig
```

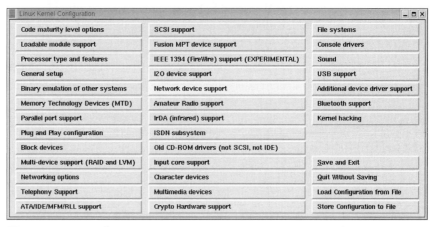

Figure 17-12   The xconfig Main menu

Each command asks the same questions and produces the same result given the same responses. The first and second commands work in character-based environments; the second and third commands work in graphical environments. For most people in most situations, the third (graphical) method is the easiest to use (Figures 17-12, and 17-13).

When you want to set all the kernel parameters back to their default values for your architecture, give the following command:

```
$ make oldconfig
```

The result of running one of the configuration scripts is a **.config** file.

The xconfig utility displays a point-and-click interface that enables you to move between configuration options, help, and saving configurations (Figure 17-12). Click one of the option buttons to display a submenu of choices relating to the option. In Figure 17-13 the system administrator can select **y** for yes (put it in the kernel), **m** for module (make it into a loadable module, page 1038, and do not put it into the kernel), or **n** for no (do not put it into the kernel or make it into a module) for each choice/module.

At any time during the configuration process, you can store the currently defined configuration to a file, load a configuration from a file, or exit with or without saving. See the last buttons on the xconfig Main menu.

The KDE Linux Kernel Configurator

Instead of using one of the preceding make commands, you can use the KDE Linux Kernel Configurator. Open the Configurator as KDE Control Center: System⇨Linux Kernel Configurator (Figure 17-14), and configure the kernel as previously described. Click Load from or Save as to load a new **.config** file, or save the one you are working

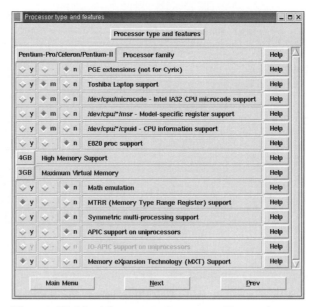

Figure 17-13   The xconfig Processor Type submenu

with. The upper frame displays a tree listing of kernel options. Click a plus sign next to one of the options to view the suboptions. Click a suboption to display information about it in the lower frame. There are three icons that can appear to the left of a suboption: a green check mark indicates that the suboption will be in the kernel, a red X indicates that it will not be in the kernel or a loadable module, and a gear icon indicates that it will be a loadable module, page 1038, and not in the kernel. Click the icon repeatedly to cycle through the three icons. When you are done, click Save as, and give your new configuration file a name.

Setting Up Dependencies

Prepare to compile the source code for the operating system by making the dependencies with the command

```
$ make dep
```

EXTRAVERSION Number

To prevent overwriting existing kernel files and to identify various compilations of the kernel, you can use the **EXTRAVERSION** variable in **Makefile**. This variable is initially set to a dash and the release number, followed by the word custom (for example –14custom). Whatever value you assign to this variable is placed at the end of the kernel name. It is a good idea to keep the original release number, but you can append the date or time to ensure a unique name for the kernel.

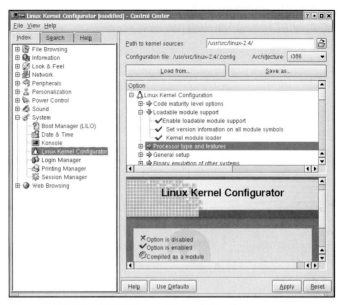

Figure 17-14   KDE Linux Kernel Configurator

Compiling the Linux Kernel

Before compiling the kernel, make sure, once again, that no files are in the source tree from previous work:

```
$ make clean
```

Then give the following command to compile the kernel:

```
$ make bzImage
```

Optional

If you want to test the new compilation of the Linux kernel, put a floppy disk in the first disk drive, and give the following command in place of **make bzImage**:

```
$ make bzdisk
```

This command compiles the kernel and puts it on the floppy. You can then reboot the system from the floppy. If the kernel fails, you can reboot your system from your hard disk, which has not changed. When you are satisfied with the new kernel, compile it with

```
$ make bzImage
```

Using Loadable Kernel Modules

A *loadable kernel module* (page 1477) (sometimes called a *module,* or *loadable module*) is an object file, part of the kernel, that is linked into the kernel at runtime. Modules are compiled separately from the kernel and can be inserted into and removed from a running kernel at almost any time except when the module is being used. This ability gives the kernel the flexibility to be as small as possible at any given time. Modules are a good way to code some kernel features, including drivers that are not used all the time (for example, usually not the hard disk driver but perhaps a tape driver).

If you are not using loadable kernel modules, skip to "Installing the Kernel and Associated Files" on page 1039. If you do not know for a fact that you are *not* using loadable modules, you probably are, so continue with this section.

When you configure the kernel to support loadable modules, you need to build and install the modules. Give the command

```
$ make modules
```

This command compiles the modules that you specified when you configured the kernel.

The next command installs the modules in **/lib/modules/*kernel-version*EXTRA-VERSION**. Run this command as **root** even when you did not build any modules:

```
# make modules_install
```

Table 17-18 lists some of the tools that can help you work with modules. Refer to the corresponding man pages for options and more information.

Tools for Working with Modules	|| table 17-18
depmod	Works with dependencies for modules.
insmod	Loads modules in a running kernel.
lsmod	Lists information about all loaded modules.
modinfo	Lists information about a module.
modprobe	Loads, unloads, and reports on modules. When it loads a module, it also loads any dependencies.
rmmod	Unloads modules from a running kernel.

Installing the Kernel and Associated Files

Next, copy the compiled kernel and associated files to the appropriate directory, usually either root (**/**) or **/boot**. When you have a **boot** partition, the files are kept in the root of this partition (**/boot**). Without a **boot** partition, the files are kept in the root directory. Run the following command as **root** to install the new kernel files in the proper directory:

```
# make install
```

Changing lilo.conf

If you are using lilo, edit **/etc/lilo.conf**, and add a section giving the absolute pathname of your kernel image and, when you use modules, the pathname of the **initrd** file. Run lilo to make your changes to **lilo.conf** take effect. Refer to "lilo: The Linux Loader" on page 1040 for details.

When You Are Not Using lilo
|| tip

The preceding step assumes that you are using lilo to boot your system. If you are booting directly from a DOS session using the **LOADLIN.EXE** program available for this purpose, you need to do things differently.

Rebooting

Reboot the computer by pressing CONTROL-ALT-DEL or giving a **reboot** command.

Boot Loader

A boot loader is a very small program that takes its place in the *bootstrap* (page 1457) process, that brings a computer from off or reset to a fully functional state. It frequently resides on the starting sectors of a hard disk called the MBR (Master Boot Record).

The *BIOS* (page 1457), which is stored in an *EEPROM* (page 1466) on the system's motherboard, gains control of a system when you turn it on or reset it. After testing the hardware, the BIOS transfers control to the MBR if the system is set up to be booted from there. This transfer of control starts the boot loader, which is responsible for locating the operating system kernel (kept in the **/** or **/boot** directory), loading that kernel into memory, and starting it running. Refer to "Booting the System" on page 943 for more information on what happens from this point on.

You can place the **/boot** directory on a very small filesystem that is near the beginning of the hard drive, where the BIOS can access it. With this setup, the root (**/**) filesystem can be anywhere on any hard drive that GNU/Linux can access and that perhaps the BIOS cannot.

Several boot loaders are available. This book discusses grub and lilo.[38]

lilo: The Linux Loader

The term lilo (Linux loader) applies to both the Linux loader utility and the boot loader that lilo writes to the start of the active partition on the hard drive or to a floppy. Although written to support GNU/Linux, lilo is a general-purpose boot loader that can start many operating systems, including DOS, OS/2, Windows, and versions of BSD. You can configure lilo to select from various operating systems and versions of the Linux kernel each time you start your system (called *dual booting*).

When you run lilo without any options, it reads **/etc/lilo.conf** to determine which operating systems are to be made available at boot time. Then it writes this information to the MBR. You must run lilo to reinstall the boot loader whenever you change the Linux kernel. Refer to "Rebuilding the Linux Kernel" on page 1031.

The **/etc/lilo.conf** file gives you a great deal of control over lilo:

```
$ cat /etc/lilo.conf
# lilo configuration file
boot=/dev/hda
map=/boot/map
install=/boot/boot.b
prompt
timeout=50
default=linux

image=/boot/vmlinuz-2.4.18-14custom
        label=linux
        initrd=/boot/initrd-2.4.18-14custom.img
        read-only
        root=/dev/hda12
```

Comments in the **lilo.conf** file start with a pound sign (#) and run through the end of the line, just as they do in a shell script. In the example, the first line that is not a comment identifies the disk that holds the Master Boot Record: **/dev/hda**. The next line gives the location of the map file. The **install** line tells lilo where to find the file it is to install as the boot loader. The **prompt** presents the user with a boot: prompt whereas **timeout** gives the time (in tenths of a second) that the system will wait before booting automatically. When you set **prompt** and do not set **timeout**, the system cannot boot automatically. Press TAB in response to the **boot:** prompt to see your choices.

---

38. Red Hat has deprecated lilo and will remove it from a future release.

The lilo boot loader allows you to specify more than one boot image. The **default** line specifies the label of the image to boot if none is specified, such as when you press RETURN in response to the **boot:** prompt. In this example, the label of the default (and only) image is **linux** (see the **label** line). The **image** line specifies the boot image of the Linux kernel. The **initrd** line initializes the boot loader *RAM disk* (page 1488), which is used in the first phase of the system boot when you use a loadable module (page 1038). Specify the **read-only** line for *every* image on a Linux system so that it is safe to run fsck automatically as you bring the system up.

Protect lilo.conf Too || security

When you protect the images specified in lilo.conf with passwords, be sure to change permissions on lilo.conf to 600, as anyone can read it with its default permissions.

This is a simple example of **lilo.conf**. You can add lines to pass arguments to the Linux kernel, adjust for strange disk geometries, require passwords to start specific kernels, and add many other options. See the **lilo.conf** man page (Section 5) for details and the **/usr/share/doc/lilo✳/doc** directory for the User and Technical Guides. View the ✳**.ps** files with gv (ghostview).

Before you modify an existing **lilo.conf** file, save the existing configuration as **lilo.conf.old** or **lilo.conf.1**. Then edit **lilo.conf** and create a new section that looks similar to the preceding example. Use your kernel version number and **EXTRAVERSION** (page 1036) in place of **2.4.18-14custom**.

When you use modules, set up the appropriate **initrd** line in **lilo.conf**:

```
initrd=/boot/initrd-2.4.18-14custom.img
```

When you are finished editing **lilo.conf**, run lilo to write the new information to the MBR. You must run lilo every time you change **lilo.conf**.

grub: The GNU/Linux Loader

The term grub[39] (www.gnu.org/software/grub) stands for Grand Unified Boot Loader. Red Hat started offering grub in version 7.2, and it will replace lilo in the future. It is a product of the GNU project and conforms to the *multiboot specification* (page 1480), which allows it to load many free operating systems directly, as well as *chain loading* (page 1459) proprietary operating systems. In many ways grub is more flexible than lilo. The grub loader can recognize various types of filesystems

---

39. There is no man page for grub; use info (page 45) instead.

and kernel executable formats, allowing it to load an arbitrary operating system: You must specify the kernel's filename and location (drive and partition). You can pass this information to grub by using either the command line or menu interface. When you boot the system, grub displays a menu of choices that is generated by the **/boot/grub/grub.conf** file or its symbolic link, **/etc/grub.conf**. At this point you can modify the menu, choose which operating system to boot, or do nothing and allow grub to boot the default system.

When you install a Red Hat Linux system, you have the choice of using grub or lilo. Whichever you choose, the installer installs both programs, allowing you to switch boot loaders without loading any new software. As with lilo, when you install grub at the time you install GNU/Linux on your machine, the installation program configures grub, and you do not have to.

The **/boot/grub/grub.conf** file is the default grub configuration file and is similar in function to **/etc/lilo.conf**. The **grub.conf** file following is from a system that had its kernel replaced using RHN (page 936). The system has a separate **boot** partition so that all kernel and **initrd** (for systems using loadable modules, page 1038) image paths are relative to **/boot/** (see the NOTICE in the file). Without a separate **boot** partition, the boot files reside in the root partition (**/**) so that kernel and **initrd** paths are relative to **/**. (Thus you would specify the kernel as *kernel* **/vmlinuz-*version*** replacing *kernel* with your system's kernel name and *version* with your version number.)

The file starts with comments that Anaconda, the graphical installer, puts there, followed by three assignments. The **default** is the section number of the default boot specification. The numbering starts with 0. The following example includes two boot specifications. The first, numbered 0, is for the 2.4.9-13 kernel, and the second, numbered 1, is for the 2.4.7-10 kernel. The **timeout** is the number of seconds that grub waits after it has prompted you for a boot specification before it boots the system with the default boot specification. The **splashimage** is the grub menu interface background that you see when you boot the system.

```
$ cat /etc/grub.conf
# grub.conf generated by anaconda
#
# Note: you do not have to rerun grub after making changes to this file
# NOTICE:
#    You have a /boot partition.  This means that
#    all kernel and initrd paths are relative to /boot/, eg.
#    root (hd0,0)
#    kernel /vmlinuz-version ro root=/dev/hda9
#    initrd /initrd-version.img

default=0
timeout=10
splashimage=(hd0,0)/grub/splash.xpm.gz
```

```
title Red Hat Linux (2.4.9-13)
    root (hd0,0)
    kernel /vmlinuz-2.4.9-13 ro root=/dev/hda9
    initrd /initrd-2.4.7-10.imginitrd /initrd-2.4.9-13.img

title Red Hat Linux (2.4.7-10)
    root (hd0,0)
    kernel /vmlinuz-2.4.7-10 ro root=/dev/hda9
    initrd /initrd-2.4.7-10.img
```

Following the **splashimage** assignment in the preceding example are two boot specifications, differentiated by the `title` lines as previously explained. The three lines following the title line in each specification specify the location of the **root** (drive 0, partition 0), **kernel**, and **initrd** images. In this case, because there is a **/boot** partition, the pathnames are relative to **/boot**. For the default boot specification (the first one, numbered 0), the absolute pathname of the kernel is `/boot/vmlinuz-2.4.9-13`, which is specified with the options `ro root=/dev/hda9`. These options tell grub that it is to be mounted readonly and that root (**/**) is mounted on **/dev/hda9**. You specify the **initrd** image in a similar manner. Substitute your kernel and **initrd** names and version numbers for the ones in the example. Make sure that when you install a new kernel manually, its **title** line is different from the others present in **grub.conf**.

LOADLIN: A DOS-Based GNU/Linux Loader

The LOADLIN loader, a DOS utility that loads GNU/Linux from DOS and some versions of MS Windows, can load big kernels (**bzImage**) and RAM disk images (**initrd**). Refer to elserv.ffm.fgan.de/~lermen, where you can find the *LOADLIN Users Guide* and other information. See also the *Loadlin+Win95/98/ME mini-HOWTO*.

PAM

PAM (actually Linux-PAM, or Linux Pluggable Authentication Modules) allows a system administrator to determine how various applications use *authentication* (page 1455) to verify the identity of a user. PAM provides shared libraries of modules (located in **/lib/security**) that, when called by an application, authenticate a user. Pluggable refers to the ease with which you can add and remove modules from the authentication stack. The configuration files that are kept in the **/etc/pam.d** directory determine the method of authentication and contain a list, or stack, of calls to the modules. PAM may also use other files, such as **/etc/passwd**, when necessary.

Instead of building the authentication code into each application, PAM allows you to use the shared libraries to keep the authentication code separate from the application code. The techniques of authenticating users stay the same from application to application. PAM permits a system administrator to change the authentication mechanism for a given application without touching the application.

PAM provides authentication for a variety of system-entry services (login, ftp, and so on). You can take advantage of PAM's ability to stack authentication modules to integrate system-entry services with different authentication mechanisms, such as RSA, DCE, Kerberos, and smart cards.

From login through using su to shutting the system down, whenever you are asked for a password (or not asked for a password because the system trusts that you are who you say you are), PAM makes it possible for systems administrators to configure the authentication process and makes the configuration process essentially the same for all applications that use PAM to do their authentication.

The configuration files stored in **/etc/pam.d** describe the authentication procedure for each application. These files usually have names that are the same as or similar to the name of the application that they configure. For example, authentication for the login utility is configured in **/etc/pam.d/login**. The name of the file is the name of the PAM service[40] that the file configures. Occasionally one file may serve two programs. PAM accepts only lowercase letters in the names of files in the **/etc/pam.d** directory. For more information on PAM, refer to the *Linux-PAM System Administrators' Guide* at www.kernel.org/pub/linux/libs/pam/Linux-PAM-html/pam.html and to the *User Authentication HOWTO*.

Do Not Lock Yourself Out of Your System || tip

Editing PAM configuration files correctly takes care and attention. It is easy to lock yourself out of your computer with a single mistake. To avoid this type of problem, always keep backup copies of the PAM configuration files you edit, test every change thoroughly, and make sure that you can still log in once the change is installed. Keep a Superuser session open until you are done testing. When a change fails and you cannot log in, use the Superuser session to replace the newly edited files with their backup copies.

PAM warns you about any errors it encounters, logging them to the **/var/log/messages** or **/var/log/secure** files. Look in these files if you are trying to figure out why a changed PAM file is not working properly. In order to prevent possibly giving unnecessary information to a malicious user, PAM sends error messages to a file rather than to the screen.

---

40. There is no relationship between PAM services and the **/etc/services** file. The name of the PAM service is an arbitrary string that each application gives to PAM; PAM then looks up the configuration file with that name and uses it to control how it does authentication. There is no central registry of PAM service names.

Configuration File, Module Type, and Control Flag

Following is an example of a PAM configuration file. Comment lines begin with a pound sign (#):

```
$ cat /etc/pam.d/login
#%PAM-1.0
auth        required     /lib/security/pam_securetty.so
auth        required     /lib/security/pam_stack.so service=system-auth
auth        required     /lib/security/pam_nologin.so
account     required     /lib/security/pam_stack.so service=system-auth
password    required     /lib/security/pam_stack.so service=system-auth
session     required     /lib/security/pam_stack.so service=system-auth
session     optional     /lib/security/pam_console.so
```

The first line is a special comment; it will become significant only if another PAM format is released. Do not use #% other than its use in the first line of the preceding example.

The rest of the lines tell PAM to do something as part of the authentication process. The first word on each line is a module type indicator: **account, auth, password,** or **session** (Table 17-19). The second is a control flag (Table 17-20), which indicates what type of action to take if authentication fails. The rest of the line contains the pathname of a PAM module and any arguments for that module. The PAM library itself uses the **/etc/pam.d** files to determine which modules to delegate work to.

Module Type	Description	Controls	table 17-19
auth	Authentication	Proving that the user is authorized to use the service. This may be done using passwords or another mechanism.	
account	Account management	Determining whether an already authenticated user is allowed to use the service he/she is trying to use. (That is, has the account expired? Is the user allowed to use this service at this time of day?)	
password	Password changing	Updates authentication mechanisms such as user passwords.	
session	Session management	Setting things up when the service is started (for example, when the user logs in) and breaking them down when the service is terminated (for example, when the user logs out).	

You can use one of the Control Flag keywords listed in Table 17-20 to set the control flags.

Control Flag   ‖ table 17-20

required	Success is required for authentication to succeed. Control and a failure result are returned after all the modules in the stack have been executed. The technique of delaying the report to the calling program until all modules have been executed may keep attackers from knowing what caused their authentication attempts to fail and tell them less about the system, making it more difficult for them to break in.
requisite	Success is required for authentication to succeed. Further module processing is aborted, and control is returned immediately after a module fails. This technique may expose information about the system to an attacker. On the other hand, if it prevents a user from giving a password over an insecure connection, it might keep information out of the hands of an attacker.
sufficient	Success indicates that this module type has succeeded, and no subsequent required modules of this type are executed. Failure is not fatal to the stack of this module type. This technique is generally used when one form or another of authentication is good enough: If one fails, PAM tries the other. For example, when you use **rsh** to connect to another computer, **pam_rhosts** first checks first to see whether your connection can be trusted without a password. If the connection can be trusted, the **pam_rhosts** module reports success, and PAM immediately reports success to the **rsh** daemon that called it. You will not be asked for a password. If your connection is not considered trustworthy, PAM starts the authentication over, asking for a password. If this second authentication succeeds, PAM ignores the fact that the **pam_rhosts** module reported failure. Of course, if both modules fail, you will not be able to log in.
optional	Result is generally ignored. An optional module is relevant only when it is the only module on the stack for a particular service.

PAM uses each of the module types as requested by the application. That is, the application will ask PAM separately to authenticate, check account status, manage sessions, and change the password. PAM will use one or more modules from the **/lib/security** directory to accomplish each of these tasks.

The configuration files in **/etc/pam.d** list the set of modules to be used for each application to do each task. Each such set of the same module types is called a *stack*. PAM calls the modules one at a time in order, from the top of the stack (the first module listed in the configuration file) to the bottom of the stack. The modules report success or failure back to PAM. When all (there are exceptions) the stacks of modules within a configuration file have been called, the PAM library reports success or failure back to the application.

Example

Part of the login service's authentication stack follows as an example:

```
$ cat /etc/pam.d/login
#%PAM-1.0
auth        required        /lib/security/pam_securetty.so
auth        required        /lib/security/pam_stack.so service=system-auth
auth        required        /lib/security/pam_nologin.so
. . .
```

The login program first asks for a user name and then asks PAM to run this stack to authenticate the user. Refer to the Table 17-19 on page 1045 and Table 17-20 on page 1046.

1. PAM first calls the **pam_securetty** (secure tty) module to make sure that the **root** user logs in only from an allowed terminal (by default, **root** is not allowed to log in over the network; this policy helps prevent security breaches). The **pam_securetty** module is *required* to succeed in order for the authentication stack to succeed. The **pam_securetty** module reports failure only if someone is trying to log in as **root** from an unauthorized terminal. Otherwise (if the user name being authenticated is not **root** or if the user name is **root** and the login attempt is being made from a secure terminal), the **pam_securetty** module reports success.

   Success and failure within PAM are opaque concepts that apply only to PAM. They do not equate to true and false as used elsewhere in the operating system.

2. The **pam_stack.so** module diverts the PAM stack to another module, returning the success or failure as the other module returns to it. The **service=system-auth** gives the name of the other module, in this case **system-auth** in /etc/pam.d. This module checks that the user who is logging in is authorized to do so, including checks on the username and password.

3. Next, the **pam_nologin** module makes sure that if the **/etc/nologin.txt** file exists, only the **root** user is allowed to log in. (That is, the **pam_nologin** module reports success only if **/etc/nologin.txt** does not exist or if the **root**

user is logging in.) Thus when a shutdown has been scheduled for some time in the near future, the system administrator can keep users from logging in to the machine only to experience a shutdown moments later. This is most useful in a multiuser environment.

The **account** module type works like the **auth** module type but is called after the user has been authenticated; it is an additional security check or requirement for a user to gain access to the system. For example, account modules can enforce a requirement that a user can log in only during business hours.

The **session** module type sets up and tears down the session (perhaps mounting and unmounting the user's home directory). One common **session** module on a Red Hat system is the **pam_console** module, which sets the system up especially for users who log in at the physical console and not for those who log in remotely. A local user is able to access the floppy and CD-ROM drives, the sound card, and sometimes other devices as defined by the system administrator.

The **password** module type is a bit unusual: All the modules in the stack are called once and told to get all the information they need to store the password to persistent memory, such as a disk, but not actually to store it. If it determines that it cannot or should not store the password, a module reports failure. If all the password modules in the stack report success, they are called a second time and told to store to persistent memory the password they obtained on the first pass. The **password** module is responsible for updating the authentication information (that is, changing the user's password).

Any one module can act as more than one module type; many modules can act as all four module types. For example, the **pam_pwdb** module is called four times in the **login** module (page 1045), working as all four module types.

Brackets ([]) in the Control Flags Field || caution

You can set the control flags in a more complex way. When you see brackets ([]) in the control flags position in a PAM configuration file, the newer, more complex method is in use. Each comma-delimited argument is a **value=action** pair. When the return from the function matches **value**, **action** is evaluated. Refer to the *PAM System Administrator's Guide* (/usr/share/doc/pam-✳/txts/pam.txt) for more information.

Modifying the PAM Configuration

Some UNIX systems require that a user be a member of the **wheel** group in order to use the su command. Although Red Hat is not configured this way by default, PAM allows you to change the default by editing the **/etc/pam.d/su** file:

```
$ cat /etc/pam.d/su
#%PAM-1.0
auth       sufficient   /lib/security/pam_rootok.so
# Uncomment the following line to implicitly trust users in the "wheel" group.
#auth      sufficient   /lib/security/pam_wheel.so trust use_uid
# Uncomment the following line to require a user to be in the "wheel" group.
#auth      required     /lib/security/pam_wheel.so use_uid
auth       required     /lib/security/pam_stack.so service=system-auth
account    required     /lib/security/pam_stack.so service=system-auth
password   required     /lib/security/pam_stack.so service=system-auth
session    required     /lib/security/pam_stack.so service=system-auth
session    optional     /lib/security/pam_xauth.so
```

The third through sixth lines of the **su** module contain comments that include the lines necessary to permit members of the **wheel** group to run su without supplying a password (sufficient) and to permit only users who are in the **wheel** group to use su (required). Uncomment one of these lines when you want your system to follow one of these rules.

Do Not Create /etc/pam.conf || caution

You may have encountered PAM on other systems where all configuration is arranged in a single file (/etc/pam.conf). This file does not exist on Red Hat. Instead the /etc/pam.d directory contains individual configuration files, one per application that uses PAM. This makes it easy to install and uninstall applications that use PAM without having to modify the /etc/pam.conf file each time. If you create a /etc/pam.conf file on a system that does not use this file, your PAM configuration may become confused. Do not use PAM documentation from a different system. Also, the **requisite** control flag is unavailable on some systems that support PAM.

Administration Utilities

This section briefly describes a few of the many utilities that can help you perform system administration tasks. You will learn about other utilities from Red Hat documents (including the Red Hat Documentation CD-ROM), from the Red Hat Web site, from other Internet resources (including newsgroups), and from other GNU/Linux users. Read the man/info pages for the utilities described in this section to learn more about using them. Some of these utilities are incorporated as part of the K or GNOME menu, and some are useful to users other than the system administrator.

kudzu: Adds or Removes a Device

The kudzu utility finds new and changed hardware and configures it. This utility finds this hardware by probing all devices on internal and external buses and comparing the results to the **/etc/sysconfig/hwconf** database. In the default configuration, the **/etc/rc.d/init.d/kudzu** script runs and calls kudzu as the machine enters runlevels 3 and 5. When it finds new or changed hardware, kudzu gives you a chance to configure it and permits you to deconfigure any hardware that you have removed.

Do Not Probe a Serial Device That Is in Use || caution

Because probing an active serial device can disturb its use, make sure that all serial devices are not being used before you run **kudzu**.

sendmail: Sends and Receives Mail

SMTP (Simple Mail Transfer Protocol) is the Internet mail protocol. Mail programs are divided into three categories: (1) MUAs (mail user agents; the user interface, graphical or otherwise); (2) MTAs (mail transfer, or transport, agents) that deliver mail to remote machines and hand off delivery of local addresses to (3) an MDA (mail/local delivery agent). Some of the MUAs that are available for GNU/Linux are elm, exmh, fastmail, mail, mailto, mh-mail, mutt, pine, and xmh. The most widely used MTA on the Internet and on Red Hat is sendmail. Other popular MTAs are qmail, exim, and postfix and come in separate rpms. MUAs are covered in earlier chapters; this section covers sendmail. MDAs are closely related to the MTA from a system standpoint; sendmail calls an MDA to get the mail into your mailbox. By default sendmail uses procmail as a local delivery agent.

You Do Not Need to Set Up sendmail to Send and Receive E-Mail || tip

Many MUAs can use the POP3 or IMAP protocols for receiving e-mail. These protocols do not require an MTA. Thus you do not need to install or configure sendmail (or other MTA) to receive e-mail. You still need SMTP to send e-mail. However, the SMTP server can be at a remote location, such as your ISP, so that you do not need to concern yourself with it.

The de facto Internet standard UNIX daemon for transferring mail between machines, **sendmail**, takes care of queuing messages, transmitting messages, handing off to a local delivery agent, relaying messages, and other necessary housekeeping. The original version of sendmail came from the University of California at Berkeley.

Should You Use an MTA Other Than sendmail? || tip

Setting up **sendmail** is not a trivial task; large books are devoted to the task. You may be better off with an MTA, such as **qmail** (www.qmail.org), which is easier to install.

To set up a sendmail server, you need both the **sendmail** and **sendmail-cf** rpms installed on your system. The **sendmail-cf** rpm contains the configuration framework for simplifying setting up your machine as a mail server.

The **/usr/share/sendmail-cf/README** file holds the *Sendmail Configuration Files* manual. This manual steps you through the configuration process and provides some examples and templates that you may wish to use or copy to set up your own system. The main thing to consider is whether you wish your machine to be a true Internet mail server (can send directly to hosts on the Internet) or an unintelligent client of another machine (forwards all mail for nonlocal users to a smart mailhost). Most likely you will choose the former, but each of these themes has numerous variations.

When you are setting up a system to send and receive mail, consider the following:

- Does the partition that holds **/var/spool/mail** have enough space for the amount of mail you expect to receive? All incoming mail for all users is stored in **/var/spool/mail**. If your users do not regularly delete mail and clean their mailboxes, the space used in this directory may fill the partition. For this reason some administrators keep **/var/spool/mail** on a separate partition.

- Does the partition that holds **/var/spool/mqueue** have enough space? The **/var/spool/mqueue** directory holds outgoing and incoming mail that has been queued for delivery. Outgoing mail may be queued because a host is temporarily unavailable. Incoming mail may be temporarily queued because a user's mailbox is too full or because the mail server is too busy to process the connection at this moment. The partition that holds **/var/spool/mqueue** must have enough space to queue the largest mail message that you would expect to receive or send. Typically the requirements for such a partition are not more than a few tens of megabytes, but some people send large attachments and may require substantially more space.

- Is your system to be a stand-alone mail server system or a client of another mail system? Many sites have one central machine that stores and delivers all mail. If **tcorp** uses a stand-alone mail server, Bill might receive e-mail as **bill@socrates.tcorp.com**, **bill@tcorp.com**, or **bill@plato.tcorp.com**; all his e-mail will go to one place. Making the decision about whether your machine is to be a client of a central server or a server by itself determines how you need to proceed.

sendmail: Mail Client

It is easier to set up sendmail on a client machine than on a server. By default sendmail configuration files are configured for client setup, with only minimal modification necessary.

A client machine needs to know the name of the mail server, or mail host. If you are running DNS, add a machine named **mailhost** to your DNS domain. If you are running NIS or NIS+, you can add an entry for **mailhost** to your name service. How you perform each of these tasks is site dependent. If neither of the preceding applies to you, add an entry for **mailhost** in **/etc/hosts**. Do not add a separate entry; simply add the word mailhost as the third (or last) column to the line referencing the mail server. The following line from **/etc/hosts** identifies the machine **achilles** as the server where mail is delivered and relayed (the **mailhost**):

```
192.168.0.5    achilles mailhost
```

The mailhost entry indicates to sendmail that this machine is the mail server and that it knows how to contact hosts; knows about special hosts, relays, and domains; and knows how to deliver and queue to these hosts. Local client machines send to **mailhost** all mail that it does not know how to deliver.

Because your machine will queue its mail to the server and because remote hosts will deliver mail to this server, you need to either log in remotely on the mail server (typically using ssh) to read your mail (tedious and inefficient) or mount the **/var/spool/mail** spool directory on your machine. To mount the file, you can add an entry to **/etc/fstab** (not recommended because you may not be able to boot the system if the mail server is down) or use autofs (page 979). If the mail server is not responding, perhaps because it is too busy, queued files will accumulate. Running sendmail periodically will scan the queue and deliver any accumulated files. Adjust the following crontab entry (page 1059) to check the queue as frequently as you like. The following entry checks the queue once an hour at 45 minutes past the hour:

```
45 * * * * /usr/sbin/sendmail -q
```

sendmail: Mail Server

Configuring a sendmail server requires more work than configuring a client. Some of the configuration files are quite complex, and some are written in the m4 macro language. Discussing all the rules, macros, and variables and what they do is enough to fill a large book. This section provides the minimum amount of information you need to get sendmail configured to send mail to and receive mail from remote hosts on the Internet.

To get started, configure your local machine as a primary mail server by modifying the default configuration files: **/etc/mail/sendmail.mc**, which is processed by m4 to generate **/etc/mail/sendmail.cf**. First, save backup copies of both files. The –p flag causes cp to preserve permissions as well as access and modification times so that you have accurate records:

```
# cp -p /etc/mail/sendmail.cf /etc/mail/sendmail.cf.0
# cp -p /etc/mail/sendmail.mc /etc/mail/sendmail.mc.0
```

By default, sendmail listens only on the local loopback address of the machine so that sendmail does not accept network SMTP requests. To cause sendmail to accept SMTP requests addressed to your local domain, comment out the following line in the **sendmail.mc** file:

```
DAEMON_OPTIONS('Port=smtp,Addr=127.0.0.1, Name=MTA')
```

by putting the characters dnl SPACE[41] at the beginning of the line so that it looks like this:

```
dnl DAEMON_OPTIONS('Port=smtp,Addr=127.0.0.1, Name=MTA')
```

Next, find the following line (toward the end of the file):

```
Cwlocalhost.localdomain.
```

Replace localhost.localdomain with the name of your domain. If your domain is **tcorp.com**, the line becomes

```
Cwtcorp.com
```

You can receive e-mail for additional domains by adding lines, each with the letters Cw followed by a domain name. When you are done making changes, save the file.

To generate **sendmail.cf**, give the following command:

```
# m4 /etc/mail/sendmail.mc > /etc/mail/sendmail.cf
```

The sendmail utility reads **/etc/mail/sendmail.cf** when it starts; restart sendmail with the following command:

```
# sh /etc/rc.d/init.d/sendmail restart
```

or

```
# service sendmail restart
```

---

41. Because this file is processed by the m4 macro processor, you cannot use the traditional pound sign to comment out a line. The dnl at the start of a line defines a macro that m4 ignores. A dnl at the end of a line does nothing.

At this point you should be able to send and receive mail. There are many options you can change: You can receive e-mail for multiple domains or multiple hosts, set up special-delivery agents, forward e-mail, and so on. For more information see the sendmail man page, the **Mail⁘** HOWTOs, the **sendmail** package documentation (see page 1396 for help finding these), www.sendmail.org, and books on sendmail.

---

sendmail Uses DNS   ‖ tip

Adding a domain name to **sendmail.mc** is not enough to get e-mail delivered to your machine. Your host must also be listed in DNS so that other hosts know how to send it e-mail. For the **tcorp** example there must be an entry in DNS for **tcorp.com** pointing to the IP address of your host.

---

aliases: Setting up E-Mail Aliases

Rather than setting up several accounts for a user, you can use aliases to allow a user to receive e-mail under several names. Frequently system administrators, postmasters, or webmasters will want to receive e-mail sent to names other than the ones they log in under. Users frequently send mail to **root, postmaster, www,** and **webmaster** without knowing the login names of the people who will receive the e-mail. Using an alias, the user does not have to log in on a specific account or use su to check e-mail; it ends up in his or her mailbox automatically. Also, if the system administrator is on vacation, it is a simple matter to send the mail to someone else for the duration. The following excerpt is a sample of an **/etc/aliases** file:

```
# cat aliases
#
#       @(#)aliases      8.2 (Berkeley) 3/5/94
#
#  Aliases in this file will NOT be expanded in the header from
#  Mail, but WILL be visible over networks or from /bin/mail.
#
#       >>>>>>>>>>       The program "newaliases" must be run after
#       >> NOTE >>       this file is updated for any changes to
#       >>>>>>>>>>       show through to sendmail.
#

# Basic system aliases -- these MUST be present.
MAILER-DAEMON:  postmaster
postmaster:     root

# General redirections for pseudo accounts.
bin:            root
daemon:         root
```

```
games:          root
ingres:         root
nobody:         root
system:         root
toor:           root
uucp:           root

# Well-known aliases.
manager:        root
dumper:         root
operator:       root

# trap decode to catch security attacks
decode:         root

# Person who should get root's mail
# replace alex with jenny when he is on vacation.
root:           alex
```

Whenever you modify **/etc/aliases**, you must run newaliases to rebuild the **aliases** database to cause the changed aliases to take effect. Rather than having to scan the **aliases** text file each time an e-mail message is received, sendmail consults a hash file in dbm format.[42] The newaliases utility rebuilds this database and informs sendmail that the database has been rebuilt so that it can deliver incoming messages to the appropriate mailbox or file. You can also specify multiple local or remote users. See the **aliases** man page for more details.

Other Utilities

Table 17-21 lists and briefly explains other system administration tools that you may find useful.

Administration Tasks

As detailed at the beginning of this chapter, the system administrator has many responsibilities. This section discusses tasks not covered elsewhere in this chapter.

---

42. Each **dbm** (a primitive internal database format) database record consists of a unique key and a value. On a call to the database, the key is looked up in a hash table, and the value is updated or returned. The value is typically made up of multiple fields that the application knows how to parse but that are meaningless to the dbm database. The most common versions of the dbm database are **dbm**, **ndbm**, and **gdbm**.

Utilities

|| table 17-21

authconfig	Configure System Authentication	A utility with a character-based/pseudographical interface that provides an easy way to configure system authentication resources including whether to use <ul><li>Cached information</li><li>NIS</li><li>LDAP</li><li>Hesiod</li><li>Shadow passwords</li><li>MD5 passwords</li><li>Kerberos 5</li><li>SMB authentication</li></ul> Refer to "Authentication" on page 985 and to the **man** page for more information, including a list of files that can be modified.

chsh	Change Login Shell	Allows you to change the login shell for a user. When you call **chsh** without an argument, you change your own login shell. Superuser can change the shell for any user by calling **chsh** with that user's login name as an argument. When changing a login shell with **chsh**, you must give a shell that is listed in the file **/etc/shells**; any other entries are rejected. Also, you must give the pathname to the shell exactly as it appears in **/etc/shells**. In the following example Superuser changes Alex's shell to **zsh**:
		
		`# chsh alex`
		`Changing the login shell for alex`
		`Enter the new value, or press return for the default`
		
		`Login Shell [/bin/bash]: /bin/zsh`

clear	Clear the Screen	Clears the screen. The value of the environment variable **TERM** is used to determine how to clear the screen.
dateconfig aka redhat-config-date	Configure Date/Time	Refer to "Date & Time" on page 985.
dmesg	Display Kernel Messages	Displays recent log messages from the system. System messages are placed in a circular (ring) buffer, so only the most recent messages appear when you run **dmesg**. Because messages that appear while booting your system are placed into this buffer, you can run **dmesg** immediately after booting and logging in on your system to see these messages, some of which may be lost if your system boot displays a lot of messages. The information that **dmesg** displays may be useful when you are trying to track down problems with your system.

Utilities (Continued)

|| table 17-21

e2label	Label a Filesystem	Displays or creates a volume label on an ext2 or ext3 disk partition. Give the command `# e2label device [newlabel]` where *device* is the name of the device (/dev/hda2, /dev/sdb1, /dev/fd0, and so on) you want to work with. When you include the optional *newlabel* parameter, e2label changes the label on *device* to *newlabel*. Without this parameter, e2label displays the label. You can also create a volume label with the −L option of tune2fs.
kbdconfig	Configure Keyboard	A utility with a character-based/pseudographical interface that specifies the type of keyboard you are using.

mkfs	Make a New Filesystem	A front end for many utilities, each of which builds a a different type of filesystem. By default mkfs builds an ext2 filesystem and works on either a hard disk partition or a floppy disk. Although it can take many options and arguments, you can use mkfs as simply
		
		`# mkfs device`
		
		where *device* is the name of the device (/dev/hda2, /dev/sdb1, /dev/fd0, and so on) you want to make a filesystem on. Use the −t option to specify a type of filesystem. The following command creates an ext3 filesystem on *device*:
		
		`# mkfs -t ext3 device`

mouseconfig	Configure Mouse	A utility with a character-based/pseudographical interface that specifies the type of mouse you are using.
netconfig	Configure Net work 2	A utility with a character-based/pseudographical interface that helps set up your network. Use redhat-config-networks (following) for more complex and complete setups when you are using a GUI interface.
ping	Send Packets to a System on the Network	The ping utility determines if you can reach a remote system through the network and the time it takes to exchange network messages with the remote system. Refer to "ping: Tests a Network Connection" on page 380.
redhat-config-network	Configure Network	Refer to "Network" on page 987.
redhat-config-services	Configure System Services	Refer to redhat-config-services: Configures Services II on page 946.

Utilities (Continued) || table 17-21

reset (link to tset)	Return Screen Characteristics to Default Values	Resets the terminal characteristics. The value of the environment variable TERM is used to determine how to reset the screen. The screen is cleared, the KILL and INTERRUPT characters are set to their default values, and character echo is turned on. The reset utility is useful to restore your screen to a sane state after it has been corrupted. Similar to the stty sane command (page 1336).

setserial	Get and Set Serial Port Information	Used by Superuser to configure a serial port. The following command sets the input address of /dev/ttys0 to 0x100, the interrupt (IRQ) to 5, and the baud rate to 115,000 baud:
		
		`# setserial /dev/ttys0 eypport 0x100 irq 5 spd_vhi`
		
		You can also check the configuration of a serial port with setserial:
		
		`# setserial /dev/ttys0`
		`/dev/ttyS0, UART: 16550A, Port: 0x0100, IRQ: 5, Flags: spd_vhi`
		
		Normally setserial is called while the system is being booted if any of the serial ports needs to be set up specially.

setup	Menu of Utilities	A utility with a character-based/pseudographical interface that provides a menu of authentication, keyboard, mouse, network, printer, timezone, and X configuration as well as system services tools. This utility simply calls other programs and does not do any of the configuration itself.
timeconfig	Configure Date/Time 2	A utility with a character-based/pseudographical interface that helps you set up the system date and time. Use dateconfig when you are using a GUI interface.

uname	Display System Information	Displays information about the system. When you run uname without any arguments, it displays the name of the operating system (linux). Giving uname a –a (all) option causes it to display the operating system name, the host name of the system, the version number and release date of the operating system, and the type of hardware you are using:
		
		`# uname -a`
		`linux bravo.tcorp.com 2.4.18-14 #2 Thu Oct 3`
		`09:30:21 PDT 2002 i686 i686 i386 GNU/Linux`

Log Files and Mail for root

Users frequently e-mail **root** and **postmaster** to communicate with the system administrator. If you do not forward **root**'s mail to yourself (a good practice; see page 1054), remember to check **root**'s mail periodically.

You will not receive reminders about mail that arrives for **root** when you use su to perform system administration tasks. However, after using su to become **root**, you can give the command **mail –u root** to look at **root**'s mail.

Look at the system log files regularly for evidence of problems. Two important files are **/var/log/messages**, where the operating system and some applications record errors, and **/var/log/maillog**, which contains errors from the mail system. You can use redhat-logviewer (GNOME/K menu:System Tools⇨System Logs) to view many of the system logs.

The logwatch utility (**/usr/sbin/logwatch** points to the **/etc/log.d/scripts/logwatch.pl** Perl script) is a report writer that sends e-mail reports on log files. By default the script is run daily (**/etc/cron.daily/00-logwatch** also points to **/etc/log.d/scripts/logwatch.pl**) and e-mails its output to **root**. Refer to the logwatch man page and to the script itself for more information.

Scheduling Tasks

It is a good practice to schedule certain routine tasks to run automatically. For example, you may want to remove old core files once a week, summarize accounting data daily, and rotate system log files monthly.

cron and crontab: Schedule Routine Tasks

Using crontab, you can submit a list of commands in a format that can be read and executed by cron. As Superuser you can put commands in one of the **/etc/cron.＊** directories to be run at intervals specified by the directory name, such as **cron.daily**. Refer to page 1129 in Part III for more information on crontab.

cron **Stops for No One; Try** anacron	‖ tip

The cron utility assumes that the machine it is running on is always running. A similar utility, anacron, does not make that assumption and is well suited to portable and home computers that are frequently turned off. The anacron utility takes its instructions from the /etc/anacrontab file unless you specify otherwise. Refer to the anacron and anacrontab (Section 5) man pages for more information.

at: Runs Occasional Tasks

Like the cron utility, at allows you to run a job sometime in the future. Unlike cron, at runs a job only once. For instance, you can schedule an at job that will reboot your system at 3 A.M. (when all users are logged off—see the following example). It is also possible to run an at job from within an at job. For instance, you could have an at job that would check for new patches every 18 days, something that would be more difficult with cron. Refer to page 1093 in Part III for more information on at.

```
# at 3am
warning: commands will be executed using (in order) a) $SHELL b) login shell c) /bin/sh
at> reboot
at> CONTROL-D <EOT>
job 1 at 2002-02-01 03:00
```

kcron: Schedules Tasks

GNOME	GNOME menu: System Tools⇨Task Scheduler
KDE	K menu: System Tools⇨Task Scheduler
graphical	**kcron**
help	kcron menubar: Help⇨KCron Handbook

The kcron utility provides an easy-to-use GUI to cron, allowing you to create and modify your own **crontab** file or a **crontab** file for any user when you are Superuser. Scheduling tasks with kcron is a matter of clicking buttons (Figure 17-15).

Run kcron when you are logged in as yourself to view and modify your personal **crontab** file. When you run kcron as **root**, you can modify any **crontab** file on the system. To start with, kcron displays a window that lists Users (when you are running as **root**), Tasks, and Variables. This Description column of this window is very wide and will probably not fit entirely on your screen. Use the right-left scroll bar to view its contents. To create a new **crontab** entry, highlight Tasks, and select New from Edit on the menubar. To modify an entry, highlight the entry, and select Modify from Edit on the menubar. From the resulting window enter the name of the program you want to run in the Program text box, and depress buttons or place check marks corresponding to the dates and times you want to run the program. Unless you redirect it, output from the program that kcron runs is mailed to you.

System Reports

Many utilities report on one thing or another. The who, finger, ls, ps, and other utilities generate simple end user reports. In some cases these reports can help you with system administration. This section describes utilities that generate more in-depth

Figure 17-15   The kcron Task Scheduler

reports that can usually be of more help with system administration tasks. GNU/Linux has many other report utilities, including sar (system activity report), iostat (input/output and CPU statistics), netstat (network report), mpstat (processor statistics), and nfsstat (NFS statistics).

vmstat: Reports Virtual Memory Statistics

The vmstat utility generates virtual memory information along with (limited) disk and CPU activity. The following example shows virtual memory statistics in 3-second intervals for seven iterations (from the arguments **3 7**). The first line covers the time since the system was last booted; the rest of the lines cover the period since the previous line:

```
$ vmstat 3 7
   procs                      memory    swap          io     system          cpu
 r  b  w   swpd   free  buff  cache   si  so    bi    bo    in    cs  us  sy  id
 1  0  0      0  14524 20776 180352    0   0     5     6    66   373  17   4  79
 2  0  0      0  16764 20792 180384    0   0     3   144  1085   194  91   8   1
 1  0  0      0   9304 20812 180400    0   0     5   127  1069   144  97   2   1
 1  0  0      0   7328 20816 180404    0   0     3     0  1056   118  99   1   0
 1  0  0      0  11236 20832 180464    0   0     4    87  1061   135  93   6   1
 2  0  0      0  17004 20832 180500    0   0     5     0  1021    54  94   5   1
 1  0  0      0  11672 20848 180516    0   0     1    92  1014    37  94   5   1
```

The following list explains the heads displayed by vmstat.

- **procs**   process information
  - **r**   number of runnable processes
  - **b**   number of blocked processes (in uninterruptable sleep)
  - **w**   number of swapped processes
- **memory** memory information in kilobytes
  - **swpd**   used virtual memory
  - **free**   idle memory
  - **buff**   memory used as buffers
- **swap**   system paging activity in kilobytes per second
  - **si**   memory swapped in from disk
  - **so**   memory swapped out to disk
- **io**   system io activity in blocks per second
  - **bi**   blocks sent to a block device
  - **bo**   blocks received from a block device
- **system** values are per second
  - **in**   interrupts (including the clock)
  - **cs**   context switches
- **cpu**   percentage of total CPU time spent in each of these states
  - **us**   user
  - **sy**   system
  - **id**   idle

top: Lists Processes Using the Most Resources

The top utility is a useful supplement to ps. At its simplest, top displays the most CPU-intensive processes and updates itself periodically. Type q to quit. Although you can use command line options, the interactive commands are often more useful. Refer to Table 17-22 and to the top man page for more information.

Interactive Commands || table 17-22

A	Sorts processes by age (newest first).
h or ?	Displays a help screen.
k	Prompts for a PID number and type of signal and sends the process that signal. Defaults to signal 15 (SIGTERM); specify 9 (SIGKILL) only when 15 does not work.

Interactive Commands (Continued)

|| table 17-22

M	Sorts processes by memory.
P	Sorts processes by CPU usage (default).
q	Quits.
s	Prompts for time between updates in seconds. Use 0 for continuous updates.
SPACE	Updates display immediately.
T	Sorts tasks by time.
W	Writes a startup file named ~/.toprc so that next time you start **top**, it uses the same parameters it is currently using.

Informing Users

One of your primary responsibilities as the system administrator is communicating with the system users. You need to make announcements, such as when the system will be down for maintenance, when a class on some new software will be held, and how users can access the new system printer. You can even start to fill the role of a small local newspaper, letting users know about new employees, RIFs, births, the company picnic, and so on.

Different communications have different priorities. Information about the company picnic in two months is not as time sensitive as the fact that you are bringing the system down in 5 minutes. To meet these differing needs, GNU/Linux provides different ways of communicating. The most common methods are described and contrasted in the following list. All these methods are generally available to everyone, except for the message of the day, which is typically reserved for Superuser.

write   Use write to communicate with any user who is logged in on your machine. You might use it to ask a user to stop running a program that is bogging down the system. The user might reply that he will be done in 3 minutes. Users can also use write to ask the system administrator to mount a tape or restore a file.

talk   The talk utility performs the same function as write but is more advanced. Although talk uses a character-based interface, it has a graphical appearance, showing what each user is typing as it is being typed. Unlike write, you can use talk to have a discussion with someone on another machine on the network.

wall The wall (write all) utility effectively communicates immediately with all users who are logged in. It works similarly to write. Users cannot use wall to write back to only you. Use wall when you are about to bring the system down or are in another crisis situation. Users who are not logged in do not get the message.

Use wall while you are Superuser *only* in crisis situations; it interrupts anything anyone is doing.

e-mail E-mail is useful for communicating less urgent information to one or more system and/or remote users. When you send mail, you have to be willing to wait for each user to read it. The e-mail utilities are useful for reminding users that they are forgetting to log out, bills are past due, or they are using too much disk space.

Users can easily make permanent records of messages they receive via e-mail, as opposed to messages received via write or talk, so that they can keep track of important details. It would be appropriate to use e-mail to inform users about a new, complex procedure, so that each user could keep a copy of the information for reference.

message of the day All users see the message of the day each time they log in. You can edit the **/etc/motd** file to change the message. The message of the day can alert users to upcoming periodic maintenance, new system features, or a change in procedures.

Creating Problems

Even experienced system administrators make mistakes. New system administrators make more mistakes. Even though you can improve your odds by carefully reading and following the documentation provided with your software, many things can still go wrong. A comprehensive list is not possible, no matter how long, as new and exciting ways to create problems are discovered every day. A few of the more common techniques are described here.

Failing to Perform Regular Backups

Few feelings are more painful to a system administrator than realizing that important information is lost forever. If your system supports multiple users, having a recent backup may be your only protection from a public lynching. If it is a single-user system, having a recent backup certainly keeps you happier when you lose a hard disk.

Not Making a Rescue Disk

Worse than permanently losing data is discovering that your system has become completely unusable. Having a rescue disk (page 920) allows you to reformat disk partitions, restore files from backup tapes, and edit or restore mangled **/etc/passwd** and other critical system files.

Not Reading and Following Instructions

Software developers provide documentation for a reason. Even when you have installed a software package before, you should carefully read the instructions again. They may have changed, or you may simply remember them incorrectly. Software changes more quickly than books are revised, so no book should be taken as offering foolproof advice; look for the latest documentation online.

Failing to Ask for Help When Instructions Are Not Clear

If something does not seem to make sense, try to find out what does make sense; do not guess. Refer to "Help" on page 1395.

Deleting or Mistyping a Critical File

One sure way to give yourself nightmares is to execute the command

```
# rm -rf /etc
```
← do not do this

Perhaps no other command renders a GNU/Linux system useless so quickly. The only recourse is to reboot from your rescue disk and restore the missing files from your recently performed backup. Although this example is extreme, many files are critical to proper operation of your system. Deleting one of these files or mistyping information in one of them is almost certain to cause problems. If you directly edit **/etc/passwd**, for example, entering the wrong information in a field can make it impossible for one or more users to log in. Do not use **rm –rf** with an argument that includes wildcard characters; do pause after typing the command, and read it before you press RETURN. Check everything you do carefully, and make a copy of a critical file before you edit it. Some files have specific editors. For example, you can use vipw to edit **/etc/passwd**.

Solving Problems

As the system administrator, it is your responsibility to keep the system secure and running smoothly. When a user is having a problem, it usually falls to the administrator to help the user get back on track. This section suggests ways to keep users happy and the system functioning at its peak.

Helping When a User Cannot Log In

When a user has trouble logging in on the system, the problem may be a user error or a problem with the system software or hardware. These steps can help you determine where the problem is.

1. Determine whether only that one user or only that user's terminal/ workstation has a problem or whether the problem is more widespread.

2. If a single user has a problem, perhaps the user does not know how to log in. The user's terminal will respond when you press RETURN, and you will be able to log in as yourself. Make sure that the user has a valid login name and password; then show the user how to log in.

3. Make sure that the user's home directory exists and corresponds to that user's entry in the **/etc/passwd** file. Verify that the user owns his or her home directory and startup files and that they are readable (and, in the case of the home directory, executable). Confirm that the entry for the user's login shell in the **/etc/passwd** file is valid (that is, that the entry is accurate and that the shell exists exactly as specified).

4. Change the user's password if there is a chance that he or she has forgotten the correct password.

5. Check the user's startup files (**.profile, .login, .bashrc,** and so on). The user may have edited one of these files and introduced a syntax error that prevents login.

6. If only that one user's terminal has a problem, other users will be using the system, but that user's terminal will not respond when you press RETURN. For a serial terminal, try pressing the BREAK and RETURN keys alternately to reestablish the proper connection rate, and make sure that the terminal is set for a legal connection rate, such as 9600 bps. For any terminal/workstation try pressing the keys listed in Table 17-23.

Key	|| table 17-23
CONTROL-Q	Unsticks the terminal if someone pressed CONTROL-S.
interrupt	Stops a runaway process that has hung the terminal. The interrupt key is usually CONTROL-C.
ESC	Helps if the user is in Input mode in **vi**.

Key (Continued) || table 17-23

CONTROL-L	Redraws the screen if the user was using **vi**.
CONTROL-M**reset**CONTROL-M	Resets a character-based terminal.
CONTROL-R	An alternative for CONTROL-L.
CONTROL-X CONTROL-C	Gets the user out of **emacs**.
ESC**:q!**RETURN	Gets the user out of **ex** or **vi**.

7. Check the terminal or monitor data cable from where it plugs into the terminal to where it plugs into the computer (or as far as you can follow it). Finally, try turning the terminal or monitor off and then turning it back on again.

8. When the problem appears to be widespread, check whether you can log in from the system console. If you can, make sure that the system is in multiuser mode. If you cannot, the system may have crashed; reboot it and perform any necessary recovery steps (the system usually does quite a bit automatically).

9. Check the **/etc/inittab** file to see that it is starting the appropriate login service (usually some form of getty, such as mingetty).

10. Check the **/var/log/messages** file. This file accumulates system errors, messages from daemon processes, and other important information. It may indicate the cause or more symptoms of a problem. Also, check the console of the machine. Occasionally messages about system problems that do not get written to **/var/log/messages** (for instance, if the disk is full) get displayed on the console.

11. If the user is logging in over a network connection, use "redhat-config-services: Configures Services II" on page 946, "chkconfig: Configures Services III" on page 947, or "ntsysv: Configures Services IV" on page 948 to make sure that the service the user is trying to use (such as telnet or ssh) is enabled.

12. Use df to check for full filesystems. Sometimes if the **/tmp** filesystem or the user's home directory is full, the login fails in unexpected ways. When applications that start when the user logs in cannot create temporary files or cannot update files in the user's home directory, the login process itself may terminate.

Speeding Up the System

When the system is running slowly for no apparent reason, perhaps a process did not exit when a user logged out. Symptoms include poor response time and a system load, as shown by w or uptime, that is greater than 1.0. Use **ps –ef** to list all processes. The top utility (page 1356) is excellent for quickly finding rogue processes. One thing to look for in **ps –ef** output is a large number in the TIME field. For example, if you find a Netscape process that has a TIME field over 100.0, this process has likely run amok. However, if the user is doing a lot of Java work and has not logged out for a long period of time, this may be normal. Look at the STIME field to see when the process was started. If the process has been running for longer than the user has been logged in, it is a good candidate to be killed.

When a user gets stuck and leaves his or her terminal unattended without notifying anyone, it is convenient to kill all processes owned by that user. If the user is running a window system, such as GNOME or KDE on the console, kill the window manager process. Manager processes to look for include **startkde, gnome-session**, or another process name that ends in wm. Usually the window manager is either the first or last thing to be run, and exiting from the window manager logs the user out. If killing the window manager does not work, try killing the X server process itself. This process is typically listed as **/etc/X11/X**. If that fails, you can kill all processes owned by a user by running **kill –1 –1**, or equivalently **kill –HUP –1** as the user. Using **–1** (one) in place of the process ID tells kill that it should send the signal to all processes that are owned by that user. For example, as **root** you could type

```
# su jenny -c 'kill -TERM -1'
```

If this does not kill all processes (sometimes TERM does not kill a process), you can use the KILL signal. The following line will definitely kill all processes owned by Jenny and will not be friendly about it:

```
# su jenny -c 'kill -KILL -1'
```

(If you do not use **su jenny –c**, the same command brings the system down.)

lsof: Finds Open Files

The name lsof is short for ls open files; this utility locates open files. Its options let you look only at certain processes, look only at certain file descriptors of a process, or show certain network connections (network connections use file descriptors just as normal files do and lsof can show those as well). Once you have identified a suspect process using **ps –ef**, run the following command:

```
# lsof -sp pid
```

Replace *pid* with the process ID of the suspect process; lsof displays a list of all file descriptors that process *n* has open. The –s option displays the size of all open files. The size information may be helpful in determining whether the process has a very large file open. If it does, contact the owner of the process or, if necessary, kill the process. The **–r***n* option redisplays the output of lsof every *n* seconds.

Keeping a Machine Log

A machine log that includes the information shown in Table 17-24 can help you find and fix system problems. Note the time and date for each entry in the log. Avoid the temptation to keep the log *only* on the computer because it will be most useful to you at times when the machine is down. Another good idea is to keep a record of all e-mail about user problems. One way to do this is to save all this mail to a separate file or folder as you read it. Another way is to set up a special mail alias that users send mail to when they have problems. This alias can then forward mail to you and also store a copy in an archive file. Following is an example of an entry in the **/etc/aliases** file that sets up this type of alias:

```
trouble: admin,/var/mail/admin.archive
```

E-mail sent to the **trouble** alias will be forwarded to the **admin** user and also stored in the file **/var/mail/admin.archive**. Remember to run the newaliases after editing **/etc/aliases**.

Condition	table 17-24
Hardware modifications	Keep track of the system hardware configuration: which interrupt is used for which device, what I/O addresses are needed by which card, which devices hold which partitions, and so on.
System software modifications	Keep track of the options used when building Linux. Print such files as /usr/include/linux/autoconf.h (Linux kernel configuration), /etc/modules.conf, and /etc/X11/XF86Config (X11 configuration). The file hierarchy under /etc/sysconfig contains valuable information about network configuration and so on.
Hardware malfunctions	Keep as accurate a list as possible of any problems with the system. Make note of any error messages or numbers that the system displays on the system console and what users were doing when the problem occurred.
User complaints	Make a list of all reasonable complaints made by knowledgeable users (for example, "machine is abnormally slow").

Keeping the System Secure

No system with dial-in lines or public access to terminals is absolutely secure. You can make your system as secure as possible by changing the Superuser password frequently and choosing passwords that are difficult to guess. Do not tell anyone who does not *absolutely* need to know the Superuser password. You can also encourage system users to choose difficult passwords and to change them periodically.

By default, passwords on Red Hat Linux use *MD5* (page 1478) hashing, which makes them more difficult to break than DES (page 1409) encrypted passwords. It makes little difference how well encrypted your password is if you make it easy for someone to find out or guess what it is.

A password that is difficult to guess is one that someone else would not be likely to think that you would have chosen. Do not use words from the dictionary (spelled forward or backward); names of relatives, pets, or friends; or words from a foreign language. A good strategy is to choose a couple of short words, include some punctuation (for example, put a ^ between them), mix the case, and replace a couple of the letters in the words with numbers. If it were not printed in this book, an example of a good password would be C&yGram5 (candygrams). Ideally you would use a random combination of ASCII characters, but that would be difficult to remember.

You can use one of several excellent password-cracking programs to find users who have chosen poor passwords. These programs work by repeatedly encrypting words from dictionaries, phrases, names, and other sources. If the encrypted password matches the output of the program, then the program has found the password of the user. Two programs that crack passwords are crack and cops. These and many other security tips and programs are available from CERT (www.cert.org), which was originally called the *computer emergency response team*. Specifically look at www.cert.org/tech_tips.

Make sure that no one except Superuser can write to files containing programs that are owned by **root** and run in setuid mode (for example, mail and su). Also make sure that users do not transfer programs that run in setuid mode and are owned by **root** onto the system by means of mounting tapes or disks. These programs can be used to circumvent system security. Refer to chmod in Part III for more information about setuid mode. One technique that prevents users from having setuid files is to use the **–nosuid** flag to mount, which you can set in the flags section in the **fstab** file. Refer to "/etc/fstab" on page 959.

The BIOS in many machines gives you some degree of protection from an unauthorized person modifying the BIOS or rebooting the system. When you set up your BIOS, look for a section named *Security*. You can probably set up a BIOS password.

Monitoring Disk Usage

Sooner or later, you will probably start to run out of disk space. Do not fill up a disk; GNU/Linux can write to files significantly faster if at least 5 percent to 30 percent of the disk space in a given filesystem is free. The result is that using more than the maximum optimal disk space in a filesystem can degrade system performance.

When the filesystem becomes full, it can become fragmented. This is similar to the DOS concept of fragmentation but is not nearly as pronounced and is typically rare on modern GNU/Linux filesystems; by design GNU/Linux filesystems are resistant to fragmentation. Keep your filesystems from running near full capacity, and you may never need to worry about fragmentation at all. If there is no space on a filesystem, you cannot write to it at all.

To check on fragmentation, you can unmount the filesystem and run fsck on it. As part of fsck execution, fragmentation is computed and displayed. You can defragment a filesystem by backing it up; using mkfs (page 1057) to make a clean, empty image; and then restoring the filesystem. The utility that you use to do your backup and restore is irrelevant and completely up to you. You can use dump/restore, tar, cpio, or a third-party backup program.

GNU/Linux provides several programs that report on who is using how much disk space on what filesystems. Refer to the du, quot, and df utilities and the **–size** option of the find utility in Part III. In addition to these utilities, you can use the disk quota system to manage disk space.

The main ways to increase the amount of free space on a filesystem are to compress files, delete files, grow filesystems, and condense directories. This section contains some ideas on ways to maintain a filesystem so that it does not get overloaded.

Files That Grow Quickly

Some files, such as log files and temporary files, grow automatically over time. Core dump files take up space and are rarely needed. Also, users occasionally run programs that accidentally generate huge files. As the system administrator, you must review these files periodically so that they do not get out of hand.

If a filesystem is running out of space quickly (that is, over a period of an hour rather than weeks or months), first figure out why it is running out of space. Use a **ps –ef** command to determine whether a user has created a runaway process that is creating a huge file. In evaluating the output of ps, look for a process that has used a large amount of CPU time. If such a process is running and creating a large file, the file will continue to grow as you free up space. If you remove the huge file, the space it occupied will not be freed until the process terminates, so you need to kill the process. Try to contact the user running the process, and ask the user to kill it. If you cannot contact the user, log in as **root** and kill the process. Refer to kill in Part III for more information.

You can also truncate a large log file rather than removing it, although you can better deal with this recurring situation with logrotate. For example, if the **/var/log/messages** file has become very large because a system daemon is misconfigured, you can use **/dev/null** to truncate it:

```
# cp /dev/null /var/log/messages
```

or

```
# cat /dev/null > /var/log/messages
```

or, without spawning a new process,

```
# : > /var/log/messages
```

If you remove **/var/log/messages**, you have to restart the **syslogd** daemon. Without restarting **syslogd**, the space on the filesystem is not released.

When no single process is consuming the disk space but it has instead been used up gradually, locate unneeded files and delete them. You can archive them by using **cpio**, **dump**, or **tar** before you delete them. You can safely remove most files named **core** that have not been accessed for several days. The following command line performs this function without removing necessary files named **core** (such as **/dev/core**, which is a symbolic link to **/proc/kcore**):

```
# find / -type f -name core | xargs file | grep 'B core file' | sed 's/:ELF.*//g' | xargs rm -f
```

The **find** command lists all ordinary files named **core** and sends its output to **xargs**, which runs **file** on each of the files in the list. The **file** utility displays a string that includes `B core file` for files created as the result of a core dump. These files need to be removed. The **grep** command filters out from **file** lines that do not contain this string. Finally, **sed** removes everything following the colon so that all that is left on the line is the pathname of the **core** file; **xargs** removes the file.

Look through the **/tmp** and **/var/tmp** directories for old temporary files and remove them. Keep track of disk usage in **/var/mail**, **/var/spool**, and **/var/log**.

logrotate: Manages Log Files

Rather than deleting or truncating log files, you may want to keep the contents around for a while in case you need to refer to them. The **logrotate** utility helps you manage system log (and other) files automatically by *rotating* (page 1490), compressing, mailing, and removing each as you specify. The **logrotate** utility is controlled by the **/etc/logrotate.conf** file, which sets default values and can optionally specify files to be rotated. Typically, **logrotate.conf** has an include statement that points to utility-specific specification files in **/etc/logrotate.d**. Following is the default **logrotate.conf** file:

```
$ cat /etc/logrotate.conf
# see "man logrotate" for details
# rotate log files weekly
weekly

# keep 4 weeks worth of backlogs
rotate 4

# create new (empty) log files after rotating old ones
create

# uncomment this if you want your log files compressed
#compress
```

```
# RPM packages drop log rotation information into this directory
include /etc/logrotate.d

# no packages own wtmp -- we'll rotate them here
/var/log/wtmp {
    monthly
    create 0664 root utmp
    rotate 1
}
# system-specific logs may be also be configured here.
```

This file sets default values for common parameters. Whenever logrotate runs into another value for one of these parameters, it resets the default value. You have a choice of rotating files **daily, weekly,** or **monthly.** The number following the **rotate** keyword specifies the number of rotated log files that you want to keep. The **create** keyword causes logrotate to create a new log file with the same name and attributes as the newly rotated log file. The **compress** keyword (commented out in the default file) causes log files to be compressed using gzip. The **include** keyword specifies the standard **/etc/logrotate.d** directory for program-specific logrotate specification files. When you install a program using rpm (page 928), rpm puts the corresponding logrotate specification file (if it is part of the package) in this directory.

The last set of instructions in **logrotate.conf** takes care of the **/var/log/wtmp** log file (**wtmp** holds login records; you can view this file with the command **who /var/log/wtmp**). The keyword **monthly** overrides the default value of **weekly** *for this utility only* (because the value is within brackets). The **create** keyword is followed by the arguments establishing the permissions, owner, and group for the new file. Finally, **rotate** establishes that one rotated log file should be kept.

The **/etc/logrotate.d/samba** file is a utility-specific logrotate specification file:

```
$ cat /etc/logrotate.d/samba
/var/log/samba/*.log {
    notifempty
    missingok
    sharedscripts
    copytruncate
    postrotate
    /bin/kill -HUP `cat /var/run/samba/smbd.pid /var/run/samba/nmbd.pid 2> /dev/null` 2>
/dev/null || true
    endscript
}
```

This file, which is incorporated in **/etc/logrotate.d** because of the **include** statement therein, works with each of the files in **/var/log/samba** that has a filename extension of **log** (*.**log**). The **notifempty** keyword causes logrotate not to rotate the log file if it is empty, overriding the default action of rotating empty log files. The **missingok** keyword means that no error will be issued when the file is missing. The **sharedscripts** keyword causes logrotate to execute the command(s) in the **prerotate** and **postrotate** sections one time only, not one time for each log that is rotated. The **copytruncate** keyword causes logrotate to truncate the original log file immediately after it copies it. This keyword is useful for programs that cannot be instructed to close and reopen their log files, as they might continue writing to the original file even after it has been moved. The commands between **postrotate** and **endscript** are executed after the rotation is complete. Similarly, commands between **prerotate** and **endscript** are executed before the rotation is started.

The logrotate utility has many keywords and many of these take arguments and have side effects. Refer to the logrotate man page for details.

Removing Unused Space from Directory

A directory with too many filenames in it is inefficient. The point at which a directory on an **ext2** or **ext3** filesystem becomes inefficient varies, depending partly on the length of the filenames it contains. Keep your directories relatively small. Having fewer than a few hundred files (or directories) in a directory is generally a good idea, and having more than a few thousand is generally a bad idea. Additionally, GNU/Linux uses a caching mechanism for frequently accessed files to speed the process of locating an inode from a filename. This caching mechanism works only on filenames of up to 30 characters in length, so avoid extremely long filenames for frequently accessed files.

When you find a directory that is too large, you can usually break it into several smaller directories by moving its contents into new directories. Make sure that you remove the original directory once you have moved its contents.

Because GNU/Linux directories do not shrink automatically, removing a file from a directory does not shrink the directory, even though it makes more space on the disk. To remove unused space and make a directory smaller, you must copy or move all the files into a new directory and remove the original directory.

The following procedure removes unused directory space. First, remove all unneeded files from the large directory. Then create a new, empty directory. Next, move or copy all the remaining files from the old large directory to the new empty directory. Remember to copy hidden files. Finally, delete the old directory and rename the new directory:

```
# mkdir /home/alex/new
# mv /home/alex/large/* /home/alex/large/.[A-z]* /home/alex/new
# rmdir /home/alex/large
# mv /home/alex/new /home/alex/large
```

Optional

Disk Quota System

The disk quota system limits the disk space and number of files owned by individual users. You can choose to limit each user's disk space, the number of files each user can own, or both. Each resource that is limited has two limits. The lower limit, or *quota*, can be exceeded by the user, although a warning is presented each time the user logs in when he or she is above the quota. After a certain number of warnings (set by the system administrator), the system will behave as if the user had reached the upper limit. Once the upper limit is reached or the user has received the specified number of warnings, the user will not be allowed to create any more files or use any more disk space. The user's only recourse at that point is to remove some files.

Users can review their usage and limits with the quota command. Superuser can use quota to obtain information about any user.

First, you must decide which filesystems to limit and how to allocate space among users. Typically, only filesystems that contain users' home directories, such as **/home**, are limited. Use the edquota command to set the quotas, and then use quotaon to start the quota system. You will probably want to put the quotaon command into the appropriate run command script so that the quota system will be enabled when you bring up the system (page 964). Unmounting a filesystem automatically disables the quota system for that filesystem.

Getting Help

Your distribution comes with extensive documentation (page 42). Red Hat maintains a page that points toward many useful support documents: www.redhat.com/apps/support. You can also find help on the System Administrator's Guild site (www.sage.org). In addition, the Internet is a rich source of information on managing a GNU/Linux system, refer to Appendix B and to the author's home page (www.sobell.com) for pointers to many useful sites.

You do not need to act as a Red Hat system administrator in isolation; a large community of GNU/Linux/Red Hat experts is willing to assist you in getting the most out of your system, although you will get better help if you have already tried to solve a problem yourself by reading the available documentation. If you are unable to solve a problem through the documentation, a well-thought-out question to the appropriate newsgroup, such as **comp.os.linux.misc**, or mailing list can often provide useful information. Be sure you describe the problem and identify your system carefully. Include information about your version of Red Hat and any software packages and hardware that you think relate to the problem. The newsgroup **comp.os.linux.answers** contains postings of solutions to common problems and periodic postings of the most up-to-date versions of the FAQ and HOWTO documents.

Red Hat provides many types and levels of support for a fee. Refer to www.redhat.com/apps/support/programs.html.

Chapter Summary

This chapter defines a system administrator as someone who keeps the system useful and convenient for its users and describes some of that person's tasks and tools. This chapter describes many of the files and programs you will work with to maintain a Red Hat system. Certain programs and files control how the system appears; many of these files are located in the /etc directory. Much of the work you do as the system administrator requires you to log in as **root**. The chapter describes the special privileges of the **root** user (called Superuser) and various ways of gaining these privileges. When you are logged in as Superuser, you have extensive systemwide powers that you do not normally have. You can read from and write to any file and execute programs that ordinary users are not permitted to execute.

When you bring up the system, it is sometimes in single-user mode. In this mode only the system console is functional, and not all the filesystems are mounted. When the system is in single-user mode, you can back up files and use fsck to check the integrity of filesystems before you mount them. The telinit utility brings the system to its normal multiuser state. With the system running in multiuser mode, you can still perform many administration tasks, such as adding users and printers.

The installation section of this chapter explains the process of installing GNU/Linux. But because of all the possible options, many of the details are left to the Red Hat documentation and the *Linux Kernel-HOWTO*.

As a system administrator you need to keep all the software on the system up-to-date: You will need to add and remove rpm software packages, as well as GNU configure and build system packages. Toward this end Red Hat and other vendors have programs that automate software update retrieval and installation. Red Hat's product is Red Hat Network.

The chapter describes system operation: booting up, running rc scripts, single-user mode, emergency mode, multiuser mode, bringing the system down, and what to do when the system crashes.

The GNU/Linux filesystem, introduced in Chapter 4, is described in detail, including a list of important files and directories, types of files, and how to maintain and work with various types of filesystems. New with the growth of the GNOME and KDE desktops are GUI system administration tools. These tools, including the GNOME System Settings and System windows, as well as KDE's Control Center's System and Network Modules, are covered in detail. Tables that parallel the menu systems help you work your way through the mazes of menus required to present all the tools and options in a GUI format.

The next sections of the chapter describe classic system administration tasks, including setting up users and groups, backing up files, and managing printers. The networking section, which delves into NFS, NIS, DNS, PPP, Samba, DHCP, OpenSSH, and GNU Privacy Guard, is followed by a description of how to rebuild the Linux kernel.

The final sections of this chapter discuss Linux-PAM, which allows you to maintain fine-grain control over who can access the system, how they can access it, and what they can do. The chapter concludes with a section on administrative tasks and discusses log files, scheduling tasks, system reports, and how to get information to system users.

Exercises

1. What option should you use with fsck if you want to review the status of your filesystems without making any changes to them? How does fsck determine what devices to check if you do not specify any on the command line?

2. How does single-user mode differ from multiuser mode?

3. How would you communicate each of the following messages?

   a. The system is coming down tomorrow at 6:00 in the evening for periodic maintenance.

   b. The system is coming down in 5 minutes.

   c. Jenny's jobs are slowing the system down drastically, and she should postpone them.

   d. Alex's wife just had a baby girl.

4. If Alex belongs to five groups—**inhouse, pubs, sys, other,** and **supers**—how would his group memberships be represented? Assume that **inhouse** is his primary group. How would Alex create a file that belongs to the group **pubs**?

5. How can you identify the user ID of another user on your system? What is the user ID of **root**?

6. How can you redirect the output of the find command so that whatever it sends to the standard error disappears?

7. How many links does a file have? What happens when you add a hard link to a file? What happens when you add a symbolic (soft) link?

8. How would you add a printer named **quark** that is on a remote machine named **physics**? How would you add a printer named **greens** if it were attached to the local machine on serial port B at 19,200 bps?

9. What are the differences between a character device and a block device?

10. What is a named pipe? Give an example of how one is used.

11. How would you mount the **/export/apps** filesystem from a server named **achilles** to a client named **perseus**? Give the commands for the client and the server machines.

12. Implement a local firewall on your system

Advanced Exercises

13. A process is using 98 percent of the CPU time. How do you identify the process and determine whether you should kill it?

14. What are the differences between a FIFO and a socket?

15. Develop a strategy for coming up with a password that an intruder would not be likely to guess but that you will be able to remember.

16. Develop a backup strategy that is executed by cron and includes the following components:

    a. A level 0 backup is done once per month.

    b. A level 2 dump is performed one day per week.

    c. A level 5 dump is performed every day that neither a level 0 nor a level 2 dump is performed.

    In the worst case how many restores would you have to perform to recover a file that was dumped using the preceding schedule?

17. How would you restrict access to a tape drive on your system so that only certain users could read and write tapes?

18. Design and implement a job that runs every night at 11:30 and removes from the **/home** filesystem all files named **core** that are more than a week old.

19. Give the command

    ```
    $ /sbin/fuser -uv /
    ```

    What is this a list of? Why is it so long? Give the same command as **root** (or ask your system administrator to do so and mail you the results). How does this list differ from the first? Why is it different?

20. When it puts files in a **lost+found** directory, fsck has lost the directory information for the files and thus has lost the names of the files. Each file is given a new name, which is the same as the inode number for the file:

    ```
    $ ls -lg lost+found
    -rw-r--r-- 1 alex pubs    110 Jun 10 10:55 51262
    ```

    What can you do to identify these files and restore them?

21. How would you allow a user to execute privileged commands without giving the user the Superuser password?

22. What do the letters of the su command stand for? (*Hint:* It is not Superuser.) What can you do with su besides give yourself Superuser privileges? How would you log in as Alex if you did not know his password but knew the **root** password? How would you establish the same environment that Alex has when he first logs on?

23. Take a look at **/usr/bin/lesspipe.sh,** and explain what it does and six ways it works.

24. Use at to reboot the system

    a. At 3 A.M. the following morning.

    b. Next Friday at 1 minute past midnight.

    c. Two weeks from tomorrow at the current time.

    d. In 30 minutes, using the TC Shell.

25. Give a command that will make a level 0 dump of the **/usr** filesystem to the first tape device on the system. What command would you use to take advantage of a drive that supports compression? What command would place a level 3 dump of the **/var** filesystem immediately after the level 0 dump on the tape?

26. How would you create a new directory **/home/shared/billken** so that users Bill and Kendra can create files in the directory? Any new files or subdirectories that either user creates should automatically be writable by either user. No one else should have access to this directory or the files within it. Modify this directory so that the group **spiffy** has readonly access to all files and directories within **billken.**

27. Why are setuid shell scripts inherently unsafe?

28. A utility named **/usr/bin/netclk** accepts a connection over the network and quits once the connection is dropped. How can you use the built-in functionality of Red Hat to make this program run so that it restarts automatically (without modifying **netclk**)? (*Hint:* It should run only in multiuser mode.)

29. A process is consuming a great deal of memory. How do you determine how much physical memory it is using and what percentage this is of the total memory?

30. When a user logs in, you would like the system to check for a login name in the local **/etc/passwd** file first and then to check NIS. How do you implement this strategy?

31. Implement a local firewall on your system without using gnome-lokkit or redhat-config-securitylevel.

PART III
The GNU/Linux Utility Programs

The following tables list the utilities grouped by function. Although most of these are true utilities (programs that are separate from the shells), some are built into the shells (builtins). The utilities in this section are listed alphabetically.

Utilities That Display and Manipulate Files

aspell	Checks a file for spelling errors—page 1089
cat	cat [options] [file-list]—page 1098
cmp	Checks whether two files differ—page 1113
comm	Compares sorted files—page 1118
cp	Copies one or more files—page 1122
cpio	Creates an archive or restores files from an archive—page 1124
cut	Selects characters or fields from input lines—page 1132
dd	Converts and copies a file—page 1144
diff	Displays the differences between two files—page 1149
find	Uses criteria to find files—page 1165
fmt	Formats text very simply—page 1174
gawk	gawk [options] [program] [file-list] gawk [options] –f program-file [file-list]—page 1185
grep	Searches for a pattern in files—page 1215
gzip	Compresses or decompresses files—page 1219
head	Displays the beginning of a file—page 1222
less	Displays text files, one screen at a time—page 1226
ln	Makes a link to a file—page 1230
lpr	Prints files—page 1232
ls	Displays information about one or more files—page 1235
man	Displays documentation for commands—page 1252

mkdir	Makes a directory—page 1255
mv	Moves (renames) a file—page 1260
od	Dumps the contents of a file—page 1265
paste	Joins corresponding lines from files—page 1270
pr	Paginates files for printing—page 1286
rm	Removes a file (deletes a link)—page 1303
rmdir	Removes a directory—page 1305
sed	Edits a file (not interactively)—page 1310
sort	Sorts and/or merges files—page 1326
tail	Displays the last part (tail) of a file—page 1340
tar	Stores or retrieves files to/from an archive file—page 1343
touch	Updates a file's modification time—page 1359
uniq	Displays lines of a file that are unique—page 1368
wc	Displays the number of lines, words, and bytes in a file—page 1372

Network Utilities

ftp	Transfers files over a network—page 1180
rcp	Copies one or more files to or from a remote computer—page 1293
rlogin	Logs in on a remote computer—page 1301
rsh	Executes commands on a remote computer—page 1306
scp	Securely copies one or more files to or from a remote computer—page 1308
ssh	Securely executes commands on a remote computer—page 1321
telnet	Connects to a remote computer over a network—page 1349

Communication Utilities

mail	Sends and receives electronic mail—page 1241
pine	Sends and receives electronic mail and news—page 1278

Utilities That Display and Alter Status

cd	Changes to another working directory—page 1100
chgrp	Changes the group associated with a file—page 1102
chmod	Changes the access mode of a file—page 1103
chown	Changes the owner of a file—page 1108
date	Displays or sets the time and date—page 1141
df	Displays disk space usage—page 1147
du	Displays information on disk usage—page 1155
file	Displays the classification of a file—page 1163
finger	Displays information about users—page 1171
kill	Terminates a process—page 1224
nice	Changes the priority of a command—page 1263
nohup	Runs a command that keeps running after you log out—page 1264
ps	Displays process status—page 1288
sleep	Creates a process that sleeps for a specified interval—page 1324
stty	Displays or sets terminal parameters—page 1335
top	Dynamically displays process status—page 1356
umask	Establishes the file-creation permissions mask—page 1366
w	Displays information on system users—page 1370

| which | Shows where in your path a command is located—page 1373 |
| who | Displays names of users—page 1375 |

Utilities That Are Programming Tools

configure	Configures source code automatically—page 1120
gcc	Compiles C and C++ programs—page 1210
make	Keeps a set of programs current—page 1247
patch	Updates source code—page 1272

Source Code Management (RCS, CVS) Utilities

ci	Creates or records changes in an RCS file—page 1110
co	Retrieves an unencoded revision of an RCS file—page 1115
cvs	Manages concurrent access to files in a hierarchy—page 1134
rcs	Creates or changes the attributes of an RCS file—page 1295
rlog	Prints a summary of the history of an RCS file—page 1298

Miscellaneous Utilities

at	Executes a shell script at a time you specify—page 1093
cal	Displays a calendar—page 1096
crontab	Maintains crontab files—page 1129
echo	Displays a message—page 1157
expr	Evaluates an expression—page 1159

fsck	Checks and repairs a filesystem—page 1176
Mtools	Uses DOS-style commands on files and directories—page 1256
tee	Copies standard input to standard output and one or more files—page 1348
test	Evaluates an expression—page 1352
tr	Replaces specified characters—page 1362
tty	Displays the terminal pathname—page 1365
xargs	Converts standard output of one command into arguments for another—page 1377

The following sample shows the format that is used throughout Part III. These descriptions of the utilities are similar to the man page descriptions (pages 42 and 1252); however, most users find the descriptions in this book easier to read and understand. These descriptions emphasize the most useful features of the utilities and often leave out the more obscure features. For information about the less commonly used features, refer to the man and info pages.

sample

Very brief description of what the utility does

*sample [**options**] **arguments***

Following the syntax-line is one or more paragraphs that describe the utility. The syntax-line shows you how to run the utility from a command line. Options and arguments enclosed in brackets (*[]*) are not required. Type words that appear in *this sans serif italic typeface* as is. Words that you must substitute when you type, appear in ***this bold sans serif italic typeface.*** Hyphenated words listed as arguments to a command identify single arguments (for example, ***source-file***) or groups of similar arguments (for example, ***directory-list***). As an example, ***file-list*** means a list of one or more files.

Arguments   This section describes the arguments that you can use when you run the utility. The argument itself, as shown in the preceding syntax-line, is printed in ***this bold sans serif italic typeface.***

Options   This section lists the common options you can use with the command. Unless otherwise specified, you must precede options with a hyphen. Most commands accept a single hyphen before multiple options (page 139). The following are some sample options:

–t toc   This is an example of a simple option preceded by a single dash and not followed with any arguments. The **toc** appearing as the first word of the description is a cue, a suggestion of what the option letter stands for. In this case **t** stands for **toc**, or table of contents.

–f *program-file*   Includes an argument. The argument is set in ***bold sans serif italic type*** in both the heading to the left and the description to the right. You substitute another word (filename, string of characters, or other value) for any arguments you see in ***this typeface.*** Type characters that are in **bold sans serif type** (such as the **–f** to the left) as is, letter for letter.

––make-directories –d   This is an example of an option that has a long and a short version. You can tell that the **–d** at the beginning of the description is *not* a cue to what the option means because it is preceded by a hyphen and does not look like a cue. In addition, the long option clearly spells out the meaning of the option—there is no need for a cue.

Discussion   This optional section contains a discussion about how to use the utility and any quirks it may have.

Notes   This section contains miscellaneous notes: some important and others merely interesting.

Examples   This section contains examples of how to use the utility. This section is tutorial and is more casual than the preceding sections of the description.

aspell

Checks a file for spelling errors

*aspell **action** [**options**] **filename***

The aspell utility checks words in a document against a standard dictionary. You can use the aspell utility interactively: It displays each misspelled word in context, together with a menu that gives you the choice of accepting the word as is, choosing one of aspell's suggested replacements for the word, inserting the word into your personal dictionary, and entering a new word. You can also use aspell so that it reads from standard input and writes to standard output. This mode is suitable when you want to redirect standard input or output or simply want a list of misspelled words, one per line.

For more information refer to **/usr/share/doc/aspell**✻ on your system (with manuals in the **man-html** and **man-text** subdirectories) and to the aspell home page at aspell.sourceforge.net.

---

aspell Is Not Like Other Utilities Regarding Its Input   ‖ tip

Unlike many other utilities, **aspell** does not accept input from standard input when you do not specify a filename on the command line. Instead, the *action* specifies where **aspell** gets its input.

Action   You can specify the aspell *action*[1] using the long form (not preceded with a hyphen) or the short form (preceded with a hyphen—not all *action*s have short forms). You must choose one and only one of the *action*s when you run aspell.

check   −c   Runs aspell as an interactive spell checker. Input comes from a single filename on the command line.

config   Displays aspell's configuration: both the default and current values. Output goes to standard output. Send the output through a pipe to less to read the whole document.

help   −?   Displays an extensive page of help. Output goes to standard output. Send the output through a pipe to less for easier viewing.

list   −l   Runs aspell noninteractively. Input comes from standard input. Output goes to standard output.

---

1. The aspell manual uses the term *commands* where its usage message uses the term *action*. This book uses *action*.

Arguments   The *filename* is the name of the file that you want to check. The aspell utility accepts this argument only when you use the **check** (**–c**) *action*.

Options   The default values of many of the options are determined when aspell is compiled (see the **config** *action*).

You can specify options on the command line, in the **ASPELL_CONF** shell variable, or in your personal configuration file (**~/.aspell.conf**). Superuser can create a global configuration file (**/etc/aspell.conf**). Put one option per line in a configuration file; separate options with a semicolon (**;**) in **ASPELL_CONF**. Options on the command line override those in **ASPELL_CONF**, which override those in your personal configuration file, which override those in the global configuration file.

As with *action*s, you can specify an *option* by using the long or short form (not all *option*s have short forms). The short form is valid only on the command line: It cannot be used in **ASPELL_CONF** or a configuration file.

---

aspell **Options and Leading Hyphens**   ‖ caution

The way you specify options differs, depending on whether you are specifying them on the command line or in the ASPELL_CONF shell variable or a configuration file.

On the command line: Prefix long options with two hyphens (for example, ––ignore-case or ––dont-ignore-case). Short options are always prefixed with a single hyphen and are allowed only on the command line.

In ASPELL_CONF or a configuration file: Drop the leading hyphens (for example, ignore-case or dont-ignore-case).

In the following list, the Boolean options turn a feature on (enable the feature) or off (disable the feature). Precede a Boolean option with **dont–** to turn it off. For example, **––ignore-case** turns this feature on, and **––dont-ignore-case** turns the feature off. Value options assign a value to a feature. Follow the option by a SPACE and an appropriate value (string or integer). For all options in a configuration file or in the **ASPELL_CONF** variable, use the long form, without leading hyphens (**ignore-case** or **dont-ignore-case**).

––backup   Creates a backup file named *filename*.**bak** (default is **––backup**).

––ignore *n*   **–W** *n*   Ignores words equal to or shorter than *n* characters (default is 1).

––ignore-case   Ignores the case of letters in words being checked (default is **––dont-ignore-case**).

––strip-accents   Removes accent marks from all the words in the dictionary before checking words (default is **––dont-strip-accents**).

Discussion When aspell finds a misspelled word, it writes the word to standard output when the *action* is **list**. When the *action* is **check**, aspell displays a screen of information and waits for your instructions. This screen allows you to control what aspell does with the word and includes information to help you. The top line of the screen shows the potentially misspelled word. If similar words are in the dictionary, they are given in a numbered list. You can enter one of the numbers to select a word in this list, or you can enter another command. The commands available in interactive mode are listed in Table III-1.

Command	**‖ table III-1**
SPACE	Takes no action and goes on to next misspelled word.
number	Selects suggested word numbered *number* to replace the misspelled word.
r or R	Replaces the misspelled word with the word that you enter at the bottom of the screen. R replaces all occurrences of this word, whereas r replaces this occurrence only.
a	Adds the word to your personal dictionary.
i or I	Ignores the word; the same as SPACE. I ignores all occurrences of this word, whereas i ignores this occurrence only.
x	Saves the file as corrected so far and exits from aspell.

The items in Table III-1 appear in a menu at the bottom of the screen. In the middle of the screen is the input line containing the potentially misspelled word (highlighted) with a few lines of context. See the "Examples."

Notes The aspell utility is not a foolproof way of finding spelling errors. It also does not check for misused but properly spelled words (such as *red* instead of *read*).

Examples The following examples use aspell to correct the spelling in the **memo.txt** file:

```
$ cat memo.txt
Here's a document for teh aspell utilitey
to check. It obviosly needs proofing
quiet badly.
```

The first example uses aspell with the **check** *action* and no options. The appearance of the screen for the first misspelled word, teh, is shown. At the bottom of the screen is the menu of commands that can be given at this point. The nine numbered words all differ slightly from the misspelled word:

```
$ aspell check memo.txt
Here's a document for teh aspell utilitey
to check. It obviosly needs proofing
quiet badly.



============================================================
1) the                             6) th
2) Te                              7) tea
3) tech                            8) tee
4) Th                              9) Ted
5) eh                              0) tel
i) Ignore                          I) Ignore all
r) Replace                         R) Replace all
a) Add                             x) Exit
============================================================
?
```

The next example uses the **list** *action* to display a list of misspelled words. The word quiet is not in the list—it is not properly used but is properly spelled:

```
$ aspell list < memo.txt
teh
aspell
utilitey
obviosly
```

The last example also uses the uses the **list** *action.* It shows a quick way to check the spelling of a word or two with a single command. The user gives the **aspell list** command and then enters **seperate temperature** into aspell's standard input (the keyboard). After the user enters RETURN and CONTROL-D (to mark the end of file), aspell writes the misspelled word to standard output (the screen):

```
$ aspell list
seperate temperatureRETURN
CONTROL-D
seperate
```

at

Executes a shell script at a time you specify

at *[options] time [date | +increment]*
atq
atrm *job-list*
batch *[options] [time]*

The **at** utility executes commands it receives from standard input as a shell script in the working directory at the time you specify. When **at** executes commands, it sends you the resulting standard output and standard error via e-mail. You can redirect the output to avoid getting mail.

The **atq** utility displays a list of **at** jobs you have queued. Normally **atq** displays only the jobs that you have scheduled using **at**. When you run **atq** as Superuser, it displays all the **at** jobs scheduled by all users on the system. The **atrm** utility cancels **at** jobs that you have queued. The **batch** utility schedules jobs so that they run when the CPU load on your system is low (that is, when it is not too busy).

Arguments

The *time* is the time of day you want **at** to execute the job. You can specify the *time* as a one-, two-, or four-digit number. One- and two-digit numbers specify an hour, and four-digit numbers specify an hour and minute. You can also give the time in the form **hh:mm**. The **at** utility assumes a 24-hour clock unless you place **am** or **pm** immediately after the number, in which case **at** uses a 12-hour clock. You can use the words **now, midnight, noon,** or **teatime** (4:00 P.M.) in place of *time*.

The *date* is the day of the week or date of the month on which you want **at** to execute the job. When you do not specify a day, **at** executes the job today if the hour you specify in *time* is greater than the current hour. If the hour is less than the current hour, **at** executes the job tomorrow.

Specify a day of the week by spelling it out or abbreviating it to three letters. You can also use the words **today** and **tomorrow.**

Use the name of a month followed by the number of the day in the month to specify a date. You can follow the month and day number with a year.

The *increment* is a number followed by one of the following (plural or singular is allowed): **minutes, hours, days,** or **weeks.** The **at** utility adds the *increment* to the *time* you specify. You cannot give an increment if you have already given a date.

When using **atrm**, *job-list* is a list of one or more job numbers for **at** jobs. You can identify job numbers by using **at** with the **–l** option or by using **atq**.

Options

The –l and –d options are not for use when you initiate a job with at. You can use them only to determine the status of a job or to a cancel job. The –f and –m options work with at and batch, not with atq or atrm.

–d delete   Cancels jobs that you previously submitted with at. The *job-list* argument is a list of one or more job numbers of the jobs you want to cancel. If you do not remember the job number, use the –l option to list your jobs and their numbers. Using this option with at is the same as running atrm.

–f *file* file   Typing commands for at from the keyboard is risky because it is difficult to correct mistakes. This option gives at the name of a *file* that contains a shell script you want to execute at the specified time.

–l list   Displays a list of all jobs that you have submitted with at. Using this option with at is the same as running atq.

–m mail   Sends you mail after a job is run, even when nothing is sent to standard output or standard error. When output is sent to standard output or standard error, at always mails it to you, regardless of this option.

Notes

The shell saves the environment variables and the working directory that are in effect at the time you submit an at job so that they are available when it executes the commands.

When the **/etc/at.deny** file exists and is empty, all users on the system can use at. When **/etc/at.deny** does not exist, Superuser must put your login name in the **/etc/at.allow** file for you to be able to use at. Superuser can also prevent you from using at by putting your login name in the **/etc/at.deny** file. When neither **/etc/at.allow** nor **/etc/at.deny** exists, only Superuser can use at.

Jobs you submit using at are run by the at daemon (**atd**). This daemon stores jobs in **/var/spool/at** and output in **/var/spool/at/spool**, both of which should be set to mode 700 and owned by the user named daemon.

Examples

You can use any of the following techniques to paginate and print **long_file** tomorrow at 2:00 A.M. The first example executes the command directly from the command line; the last two examples use a file containing the necessary command (**pr_tonight**) and execute it using at:

```
$ at 2am
warning: commands will be executed using (in order) a) $SHELL b) login shell c) /bin/sh
at> pr long_file | lpr
at>CONTROL-D<EOT>
job 7 at 2003-08-17 02:00
```

```
$ cat pr_tonight
#!/bin/bash
pr long_file | lpr

$ at -f pr_tonight 2am
warning: commands will be executed using (in order) a) $SHELL b) login shell c) /bin/sh
job 9 at 2003-08-17 02:00

$ at 2am < pr_tonight
warning: commands will be executed using (in order) a) $SHELL b) login shell c) /bin/sh
job 10 at 2003-08-17 02:00
```

If you execute the command directly from the command line, you must signal the end of the list of commands by pressing CONTROL-D at the beginning of a line. The line that begins with Job contains the job number and the time at will execute the job.

If you run atq after the preceding commands, it displays a list of jobs in its queue:

```
$ atq
7          2003-08-17 02:00 a
9          2003-08-17 02:00 a
10         2003-08-17 02:00 a
```

The following command removes one of the jobs from the queue:

```
$ atrm 9
$ atq
7          2003-08-17 02:00 a
10         2003-08-17 02:00 a
```

The next example executes **cmdfile** at 3:30 P.M. (1530 hours) one week from today:

```
$ at -f cmdfile 1530 +1 week
warning: commands will be executed using (in order) a) $SHELL b) login shell c) /bin/sh
job 12 at 2003-08-23 15:30
```

The final example executes a find job at 7 P.M. on Friday. It creates an intermediate file, redirects the output sent to standard error, and prints the file:

```
$ at 7pm Friday
warning: commands will be executed using (in order) a) $SHELL b) login shell c) /bin/sh
at> find / -name "core" -print >report.out 2>report.err
at> lpr report.out
at>CONTROL-D<EOT>
job 13 at 2003-08-18 19:00
```

cal

Displays a calendar

*cal [[**month**] **year**]*

The cal utility displays a calendar for a month or year.

Arguments   The arguments specify the month and year for which cal displays a calendar. The *month* is a decimal integer from 1 to 12, and the *year* is a decimal integer. Without any arguments cal displays a calendar for the current month. When you specify a single argument, it is taken to be the year.

Options

–j Julian   Displays a Julian calendar: a calendar that numbers the days consecutively from January 1 (1) through December 31 (365 or 366). See the second example.

–m Monday   Makes Monday the first day of the week. Without this option, Sunday is the first day of the week.

–y year   Displays a calendar for the current year.

Notes   Do not abbreviate the year. The year 97 does not represent the same year as 1997 and 03 is not the same as 2003.

Examples   The following command displays a calendar for August 2007:

```
$ cal 8 2007
     August 2007
Su Mo Tu We Th Fr Sa
          1  2  3  4
 5  6  7  8  9 10 11
12 13 14 15 16 17 18
19 20 21 22 23 24 25
26 27 28 29 30 31
```

The next command displays a Julian calendar for 1949 with Monday as the first day of the week:

```
$ cal -jm 1949
```

```
                              1949

            January                          February
Mon Tue Wed Thu Fri Sat Sun      Mon Tue Wed Thu Fri Sat Sun
                      1   2            32  33  34  35  36  37
  3   4   5   6   7   8   9       38  39  40  41  42  43  44
 10  11  12  13  14  15  16       45  46  47  48  49  50  51
 17  18  19  20  21  22  23       52  53  54  55  56  57  58
 24  25  26  27  28  29  30       59
 31
             March                            April
Mon Tue Wed Thu Fri Sat Sun      Mon Tue Wed Thu Fri Sat Sun
     60  61  62  63  64  65                        91  92  93
 66  67  68  69  70  71  72       94  95  96  97  98  99 100
 73  74  75  76  77  78  79      101 102 103 104 105 106 107
 80  81  82  83  84  85  86      108 109 110 111 112 113 114
 87  88  89  90                  115 116 117 118 119 120
              May                             June
Mon Tue Wed Thu Fri Sat Sun      Mon Tue Wed Thu Fri Sat Sun
                        121           152 153 154 155 156
122 123 124 125 126 127 128      157 158 159 160 161 162 163
129 130 131 132 133 134 135      164 165 166 167 168 169 170
136 137 138 139 140 141 142      171 172 173 174 175 176 177
143 144 145 146 147 148 149      178 179 180 181
150 151
              July                           August
Mon Tue Wed Thu Fri Sat Sun      Mon Tue Wed Thu Fri Sat Sun
                182 183 184      213 214 215 216 217 218 219
185 186 187 188 189 190 191      220 221 222 223 224 225 226
192 193 194 195 196 197 198      227 228 229 230 231 232 233
199 200 201 202 203 204 205      234 235 236 237 238 239 240
206 207 208 209 210 211 212      241 242 243
           September                         October
Mon Tue Wed Thu Fri Sat Sun      Mon Tue Wed Thu Fri Sat Sun
            244 245 246 247                           274 275
248 249 250 251 252 253 254      276 277 278 279 280 281 282
255 256 257 258 259 260 261      283 284 285 286 287 288 289
262 263 264 265 266 267 268      290 291 292 293 294 295 296
269 270 271 272 273              297 298 299 300 301 302 303
                                 304
           November                          December
Mon Tue Wed Thu Fri Sat Sun      Mon Tue Wed Thu Fri Sat Sun
    305 306 307 308 309 310                       335 336 337 338
311 312 313 314 315 316 317      339 340 341 342 343 344 345
318 319 320 321 322 323 324      346 347 348 349 350 351 352
325 326 327 328 329 330 331      353 354 355 356 357 358 359
332 333 334                      360 361 362 363 364 365
```

cat

Joins or displays files

cat [options] [file-list]

The cat utility joins files end to end. It takes its input from files you specify on the command line or from standard input. You can use cat to display the contents of one or more ASCII files on the screen.

Arguments   The *file-list* is composed of pathnames of one or more files that cat displays. You can use a hyphen in place of a filename to cause cat to read standard input.

Options

––number **–n**   Numbers all lines as they are written to standard output.

––show-ends **–E**   Marks with dollar signs the ends of lines.

––show-nonprinting **–v**   Displays CONTROL characters with the caret notation (^M) and displays characters that have the high bit set (META characters) with the M- notation. This option does not convert TABs and LINEFEEDs. Use **––show-tabs** if you want to display TABs. LINEFEEDs cannot be displayed as anything but themselves; otherwise, the line would be too long.

––show-tabs **–T**   Marks each TAB with a ^I.

––squeeze-blank **–s**   Removes extra blank lines so that there is never more than a single blank line in a row.

–e Same as –vE.

–t Same as –vT.

––show-all **–A**   Same as –vET.

Notes   Use the od utility (page 1265) to display the contents of a file that does not contain text (for example, an executable program file).

The name cat is derived from one of the functions of this utility, *catenate*, which means to join together sequentially, or end to end.

NOCLOBBER || caution

Despite cat's warning message, the shell destroys the input file (**letter**) before invoking **cat** in the following example:

```
$ cat memo letter > letter
cat: letter: input file is output file
```
You can prevent this problem by setting the **noclobber** variable (pages 554 and 713).

Examples   The following command line displays on the terminal the contents of the text file named **memo**:

```
$ cat memo
.
.
```

The next example catenates three files and redirects the output to the **all** file:

```
$ cat page1 letter memo > all
```

You can use cat to create short text files without using an editor. Enter the following command line, type (or paste) the text that you want in the file, and then press CONTROL-D on a line by itself:

```
$ cat > new_file
.
.
(text)
.
.
CONTROL-D
```

The cat utility takes its input from standard input (the terminal), and the shell redirects standard output (a copy of the input) to the file you specify. The CONTROL-D signals the EOF (end of file) and causes cat to return control to the shell (page 144).

Following, a pipe sends the output from who to standard input of cat. The shell redirects cat's output to the file named **output** that, after the line has finished executing, contains the contents of the **header** file, the output of who, and, finally, **footer**. The hyphen on the command line causes cat to read standard input after reading **header** and before reading **footer**:

```
$ who | cat header - footer > output
```

cd

cd

Changes to another working directory

*cd [**directory**]*

Without an argument cd makes your home directory the working directory. With a directory pathname as an argument, cd makes that directory the working directory.

Argument
The *directory* is the pathname of the directory you want to become your new working directory.

Notes
The cd program is a builtin in bash, tcsh, and zsh. Refer to the discussions of the **HOME** shell variable on pages 576 and 708. Chapter 4 contains a discussion of cd on page 108.

Each of the three shells has a variable (**CDPATH** `bash` `zsh` or **cdpath** `tcsh`) that affects the operation of cd. The **CDPATH** variable contains a list of directories cd searches in addition to the working directory. If **CDPATH** is not set, cd searches only the working directory. If **CDPATH** is set, cd searches each of the directories in **CDPATH**'s directory list. Refer to page 580 for more information about **CDPATH** or to page 707 for more information about **cdpath**.

The Z Shell cd builtin has features in addition to those common to all three shells.

Examples
The following command makes your home directory become the working directory:

```
$ cd
```

The next command makes the **/home/alex/literature** directory the working directory. The pwd builtin verifies the change:

```
$ cd /home/alex/literature
$ pwd
/home/alex/literature
```

Next, the cd utility makes a subdirectory of the working directory the new working directory:

```
$ cd memos
$ pwd
/home/alex/literature/memos
```

Finally, cd uses the **..** reference to the parent of the working directory to make the parent the new working directory:

```
$ cd ..
$ pwd
/home/alex/literature
```

chgrp

Changes the group associated with a file

*chgrp [**options**] **group file-list***
*chgrp [**options**] --reference=**rfile file-list***

The chgrp utility changes the group associated with a file. See page 1108 for information on how chown can change the group associated with, as well as the owner of, a file.

Arguments   The **group** is the name or numeric group ID of the new group. The **file-list** is a list of pathnames of the files whose group association you want to change. The **rfile** is the pathname of a file whose group is to become the new group associated with **file-list**.

Options

--changes –c   Displays a message for each file whose group was changed.

--quiet *or* –f   Causes chgrp not to display warning messages about files whose permissions
--silent   prevent you from changing the group.

--recursive –R   When you include a directory in the **file-list**, descends the directory hierarchy, setting the group ID on all the files it encounters.

--verbose –v   Displays for each file a message saying whether its group was retained or changed.

--reference=rfile   Changes the group of the files in **file-list** to that of **rfile**.

Notes   Only the owner of a file or Superuser can change the group association of a file. Also, unless you are Superuser, you must belong to the specified **group**.

Example   The following command changes the group that the **manuals** file is associated with; the new group is **pubs**.

```
$ chgrp pubs manuals
```

chmod

Changes the access mode of a file

chmod [**options**] **who operation permission file-list** (symbolic)
chmod [**options**] **mode file-list** (absolute)
chmod [**options**] --reference=**rfile file-list** (referential)

The chmod utility changes the ways in which a file can be accessed by the owner of the file, the group to which the file belongs, and/or all other users. Only the owner of a file or Superuser can change the access mode, or permissions, of a file. You can specify the new access mode absolutely, symbolically, or referentially.

Arguments   Arguments specify which files are to have their modes changed in what ways.

Symbolic

The chmod utility changes the access permission for the class of user specified by **who.** The class of user is designated by one or more of the letters specified in the **who** column of Table III-2.

who	**User Class**	**Meaning**	‖ table III-2
u	User	Owner of the file	
g	Group	Group to which the owner belongs	
o	Other	All other users	
a	All	Can be used in place of u, g, and o	

The **operation** to be performed is defined by the list in Table III-3.

operation		‖ table III-3
+		Adds permission for the specified user class
−		Removes permission for the specified user class
=		Sets permission for the specified user—resets all other permissions for that user class

The access *permission* is defined by the list Table III-4.

permission	|| table III-4
r	Sets read permission
w	Sets write permission
x	Sets execute permission
s	Sets user ID or sets group ID (depending on the *who* argument) to that of the owner of the file while the file is being executed
t	Sets the sticky bit (only Superuser can set the sticky bit, and it can be used only with u)—page 1495
X	Makes the file executable only if it is a directory or if another user has execute permission (that is, the owner or others if setting the group permission, the group or owner if setting permission for others, and the group or others if setting the owner's permission)
u	Makes the permissions you are setting match those already present for the owner
g	Makes the permissions you are setting match those already present for the group
o	Makes the permissions you are setting match those already present for others

Absolute

In place of the symbolic method of changing the access permissions for a file, you can use an octal number to represent the mode. Construct the number by ORing the appropriate values from Table III-5. (To OR two octal numbers from Table III-5, just add them. Refer to Table III-6 for examples.)

Number	|| table III-5
4000	Sets user ID when the program is executed
2000	Sets group ID when the program is executed

Number (Continued) || table III-5

1000	Sticky bit
0400	Owner can read the file
0200	Owner can write to the file
0100	Owner can execute the file
0040	Group can read the file
0020	Group can write to the file
0010	Group can execute the file
0004	Others can read the file
0002	Others can write to the file
0001	Others can execute the file

Table III-6 lists some typical modes.

Example Modes || table III-6

0777	Owner, group, and public can read, write, and execute file.
0755	Owner can read, write, and execute; group and public can read and execute file.
0711	Owner can read, write, and execute; group and public can execute file.
0644	Owner can read and write; group and public can read file.
0640	Owner can read and write, group can read, and public has no access to file.

Options

--changes **−c** For each file whose mode is changed, displays a message saying that its mode was changed and giving the value of the mode absolutely and symbolically.

--quiet *or* **−f** Prevents chmod from displaying error messages when it is unable to change the
--silent permissions of a file.

--recursive **−R** When you include a directory in *file-list*, descends the directory hierarchy, setting the specified modes on all the files it encounters.

--verbose **−v** Displays for each file a message saying that its mode was changed—even if it was not changed—and giving the value of the mode absolutely and symbolically.

--reference=*rfile* Changes the access mode of the files in *file-list* to that of *rfile.*

Notes

When you are using symbolic arguments, you can omit the *permission* from the command line only when the *operation* is =. This omission takes away all permissions.

Examples

The following examples show how to use the chmod utility to change permissions on a file named **temp**. The initial access mode of **temp** is shown by ls:

```
$ ls -l temp
-rw-rw-r-- 1 alex  pubs     57  Jul 12 16:47 temp
```

The following command line removes all access permissions for the group and all other users so that only the owner has access to the file:

```
$ chmod go= temp
$ ls -l temp
-rw------- 1 alex  pubs     57  Jul 12 16:47 temp
```

When you do not follow an equal sign with a permission, chmod removes all permissions for the specified user class. The ls utility verifies the change.

The next command changes the access modes for all users (owner, group, and all others) to read and write. Now anyone can read from or write to the file.

```
$ chmod a=rw temp
$ ls -l temp
-rw-rw-rw- 1 alex  pubs     57  Jul 12 16:47 temp
```

Using an absolute argument, the **a=rw** becomes **666**. The next command performs the same function as the previous **chmod** command:

```
$ chmod 666 temp
```

The next command removes the write access privilege for other users. This change means that members of the **pubs** group can still read from and write to the file, but other users can only read from the file:

```
$ chmod o-w temp
```

```
$ ls -l temp
-rw-rw-r-- 1 alex   pubs      57  Jul 12 16:47 temp
```

The following command yields the same result, using an absolute argument:

```
$ chmod 664 temp
```

The final command adds execute access privilege for all users:

```
$ chmod a+x temp
```

```
$ ls -l temp
-rwxrwxr-x 1 alex   pubs      57  Jul 12 16:47 temp
```

If **temp** is a shell script or other executable file, all users can now execute it.[2] Again, the absolute command that yields the same result is

```
$ chmod 775 temp
```

2. You need read and execute access to run a shell script but only execute access to run a binary file. The script requires read access because the shell has to read and interpret the file before it can execute it.

chown

Changes the owner of a file

*chown [**options**] **owner:group file-list***
*chown [**options**] --reference=**rfile file-list***

The chown utility changes the owner of a file.

Arguments   The *owner:group* is the name or numeric user ID of the new owner of the file and/or the name or numeric group ID of the new group that the file is associated with, as specified following:

- *owner*   The new owner of *file-list*; the group is not changed

- *owner:group*   The new owner and new group association of *file-list*

- *owner:*   The new owner of *file-list*; the group association is changed to that of the new owner's login group

- *:group*   The new group associated with *file-list*; the owner is not changed

The *file-list* is a list of pathnames of the files whose ownership you want to change.

Options

--changes −c   Displays a message for each file whose ownership/group was changed.

--quiet *or* −f   Prevents chown from displaying error messages when it is unable to change the
--silent ownership/group of a file.

--recursive −R   When you include directories in the *file-list*, this option descends the directory hierarchy, setting the specified ownership/group on all files encountered.

--verbose −v   Displays for each file a message saying whether its ownership/group was retained or changed.

--reference=*rfile*   Changes the ownership and group association of the files in the *file-list* to that of *rfile*.

Note   The GNU version of chown, which is supplied with Red Hat, has many more options than specified here. Refer to the info page for details.

Examples   The following command changes the owner of the **chapter1** file in the **manuals** directory. The new owner is Jenny:

```
$ chown jenny manuals/chapter1
```

The following command makes Alex the owner of, and Alex's login group (presumably **alex**) the group associated with, all files in the **/home/alex/literature** directory and in all its subdirectories:

```
$ chown --recursive alex: /home/alex/literature
```

The next command changes the ownership of the files in **literature** to **alex** and the group association of the same files to **pubs**:

```
$ chown alex:pubs /home/alex/literature/*
```

The final example changes the group association of the files in **manuals** to **pubs** without altering their ownership:

```
$ chown :pubs manuals/*
```

ci

Creates or records changes in an RCS file

*ci [**options**] **file-list***

The ci (check in) utility creates or records changes in RCS-encoded files. It is part of RCS (Revision Control System—page 871), a group of related utilities that manages the storage, retrieval, and updating of source files. The RCS utilities covered in Part III are ci, co, rcs, and rlog.

Arguments

The *file-list* is a list of filenames, typically working filenames. For each of the named files, ci creates or changes the corresponding RCS file in the subdirectory **RCS** of the working file's directory, if one exists, or in the working file's directory otherwise. See the following "Notes" for more about RCS and working filenames.

Options

–d[*date*] **date**   Specifies the check-in date and time. Many different formats are accepted for *date*. Enclose *date* within quotation marks if it contains any blanks.

–k[*revision-number*] **keyword**   Checks in revision with existing keyword values for author, date, and revision. This method preserves identifying information attached to source files obtained from other sites. This option is usually used for initial checkin only.

–l[*revision-number*] **lock**   After checking in the revision, retrieves a locked (editable) copy at the next revision level. This is a one-step equivalent to running **ci** followed by **co –l**.

–m[*comments*] **messages**   Allows you to enter the reason for checking in a revision to the file. If you do not use the **–m** option and standard input is a terminal, ci prompts you for comments. To create a null comment, do not enter anything after the **–m** option or enter a period (.) in response to the prompt for comments.

–n[*name*] **name**   Assigns the symbolic name *name* to the revision. This option allows you to give meaningful names to revisions so that you can access them more easily.

–r[*revision-number*] **revision**   Specifies the revision number for the RCS-encoded file that is being checked in. This option is needed only if you do not want to use the default *revision-number*.

–u[*revision-number*] **unlock**   After checking in the revision, retrieves an unlocked (unwritable) copy at the current revision level. This is a one-step equivalent to running **ci** followed by **co –u**.

Notes   The name of an RCS-encoded file ends in the two characters **,v**. The simple filename component of the working file must be the same as that of the RCS file, except for the characters **,v** terminating the RCS filename. The working filename corresponding to the RCS file **RCS/mergecases.c,v** may be **mergecases.c** but not **mergetests.c**. Refer to the rcs man page and other RCS documentation to learn more about naming files, including RCS files, in the *file-list*. Although you can store RCS and working files anywhere, the RCS file is usually stored in a subdirectory (named **RCS**) of the directory storing the working file. Sometimes both are stored in the same directory.

You can identify a revision by its revision number, which consists of an even number of period-separated integers. Revision numbers on the trunk consist of two integers, whereas branch revision numbers have at least four integers. You can also use symbolic names to identify revisions.

If source files are expected to undergo modification by more than one developer at a time or if you have a large number of source files organized in a directory hierarchy, you may want to consider using cvs (page 879) instead of the utilities of RCS. The cvs utility extends the functionality of RCS to accommodate large-project development. The cvs interface closely resembles that of RCS and is easy for RCS users to learn and use.

If you want identifying information about each revision to appear within the revision itself, you may place one or more *keyword strings* inside the working file. These strings are expanded into meaningful replacement strings when the revision is subsequently checked out. A dollar sign ($) must appear on either side of the keyword string. Table III-7 lists some of the valid keyword strings.

Keyword String	**‖ table III-7**
$Author$	The user who checked in the revision
$Date$	When the revision was checked in
$Revision$	The revision number of the revision
$Header$	The information given by the preceding items, along with the full pathname of the RCS file, the state of the revision, and the locker for locked revisions

Keyword strings usually appear as comments inside source files; this may be necessary to avoid compilation errors, for instance. In C source files keyword strings may also be assigned to string variables. Refer to the following examples.

Examples   The first example demonstrates the use of the ci utility to create a new RCS file:

```
$ ci thesis
RCS/thesis,v  <--  thesis
enter description, terminated with a single '.' or end of file:
NOTE: This is NOT the log message!
>> Master copy of my thesis.
>> .
initial revision: 1.1
done
$
```

The following examples illustrate the use of the ci utility after co has been used with the –l option to retrieve the highest revision on the trunk. In this example, the user enters comments directly on the command line with the –m option and uses the –l option to retrieve the next revision for editing:

```
$ ci -l -m"first pass at chapter one" thesis
RCS/thesis,v  <--  thesis
new revision: 1.2; previous revision: 1.1
done
```

The next example starts a new revision level, using the –r option:

```
$ ci -r2 thesis
RCS/thesis,v  <--  thesis
new revision: 2.1; previous revision: 1.2
enter log message, terminated with a single '.' or end of file:
>> major reorganization
>> .
done
```

The following example is identical to the preceding one, except that the new revision is available for reading (only) after it is checked in:

```
> ci -u2 thesis
RCS/thesis,v  <--  thesis
new revision: 2.1; previous revision: 1.2
enter log message, terminated with single '.' or end of file:
>> major reorganization
>> .
done
```

The last example shows the top few lines of a C source file that Alex is about to check in for the first time. It contains two keyword strings inside a comment:

```
/*
$Author$
$Revision$
*/
```

cmp

Checks whether two files differ

*cmp [**options**] **file1** [**file2**]*

The cmp utility does a byte-by-byte comparison of **file1** and **file2.** If the files differ, cmp outputs the location at which the first difference occurs. Unlike diff (page 1149), cmp works with binary as well as ASCII files.

The cmp utility returns an exit status of 0 if the files are the same and 1 if they are different. An exit status > 2 means that an error occurred.

Arguments   The **file1** and **file2** arguments identify the two files to compare. If **file2** is omitted, cmp uses standard input instead. Using a filename of – for either **file1** or **file2** causes cmp to read standard input in place of that file.

Options

--ignore--initial=*n* –i *n*   Skips the first *n* bytes in both files before beginning the comparison.

--print-chars –c   Shows the bytes at the first location where the files differ. The byte at that location in each file is displayed as an octal value and an ASCII character. Nonprinting ASCII characters are displayed symbolically.

--silent *or* –s   Suppresses output from cmp. Use this option when you are interested in only
--quite   the exit status resulting from the comparison.

--verbose –1   Instead of stopping at the first byte that differs, continues comparing the two files and displays both the locations and values of every byte that differs in the two files. Locations are displayed as decimal offsets from the beginning of the files, and byte values are displayed in octal. The comparison terminates when an EOF is encountered on either file.

Notes   The cmp utility only sets the exit status; it does not display any output if the files are identical.

When cmp displays the bytes that are different in the two files (with either the **--print-chars** or the **--verbose** option), the byte from *file1* is shown first, followed by the byte from *file2*.

Examples

The examples use the files **a** and **b** shown following. These files have two differences. The first difference is that the word lazy in file **a** is replaced by lasy in file **b**. The second difference is more subtle; a TAB character is just before the NEWLINE character in file **b**:

```
$ cat a
The quick brown fox jumped over the lazy dog's back.
$ cat b
The quick brown fox jumped over the lasy dog's back.TAB
```

The first example uses cmp without any options to compare the two files. The cmp utility reports that the files are different and identifies the offset from the start of the files where the first difference is found:

```
$ cmp a b
a b differ: char 39, line 1
```

You can see the values of the bytes at that location by adding the **--print-chars** option:

```
$ cmp --print-chars a b
a b differ: char 39, line 1 is 172 z 163 s
```

The –l option displays all the bytes that differ in the two files. (Because this option creates a lot of output if the files have many differences, you may want to redirect it to a file.) Following, the two differences are shown. The –c option displays the values for the bytes as well. Where file **a** has a CONTROL-J (NEWLINE), file **b** has a CONTROL-I (TAB). Then cmp displays a message saying that it has reached the end of file on file **a**, indicating that file **b** is longer than file **a**:

```
$ cmp -lc a b
39 172 z     163 s
53  12 ^J     11 ^I
cmp: EOF on a
```

In the final example, the **--ignore-initial** option is used to skip over the first difference in the files. The cmp utility now reports on the second difference:

```
$ cmp --ignore-initial=39 a b
a b differ: char 53, line 1
```

CO

Retrieves an unencoded revision of an RCS file

*co [**options**] file-list*

The co (check out) utility creates or records changes in RCS-encoded files. It is part of RCS (Revision Control System—page 871), which is a group of related utilities that manage the storage, retrieval, and updating of source files. The RCS utilities covered in Part III are ci, co, rcs, and rlog.

Arguments   The *file-list* is a list of filenames—typically working filenames. For each, co looks for the corresponding RCS file in the subdirectory **RCS** of the working file's directory and then in the working file's directory. See "Notes" following for more about RCS and working filenames.

Options

–d*date*   **date**   Retrieves the latest revision of the file made on or before *date*.

–l[*revision-number*]   **lock**   Retrieves a locked (editable) copy of the file. When you do not specify a *revision-number*, co retrieves the latest revision; otherwise, it retrieves the latest revision less than or equal to the *revision-number*.

–p[*revision-number*]   **print**   Sends a copy of the file to standard output. When you do not specify a *revision-number*, co uses the latest revision; otherwise, it uses the latest revision less than or equal to the *revision-number* you specify.

–r[*revision-number*]   **revision**   Identifies the *revision-number* of the RCS-encoded file that you are checking out. With this option, co retrieves the latest revision less than or equal to the *revision-number* you specify. When you do not specify a *revision-number* (or if you do not use this option), co retrieves the latest revision.

–u[*revision-number*]   **unlock**   Retrieves the latest revision less than or equal to the *revision-number*, unlocking the revision if locked. Without a *revision-number*, this option causes co to retrieve the latest revision that you locked, if such a revision exists; otherwise, co retrieves the latest unlocked revision.

Notes

The name of an RCS-encoded file ends in the two characters **,v**. The simple filename component of the working file must have the same name as the RCS file except for the characters **,v** terminating the RCS filename. The working filename corresponding to the RCS file **RCS/mergecases.c,v** may be **mergecases.c** but not **mergetests.c**. Refer to the rcs man page and other RCS documentation to learn more about naming files, including RCS files, in the *file-list*. Although you can store RCS and working files anywhere, the RCS file is usually stored in a subdirectory (named **RCS**) of the directory storing the working file. Sometimes both are stored in the same directory.

You can identify a revision by its revision number, which consists of an even number of period-separated integers. Revision numbers on the trunk consist of two integers, whereas branch revision numbers have at least four integers. You can also use symbolic names to identify revisions.

When specifying a date, the default time zone is Universal Coordinated Time (UTC), also known as Greenwich Mean Time (GMT). The RCS commands recognize dates in a variety of formats, such as

```
5:00 PM LT
1:00am, Jul. 11, 2003
Thu Aug 21 17:00:00 PDT 2003
```

In the first example preceding, LT represents the local time (which is PDT, or Pacific Daylight Time, in this case).

If source files are expected to undergo modification by more than one developer at a time or if you have a large number of source files organized in a directory hierarchy, you may want to consider using cvs (page 879) instead of the utilities of RCS. The cvs utility extends the functionality of RCS to accommodate large-project development. The cvs interface closely resembles RCS and is easy for RCS users to learn and use.

If the RCS file contains keyword strings, the working file that you check out will contain their expanded values. See the "Notes" section of the ci utility (page 1111) for details.

Examples

The first command retrieves the latest revision but not for editing:

```
$ co thesis
RCS/thesis,v  -->  thesis
revision 1.4
done
```

The next command retrieves a writable copy of the file, setting a lock that prevents other users from retrieving a writable copy of the same file at this revision level:

```
$ co -l thesis
RCS/thesis,v  -->  thesis
revision 1.4 (locked)
done
```

The next command displays revision 1.3 of **thesis** (without storing it in a new file):

```
$ co -r1.3 -p thesis
RCS/thesis,v  -->  stdout
revision 1.3
.
.
.
```

The last command retrieves the latest revision of **thesis** that was checked in at or before the specified time:

```
$ co -d'Thu Jul 14 2 pm lt' thesis
```

comm

Compares sorted files

comm [options] file1 file2

The comm utility displays a line-by-line comparison of two sorted files. (If the files have not been sorted, comm will not work properly.) The display is in three columns. The first column lists all the lines found only in *file1*, the second column lists lines found only in *file2*, and the third lists those common to both files. Lines in the second column are preceded by one TAB, and those in the third column are preceded by two TABs.

Arguments   The *file1* and *file2* are pathnames of the files that comm compares. You can use a hyphen in place of either *file1* or *file2* (but not both) to cause comm to read standard input.

Options   You can use the options –1, –2, and –3 individually or in combination.

–1 Does not display column 1 (does not display lines it finds only in **file1**).

–2 Does not display column 2 (does not display lines it finds only in **file2**).

–3 Does not display column 3 (does not display lines it finds in both files).

Examples   The following examples use two files (**c** and **d**) in the working directory. The contents of these files follow. As with all input to comm, the files are in sorted order:

File c	File d
bbbbb	aaaaa
ccccc	ddddd
ddddd	eeeee
eeeee	ggggg
fffff	hhhhh

Refer to sort on page 1326 for information on sorting files.

The first command following calls comm without any options, so it displays three columns. The first column lists those lines found only in file **c**, the second column lists those found in **d**, and the third lists the lines found in both **c** and **d**:

```
$ comm c d
              aaaaa
bbbbb
ccccc
                        ddddd
                        eeeee
fffff
              ggggg
              hhhhh
```

The next example shows the use of options to prevent comm from displaying columns 1 and 2. The result is column 3, a list of the lines common to files **c** and **d**.

```
$ comm -12 c d
ddddd
eeeee
```

configure

Configures source code automatically

./configure **options**

This utility is part of the GNU Configure and Build System (page 931). Software developers who supply source code for their products are faced with the problem of making it easy for relatively naive users to build and install their software package on a wide variety of machine architectures, operating systems, and system software. Toward this end many software developers supply a shell script named configure with their source code. They create the configure script from a file named **configure.in**. The **configure.in** file contains information on the system requirements for the software package.

When you run configure, it determines the capabilities of your system. The data collected by configure is used to build the makefiles that make uses to build the executables and libraries. You can adjust the behavior of configure with command line options and environment variables.

Options

The configure utility accepts a wide variety of options. The more commonly used options are listed here.

––prefix=*directory* By default configure builds makefiles that install software in the **/usr/local** directory (when you give the command **make install**). To install into a different directory, replace *directory* with the name of the directory you want to install the software in.

––with-*package* Replace *package* with the name of an optional package that can be included with the software you are configuring. For example, if you configure the source code for the Windows emulator wine with the command **configure ––with-dll**, the source code is configured to build a shared library of Windows emulation support. Check the **README** file supplied with the software distribution to see what choices you have for *package*. Also, **configure ––help** usually shows you your choices for *package*.

––enable-*feature* Replace *feature* with the name of a feature that can be supported by the software being configured. For example, configuring the Z Shell source code with the command **configure ––enable-zsh-mem** configures the source code to use special memory allocation routines provided with zsh instead of using the system memory allocation routines. Check the **README** file supplied with the software distribution to see what choices you have for *feature*.

––disable-*feature* Works in the same manner as ––*enable-feature* but disables support for *feature*.

--help Displays a detailed list of all the options available for use with configure. The contents of this list depends on the software distribution being configured.

Discussion

The GNU Configure and Build System allows software developers to distribute software that can configure itself to be built on a variety of systems. This package builds a shell script named configure, which prepares the software distribution to be built and installed on your system. Then configure searches your system to find the various dependencies for the software distribution and constructs the appropriate makefiles. Once you have run configure, you can build the software with a **make** command and install the software with a **make install** command.

The configure script determines which C compiler to use (usually gcc) and specifies a set of flags to pass to that compiler. You can set the environment variables **CC** and **CFLAGS** to override these values with your own choices. See the "Examples" section.

Notes

Each package that uses the GNU autoconfiguration utility provides its own custom copy of configure, which the software developer created using the GNU autoconf utility. Read the **README** and **INSTALL** files that are provided with these packages for detailed information about the options that are available.

The configure scripts are self-contained and run correctly on a wide variety of systems. You need no special system resources to use configure.

Examples

The simplest way to call configure is to cd to the base directory for the software distribution you want to configure and run the following command:

```
$ ./configure
```

The ./ is prepended to the command name to ensure that you are running the configure script that was supplied with the software distribution. To cause configure to build makefiles that pass the flags **-Wall** and **-O2** to gcc, use the following command from either bash or zsh:

```
$ CFLAGS="-Wall -O2" ./configure
```

If you are using tcsh, use the following command:

```
> env CFLAGS="-Wall -O2" ./configure
```

cp

Copies one or more files

cp [options] source-file destination-file
cp [options] source-file-list destination-directory

The cp utility copies one or more files and has two modes of operation. The first copies one file to another; the second copies one or more files to a directory. The cp utility copies directories only with the **–r** or **–R** options.

Arguments   The *source-file* is the pathname of the file that cp is going to copy. The *destination-file* is the pathname that cp assigns to the resulting copy of the file.

The *source-file-list* is one or more pathnames of files that cp is going to copy. The *destination-directory* is the pathname of the directory in which cp places the copied files.

When you specify a *destination-directory*, cp gives each of the copied files the same simple filename as its *source-file*. For example, when you copy **/home/jenny/memo.416** to the **/home/jenny/archives** directory, the copy has the simple filename **memo.416**, but the new pathname is **/home/jenny/archives/memo.416**.

When you use the **–r** option, the *source-file* or *source-file-list* can contain directories.

Options

--backup   **–b**   If copying a file would overwrite an existing file, this option makes a backup copy of the file that would be overwritten. The cp utility gives the backup copy the same name as the destination file but with a tilde (~) appended to it.

--force   **–f**   When the *destination-file* exists and cannot be opened for writing, cp tries to remove it before starting to copy the *source-file*. This option is useful when the user copying a file does not have write permission to an existing *destination-file* but has write permission to the directory containing the *destination-file*.

--interactive   **–i**   Prompts the user whenever cp would overwrite an existing file. If you enter **y**, cp continues. If you enter anything other than **y**, cp does not make the copy.

--preserve   **–p**   Preserves each file's owner, group, permissions, and modification dates when copying it.

--recursive   **–R**   Recursively copies directories as well as ordinary files.

--update   **–u**   Copies only when the *destination-file* does not exist or when it is older than the *source-file*.

--verbose   **–v**   Explains what cp is doing.

Notes   If the *destination-file* exists before you execute cp, cp overwrites the file, destroying the contents but leaving the access privileges, owner, and group associated with the file as they were.

If the *destination-file* does not exist, cp uses the access privileges of the *source-file*. The user becomes the owner of the *destination-file*, and the user's group becomes the group associated with the *destination-file*.

With the **–p** option cp attempts to set the access privileges, owner, and group to match those of the *source-file*.

Examples   The first command makes a copy of the file **letter** in the working directory. The name of the copy is **letter.sav**:

```
$ cp letter letter.sav
```

The next command copies all the files with filenames ending in **.c** into the **archives** directory, a subdirectory of the working directory. Each copied file retains its simple filename but has a new absolute pathname:

```
$ cp *.c archives
```

The next example copies **memo** from **/home/jenny** to the working directory:

```
$ cp /home/jenny/memo .
```

The following command copies the files named **memo** and **letter** into another directory. The copies have the same simple filenames as the source files (**memo** and **letter**) but have different absolute pathnames. The absolute pathnames of the copied files are **/home/jenny/memo** and **/home/jenny/letter**:

```
$ cp memo letter /home/jenny
```

The final command demonstrates one use of the **–f** option. Alex owns the working directory and tries unsuccessfully to copy **one** onto a file (**me**) that he does not have write permission for. Because he has write permission to the directory that holds **me**, he can remove the file but not write to it. The **–f** option unlinks, or removes, **me** and then copies **one** to the new file named **me**.

```
$ ls -ld
drwxrwxr-x    2 alex      alex           4096 Oct 21 22:55 .
$ ls -l
-rw-r--r--    1 root      root           3555 Oct 21 22:54 me
-rw-rw-r--    1 alex      alex           1222 Oct 21 22:55 one
$ cp one me
cp: cannot create regular file `me': Permission denied
$ cp -f one me
$
```

Refer to "Directory Access Permissions" on page 121 for more information.

cpio

Creates an archive or restores files from an archive

cpio −o [**options**]
cpio −i [**options**] [**patterns**]
cpio −p [**options**] **directory**

The cpio utility has three modes of operation. It allows you to place multiple files into a single archive file (create or copy-out), restore files from an archive (extract or copy-in), and copy a directory hierarchy to another location (pass-through or copy-pass). The archive file used by cpio may be saved on disk, tape, other removable media, or a remote system.

Create mode reads a list of ordinary or directory filenames from standard input and writes the resulting archive file to standard output. Use this mode to create an archive. Extract mode reads the name of an archive from standard input and extracts files from the archive. You can decide to restore all the files from the archive or only those whose names match specific **patterns**. Pass-through mode reads ordinary or directory filenames from standard input and copies the files to another location on disk.

Arguments   The default action of cpio when extracting files from an archive (−**i** option) is to extract all the files found in the archive. You can choose to extract files selectively by supplying one or more **patterns** to cpio. Each **pattern** is treated as a separate regular expression. If the name of a file in the archive matches one of the **patterns**, that file is extracted; otherwise, it is ignored.

When using cpio to copy files into a **directory**, you must give the name of the target **directory** as an argument to cpio.

Options

Major Options

Three options determine the mode in which cpio operates. You must include exactly one of these options, in either its long or short form, whenever you use cpio.

−−**create** −**o** (**copy-out** mode)   Constructs an archive from the files named on standard input. The files may be ordinary or directory files, and each must appear on a separate line. The archive is written to standard output as it is built. The find utility frequently generates the filenames that cpio uses. The following command builds an archive of your entire system and writes it to the SCSI tape at **/dev/st0**:

```
$ find / -depth -print | cpio -o >/dev/st0
```

The **−depth** option causes find to search for files in a depth-first search, reducing the likelihood of permission problems on a file or directory. See the discussion of this option on page 1127.

−−extract   **−i** (**copy-in** mode)   Reads the archive from standard input and extracts files. Without any **patterns** on the command line, cpio extracts all the files from the archive. With **patterns** cpio extracts only files whose names match the **patterns** (regular expressions). The following example extracts only files whose names end in **.c**:

```
$ cpio -i \*.c </dev/st0
```

The backslash prevents the shell from expanding the * before passing the argument to cpio.

−−pass-through   **−p** (**copy-pass** mode)   Copies files from one place on your system to another. Instead of constructing an archive file containing the files named on standard input, cpio copies them into the **directory** (the last argument given to cpio). The effect is the same as if you had created an archive with copy-out mode and then extracted the files with copy-in mode, but using pass-through mode avoids creating an actual archive. The following example copies the working directory and all subdirectories into **/home/alex/code**:

```
$ find . -depth -print | cpio -pdm ~alex/code
```

Other Options

The remaining options alter the behavior of cpio. These options work with one or more of the preceding major options.

−−reset−access−tim
e   **−a**   Sets the access times of input files to the access time of the source files after copying them.

−B   **block**   Sets the block size to 5,120 bytes instead of the default 512 bytes.

−−block−size=_n_   Sets the block size used for input and output to _n_ 512-byte blocks.

−c   **compatible**   Writes header information in ASCII so that older (incompatible) cpio utilities on other machines can read the file. This option is rarely needed.

−−make−directories   **−d**   Creates directories as needed when it is copying files. For example, you need this option when extracting files from an archive with a file list generated by find with the **−depth** option. This option can be used only with the **−−extract** and **−−pass−through** options.

--pattern-file=filename

−E *filename*   Giving *patterns* as arguments to cpio when extracting selected files is tedious and error prone if done repeatedly. This option reads *patterns* from *filename*. You can specify additional *patterns* on the command line. Each line in the *filename* must contain a single *pattern*.

--nonmatching   −f   Reverses the sense of the test done on *patterns* when extracting files from an archive. Files are extracted from the archive only if they do not match any of the *patterns*.

--file=archive   −F *archive*   Uses *archive* as the archive file instead of reading its name from standard input (when extracting files from an archive) or writing to standard output (when creating an archive). You can use this option to access a device on another system on your network, in the same way that the −f option allows you to do with tar (page 1343).

--link   −l   When possible, this option links files instead of copying them.

--list   −t **table of contents**   Displays a table of contents of the archive. This option works only when you use the −−extract option, although no files are actually extracted from the archive. With the −−verbose option this option causes cpio to display the same information as ls −l.

--preserve-modification-time

−m   Preserves the modification times of files that are extracted from an archive. Without this option the files show the time they were extracted. With this option the created files show the time they had when they were copied into the archive.

--rename   −r   Allows you to rename files as cpio copies them. When cpio prompts you with the name of a file, you respond with the new name. The file is then copied with the new name. If you press RETURN instead, cpio does not copy the file.

--unconditional   −u   Overwrites existing files regardless of their modification times. Without this option cpio will not overwrite a more recently modified file with an older one; it simply displays a warning message.

--verbose   −v   Lists all the files as they are processed. With −−list, it displays a detailed table of contents in a format similar to that used by ls −l.

--help   Displays a list of all options.

Discussion   You can use both ordinary and directory filenames as input when you create an archive. If the name of an ordinary file appears in the input list before the name of its parent directory, the ordinary file appears before its parent directory in the archive as well. This can lead to an avoidable error: When you extract files from the archive, the child has nowhere to go in the file structure if its parent has not yet been extracted.

Making sure that files appear after their parent directories in the archive is not always a solution. One problem occurs if the **−−preserve−modification−time** option is used when extracting files. Because the modification time of a parent directory is updated each time a file within it is created, the original modification time of the parent directory is lost when the first file is written to it.

The solution to this potential problem is to make sure that all the files appear *before* their parent directories when creating an archive *and* to create directories as needed when extracting files from an archive. When you use this technique, directories are extracted only after all the files have been written to them and their modification times are preserved.

With the **−depth** option the find utility generates a list of files with all children appearing in the list before their parent directories. Using this list as input to cpio when you are creating an archive gives you just what you need. (Refer to the first example following.) The **−−make−directories** option causes cpio to create parent directories as needed while it is extracting files from an archive. The **−−preserve−modification−time** option does just what its name says. Using this combination of utilities and options preserves directory modification times through a create/extract sequence.

This way of doing things solves another potential problem. Sometimes a parent directory may not have permissions set so you can extract files into it. When cpio automatically creates the directory with **−−make−directories**, you can be assured of write permission to the directory. When the directory is extracted from the archive (after all the files are written into the directory), it is extracted with its original permissions.

Examples   The first example creates an archive of all the files in Jenny's account, writing the archive to a tape drive supported by the **ftape** driver:

```
$ find /home/jenny -depth -print | cpio -oB >/dev/ftape
```

The find utility produces the filenames that cpio uses to build the archive. The **−depth** option to find causes all entries in a directory to be listed before listing the directory name itself, making it possible for cpio to preserve the original modification times of directories. Use the **−−make-directories** and the **−−preserve-modification-time** when you extract files from this archive (see the following examples). The **−B** option blocks the tape at 5,120 bytes/block.

To check the contents of the archive file and get a detailed listing of all of the files it contains, use

```
$ cpio -itv < /dev/ftape
```

To restore the files that formerly were in the **memo** subdirectory in Jenny's account, use the following command:

```
$ cpio -idm /home/jenny/memo/\* < /dev/ftape
```

The **–d** (**––make-directories**) option is used with cpio in the preceding example to make sure that any subdirectories that were in the **memo** directory are recreated as needed; the **–m** (**––preserve-modification-time**) option preserves the modification times of files and directories. The asterisk in the regular expression is escaped to keep the shell from expanding it.

The final example uses the **–f** option to restore all the files in the archive except those that were formerly in the **memo** subdirectory:

```
$ cpio -ivmdf /home/jenny/memo/\* < /dev/ftape
```

The **–v** option lists the extracted files as cpio processes the archive. This is useful to verify that the expected files are extracted.

crontab

Maintains crontab files

*crontab [–u **user-name**] **filename***
*crontab [–u **user-name**] **options***

A crontab file associates periodic times (such as 14:00 on Wednesdays) with commands. The cron utility executes each command at the specified time. The crontab utility installs, removes, lists, and edits your crontab file.[2] Superuser can process any user's crontab file.

Arguments   The first format copies the contents of ***filename*** (which contains crontab commands) into the crontab file of the user who runs the command. When the user does not have a crontab file, this process creates a new one; when the user has a crontab file, this process overwrites the file. Always use the **–u** option when you run crontab as **root,** even when you are creating a crontab file for **root.** When you replace ***filename*** with a hyphen, crontab reads commands from standard input as you type them or redirect them; end with CONTROL-D.

Options

–u *user-name* user   Specifies the user whose crontab file the command is to work on. Only Superuser can use this option, and Superuser should always use this option.

–e edit   Runs a text editor on the crontab file, enabling you to add, change, or delete entries.

–l list   Displays the contents of the crontab file.

–r remove   Deletes the crontab file.

Notes   This section covers the versions of cron, (**crond**), crontab, and crontab files that were written by Paul Vixie; hence the term *Vixie cron.* This differs from an earlier version of Vixie cron and from the classic SVR3 syntax of cron. This version is POSIX compliant.

---

3. A point of confusion here: There is a utility named crontab. There are files referred to as *crontab files.* But the crontab files are not named crontab; they are named using users' login names. So the file named **alex** could be a crontab file that is edited using crontab.

User crontab files are kept in the **/var/spool/cron** directory, each named with the login name of the user who owns it. Other crontab files are kept in the **/etc/cron.d** directory.

The system utility named cron reads the crontab files and runs the commands. If a command line in a crontab file does not redirect its output, output sent to standard output and error output are mailed to the owner of the file unless you set the **MAILTO** variable within the crontab file. Refer to the example on page 1131.

To make a system administrator's job easier there are directories named **/etc/cron.hourly, /etc/cron.daily, /etc/cron.weekly**, and **/etc/cron.monthly**, each of which holds crontab files which are run by run-parts which in turn are run by the **/etc/crontab** file. Each of these directories has files in it, each of which executes system tasks at the interval named by the directory. Superuser can add files to these directories instead of adding lines to **root**'s crontab file. The **/etc/crontab** file looks like this:

```
$ cat /etc/crontab
SHELL=/bin/bash
PATH=/sbin:/bin:/usr/sbin:/usr/bin
MAILTO=root
HOME=/

# run-parts
01 * * * * root run-parts /etc/cron.hourly
02 4 * * * root run-parts /etc/cron.daily
22 4 * * 0 root run-parts /etc/cron.weekly
42 4 1 * * root run-parts /etc/cron.monthly
```

Each entry in a crontab file begins with five fields that specify when the command is to run (minute, hour, day of the month, month, and day of the week). An asterisk appearing in place of a number is interpreted by cron as a wildcard representing all possible values. In the day-of-the-week field, you can use either 7 or 0 to represent Sunday.

It is a good practice to start cron jobs a variable number of minutes before or after the hour, half hour, or quarter hour. When you start them at these times, it is less likely that many processes will start at the same time and thus overload the machine.

When cron starts (usually when the system is booted), it reads into memory all the crontab files. The cron utility mostly sleeps but wakes up once a minute, reviews all the crontab entries it has stored in memory, and runs whichever ones are due to be run that minute.

Superuser determines which users can run crontab by creating and removing the **/etc/cron.allow** and **/etc/cron.deny** files and putting entries in and removing entries from these files. When you create a **cron.deny** file with no entries and there is no **cron.allow** file, everyone will be able to use crontab. When the **cron.allow** file exists, only users listed therein can use crontab, regardless of **cron.deny**. Otherwise, list in the **cron.allow** file the users you want to be able to use crontab and in **cron.deny** those you do not want to be able to use it.[4]

Example   The following example lists the contents of Jenny's crontab file (**/var/spool/cron/jenny**) by using a **crontab –l** command. All the scripts that Jenny runs are in her **~/bin** directory. The first line sets the **MAILTO** variable to a l ex so that Alex gets all output (from Jenny's crontab file) that is not redirected. The **satjob** script runs every Saturday (day 6) at 2:05 A.M., **twice.week** runs at 12:02 on Sunday and Thursday mornings, and **twice.day** runs twice a day, every day, at 10 A.M. and 4 P.M.

```
$ who am i
jenny

$ crontab -l
MAILTO=alex
05 02 * * 6        $HOME/bin/sat.job
00 02 * * 0,4      $HOME/bin/twice.week
05 10,16 * * *     $HOME/bin/twice.day
```

To add an entry to your crontab file, run the crontab utility with the **–e** (edit) option.

---

4. Listing a user in **cron.deny** is not necessary because, if there is a **cron.allow** file and the user is not listed in it, the user will not be able to use crontab anyway.

cut

Selects characters or fields from input lines

cut [**options**] [**file–list**]

The cut utility selects characters or fields from lines of input and writes them to standard output. Characters and fields are numbered starting with 1.

Arguments   The **file–list** is a list of ordinary files. If omitted, cut reads from standard input.

Options

––characters=clist –c **clist**   Selects the characters given by the column numbers in **clist**. The value of **clist** is one or more comma-separated column numbers or column ranges. A range is specified by separating two column numbers with a hyphen.

––fields=flist –f **flist**   Selects the fields specified in **flist**. The value of **flist** is one or more comma-separated field numbers or field ranges. A range is specified by separating two field numbers with a hyphen. The field delimiter is a TAB character unless you use the **–d** option to change it.

––delimiter=dchar –d **dchar**   Use character **dchar** as a delimiter when using the **–f** option. The default delimiter is the TAB character. Quote characters as necessary to protect them from shell expansion. If this option is used and more than one field is selected from the input lines, cut uses **dchar** to separate the output fields.

Notes   Although limited in functionality, cut is easy to learn and use and is a good choice when columns and fields can be selected without pattern matching. Sometimes cut is used with paste (page 1270).

Examples   For the following two examples, assume that the ls command with the **–l** option produces the following output in the working directory:

```
$ ls -l
total 148
-rwxrwxrwx   1 alex      group        123 Jan 31  2001 countout
-rwxrw-r--   1 alex      group       2065 Aug 16 14:48 headers
```

```
-rw-rw-r--   1 root    root         72 May 24 11:44 memo
-rwxrw-r--   1 alex    group       715 Mar  2 16:30 memos_save
-rw-rw-rw-   1 alex    group        14 Jan  8 2001 tmp1
-rw-rw-rw-   1 alex    group        14 Jan  8 2001 tmp2
-rw-rw-r--   1 alex    group       218 Nov 27 2002 typescript
```

The following command outputs the permissions of the files in the working directory. The cut utility with the **–c** option specifies that characters 2 through 10 be selected from each input line. The characters in this range are written to standard output:

```
$ ls -l | cut -c2-10
otal 148
rwxrwxrwx
rwxrw-r--
rw-rw-r--
rwxrw-r--
rw-rw-rw-
rw-rw-rw-
rw-rw-r--
```

The next command outputs the size and name of each file in the working directory. This time the **–f** option selects the fifth and ninth fields from the input lines. The **–d** option tells cut that SPACEs, not TABs, delimit fields in the input. The tr command (page 1362) with the **–s** option changes sequences of more than one SPACE character into a single SPACE; otherwise, cut counts the extra SPACE characters as separate fields:

```
$ ls -l | tr -s ' ' ' ' | cut -f5,9 -d' '
123 countout
2065 headers
72 memo
715 memos_save
14 tmp1
14 tmp2
218 typescript
```

The last example displays a list of full names as stored in the fifth field of the **/etc/passwd** file. The **–d** option specifies that the colon character be used as the field delimiter:

```
$ cat /etc/passwd
root:x:0:0:Root:/:/bin/sh
jenny:x:401:50:Jenny Chen:/home/jenny:/bin/zsh
alex:x:402:50:Alex Watson:/home/alex:/bin/bash
scott:x:504:500:Scott Adams:/home/scott:/bin/tcsh
hls:x:505:500:Helen Simpson:/home/hls:/bin/bash
$ cut -d: -f5 /etc/passwd
Root
Jenny Chen
Alex Watson
Scott Adams
Helen Simpson
```

CVS

Manages concurrent access to files in a hierarchy

*cvs [**general-options**]*
*cvs-command [**specific-options**] [**file-list**]*

The cvs (Concurrent Versions System) utility is built on RCS. Like RCS, cvs stores successive revisions of files efficiently. It also ensures that access to files by multiple developers is done in a controlled manner that produces predictable results.

RCS has been extended by cvs in two significant ways that make it attractive for large-project development. One extension shifts the unit of focus from individual files to entire directories of files. This makes cvs a better choice when the project files are naturally organized in a tree structure and when groups of files corresponding to subtrees are conveniently treated together. Another extension permits more than one user to work simultaneously on a given file. This makes it unnecessary to wait for a file to become unlocked and encourages the independent development of separate portions of a source file.

See page 879 and the cvs man page for more information about the cvs utility. The authoritative work on cvs is *Version Management with CVS* by Per Cederqvist et al. Use a search engine to look up Cederqvist to find it.

Arguments   The *cvs-command* can be any one of the following commands (refer to "The cvs-commands" on page 1136). The *file-list* is a list of one or more directories or ordinary files. In most cases directory filenames represent all files and subdirectories within the directory.

Options   The two kinds of options in cvs are *general-options*, which pertain to the overall behavior of the cvs utility, and *specific-options*, which alter the behavior of an individual *cvs-command*. The *general-options* must appear on the command line before the *cvs-command*, whereas *specific-options* follow the *cvs-command*. Many of the *specific-options* are applicable to more than one *cvs-command* (for example, –m message).

General Options

--help [*command*]   –H   Displays information about a *cvs-command*. Without *command* displays information on how to get more help.

−n   **no change**   Does *not* modify the source repository or any other directories or files but does attempt to display the same information as if the command were run without the **−n** option. This allows you to preview the effects of a command without the risk of unexpected changes. Use with the **−t** option for a detailed trace of the execution of the *cvs-command*.

−q   **quiet**   Suppresses output that is informative only; output that flags errors or potential errors is still displayed. Use **−Q** if you want even less information.

−d *dir*   **directory**   Specifies the absolute pathname of a directory to use as the root of the source repository. Without this option, cvs assumes that the root of the repository is the value of the environment variable **CVSROOT**.

−t   **trace**   Causes cvs to trace the execution of a *cvs-command*. This option displays information detailing the various steps during execution. You can use this option to learn about the effects of a *cvs-command*. If you want to protect your files from unexpected changes while using this option, use the **−n** option as well.

Specific Options

These options work with the *cvs-commands* described in the next section.

−m *message*   **message**   Allows you to enter a message on the command line. With the **add** command, you enter a description of the file. With the **commit** and **import** commands, you enter a log message. Without this option, cvs uses an empty description.

−D *datestr*   **date**   With the **checkout, diff, export,** or **update** commands, specifies that a revision be dated on or before the date given by *datestr*. Most familiar formats are accepted for *datestr*, which should be quoted to protect it from the shell. This option implies the **−P** option.

−d   **delete**   With the **release** command causes cvs to delete files from the source repository but warns you if any files need updating first and prompts for your consent. The deletion is performed only if you enter **y** or **yes**.

−l   **local**   Suppresses the default recursive behavior of the **checkout, commit, diff, export, remove,** and **update** commands.

−r *revision*   With the **add, checkout, commit,** and **diff** commands, specifies a *revision*.

−P   **prune**   When you check out or update a module, the source repository may contain directories that once contained files but that have since become empty. With the **checkout** or **update** command, this option causes cvs to remove your copies of empty directories in the hierarchy. This option is implied if the **−D date** option is present.

The *cvs-commands*

The common *cvs-commands* follow, along with a brief description of each. The only *cvs-commands* that modify the source repository are **import** and **commit**; all others affect copies of files belonging to individual users.

add *file-list*   Marks one or more directory or ordinary files for addition to the source repository. The addition of a marked file is reflected in the source repository only when the filename is given as an argument to a **commit** command. This can occur anytime after the file has been marked with **add**.

Files marked for addition to the source repository must reside in a module that has been checked out from the source repository; the new file assumes the same relative position in the repository hierarchy as its counterpart in the user's working copy of the module.

To execute **add**, you must be in the directory containing the file that you want to add. The **add** command is not recursive, so the name of each file you want to add must appear in the *file-list* of an **add** command. Without the **–m** option, **add** uses an empty description.

checkout *module-list*   Checks out a module or modules from the source repository. By default, **checkout** recursively creates all subdirectories and files in a module in the working directory. All names in *module-list* must be given relative to **CVSROOT** unless you use **–d** to specify another source repository.

A synonym for **checkout**, **co**, is usually called with a single nonoption argument.

commit [*file-list*]   Modifies the source repository. This option adds files that have been marked for addition with the **add** command, removes files that have been marked for removal with the **remove** command, and incorporates the changes in your working copies into the source repository. The *file-list* is optional; without it **commit** looks at all the files in the working directory, committing only those that have been marked for addition or marked for removal (provided they have also been physically removed) and those that have undergone changes. The **commit** command aborts if your copy of the source repository needs updating; in this case you must first execute an **update** command to make your copies current. Unless you give a **–m** option with the **commit** command, you are put into the editor to enter a log message.

A synonym for **commit** is **ci**.

diff [*file-list*]   With no *file-list* compares each working file in the working directory with the revision in the source repository used during checkout of the file. Giving a file in *file-list* tells **diff** to compare that file with the copy in the source repository used during checkout. The **diff** command is based on the RCS command **rcsdiff**, which itself calls the GNU/Linux **diff** utility. See **rcsdiff** (page 878) for more information about other options that you can use with the **cvs diff** command.

export *module-list* Similar to **checkout** except that no administrative directories are included with the module. The option **–D datestr** is required with this command. See the following "Discussion" section.

import *repository ventag reltag*

Initializes the source repository with a directory hierarchy or installs a modified module. Before you give the **import** command, you must be in the root of the directory containing the files in the new module. When this command is given, the working directory hierarchy is stored in **CVSROOT/***repository*; *repository* is often a subdirectory of **CVSROOT** but may be an arbitrary pathname relative to **CVSROOT**.

An error results if you do not give the two arguments *ventag* (vendor tag) and *reltag* (release tag)—both on page 1138. However, the values given for these arguments are usually insignificant unless you are importing a module from an outside source.

release *module-list* Provides a safe way to remove CVS files from a directory module, without the unexpected removal of files that have been added to a directory since checkout or that have been modified but not updated. Running **release** without the **–d** option amounts to a "dry run"; no files are deleted, but the same information is displayed on the screen.

If a file needs updating or if a file has been added to the module since the last checkout, you must give your consent before **release** deletes the file.

remove *file-list* Marks one or more directory or ordinary files for removal from the source repository. The file is removed from the repository only when the file is given as an argument to **commit**; this can occur anytime after the file has been marked for removal. At the point that the **commit** command is given, the designated files must have been physically removed from the user's directory.

Unlike the **add** command, the **remove** command is recursive. To restrict the operation of the **remove** command to the working directory, use the **–l** (local) option.

update [*file-list*] Incorporates changes made to the source repository into your working copies. If no changes have been made to the source repository since you checked out your copies, **update** does nothing. Otherwise, **update** attempts to incorporate the changes into your working copies. This is straightforward if you have made no changes to your working copies. If you have modified your module, **update** attempts to **merge** the changes in the repository with your modified working copies. If this is not possible because of overlapping changes, **update** displays the differences between your copy and the one in the source repository. The files in *file-list* may be directory or ordinary files. An empty *file-list* defaults to the working directory.

The **update** display usually includes filenames preceded by single *status* letters. The letter **U** signifies that the working copy is up-to-date, the letter **M** means that the working copy has been modified, and the letter **C** means that an overlap has occurred during an attempt to merge.

Discussion   The cvs utility keeps track of multiple versions of files by maintaining a *central copy* of each file in a directory called the *source repository*. The source repository is a GNU/Linux directory and is generally given by the environment variable **CVS-ROOT**. For example, if you are using bash, you might include the following line in your **.profile** file to define **CVSROOT**:

```
export CVSROOT="/usr/local/src/master"
```

(Any pathname may be assigned to **CVSROOT**; the value given here is not required.) If **CVSROOT** is undefined, you need to use **–d** to name a source repository. The **–d** option can also be used if you want to override **CVSROOT**.

Although built on RCS (pages 871 and 1295), cvs does not use the RCS locking mechanism to ensure exclusive access to files; instead, users modify copies of cvs source files that the cvs **checkout** command creates in their own directory hierarchy. Usually the unit checked out is a *module*—a group of related files stored in a directory within the source repository hierarchy. Users submit periodic changes to the source repository by using the **commit** command. Automatic merging of source repository files with the user's working copies is done when necessary.

Revisions in cvs are named in the same way as revisions in RCS—with digits separated by a period(.). The rightmost digit of the revision number is incremented when a **commit** occurs, and such terms as *trunk* and *branch* (page 871) retain the meaning they have in RCS. The RCS functions also have counterparts in cvs.

When you create a module, you can identify the source of the module through a *vendor tag*, a name you create to help you keep track of the source of the module. This is particularly useful to keep track of the sources of software you get from other places. For example, if you want to import a module consisting of the source code for nvi, you might choose to assign a vendor tag of **Bostic** (Keith Bostic is the author of nvi). Although the choice of the vendor tag is completely arbitrary, you could use this same vendor tag for any other software that Keith has written that you decide to import into your directory.

A second tag, called the *release tag*, allows you to name versions of a software package in a similar manner. For example, if the version of nvi that you want to import into the repository is 1.71, you can give a release tag such as **NVI_1_71**. Then, if you later decide to add version 1.75 of nvi to the repository, you could import that version with vendor tag **Bostic** and release tag **NVI_1_75**.

There is a difference between *checking out* and *exporting* a module. When you check out a module, cvs assumes that you are doing so in order to work on the module and that you plan on checking in a new revision at a later time. The cvs utility includes in the working directory for the checked-out module some administrative files that make it easier to check the work back in later. (These files are particularly important to cvs if several people have checked out the same revision to work on at the same time.) When you export a module, cvs assumes that you are doing so in order to send that particular revision to someone else and that you do not plan on checking it back in later. In this case cvs does not include the administrative files as part of the working directory.

Notes   In the source repository the **modules** file is an administrative file that stores the definitions for all the modules in the repository. This file—itself defined as a module—should be checked out of the source repository and edited when defining a new module. See the cvs documentation for more information.

You can set the environment variable **CVSEDITOR** to specify an editor to use when entering log messages. If **CVSEDITOR** is undefined, the environment variable **EDITOR** is used instead.

When a file is removed by using **remove**, it is copied to the **Attic** directory within the source repository. This makes it possible to retrieve a file that was removed earlier from the repository.

Examples   For the following examples assume that the environment variable **CVSROOT** gives the pathname of the source repository and that the directory in which the user stores working copies of cvs modules has been assigned to the variable **CVSWORK**.

The following commands show what modules are stored in the source repository and which ones are currently checked out by the user:

```
$ ls $CVSROOT
CVSROOT         Project2        dulce           testgen
Project1        cvs             laptop          workshop_demos
$ cd $CVSWORK
$ ls
Project1  Project2  dulce     testgen
```

Following, **checkout** copies the module **workshop_demos** to the user's working directory. Because this is the first checkout of **workshop_demos** in the **CVSWORK** directory, the **workshop_demos** subdirectory is created, and each file within it is listed after its parent directory. The letter **U** to the left of each file signifies that the file is up-to-date (with respect to the source repository) after the checkout.

An ls command following the checkout shows that the directory **workshop_demos** has been created:

```
$ cvs checkout workshop_demos
cvs checkout: Updating workshop_demos
U workshop_demos/.transmit
U workshop_demos/README
...
cvs checkout: Updating workshop_demos/present.3
U workshop_demos/present.3/demo2_a.c
U workshop_demos/present.3/demo2_b.c
U workshop_demos/present.3/demo2_c.c
$ ls
Project1        Project2        dulce           testgen
workshop_demos
```

In the next example the user changes directories to the **workshop_demos** directory. The ls command lists the **newdemo4** file, and the user edits it. After the file is edited, the version of **newdemo4** differs from the one in the source repository.

The cvs **update** command displays the letter **M** to the left of **newdemo4**, signifying that the user's working copy has undergone modification. In this case the copy of **newdemo4** in the source repository has not changed since the user checked it out. When the copy of a file in the source repository also undergoes modification, the **update** command attempts to merge the changes into the user's working copy, displaying a message if the merge succeeds.

After the **update** command, the cvs **commit** command checks in the changes to **newdemo4** into the source repository.

```
$ cd workshop_demos
$ ls
CVS          newdemo3    newdemo5    present.2
README       newdemo4    present.1   present.3
$ vi newdemo4
...
newdemo4: 92 lines, 1483 characters.
$ cvs update newdemo4
M newdemo4
$ cvs commit -m "added side dirs." newdemo4
Checking in newdemo4;
/usr/local/src/master/workshop_demos/newdemo4,v  <--  newdemo4
new revision: 1.4; previous revision: 1.3
done
```

In the next example the file **newdemo3** is deleted. An error occurs the first time the cvs **remove** command is given because cvs requires that the file be physically deleted from the directory first. The rm utility does this, and then the cvs **remove** command is given again. The **commit** command removes the file from the source repository. The final ls command displays the contents of the **workshop_demos** module in the source repository after the removal of **newdemo3**:

```
$ cvs remove newdemo3
cvs remove: file 'newdemo3' still in working directory
cvs remove: 1 file exists; use 'rm' to remove it first
$ rm newdemo3
$ ls
CVS          README      newdemo4    newdemo5    present.1   present.2
present.3
$ cvs remove newdemo3
cvs remove: scheduling 'newdemo3' for removal
cvs remove: use 'cvs commit' to remove this file permanently
$ cvs commit newdemo3
/tmp/10806aaa: 10 lines, 316 characters.
$ ls $CVSROOT/workshop_demos
Attic        README,v    newdemo4,v  newdemo5,v  present.1   present.2
present.3
```

date

Displays or sets the time and date

*date [**options**] [+**format** |**newdate**]*

The date utility displays the time and date. Superuser can use this utility to change the system clock.

Arguments   When Superuser specifies a *newdate*, the system changes the system clock to reflect the new date. The *newdate* argument has the format

> *nnddhhmm[[cc]yy][.ss]*

Where *nn* is the number of the month (01–12), *dd* is the day of the month (01–31), *hh* is the hour based on a 24-hour clock (00–23), and *mm* is the minutes (00–59). When you change the date, you must specify at least these fields.

The optional *cc* specifies the first two digits of the year (the value of the century minus 1), and *yy* specifies the last two digits of the year. You can specify *yy* or *ccyy* following *mm*. When you do not specify a year, date assumes that the year has not changed.

You can specify the number of seconds past the start of the minute with *.ss*.

The *+format* argument specifies the format of the output of date. Following the + sign, you can specify a format string consisting of field descriptors and text. The field descriptors are preceded by percent signs, and each one is replaced by its value in the output. See the Table III-8 for a list of the field descriptors.

Field Descriptor	**‖ table III-8**
%a	Abbreviated weekday—Sun to Sat
%A	Unabbreviated weekday—Sunday to Saturday
%b	Abbreviated month—Jan to Dec
%B	Unabbreviated month—January to December
%c	Date and time in default format used by date

Field Descriptor (Continued) || table III-8

%d	Day of the month—01 to 31
%D	Date in mm/dd/yy format
%H	Hour—00 to 23
%I	Hour—00 to 12
%j	Julian date (day of the year—001 to 366)
%m	Month of the year—01 to 12
%M	Minutes—00 to 59
%n	NEWLINE character
%P	A.M. or P.M.
%r	Time in A.M./P.M. notation
%S	Seconds—00 to 59
%s	Number of seconds since the beginning of Jan. 1, 1970
%t	TAB character
%T	Time in HH:MM:SS format
%w	Day of the week—0 to 6 (0=Sunday)
%y	Last two digits of the year—00 to 99
%Y	Year in four-digit format (for example, 2005)
%Z	Time zone (for example, PDT)

By default date zero fills numeric fields. Place an underscore (_) immediately following the percent sign (%) for a specific field to cause date to blank fill the field and with a hyphen (–) to cause date not to fill the field at all.

The date utility assumes that in a format string, any character that is not a percent sign, an underscore or a hyphen following the percent sign, or a field descriptor is ordinary text and copies it to standard output. You can use ordinary text to add punctuation to the date and to add labels (for example, you can put the word DATE:

in front of the date). Surround the format argument with single quotation marks if it contains SPACEs or other characters that have a special meaning to the shell.

Options

--date=*datestring* –d *datestring*   Displays the date specified by ***datestring***, not the current date. Does not change the system clock.

--utc *or*--universal –u   Displays or sets the date in Universal Coordinated Time (*UTC* (page 1500)—also called Greenwich Mean Time—GMT). The system operates in UTC, and date converts it to and from the local standard time and daylight saving time.

--help help   Summarizes how to use the date command, including a complete list of the field descriptors and their meanings.

Note

If you set up a locale database, date uses that database to substitute terms appropriate to your *locale* (page 1477).

Examples

The first example shows how to set the date for 2:07:30 P.M. on August 19 without changing the year:

```
# date 08191407.30
Sat Aug 19 14:07:30 PDT 2006
```

The next example shows the *format* argument, which causes date to display the date in a commonly used format:

```
$ date '+Today is %h %d, %Y'
Today is Aug 19, 2006
```

dd

Converts and copies a file

*dd [**arguments**]*

The dd (device-to-device copy) utility converts and copies a file. The primary use of dd is to copy files to and from such devices as tape and floppy drives. Often dd can handle the transfer of information to and from other operating systems when other methods fail. This utility is often used to create a GNU/Linux boot disk from a file containing an image of the boot disk. A rich set of arguments gives you precise control over the characteristics of the transfer.

Arguments   By default dd copies standard input to standard output.

if=*filename*   **input file**   Reads from *filename* instead of from standard input. You can use a device name for *filename* to read directly from that device.

of=*filename*   **output file**   Writes to *filename* instead of to standard output. You can use a device name for filename to write directly to that device.

bs=*n*   **block size**   Reads and writes *n* bytes at a time. This argument overrides the **ibs** and **obs** arguments.

ibs=*n*   **input block size**   Reads *n* bytes at a time.

obs=*n*   **output block size**   Writes *n* bytes at a time.

cbs=*n*   **conversion block size**   When performing data conversion during the copy, converts *n* bytes at a time.

skip=*numblocks*   Skips *numblocks* blocks of input before starting to copy. The size of each block is the number of bytes given in the **ibs** argument.

seek=*numblocks*   Skips *numblocks* blocks of output before writing any output. The size of each block is the number of bytes given in the **obs** argument.

count=*numblocks*   Restricts to *numblocks* the number of blocks of input that dd copies. The size of each block is the number of bytes given in the **ibs** argument.

conv=*type*[,*type*...]   By applying conversion types in the order given on the command line, converts the data that is being copied. The types of conversions are shown in Table III-9

type	|| table III-9
ascii	Converts EBCDIC-encoded characters to ASCII, allowing you to read tapes written on IBM mainframe and similar computers.
block	Each time a line of input is read (that is, a sequence of characters terminated with a NEWLINE character), outputs a block of text without the NEWLINE. Each output block has the size given in the **obs** or **bs** argument and is created by adding trailing SPACE characters to the text until it is the proper size.
ebcdic	Converts ASCII-encoded characters to EBCDIC, allowing you to write tapes for use on IBM mainframe and similar computers.
unblock	Performs the opposite of the block conversion.
lcase	Converts uppercase letters to lowercase while copying data.
noerror	If a read error occurs, **dd** normally terminates. This conversion allows **dd** to continue processing data. This is useful when trying to recover data from bad media.
ucase	Converts lowercase letters to uppercase while copying data.

Notes   The dd utility allows you to use a shorthand notation to give large numbers as arguments. Appending **c** to a number indicates that the number is multiplied by 512, appending **k** multiplies the number by 1,024, and appending **M** multiplies by 1,048,576. Refer to the man page for a complete list of multipliers.

Examples   The first example shows how to use the dd utility to make an exact copy of a floppy disk by first copying the disk's contents to a file on a hard drive and then, after inserting a fresh disk into the floppy disk drive, copying that file to the floppy disk. This works regardless of what is on the floppy disk. In this case it is a DOS-formatted disk. The copy that results from the second call to dd is also a DOS-formatted disk. The mount, ls, umount sequences at the beginning and end of the example verify that the original disk and the copy hold the same files. The **floppy.copy** file is also an exact copy of the original floppy disk.

```
# mount -t msdos /dev/fd0H1440 /mnt
# ls /mnt
abprint.dat  bti.ini      setup.ins    supfiles.z   wbt.z
adbook.z     setup.exe    setup.pkg    telephon.z
# umount /mnt
# dd if=/dev/fd0 ibs=512 >floppy.copy
2880+0 records in
2880+0 records out
# ls -l floppy.copy
-rw-rw-r--   1 alex       speedy     1474560 Oct 11 05:43 floppy.copy
# dd if=floppy.copy bs=512 of=/dev/fd0
2880+0 records in
2880+0 records out
# mount -t msdos /dev/fd0H1440 /mnt
# ls /mnt
abprint.dat  bti.ini      setup.ins    supfiles.z   wbt.z
adbook.z     setup.exe    setup.pkg    telephon.z
# umount /mnt
```

The second example shows a simple shell script to do a full system backup to a remote system. The shell script uses the ssh utility to run dd on the remote system:

```
# cat backmeup
#! /bin/bash
# Do a full backup to remote tape drive on bravo

machine=bravo
device=/dev/rst0

echo -n "Backing up to $machine using device $device...(be patient)..."
cd /
tar -cf - . | ssh -l hls $machine "dd obs=256k of=$device"
echo "Full backup to $machine ($device) on " $(date) > /etc/last.backup
echo "done."
```

df

Displays disk space usage

df [*options*] [*filesystem-list*]

The df (disk free) utility reports on total and free space on each mounted device. By default, the report is in terms of 1-kilobyte blocks.

Arguments   When you call df without an argument, it reports on the free space on each of the currently mounted devices.

The *filesystem-list* is an optional list of one or more pathnames that specify the filesystems you want a report on. The df utility permits you to refer to a mounted filesystem by its device pathname *or* by the pathname of the directory it is mounted on.

Options

—type=*fstype* –t *fstype*   Reports information only about the filesystems of type *fstype*, such as DOS or NFS.

—inodes –i   Reports the number of inodes that are used and free instead of reporting on blocks.

—human-readable –h   Displays sizes in K (kilobyte), M (megabyte), and G (gigabyte) blocks.

—megabytes –m   Displays sizes in 1-megabyte blocks.

—local –l   Displays local filesystems only.

Examples   Following, df displays information about all the mounted filesystems on a machine:

```
$ df
Filesystem          1k-blocks     Used Available Use% Mounted on
/dev/hda12           1517920     53264   1387548   4% /
/dev/hda1              15522      4846      9875  33% /boot
/dev/hda8            1011928    110268    850256  11% /free1
/dev/hda9            1011928     30624    929900   3% /free2
/dev/hda10           1130540     78992    994120   7% /free3
/dev/hda5            4032092   1988080   1839188  52% /home
/dev/hda7            1011928        60    960464   0% /tmp
/dev/hda6            2522048    824084   1569848  34% /usr
zach:/c              2096160   1811392    284768  86% /zach_c
zach:/d              2096450   1935097    161353  92% /zach_d
```

Next, df is called with the **–l** and **–h** options, generating a human-readable list of local filesystems. All the sizes in this listing are given in terms of megabytes and gigabytes. The NFS mounted filesystems (from **zach**) are not visible:

```
$ df -lh
Filesystem        Size  Used Avail Use% Mounted on
/dev/hda12        1.4G   52M  1.3G   4% /
/dev/hda1          15M  4.7M  9.6M  33% /boot
/dev/hda8         988M  108M  830M  11% /free1
/dev/hda9         988M   30M  908M   3% /free2
/dev/hda10        1.1G   77M  971M   7% /free3
/dev/hda5         3.8G  1.9G  1.8G  52% /home
/dev/hda7         988M   60k  938M   0% /tmp
/dev/hda6         2.4G  805M  1.5G  34% /usr
```

The next example uses 1-megabyte blocks to display information about the **/free2** partition.

```
$ df -m /free2
Filesystem        1M-blocks     Used Available Use% Mounted on
/dev/hda9               988       30       908   3% /free2
```

The final example displays information about NFS filesystems in human-readable terms:

```
$ df -ht nfs
Filesystem        Size  Used Avail Use% Mounted on
zach:/c           2.0G  1.7G  278M  86% /zach_c
zach:/d           2.0G  1.8G  157M  92% /zach_d
```

diff

Displays the differences between two files

*diff [**options**] **file1 file2***
*diff [**options**] **file1 directory***
*diff [**options**] **directory file2***
*diff [**options**] **directory1 directory2***

The diff utility displays line-by-line differences between two files. By default diff displays the differences as instructions that you can use to edit one of the files to make it the same as the other.

Arguments

The *file1* and *file2* are pathnames of the files that diff works on. When the *directory2* argument is used in place of *file2*, diff looks for a file in *directory2* with the same name as *file1*. Similarly, when the directory argument is used in place of *file1*, diff looks for a file in *directory1* with the same name as *file2*. You can use a hyphen in place of *file1* or *file2* to cause diff to use standard input. When you specify two directory arguments, diff compares all the files in *directory1* with the files that have the same simple filenames in *directory2*.

Options

--brief −q   Does not display the differences between lines in the files. Instead, diff reports only that the files differ.

--context [=*lines*] −C *lines* or −c   Displays the sections of the two files that differ, including *lines* lines (default is 3) around each line that differs to show the context. Each line in *file1* that is missing from *file2* is preceded by −; each extra line in *file2* is preceded by +; and lines that have different versions in the two files are marked with !. When lines that differ are within three lines of each other, they are grouped together in the output.

--ed −e   Creates a script for the ed editor, which will edit *file1* to make it the same as *file2*, and sends it to standard output. You must add **w** (write) and **q** (quit) instructions to the end of the script if you are going to redirect input to ed from the script. When you use **--ed**, diff displays the changes in reverse order—changes to the end of the file are listed before changes to the top. This prevents early changes from affecting later changes when the script is used as input to ed. If ed made changes to the top of the file first, the changes might affect later changes to the end of the file. For example, if a line near the top were deleted, subsequent line numbers in the script would be wrong.

--ignore--blank--lines

        −B   Ignores differences that involve only numbers of blank lines.

--ignore-case **−i**   Ignores differences in case when comparing files.

--ignore--space-change

        −b   Ignores blanks (SPACEs and TABs) at the ends of lines and considers other strings of blanks equal.

      −p Shows which C function each change is in.

--recursive **−r**   When using diff to compare the files in two directories, causes the comparisons to extend through subdirectories as well.

--side-by-side **−y**   Displays output in a side-by-side format. This option generates the same output as sdiff. Use the **--width=***columns* option with this option.

--unified[=*lines***]** **−u**   Uses the easier-to-read unified output format. See the discussion of diff on page 67 for more detail and an example. The *lines* is the number of lines of context; the default is three.

      −w **whitespace**   Ignores whitespace when comparing lines.

--width=*columns* **−W** *columns*   Sets the number of columns that diff uses to display the output to *columns*. This option is useful with the **--side-by-side** option. The sdiff utility uses a lowercase w to perform the same function: **−w columns**.

Notes

The sdiff utility is similar to diff, but the output may be easier to read. The **--side-by-side** option to diff produces the same output as sdiff. If you experiment with sdiff, make sure that you use the **−w** *columns* option, which sets the page width to *columns* characters (the default is 130). See the "Examples" section and refer to the diff and sdiff info pages for more information.

Discussion

When you use diff without any options, it produces a series of lines containing Add (**a**), Delete (**d**), and Change (**c**) instructions. Each of these lines is followed by the lines from the file that you need to add, delete, or change. A *less than* symbol (**<**) precedes lines from **file1**. A *greater than* symbol (**>**) precedes lines from **file2**. The diff output is in the format shown Table III-10. A pair of line numbers separated by a comma represents a range of lines; diff uses a single line number to represent a single line.

    The diff utility assumes that you are going to convert *file1* to *file2*. The line numbers to the left of each of the **a**, **c**, or **d** instructions always pertain to *file1*; numbers to the right of the instructions apply to *file2*. To convert *file1* to *file2*, ignore the line numbers to the right of the instructions. (To convert *file2* to *file1*, run diff again, reversing the order of the arguments.)

Instruction	Meaning (to change file1 to file2) table III-10
`line1 a line2,line3` `> lines from file2`	Appends lines from **file2** after line1 in **file1**
`line1,line2 d line3` `< lines from file1`	Deletes line1 through line2 from **file1**

`line1,line2 c`
`line3,line4`
`< lines from file1`
    `---`
`> lines from file 2`
	Changes line1 through line2 in **file1** to lines from **file2**

Examples

The first example shows how diff displays the differences between two short, similar files:

```
$ cat m
aaaaa
bbbbb
ccccc

$ cat n
aaaaa
ccccc

$ diff m n
2d1
< bbbbb
```

The difference between files **m** and **n** is that the second line from file **m** (bbbbb) is missing from file **n**. The first line that diff displays (2d1) indicates that you need to delete the second line from file 1 (**m**) to make it the same as file 2 (**n**). Ignore the numbers following the letters on the instruction lines. (They would apply if you were converting **file2** to **file1**.) The next line diff displays starts with a less than symbol (<), indicating that this line of text is from **file1**. In this example you do not need this information—all you need to know is the line number so that you can delete the line.

The **‑‑side‑by‑side** option and the sdiff utility, both with the output width set to 30 columns (characters), display the same output. In the output a less than symbol points to the extra line in **m** whereas diff/sdiff leaves a blank line in **n** where the extra line would go to make the files the same.

```
$ diff --side-by-side --width=30 m n
aaaaa           aaaaa
bbbbb         <
ccccc           ccccc

$ sdiff -w 30 m n
aaaaa           aaaaa
bbbbb         <
ccccc           ccccc
```

The next example uses the same **m** file and a new file, **p**, to show diff issuing an **a** (append) instruction:

```
$ cat p
aaaaa
bbbbb
rrrrr
ccccc
$ diff m p
2a3
> rrrrr
```

In this example diff issues the instruction 2a3 to indicate that you must append a line to file **m**, after line 2, to make it the same as file **p**. The second line that diff displays indicates that the line is from file **p** (the line begins with **>**, indicating **file2**). In this example you need the information on this line; the appended line must contain the text rrrrr.

The next example uses **m** again, this time with file **r**, to show how diff indicates a line that needs to be changed:

```
$ cat r
aaaaa
-q
ccccc

$ diff m r
2c2
< bbbbb
---
> -q
```

The difference between the two files is in line 2: File **m** contains bbbbb, and file **r** contains -q. Preceding, diff displays 2c2 to indicate that you need to change line 2. After indicating that a change is needed, diff shows that you must change line 2 in file **m** (bbbbb) to line 2 in file **r** (-q) to make the files the same. The three hyphens indicate the end of the text in file **m** that needs to be changed and the start of the text in file **r** that is to replace it.

Comparing the same files using the short forms of the side-by-side and width options (–y and **–W**) yields an easier-to-read result. The pipe symbol (l) indicates that the line on one side has to replace the line on the other side to make the files the same:

```
$ diff -y -W 30 m r
aaaaa                aaaaa
bbbbb            |   -q
ccccc                ccccc
```

The next examples compare the two files **q** and **v**:

```
$ cat q              $ cat v
Monday               Monday
Tuesday              Wednesday
Wednesday            Thursday
Thursday             Thursday
Saturday             Friday
Sunday               Saturday
                     Sundae
```

Running diff in side-by-side mode you can see that Tuesday is missing from file **v** and that Thursday (there are two in file **v**) and Friday are missing from file **q**. The last line of file **q** is Sunday and in **v** it is Sundae: diff indicates that the lines are different. You can change file **q** to be the same as file **v** by removing Tuesday, adding Thursday and Friday, and substituting Sundae from file **v** for Sunday from file **q**. Or you can change file **v** to be the same as file **q** by adding Tuesday, removing Thursday and Friday, and substituting Sunday from file **q** for Sundae from file **v**:

```
$ diff -y -W 30 q v
Monday               Monday
Tuesday          <
Wednesday
Thursday
                 >   Thursday
                 >   Friday
Saturday
Sunday           |   Sundae
```

With the **––context** option (called a *context diff*), diff gives you output that tells you how to turn the first file into the second. The top two lines identify the files and show that **q** is represented by asterisks, whereas **v** is represented by dashes. Following a row of asterisks that indicates the start of a hunk of text is a row of asterisks with the numbers 1,6 in the middle. This line indicates that the instructions in the first section tell you what to remove from or change in file **q**, lines 1 through 6 (that is, all the lines of file **q**; in a longer file it would mark the first hunk). The dash on the second line means that you need to remove the line with Tuesday on it. The line with an exclamation point indicates that you need to replace the line with Sunday on it with the corresponding line from file **v**. The row of dashes with the numbers 1,7 in the middle indicates that the next section tells you which lines from file **v**, lines 1 through 7, you need to add or change in file **q**. You need to add a second line with Thursday and a line with Friday. Again you need to change Sunday in file q to Sundae (from file **v**):

```
$ diff --context q v
*** q   Mon Aug 21 18:26:45 2006
--- v   Mon Aug 21 18:27:55 2006
***************
*** 1,6 ****
  Monday
- Tuesday
  Wednesday
  Thursday
  Saturday
! Sunday
--- 1,7 ----
  Monday
  Wednesday
  Thursday
+ Thursday
+ Friday
  Saturday
! Sundae
```

du

Displays information on disk usage

*du [**options**] [**path-list**]*

The du (disk usage) utility reports how much disk space is occupied by a directory (along with all its subdirectories and files) or a file. By default du displays the number of 1,024-byte blocks that are occupied by the directory or file.

Arguments   Without an argument du displays information about the working directory and its subdirectories and files therein. The **path-list** specifies the directories and files you want information on.

Options   Without any options du displays the total storage used for each argument in **path-list.** For directories du displays this total only after recursively listing the totals for each subdirectory.

--all −a   Displays the space used by all ordinary files along with the totals for each directory.

--total −c   Displays a grand total.

--human-readable −h   Displays sizes in K (kilobyte), M (megabyte), and G (gigabyte) blocks.

--kilobytes −k   Displays sizes in 1-kilobyte blocks.

--megabytes −m   Displays sizes in 1-megabyte blocks.

--one-file-system −x   Reports only on files and directories on the same filesystem as that of the argument being processed.

--summarize −s   Displays only the total for each directory or file you specify on the command line; subdirectory totals are not displayed.

Examples   The following use of du displays size information about subdirectories in the working directory. The last line contains the grand total for the working directory and its subdirectories.

```
$ du
26      ./Postscript
4       ./RCS
47      ./XIcon
4       ./Printer/RCS
12      ./Printer
105     .
```

The total (105) is the number of blocks occupied by all the plain files and directories under the working directory. All files are counted, even though du displays only the sizes of directories.

Next, using the **--summarize** option, du displays only the totals for each of the directories in **/home**:

```
# du --summarize /home/*
68       /home/Desktop
1188     /home/doug
100108   /home/dump
62160    /home/ftp
6540     /home/httpd
16       /home/lost+found
1862104  /home/alex
176      /home/max
88       /home/jenny
4        /home/samba
4        /home/tom
```

Add to the previous example the **--total** option and you get the same listing with a grand total at the end:

```
# du --summarize --total /home/*
68       /home/Desktop
...
4        /home/tom
2032456 total
```

If you do not have read permission for a file or directory that du encounters, du sends a warning to standard error and skips that file or directory. The following example uses the **s** (summarize), **h** (human-readable) and **c** (total) options:

```
$ du -shc /usr/*
112M    /usr/X11R6
161M    /usr/bin
4.0K    /usr/dict
4.0K    /usr/doc
4.0K    /usr/etc
3.9M    /usr/games
...
du: cannot change to directory '/usr/lost+found': Permission denied
30M     /usr/sbin
du: cannot change to directory '/usr/share/ssl/CA': Permission denied
797M    /usr/share
188M    /usr/src
2.2G    total
```

The final example displays, in human-readable format, the total size of all the files the user can read in the **/usr** filesystem. Redirecting standard error to **/dev/null** discards all warnings about files and directories that are unreadable.

```
$ du --human-readable --summarize /usr 2>/dev/null
2.2G    /usr
```

echo

Displays a message

*echo [**options**] **message***

The echo utility copies its arguments, followed by a NEWLINE, to standard output. Each of the shells has an echo builtin ^{bash tcsh zsh} that works similarly to the echo utility.

Arguments   The ***message*** is one or more arguments, which can include quoted strings, ambiguous file references, and shell variables. A SPACE separates each argument from the others. The shell recognizes unquoted special characters in the arguments, for example, the shell expands an asterisk into a list of filenames in the working directory.

Options

–n   Suppresses the NEWLINE terminating the message ^{bash tcsh zsh}.

–e   Enables the interpretation of backslash-escaped characters ^{bash zsh}.

–E   Suppresses the interpretation of backslash-escaped characters (default).

––help   Gives a short summary of how to use echo. The summary includes a list of the escape sequences interpreted by echo. Works only with echo utility (**/bin/echo**) and not with the echo builtins ^{bash tcsh zsh}.

Notes   You can use echo to send messages to the screen from a shell script (refer to Chapter 12). For other uses of echo, see the discussion of echo starting on page 158.

The echo utility and builtins provide an escape notation to represent certain non-printing characters in ***message*** (Table III-11). You must use the **–e** option to get these escape sequences to work with the echo utility and builtin ^{bash zsh}. Do not use the **–e** option with the tcsh echo builtin. Refer to the Optional Section on page 781 if you are using the \c escape sequence or the **–n** option to suppress a trailing NEWLINE in zsh.

Examples   The following examples show how the echo command can be used:

```
$echo "This echo command has one argument."
This echo command has one argument.
```

```
$echo This echo command has six arguments.
This echo command has six arguments.

$ echo -e "This message contains\v a vertical tab."
This message contains
                 a vertical tab
```

Escape Sequence   ‖ table III-11

\a	Bell
\c	Suppress trailing NEWLINE
\n	NEWLINE
\t	HORIZONTAL TAB
\v	VERTICAL TAB
\\	BACKSLASH

The following examples contain messages with the escape sequence **\c**. In the first example, the shell processes the arguments before calling echo. When the shell sees the **\c**, it replaces the **\c** with the character **c**. The last three examples show how to quote the **\c** so that the shell passes it to echo to prevent echo from appending a NEWLINE to the end of the message. The first four examples are run under bash and require the **–e** option. The final example runs under tcsh, which does not use this option:

```
$ echo There is a newline after this.\c
There is a newline after this.c

$ echo -e 'There is no newline after this.\c'
There is no newline after this.$

$ echo -e "There is no newline after this.\c"
There is no newline after this.$

$ echo -e There is no newline after this.\\c
There is no newline after this.$

$ tcsh
tcsh $ echo 'There is no newline after this.\c'
There is no newline after this.$
```

Any of the examples could have used the **–n** option in place of **–e** and **\c**.

expr

Evaluates an expression

expr **expression**

The expr utility evaluates an expression and displays the result. The utility evaluates character strings that represent either numeric or nonnumeric values. Operators are used with the strings to form expressions.

Arguments   The **expression** is composed of strings with operators in between. Each string and operator constitute a distinct argument that you must separate from other arguments with a SPACE. You must quote operators that have special meanings to the shell (for example, the multiplication operator, ✻).

The following list of expr operators is in order of decreasing precedence. Each group of operators has the same precedence. You can change the order of evaluation with parentheses.

: **comparison**   Compares two strings, starting with the first character in each string and ending with the last character in the second string. The second string is a regular expression with an implied caret (^) as its first character. If there is a match, the number of characters in the second string is displayed. If there is no match, zero is displayed.

✻ **multiplication**
/ **division**
% **remainder**   Work only on strings that contain the numerals 0 through 9 and optionally a leading minus sign. Convert strings to integer numbers, perform the specified arithmetic operation on numbers, and convert the result back to a string before displaying it.

+ **addition**
− **subtraction**   Function in the same manner as the preceding group of operators.

< **less than**
<= **less than or equal to**
= *or* == **equal to**
!= **not equal to**
>= **greater than or equal to**
> **greater than**   Relational operators that work on both numeric and nonnumeric arguments. If one or both of the arguments is nonnumeric, the comparison is

nonnumeric, using the machine collating sequence (usually ASCII). If both arguments are numeric, the comparison is numeric. The expr utility displays a 1 (one) if the comparison is true and a 0 (zero) if it is false.

& AND   Evaluates both of its arguments. If neither is 0 or a null string, the value of the first argument is displayed. Otherwise, it displays a 0. You must quote this operator.

| OR   Evaluates the first argument. If it is neither 0 nor a null string, the value of the first argument is displayed. Otherwise, the value of the second argument is displayed. You must quote this operator.

Notes   The expr utility returns an exit status of 0 (zero) if the expression is neither a null string nor the number 0, a status of 1 if the expression is null or 0, and a status of 2 if the expression is invalid.

The expr utility is useful in bash scripts. Because tcsh and zsh have the equivalent of expr built in, tcsh and zsh scripts do not normally use expr.

Although expr and this discussion distinguish between numeric and nonnumeric arguments, all arguments to expr are nonnumeric (character strings). When applicable, expr attempts to convert an argument to a number (for example, when using the + operator). If a string contains characters other than 0 through 9 with an optional leading minus sign, expr cannot convert it. Specifically, if a string contains a plus sign or a decimal point, expr considers it to be nonnumeric. If both arguments are numeric the comparison is numeric. If one is nonnumeric, the comparison is lexicographic.

Examples   The following examples show command lines that call expr to evaluate constants. You can also use expr to evaluate variables in a shell script. In the fourth example, expr displays an error message because of the illegal decimal point in 5.3:

```
$ expr 17 + 40
57
$ expr 10 - 24
-14
$ expr -17 + 20
3
$ expr 5.3 \* 4
expr: non-numeric argument
```

The multiplication (*), division (/), and remainder (%) operators provide additional arithmetic power, as the following examples show. You must quote the multiplication operator (precede it with a backslash) so that the shell does not treat it as a special character (an ambiguous file reference). You cannot put quotation marks around the entire expression because each string and operator must be a separate argument:

```
$ expr 5 \* 4
20
$ expr 21 / 7
3
$ expr 23 % 7
2
```

The next two examples show how you can use parentheses to change the order of evaluation. You must quote each parenthesis and surround the backslash/parenthesis combination with SPACEs:

```
$ expr 2 \* 3 + 4
10
$ expr 2 \* \( 3 + 4 \)
14
```

You can use relational operators to determine the relationship between numeric or nonnumeric arguments. The following command compares two strings to see if they are equal. The expr utility displays a 0 when the relationship is false and a 1 when it is true:

```
$ expr fred == mark
0
$ expr mark == mark
1
```

In the following examples the relational operators which must be quoted, can establish order between numeric or nonnumeric arguments. Again, if a relationship is true, expr displays a 1:

```
$ expr fred \> mark
0
$ expr fred \< mark
1
$ expr 5 \< 7
1
```

The next command compares 5 with **m**. When one of the arguments that expr is comparing with a relational operator is nonnumeric, expr considers the other to be nonnumeric. In this case, because **m** is nonnumeric, expr treats 5 as a nonnumeric argument. The comparison is between the ASCII (on most machines) values of **m** and 5. The ASCII value of **m** is 109 and 5 is 53, so expr evaluates the relationship as true:

```
$ expr 5 \< m
1
```

The next example shows the matching operator determining that the four characters in the second string match four characters in the first string. The expr utility displays a 4:

```
$ expr abcdefghijkl : abcd
4
```

The & operator displays a 0 if one or both of its arguments are 0 or a null string; otherwise it displays the first argument:

```
$ expr '' \& book
0

$ expr magazine \& book
magazine

$ expr 5 \& 0
0

$ expr 5 \& 6
5
```

The | operator displays the first argument if it is not 0 or a null string; otherwise it displays the second argument:

```
$ expr '' \| book
book

$ expr magazine \| book
magazine

$ expr 5 \| 0
5

$ expr 0 \| 5
5

$ expr 5 \| 6
5
```

file

Displays the classification of a file

*file [**option**] **file-list***

The file utility classifies files according to their contents.

Arguments   The *file-list* contains the pathnames of one or more files that file classifies. You can specify any kind of file, including ordinary, directory, and special files, in the *file-list*.

Option

–f *file*   **file**   Takes the names of files to be examined from *file* rather than from the command line. The names of the files must be listed one per line in *file*.

–z   **zip**   Attempts to classify files within a compressed file.

Notes   The file utility can classify more than 5000 file types. Some of the more common file types found on GNU/Linux systems, as displayed by file, are

```
archive
ascii text
c program text
commands text
core file
cpio archive
data
directory
ELF 32-bit LSB executable
empty
English text
executable
```

The file utility uses up to three tests when it attempts to classify a file: filesystem, magic number, and language tests. When file identifies the type of file, it ceases testing. The first test, the filesystem test, examines the return from a **stat** system call to see whether the file is empty or a special file. The *magic number* (page 1478) test looks for data in particular fixed formats near the beginning of the file. The last test, if needed, determines whether the file is a text file, what encoding it uses, and what language it is written in. Refer to the file man page for a more detailed description of how file works. The results of file are not always correct.

Examples

Some examples of file identification follow:

```
/etc/a2ps.cfg:              ASCII English text
/etc/aep:                   directory
/etc/aliases.db:            can't read '/etc/aliases.db' (Permission denied).
/etc/dumpdates:             empty
/etc/grub.conf:             symbolic link to ../boot/grub/grub.conf
/etc/mime-magic:            ASCII C++ program text
/usr/bin/4odb:              a /usr/bin/python script text executable
/usr/bin/a2p:               ELF 32-bit LSB executable, Intel 80386, version 1 (SYSV),
    dynamically linked (uses shared libs), not stripped
/usr/bin/AbiWord:           Bourne shell script text executable
/usr/bin/aclocal:           perl script text executable
/usr/bin/addr2name.awk:     awk script text executable
/usr/bin/authconfig:        symbolic link to consolehelper
/usr/share/aclocal-1.4/error.m4:                ASCII M4 macro language pre-processor text
/usr/share/aclocal-1.5/termios.m4:              ASCII C program text
/usr/share/aclocal/esd.m4:                      ASCII M4 macro language pre-processor text
/usr/share/apacheconf/ApacheBase.py:            ASCII Java program text
/usr/share/apacheconf/apache-config.glade:      XML document text
/usr/share/apacheconf/ApacheConf.py:            a /usr/bin/python script text executable
/usr/share/apacheconf/ApacheControl.pyc:        data
/usr/share/application-registry/gnome-vfs.applications: ASCII text, with very long lines
/usr/share/applications/apacheconf.desktop:     UTF-8 Unicode English text
/usr/share/doc/w3c-libwww-5.4.0/Bug48x.gif:     GIF image data, version 89a, 48 x 48,
/usr/share/doc/w3c-libwww-5.4.0/COPYRIGHT.html: HTML document text
/usr/share/doc/xmltex-20000118/readme.txt.gz:   gzip compressed data, deflated, last
    modified: Wed Dec 31 16:00:00 1969, max compression, os: Unix
/usr/share/doc/zlib-devel-1.1.4/example.c:      ASCII C program text
```

find

Uses criteria to find files

*find [**directory-list**] [**expression**]*

The find utility selects files that are located in specified directory hierarchies and meet criteria specified in an expression.

Arguments   The *directory-list* specifies the directories that find is to search. When find searches a directory, it searches all subdirectories to all levels. When you do not specify a *directory-list*, find searches the working directory.

The *expression* contains criteria, as described in "Criteria," following. The find utility tests each of the files in each of the directories in the *directory-list* to see whether it meets the criteria described by the *expression*. When you do not specify an *expression*, the *expression* defaults to **–print**.

A SPACE separating two criteria is a Boolean AND operator: The file must meet *both* criteria to be selected. A **–or** or **–o** separating the criteria is a Boolean OR operator: The file must meet one or the other (or both) of the criteria to be selected.

You can negate any criterion by preceding it with an exclamation point. The find utility evaluates criteria from left to right unless you group them using parentheses.

Within the *expression* you must quote special characters so that the shell does not interpret them but passes them to find. Special characters that you may frequently use with find are parentheses, brackets, question marks, and asterisks.

Each element within the *expression* is a separate argument. You must separate arguments from each other with SPACEs. There must be a SPACE on both sides of each parenthesis, exclamation point, criterion, or other element. When you use a backslash to quote a special character, the SPACEs go on each side of the pair of characters (for example, " \[").

Criteria   You can use the following criteria within the *expression*. As used in this list, $\pm n$ is a decimal integer that can be expressed as **+n** (more than *n*), **–n** (less than *n*), or *n* (exactly *n*).

–name *filename*   The file being evaluated meets this criterion if *filename* matches its name. You can use ambiguous file references, but you must quote them.

–type *filetype*   The file being evaluated meets this criterion if its file type is the specified *filetype*. You can select a file type from the following list:

b	Block special file
c	Character special file
d	Directory file
f	Ordinary file
l	Symbolic link
p	FIFO (named pipe)
s	Socket

–links ± *n*   The file being evaluated meets this criterion if it has the number of links specified by ± *n*.

–user *name*   The file being evaluated meets this criterion if it belongs to the user with the specified login name, *name*. You can use a numeric user ID in place of *name*.

–group *name*   The file being evaluated meets this criterion if it belongs to the group with the specified group name, *name*. You can use a numeric group ID in place of *name*.

–perm [±]*mode*   The file being evaluated meets this criterion if it has the access permissions given by *mode*. If *mode* is preceded by a minus sign (–), the file access permissions must include all the bits in *mode*. If *mode* is preceded by a plus sign (+), the file access permissions must include at least one of the bits in *mode*. If no plus or minus sign precedes *mode*, the mode of the file must exactly match *mode*. Use either symbolic or octal representation for *mode* (see chmod on page 1103).

–inum *n*   The file being evaluated meets this criterion if its inode number is *n*.

–size ± *n*[c|k]   The file being evaluated meets this criterion if it is the size specified by ± *n*, measured in 512-byte blocks. Follow *n* with the letter **c** to measure files in characters or **k** to measure in kilobytes.

–atime ± *n*   The file being evaluated meets this criterion if it was last accessed the number of days ago specified by ± *n*. When you use this option, find changes the access times of directories it searches.

–mtime ± *n*   The file being evaluated meets this criterion if it was last modified the number of days ago specified by ± *n*.

–newer *filename*   The file being evaluated meets this criterion if it was modified more recently than *filename*.

–print   The file being evaluated always meets this action criterion. When evaluation of the *expression* reaches this criterion, find displays the pathname of the file it is evaluating. If this is the only criterion in the *expression*, find displays the names of all the files in the *directory-list*. If this criterion appears with other criteria, find displays the name only if the preceding criteria are met. If no action criteria appear in the *expression*, **–print** is assumed by default. Refer to the following "Discussion" and "Notes" sections.

–exec *command* \; The file being evaluated meets this action criterion if the *command* returns a zero (*true* value) as an exit status. You must terminate the *command* with a quoted semicolon. A pair of braces ({}) within the *command* represents the name of the file being evaluated. You can use the **–exec** action criterion at the end of a group of other criteria to execute the *command* if the preceding criteria are met. Refer to "Discussion." See xargs on page 1377 for a more efficient way of doing what this option does.

–ok *command* \; This action criterion is the same as **–exec** but displays each *command* to be executed enclosed in angle brackets and executes the *command* only if it receives a **y** or **Y** from standard input.

–depth The file being evaluated always meets this action criterion. It causes find to take action on entries in a directory before it acts on the directory itself. When you use find to send files to the cpio utility, the **–depth** criterion enables cpio to preserve modification times of directories (assuming that you use the **––preserve–modification–time** option to cpio). See "Discussion" and "Examples" under cpio on pages 1126 and 1127.

–xdev The file being evaluated always meets this action criterion. It causes find not to search directories in filesystems other than the one in which the working directory (from the *directory-list* argument) resides. Also **–mount**.

–nouser The file being evaluated meets this criterion if it does not belong to a user who is in the **/etc/passwd** file (that is, the user ID associated with the file does not correspond to a known user of the system).

–nogroup The file being evaluated meets this criterion if it does not belong to a group that is listed in the **/etc/group** file.

–follow When this criterion is specified and find encounters a symbolic link pointing to a directory file, find follows the link.

Discussion   Assume that **x** and **y** are criteria. The following command line never tests whether the file meets criterion **y** if it does not meet criterion **x**. Because the criteria are separated by a SPACE (the Boolean AND operator), once find determines that criterion **x** is not met, the file cannot meet the criteria, so find does not continue testing. You can read the expression as "(test to see) whether the file meets criterion **x** *and* (SPACE means *and*) criterion **y**":

        $ **find dir x y**

The next command line tests the file against criterion **y** if criterion **x** is not met. The file can still meet the criteria, so find continues the evaluation. It is read as "(test to see) whether criterion **x** *or* criterion **y** is met." If the file meets criterion **x**, find does not evaluate criterion **y**, as there is no need:

```
$ find dir x -or y
```

Certain "criteria" do not select files but cause find to take action. The action is triggered when find evaluates one of these *action criteria*. Therefore, the position of an action criterion on the command line, not the result of its evaluation, determines whether find takes the action.

The **–print** action criterion causes find to display the pathname of the file it is testing. The following command line displays the names of *all* the files in the **dir** directory (and all its subdirectories), whether they meet the criterion **x**:

```
$ find dir -print x
```

The following command line displays only the names of the files in the **dir** directory that meet criterion **x**:

```
$ find dir x -print
```

This common use of **–print** after the testing criteria is the default action criterion. The following command line does the same thing as the previous one:

```
$ find dir x
```

Note   You can use the **–a** operator between criteria for clarity. This operator is a Boolean AND operator, just as the SPACE is.

Examples   The following command line finds the files in the working directory and subdirectories that have filenames that begin with **a**. The command uses a period to designate the working directory. To prevent the shell from interpreting the ambiguous file reference, it is enclosed within quotation marks:

```
$ find . -name 'a*'
```

If you omit the *directory-list* argument, find searches the working directory. The following command line performs the same function as the preceding one without specifying the working directory:

```
$ find -name 'a*'
```

The following command line sends a list of selected filenames to the cpio utility, which writes them to tape. The first part of the command line ends with a pipe symbol, so the shell expects another command to follow and displays a secondary prompt (**>**) before accepting the rest of the command line. You can read this find command as "find, in the root directory and all subdirectories (**/**), ordinary files (**–type f**) that have been modified within the past day (**–mtime –1**), with the exception of files whose names are suffixed with .o (**! –name '∗.o'**)." (An object file carries a **.o** suffix and usually does not need to be preserved as it can be recreated from the corresponding program source file.)

```
$ find / -type f -mtime -1 ! -name '*.o' -print |
> cpio -oB > /dev/ftape
```

The following command line finds, displays the filenames of, and deletes the files in the working directory and subdirectories named **core** or **junk**:

```
$ find . \( -name core -o -name junk \) -print -exec rm {} \;
.
.
```

The parentheses and the semicolon following **–exec** are quoted so that the shell does not treat them as special characters. SPACEs separate the quoted parentheses from other elements on the command line. Read this find command as "find, in the working directory and subdirectories (**.**), files named **core** (**–name core**) *or* (**–o**) **junk** (**–name junk**) [if a file meets these criteria, continue with] *and* (SPACE) print the name of the file (**–print**) *and* (SPACE) delete the file (**–exec rm {}**)."

The next shell script uses find with grep to identify files that contain a particular string. This script enables you to look for a file when you remember its contents but cannot remember its filename. The **finder** script locates files in the working directory and subdirectories that contain the string specified on the command line. The **–type f** criterion is necessary so that find passes grep only the names of ordinary files, not directory files:

```
$ cat finder
find . -type f -exec grep -l "$1" {} \;
$ finder "Executive Meeting"
./january/memo.0102
./april/memo.0415
```

When called with the string Executive Meeting, **finder** locates two files containing that string: **./january/memo.0102** and **./april/memo.0415**. The period (**.**) in the pathnames represents the working directory; that is, **january** and **april** are subdirectories of the working directory.

The next command finds in two user directories the files that are larger than 100 blocks (**–size +100**) and have been accessed only more than five days ago—that is, have not been accessed within the past five days (**–atime +5**). This **find** command then asks whether you want to delete the file (**–ok rm {}**). You must respond to each of these queries with a **y** (for *yes*) or **n** (for *no*). The rm command works only if you have execute and write access permission to the directory:

```
$ find /home/alex /home/barbara -size +100 -atime +5 -ok rm {} \;
< rm ... /home/alex/notes >? y
< rm ... /home/alex/letter >? n
.
.
.
```

In the next example, **/home/alex/memos** is a symbolic link to Jenny's directory named **/home/jenny/memos**. When you use the **–follow** option with find, the symbolic link is followed, and the contents of that directory are searched:

```
$ ls -l /home/alex
lrwxrwxrwx  1 alex    pubs     17 Aug 19 17:07 memos -> /home/jenny/memos
-rw-r--r--  1 alex    pubs   5119 Aug 19 17:08 report

$ find /home/alex -print
/home/alex
/home/alex/memos
/home/alex/report
/home/alex/.profile

$ find /home/alex -follow -print
/home/alex
/home/alex/memos
/home/alex/memos/memo.817
/home/alex/memos/memo.710
/home/alex/report
/home/alex/.profile
```

finger

Displays information about users

*finger [**options**] [**user-list**]*

The finger utility displays the login names of users, together with their full names, terminal device numbers, the times they logged in, and other information. The *options* control how much information finger displays, and the *user-list* specifies which users finger displays information about. The finger utility can retrieve information from local and remote systems.

Arguments   Without any arguments, finger provides a short (–s) report on users who are logged in on the local system. When you specify a *user-list*, finger provides a long (–l) report on each of the users in the *user-list*.

   If the name includes an at sign (@), the finger utility interprets the name following the @ as the name of a remote host to contact over the network. If there is also a name in front of the @ sign, finger provides information on that particular user on the remote system.

Options

   –l long   Displays detailed information (the default display when *user-list* is present).

   –m match   If a *user-list* is specified, displays entries only for those users whose *login* names match the names given in *user-list*. Without this option the *user-list* names match *login* and *full* names.

   –p plan and project   Does not display the contents of **.plan** and **.project** files for users. Because these files may contain escape sequences that can change the behavior of your display, you may not wish to view them. Normally the long listing of finger shows you the contents of these files if they exist in the user's home directory.

   –s short   Provides a short report for each user. Same as no *options* and no *user-list*.

Discussion   The long report provided by the finger utility includes the user's login name, full name, home directory location, and login shell, followed by information about when the user last logged in on the system and how long it has been since the user last typed on the keyboard or received and read electronic mail. After extracting this information from various system files, the finger utility then displays the contents of files named **.plan** and **.project** in the user's home directory. It is up to each user to create and maintain these files, which usually provide more information about the user (such as telephone number, postal mail address, schedule, interests, and so forth).

The short report generated by finger is similar to that provided by the w utility; it includes the user's login name, full name, the device number of the user's terminal, how much time has elapsed since the user last typed on the terminal keyboard, the time the user logged in, and the location of the user's terminal. If the user has logged in over the network, the name of the remote system is identified as the user's location.

Notes

When you specify a network address, the finger utility works by querying a standard network service that runs on the remote system. Although this service is supplied with Red Hat Linux, some sites choose not to run it (to minimize load on their systems, as well as possible security risks, or simply to maintain privacy). If you try to use finger to get information on someone at such a site, the result may be an error message or nothing at all. The remote system determines how much information to share with your system and in what format. As a result, the report displayed for any given system may differ from the examples shown. See also "finger: Lists Users on the System" on page 81.

Examples

The first example displays information on all the users currently logged in on the system:

```
$ finger
Login    Name                  Tty    Idle  Login Time    Office      Office
Phone
alex     Alex Watson           tty1   13:29 Jun 22 21:03
hls      Helen Simpson        *pts/1  13:29 Jun 22 21:02 (:0)
jenny    Jenny Chen            pts/2        Jun 23 07:47 (bravo.tcorp.com)
```

In the example, the asterisk (*) in front of the name of Helen's terminal (TTY) line indicates that she has blocked others from sending messages directly to her terminal (see mesg, page 87). A long report displays the string messages off for users who have disabled messages.

The next two examples cause finger to contact the remote system named **kudos** over the network for information:

```
$ finger @kudos
[kudos]
Login    Name                  Tty     Idle  Login Time   Office     Office
Phone
alex     Alex Watson           tty1    23:15  Jun 22 11:22
roy      Roy Wong              pts/2          Jun 22 11:22

$ finger watson@kudos
[kudos]
Login: alex                          Name: Alex Watson
Directory: /home/alex                Shell: /bin/zsh
On since Sat Jun 22 11:22 (PDT) on tty1,  idle 23:22
Last login Sun Jun 23 06:20 (PDT) on ttyp2 from speedy
Mail last read Thu Jun 20 08:10 2002 (PDT)
Plan:
For appointments contact Jenny Chen, x1963.
```

fmt

Formats text very simply

*fmt [**option**] [**file-list**]*

The fmt utility does simple text formatting by attempting to make all nonblank lines nearly the same length.

Arguments The fmt utility reads all the files in *file-list* and prints a formatted version of their contents to standard output. If you do not give any filenames, fmt reads standard input.

Options

--uniform-spacing –u Changes the output so that one SPACE is between words; and two SPACES are between sentences.

--width=n –n Changes the output line width to *n* characters. Without this option, fmt tries to keep output lines close to 75 characters wide.

Notes The fmt utility works by moving NEWLINE characters. The indentation of lines, as well as the spacing between words, is left intact.

This utility is often used to format text while you are using an editor, such as vi. For example, you can format a paragraph in command mode of the vi editor by positioning the cursor at the top of the paragraph and then entering !}fmt –60. This replaces the paragraph with the result of feeding it through fmt, specifying a width of 60 characters.

Example The following example shows how fmt attempts to make all the lines the same length. The –50 option gives a target line length of 50 characters:

```
$ cat memo
One factor that is important to remember while administering the dietary
intake of Charcharodon carcharias is that there is, at least from
the point of view of the subject,
```

very little
differentiating the prepared morsels being proffered from your digits.

In other words, don't feed the sharks!

```
$ fmt -50 memo
```
One factor that is important to remember while
administering the dietary intake of Charcharodon
carcharias is that there is, at least from the
point of view of the subject, very little
differentiating the prepared morsels being
proffered from your digits.

In other words, don't feed the sharks!

fsck

Checks and repairs a filesystem

*fsck [**options**] [**filesystem-list**]*

The fsck utility verifies the integrity of a filesystem and reports on problems it finds. This utility is a front end for filesystem checkers specific to a filesystem type (each checker is named **fsck.***type*, where *type* is the filesystem type).

Arguments   The *filesystem-list* is required unless you use the **−A** option, in which case fsck checks all the filesystems listed in the **/etc/fstab** file.[5]

On the command line there are two ways to list the filesystems you want fsck to check. You can either use the name of the device that holds the filesystem (for example, **/dev/hda2**) or, if the filesystem appears in **/etc/fstab**, specify the mount point (for example, **/usr2**) for the filesystem.

Options   Without the **−A** option fsck checks the filesystems in the *filesystem-list*. When a filesystem is consistent, you see a report such as the following:

```
# /sbin/fsck -f /dev/hda8
fsck 1.27 (8-Mar-2002)
e2fsck 1.27 (8-Mar-2002)
Pass 1: Checking inodes, blocks, and sizes
Pass 2: Checking directory structure
Pass 3: Checking directory connectivity
Pass 4: Checking reference counts
Pass 5: Checking group summary information
/dev/hda8: 26/128768 files (7.7% non-contiguous), 62361/257032 blocks
```

If fsck finds problems with a filesystem, it reports on each problem, allowing you to choose whether to repair it or ignore it.

When you run fsck, you specify both fsck options and options specific to the filesystem type that fsck is checking (for example, **ext2**, **ext3**, **msdos**, **reiserfs**). The fsck options precede the type-specific options.

---

5. The fsck utility does not check those entries in **fstab** that have a zero in the fifth (next-to-last) column.

fsck Options

–A   **all**   Processes all the filesystems found in the **/etc/fstab** file. Do not specify a *filesystem-list* when you use this option.

–t *fstype* **type**   Specifies the filesystem type(s) to check. With the **–A** option fsck checks all the filesystems in **/etc/fstab** that match *fstype*. Table 17-8 on page 973 lists common filesystem types.

–N   **no**   Assumes a *no* response to any questions that arise while processing a filesystem.

–R   **root-skip**   With the **–A** option skips the root filesystem.

–V   **verbose**   Displays more output, including filesystem-specific commands.

Filesystem-Specific Options

The following options apply to many common filesystem types, including **ext2** and **ext3**. Refer to the man page for a specific filesystem checker for a complete list. Give the command **ls /sbin/fsck**✳ for a list of common filesystem checkers.

–a   **automatic**   Same as the **–p** option; kept for backward compatibility.

–f   **force**   The fsck utility keeps track of whether a filesystem is *clean*. (A clean filesystem is one that was either just successfully checked with fsck or successfully unmounted and has not been mounted since.) Clean filesystems are skipped by fsck, greatly speeding up system booting under normal conditions. The **–f** option forces fsck to check the filesystems even if they are considered clean.

–p   **preen**   Attempts to repair all minor inconsistencies it finds when processing a filesystem. If any problems are not repaired, fsck terminates with a nonzero exit status. Without the **–p** option fsck asks you whether to correct or ignore each problem it finds. The **–p** option is commonly used with the **–A** option when checking filesystems while booting GNU/Linux.

–r   **interactive**   Asks whether to correct or ignore each problem that is found. For many filesystem types this behavior is the default.

–y   **yes**   Assumes a *yes* response to any questions that fsck asks while processing a filesystem.

Notes   Use the **–p** option cautiously: It causes fsck to repair the filesystem automatically (without asking you to confirm changes).

The fsck utility is a front end that calls other utilities to handle various types of filesystems. For example, fsck calls e2fsck (which is linked to **/sbin/fsck.ext2** and

/sbin/fsck.ext3) to check the widely used **ext2** and **ext3** filesystems. Refer to the e2fsck man page for more information. By splitting fsck in this manner, filesystem developers can provide programs to check their filesystems without impacting the development of other filesystems or changing how system administrators use fsck.

Run fsck on filesystems that are unmounted or mounted readonly. When GNU/Linux is booting, the root filesystem is first mounted readonly to allow it to be processed by fsck. If fsck finds no problems with the root filesystem, it is then remounted (using the **remount** option to the mount utility) read-write. If you ever run fsck on the root filesystem while it is mounted read-write and fsck finds any problems, halt your system immediately, after fsck finishes, without running sync (that is, reset the machine or turn off the power without bringing the system down "properly"); then reboot.

Although it is technically feasible to repair files that are damaged and that fsck says you should remove, it is usually not practical. The best insurance against significant loss of data is frequent backups. Refer to page 997 for more information on backing up the system.

When it encounters a file that has lost its link to its filename, fsck asks whether you want to reconnect it. If you choose to reconnect it and fix the problem, the file is put in a directory named **lost+found** in the root directory of the filesystem that the file was found in and is given its inode number as a name. In order for fsck to restore files in this way, a **lost+found** directory must be in the root directory of each filesystem. For example, if your filesystems are **/**, **/usr**, and **/tmp**, you should have the following three **lost+found** directories: **/lost+found**, **/usr/lost+found**, and **/tmp/lost+found**. Each of the **lost+found** directories must be *slotted*. To put slots in a directory, add many files to the directory (for example, 500) and then remove them. Or you can use the mklost+found utility to create a slotted **lost+found** directory. Either of these procedures creates unused entries in the directory that fsck can use to store the inode numbers for files that have lost their links. For **ext2** and **ext3** filesystems, mkfs (page 1057) creates appropriately slotted **lost+found** directories when you create a filesystem.

Messages   This section explains fsck's standard messages, not every message that fsck produces (Table III-12). In general, fsck suggests the most logical way of dealing with a problem in the file structure. Unless you have information that suggests another response, respond to its prompts with **yes**. Use the system backup tapes or disks to restore any data that is lost as a result of this process.

Phase	What Is Checked	‖ table III-12
Phase 1 - Check inodes, blocks, and sizes	Checks inode information.	
Phase 2 - Check directory structures	Looks for directories that point to bad inodes that **fsck** found in Phase 1.	
Phase 3 - Check directory connectivity	Looks for unreferenced directories and a nonexistent or full **lost+found** dirctory.	
Phase 4 - Check reference counts	Checks for unreferenced files, a nonexistent or full **lost+found** directory, bad link counts, bad blocks, duplicated blocks, and incorrect inode counts.	
Phase 5 - Check group summary information	Checks whether the free list and other filesystem structures are OK. If any problems are found with the free list, Phase 6 is run.	
Phase 6 - Salvage free list	If Phase 5 found any problems with the free list, Phase 6 fixes them.	

Cleanup

Once it has repaired the filesystem, fsck informs you about the status of the filesystem and tells you what you must do. The fsck utility displays the following message if it has repaired the filesystem:

```
*****File System Was Modified*****
```

On **ext2** and **ext3** filesystems fsck displays messages such as the following when it has finished checking the filesystem:

```
filesys: used/maximum files (percent non-contiguous), used/maximum blocks
```

This message tells you how many files and disk blocks you have used, as well as how many files and disk blocks the filesystem can hold. The percent noncontiguous tells you how fragmented the disk is. Refer to "Monitoring Disk Usage" on page 1070.

ftp

Transfers files over a network

*ftp [**options**] [**remote-computer**]*

The ftp utility is a user interface to the standard File Transfer Protocol (FTP), which transfers files between systems that can communicate over a network. To establish an FTP connection, you must have an account (personal, guest, or anonymous) on the remote system.

Arguments   The *remote-computer* is the name or network address of the remote system (the server that runs an **ftpd** daemon) that you want to exchange files with.

Options

   –v verbose   Tells you more about how ftp is working. Responses from the remote computer are displayed, and ftp reports information on how quickly files are transferred.

   –n no auto login   You can configure ftp so that it automatically logs in on some remote computers. If you have set ftp to do automatic logins, this option disables that behavior. A discussion on configuring ftp for automatic logins follows.

Discussion   This utility is interactive; after you start ftp, it prompts you to enter commands to transfer files or set parameters. You can use a number of commands in response to the ftp> prompt; following are some of the more common ones.

   !   Escapes to a shell on your local system (use CONTROL-D or **exit** to return to ftp when you are through).

   ascii   Sets the file transfer type for ASCII files; allows you to transfer text files from systems that end lines with a RETURN/LINEFEED combination and automatically strip off the RETURN. This type of transfer is useful when the remote computer is a DOS or MS Windows machine.

   binary   Sets the file transfer type so that you can transfer files that contain non-ASCII (unprintable) characters correctly. Also works for ASCII files that do not require changes to the ends of lines.

   bye   Closes the connection to a remote computer and terminates ftp. Same as **quit**.

cd *directory*   Changes to a working directory named *directory* on the remote system.

close   Closes the connection with the remote system without exiting from ftp.

dir [*directory*] [*file*]   Displays a listing of *directory* from the remote system. When you do not specify *directory*, the working directory is displayed. When you specify *file*, the listing is saved on the local system in that *file*; if not, it goes to standard output.

get *remote-file* [*local-file*]

Copies *remote-file* to the local system under the name *local-file*. Without *local-file*, ftp uses *remote-file* as the filename on the local system. The *remote-file* and *local-file* names can be pathnames.

glob   Toggles filename expansion for **mget** and **mput** commands and tells you what the current state is (Globbing on or Globbing off).

help   Displays a list of commands recognized by the ftp utility on the local system.

lcd [*local_directory*]   Changes the working directory on the local machine to *local_directory*. Without an argument this command changes the working directory on the local machine to your home directory (just as cd does without an argument).

ls [*directory*] [*file*]   Similar to **dir** but produces a more concise listing on some remote computers.

mget *remote-file-list*   multiple get   Unlike the **get** command, the **mget** command allows you to retrieve multiple files from the remote system. You can name the remote files literally or use wildcards (see **glob**). See also **prompt**.

mput *local-file-list*   multiple put   The **mput** command allows you to put multiple files from the local system onto the remote system. You can name the local files literally or use wildcards (see **glob**). See also **prompt**.

open   Interactively specifies the name of the remote system. Useful if you did not specify a remote system on the command line or if the attempt to connect to the system failed.

prompt   When using **mget** or **mput** to receive or send multiple files, ftp asks for verification (by default) before transferring each file. This command toggles that behavior and tells you what the current state is (Interactive mode off or Interactive mode on).

pwd   Causes ftp to display the pathname of the working directory on the remote computer. Use **!pwd** to display the name of the local working directory.

put *local-file* [*remote-file*]

Copies *local-file* to the remote system under the name *remote-file*. Without *remote-file*, ftp uses *local-file* as the filename on the remote system. The *remote-file* and *local-file* names can be pathnames.

quit   Quits the ftp session. Same as **bye**.

user *user-name*   If the ftp utility did not log you in automatically, you can specify your account name interactively with this command.

Notes   Many computers, including non-GNU/Linux systems, support FTP. The ftp utility, an implementation of this protocol, exchanges files with various types of systems.

By convention many sites offer archives of free information on an ftp-based system (for example, ftp://metalab.unc.edu/pub/Linux).[6] You can use the guest account **anonymous** on many systems. When you log in as **anonymous**, you are prompted to enter a password. Although any password may be accepted, by convention you are expected to supply your e-mail address. This information helps the remote site to know who uses its services. Most systems that support anonymous logins accept the name **ftp** as an easier-to-spell and quicker-to-enter synonym for **anonymous**. On many machines that permit anonymous FTP access, the interesting files are in a directory named **pub**.

If you visit some sites regularly with ftp, you can set up your local account so that you can log in on those machines automatically. The ftp utility reads the **~/.netrc** file to determine whether you have an automatic login set up for a remote machine. The following is a typical **~/.netrc** file:

```
$ cat ~/.netrc
machine bravo login alex password mypassword
default login anonymous password alex@tcorp.com
```

Each line identifies a remote machine. The keywords `machine`, `login`, and `password` precede the appropriate login elements. The last line in this example replaces the word `machine` with `default`. When you connect to a remote system that is not mentioned in **.netrc**, ftp uses the information on this line to try to log in. Make the file **.netrc** unreadable by everyone except yourself to protect the account information that is kept in it. Refer to the **netrc** man page for more information.

Example   The ftp utility displays various messages to let you know how your requests are proceeding. To keep the following example clear and brief, the progress messages from ftp are not shown.

In the following example Alex gives the command **ftp bravo** to connect to the remote system **bravo**. The ftp server on **bravo** responds with a couple of lines identifying the server and the version of the ftp software it is using. Then it prompts Alex with `Name (bravo:alex):`. Because Alex wants to log in as **alex**, he presses RETURN in response to the prompt. He could have typed another name instead. Then he types his password (on bravo) in response to the `Password:` prompt. The remote server tells Alex that he has logged on and gives him some additional information:

```
$ ftp bravo
Connected to bravo.tcorp.com.
220 bravo.tcorp.com FTP server (Version wu-2.6.0(1) Mon Feb 28 10:30:36 EST 2000) ready.
```

---

6. Today you can view the contents of many ftp sites on a parallel Web site: Point your browser to www.ibiblio.org/pub/Linux to see a graphical representation of the same information.

```
Name (bravo:alex): RETURN
331 Password required for alex.
Password:
230 User alex logged in.
Remote system type is UNIX.
Using binary mode to transfer files.
ftp>
```

The first thing that Alex does once he has logged on is to **cd** to the **xfer** directory on the remote machine and list its contents. Then Alex uses **cd** to change to the **incoming** directory on the remote system. He knows that he wants to transfer the files from the working directory on the local system to the **incoming** directory on the remote system. Before he makes the transfer, he uses a local shell command to list the files in the working directory on the local system (**!ls –l**).

```
ftp> cd xfer
250 CWD command successful.
ftp> ls
200 PORT command successful.
150 Opening ASCII mode data connection for /bin/ls.
total 960
-rw-rw-r--    1 alex       alex          606736 Oct   2 13:23 fileutils-4.0-21.i386.rpm
-rw-rw-r--    1 alex       alex          170825 Oct   2 13:21 grep-2.4-3.i386.rpm
drwxrwxr-x    2 alex       alex            4096 Oct   2 13:27 incoming
-rw-rw-r--    1 alex       alex          180669 Oct   2 13:24 sh-utils-2.0-5.i386.rpm
226 Transfer complete.
ftp> cd incoming
250 CWD command successful.
ftp> !ls -l
total 1090
-rw-rw-r--    1 alex       alex           39150 Oct   2 13:26 187a.txt
-rw-rw-r--    1 alex       alex           37950 Oct   2 13:27 191g.txt
-rw-rw-r--    1 alex       alex           26730 Oct   2 13:28 205b.txt
-rw-rw-r--    1 alex       alex           38955 Oct   2 13:28 211r.txt
ftp>
```

Before starting the transfer, Alex turns prompt mode off and globbing on. After giving the **glob** command, ftp reports that globbing is off, so Alex gives another **glob** command to turn it on. Then he gives an **mput** command with an ambiguous file reference, and ftp reports on each of the transfers:

```
ftp> prompt
Interactive mode off.
ftp> glob
Globbing off.
ftp> glob
Globbing on.
ftp> mput *.txt
local: 187a.txt remote: 187a.txt
200 PORT command successful.
150 Opening BINARY mode data connection for 187a.txt.
226 Transfer complete.
39150 bytes sent in 0.00292 secs (1.3e+04 Kbytes/sec)
```

```
  ...
  local: 211r.txt remote: 211r.txt
  200 PORT command successful.
  150 Opening BINARY mode data connection for 211r.txt.
  226 Transfer complete.
  38955 bytes sent in 0.00426 secs (8.9e+03 Kbytes/sec)
  ftp>
```

Next, Alex wants to bring some files from the remote system back to the local system. He changes the working directory on the remote system (**cd ..**), makes sure that he is in the directory that he wants to be in (**pwd**), and lists the files in the working directory (**ls**). As a matter of habit, Alex makes sure that ftp is set up for a binary transfer (**bin**) and uses **mget** to transfer all the files whose names end in **.rpm** from the working directory on the remote system.

```
ftp> cd ..
250 CWD command successful.
ftp> pwd
257 "/home/alex/xfer" is current directory.
ftp> ls
200 PORT command successful.
150 Opening ASCII mode data connection for /bin/ls.
total 960
-rw-rw-r--    1 alex      alex        606736 Oct  2 13:23 fileutils-4.0-21.i386.rpm
-rw-rw-r--    1 alex      alex        170825 Oct  2 13:21 grep-2.4-3.i386.rpm
drwxrwxr-x    2 alex      alex          4096 Oct  2 13:32 incoming
-rw-rw-r--    1 alex      alex        180669 Oct  2 13:24 sh-utils-2.0-5.i386.rpm
226 Transfer complete.
ftp> bin
200 Type set to I.
ftp> mget *rpm
local: fileutils-4.0-21.i386.rpm remote: fileutils-4.0-21.i386.rpm
200 PORT command successful.
150 Opening BINARY mode data connection for fileutils-4.0-21.i386.rpm (606736 bytes).
226 Transfer complete.
606736 bytes received in 46.8 secs (13 Kbytes/sec)
local: grep-2.4-3.i386.rpm remote: grep-2.4-3.i386.rpm
200 PORT command successful.
150 Opening BINARY mode data connection for grep-2.4-3.i386.rpm (170825 bytes).
226 Transfer complete.
170825 bytes received in 12.8 secs (13 Kbytes/sec)
  ...
ftp>
```

When Alex is finished with his transfers, he gives a **quit** command, and ftp summarizes the session and returns him to the local shell prompt:

```
ftp> quit
221-You have transferred 1101015 bytes in 7 files.
221-Total traffic for this session was 1103813 bytes in 10 transfers.
221-Thank you for using the FTP service on bravo.tcorp.com.
221 Goodbye.
```

See page 378 for additional information on using ftp.

gawk

Searches for and processes patterns in a file

gawk *[options] [program] [file-list]*
gawk *[options]* –f *program-file [file-list]*

The gawk (GNU awk) utility is a pattern-scanning and processing language that searches one or more files to see whether they contain records (usually lines) that match specified patterns and then performs actions, such as writing the record to standard output or incrementing a counter, each time it finds a match. You can use gawk to generate reports or filter text. It works equally well with numbers and text; when you mix the two, gawk usually comes up with the right answer.

The authors of awk (Alfred V. Aho, Peter J. Weinberger, and Brian W. Kernighan), on which gawk is based, designed awk to be easy to use, and to this end they sacrificed execution speed.

The gawk utility takes many of its constructs from the C programming language and includes the following features:

- Flexible format

- Conditional execution

- Looping statements

- Numeric variables

- String variables

- Regular expressions

- Relational expressions

- C's **printf**

The gawk utility takes its input from files you specify on the command line or from standard input.

Arguments   The *program* is a gawk program that you include on the command line. The *program-file* is the name of the file that holds the gawk program. Putting the program on the command line allows you to write simple, short gawk programs without having to create a separate *program-file.* To prevent the shell from interpreting the gawk commands as shell commands, it is a good idea to enclose the *program* within single quotation marks. Putting the program in a file reduces typing and the chance for errors when the program is long or complex. See the –f option and "Discussion" following.

The *file-list* contains pathnames of the ordinary files that gawk processes. These files are the input files.

Options

--assign *var=value* **−v** *var=value* Assigns *value* to the variable *var*. The assignment takes place prior to execution of the gawk program and is available within the BEGIN pattern (see the next section). You can repeat this option as many times as needed.

--field-separator *fs* **−F** *fs* Uses *fs* as the value of the input field separator (FS variable).

--file *program* **−f** *program* Reads its program from the file named *program*. You can use this option more than once on the command line.

--help **−W help** Summarizes how to use gawk.

--lint **−W lint** Warns about constructs that may not be correct or ones that may not be portable.

--posix **−W posix** Runs a POSIX-compliant version of gawk. This option introduces some restrictions: See the gawk man page for details.

--traditional **−W traditional** Ignores the new GNU features in a gawk program, making the program conform to UNIX awk.

Notes

The gawk utility is the GNU version of UNIX awk that is provided with GNU/Linux. For convenience Red Hat Linux systems provide a link from **/bin/awk** to **/bin/gawk** so that you can run the program using either name.

See page 1208 for examples of gawk error messages.

Discussion

A gawk program consists of one or more program lines containing a *pattern* and/or *action* in the following format:

pattern { action }

The *pattern* selects lines from the input file. The gawk utility performs the *action* on all lines that the *pattern* selects. You must enclose the *action* within braces so that gawk can differentiate it from the *pattern*. If a program line does not contain a *pattern*, gawk selects all lines in the input file. If a program line does not contain an *action*, gawk copies the selected lines to standard output.

To start, gawk compares the first line in the input file (from the *file-list*) with each *pattern* in the *program-file* or *program*. If a *pattern* selects the line (if there is a match), gawk takes the *action* associated with the *pattern*. If the line is not selected, gawk takes no *action*. When gawk has completed its comparisons for the first line of the input file, it repeats the process for the next line of input, continuing this process, comparing subsequent lines in the input file, until it has read the entire *file-list*.

If several *patterns* select the same line, gawk takes the *actions* associated with each of the *patterns* in the order in which they appear. It is, therefore, possible for gawk to send a single line from the input file to standard output more than once.

Patterns

You can use a regular expression (Appendix A), enclosed within slashes, as a *pattern*. The ~ operator tests whether a field or variable matches a regular expression. The !~ operator tests for no match. You can perform both numeric and string comparisons by using the relational operators listed in Table III-13.

Operator	|| table III-13
<	Less than
<=	Less than or equal to
==	Equal to
!=	Not equal to
>=	Greater than or equal to
>	Greater than

You can combine any of the *patterns* described above using the Boolean operators || (OR) or && (AND).

The comma is the range operator. If you separate two *patterns* with a comma on a single gawk program line, gawk selects a range of lines, beginning with the first line that matches the first *pattern*. The last line gawk selects is the next subsequent line that matches the second *pattern*. After gawk finds the second *pattern*, it starts the process over by looking for the first *pattern* again.

Two unique *patterns*, **BEGIN** and **END**, execute commands before gawk starts its processing and after it finishes. The gawk utility executes the *actions* associated with the **BEGIN** *pattern* before, and with the **END** *pattern* after, it processes all the files in the *file-list*.

Actions

The *action* portion of a gawk command causes gawk to take *action* when it matches a *pattern*. When you do not specify an *action*, gawk performs the default *action*, which is the **print** command (explicitly represented as {print}). This *action* copies the record (normally a line—see "Variables," following) from the input file to gawk's standard output.

You can follow a **print** command with arguments, causing gawk to print only the arguments you specify. The arguments can be variables or string constants. Using gawk, you can send the output from a **print** command to a file (>), append it to a file (>>), or pipe it to the input of another program (|).

Unless you separate items in a **print** command with commas, gawk catenates them. Commas cause gawk to separate the items with the output field separator (normally a SPACE—see "Variables," following).

You can include several *actions* on one line within a set of braces by separating them with semicolons.

Comments

The gawk utility disregards anything on a program line following a pound sign (#). You can document a gawk program by preceding comments with this symbol.

Variables

Variables in gawk are not declared prior to their use. You can optionally give a variable an initial value. Numeric variables that you do not initialize are automatically initialized to 0; string variables, to the null string. In addition to user variables, gawk maintains program variables for your use. You can use both user and program variables in the *pattern and* in the *action* portion of a gawk program. Table III-14 lists a few of the available program variables.

Variable	‖ table III-14
$0	The current record (as a single variable)
$1-$n	Fields in the current record
FILENAME	Name of the current input file
FS	Input field separator (default: SPACE or TAB)
NF	Number of fields in the current record
NR	Record number of current record
OFS	Output field separator (default: SPACE)
ORS	Output record separator (default: NEWLINE)
RS	Input record separator (default: NEWLINE)

In addition to initializing variables within your gawk program, you can use the **−v** option to initialize variables on the command line. Initializing variables in this manner can be useful if the value of a variable changes from one run of gawk to the next.

The input and output record separators are, by default, NEWLINE characters. Thus gawk takes each line in the input file to be a separate record and appends a NEWLINE to the end of each record that it sends to standard output. The input field separators are, by default, SPACEs and TABs. The output field separator is a SPACE. You can change the value of any of the separators at any time by assigning a new value to its associated variable. This assignment can be done either within a gawk program or on the command line by using the **−v** option.

Functions

Table III-15 lists a few of the functions that gawk provides for manipulating numbers and strings.

Name	**‖ table III-15**
length(**str**)	Returns the number of characters in *str;* if you do not supply an argument, it returns the number of characters in the current input record
int(**num**)	Returns the integer portion of *num*
index(**str1,str2**)	Returns the index of *str2* in *str1* or 0 if *str2* is not present
split(**str,arr,del**)	Places elements of *str,* delimited by *del*, in the array *arr*[1]...*arr*[*n*]; returns the number of elements in the array
sprintf(**fmt,args**)	Formats *args* according to *fmt* and returns the formatted string; mimics the C programming language function of the same name
substr(**str,pos,len**)	Returns a substring of *str* that begins at *pos* and is *len* characters long
tolower(**str**)	Returns a copy of *str* in which all uppercase letters are replaced with their lowercase counterparts
toupper(**str**)	Returns a copy of *str* in which all lowercase letters are replaced with their uppercase counterparts

Operators

The gawk arithmetic operators listed in Table III-16 are from the C programming language.

Operator		table III-16
*	Multiplies the expression preceding the operator by the expression following it
/	Divides the expression preceding the operator by the expression following it
%	Takes the remainder after dividing the expression preceding the operator by the expression following it
+	Adds the expression preceding the operator to the expression following it
–	Subtracts the expression following the operator from the expression preceding it
=	Assigns the value of the expression following the operator to the variable preceding it
++	Increments the variable preceding the operator
––	Decrements the variable preceding the operator
+=	Adds the expression following the operator to the variable preceding it and assigns the result to the variable preceding the operator
–=	Subtracts the expression following the operator from the variable preceding it and assigns the result to the variable preceding the operator
*=	Multiplies the variable preceding the operator by the expression following it and assigns the result to the variable preceding the operator
/=	Divides the variable preceding the operator by the expression following it and assigns the result to the variable preceding the operator
%=	Takes the remainder, after dividing the variable preceding the operator by the expression following it, and assigns the result to the variable preceding the operator

Associative Arrays

An associative array is one of gawk's most powerful features. An associative array uses strings as its indexes. Using an associative array, you can mimic a traditional array by using numeric strings as indexes.

You assign a value to an element of an associative array just as you would assign a value to any other gawk variable. The syntax is

array[string] = *value*

The *array* is the name of the array, *string* is the index of the element of the array you are assigning a value to, and *value* is the value you are assigning to the element of the array.

You can use a special **for** structure with a gawk array. The syntax is

for (elem in array) action

The *elem* is a variable that takes on the values of each of the elements in the array as the **for** structure loops through them, *array* is the name of the array, and *action* is the action that gawk takes for each element in the array. You can use the *elem* variable in this *action*.

The "Examples" section contains programs that use associative arrays.

printf

You can use the **printf** command in place of **print** to control the format of the output that gawk generates. The gawk version of **printf** is similar to that of the C language. A **printf** command takes the following syntax:

printf "*control-string*", *arg1, arg2, ..., argn*

The *control-string* determines how **printf** formats *arg1-n*. The *arg1-n* can be variables or other expressions. Within the *control-string* you can use \n to indicate a NEWLINE and \t to indicate a TAB.

The *control-string* contains conversion specifications, one for each argument (*arg1-n*). A conversion specification has the following syntax:

%[–][x[.y]]conv

The – causes **printf** to left justify the argument. The *x* is the minimum field width, and the *.y* is the number of places to the right of a decimal point in a number. The *conv* is a letter from the list in Table III-17.

Refer to the following "Examples" section for examples of how to use **printf**.

conv	|| table III-17
d	Decimal
e	Exponential notation
f	Floating-point number
g	Use **f** or **e**, whichever is shorter
o	Unsigned octal
s	String of characters
x	Unsigned hexadecimal

Examples

A simple gawk program is

```
{ print }
```

This program consists of one program line that is an *action*. It uses no *pattern*. Because the *pattern* is missing, gawk selects all lines in the input file. Without any arguments the **print** command prints each selected line in its entirety. This program copies the input file to standard output.

The following program has a *pattern* part without an explicit *action*:

```
/jenny/
```

In this case gawk selects from the input file all lines that contain the string jenny. When you do not specify an *action*, gawk assumes the *action* to be **print**. This program copies to standard output all the lines in the input file that contain jenny.

The following examples work with the **cars** data file. From left to right the columns in the file contain each car's make, model, year of manufacture, mileage in 1,000s, and price. All whitespace in this file is composed of single TABs (there are no SPACEs in the file):

```
$ cat cars
plym    fury    77      73      2500
chevy   nova    79      60      3000
ford    mustang 65      45      10000
volvo   gl      78      102     9850
ford    ltd     83      15      10500
chevy   nova    80      50      3500
fiat    600     65      115     450
honda   accord  81      30      6000
```

```
ford    thundbd 84      10      17000
toyota  tercel  82      180     750
chevy   impala  65      85      1550
ford    bronco  83      25      9500
```

The following example selects lines that contain the string chevy. The slashes indicate that chevy is a regular expression. This example has no *action* part:

```
$ gawk '/chevy/' cars
chevy   nova    79      60      3000
chevy   nova    80      50      3500
chevy   impala  65      85      1550
```

Although neither gawk nor shell syntax requires single quotation marks on the command line, it is a good idea to use them because they prevent many problems. If the gawk program you create on the command line includes SPACEs or any special characters that the shell interprets, you must quote them. Always enclosing the program in single quotation marks is the easiest way of making sure that you have quoted any characters that need to be quoted.

The next example selects all lines from the file (it has no *pattern* part). The braces enclose the *action* part; you must always use braces to delimit the *action* part so that gawk can distinguish the *pattern* part from the *action* part. This example prints the third field ($3), a SPACE (the output field separator, indicated by the comma), and the first field ($1) of each selected line:

```
$ gawk '{print $3, $1}' cars
77 plym
79 chevy
65 ford
78 volvo
83 ford
80 chevy
65 fiat
81 honda
84 ford
82 toyota
65 chevy
83 ford
```

The next example, which includes both a *pattern* and an *action* part, selects all lines that contain the string chevy and prints the third and first fields from the lines it selects:

```
$ gawk '/chevy/ {print $3, $1}' cars
79 chevy
80 chevy
65 chevy
```

The next example selects lines that contain a match for the regular expression h. Because there is no explicit action, it prints all the lines it selects.

```
$ gawk '/h/' cars
chevy    nova     79        60        3000
chevy    nova     80        50        3500
honda    accord   81        30        6000
ford     thundbd  84        10        17000
chevy    impala   65        85        1550
```

The next *pattern* uses the matches operator (~) to select all lines that contain the letter h in the first field:

```
$ gawk '$1 ~ /h/' cars
chevy    nova     79        60        3000
chevy    nova     80        50        3500
honda    accord   81        30        6000
chevy    impala   65        85        1550
```

The caret (^) in a regular expression forces a match at the beginning of the line or, in this case, the beginning of the first field:

```
$ gawk '$1 ~ /^h/' cars
honda    accord   81        30        6000
```

A pair of brackets surrounds a character-class definition (page 1385). Next, gawk selects lines that have a second field that begins with t or m and then prints the third and second fields, a dollar sign, and the fifth field.

```
$ gawk '$2 ~ /^[tm]/ {print $3, $2, "$"  $5}' cars
65 mustang $10000
84 thundbd $17000
82 tercel $750
```

The next example shows three roles that a dollar sign can play in a gawk program. A dollar sign followed by a number forms the name of a field. Within a regular expression a dollar sign forces a match at the end of a line or field (5$). Within a string you can use a dollar sign as itself:

```
$ gawk '$3 ~ /5$/ {print $3, $1, "$"  $5}' cars
65 ford $10000
65 fiat $450
65 chevy $1550
```

In the next example the equal-to relational operator (==) causes gawk to perform a numeric comparison between the third field in each line and the number 65. The gawk command takes the default *action*, **print**, on each line where the comparison is *true:*

```
$ gawk '$3 == 65' cars
ford     mustang 65        45        10000
fiat     600      65       115       450
chevy    impala   65        85        1550
```

The next example finds all cars priced at or under $3,000:

```
$ gawk '$5 <= 3000' cars
plym    fury    77      73      2500
chevy   nova    79      60      3000
fiat    600     65      115     450
toyota  tercel  82      180     750
chevy   impala  65      85      1550
```

When you use double quotation marks, gawk performs textual comparisons, using the ASCII (or other local) collating sequence as the basis of the comparison. Following, gawk shows that the *strings* 450 and 750 fall in the range that lies between the *strings* 2000 and 9000:

```
$ gawk '$5 >= "2000" && $5 < "9000"' cars
plym    fury    77      73      2500
chevy   nova    79      60      3000
chevy   nova    80      50      3500
fiat    600     65      115     450
honda   accord  81      30      6000
toyota  tercel  82      180     750
```

When you need a numeric comparison, do not use quotation marks. The next example gives the correct results. It is the same as the previous example but omits the double quotation marks:

```
$ gawk '$5 >= 2000 && $5 < 9000' cars
plym    fury    77      73      2500
chevy   nova    79      60      3000
chevy   nova    80      50      3500
honda   accord  81      30      6000
```

Next, the range operator (,) selects a group of lines. The first line it selects is the one specified by the *pattern* before the comma. The last line is the one selected by the *pattern* after the comma. If no line matches the *pattern* after the comma, gawk selects every line up to the end of the file. The next example selects all lines, starting with the line that contains volvo and concluding with the line that contains fiat:

```
$ gawk '/volvo/ , /fiat/' cars
volvo   gl      78      102     9850
ford    ltd     83      15      10500
chevy   nova    80      50      3500
fiat    600     65      115     450
```

After the range operator finds its first group of lines, it starts the process over, looking for a line that matches the *pattern* before the comma. In the following example gawk finds three groups of lines that fall between chevy and ford. Although the fifth line in the file contains ford, gawk does not select it because at the time it is processing the fifth line; it is searching for chevy:

```
$ gawk '/chevy/ , /ford/' cars
chevy    nova     79      60      3000
ford     mustang 65       45      10000
chevy    nova     80      50      3500
fiat     600      65      115     450
honda    accord   81      30      6000
ford     thundbd 84       10      17000
chevy    impala   65      85      1550
ford     bronco   83      25      9500
```

When you are writing a longer gawk program, it is convenient to put the program in a file and reference the file on the command line. Use the –f option, followed by the name of the file containing the gawk program.

The following gawk program, named **pr_header**, has two *actions* and uses the BEGIN *pattern*. The gawk utility performs the *action* associated with **BEGIN** before processing any lines of the data file: It prints a header. The second *action*, {print}, has no *pattern* part and prints all the lines in the file:

```
$ cat pr_header
BEGIN   {print "Make     Model    Year    Miles    Price"}
        {print}

$ gawk -f pr_header cars
Make     Model    Year    Miles    Price
plym     fury     77      73       2500
chevy    nova     79      60       3000
ford     mustang 65       45       10000
volvo    gl       78      102      9850
ford     ltd      83      15       10500
chevy    nova     80      50       3500
fiat     600      65      115      450
honda    accord   81      30       6000
ford     thundbd 84       10       17000
toyota   tercel   82      180      750
chevy    impala   65      85       1550
ford     bronco   83      25       9500
```

In the previous and following examples, the whitespace in the headers is composed of single TABs, so that the titles line up with the columns of data:

```
$ cat pr_header2
BEGIN   {
print "Make     Model    Year    Miles    Price"
print "------------------------------------------"
}
        {print}

$ gawk -f pr_header2 cars
Make     Model    Year    Miles    Price
------------------------------------------
plym     fury     77      73       2500
chevy    nova     79      60       3000
```

```
ford     mustang 65        45         10000
volvo    gl        78       102        9850
ford     ltd       83       15         10500
chevy    nova      80       50         3500
fiat     600       65       115        450
honda    accord   81        30         6000
ford     thundbd 84         10         17000
toyota   tercel   82        180        750
chevy    impala   65        85         1550
ford     bronco   83        25         9500
```

When you call the **length** function without an argument, it returns the number of characters in the current line, including field separators. The $0 variable always contains the value of the current line. In the next example gawk prepends the length to each line, and then a pipe sends the output from gawk to sort so that the lines of the **cars** file appear in order of length:

```
$ gawk '{print length, $0}' cars | sort
19 fiat 600      65       115        450
20 ford ltd      83       15         10500
20 plym fury     77       73         2500
20 volvo         gl       78         102     9850
21 chevy         nova     79         60      3000
21 chevy         nova     80         50      3500
22 ford bronco  83        25         9500
23 chevy         impala   65         85      1550
23 honda         accord   81         30      6000
24 ford mustang 65        45         10000
24 ford thundbd 84        10         17000
24 toyota        tercel   82         180     750
```

The formatting of this report depends on TABs for horizontal alignment. The three extra characters at the beginning of each line throw off the format of several lines, including the last. A remedy for this situation is covered shortly.

The **NR** variable contains the record (line) number of the current line. The following *pattern* selects all lines that contain more than 23 characters. The *action* prints the line number of all the selected lines:

```
$ gawk 'length > 23 {print NR}' cars
3
9
10
```

You can combine the range operator (,) and the **NR** variable to display a group of lines of a file, based on their line numbers. The next example displays lines 2 through 4:

```
$ gawk 'NR == 2 , NR == 4' cars
chevy    nova      79       60         3000
ford     mustang 65        45         10000
volvo    gl        78       102        9850
```

The **END** *pattern* works in a manner similar to the **BEGIN** *pattern*, except that gawk takes the *actions* associated with it after it has processed the last of its input lines. The following report displays information only after it has processed the entire data file. The **NR** variable retains its value after gawk has finished processing the data file, so that an *action* associated with an **END** *pattern* can use it:

```
$ gawk 'END {print NR, "cars for sale." }' cars
12 cars for sale.
```

The next example uses **if** commands to change the values of some of the first fields. As long as gawk does not make any changes to a record, it leaves the entire record, including separators, intact. Once it makes a change to a record, gawk changes all separators in that record to the value of the output field separator. The default output field separator is a SPACE:

```
$ cat separ_demo
        {
        if ($1 ~ /ply/)  $1 = "plymouth"
        if ($1 ~ /chev/) $1 = "chevrolet"
        print
        }

$  gawk -f separ_demo cars
plymouth fury 77 73 2500
chevrolet nova 79 60 3000
ford    mustang 65      45      10000
volvo   gl      78      102     9850
ford    ltd     83      15      10500
chevrolet nova 80 50 3500
fiat    600     65      115     450
honda   accord  81      30      6000
ford    thundbd 84      10      17000
toyota  tercel  82      180     750
chevrolet impala 65 85 1550
ford    bronco  83      25      9500
```

You can change the default value of the output field separator by assigning a value to the **OFS** variable. The following example assigns a TAB character to **OFS**, using a common escape sequence notation. This fix improves the appearance of the report but does not properly line up the columns:

```
$ cat ofs_demo
BEGIN   {OFS = "\t"}
        {
        if ($1 ~ /ply/)  $1 = "plymouth"
        if ($1 ~ /chev/) $1 = "chevrolet"
        print
        }
```

```
$ gawk -f ofs_demo cars
plymouth          fury     77      73      2500
chevrolet         nova     79      60      3000
ford      mustang 65       45      10000
volvo     gl       78       102     9850
ford      ltd      83       15      10500
chevrolet         nova     80      50      3500
fiat      600      65       115     450
honda     accord   81       30      6000
ford      thundbd 84       10      17000
toyota    tercel   82       180     750
chevrolet         impala   65      85      1550
ford      bronco   83       25      9500
```

You can use **printf** (page 1191) to refine the output format. The following example uses a backslash at the end of a program line to mask the following NEWLINE from gawk. You can use this technique to continue a long line over one or more lines without affecting the outcome of the program.

```
$ cat printf_demo
BEGIN   {
    print "                                    Miles"
    print "Make        Model       Year     (000)       Price"
    print \
    "----------------------------------------------------"
    }
    {
    if ($1 ~ /ply/)  $1 = "plymouth"
    if ($1 ~ /chev/) $1 = "chevrolet"
    printf "%-10s %-8s    19%2d    %5d       $ %8.2f\n",\
        $1, $2, $3, $4, $5
    }
```

```
$ gawk -f printf_demo cars
                          Miles
Make        Model     Year     (000)        Price
----------------------------------------------------
plymouth    fury      1977      73      $  2500.00
chevrolet   nova      1979      60      $  3000.00
ford        mustang   1965      45      $ 10000.00
volvo       gl        1978      102     $  9850.00
ford        ltd       1983      15      $ 10500.00
chevrolet   nova      1980      50      $  3500.00
fiat        600       1965      115     $   450.00
honda       accord    1981      30      $  6000.00
ford        thundbd   1984      10      $ 17000.00
toyota      tercel    1982      180     $   750.00
chevrolet   impala    1965      85      $  1550.00
ford        bronco    1983      25      $  9500.00
```

The next example creates two new files: one with the lines that contain chevy and the other with lines containing ford:

```
$ cat redirect_out
/chevy/     {print > "chevfile"}
/ford/      {print > "fordfile"}
END         {print "done."}
$ gawk -f redirect_out cars
done.
$ cat chevfile
chevy   nova    79      60      3000
chevy   nova    80      50      3500
chevy   impala  65      85      1550
```

The **summary** program produces a summary report on all cars and newer cars. The first two lines of declarations are not required; gawk automatically declares and initializes variables as you use them. After reading all the input data, gawk computes and displays averages:

```
$ cat summary
BEGIN   {
        yearsum = 0 ; costsum = 0
        newcostsum = 0 ; newcount = 0
        }
        {
        yearsum += $3
        costsum += $5
        }
$3 > 80 {newcostsum += $5 ; newcount ++}
END     {
        printf "Average age of cars is %4.1f years\n",\
            90 - (yearsum/NR)
        printf "Average cost of cars is $%7.2f\n",\
            costsum/NR
            printf "Average cost of newer cars is $%7.2f\n",\
                newcostsum/newcount
        }
$ gawk -f summary cars
Average age of cars is 13.2 years
Average cost of cars is $6216.67
Average cost of newer cars is $8750.00
```

In the following example, grep shows the format of a line from the **passwd** file that the next example uses:

```
$ grep 'mark' /etc/passwd
mark:x:107:100:ext 112:/home/mark:/bin/tcsh
```

The next example demonstrates a technique for finding the largest number in a field. Because it works with the **passwd** file, which delimits fields with colons (:), the example changes the input field separator (**FS**) before reading any data. (Alternatively, the assignment to **FS** could be made on the command line, using the **–v** option.) This example reads the **passwd** file and determines the next available user ID number (field 3). The numbers do not have to be in order in the **passwd** file for this program to work.

The *pattern* causes gawk to select records that contain a user ID number greater than any previous user ID number that it has processed. Each time it selects a record, gawk assigns the value of the new user ID number to the **saveit** variable. Then gawk uses the new value of **saveit** to test the user ID of all subsequent records. Finally, gawk adds 1 to the value of **saveit** and displays the result:

```
$ cat find_uid
BEGIN           {FS = ":"
                saveit = 0}
$3 > saveit     {saveit = $3}
END             {print "Next available UID is " saveit + 1}

$ gawk -f find_uid /etc/passwd
Next available UID is 192
```

The next example shows another report based on the **cars** file. This report uses nested **if else** statements to substitute values based on the contents of the price field. The program has no *pattern* part; it processes every record:

```
$ cat price_range
{
if ($5 <= 5000) $5 = "inexpensive"
else if ($5 > 5000 && $5 < 10000) $5 = "please ask"
else if ($5 >= 10000) $5 = "expensive"
printf "%-10s %-8s   19%2d    %5d    %-12s\n",\
    $1, $2, $3, $4, $5
}

$ gawk -f price_range cars
plym      fury      1977      73     inexpensive
chevy     nova      1979      60     inexpensive
ford      mustang   1965      45     expensive
volvo     gl        1978     102     please ask
ford      ltd       1983      15     expensive
chevy     nova      1980      50     inexpensive
fiat      600       1965     115     inexpensive
honda     accord    1981      30     please ask
ford      thundbd   1984      10     expensive
toyota    tercel    1982     180     inexpensive
chevy     impala    1965      85     inexpensive
ford      bronco    1983      25     please ask
```

Following, the **manuf** associative array uses the contents of the first field of each record in the **cars** file as an index. The array is composed of the elements **manuf[plym]**, **manuf[chevy]**, **manuf[ford]**, and so on. The C language operator **++** increments the variable that it follows.

The *action* following the **END** *pattern* is the special **for** structure that loops through the elements of an associative array. A pipe sends the output through sort to produce an alphabetical list of cars and the quantities in stock:

```
$ cat manuf
gawk ' {manuf[$1]++}
END    {for (name in manuf) print name, manuf[name]}
' cars |
sort

$ manuf
chevy 3
fiat 1
ford 4
honda 1
plym 1
toyota 1
volvo 1
```

The **manuf.sh** program is a more complete shell script that includes error checking. This script lists and counts the contents of a column in a file, with both the column number and the name of the file specified on the command line.

The first gawk *action* (the one that starts with {count) uses the shell variable **$1** in the middle of the gawk program to specify an array index. Because of the way the single quotation marks are paired, the **$1** that appears to be within single quotation marks is actually not quoted: The two quoted strings in the gawk program surround, but do not include, the **$1**. Because the **$1** is not quoted, the shell substitutes the value of the first command line argument in place of **$1**, so that **$1** is interpreted before the gawk command is invoked. The leading dollar sign (the one before the first single quotation mark on that line) causes gawk to interpret what the shell substitutes as a field number:

```
$ cat manuf.sh
if [ $# != 2 ]
    then
        echo "Usage: manuf.sh field file"
        exit 1
fi
gawk < $2 '
        {count[$'$1']++}
END     {for (item in count) printf "%-20s%-20s\n",\
            item, count[item]}' |
sort
$ manuf.sh
Usage: manuf.sh field file

$ manuf.sh 1 cars
chevy                   3
fiat                    1
```

```
ford            4
honda           1
plym            1
toyota          1
volvo           1

$ manuf.sh 3 cars
65              3
77              1
78              1
79              1
80              1
81              1
82              1
83              2
84              1
```

Refer to Chapters 13 through 15 for more information on shell scripts.

The **word_usage** script displays a word usage list for a file you specify on the command line. The tr utility lists the words from standard input, one to a line. The sort utility orders the file, with the most frequently used words at the top of the list. This script sorts groups of words that are used the same number of times in alphabetical order:

```
$ cat word_usage
tr -cs 'a-zA-Z' '[\n*]' < $1 |
gawk     '
        {count[$1]++}
END     {for (item in count) printf "%-15s%3s\n", item, count[item]}' |
sort +1nr +0f -1

$ word_usage textfile
the             42
file            29
fsck            27
system          22
you             22
to              21
it              17
SIZE            14
and             13
MODE            13
.
.
.
.
```

Refer to sort (page 1326) and tr (page 1362) for more information.

Following is a similar program in a different format. The style mimics that of a C program and may be easier to read and work with for more complex gawk programs:

```
$ cat word_count
tr -cs 'a-zA-Z' '[\n*]' < $1 |
gawk ' {
        count[$1]++
}
END    {
        for (item in count)
            {
            if (count[item] > 4)
                {
                printf "%-15s%3s\n", item, count[item]
                }
            }
} ' |
sort +1nr +0f -1
```

The tail utility displays the last ten lines of output, illustrating that words occurring fewer than five times are not listed:

```
$ word_count textfile | tail
directories     5
if              5
information     5
INODE           5
more            5
no              5
on              5
response        5
this            5
will            5
```

The next example shows one way to put a date on a report. The first line of input to the gawk program comes from date. The gawk program reads this line as record number 1 (NR == 1), processes it accordingly, and processes all subsequent records with the *action* associated with the next *pattern* (NR > 1):

```
$ cat report
if (test $# = 0) then
    echo "You must supply a filename."
    exit 1
fi
(date; cat $1) |
gawk '
NR == 1    {print "Report for", $1, $2, $3 ", " $6}
NR > 1     {print $5 "        " $1}'

$ report cars
Report for Mon Jul 12, 2004
2500     plym
3000     chevy
10000    ford
9850     volvo
10500    ford
3500     chevy
```

```
450     fiat
6000    honda
17000   ford
750     toyota
1550    chevy
9500    ford
```

The next example uses the **numbers** file and sums each of the columns in a file you specify on the command line. The example performs error checking, reporting on and discarding rows that contain nonnumeric entries. The **next** command (thirteenth line) causes gawk to skip the rest of the commands for the current record and to read in another. At the end of the program, gawk displays a grand total for the file:

```
$ cat numbers
10      20       30.3    40.5
20      30       45.7    66.1
30      xyz      50      70
40      75       107.2   55.6
50      20       30.3    40.5
60      30       45.0    66.1
70      1134.7   50      70
80      75       107.2   55.6
90      176      30.3    40.5
100     1027.45  45.7    66.1
110     123      50      57a.5
120     75       107.2   55.6

$ cat tally
gawk ' BEGIN   {
                ORS = ""
                }

NR == 1 {
    nfields = NF
    }
    {
    if ($0 ~ /[^0-9. \t]/)
        {
        print "\nRecord " NR " skipped:\n\t"
        print $0 "\n"
        next
        }
    else
        {
        for (count = 1; count <= nfields; count++)
            {
            printf "%10.2f", $count > "tally.out"
            sum[count] += $count
            gtotal += $count
            }
        print "\n" > "tally.out"
        }
    }
```

```
END     {
    for (count = 1; count <= nfields; count++)
        {
        print "   -------" > "tally.out"
        }
    print "\n" > "tally.out"
    for (count = 1; count <= nfields; count++)
        {
        printf "%10.2f", sum[count] > "tally.out"
        }
    print "\n\n        Grand Total " gtotal "\n" > "tally.out"
} ' < numbers

$ tally
Record 3 skipped:
        30      xyz     50      70

Record 6 skipped:
        60      30      45.0    66.1

Record 11 skipped:
        110     123     50      57a.5

$ cat tally.out
    10.00     20.00     30.30     40.50
    20.00     30.00     45.70     66.10
    40.00     75.00    107.20     55.60
    50.00     20.00     30.30     40.50
    70.00   1134.70     50.00     70.00
    80.00     75.00    107.20     55.60
    90.00    176.00     30.30     40.50
   100.00   1027.45     45.70     66.10
   120.00     75.00    107.20     55.60
   -------   -------   -------   -------
   580.00   2633.15    553.90    490.50

        Grand Total 4257.55
```

The next gawk example reads the **passwd** file, listing users who do not have passwords and users who have duplicate user ID numbers:

```
$ cat /etc/passwd
bill::102:100:ext 123:/home/bill:/bin/bash
roy:x:104:100:ext 475:/home/roy:/bin/bash
tom:x:105:100:ext 476:/home/tom:/bin/bash
lynn:x:166:100:ext 500:/home/lynn:/bin/bash
mark:x:107:100:ext 112:/home/mark:/bin/bash
sales:x:108:100:ext 102:/m/market:/bin/bash
anne:x:109:100:ext 355:/home/anne:/bin/bash
toni::164:100:ext 357:/home/toni:/bin/bash
ginny:x:115:100:ext 109:/home/ginny:/bin/bash
chuck:x:116:100:ext 146:/home/chuck:/bin/bash
neil:x:164:100:ext 159:/home/neil:/bin/bash
```

```
rmi:x:118:100:ext 178:/home/rmi:/bin/bash
vern:x:119:100:ext 201:/home/vern:/bin/bash
bob:x:120:100:ext 227:/home/bob:/bin/bash
janet:x:122:100:ext 229:/home/janet:/bin/bash
maggie:x:124:100:ext 244:/home/maggie:/bin/bash
dan::126:100::/home/dan:/bin/bash
dave:x:108:100:ext 427:/home/dave:/bin/bash
mary:x:129:100:ext 303:/home/mary:/bin/bash
```

```
$ cat passwd_check
gawk < /etc/passwd '      BEGIN    {
    uid[void] = ""          # tell gawk that uid is an array
    }
    {                       # no pattern indicates process all records
    dup = 0                 # initialize duplicate flag
    split($0, field, ":")   # split into fields delimited by ":"
    if (field[2] == "")     # check for null password field
        {
        if (field[5] == "")# check for null info field
            {
            print field[1] " has no password."
            }
        else
            {
            print field[1] " ("field[5]") has no password."
            }
        }

    for (name in uid)       # loop through uid array
        {
        if (uid[name] == field[3])# check for 2nd use of UID
            {
            print field[1] " has the same UID as " name " : UID = "
uid[name]
            dup = 1  # set duplicate flag
            }
        }
    if (!dup)  # same as: if (dup == 0)
            # assign UID and login name to uid array
        {
        uid[field[1]] = field[3]
        }
    }'
```

```
$ passwd_check
bill (ext 123) has no password.
toni (ext 357) has no password.
neil has the same UID as toni : UID = 164
dan has no password.
dave has the same UID as sales : UID = 108
```

(The pwck utility also performs these checks, as well as a few more.)

The final example shows a complete interactive shell script that uses gawk to generate a report:

```
$ cat list_cars
trap 'rm -f $$.tem > /dev/null;echo $0 aborted.;exit 1' 1 2 15
echo -n "Price range (for example, 5000 7500):"
read lowrange hirange

echo '
                                        Miles
Make           Model          Year      (000)         Price
------------------------------------------------------' > $$.tem
gawk < cars '
$5 >= '$lowrange' && $5 <= '$hirange' {
    if ($1 ~ /ply/)  $1 = "plymouth"
    if ($1 ~ /chev/) $1 = "chevrolet"
    printf "%-10s %-8s    19%2d    %5d    $ %8.2f\n", $1, $2, $3, $4, $5
    }' | sort -n +5 >> $$.tem
cat $$.tem
rm $$.tem

$ list_cars
Price range (for example, 5000 7500): 3000 8000

                                      Miles
Make           Model        Year      (000)          Price
--------------------------------------------------------
chevrolet   nova            1979        60     $    3000.00
chevrolet   nova            1980        50     $    3500.00
honda       accord          1981        30     $    6000.00

$ list_cars
Price range (for example, 5000 7500): 0 2000

Make           Model        Year      (000)          Price
--------------------------------------------------------
fiat        600             1965       115     $     450.00
toyota      tercel          1982       180     $     750.00
chevrolet   impala          1965        85     $    1550.00

$ list_cars
Price range (for example, 5000 7500): 15000 100000

                                      Miles
Make           Model        Year      (000)          Price
--------------------------------------------------------
ford        thundbd         1984        10     $ 17000.00
```

Error Messages

The following examples show some of the more common causes of gawk's infamous error messages (and nonmessages). The examples are run under bash. (When using gawk with other shells, the error message you get may be different.)

The first example leaves the single quotation marks off the command line, so the shell interprets $3 and $1 as shell variables. Another problem is that because there are no single quotation marks, the shell passes gawk four arguments instead of two:

```
$ gawk {print $3, $1} cars
gawk: cmd. line:2: (END OF FILE)
gawk: cmd. line:2: parse error
```

The next command line includes a typo (prinnt) that gawk does not catch. Instead of issuing an error message, gawk simply does not do anything useful:

```
$ gawk '$3 >= 83 {prinnt $1}' cars
```

The next example has no braces around the *action:*

```
$ gawk '/chevy/ print $3, $1' cars
gawk: cmd. line:1: /chevy/ print $3, $1
gawk: cmd. line:1:            ^ parse error
```

There is no problem with the next example; gawk did just what you asked it to (none of the lines in the file contained a z).

```
$ gawk '/z/' cars
```

The following program contains a useless *action* (the **print** command is missing):

```
$ gawk '{$3}' cars
gawk: illegal statement 56250
 record number 1
```

The next example shows an improper *action* which generates no error message:

```
$ gawk '{$3  " made by "  $1}' cars
```

The heading in the following example is not displayed, because there is no backslash after the **print** command in the **BEGIN** block. The backslash is needed to quote the following NEWLINE so that the line can be continued. Without it, gawk sees two separate statements; the second does nothing:

```
$ cat print_cars
BEGIN    {print
"Model   Year    Price"}
/chevy/ {printf "%5s\t%4d\t%5d\n", $2, $3, $5}

$gawk -f print_cars cars

nova    79      3000
nova    80      3500
impala  65      1550
```

You must use double quotation marks, not single ones, to delimit strings.

```
$ cat print_cars2
BEGIN {OFS='\t'}
$3 ~ /5$/   {print $3, $1, "$" $5}

$ gawk -f print_cars2 cars
gawk: print_cars2:2: BEGIN {OFS='\t'}
gawk: print_cars2:2:                 ^ Invalid char ''' in expression
```

gcc

Compiles C and C++ programs

*gcc [**options**] **file-list** [–**/arg**]*
*g++ [**options**] **file-list** [–**/arg**]*

The GNU/Linux operating system uses the GNU C compiler, gcc, to preprocess, compile, assemble, and link C language source files. The same compiler with a different front end, g++, processes C++ source code. The gcc and g++ compilers can also assemble and link assembly language source files, link object files only, or build object files for use in shared libraries.

These compilers take input from files you specify on the command line. Unless you use the –o option, they store the executable program in **a.out**.

The gcc and g++ compilers are part of GCC, the *GNU Compiler Collection,* which includes front ends for C, C++, Objective C, Fortran, Java, and Ada as well as libraries for these languages. Go to gcc.gnu.org for more information.

---

gcc and g++ || tip

Although this section specifies the **gcc** compiler, it is mostly applicable to **g++** also.

Arguments   The **file-list** contains the pathnames of the files that gcc is to compile, assemble, and/or link.

Options   Without any options gcc accepts C language source files, assembly language files, object files, and other files as described in Table III-18 on page 1213. The gcc utility preprocesses, compiles, assembles, and links these files as appropriate, producing an executable file named **a.out**. If gcc is used to create object files without linking them to produce an executable file, each object file is named by adding the extension .o to the basename of the corresponding source file. If gcc is used to create an executable file, any object files created are deleted.

Some of the most commonly used options are listed following. When certain filename extensions are associated with an option, you can assume that the extension is added to the basename of the source file.

–c **compile**   Suppresses the linking step of compilation. The gcc utility compiles and/or assembles source code files and leaves the object code in files with the extension .o.

–o *file* **output**   Places the executable program that results from linking into *file* instead of **a.out**.

–O*n* **optimize**   Attempts to improve (optimize) the object code produced by the compiler. The value of *n* may be 0, 1, 2, or 3 (or 06 if you are compiling code for the Linux kernel). The default value of *n* is 1. Larger values of *n* result in better optimization but may increase both the size of the object file and the time it takes gcc to run. Using –O0 turns off optimization. Many related options control precisely the types of optimizations attempted by gcc when you use –O. Refer to the gcc info page for details.

–S **suppress**   Suppresses the assembling and linking steps of compilation on source code files. The resulting assembly language files use the .s filename extension.

–E **everything**   On source code files suppresses all steps of compilation *except* preprocessing and writes the result to standard output. By convention the extension .i is used for preprocessed C source and .ii for preprocessed C++ source.

–g **gdb**   Embeds diagnostic information in the object files. This information is used by symbolic debuggers, such as gdb. Although it is necessary only if you later use a debugger, it is a good practice to include this option as a matter of course.

–I*directory*   Looks for include files in *directory* before looking in the standard locations. You can give this option multiple times to look in more than one directory.

–L*directory*   Adds *directory* to the list of directories to search for libraries given with the –l option. Directories that are added to the list with –L are searched before looking in the standard locations for libraries.

–l*arg*   Searches the directories **/lib** and **/usr/lib** for a library file named **lib***arg***.a**. If this library is found, gcc then searches this library for any required functions. You must replace *arg* with the name of the library you want to search. For example, the –lm option normally links the standard math library **libm.a**. The position of this option is significant; it generally needs to go at the end of the command line but can be repeated multiple times to search different libraries. Libraries are searched in the order in which they appear on the command line. The linker uses the library only to resolve undefined symbols from modules that *precede* the library option on the command line. You can add other library paths to search for **lib***arg***.a**, using the –L option shown earlier.

–Wall   Causes gcc to warn you about questionable code in the source code files. Many related options control warning messages more precisely.

–pedantic The C language accepted by the GNU C compiler includes features that are not part of the ANSI standard for the C language. Using this option forces gcc to reject these *language extensions* and accept only standard C programming language features.

–traditional Causes gcc to accept only C programming language features that existed in the traditional Kernighan and Ritchie C programming language. This option allows you to compile correctly older programs written using the traditional C language that existed before the ANSI standard C language was defined.

–D*name*[=*value*] Usually #define preprocessor directives are given in header, or include, files. You can use this option to define symbolic names on the command line instead. For example, **–DLinux** is equivalent to having the line #define Linux in an include file, and **–DMACH=i586** is the same as #define MACH i586.

–fpic Causes gcc to produce *position-independent* code, which is suitable for installing into a shared library.

–fwritable-strings By default, the GNU C compiler places string constants into *protected memory*, where they cannot be changed. Some (usually older) programs assume that you can modify string constants. This option changes the behavior of gcc so string constants can be modified.

Notes

The preceding list of options is only a small fraction of the full set of options available with the GNU C compiler. See the gcc info page for a complete list.

Although the **–o** option is generally used to specify a filename to store object code, this option can also be used to name files resulting from other compilation steps. In the following example the **–o** option causes the assembly language produced by the following gcc command to be stored in the file **acode** instead of **pgm.s**, the default:

```
$ gcc -S -o acode pgm.c
```

The lint utility found in many UNIX systems is not available on GNU/Linux. However, the **–Wall** option performs many of the same checks and can be used in place of lint (page 859).

The conventions used by the C compiler for assigning filename extensions are summarized in Table III-18.

Examples

The first example compiles, assembles, and links a single C program, **compute.c**. The executable output is put in **a.out**. The gcc utility deletes the object file:

```
$ gcc compute.c
```

Filename Extension	**‖ table III-18**
.a	Library of object modules
.c	C language source file
.C, .cc, or .cxx	C++ language source file
.i	Preprocessed C language source file
.ii	Preprocessed C++ language source file
.o	Object file
.s	Assembly language source file
.S	Assembly language source file that needs preprocessing

The next example compiles the same program, using the C optimizer (–**O** option). It assembles and then links the optimized code. The –**o** option causes gcc to put the executable output in **compute**:

```
$ gcc -O -o compute compute.c
```

Next, a C source file, an assembly language file, and an object file are compiled, assembled, and linked. The executable output goes to **progo**:

```
$ gcc -o progo procom.c profast.s proout.o
```

In the next example gcc searches the standard math library stored in **/lib/libm.a** when it is linking the **himath** program and places the executable output in **a.out**:

```
$ gcc himath.c -lm
```

In the next example, the C compiler compiles **topo.c** with options that check the code for questionable source code practices (the –**Wall** option) and violations of the ANSI C standard (the –**pedantic** option). The –**g** option embeds debugging support in the executable file, which is saved in **topo** with the –**o topo** option. Full optimization is enabled with the –**O3** option.

The warnings produced by the C compiler are displayed on standard output. In this example the first and last warnings result from the –**pedantic** option; the other warnings result from the –**Wall** option:

```
$ gcc -Wall -g -O3 -pedantic -o topo topo.c
In file included from topo.c:2:
/usr/include/ctype.h:65: warning: comma at end of enumerator list
topo.c:13: warning: return-type defaults to 'int'
topo.c: In function 'main':
topo.c:14: warning: unused variable 'c'
topo.c: In function 'getline':
topo.c:44: warning: 'c' might be used uninitialized in this function
```

When compiling programs that use the X11 include files and libraries, you may need to use the –I and –L options to tell gcc where to locate those include files and libraries. The next example uses those options and also instructs gcc to link the program with the basic X11 library:

```
$ gcc -I/usr/X11R6/include plot.c -L/usr/X11R6/lib -lX11
```

grep

Searches for a pattern in files

*grep [**options**] **pattern** [**file-list**]*

The grep utility searches one or more files, line by line, for a ***pattern***, which can be a simple string or another form of a regular expression. The grep utility takes various actions, specified by options, each time it finds a line that contains a match for the ***pattern***. The grep utility takes its input from files you specify on the command line or from standard input.

Arguments   The ***pattern*** is a regular expression, as defined in Appendix A. You must quote regular expressions that contain special characters, SPACEs, or TABs. An easy way to quote these characters is to enclose the entire expression within single quotation marks.
The ***file-list*** contains pathnames of ordinary files that grep searches.

Options   Without any options grep sends lines that contain a match for ***pattern*** to standard output. When you specify more than one file on the command line, grep precedes each line that it displays with the name of the file that it came from and a colon.

Major Options

You can use only one of the following three options at a time. Normally you do not need to use any, as grep defaults to **–G**, which is regular grep.

–G   grep   Interprets ***pattern*** as a basic regular expression. This is the default major option if none is specified.

–E   extended   Interprets ***pattern*** as an extended regular expression (page 1392). The command **grep –E** is the same as egrep. See "Notes," following.

–F   fixed   Interprets ***pattern*** as a fixed string of characters. The command **grep –F** is the same as fgrep.

Other Options

––count –c   Displays only the number of lines that contain a match in each file.

––no-filename –h   If more than one file is given on the command line, does not precede each line of output with the name of the file containing it.

--ignore-case **–i** Causes lowercase letters in the pattern to match uppercase letters in the file and vice versa. Use this option when searching for a word that may be at the beginning of a sentence (that is, may or may not start with an uppercase letter).

--files-with-matches

–l Displays only the name of each file that contains one or more matches. It displays each filename only once, even if the file contains more than one match.

--line-number **–n** Precedes each line by its line number in the file. The file does not need to contain line numbers. This number represents the number of lines in the file up to and including the displayed line.

--quiet **–q** Does not send anything to standard out; only sets the exit code.

--recursive **–r** Recursively descends and processes directories in *file-list.*

--no-messages **–s** Does not display an error message if a file in *file-list* does not exist or is not readable.

--invert-match **–v** Causes lines *not* containing a match to satisfy the search. When you use this option by itself, grep displays all lines that do not contain a match for the *pattern.*

--word-regexp **–w** With this option, the *pattern* must match a whole word. This option is helpful if you are searching for a specific word that may also appear as a substring of another word in the file.

Notes

The grep utility returns an exit status of 0 if it finds a match, 1 if it does not find a match, and 2 if the file is not accessible or there is a syntax error.

Two utilities perform functions similar to that of grep. The egrep utility (same as **grep –E**) allows you to use *extended regular expressions* (page 1392), which include a different set of special characters than basic regular expressions do (page 1390). The fgrep utility (same as **grep –F**) is fast and compact but processes only simple strings, not regular expressions.

GNU grep, which is the grep that is included with Red Hat Linux, uses extended regular expressions in place of regular expressions. Thus egrep is virtually the same as grep. Refer to the grep info page for a minimal distinction.

Examples

The following examples assume that the working directory contains three files: **testa**, **testb**, and **testc**. The contents of each file are

File testa	File testb	File testc
aaabb	aaaaa	AAAAA
bbbcc	bbbbb	BBBBB
ff–ff	ccccc	CCCCC
cccdd	ddddd	DDDDD
dddaa		

The grep utility can search for a pattern that is a simple string of characters. The following command line searches **testa** for and displays each line containing the string bb:

```
$ grep bb testa
aaabb
bbbcc
```

The **–v** option reverses the sense of the test. The following example displays all the lines *without* bb:

```
$ grep -v bb testa
ff-ff
cccdd
dddaa
```

The **–n** option displays the line number of each displayed line:

```
$ grep -n bb testa
1:aaabb
2:bbbcc
```

The grep utility can search through more than one file. Here grep searches through each file in the working directory. (The ambiguous file reference * matches all filenames.) The name of the file containing the string precedes each line of output.

```
$ grep bb *
testa:aaabb
testa:bbbcc
testb:bbbbb
```

When the search for the string bb is done with the **–w** option, grep produces no output because none of the files contains the string bb as a separate word:

```
$ grep -w bb *
$
```

The search that grep performs is case sensitive. Because the previous examples specified lowercase bb, grep did not find the uppercase string, BBBBB, in **testc**. The **–i** option causes both uppercase *and* lowercase letters to match either case of letter in the pattern:

```
$ grep -i bb *
testa:aaabb
testa:bbbcc
testb:bbbbb
testc:BBBBB
$ grep -i BB *
testa:aaabb
testa:bbbcc
testb:bbbbb
testc:BBBBB
```

The **–c** option displays the number of lines in each file that contain a match:

```
$ grep -c bb *
testa:2
testb:1
testc:0
```

The following command line displays from the file **text2** lines that contain a string of characters starting with st, followed by zero or more characters (.* represents zero or more characters in a regular expression—see Appendix A) and ending in ing:

```
$ grep 'st.*ing' text2
...
```

The ^ regular expression, which matches the beginning of a line, can be used alone to match every line in a file. Together with the **–n** option, ^ can be used to display the lines in a file, preceded by their line numbers.

```
$ grep -n '^' testa
1:aaabb
2:bbbcc
3:ff-ff
4:cccdd
5:dddaa
```

The next command line counts the number of times #include statements appear in C source files in the working directory. The **–h** option causes grep to suppress the filenames from its output. The input to sort is all lines from *.c that match #include. The output from sort is an ordered list of lines that contains many duplicates. When uniq with the **–c** option processes this list, it outputs repeated lines only once, along with a count of the number of repetitions in its input:

```
$ grep -h '^#include' *.c | sort | uniq -c
9 #include "buff.h"
2 #include "poly.h"
1 #include "screen.h"
6 #include "window.h"
2 #include "x2.h"
2 #include "x3.h"
2 #include <math.h>
3 #include <stdio.h>
```

The final command line calls the vi editor with a list of files in the working directory that contain the string Sampson. The $(...) command substitution structure (page 575) causes the shell to execute grep in place and supply vi with a list of filenames that you want to edit:

```
$ vi $(grep -l 'Sampson' *)
...
```

The single quotation marks are not necessary in this example, but they are required if the string you are searching for contains special characters or SPACEs. It is generally a good habit to quote the pattern so that the shell does not interpret any special characters it may contain.

gzip

Compresses or decompresses files

*gzip [**options**] [**file-list**]*
*gunzip [**options**] [**file-list**]*

The gzip utility compresses files, reducing disk space requirements and the time needed to transmit files between computers. When gzip compresses a file, it adds the extension **.gz** to the filename: Compressing the file **fname** creates the file **fname.gz** and deletes the original file. To restore **fname**, use the command **gunzip** with the argument **fname.gz**. The **.gz** extension is optional.

Arguments

The *file-list* is a list of one or more files that are to be compressed or decompressed. If a directory appears in *file-list* with no **--recursive** option, gzip issues an error message and ignores the directory. With the **--recursive** option, gzip recursively compresses files within the directory and subdirectories to any level.

If *file-list* is empty or if the special option – is present, gzip reads from standard input. The **--force** option permits standard input to come from the terminal and causes gzip to write to standard output.

The information in this section is also true of gunzip, a link to gzip.

Options

--decompress *or* **–d**   Decompresses a file compressed with gzip. This option with gzip is equivalent
--uncompress   to the gunzip command.

--fast *or* **–#**   Gives you control over the tradeoff between the speed of compression and the
--best   amount of compression. In the form –#, replace the # with a digit from 1 to 9; level 1 is the fastest compression and level 9 the best. The default level is 6. The options **--fast** and **--best** are synonyms for –1 and –9, respectively.

--force **–f**   Forces compression even if a file already exists, has multiple links, or comes directly from a terminal. The option has a similar effect with gunzip.

--recursive **–r**   For directories in *file-list*, descends tree rooted at the directory, compressing all files recursively. Used with gunzip, recursively decompresses files.

--stdout **–c**   Writes the results of compression or decompression to standard output instead of overwriting the original file.

--verbose **–v**   For each file, displays the name of the file, the name of the compressed file, and the amount of compression. Displays similar information with gunzip.

Discussion   Almost all files become much smaller when compressed with gzip. Rarely a file becomes larger, but only by a slight amount. The type of a file and its contents (as well
as the –# option) determine how much reduction is done; text files are often reduced by 60 percent to 70 percent.

The attributes of a file, such as owner, permissions, and modification and access
times, are left intact when gzip compresses a file.

If the compressed version of a file already exists, gzip reports that fact and asks
for your confirmation before overwriting the existing file. If a file has multiple links
to it, gzip issues an error message and terminates. The ––force option overrides the
default behavior in both of these situations.

Notes   In addition to the gzip format, gunzip recognizes several other compressed-file formats, enabling gunzip to decompress files compressed with compress.

To see an example of a file that gets larger when compressed with gzip, compare
the size of a file that has been compressed once with the same file compressed with
gzip again. Because gzip complains when you give it an argument with the extension
.gz, you need to rename the file before compressing it a second time.

The tar utility with the –z option calls gzip (page 1219).

The following related utilities display and manipulate compressed files. None of
these utilities changes the files that it works on.

zcat *file-list*   Works like cat except that *file-list* contains compressed files that are decompressed
with gunzip as each is output.

zdiff [*options*] *file1*   Works like diff except that *file1* and *file2* are decompressed with gunzip as needed. The
[*file2*]   zdiff utility accepts the same options as diff (page 1149). If you omit *file2*, zdiff compares *file1* with the compressed version of *file1* (assuming that it exists).

zless *file-list*   Works like less except that *file-list* contains compressed files that are decompressed
with gunzip as each is displayed by less.

Examples   In the first example, gzip compresses two files. Next, gunzip decompresses one of the
files. When a file is compressed and decompressed, its size changes, but its modification time remains the same:

```
$ ls -l
total 175
-rw-rw-r-- 1 alex group 33557 Jul 20 17:32 patch-2.0.7
-rw-rw-r-- 1 alex group 143258 Jul 20 17:32 patch-2.0.8
$ gzip *
```

```
$ ls -l
total 51
-rw-rw-r-- 1 alex group 9693 Jul 20 17:32 patch-2.0.7.gz
-rw-rw-r-- 1 alex group 40426 Jul 20 17:32 patch-2.0.8.gz
$ gunzip patch-2.0.7.gz
$ ls -l
total 75
-rw-rw-r-- 1 alex group 33557 Jul 20 17:32 patch-2.0.7
-rw-rw-r-- 1 alex group 40426 Jul 20 17:32 patch-2.0.8.gz
```

In the next example the files in Jenny's home directory are archived by using the cpio utility. The archive is compressed with gzip before it is written to tape:

```
$ find /home/jenny -depth -print | cpio -oBm | gzip >/dev/ftape
```

For more information, refer to cpio on page 1124.

head

Displays the beginning of a file

*head [**options**] [**file-list**]*

The head utility displays the beginning (head) of a file. The utility takes its input from one or more files you specify on the command line or from standard input.

Arguments   The *file-list* contains pathnames of the files that head displays. When you specify more than one file, head displays the filename of each file before displaying the first few lines. When you do not specify a file, head takes its input from standard input.

Options

--bytes [*n*[*u*]] −c   Counts by bytes (characters). The *n* is an optional nonzero integer. The *u* is an optional unit of measure that can be **b** (512-byte blocks), **k** (1,024-byte blocks), or **m** (1-megabyte blocks). If you include the unit of measure, head counts by this unit in place of bytes.

--lines[[+]*n*] −*n*   Counts by lines (the default). You can use −*n* to specify *n* lines without using the **lines** keyword.

--quiet −q   Suppresses header information when you specify more than one filename on the command line.

--help   Summarizes how to use head.

Note   The head utility displays ten lines by default.

Examples   The examples are based on the following **eleven** file:

```
$ cat eleven
line one
line two
line three
line four
line five
line six
line seven
line eight
line nine
line ten
line eleven
```

In this example head displays the first ten lines of the **eleven** file (no arguments):

```
$ head eleven
line one
line two
line three
line four
line five
line six
line seven
line eight
line nine
line ten
```

The next example displays the first three lines (**--lines 3**) of the file:

```
$ head --lines 3 eleven
line one
line two
line three
```

The following example is equivalent to the preceding one:

```
$ head -3 eleven
line one
line two
line three
```

The next example displays the first six characters (**--bytes 6**) in the file:

```
$ head --bytes 6 eleven
line o$
```

kill

Terminates a process

kill [option] PID-list
kill –l

The kill builtin **bash tcsh zsh** terminates one or more processes by sending them signals. By default, kill sends software termination signals (signal number 15). The process must belong to the user executing kill, except that Superuser can terminate any process.

In the second form of the command, kill displays a list of all the available signal names. You can use either a signal number or the signal name with the kill builtin.

Arguments   The *PID-list* contains process identification (PID) numbers of processes kill is to terminate.

Options   You can specify a signal number or name, preceded by a hyphen, as an option before the *PID-list* to cause kill to send the signal you specify to the process.

Notes   The shell displays the PID number of a background process when you initiate the process. You can also use the ps utility to determine PID numbers.

If the software termination signal does not terminate the process, try using a KILL signal (signal number 9). A process can choose to ignore any signal except KILL.

The kill builtin **bash tcsh zsh** accepts job identifiers in place of the *PID-list*. Job identifiers consist of a percent sign (%) followed by either a job number or a string that uniquely identifies the job. The builtin versions of kill also allow you to specify signals by name rather than number. You can use the **kill –l** command to list the signal names.

To terminate all processes that the current login process initiated and have the operating system log you out, give the command **kill –9 0**.

---

root: Do Not Run kill with Arguments of –9 0 *or* KILL 0 || caution

If you run the command **kill –9 0** while you are logged in as Superuser, you will bring the system down.

Examples   The first example shows a command line executing the file **compute** as a background process and the kill utility terminating it:

```
$ compute &
[2] 259
$ kill 259
$
[2]  + terminated  compute
```

The next example shows the ps utility determining the PID number of the background process running a program named **xprog** and the kill utility terminating **xprog** with the TERM signal:

```
$ ps
PID TTY STAT  TIME COMMAND
116   1 S     0:00 -zsh
128   1 S N   0:00 xinit /home/alex/.xinitrc --
137   1 S N   0:01 fvwm
138  p0 S N   0:00 -zsh
161  p0 S N   0:10 xprog
262  p0 R N   0:00 ps
$ kill -TERM 161
[1]  + killed      xprog
$
```

less

Displays text files, one screen at a time

less **[options]** **[file-list]**

The less utility displays text files, one screen at a time and is similar to more but includes many enhancements. After displaying a screen of text, less displays a prompt and waits for you to enter a command. You can skip forward and backward in the file, invoke an editor, search for a pattern, or perform a number of other tasks. This utility takes its input from files you specify on the command line or from standard input.

Arguments The **file-list** is the list of files you want to view. If there is no **file-list**, less reads from standard input.

Options This section describes only some of the more commonly used options. Refer to the less man page for a complete list of options.

–e exit Normally less requires you to enter **q** to terminate. This option exits automatically the *second* time less reads the end of file.

–E Exit Similar to **–e**, except that less exits automatically the *first* time it reads the end of file.

–i ignore case Causes a search for a string of lowercase letters to match both upper- and lowercase. If you give a pattern that includes any uppercase letters, this option is ignored.

–I IGNORE CASE Causes a search for a string of letters of any case to match both upper- and lowercase.

–m Reports the percentage of the file that you have viewed with each prompt. This is similar to the prompt used by more. Does not work when reading from standard input, as less has no way of determining how large the input is.

–N number Displays a line number at the start of each line.

–P*prompt* Changes the prompt string to **prompt**. Enclose **prompt** in quotation marks if it contains any SPACES. There are special symbols you can use in **prompt** that less replaces with other values when it displays the prompt. For example, less displays the current filename in place of **%f** in **prompt**. See the less man page for a full list of these special symbols. Custom prompts are useful if you are running less from within another program and want to give instructions or information to the person using the program. The default prompt is the name of the file in reverse video.

–s squeeze blanks Displays multiple, adjacent blank lines as a single blank line. When you use less to display text that has been formatted for printing with blank space at the top and bottom of each page, this option shortens these headers and footers to a single line.

–x*n* Sets tab stops *n* characters apart. The default is eight characters.

–[z]*n* Sets the scrolling size to *n* lines. The default is the size of the display. Each time you move forward or backward a page, you move *n* lines.

+*command* Any command you can give less while it is running can also be given as an option by preceding it with a plus sign (**+**) on the command line. See the "Commands" section following. A command preceded by a plus sign on the command line is executed as soon as less starts and applies only to the first file.

++*command* Similar to **+***command* except that *command* is applied to every file in *file–list*, not just the first.

Notes

The phrase *less is more* explains the origin of this utility; more is the original Berkeley UNIX pager (also available under GNU/Linux).

You can set the options to less either from the command line when you call less or by setting the **LESS** environment variable. For example, you can use the following command from bash to use less with the **–x4** and **–s** options.

```
$ export LESS="-x4 -s"
```

Normally you would set **LESS** in **.profile** if you are using bash or **.zprofile** if you are using zsh. If you use tcsh, set it in your **.login** file. Once you have set the **LESS** variable, less is invoked with the specified options each time you call it. (Any options you give on the command line override the settings in the **LESS** variable.) The **LESS** variable is used both when you directly call less from the command line and when less is invoked by another program, such as man. You can specify less as the pager to use with man and other programs by setting the environment variable **PAGER** to **less**. For example, with bash you can add the following line to **.profile**:

```
export PAGER=less
```

Commands

Whenever less pauses, you can enter any of a large number of commands. The following list gives the commonly used commands. Refer to the less man page to see the full list of commands. The *n*, an optional numeric argument, defaults to 1, with exceptions as noted. You do not need to follow these commands with RETURN.

h *or* H	**help**	Displays a summary of all available commands. The summary is displayed using less, as the list of commands extends across several screens of a typical display.
*n*SPACE		Displays the next *n* lines of text. Because the value of *n* defaults to the size of the screen, SPACE by itself displays the next screen of text.
*n*z		Works like *n*SPACE except that the value of *n*, if present, becomes the new default value for the z and SPACE commands.
*n*RETURN or *n*j	**jump**	Scrolls forward *n* lines. The default value of *n* is 1.
*n*d or *n*CONTROL-D	**down**	Scrolls forward *n* lines. The default value of **n** is one-half the screen size. When you specify *n*, it becomes the new default value for this command.
*n*b or *n*CONTROL-B	**backward**	Scrolls backward *n* lines. The default value of *n* is the size of the screen.
*n*w		Scrolls backward as in the previous command, except that the value of *n* becomes the new default value for this command.
*n*y or *n*k		Scrolls backward *n* lines. The default value of *n* is 1.
*n*u or *n*CONTROL-U		Scrolls backward *n* lines. The default value of *n* is half the screen size. When you specify *n*, it becomes the default value for this command.
*n*g	**go**	Goes to line number *n*. This command may not work if the file is read from standard input and you have moved too far down into the file already. The default value of *n* is 1.

/*regular-expression*   Skips forward in the file, looking for strings matching *regular-expression*. If you begin *regular-expression* with an exclamation point (!), this command looks for strings that *do not match* *regular-expression*. If *regular-expression* begins with an asterisk (*), this command continues the search through *file-list*. If *regular-expression* begins with an at sign (@), this command begins the search at the start of *file-list* and continues to the end of *file-list*.

?*regular-expression*   This command is similar to the previous one but searches backward through the file (and *file-list*). An asterisk (*) as the first character in *regular-expression* causes the search to continue backward, through *file-list*, through the first file. An at sign (@) causes the search to start with the last line of the last file in *file-list* and progress toward the first line of the first file.

{ *or* (*or* [If one of these characters appears in the top line of the display, this command scrolls forward to the matching right brace, parenthesis, or bracket (that is, typing { causes less to move to the matching }).

} *or*) *or*]   Similar to the preceding commands, these commands move you backward to the matching left brace, parenthesis, or bracket.

CONTROL-L   Redraws the screen. This command is useful if the text on the screen has become garbled.

F **forward** Scrolls forward. If the end of the input file is reached, this option waits for more input and then continues scrolling. This option allows you to use less in a manner similar to **tail –f** (page 1340), except that less paginates the output as it appears.

n:**n** Skips to the next file in *file-list*. If *n* is given, skips to the *n*[th] next file in *file-list*.

v This command brings the current file into an editor with the cursor on the current line. The less utility uses the editor specified in the **EDITOR** environment variable. If **EDITOR** is unset, less uses vi.

![*command line*] Executes *command line* under the shell specified by the **SHELL** environment variable, or sh (usually linked to bash) by default. A percent sign (%) in *command line* is replaced by the name of the current file. If *command line* is omitted, less starts an interactive shell.

q *or* **:q** Terminates less.

Examples

The following example displays the file **memo.txt**. To see more of the file, the user presses the SPACE bar in response to the less prompt at the bottom left of the screen:

```
$ less memo.txt
.
.
memo.txt SPACE
.
.
```

In the next example the user has changed the prompt to a more meaningful message and has used the **–N** option to display line numbers. Finally, the user has instructed less to skip forward to the first line containing the string procedure:

```
$ less -P"Press SPACE to continue, q to quit" -N +/procedure ncut.icn
   28   procedure main(args)
   29       local filelist, arg, fields, delim
   30
   31       filelist:=[]
.
.
   45       # Check for real field list
   46       #
   47       if /fields then stop("-fFIELD_LIST is required.")
   48
   49       # Process the files and output the fields
Enter SPACE to continue, q to quit
```

ln

Makes a link to a file

*ln [**options**] **existing-file new-link***
*ln [**options**] **existing-file-list directory***

The first format creates a link between an existing file and a new filename. The second format links existing files into a different directory. The new links have the same simple filenames as the original files but have different full pathnames.

By default ln makes *hard links*. A hard link to a file is indistinguishable from the original filename. All hard links to a file must be in the same filesystem as the original file.

You can also use ln to create *symbolic links*. Unlike a hard link, a symbolic link can exist in a different filesystem from the linked-to file. Also, a symbolic link can connect to a directory. Refer to page 126 for more information about symbolic links.

Arguments

The *existing-file* is the pathname of the file you want to make a link to. The *new-link* is the pathname of the new link. When you are making a symbolic link, the *existing-file* can be a directory.

Using the second format, the *existing-file-list* contains the pathnames of the ordinary files you want to make links to. The ln utility establishes the new links so that they appear in the *directory*. The simple filenames of the entries in the *directory* are the same as the simple filenames of the files in the *existing-file-list*.

Options

--backup –b If the ln utility is going to remove a file, this option makes a backup by appending ~ to the filename. This option works only with **--force**.

--force –f Normally ln does not create the link if *new-link* already exists. This option removes *new-link* before creating the link. With the **--backup** option, a copy of *new–link* is made before removing it.

--interactive –i If *new-link* already exists, this option prompts you before removing *new-link*. If you enter **y** or **yes**, ln removes *new-link* before creating the link. If you answer **n** or **no**, no new link is made.

--symbolic –s Creates a symbolic link. When you use this option, the *existing-file* and *new-link* may be directories and may be on different filesystems. Refer to "Symbolic Links" on page 126.

Notes   The ls utility with the **–l** option shows you how many hard links a file has. Refer to "Links" on page 123.

    If *new-link* is the name of an existing file, ln does not create the link unless you use the **––force** option or answer **yes** when using the **––interactive** option.

    You can use symbolic links to link across filesystems and to create links to directories. When you use the ls **–l** command to list information about a symbolic link, ls displays -> and the name of the linked-to file after the name of the link.

Examples   The following command makes a link between **memo2** in the **/home/alex/literature** directory and the working directory. The file appears as **memo2** (the simple filename of the existing file) in the working directory:

```
$ ln /home/alex/literature/memo2 .
```

The next command makes a link to the same file. This time the file appears as **new_memo** in the working directory:

```
$ ln /home/alex/literature/memo2 new_memo
```

The following command makes a link that causes the file to appear in another user's directory:

```
$ ln /home/alex/literature/memo2 /home/jenny/new_memo
```

You must have write and execute access permission to the other user's directory for this command to work. If you own the file, you can use chmod to give the other user write access permission to the file.

    The next command makes a symbolic link to an existing file, **memo3**, in the directory **/home/alex/literature**. The symbolic link is in a different filesystem, **/tmp**. The ls **–l** command shows the linked-to filename:

```
$ pwd
/home/alex/literature
$ ln -s memo3 /tmp/memo
$ ls -l /tmp/memo
lrwxrwxrwx 1 alex  pubs 5  Jul 13 11:44 /tmp/memo -> memo3
```

The final example attempts to make a symbolic link named **memo1** to the file **memo2**. Because the file **memo1** exists, ln refuses to make the link. If you use the **––interactive** option, ln asks whether you want to replace the existing **memo1** file with the symbolic link. If you enter **y** or **yes**, the link is made, and the old **memo1** disappears:

```
$ ls -l memo?
-rw-rw-r--   1 alex       group           224 Jul 31 14:48 memo1
-rw-rw-r--   1 alex       group           753 Jul 31 14:49 memo2
$ ln --symbolic memo2 memo1
ln: memo1: File exists
$ ln --symbolic --interactive memo2 memo1
ln: replace 'memo1'? y
$ ls -l memo?
lrwxrwxrwx   1 alex       group             5 Jul 31 14:49 memo1 -> memo2
-rw-rw-r--   1 alex       group           753 Jul 31 14:49 memo2
```

lpr

Prints files

lpr [options] [file-list]
lpq [options] [job-identifiers]
lprm [options] [job-identifiers]

The lpr utility places one or more files into a print queue, providing orderly access to printers for several users or processes. The utility can work with printers attached to remote systems. You can use the lprm utility to remove files from the print queues and the lpq utility to check the status of files in the queues. Refer to the "Notes" section.

The lpr utility takes its input from files you specify on the command line or from standard input and adds them to the print queue as *print jobs*. The utility assigns a unique identification number to each print job. You can use the lprm utility to remove a print job from the print queue; the lpq utility displays the job numbers of the print jobs that lpr set up.

Arguments   The *file-list* is a list of one or more filenames for lpr to print. Often these files are text files, but many systems are configured so that lpr can accept and properly print a variety of file types.

The *job-identifiers* is a list of job numbers or user names. If you don't know a printer job number, use lpq to display it.

Options   Some of the following options depend on the type of file being printed, as well as on how your system is configured for printing. To see which options are available, check with the person who set up lpr.

–P*printer*   Routes the print jobs to the queue for the printer named *printer*. If you do not use this option, print jobs are routed to the default printer for your system. The acceptable values for *printer* are found in the file **/etc/printcap** and vary from system to system.

–h   Suppresses printing of the header, or burst, page. This page is useful for identifying the owner of the output in a multiuser setup, but printing it is a waste of paper when there is only one user.

–m *user*   Sends mail to *user* (for example, **alex@bravo.com**) when the print jobs complete successfully. This option is useful on systems that have many people sharing the same printer or when the printer is not located near you.

–#*n*   Prints *n* copies of each file. Depending on your shell, you may need to escape the **#** with a backslash to pass it to lpr.

Discussion The lpr utility works with the **lpd** line printer daemon and is generally part of the **LPRng** or **CUPS** printing system. The **lpd** daemon manages the print queues and routes jobs to the printers when they become available.

The lpq utility displays information about jobs in a print queue. When called without any arguments, lpq lists all the print jobs queued for the default printer. Use the **−P***printer* option (see the description in the preceding "Options" section) with lpq to look at other print queues, even those for printers connected to other computers. With the **−l** option lpq displays more information about each job. If you give the login name of a user as an argument, lpq displays only the printer jobs belonging to that user.

One of the items displayed by lpq is the job number for each print job in the queue. To remove a job from the print queue, use the job number as an argument to lprm. Unless you are Superuser, you can remove only your own jobs. Even as Superuser you may not be able to remove a job from a queue for a remote printer. You can remove all jobs from a selected queue with **lprm −P***printer* **all**. If you do not give any arguments to lprm, it removes the currently active printer job (that is, the job that is now printing) from the queue, if you own that job. You can remove all your print jobs by using your login name or the word **all** as the argument. Using a login name is a useful way for Superuser to remove all printer jobs that belong to a particular user.

Notes If you normally use a printer other than the system default printer, you can set up lpr to use another printer as your personal default by assigning the name of this printer to the environment variable **PRINTER**. For example, if you use bash, you can add the following line to **~/.profile** to set your default printer to the printer named **ps**:

```
export PRINTER=ps
```

Examples The first command sends the file named **memo2** to the default printer:

```
$ lpr memo2
```

Next, a pipe sends the output of ls to the printer named **deskjet**:

```
$ ls | lpr -Pdeskjet
```

The next example paginates and sends the file **memo** to the printer:

```
$ pr -h "Today's memo" memo | lpr
```

The next example shows a number of print jobs queued for the default printer. All the jobs are owned by Alex, and the first one is currently being printed (active).

Jobs 635 and 639 were created by sending input to lpr standard input, whereas job 638 was created by giving **ncut.icn** as an argument to the lpr command. The last column gives the size of each print job:

```
$ lpq
lp is ready and printing
Rank    Owner      Job  Files                        Total Size
active  alex       635  (standard input)             38128 bytes
1st     alex       638  ncut.icn                      3587 bytes
2nd     alex       639  (standard input)              3960 bytes
```

The next command removes job 638 from the default print queue. The lpr command responds by identifying the data file and control file that **lpd** uses to keep track of the print job. The data file contains the data to send to the printer, and the control file contains any special information (such as the number of copies to make) required when printing the file:

```
$ lprm 638
dfA638Aa28156 dequeued
cfA638Aa28156 dequeued
```

Finally, Alex removes all his jobs from the print queue by giving lprm an argument of **all**:

```
$ lprm all
dfA635Aa28141 dequeued
cfA635Aa28141 dequeued
dfA639Aa28159 dequeued
cfA639Aa28159 dequeued
```

ls

Displays information about one or more files

ls [options] [file-list]

The ls utility displays information about one or more files. It lists the information alphabetically by filename unless you use an option to change the order.

Arguments   When you do not use an argument, ls displays the names of the visible files in the working directory (those files whose filenames do not begin with a period [.]).

The *file-list* contains one or more pathnames of files. You can use the pathname of any ordinary, directory, or device file. These pathnames can include ambiguous file references.

When you specify a directory, ls displays the contents of the directory. It displays the name of the directory only when needed to avoid ambiguity, such as when more than one directory is included in the listing. When you specify an ordinary file, ls displays information about that one file.

Options   The options determine the type of information ls displays, how it displays it, and the order in which it is displayed. When you do not use an option, ls displays a short list that contains only the names of files.

--all -a   Without a *file-list* (no arguments on the command line), this option displays information about all the files in the working directory, including invisible files (those with filenames that begin with a period). Without this option ls does not list information about invisible files unless you list the name of an invisible file in *file-list.*

When you use this option with a *file-list* that includes an appropriate ambiguous file reference, ls displays information about invisible files. (The ✳ ambiguous file reference does not match a leading period in a filename—see page 158.)

--almost-all -A   The same as **--all** but does not list the . and .. entries.

--escape -b   Displays nonprinting characters in a filename, using escape sequences similar to those used in C language strings. A partial list is given in Table III-19. Other nonprinting characters are displayed with a backslash followed by an octal number.

Escape Sequence	**‖ table III-19**
\b	BACKSPACE
\n	NEWLINE
\r	RETURN
\t	HORIZONTAL TAB
\v	VERTICAL TAB
\\	BACKSLASH

--directory –d Displays the names of directories without displaying their contents. Without an argument this option displays information about the working directory. Normally this option displays ordinary files in the directory you are displaying, as well as directory files.

--classify –F Displays a slash after each directory, an asterisk after each executable file, and an at sign (@) after symbolic links.

--color[=*when*] The ls utility can display various types of files in different colors but normally does not use colors (same as using **never** for *when*). If you do not specify *when* or if you specify *when* as **always**, ls uses colors. When you use **auto** or **tty** for *when*, ls uses colors only when the output goes to a screen. The default Red Hat setup creates an alias for ls that substitutes **ls --color=tty** when you call ls. Give the command **unalias ls** to remove the alias. See "Notes."

--human-readable –h Displays file sizes using K, M, and G as appropriate. Uses powers of 1,024; use **--si** for powers of 1,000.

--inode –i Displays the inode number of each file. With the –l option this option displays the inode number in column 1 and shifts all other items one column to the right.

--format=long –l ("ell") Lists more information about each file. Use with –h to make file sizes more readable. See "Discussion."

--dereference –L Lists information about the file referenced by each symbolic link rather than information about the link itself.

--hide-control-chars –q Displays nonprinting characters in a filename as question marks. When output is going to the screen, this is the default behavior.

--reverse –r Displays the list of filenames in reverse sorted order.

--recursive –R Recursively lists subdirectories.

--size -s   Displays the size of each file in 1,024-byte blocks. The size precedes the filename. With the **-l** option this option displays the size in column 1 and shifts each of the other items one column to the right. You can include the **-h** option to make the file sizes easier to read.

--format=*word*   By default ls displays files sorted vertically. This option sorts files based on *word*: **across** (**-x**), separated by **commas** (**-m**), **horizontal** (**-x**), **long** (**-l**), **single-column** (**-1**).

--sort=*word*   By default ls displays files in ASCII order. This option sorts the files based on *word*: filename **extension** (**-X**), **none** (**-U**), file **size** (**-S**), **access** time (**-u**), modification **time** (**-t**), except see **--time**, following.

--time=*word*   By default the time that ls displays is the modification time of a file. Set *word* to **atime** to display access time (or use the **-t** option) or to **ctime** to display creation time. The list is sorted by *word* when you also give the **--sort=time** option.

Discussion   The ls long listing (**--format=long** or **-l** options) displays the seven columns shown in Figure 4-12 on page 119. The first column, which contains 11 characters, is divided as described in the following paragraphs. The first character describes the type of file, as shown in Table III-20. Refer to pages 103 and 968 for more information on types of files.

First Character   **|| table III-20**

–	Ordinary
b	Block device
c	Character device
d	Directory
p	FIFO (named pipe)
l	Symbolic link

The next nine characters of the first column represent all the access permissions associated with the file. These nine characters are divided into three sets of three characters each.

The first three characters represent the owner's access permissions. If the owner has read access permission to the file, an **r** appears in the first character position. If the owner is not permitted to read the file, a hyphen appears in this position. The next two positions represent the owner's write and execute access permissions. A **w** appears in the second position if the owner is permitted to write to the file, and an **x** appears in the third position if the owner is permitted to execute the file. An **s** in the third position indicates that the file has setuid permission and execute permission. An **S** indicates setuid without execute permission. A hyphen indicates that the owner does not have the access permission associated with the character position.

In a similar manner the second and third sets of three characters represent the access permissions of the user's group and other users. An **s** in the third position of the second set of characters indicates that the file has setgid permission with execute permission, and an **S** indicates setgid without execute permission.

The last character is **t** if the sticky bit is set with execute permission and **T** if it is set without execute permission. Refer to chmod on page 1103 for information on changing access permissions.

The second column indicates the number of hard links to the file. Refer to page 123 for more information on links.

The third and fourth columns display the name of the owner of the file and the name of the group the file belongs to.

The fifth column indicates the size of the file in bytes or, if information about a device file is being displayed, the major and minor device numbers. In the case of a directory, this number is the size of the directory file, not the size of the files that are entries within the directory. (Use du to display the sum of the sizes of all the files in a directory.) Include the **–h** option to display the size of files in kilobytes, megabytes, or gigabytes.

The last two columns display the date and time the file was last modified and the filename, respectively.

Notes

Refer to page 157 for examples of using ls with ambiguous file references.

With the **––color** option ls can display filenames of various types of files in different colors. By default, executable files are green, directory files are blue, symbolic links are cyan, archives and compressed files are red, and ordinary text files are black. The manner in which ls colors each of the different file types is specified in the **/etc/DIR_COLORS** file. If this file does not exist on your system, ls will not color filenames. You can modify **/etc/DIR_COLORS** to alter the default color/file-type mappings on a systemwide basis. For your personal use, you can copy **/etc/DIR_COLORS** to **~/.dir_colors** file in your home directory and modify **~/.dir_colors**. For your login, **~/.dir_colors** overrides the systemwide colors established in **/etc/DIR_COLORS**. Refer to the **dir_colors** and dircolors man pages for more information.

Examples   The first command line shows the ls utility with the **–x** option. You see an alphabetical list of the names of the files in the working directory:

```
$ ls -x
bin         c           calendar
execute     letters     shell
```

The **–F** option appends a slash (**/**) to files that are directories, an asterisk to files that are executable, and an at sign (**@**) after symbolic links:

```
$ ls -Fx
bin/        c/          calendar
execute*  letters/    shell@
```

The **–l** (**long**) option displays a long list. The files are still in alphabetical order:

```
$ ls -l
total 8
drwxrwxr-x  2 jenny    pubs    80  May 20 09:17 bin
drwxrwxr-x  2 jenny    pubs   144  Mar 26 11:59 c
-rw-rw-r--  1 jenny    pubs   104  May 28 11:44 calendar
-rwxrw-r--  1 jenny    pubs    85  May  6 08:27 execute
drwxrwxr-x  2 jenny    pubs    32  Oct  6 22:56 letters
drwxrwxr-x 16 jenny    pubs  1296  Jun  6 17:33 shell
```

The **–a** (**all**) option lists all files, including invisible ones:

```
$ ls -a
.           .profile    c           execute     shell
..          bin         calendar    letters
```

Combining the **–a** and **–l** options displays a long listing of all files, including invisible files, in the working directory. This list is still in alphabetical order:

```
$ ls -al
total 12
drwxrwxr-x  6 jenny    pubs   480 Jun  6 17:42 .
drwxrwx---  26 root    root   816 Jun  6 14:45 ..
-rw-rw-r--  1 jenny    pubs   161 Jun  6 17:15 .profile
drwxrwxr-x  2 jenny    pubs    80 May 20 09:17 bin
drwxrwxr-x  2 jenny    pubs   144 Mar 26 11:59 c
-rw-rw-r--  1 jenny    pubs   104 May 28 11:44 calendar
-rwxrw-r--  1 jenny    pubs    85 May  6 08:27 execute
drwxrwxr-x  2 jenny    pubs    32 Oct  6 22:56 letters
drwxrwxr-x 16 jenny    pubs  1296 Jun  6 17:33 shell
```

When you add the **–r** (reverse) option to the command line, ls produces a list in reverse alphabetical order:

```
$ ls -ral
total 12
drwxrwxr-x 16 jenny    pubs  1296 Jun  6 17:33 shell
drwxrwxr-x  2 jenny    pubs    32 Oct  6 22:56 letters
```

```
-rwxrw-r--   1 jenny    pubs     85 May   6 08:27 execute
-rw-rw-r--   1 jenny    pubs    104 May  28 11:44 calendar
drwxrwxr-x   2 jenny    pubs    144 Mar  26 11:59 c
drwxrwxr-x   2 jenny    pubs     80 May  20 09:17 bin
-rw-rw-r--   1 jenny    pubs    161 Jun   6 17:15 .profile
drwxrwx--- 26 root     root     816 Jun   6 14:45 ..
drwxrwxr-x   6 jenny    pubs    480 Jun   6 17:42 .
```

Use the −t and −l options to list files so that the most recently modified file appears at the top of the list:

```
$ ls -tl
total 8
drwxrwxr-x 16 jenny    pubs   1296 Jun   6 17:33 shell
-rw-rw-r--   1 jenny    pubs    104 May  28 11:44 calendar
drwxrwxr-x   2 jenny    pubs     80 May  20 09:17 bin
-rwxrw-r--   1 jenny    pubs     85 May   6 08:27 execute
drwxrwxr-x   2 jenny    pubs    144 Mar  26 11:59 c
drwxrwxr-x   2 jenny    pubs     32 Oct   6 22:56 letters
```

Together, the −r and −t options cause ls to list files with the file you modified least recently at the top of the list:

```
$ ls -trl
total 8
drwxrwxr-x   2 jenny    pubs     32 Oct   6 22:56 letters
drwxrwxr-x   2 jenny    pubs    144 Mar  26 11:59 c
-rwxrw-r--   1 jenny    pubs     85 May   6 08:27 execute
drwxrwxr-x   2 jenny    pubs     80 May  20 09:17 bin
-rw-rw-r--   1 jenny    pubs    104 May  28 11:44 calendar
drwxrwxr-x 16 jenny    pubs   1296 Jun   6 17:33 shell
```

The next example shows ls with a directory filename as an argument. The ls utility lists the contents of the directory in alphabetical order:

```
$ ls bin
c        e        lsdir
```

To display information about the directory file itself, use the −d (**directory**) option. This option lists information only about the directory:

```
$ ls -dl bin
drwxrwxr-x 2 jenny    pubs          80 May 20 09:17 bin
```

You can use the following command from bash to display a list of all the invisible filenames (those starting with a period) in your home directory. This is a convenient way to list all the initialization files in your home directory:

```
$ ls -d ~/.*
```

mail

Sends and receives electronic mail

*mail [–s **subject**] **user-list***
*mail –f [**filename**]*

The mail utility sends and receives electronic mail in a text environment. Although there are many newer MUAs (mail user agents), mail remains useful in specific situations, especially for a system administrator.

When you use mail to send someone a message, the system puts the message in that user's mailbox, typically **/var/spool/mail/*login-name***, where ***login-name*** is the login name of the user you are sending the message to. When you use mail to read messages, mail normally reads from your mailbox and stores the messages you have read in **~/mbox**.

The way mail appears and functions depends to a large extent on the mail *environment*. When you call mail, it establishes an environment based on variables set in **/etc/mail.rc** and **~/.mailrc**. You can change any aspect of your mail environment that is established by **/etc/mail.rc** by setting variables in your **~/.mailrc** file.

Arguments

Without any arguments, mail displays any messages that are waiting for you. With one or more arguments, mail sends messages. The ***user-list*** is a list of the users you are sending messages to.

Options

–f [*filename*]   Reads messages from ***filename*** instead of from your system mailbox. The ***filename*** defaults to **~/mbox**.

–s *subject*   Sets the subject field to ***subject***. If ***subject*** contains SPACEs, enclose it within quotation marks.

Sending Messages

To send a message, give the command **mail** followed by the login names of the recipients. Now mail is in Input mode, and you can enter the text of your message. When you are done, enter CONTROL-D on a line by itself to terminate the message. Depending on your mail environment, you may get a prompt to enter the names of users who are to receive copies of your message. Enter any names you want and press RETURN; mail sends your message to the recipients.

You can run mail commands while mail is in Input mode—all Input mode commands start with a tilde (~). They are called *tilde escapes* because they temporarily escape from Input mode so that you can give a command. The tilde must appear as the first character on a line.

The following list describes some of the more important tilde escapes.

~! command   Gives the shell *command* as a command line while you are composing a message.

~?   Displays a list of all tilde escapes.

~| command   Replaces the message you are composing with the result of piping the message through *command*.

~b name-list   blind   Sends blind copies (Bcc) to *name-list*. The users who receive blind copies are not listed on the copy of the message that goes to the addressee; the people who receive regular copies (Cc) are, see ~c following.

~c name-list   carbon copy   Sends copies (Cc) to *name-list*.

~d   dead letter   Retrieves ~/dead.letter so you can continue writing it, or you can modify it. This file is created when you quit mail while composing a message.

~h   header   Prompts you for the Subject, To, Cc, and Bcc fields. Each prompt includes the current entries for that field; you can use the erase and line kill keys to back up over and edit the entries.

~m [msg-list]   message   Includes the messages specified by the *msg-list* in a message you are composing, placing a TAB at the beginning of each line. (Refer to "Reading Messages," which follows, for a description of *msg-list*.) You can use ~m only when you are sending a message while reading your messages (see the **m** and **r** commands, also in "Reading Messages").

~p   print   Displays the message you are currently composing.

~q   quit   Quits, saving the message you are composing in the file **dead.letter** in your home directory. See ~d for retrieving this file.

~r filename   read   Reads *filename* into the message you are composing.

~s subject   subject   Sets the subject field for the message you are composing to *subject*, replacing the current subject if there is one.

~t name-list   to   Adds *name-list* to the list of recipients.

~v   vi   Calls the vi editor so that you can edit the message you are composing.

Reading Messages

When you have mail to read, call mail without any arguments. The mail utility displays a list of headers of messages waiting for you. Each line of the display has the following format:

[>] status message-# from-name date lines/characters [subject]

The > indicates that the message is the *current message*. The *status* is **N** if the message is new or **U** (for unread) if the message is not new (that is, you have seen its header before), but you have not read the message yet. The *message-#* is the sequential number of the message in your mailbox. The *from-name* is the name of the person who sent you the message. The *date* and *lines/characters* are the date the message was sent and its size. The *subject* is the optional subject field for the message.

After the list of headers, mail displays its prompt, usually an ampersand (&). The mail utility is in Command mode, waiting for a command. The easiest way to read your messages is to press RETURN. After each message, mail prompts you. Pressing RETURN is a shorthand for displaying the next message. Keep pressing RETURN to read each message in turn. The characters **+** and **–** can also be used to move forward and backward among the mail messages. If you want to read a message out of sequence, you can enter a number followed by RETURN. Usually you give mail commands to manipulate and respond to a message before reading another.

In the following summary of commands, *msg-list* is a message number or a range of message numbers (use a dash to indicate a range, as in **a–b**). In *msg-list*, an asterisk (✳) stands for all messages, and a dollar sign (**$**) stands for the last message.

When you do not specify a *msg-list* where one is called for, mail responds as though you had specified the current message. The current message is the message that is preceded by a > in the header list.

Most of the following commands can appear in your **.mailrc** file; however, it usually makes sense to use only **alias** and **set** there.

!command   Runs a shell *command* while you are reading messages.

| command   Pipes the current message through *command*. This command works only when you are composing a message, not when you are reading one.

?   Displays a list of all mail commands.

a [a-name] [name-list]

You can declare *a-name* (alias name) to represent all the login names in *name-list*. When you want to send a message to everyone in *name-list*, send a message to *a-name*. The mail utility expands *a-name* into the *name-list*. Without any arguments this command displays the currently defined aliases. With only an *a-name*, the command displays the corresponding alias.

d [*msg-list*] **delete** Deletes the messages in the *msg-list* from your mailbox. Without *msg-list* it deletes the current message.

ex *or* **x** **exit** Exits from mail without changing your mailbox. If you deleted any messages during this session with mail, they are not removed from your mailbox.

h **header** Displays a list of headers. Refer to the **z** command (following) if you want to scroll the list of headers.

m *name* **mail** Sends a message to *name*. Using this command is similar to calling mail with *name* from the command line.

p [*msg-list*] **print** Displays the messages in the *msg-list*.

pre [*msg-list*] **preserve** Preserves messages in the *msg-list* in your mailbox. Use this command after you have read a message but do not want to remove it from your mailbox. Refer to the **q** command.

q **quit** Exits from mail, saving in your **mbox** file messages that you read and did not delete and leaving in your mailbox messages that you have not read. You can use the **pre** command to force mail to leave a message in your mailbox even though you have read it.

r [*message*] **reply** Replies to a *message*. This command copies the subject line of the *message* and addresses a reply message to the person who sent you the *message*. Everyone who got a copy of the original *message* also gets a copy of the new message. The **r** command puts mail in Input mode so you can compose a message.

R [*message*] **reply** Replies to a *message*. This command is like the **r** command, but it sends a reply only to the person who sent you the message.

s [*msg-list*] *filename* **save** Saves the messages in *msg-list* in file *filename*. When you use this command, mail does *not* save *msg-list* in your **mbox** file when you exit from mail with the **q** command. This command appends to *filename* if it already exists; otherwise, it creates it.

set See the introduction to the following section, "The mail Environment," for a description of this command. Although you can give the **set** command in response to a mail prompt, **set** is typically used in **.mailrc** files.

t [*msg-list*] Displays the messages in the *msg-list*. This command is a synonym for **p**.

top [*msg-list*] Displays the top few lines of the specified messages.

u [*msg-list*] **undelete** Restores the specified messages. You can restore a deleted message only if you have not quit from mail since you deleted the message.

unset Like the command **set**, this command modifies the mail environment. This command can be given in response to the mail prompt to remove the value of an environment variable, but it is usually given in **.mailrc**. See the following section for a discussion.

v [*msg-list*] **vi** Edits the specified messages with vi.

z± Scrolls the list of headers (see the **h** command) forward (+) or backward (–).

The mail Environment

You can establish your mail environment by assigning values to mail variables by using the **set** command in **~/.mailrc**. The **set** command has the following format:

  set [name[=value]]

The *name* is the name of the mail variable that you are setting, and the *value* is the optional value you are assigning to the variable. The *value* may be either a string or a number. If you use **set** without a *value*, mail assigns the variable a null value (the values of some mail variables are not relevant; it is important only that they are set).

The following is a list of some of the more important mail variables.

ask Prompts you for the subject of each message.

askcc Prompts you for the names of people to receive copies of messages you send.

crt=*number* Assign *number* to this variable if you want messages containing *number* or more lines to be piped through **PAGER**. If you are using a standard ASCII terminal, set *number* to 24. See the variable **PAGER**, following.

dot If set, you can terminate mail messages by entering a period (.) on a line by itself. Unless **ignoreeof** is also set, entering CONTROL-D on a line by itself still serves to terminate mail messages.

ignore Ignores interrupts while you are composing and sending messages. Setting **ignore** can make your job easier if you are working over a noisy telephone line.

record=*filename* Copies outgoing messages to **filename**.

ignoreeof Causes CONTROL-D not to terminate mail messages.

nosave Causes mail not to save your messages in **dead.letter** when you quit mail while composing a message.

PAGER=*pathname* Sets the location to *pathname* for the pager you want mail to use for messages that do not fit on your screen. The default pager is more.

VISUAL=*editor* Sets the *editor* you want mail to use when you give the ~v command while composing a message. The default editor is vi.

Notes By default the Bourne Again Shell checks every 60 seconds for new mail. If mail has arrived, bash presents a message before the next prompt. You can change the frequency of the checks by setting the **MAILCHECK** variable (page 578) to the number of seconds you want the shell to wait between checks for new mail. The shell does not check for new mail if **MAILCHECK** is not set.

Examples

The following example shows Alex using mail to read his messages. After calling mail and seeing that he has two messages, he gives the command **p 2** (simply **2** is enough), followed by a RETURN, to display the second message. After displaying the message, mail displays a prompt, and Alex deletes the message with a **d** command:

```
$ mail
Mail version 8.1 6/6/93.  Type ? for help.
"/var/spool/mail/alex": 2 messages 2 new
 N  1 hls                 Wed Oct 11 00:15  14/327  "your trip"
>N  2 jenny               Tue Oct 10 06:32  22/614  "our meeting"
& p 2
(text of message 2)
  .
  .
& d
```

After reading his second message, Alex tries to read his first message by pressing RETURN. The mail utility tells him he is at the end of his mailbox (At EOF), so he gives the command **p 1** (or **1**), followed by RETURN, to view his first piece of mail. After reading it, he chooses to save a copy in the file **hls_msgs**. Because the file already exists, the message is appended to it. Finally, he decides that he did not really want to delete his second message and that he wants to read both messages again later, so he exits from mail with an **x** command, leaving both messages in his mailbox:

```
& RETURN
At EOF
& p 1
(text of message 1)
  .
  .
& s hls_msgs
"hls_msgs" [Appended] 14/327
& x
$
```

make

Keeps a set of programs current

*make [**options**] [**target-files**] [**arguments**]*

The GNU make utility keeps a set of executable programs current, based on differences in the modification times of the programs and the source files that each is dependent on. The executable programs, or *target-files*, are dependent on one or more prerequisite files. The relationships between *target-files* and prerequisites are specified on *dependency lines* in a makefile. Construction commands follow the dependency line, specifying how make can update the *target-files*.

Refer to page 849 for more information about makefiles. For further information about make, refer to the make info page and the *GNU Make Manual* at www.gnu.org/manual/make.

Arguments   The *target-files* refer to targets on dependency lines in the makefile. When you do not specify a *target-file*, make updates the target on the first dependency line in the makefile. Arguments of the form **name=value** set the variable **name** to **value** inside the makefile. See "Discussion" for more information.

Options   If you do not use the –**f** option, make takes its input from a file named **GNUmakefile**, **makefile**, or **Makefile** (in that order) in the working directory. Following, this file is referred to as **makefile**. Many users prefer to use the name **Makefile** because it shows up earlier in directory listings.

–**f** *file*   **input file**   Uses *file* as input in place of **makefile**.

–**j** *n*   **jobs**   Runs up to *n* commands at the same time instead of the default of one. This is especially effective if you are running GNU/Linux on a multiprocessor system.

–**k**   Continues with the next file from the list of *target-files* instead of quitting when a construction command fails.

–**n**   **no execution**   Displays the commands it would execute to bring the *target-files* up-to-date but does not execute the commands.

–**s**   **silent**   Does not display the names of the commands being executed.

–**t**   **touch**   Updates modification times of target files but does not execute any construction commands. Refer to touch on page 1359.

Discussion Although the most common use of make is to build programs from source code, it is also a general-purpose build utility suitable for a wide range of uses. Any place where you can define a set of dependencies to get from one state to another can be an ideal candidate for make.

Much of the power of make comes from the features you can use inside a makefile. For example, you can define variables using the same syntax found in the Bourne Again Shell. *Always* define the variable **SHELL** inside a makefile; set it to the pathname of the shell you want to use when running construction commands. To define the variable and assign it a value, place the following line near the top of your makefile:

```
SHELL=/bin/sh
```

Assigning the value **/bin/sh** to **SHELL** allows you to use the makefile on other computer systems. On GNU/Linux systems **/bin/sh** is generally linked to **/bin/bash**. The make utility uses the value of the *environment variable* **SHELL** if you do not set **SHELL** inside the makefile. If this is not the shell you intended to use, this feature may cause your construction commands to fail.

Other features perform the following tasks.

- Run specific construction commands silently by preceding them with the @ sign. For example, the following lines will display a short help message when you run the command **make help**:

  ```
  help:
      @echo "You may make the following:"
      @echo " "
      @echo "libbuf.a        -- the buffer library"
      @echo "Bufdisplay      -- display any-format buffer"
      @echo "Buf2ppm         -- convert buffer to pixmap"
  ```

  (This technique works because no file is named **help** in the working directory, so make runs the construction commands in an attempt to build this file. Because the construction commands only print messages and do not, in fact, build the file **help**, you can run **make help** repeatedly with the same result.)

- Ignore the exit status of specific commands by preceding them with a – character. For example, the following line allows make to continue whether the call to **/bin/rm** is successful (the call to **/bin/rm** fails if **libbuf.a** does not exist):

  ```
  -/bin/rm libbuf.a
  ```

- Use special variables to refer to information that might change from one use of make to the next. Such information might include the files that need updating, the files that are newer than the target, or the files that match a pattern. For example, you can use the variable **$?** in a construction command to identify all prerequisite files that are newer than the target file. This allows you to print any files that have changed since the last time you printed files out:

```
list:       .list
.list:      Makefile buf.h xtbuff_ad.h buff.c buf_print.c xtbuff.c
pr $? | lpr
date >.list
```

In this example the target list depends on the source files that might be printed. The construction command **pr $? | lpr** prints only those source files that are newer than the file list. Finally, the line **date > .list** modifies **.list** so that it is newer than any of the source files (so that the next time you run the command **make list**, only the files that have been changed again are printed).

- Include other makefiles as if they were part of the current makefile. The following line causes make to read **Make.config** and treat the contents of that file as though it were part of the current makefile, allowing you to put information common to more than one makefile in a single place:

```
include Make.config
```

Red Hat Linux comes with GNU make, which includes a number of additional features that are described in the GNU make documentation. Although these new features of GNU make are powerful and useful, they can limit the portability of your makefiles. You can learn more about how to use all of the features listed here, as well as many other features, from the sources cited on page 1247.

Examples

The first example causes make to bring the *target-file* named **analysis** up-to-date by issuing the three **cc** commands shown here. The example uses a file named **GNU-makefile**, **makefile**, or **Makefile** in the working directory:

```
$ make analysis
cc -c analy.c
cc -c stats.c
cc -o analysis analy.o stats.o
```

The following example also updates **analysis** but uses a makefile named **analysis.mk** in the working directory:

```
$ make -f analysis.mk analysis
'analysis' is up to date.
```

The next example lists the commands make would execute to bring the *target-file* named **credit** up-to-date. Because of the **–n** option, make does not execute the commands:

```
$ make -n credit
cc -c -O credit.c
cc -c -O accounts.c
cc -c -O terms.c
cc -o credit credit.c accounts.c terms.c
```

The next example uses the **–t** option to update the modification time of the *target-file* named **credit**. After you use the **–t** option, make thinks that **credit** is up-to-date:

```
$ make -t credit
$ make credit
'credit' is up to date.
```

The next example shows a simple makefile for building a utility named **ff**. Because the **cc** command needed to build **ff** is complex, using a makefile allows you to rebuild **ff** easily, without having to retype (let alone remember) the **cc** command:

```
$ cat Makefile
# Build the ff command from the fastfind.c source
SHELL=/bin/sh

ff:
cc -traditional -O2 -g -DBIG=5120 -o ff fastfind.c myClib.a

$ make ff
cc -traditional -O2 -g -DBIG=5120 -o ff fastfind.c myClib.a
```

The final example shows a much more sophisticated makefile that uses features not discussed in this section. Refer to the sources cited on page 1247 for information about these and other advanced features:

```
$ cat Makefile
#########################################################
## build and maintain the buffer library
#########################################################
SHELL=/bin/sh

#########################################################
## Flags and libraries for compiling. The XLDLIBS are needed
#   whenever you build a program using the library. The CCFLAGS
#   give maximum optimization.
CC=gcc
CCFLAGS=-O2 $(CFLAGS)
XLDLIBS= -lXaw3d -lXt -lXmu -lXext -lX11 -lm
BUFLIB=libbuf.a

#########################################################
## Miscellaneous
INCLUDES=buf.h
XINCLUDES=xtbuff_ad.h
OBJS=buff.o buf_print.o xtbuff.o
```

```
#########################################################
## Just a 'make' generates a help message
help    Help:
        @echo "You can make the following:"
        @echo " "
        @echo " libbuf.a        -- the buffer library"
        @echo " bufdisplay      -- display any-format buffer"
        @echo " buf2ppm         -- convert buffer to pixmap"
#########################################################
## The main target is the library
libbuf.a:   $(OBJS)
    -/bin/rm libbuf.a

    ar rv libbuf.a $(OBJS)
    ranlib libbuf.a
#########################################################
## Secondary targets -- utilities built from the library
bufdisplay: bufdisplay.c libbuf.a
    $(CC) $(CCFLAGS) bufdisplay.c -o bufdisplay $(BUFLIB) $(XLDLIBS)

buf2ppm: buf2ppm.c libbuf.a
    $(CC) $(CCFLAGS) buf2ppm.c -o buf2ppm $(BUFLIB)


#########################################################
## Build the individual object units
buff.o: $(INCLUDES) buff.c
    $(CC) -c $(CCFLAGS) buff.c

buf_print.o:$(INCLUDES) buf_print.c
    $(CC) -c $(CCFLAGS) buf_print.c

xtbuff.o: $(INCLUDES) $(XINCLUDES) xtbuff.c
    $(CC) -c $(CCFLAGS) xtbuff.c
```

The make utility can be used for tasks other than compiling code. As a final example, assume that you have a database that lists IP addresses and the corresponding hostnames in two columns and that the database dumps these values to a file named **hosts.tab**. You need to extract only the hostnames from this file and generate a Web page named **hosts.html** containing these names. The following makefile is a simple report writer:

```
$ cat makefile
#
SHELL=/bin/sh
#

hosts.html: hosts.tab
    @echo "<HTML><BODY>" > hosts.html
    @awk '{print $$2, "<br>"}' hosts.tab >> hosts.html
```

man

Displays documentation for commands

*man [**options**] [**section**] **command***
*man –k **keyword***

The man utility provides online documentation for GNU/Linux commands. In addition to user commands, documentation is available for many other commands and details that relate to use of GNU/Linux. Because many of the commands are from GNU, the GNU info utility (page 45) frequently provides additional information.

A one-line header is associated with each manual page. This header consists of a command name, the section of the manual in which the command is found, and a brief description of what the command does. These headers are stored in a database so that you can perform quick searches on keywords associated with each man page.

Arguments

The ***section*** argument tells man to limit its search to the specified section of the manual (see page 44 for a listing of manual sections). Without this argument man searches the sections in numerical order until it locates a man page. In the second form of the man command, the **–k** option enables a search for a keyword in the database of headers; man displays a list of headers that contain the specified keyword. A **man –k** command performs the same function as apropos (page 79).

Options

–a Displays manual pages for all sections. Use this option when you are not sure which section contains the information you are looking for.

–k *keyword* Displays manual page headers that contain the string ***keyword***. You can scan this list for commands of interest. This option is equivalent to the apropos command (page 79).

–t Formats the page for display on a PostScript printer. Output goes to standard output.

Discussion

The manual pages are organized as a set of sections, each pertaining to a separate aspect of the GNU/Linux system. Section 1 contains user-callable commands and is the section most likely to be accessed by users who are not system administrators or programmers. Contained in some of the other sections of the manual are system calls, library functions, and commands used only by the system administrator. See page 44 for a listing of the manual sections.

The less utility displays manual pages that fill more than one screen. You can change to another pager by setting the environment variable **PAGER** to the name of the pager you want to use. For example, adding the following line to **.profile** allows bash users to use more in place of less:

```
export PAGER=/bin/more
```

You can tell man where to look for man pages by setting the environment variable **MANPATH** to a colon-separated list of directories. For example, bash users can add the following line to **.profile** to cause man to search the **/usr/man**, **/usr/local/man**, and **/usr/X11R6/man** directories:

```
export MANPATH=/usr/man:/usr/local/man:/usr/X11R6/man
```

Notes

The argument to man is not always a command name. For example, the command **man ascii** lists all the ASCII characters and their various representations.

The man pages are commonly stored in unformatted, compressed form. When a man page is requested, it has to be decompressed and formatted before it is displayed. To speed up subsequent requests for that man page, man attempts to save the formatted version of the page.

Some utilities described in the manual pages have the same name as shell builtin commands. The behavior of the shell builtin may be slightly different from the behavior of the utility as described in the manual page.

Examples

The following example uses man to display the documentation for the command write, which sends messages to another user's terminal:

```
$ man write

WRITE(1)            Linux Programmer's Manual            WRITE(1)

NAME
     write - send a message to another user
SYNOPSIS
     write user [ttyname]
DESCRIPTION
     Write allows you to communicate with other users, by copy-
     ing lines from your terminal to theirs.

     When you run the write command, the user you are writing
     to gets a message. . .
```

The next example displays the man page for another command—the man command itself, a good starting place for someone learning about the system:

```
$ man man
man(1)                                                           man(1)


NAME
       man - format and display the online manual pages
       manpath - determine users search path for man pages

SYNOPSIS
       man  [-acdfFhkKtwW]  [--path]  [-m system] [-p string] [-C
       config_file] [-M pathlist] [-P  pager]  [-S  section_list]
       [section] name ...


DESCRIPTION
       man formats and displays the online manual pages.  If you
       specify section, man only looks in  that  section  of  the
       ...
```

The next example shows how the man utility can be used to find the man pages that pertain to a certain topic. In this case **man –k**[7] displays man page headers containing the string latex:

```
$ man -k latex
Pod::LaTeX          (3pm)  - Convert Pod data to formatted Latex
einitex [elatex]    (1)    - extended TeX
elatex [latex]      (1)    - structured text formatting and typesetting
etex [elatex]       (1)    - extended TeX
evirtex [elatex]    (1)    - extended TeX
lambda [latex]      (1)    - structured text formatting and typesetting
latex               (1)    - structured text formatting and typesetting
...
```

The search for the keyword entered with the **–k** option is not case sensitive. Although the keyword entered on the command line is all lowercase, it matches the first header, which contains the string LaTeX (upper- and lowercase). The 3pm on the first line indicates that the man page is from Section 3 (Subroutines) of the GNU/Linux System Manual and comes from the *Perl Programmers Reference Guide* (it is a Perl[8] subroutine).

---

7. The apropos utility (a shell script stored in **/usr/bin/apropos**) functions similarly to **man –k**.

8. See www.perl.org for more information on the Perl programming language.

mkdir

Makes a directory

*mkdir [**option**] **directory-list***

The mkdir utility creates one or more directories.

Arguments   The ***directory-list*** contains one or more pathnames of directories that mkdir creates.

Options

--mode *mode* **–m *mode***   Sets the permission to ***mode.*** You may use either the symbolic form or an octal number to represent the mode. Refer to page 1103 for more information on chmod.

--parents **–p**   Creates any directories that do not exist in the path to the directory you wish to create.

Notes   You must have permission to write to and search (execute permission) the parent directory of the directory you are creating. The mkdir utility creates directories that contain the standard invisible entries . and .. .

Examples   The following command creates a directory named **accounts** as a subdirectory of the working directory and a directory named **prospective** as a subdirectory of **accounts**:

```
$ mkdir --parents accounts/prospective
```

Without changing working directories, the same user creates another subdirectory within the **accounts** directory:

```
$ mkdir accounts/existing
```

Next, the user changes the working directory to the **accounts** directory and creates one more subdirectory:

```
$ cd accounts
$ mkdir closed
```

The last example shows the user creating another subdirectory. This time the **--mode** option removes all access permissions for group and others:

```
$ mkdir --mode go= accounts/past_due
```

Mtools

Uses DOS-style commands on files and directories

mcd [**directory**]
mcopy [**options**] **file-list target**
mdel **file-list**
mdir [–w] **directory**
mformat [**options**] **device**
mtype [**options**] **file-list**

These utilities mimic DOS commands and manipulate GNU/Linux files or DOS files. The mcopy utility provides an easy way to move files between a GNU/Linux filesystem and a DOS disk. The default drive for all commands is **/dev/fd0** or **a:**.

Summary

Table III-21 lists each of the utilities in the Mtools collection.

Utility	‖ table III-21
mcd	Changes the working directory on the DOS disk
mcopy	Copies DOS files from one directory to another
mdel	Deletes DOS files
mdir	Lists contents of DOS directories
mformat	Adds DOS formatting information to a disk
mtype	Displays the contents of DOS files

Arguments

The *directory*, used with mcd and mdir, must be the name of a directory on a DOS disk. The *file-list*, used with mcopy and mtype, is a list of one or more SPACE-separated filenames. The *target*, used with mcopy, is the name of a regular file or a directory. If you give mcopy a *file-list* with more than one filename, *target* must be the name of a directory. The *device*, used with mformat, is the DOS drive letter containing the disk to be formatted (for example, A:).

Options

mcopy

-n   Automatically replaces existing files without asking. Normally mcopy asks for verification before overwriting a file.

-p   preserve   Preserves the attributes of files when they are copied.

-s   recursive   Copies directories and their contents recursively.

-t   text   Converts DOS text files for use on a GNU/Linux system. Lines in DOS text files are terminated with the character pair RETURN-NEWLINE. This option causes mcopy to remove the RETURN character while copying.

mdir

-w   wide   Displays only filenames and fits as many as possible on each line. By default mdir lists information about each file on a separate line, showing filename, size, and creation time.

mformat

-f 1440   1,440K 3.5 inch HD diskette.

-f 2880   2,880K 3.5 inch ED diskette.

-l vol   label   Puts *vol* as the volume label on the newly formatted disk.

mtype

-t   text   Similar to the –t option for mcopy, this option replaces each RETURN-NEWLINE character pair in the DOS file with a single NEWLINE character before displaying the file.

Discussion

Although these utilities mimic their DOS counterparts, they do not attempt to match those tools exactly. In most cases this means that restrictions imposed by DOS are removed. For example, the asterisk ambiguous file reference (*) matches all filenames (as it does under GNU/Linux), including those filenames that DOS would require *.* to match.

Notes

If your kernel is configured to support DOS filesystems, you can mount DOS disks onto your GNU/Linux filesystem and manipulate the files by using GNU/Linux utilities. Although this is very handy and has reduced the need for Mtools, it is sometimes not practical or efficient to mount and unmount a DOS filesystem, as these tasks can be time-consuming, and some systems are set up so that regular users cannot mount or unmount filesystems.

Use caution when using Mtools. These utilities do not warn you if you are about to overwrite a file. Using explicit pathnames, not ambiguous file references, reduces the chance of having this type of accident.

The most common uses of the Mtools utilities are to examine files on DOS floppy disks (mdir) and to copy files between a DOS floppy disk and the GNU/Linux filesystem (mcopy). You can identify DOS disks by using the usual DOS drive letters: A: for the first floppy drive, C: for the first hard disk, and so on. Also, you can separate filenames in paths by using either the GNU/Linux forward slash (/) or the DOS backslash (\). You need to escape the backslash to prevent the shell from interpreting it before passing the pathname on to the utility you are using.

Examples

In the first example the mdir utility is used to examine the contents of a DOS floppy disk that is in **/dev/fd0**:

```
$ mdir
 Volume in drive A is DOS UTY
 Directory for A:/

ACAD     LIF     419370    5-10-03    1:29p
CADVANCE LIF      40560    2-08-04   10:36a
CHIPTST  EXE       2209    4-26-03    4:22p
DISK     ID          31   12-27-03    4:49p
GENERIC  LIF      20983    2-08-04   10:37a
INSTALL  COM        896    7-03-03   10:23a
INSTALL  DAT      45277   12-27-03    4:49p
KDINSTAL EXE     110529    8-13-03   10:50a
LOTUS    LIF      44099    1-18-03    3:36p
PCAD     LIF      17846    5-01-03    3:46p
READID   EXE      17261    5-07-03    8:26a
README   TXT       9851    4-30-03   10:32a
UTILITY  LIF      51069    5-03-03    9:13a
WORD     LIF      16817    7-01-03    9:58a
WP       LIF      57992    8-29-03    4:22p
       15 File(s)     599040 bytes free
```

Next, the *.TXT files are copied from the DOS disk to the working directory on the GNU/Linux filesystem by using mcopy. Because only one file has the extension .TXT, only one file is copied. Because .TXT files are usually text files under DOS, the **–t** option is used to strip off the unnecessary RETURN characters at the end of each line. The ambiguous file reference * is escaped on the command line to prevent the shell from attempting to expand it before passing the argument to mcopy. The mcopy utility locates the file **README.TXT** when given the pattern *.**txt** because DOS does not differentiate between uppercase and lowercase letters in filenames:

```
$ mcopy -t a:\*.txt .
Copying README.TXT
```

Finally, the DOS floppy disk is reformatted using mformat. If the disk has not been low-level formatted, you need to use fdformat before giving the following commands:

```
$ mformat a:
$ mdir a:
 Volume in drive A has no label
 Directory for A:/

File "*" not found
```

A check with mdir shows it is empty after formatting.

mv

Moves (renames) a file

*mv [**options**] **existing-file new-filename***
*mv [**options**] **existing-file-list directory***
*mv [**options**] **existing-directory new-directory***

The mv utility, which moves or renames one or more files, has three formats. The first renames a single file with a new filename that you supply. The second renames one or more files so that they appear in a specified directory. The third renames a directory. The mv utility physically moves the file if it is not possible to rename it (that is, if you move it from one filesystem to another).

Arguments

In the first form, the *existing-file* is a pathname that specifies the ordinary file that you want to rename. The *new-filename* is the new pathname of the file.

In the second form, the *existing-file-list* contains the pathnames of the files that you want to rename, and the *directory* specifies the new parent directory for the files. The files you rename will have the same simple filenames as the simple filenames of each of the files in the *existing-file-list* but new absolute pathnames.

The third form renames the *existing-directory* with the *new-directory* name. This form works only when the *new-directory* does not already exist and when the *existing-directory* and the *new-directory* are on the same filesystem.

Options

––backup –b   Makes a backup copy (by appending a ~ to the filename) of any file that would be overwritten.

––force –f   Causes mv *not* to prompt you if a move would overwrite an existing file that you do not have write permission for. You must have write permission for the directory holding the target file.

––interactive –i   Prompts you for confirmation if a move would overwrite an existing file. If your response begins with a y or Y, the move proceeds; otherwise, the file is not moved.

––update –u   If a move would overwrite an existing file, this option causes mv to compare the modification times of the source and target files. If the target file has a more recent modification time (the target is newer than the source), mv does not replace it with the source file.

-- Marks the end of the options and the beginning of the filenames on the command line. This option makes it possible to move a file whose name begins with a hyphen. Without this option mv complains that the file is an invalid option.

Notes GNU mv is implemented as ln and rm. When you execute the mv utility, it first makes a link (ln) to the *new-file* and then deletes (rm) the *existing-file*. If the *new-file* already exists, mv may delete it before creating the link.

As with rm, you must have write and execute access permission to the parent directory of the *existing-file*, but you do not need read or write access permission to the file itself. If the move would overwrite an existing file that you do not have write permission for, mv displays the access permission and waits for a response. If you enter **y** or **yes**, mv renames the file; otherwise, it does not. If you use the **–f** option, mv does not prompt you for a response but simply overwrites the file.

If the *existing-file* and the *new-file* or *directory* are on different filesystems, GNU mv is implemented as cp and rm. In this case, mv copies the file instead of renaming it. After a file is copied, the user who moved the file becomes the owner of the file.

Although earlier versions of mv could move only ordinary files between filesystems, mv can now move any type of file, including directories and device files, from one filesystem to another.

Examples The first command line renames **letter**, a file in the working directory, as **letter.1201**:

```
$ mv letter letter.1201
```

The next command line renames the file so that it appears, with the same simple filename, in the **/usr/archives** directory:

```
$ mv letter.1201 /usr/archives
```

The following command line renames all the files in the working directory whose names begin with **memo** so they appear in the **/usr/backup** directory:

```
$ mv memo* /usr/backup
```

The next example shows how using the **–u** option prevents mv from replacing a file with an older file. The file **memo** is newer in the directory **memos** than it is in the parent directory, and so it is not replaced by the mv command. This example also shows how mv prompts Alex (who is executing the command) before replacing the file **memos/memo1**, which is owned by Jenny:

```
$ ls -l
total 4
-rw-rw-r--   1 alex      group            14 Jul 30 01:38 memo1
-rw-rw-r--   1 alex      group            14 Jul 30 01:38 memo2
-rw-rw-r--   1 alex      group            14 Jul 30 01:35 memo3
drwxrwxr-x   2 alex      group          1024 Jul 30 01:08 memos

$ ls -l memos
total 3
-rw-r--r--   1 jenny     group            14 Jul 30 01:34 memo1
-rw-rw-r--   1 alex      group            14 Jul 30 01:35 memo2
-rw-rw-r--   1 alex      group            20 Jul 30 01:36 memo3

$ mv -u memo[1-3] memos
mv: replace `memos/memo1', overriding mode 0644? y

$ ls -l
total 2
-rw-rw-r--   1 alex      group            14 Jul 30 01:35 memo3
drwxrwxr-x   2 alex      group          1024 Jul 30 01:08 memos

$ ls -l memos
total 3
-rw-rw-r--   1 alex      group            14 Jul 30 01:38 memo1
-rw-rw-r--   1 alex      group            14 Jul 30 01:38 memo2
-rw-rw-r--   1 alex      group            20 Jul 30 01:36 memo3
```

nice

Changes the priority of a command

nice [option] [command line]

The nice utility reports the priority of the shell or alters the priority of a command line. An ordinary user can decrease the priority of a command. Only Superuser can increase the priority of a command. The TC Shell has a nice builtin that has a different syntax. Refer to "Notes."

Arguments   The ***command line*** is the command line you want to execute at a different priority. Without any options or arguments, nice reports the priority of the shell running the nice command.

Options   Without an option, nice defaults to an adjustment of 10, lowering the priority of the command by 10, typically from 0 to 10. (As you raise the priority value, the command is run at a lower priority.)

–n *value*   Changes the priority by an adjustment of ***value***. The range of priorities is from –20 (the highest priority) to 19 (the lowest priority). A positive ***value*** lowers the priority, whereas a negative ***value*** raises the priority. Only Superuser can specify a negative ***value***. When you specify a value past either end of this range, the priority is set to the limit of the range.

Notes   The TC Shell has a nice builtin. Under tcsh, use **nice ±*value command line*** to change the priority at which ***command line*** is run. You must include the plus sign for positive values.

Higher (more positive) priority values mean that the kernel schedules a job less often, whereas lower (more negative) values cause the job to be scheduled more often.

When Superuser schedules a job to run at the highest priority, it can impact the performance of the system for all other jobs, including the operating system itself. For this reason use nice with negative values carefully.

Example   The following command executes find in the background at the lowest possible priority. The **ps –l** command displays the nice value of the command in the NI column:

```
# nice -n 19 find / -name core -print > corefiles.out &
[1] 2610
# ps -l
  F S   UID   PID  PPID  C PRI  NI ADDR    SZ WCHAN  TTY          TIME CMD
100 S     0  1099  1097  0  75   0    -   605 wait4  pts/0    00:00:00 bash
100 R     0  2610  1099  0  99  19    -   634 -      pts/0    00:00:03 find
100 R     0  2611  1099  0  76   0    -   747 -      pts/0    00:00:00 ps
```

nohup

Runs a command that keeps running after you log out

nohup **command line**

The nohup utility executes a command line so that the command keeps running after you log out. Normally when you log out, the system kills all processes you have started. The TC Shell has a nohup builtin. Refer to "Notes."

Arguments   The **command line** is the command line you want to execute.

Notes   The nohup utility automatically lowers the priority of the command it executes by 5. See nice (page 1263) for information about priorities.

If you do not redirect the output from a process that you execute with nohup, both standard output *and* standard error are sent to the file named **nohup.out** in the working directory. If you do not have write permission for the working directory, nohup opens a **nohup.out** file in your home directory.

Unlike the nohup utility, the TC Shell's nohup builtin does not send output to **nohup.out**. Background jobs started from tcsh automatically continue to run after you log out.

Example   The following command executes find in the background, using nohup:

```
$ nohup find / -name core -print > corefiles.out &
[1] 14235
```

od

Dumps the contents of a file

od [options] [file-list]

The od (octal dump) utility dumps the contents of a file, which is useful for viewing executable (object) files and text files with embedded nonprinting characters.

This utility takes its input from the file you specify on the command line or from standard input.

Arguments   The *file-list* includes the pathnames of the files that od displays. When you do not specify a *file-list*, od reads from standard input.

Options

--address-radix=*base*

−A *base*   Specifies the base used when displaying the offsets shown for positions in the file. By default, offsets are given in octal. The values for *base* are **d** (decimal), **o** (octal), **x** (hexadecimal), and **n** (no offsets printed).

--format=*type*   **−t *type***   Determines the output format to use when displaying data from the file. You can repeat this option with different format types to see the file in several different formats. The possible values for *type* are

a   Named character. Nonprinting control characters are displayed using their official ASCII names. For example, FORMFEED is displayed as **ff**.

c   ASCII character.

d   Signed decimal.

f   Floating point.

o   Octal (default).

u   Unsigned decimal.

x   Hexadecimal.

The od utility displays certain nonprinting characters as printing characters preceded by a backslash (Table III-22). It displays nonprinting characters that are not in the table as three-digit octal numbers.

Symbol	|| table III-22
\0	NULL
\a	BELL
\b	BACKSPACE
\f	FORMFEED
\n	NEWLINE
\r	RETURN
\t	HORIZONTAL TAB
\v	VERTICAL TAB

By default od dumps a file as 2-byte octal numbers. You can change both the *type* of number it dumps and the number of bytes it reads to compose each number. The types in Table III-23 can be suffixed by length indicators from Table III-24.

type	|| table III-23
d (decimal)	Displays data as signed decimal values
o (octal)	Displays data as unsigned octal values
u (unsigned decimal)	Displays data as unsigned decimal values
x (hex)	Displays data as unsigned hexadecimal values

The length indicators in Table III-24 can follow any of the **d, o, u,** or **x** types to indicate how many bytes should be read to compose each number.

Length Indicator	|| table III-24
F	Uses 4 bytes.
D	Uses 8 bytes.
L	Uses the number of bytes that the C compiler uses for long double values. On most machines this is 8 bytes.
f (float)	Displays data as floating-point values. You can follow f with one of the following characters to tell **od** how many bytes to read from the file to build each floating point value.
C (character)	Uses single characters for each decimal value.
S (short integer)	Uses 2 bytes.
I (integer)	Uses 4 bytes.
L (long)	Uses 4 bytes on 32-bit machines and 8 bytes on 64-bit machines.

--strings=*n*   **-s *n***   Outputs from the file only those bytes that contain runs of *n* or more printable ASCII characters that are terminated by a NULL byte. The default value for *n* is 3.

--help   Gives a short summary of how to use od.

Notes   To retain backward compatibility with older, non-POSIX versions of od, the GNU/Linux od utility also includes the options listed in Table III-25 as shorthand versions of many of the preceding options.

Old Form	Equivalent New Form	‖ table III-25
−a	−t a	
−b	−t oC	
−c	−t c	
−d	−t u2	
−f	−t fF	
−h	−t x2	
−i	−t d2	
−l	−t d4	
−o	−t o2	
−x	−t x2	

Examples   The file **ac**, used in the following examples, contains all the ASCII characters. In the first example the bytes in this file are displayed as named characters. The first column shows the offset of each byte from the start of the file. The offsets are given as octal values:

```
$ od -t a ac
0000000 nul soh stx etx eot enq ack bel bs ht nl vt ff cr so si
0000020 dle dc1 dc2 dc3 dc4 nak syn etb can em sub esc fs gs rs us
0000040 sp ! " # $ % & ' ( ) * + , - . /
0000060 0 1 2 3 4 5 6 7 8 9 : ; < = > ?
0000100 @ A B C D E F G H I J K L M N O
0000120 P Q R S T U V W X Y Z [ \ ] ^ _
0000140 ` a b c d e f g h i j k l m n o
0000160 p q r s t u v w x y z { | } ~ del
0000200 nul soh stx etx eot enq ack bel bs ht nl vt ff cr so si
0000220 dle dc1 dc2 dc3 dc4 nak syn etb can em sub esc fs gs rs us
0000240 sp ! " # $ % & ' ( ) * + , - . /
0000260 0 1 2 3 4 5 6 7 8 9 : ; < = > ?
0000300 @ A B C D E F G H I J K L M N O
0000320 P Q R S T U V W X Y Z [ \ ] ^ _
0000340 ` a b c d e f g h i j k l m n o
0000360 p q r s t u v w x y z { | } ~ del
0000400 nl
0000401
```

In the next example the bytes are displayed as octal numbers, ASCII characters, or printing characters preceded by a backslash (refer to Table III-22 on page 1266):

```
$ od -t c ac
0000000 \0 001 002 003 004 005 006 \a \b \t \n \v \f \r 016 017
0000020 020 021 022 023 024 025 026 027 030 031 032 033 034 035 036 037
0000040  !  "  #  $  %  &  '  (  )  *  +  ,  -  .  /
0000060  0  1  2  3  4  5  6  7  8  9  :  ;  <  =  >  ?
0000100  @  A  B  C  D  E  F  G  H  I  J  K  L  M  N  O
0000120  P  Q  R  S  T  U  V  W  X  Y  Z  [  \  ]  ^  _
0000140  `  a  b  c  d  e  f  g  h  i  j  k  l  m  n  o
0000160  p  q  r  s  t  u  v  w  x  y  z  {  |  }  ~  177
0000200 200 201 202 203 204 205 206 207 210 211 212 213 214 215 216 217
0000220 220 221 222 223 224 225 226 227 230 231 232 233 234 235 236 237
0000240 240 241 242 243 244 245 246 247 250 251 252 253 254 255 256 257
0000260 260 261 262 263 264 265 266 267 270 271 272 273 274 275 276 277
0000300 300 301 302 303 304 305 306 307 310 311 312 313 314 315 316 317
0000320 320 321 322 323 324 325 326 327 330 331 332 333 334 335 336 337
0000340 340 341 342 343 344 345 346 347 350 351 352 353 354 355 356 357
0000360 360 361 362 363 364 365 366 367 370 371 372 373 374 375 376 377
0000400 \n
0000401
```

The final example finds in the file **myprog** all strings that are at least three characters long (the default) and terminated by a null byte. The offset positions are given as decimal offsets instead of octal offsets:

```
$ od -A d --strings myprog
0000236 I9.0.00/32
0000472 main
0000477 write
0000483 myprog.icn
```

paste
==========

paste

Joins corresponding lines from files

paste [option] [file-list]

The paste utility reads lines from the *file-list* and joins corresponding lines in its output. By default output lines are separated by a TAB character.

Arguments   The *file-list* is a list of ordinary files. When you omit *file-list*, paste reads from standard input.

Options

--delimiter=*dlist*   −d *dlist*   The *dlist* is a list of characters to be used to separate output lines. If *dlist* contains a single character, paste uses that character instead of the default TAB character to separate lines of output. If *dlist* contains more than one character, the characters are used in turn to separate output lines and are then reused from the beginning of the list as necessary.

Notes   A common use of paste is to rearrange the columns of a table. A utility, such as cut, can get the desired columns in separate files, and then paste can join them in any order.

Examples   The following example uses the files **fnames** and **accntinfo**. These files can easily be created by using cut (page 1132) and the **/etc/passwd** file. The paste command puts the full-name field first, followed by the remaining user account information. A TAB character separates the two output fields:

```
$ cat fnames
Jenny Chen
Alex Watson
Scott Adams
Helen Simpson
```

```
$ cat accntinfo
jenny:x:401:50:/home/jenny:/bin/zsh
alex:x:402:50:/home/alex:/bin/bash
scott:x:504:500:/home/scott:/bin/tcsh
hls:x:505:500:/home/hls:/bin/bash

$ paste fnames accntinfo
Jenny Chen      jenny:x:401:50:/home/jenny:/bin/zsh
Alex Watson     alex:x:402:50:/home/alex:/bin/bash
Scott Adams     scott:x:504:500:/home/scott:/bin/tcsh
Helen Simpson   hls:x:505:500:/home/hls:/bin/bash
```

The next examples use the files **p1**, **p2**, **p3**, and **p4**; the last example uses the **−d** option to give paste a list of characters to use to separate output fields:

```
$ cat p1
1
one
ONE
$ cat p2
2
two
TWO
$ cat p3
3
three
THREE
$ cat p4
4
four
FOUR

$ paste p1 p2 p3 p4
1       2       3       4
one     two     three   four
ONE     TWO     THREE   FOUR

$ paste p4 p3 p2 p1
4       3       2       1
four    three   two     one
FOUR    THREE   TWO     ONE

$ paste -d "+-=" p3 p2 p1 p4
3+2-1=4
three+two-one=four
THREE+TWO-ONE=FOUR
```

patch

Updates source code

*patch [**options**] target-file patch-file*
*patch [**options**]*

The patch utility updates a file from a file of change information, or patches, created by diff. The patch utility can read many forms of diff output, including context diffs, ed scripts, and the default diff output. See page 1149 and the diff info page for more information on these and other output forms.

Useful when making changes to large software applications, including the Linux kernel, the patch utility allows one version of the application source to be changed into another simply by applying patches. The presence of the utility is often assumed by software developers who e-mail patches so users can install updates.

Today patches are used less frequently than they used to be: Many developers give users access to raw development trees via anonymous CVS or such Web sites as www.sourceforge.net. But patches are still used in some situations, such as the Linux kernel where the size of the file is large relative to the size of the patch required to go from one minor revision to the next.

Arguments   In the first form, the patch utility applies the changes detailed in the *patch-file* to the *target-file*. Before any changes are made, a copy of the *target-file* is created by adding the extension **.orig** to the name of the original file. This allows you to restore the *target-file* if necessary.

In the second form, patch reads the change information from standard input, usually redirected from a file or a pipe, and attempts to identify the name of the file to be updated from the change information. If the filename cannot be determined from the patch, patch prompts you for a filename. If there are changes to multiple files in the change information, patch updates all the files. This second form is used more commonly.

Options

–d directory   directory   Makes *directory* the working directory before further processing.

–E   empty   Removes a file if the changes made by patch cause a file to become empty.

-l loose Performs *loose* pattern matching when trying to locate where patches should go in *target-file*. In particular, any sequence of whitespace in the patch also matches any sequence of whitespace in *target-file*.

-p*n* prefixes Strips prefixes from the paths to files to be patched. The value *n* is the number of slashes to remove from the start of pathnames (any directory names between these slashes are also removed). Using 0 for *n* or using **-p** without *n* causes the pathnames to be unchanged. If you omit this option entirely, the entire pathname up to the simple filename is removed. This option makes it possible for you to patch files that you have in a location other than the location used by the person who built the *patch-file*.

-R reverse Attempts to apply the patch in reverse. See "Discussion."

-s silent Reports only errors. Normally patch displays quite a bit of information about the work it is doing.

Discussion

The patch utility is designed to simplify the task of keeping the source code for large software applications up-to-date. If you are a software developer, this makes it easier for you to provide updates to users. If you are a user, patch makes it easier for you to obtain and install updates. For example, the entire software distribution for version 2.4.18 of the Linux kernel can be obtained as a compressed tar archive file of nearly 30 megabytes. However, the patch to change version 2.4.17 into version 2.4.18 is a compressed file smaller than 1 megabyte. If you have version 2.4.17 installed and wish to upgrade to version 2.4.18, using the patch file is much faster and simpler than downloading and installing the entire source for 2.4.18.

The patch utility works by reading the *patch-file* and locating *hunks*. Each hunk describes the changes needed to change part of a file into the new version. When it finds a hunk, patch locates the affected portion of the target file and performs the changes indicated in the hunk. The patch utility is able to extract hunks that are embedded in mail messages and other text, making it easy to apply patches: Simply feed the mail message as standard input to the patch program.

If patch finds a hunk that cannot be applied to the target file, that hunk is rejected. All rejected hunks are saved in a file named by adding the filename extension **.rej** to the name of the target file. When patch is successful in making changes to a file, a copy of the original target file is kept with the extension **.orig**. This makes it possible for you to compare the original and changed versions to examine the changes that were made.

While locating the place where a hunk applies to *target-file*, patch checks whether the change has already been made. If the change has been made, it may be because the person who built *patch-file* accidently reversed the old and new files when building the patch. In this case, patch asks whether you would like to apply the patch in reverse. If you know that *patch-file* contains reversed patches, you can give patch the –R option to apply patches in reverse automatically.

Notes

The patch utility reports on how many changes were successfully applied and how many were rejected. If you do not use the –s option, patch displays a great deal of information as it processes the patch file.

You can create a patch file by keeping a directory holding the previous version of an application and making your changes to a copy of that application in another directory. Using the ––recursive option with diff allows you to build a patch file containing all the differences between the old and new versions. See "Examples."

If you are a distributor of software source code, you can help your users by keeping a file named **patchlevel.h** that holds the current version number and patch number of your software.

If you are building a patch file and want to add a file, you need to create an empty file with the same name as the new file to serve as the *target-file* before comparing with diff.

Examples

In the following example, the distributor is building a patch file for a small software application. The new version of the application source code is in the directory **pi**, whereas the directory **Old_pi** holds the previous version:

```
$ ls -l Old_pi
total 8
-rw-rw-r--   1 alex      group          132 Jul  3 14:13 Makefile
-rw-rw-r--   1 alex      group            0 Aug  4 08:16 patchlevel.h
-rw-r--r--   1 alex      group         5917 Jul 14 09:43 pi.c
-rw-rw-r--   1 alex      group          605 Jul 23 11:08 piform.icn
$ ls -l pi
total 9
-rw-rw-r--   1 alex      group          167 Aug  4 08:12 Makefile
-rw-rw-r--   1 alex      group           42 Aug  4 10:24 patchlevel.h
-rw-r--r--   1 alex      group         5988 Aug  4 08:09 pi.c
-rw-rw-r--   1 alex      group          605 Jul 23 11:08 piform.icn
```

The developer uses the following command to build a patch file using the context (–c) option to diff (page 1149). (In this example the ––recursive option is not needed because no subdirectories are in **pi** and **Old_pi**, but the developer included it anyway):

```
$ diff --recursive -c Old_pi pi >patch.1.1
```

The **patch.1.1** patch file contains all the information needed to change the old version of the **pi** application into the new version:

```
$ cat patch.1.1
diff --recursive -c Old_pi/Makefile pi/Makefile
*** Old_pi/MakefileWed Jul  3 14:13:20 2002
--- pi/MakefileSun Aug  4 08:12:41 2002
***************
*** 2,10 ****
  # makefile
  #
  CC = gcc
! CFLAGS = -O3 -fomit-frame-pointer -fwritable-strings

  all: pi

  pi:  pi.c
    $(CC) $(CFLAGS) -o pi $? -lm
--- 2,13 ----
  # makefile
  #
  CC = gcc
! CFLAGS = -O3 -fomit-frame-pointer -ffast-math -fwritable-strings

  all: pi

  pi:  pi.c
    $(CC) $(CFLAGS) -o pi $? -lm
+
+ clean:
+   -rm -f *.o pi
diff --recursive -c Old_pi/patchlevel.h pi/patchlevel.h
*** Old_pi/patchlevel.hSun Aug  4 08:16:08 2002
--- pi/patchlevel.hSun Aug  4 10:24:29 2002
***************
*** 0 ****
--- 1,4 ----
+
+ #define VERSION1
+ #define PATCHLEVEL1
+
diff --recursive -c Old_pi/pi.c pi/pi.c
*** Old_pi/pi.cSun Jul 14 09:43:43 2002
--- pi/pi.cSun Aug  4 08:09:45 2002
***************
*** 17,22 ****
--- 17,23 ----
    *              486dx2/66  [Linux 1.2.13]: 126 cpu seconds,
    *              486dx4/100 [Linux 1.2.13]:  92 cpu seconds)
    *      Cyrix  586dx4/100 [Linux 1.2.13]:  85 cpu seconds) [no
speedups]
+   *      Cyrix  586dx4/120 [Linux 2.0.00]:  77 cpu seconds) [speedups]
    *
    */

***************
*** 171,176 ****
--- 172,179 ----
      {
      int i;
```

```
        char *s = "        ";
+       sprintf(s,"%%%dd.",NDS);
+       printf(s,(int)a[0]);
        sprintf(s,"%%%d.%dd ",NDS,NDS);
        for (i = 1; i < nwd; i++) {
            printf(s,(int)a[i]);
```

This patch file is then mailed out to all users:

```
$ mail pi-users
To: pi_users
Subject: New version of pi available


Hi - Here are the patches you need to upgrade to version 1.1
of the pi program:

~r patch.1.1
patch.1.1: 61 lines
(continue editing letter)
CONTROL-D
```

If you receive this mail, you can save the message to a file and then move to the directory holding the old version of **pi** and run patch to upgrade your source code. (Some mail programs can pipe the message directly into patch without having to save it to a file.) There is no need to extract the patches from the mail file. While running, patch shows you all the processing that is taking place. Three hunks are successfully processed:

```
$ cd pi
$ patch <../mail.pi
Hmm...  Looks like a new-style context diff to me...
The text leading up to this was:
--------------------------
|
|Hi - Here are the patches you need to upgrade to version 1.1
|  of the pi program:
|
|diff --recursive -c Old_pi/Makefile pi/Makefile
|*** Old_pi/MakefileWed Jul  3 14:13:20 2002
|--- pi/MakefileSun Aug  4 08:12:41 2002
--------------------------
Patching file Makefile using Plan A...
Hunk #1 succeeded at 2.
Hmm...  The next patch looks like a new-style context diff to me...
The text leading up to this was:
--------------------------
|diff --recursive -c Old_pi/patchlevel.h pi/patchlevel.h
|*** Old_pi/patchlevel.hSun Aug  4 08:16:08 2002
|--- pi/patchlevel.hSun Aug  4 10:24:29 2002
--------------------------
Patching file patchlevel.h using Plan A...
```

```
Hunk #1 succeeded at 1.
Hmm...  The next patch looks like a new-style context diff to me...
The text leading up to this was:
--------------------------
|diff --recursive -c Old_pi/pi.c pi/pi.c
|*** Old_pi/pi.cSun Jul 14 09:43:43 2002
|--- pi/pi.cSun Aug  4 08:09:45 2002
--------------------------
Patching file pi.c using Plan A...
Hunk #1 succeeded at 17.
Hunk #2 succeeded at 172.
Hmm...  Ignoring the trailing garbage.
done
```

The last example shows how you might apply the patch needed to upgrade version 2.4.17 of the GNU/Linux operating system to version 2.4.18:

> `$ gunzip <patch.2.4.18.gz | patch -d /usr/src -p0`

Because Linux kernel patches are compressed with gzip before being distributed, gunzip decompresses the *patch-file* before feeding it to patch. Also, kernel patches are distributed, assuming that your kernel sources are kept in the directory named **linux**. The **–p0** option to patch allows you to run patch from the parent directory of **linux**; usually this is **/usr/src**. The **–d /usr/src** option causes patch to change to this directory before applying the patches. You should be Superuser to upgrade the kernel source. (Allowing other users write permission to kernel source files is a large security hole.)

pine

Sends and receives electronic mail and news

pine –i
pine [options] [recipient–list]

You can send and receive electronic mail messages with pine, a screen-based mailer. The primary design objective in the early releases of pine was ease of use. To this end pine was endowed with extensive built-in documentation, safeguards against mishaps, and a clean and forgiving user interface.

Since the early releases, a number of advanced features have been added to the mailer, making it attractive to both the sophisticated and the naive user. Advanced features that are now available in pine include

- MIME support for sending and receiving binary files in mail messages.

- The ability to read and post network news.

- Maintenance of an address book of mail recipients.

- Spell checking during message composition.

- Mouse support when using xterm on an X Window System.

- A highly configurable environment that can be easily customized to suit the needs of a wide range of users.

The basic unit of storage for pine mail is the Message Folder. Initially there are three Message Folders: pine stores messages you receive in **INBOX**, copies of messages you send in **sent-mail**, and messages you explicitly save in **saved-messages**. You can change the defaults for these folders, and you can create as many new folders as you wish. See also "Tutorial: Using pine to Send and Receive E-Mail" on page 88, "Tutorial: Using pine as a Newsreader" on page 401, and mail on page 1241.

Arguments   Without any options or arguments, pine displays the Main menu. With the **–i** option (first form), **pine** displays the Message Index screen, bypassing the Main menu. Here you can view mail headers and select incoming messages that you want to read. When you have finished reading your messages, pine returns you to the shell, again bypassing the Main menu.

In the second form, *recipient-list* is a list of recipients of the mail message you have yet to compose. When the *recipient-list* is present on the command line, pine displays the Compose Message screen, bypassing the Main menu. When you are finished composing and sending your message, you are returned to the shell.

The *recipient-list* may contain e-mail addresses, user names (for users on your system), or nicknames that you establish when setting up your address book. You may also use a nickname to refer to a set of addresses.

Options

–conf   Sends information about the current configuration to standard output.

–feature-list=[no–]*feature-list-option*

Sets a *feature-list-option*. For example, including **–feature-list=enable-flag-cmd** on the command line provides you with a Message Index screen menu item that changes the message status flags. Prepending *no–* to the *feature-list-option* unsets the option. Refer to "Configuring pine" on page 1282 for a discussion of *feature-list* options.

–f *folder*   Opens the folder given by *folder*. Without this option pine opens the **INBOX** folder.

–i   Enters the Message Index screen directly to read your mail.

–variable=*variable-value*

Assigns the value *variable-value* to the variable named *variable*. This value overrides the value given in the **/etc/pine.conf** file or the **.pinerc** file in your home directory. For example, giving the option **–signature-file=~/.funsig** causes pine to insert the contents of the **~/.funsig** file in each message you send.

–sort *sort-type*[**/reverse**]

Sorts message headers. By default the message headers displayed in the Message Index screen are sorted by arrival time. You can have pine sort on a different field by giving the **–sort** option on the command line. The argument *sort-type* identifies the sort field. In addition to **arrival**, you can specify **subject, from, date,** and **size**. To reverse the order of the sort, append **/reverse** to the *sort-type*.

–h   help   Displays a list of options that you can use with the pine command, along with a brief summary of each.

Discussion

At the top of all pine screens is a status line that includes the name of the current screen and other status information. At the bottom of each pine screen is a two-line menu of commands that are defined for that screen. If there are too many commands to fit in two lines, pine displays a command that enables you to cycle through two or more partial menus.

Every pine screen allows you to use an aspect of pine's functionality. Help is available when you need to make decisions.

The following items appear in the Main menu (see Figure 3-17 on page 89):

- Help

- Compose Message

- Message Index

- Folder List

- Address Book

- Setup

- Quit

Except for Setup and Quit, when you select an item in the preceding list, pine displays a screen for that item. When you select Setup, pine prompts you first for a setup task; one choice you have is Config, which modifies the behavior of pine (refer to "Configuring pine" on page 1282). Selecting Quit returns you to the shell.

Selecting Help in the Main menu displays the Help For Main menu screen, which gives an overview of the pine mailer. This is a good place to start if you are new to pine.

Sending Messages

Having a pine address book makes sending mail messages much easier. To set up your address book or to add, delete, or edit an entry, select Address Book from the Main menu. For each user you add to your address book, pine prompts you for the user's full name, nickname, and e-mail address. In the Address Book screen, you may also select Create List to define a *distribution list*—a group of users you can reference with a single nickname. (A nickname is an alias that easily allows you to remember and reference a recipient or set of recipients.)

Specifying *recipient-list* on the pine command line puts you directly into the Compose Message screen (see Figure 3-18 on page 90). If you use a full name or a nickname as an address, pine attempts to map the name to a proper e-mail address (or list of e-mail addresses), using your address book. If you give a name that is not in your address book, pine assumes that the name is a user on your machine. Of course, you can specify any address on the command line; the recipient does not have to be in your address book or on your machine.

You can also enter the message composer by selecting Compose from the Main menu. Having access to the Main menu permits you to use other pine functions during your pine session.

The fields for the header of the message are displayed at the top of the Compose Message screen. If you have included a *recipient-list* on the command line, the To: field is already be filled in; otherwise, you need to enter an e-mail address in this field or a full name or nickname as it appears in your address book. Other fields are Cc:, for recipients of "carbon copies" of your message; Attchmnt:, for attaching binary files to your message; and Subject:, for entering the subject of your message. After completing the fields in the header, you can compose your mail message by using the built-in pine editor. (Help is available to learn the editor commands.)

If you are in the middle of composing a message and want to finish it later, you can select Postpone. The pine utility stores the message in the folder named **postponed-msgs**, and the next time you run pine, it gives you the opportunity to continue with the postponed message.

Reading Messages

If you simply want to read your mail, the easiest way is to use the –i option on the command line. This option takes you directly to the Message Index screen (see Figure 3-19 on page 92), where a list of message headers is displayed. The highlighted message is the current message; you can highlight any other message by using the control characters given in the screen menu.

Another way to read messages in pine is to select Message Index from the Main menu. This is appropriate if you plan to remain in the mailer after reading your incoming messages.

By default each message header contains the following fields:

flags   message-#   date-sent   from-name   size   [subject]

The first field lists the possible status flags for each message (Table III-26).

Flag	**‖ table III-26**
A	You have replied to the mail message.
D	You have marked the message for deletion.
N	The message is new.
+	The message was sent directly to you (that is, not a carbon copy).
*	You have marked the message as important.

Once you have read a mail message, you can reply to the message, forward it to another person, save it in a folder, or export the message to a file. If you do not wish to keep a message, you can also select Delete to mark the message for deletion; the message is not deleted until you give the eXpunge command or terminate your pine session. Exporting a message to a file automatically marks that message for deletion.

To mark a message as important (*), set the pine variable **enable-flag-cmd**.

Attachments

The types of binary files that you may want to attach to a mail message include executable files, image files, audio files, and word processing documents. Unlike ASCII text files, these files contain characters that require special handling, which is provided by pine's MIME (Multipurpose Internet Mail Extensions) software. To attach a file to a pine message, select Attach in the Compose Message screen while the Attchmnt line in the header is highlighted. When you receive a message that has an attachment, it is listed in the header; you can view an attachment that you have the software to display.

Reading and Posting News

The pine utility also acts as a newsreader if you have access to newsgroups. You can ask your Internet service provider whether Usenet news is available for your system. If Usenet news is provided to your system from an NNTP (Network News Transfer Protocol) server, you can use pine to access newsgroups by setting the pine variable **nntp-server** to the hostname of the NNTP server (see "Configuring pine," following).

Once the name of your news server has been assigned to **nntp-server**, pine creates a separate directory, or *collection*, to store newsgroup folders. Each newsgroup that you subscribe to appears as a separate folder in this collection. At this point you probably have at least two collections, counting the default collection, with folders **INBOX, sent-mail**, and **saved-messages**. When you have more than one collection, the Folder List screen displays a list of collections instead of a list of folders; you need to highlight the newsgroup collection before viewing the folders within it. When a collection is highlighted, you can also subscribe and unsubscribe to newsgroups.

In most ways pine manages news as it does mail. You can mark news messages for deletion, reply to news messages, and so on.

To use pine to post a message to a newsgroup, select Rich Hdr (Rich Headers) from the menu in the Compose Message screen. This displays header fields that are normally hidden, including the field Newsgrps. This is where you enter the name of the newsgroup you want to post a message to.

Configuring pine

Changing the default configuration of pine changes the behavior of the utility. Some pine variables take on the value of a string, whereas others are either set or unset. The latter are called feature-list options.

Superuser can establish the values of some pine variables in the **/etc/pine.conf** file. To display these values, give the option **–conf** on the pine command line. If there are values you wish to override, redefine the variables in your pine startup file, ~/.pinerc, or select Setup from the pine Main menu, followed by Config, to enter the Setup Configuration screen.

String-Valued Variables

editor
: Specifies the editor to use in the message composer: defaults to the pine builtin editor, pico.

personal-name
: Appears in the From: line of messages you send; defaults to your full name from the /etc/passwd file.

signature-file
: Specifies the pathname of the file to insert into messages that you are replying to or composing; defaults to ~/.signature. This file usually includes at least your full name and e-mail address.

nntp-server
: Specifies the address of your news server.

Feature-list Options

enable-flag-cmd
: Enables you to specify flags for mail messages in your Message Folder. When this option is set, the menu item Flag is included in the menu for the Message Index screen.

enable-unix-pipe-cmd
: Causes the menu item Pipe to appear in the pine Message Text screen. Selecting this item causes pine to send the text of the message as standard input to the command you enter.

expunge-without-confirm
: Causes pine not to request confirmation before permanently deleting messages.

quit-without-confirm
: Causes pine not to ask for confirmation when you select Quit to exit from pine.

save-will-not-delete
: Normally, when you copy a message to a folder by choosing Save in the Message Index screen, the message is automatically marked for deletion. Setting this option suppresses this behavior.

signature-at-bottom
: By default, when you include the original mail message in your reply to it, pine puts the contents of your signature file (~/.signature) *above the original message*. Setting this option tells pine to put your signature below the text of the original message instead.

use-current-dir
: When you enter a relative pathname within the mailer to export a mail message or read the contents of a file into a mail message, pine assumes that the pathname is relative to your home directory. This option tells pine to use the working directory instead.

Examples

Normally the Message Folder **INBOX** is opened when you start pine. In the following example the **–f** option opens the folder **project_may03** instead:

```
$ pine -f project_may03
```

In the next example Alex gives the command to run pine with the **–i** option:

```
$ pine -i
```

This option displays the Message Index screen, bypassing the Main menu. The headers in the display summarize the messages in the folder **~alex/mail/INBOX**, which is open by default. Each message remains in the INBOX folder until Alex marks it for deletion. Once marked for deletion, a message remains in the INBOX folder until it is expunged. The status flag **N** to the left of the recent messages means that those messages are unread, messages marked with the flag **+** were sent directly to Alex, and those replied to by Alex are marked with the flag **A**. Alex has given one message the flag **✻**, to signify its importance:

```
+ A 1   Oct  8 Colleen Steiner     (448) reminder
    2   Oct  9 John L. Davis    (10,798) Re: papers
✻ A 3   Oct  9 John L. Davis     (1,803) New Schedule
    4   Oct  9 John L. Davis     (1,560) Re: bundle 11
+   5   Oct 10 Colleen Steiner  (29,408) edge-meshes
+ N 6   Oct 11 Steve Walters     (1,375) Re: ponder this
+ N 7   Oct 11 Steve Walters       (603) Re: check
  N 8   Oct 11 Jenny Chen        (2,135) Newsletters
  N 9   Oct 11 Wanda Hayes       (1,079) conference
+ N 10  Oct 11 Steve Walters       (553) seminar 9/25
```

The flags in the headers change after Alex reads the Oct. 11 messages and marks the one from Jenny for deletion:

```
+ A 1   Oct  8 Colleen Steiner     (448) reminder
    2   Oct  9 John L. Davis    (10,798) Re: papers
✻ A 3   Oct  9 John L. Davis     (1,803) New Schedule
    4   Oct  9 John L. Davis     (1,560) Re: bundle 11
+   5   Oct 10 Colleen Steiner  (29,408) edge-meshes
+   6   Oct 11 Steve Walters     (1,375) Re: ponder this
+   7   Oct 11 Steve Walters       (603) Re: check
  D 8   Oct 11 Jenny Chen        (2,135) Newsletters
    9   Oct 11 Wanda Hayes       (1,079) conference
+   10  Oct 11 Steve Walters       (553) seminar 9/25
```

If Alex exits from pine and calls it again as

```
$ pine -i -sort from
```

the Message Index screen looks like this:

```
      1    Oct  9 John L. Davis      (10,798) Re: papers
*  A  2    Oct  9 John L. Davis       (1,803) New Schedule
      3    Oct  9 John L. Davis       (1,560) Re: bundle 11
   N  4    Oct 11 Wanda Hayes         (1,079) conference
+  A  5    Oct  8 Colleen Steiner       (448) reminder
+     6    Oct 10 Colleen Steiner    (29,408) edge-meshes
+  N  7    Oct 11 Steve Walters        (1,375) Re: ponder this
+  N  8    Oct 11 Steve Walters          (603) Re: check
+  N  9    Oct 11 Steve Walters          (553) seminar 9/25
```

The –i option puts Alex directly in the Message Index screen. The –**sort** option specifies that the headers be sorted by the sender's name. The message from Jenny Chen is no longer in the folder, and the remaining messages are sorted by sender's name, not by arrival time.

In the final example Alex displays the contents of his signature file. The text from this file appears in the messages that Alex sends to others. Some people (such as Alex) make their ~/**.signature** files ornate, whereas others keep them simple:

```
$ cat ~/.signature

      [ A ][ L ][ E ][ X ]
     ][ ][ ][ ][ ][
 [ W ][ A ][ T ][ S ][ O ][ N ]

      alex@bravo.tcorp.com
```

pr

Paginates files for printing

*pr [**options**] [**file-list**]*

The pr utility breaks files into pages, usually in preparation for printing. Each page has a header with the name of the file, date, time, and page number.

The pr utility takes its input from files you specify on the command line or from standard input. The output from pr goes to standard output and is frequently redirected by a pipe to a printer.

Arguments   The *file-list* contains the pathnames of text files that you want pr to paginate. When you do not specify a file, pr reads standard input.

Options   You can embed options within the *file-list*. An embedded option affects only files following it on the command line.

+page   Causes output to begin with the specified *page*. This option begins with a plus sign, not a hyphen. Replace *page* with the page number you want to start with.

–columns   **columns**   Displays output in *column* columns. This option cannot be used with **–m**.

–c   **control**   Uses a caret (^) to represent control characters. For example, a BACKSPACE is represented as ^H.

–d   **double space**   Double spaces the output.

–f   **formfeed**   Uses a FORMFEED character to skip to the next page rather than filling the current page with NEWLINE characters.

–h *header*   **header**   The pr utility displays the *header* at the top of each page in place of the filename. If *header* contains SPACEs, you must enclose it within quotation marks.

–l *lines*   **length**   Changes the page length from the default 66 lines to *lines* lines.

–m   **merge**   Displays all specified files simultaneously in multiple columns. This option cannot be used with **–columns**.

–n[c[k]]   **number**   Numbers the lines of the file. The *c* is a character that pr appends to the number to separate it from the contents of the file. When you do not specify *c*, TAB is used. The *k* argument specifies the number of digits in each line number. By default *k* is five.

−o *spaces* offset   Specifies the number of ***spaces*** to skip before displaying the first character of each output line (the left margin).

−s[*x*] separate   Separates columns with the single character *x*. By default pr uses TABs as separation characters unless you use the **−w** option, in which case nothing separates columns.

−t no header or trailer   Causes pr not to display its five-line page header and trailer. The header that pr normally displays includes the name of the file, the date, time, and page number. The trailer is five blank lines.

−w *n* width   Changes the page width from standard 72 columns to *n* columns. Replace *n* with the number of columns you want. This option is effective only with multicolumn output (that is, the **−m** or **−columns** options).

Notes   When you use the **−columns** option to display the output in multiple columns, pr displays the same number of lines in each column (with the possible exception of the last).

The write utility cannot send messages to your terminal while you are running pr with its output going to the terminal. The pr utility disables messages to prevent another user from sending you a message and disrupting pr's output to your screen.

Examples   The first command line shows pr paginating a file named **memo** and sending its output through a pipe to lpr for printing:

```
$ pr memo | lpr
```

Next, **memo** is sent to the printer again, this time with a special heading at the top of each page. The job is run in the background.

```
$ pr -h 'MEMO RE: BOOK' memo | lpr&
[1] 4904
```

Next, pr displays the **memo** file on the terminal, without any header, starting with page 3:

```
$ pr -t +3 memo
.
.
```

sp

ps

Displays process status

ps [options][process-list]

The ps utility displays status information about processes.

Arguments   The *process-list* is a comma- or SPACE-separated list of PID numbers. When you specify a *process-list*, ps reports only on processes in that list. The *process-list* must follow all options on the command line.

Options   The version of ps that Red Hat includes takes three types of options, each preceded by a different prefix. You can intermix the options.

1. Two hyphens: GNU options

2. One hyphen: UNIX98 options

3. No hyphens: BSD options

−A all   Reports on all processes. Also **−e**.

−e everything   Reports on all processes. Also **−A**.

−f full   Displays a listing with more columns of information.

−−forest   Displays the process tree.

−l long   Produces a long listing showing more information about each process. See the "Discussion" section for a description of all the columns that this option displays.

−−no-headers   Omits the header; useful if you are sending the output to another program for further processing.

u user-oriented   Adds to the display the username, time that the process was started, the percentage of CPU and memory, and other information.

−−User *username*   Specifies a real *username* or UID to report on.

−w wide   Without this option ps truncates output lines at the right side of the display. This option extends the display so it wraps around one more line, if needed.

Discussion   Without any options, ps displays the statuses of all active processes that your terminal controls. Table III-27 lists the heading and content of each of the four columns that ps displays.

Heading I || table III-27

PID	The process identification number.
TTY (terminal)	The name of the terminal that controls the process.
TIME	The number of minutes and seconds the process has been running.
CMD	The command line the process was called with. The command is truncated to fit on one line. Use the −w option to see more of the command line (see "Options").

The columns that ps displays depend on your choice of options. Table III-28 lists the headings and contents of the most common columns.

Heading II || table III-28

The exact column title differs, depending on the type of option you use. This table shows the headings for UNIX98 (one hyphen) options.

%CPU	The percentage of total CPU time that the process is using. Owing to the way that GNU/Linux does process accounting, this is only approximate, and the total of all the %CPU values for all the processes may exceed 100%.
%MEM (memory)	The percentage of RAM memory that the process is using.
CMD	The command line that started the process. This column is always displayed last on a line.
F (flags)	The flags associated with the process.
PID	The process identification number.
PPID (parent PID)	The process identification number of the parent process.
PRI (priority)	The priority of the process.

Heading II (Continued)

The exact column title differs, depending on the type of option you use. This table shows the headings for UNIX98 (one hyphen) options.

RSS (resident set size)	The number of blocks of memory that process is using.
SIZE	The size, in blocks, of the core image of the process.
STIME or START	The date the process started.
STAT or S (status)	The status of the process as specified by one or more letters from the following list:

	< High priority
	    D Sleeping and cannot be interrupted
	    L Pages locked in memory (real-time and custom I/O)
	    N Low priority
	    R Available for execution (on run queue)
	    S Sleeping
	    T Either stopped or being traced
	    W Has no pages resident in RAM memory
	    Z Zombie process that is waiting for its child processes to terminate before it terminates

TIME	The number of minutes and seconds that the process has been running.
TTY (terminal)	The name of the terminal controlling the process.
UID (user ID)	The user ID of the user who owns the process.
USER	The username of the user who owns the process.
WCHAN (wait channel)	If the process is waiting for an event, this column gives the address of the kernel function that caused the process to wait. It is 0 for processes that are not waiting or sleeping.

Examples   The first example shows ps, without any options, displaying the user's active processes. The first process is the shell (zsh), and the second is the process executing the ps utility:

```
$ ps
  PID TTY          TIME CMD
 2697 pts/0    00:00:02 bash
 3299 pts/0    00:00:00 ps
```

With the –l (long) option, ps displays more information about the processes:

```
$ ps -l
  F S   UID   PID  PPID  C PRI  NI ADDR    SZ WCHAN  TTY          TIME CMD
000 S   500  2697  2696  0  75   0    -   639 wait4  pts/0    00:00:02 bash
000 R   500  3300  2697  0  76   0    -   744 -      pts/0    00:00:00 ps
```

The –u option shows various types of information about the processes, including how much of your system CPU and memory each one is using:

```
$ ps -u
USER        PID %CPU %MEM   VSZ  RSS TTY      STAT START   TIME COMMAND
alex       2697  0.0  0.5  2556 1460 pts/0    S    Jul31   0:02 -bash
alex       3303  0.0  0.2  2476  616 pts/0    R    Jul31   0:00 ps -u
```

The ––forest option causes ps to display what the man page describes as an "ASCII art process tree." It displays processes that are children of other processes indented under their parents, making the process hierarchy, or tree, easier to see:

```
$ ps -ef --forest
UID        PID  PPID  C STIME TTY          TIME CMD
root         1     0  0 Jul22 ?        00:00:03 init
root         2     1  0 Jul22 ?        00:00:00 [keventd]
. . .
root       785     1  0 Jul22 ?        00:00:00 /usr/sbin/apmd -p 10 -w 5 -W -P
root       839     1  0 Jul22 ?        00:00:01 /usr/sbin/sshd
root      3305   839  0 Aug01 ?        00:00:00  \_ /usr/sbin/sshd
alex      3307  3305  0 Aug01 ?        00:00:00      \_ /usr/sbin/sshd
alex      3308  3307  0 Aug01 pts/1    00:00:00          \_ -bash
alex      3774  3308  0 Aug01 pts/1    00:00:00              \_ ps -ef --forest
. . .
root      1040     1  0 Jul22 ?        00:00:00 login -- root
root      3351  1040  0 Aug01 tty2     00:00:00  \_ -bash
root      3402  3351  0 Aug01 tty2     00:00:00      \_ make modules
root      3416  3402  0 Aug01 tty2     00:00:00          \_ make -C drivers CFLA
root      3764  3416  0 Aug01 tty2     00:00:00              \_ make -C scsi mod
root      3773  3764  0 Aug01 tty2     00:00:00                  \_ ld -m elf_i3
```

The next sequence of commands shows how to use ps to determine the process number of a process running in the background and how to terminate that process by using the kill command. In this case it is not necessary to use ps, because the shell displays the process number of the background processes. The ps utility verifies the PID number.

The first command executes find in the background. The shell displays the job and PID numbers of the process, followed by a prompt:

```
$ find ~ -name memo -print > memo.out &
[1] 3343
```

Next, ps confirms the PID number of the background task. If you did not already know this number, using ps would be the only way to find it out:

```
$ ps
  PID TTY          TIME CMD
 3308 pts/1    00:00:00 bash
 3343 pts/1    00:00:00 find
 3344 pts/1    00:00:00 ps
```

Finally, kill (page 1224) terminates the process:

```
$ kill 3343
$ RETURN
[1]+  Terminated              find ~ -name memo -print >memo.out
$
```

rcp

Copies one or more files to or from a remote computer

*rcp [**options**] **source-file destination-file***
*rcp [**options**] **source-file-list destination-directory***

The rcp utility copies one or more ordinary files between two computers that can communicate over a network. Like cp, rcp has two modes of operation: The first copies one file to another, and the second copies one or more files to a directory.

---

rcp Is Not Secure   ‖ security

The rcp utility uses host-based trust, which is not secure, to authorize files to be copied. Refer to "Trusted Hosts" on page 373. Use scp (page 1308) when it is available.

Arguments   The *source-file*, *source-file-list*, and *destination-file* are pathnames of the ordinary files, and the *destination-directory* is the pathname of a directory file. A pathname that does not contain a colon (:) is the name of a local file. A pathname of the form *name@host:path* names a file on the remote computer named *host*. The *path* is relative to the home directory of user *name* (unless *path* is an absolute pathname). When you omit the *name@* portion of the destination, a relative pathname is relative to the home directory on *host* of the user giving the rcp command.

The *source-file[-list]* is the name of the file(s) that rcp is going to copy; *destination-file* is the name that rcp assigns to the resulting copy of the file, or the *destination-directory* is the name of the directory that rcp puts the copied files in. When rcp copies files to a *destination-directory*, the files maintain their original simple filenames.

Options

–p   **preserve**   Sets the modification times and file access permissions of each copy to match those of the *source-file*. When you do not use –p, rcp uses the file-creation mask (umask, page 1366) on the remote system to modify the access permissions.

–r   **recursive**   When a file in the *source-file-list* is a directory, this option copies the contents of that directory and any subdirectories into the *destination-directory*. You can use this option only when the destination is a directory.

Notes   You must have a login account on the remote computer to copy files to or from it using rcp. The rcp utility does not prompt for a password but uses several alternative methods to verify that you have the authority to read or write files on the remote system. One common method requires that the name of your local computer be specified in the **/etc/hosts.equiv** file on the remote computer. If the name of your computer is there, rcp allows you to copy files *if* your login names are the same on both computers and your account on the remote computer has the necessary permissions to access files there. Authorization can also be specified on a per user basis: The remote user's home directory must contain a file named **.rhosts** that lists trusted remote systems and users. With the second method, your local and remote user names do not have to match, but your local user name must appear on the line in the remote **.rhosts** file that starts with the name of your local machine. See the description of rsh on page 1306 for more details.

If you use a wildcard (such as *****) in a remote pathname, you must quote the wildcard character or pathname so that the wildcard is interpreted by the shell on the remote computer and not by the local shell. As with cp, if the ***destination-file*** exists before you execute rcp, rcp overwrites the file.

Examples   The first example copies all the files with filenames ending in **.c** into the **archives** directory on the remote computer named **bravo**. Because the full pathname of the **archives** directory is not specified, rcp assumes that it is a subdirectory of the user's home directory on **bravo**. Each of the copied files retains its simple filename.

```
$ rcp *.c bravo:archives
```

The next example copies **memo** from the **/home/jenny** directory on **bravo** to the working directory on the local computer:

```
$ rcp bravo:/home/jenny/memo .
```

The next command copies two files named **memo.new** and **letter** to Jenny's home directory on the remote computer **bravo**. The absolute pathnames of the copied files on **bravo** are **/home/jenny/memo.new** and **/home/jenny/letter**:

```
$ rcp memo.new letter bravo:/home/jenny
```

The final command copies all the files in Jenny's **reports** directory on **bravo** to the **oldreports** directory on the local computer, preserving the original modification dates and file access permissions on the copies:

```
$ rcp -p 'bravo:reports/*' oldreports
```

rcs

Creates or changes the attributes of an RCS file

rcs [options] file-list

The rcs utility creates or changes the attributes of RCS files. The options control the operations performed on the files. The rcs utility is part of RCS (Revision Control System—page 871), which is a group of related utilities that manage the storage, retrieval, and updating of the source files. The RCS utilities covered in Part III are ci, co, rcs, and rlog.

Arguments   The *file-list* is a list of filenames—typically working filenames. For each, rcs looks for the corresponding RCS file in the subdirectory **RCS** of the working file's directory and then in the working file's directory. See "Notes" following for more about RCS and working filenames.

Options

–a*login-list* **add**   Adds to the list of users who are allowed to make changes to an RCS file. Replaces *login-list* with a comma-separated list of user login names. Before any users are added to the access list, the list is empty, and any user can check in changes to the file.

–e[*login-list*] **erase**   Deletes from the list of users who are allowed to make changes to an RCS file. Replaces *login-list* with a comma-separated list of user login names. If the *login-list* is not specified, all users are deleted, and any user can check in changes to the file.

–i **initialize**   Creates an empty (null) RCS file.

–l[*revision-number*]

lock   Sets a lock for an RCS file. Normally, when you want to edit a revision of an RCS file, you set the lock when you check out the file. If you forget to do so, you can use the –l option with the rcs command to set the lock retroactively. When you do not specify a *revision-number*, rcs locks the latest revision; otherwise, it sets the lock for the specified revision.

–o*revision-list* **outdate**   Removes a revision or range of revisions from an RCS file. The *revision-list* can include one revision number (for example, **–o1.4**) or a pair of revision numbers separated by a colon (for example, **–o1.4:1.6**).

–u[*revision-number*] unlock Unlocks an RCS file. A lock on an RCS file is normally released when the file is checked in. Use this option to release the lock without checking in the file or to release a lock that was set by another user. When you do not specify a *revision-number*, rcs unlocks the latest revision; otherwise, it removes the lock for the specified revision.

Notes The name of an RCS-encoded file ends in the two characters **,v**. The simple filename component of the working file must agree with that of the RCS file, except for the characters **,v** terminating the RCS filename. The working filename corresponding to the RCS file **RCS/mergecases.c,v** may be **mergecases.c** but not **mergetests.c**. Refer to the rcs man page and other documentation to learn more about naming files, including RCS files, in the *file-list*. Although you can store RCS and working files anywhere, the RCS file is usually stored in a subdirectory (named **RCS**) of the directory storing the working file. Sometimes both are stored in the same directory.

A revision may be identified by a number consisting of an even number of period-separated integers. Revision numbers on the trunk consist of two integers, whereas branch revision numbers consist of at least four integers. You can also use symbolic names to identify revisions.

If source files are expected to undergo modification by more than one developer at a time or if you have a large number of source files organized in a directory hierarchy, you may want to consider using cvs (page 879) instead of the utilities of RCS. The cvs utility extends the functionality of RCS to accommodate large project development. The cvs interface closely resembles RCS and is easy for RCS users to learn and use.

Examples The following command creates a new RCS-encoded file with the name of **RCS/menu1,v**:

```
$ rcs -i menu1
RCS file: RCS/menu1,v
enter description, terminated with single '.' or end of file:
NOTE: This is NOT the log message!
>> basic menu
>> .
done
```

The next example adds Alex and Barbara to the list of users who are authorized to make changes to the file **menus_march**:

```
$ rcs -aalex,barbara menus_march
```

Having added Barbara to the list, you can revoke her access with the following command:

```
$ rcs -ebarbara menus_march
```

The next command line removes revision 1.5 from the file **menu1**:

```
$ rcs -o1.5 menu1
RCS file: RCS/menu1,v
deleting revision 1.5
done
```

The last example deletes revisions 1.5 through 1.8 from the file **menus_march**:

```
$ rcs -o1.5:1.8 menus_march
RCS file: RCS/menus_march,v
deleting revision 1.8
deleting revision 1.7
deleting revision 1.6
deleting revision 1.5
done
```

rlog

Prints a summary of the history of an RCS file

*rlog [**options**] file-list*

The rlog utility displays a summary of the history of RCS files. The options control how much information rlog displays. The rlog utility is part of RCS (Revision Control System—page 871), which is a group of related utilities that manage the storage, retrieval, and updating of the source files. The RCS utilities covered in Part III are ci, co, rcs, and rlog.

Arguments   The *file-list* is a list of filenames—typically working filenames. For each, rlog looks for the corresponding RCS file in the **RCS** subdirectory of the working file's directory and then in the working file's directory. See "Notes" following for more about RCS and working filenames.

Options

–ddates[;*dates*]   **date**   Uses file check-in dates to restrict the information displayed by rlog. You can select more than one range of dates by separating each range with a semicolon. Each range of dates is specified using greater than (>) and less than (<) symbols and must be quoted to prevent the shell from interpreting those symbols as redirections. To see the history of a file during the month of October 2003, you would use

    "Oct 1 2003 8:00 am LT < Oct 31 2003 12:00 pm LT"

–r[*revision-list*]   **revision**   Restricts the information reported by rlog to the specified revision number or range of revisions. When you specify the **–r** option without a revision number, rlog reports on the latest revision. A range of revisions can be specified by including a colon. For example, to restrict the display to revisions 1.2 through 1.4, use **–r1.2:1.4**. To see information on revisions 1.2 through the current revision, use **–r1.2:**. For information on revision 1.4 and all earlier revisions, use **–:r1.4**.

Notes   The name of an RCS-encoded file ends in the two characters **,v**. The simple filename component of the working file must agree with that of the RCS file except for the characters **,v** terminating the RCS filename. The working filename corresponding to the RCS file **RCS/mergecases.c,v** may be **mergecases.c** but not **mergetests.c**. Refer to the rcs man page and other documentation to learn more about naming files, including RCS files, in the *file-list*. Although you can store RCS and working files anywhere, the RCS file is usually stored in a subdirectory (named **RCS**) of the directory storing the working file. Sometimes both are stored in the same directory.

A revision may be identified by a number consisting of an even number of period-separated integers. Revision numbers on the trunk consist of two integers, whereas branch revision numbers consist of at least four integers. You can also use symbolic names to identify revisions.

When specifying a date, the default time zone is Coordinated Universal Time (UTC), also known as Greenwich Mean Time (GMT). The RCS commands recognize dates in a variety of formats, such as

```
5:00 PM LT
1:00am, Jul. 16, 2004
Fri Jul 16 17:00:00 PDT 2004
```

In this example LT represents the local time, which in this case is PDT, Pacific Daylight Time.

If source files are expected to undergo modification by more than one developer at a time or if you have a large number of source files organized in a directory hierarchy, you may want to consider using cvs (page 879) instead of the utilities of RCS. The cvs utility extends the functionality of RCS to accommodate large-project development. The cvs interface closely resembles RCS and is easy for RCS users to learn and use.

Examples   Following, rlog displays standard information about the changes that have been made to the file **RCS/thesis,v**:

```
$ rlog thesis

RCS file: thesis,v
Working file: thesis
head: 2.7
branch:
locks: strict
alex: 2.7
access list:
symbolic names:
comment leader: "# "
keyword substitution: kv
total revisions: 14;    selected revisions: 14
description:
Alex Watson's thesis
---------------------------
```

```
revision 2.7     locked by: alex;
date: 2003/08/08 21:15:47;   author: alex;   state: Exp;   lines: +663 −0
add examples
----------------------------
.
.
```

The next example prints information only about revision 1.3:

```
$ rlog -r1.3 thesis
.
```

The final example displays information about the changes made during the last two weeks of July:

```
$ rlog -d"Jul 15 2003 8:00 am LT < Jul 31 2003 5:00 pm LT" thesis
.
```

rlogin

Logs in on a remote computer

*rlogin [**option**] **remote-computer***

The rlogin utility establishes a login session on a remote computer over a network.

rlogin **Is Not Secure** || security

The rlogin utility uses host-based trust, which is not secure, to authorize your login. Alternatively, it sends your password over the network as cleartext, which is not a secure practice. Refer to "Trusted Hosts" on page 373. Use **ssh** (page 1321) when it is available.

Arguments   The ***remote-computer*** is the name of a computer that your system can reach by using a network.

Options

–l *login-name* **login**   Logs you in on the remote computer as the user specified by *login-name* rather than as yourself.

Notes   If the file named **/etc/hosts.equiv** located on the remote computer specifies the name of your local computer, the remote computer will not prompt you to enter your password. Computer systems that are listed in the **/etc/hosts.equiv** file are considered as secure as your local machine.

An alternative way to specify a trusted relationship is on a per user basis. Each user's home directory can contain a file named **.rhosts** that contains a list of trusted remote systems and users.

Examples   The following example illustrates the use of rlogin. On the local system, Alex's login name is **alex,** but on the remote computer **bravo,** his login name is **watson.** The remote system prompts Alex to enter a password because he is logging in using a user name different from the one he uses on the local system.

```
$ who am i
alex        tty06         Oct 14 13:26
$ rlogin -l watson bravo
Password:
```

If the local computer is named **hurrah**, a .rhosts file on **bravo** like the following one allows the user **alex** to log in as the user **watson** without entering a password:

```
$ cat /home/watson/.rhosts
hurrah alex
```

rm

Removes a file (deletes a link)

*rm [**options**] **file-list***

The rm utility removes hard and/or symbolic links to one or more files. When you remove the last hard link to a file, the file is deleted. Refer to Chapter 4 for more information about hard and symbolic links.

Use Caution When You Use rm with Wildcards ‖ caution

Because you can remove a large number of files with a single command, use **rm** cautiously, especially when you are using an ambiguous file reference. If you are in doubt as to the effect of an **rm** command with an ambiguous file reference, first use **echo** with the same file reference to evaluate the list of files the reference generates.

Arguments   The *file-list* contains the list of files that rm deletes.

Options

--force –f   Without asking for your consent, this option removes files for which you do not have write access permission. It also suppresses informative output if a file does not exist.

--interactive –i   Asks before removing each file. If you use **--recursive** with this option, rm also asks you before examining each directory.

–r recursive   Deletes the contents of the specified directory, including all its subdirectories, and the directory itself. Use this option cautiously.

Notes   To delete a file, you must have execute and write access permission to the parent directory of the file, but you do not need read or write access permission to the file itself. If you are running rm interactively (that is, rm's standard input is coming from a keyboard) and you do not have write access permission to the file, rm displays your access permission and waits for you to respond. If you enter **y** or **yes**, rm deletes the file; otherwise, it does not. If standard input is not coming from a keyboard, rm deletes the file without question.

The section on ln (page 130) contains a discussion about removing links. Refer to the rmdir utility (page 1305) if you need to remove an empty directory.

When you want to remove a file that begins with a hyphen, you must prevent rm from interpreting the filename as an option. One way to do this is to give the special option -- before the name of the file. This special option tells rm that no more options follow—arguments that come after it are filenames, even if they look like options.

Examples

The following command lines delete files both in the working directory and in another directory:

```
$ rm memo
$ rm letter memo1 memo2
$ rm /home/jenny/temp
```

The next example asks the user before removing each file in the working directory and its subdirectories:

```
$ rm -ir .
```

This command is useful for removing filenames that contain special characters, especially SPACEs, TABs, and NEWLINEs. (You should not create filenames containing these characters on purpose, but it may happen accidentally.)

rmdir

Removes a directory

rmdir **directory-list**

The rmdir utility deletes empty directories from the filesystem by removing links to those directories.

Arguments   The **directory-list** contains pathnames of empty directories that rmdir removes.

Notes   Refer to the rm utility with the **–r** option if you need to remove directories that are not empty, together with their contents.

Examples   The following command line deletes the empty **literature** directory from the working directory:

```
$ rmdir literature
```

The next command line removes the **letters** directory, using an absolute pathname:

```
$ rmdir /home/jenny/letters
```

rsh

Executes commands on a remote computer

rsh [option] host [command line]

The rsh utility runs *command line* on *host* by starting a shell on the remote system. Without a *command line* rsh calls rlogin, which logs you in on the remote computer.

---

rsh Is Not Secure || security

The **rsh** utility uses host-based trust, which is not secure, to authorize your login. Alternatively, it sends your password over the network as cleartext, which is not a secure practice. Refer to "Trusted Hosts" on page 373. Use **ssh** (page 374) when it is available.

Arguments The name of the remote computer must be given as *host.* Any arguments following *host* are part of *command line*, which is run on the remote system. You must quote special characters in *command line* if you do not want them expanded by the local shell prior to passing them to rsh.

Options

–l *login-name* If your login name on the remote computer is different from your local login name, you can use this option to give the remote login name.

Notes Your local login name and the name of your local computer should appear in the file **.rhosts** in the home directory for the account used on the remote computer. See "Examples" for rlogin (page 1302) for a sample **.rhosts** file.

Examples In the first example, Alex uses rsh to obtain a listing of the files in his home directory on **bravo**:

```
$ rsh bravo ls
Cost-of-living
Info
Work
preferences
```

In the second example, the output of the previous command is redirected into the file **bravo.ls**. Because the redirection character **>** is not escaped, it is interpreted by the local shell, and the file **bravo.ls** is created on the local machine.

```
$ rsh bravo ls > bravo.ls
$ cat bravo.ls
Cost-of-living
Info
Work
preferences
```

The next example quotes the redirection character **>**. The file **bravo.ls** is created on the remote computer (**bravo**), as shown by ls run on **bravo**.

```
$ rsh bravo ls ">" bravo.ls
$ rsh bravo ls
Cost-of-living
Info
Work
bravo.ls
preferences
```

In the final example, rsh without *command line* logs in on the remote computer. Here Alex has used the **–l watson** option to log in on **bravo** as **watson**. The **/home/watson/.rhosts** file must be configured to allow Alex to log in on the account in this manner:

```
$ rsh -l watson bravo
Last login: Sat Jul 27 16:13:53 from :0.0
Linux 2.0.18. (POSIX).
$ hostname
bravo
$ exit
rlogin: connection closed.
```

scp

Securely copies one or more files to or from a remote computer

*scp [[**user@**]**from-host:**]**source-file** [[**user@**]**to-host:**][**destination-file**]*

The scp (secure copy) utility copies an ordinary or directory file from one computer to another on a network. This utility uses ssh to transfer files and the same authentication mechanism as ssh; therefore, it provides the same security. The scp utility asks you for a password when it is needed for security.

Arguments
The *from-host* is the name of the machine you are copying files from, and *to-host* is the machine you are copying to. When you do not specify a host, scp assumes the local machine. The user on either host defaults to the user on the local machine who is giving the command; specify a different user with *user@*. The scp utility permits you to copy between two remote machines.

The *source-file* is the file you are making a copy of, and the *destination-file* is the resulting copy. You can specify plain or directory files as relative or absolute pathnames. A relative pathname is relative to the specified or implicit user's home directory. When the *source-file* is a directory, you must use the –r option to copy its contents. When the *destination-file* is a directory, each of the source files maintains its simple filename.

Options

–p preserve Sets the modification times, access times, and file access permissions of each copy to match those of the *source-file*. When you do not use –p, scp uses the file-creation mask (umask, page 1366) on the remote system to modify the access permissions.

–r recursive When a file in the *source-file-list* is a directory, this option copies the contents of that directory and any subdirectories into the *destination-file*.

Notes
You can copy from or to your local machine or between two remote machines. Make sure that you have read permission for the file you are copying and write permission for the directory you are copying it into.

When you use a wildcard character (such as *) in a remote pathname, you must quote the wildcard character so that it is interpreted by the shell on the remote machine and not by the local shell.

As with cp, if the **_destination-file_** exists before you run scp, scp overwrites the file.

Examples   The first example copies the files with filenames ending in **.c** from the working directory on the local machine into the ~**jenny/archives** directory on **bravo**. The wildcard character is not quoted, because it is to be expanded by the local shell. Because **archives** is a relative pathname, scp assumes that it is a subdirectory of Jenny's home directory on **bravo**. Each of the copied files retains its simple filename:

```
$ scp *.c jenny@bravo:archives
```

Next, Alex copies the directory structure under ~**alex/memos** on **bravo** to ~**jenny/alex.memos.bravo** on **kudos**. Alex must have the necessary permissions to write to Jenny's home directory on **kudos**:

```
$ scp -r bravo:memos jenny@kudos:alex.memos.bravo
```

Finally, Alex copies the files with filenames ending in **.c** from Jenny's **archives** directory on **bravo** to the **jenny.c.bravo** directory in his working directory. The wildcard character is quoted because it is to be interpreted by the remote machine, **bravo**:

```
$ scp -r 'jenny@bravo:archives/*.c' jenny.c.bravo
```

It is important to remember that whenever you copy multiple files or directories, the destination—either local or remote—must be an existing directory and not an ordinary or nonexistent file.

sed

sed

Edits a file (not interactively)

sed [–n] –f **script-file** [**file-list**]
sed [–n] **script** [**file-list**]

The sed (stream editor) utility is a batch (noninteractive) editor. The sed commands are usually stored in a *script-file* (the first format), although you can give simple sed commands from the command line (second format). By default, sed copies lines from the *file-list* to standard output, editing the lines in the process. This utility selects lines to be edited by position within the file (line number) or context (pattern matching). Refer to the sed info page for complete documentation.

The sed utility takes its input from files you specify on the command line or from standard input. Unless you direct output from a sed script elsewhere, it goes to standard output.

Arguments

The *script-file* is the pathname of a file containing a sed script (see "Discussion," following).

The *script* is a sed script, included on the command line. This format allows you to write simple, short sed scripts without creating a separate *script-file*.

The *file-list* contains pathnames of the ordinary files that sed processes. These are the input files. When you do not specify a file, sed takes its input from standard input.

Options

If you do not use the –f option, sed uses the first command line argument as its script.

–f file Causes sed to read its script from the *script-file* given as the first command line argument.

–n no print Causes sed not to copy lines to standard output except as specified by the Print (p) instruction or flag.

Discussion

A sed script consists of one or more lines in the following format:

[*address*[*, address*]] *instruction* [*argument-list*]

The *address*es are optional. If you omit the *address*, sed processes all lines from the input file. The *address*es·select the line(s) the *instruction* part of the command operates on. The *instruction* is the editing instruction that modifies the text. The number and kinds of arguments in the *argument-list* depend on the instruction.

The sed utility processes an input file as follows:

1. Reads one line from the input file (*file-list*).

2. Reads the first instruction from the *script-file* (or command line), and, if the address selects the input line, acts on the input line as the *instruction* specifies.

3. Reads the next instruction from the *script-file*; if the address selects the input line, acts on the input line (as possibly modified by the previous instruction) as the new *instruction* specifies.

4. Repeats step 3 until it has executed all the instructions in the *script-file*.

5. Starts over again with step 1 if another line is in the input file; otherwise, it is finished.

Addresses

A line number is an address that selects a line. As a special case, the line number $ represents the last line of the last file in the *file-list*.

A regular expression (refer to Appendix A) is an address that selects the lines that contain a string that the expression matches. Although slashes are often used to delimit these regular expressions, sed permits you to use any character other than a backslash or NEWLINE.

Except as noted, zero, one, or two addresses (either line numbers or regular expressions) can precede an instruction. If you do not use an address, sed selects all lines, causing the instruction to act on every input line. One address causes the instruction to act on each input line that the address selects. Two addresses cause the instruction to act on groups of lines. The first address selects the first line in the first group. The second address selects the next subsequent line that it matches; this line is the last line in the first group. After selecting the last line in a group, sed starts the selection process over again, looking for the next line that the first address matches. This line is the first line in the next group. The sed utility continues this process until it has finished going through the file.

Instructions

d delete The Delete instruction causes sed not to write out the lines it selects and not to finish processing the lines. After sed executes a Delete instruction, it reads the next input line from the *file-list* and begins over again with the first instruction in the *script-file*.

n   next   The Next instruction reads the next input line from the *file-list*, writing out the currently selected line, if appropriate, and starts processing the new line with the next instruction in the *script-file*.

a   append   The Append instruction appends one or more lines to the currently selected line. If you do not precede the Append instruction with an address, it appends to each input line from the *file-list*. You cannot precede an Append instruction with two addresses. An Append instruction has the following format:

> *[address]* *a*\
> *text* \
> *text* \
> .
>
> .
>
> *text*

You must end each line of appended text, except the last, with a backslash (the backslash quotes the following NEWLINE). The appended text concludes with a line that does not end with a backslash. The sed utility *always* writes out appended text, regardless of whether you set the **–n** flag on the command line, and even writes out the text if you delete the line to which you appended the text.

i   insert   The Insert instruction is identical to the Append instruction but places the new text *before* the selected line.

c   change   The Change instruction is similar to Append and Insert but changes the selected lines so that they contain the new text. You can use this instruction with two addresses. When you specify an address range, Change replaces the entire range of lines with a single occurrence of the new text.

s   substitute   The Substitute instruction is similar to that of vi and has the following format:

> *[address[,address]]* *s/pattern/replacement-string/[g][p][w file]*

The *pattern* is a regular expression that is delimited by any character other than a SPACE or NEWLINE; however, slash (/) is traditionally used. The *replacement-string* starts immediately following the second delimiter and must be terminated by the same delimiter. The final (third) delimiter is required. The *replacement-string* can contain an ampersand (&), which sed replaces with the matched *pattern*. Unless you use the **g** flag, the Substitute instruction replaces only the first occurrence of the *pattern* on each selected line.

The **g** (global) flag causes the Substitute instruction to replace all nonoverlapping occurrences of the *pattern* on the selected lines.

The **p** (print) flag causes sed to send all lines on which it makes substitutions to standard output. This flag overrides the **–n** option on the command line.

The **w** (write) flag is similar to the **p** flag but sends the output to a specified file. A single SPACE and the name of a file must follow the write flag.

p **print**   The Print instruction writes the selected lines to standard output, writing the lines immediately, and does not reflect the effects of subsequent instructions. This instruction overrides the **–n** option on the command line.

w *file* **write**   This instruction is similar to the Print instruction but sends the output to a specified file. A single SPACE and the name of a file (*file*) must follow the Write instruction.

r *file* **read**   The Read instruction reads the contents of the specified file and appends it to the selected line. You cannot precede a Read instruction with two addresses. A single SPACE and the name of a file must follow a Read instruction.

q **quit**   The Quit instruction causes sed to stop processing.

Control Structures

! **NOT**   The NOT structure causes sed to apply the following instruction, located on the same line, to each of the lines *not* selected by the address portion of the instruction.

{ } **group instructions**   When you enclose a group of instructions within a pair of braces, a single address (or address pair) selects the lines on which the group of instructions operates.

Examples   The following examples use the input file **new**:

```
$ cat new
Line one.
The second line.
The third.
This is line four.
Five.
This is the sixth sentence.
This is line seven.
Eighth and last.
```

Unless you instruct it not to, sed copies all lines, selected or not, to standard output. When you use the **–n** option on the command line, sed copies only selected lines.

The command line that follows displays all the lines in the **new** file that contain the word **line** (all lowercase):

```
$ sed '/line/ p' new
Line one.
The second line.
The second line.
The third.
This is line four.
This is line four.
Five.
This is the sixth sentence.
This is line seven.
This is line seven.
Eighth and last.
```

The command uses the address /line/, a regular expression. The sed utility selects each of the lines that contains a match for that pattern. The Print (**p**) instruction displays each of the selected lines.

The preceding command does not use the **–n** option, so it displays all the lines in the input file at least once. It displays the selected lines an additional time because of the Print instruction.

The following command uses the **–n** option so that sed displays only the selected lines:

```
$ sed -n '/line/ p' new
The second line.
This is line four.
This is line seven.
```

Next, sed copies part of a file based on line numbers. The Print instruction selects and displays lines 3 through 6:

```
$ sed -n '3,6 p' new
The third.
This is line four.
Five.
This is the sixth sentence.
```

The next command line uses the Quit instruction to cause sed to display only the top of a file, in this case the first five lines of **new** enabling you to look at the top of a file in the same way the head utility does:

```
$ sed '5 q' new
Line one.
The second line.
The third.
This is line four.
Five.
```

When you need to give sed more complex or lengthy instructions, you can use a script file. The following script file (**print3_6**) and command line perform the same function as the command line in a previous example (**sed -n '3,6 p' new**):

```
$ cat print3_6
3,6 p

$ sed -n -f print3_6 new
The third.
This is line four.
Five.
This is the sixth sentence.
```

The following sed script, **append_demo**, demonstrates the Append instruction. The instruction in the script file selects line 2 and appends a NEWLINE and the text AFTER. to the selected line. Because the command line does not include the **–n** option, sed copies all the lines from the input file **new**:

```
$ cat append_demo
2 a\
AFTER.

$ sed -f append_demo new
Line one.
The second line.
AFTER.
The third.
This is line four.
Five.
This is the sixth sentence.
This is line seven.
Eighth and last.
```

The **insert_demo** script selects all the lines containing the string This and inserts a NEWLINE and the text BEFORE. before the selected lines:

```
$ cat insert_demo
/This/ i\
BEFORE.

$ sed -f insert_demo new
Line one.
The second line.
The third.
BEFORE.
This is line four.
Five.
BEFORE.
This is the sixth sentence.
BEFORE.
This is line seven.
Eighth and last.
```

The next example demonstrates a Change instruction with an address range. When you give a Change instruction a range of lines, it does not change each line within the range but changes the block of text to a single occurrence of the new text:

```
$ cat change_demo
2,4 c\
SED WILL INSERT THESE\
THREE LINES IN PLACE\
OF THE SELECTED LINES.

$ sed -f change_demo new
Line one.
SED WILL INSERT THESE
THREE LINES IN PLACE
OF THE SELECTED LINES.
Five.
This is the sixth sentence.
This is line seven.
Eighth and last.
```

The next example demonstrates a Substitute instruction. The sed utility selects all lines because the instruction has no address, replacing the first occurrence on each line of the string line with sentence and displaying the resulting line. The **p** flag displays each line where a substitution occurs. The command line calls sed with the **–n** option, so that sed displays only the lines that the script explicitly requests it to display:

```
$ cat subs_demo
s/line/sentence/p

$ sed -n -f subs_demo new
The second sentence.
This is sentence four.
This is sentence seven.
```

The next example is similar to the preceding one except that a **w** flag and file-name (**temp**) at the end of the Substitute instruction cause sed to create the file **temp**. The command line does not include the **–n** option, so it displays all lines, including those that sed changes. The cat utility displays the contents of the file **temp**. The word Line (starting with an uppercase L) is not changed:

```
$ cat write_demo1
s/line/sentence/w temp

$ sed -f write_demo1 new
Line one.
The second sentence.
The third.
This is sentence four.
Five.
This is the sixth sentence.
This is sentence seven.
Eighth and last.
```

```
$ cat temp
The second sentence.
This is sentence four.
This is sentence seven.
```

The following is a Bourne Again Shell script named **sub** that changes all occurrences of REPORT to report, FILE to file, and PROCESS to process in a group of files. The **For** structure loops through the list of files supplied on the command line. (See page 640 for more information on the **For** structure.) As it processes each file, **sub** displays the filename before running sed on the file. This script uses a multiline embedded sed instruction; as long as the NEWLINEs within the instruction are quoted (that is, placed between single quotation marks), sed accepts the multiline instruction as though it appeared on a single line. Each Substitute instruction includes a **g** (global) flag to take care of the case in which one of the strings occurs more than one time on a line:

```
$ cat sub
for file
do
        echo $file
        mv $file $$.subhld
        sed 's/REPORT/report/g
            s/FILE/file/g
            s/PROCESS/process/g' $$.subhld > $file
done
rm $$.subhld

$ sub file1 file2 file3
file1
file2
file3
```

Following, sed uses the Write instruction to copy part of a file to another file (**temp2**). The line numbers 2 and 4, separated by a comma, select the range of lines sed is to copy. This script does not alter the lines:

```
$ cat write_demo2
2,4 w temp2

$ sed -n -f write_demo2 new

$ cat temp2
The second line.
The third.
This is line four.
```

The script **write_demo3** is very similar to **write_demo2** but precedes the Write instruction with the NOT operator (!), causing sed to write to the file the lines *not* selected by the address:

```
$ cat write_demo3
2,4 !w temp3

$ sed -n -f write_demo3 new

$ cat temp3
Line one.
Five.
This is the sixth sentence.
This is line seven.
Eighth and last.
```

Following, **next_demo1** demonstrates the Next instruction. When it processes the selected line (line 3), sed immediately starts processing the next line without printing line 3 and so does not display line 3:

```
$ cat next_demo1
3 n
p

$ sed -n -f next_demo1 new
Line one.
The second line.
This is line four.
Five.
This is the sixth sentence.
This is line seven.
Eighth and last.
```

The next example uses a textual address. The sixth line contains the string the, so the Next instruction causes sed not to display it:

```
$ cat next_demo2
/the/ n
p

$ sed -n -f next_demo2 new
Line one.
The second line.
The third.
This is line four.
Five.
This is line seven.
Eighth and last.
```

The next set of examples uses the file **compound.in** to demonstrate how sed instructions work together:

```
$ cat compound.in
1. The words on this page...
2. The words on this page...
3. The words on this page...
4. The words on this page...
```

The first example that uses **compound.in** instructs sed to substitute the string words with text on lines 1, 2, and 3 and the string text with TEXT on lines 2, 3, and 4. The example also selects and deletes line 3. The result is text on line 1, TEXT on line 2, no line 3, and words on line 4. The sed utility made two substitutions on lines 2 and 3: text for words and TEXT for text. Then sed deleted line 3:

```
$ cat compound
1,3 s/words/text/
2,4 s/text/TEXT/
3 d

$ sed -f compound compound.in
1. The text on this page...
2. The TEXT on this page...
4. The words on this page...
```

The next example shows that the ordering of instructions within a sed script is critical. Both Substitute instructions are applied to the second line, as in the previous example, but the order in which the substitutions occur changes the result:

```
$ cat compound2
2,4 s/text/TEXT/
1,3 s/words/text/
3 d

$ sed -f compound2 compound.in
1. The text on this page...
2. The text on this page...
4. The words on this page...
```

Next, **compound3** appends two lines to line 2. The sed utility displays all the lines from the file once, because no **–n** option appears on the command line. The Print instruction at the end of the script file displays line 3 an additional time:

```
$ cat compound3
2 a\
This is line 2a.\
This is line 2b.
3 p

$ sed -f compound3 compound.in
1. The words on this page...
2. The words on this page...
This is line 2a.
This is line 2b.
3. The words on this page...
3. The words on this page...
4. The words on this page...
```

The next example shows that sed always displays appended text. Here line 2 is deleted, but the Append instruction still displays the two lines that were appended to it. Appended lines are displayed even if you use the **–n** option on the command line:

```
$ cat compound4
2 a\
This is line 2a.\
This is line 2b.
2 d

$ sed -f compound4 compound.in
1. The words on this page...
This is line 2a.
This is line 2b.
3. The words on this page...
4. The words on this page...
```

The final examples use regular expressions in addresses. The regular expression in the following instruction (^.) matches one character at the beginning of a line (that is, it matches every line that is not empty). The replacement string (between the second and third slashes) contains a TAB character followed by an ampersand (&). The ampersand takes on the value of whatever the regular expression matched:

```
$ sed 's/^./    &/' new
        Line one.
        The second line.
        The third.
    .
    .
```

This type of substitution is useful for indenting a file to create a left margin. See Appendix A for more information on regular expressions.

You may want to put the preceding sed instruction into a shell script so that you do not have to remember it (and retype it) every time you want to indent a file:

```
$ cat indent
sed 's/^./    &/' $*
$ chmod u+x indent
$ indent new
        Line one.
        The second line.
        The third.
    ...
```

When you create a sed instruction that you think you may want to use again, it is generally a good idea to put it into a shell script or a *script-file* to save yourself the effort of trying to reconstruct it.

In the following shell script, the regular expression (two SPACEs followed by an *$) matches one or more spaces at the end of a line. This script removes trailing spaces at the end of a line, which is useful for cleaning up files that you created using vi:

```
$ cat cleanup
sed 's/ *$//' $*
```

ssh

Securely executes commands on a remote computer

ssh [option] [user@]host [command line]

The ssh utility runs *command line* on *host* by starting a shell on the remote system. Without a *command line* ssh logs you in on the remote computer.

The ssh utility, which can replace rsh and rlogin, provides secure encrypted communications between two machines on an insecure network. For more information, refer to "ssh: Logs in or Runs a Command on a Remote Computer" on page 374.

Arguments   The *host* is the machine that you want to log in or run a command on. Unless you have one of several kinds of authentication established, ssh prompts you for a username and password for the remote system. When ssh is able to log in automatically, it logs in as the user running the ssh command or as *user* if *user@* is present on the ssh command line.

The *command line* runs on the remote system. Without *command line*, ssh logs you in on the remote system. You must quote special characters in *command line* if you do not want them expanded by the local shell prior to passing them to ssh.

Options

–l *login-name*   If your login name on the remote computer is different from your local login name, you can use this option to give the remote login name. This is an alternative to using *user@* on the command line.

–l *login-name*   **–t**   **tty** Allocates a pseudo tty to the ssh process on the remote machine. Without this option, when you run a command on a remote system using ssh, ssh does not allocate a tty (terminal) to the process. Instead, ssh attaches standard input and standard output of the remote process to the ssh session: normally, but not always, what you want. This option forces ssh to allocate a tty on the remote machine so that programs that require a tty work.

Notes   Refer to "ssh: Logs in or Runs a Command on a Remote Computer" on page 374 for more information on ssh. See also the optional section on page 375 for an example of how to use ssh to create a VPN by tunneling.

Examples   In the first example, Alex uses ssh to obtain a listing of the files in his home directory on **kudos**:

```
$ ssh kudos ls
alex@kudos's password:
reports
graphs
Work
code
```

In the second example, the output of the previous command is redirected into
the file **kudos.ls**. Because the redirection character > is not escaped, it is interpreted
by the local shell, and the file **kudos.ls** is created on the local machine:

```
$ ssh kudos ls > kudos.ls
alex@kudos's password:
$ cat kudos.ls
reports
graphs
Work
code
```

The next example quotes the entire command that is to be run on the remote
system, so that the local shell does not interpret the redirection character (>) but
passes it to the remote shell. The file **kudos.ls** is created on the remote computer
(**kudos**), as shown by ls run on **kudos**:

```
$ ssh kudos "ls > kudos.ls"
alex@kudos's password:
$ ssh kudos ls
alex@kudos's password:
reports
graphs
Work
kudos.ls
code
```

The next command does not quote the pipe symbol (|), so the pipe is interpreted
by the local shell, which sends the output of the remote ls to standard input of less
on the local system:

```
$ ssh kudos ls | less
```

Next, ssh executes a series of commands, connected with pipes, on a remote
machine. The series of commands is enclosed within single quotation marks so that
the local shell does not interpret the pipe symbols and all the commands are run on
the remote system:

```
$ ssh kudos 'ps -ef | grep nmbd | grep -v grep | cut -c10-15 |xargs kill -1'
```

First, the output of ps is piped through grep, which passes all lines containing the string nmbd to another invocation of grep. The second grep passes all lines *not* containing the string grep to cut (page 1132), which extracts the process ID numbers and passes them to xargs, which kills the listed processes with a HUP signal (**kill –1**). Refer to page 1377 in Part III for more information on xargs, a very useful utility.

In the following example, ssh without *command line* logs in on the remote computer. Here Alex has used **watson@kudos** to log in on **kudos** as **watson**:

```
$ ssh watson@kudos
watson@kudos's password:
Last login: Sat Sep 14 06:51:59 from bravo
$ hostname
kudos
$ exit
```

Next, Alex wants to change the password for his **watson** login on **kudos**:

```
$ ssh watson@kudos passwd
watson@kudos's password:
(current) UNIX password: por
```

Alex stops as soon as he sees passwd (running on **kudos**) displaying his password: He knows that something is wrong. In order for the passwd to work, it must run with a tty (terminal) so that it can turn off character echo (**stty –echo**) in order not to display passwords as the user enters them. The –t option solves the problem by associating a pseudo tty with the process running passwd on the remote machine:

```
$ ssh -t watson@kudos passwd
watson@kudos's password:
Changing password for watson
(current) UNIX password:
New UNIX password:
Retype new UNIX password:
passwd: all authentication tokens updated successfully
Connection to kudos closed.
$
```

The –t option is also useful when you are running programs that display a character-based/pseudographical interface.

sleep

Creates a process that sleeps for a specified interval

*sleep **time***
*sleep **time-list***

The sleep utility causes the process executing it to go to sleep for the time specified. Refer to the sleep info page for complete documentation.

Arguments

Typically the amount of time that a process sleeps is given as a single integer argument, **time**, which represents seconds. You can append a unit specification to the integer: **s** (seconds), **m** (minutes), **h** (hours), and **d** (days).

You can construct a **time-list** by including several times on the command line: The total time that the process sleeps is the sum of the times. For example, if you specify 1h 30m 100s, the process sleeps for 91 minutes and 40 seconds.

Examples

You can use sleep from the command line to execute a command after a period of time. The following example executes in the background a process that reminds you to make a phone call in 20 minutes (1,200 seconds):

```
$ (sleep 1200; echo "Remember to make call.") &
[1] 4660
```

Alternatively, you could give the following command to get the same reminder:

```
$ (sleep 20m; echo "Remember to make call.") &
[2] 4667
```

You can also use sleep within a shell script to execute a command at regular intervals. The following **per** shell script executes a program named **update** every 90 seconds:

```
$ cat per
#!/bin/sh
while true
do
    update
    sleep 90
done
```

If you execute a shell script such as **per** in the background, you can terminate it only by using kill.

The final example shows a shell script that accepts the name of a file as an argument and waits for that file to appear on the disk. If the file does not exist, the script sleeps for 1 minute and 45 seconds before checking for the file again:

```
$ cat wait_for_file
#!/bin/sh

if [ $# != 1 ]; then
echo "Use: wait_for_file filename"
exit 1
fi

while true
do
if [ -f "$1" ]; then
echo "$1 is here now"
exit 0
fi
sleep 1m 45
done
```

sort

Sorts and/or merges files

*sort [**options**] [**field-specifier-list**] [**file-list**]*

The sort utility merges and sorts one or more text files. The sort utility takes its input from files you specify on the command line or from standard input. Without the –o option sort sends its output to standard output.

Arguments   The *field-specifier-list* specifies one or more sort fields within each line. The sort utility uses the sort fields to sort the lines from the *file-list*. The *file-list* contains pathnames of one or more ordinary files that contain the text to be sorted. The sort utility sorts and merges the files unless you use the –m option, in which case sort only merges the files.

Options   When you do not specify an option, sort orders the file in the machine collating (usually ASCII) sequence. You can embed options within the *field-specifier-list* by following a field specifier with an option without a leading hyphen; see "Discussion."

–b blanks   Blanks (TAB and SPACE characters) are normally field delimiters in the input file. Unless you use this option, sort *also* considers leading blanks to be part of the field they precede. This option considers multiple blanks as single-field delimiters with no intrinsic value, so sort does not consider these characters in sort comparisons.

–c check only   Checks whether the file is properly sorted. The sort utility does not display anything if everything is in order. It displays a message if the file is not in sorted order and returns an exit status of 1.

–d dictionary order   Ignores all characters that are not alphanumeric characters or blanks. For example, with this option sort does not consider punctuation.

–f fold lowercase into uppercase   Considers all lowercase letters to be uppercase letters. Use this option when you are sorting a file that contains both uppercase and lowercase text.

–i ignore   Ignores nonprinting characters when you perform a nonnumeric sort.

–m merge   Assumes that multiple input files are in sorted order and merges them without verifying that they are sorted.

−n   **numeric sort**   When you use this option, minus signs and decimal points take on their arithmetic meaning. The sort utility does not order lines or order sort fields in the machine collating sequence but rather in arithmetic order.

−o *filename*   **output**   Sends output to *filename* instead of standard output. Replace *filename* with a filename of your choice; it can be the same as one of the names in the *file-list*.

−r   **reverse**   Reverses the sense of the sort (for example, **z** precedes **a**).

−t*x*   **set delimiter**   Replace *x* with the character that is the field delimiter in the input file. This character replaces SPACEs, which become regular (nondelimiting) characters.

−u   **unique**   Outputs repeated lines only once. When you use the **−c** and **−u** options together, sort displays a message if the same line appears more than once in the input file, even if the file is in sorted order.

Discussion   In the following description, a *field* is a sequence of characters on a line in an input file. These sequences are bounded by blanks or by a blank and the beginning or end of the line. These fields are used to define sort fields.

A *sort field* is a sequence of characters that sort uses to put lines in order. A sort field can contain part or all of one or more fields in the input file. Refer to Figure III-1.

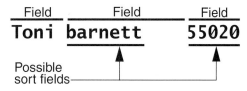

Figure III-1   Fields and sort fields

The *field-specifier-list* contains pairs of pointers that define subsections of each line (sort fields) for comparison. A pointer is in the form **±f.c**. The first of each pair of pointers begins with a plus sign, and the second begins with a hyphen or minus sign.

You can make a pointer point to any character on a line. Pointers having the form **±f.c** skip **f** fields and **c** characters. The plus sign that precedes the first of each pair of pointers indicates that all characters to the right of the pointer, up to the other pointer in the pair, are to be included in the sort field. If there is no second pointer in the pair, all characters up to the end of the line are included. The hyphen or minus sign that precedes the second pointer in the pair indicates that all characters to the left of the pointer, back to the first pointer in the pair, are to be included in the sort field.

The **–b** option causes sort to count multiple leading blanks as a *single* field-delimiter character. If you do not use this option, sort considers each leading blank to be a character in the sort field and includes it in the sort comparison.

You can specify options that pertain only to a given sort field by immediately following the field specifier by one of the options **b**, **d**, **f**, **i**, **n**, or **r**. In this case you must *not* precede the options with a hyphen.

When you specify more than one sort field, sort examines them in the order you specify them on the command line. If the first sort field of two lines is the same, sort examines the second sort field. If these are again the same, sort looks at the third field. This process continues for all the sort fields you specify. If all the sort fields are the same, sort examines the entire line.

If you do not use any options or arguments, the sort is based on entire lines.

Examples

The examples in this section demonstrate some of the features and uses of the sort utility. The examples assume that the **list** file is in the working directory:

```
$ cat list
Tom Winstrom        94201
Janet Dempsey       94111
Alice MacLeod       94114
David Mack          94114
Toni Barnett        95020
Jack Cooper         94072
Richard MacDonald   95510
```

This file contains a list of names and zip codes. Each line of the file contains three fields: the first name field, the last name field, and the zip code field. For the examples to work, make sure all the blanks in the file are SPACEs, and not TABs.

The first example demonstrates sort without any options or arguments other than a filename. Following, sort sorts the file on a line-by-line basis. If the first characters on two lines are the same, sort looks at the second characters to determine the proper sorted order. If the second characters are the same, sort looks at the third characters. This process continues until sort finds a character that differs between the lines. If the lines are identical, it does not matter which one sort puts first. In this example sort needs to examine only the first three letters (at most) of each line. The sort utility displays a list that is in alphabetical order by first name:

```
$ sort list
Alice MacLeod       94114
David Mack          94114
Jack Cooper         94072
Janet Dempsey       94111
Richard MacDonald   95510
Tom Winstrom        94201
Toni Barnett        95020
```

You can instruct sort to skip any number of fields and characters on a line before beginning its comparison. Blanks normally separate one field from another. The next example sorts the same list by last name, the second field. The **+1** argument indicates that sort is to *skip one field* before beginning its comparison; sort skips the first-name field. Because there is no second pointer, the sort field extends to the end of the line. Now the list is almost in last-name order, but there is a problem with Mac:

```
$ sort +1 list
Toni Barnett         95020
Jack Cooper          94072
Janet Dempsey        94111
Richard MacDonald    95510
Alice MacLeod        94114
David Mack           94114
Tom Winstrom         94201
```

In the preceding example, MacLeod comes before Mack. After finding that the sort fields of these two lines were the same through the third letter (Mac), sort put L before k because it arranges lines in the order of ASCII character codes, in which uppercase letters come before lowercase.

The **–f** option makes sort treat uppercase and lowercase letters as equals and thus fixes the problem with MacLeod and Mack:

```
$ sort -f +1 list
Toni Barnett         95020
Jack Cooper          94072
Janet Dempsey        94111
Richard MacDonald    95510
David Mack           94114
Alice MacLeod        94114
Tom Winstrom         94201
```

The next example attempts to sort **list** on the third field, the zip code. Following, sort does not put the numbers in order but puts the shortest name first in the sorted list and the longest name last. With the argument of **+2**, sort *skips* two fields and counts the SPACEs after the second field (last name) as part of the sort field. The ASCII value of a SPACE character is less than that of any other printable character, so sort puts the zip code that is preceded by the greatest number of SPACEs first and the zip code that is preceded by the fewest SPACEs last:

```
$ sort +2 list
David Mack           94114
Jack Cooper          94072
Tom Winstrom         94201
Toni Barnett         95020
Janet Dempsey        94111
Alice MacLeod        94114
Richard MacDonald    95510
```

The **–b** option causes sort to ignore leading SPACEs. With the **–b** option, the zip codes come out in the proper order, as shown next. When sort determines that MacLeod and Mack have the same zip codes, it compares the entire lines, putting Alice MacLeod before David Mack (because A comes before D):

```
$ sort -b +2 list
Jack Cooper          94072
Janet Dempsey        94111
Alice MacLeod        94114
David Mack           94114
Tom Winstrom         94201
Toni Barnett         95020
Richard MacDonald    95510
```

To sort alphabetically by last name when zip codes are the same, you need a second pass that sorts on the last-name field. The next example shows how to make this second pass by specifying a second sort field and uses the **–f** option to keep the Mack/MacLeod problem from cropping up again:

```
$ sort -b -f +2 +1 list
Jack Cooper          94072
Janet Dempsey        94111
David Mack           94114
Alice MacLeod        94114
Tom Winstrom         94201
Toni Barnett         95020
Richard MacDonald    95110
```

The **–f** option does not fix the MacLeod and Mack problem because sort never compares *last names*. When it determines that the last two digits of MacLeod and Mack's zip codes are the same, it compares the *entire lines*, starting with the first names. These two lines are in first-name order. The problem is fixed in the next example, in which two sort options are combined after a single hyphen.

The next example shows a **sort** command that skips not only fields but also characters. The **+2.3** causes sort to skip two fields and then skip three characters before starting its comparisons. Because the command does not define an end to the sort field, it is taken to be the end of the line. The sort field is the last two digits in the zip code:

```
$ sort -fb +2.3 list
Tom Winstrom         94201
Richard MacDonald    95510
Janet Dempsey        94111
Alice MacLeod        94114
David Mack           94114
Toni Barnett         95020
Jack Cooper          94072
```

The problem of how to sort by last name within zip code is solved by a second pass covering the last-name field. Although the second element in the pair of pointers for the second pass is not necessary (you already know from the first pass that the zip codes match), it is included for its instructional value. A third pass, in case zip code and last names are the same, is also not required. After the second pass, sort compares entire lines, so it automatically sorts on first name within last name:

```
$ sort -fb +2.3 +1 -2 list
Tom Winstrom            94201
Richard MacDonald       95110
Janet Dempsey           94111
David Mack              94114
Alice MacLeod           94114
Toni Barnett            95020
Jack Cooper             94072
```

The next set of examples uses the **cars** data file. From left to right the columns in the file contain each car's make, model, year of manufacture, mileage, and price:

```
$ cat cars
plym     fury     77    73     2500
chevy    nova     79    60     3000
ford     mustang  65    45     10000
volvo    gl       78    102    9850
ford     ltd      83    15     10500
chevy    nova     80    50     3500
fiat     600      65    115    450
honda    accord   81    30     6000
ford     thundbd  84    10     17000
toyota   tercel   82    180    750
chevy    impala   65    85     1550
ford     bronco   83    25     9500
```

Without any options sort displays a sorted copy of the file:

```
$ sort cars
chevy    impala   65    85     1550
chevy    nova     79    60     3000
chevy    nova     80    50     3500
fiat     600      65    115    450
ford     bronco   83    25     9500
ford     ltd      83    15     10500
ford     mustang  65    45     10000
ford     thundbd  84    10     17000
honda    accord   81    30     6000
plym     fury     77    73     2500
toyota   tercel   82    180    750
volvo    gl       78    102    9850
```

Unless you specify otherwise, a sort field extends to the end of the line. To sort from the beginning of the line (and skip zero fields), use a **+0** sort field specifier, as shown in the next example, which also shows one problem to avoid when you are using sort. In this example the objective is to sort by manufacturer and then by price within manufacturer. The command line instructs sort to sort on the entire line (**+0**) and then make a second pass, sorting on the fifth field all lines whose first-pass sort fields were the same (**+4**):

```
$ sort +0 +4 cars
chevy    impala  65      85      1550
chevy    nova    79      60      3000
chevy    nova    80      50      3500
fiat     600     65      115     450
ford     bronco  83      25      9500
ford     ltd     83      15      10500
ford     mustang 65      45      10000
ford     thundbd 84      10      17000
honda    accord  81      30      6000
plym     fury    77      73      2500
toyota   tercel  82      180     750
volvo    gl      78      102     9850
```

Because no two lines are the same, sort makes only one pass, sorting on each entire line. (If two lines differed only in the fifth field, they would be sorted properly on the first pass anyway, so the second pass would be unnecessary.) Look at the lines with the ltd and mustang. They are sorted by the second field rather than the fifth, demonstrating that sort never made a second pass and never sorted by the fifth field.

The next example forces the first-pass sort to stop just before the second field by defining the end of the first sort field (**-1**). Now the ltd and mustang are properly sorted by price. But look at the bronco. It is less expensive than the other Fords, but sort has it positioned as the most expensive. The sort utility put the list in ASCII collating sequence order, not in numeric order: 9500 comes after 10000 because 9 comes after 1:

```
$ sort +0 -1 +4 cars
chevy    impala  65      85      1550
chevy    nova    79      60      3000
chevy    nova    80      50      3500
fiat     600     65      115     450
ford     mustang 65      45      10000
ford     ltd     83      15      10500
ford     thundbd 84      10      17000
ford     bronco  83      25      9500
honda    accord  81      30      6000
plym     fury    77      73      2500
toyota   tercel  82      180     750
volvo    gl      78      102     9850
```

The **–n** (numeric) option on the second pass puts the list in the proper order:

```
$ sort +0 -1 +4n cars
chevy    impala   65      85      1550
chevy    nova     79      60      3000
chevy    nova     80      50      3500
fiat     600      65      115     450
ford     bronco   83      25      9500
ford     mustang  65      45      10000
ford     ltd      83      15      10500
ford     thundbd  84      10      17000
honda    accord   81      30      6000
plym     fury     77      73      2500
toyota   tercel   82      180     750
volvo    gl       78      102     9850
```

The next example again shows that, unless you instruct it otherwise, sort orders a file starting with the field you specify and continuing to the end of the line. It does not make a second pass unless two of the first sort fields are the same. Although this example sorts the cars by years, it does not sort the cars by manufacturer within years:

```
$ sort +2 +0 cars
fiat     600      65      115     450
ford     mustang  65      45      10000
chevy    impala   65      85      1550
plym     fury     77      73      2500
volvo    gl       78      102     9850
chevy    nova     79      60      3000
chevy    nova     80      50      3500
honda    accord   81      30      6000
toyota   tercel   82      180     750
ford     ltd      83      15      10500
ford     bronco   83      25      9500
ford     thundbd  84      10      17000
```

Specifying an end to the sort field for the first pass allows sort to perform its secondary sort properly:

```
$ sort +2 -3 +0 cars
chevy    impala   65      85      1550
fiat     600      65      115     450
ford     mustang  65      45      10000
plym     fury     77      73      2500
volvo    gl       78      102     9850
chevy    nova     79      60      3000
chevy    nova     80      50      3500
honda    accord   81      30      6000
toyota   tercel   82      180     750
ford     bronco   83      25      9500
ford     ltd      83      15      10500
ford     thundbd  84      10      17000
```

The next examples demonstrate an important sorting technique: putting a list in alphabetical order, merging upper- and lowercase entries, and eliminating duplicates. The unsorted list is

```
$ cat short
Pear
Pear
apple
pear
Apple
```

The following is a plain sort:

```
$ sort short
Apple
Pear
Pear
apple
pear
```

The following folded sort is a good start, but it does not eliminate duplicates:

```
$ sort -f short
Apple
apple
Pear
Pear
pear
```

The **–u** (unique) option eliminates duplicates but causes all the uppercase entries to come first:

```
$ sort -u short
Apple
Pear
apple
pear
```

When you attempt to use both **–u** and **–f**, the lowercase entries get lost:

```
$ sort -uf short
Apple
Pear
```

Two passes are the answer. Both passes are unique sorts, and the first folds uppercase letters onto lowercase ones:

```
$ sort -u +0f +0 short
Apple
apple
Pear
pear
```

stty

Displays or sets terminal parameters

stty **[options]** **[arguments]**

Without any arguments, stty displays certain parameters affecting the operation of the terminal. For a list of some of these parameters and an explanation of each, see "Arguments." The arguments establish or change the parameter(s) you specify.

Options

Without an option or argument, stty displays a summary report that includes only a few of its parameters.

--all **−a**   Reports on all parameters. This option does not take any arguments.

--file=/dev/device **−F /dev/device**   Without this option stty affects the device attached to standard input. With this option stty affects *device*. You can change the characteristics of a device only if you own its device file or if you are Superuser.

--save **−g**   Generates a report of the current settings in a format you can use as arguments to another stty command. This option does not take any arguments.

Arguments

The arguments to stty specify which terminal parameters stty is to alter. Turn on each of the parameters that is preceded by an optional hyphen (indicated in the following list as [−]) by specifying the parameter without the hyphen. Turn it off by using the hyphen. Unless specified otherwise, this section describes the parameters in their *on* states.

Special Keys and Characteristics

columns *n* Sets the line width to *n* columns.

ek Sets the erase and line kill keys to their default values. Most GNU/Linux systems use DELETE and CONTROL-U as the defaults.

erase *x* Sets the erase key to *x*. To specify a control character, precede *x* with CONTROL-V (for example, use CONTROL-V CONTROL-H to indicate CONTROL-H) or use the notation ^h, where ^ is a caret (SHIFT 6 on most keyboards).

kill *x* Sets the line kill key to *x*. See **erase *x*** for conventions.

intr *x* Sets the interrupt key to *x*. See **erase** *x* for conventions.

susp *x* Sets the suspend key to *x*. See **erase** *x* for conventions.

rows *n* Sets the number of screen rows to *n*.

sane Sets the terminal parameters to values that are usually acceptable. The **sane** argument is useful when several stty parameters have changed, making it difficult to use the terminal even to run stty to set things right. If **sane** does not appear to work, try entering

> CONTROL-J **stty sane** CONTROL-J

werase *x* Sets the word erase key to *x*. See **erase** *x* for conventions.

Modes of Data Transmission

[–]raw The normal state is **–raw**. When the system reads input in its raw form, it does not interpret the following special characters: erase (usually DELETE), line kill (usually CONTROL-U), interrupt execution (CONTROL-C), and EOF (CONTROL-D). In addition, the system does not use parity bits. With humor typical of GNU/Linux's heritage, you can specify **–raw** as **cooked**.

[–]parenb **parity enable** When you specify **–parenb**, the system does not use or expect a parity bit when communicating with the terminal.

[–]parodd Selects odd parity (**–parodd** selects even parity).

[–]cstopb Selects two stop bits (**–cstopb** specifies one stop bit).

Treatment of Characters

[–]nl Accepts only a NEWLINE character as a line terminator. With **–nl** in effect, the system accepts a RETURN character from the terminal as a NEWLINE but sends a RETURN followed by a NEWLINE to the terminal in place of a NEWLINE.

[–]echo Echoes characters as they are typed (full-duplex operation). If a terminal is half duplex and displays two characters for each one it should display, turn the **echo** parameter off (**–echo**).

[–]echoe The normal setting is **echoe**, which causes GNU/Linux to echo the character sequence BACKSPACE SPACE BACKSPACE when you use the erase key to delete a character. The effect is to move the cursor backward across the line, removing characters as you delete them.

[–]echoprt The normal setting is **–echoprt**, causing characters to disappear as you erase them. When you set **echoprt**, characters that you erase are displayed between a backslash (\) and a slash (/). For example, if you type the word sort and then erase it by pressing BACKSPACE four times, you see sort\tros/ when **echoprt** is set. Also, if you use the kill character to delete the entire line, having **echoprt** set causes the entire line to be displayed as if you had BACKSPACEd to the beginning of the line.

[–]**echoke**   The normal setting is **echoke**. When you use the kill character to delete a line while this option is set, all characters back to the prompt are erased on the current line. When this option is negated, pressing the kill key moves the cursor to the beginning of the next line instead.

[–]**lcase**   For uppercase-only terminals, translates all uppercase characters into lowercase as they are entered (also [–]**LCASE**).

[–]**tabs**   Transmits each TAB character to the terminal as a TAB character. When **tabs** is turned off (**–tabs**), the system translates each TAB character into the appropriate number of SPACEs and transmits them to the terminal (also [–]**tab3**).

Job Control Parameters

[–]**tostop**   Stops background jobs if they attempt to send output to the terminal (**–tostop** allows background jobs to send output to the terminal).

Notes   The shells ⬚ all retain some control over standard input if you are using the shell interactively. This control means that a number of the options available with stty appear to have no effect. For example, the command **stty –echo** appears to have no effect under zsh:

```
zsh % stty -echo
zsh % date
Fri Jul 19 18:09:10 PDT 2002
```

Also, while **stty –echo** does work when using bash interactively, **stty –echoe** does not. You can, however, still use these options to affect shell scripts and other utilities:

```
$ cat testit
#!/bin/zsh
stty -echo
echo -n "Enter a value: "
read a
echo "You entered: $a"
stty echo
$ testit
Enter a value: You entered: this is a value
```

In the preceding example the input typed at the Enter a value: prompt is not displayed as it is typed. The value is, however, retained by the **a** variable and is displayed by the echo "You entered: $a" statement.

You can always change the values of the special characters, such as kill and erase.

The *stty* is short for set teletypewriter, which is also referred to as a *TTY* (page 1499).

Examples

The first example shows stty without any arguments, displaying several terminal operation parameters. (Your system may display more or different parameters.) The character following the erase = is the erase key. A ∧ preceding a character indicates a CONTROL key. The example shows the erase key set to CONTROL-H.

If stty does not display the erase character, it is set to its default value, DELETE. If you do not see a kill character, it is set to its default, ∧U:

```
$ stty
speed 9600 baud; line = 0;
erase = ^H;
```

Next, the **ek** argument returns the erase and line kill keys to their default values:

```
$ stty ek
```

The next display verifies the change. The stty utility does not display either the erase character or the line kill character, indicating that they are both set to their default values:

```
$ stty
speed 38400 baud; line = 0;
```

The next example sets the erase key to CONTROL-H. The CONTROL-V quotes the CONTROL-H so that the shell does not interpret it, and it gets passed to stty:

```
$ stty erase  CONTROL-V CONTROL-H
$ stty
speed 9600 baud; line = 0;
erase = ^H;
```

Following, stty sets the line kill key to CONTROL-X. This time the user entered a caret (∧) followed by an **x** to represent CONTROL-X. You can use either a lower- or uppercase letter:

```
$ stty kill ^X
$ stty
speed 38400 baud; line = 0;
erase = ^H; kill = ^X;
```

Next, stty changes the interrupt key to CONTROL-C:

```
$ stty intr CONTROL-V CONTROL-C
```

Following, stty turns off TABs so the appropriate number of SPACEs is sent to the terminal in place of a TAB. Use this command if a terminal does not automatically expand TABs:

```
$ stty -tabs
```

If you log in and everything that appears on the terminal is in uppercase letters, give the following command, and then check the CAPS LOCK key; if it is set, turn it off:

```
$ STTY -LCASE
```

Turn on **lcase** if the terminal you are using cannot display lowercase characters. Although no one usually changes the suspend key from its default, CONTROL-Z, you can. Give the following command to change the suspend key to CONTROL-T:

```
$ stty susp ^T
```

tail

Displays the last part (tail) of a file

*tail [**options**] [**file-list**]*

The tail utility displays the last part, or end, of a file. This utility takes its input from one or more files you specify on the command line or from standard input.

Arguments   The *file-list* contains pathnames of the files that tail displays. When you specify more than one file, tail displays the filename of each file before displaying the lines of the file. When you do not specify a file, tail takes its input from standard input.

Options

--bytes=[[+]n[u]] –c   Counts by bytes (characters). The *n* is an optional nonzero integer. The *u* is an optional unit of measure that can be **b** (512-byte blocks), **k** (1,024-byte or 1-kilobyte blocks), or **m** (1-megabyte blocks). If you include the unit of measure, tail counts by this unit in place of bytes. You can put a plus sign (**+**) in front of *n* to cause tail to count from the start of the file instead of the end. The tail utility still counts *to the end* of the file, even if you *start* counting from the beginning, so +10 causes tail to display from the tenth line through the last line of the file.

--follow –f   After copying the last line of the file, tail enters an endless loop, waiting and copying additional lines from the file if the file grows. This feature is useful for tracking the progress of a process that is running in the background and sending its output to a file. The tail utility continues to wait indefinitely, so you must use the interrupt key to terminate it.

–n *or* –n   Counts by lines (the default). The *u* is an optional unit of measure (see **--bytes**
--lines=[[+]n[u]] for an explanation). You can put a plus sign (**+**) in front of *n* to cause tail to count from the start of the file instead of the end. You can use **–n** to specify a number of lines without using the **lines** keyword.

--quiet –q   Suppresses header information when you specify more than one filename on the command line.

Notes   The tail utility displays ten lines by default.

Examples   The examples are based on the following **eleven** file:

```
$ cat eleven
line one
line two
line three
line four
line five
line six
line seven
line eight
line nine
line ten
line eleven
```

First, tail displays the last ten lines of the **eleven** file (no options):

```
$ tail eleven
line two
line three
line four
line five
line six
line seven
line eight
line nine
line ten
line eleven
```

The next example displays the last three lines (**−−lines 3**) of the file:

```
$ tail --lines 3 eleven
line nine
line ten
line eleven
```

The next example displays the file, starting at line eight (**+8**):

```
$ tail +8 eleven
line eight
line nine
line ten
line eleven
```

The next example displays the last six characters in the file (**−−bytes 6**). Only five characters are evident (1even); the sixth is a NEWLINE:

```
$ tail --bytes 6 eleven
leven
```

The final example demonstrates the –f option; following, tail tracks the output
of a make command, which is being sent to the file **accounts.out**:

```
$ make accounts > accounts.out &
$ tail -f accounts.out
        cc -c trans.c
        cc -c reports.c
   .
   .
   .
CONTROL-C
$
```

In the preceding example, using tail with –f has the same effect as running make
in the foreground and letting its output go to the terminal; however, using tail has
some advantages. First, the output of make is saved in a file. (The output would not
be saved if you simply let it go to the terminal.) Also, if you decide to do something
else while make is running, you can kill tail, and the terminal will be free for you to
use while make continues in the background. When you are running a large job,
such as compiling a large program, you can use tail with the –f option to check on its
progress periodically.

tar

Stores or retrieves files to/from an archive file

*tar **option** [**modifiers**] [**file-list**]*

The tar (tape archive) utility creates, adds to, lists, and retrieves files from an archive file.

Options

Use only one of the following options to indicate what type of action you want tar to take. You can affect the action of the option by following it with one or more modifiers.

--append   −r   Writes the *file-list* to the end of the archive. This option leaves files that are already in the archive intact, so duplicate copies of files may be in the archive after tar finishes. When tar extracts the files, the last copy of a file in the archive is the one that ends up on the disk.

--create   −c   This option takes the *file-list* given on the command line and stores the named files in a new archive. If the archive already exists, it is destroyed before the new archive is created. If a *file-list* argument is a directory, tar recursively copies the files within the directory into the archive. The following command copies all the files on your system to the archive. Without the −f option the archive is created on /dev/rmt0:

```
$ tar -c /
```

--extract *or*   −x   Extracts the *file-list* from the archive and writes it to the disk. Any existing files
--get   with the same name are overwritten. Without a *file-list*, all the files in the archive are extracted. If the *file-list* includes a directory, tar extracts that directory and all the files below it. The tar utility attempts to keep the owner, modification time, and access privileges the same as those of the original file. If tar reads the same file more than once, the later versions of the file overwrite any previous versions.

--list   −t) **table of contents**   Without a *file-list*, this option produces a table of contents of all the files in an archive. With a *file-list*, it displays the name of each of the files in the *file-list* each time it occurs in the archive. You can use this option with the −−**verbose** option to display detailed information about each file in the archive.

--update   −u   Adds the files from *file-list* if they are not already in the archive or if they have been modified since they were last written to the archive. Because of the additional checking that this requires, tar runs more slowly when you use this option.

--help   Displays a complete list of options and modifiers, with short descriptions of each.

Modifiers

You can specify one or more modifiers following an option. If you use the single-character form of the modifier, a leading hyphen is not required. However, it is good practice to use the hyphen unless you combine the modifier with other single-character modifiers.

If a modifier takes an argument, that modifier must be the last one in a group. For example, the arguments are arranged legally in the following tar command:

```
$ tar -cb 10 -f /dev/ftape
```

On the other hand, the following tar command generates an error:

```
$ tar -cbf 10 /dev/ftape
tar: Invalid value for blocksize
```

The error is generated because the –b modifier takes an argument but is not the last modifier in a group. This is different from the original version of tar, used with many UNIX systems, that allowed this construct.

--absolute-paths –P The default behavior of tar is to force all pathnames to be relative paths by stripping any leading slashes. This option disables this feature, so any absolute pathnames remain as absolute paths.

--block-compress Normally tar compresses (gzip) or decompresses (gunzip) the entire archive at once. This technique does not work with archives that are on tape devices. This option, when used with one of the preceding compression or decompression options, causes tar to compress the archive on a block-by-block basis, which works well with tape archives.

--block-size [*n*] –b Uses *n* as the blocking factor for creating an archive. Use this option only when tar is creating an archive directly to a tape. (When tar reads a tape archive, it automatically determines the blocking factor.) The value of *n* is the number of 512-byte blocks to write as a single block on the tape. When you do not specify *n*, it defaults to 20.

--bzip –j Uses bzip2 (page 74) when creating the archive and extracting files from the archive.

--checkpoint Displays the names of directories it extracts from an archive.

--compress *or* –Z Uses compress when creating the archive and uncompress when extracting files
--uncompress from the archive.

--dereference –h Follows symbolic links and includes the linked-to files as if they were normal files and directories.

--directory *directory* –C Changes the working directory to *directory* before processing.

--exclude *filename* Does not process the file given as *filename*. If *filename* is a directory, no files or directories within that directory are processed.

—exclude-from *filename*

     −X   Similar to the **—exclude** option except that *filename* identifies a file that contains a list of files to exclude from processing. Each file listed in *filename* must be on a separate line.

—file *filename* **−f**   Uses *filename* as the name of the file (device) to hold the archive. The *filename* can be the name of an ordinary file, a device (such as a tape drive), or a device on another computer on your network. To give the name of a device on another computer, put the domain name of the other computer and a colon (:) in front of the device name. If your username on the other machine is different from the one you are using, you can precede the domain name with the username on the remote machine, followed by an @. The following command, given by Alex on **kudos**, causes tar to use tape device **/dev/st0** on **bravo** to hold the archive, using the account for Scott on **bravo** to access the tape device:

```
$ tar -cf scott@bravo:/dev/st0 /
```

For the preceding tar command to work, the remote machine must be running the **rshd** daemon (see footnote 15 on page 373), Alex (working from **kudos**) must have permission to use Scott's account on **bravo** with rsh, Scott must be able to execute the rmt utility on **bravo** (rmt on the remote machine accepts the tar output and writes it to tape), and Scott must have write permission to **/dev/st0** on **bravo**.[9]

You can use a hyphen (−) in place of a filename as a way to refer to standard input when creating an archive and standard output when extracting files from an archive. The following two commands are equivalent ways of creating an archive of the files under the **/home** directory on **/dev/st0**:

```
$ tar -zcf /dev/st0 /home
$ tar -cf - /home | gzip > /dev/st0
```

—gzip **−z**   Causes tar to use gzip to compress the archive while it is being created and to
—ungzip decompress the archive when extracting files from it. When reading from an archive, this option also causes tar to detect when an archive has been compressed with the compress utility. If compress was used, tar uses uncompress instead of gunzip as the files are extracted.

—ignore-failed-read When creating an archive, tar normally quits with a nonzero exit status if any of the files in *file-list* is unreadable. This option causes tar to continue processing, skipping unreadable files.

—interactive *or* **−w**   Asks you for confirmation before reading or writing each file. Respond with **y** if
—confirmation you want tar to take the action. Any other response causes tar not to take the action.

---

9. A more secure way of accomplishing the same task is to send the output of tar to ssh, which runs a command on the remote machine that writes tar's output to the remote tape.

--modification-time **–m**   Sets the modification time to the time of extraction. Without this option tar attempts to maintain the modification time of the original file.

--one-file-system **–l**   When a directory name appears in *file-list* while reading files for an archive, tar recursively processes the files and directories below the named directory. With this option tar stays in the filesystem that the named directory is in and does not read files and directories that exist on other filesystems.

--sparse **–S**   GNU/Linux allows you to have sparse files on disk. These are large, mostly empty files. The empty sections of sparse files do not take up any disk space. When tar copies one of these sparse files out of an archive, it normally expands it to its full size. This means that when you restore a sparse file from a tar backup, the file takes up its full space and may no longer fit in the same disk space as the original. This option causes tar to handle sparse files efficiently so that they do not take up unnecessary space either in the archive or when they are extracted.

--tape–length *n* **–L**   Asks for a new tape after writing *n* ∗ 1,024 bytes to the current tape. This feature is useful when building archives that are too big to fit on a single tape.

--verbose **–v**   Lists each file as tar reads or writes it. When combined with the **–t** option, **–v** causes tar to display a more detailed listing of the files, showing ownership, permissions, size, and other useful information for files in the archive.

Notes

The GNU/Linux version of tar was developed by the GNU project and includes a large number of options and modifiers. Only the most commonly used options and modifiers are presented here. The **--help** option displays all the options and modifiers. The info page on tar is extensive, including a tutorial.

You can use ambiguous file references when you write files but not when you read them.

The name of a directory file within the *file-list* references all files and subdirectories within that directory.

The file that tar sends its output to by default is compilation specific; typically it goes to standard output. Use the **–f** option to specify a different filename or device that is to hold the archive.

If you write a file using a simple filename, the file appears in the working directory when you read it back. If you write a file using a relative pathname, the file appears with that relative pathname, starting from the working directory when you read it back. If you use the **–P** option and an absolute pathname to write a file, tar reads it back in with the same pathname.

As you read and write files, tar attempts to preserve links between files. Unless you use the **–h** option, tar does not inform you when it fails to maintain a link.

Examples

The following example makes a copy of the **/home/alex** directory and all files and subdirectories within that directory onto a floppy tape device. The v modifier causes the command to list all the files it writes to the tape as it proceeds. This command erases anything that was already on the tape. The message from tar explains that the default action is to store all pathnames as relative paths instead of absolute paths, allowing you to extract the files into a different place on your disks:

```
$ tar -cvf /dev/ftape /home/alex
tar: Removing leading / from absolute path names in the archive.
home/alex/
home/alex/.zprofile
home/alex/.zshenv
.
.
```

In the next example, the same directory is saved on the tape device **/dev/st0** with a blocking factor of 100. Without the v modifier, tar does not display the list of files it is writing to the tape. The command runs in the background and displays any messages after the shell issues a new prompt:

```
$ tar -cb 100 -f /dev/st0 /home/alex &
[1] 4298
$ tar: Removing leading / from absolute path names in the archive.
```

The next command displays the table of contents of the archive on tape device **/dev/ftape**:

```
$ tar -tvf /dev/ftape
drwxrwxrwx alex/group         0 Jun 30 21:39 2004 home/alex/
-rw-r--r-- alex/group       678 Aug  6 14:12 2003 home/alex/.zprofile
-rw-r--r-- alex/group       571 Aug  6 14:06 2003 home/alex/.zshenv
drwx------ alex/group         0 Nov  6 22:34 2003 home/alex/mail/
-rw------- alex/group      2799 Nov  6 22:34 2003 home/alex/mail/sent-mail
```

In the last example, Alex creates a gzipped tar archive in **/tmp/alex.tgz**. This is a common way to bundle together files that you want to transfer over a network or otherwise share with others. Ending a filename with **.tgz** is a common convention for identifying gzipped tar archives. Another common convention is to end the filename with **.tar.z**:

```
$ tar -czf /tmp/alex.tgz literature
```

The next command lists the files in the compressed archive **alex.tgz**:

```
$ tar -tzvf /tmp/alex.tgz
...
```

tee

Copies standard input to standard output and one or more files

tee [options] file-list

The tee utility copies standard input to standard output *and* to one or more files you specify on the command line.

Arguments   The *file-list* contains the pathnames of files that receive output from tee.

Options   Without any options, tee overwrites the output files if they exist and responds to interrupts. If a file in *file-list* does not exist, tee creates it.

--append **−a**   Appends output to existing files rather than overwrites them.

--ignore-interrupts **−i**   Causes tee not to respond to interrupts.

Example   In the following example, a pipe sends the output from make to tee, which copies it to standard output and the file **accounts.out**. The copy that goes to standard output appears on the screen. The cat utility displays the copy that was sent to the file:

```
$ make accounts | tee accounts.out
        cc -c trans.c
        cc -c reports.c
     .
     .
     .

$ cat accounts.out
        cc -c trans.c
        cc -c reports.c
     .
     .
     .
```

Refer to page 1342 for a similar example that uses **tail −f** rather than tee.

telnet

Connects to a remote computer over a network

*telnet [**options**] [**remote-computer**]*

The telnet utility implements the TELNET protocol to connect to a remote system over a network. The *remote-computer* is the name or IP address of the remote system. You can use telnet to establish a login session on a remote system that you have an account on.

telnet **Is Not Secure** || security

> The telnet utility is not secure. It sends your username and password over the network as cleartext, which is not a secure practice. Use **ssh** (page 374) when it is available and the remote system supports it.

Arguments   When you specify *remote-computer* on the command line, telnet tries to establish a connection to that system. When you do not specify *remote-computer,* telnet works interactively, prompting you to enter one of the commands described next.

Options

–e *c* escape   Changes the escape character from CONTROL-] to the character *c*.

–l *login-name* login   Attempts an automatic login to the remote computer using *login-name*. If the remote computer understands how to handle automatic login with telnet, you are prompted for that user's password.

Discussion   After you are connected to a remote computer, you can put telnet into command mode by typing the escape character. On GNU/Linux systems, the escape character is usually CONTROL-]. When you connect to a remote system, it should report the escape character it recognizes. To leave command mode, type a RETURN on a line by itself.

In response to a `telnet>` prompt, you can use the following commands:

? help   Displays a list of commands recognized by the telnet utility on the local system.

close   Closes the connection to the remote system. If you specified the name of a system on the command line when you started telnet, **close** has the same effect as **quit**: The telnet program quits, and you are returned to the shell. If you used the **open** command instead of specifying a remote system on the command line, **close** returns telnet to command mode.

open *remote-computer*

If you did not specify a remote system on the command line or if the attempt to connect to the system failed, you can specify the name of a remote system interactively with the **open** command.

quit   Quits the telnet session.

z   You can suspend your session with the remote system by using the **z** command. When you suspend a session, you return to your login shell on your local system. To resume your telnet session with the remote system, type **fg** at a shell prompt.

Notes

Many computers, including non-GNU/Linux systems, support the TELNET protocol. The telnet utility is a user interface to this protocol for GNU/Linux systems, allowing you to connect to many different types of systems. Although you typically use telnet to log in, the remote computer may offer other services through telnet, such as access to special databases.

Examples

In the following example the user connects to a remote system named **bravo**. After running a few commands, the user escapes to command mode and uses the **z** command to suspend the telnet session in order to run a few commands on the local system. The user gives the shell an **fg** command to resume using telnet. Finally, the **logout** command on the remote system ends the telnet session, and a prompt from the local system appears:

```
kudos% telnet bravo
Trying 192.168.0.55 ...
Connected to bravo.
Escape character is '^]'.

Red Hat Linux Release 7.2 (Enigma)
Kernel 2.4.7-10 on an i686

login: watson
Password:
Last login: Wed Jul 31 10:37:16 from kudos
```

```
bravo $
.
.
bravo $CONTROL-]
telnet> z

[1]+ Stopped   telnet bravo
kudos $
.
.
kudos $fg
telnet bravo

bravo$ logout
Connection closed by foreign host.
kudos $
```

test

Evaluates an expression

test **expression**
[**expression** *]*

The test utility evaluates an expression and returns a condition code indicating that the expression is either *true* (0) or *false* (not 0). You can use brackets ([]) around the expression instead of using the word test (second format).

Arguments   The *expression* contains one or more criteria (see the following list) that test evaluates. A –a separating two criteria is a Boolean AND operator: Both criteria must be true for test to return a condition code of *true*. A –o is a Boolean OR operator. When –o separates two criteria, one or the other (or both) of the criteria must be true in order for test to return a condition code of *true*.

You can negate any criterion by preceding it with an exclamation point (!). You can group criteria with parentheses. If there are no parentheses, –a takes precedence over –o, and test evaluates operators of equal precedence from left to right.

Within the *expression* you must quote special characters, such as parentheses, so that the shell does not interpret them but passes them on to test.

Because each element, such as a criterion, string, or variable within the **expression** is a separate argument, you must separate each element from other elements with a SPACE. Table III-29 lists the criteria you can use within the *expression*. Relational operators you can use within the criteria are listed in Table III-30.

Criteria	‖ table III-29
string	True if *string* is not a null string.
–n *string*	True if *string* has a length greater than zero.
–z *string*	True if *string* has a length of zero.
string1 = *string2*	True if *string1* is equal to *string2*.
string1 != *string2*	True if *string1* is not equal to *string2*.

Criteria (Continued)

|| table III-29

int1 relop int2	True if integer *int1* has the specified algebraic relationship to integer *int2*. The *relop* is a relational operator from Table III-30. As a special case, —l *string*, which gives the length of *string*, may be used for *int1* or *int2*.
file1 —ef *file2*	True if *file1* and *file2* have the same device and inode numbers.
file1 —nt *file2*	True if *file1* was modified after *file2* (the modification time of *file1* is newer than that of *file2*).
file1 —ot *file2*	True if *file1* was modified before *file2* (the modification time of *file1* is older than that of *file2*).
—e *filename*	True if the file named *filename* exists.
—b *filename*	True if the file named *filename* exists and is a block special file.
—c *filename*	True if the file named *filename* exists and is a character special file.
—d *filename*	True if the file named *filename* exists and is a directory.
—f *filename*	True if the file named *filename* exists and is an ordinary file.
—g *filename*	True if the file named *filename* exists and its setgid bit is set.
—k *filename*	True if the file named *filename* exists and its sticky bit is set.
—L *filename*	True if the file named *filename* exists and is a symbolic link.
—p *filename*	True if the file named *filename* exists and is a named pipe.
—r *filename*	True if the file named *filename* exists and you have read access permission to it.
—s *filename*	True if the file named *filename* exists and contains information (has a size greater than 0 bytes).
—t *file-descriptor*	True if *file-descriptor* is associated with a terminal. The *file-descriptor* for standard input is 0, for standard output is 1, and for standard error is 2.
—u *filename*	True if the file named *filename* exists and its setuid bit is set.
—w *filename*	True if the file named *filename* exists and you have write access permission to it.
—x *filename*	True if the file named *filename* exists and you have execute access permission to it.

Relop	|| table III-30
−gt	Greater than
−ge	Greater than or equal to
−eq	Equal to
−ne	Not equal to
−le	Less than or equal to
−lt	Less than

Note   The test command is built into bash, tcsh, and zsh.

Examples   The following examples show how to use the test utility in Bourne Again Shell scripts. Although test works from a command line, it is more commonly used in shell scripts to test input or verify access to a file.

The first two examples show incomplete shell scripts. They are not complete because they do not test for upper- as well as lowercase input or inappropriate responses and do not acknowledge more than one response.

The first example prompts the user, reads a line of input into the user variable **user_input**, and uses test to see whether the user variable **user_input** matches the string yes:

```
$ cat user_in
echo -n "Input yes or no: "
read user_input
if [ "$user_input" = yes ]
    then
        echo You input yes.
fi
```

Refer to Chapters 12 and 13 for more information on variables, read, and **if**.

The next example prompts for a filename and then uses test to see whether the user has read access permission (−r) for the file *and* (−a) whether the file contains information (−s):

```
$ cat validate
echo -n "Enter filename: "
read filename
if [ -r "$filename" -a -s "$filename" ]
    then
        echo File $filename exists and contains information.
        echo You have read access permission to the file.
fi
```

The **–t 1** criterion checks whether the process running test is sending output to a terminal. If it is, the test utility returns a value of *true* (0). Following is a listing of the shell script **term** that runs test:

```
$ cat term
test -t 1
echo "This program is (=0) or is not (=1)
sending its output to a terminal:" $?
```

First, **term** is run with the output going to the terminal; that is, the output is not redirected to a file. The test utility returns a 0. The shell stores this value in the shell variable that records the condition code of the last process, **$?**. The echo utility displays this value:

```
$ term
This program is (=0) or is not (=1)
sending its output to a terminal: 0
```

The next example runs **term** and redirects the output to a file. The contents of the file **temp** show that test returned a 1, indicating that its output was not going to a terminal:

```
$ term > temp
$ cat temp
This program is (=0) or is not (=1)
sending its output to a terminal: 1
```

top

Dynamically displays process status

*top [**options**]*

The top utility displays information about the status of your GNU/Linux system, including information about all the current processes. This utility is similar to ps but periodically updates the display, enabling you to watch the behavior of your system over time.

Options
Although top does not require the use of hyphens with options, it is a good idea to include them for clarity and consistency.

–d*n* Specify *n* as the delay from one display update to the next. The default is 5 seconds.

–n*n* Number of updates: top updates the display *n* times and exits.

–q Runs top without any delay. When Superuser uses this option, top runs at the highest priority.

–s Runs top in Secure mode. This restricts the commands that you can use while top is running to those commands that pose no security risk.

–S Causes top to run in Cumulative mode. When you use this option, CPU times reported for processes include any CPU times accumulated by child processes that are now dead.

Discussion
The first few lines that top displays provide a summary of the status of your system. You can turn each of these lines on or off with the toggle switches (interactive command keys) specified in the following sentences. The first line is the same as the output of the uptime utility and displays the current time, how long your system has been running since it was last booted, the number of users logged in, and the load averages from the last 1, 5, and 15 minutes (toggle l—"ell"). The second line displays information on the number of processes that are currently running (toggle **t**). The next three lines report on CPU (toggle **t**), memory (toggle **m**), and swap space (toggle **m**) use.

The rest of the display reports on individual processes, listed in descending order by current CPU usage (the most CPU-intensive process is first). By default top displays only the number of processes that fit on your display.

Table III-31 describes the meaning of the fields displayed for each process.

Field Name	|| table III-31
PID	Process identification number
USER	Login name of the owner of the process
PRI	Current priority
NI	Nice value (see page 1263)
SIZE	Current size of process, measured in kilobytes
RSS	Number of kilobytes of physical memory currently used
SHARE	Number of kilobytes of shared memory currently used
STAT	Status of the process (see **STAT** on page 1290)
%CPU	Percentage of the total CPU time that the process is using
%MEM	Percentage of physical memory that the process is using
TIME	Total CPU time used so far by the process
COMMAND	Command line used to start the process

While top is running, you can use the following commands to modify its behavior. Some of the commands are disabled when running top in Secure mode (−s option).

A **age**   Sorts processes by age.

h *or* **?** **help**   Displays a summary of the commands you can use while top is running.

k **kill**   Allows you to kill a process. Unless you are Superuser, you can kill a process only if you own it. When you use this command, top prompts you for the PID of the process and the signal to send to the process. You can enter either a signal number (for example, 9) or a signal name (for example, KILL). This command is disabled when running in Secure mode.

M **memory**   Sorts processes by resident memory usage.

n *or* **#** **number**   When you give this command, the top utility asks you to enter the number of processes you want it to display. If you enter 0, the default, top shows as many processes as it can fit on the screen.

P **CPU**   Sorts processes by CPU usage. This is the default sort.

q **quit**   Terminates top.

r   renice   Changes the priority of a running process. (Refer to **nice** on page 1263.) Unless you are Superuser, you can change the priority only of your own processes and even then only to lower the priority by entering a positive value. Superuser can enter a negative value, increasing the priority of the process. This command is not available when **top** is running in Secure mode.

s   seconds   Prompts you for the number of seconds to delay between updates to the display—5 seconds by default. You may enter an integer, a fraction, or 0 (for continuous updates). This command is unavailable when **top** is running in Secure mode.

S   switch   Switches **top** back and forth between Cumulative mode and Regular mode. See the **–S** option for details.

W   write   Writes **top**'s current configuration to **~/.toprc**. This is a good way to write a configuration file for **top**.

Notes   The **top** utility shows only as much of the command line for each process as fits on the current line of the display. If a process is swapped out, **top** replaces the command line by the name of the command in parentheses.

The **top** utility uses the **proc** filesystem: When **proc** is not mounted, **top** does not work.

Requesting continuous updates is almost always a mistake: The display updates too quickly, and the system load goes up dramatically.

Example   The following display is the result of a typical execution of **top**:

```
 9:21am  up 2 days,  3:21, 12 users,  load average: 1.51, 1.20, 1.09
77 processes: 73 sleeping, 2 running, 2 zombie, 0 stopped
CPU states: 61.2% user, 35.7% system,  0.2% nice,  3.5% idle
Mem:  30940K av, 27592K used,  3348K free, 13040K shrd,  5448K buff
Swap: 385508K av, 16868K used, 368640K free              9128K cached

  PID USER      PRI  NI SIZE  RSS SHARE STAT %CPU %MEM   TIME COMMAND
20022 jenny      12   0 2772 1304   464 R    56.3  4.2   3:26 gimp
18658 root        6   0 4856 2116   992 S    33.3  6.8  31:09 X
20054 alex       12   0  972  372   192 R     6.4  1.2   0:03 top
   13 root        0   0  840   32    20 S     0.1  0.1   0:02 update
13910 root        0   0  904  104    84 S     0.1  0.3   0:01 in.telnetd
15046 alex        5   5 2372  808   368 S N   0.1  2.6   0:52 tkmail.tcl
15047 alex        5   5 2968 1004   520 S N   0.1  3.2   1:14 wish3
18666 jenny       0   0 2348  600   420 S     0.1  1.9   0:01 wish
    1 root        0   0  864   80    60 S     0.0  0.2   0:50 init
    2 root        0   0    0    0     0 SW    0.0  0.0   0:00 kflushd
    3 root      -12 -12    0    0     0 SW<   0.0  0.0   0:01 kswapd
    4 root        0   0    0    0     0 SW    0.0  0.0   0:00 nfsiod
  123 alex        0   0 1268    0     0 SW    0.0  0.0   0:00 zsh
```

touch

Updates a file's modification time

*touch [**options**] **file-list**

The touch utility updates the time a file was last accessed and the time it was last modified and also allows you to specify these times on the command line. This utility is frequently used with make.

Arguments   The *file-list* contains the pathnames of the files touch is to update.

Options   When you do not specify the –c option, touch creates files that do not already exist. If touch is used without the –d or –t options, touch uses the current date and time.

––date *datestring*   –d *datestring*   Updates times with the date specified by *datestring*. Most familiar formats are permitted for *datestring*. Components of the date and time not included in *datestring* are assumed to be the current date and time. This option may not be used with –t.

––no-create   –c   Does not create files that do not already exist.

––reference=*file*   –r *file*   Updates times with the dates of *file*.

–t *nnddhhmm*[*cc*[*yy*]][.*ss*]

Updates times with the date specified by the argument. The *nn* is the number of the month (01–12), *dd* is the day of the month (01–31), *hh* is the hour based on a 24-hour clock (00–23), and *mm* is the minutes (00–59). The year, *yy*, is optional and specifies the last two digits of the year. If *yy* is given, the century, *cc*, may also be given and specifies the first two digits of the year. The optional portion, .*ss*, gives seconds (.00–.59); the number of seconds must be preceded by a period. Any optional portion missing from the time specification is assumed to be unchanged. This option may not be used with –d.

––time=atime *or*   –a   Updates the access time only, leaving the modification time unchanged.
––time=access

––time=mtime *or*   –m   Updates the modification time only, leaving the access time unchanged.
––time=modify

Examples

The following commands demonstrate how touch functions. The first commands show touch updating an existing file. The ls utility with the –l option displays the modification time of the file. The last three command lines show touch creating a file:

```
$ ls -l program.c
-rw-r--r--   1 alex      group               5860 Apr 21 09:54 program.c

$ touch program.c

$ ls -l program.c
-rw-r--r--   1 alex      group               5860 Aug 13 19:01 program.c

$ ls -l read.c
ls: read.c: No such file or directory

$ touch read.c

$ ls -l read.c
-rw-rw-r--   1 alex      group                  0 Aug 13 19:01 read.c
```

The next example demonstrates the use of the –a option to change access time only and the –d option to specify a date for touch to use instead of the current date and time.

The first ls command displays the file *modification* times, and the second ls (with the –u option) displays file *access* times. The touch command does not have the intended effect. The pair of ls commands show that the access times of the files **cases** and **excerpts** have been changed to 7:00 on the current date and that three unwanted files have been created. Because the date was not quoted (by surrounding it with double quotation marks), touch assumed that the 7:00 goes with the –d option and creates the **pm**, **Jul**, and **30** files:

```
$ ls -l
-rw-rw-r--   1 alex      group                 45 Nov 30   2003 cases
-rw-rw-rw-   1 alex      group                 14 Jan  8   2004 excerpts

$ ls -lu
-rw-rw-r--   1 alex      group                 45 Jul 17 19:47 cases
-rw-rw-rw-   1 alex      group                 14 Jul 17 19:47 excerpts

$ touch -a -d 7:00 pm Jul 30 cases excerpts

$ ls -l
-rw-rw-r--   1 alex      group                  0 Aug 11 12:23 30
-rw-rw-r--   1 alex      group                  0 Aug 11 12:23 Jul
-rw-rw-r--   1 alex      group                 45 Nov 30   2003 cases
-rw-rw-rw-   1 alex      group                 14 Jan  8   2004 excerpts
-rw-rw-r--   1 alex      group                  0 Aug 11 12:23 pm
```

```
$ ls -lu
-rw-rw-r--    1 alex      group              0 Aug 11 07:00 30
-rw-rw-r--    1 alex      group              0 Aug 11 07:00 Jul
-rw-rw-r--    1 alex      group             45 Aug 11 07:00 cases
-rw-rw-rw-    1 alex      group             14 Aug 11 07:00 excerpts
-rw-rw-r--    1 alex      group              0 Aug 11 07:00 pm
```

The final example is the same as the preceding one but correctly encloses the date within double quotation marks. After the touch command, ls shows that the access times of the files **cases** and **excerpts** have been updated as expected:

```
$ ls -l
-rw-rw-r--    1 alex      group             45 Nov 30  2003 cases
-rw-rw-rw-    1 alex      group             14 Jan  8  2003 excerpts
$ ls -lu
-rw-rw-r--    1 alex      group             45 Jul 17 19:47 cases
-rw-rw-rw-    1 alex      group             14 Jul 17 19:47 excerpts

$ touch -a -d "7:00 pm Jul 30" cases excerpts

$ ls -l
-rw-rw-r--    1 alex      group             45 Nov 30  2003 cases
-rw-rw-rw-    1 alex      group             14 Jan  8  2004 excerpts
$ ls -lu
-rw-rw-r--    1 alex      group             45 Jul 30 19:00 cases
-rw-rw-rw-    1 alex      group             14 Jul 30 19:00 excerpts
```

tr

Replaces specified characters

tr [options] string1 [string2]

The tr utility reads standard input and, for each input character, maps it to an alternate character, deletes the character, or leaves the character alone. The utility writes the result to standard output.

Arguments   The tr utility is typically used with two arguments, *string1* and *string2*. The position of each character in the two strings is important; tr replaces each character from *string1* with the corresponding character in *string2*.

With one argument, *string1*, and the **--delete** option, tr deletes the characters specified in *string1*. The option **--squeeze-repeats** replaces multiple sequential occurrences of characters in *string1* with single occurrences (for example, abbc becomes abc).

Range

A range of characters is similar in function to a character class within a regular expression (page 1385). GNU tr does not support ranges (character classes) enclosed within brackets. You can specify a range of characters by following the character that is earlier in the collating sequence with a hyphen and then the character that is later in the collating sequence. For example, 1-6 expands to 123456. Although the range A-Z expands as you would expect in ASCII, it does not when you use the EBCDIC collating sequence, as these characters are not sequential in EBCDIC. See "Character Class," following, for a solution to this issue.

Character Class

As mentioned earlier, a tr character class is not the same as described elsewhere in this book. (GNU documentation uses the term *list operator* for what this book calls a *character class*.) You specify a character class as '[:*class*:]' where *class* is a character class from Table III-32. You must specify a character class in *string1* unless you are performing case conversion (see "Examples," following) or are using the –d and –s options together.

Character Classes

|| table III-32

alnum	Letters and digits
alpha	Letters
cntrl	CONTROL characters
digit	Digits
graph	Printable characters but not SPACES
lower	Lowercase letters
print	Printable characters, including SPACES
punct	Punctuation characters
space	Horizontal or vertical whitespace
upper	Uppercase letters
xdigit	Hexidecimal digits

Options

--delete -d   Deletes characters that match those specified in *string1*. If used with the **--squeeze-repeats** option, both *string1* and *string2* must be given (see "Notes").

--squeeze-repeats -s   Replaces multiple sequential occurrences of a character in *string1* with a single occurrence of the character when you call tr with only one string argument. If you use both *string1* and *string2*, the tr utility first translates the characters in *string1* to those in *string2* and then reduces multiple sequential occurrences of characters in *string2*.

--complement -c   Complements *string1*, causing tr to match all characters *except* those in *string1*.

--help   Gives a summary of how to use tr, including the special symbols you can use in *string1* and *string2*.

Notes

When *string1* is longer than *string2*, the initial portion of *string1* (equal in length to *string2*) is used in the translation. When *string1* is shorter than *string2*, the GNU version of tr (described here) uses the last character of *string1* to extend *string1* to the length of *string2*. In this case the GNU version of tr departs from the POSIX standard, which does not define a result.

If you use the **--delete** and **--squeeze-repeats** options at the same time, tr deletes the characters in *string1* and then reduces multiple sequential occurrences of characters in *string2*.

Examples

You can use a hyphen to represent a range of characters in *string1* or *string2*. The two command lines in the following example produce the same result:

```
$ echo abcdef | tr 'abcdef' 'xyzabc'
xyzabc
$ echo abcdef | tr 'a-f' 'x-za-c'
xyzabc
```

The next example demonstrates a popular method for disguising text, often called *rotate 13* because it replaces the first letter of the alphabet with the thirteenth, the second with the fourteenth, and so forth:

```
$ echo The punchline of the joke is ... |
> tr '[A-M][N-Z][a-m][n-z]' '[N-Z][A-M][n-z][a-m]'
Gur chapuyvar bs gur wbxr vf ...
```

To make the text intelligible again, reverse the order of the arguments to tr:

```
$ echo Gur chapuyvar bs gur wbxr vf ... |
> tr '[N-Z][A-M][n-z][a-m]' '[A-M][N-Z][a-m][n-z]'
The punchline of the joke is ...
```

The **--delete** option causes tr to delete selected characters:

```
$ echo If you can read this, you can spot the missing vowels! |
> tr --delete 'aeiou'
If y cn rd ths, y cn spt th mssng vwls!
```

In the following example tr replaces characters and reduces pairs of identical characters to single characters:

```
$ echo tennessee | tr -s 'tnse' 'srne'
serene
```

The following example replaces each sequence of nonalphabetic characters (the complement of all the alphabetic characters as specified by the character class **alpha**) in the file **draft1** with a single NEWLINE character. The output is a list of words, one per line:

```
$ tr --complement --squeeze-repeats '[:alpha:]' '\n' < draft1
```

The next example uses character classes to upshift the string hi there:

```
$ echo hi there | tr '[:lower:]' '[:upper:]'
HI THERE
```

tty

Displays the terminal pathname

tty [option]

The tty utility displays the pathname of standard input if it is a terminal and displays not a tty if it is not. The exit status is 0 if standard input is a terminal and 1 if it is not.

Arguments   There are no arguments.

Options

--silent *or* **-s**   Causes tty not to print anything. The exit status of tty is still set, however.
--quiet

Notes   The term tty is short for teletypewriter, the terminal device that UNIX was first run from. This command appears in UNIX, and GNU/Linux has kept it for the sake of consistency and tradition.

Example   The following example illustrates the use of tty:

```
$ tty
/dev/tty11
$ echo $?
0
$ tty < memo
not a tty
$ echo $?
1
```

umask

Establishes the file-creation permissions mask

*umask [**mask**]*

The umask builtin specifies a mask that the system uses to set up access permissions when you create a file. This builtin works slightly differently in each of the shells.

Arguments   The ***mask*** can be a three-digit octal number `bash tcsh zsh` or a symbolic value `bash zsh` such as you would use with chmod (page 1103). The ***mask*** specifies the permissions that are *not* allowed.

When ***mask*** is an octal number, the digits correspond to permissions for the owner of the file, members of the group the file is associated with, and everyone else. Because the ***mask*** specifies the permissions that are *not* allowed, the system subtracts each of these digits from 7 when you create a file. The result is three octal numbers that specify the access permissions for the file (the numbers you would use with chmod). A ***mask*** that you specify as a symbolic value also specifies the permissions that are *not* allowed. See "Notes."

Without any arguments, umask displays the file-creation permissions ***mask***.

Notes   Most utilities and applications do not attempt to create files with execute permissions, regardless of the value of ***mask***; they assume that you do not want an executable file. The effective result is that when a utility or application, such as touch, creates a file, the system subtracts each of the digits in ***mask*** from 6. An exception is mkdir, which does assume that you want the execute (access in the case of a directory) bit set. See the "Examples" section.

The umask program is a builtin in bash, tcsh, and zsh and generally goes in the initialization file for your shell (**.profile** `bash`, **.zprofile** `zsh`, or **.login** `tcsh`).

Under bash and zsh the argument **g=r,o=r** turns *on* the write bit in the ***mask*** for groups and other users (the mask is 0033), causing those bits to be *off* in file permissions (744 or 644). Refer to chmod on page 1103 for more information about symbolic permissions.

Examples The following commands set the file-creation permissions mask and display the mask and its effect when you create a file and a directory. The mask of 022, when subtracted from 777, gives permissions of 644 (rw–r––r––) for a file and 755 (rwxr–xr–x) for a directory:

```
$ umask 022
$ umask
022
$ touch afile
$ mkdir adirectory
$ ls -ld afile adirectory
drwxr-xr-x   2 mark     mark             4096 Jul 24 11:25 adirectory
-rw-r--r--   1 mark     mark                0 Jul 24 11:25 afile
```

The next example sets the same mask value symbolically:

```
$ umask g=rx,o=rx
$ umask
022
```

uniq

Displays lines of a file that are unique

*uniq [**options**] [**input-file**] [**output-file**]*

The uniq utility displays a file, removing all but one copy of successive repeated lines. If the file has been sorted (refer to the sort utility), uniq ensures that no two lines that it displays are the same.

Arguments   When you do not specify the *input-file*, uniq uses standard input. When you do not specify the *output-file*, uniq uses standard output.

Options   A *field* is a sequence of characters bounded by SPACEs, TABs, NEWLINEs, or a combination of these.

--count   **−c**   Precedes each line with the number of occurrences of the line in the input file.

--ignore-case   **−i**   Ignores case when comparing lines.

--repeated   **−d**   Displays one copy of lines that are repeated; does not display lines that are not repeated.

--skip-chars=*nchar*   **−s** *nchar*   Ignores the first *nchar* characters of each line. If you also use the **--skip-fields** option (see following), uniq ignores the first *nfield* fields followed by *nchar* characters. This option can be used to skip over the leading blanks of a field. An abbreviated form of this option, **+***nchar*, is recognized by uniq.

--skip-fields=*nfield*   **−f** *nfield*   Ignores the first *nfield* blank-separated fields of each line. The uniq utility bases its comparison on the remainder of the line, including the leading blanks of the next field on the line (see the **--skip-chars** option). An abbreviated form of this option, **−***nfield*, is recognized by uniq.

--unique   **−u**   Displays only lines that are *not* repeated.

Examples   These examples assume that the file named **test** in the working directory contains the following text:

```
$ cat test
boy took bat home
boy took bat home
girl took bat home
dog brought hat home
dog brought hat home
dog brought hat home
```

Without any options, uniq displays only one copy of successive repeated lines:

```
$ uniq test
boy took bat home
girl took bat home
dog brought hat home
```

The **––count** option displays the number of consecutive occurrences of each line in the file:

```
$ uniq --count test
   2 boy took bat home
   1 girl took bat home
   3 dog brought hat home
```

The **––repeated** option displays only lines that are consecutively repeated in the file:

```
$ uniq --repeated test
boy took bat home
dog brought hat home
```

The **––unique** option displays only lines that are *not* consecutively repeated in the file:

```
$ uniq --unique test
girl took bat home
```

Next, the *–nfields* argument (**–1**) skips the first field in each line, causing the lines that begin with boy and the one that begins with girl to appear to be consecutive repeated lines. The uniq utility displays only one occurrence of these lines:

```
$ uniq --skip-fields=1 test
boy took bat home
dog brought hat home
```

The next example uses both the *–nfields* and *+nchars* arguments (–2 and +2) first to skip two fields and then to skip two characters. The two characters this command skips include the SPACE that separates the second and third fields and the first character of the third field. Ignoring these characters, all the lines appear to be consecutive repeated lines containing the string at home. The uniq utility displays only the first of these lines:

```
$ uniq -2 +2 test
boy took bat home
```

The following example is equivalent to the previous one but uses the abbreviated form of the **–f** *nfields* and **–s** *nchars* options:

```
$ uniq -2 +2 test
boy took bat home
```

w

Displays information on system users

*w [**options**] [**login-name**]*

The w utility displays the names of users who are currently logged in, together with their terminal device numbers, the times they logged in, which commands they are running, and other information.

Options

−f from   Removes the FROM column. For users who are directly connected, this field contains a dash.

−h no header   Suppresses the output of the header line that is normally displayed by the w utility.

−s short   Displays less information: user name, terminal device, idle time, and the command names.

Arguments

If a *login-name* is supplied as an argument to the w utility, the display is restricted to information about that user.

Discussion

The first line that w displays is the same as that displayed by uptime. This line includes the current time of day, how long the computer has been running (in days, hours, and minutes), how many users are logged in, and how busy the system is (load average). From left to right, the load averages indicate the number of processes that have been waiting to run in the past 1 minute, 5 minutes, and 15 minutes.

The columns of information that w displays for each user have the following headings:

```
USER TTY FROM LOGIN@ IDLE JCPU PCPU WHAT
```

The USER is the login name of the user. The TTY is the device name for the line that the user is on. The FROM is the machine name that a remote user is logged in from; it is a hyphen for a local user. The LOGIN@ is the date and time the user logged in. The

IDLE indicates how many minutes have elapsed since the user last used the keyboard or mouse. The JCPU is the CPU time used by all processes attached to the user's tty, not including completed background jobs. The PCPU is the time used by the process named in the WHAT column. The WHAT is the command that user is running.

Examples

The first example shows the full list produced by the w utility:

```
$ w
 10:26am  up 1 day, 55 min,  6 users,  load average: 0.15, 0.03, 0.01
 USER      TTY      FROM           LOGIN@   IDLE    JCPU   PCPU   WHAT
 alex      tty1     -              Fri 9am  20:39m  0.22s  0.01s  vim td
 alex      tty2     -              Fri 5pm  17:16m  0.07s  0.07s  -bash
 root      pts/1    -              Fri 4pm  14:28m  0.20s  0.07s  -bash
 jenny     pts/2    -              Fri 5pm   3:23   0.08s  0.08s  /bin/bash
 hls       pts/3    potato         10:07am  0.00s  0.08s  0.02s  w
```

The next example shows the –s option producing an abbreviated listing:

```
$ w -s
 10:30am  up 1 day, 58 min,  6 users,  load average: 0.15, 0.03, 0.01
 USER      TTY      FROM            IDLE   WHAT
 alex      tty1     -              20:43m  vim td
 alex      tty2     -              17:19m  -bash
 root      pts/1    -              14:31m  -bash
 jenny     pts/2    -               0.20s  vim memo.030125
 hls       pts/3    potato          0.00s  w -s
```

The final example requests information only about Alex:

```
$ w alex
 10:35am  up 1 day,  1:04,  6 users,  load average: 0.06, 0.01, 0.00
 USER      TTY      FROM           LOGIN@   IDLE    JCPU   PCPU   WHAT
 alex      tty1     -              Fri 9am  20:48m  0.22s  0.01s  vim td
 alex      tty2     -              Fri 5pm  17:25m  0.07s  0.07s  -bash
```

wc

Displays the number of lines, words, and bytes in a file

wc [options] [file-list]

The wc utility displays the number of lines, words, and bytes contained in one or more files. When you specify more than one file on the command line, wc displays totals for each file and totals for the group of files. The wc utility takes its input from files you specify on the command line or from standard input.

Arguments   The *file-list* contains the pathnames of one or more files that wc analyzes.

Options

––bytes –c   Displays only the number of bytes in the file.

––lines –l ("ell")   Displays only the number of lines (that is, NEWLINE characters) in the file.

––words –w   Displays only the number of words in the file.

Notes   A *word* is a sequence of characters bounded by SPACEs, TABs, NEWLINEs, or a combination of these.

Examples   The following command line displays an analysis of the file named **memo**. The numbers represent the number of lines, words, and characters in the file:

```
$ wc memo
      5      31     146 memo
```

The next command displays the number of lines and words in three files. The line at the bottom, with the word total in the right column, contains the sum of each column:

```
$ wc -lw memo1 memo2 memo3
     10      62 memo1
     12      74 memo2
     12      68 memo3
     34     204 total
```

which

Shows where in your path a command is located

which **command-list**

The which utility searches the directories listed in the **PATH** variable and displays the absolute pathname of each file in *command-list* that it finds.

Arguments   The *command-list* contains one or more commands (utilities) that which searches for. For each command which searches the directories listed in your **PATH** environment variable, in order, and displays the full pathname of the first command (executable file) it finds. If which does not locate a command, it displays an error message.

Options

--all **−a** **all**   Displays all matching executable files in **PATH**, not just the first.

--read-alias **−i**   Reads aliases from standard input and reports on matching aliases in addition to executable files in **PATH** (turn off with **--skip-alias**).

--show-tilde   Displays a tilde (~) in place of the absolute pathname of the user's home directory where appropriate. This option is ignored when which is run by Superuser.

--show-dot   Displays a period (.) in place of the absolute pathname when a directory in **PATH** starts with a period and a matching executable file is in that directory (turn off with **--skip-dot**).

---show-functions   Reads shell functions from standard input and reports on matching functions in addition to executable files in **PATH** (turn off with **--skip-functions**).

--tty-only   Do not process more options (to the right of this option) if the process running which is not attached to a tty (keyboard and screen).

Notes   By default, Red Hat Linux defines an alias for which:

```
alias which='alias | /usr/bin/which --tty-only --read-alias --show-dot --show-tilde'
```

This alias is effective only when a which command is given interactively (**--tty-only**) and causes which to display aliases, display the working directory as a period when appropriate, and display the name of the user's home directory as a tilde.

The TC and Z Shells have which builtins (see the tcsh and **zshbuiltins** man pages) that work slightly differently from the which utility (**/usr/bin/which**). Without any options which does not locate aliases, functions, and shell builtins, because these do not appear in **PATH** (the tcsh and zsh which builtins locate aliases, functions, and shell builtins).

Examples   The first example quotes the first letter of the command (**\which**) to prevent the shell from invoking the alias (page 603) for which:

```
$ \which vim dir which
/usr/bin/vim
/usr/bin/dir
/usr/bin/which
```

The next example is the same as the first but uses the alias for which (which it displays):

```
$ which vim dir which
alias which='alias | /usr/bin/which --tty-only --read-alias --show-dot --show-tilde'
/usr/bin/which
/usr/bin/vim
/usr/bin/dir
```

The final example is the same as the previous one but is given from tcsh. This time the which builtin [tcsh zsh] is used instead of the which utility.

```
tcsh $ which vim dir which
/usr/bin/vim
/usr/bin/dir
which: shell built-in command.
```

who

Displays names of users

*who [**options**]*
who am i

The who utility displays the names of users currently logged in, their terminal device numbers, the times they logged in, and, if applicable, the corresponding remote hostname or X display.

Arguments

When given two arguments (traditionally, **am i**), who displays information about the user giving the command. If applicable, the user's login name is preceded by the hostname of the system running who (as in **kudos!alex**).

Options

--count –q **quick** Lists the user names only, followed by the number of users logged in on the system.

--heading –H Displays a header.

--idle –i **idle** Includes each user's idle time in the display. If there has been input at the user's terminal in the past minute, who puts a period (**.**) in this field. If there has been no input at the terminal for more than one day, who displays the string **old**.

–m Equivalent to giving two arguments.

--message *or* –T Appends after each user's login name a character that shows whether that user
--mesg has messages enabled. A plus (**+**) means that messages are enabled, a hyphen (**–**) means they are disabled, and a question mark (**?**) indicates that it cannot find the device. If messages are enabled, you can use write to communicate with the user. Refer to "**mesg**: Denies or Accepts Messages" on page 87.

Discussion

The syntax of the line that who displays is

user [messages] line login-time [idle] from

The *user* is the login name of the user. The *messages* indicates whether messages are enabled or disabled (see the **--message** option). The *line* is the device name associated with the line the user is logged in on. The *login-time* is the date and time that the user logged in. The *idle* is the length of time since the terminal was last used (the *idle time*—see the --**idle** option). The *from* is the remote machine or X display that the user is logged in from (blank for local users).

Notes

The finger utility (page 1171) provides information similar to the information who provides.

Examples

The following examples demonstrate the use of the who utility:

```
$ who
hls        tty1      Jul 30 06:01
jenny      tty2      Jul 30 06:02
alex       ttyp3     Jul 30 14:56 (bravo)

$ who am i
bravo!alex      ttyp3     Jul 30 14:56 (bravo)

$ who --heading --idle -T
USER      MESG LINE      LOGIN-TIME    IDLE   FROM
hls        -   tty1      Jul 30 06:01 03:53
jenny      +   tty2      Jul 30 06:02 14:47
alex       +   ttyp3     Jul 30 14:56   .    (bravo)
```

xargs

Converts standard output of one command into arguments for another

*xargs [**options**] [**command**]*

The xargs utility is a convenient, efficient way to convert standard output of one command into arguments for another command. This utility reads from standard input, keeps track of the maximum allowable length of a command line, and avoids exceeding that limit by repeating *command* as necessary.

Arguments

You can give xargs a command line as the argument *command*. If any arguments to *command* should precede the arguments from standard input, they must be included as part of *command*. By default xargs assumes that standard input is to be appended to *command* to form a complete command line. If you omit *command*, it defaults to echo.

Options

--interactive –p Prompts the user prior to each execution of *command*.

--max–args=*maxargs*

–n *maxargs* Executes *command* once for every *maxargs* arguments in the input line.

--max–lines[=*maxlines*]

–l[*maxlines*] Executes *command* once for every *maxlines* of input. If *maxlines* is omitted, it defaults to 1.

--max–procs=*maxprocs*

–P *maxprocs* Allows xargs to run up to *maxprocs* instances of *command* simultaneously. (The default is to run them sequentially.) May improve the throughput if you are running GNU/Linux on a multiprocessor computer.

--no–run–if–empty –r Ordinarily xargs executes *command* at least once, even if only blanks are in standard input. This option tells xargs not to execute *command* if standard input is empty.

--replace[=*marker*] –i[*marker*] Allows you to place arguments from standard input anywhere within *command*. All occurrences of *marker* in *command* for xargs are replaced by the arguments generated from standard input of xargs. If you omit *marker*, it defaults to the string {}, which matches the syntax used in the find command's **–exec** option. With this option *command* is executed for each input line. The option **--max–lines** is ignored when you use **--replace**.

Discussion

The xargs utility reads arguments to *command* from standard input, interpreting each whitespace-delimited string as a separate argument. The xargs utility constructs a command line from *command* and a series of arguments. When the maximum command line length would be exceeded by adding another argument, xargs runs the command line it has built. If there is more input, xargs repeats the process of building a command line and running it. This process continues until all the input has been read.

Notes

The most common use of xargs is as an efficient alternative to using the **–exec** option of find (refer to "–exec command \;" on page 1167). If you call find with the **–exec** option to run a command, it runs each command individually, once for each file that is processed. This is often inefficient, as every execution of a command requires the creation of a new process. By accumulating as many arguments as possible, xargs can greatly reduce the number of processes needed. The first example following shows how to use xargs with find.

Using xargs is safer than using command substitution—the $(**command**) ^{bash} ^{zsh} or ` **command** ` ^{bash tcsh zsh}. When you use command substitution to build an argument list for another command, you may exceed the command length limit imposed by GNU/Linux. When you exceed this limit, GNU/Linux issues an error message and does not run the command. As xargs avoids exceeding this limit by splitting up the list of arguments and repeating *command* as many times as necessary, you are assured that GNU/Linux will always run *command*.

The **––replace** option changes how xargs handles whitespace in standard input. Without this option xargs treats sequences of blanks, TABS, and NEWLINES as equivalent. With this option xargs treats NEWLINE characters specially. If a NEWLINE is encountered in standard input when using the **––replace** option, xargs runs *command* using the argument list that has been built up to that point.

Examples

If you want to locate and remove all the files whose names end in .o from the working directory and its subdirectories, you can do so with the **–exec** option of find:

```
$ find . -name \*.o -exec rm --force {} \;
```

This approach calls the rm utility once for each .o file that find locates. Each invocation of rm requires a new process. If there are a lot of .o files, a significant amount of time is spent creating, starting, and then cleaning up these processes. You can reduce the number of processes by allowing xargs to accumulate as many filenames as possible before calling rm:

```
$ find . -name \*.o -print | xargs rm --force
```

In the next example the contents of all the ***.txt** files located by find are searched for lines containing the word `login`. All the filenames that contain `login` are displayed by grep:

```
$ find . -name \*.txt -print | xargs grep -w -l login
```

The next example shows how you can use the **--replace** option to have xargs embed standard input within **command** instead of appending it to **command**. This option also causes **command** to be executed each time a NEWLINE character is encountered in standard input; the option **--max-lines** cannot be used to override this behavior:

```
$ cat names
Tom,
Dick,
and Harry
$ xargs echo "Hello, " <names
Hello, Tom, Dick, and Harry
$ xargs --replace echo "Hello {}.  Join me for lunch?" <names
Hello Tom,. Join me for lunch?
Hello Dick,. Join me for lunch?
Hello and Harry. Join me for lunch?
```

The final example uses the same input file as the previous example and also uses the options **--max-args** and **--max-lines**:

```
$ xargs echo "Hi there" < names
Hi there Tom, Dick, and Harry
$ xargs --max-args=1 echo "Hi there" < names
Hi there Tom,
Hi there Dick,
Hi there and
Hi there Harry
$ xargs --max-lines=2 echo "Hi there" < names
Hi there Tom, Dick,
Hi there and Harry
```

See pages 1322 and 1072 for more examples of the use of xargs.

PART IV
Appendixes

IN THIS APPENDIX

Regular
Expressions

A

A regular expression defines a set of one or more strings of characters. Several of the GNU/Linux utilities, including vi, emacs, grep, gawk, and sed, use regular expressions to search for and replace strings. A simple string of characters is a regular expression that defines one string of characters: itself. A more complex regular expression uses letters, numbers, and special characters to define many different strings of characters. A regular expression is said to *match* any string it defines.

This appendix describes the regular expressions used by ed, vi, emacs, grep, gawk, and sed. The regular expressions used in ambiguous file references with the shell are somewhat different and are described in Chapter 5. Chapter 15 covers additional expressions that are used by the Z Shell.

Characters

As used in this appendix, a *character* is any character *except* a NEWLINE. Most characters represent themselves within a regular expression. A *special character* is one that does not represent itself. If you need to use a special character to represent itself, refer to "Quoting Special Characters" on page 1387.

Delimiters

A character called a *delimiter* usually marks the beginning and end of a regular expression. The delimiter is always a special character for the regular expression it delimits (that is, it does not represent itself but marks the beginning and end of the expression). Although vi permits the use of other characters as a delimiter and grep does not use delimiters at all, the regular expressions in this appendix use a forward slash (/) as a delimiter. In some unambiguous cases, the second delimiter is not required. For example, you can sometimes omit the second delimiter when it would be followed immediately by RETURN.

Simple Strings

The most basic regular expression is a simple string that contains no special characters except the delimiters. A simple string matches only itself (Table A-1). In the examples in this appendix, the strings that are matched look like this.

Regular Expression	Matches	Table A-1 Examples
/ring/	ring	ring, spring, ringing, stringing
/Thursday/	Thursday	Thursday, Thursday's
/or not/	or not	or not, poor nothing

Special Characters

You can use special characters within a regular expression to cause the regular expression to match more than one string. A regular expression that includes a special character always matches the longest possible string, starting as far toward the beginning (left) of the line as possible.

Period

A period (.) matches any character (Table A-2).

Regular Expression	Matches	**Table A-2** Examples
/ .alk/	All strings consisting of a SPACE followed by any character followed by <u>alk</u>	will<u> talk</u>, may<u> balk</u>
/.ing/	All strings consisting of any character preceding <u>ing</u>	<u>sing</u> song, <u>ping</u>, before <u>inglenook</u>

Brackets

Brackets ([]) define a *character class*[1] that matches any single character within the brackets (Table A-3). If the first character following the left bracket is a caret (^), the brackets define a character class that matches any single character not within the brackets. You can use a hyphen to indicate a range of characters. Within a character class definition, backslashes and asterisks (described in the following sections) lose their special meanings. A right bracket (appearing as a member of the character class) can appear only as the first character following the left bracket. A caret is special only if it is the first character following the left bracket, and a dollar sign is special only if it is followed immediately by a right bracket.

Regular Expression	Matches	**Table A-3** Examples
/[bB]ill/	Member of the character class <u>b</u> and <u>B</u> followed by <u>ill</u>	<u>bill</u>, <u>Bill</u>, <u>bill</u>ed
/t[aeiou].k/	<u>t</u> followed by a lowercase vowel, any character, and a <u>k</u>	<u>talk</u>ative, <u>stink</u>, <u>teak</u>, <u>tank</u>er
/# [6–9]/	<u>#</u> followed by a SPACE and a member of the character class <u>6</u> through <u>9</u>	<u># 6</u>0, <u># 8</u>:, get <u># 9</u>
/[^a–zA–Z]/	Any character that is not a letter (ASCII character set only)	<u>1</u>, <u>7</u>, <u>@</u>, <u>,</u> <u>}</u>, Stop<u>!</u>

---

1. GNU documentation calls these List Operators and defines Character Class operators as expressions that match a predefined group of characters, such as all numbers. Refer to "Character Class" on page 1362 for more information.

Regular Expression	Matches	**‖ Table A-4** Examples
/ab*c/	a followed by zero or more b's followed by a c	ac, abc, abbc, debbcaabbbc
/ab.*c/	ab followed by zero or more characters followed by c	abc, abxc, ab45c, xab 756.345 x cat
/t.*ing/	t followed by zero or more characters followed by ing	thing, ting, I thought of going
/[a–zA–Z]*/	A string composed only of letters and SPACEs	1. any string without numbers or punctuation!
/(.*)/	As long a string as possible between (and)	Get (this) and (that);
/([^)]*)/	The shortest string possible that starts with (and ends with)	(this), Get (this and that)

Asterisk

An asterisk can follow a regular expression that represents a single character (Table A-4). The asterisk represents *zero* or more occurrences of a match of the regular expression. An asterisk following a period matches any string of characters. (A period matches any character, and an asterisk matches zero or more occurrences of the preceding regular expression.) A character class definition followed by an asterisk matches any string of characters that are members of the character class.

Regular Expression	Matches	**‖ Table A-5** Examples
/^T/	A T at the beginning of a line	This line..., That Time..., In Time
/^+[0–9]/	A plus sign followed by a digit at the beginning of a line	+5 +45.72, +759 Keep this...
/:$/	A colon that ends a line	...below:

Caret and Dollar Sign

A regular expression that begins with a caret (^) can match a string only at the beginning of a line. In a similar manner a dollar sign at the end of a regular expression matches the end of a line. The caret and dollar sign are called anchors because they force (anchor) a match to the beginning or end of a line (Table A-5).

Quoting Special Characters

You can quote any special character (but not a digit or a parenthesis) by preceding it with a backslash (Table A-6). Quoting a special character makes it represent itself.

Regular Expression	Matches	Table A-6 Examples
/end\./	All strings that contain <u>end</u> followed by a period	The <u>end.</u>, <u>send.</u>, pr<u>etend.</u>mail
/ \\/	A single backslash	\
/ */	An asterisk	<u>*</u>.c, an asterisk (<u>*</u>)
/ \[5\]/	<u>[5]</u>	it was five <u>[5]</u>
/and \/or/	<u>and/or</u>	<u>and/or</u>

Rules

The following rules govern the application of regular expressions.

Longest Match Possible

As stated previously, a regular expression always matches the longest possible string, starting as far toward the beginning of the line as possible. For example, given the following string,

```
This (rug) is not what it once was (a long time ago), is it?
```

the expression /Th.*is/ matches

```
This (rug) is not what it once was (a long time ago), is
```

and /(.*)/ matches

> (rug) is not what it once was (a long time ago)

However, /([^)]*)/ matches

> (rug)

> Given the following string,

> singing songs, singing more and more

the expression /s.*ing/ matches

> singing songs, singing

and /s.*ing song/ matches

> singing song

Empty Regular Expressions

Within some utilities, such as vi and less, but not grep, an empty regular expression represents the last regular expression that you used. For example, if you give vi the following Substitute command:

> :s/mike/robert/

and then want to make the same substitution again, you can use the following command:

> :s//robert/

Alternatively, you can use the following commands to search for the string mike and then make the substitution

> /mike/
> :s//robert/

The empty regular expression (//) represents the last regular expression you used (/mike/).

Bracketing Expressions

You can use quoted parentheses, \(and \), to *bracket* a regular expression. The string that the bracketed regular expression matches can be recalled, as explained in "Quoted Digit," following. A regular expression does not attempt to match quoted parentheses. Thus a regular expression enclosed within quoted parentheses matches what the same regular expression without the parentheses would match. The expression /\(rexp\)/ matches what /rexp/ would match, and /a\(b*\)c/ matches what /ab*c/ would match.

You can nest quoted parentheses. The bracketed expressions are identified only by the opening \(, so there is no ambiguity in identifying them. The expression /\([a-z]\([A-Z]*\)x\)/ consists of two bracketed expressions, one within the other. In the string 3 t dMNORx7 1 u, the preceding regular expression matches dMNORx, with the first bracketed expression matching dMNORx and the second matching MNORx.

The Replacement String

The vi and sed editors use regular expressions as search strings within Substitute commands. You can use the ampersand (&) and quoted digits (\n) special characters to represent the matched strings within the corresponding replacement string.

Ampersand

Within a replacement string, an ampersand (&) takes on the value of the string that the search string (regular expression) matched. For example, the following vi Substitute command surrounds a string of one or more digits with **NN**. The ampersand in the replacement string matches whatever string of digits the regular expression (search string) matched:

    :s/[0-9][0-9]*/NN&NN/

Two character class definitions are required because the regular expression [0–9]* matches *zero* or more occurrences of a digit, and *any* character string is zero or more occurrences of a digit.

Quoted Digit

Within the search string, a quoted regular expression, \(**xxx**\), matches what the regular expression would have matched without the quotes. Within the replacement string, a quoted digit, *n*, represents the string that the bracketed regular expression (portion of the search string) beginning with the *n*th \(matched. For example, you can take a list of people in the form

> ```
> last-name, first-name initial
> ```

and put it in the following form:

> ```
> first-name initial last-name
> ```

with the following vi command:

> ```
> :1,$s/\([^,]*\), \(.*\)/\2 \1/
> ```

This command addresses all the lines in the file (**1,$**). The Substitute command (**s**) uses a search string and a replacement string delimited by forward slashes. The first bracketed regular expression within the search string, \([^,]*\), matches what the same unbracketed regular expression, [^,]*, would match: zero or more characters not containing a comma (the **last-name**). Following the first bracketed regular expression are a comma and a SPACE that match themselves. The second bracketed expression, \(.*\), matches any string of characters (the **first-name** and **initial**).

The replacement string consists of what the second bracketed regular expression matched (**\2**) followed by a SPACE and what the first bracketed regular expression matched (**\1**).

Extended Regular Expressions

The three utilities egrep, grep when run with the **–E** option (similar to egrep), and gawk provide all the special characters that are included in ordinary regular expressions, except for \(and \), as well as several others. The vi (vim) editor includes the additional characters as well as \(and \). Patterns using the extended set of special characters are called *full regular expressions,* or *extended regular expressions.*

Two of the additional special characters are the plus sign (**+**) and question mark (**?**). They are similar to the *, which matches *zero* or more occurrences of the previous character. The plus sign matches *one* or more occurrences of the previous character, whereas the question mark matches *zero* or *one* occurrence. You can use any one of the special characters *, +, and ? following parentheses, causing the special character to apply to the string surrounded by the parentheses. Unlike the parentheses in bracketed regular expressions, these parentheses are not quoted (Table A-7).

Regular Expression	Matches	Table A-7 Examples
/ab+c/	<u>a</u> followed by one or more <u>b</u>'s followed by a <u>c</u>	y<u>abc</u>w, <u>abbc</u>57
/ab?c/	<u>a</u> followed by zero or one <u>b</u> followed by <u>c</u>	b<u>ac</u>k, <u>abc</u>def
/(ab)+c/	One or more occurrences of the string <u>ab</u> followed by <u>c</u>	z<u>abc</u>d, <u>ababc</u>!
/(ab)?c/	Zero or one occurrences of the string <u>ab</u> followed by <u>c</u>	x<u>c</u>, <u>abc</u>c

In full regular expressions, the vertical bar (I) special character is an OR operator. Within vim you must quote the vertical bar by preceding it with a backslash to make it special (\I). A vertical bar between two regular expressions causes a match with strings that match either the first expression or the second or both. You can use the vertical bar with parentheses to separate from the rest of the regular expression the two expressions that are being ORed (Table A-8).

Regular Expression	Meaning	Table A-8 Examples
/ab|ac/	Either <u>ab</u> or <u>ac</u>	<u>ab</u>, <u>ac</u>, <u>abac</u> *(abac is two matches of the regular expression)*
/^Exit|^Quit/	Lines that begin with <u>Exit</u> or <u>Quit</u>	<u>Exit</u>, Quit, No Exit
/(D|N)\. Jones/	<u>D. Jones</u> or <u>N. Jones</u>	P.<u>D. Jones</u>, <u>N. Jones</u>

Appendix Summary

A regular expression defines a set of one or more strings of characters. A regular expression is said to match any string it defines.

Special Characters

.	Matches any single character
*	Matches zero or more occurrences of a match of the preceding character
^	Forces a match to the beginning of a line
$	A match to the end of a line
\	Used to quote special characters
\<	Forces a match to the beginning of a word
\>	Forces a match to the end of a word

Character Classes and Bracketed Regular Expressions

[*xyz*]	Defines a character class that matches *x*, *y*, or *z*
[^ *xyz*]	Defines a character class that matches any character except *x*, *y*, or *z*
[*x–z*]	Defines a character class that matches any character *x* through *z* inclusive
\(*xyz*\)	Matches what *xyz* matches (a bracketed regular expression)

Extended Regular Expression

In addition to the preceding special characters and strings (excluding quoted parentheses, except in vim), the following characters are special within full, or extended, regular expressions.

+	Matches one or more occurrences of the preceding character
?	Matches zero or one occurrence of the preceding character
(*xyz*)+	One or more occurrences of what *xyz* matches
(*xyz*)?	Zero or one occurrence of what *xyz* matches
(*xyz*)✳	Zero or more occurrences of what *xyz* matches
xyz|*abc*	Either what *xyz* or what *abc* matches (use \\| in **vim**)
(*xy*|*ab*)*c*	Either what *xyc* or what *abc* matches (use \\| in **vim**)

Replacement String

Refer to page 439 for a description of regular expressions in **vim**. The following characters are special within a replacement string in **sed** and **vim**.

&	Represents what the regular expression (search string) matched
n	A quoted number, *n*, represents what the *n*th bracketed regular expression in the search string matched

IN THIS APPENDIX

Help

You need not act as a Red Hat user or administrator in isolation; a large community of GNU/Linux/Red Hat experts is willing to assist you in learning about, helping you solve your problems with, and getting the most out of your GNU/Linux system. Before you ask for help, make sure that you have done everything you can do to solve the problem by yourself. No doubt, someone has had the same problem before you and the answer to your question is written down somewhere on the Internet. Your job is to find it. This appendix lists resources and describes methods that can help you in that task.

Solving a Problem

Following is a list of steps that can help you solve a problem without asking someone else for help. Depending on your understanding of and experience with the hardware and software involved, these steps may lead you to a solution.

1. Red Hat Linux comes with extensive documentation (page 42). Read the documentation on the specific hardware/software you are having a problem with. If it is a GNU product, use info; otherwise use man to find local information.

2. When the problem involves some type of error or other message, use a search engine, such as Google (www.google.com) or Google Groups (groups.google.com), to look up the message on the Internet. If the message is long, pick a unique part of the message to search for; 10 to 20

characters should be enough. Always enclose the search string within double quotation marks.

3. Check whether the Linux Documentation Project home page (www.tldp.org) has a HOWTO or mini-HOWTO on the subject in question. Search on keywords that relate directly to the product and your problem. Read the FAQs.

4. See Table B-1 on page 1397 for other sources of documentation.

5. Use Google or Google Groups to search on keywords that relate directly to the product and your problem.

6. When all else fails, or perhaps before you try anything else, look at the system logs in **/var/log**. Running as Superuser, first look at the end of the **messages** file using the following command:

```
# tail -20 /var/log/messages
```

If **messages** contains nothing useful, run the following command, which displays the most recent log files at the bottom of the list:

```
$ ls -ltr /var/log
```

If your problem involves a network connection, look at the **secure** log file on the local and remote machines. Also look at **messages** on the remote machine.

7. The **/var/spool** directory contains subdirectories with useful information: **lpd** holds the print queues, **mail** holds the user's mail files, and so on.

If you are unable to solve a problem yourself, a well-thought-out question to an appropriate newsgroup (page 1399) or mailing list (page 1399) can elicit useful information. When you send or post a question, make sure that you describe the problem and identify your system carefully. Include the version numbers of Red Hat and any software packages you think relate to the problem. Describe your hardware, if appropriate. For a fee, Red Hat provides many different types of support. Refer to www.redhat.com/apps/support/programs.html.

The author's home page (www.sobell.com) contains an up-to-date version of the tables in this appendix, corrections to this book, as well as pointers to many other GNU/Linux sites.

Finding GNU/Linux-Related Information

Distributions of GNU/Linux come with reference pages stored online. You can read these documents by using the info, man, or xman utilities (page 42). You can read man and info pages to get more information about specific topics while reading this book or to determine what features are available with GNU/Linux. You can search for topics by using apropos (see page 79 or give the command **man apropos**).

Documentation

Good books are available on various aspects of using and administrating UNIX systems in general and GNU/Linux systems in particular. In addition, you may find the sites listed in Table B-1useful.[1]

Site Name	What It Does	Table B-1 Finding Documentation
FAQ Archives	FAQ archives.	tldp.org/FAQ/Linux-FAQ
GNU Manuals Online	GNU manuals.	www.gnu.org/manual
Internet FAQ Archives	Searchable FAQ archives.	www.faqs.org
Info	Instructions for using the info utility.	www.gnu.org/manual/info/html_mono/info.html
Red Hat Documentation and Support	This site has a search engine that looks through the Red Hat Knowledgebase to help answer your questions. The site also has links to online documentation for Red Hat products, and a section named Quickhelp that links to common topics of interest.	www.redhat.com/apps/support
RFCs	Request for Comments; see *RFC (continued)* (page 1490). Download **rfc-index** for a list of RFCs.	ftp://ftp.uu.net/inet/rfc
System Administrators Guild (SAGE)	SAGE is a group for system administrators. Click on **Resources for SysAdmins** or follow the system administrator *Web ring* (page 1501).	www.sage.com

---

1. The right-hand columns of most of the tables in this appendix show Internet addresses (URLs). All sites have an implicit http:// prefix unless ftp:// or https:// is shown. Refer to "URLs (Web Addresses)" on page 27.

Site Name	What It Does	Table B-1 Finding Documentation (Continued)
The Linux Documentation Project	All things related to GNU/Linux documentation (in many languages): HOWTOs, guides, FAQs, man pages, and magazines. This is the best overall source for GNU/Linux documentation. Make sure to visit their Links page.	www.tldp.org www.tldp.org/linkswww.tldp.org/FAQ/Linux-FAQ
Woven Goods for Linux	The usual along with e-zines, books, journals, standards, and logos. In English and German.	www.fokus.gmd.de/linux/linux-doc.html

Useful GNU/Linux Sites

Sometimes the sites listed in Table B-2 are so busy that you cannot log in. When this happens, you are usually given a list of alternative, or *mirror*, sites to try. For a more current list of sites that have GNU/Linux-related information, use a browser to visit www.sobell.com.

Site Name	What It Does	Table B-2 Finding Miscellaneous
GNU	GNU Project web server.	www.gnu.org
ibiblio	A large library and digital archive. Formerly Metalab, formerly Sunsite.	www.ibiblio.org www.ibiblio.org/pub/Linux www.ibiblio.org/pub/historic-linux
Linux Knowledge Portal	A configurable site that gathers information from other sites and sources and presents it in a well-organized format. Sources include KDE News, GNOME News, slashdot, and many more. In English and German.	www.linux-knowledge-portal.org
Linux Standard Base (LSB)	A group dedicated to standardizing GNU/Linux	www.linuxbase.org
Sobell	The author's home page contains useful links, errata for this book, code for many of the examples in this book, and so on.	www.sobell.com

Site Name	What It Does	Table B-2 Finding Miscellaneous (Continued)
USENIX	A large, well-established UNIX group. This site has many links, including a list of conferences.	www.usenix.org
X.Org	The X Window System home. Click **Download** for software.	www.x.org

GNU/Linux Newsgroups

One of the best ways of getting specific information is through a newsgroup (pages 401 and 405). Frequently you can find the answer to your question just by reading postings to the newsgroup. Try using Google Groups to search through newsgroups (groups.google.com) to see whether your question has already been asked and answered. Or open a newsreader program and subscribe to appropriate newsgroups. If necessary, you can post your question for someone to answer. Before you post it, make sure that your question has not been answered Refer to "Usenet" on page 399 and "Tutorial: Using pine as a Newsreader" on page 401.

The newsgroup `comp.os.linux.answers` contains postings of solutions to common problems and periodic postings of the most up-to-date versions of the FAQ and HOWTO documents. The `comp.os.linux.misc` newsgroup has answers to miscellaneous GNU/Linux-related questions.

Mailing Lists

Subscribing to a mailing list (page 372) allows you to participate in an electronic discussion. With most lists, you can send and receive e-mail dedicated to a specific topic to and from a group of users. Moderated lists do not tend to stray as much as unmoderated lists, assuming that the list has a good moderator. The disadvantage of a moderated list is that some discussions may be cut off when they get interesting if the moderator deems that the discussion has gone on for too long. Mailing lists described as bulletins are strictly unidirectional: You cannot post information to these lists but can only receive periodic bulletins. If you have the subscription address for a mailing list but are not sure how to subscribe, put the word `help` in the body and/or header of e-mail that you send to the address. You will usually receive instructions via return e-mail. Red Hat hosts several mailing lists; go to www.redhat.com/mailing-lists for more information. You can also use a search engine to search for `mailing list linux`.

Words

Many dictionaries, thesauruses, and glossaries are online. Table B-3 lists a few of them.

Site Name	What It Does	Table B-3 Looking Up Words
ARTFL Project: ROGET'S Thesaurus	Thesaurus	humanities.uchicago.edu/forms_unrest/ROGET.html
Dictionary.com	Everything related to words	www.dictionary.com
DNS Glossary	DNS Glossary	www.menandmice.com/online_docs_and_faq/glossary/glossarytoc.htm?dynamic.ip.address.htm
FOLDOC (The Free On-line Dictionary of Computing)	Computer terms	foldoc.doc.ic.ac.uk/foldoc
Merriam-Webster	English language	www.m-w.com
OneLook	Multiple-site word search with a single query	www.onelook.com
The Jargon File	An online version of *The New Hacker's Dictionary*	www.tuxedo.org/~esr/jargon
Webopedia	Commercial technical dictionary	www.webopedia.com
Wordsmyth	Dictionary and thesaurus	www.wordsmyth.net
Yahoo Reference	Search multiple sources at the same time	education.yahoo.com/reference

Programs

There are many ways to learn of interesting software packages and where they are available on the Internet. Table B-4 list many sites that you can download software from. For security-related programs refer to Table C-1 on page 1421. Another way to learn about software packages is through a newsgroup (page 1399).

Site Name	What It Does	**‖ Table B-4** **Finding Programs**
Free Software Directory	Categorized, searchable lists of free software.	www.gnu.org/directory savannah.gnu.org
freshmeat	A large index of UNIX and cross-platform software, themes, and Palm OS software	freshmeat.net
IceWALKERS	Categorized, searchable lists of free software	www.icewalkers.com
Linux Software Map	A database of packages written for, ported to, or compiled for Linux	www.boutell.com/lsm
linuxapps	Categorized, searchable list of free software	www.linuxapps.com
Network Calculators	Subnet mask calculator and more	www.telusplanet.net/public/sparkman/netcalc.htm
rpmfind.net	Searchable list of **rpm** files for various GNU/Linux distributions and versions	rpmfind.net/linux/RPM
SourceForge	A development website with a large repository of Open Source code and applications	sourceforge.net
Tucows-Linux	Commercial, categorized, searchable list of free software	linux.tucows.com

Office Suites and Word Processors

Several office suites and many word processors are available for GNU/Linux. Table B-5 lists a few of them. If you are exchanging documents with people using MS Windows make sure the import from/export to MS Word functionality covers your needs.

Product Name	What It Does	**‖ Table B-5** **Finding Word Processors**
AbiWord	Word processor (free)	www.abisource.com
Applixware Office	Integrated suite of office applications including the Words word processing program (commercial)	www.vistasource.com/products/axware

Product Name	What It Does	**Table B-5** **Finding Word Processors (Continued)**
KOffice	Integrated suite of office applications including the Kword word processing program (free, KDE based)	www.koffice.org
OpenOffice	An open source version of StarOffice	www.openoffice.org
WordPerfect	A port of the popular MS Windows word processor to GNU/Linux (commercial)	linux.corel.com/products/wpo2000_linux
Xcoral	A programmer's multiwindow mouse-based editor that runs under X (free)	xcoral.free.fr

Specifying Your Terminal

Because vi, emacs, konsole, and other programs take advantage of features that are specific to various kinds of terminals and terminal emulators, you must tell these programs the name of the terminal you are using or the terminal that your terminal emulator is emulating. On many systems your terminal name is set for you. If your terminal name is not specified or is not specified correctly, your screen will look strange, or, when you start a program, you will get a message that requires this information: You need to specify your terminal name.

Terminal names describe the functional characteristics of your terminal or terminal emulator to programs that require this information. Although terminal names are referred to as either Terminfo or Termcap names, the difference is in the method the two systems use to store the terminal characteristics internally, not in the manner that you specify the name of your terminal. Terminal names that are often used with GNU/Linux terminal emulators and with graphical monitors while they are run in text mode are **ansi**, **linux**, **vt100**, **vt102**, **vt220**, and **xterm**.

When you are running a terminal emulator, you can specify the type of terminal you want to emulate. Set the emulator to either **vt100** or **vt220** and set **TERM** to the same value (following).

When you log in, you may be prompted to identify the type of terminal you are using:

```
TERM = (vt100)
```

There are two ways to respond to this prompt: You can press RETURN to set your terminal type to the name in parentheses. When that name does not describe the terminal you are using, you can enter the correct name before you press RETURN:

```
TERM = (vt100) ansi
```

You can also receive the following prompt:

```
TERM = (unknown)
```

This prompt indicates that the system does not know what type of terminal you are using. If you are going to be running programs that require this information, enter the name of your terminal or terminal emulator before you press RETURN.

If you do not receive a prompt, you can give the following command to check whether your terminal type has been set:

```
$ echo $TERM
```

If the system responds with the wrong name, a blank line, or an error message, set or change the terminal name. If you are using the Bourne Again or Z Shell, enter a command similar to the following to identify the type of terminal you are using:

export TERM=name

Replace **name** with the terminal name for your terminal, making sure that you do not put a SPACE before or after the equal sign. If you always use the same type of terminal, you can place this command in your **.profile** file. This causes the shell to set the terminal type each time you log in (page 109).

For example, give the following command to set your terminal name to **vt100**:

```
$ export TERM=vt100
```

The TC Shell requires the following command syntax:

setenv TERM name

When the automatic terminal determination fails, you can place a command with this syntax in your **.login** file for automatic execution.

IN THIS APPENDIX

Security

Security is a major part of the foundation of any system that is not totally cut off from other machines and users. Some aspects of security have a place even on isolated machines. Examples are periodic system backups, BIOS or power-on passwords, and self-locking screensavers.

A system that is connected to the outside world requires other mechanisms to secure it: tools to check files (tripwire), audit tools (tiger/cops), secure access methods (kerberos/ssh), services that monitor logs and machine states (swatch/watcher), packet-filtering and routing tools (ipfwadm/iptables/ipchains), and more.

System security has many dimensions. The security of your system as a whole depends on the security of individual components, such as your e-mail, files, network, login and remote access policies, as well as the physical security of the host itself. These dimensions frequently overlap, and their borders are not always static or clear. For instance, e-mail security is affected by the security of files and your network. If the medium (the network) over which you send and receive your e-mail is not secure, you must take extra steps to ensure the security of your messages. If you save your secure e-mail into a file on your local system, you rely on the filesystem and host access policies for file security. A failure in any one of these areas can start a domino effect, diminishing reliability and integrity in other areas and potentially compromising system security as a whole.

This short appendix cannot cover all the facets of system security but does provide an overview of the complexity of setting up and maintaining a secure system. This appendix provides some specifics, concepts, guidelines to consider, and many pointers to security resources (Table C-1 on page 1421).

> ### Other Sources of System Security Information ▐▐ security
>
> Depending on how important system security is to you, you may want to purchase one or more of the books dedicated to system security, read from some of the Internet sites that are dedicated to security, or hire someone who is an expert in the field.
>   *Do not rely on this appendix as your sole source of information on system security.*

Encryption

One of the building blocks of security is encryption, which provides a means of scrambling data for secure transmission to other parties. In cryptographic terms, the data or message to be encrypted is referred to as *plaintext,* and the resulting encrypted block of text as *ciphertext.* A number of processes exist for converting plaintext into ciphertext through the use of *keys,* which are essentially random numbers of a specified length used to *lock* and *unlock* data. This conversion is achieved by applying the keys to the plaintext by following a set of mathematical instructions, referred to as the *encryption algorithm.*

Developing and analyzing strong encryption software is extremely difficult. There are many nuances and standards governing encryption algorithms, and a background in mathematics is requisite. Also, unless an algorithm has undergone public scrutiny for a significant period of time, it is generally not considered secure; it is often impossible to know that an algorithm is completely secure but possible to know that one is not secure. Time is the best test of an algorithm. Also, a solid algorithm does not guarantee an effective encryption mechanism, as the fallibility of an encryption scheme frequently lies in problems with implementation and distribution.

An encryption algorithm uses a key that is a certain number of bits long. Each bit you add to the length of a key effectively doubles the *key space* (the number of combinations allowed by the number of bits in the key—2 to the power of the length of the key in bits[1]) and means that it will take twice as long for an attacker to decrypt your message (assuming that there are no inherent weaknesses or vulnerabilities to exploit in the scheme). However, it is a mistake to compare algorithms based only on the number of bits used. An algorithm that uses a 64-bit key can be more secure than an algorithm that uses a 128-bit key.

---

1. A 2-bit key would have a key space of 4 (2^2), a 3-bit key would have a key space of 8 (2^3), and so on.

The two primary classifications of encryption schemes are *public key encryption* and *symmetric key encryption*. Public key encryption, also called *asymmetric encryption,* uses two keys: a public key and a private key; these keys are uniquely associated with a specific individual user. Symmetric key encryption, also called *symmetric encryption,* or *secret key encryption,* uses one key that you and the person you are communicating with (hereafter, referred to as your *friend*) share as a secret. Public key algorithm keys typically have a length of 512 bits to 2,048 bits, whereas symmetric key algorithms use keys in the range of 64 bits to 512 bits.

When you are choosing an encryption scheme, realize that security comes at a price. There is usually a trade-off between resilience of the cryptosystem and ease of administration.

Hard to Break? Hard to Use! || security

The more difficult an algorithm is to crack, the more difficult it is to maintain and to get people to use properly. The paramount limitations of most respectable cryptosystems lie not in weak algorithms but rather in users' failure to transmit and store keys in a secure manner.

The practicality of a security solution is a far greater factor in encryption, and in security in general, than most people realize. With enough time and effort, nearly every algorithm can be broken. In fact, you can often unearth the mathematical instructions for a widely used algorithm by flipping through a cryptography book, reviewing a vendor's product specifications, or performing a quick search on the Internet. The challenge is to ensure that the effort required to follow the twists and turns taken by an encryption algorithm and its resulting encryption solution outweighs the worth of the information it is protecting.

How Much Time and Money Should You Spend on Encryption? || tip

When the cost of obtaining the information exceeds the value realized by its possession, the solution is an effective one.

Public Key Encryption

In order to use public key encryption, you must generate two keys: a public key and a private key. You keep the private key for yourself and give the public key to the world. In a similar manner your friends will generate a pair of keys and give you their public keys. Public key encryption is marked by two distinct features.

1. When you encrypt data with someone's public key, only that person's private key can decrypt it.

2. When you encrypt data with your private key, anyone else can decrypt it with your public key.

You may wonder why the second point is useful at all: Why would you want everybody else to be able to decrypt something you just encrypted? The answer lies in the purpose of the encryption. Although encryption changes the original message into unreadable ciphertext, the purpose of this encryption is to provide a *digital signature*. If the message decrypts properly with your public key, *only you* could have encrypted it with your private key, proving that the message is authentic. Combining these two modes of operation yields privacy and authenticity. You can sign something with your private key so that it is verified as authentic, and then you can encrypt it with your friend's public key so that only your friend can decrypt it.

Public key encryption has three major shortcomings.

1. Public key encryption algorithms are generally much slower than symmetric key algorithms and usually require a much larger key size and a way to generate large prime numbers to use as components of the key, making them more resource intensive.

2. The private key must be stored securely and its integrity safeguarded. If a person's private key is obtained by another party, that party can encrypt, decrypt, and sign messages impersonating the original owner of the key. If the private key is lost or becomes corrupted, any messages previously encrypted with it are also lost, and a new keypair must be generated.

3. It is difficult to authenticate the origin of a key, that is, to prove who it originally came from. This is known as the key-distribution problem and is the raison d'être for such companies as VeriSign (www.verisign.com).

Algorithms such as RSA, Diffie-Hellman, and El-Gamal implement public key encryption methodology. Today a 512-bit key is considered barely adequate for RSA encryption and offers marginal protection; 1,024-bit keys are expected to withhold determined attackers for several more years. Keys that are 2,048 bits long are now becoming commonplace and rated as *espionage strength*. A mathematical paper published in late 2001 and reexamined in the spring of 2002 describes how a machine can be built—for a very large sum of money—that could break 1,024-bit RSA encryption in seconds to minutes (www.counterpane.com/crypto-gram-0203.html#6). Although the cost of such a machine is beyond the reach of most individuals and smaller corporations, it is well within the reach of large corporations and governments.

Symmetric Key Encryption

Symmetric key encryption is generally fast and simple to deploy. First, you and your friend agree on which algorithm to use and a key that you will share. Then either of you can decrypt or encrypt a file with the same key. Behind the scenes, symmetric key encryption algorithms are most often implemented as a network of black boxes, which can involve hardware components, software, or a combination of the two. Each box imposes a reversible transformation on the plaintext and passes it on to the next box, where another reversible transformation further alters the data. The security of a symmetric key algorithm relies on the difficulty of determining which boxes were used and the number of times the data was fed through the set of boxes. A good algorithm will cycle the plaintext through a given set of boxes many times before yielding the result, and there will be no obvious mapping from plaintext to ciphertext.

The disadvantage of symmetric key encryption is that it depends heavily on a secure channel to send the key to your friend. For example, you would not use e-mail to send your key; if your e-mail is intercepted, a third party is in possession of your secret key, and your encryption is useless. You could relay the key over the phone, but your call could be intercepted if your phone were tapped or someone overheard your conversation.

Common implementations of symmetric key algorithms are DES (Data Encryption Standard), 3-DES (triple DES), IDEA, RC5, Blowfish, and AES (Advanced Encryption Standard). AES is the new Federal Information Processing Standard (FIPS-197) algorithm endorsed for governmental use and chosen to replace DES as the de facto encryption algorithm. AES uses the Rijndael algorithm (www.rijndael.com), chosen after a thorough evaluation of 15 candidate algorithms by the cryptographic research community.

None of the aforementioned algorithms has undergone more scrutiny than DES, which has been in use since the late 1970s. However, the use of DES has drawbacks, and it is no longer considered secure, as the weakness of its 56-bit key makes it unreasonably easy to break. With advances in computing power and speed since DES was developed, the small size of its key renders it inadequate for operations requiring more than basic security for a relatively short period of time. For a few thousand U.S. dollars, you can link off-the-shelf computer systems so that they can crack DES keys in a few hours.

The 3-DES application of DES is intended to combat its degenerating resilience by running the encryption three times; it is projected to be secure for years to come. DES is probably sufficient for such tasks as sending e-mail to a friend when you need it to be confidential, or secure, for only a few days (for example, to send a notice of a meeting that will take place in a few hours). It is unlikely that anyone is sufficiently interested in your e-mail to invest the time and money to decrypt it. Because of 3-DES's wide availability and ease of use, it is advisable to use it instead of DES.

Encryption Implementation

In practice, most commercial software packages use both public and symmetric key encryption algorithms, taking advantage of the strengths of each and avoiding the weaknesses. The public key algorithm is used first, as a means of negotiating a randomly generated secret key and providing for message authenticity. Then a secret key algorithm, such as 3-DES, IDEA, AES, or Blowfish, encrypts and decrypts the data on both ends for speed. Finally, a hash algorithm, such as DSA (Digital Signature Algorithm), generates a message digest that provides a signature that can alert you to tampering. The digest is digitally signed with the sender's private key.

GnuPG/PGP

The most popular personal encryption packages available today are GnuPG (GNU Privacy Guard—www.gnupg.org, see page 1030) and PGP (Pretty Good Privacy—www.pgp.com). GNU Privacy Guard was designed as a free replacement for PGP, a security tool that made its debut during the early 1990s. Phil Zimmerman developed PGP as a Public Key Infrastructure (PKI) featuring a convenient interface, ease of use and management, and the security of digital certificates. One critical characteristic set PGP apart from the majority of cryptosystems then available: PGP functions entirely without certification authorities (CA). Until the introduction of PGP, PKI implementations were built around the concept of CAs and centralized key management controls.

PGP and GnuPG use the notion of a ring of trust:[2] If you trust someone and that person trusts someone else, the person you trust can provide an introduction to the third party. When you trust someone, you perform an operation called *key signing*. By signing someone else's key, you are verifying that that person's public key is authentic and safe for you to use to send e-mail. When you sign a key, you are asked whether you trust this person to introduce other keys to you. It is common practice to assign this trust based on several criteria, including your knowledge of a person's character or a lasting professional relationship with the person. The best practice is to sign someone's key only after you have met face to face to avert any chance of a person-in-the-middle[3] scenario. The disadvantage of this scheme is the lack of a central registry for associating with people you do not already know.

---

2. For more information, see the section of *The GNU Privacy Handbook* (www.gnupg.org/docs.html) titled "Validating Other Keys on Your Public Keyring."

3. Person in the middle: If Alex and Jenny try to carry on a secure e-mail exchange over a network, Alex first sends Jenny his public key. However, suppose that Mr. X sits between Alex and Jenny on the network and intercepts Alex's public key. Mr. X then sends *his own* public key to Jenny. Jenny then sends her public key to Alex, but once again Mr. X intercepts it and substitutes *his* public key and sends that to Alex. Without some kind of active protection (a piece of shared information), Mr. X, the *person in the middle*, can decrypt all traffic between Alex and Jenny, reencrypt it, and send it on to the other party.

PGP is available without cost for personal use,[4] but its deployment in a commercial environment requires you to purchase a license. This was not always the case: Soon after its introduction, PGP was available on many bulletin board systems, and users could implement it in any manner they chose. PGP rapidly gained popularity in the networking community, which capitalized on its encryption and key management capabilities for secure transmission of e-mail.

After a time, attention turned to the two robust cryptographic algorithms RSA and IDEA, which are an integral part of PGP's code. These algorithms are privately owned. The wide distribution and growing user base of PGP sparked battles over patent violation and licenses, resulting in the eventual restriction of PGP's use.

Enter GnuPG, which supports most of the features and implementations made available by PGP and complies with the OpenPGP Message Format standard. Because GnuPG does not use the patented IDEA algorithm but uses BUGS (www.gnu.org/directory/bugs.html) instead, you can use it almost without restriction: It is released under the GNU GPL (refer to "The Code Is Free" on page 6). The two tools are considered to be interchangeable and interoperable. The command sequences for and internal workings of PGP and GnuPG are very similar.

> ### The GnuPG System Includes the gpg Program   ‖ tip
>
> GnuPG is frequently referred to as **gpg**, but **gpg** is actually the main program for the GnuPG system. See page 1030 for an example of how to use **gpg**.

GNU has a good introduction to privacy, *The GNU Privacy Handbook*, available in several languages listed at www.gnupg.org/docs.html. Listed on the same Web page is the *Gnu Privacy Guard (GnuPG) Mini Howto*, which steps through the setup and use of **gpg**. And, of course, there is a **gpg** info page.

File Security

From an end user's perspective, file security is one of the most critical areas of security. Some file security is built into GNU/Linux: chmod (pages 119 and 1103) gives you basic security control. ACLs (Access Control Lists) allow more fine-grained control of file access permissions. ACLs are part of Solaris, Windows NT/2000/XP, VAX/VMS, and mainframes OSs. Red Hat 8.0 includes the getfacl and setfacl utilities

---

4. Download the free version of PGP by following the menu at for PGP and then for UNIX; you will eventually get to a Red Hat rpm file that you can download.

but does not activate ACLs in the kernel. Refer to the **acl** man page for more information. Even these tools are insufficient when your account is compromised (for example, by someone watching your fingers on the keyboard as you type your password). To provide maximum file security, you must encrypt your files. Then even someone who knows your password cannot read your files. (Of course, if someone knows your key, that person can decrypt your files if he or she can get to them.)

E-mail Security

E-mail security overlaps file security and, as discussed later, network security. GnuPG is the most frequently used tool for e-mail security, although you can also use PGP. PEM (Privacy Enhanced Mail) is a standard rather than an algorithm and is used less frequently.

MTAs (Mail Transfer Agents)

MTA Increasingly commonplace is STARTTLS (Start Transport Layer Security—www.sendmail.org/~ca/email/starttls.html). TLS itself usually refers to SSL (Secure Socket Layer) and has become the de facto method for encrypting TCP/IP traffic on the Internet. The sendmail utility can be built to support STARTTLS, and much documentation exists on how to do so. STARTTLS enhancements also exist for qmail and postfix and other popular MTAs. It is important to note that this capability provides encryption between two mail servers but not necessarily between your machine and the mail server.

MUAs (Mail User Agents)

Many popular mail user agents, such as pine, mutt, elm, and emacs, include the ability to use PGP or GnuPG for encryption. This has become the default way to exchange secure e-mail.

Network Security

Network security is vital to the security of a computing site. However, without the right infrastructure, providing network security is difficult, if not impossible. For example, if you run a shared network topology,[5] such as Ethernet, and have in public

---

5. Shared network topology: A network in which each packet may be seen by machines other than its destination. "Shared" means that the 100 megabits per second bandwidth is shared by all users.

locations jacks that allow anyone to plug in to the network at will, how can you prevent someone from plugging in a machine and capturing all the *packets* (page 1483) that traverse the network?[6] You cannot, so you have a potential security hole. Another common security hole is the use of telnet for logins. Because telnet sends and receives cleartext, anyone "listening in" on the line can easily capture login names and passwords, compromising security.

Do not allow unauthenticated PCs (any PC that does not require users to supply a local name and password) on your network. With a Windows 9x PC, any user on the network is effectively Superuser for the following reasons:

- On a PC there is no concept of **root**; all users, by default, have access to and can watch the network, capture packets, and send packets.

- On UNIX/Linux only Superuser can put the network interface in promiscuous mode and collect packets. On UNIX and GNU/Linux, ports numbered less than 1,024[7] are privileged. That is, normal user protocols cannot bind to these ports. This is an important but regrettable means of security for some protocols, such as NIS, NFS, RSH, and LPD. Normally a data switch on your LAN automatically protects your machines from people snooping on your network for data. In high-load situations switches have been known to behave unpredictably, directing packets to the wrong ports. There are programs that can overload the switch tables that hold information about which machine is on which port. When these tables are overloaded, the switch becomes a repeater and broadcasts all packets to all ports. The attacker on the same switch as you can potentially see all the traffic your system sends and receives.

Network Security Solutions

One solution to the shared-network problems is to encrypt messages that travel between machines. IPSec (Internet Protocol Security Protocol) provides just such a technology and is commonly used to establish a secure point-to-point virtual network, called a *VPN* (page 1501), that allows two hosts to communicate securely over an insecure channel, such as the Internet. IPSec provides integrity, confidentiality, authenticity, and flexibility of implementation that supports multiple vendors.

---

6. Do not make the mistake of assuming that you have security just because you have a switch. Switches are designed to allocate bandwidth, not to guarantee security.

7. The term *port* has many meanings. Here it is a number assigned to a program. The number links incoming data with a specific service. For example, port 21 is used by ftp traffic, and port 23 is used by telnet.

IPSec is an amalgamation of protocols (IPsec = AH + ESP + IPComp + IKE):

- **Authentication Header**   (AH) A cryptographically secure, irreversible *checksum* (page 1460) for an entire packet. AH guarantees that the packet is authentic.

- **Encapsulating Security Payload**   (ESP) Encrypts a packet to make the data unreadable.

- **IP Payload Compression**   (IPComp) Compresses a packet. Encryption can increase the size of a packet, and IPComp counteracts this increase in size.

- **Internet Key Exchange**   (IKE) Provides a way for the endpoints to negotiate a common key securely. For AH to work, the two ends must use the same key to prevent a "person in the middle" (see footnote 3 on page 1410) from spoofing the connection.

IPv6 (page 369) also has provisions for encryption. However, it may be quite some time before IPv6 is widely implemented.

Network Security Guidelines

Some general guidelines for establishing and maintaining a secure system follow. The list is not complete but rather is only a guide.

- Fiberoptic cable is more secure than copper cable. Copper is subject to active and passive eavesdropping. With access to copper cable, all a data thief needs to monitor your network traffic is a passive device for measuring magnetic fields. It is much more difficult to tap a fiberoptic cable without interrupting the signal. Sites requiring top security keep fiberoptic cable in pressurized conduits, where a change in pressure signals that the physical security of the cable has been breached.

- Avoid leaving unused ports in public areas. If a malicious user can plug a laptop into the network without being detected, you are at risk of a serious security problem. Network drops that are to remain unused for extended periods should be disabled at the switch, preventing them from accepting or passing network traffic.

- Many network switches have provisions for binding a hardware address to a port for enhanced security. If someone unplugs a machine and plugs in another machine to capture traffic, chances are that that machine will have a different hardware address. When it detects a device with a different hardware address, the switch can disable the port. Even this solution is no guarantee, as there are programs that enable you to change or mask the hardware address of a network interface.

Install a Small Kernel and Run Only the Programs You Need || security

GNU/Linux systems contain a huge number of programs that, although useful, significantly reduce the security of the host. Install the smallest operating system kernel that meets your needs. For Web and FTP servers, install only the needed components. Users usually require additional packages.

- Do not allow NFS or NIS access outside of your network. Otherwise, it is a simple matter for a malicious user to steal your entire password map. Default NFS security is marginal to nonexistent and should not be allowed outside your network to machines that you do not trust. Experimental versions of NFS for GNU/Linux that support much better authentication algorithms are now becoming available. A common joke is that NFS stands for No File Security. Use IPSec, an experimental NFSv4 with improved authentication, or firewalls to provide access outside of your domain.

    Support for VPN configuration is often built into new firewalls or provided as a separate product, enabling you to join securely with customers or partners. If you must allow business partners, contractors, or other outside parties to access your files, consider using a secure filesystem, such as NFS with *Kerberos* (page 1475), secure NFS (encrypts authentication, not traffic), NFS over a VPN such as IPSec, or cfs (cryptographic filesystem).

- Specify **/usr** as readonly (ro) in **/etc/fstab**. This may cause your machine to be difficult to update, so use this tactic with care. For example,

    ```
    /dev/hda6      /usr     ext2     ro     0    0
    ```

- Mount filesystems other than **/** and **/usr** nosuid to prevent setuid programs from executing on this filesystem. For example,

    ```
    /dev/hda4      /var       ext3     nosuid   0    0
    /dev/hda5      /usr/local ext3     nosuid   0    0
    ```

- Use a barrier or firewall product between your network and the Internet. Several valuable mailing lists cover firewalls: the **comp.security.firewalls** newsgroup and the free firewalls Web site, www.freefire.org. Red Hat Linux includes ipchains, which allows you to implement a firewall. See "redhat-config-securitylevel: Sets up a Firewall" on page 924 and the *Linux IPCHAINS-HOWTO*.

Host Security

Your host must be secure. Simple security steps include preventing remote logins and leaving the **/etc/hosts.equiv** and individual users' **~/.rhosts** files empty (or not having them at all). Complex security steps include installing IPSec for VPNs between hosts. Many common security measures are between these two extremes. A few of these follow. See Table C-1 on page 1421 for URLs.

- Although potentially tricky to implement and manage, Intrusion Detection Systems (IDSs) are an excellent way to keep an eye on the integrity of a device. An IDS can warn of possible attempts at subverting security on the host on which it runs. The great-granddaddy of intrusion detection systems is tripwire. This host-based system checks modification times and integrity of files by using strong algorithms (cryptographic checksums or signatures) that can detect even the most minor modification. There is also a commercial version of tripwire. Another commercial IDS is DragonSquire. Other free, popular, and flexible IDSs include samhain and AIDE. These last two offer even more features and means of remaining invisible to users than tripwire does. Commercial IDSs that are popular in enterprise environments include Cisco Secure IDS (formerly NetRanger), Enterasys Dragon, and ISS RealSecure.

- The archives for the **redhat-watch-list** mailing list (note the s following http in this URL: https://listman.redhat.com/pipermail/redhat-watch-list), can keep you up-to-date on security and bugfix announcements. Go to https://listman.redhat.com/mailman/listinfo/redhat-watch-list to subscribe to this list.

- Red Hat Network (RHN) can automatically or semiautomatically keep one or more systems up-to-date (page 936), preventing your system from becoming prey to fixed security bugs.

- Complementing host-based intrusion detection systems are network-based intrusion detection systems. These programs monitor the network and nodes on the network and report suspicious occurrences (attack signatures) via user-defined alerts. These signatures can be matches on known worms, overflow attacks against programs, or unauthorized scans of network ports. Such programs as snort, klaxon, and NFR are used in this capacity. Commercial programs, such as DragonSentry, also fill this role.

- Provided with Red Hat Linux is PAM, which allows you to set up different methods and levels of authentication in many ways (page 1043).

- Process accounting, a good supplement to system security, can provide a continuous record of user actions on your system. See the accton man page for more information.

- Emerging standards for such things as Role Based Access Control (RBAC) allow tighter delegation of privileges along defined organizational boundaries. You can delegate each user a role or roles appropriate to the access required.

- General mailing lists and archives are an extremely useful repository of security information, statistics, and papers. The most useful are the bugtraq mailing list and CERT[8]. The bugtraq site and e-mail provide immediate notifications about specific vulnerabilities, whereas CERT provides notice of widespread vulnerabilities and useful techniques to fix them, as well as links to vendor patches.

- The syslog facility (provided with Red Hat Linux) can direct messages from system daemons to specific files such as those in **/var/log**. On larger groups of systems, you can send all important syslog information to a secure host, where that host's only function is to store syslog data so that it cannot be tampered with. See page 396 and the **syslogd** man page.

Login Security

Without a secure host, good login security cannot add much protection. Table C-1, "Where to Get It," on page 1421 lists some of the best login security tools, including replacement daemons for **telnetd**, **rlogind**, and **rshd**. The current choice of most sites is ssh, which comes as both freeware and a commercially supported package that works on UNIX/Linux, MS Windows, and Macintosh platforms.

The PAM facility (page 1043) allows you to set up multiple authentication methods for users in series or in parallel. In-series PAM requires multiple methods of authentication for a user. In-parallel PAM uses any one of a number of methods for authentication.

Although not a frequent choice, you can configure your system to take advantage of one-time passwords. S/Key is the original implementation of one-time passwords by Bellcore. OPIE (one-time passwords in everything), developed by the U.S. Naval Research Labs, is an improvement over the original Bellcore system. In one permutation of one-time passwords, the user gets a piece of paper listing a set of one-time passwords. Each time a user logs in, the user enters a password from the piece of paper. Once used, a password becomes obsolete, and the next password in the list is the only one that will work. Even if a malicious user compromises the network and sees your password, it will be of no use because the password can be used only one time. This setup makes it very difficult for someone to log in as you but does nothing about protecting the data you type at the keyboard. One-time

---

8. CERT is slow but useful as a medium for coordination between sites. It acts as a tracking agency to document the spread of security problems.

passwords are a good solution if you are at a site where no encrypted login is available. A truly secure (or paranoid) site will combine one-time passwords and encrypted logins.

Another type of secure login that is becoming more common is facilitated by a token or a *smart card*. Smart cards are credit-card-like devices that use a challenge-response method of authentication. Smart card and token authentication rely on something you have (the card) and something you know (a pass phrase, user ID, or pin). For example, you might enter your login name in response to the login prompt and get a password prompt. In response, you enter your PIN and the number displayed on the access token. The token has a unique serial number that is stored in a database on the authentication server. The token and the authentication server use this serial number as a means of computing a challenge every 30 to 60 seconds. If the pin and token number you enter match what it should be as computed by the access server, you are granted access to the system.

Remote Access Security

Issues and solutions surrounding remote access security overlap those pertaining to login and host security. Local logins may be secure with simply a login name and password, whereas remote logins (and all remote access) should be made more secure. Many breakins can be traced back to reusable passwords. It is a good idea to use an encrypted authentication client, such as ssh or kerberos. You can also use smart cards for remote access authentication.

Modem pools can also be an entry point. Most people are aware of how easy it is to monitor a network line. But people take for granted the security of the public switched telephone network (PSTN, aka POTS—plain old telephone service). You may want to set up an encrypted channel after dialing in to a modem pool. One way to do this is by running ssh over PPP.

There are ways to provide stringent modem authentication policies so that unauthorized users are not able to use your modems. The most common techniques are PAP (password authentication protocol), CHAP (challenge handshake authentication protocol), and Radius. PAP and CHAP are relatively weak when compared to Radius, so the latter has rapidly gained in popularity. Cisco also provides a method of authentication called TACACS/TACACS+ (Terminal Access Controller Access Control System).

One or more of these authentication techniques is available in a RAS (remote access server—in a network a computer that provides network access to remote users via modem). Before purchasing a RAS, check what kind of security it provides and decide whether that level of security meets your needs.

Two other techniques for remote access security can be built into a modem (or RAS if it has integrated modems). One is callback: After you dial in, you get a password prompt. Once you type in your password, the modem hangs up and calls you back at a phone number it has stored internally. But this technique is not foolproof.

Some modems have a built-in callback table with about ten entries. This works for small sites with only a few modems. If you use more modems, you will need to have callback provided by the RAS software.

The second technique is to use CLID (caller ID) or ANI (automatic number identification) to decide whether to answer the call. Depending on your wiring and the local phone company, you may or may not be able to use ANI. ANI information is provided before the call, whereas CLID information is provided along with the call.

Viruses and Worms

Examples of UNIX/Linux viruses are the Bliss virus/worm released in 1997 and the RST.b virus discovered in December 2001. Both are discussed in detail in articles on the Web. Viruses spread through systems by infecting executable files. In the cases of Bliss and RST.b, the GNU/Linux native executable format, ELF, was used as a propagation vector.

Just after 5 P.M. on November 2, 1988, Robert T. Morris Jr., a graduate student at Cornell University, released the first big virus onto the Internet. This virus was called an Internet worm and was designed to propagate copies of itself over many machines on the Internet. The worm was a piece of code that exploited four vulnerabilities, including one in finger, to get a buffer to overflow on a system. Once the buffer overflowed, the code was able to get a shell and then to recompile itself on the remote machine. The worm spread around the Internet very quickly and was not disabled, despite many people's efforts, for 36 hours.

The chief characteristic of a worm is propagation over a public network, such as the Internet. Whereas a virus propagates by infecting executables on the machine, a worm tends to prefer exploiting known security holes in network servers to gain **root** access and then trying to infect other machines in the same way.

UNIX/Linux file permissions help to inoculate against many viruses. Windows NT is resistant for similar reasons. You can easily protect your system against many viruses and worms by keeping your system patches up-to-date, not executing untrusted binaries from the Internet, limiting your path to include only necessary system directories, and doing as little as possible while enabled with Superuser privileges. You can prevent a disaster in case of a virus by backing up your system frequently.

Physical Security

Physical security, often overlooked as a defense against intrusion, covers access to the computer itself and to the console or terminal attached to the machine. If the machine is unprotected in an unlocked room, there is very little hope for physical security. (A simple example of physical vulnerability is someone walking into the room where the computer is, removing the hard drive from the computer, taking it home, and analyzing it.) You can take certain steps to improve the physical security of your computer.

- Keep servers in a locked room with limited access. A key, a combination, or a swipe card should be required to gain access. Protect windows as well as doors. Maintain a single point of entry. (Safety codes may require multiple exits, but only one must be an entry.)

- For public machines use a security system, such as a fiberoptic security system, which can secure a lab full of machines. With this system you run a fiberoptic cable through each of the machines such that the machine cannot be removed (or opened) without cutting the cable. When the cable is cut, an alarm goes off. Some machines are much more difficult to secure than others. PCs with plastic cases are difficult to secure. Although this is not a perfect solution, it may improve your security enough to cause a would-be thief to go somewhere else.

- Most modern PCs have a BIOS password. You can set the order in which a PC searches for a boot device, preventing the PC from being booted from a floppy disk or CD-ROM. Some BIOSs can prevent the machine from booting altogether without a proper password. The password protects the BIOS from unauthorized modification. Beware, however; many BIOSs have well-known *back door (continued)s* (page 1456). Research this issue if the BIOS password is an important feature for you.

- Run only fiberoptic cable between buildings. This is not only more secure but also safer in the event of lightning strikes and is required by many commercial building codes.

- Maintain logs of who goes in and out of secure areas. Sign-in/out sheets are useful only if everyone uses them. Sometimes a guard is warranted. Often, a simple proximity badge or smart card can tell when anyone has entered or left an area and keep logs, although these can be expensive to procure and install.

- Anyone who has access to the physical hardware has the keys to the palace. Someone with direct access to a computer system can do such things as swap components, insert boot media, and so on, that are security threats.

- Avoid activated, unused network jacks in public places. Such jacks provide unnecessary risk.

- Many modern switches can lock a particular switch port so that it accepts only traffic from an NIC (network interface card) with a particular hardware address and shuts down the port if another address is seen. However, commonly available programs allow one to reset this address.

- Make periodic security sweeps. Check doors for proper locking. If you must have windows, make sure that they are locked or are permanently sealed.

- Waste receptacles are a common source of information for intruders. Have policies for containment and disposal of sensitive documents.

- Use a UPS (uninterruptable power supply). Without a clean source of power, your system is vulnerable to corruption.

Security Resources

Many free and commercial programs can enhance system security. Some of these are listed in Table C-1.

Tool	What It Does	Where to Get It	‖ Table C-1
AIDE	Advanced Intrusion Detection Environment. Similar to **tripwire** with extensible verification algorithms.	www.cs.tut.fi/~rammer/aide.html	
Argus	Audits network transactions.	ciac.llnl.gov/ciac/ToolsUnixNetMon.html#Argus	
bugtraq	A moderated mailing list for the announcement and detailed discussion of all aspects of computer security vulnerabilities.	www.securityfocus.com	
CERT	Computer Emergency Response Team. A repository of papers and data about major security events and a list of security tools.	www.cert.org http://www.cert.org/tech_tips/security_tools.html	
chkrootkit	Checks for signs of a rootkit indicating that the machine has been compromised.	www.chkrootkit.org	
cops	Checks password file for bad passwords and other vulnerabilities.	www.fish.com/cops	
courtney	Identifies signatures of network attacks (requires Perl, **tcpdump**, and **libpcap**).	libpcap-0.0: ftp://ftp.ee.lbl.gov:/libpcap.tar.gz tcpdump-3.0: ftp://ftp.ee.lbl.gov:/tcdump.tar.gz courtney: ciac.llnl.gov/ciac/ToolsUnixNetMon.html#Courtney	
dsniff	Sniffing and network audit tool suite. Free.	naughty.monkey.org/~dugsong/dsniff/	

Tool	What It Does	Where to Get It (Continued)	‖ Table C-1
ethereal	Network protocol analyzer. Free.	www.ethereal.com	
freefire	Supplies free security solutions and supports developers of free security solutions.	www.freefire.org	
fwtk	Firewall toolkit. A set of proxies that can be used to construct a firewall.	www.fwtk.org	
GIAC	A security certification and training Web site.	www.giac.org/	
hping	Multipurpose network auditing and packet analysis tool. Free.	www.hping.org	
John	John the Ripper: a fast, flexible, weak password detector.	www.openwall.com/john	
Kerberos	Complete, secure network authentication system.	web.mit.edu/kerberos/www	
klaxon	Launches out of **xinetd** and allows you to put alarms on unused services.	ftp://ftp.cerias.purdue.edu/pub/tools/unix/logutils/klaxon	
L6	Verifies file integrity; similar to **tripwire**.	www.pgci.ca/l6.html	
LIDS	Intrusion detection and active defense system.	www.lids.org	
logdaemon	Has portable, secure replacements for **telnetd**, **login**, **ftpd**, **rexecd**. Requires **tcp_wrappers**.	ftp://ftp.cerias.purdue.edu/pub/tools/unix/logutils/logdaemon	
mason	Builds GNU/Linux firewalls.	www.dreamwvr.com/fwtk.org/mason/	
nat	Netbios Audit Tool. Shows what services an MS Windows machine is exporting. Do not confuse with *NAT* (page 1481).	www.singcert.org.sg/archive/tools_ciac/cert.org/tools/NetBIOS	
nessus	A plugin-based remote security scanner that can perform more than 370 security checks. Free.	www.nessus.org	

Tool	What It Does	Where to Get It (Continued)	Table C-1
netcat	Explores, tests, and diagnoses networks.	freshmeat.net/projects/netcat	
netsys	A full-disclosure unmoderated security mailing list.	lists.netsys.com	
nmap	Scans hosts to see what ports are available. It can perform stealth scans, determine OS type, find open ports, and so on.	www.insecure.org/nmap	
OPIE	Provides one-time passwords for system access.	inner.net/opie	
papers	Miscellaneous computer security papers.	www.fish.com	
Psionic (Abacus) Portsentry	Monitors for and reacts to port scans.	www.psionic.com/products/portsentry.html	
RBAC	Role Based Access Control. Assigns roles and privileges associated with the roles.	csrc.nist.gov/rbac	
SAINT	Security Administrator's Integrated Network Tool. Assesses and analyzes network vulnerabilities. This tool follows satan.	www.wwdsi.com/saint	
samhain	A file integrity checker. Has a GUI configurator, client/server capability, and real-time reporting capability.	samhain.sourceforge.net	
SARA	The Security Auditor's Research Assistant security analysis tool.	www-arc.com/sara	
SATAN	Security Administrator's Tool for Analyzing Networks. Scans your host and network for vulnerabilities. This program is starting to show its age.	www.fish.com/satan	
SecurityFocus	Home for security tools, mail lists, libraries, and cogent analysis.	www.securityfocus.com	

Tool	What It Does	Where to Get It (Continued) || Table C-1
sentry	Detects port scans.	ftp.cerias.purdue.edu/pub/tools/unix/logutils/sentry
sfingerd	A secure, configurable replacement for the **fingerd** daemon.	ftp.cerias.purdue.edu/pub/tools/unix/daemons/sfingerd
skey	One-time disposable passwords for login.	See logdaemon earlier in this list.
snort	A flexible IDS.	www.snort.org
srp	Secure Remote Password. Upgrades common protocols, such as TELNET and FTP to use secure password exchange.	srp.stanford.edu
ssh	A secure **rsh**, **rdist**, **rlogin** replacement with encrypted sessions and other options. Supplied with Red Hat Linux.	www.ssh.org openssh.org
sudo	Gives very limited Superuser capabilities on an as-needed basis to system operators.	ftp://ftp.courtesan.com/pub/sudo
swatch	A Perl-based log parser and analyzer.	www.oit.ucsb.edu/~eta/swatch
syslog-ng	A cryptographically secure replacement for **syslog**.	www.balabit.hu/en/downloads/syslog-ng
tcp_wrappers	Monitor, filter, and log incoming requests for the **systat**, **finger**, **ftp**, **telnet**, **rlogin**, **rsh**, **exec**, **tftp**, **talk**, and other network services by wrapping system daemons.	ftp://ftp.porcupine.org/pub/security/index.html
tct	The Coroner's Toolkit. Performs post-breakin forensic analysis.	www.fish.com/tct
titan	Audits and fixes potential security issues. Originally coded for Solaris, it is being ported to GNU/Linux.	www.fish.com/titan
tklogger	Visualizes logs. Requires Tcl/Tk.	ftp://ftp.cerias.purdue.edu/pub/tools/unix/logutils/tklogger
Treachery	A collection of tools for security and auditing.	www.treachery.net/tools
tripwire	Checks for possible signs of intruder activity. Supplied with Red Hat Linux.	ftp://ftp.cerias.purdue.edu/pub/tools/unix/ids/tripwire

Appendix Summary

Security is inversely proportional to usability. There must be a balance between the requirements that your users have to get their work done and the amount of security that is implemented. It is often unnecessary to provide top security for a small business with only a few employees. On the other hand, if you work for a government military contractor, you are bound to have extreme security constraints and an official audit policy to determine whether your security policies are being implemented correctly.

Review your own security requirements periodically. Several of the tools mentioned in this appendix are designed to help you do this. Such tools as nessus, samhain, and SAINT all provide an auditing mechanism.

Some companies specialize in security and auditing. Hiring one of them to examine your site can be costly but may result in specific recommendations for areas that you may have overlooked in your initial setup. When you hire someone to audit your security, you may be providing both physical and Superuser access to your systems. Make sure the company that you hire has a good history, has been in business for several years, and has impeccable references. Check on them periodically: Things change over time. Avoid the temptation to hire former system crackers as consultants. Security consultants should have an irreproachable ethical background, or you will always have doubts about their intentions.

Your total security package is based on your risk assessment of your vulnerabilities. Strengthen those areas that are most important for your business. For example, many sites will rely on a firewall to protect them completely from the Internet, whereas internal hosts receive little or no security attention. Crackers refer to this as "the crunchy outside surrounding the soft chewy middle." Yet this is entirely sufficient to protect some sites. Perform your own risk assessment and address your needs accordingly. If need be, hire a full-time security administrator whose job it is to design and audit your security policies.

IN THIS APPENDIX

The POSIX Standards

In the past, the existence of various versions of the UNIX system was a fruitful source of creative and innovative software. However, it has also been a persistent source of frustration for users and programmers. Users who moved between the BSD and System V versions of the system, for example, discovered that commands that worked on one system did not work, or worked differently, on the other. Programmers found a similar phenomenon: Programs that worked on one system behaved differently, or even failed to compile, on another. In 1984 the user's group **/usr/group** (now called UniForum) started an effort to specify a "standard UNIX." This effort has expanded beyond the wildest dreams of its initiators as the POSIX series of standards.

POSIX standards specify interfaces for application programs but say nothing about how the interfaces are to be implemented. Thus a wide variety of systems, including most varieties of UNIX, GNU/Linux, and many systems that are unrelated to either, now supply versions of these interfaces. As an example, you can run bash with the **--posix** option to make it conform more closely with the POSIX.2 standard (page 1430). As a consequence, GNU/Linux can support more and more application programs that run on other POSIX systems.

Richard Stallman[1] provides a connection between GNU and POSIX as he started GNU and was involved in the start of POSIX. The Introduction to POSIX.1 states that "The name POSIX was suggested by Richard Stallman." POSIX is almost an acronym for Portable Operating System Interface and Stallman probably put the X on the end to give it that UNIX "ring."

---

1. Refer to "The GNU/Linux Connection" on page 4 for more information on Richard Stallman.

Background

POSIX is the name for a collection of software standards based on but not limited to the UNIX system. The standards are developed by working groups of the Institute for Electrical and Electronics Engineering (IEEE); participation in these groups is open to everyone. For this and other reasons, the POSIX standards are referred to as Open Systems Standards.

The explicit goal of the POSIX effort is to promote application portability. Thus the standards specify both program and user interfaces but not implementations. Refer to www.pasc.org/standing/sd11.html#statustable for the most recent information on the status of the POSIX standards.

POSIX.1

POSIX.1 (POSIX 1003.1), the original POSIX standard, was adopted in 1988. POSIX.1 is a C programming language interface standard. In its original form it specified the syntax and semantics of 203 C language functions and the contents of various *data structures* (page 1463). Subsequent revisions have greatly expanded its scope (Table D-1). In 1993 interfaces for supporting real-time programming were added, and in 1995 interfaces for supporting multithreaded application programs were added.

POSIX.1 specifies the abstract structure of a filesystem. For example, a system that conforms to POSIX.1 must have a hierarchical filesystem with directories, FIFO files, and regular files. Each file must have attributes typical of UNIX system files, such as permission bits, owner and group IDs, and link counts. The programming interfaces refer to filenames using familiar UNIX-style pathnames, such as **/home/alex/src/load.c.**

Name	|| Table D-1
POSIX 1003.1 (POSIX.1)	Base system interfaces in the C language. Includes real-time extensions, threads, protocol independent interfaces, and more.
POSIX 1003.2 (POSIX.2)	Shell and utilities, including interactive utilities.
POSIX 2003 (POSIX.3)	Test methods for measuring conformance to POSIX standards.
POSIX 2003.1 (POSIX.3.1)	Test methods for POSIX 1003.1.

Name (Continued)		Table D-1
POSIX 2003.2	(POSIX.3.2)	Test methods for POSIX 1003.2.
POSIX 1003.5	(POSIX.5)	Ada language binding to 1990 version of 1003.1.
POSIX 1003.9	(POSIX.9)	FORTRAN binding to 1990 version of 1003.1.
POSIX 1003.17	(POSIX.17)	Standard for X.500 Directory Services, a protocol that allows multiple distributed "directories" to be searched as a single entity. The word "directory" does not refer to a GNU/Linux filesystem directory but to a generic database.
POSIX 1387.2		System administration: software management (principally a software installation standard).

Issues related to system administration are specifically excluded from POSIX.1, as are implementation details. After all, an application program does not need to know how to create a new device special file and does not care how the **open**() function (which opens a file) works internally. By avoiding implementation issues, the standard allows systems that are not based on UNIX to conform to POSIX.1.

The POSIX.1 committee was responsible for codifying existing practice, not engineering a new version of the UNIX system. During the development of the POSIX.1 standard, partisans of BSD and System V were forced to try to reconcile their differences. In some cases this meant standardizing on behavior from one or the other version. In a few cases the working group decided that both the BSD and System V implementations of some features were deficient and created new interfaces (such as terminal control) based on existing practice but with new syntax and semantics. Where no compromise seemed to be reachable, the working group adopted optional behavior. For example, BSD has had job control at least since release 4.1, whereas SVR3 does not support job control. POSIX.1 makes job control an option.

One compromise took a unique form. POSIX.1 specifies formats for file archives. On UNIX System V, the preferred archive format is cpio (page 1124). On BSD the preferred format is tar (page 1343). POSIX.1 requires that both formats be supported, in slightly modified forms. Because the specification of utilities is outside the scope of POSIX.1, neither the cpio nor the tar utility is mentioned; only the file formats for the archives are part of the standard. POSIX.1 requires that the implementation provide unnamed archive creation and archive reading utilities. See page 1439 for a discussion of the pax utility specified by POSIX.2.

The POSIX.1 standard is available from the American National Standards Institute (ANSI) or from the IEEE. In addition, the standard has been adopted as an international standard by the International Standards Organization (ISO) and the International Electrotechnical Commission (IEC), which jointly coordinate international computing standards.

POSIX.2

POSIX.2, the shell and utilities standard, is most important for users, as opposed to application developers. Its principal purpose is to specify the semantics of a shell (based on the Korn Shell) and a collection of utilities that you can use to develop portable shell scripts. A secondary purpose is to promote user portability. This term refers to a standard specification for utilities, such as vi, man, and who, that are not very useful for scripts but are typically used interactively.

POSIX.2 is independent of POSIX.1, and a system can claim conformance to POSIX.2 without claiming conformance to POSIX.1. This is not true of most of the other POSIX standards, which take POSIX.1 as a base. In practice you can expect virtually all UNIX systems to comply with both POSIX.1 and POSIX.2 within a few years. Many non-UNIX systems will also comply, making them "UNIX-like," at least on the outside. Although it has not been formally certified, GNU/Linux conforms to the requirements of POSIX.2 in many respects. For example, the GNU Bourne Again Shell info page states: "It is intended to be a conformant implementation of the IEEE POSIX Shell and Tools specification."

Localization

One of the most important features of POSIX.2 is that it is fully localized. That is, it describes the behavior of the shell and utilities in the context of different character sets and locale-specific information (such as date and time formats). For example, the grep utility has a –i option that causes grep to ignore case in determining matches. POSIX.2 specifies what this means for alphabets in which the uppercase-to-lowercase mapping is either not defined or not one-to-one.

The general idea behind localization is that every process executes in a particular locale. The POSIX.2 standard defines a locale as "the definition of the subset of the environment of a user that depends on language and cultural conventions." The locale describes how the process should display or interpret information that depends on the language and culture, including character set and the method of writing times, dates, numbers, and currency amounts. Localization is not unique to POSIX.2; both the C standard and POSIX.1 support it to a limited degree. However, POSIX.2 is much more specific in its description of how locale-specific information is provided to the system and how it affects the system's operation.

An important feature of POSIX.2 locales is that they are fragmented into categories. The standard specifies six locale categories and defines six environment variables corresponding to these categories (Table D-2).

Environment Variable	Table D-2
LC_CTYPE	Describes which characters are considered alphabetic, numeric, punctuation, blank, and so on, and describes the mapping of uppercase to lowercase and vice versa
LC_COLLATE	Describes the order of characters for sorting
LC_TIME	Describes abbreviated and full names for months and days of the week, local equivalents of A.M. and P.M., appropriate date representation, and appropriate 12- and 24-hour time representation
LC_NUMERIC	Describes the character to use as a decimal point, the character to separate groups of digits (such as the comma in 65,536), and the number of digits in a group
LC_MONETARY	Describes the currency symbol, where it is positioned, how negative values are written, the currency decimal-point character, the number of fractional digits, and other details of how currency values are written
LC_MESSAGES	Describes the formats of informative and diagnostic messages and interactive responses, and expressions to be interpreted as *yes* and *no* responses for those utilities that query the user

Two more environment variables (**LC_ALL** and **LANG**) interact with these six to provide overrides and defaults. If **LC_ALL** is set, then its value is used in place of the value of any of the other six **LC_*** variables. If **LANG** is set, then its value is used in place of any **LC_*** variable that is not set.

Each of these environment variables can be set to a value that is the name of a locale and that will cause features of the shell and some utilities to change behavior. For example, here is a fragment of a shell session on a system with POSIX.2 internationalization:

```
$ LC_TIME=POSIX
$ date
Thu Aug 21 21:21:03 2003
$ LC_TIME=Fr_FR # French
$ date
Jeu 21 Ao 21:21:12 PDT 2003
```

In this and the following examples, assume that **LANG** and the **LC_∗** variables have been exported. They must be exported because they affect the standard utilities only when they are in the environment of those utilities.

The two standard locale names are POSIX and C. They describe the identical locale, which is a generic UNIX locale; setting all the locale environment variables to **POSIX** will result in traditional UNIX system behavior. Other locale names are implementation defined. There is no standard format. Common conventions include the abbreviated language and country in the locale name. Thus **En_US** and **Fr_CA** might be locale names for locales describing English in the United States and French in Canada.

An example that was run on a system that supports POSIX.2 style localization shows the results of mixing locales:

```
$ LC_TIME=Fr_FR
$ LANG=De_DE
$ cal 1 2006

       Janvier 2006
Dim Lun Mar Mer Jeu Ven Sam
  1   2   3   4   5   6   7
  8   9  10  11  12  13  14
 15  16  17  18  19  20  21
 22  23  24  25  26  27  28
 29  30  31

$ rm NoSuchFile
rm: NoSuchFile: Verzeichnis/Datei im Pfadnamen existiert nicht.
```

On some POSIX.2 systems it is possible for users to define their own locales in addition to those provided by the system; see the definition of the localedef utility on page 1438.

The POSIX Shell

POSIX.2 specifies the syntax and semantics of a shell command language. The POSIX shell is generically named sh but is most closely based on the Korn Shell, ksh. The GNU/Linux Z Shell (Chapter 15) also closely resembles ksh. The POSIX shell is almost a subset of the 1988 version of ksh. Both the GNU/Linux zsh and newer versions of ksh have been designed as supersets of the POSIX shell. If you want to write shell scripts that are portable across all POSIX shell implementations, you should try to avoid using constructs that are not supported by the POSIX shell. Here is a brief description of some of the differences between the POSIX shell and its relatives, ksh and zsh.

- The POSIX shell does not support the **typeset** keyword or the zsh's **declare** keyword.

- The POSIX shell does not support the **select** command.

- The POSIX shell does not support the two-argument form of the cd command.

- The POSIX shell does not automatically define and maintain the value of the **PWD** environment variable.

- The POSIX shell has a different syntax for doing integer arithmetic. It does not use the **let** keyword. Arithmetic expressions are initiated by the symbols $((and are terminated by)). Within the parentheses you must refer to shell variables by using a **$** sign. For example, the following brief POSIX shell dialog will display the value 7:

```
$ x=3
$ y=4
$ z=$(($x + $y))
$ echo $z
7
```

The equivalent zsh or ksh sequence would be

```
$ x=3
$ y=4
$ let z="x + y"
$ echo $z
7
```

- In zsh or ksh you can also use double parentheses for arithmetic instead of **let**, but the syntax is different. Two ways to write the **let** statement in zsh or ksh are

$$z=\$((x + y))$$

and

$$\$ ((z=x + y))$$

- You can define shell functions in the POSIX shell, just as you can in zsh or ksh. However, both zsh and ksh support multiple syntaxes to define functions. The POSIX shell supports only one of these; it does not support the **function** keyword, and it requires braces ({}) even if the function body is a single command. The following function definition style is valid in the POSIX shell, zsh, and ksh:

```
parent()
{
_dir=$(dirname $1)
echo $(basename $_dir)
}
```

The preceding function will print the name of the parent (last-but-one) component of a pathname argument:

```
$ parent /home/alex/literature/moby_dick
literature
```

- Functions in the POSIX shell execute in the caller's execution environment. This is largely but not entirely true for zsh and ksh. The principal exception is that in both of these shells, traps that are set within functions apply to the execution of the function only. For example, consider the following shell dialog:

```
$ side_effect()
> {
> trap "rm /tmp/foo" 0 # on exit, remove it
> }
$ trap - 0              # on exit, no action
$ side_effect
```

If the POSIX shell executes the **side_effect** function and then returns from the function, the trap has been set for when the calling shell exits. In the zsh and the 1988 ksh, the trap is set for execution of the function and occurs when the function exits. (The 1993 version of ksh follows the POSIX semantics.)

- In zsh you can set many parameters as environment variables and, in effect, customize the shell environment. These include such parameters as **NO_SHORT_LOOPS, NULLCMD, KEYTIMEOUT,** and so forth. Most of these are not special to the POSIX shell, and in some cases they must be set to particular values to get POSIX shell semantics. For example, **NULLCMD** should be set to : (which is not its default) to get POSIX semantics. See the **zshparam** man page for details.

Utilities for Portable Shell Applications

POSIX.2 specifies 72 required utilities, referred to as Execution Environment Utilities. Most of them are familiar from SVR3 or Berkeley UNIX or are derived from UNIX utilities. A few, such as pathchk and printf (see the following list), are inventions of the POSIX.2 committee and were created to satisfy requirements that specifically relate to portability. Other utilities are adopted from the UNIX system but have changed semantics to resolve conflicts between SVR3 and Berkeley UNIX, to remove behavior that does not make sense in an internationalized context, or to fix inconsistencies (especially with the syntax of options).

The Execution Environment Utilities follow. Utilities that are not described in the main part of this text are marked with an asterisk (✳). Utilities that have significant differences from their traditional UNIX semantics are marked with a dagger (†). Utilities that are new (that is, inventions of the POSIX.2 working group) are marked with a double dagger (‡). Following the list are brief descriptions of the utilities that are new with POSIX.2.

awk	basename	bc*	cat	cd
chgrp	chmod	chown	cksum*‡	cmp*
comm	command*‡	cp	cut*	date
dd*	diff	dirname*	echo†	ed
env*	expr	false	find	fold*
getconf*‡	getopts	grep†	head	id*
join*	kill†	ln	locale*‡	localedef*‡
logger*‡	logname*	lp*	ls	mailx*
mkdir	mkfifo*‡	mv	nohup	od†
paste	pathchk*‡	pax*‡	pr	printf*‡
pwd	read	rm	rmdir	sed
sh	sleep	sort	stty	tail
tee	test	touch	tr	true
tty	umask	uname*	uniq	wait
wc	xargs			

cksum

The cksum utility computes a checksum for a file. This utility is useful when you are sending or receiving a file and want to ensure that it was not corrupted in transmission. The cksum utility replaces a utility named sum that was present in both BSD and SVR4. The POSIX.2 committee did not use sum; BSD and System V had differing, incompatible implementations. The algorithm used by cksum is based on a cyclic redundancy check from the Ethernet standard ISO 8802-3.

The syntax is

*cksum [**file...**]*

You can name zero or more files on the command line. If you do not specify a filename, cksum computes a checksum for standard input. For each input file, cksum writes to standard output the file's checksum, byte count (or rather octet count), and name. On those rare systems where a byte is not 8 bits, these will differ.

command

The command utility executes any command line in a manner designed to guarantee that you are executing the version of the command that you would expect. If you type

*command **command_name** [**arguments...**]*

the shell executes ***command_name*** without looking for a shell function of that name. If you use the **–p** option, as in

*command –p **command_name** [**arguments...**]*

the shell searches for ***command_name***, using a special value for **PATH**, one that is guaranteed to find all the standard utilities. This protects you from accidentally invoking local utilities or functions with the same names as standard utilities.

If the system supports POSIX.2's User Portability Utilities Option (UPE, page 1440), command has two more option flags. With the **–v** option, command reports the absolute pathname of ***command_name*** without running it, using your **PATH** variable for the search. If ***command_name*** is a built-in shell utility, a reserved word, or a function, only its name is written. If ***command_name*** is an alias, the command line representing its alias definition is written. The **–V** option is similar but distinguishes among functions, reserved words, and built-in utilities.

getconf

The getconf utility lets you determine the values of various options and configuration-dependent parameters, such as whether the system supports the User Portability Utilities Option or what maximum-length filename the system supports. Some of these parameters may vary, depending on where you are in the filesystem. For example, a UNIX system might support both traditional System V filesystems (in which filenames are limited to 14 characters) and BSD filesystems (in which filenames can be as long as 255 characters).

You invoke getconf in either of the following ways:

getconf system_var

getconf path_var pathname

The first syntax is used for systemwide variables. For example, you can determine the maximum number of simultaneous processes that any one user ID can own with the call

```
$ getconf CHILD_MAX
40
```

The second syntax is used to determine the values of variables that may vary from place to place in the file hierarchy. For example, you can determine the maximum permissible length of a filename in the **/tmp** directory with the command

```
$ getconf NAME_MAX /tmp
255
```

The set of symbols that you can query, which is too long to be listed here, can be found in the POSIX.2 standard (which refers directly to POSIX.1 for some of these symbols). Table D-3 lists some of the more useful symbols.

Symbol	|| Table D-3
PATH	Reports a value of the **PATH** variable that will find all standard utilities.
LINE_MAX	Reports the maximum length of an input line that you can reliably pass to a standard utility that processes text files. The length must be at least 2,048.
POSIX2_UPE	Displays the value 1 if the system supports the User Portability Utilities Option (page 1440).
POSIX2_LOCALEDEF	Displays the value 1 if the system supports the ability to define new locales, using the **localedef** utility (page 1438).
PATH_MAX dir	Reports the length of the longest pathname that you can reliably use relative to directory **dir**. This length may vary from place to place in the filesystem.
NAME_MAX dir	Reports the length of the longest filename that you can use in **dir**. This length may vary from place to place in the filesystem.

locale

The locale utility is part of POSIX.2's effort to internationalize the UNIX environment. The locale utility exports information about the current locale. If invoked with no arguments or options, locale writes to standard output the values of the **LANG** and **LC_*** environment variables. This utility can also take options or arguments that write information about all available public locales or the names and values of selected keywords used in defining locales. The description of these keywords is beyond the scope of this book, but an example will illustrate their use. Refer to the locale man page for more information.

Suppose that a user has typed a response to a question, and you want to determine, in a localized way, whether the response is affirmative or negative. The definition of the **LC_MESSAGES** locale category contains the keyword **yesexpr**. The value associated with this keyword is a regular expression describing the responses that should be treated as *yes* in the current locale. If the user's response is in a shell variable named **response**, the following shell fragment will work:

```
yes=`locale yesexpr`
echo $response | grep "$yes" > /dev/null
if [ $? -eq 0 ]
then
echo "Answer was yes"
else
echo "Answer was no"
fi
```

localedef

The localedef utility allows users to define their own locales if the implementation supports this facility. Such support is an option in POSIX.2. The information required to define a locale is voluminous, and its description is beyond the scope of this book. You can find a sample set of locale definition files, provided by the Danish Standards Association, in Annex G of the POSIX.2 standard. Refer also to the localedef man page.

logger

The logger utility provides a means for scripts to write messages to an unspecified system log file. The intended purpose of the logger utility is for noninteractive scripts that encounter errors to record them in a place where system administrators can later examine them. Refer to the logger man page for more information.

The format and method of reading these messages are unspecified by POSIX.2 and will vary from one system to another. The syntax of logger is

logger string ...

mkfifo

POSIX.1 includes a **mkfifo( )** function that allows programs to create FIFO special files (named pipes that persist in the filesystem even when not in use). This utility provides the same functionality at the shell level. The syntax is

mkfifo [–m mode] file ...

By default the mode of the created FIFOs is 660 (**rw–rw––––**), modified by the caller's umask. If the **–m** option is used, the mode argument (in the same format as that used by chmod) is used instead. Refer to the mkfifo man page for more information.

pathchk

The pathchk utility allows portable shell scripts to determine whether a given pathname is valid on a given system. The problem arises because the character set used in the pathname may not be supported on the system, or the pathname may be longer than the maximum **PATH_MAX** for this filesystem or may have components (filenames) longer than the maximum **FILE_MAX** for this filesystem. The syntax of pathchk is

pathchk [–p] pathname ...

For each pathname argument, pathchk will check that the length is no greater than **PATH_MAX**, that the length of each component is no greater than **NAME_MAX**, that each existing directory in the path is searchable, and that every character in the pathname is valid in its containing directory. If any of these fail pathchk writes a diagnostic message to standard error. If you use the **–p** option, pathchk performs a more stringent portability check: Pathnames are checked against a maximum length of 255 bytes, filenames against a maximum length of 14 bytes, and characters against the portable filename character set (which consists of the lowercase and uppercase letters of the Roman alphabet, the digits 0–9, period, underscore, and hyphen). The limits of 255 for **PATH_MAX** and 14 for **NAME_MAX** are the minimum that any POSIX-conforming system can support. Refer to the pathchk man page for more information.

pax

The name pax is ostensibly an acronym for Portable Archive eXchange, but it is also a bilingual pun. The disputes between the advocates of the tar and cpio formats were referred to as the tar wars (in which 3-cpio did battle with tar-2-d-2), and pax is the peace treaty. The pax utility can read and write archives in several formats. These specifically include, but are not limited to, the POSIX.1 tar and cpio formats. Other formats are implementation defined. It is the stated intent of the POSIX.2 committee to define a new archive format in a future revision of the standard. That format will become the default for pax.

The syntax of the pax command is too complex to describe here (as you might expect from looking at all the options available to tar and cpio). If it exists in your system, consult the manual pages. The USENIX Association funded the development of a portable implementation of pax and placed it in the public domain, so this utility is now widely available. Refer to the pax man page for more information.

printf

The printf utility was invented largely to deal with the incompatibility between the BSD and System V versions of echo (page 1157). BSD echo treats a first argument of –n in a special fashion, whereas System V will echo it. System V echo treats certain strings starting with \ in a special fashion, whereas BSD will echo them. POSIX.2 states that any echo command line in which –n is the first argument or in which any argument starts with \ will have implementation-defined behavior. To print portably any but the simplest strings, you should use printf.

The *f* in printf stands for formatted, and the printf utility allows you to print strings to standard output under the control of a formatting argument. The syntax is

> *printf format [string ...]*

Both the name printf and the syntax of the format string are borrowed from C. Refer to the printf man page for more information.

The User Portability Utilities Option (UPE)

The UPE is a collection of 37 utilities and shell built-in commands for interactive use. This portion of the standard is an option; that is, a system can conform to POSIX.2 without providing these. Their purpose is to promote user portability by creating a uniform interactive command environment. Following is a list of the UPE utilities. Those that are not described in the main part of this text are marked with an asterisk (*).

| alias | at | batch* | bg | crontab |
| csplit* | ctags* | df | du | ex |

expand*	fc	fg	file	jobs
man	mesg	more	newgrp	nice
nm*	patch	ps	renice*	split*
strings*	tabs*	talk	time	tput*
unalias	unexpand*	uudecode*	uuencode*	vi
who	write			

Three of these utilities (bg, fg, and jobs) need be supported only if the system also supports job control. Two others (ctags and nm) need be supported only if the system also supports the Software Development Utilities option.

Many of the UPE utilities are affected by localization. For example, the at utility can accept names of days of the week as part of its time specification. The way one writes these names depends on the value of **LC_TIME**.

Software Development Utilities

As an option, POSIX.2 specifies the behavior of some utilities, such as make, lex, and yacc, useful to software developers. In fact, three separate options in POSIX.2 cover three distinct sets of development tools.

- The Software Development Utilities Option specifies the behavior of the ar, make, and strip utilities. These utilities are useful for software development in any programming language.

- The C-Language Development Utilities Option specifies the behavior of the c89, lex, and yacc utilities. The c89 command invokes a C compiler that conforms to the 1989 C standard (ANSI X3.159-1989, also ISO/IEC 9899-1990.) The lex and yacc utilities are useful high-level tools that parse input streams into tokens and take actions when a particular token is recognized. These utilities have historically been available on UNIX systems.

- The FORTRAN Development and Runtime Utilities Option specifies the behavior of the asa and fort77 utilities. The asa utility converts between FORTRAN's arcane printer control commands and ASCII output. The fort77 command invokes a FORTRAN compiler that conforms to the FORTRAN 77 standard (ANSI X3.9-1978).

POSIX.3

The POSIX standards developers recognized early in the process that testing systems for conformance to the standards was going to be essential. In the past, other standards efforts have suffered from lack of appropriately specified conformance tests or from conflicting conformance tests with different measures of conformance. The POSIX.3 standard specifies general principles for test suites that measure conformance to POSIX standards. A set of assertions (individual items to be tested) is developed for each standard. For POSIX.1 a test methods standard with more than 2,400 assertions has been adopted as POSIX.3.1. For POSIX.2 a test methods standard contains almost 10,000 assertions.

GNU/Linux users who are involved in testing or procuring systems that must conform to standards need to be familiar with POSIX.3 and its associated test methods standards. For other GNU/Linux users these standards have little importance.

POSIX.4

The POSIX.4 standard, an addition to and modification of the POSIX.1 standard, describes C language interfaces for real-time applications. The standard defines real time as "the ability of the operating system to provide a required level of service in a bounded response time." Real-time systems have historically been implemented as stand-alone systems controlling processes or machines or as embedded systems (such as inside a microwave oven). However, there has always been a need for combined interactive and real-time systems, and the UNIX system has served as the base for many implementations of real-time facilities.

The facilities specified in POSIX.4 are those commonly used by real-time applications, such as semaphores, timers, interprocess communication, shared memory, and so on. Although quite a few of these and related facilities have been implemented in various UNIX systems, there was no well-established and widely accepted set of UNIX real-time interfaces. Thus the routines specified in POSIX.4 are largely the invention of the POSIX.4 committee and have already been implemented on a number of UNIX systems.

POSIX.4 is structured as a collection of optional extensions to POSIX.1. Thus a system can claim conformance to some parts of the standard and not others but must claim conformance to POSIX.1. This has been a subject of some controversy, as many real-time applications, particularly for embedded systems, do not need the support of an operating system with all the POSIX.1 machinery. Currently GNU/Linux supports some subset of the POSIX.1b interfaces. These interfaces include memory locking (the ability of a process with suitable privileges to lock itself in memory), some portion of synchronous I/O, and multiple schedulers. There is considerable interest within the GNU/Linux community in providing the remaining POSIX.1b interfaces.

Most real-time applications have traditionally been implemented as sets of co-operating, closely coordinated processes. In many cases this cooperation extends to the use of shared data, and one convenient way to do this is to use multiple threads of control in a single process. Support for threads allows a single process to have multiple execution paths active at once, and—on hardware with multiple processors—to execute those paths simultaneously. The original POSIX real-time project included an attempt at standardizing threads interfaces. It was soon recognized that this was sufficiently complicated to be a separate standard, and a new committee was formed. The resulting POSIX threads standard, POSIX.1c, was adopted in 1995.

POSIX.5

POSIX.5, an Ada language version of POSIX.1, specifies Ada routines that provide essentially the same functionality as the C routines of POSIX.1. The UNIX system itself is written in C, and C has always been the most widely used programming language on UNIX systems, but the Ada community has always been interested in the UNIX system and in providing a standard way for Ada programs to access UNIX system services. POSIX.5 provides that standard. In principle POSIX.5 provides the exact functionality provided by POSIX.1. This does not mean that there is a precise one-to-one correlation between the interfaces in POSIX.1 and POSIX.5 because differences in the languages make that correlation impossible.

The POSIX.5 working group is tracking changes to POSIX.1 and will keep the Ada version of the standard synchronized with the C version. The POSIX.20 working group, which works in concert with POSIX.5, is developing an Ada language version of POSIX.4 and POSIX.4a; this will provide Ada programmers with the ability to use standard interfaces for real-time applications on the UNIX system and UNIX-like systems. This is important to the Ada community, as Ada has from its inception been used heavily in the development of real-time systems.

Security

Since early in its development, the UNIX system has had a simple and relatively effective security paradigm. File access permissions are assigned according to three levels of granularity (owner, group, and other—page 118), and certain actions require privileges. The privileges are monolithic; that is, either a process has all the privileges that the system supports (such as adding users, changing the ownership of files, changing its user ID), or it has none. One user ID is reserved for a privileged user, Superuser.

For most ordinary purposes this paradigm works well, particularly in organizations where small groups cooperate on projects. However, it does not provide the level of security that some users need. The Department of Defense has defined several levels of security in a document commonly referred to as the *Orange Book*. Some vendors have layered additional security features on top of UNIX systems to conform to the more secure levels of the *Orange Book*.

An important feature of all the POSIX standards is that they support an abstract privilege model in which privileges are discrete. Each time a POSIX standard describes an action that requires some privilege, the phrase *appropriate privileges* is used. Thus POSIX.2 states that chmod can be used to change the mode of a file by the owner of the file or by a process with appropriate privileges. One model of these privileges is the Superuser model, but there can be others. Thus POSIX allows many security paradigms.

Areas under discussion include user interfaces, program interfaces, and structures to define higher levels of security. Some of the general issues are described following.

Least Privilege

This is the idea that a process should have only the privileges that are absolutely necessary for its function. The monolithic nature of traditional UNIX system privileges is considered a security hazard. You may recall that in 1988, a worm program traveled across the Internet, crippling computers around the world (page 1419). The worm exploited a feature of the sendmail program. Because sendmail has to write to all users' mail files, it must have some privileges. On a classical UNIX system, this means that it has all privileges, and the worm used this fact to acquire all privileges itself.

Discretionary Access Controls (DACs)

These are additional access restrictions under the control of the creator of an object (such as a file). A typical DAC is an ACL (Access Control List), a list of user IDs permitted access to the file. This acts as an additional restriction to that imposed by the file's mode. See also "File Security" on page 1411.

Mandatory Access Controls (MACs)

These are like two security levels. An object is created at some level, not under the control of its creator, and can be accessed only by processes at the same or a higher level. The level can be determined by the process's user or group ID or by the nature of the process itself.

Auditability Mechanism

This covers which types of objects or actions need to be audited and the mechanisms for keeping track of the audit trail. In all these areas there is existing practice for UNIX systems; that is, you can find DACs, MACs, partitioned privilege, and audit mechanisms on secure UNIX systems. The goal of POSIX.1e is to standardize the practices.

The POSIX.22 committee is addressing similar issues in a distributed environment. Clearly network security adds its own layer of difficulties, including file access on remotely mounted systems.

Networks

A number of POSIX groups are working on various standards related to networks. The areas that need to be standardized occur at many different levels. Some are visible to users, some to application programs, and some only to the operating system.

The most visible network feature to a user is the availability of remote filesystems. There is a well-established existing practice for this on UNIX systems, via such packages as NFS (page 391) and RFS. The purpose of remote filesystems is to enable file hierarchies on remote hosts to behave, to the extent possible, as if they were mounted on the local host. That is, the presence of the network should be transparent to the user and the user's programs. The POSIX.1f committee is charged with standardizing transparent file access.

There is also existing practice for allowing programs on two different hosts to communicate with each other, much as pipes or FIFOs allow programs on the same host to communicate. In fact, there are at least two competing approaches: Berkeley sockets and the XTI interface from X/Open. The POSIX.1g committee is trying to resolve the differences between these approaches. Sockets and XTI are referred to as protocol-independent interfaces, as they are above the level of the network protocol, the convention that describes precisely how hosts on the network communicate.

That protocol is also the subject of considerable standards effort. There is already an international standard for network protocols: the ISO OSI. However, most UNIX systems have historically used a different protocol: TCP/IP. Trying to resolve the differences among OSI, TCP/IP, and other network protocols will be difficult.

Profiles and POSIX Standards

An important concept in the POSIX lexicon is that of a profile. As the number of standards grows, the number of combinations of standards grows exponentially. However, the number of sensible, coherent combinations is much smaller. Many of the POSIX committees are developing AEPs (application environment profiles) rather than standards. An AEP is a "standard collection of standards" suitable for a particular application area. For example, the POSIX.10 developed a supercomputing AEP. This profile references a number of standards that would be useful for applications that run on supercomputers. These standards include POSIX.1, POSIX.2, the ISO Fortran (Fortran 90) standard, and the C standard. A user who needs the resources of a supercomputer will typically also need the features provided by most or all of these standards.

Profiles are most useful as tools for procurements, particularly by large organizations, such as government agencies. Typically such organizations find that requiring conformance to one or two standards does not adequately specify their needs. For example, although the POSIX.1 standard is quite useful and widely referenced, knowing that your system conforms to POSIX.1 does not by itself guarantee you much; most complex applications require facilities well outside the scope of POSIX.1.

If you are going to ask hardware vendors to propose systems to satisfy a complex set of requirements, using a profile makes your job much simpler. Thus it is not surprising that the U.S. government and the European Commission are actively involved in the development of POSIX profiles and also develop profiles for their own purposes. As the number of POSIX standards grows, these standards are taking a more central place in government profiles.

Appendix Summary

The IEEE POSIX committees have developed standards for programming and user interfaces, based on historical UNIX practice and new standards. Most of the standards are compromises between versions of System V and versions of BSD, with a few innovations where compromise was not possible or was technically inadvisable. The standards have met with broad acceptance from government bodies and industry organizations.

POSIX.1 standardizes C language interfaces to the core UNIX system facilities; Ada and FORTRAN versions of these interfaces are specified by POSIX.5 and POSIX.9. POSIX.2 standardizes a shell and a collection of utilities useful for scripts and interactive use, specifying how these tools should behave in international environments in which character sets and local conventions differ from those in the original UNIX environment. POSIX.4 specifies interfaces for real-time programs executing in UNIX-like environments.

Standards under development will cover parts of system administration, extended system security, networks, and user interfaces. Existing UNIX (and therefore GNU/Linux) system practice in all these areas forms the basis of new standards. In turn, innovations from these standards will find their way into future UNIX and GNU/Linux systems.

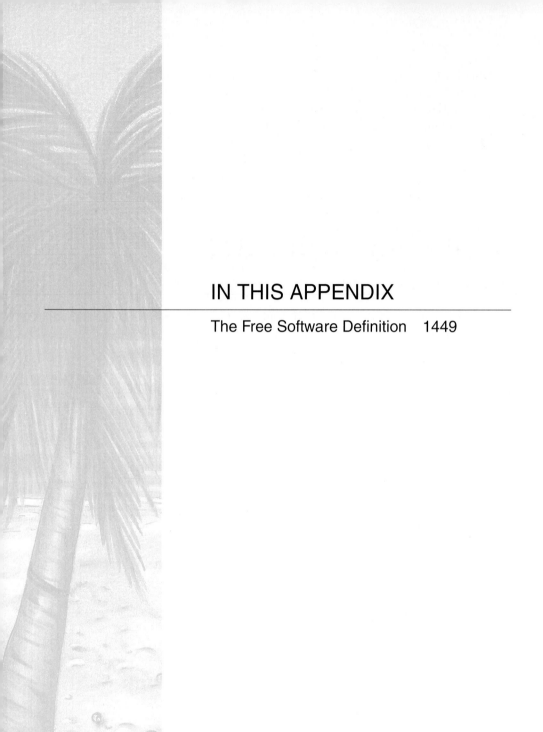

IN THIS APPENDIX

The Free Software Definition

[Croatian | Czech | Danish | Dutch | English | French | Galician | German | Hungarian | Indonesian | Italian | Japanese | Korean | Norwegian | Polish | Portuguese | Russian | Slovenian | Spanish | Turkish] [1]

We maintain this free software definition to show clearly what must be true about a particular software program for it to be considered free software.

"Free software" is a matter of liberty, not price. To understand the concept, you should think of "free" as in "free speech," not as in "free beer."

Free software is a matter of the users' freedom to run, copy, distribute, study, change and improve the software. More precisely, it refers to four kinds of freedom, for the users of the software:

- The freedom to run the program, for any purpose (freedom 0).

- The freedom to study how the program works, and adapt it to your needs (freedom 1). Access to the source code is a precondition for this.

- The freedom to redistribute copies so you can help your neighbor (freedom 2).

- The freedom to improve the program, and release your improvements to the public, so that the whole community benefits. (freedom 3). Access to the source code is a precondition for this.

---

1. This material is at www.gnu.org/philosophy/free-sw.html on the GNU Web site. Because GNU requests a verbatim copy, links remain in place (underlined). View the document on the Web to ensure you are reading the latest copy and to follow the links.

A program is free software if users have all of these freedoms. Thus, you should be free to redistribute copies, either with or without modifications, either gratis or charging a fee for distribution, to <u>anyone anywhere</u>. Being free to do these things means (among other things) that you do not have to ask or pay for permission.

You should also have the freedom to make modifications and use them privately in your own work or play, without even mentioning that they exist. If you do publish your changes, you should not be required to notify anyone in particular, or in any particular way.

The freedom to use a program means the freedom for any kind of person or organization to use it on any kind of computer system, for any kind of overall job, and without being required to communicate subsequently with the developer or any other specific entity.

The freedom to redistribute copies must include binary or executable forms of the program, as well as source code, for both modified and unmodified versions. (Distributing programs in runnable form is necessary for conveniently installable free operating systems.) It is ok if there is no way to produce a binary or executable form (since some languages don't support that feature), but you must have the freedom to redistribute such forms should you find or develop a way to make them.

In order for the freedoms to make changes, and to publish improved versions, to be meaningful, you must have access to the source code of the program. Therefore, accessibility of source code is a necessary condition for free software.

In order for these freedoms to be real, they must be irrevocable as long as you do nothing wrong; if the developer of the software has the power to revoke the license, without your doing anything to give cause, the software is not free.

However, certain kinds of rules about the manner of distributing free software are acceptable, when they don't conflict with the central freedoms. For example, copyleft (very simply stated) is the rule that when redistributing the program, you cannot add restrictions to deny other people the central freedoms. This rule does not conflict with the central freedoms; rather it protects them.

Thus, you may have paid money to get copies of GNU software, or you may have obtained copies at no charge. But regardless of how you got your copies, you always have the freedom to copy and change the software, even to <u>sell copies</u>.

"Free software" does not mean "non-commercial". A free program must be available for commercial use, commercial development, and commercial distribution. Commercial development of free software is no longer unusual; such free commercial software is very important.

Rules about how to package a modified version are acceptable, if they don't effectively block your freedom to release modified versions. Rules that "if you make the program available in this way, you must make it available in that way also" can be acceptable too, on the same condition. (Note that such a rule still leaves you the choice of whether to publish the program or not.) It is also acceptable for the license to require that, if you have distributed a modified version and a previous developer asks for a copy of it, you must send one.

In the GNU project, we use "copyleft" to protect these freedoms legally for everyone. But non-copylefted free software also exists. We believe there are important reasons why it is better to use copyleft, but if your program is non-copylefted free software, we can still use it.

See Categories of Free Software (18k characters) for a description of how "free software," "copylefted software" and other categories of software relate to each other.

Sometimes government export control regulations and trade sanctions can constrain your freedom to distribute copies of programs internationally. Software developers do not have the power to eliminate or override these restrictions, but what they can and must do is refuse to impose them as conditions of use of the program. In this way, the restrictions will not affect activities and people outside the jurisdictions of these governments.

When talking about free software, it is best to avoid using terms like "give away" or "for free", because those terms imply that the issue is about price, not freedom. Some common terms such as "piracy" embody opinions we hope you won't endorse. See Confusing Words and Phrases that are Worth Avoiding for a discussion of these terms. We also have a list of translations of "free software" into various languages.

Finally, note that criteria such as those stated in this free software definition require careful thought for their interpretation. To decide whether a specific software license qualifies as a free software license, we judge it based on these criteria to determine whether it fits their spirit as well as the precise words. If a license includes unconscionable restrictions, we reject it, even if we did not anticipate the issue in these criteria. Sometimes a license requirement raises an issue that calls for extensive thought, including discussions with a lawyer, before we can decide if the requirement is acceptable. When we reach a conclusion about a new issue, we often update these criteria to make it easier to see why certain licenses do or don't qualify.

If you are interested in whether a specific license qualifies as a free software license, see our list of licenses. If the license you are concerned with is not listed there, you can ask us about it by sending us email at <licensing@gnu.org>.

Other Texts to Read

Another group has started using the term "open source" to mean something close (but not identical) to "free software". We prefer the term "free software" because, once you have heard it refers to freedom rather than price, it calls to mind freedom.

[Croatian | Czech | Danish | Dutch | English | French | Galician | German | Hungarian | Indonesian | Italian | Japanese | Korean | Norwegian | Polish | Portuguese | Russian | Slovenian | Spanish | Turkish]

Return to GNU's home page.

Please send FSF & GNU inquiries & questions to gnu@gnu.org. There are also other ways to contact the FSF.

Please send comments on these web pages to webmasters@gnu.org, send other questions to gnu@gnu.org.

Updated: $Date: 2002/08/26 22:02:14 $ $Author: rms $

Glossary

All entries marked with ᶠᵒˡᵈᵒᶜ are based on definitions in the Free Online Dictionary of Computing (www.foldoc.org), Denis Howe, editor. Used with permission.

10.0.0.0	See *private address space* on page 1486.
172.16.0.0	See *private address space* on page 1486.
192.168.0.0	See *private address space* on page 1486.
absolute pathname	A pathname that starts with the root directory (*/*). An absolute pathname locates a file without regard to the working directory.
access	In computer jargon a verb meaning to use, read from, or write to. To access a file means to read from or write to the file.
Access Control List	See *ACL*.
access permission	Permission to read from, write to, or execute a file. If you have write access permission to a file, you can write to the file. Also, *access privilege*.
ACL	Access Control List. A system that performs a function similar to file permissions but with much finer-grain control. Refer to "File Security" on page 1411.
active window	On a desktop the window that receives the characters you type on the keyboard. Same as *focus, desktop* (page 1468).

address mask   See *subnet mask* on page 1495.

alias   In the TC and Z Shells a mechanism that enables you to define new commands.

alphanumeric character   One of the characters, either upper- or lowercase, from A to Z and 0 to 9, inclusive.

ambiguous file reference   A reference to a file that does not necessarily specify any one file but can be used to specify a group of files. The shell expands an ambiguous file reference into a list of filenames. Special characters represent single characters (?), strings of zero or more characters (*), and character classes ([]) within ambiguous file references. An ambiguous file reference is a type of *regular expression*.

angle bracket   A left angle bracket (<) and a right angle bracket (>). The shell uses < to redirect a command's standard input to come from a file and > to redirect the standard output. Also, the shell uses the characters << to signify the start of a here document and >> to append output to a file.

animate   When referring to a window action, means that the action is slowed down so the user can view it. For example, when you minimize a window, it can disappear all at once (not animated), or it can slowly telescope into the panel so you can get a visual feel for what is happening (animated).

antialiasing   Adding gray pixels at the edge of a diagonal line to get rid of the jagged appearance and thereby make the line look smoother. Antialiasing sometimes makes type on a screen look better and sometimes worse; it works best on small and large fonts and is less effective on fonts from 8–15 points. See also *subpixel hinting* (page 1495).

append   To add something to the end of something else. To append text to a file means to add the text to the end of the file. The shell uses >> to append a command's output to a file.

argument   A number, letter, filename, or another string that gives some information to a command and is passed to the command when it is called. A command line argument is anything on a command line following the command name that is passed to the command. An option is a kind of argument.

arithmetic expression   A group of numbers, operators, and parentheses that can be evaluated. When you evaluate an arithmetic expression, you end up with a number. The Bourne Again Shell uses the expr command to evaluate arithmetic expressions; the TC Shell uses @, and the Z Shell uses let.

array   An arrangement of elements (numbers or strings of characters) in one or more dimensions. The TC and Z Shells and gawk can store and process arrays.

ASCII	American Standard Code for Information Interchange. A code that uses seven bits to represent both graphic (letters, numbers, and punctuation) and CONTROL characters. You can represent textual information, including program source code and English text, in ASCII code. Because ASCII is a standard, it is frequently used when exchanging information between computers. See the file **/usr/pub/ascii**, or give the command **man ascii** to see a list of ASCII codes.

Extensions of the ASCII character set use eight bits. The seven-bit set is common; the eight-bit extensions are still coming into popular use. The eighth bit is sometimes referred to as the metabit. |
ASCII terminal	A text-based terminal. Contrast to *graphical display* (page 1469).
ASP	Application service provider. A company that provides applications over the Internet.
asynchronous event	An event that does not occur regularly or synchronously with another event. GNU/Linux system signals are asynchronous; they can occur at any time because they can be initiated by any number of nonregular events.
attachment	A file that is attached to, but is not part of, a piece of e-mail. Attachments are frequently opened by programs (including your Internet browser) that are called by your mail program so you may not be aware that they are not an integral part of an e-mail message.
authentication	The verification of the identity of a person or process. In a communication system, authentication verifies that a message comes from its stated source. Some of the methods of authentication on a GNU/Linux system include the **/etc/passwd** and **/etc/shadow** files, LDAP, Kerberos 5, and SMB authentication.FOLDOC
automatic mounting	A way of demand mounting directories from remote hosts without having them hard-configured into **/etc/vfstab**. Also called *automounting*.
avoided	An object, such as a panel, that should not normally be covered by another object, such as a window.
back door	A security hole deliberately left in place by designers or maintainers of a system. The motivation for such holes is not always sinister; some operating systems, for example come out of the box with privileged accounts intended for use by field service technicians or the vendor's maintenance programmers.

Ken Thompson's 1983 Turing Award lecture to the ACM revealed the existence in early UNIX versions of a back door that may be the most fiendishly clever security hack of all time. The C compiler contained code that would recognize when the `login` command was being recompiled and would insert some code recognizing a password chosen by Thompson, giving him entry to the system whether or not an account had been created for him. |

back door (continued) Normally such a back door could be removed by removing it from the source code for the compiler and recompiling the compiler. But to recompile the compiler, you have to *use* the compiler, so Thompson also arranged that the compiler would *recognize when it was compiling a version of itself* and would insert into the recompiled compiler the code to insert into the recompiled `login` the code to allow Thompson entry, and, of course, the code to recognize itself and do the whole thing again the next time around. Having done this once, he was then able to recompile the compiler from the original sources; the hack perpetuated itself invisibly, leaving the back door in place and active but with no trace in the sources. Sometimes called a wormhole. Also *trap door*.FOLDOC

background process A process that is not run in the foreground. Also called a *detached process*, a background process is initiated by a command line that ends with an ampersand (&). You do not have to wait for a background process to run to completion before giving the shell additional commands. If you have job control, you can move background processes to the foreground, and vice versa.

basename The name of a file that, in contrast to a pathname, does not mention any of the directories containing the file (and therefore does not contain any slashes [/]). For example, **hosts** is the basename of **/etc/hosts**.FOLDOC

baud The maximum information-carrying capacity of a communication channel in symbols (state-transitions or level-transitions) per second. This coincides with bits per second only for two-level modulation with no framing or stop bits. A symbol is a unique state of the communication channel, distinguishable by the receiver from all other possible states. For example, it may be one of two voltage levels on a wire for a direct digital connection, or it might be the phase or frequency of a carrier.FOLDOC
Baud is often mistakenly used as a synonym for bits per second.

baud rate Transmission speed. Usually used to measure terminal or modem speed. Common baud rates range from 110 to 19,200 baud. See *baud*.

Berkeley UNIX One of the two major versions of the UNIX operating system. Berkeley UNIX was developed at the University of California at Berkeley by the Computer Systems Research Group and is often referred to as *BSD* (Berkeley Software Distribution).

BIND Berkeley Internet Name Domain. An implementation of a *DNS* (page 1465) server developed and distributed by the University of California at Berkeley

BIOS   Basic input/output system. On PCs, *EEPROM*-based (page 1466) system soft-ware that provides the lowest-level interface to peripheral devices and controls the first stage of the *bootstrap* (page 1457) process, which loads the operating system. The BIOS can be stored in different types of memory. The memory must be nonvolatile so that it remembers the systems settings even when the system is turned off. Also BIOS ROM. Refer to footnote 10 on page 921 for instructions on how to open the BIOS screens for maintenance.

bit   The smallest piece of information a computer can handle. A *bit* is a binary digit: either 1 or 0 (*on* or *off*).

bit-mapped display   A graphical display device in which each pixel on the screen is controlled by an underlying representation of zeros and ones.

blank character   Either a SPACE or a TAB character, also called *whitespace* (page 1501). Also, in some contexts, NEWLINEs are considered blank characters.

block   A section of a disk or tape (usually 1,024 bytes long but shorter or longer on some systems) that is written at one time.

block device   A disk or tape drive. A block device stores information in blocks of characters. A block device is represented by a block device (block special) file. Contrast to *character device* (page 1460).

block number   Disk and tape *blocks* (page 1457) are numbered so that GNU/Linux can keep track of the data on the device.

blocking factor   The number of logical blocks that make up a physical block on a tape or disk. When you write 1K logical blocks to a tape with a physical block size of 30K, the blocking factor is 30.

boot   See *bootstrap*.

boot loader   A very small program that takes its place in the *bootstrap* process that brings a computer from off or reset to a fully functional state. See *Boot Loader* on page 1039.

bootstrap   Derived from "Pull oneself up by one's own bootstraps," the incremental process of loading an operating system kernel into memory and starting it running without any outside assistance. Frequently shortened to *boot*.

Bourne Again Shell   bash. GNU's command interpreter for UNIX, bash is a POSIX-compliant shell with full Bourne Shell syntax and some C Shell commands built in. The Bourne Again Shell supports emacs-style command line editing, job control, functions, and online help.FOLDOC

Bourne Shell   sh. A UNIX command processor. It was developed by Steve Bourne at AT&T Bell Laboratories. See *shell* on page 1492.

brace   A left brace ({) and a right brace (}). Braces have special meanings to the shell.

bracket   Either a *square bracket* (page 1494) or an *angle bracket* (page 1454).

branch   In a tree structure a branch connects nodes, leaves, and the root. The GNU/Linux filesystem hierarchy is often conceptualized as an upside-down tree. The branches connect files and directories. In a source code control system, such as SCCS or RCS, a branch occurs when a revision is made to a file and is not included in other, subsequent revisions to the file.

bridge   Typically a two-port device originally used for extending networks at layer 2 (data link) of the Internet Protocol model.

broadcast   A transmission to multiple, unspecified recipients. On Ethernet a broadcast packet is a special type of multicast packet that has a special address indicating that all devices that receive it should process it. Broadcast traffic exists at several layers of the network stack, including Ethernet and IP. Broadcast traffic has one source but indeterminate destinations (all hosts on the local network).

broadcast address   The last address on a subnet (usually 255), reserved as shorthand to mean all hosts.

broadcast network   A type of network, such as Ethernet, in which any system can transmit information at any time, and all systems receive every message.

BSD   See *Berkeley UNIX* on page 1456.

buffer   An area of memory that stores data until it can be used. When you write information to a file on a disk, GNU/Linux stores the information in a disk buffer until there is enough to write to the disk or until the disk is ready to receive the information.

builtin (command)   A command that is built into a shell. Each of the three major shells—the Bourne Again, TC, and Z Shells—has its own set of builtins. Refer to "Builtins" on page 161.

byte   A component in the machine data hierarchy usually larger than a bit and smaller than a word; now most often eight bits and the smallest addressable unit of storage. A byte typically holds one character.^{FOLDOC}

C programming language   A modern systems language that has high-level features for efficient, modular programming, as well as lower-level features that make it suitable as a systems programming language. It is machine independent, so that carefully written C programs can be easily transported to run on different machines. Most of the GNU/Linux operating system is written in C, and GNU/Linux provides an ideal environment for programming in C.

C Shell   csh. The C Shell is a UNIX command processor. Developed by Bill Joy for Berkeley UNIX. It was named for the C programming language because its programming constructs are similar to those of C. See *shell* on page 1492.

cable modem   A type of modem that allows you to access the Internet by using your cable television connection.

cache   Holding recently accessed data, a small fast memory designed to speed up subsequent access to the same data. Most often applied to processor-memory access but also used for a local copy of data accessible over a network, from a hard disk, and so on.ᶠᴼᴸᴰᴼᶜ

calling environment   A list of variables and their values that is made available to a called program. Refer to "Executing a Command" on page 562 and "Variable Substitution" on page 699.

cascading stylesheet   See *CSS* on page 1463.

cascading windows   An arrangement of windows such that they overlap, generally with at least part of the title bar visible. Opposite of *tiled windows* (page 1498).

case sensitive   Able to distinguish between upper- and lowercase characters. Unless you set the **ignorecase** parameter, vi performs case-sensitive searches. The grep utility performs case-sensitive searches unless you use the **–i** option.

catenate   To join sequentially, or end to end. The GNU/Linux cat utility catenates files: it displays them one after the other. Also *concatenate*.

chain loading   The technique used by a boot loader to load unsupported operating systems. Used for loading such operating systems as DOS or MS Windows, it works by loading another boot loader.

character-based   A program, utility, or interface that works only with *ASCII* (page 1455) characters. This set of characters includes some simple graphics, such as lines and corners, and can display colored characters but cannot display true graphics. Contrast to *GUI* (page 1469).

character-based terminal	A terminal that displays only characters and very limited graphics. See *character-based*.
character class	In a regular expression, a group of characters that defines which characters can occupy a single character position. A character class definition is usually surrounded by square brackets. The character class defined by [**abcr**] represents a character position that can be occupied by **a**, **b**, **c**, or **r**. Also *list operator*, see "Character Class" on page 1362.
character device	A terminal, printer, or modem. A character device stores or displays characters one at a time. A character device is represented by a character device (character special) file. Contrast to *block device* (page 1457).
checksum	A computed value that depends on the contents of a block of data and is transmitted or stored along with the data in order to detect corruption of the data. The receiving system recomputes the checksum based on the received data and compares this value to the one sent with the data. If the two values are the same, the receiver has some confidence that the data was received correctly. The checksum may be 8 bits (modulo 256 sum), 16, 32, or some other size. It is computed by summing the bytes or words of the data block ignoring overflow. The checksum may be negated so that the total of the data words plus the checksum is zero. Internet packets use a 32-bit checksum.^{FOLDOC}
child process	A process that was created by another process, the parent process. Every process is a child process except for the first process, which is started when GNU/Linux begins execution. When you run a command from the shell, the shell spawns a child process to run the command. See *process* on page 1486.
CIDR	Classless Inter-Domain Routing. A scheme that allocates blocks of Internet addresses in a way that allows summarization into a smaller number of routing table entries. A CIDR block is a block of Internet addresses assigned to an ISP by the Internic (page 362).^{FOLDOC} Refer to "CIDR: Classless Inter-Domain Routing" on page 367.
CIPE	Crypto IP Encapsulation. This protocol tunnels IP packets within encrypted UDP packets, is lightweight and simple, and works over dynamic addresses, NAT, and SOCKS proxies.
cipher (cypher)	A cryptographic system that uses a key to transpose/substitute characters within a message, the key itself, or the message.
ciphertext	Text that is encrypted. Contrast to *plaintext* (page 1485). See also "Encryption" on page 1406.
Classless Inter-Domain Routing	See *CIDR*.

cleartext   Text that is not encrypted; also *plaintext*. Contrast to *ciphertext*.

CLI   Command line interface. See also *character-based* (page 1459).

client   A computer or program that requests one or more services from a server.

CODEC   Coder/decoder or compressor/decompressor. A hardware and/or software technology that codes and decodes data. MPEG is a popular CODEC for computer video.

command   What you give the shell in response to a prompt. When you give the shell a command, it executes a utility, another program, a builtin command, or a shell script. Utilities are often referred to as commands. When you are using an interactive utility, such as vi or mail, you use commands that are appropriate to that utility.

command line   A line of instructions and arguments that executes a command. This term usually refers to a line that you enter in response to a shell prompt on a character-based terminal or terminal emulator. For more information see the tip "GUI? Use a Terminal Emulator to Run Command Line Examples" on page 28.

command substitution   Replacing a command with its output. The shells perform command substitution when you enclose a command between $(and) or between a pair of backquotes (`), also called grave accent marks.

concatenate   See *catenate* on page 1459.

condition code   See *exit status* on page 1466.

connectionless protocol   The data communication method in which communication occurs between hosts with no previous setup. Packets sent between two hosts may take different routes. There is no guarantee that packets will arrive as transmitted or that they will arrive at the destination at all. *UDP* (page 1499) is a connectionless protocol. Also called packet switching. Contrast circuit switching and *connection-oriented protocol*. FOLDOC

connection-oriented protocol   A type of transport layer data communication service that allows a host to send data in a continuous stream to another host. The transport service guarantees that all data will be delivered to the other end in the same order as sent and without duplication. Communication proceeds through three well-defined phases: connection establishment, data transfer, connection release. The most common example is *TCP* (page 1497).

    Also called connection-based protocol and stream-oriented protocol. Contrast *connectionless protocol* and *datagram* (page 1464). FOLDOC

console	See *system console* on page 1496.
console terminal	See *system console* on page 1496.
control character	A character that is not a graphic character, such as a letter, number, or punctuation mark. Such characters are called control characters because they frequently act to control a peripheral device. RETURN and FORMFEED are control characters that control a terminal or printer.
	The word CONTROL is shown in this book in THIS FONT because it is a key that appears on most terminal keyboards. control characters are represented by ASCII codes less than 32 (decimal). See also *nonprinting character* on page 1482.
control flow commands	Commands that alter the order of execution of commands within a shell script or other program. Each one of the shells provides control structures, such as **If** and **While**, as well as other commands that alter the order of execution (for example, exec).
control structure	A statement used to change the order of execution of commands in a shell script or other program. Control structures are among the commands referred to as control flow commands. See *control flow commands*.
cookie	Data stored on a client system by a server. The client system browser sends the cookie back to the server each time it accesses that server. For example, a catalog shopping service may store a cookie on your system when you place your first order. When you return to the site, it knows who you are and can supply your name and address for subsequent orders. You may consider cookies an invasion of privacy.
CPU	Central processing unit. The part of a computer that controls all the other parts. The CPU includes the control unit and the arithmetic and logic unit (ALU). The control unit fetches instructions from memory and decodes them to produce signals that control the other parts of the computer. These signals can cause data to be transferred between memory and ALU or peripherals to perform input or output. A CPU that is housed on a single chip is called a microprocessor. Also *processor* and *central processor*.
cracker	An individual who attempts to gain unauthorized access to a computer system. These individuals are often malicious and have many means at their disposal for breaking into a system. Contrast to *hacker* (page 1470). FOLDOC
crash	The system suddenly stops/fails when you do not intend it to. Derived from the action of the hard disk heads on the surface of the disk when the air gap between the two collapses.

cryptography   The practice and study of encryption and decryption—encoding data so that only a specific individual/machine can decode it. A system for encrypting and decrypting data is a cryptosystem. These usually involve an algorithm for combining the original data (plaintext) with one or more keys—numbers or strings of characters known only to the sender and/or recipient. The resulting output is called ciphertext.

The security of a cryptosystem usually depends on the secrecy of keys rather than on the supposed secrecy of an algorithm. Because a strong cryptosystem has a large range of keys, it is not possible to try all of them. Ciphertext appears random to standard statistical tests and resists known methods for breaking codes.FOLDOC

.cshrc file   In your home directory, a file that the TC Shell executes each time you invoke a new TC Shell. You can use this file to establish variables and aliases.

CSS   Cascading stylesheet. Describes how documents are presented on screen and in print. Attaching a stylesheet to a structured document can affect the way it looks without adding new HTML (or other) tags and without giving up device independence. Also *stylesheet*.

current (process, line, character, directory, event, and so on)   The item that is immediately available, working, or being used. The current process controls the program you are running; the current line or character is the one the cursor is on; the current directory is the working directory.

cursor   A small lighted rectangle, underscore, or vertical bar that appears on the terminal screen and indicates where the next character is going to appear. Differs from the *mouse pointer* (page 1480).

daemon   A program that is not invoked explicitly but lies dormant, waiting for some condition(s) to occur. The idea is that the perpetrator of the condition need not be aware that a daemon is lurking (although often a program will commit an action only because it knows that it will implicitly invoke a daemon). From the mythological meaning, later rationalized as the acronym Disk And Execution MONitor.FOLDOC See Table on page 394 for a list of daemons.

data structure   A particular format for storing, organizing, working with, and retrieving data. Frequently data structures are designed to work with specific algorithms that facilitate these tasks. Common data structures include trees, files, records, tables, arrays, and so on.

datagram	A self-contained, independent entity of data carrying sufficient information to be routed from the source to the destination computer without reliance on earlier exchanges between this source and destination computer and the transporting network.^{FOLDOC} See also *frame* (page 1468) and *packet* (page 1483).
dataless	A computer, usually a workstation, that uses a local disk to boot a copy of the operating system and access system files but does not use a local disk to store user files.
debug	To correct a program by removing its bugs (that is, errors).
default	Something that is selected without being explicitly specified. For example, when used without an argument, ls displays a list of the files in the working directory by default.
delta	A set of changes made to a file that has been encoded by the Source Code Control System (SCCS).
denial of service	An attack that attempts to make the target host or network unusable.
dereference	When speaking of symbolic links, follow the link rather than working with the reference to the link. For example, the –L or ––dereference option causes ls to list the entry that a symbolic link points to rather than the symbolic link (the reference) itself.
desktop	A collection of windows, toolbars, and icons/buttons, some or all of which appear on your display. A desktop comprises one or more *workspaces* (page 1502). Refer to "Desktop" on page 174.
detached process	See *background process* on page 1456.
device	A disk drive, printer, terminal, plotter, or other input/output unit that can be attached to the computer.
device driver	Part of the GNU/Linux kernel that controls a device, such as a terminal, disk drive, or printer.
device file	A file that represents a device. Also *special file*.
device filename	The pathname of a device file. All GNU/Linux systems have two kinds of device files: block and character device files. GNU/Linux also has FIFOs (named pipes) and sockets. Device files are traditionally located in the **/dev** directory.
device number	See *major device number* (page 1478) and *minor device number* (page 1480).

DHCP	Dynamic Host Configuration Protocol. A protocol that dynamically allocates IP addresses to computers on a LAN.^{FOLDOC} Refer to "DHCP Client" on page 1028.
directory	Short for *directory file*. A file that contains a list of other files.
directory service	A structured repository of information on people and resources within an organization, facilitating management and communication.^{FOLDOC}
disk partition	See *partition* on page 1484.
diskless	A computer, usually a workstation, that has no disk and must contact another computer (a server) to boot a copy of the operating system and access the necessary system files.
distributed computing	A style of computing in which tasks or services are performed by a network of cooperating systems, some of which may be specialized.
DNS	Domain Name Service. A distributed service that manages the correspondence of full hostnames (those that include a domain name) to IP addresses and other system characteristics.
document object model	See *DOM*.
DOM	Document Object Model. A platform-/language-independent interface that enables a program dynamically to update the content, structure, and style of a document. The changes can then be made part of the displayed document. Go to www.w3.org/DOM for more information.
domain	A name associated with an organization, or part of an organization, to help identify systems uniquely. Domain names are assigned hierarchically; the domain Berkeley.EDU refers to the University of California at Berkeley, for example (part of the higher-level education domain).
Domain Name Service	See *DNS*.
door	An evolving filesystem-based *RPC* (page 1491) mechanism.
drag	To move an icon from one position or application to another, usually in the context of a window manager. The motion part of drag-and-drop.
DSA	Digital Signature Algorithm. A public key cipher used to generate digital signatures.

DSL   Digital subscriber line/loop. Provides high-speed digital communication over a specialized, conditioned telephone line. See also *xDSL* (page 1502).

Dynamic Host Configuration Protocol   See *DHCP* on page 1465.

editor   A utility, such as vim or emacs, that creates and modifies text files.

EEPROM   Electrically erasable, programmable read-only memory. A *PROM* (page 1486) that can be written to.

effective user ID   The user ID that a process appears to have; usually the same as the user ID. For example, while you are running a setuid program, the effective user ID of the process running the program is that of the owner of the program.

element   One thing, usually a basic part of a group of things. An element of a numeric array is one of the numbers that are stored in the array.

emergency boot floppy   See *rescue disk* on page 1489.

emoticon   See *smiley* on page 1492.

environment   See *calling environment* on page 1459.

EOF   End of file.

EPROM   Erasable programmable read-only memory. A *PROM* (page 1486) that can be written to by applying a higher than normal voltage.

escape   See *quote* on page 1487.

Ethernet   A type of *LAN* (page 1476) capable of transfer rates up to 1,000 megabits per second. Refer to "Ethernet" on page 355.

event   An occurrence, or happening, of significance to a task or program, such as the completion of an asynchronous input/output operation, such as a keypress or mouse click.FOLDOC

exit status   The status returned by a process; either successful (usually 0) or unsuccessful (usually 1).

expression   See *logical expression* (page 1477) and *arithmetic expression* (page 1454).

extranet	A network extension for a subset of users (such as students at a particular school or engineers working for the same company), an extranet limits access to private information even though it travels on the public Internet.
failsafe session	A session that allows you to log in on a minimal desktop in case your standard login does not work well enough to allow you to log in to fix a login problem.
FDDI	Fiber Distributed Data Interface. A type of *LAN* (page 1476) designed to transport data at the rate of 100 million bits per second over fiberoptic cable.
file	A collection of related information referred to with a *filename* and frequently stored on a disk. Text files typically contain memos, reports, messages, program source code, lists, or manuscripts. Binary or executable files contain utilities or programs that you can run. Refer to "Directory and Ordinary Files" on page 103.
filename	The name of a file. A filename refers to a file.
filename completion	Automatic completion of a filename after you specify a unique prefix.
filename extension	The part of a filename following a period.
filename generation	What occurs when the shell expands ambiguous file references. See *ambiguous file reference* on page 1454.
filesystem	A *data structure* (page 1463) that usually resides on part of a disk. All GNU/Linux systems have a root filesystem, and most have at least a few other filesystems. Each filesystem is composed of some number of blocks, depending on the size of the disk partition that has been assigned to the filesystem. Each filesystem has a control block, named the superblock, that contains information about the filesystem. The other blocks in a filesystem are inodes, which contain control information about individual files, and data blocks, which contain the information in the files.
filling	A variant of maximizing in which window edges are pushed out as far as they can go without overlapping another window.
filter	A command that can take its input from standard input and send its output to standard output. A filter transforms the input stream of data and sends it to standard output. A pipe usually connects a filter's input to standard output of one command, and a second pipe connects the filter's output to standard input of another command. The grep and sort utilities are commonly used as filters.

firewall
A device for policy-based traffic management used to keep a network secure. A firewall can be implemented in a single router that filters out unwanted packets, or it can use a combination of routers, proxy servers, and other devices. Firewalls are widely used to give users access to the Internet in a secure fashion and to separate a company's public WWW server from its internal network. Firewalls are also used to keep internal network segments more secure.

Recently the term has come to be more loosely defined to include a simple packet filter running on an endpoint machine.

See also *proxy server* on page 1487.

focus, desktop
On a desktop the window that is active. The window with the desktop focus receives the characters you type on the keyboard. Same as *active window* (page 1453).

footer
The part of a format that goes at the bottom (or foot) of a page. Contrast to *header*.

foreground process
When you run a command in the foreground, the shell waits for the command to finish before giving you another prompt. You must wait for a foreground process to run to completion before you can give the shell another command. If you have job control, you can move background processes to the foreground, and vice versa. See *job control* on page 1475. Contrast with *background process* (page 1456).

fork
To create a process. When one process creates another process, it forks a process. Also *spawn*.

FQDN
Fully qualified domain name. The full name of a system, consisting of its local hostname and its domain name, including a top-level domain. For example, **sobell** is a hostname and **sobell.com** is an FQDN. An FQDN is sufficient to determine a unique Internet address for a machine on the Internet.FOLDOC

frame
A data link layer packet that contains, in addition to data, the header and trailer information required by the physical medium. Network layer packets are encapsulated to become frames.FOLDOC See also *datagram* (page 1464) and *packet* (page 1483).

free list
In a filesystem the list of blocks that are available for use. Information about the free list is kept in the superblock of the filesystem.

free software
Refer to Appendix E, "The Free Software Definition" (page 1449).

full duplex
The ability to receive and transmit data simultaneously. A *network switch* (page 1482) is typically a full-duplex device. Contrast to *half duplex* (page 1470).

fully qualified domain name	See *FQDN* on page 1468.
function	See *shell function* on page 1492.
gateway	A generic term for a computer or a special device connected to more than one dissimilar type of network to pass data between them. Unlike a router, a gateway often must convert the information into a different format before passing it on. The historical usage of gateway to designate a router is deprecated.
giga-	In the binary system the giga- prefix multiplies by 2^{30}, or 1,073,741,824. Gigabit and gigabyte are common uses of this prefix. Abbreviated as G.
glyph	A symbol that communicates a specific piece of information nonverbally. A *smiley* (page 1492) is a glyph.
GMT	Greenwich Mean Time. See *UTC* on page 1500.
graphical display	A bitmapped monitor that can display graphical images. Contrast to *ASCII terminal* (page 1455).
graphical user interface	See *GUI* on page 1469.
group (of users)	A collection of users. Groups are used as a basis for determining file access permissions. If you are not the owner of a file and you belong to the group the file is assigned to, you are subject to the group access permissions for the file. A user can simultaneously belong to several groups.
group (of windows)	A way to identify similar windows so that they can be displayed and acted on similarly. Typically windows started by a given application belong to the same group. You can change the group a window belongs to with Window Operations menu: In group (page 257).
group ID	A unique number that identifies a set of users. It is stored in the password and group databases (**/etc/passwd** and **/etc/group** files or their NIS equivalents). The group database associates group IDs with group names.
GUI	Graphical user interface. A GUI provides a way to interact with a computer system by choosing items from menus or manipulating pictures drawn on a display screen instead of by typing command lines. Under GNU/Linux, the X Window System provides a graphical display and mouse/keyboard input. GNOME and KDE are two popular desktop managers that run under X. Contrast to *character-based* (page 1459).

hacker
A person who enjoys exploring the details of programmable systems and how to stretch their capabilities, as opposed to users, who prefer to learn only the minimum necessary. One who programs enthusiastically (even obsessively) or who enjoys programming rather than just theorizing about programming.ᶠᴼᴸᴰᴼᶜ Contrast to *cracker* (page 1462).

half duplex
A half-duplex device can only receive or transmit at a given moment; it cannot do both. A *hub* (page 1472) is typically a half-duplex device. Contrast to *full duplex* (page 1468).

hard link
A directory entry that contains the filename and inode number for a file. The inode number identifies the location of control information for the file on the disk, which in turn identifies the location of the file's contents on the disk. Every file has at least one hard link, which locates the file in a directory. When you remove the last hard link to a file, you can no longer access the file. See *link* (page 1477) and *symbolic link* (page 1496).

hash
A string that is generated from another string. See *one-way hash function* on page 1483. When used for security a hash can prove, almost to a certainty, that a message has not been tampered with during transmission: The sender generates a hash of a message; encrypts the message and hash; sends the encrypted message and hash to the recipient, who decrypts the message and hash; generates a second hash from the message; and compares the hash that the sender generated to the new hash. When they are the same, the message has probably not been tampered with. A hash can also be used to create an index called a *hash table* (next). Also *hash value*.

hash table
An index created from hashes of the items to be indexed. The hash function makes it highly unlikely that two items will create the same hash. To look up an item in the index, create a hash of the item and search for the hash. Because the hash is typically shorter than the item, the search is more efficient.

header
When you are formatting a document, the header goes at the top, or head, of a page. In electronic mail the header identifies who sent the message, when it was sent, the subject of the message, and so forth.

here document
A shell script that takes its input from the file that contains the script.

hesiod
The name server of project Athena. Hesiod is a name service library that is derived from *BIND* (page 1456) and leverages a DNS infrastructure.

heterogeneous
Consisting of different parts; a heterogeneous network includes systems produced by different manufacturers and/or running different operating systems.

hexadecimal number

A base 16 number. Hexadecimal (or *hex*) numbers are composed of the hexadecimal digits 0–9 and A–F.

Decimal	Octal	Hex	Decimal	Octal	Hex
1	1	1	17	21	11
2	2	2	18	22	12
3	3	3	19	23	13
4	4	4	20	24	14
5	5	5	21	25	15
6	6	6	31	37	1F
7	7	7	32	40	20
8	10	8	33	41	21
9	11	9	64	100	40
10	12	A	96	140	60
11	13	B	100	144	64
12	14	C	128	200	80
13	15	D	254	376	FE
14	16	E	255	377	FF
15	17	F	256	400	100
16	20	10	257	401	101

hidden file

See *invisible file* on page 1474.

hierarchy

An organization with a few things, or thing, one at the top and with several things below each other thing. An inverted tree structure. Examples in computing include a directory hierarchy where each directory may contain files or other directories; a hierarchical network; a class hierarchy in object-oriented programming.^{FOLDOC} Refer to "The Hierarchical Filesystem" on page 101.

history

Provided by the TC and Z Shells, a mechanism that enables you to modify and reexecute recent commands.

home directory

The directory that is your working directory when you first log in. The pathname of this directory is stored in the **HOME** shell variable.

hover

To leave the mouse pointer stationary for a moment over an object. In many cases this displays a *tooltip* (page 1498).

HTML   Hypertext Markup Language. A *hypertext* document format used on the World Wide Web. Tags, which are embedded in the text, consist of a less than sign (<), a directive, zero or more parameters, and a greater than sign (>). Matched pairs of directives, such as <TITLE> and </TITLE> delimit text that is to appear in a special place or style.^{FOLDOC} For more information on HTML go to www.html-help.com/faq/html/all.html.

HTTP   Hypertext Transfer Protocol. The client/server TCP/IP protocol used on the World Wide Web for the exchange of *HTML* documents.

hub   A multiport repeater. A hub rebroadcasts all packets it receives on all ports. This term is frequently used to refer to small hubs and switches regardless of device intelligence. A generic term for a layer -2 shared-media networking device. Today the term *hub* is sometimes used to refer to small intelligent devices, although that was not its original meaning. Contrast with *network switch* (page 1482).

hypertext A collection of documents/nodes containing (usually highlighted or underlined) cross-references or links which, with the aid of an interactive browser program, allow the reader to move easily from one document to another.^{FOLDOC}

Hypertext Markup Language See *HTML* on page 1472.

Hypertext Transfer Protocol See *HTTP* on page 1472.

i/o device Input/output device. See *device* on page 1464.

IANA   Internet Assigned Numbers Authority.   A group that maintains a database of all permanent, registered system services (www.iana.org).

icon   In a GUI, a small picture representing a file, directory, action, program, and so on. When you click an icon, an action, such as opening a window and starting a program or displaying a directory or Web site, takes place. From miniature religious statues.^{FOLDOC}

iconify The process of changing a window into an *icon*. Contrast with *restore* (page 1489).

ignored window A state in which a window has no decoration and therefore no buttons or a titlebar to control it with. This state is turned on and off by Window Operations menu: Toggle⇨Ignored (page 256). Same as *unmanaged window*.

indentation   See *indention*.

indention   The blank space between the margin and the beginning of a line that is set in from the margin.

inode   A *data structure* (page 1463) that contains information about a file. An inode for a file contains the file's length, the times the file was last accessed and modified, the time the inode was last modified, owner and group IDs, access privileges, number of links, and pointers to the data blocks that contain the file itself. Each directory entry associates a filename with an inode. Although a single file may have several filenames (one for each link), it has only one inode.

input   Information that is fed to a program from a terminal or other file. See *standard input* on page 1494.

installation   A computer at a specific location. Some aspects of the GNU/Linux system are installation dependent. Also *site*.

interactive   A program that allows ongoing dialog with the user. When you give commands in response to shell prompts, you are using the shell interactively. Also, when you give commands to utilities, such as vi and mail, you are using the utilities interactively.

interface   The meeting point of two subsystems. When two programs work together, their interface includes every aspect of either program that the other deals with. The *user interface* (page 1500) of a program includes every program aspect the user comes into contact with: the syntax and semantics involved in invoking the program, the input and output of the program, and its error and informational messages. The shell and each of the utilities and built-in commands have a user interface.

International Organization for Standardization   See *ISO* on page 1475.

internet   A large network that encompasses other, smaller networks.

Internet   The largest internet in the world. The Internet (capital I) is a multilevel hierarchy composed of backbone networks (ARPAnet, NSFNet, MILNET, and others), midlevel networks, and stub networks. These include commercial (**.com** or **.co**), university (**.ac** or **.edu**), research (**.org** or **.net**), and military (**.mil**) networks and span many different physical networks around the world with various protocols, including the Internet Protocol (IP). Outside the United States, country code domains are popular (**.us**, **.es**, **.mx**, **.de**, and so forth), although you will see them used within the United States too.

Internet Protocol   See *IP*.

Internet Service   See *ISP*.
Provider

intranet   An inhouse network designed to serve a group of people such as a corporation or school. The general public on the Internet does not have access to the intranet. See page 352.

invisible file   A file whose filename starts with a period. These files are called invisible because the ls utility does not normally list them. Use the –a option of ls to list all files, including invisible ones. Also, the shell does not expand a leading asterisk (✳) in an ambiguous file reference to match the filename of an invisible file. Also *hidden file*.

IP   Internet Protocol. The network layer for TCP/IP. IP is a best-effort, packet-switching, *connectionless protocol* (page 1461) that provides packet routing, fragmentation, and reassembly through the data link layer. Version IPv4 is slowly giving way to version *IPv6* (page 1474).FOLDOC

IP address   Internet Protocol address. A four-part address associated with a particular network connection for a system using the Internet Protocol (IP). A system that is attached to multiple networks that use the IP will have a different IP address for each network interface.

IP multicast   See *multicast* on page 1480.

IP spoofing   A technique used to gain unauthorized access to a computer. The would-be intruder sends messages to the target machine. These messages contain an IP address indicating that the messages are coming from a trusted host. The target machine responds to the messages, giving the intruder (privileged) access to the target.

IPv4   See *IP* and *IPv6*.

IPv6   *IP* version 6. The next generation of Internet Protocol, which provides a much larger address space (2^{128} bits versus 2^{32} for IPv4) that is designed to accommodate the rapidly growing number of Internet addressable devices. IPv6 also has built-in autoconfiguration, enhanced security, better multicast support, and many other features.

ISDN   Integrated Services Digital Network.   A set of communications standards that allows a single pair of digital or standard telephone wires to carry voice, data, and video at a rate of 64 kilobits per second.

ISO International Organization for Standardization. A voluntary, nontreaty organization founded in 1946. It is responsible for creating international standards in many areas, including computers and communications. Its members are the national standards organizations of 89 countries, including the American National Standards Institute.FOLDOC

ISO9660 The *ISO* standard defining a filesystem for CD-ROMs.

ISP Internet service provider. Provides Internet access to its customers.

job control A facility that enables you to move commands from the foreground to the background and vice versa. TC and Z Shell job control enables you to stop commands temporarily.

journaling filesystem A filesystem that maintains a noncached log file, or journal, which records all transactions involving the filesystem. When a transaction is complete, it is marked as complete in the log file.

 The log file results in greatly reduced time spent recovering a filesystem after a crash, making it particularly valuable in systems where high availability is an issue.

JPEG Joint Photographic Experts Group. The name of the committee that designed the standard image-compression algorithm. JPEG is designed for compressing either full-color or gray-scale digital images of natural, real-world scenes and does not work as well on nonrealistic images, such as cartoons or line drawings. Filename extensions: **.jpg**, **.jpeg**.FOLDOC

justify To expand a line of type to the right margin in the process of formatting text. A line is justified by increasing the space between words and sometimes between letters on the line.

Kerberos An MIT-developed security system that authenticates users and machines. It does not provide authorization to services or databases; it establishes identity at logon, which is used throughout the session. Once you are authenticated, you can open as many terminals, windows, services, or other network accesses until your session expires.

kernel The part of the operating system that allocates machine resources, including memory, disk space, and *CPU* (page 1462) cycles, to all the other programs that run on a computer. The kernel includes the low-level hardware interfaces (drivers) and manages *processes* (page 1486), the means by which GNU/Linux executes programs. The kernel is the part of the GNU/Linux system that Linus Torvalds originally wrote (see the beginning of Chapter 1).

key binding	A *keyboard* key is said to be bound to the action that results from pressing it. Typically keys are bound to the letters that appear on the keycaps: When you press **A**, an A appears on the screen. Key binding usually refers to what happens when you press a combination of keys, one of which is CONTROL, ALT, META, or SHIFT, or when you press a series of keys, the first of which is typically ESCAPE.
keyboard	A hardware input device consisting of a number of mechanical buttons (keys) that the user presses to input characters to a computer. By default a keyboard is connected to standard input of a shell.ᶠᵒˡᵈᵒᶜ
kilo-	In the binary system the kilo- prefix multiplies by 2^{10}, or 1,024. Kilobit and kilobyte are common uses of this prefix. Abbreviated as k.
Korn Shell	ksh. A command processor, developed by David Korn at AT&T Bell Laboratories, that is compatible with the Bourne Shell but includes many extensions. See also *shell* on page 1492.
LAN	Local area network. A network that connects computers within a localized area (such as a single site, building, or department).
large number	Go to mathworld.wolfram.com/LargeNumber.html for a comprehensive list.
LDAP	Lightweight Directory Access Protocol. A protocol for accessing online directory services.ᶠᵒˡᵈᵒᶜ See *directory service* on page 1465.
leaf	In a tree structure the end of a branch that cannot support other branches. When the GNU/Linux filesystem hierarchy is conceptualized as a tree, files that are not directories are leaves. See *node* on page 1482.
least privilege, concept of	Mistakes that Superuser makes can be much more devastating than those made by an ordinary user. When you are working on the computer, especially when you are working as the system administrator, always perform any task using the least privilege possible. If you can perform a task logged in as an ordinary user, do so. If you must be logged in as Superuser, do as much as you can as an ordinary user, log in or su so you are Superuser, do as much of the task that has to be done as Superuser, and revert to being an ordinary user as soon as you can. Because you are more likely to make a mistake when you are rushing, this concept becomes more important when you have less time to apply it.
Lightweight Directory Access Protocol	See *LDAP*.

link	A pointer to a file. There are two kinds of links: hard links and symbolic (soft) links. A hard link associates a filename with a place on the disk where the contents of the file is located. A symbolic link associates a filename with the pathname of a hard link to a file. See *hard link* (page 1470) and *symbolic link* (page 1496).
Linux-PAM	See *PAM* on page 1484.
Linux-Pluggable Authentication Modules	See *PAM* on page 1484.
loadable kernel module	See *loadable module*.
loadable module	A portion of the operating system that controls a special device and that can be loaded automatically into a running kernel as needed to access that device. See "Using Loadable Kernel Modules" on page 1038.
local area network	See *LAN* on page 1476.
locale	The language; date, time, and currency formats; character sets; and so forth that pertain to a geopolitical place or area. For example, en_US specifies English as spoken in the United States and dollars; en_UK specifies English as spoken in the United Kingdom and pounds. See the **locale** (5) man page for more information.
log in	To gain access to a computer system by responding correctly to the login: and Password: prompts. Also, *log on, login*.
log out	To end your session by exiting from your login shell. Also *log off*.
logical expression	A collection of strings separated by logical operators (>, >=, =, !=, <=, and <) that can be evaluated as *true* or *false*. Also *Boolean expression*.
.login file	A file that the TC Shell executes when you log in. You can use this file to set environment variables and to run commands that you want executed at the beginning of each session.
login name	The name you enter in response to the login: prompt. Other users use your login name when they send you mail or write to you. Each login name has a corresponding user ID, which is the numeric identifier for the user. Both the login name and the user ID are stored in the **passwd** database (**/etc/passwd** or the NIS equivalent).

login shell	The shell that you are using when you log in. The login shell can fork other processes that can run other shells, utilities, and programs.
.logout file	A file that the TC Shell executes when you log out, assuming that the TC Shell is your login shell. You can put in the **.logout** file commands that you want run each time you log out.
MAC address	Media access control address. The unique hardware address of a device connected to a shared network medium.^{FOLDOC}
machine collating sequence	The sequence in which the computer orders characters. The machine collating sequence affects the outcome of sorts and other procedures that put lists in alphabetical order. Many computers use ASCII codes so their machine collating sequences correspond to the ordering of the ASCII codes for characters.
macro	A single instruction that a program replaces by several (usually more complex) instructions. The C compiler recognizes macros, which are defined using a **#define** instruction to the preprocessor.
magic number	A magic number, which occurs in the first 512 bytes of a binary file, is a 1-, 2-, or 4-byte numeric value or character string that uniquely identifies the type of file (much like a DOS 3-character filename extension). See **/usr/share/magic** and the **magic** man page (5) for more information. See also file on page 1163 in Part III.
main memory	Random access memory (RAM), an integral part of the computer; contrasted with disk storage. Although disk storage is sometimes referred to as memory, it is never referred to as main memory.
major device number	A number assigned to a class of devices, such as terminals, printers, or disk drives. Using the ls utility with the –l option to list the contents of the /dev directory displays the major and minor device numbers of many devices (as major, minor).
MAN	Metropolitan area network. A network that connects computers and *LANs* (page 1476) at multiple sites in a small regional area, such as a city.
MD5	Message Digest 5. A *one-way hash function* (page 1483).
mega-	In the binary system the mega- prefix multiplies by 2^{20}, or 1,048,576. Megabit and megabyte are common uses of this prefix. Abbreviated as M.

menu	A list from which the user may select an operation to be performed. This is often done with a mouse or other pointing device under a GUI but may also be controlled from the keyboard. Very convenient for beginners, menus show what commands are available and make experimenting with a new program easy, often reducing the need for user documentation. Experienced users, however, usually prefer keyboard commands, especially for frequently used operations, because they are faster to use.^{FOLDOC}
merge	To combine two ordered lists so that the resulting list is still in order. The sort utility can merge files.
META **key**	On the keyboard, a key that is labeled META or ALT. Use this key as you would the SHIFT key. While holding it down, press another key. The emacs editor makes extensive use of the META key.
metacharacter	A character that has a special meaning to the shell or another program in a particular context. Metacharacters are used in the ambiguous file references recognized by the shell and in the regular expressions recognized by several utilities. You must quote a metacharacter if you want to use it without invoking its special meaning. See *regular character* (page 1489) and *special character* (page 1493).
metadata	Data about data. In data processing metadata is definitional data that provides information about or documentation of other data managed within an application or environment. For example, metadata can document data about data elements or attributes (name, size, data type, and so on), records or *data structures* (page 1463) (length, fields, columns, and so on), and data itself (where it is located, how it is associated, who owns it, and so on). Metadata can include descriptive information about the context, quality and condition, or characteristics of the data.^{FOLDOC}
metropolitan area network	See *MAN* on page 1478.
MIME	Multipurpose Internet Mail Extension. Originally used to describe how specific types of files that were attached to e-mail were to be handled. Today MIME types describe how a file is to be opened or worked with, based on its filename extension.

minimize   See *iconify* on page 1472.

minor device number   A number assigned to a specific device within a class of devices. See *major device number* on page 1478.

modem   Modulate/demodulate. A peripheral device that modulates digital data into analog data for transmission over a voice-grade telephone line. Another modem demodulates the data at the other end.

module   See *loadable module* on page 1477.

mount   To make a filesystem accessible to system users. When a filesystem is not mounted, you cannot read from or write to files it contains.

mount point   A directory that you mount a local or remote filesystem on (page 974).

mouse   A device you use to point to a particular location on a display screen, typically so you can choose a menu item, draw a line, or highlight some text. You control a pointer on the screen by sliding a mouse around on a flat surface; the position of the pointer moves relative to the movement of the mouse. You select items by pressing one or more buttons on the mouse.

mouse pointer   In a GUI a marker that moves in correspondence with the mouse. It is usually a small black **X** with a white border or an arrow. Differs from the *cursor* (page 1463).

mouseover   The action of passing the mouse pointer over an icon or other object on the screen.

multiboot specification   Specifies an interface between a boot loader and an operating system. With compliant boot loaders and operating systems, any boot loader should be able to load any operating system. The object of this specification is to get different operating systems to work on a single machine. For more information, go to odin-os.sourceforge.net/guides/multiboot.html.

multicast   A multicast packet has one source and multiple destinations. In multicast, source hosts register at a special address to transmit data. Destination hosts register at the same address to receive data. In contrast to *broadcast* (page 1458), which is LAN based, multicast traffic is designed to work across routed networks on a subscription basis. Multicast reduces network traffic by transmitting a packet one time, with the router at the end of the path breaking it apart as needed for multiple recipients.

multitasking A computer system that allows a user to run more than one job at a time. One trait of a multitasking system, such as GNU/Linux, is that it allows you to run a job in the background while running a job in the foreground.

multiuser system A computer system that can be used by more than one person at a time. GNU/Linux is a multiuser operating system. Contrast to *single-user system*.

NAT Network Address Translation. A scheme that enables a LAN to use one set of IP addresses internally and a different set externally. The internal set is for LAN-private use. The external set is typically used on the Internet and is Internet unique.

netboot To boot a computer over the network as opposed to booting from a local disk.

netiquette The conventions of politeness recognized on Usenet and in mailing lists, such as not (cross-)posting to inappropriate groups and refraining from commercial advertising outside the business groups.

The most important rule of netiquette is "Think before you post." If what you intend to post will not make a positive contribution to the newsgroup and be of interest to several readers, do not post it. Personal messages to one or two individuals should not be posted to newsgroups; use private e-mail instead.FOLDOC

netmask A 32-bit mask (for IPv4), which shows how an Internet address is to be divided into network, subnet, and host parts. The netmask has 1s in the bit positions in the 32-bit address that are to be used for the network and subnet parts; 0s, for the host part. The mask should contain at least the standard network portion (as determined by the address class), and the subnet field should be contiguous with the network portion.FOLDOC

network address The network portion (**netid**) of an IP address. For a class A network, this is the first byte, or segment, of the IP address; for class B it is the first two bytes; and for class C it is the first three bytes. In each case the balance of the IP address is the host address (**hostid**). Assigned network addresses are globally unique within the Internet. Also *network number*. See also "Host Address" on page 362.

Network Filesystem See *NFS*.

Network Information Service See *NIS*.

network number   See *network address*.

network segment   A part of an Ethernet or other network on which all message traffic is common to all nodes; that is, it is broadcast from one node on the segment and received by all others. This is normally because the segment is a single continuous conductor. Communication between nodes on different segments is via one or more routers.FOLDOC

network switch   A connecting device in networks. Switches are increasingly replacing shared media hubs in order to increase bandwidth. For example, a 16-port 10BaseT hub shares the total 10 megabits per second bandwidth with all 16 attached nodes. By replacing the hub with a switch, each sender and receiver has the full 10 megabits per second capacity. Each port on the switch can give full bandwidth to a single server or client station or to a hub with several stations. Network switch refers to a device with intelligence. Contrast to *hub* (page 1472).

Network Time Protocol   See *NTP*.

NFS   Network Filesystem. A remote filesystem designed by Sun Microsystems, available on computers from most UNIX system vendors.

NIC   Network interface card (or controller). An adapter circuit board installed in a computer to provide a physical connection to a network.FOLDOC

NIS   Network Information Service. A distributed service built on a shared database to manage system-independent information (such as login names and passwords).

NNTP   Network News Transfer Protocol. Refer to "Usenet" on page 399.

node   In a tree structure, the end of a branch that can support other branches. When the GNU/Linux filesystem hierarchy is conceptualized as a tree, directories are nodes. See *leaf* on page 1476.

nonprinting character   See *control character* on page 1462. Also *nonprintable character*.

nonvolatile storage   A storage device whose contents are preserved when its power is off. Also NVS and persistent storage. Some examples are CD-ROM, paper punch tape, hard disk, *ROM* (page 1490), *PROM* (page 1486), *EPROM* (page 1466), and *EE-PROM* (page 1466). Contrast to *RAM* (page 1487).

NTP   Network Time Protocol. Built on top of TCP/IP, NTP maintains accurate local time by referring to known accurate clocks on the Internet.

null string   A string that could contain characters but does not. A string of zero length.

octal number   A base 8 number. Octal numbers are composed of the digits 0–7, inclusive. Refer to the table under *hexadecimal number* (page 1471).

one-way hash function   A one-way function that takes a variable-length message and produces a fixed-length hash. Given the hash, it is computationally infeasible to find a message with that hash; in fact, you cannot determine any usable information about a message with that hash. Also *message digest function*. See also *hash* (page 1470).

OpenSSH   A free version of the SSH (secure shell) protocol suite that replaces TELNET, rlogin, and more with secure programs that encrypt all communication, even passwords, over a network. Refer to "OpenSSH: Provides Secure Network Tools" on page 1029.

operating system   A control program for a computer that allocates computer resources, schedules tasks, and provides the user with a way to access resources.

option   A command line argument that modifies the effects of a command. Options are usually preceded by hyphens on the command line and traditionally have single-character names (such as **–h**, **–n**). Some commands allow you to group options following a single hyphen (for example **–hn**). GNU utilities frequently have two arguments that do the same thing: a single-character argument and a longer, more descriptive argument that is preceded by two hyphens (such as **––show-all**, **––invert-match**).

ordinary file   A file that is used to store a program, text, or other user data. See *directory* (page 1465) and *device file* (page 1464).

output   Information that a program sends to the terminal or another file. See *standard output* on page 1494.

packet   A unit of data sent across a network. *Packet* is a generic term used to describe a unit of data at any layer of the OSI protocol stack, but it is most correctly used to describe network- or application-layer (page 361) data units ("application protocol data unit," APDU).ᶠᵒᴸᴰᴼᶜ See also *frame* (page 1468) and *datagram* (page 1464).

packet filtering   A technique used to block network traffic based on specified criteria, such as the origin, destination, or type of each packet. See also *firewall* (page 1468).

pager   A utility that allows you to view a file one screen at a time (for example, less and more).

paging	The process by which virtual memory is maintained by the operating system. The contents of process memory is moved (paged out) to the *swap space* (page 1496) as needed to make room for other processes.
PAM	Linux-PAM or Linux Pluggable Authentication Modules. These modules allow a system administrator to determine how various applications authenticate users. Refer to "PAM" on page 1043.
parent process	A process that forks other processes. See *process* (page 1486) and *child process* (page 1460).
partition	A section of a (hard) disk that has a name so you can address it separately from other sections. A disk partition can hold a filesystem or another structure, such as the swap area. Under DOS/MS Windows partitions (and sometimes whole disks) are labeled **C:**, **D:**, and so on. Also, *disk partition* and *slice*.
passive FTP	Allows FTP to work through a firewall by allowing the flow of data to be initiated and controlled by the client FTP program instead of the server. Also called PASV FTP because it uses the FTP PASV command.
passphrase	A string of words and characters that you type in to authenticate yourself. A passphrase differs from *password* only in length. A password is usually short—6 to 10 characters. A passphrase is usually much longer—up to 100 characters or more. The greater length makes a passphrase harder to guess or reproduce than a password and therefore more secure.ᶠᴼᴸᴰᴼᶜ
password	In order to prevent unauthorized access to a user's account, an arbitrary string of characters chosen by the user or system administrator and used to authenticate the user when attempting to log in.ᶠᴼᴸᴰᴼᶜ See also *passphrase*.
PASV FTP	See *passive FTP*.
pathname	A list of directories separated by slashes (/) and ending with the name of a file, which can be a directory. A pathname is used to trace a path through the file structure to locate or identify a file.
pathname, last element of a	The part of a pathname following the final /, or the whole filename if there is no /. A simple filename. Also *basename*.
pathname element	One of the filenames that forms a pathname.

peripheral device   See *device* on page 1464.

persistent   Data that is stored on nonvolatile media, such as a hard disk.

physical device   A tangible device, such as a disk drive, that is physically separate from other, similar devices.

PID   Process identification, usually followed by the word *number*. GNU/Linux assigns a unique PID number as each process is initiated.

pipe   A connection between programs such that standard output of one is connected to standard input of the next. Also *pipeline*.

pixel   The smallest element of a picture, typically a single dot on a display screen.

plaintext   Text that is not encrypted. Contrast to *ciphertext* (page 1460). See also "Encryption" on page 1406.

Pluggable Authentication Modules   See *PAM* on page 1484.

point-to-point link   A connection limited to two endpoints, such as the connection between a pair of modems.

port   A logical channel or channel endpoint in a communications system. The *TCP* (page 1497) and *UDP* (page 1499) transport layer protocols used on Ethernet use port numbers to distinguish between different logical channels on the same network interface on the same computer.

The **/etc/services** file (see the beginning of this file for more information) or the *NIS* (page 1482) **services** database specifies a unique port number for each application program. The number links incoming data to the correct service (program). Standard, well-known ports are used by everyone: Port 80 is used for HTTP (Web) traffic. Some protocols, such as TELNET and HTTP (which is a special form of TELNET), have default ports specified as mentioned earlier but can use other ports as well.ꜰᴏʟᴅᴏᴄ

portmapper   A server that converts TCP/IP port numbers into *RPC* (page 1491) program numbers. See "RPC Network Services" on page 398.

printable character   One of the graphic characters: a letter, number, or punctuation mark; contrasted with a nonprintable, or ᴄᴏɴᴛʀᴏʟ, character. Also *printing character*.

private address
space

IANA (page 1472) has reserved three blocks of IP addresses for private internets or LANs. The blocks are

```
10.0.0.0 - 10.255.255.255
172.16.0.0 - 172.31.255.255
192.168.0.0 - 192.168.255.255
```

You can use these addresses without coordinating with anyone outside of your LAN (you do not have to register the system name or address). Systems using these IP addresses cannot communicate directly with hosts using the global address space but must go through a gateway. Because private addresses have no global meaning, routing information is not stored by DNSs, and most ISPs reject privately addressed packets. Make sure that your router is set up not to forward these packets onto the Internet.

procedure

A sequence of instructions for performing a particular task. Most programming languages, including machine languages, enable a programmer to define procedures that allow the procedure code to be called from multiple places. Also *subroutine*.FOLDOC

process

The execution of a command by GNU/Linux. See "Processes" on page 560.

.profile file

A startup file that a Bourne Again or Z login shell executes when you log in. The TC Shell executes **.login** instead. You can use the **.profile** file to run commands, set variables, and define functions.

program

A sequence of executable computer instructions contained in a file. GNU/Linux utilities, applications, and shell scripts are all programs. Whenever you run a command that is not built into a shell, you are executing a program.

PROM

Programmable read-only memory. A kind of nonvolatile storage. *ROM* (page 1490) that can be written to using a PROM programmer.

prompt

A cue from a program, usually displayed on the screen, indicating that it is waiting for input. The shell displays a prompt, as do some of the interactive utilities, such as mail. By default the Bourne Again and Z Shells use a dollar sign ($) as a prompt, and the TC Shell uses a percent sign (%).

protocol

A set of formal rules describing how to transmit data, especially across a network. Low-level protocols define the electrical and physical standards, bit and byte ordering, and transmission, error detection, and correction of the bit stream. High-level protocols deal with the data formatting, including message syntax, terminal-to-computer dialog, character sets, sequencing of messages, and so forth.FOLDOC

proxy   A service that is authorized to act for a system while not being part of that system. See also *proxy gateway* and *proxy server*.

proxy gateway   A computer that separates clients (such as browsers) from the Internet, working as a trusted agent that accesses the Internet on their behalf. A proxy gateway passes a request for data from an Internet service, such as HTTP from a browser/client, to a remote server. The data that the server returns goes back through the proxy gateway to the requesting service. A proxy gateway should be transparent to the user.

A proxy gateway often runs on a *firewall* (page 1468) machine as a barrier to malicious users. A proxy gateway hides the IP addresses of the local computers inside the firewall from Internet users outside the firewall.

You can configure browsers, such as Mozilla and Netscape, to use a different proxy gateway or use no proxy for each URL access method including FTP, netnews, SNMP, HTTPS, and HTTP. See also *proxy*.

proxy server   A *proxy gateway* that usually includes a *cache* (page 1459) that holds frequently used Web pages so that the next request for that page is available locally (and therefore more quickly). See also *proxy*. The terms proxy server and proxy gateway are frequently interchanged so that the use of cache does not rest exclusively with the proxy server.

Python   A simple, high-level, interpreted, object-oriented, interactive language that bridges the gap between C and shell programming. Suitable for rapid prototyping or as an extension language for C applications, Python supports packages, modules, classes, user-defined exceptions, a good C interface, and dynamic loading of C modules and has no arbitrary restrictions. www.python.org ᶠᴼᴸᴰᴼᶜ

quote   When you quote a character, you take away any special meaning that it has in the current context. You can quote a character by preceding it with a backslash. When you are interacting with the shell, you can also quote a character by surrounding it with single quotation marks. For example, the command **echo *** or **echo '*'** displays *. The command **echo** * displays a list of the files in the working directory. See also *escape* on page 1466. See *ambiguous file reference* (page 1454), *metacharacter* (page 1479), *regular character* (page 1489), *regular expression* (page 1489), and *special character* (page 1493).

RAM   Random access memory. A kind of volatile storage. A data storage device for which the order of access to different locations does not affect the speed of access. Contrast to a hard disk or tape drive, which provides quicker access to sequential data because accessing a nonsequential location requires physical movement of the storage medium and/or read-write head rather than just electronic switching. Contrast to *nonvolatile storage* (page 1482).ᶠᴼᴸᴰᴼᶜ

RAM disk   *RAM* that is made to look like a (floppy) disk. RAM disk is frequently used as part of the *boot* (page 1457) process.

RAS   Remote access server. In a network, a computer that provides access to remote users via analog modem or ISDN connections. RAS includes the dial-up protocols and access control (authentication) and may be a regular file server with remote access software or a proprietary system, such as Shiva's LANRover. The modems may be internal or external to the device.

RDF   Resource Description Framework. Being developed by W3C (the main standards body for the World Wide Web), a standard that specifies a mechanism for encoding and transferring *metadata* (page 1479). RDF does not specify what the metadata should or can be. RDF can integrate many kinds of applications and data, using XML as an interchange syntax. Some examples of the kinds of data that can be integrated are library catalogs and worldwide directories, syndication and aggregation of news, software, and content, and collections of music and photographs. Go to www.w3.org/RDF for more information.

redirection   The process of directing standard input for a program to come from a file rather than from the keyboard. Also, directing standard output or standard error to go to a file rather than to the screen.

reentrant   Code that can have multiple simultaneous, interleaved, or nested invocations that do not interfere with one another. Noninterference is important for parallel processing, recursive programming, and interrupt handling.

It is usually easy to arrange for multiple invocations (that is, calls to a subroutine) to share one copy of the code and any readonly data. But for the code to be reentrant, each invocation must use its own copy of any modifiable data (or synchronized access to shared data). This is most often achieved by using a stack and allocating local variables in a new stack frame for each invocation. Alternatively the caller may pass in a pointer to a block of memory that that invocation can use (usually for output), or the code may allocate some memory on a heap, especially if the data must survive after the routine returns.

Reentrant code is often found in system software, such as operating systems and teleprocessing monitors. It is also a crucial component of multithreaded programs, where the term *thread-safe* is often used instead of reentrant.FOLDOC

regular character   A character that always represents itself in an ambiguous file reference or another type of regular expression. Contrast to *special character*.

regular expression   A string—composed of letters, numbers, and special symbols—that defines one or more strings. See Appendix A.

relative pathname   A pathname that starts from the working directory. Contrast to *absolute pathname*.

remote access server   See *RAS* on page 1488.

remote filesystem   A filesystem on a remote computer that has been set up so that you can access (usually over a network) its files as though they were stored on your local computer's disks. An example of a remote filesystem is NFS.

Remote procedure call   See *RPC* on page 1491.

rescue disk   One or two floppy disks that contain a version of the GNU/Linux kernel for your system and a few basic system administration utilities. A rescue disk is invaluable when you are unable to boot your system in the normal manner. Refer to "**mkbootdisk**: Creates a Rescue/Emergency/Boot Floppy Disk" on page 920.

resolver   The TCP/IP library software that formats requests to be sent to the *DNS* (page 1465) for hostname-to-Internet address conversion.FOLDOC

Resource Description Framework   See *RDF* on page 1488.

restore   The process of turning an icon into a window. Contrast to *iconify*.

return code   See *exit status* on page 1466.

RFC   Request for Comments. Begun in 1969, one of a series of numbered Internet informational documents and standards widely followed by commercial software and freeware in the Internet and UNIX/GNU/Linux communities. Few RFCs are standards, but all Internet standards are recorded in RFCs. Perhaps the single most influential RFC has been RFC 822, the Internet electronic mail format standard.

RFC (continued) The RFCs are unusual in that they are floated by technical experts acting on their own initiative and reviewed by the Internet at large rather than formally promulgated through an institution such as ANSI. For this reason, they remain known as RFCs even once adopted as standards. The RFC tradition of pragmatic, experience-driven, after-the-fact standard writing done by individuals or small working groups has important advantages over the more formal, committee-driven process typical of ANSI or ISO.FOLDOC

ROM Read-only memory. A kind of nonvolatile storage. A data storage device that is manufactured with fixed contents. In general, ROM describes any storage system whose contents cannot be altered, such as a gramophone record or printed book. When used in reference to electronics and computers, ROM describes semiconductor integrated circuit memories, of which there are several types, and CD-ROM.

ROM is nonvolatile storage—it retains its contents even after power has been removed; contrast to *RAM* (page 1487). ROM is often used to hold programs for embedded systems, as these usually have a fixed purpose. ROM is also used for storage of the *BIOS* (page 1457) in a computer.FOLDOC

root directory The ancestor of all directories and the start of all absolute pathnames. The name of the root directory is */*.

root filesystem The filesystem that is available when the system is brought up in single-user mode. The name of this filesystem is always */*. You cannot unmount or mount the root filesystem. You can remount root to change its mount options (page 949).

root login Usually the login name of *Superuser* (page 1496).

rotate When a file, such as a log file, gets indefinitely larger, you must keep it from taking up too much space on the disk. Because you may need to refer to the information in the log files in the near future, it is generally not a good idea to delete the contents of the file until it has aged. Toward this end you can periodically save the current log file under a new name and create a new, empty file as the current log file. You can keep a series of these files, renaming each as a new one is saved. You will then *rotate* the files as, for example, remove **xyzlog.4**, **xyzlog.3**→**xyzlog.4**, **xyzlog.2**→**xyzlog.3**, **xyzlog.1**→**xyzlog.2**, **xyzlog**→**xyzlog.1**, create a new **xyzlog** file. By the time you remove **xyzlog.4**, it will not contain any information more recent than you want to remove.

router A device, often a computer, that is connected to more than one similar type of network to pass data between them. See *gateway* on page 1469.

RPC Remote procedure call. A call to a *procedure* (page 1486) that acts transparently across a network. The procedure itself is responsible for accessing and using the network. The RPC libraries make sure that network access is transparent to the application. RPC runs on top of TCP/IP or UDP/IP.

RSA A public key encryption (page 1407) technology that is based on the lack of an efficient way to factor very large numbers. Because of this lack, it takes an extraordinary amount of computer processing time and power to deduce an RSA key. The RSA algorithm is the de facto standard for data sent over the Internet.

run To execute a program.

Samba A free suite of programs that implement the Server Message Block (SMB) protocol. See *SMB* (page 1492) and *Samba/swat* (page 1025).

schema Within a GUI a pattern that helps you see and interpret the information that is presented in a window, making it easier to understand new information that is presented using the same schema.

scroll To move lines on a terminal or window up and down or left and right.

server A powerful centralized computer (or program) designed to provide information to clients (smaller computers or programs) on request.

session The lifetime of a process. For a desktop it is the desktop session manager. For a character-based terminal it is the user's login shell process. In KDE it is launched by kdeinit. Or the sequence of events between when you start using a program, such as an editor, and when you finish.

setgid When you execute a file that has setgid (set group ID) permission, the process executing the file takes on the privileges of the group the file belongs to. The ls utility shows setgid permission as an s in the group's executable position. See also *setuid*.

setuid When you execute a file that has setuid (set user ID) permission, the process executing the file takes on the privileges of the owner of the file. As an example, if you run a setuid program that removes all the files in a directory, you can remove files in any of the file owner's directories even if you do not normally have permission to do so. When the program is owned by **root**, you can remove files in any directory that **root** can remove files from. The ls utility shows setuid permission as an s in the owner's executable position. See also *setgid*.

sexillion In the British system 10^{36}. In the American system this number is named *undecillion*. See also *large number* (page 1476).

share	A directory and the filesystem hierarchy below it that is shared with another system using Samba. See *Samba/swat* on page 1025. Also *window share*.
shared network topology	A network, such as Ethernet, in which each packet may be seen by systems other than its destination system. *Shared* means that the network bandwidth is shared by all users.
shell	A GNU/Linux system command processor. The three major shells are the *Bourne Again Shell* (page 1457), the *TC Shell* (page 1497), and the *Z Shell* (page 1503).
shell function	A series of commands that the shell stores for execution at a later time. Shell functions are like shell scripts but run more quickly because they are stored in the computer's main memory rather than in files. Also, a shell function is run in the environment of the shell that calls it (unlike a shell script, which is typically run in a subshell).
shell script	An ASCII file containing shell commands. Also *shell program*.
signal	A very brief message that the UNIX system can send to a process, apart from the process's standard input. Refer to "**trap**: Catches a Signal" on page 667.
simple filename	A single filename containing no slashes (*/*). A simple filename is the simplest form of pathname. Also the last element of a pathname. Also *basename*.
single-user system	A computer system that only one person can use at a time. Contrast to *multi-user system*.
SMB	Server Message Block. A client/server protocol that provides file and printer sharing between computers. In addition, SMB can share serial ports and communications abstractions, such as named pipes and mail slots. SMB is similar to remote procedure call, *RPC* (page 1491), specialized for filesystem access.^{FOLDOC} See *Samba/swat* on page 1025.
smiley	A character-based *glyph* (page 1469), typically used in e-mail, that conveys an emotion. The characters :-) in a message portray a smiley face (look at it sideways). Because it can be difficult to tell when the writer of an electronic message is saying something in jest or in seriousness, e-mail users often use :-) to indicate humor. The two original smileys, designed by Scott Fahlman, were :-) and :-(. Also *emoticon, smileys,* and *smilies*. For more information search on `smiley` on the Internet.
smilies	See *smiley*.

SMTP Simple Mail Transfer Protocol. A protocol used to transfer electronic mail between computers. It is a server-to-server protocol, so other protocols are used to access the messages. The SMTP dialog usually happens in the background under the control of a message transport system such as sendmail.FOLDOC

snap (windows) As you drag a window toward another window or edge of the workspace, it can move suddenly so that it is adjacent to the other window/edge. Thus the window *snaps* into position.

sneakernet Using hand-carried magnetic media to transfer files between machines.

SOCKS A networking proxy protocol embodied in a SOCKS server, which performs the same functions as a *proxy gateway* (page 1487) or *proxy server* (page 1487). The difference is that SOCKS works at the application level, requiring that an application be modified to work with the SOCKS protocol, whereas a *proxy* (page 1487) makes no demands on the application.

SOCKSv4 does not support authentication or UDP proxy. SOCKSv5 supports a variety of authentication methods and UDP proxy.

sort To put in a specified order, usually alphabetic or numeric.

SPACE character A character that appears as the absence of a visible character. Even though you cannot see it, a SPACE is a printable character. It is represented by the ASCII code 32 (decimal). A SPACE character is considered a *blank*, or *whitespace* (page 1501).

spam Posting irrelevant or inappropriate messages to one or more Usenet newsgroups or mailing lists in deliberate or accidental violation of *netiquette* (page 1481). Also, sending large amounts of unsolicited e-mail indiscriminately. This e-mail usually promotes a product or service. Spam is the electronic equivalent of junk mail. From the Monty Python "Spam" song.FOLDOC

sparse file A file that is large but takes up little disk space. The data in a sparse file is not dense (thus its name). Examples of sparse files are core files, dbm files, and /etc/utmp ($\rightarrow$ /var/adm/utmp).

spawn See *fork* on page 1468.

special character A character that has a special meaning when it occurs in an ambiguous file reference or another type of regular expression, unless it is quoted. The special characters most commonly used with the shell are ❋ and ?. Also *metacharacter* and *wildcard*.

special file See *device file* on page 1464.

spinner	In a GUI a type of *text box* (page 1497) that holds a number that you can change by typing over it or using the up and down arrows at the end of the box.
spoofing	See *IP spoofing* on page 1474.
spool	To place items in a queue, each waiting its turn for some action. Often used when speaking about the lp utility and the printer; that is, lp spools files for the printer.
SQL	Structured Query Language. A language that provides a user interface to relational database management systems (RDBMS). SQL, the de facto standard, is also an ISO and ANSI standard and is often embedded in other programming languages.FOLDOC
square bracket	There is a left square bracket ([) and a right square bracket (]). They are special characters that define character classes in ambiguous file references and other regular expressions.
SSH Communications Security	The company that created the original SSH (secure shell) protocol suite (www.ssh.com). GNU/Linux uses openSSH. See *OpenSSH* on page 1483.
standard error	A file to which a program can send output. Usually only error messages are sent to this file. Unless you instruct the shell otherwise, it directs this output to the screen (that is, to the device file that represents the screen).
standard input	A file from which a program can receive input. Unless you instruct the shell otherwise, it directs this input so that it comes from the keyboard (that is, from the device file that represents the keyboard).
standard output	A file to which a program can send output. Unless you instruct the shell otherwise, it directs this output to the screen (that is, to the device file that represents the screen).
startup file	A file that the login shell runs when you log in. The Bourne Again and Z Shells run **.profile**, and the TC Shell runs **.login**. The TC Shell also runs **.cshrc** whenever a new TC Shell or a subshell is invoked. The Z Shell runs an analogous file whose name is identified by the **ENV** variable.
status line	The bottom (usually the twenty-fourth) line of the terminal. The vi editor uses the status line to display information about what is happening during an editing session.

sticky bit   An access permission bit that causes an executable program to remain on the swap area of the disk. It takes less time to load a program that has its sticky bit set than one that does not. Only Superuser can set the sticky bit. If the sticky bit is set on a directory that is publicly writable, only the owner of a file in that directory can remove the file.

streaming tape   A tape that moves at a constant speed past the read/write heads rather than speeding up and slowing down, which can slow the process of writing to or reading from the tape. A proper blocking factor helps ensure that the tape device will be kept streaming.

streams   See *connection-oriented protocol* on page 1461.

string   A sequence of characters.

stylesheet   *See CSS* on page 1463.

subdirectory   A directory that is located within another directory. Every directory except the root directory is a subdirectory.

subnet   Subnetwork.   A portion of a network, which may be a physically independent network segment, that shares a network address with other portions of the network and is distinguished by a subnet number. A subnet is to a network what a network is to an internet.^FOLDOC

subnet address   The subnet portion of an IP address. In a subnetted network the host portion of an IP address is split into a subnet portion and a host portion using a subnet mask (also address mask).

subnet mask   A bit mask used to identify which bits in an IP address correspond to the network address and subnet portions of the address. Called a subnet mask because the network portion of the address is determined by the number of bits that are set in the mask. The subnet mask has ones in positions corresponding to the network and subnet numbers and zeros in the host number positions. Also *address mask*.

subnet number   The subnet portion of an IP address. In a subnetted network the host portion of an IP address is split into a subnet portion and a host portion using a *subnet mask* (also address mask).

subpixel hinting   Similar to *antialiasing* (page 1454) but takes advantage of colors to do the antialiasing. Particularly useful on LCD screens.

subroutine   See *procedure* on page 1486.

subshell   A shell that is forked as a duplicate of its parent shell. When you run an executable file that contains a shell script by using its filename on the command line, the shell forks a subshell to run the script. Also, commands surrounded with parentheses are run in a subshell.

superblock   A block that contains control information for a filesystem. The superblock contains housekeeping information, such as the number of inodes in the filesystem and free list information.

superserver   The extended Internet services daemon. Refer to xinetd on page 397.

Superuser   A privileged user having access to anything any other system user has access to and more. The system administrator must be able to become Superuser in order to establish new accounts, change passwords, and perform other administrative tasks. The login name of Superuser is typically **root**.

swap   The operating system moving a process from main memory to a disk, or vice versa. Swapping a process to the disk allows another process to begin or continue execution. Refer to "swap" on page 967.

swap space   An area of a disk (that is, a swap file) used to store the portion of a process's memory that has been paged out. Under a virtual memory system, it is the amount of swap space rather than the amount of physical memory that determines the maximum size of a single process and the maximum total size of all active processes. Also, *swap area* or *swapping area.*^{FOLDOC}

switch   See *network switch* on page 1482.

symbolic link   A directory entry that points to the pathname of another file. In most cases a symbolic link to a file can be used in the same ways a hard link can be used. Unlike a hard link, a symbolic link can span filesystems and can connect to a directory.

system administrator   The person responsible for the upkeep of the system. The system administrator has the ability to log in as Superuser. See *Superuser.*

system console   The main system terminal, usually directly connected to the computer and the one that receives system error messages. Also *console, console terminal.*

system mode   The designation for the state of the system while it is doing system work. Some examples are making system calls, running NFS and autofs, processing network traffic, and performing kernel operations on behalf of system. Contrast to *user mode* (page 1500).

System V	One of the two major versions of the UNIX system.
TC Shell	tcsh. An enhanced but completely compatible version of the Berkeley UNIX C shell, csh.
TCP	Transmission Control Protocol. The most common transport layer protocol used on the Internet. It is the connection-oriented protocol built on top of *IP* (page 1474) and is nearly always seen in the combination TCP/IP (TCP over *IP*). TCP adds reliable communication, sequencing, and flow-control and provides full-duplex, process-to-process connections. *UDP* (page 1499), although connectionless, is the other protocol that runs on top of *IP*.^{FOLDOC}
tera-	In the binary system the tera- prefix multiplies by 2^{40}, or 1,099,511,627,776. Terabyte is a common use of this prefix. Abbreviated as T.
termcap	Terminal capability. The **/etc/termcap** file contains a list of various types of terminals and their characteristics. *System V* (page 1497) replaced the function of this file with the *terminfo* system.
terminal	Differentiated from a *workstation* (page 1502) by its lack of intelligence, a terminal connects to a computer that runs GNU/Linux. A workstation runs GNU/Linux on itself.
terminfo	Terminal information. The **/usr/lib/terminfo** directory contains many subdirectories, each containing several files, each of which is named for, and contains a summary of the functional characteristics of, a particular terminal. Visually oriented text-based programs, such as vi, use these files. An alternative to the *termcap* file.
text box	In a GUI a box that you can type in.
theme	Defined as an implicit or recurrent idea, *theme* is used in a GUI to describe a look that is consistent for all elements of a desktop. Go to www.themes.org for examples.
thicknet	A type of coaxial cable (thick) used for an Ethernet network. Devices are attached to thicknet by tapping the cable at fixed points.
thinnet	A type of coaxial cable (thin) used for an Ethernet network. Thinnet cable is smaller in diameter and more flexible than *thicknet* cable. Each device is typically attached to two separate cable segments by using a T-shaped connector; one segment leads to the device ahead of it on the network and one to the device that follows it.

thread-safe   See *reentrant* on page 1488.

tiff   Tagged Image File Format. A file format used for still-image bitmaps, stored in tagged fields. Application programs can use the tags to accept or ignore fields, depending on their capabilities.ꜰᴏʟᴅᴏᴄ

tiled windows   An arrangement of windows such that no window overlaps another. Opposite of *cascading windows* (page 1459).

time to live   See *TTL* on page 1499.

toggle   To switch between one of two positions. For example, the ftp **glob** command toggles the **glob** feature: Give the command once, and it turns the feature on or off; give the command again, and it sets the feature back to its original state.

token ring   A type of *LAN* (page 1476) in which computers are attached to a ring of cable. A token packet circulates continuously around the ring; a computer can transmit information only when it holds the token.

tooltip   A minicontext help system that you activate by allowing your mouse pointer to *hover* (page 1471) over a button, icon, or applet (such as those on a panel).

transient window   A dialog or other window that is displayed for only a short time.

Transmission Control Protocol   See *TCP* on page 1497.

Trojan horse   A program that does something destructive or disruptive to your system. Its action is not documented, and the system administrator would not approve of it if he or she were aware of it. See "Avoiding a Trojan Horse" (page 903).

The term *Trojan horse* was coined by MIT-hacker-turned-NSA-spook Dan Edwards. A malicious security-breaking program that is disguised as something benign, such as a directory lister, archive utility, game, or (in one notorious 1990 case on the Mac) a program to find and destroy viruses. Similar to *back door (continued)* (page 1456).ꜰᴏʟᴅᴏᴄ

TTL	Time to live.

1. All DNS records specify how long they are good for, usually up to a week at most. This time is called the record's *time to live*. When a DNS server or an application stores this record in *cache* (page 1459), it decrements the TTL value and removes the record from cache when the value reaches zero. A DNS server passes a cached record to another server with the current (decremented) TTL guaranteeing the proper TTL no matter how many servers the record passes through.

2. In the IP header, a field that indicates how many more hops the packet should be allowed to make before being discarded or returned.

TTY	Teletypewriter. The terminal device that UNIX was first run from. Today TTY refers to the screen (or window in the case of a terminal emulator), keyboard, and mouse that are connected to a computer. This term appears in UNIX, and GNU/Linux has kept the term for the sake of consistency and tradition.
tunneling	Encapsulation of protocol A within packets carried by protocol B, such that A treats B as though it were a data link layer. Tunneling is used to get data between administrative domains that use a protocol not supported by the internet connecting those domains. See also *VPN* (page 1501).
UDP	User Datagram Protocol. The Internet standard transport layer protocol that provides simple but unreliable datagram services. UDP is a connectionless protocol that, like *TCP* (page 1497), is layered on top of *IP* (page 1474).
	Unlike *TCP*, UDP neither guarantees delivery nor requires a connection. As a result it is lightweight and efficient, but all error processing and retransmission must be taken care of by the application program. UDP is often used for sending time-sensitive data that is not particularly sensitive to minor loss, such as audio and video data. FOLDOC
UID	A number that the **passwd** database associates with a login name.
undecillion	In the American system 10^{36}. In the British system, this number is named *sexillion*. See also *large number* (page 1476).
Unicast	A packet sent from one host to another host. Unicast means one source and one destination.
unmanaged window	See *ignored window* on page 1472.

usage message   A message displayed by a command when you call the command using incorrect command line arguments.

User Datagram Protocol   See *UDP*.

User ID   See *UID*.

user interface   See *interface* on page 1473.

user mode   The designation for the state of the system while it is doing user work, such as running a user program (but not the system calls made by the program). Contrast to *system mode* (page 1496).

UTC   Coordinated Universal Time. UTC is equivalent to the mean solar time at the prime meridian (0 degrees longitude). Also called Zulu time (Z stands for longitude zero) and GMT (Greenwich Mean Time).

utility   A program included as a standard part of GNU/Linux. You typically invoke a utility either by giving a command in response to a shell prompt or by calling it from within a shell script. Utilities are often referred to as commands. Contrast to *builtin (command)* (page 1458).

variable   A name and an associated value. The shell allows you to create variables and use them in shell scripts. Also, the shell inherits several variables when it is invoked, and it maintains those and other variables while it is running. Some shell variables establish characteristics of the shell environment, whereas others have values that reflect different aspects of your ongoing interaction with the shell.

viewport   Same as *workspace* (page 1502).

virtual console   Additional consoles, or displays, that you can view on the system, or physical, console. See page 36 for more information.

virus   A *cracker* (page 1462) program that searches out other programs and "infects" them by embedding a copy of itself in them, so that they become *Trojan horses* (page 1498). When these programs are executed, the embedded virus is executed too, propagating the "infection," usually without the user's knowledge. By analogy with biological viruses.^{FOLDOC}

VLAN   A logical grouping of two or more nodes that are not necessarily on the same physical network segment but that share the same network number. A VLAN is often associated with switched Ethernet.^{FOLDOC}

VPN   Virtual private network. A private network that exists on a public network, such as the Internet. A VPN is a less expensive substitute for company-owned/leased lines and uses encryption (page 1406) to ensure privacy. A nice side effect is that you can send non-Internet protocols, such as Appletalk, IPX, or Netbios, over the VPN connection by *tunneling* (page 1499) them through the VPN IP stream.

W3C   World Wide Web Consortium (www.w3.org).

WAN   Wide area network. A network that interconnects *LANs* (page 1476) and *MANs* (page 1478), spanning a large geographic area (typically states or countries).

Web ring   A collection of Web sites that provide information on a single topic or group of related topics. Each home page that is part of the Web ring has a series of links that let you go from site to site. An example is the emacs ring whose home is at www.gnusoftware.com/WebRing.

whitespace   A collective name for SPACEs and/or TABs and occasionally NEWLINEs. Also, *white space*.

wide area network   See *WAN*.

widget   A user-interface element, such as a button, menu, scrollbar, and so on.

wild card   See *metacharacter* on page 1479.

window   On a display screen a region that runs or is controlled by a particular program.

window manager   A program that controls how windows appear on a display screen and how you manipulate them.

window share   See *share* on page 1492.

word   A sequence of one or more nonblank characters separated from other words by TABs, SPACEs, or NEWLINEs. Used to refer to individual command line arguments. In vi a word is similar to a word in the English language—a string of one or more characters bounded by a punctuation mark, a numeral, a TAB, a SPACE, or a NEWLINE.

work buffer   A location where vi stores text while it is being edited. The information in the Work buffer is not written to the file on the disk until you give the editor a command to write it.

working directory
The directory that you are associated with at any given time. The relative pathnames you use are *relative to* the working directory. Also *current directory*.

workspace
A subdivision of a *desktop* (page 1464) that occupies the entire display. Refer to "Desktop" on page 174.

workstation
A small computer, typically designed to fit in an office and be used by one person and usually equipped with a bit-mapped graphical display, keyboard, and mouse. Differentiated from a *terminal* (page 1497) by its intelligence. A workstation runs GNU/Linux on itself while a terminal connects to a computer that runs GNU/Linux.

worm
A program that propagates itself over a network, reproducing itself as it goes. Today the term has negative connotations, as it is assumed that only *crackers* (page 1462) write worms. Compare to *virus* (page 1500), *Trojan horse* (page 1498). From *Tapeworm* in John Brunner's novel, *The Shockwave Rider*, Ballantine Books, 1990. (via XEROX PARC)FOLDOC

X terminal
A graphics terminal designed to run the X Window System.

X Window System
A design and set of tools for writing flexible, portable windowing applications, created jointly by researchers at MIT and several leading computer manufacturers.

XDMCP
X Display Manager Control Protocol. XDMCP allows the login server to accept requests from network displays. XDMCP is built into many X terminals.

xDSL
Different types of *DSL* (page 1466) are identified by a prefix, for example, ADSL, HDSL, SDSL, and VDSL.

Xinerama
An extension to XFree86 Release 6 Version 4.0 (X4.0). Xinerama allows window managers and applications to use the two or more physical displays as one large virtual display. Refer to the Xinerama-HOWTO.

XML
Extensible Markup Language.   A universal format for structured documents and data on the Web. Developed by *W3C* (page 1501), XML is a pared-down version of SGML. See www.w3.org/XML and www.w3.org/XML/1999/XML-in-10-points.

XSM   X Session Manager allows you to create a session that includes certain applications. While the session is running, you can perform a *checkpoint* (saves the application state) or a *shutdown* (saves the state and exits from the session). When you log back in, you can load your session so that everything in your session is running just as it was when you logged off.

Z Shell   zsh. A *shell* (page 1492) that incorporates many of the features of the *Bourne Again Shell* (page 1457), *Korn Shell* (page 1476), and *TC Shell* (page 1497), as well as many original features.

Zulu time   See *UTC* on page 1500.

Index

Italic numbers indicate definitions; bold numbers indicate entries in Part III.

Italic numbers indicate definitions; bold numbers indicate entries in Part III.

Italic numbers indicate definitions; bold numbers indicate entries in Part III.

Italic numbers indicate definitions; bold numbers indicate entries in Part III.

Italic numbers indicate definitions; bold numbers indicate entries in Part III.

Italic numbers indicate definitions; bold numbers indicate entries in Part III.

Italic numbers indicate definitions; bold numbers indicate entries in Part III.

Italic numbers indicate definitions; bold numbers indicate entries in Part III.

Italic numbers indicate definitions; bold numbers indicate entries in Part III.

Italic numbers indicate definitions; bold numbers indicate entries in Part III.

Italic numbers indicate definitions; bold numbers indicate entries in Part III.

Italic numbers indicate definitions; bold numbers indicate entries in Part III.

Italic numbers indicate definitions; bold numbers indicate entries in Part III.

Italic numbers indicate definitions; bold numbers indicate entries in Part III.

Italic numbers indicate definitions; bold numbers indicate entries in Part III.

Italic numbers indicate definitions; bold numbers indicate entries in Part III.

Italic numbers indicate definitions; bold numbers indicate entries in Part III.

Italic numbers indicate definitions; bold numbers indicate entries in Part III.

Italic numbers indicate definitions; bold numbers indicate entries in Part III.

Italic numbers indicate definitions; bold numbers indicate entries in Part III.

Italic numbers indicate definitions; bold numbers indicate entries in Part III.

Italic numbers indicate definitions; bold numbers indicate entries in Part III.

Italic numbers indicate definitions; bold numbers indicate entries in Part III.

Register
Your Book

at www.awprofessional.com/register

You may be eligible to receive:

- Advance notice of forthcoming editions of the book
- Related book recommendations
- Chapter excerpts and supplements of forthcoming titles
- Information about special contests and promotions throughout the year
- Notices and reminders about author appearances, tradeshows, and online chats with special guests

Contact us

If you are interested in writing a book or reviewing manuscripts prior to publication, please write to us at:

Editorial Department
Addison-Wesley Professional
75 Arlington Street, Suite 300
Boston, MA 02116 USA
Email: AWPro@aw.com

Visit us on the Web: http://www.awprofessional.com

CD-ROM Warranty

Addison-Wesley warrants the enclosed discs to be free of defects in materials and faulty workmanship under normal use for a period of ninety days after purchase. If a defect is discovered in the discs during this warranty period, replacement discs can be obtained at no charge by sending the defective discs, postage prepaid, with proof of purchase to:

Editorial Department
Addison-Wesley Professional
Pearson Technology Group
75 Arlington Street, Suite 300
Boston, MA 02116
Email: AWPro@awl.com

Addison-Wesley makes no warranty or representation, either expressed or implied, with respect to this software, its quality, performance, merchantability, or fitness for a particular purpose. In no event will Addison-Wesley, its distributors, or dealers be liable for direct, indirect, special, incidental, or consequential damages arising out of the use or inability to use the software. The exclusion of implied warranties is not permitted in some states. Therefore, the above exclusion may not apply to you. This warranty provides you with specific legal rights. There may be other rights that you may have that vary from state to state. The contents of these CD-ROMs are intended for personal use only.

This book includes a copy of the Publisher's Edition of Red Hat® Linux® from Red Hat, Inc., which you may use in accordance with the license agreement found at http://www.redhat.com/licenses/. Official Red Hat® Linux®, which you may purchase from Red Hat, includes the complete Red Hat® Linux® distribution, Red Hat's documentation, and may include technical support for Red Hat® Linux®. You also may purchase technical support from Red Hat. You may purchase Red Hat® Linux® and technical support from Red Hat through the company's Web site (www.redhat.com) or its toll-free number 1.888.REDHAT1.

More information and updates are available at:
http://www.awprofessional.com/